THE ENCYCLOPEDIA OF AMERICAN FOOD AND DRINK

Menu Design in America (with Steven Heller)

How Italian Food Conquered the World

The Italian-American Cookbook (with Galina Mariani)

Almost Golden (with Robert Mariani)

The Dictionary of Italian Food and Drink

The Four Seasons (with Alex von Bidder)

America Eats Out

Mariani's Coast-to-Coast Dining Guide

Eating Out

Vincent's Cookbook (with Vincent Guerithault)

The Dictionary of American Food and Drink

THE ENCYCLOPEDIA OF

FOOD AND DRINK

JOHN F. MARIANI

BLOOMSBURY

NEW YORK · LONDON · NEW DELHI · SYDNEY

Published by Bloomsbury USA, New York

All papers used by Bloomsbury USA are natural, recyclable
products made from wood grown in well-managed forests.
The manufacturing processes conform to the
environmental regulations of the country of origin.

LIBRARY OF CONGRESS CATALOGING-IN-PUBLICATION DATA
Mariani, John F.
The encyclopedia of American food and drink / John F. Mariani.
pages cm
Includes bibliographical references and index.
ISBN 978-1-62040-160-6 (alk. paper)
1. Cooking, American—Encyclopedias. 2. Food—
Encyclopedias. 3. Beverages—Encyclopedias. I. Title.
TX349.M266 2013
641.5973—dc23
2013029975

This revised and updated edition published by
Bloomsbury USA 2013

1 3 5 7 9 10 8 6 4 2

Designed by Sara Stemen
Printed in the United States of America
by RR Donnelley, Willard, Ohio

As ever,

for Galina

CONTENTS

PREFACE

IN SEARCH OF AMERICAN FOOD

THREE DECADES AGO, when the first edition of this book was published, the question of what is American food was rarely a subject of serious consideration. Indeed, many observers of the food scene back then sniffed at the idea that American food was anything other than a mongrel cuisine that was never as good as the European or Asian originals and that, after all, most Americans ate processed food promoted by agribusiness and huge food corporations.

Now, in 2013, American food has become one of the most studied, written-about, and argued-over subjects of our culture. Food magazines abound, many with a special focus on a regional cuisine, others aimed at specific diets. Food sections in newspapers have expanded from being mere showcases for their advertisers, who always provided the recipes, to include everything from "listicles" of the ten best pizzerias to "classic" recipes for making whoopie pies. Food polemics top the bestseller lists, and television has found food shows to attract huge audiences devoted to "celebrity star chefs" and cooking competitions and reality shows in which egos are exalted and demolished every half hour. Restaurants have become topics of raging dissension on the Internet, and restaurant critics have been both deified and defiled on all sides.

None of this, I can assure you, was the case in 1977 when my wife and I drove cross-country for eleven weeks, with no firmer commitment than to see what we had not seen, learn what we did not know, and savor what we had not tasted. We began in NYC, went south, then west across Texas and over the mountains to California. Our return took us through the Grand Canyon, the flatlands of Kansas, and the snowy hills of the Midwest before ending on the edges of New England.

At that time I had no intention of compiling a gastronomic encyclopedia, nor of writing a book of any kind about American food. In fact, most of our meals on the road were disappointing, consumed in restaurants recommended by friends, editors, and guidebooks, the most thorough of which was the multivolume *Mobil Travel Guide*, an oil company's Baedeker with the uncanny ability to choose the most restaurants specializing in steaks, chops, and prime ribs. Depending on such a guide would lead a traveler to believe that Americans live on nothing but steak and potatoes—a prevailing view in most people's minds anyhow, and one the compilers of the *Mobil Travel Guide* took to heart.

One can hardly blame them, since even in the large cities and small towns of the South and the West, our request for a good meal was usually answered with directions to the nearest steak house. The "best" restaurant in town was invariably the kind of place peripatetic author Calvin Trillin spoke of when he described "some purple palace that serves 'Continental cuisine' and has as its chief creative employee a menu-writer rather than a chef." My wife was almost brought to tears at a penthouse restaurant atop a hotel in Birmingham, Alabama, when a waiter tried to make up for some stale shrimp cocktail with a sweet lime sherbet intended to "clear the palate" before moving on to a tough, burned steak.

What we found difficult to believe was that restaurants serving traditional, fine American cuisine were exceedingly difficult to find. The board members of local chambers of commerce, the businesspeople, and the tourist-information agents may eat in a wonderful little barbecue place on the outskirts of town, but without fail they would send the traveler to one of those hotel dining rooms where decor and situation mean far more than quality or integrity of food. So we'd ply our way through a wretchedly made béarnaise, wilted string beans *amandine*, filet mignon topped with canned liver pâté, and *mousse au chocolat* with all the taste and texture of shaving cream.

Only with the greatest and most insistent effort did we ferret out a good American restaurant serving old-fashioned fare or just plain, well-made contemporary cookery. We found that most of the cooking of this sort, as the Time-Life *American Cooking* series indicated, was being done in the homes of Americans who were upholding a long and honorable heritage of baking, roasting, grilling, barbecuing, and mixing—from frosted silver mugs of mint julep to tortillas with a *salsa cruda* more complex than any Gallic rouille.

We sampled excellent corn bread, made without sugar in the South, crabmeat dishes in Charleston that were creamy and full of the flavor of the Caribbean, and in the Southwest a bowl of fresh, fragrant guacamole.

But it was not only in the homes that we began to find American food: there were cafeterias serving well-made stews and perfect pies, diners where the German chocolate cake was hot out of the oven, a barbecue pit set up in what had once been an Army barracks, and pastry shops that served up the best muffins I've ever had.

In New Orleans, we had red beans and rice and sampled beignets and chicory coffee in the French Market. There were walnut waffles in Greensboro and deep-fried, cornmeal-dusted catfish at a Vicksburg restaurant where we were entertained by an organ player wearing a VFW cap. We couldn't get enough of those succulent Gulf shrimp or of the pecan pie with peach ice cream in Georgia, and in Texas a meal of chili and ice-cold beer seemed one of the best things in the world as we listened to a jukebox full of Hank Williams classics. We were introduced to chimichangas in Arizona, enjoyed fresh game in Nevada, burgers of real substance in Los Angeles, and exquisite wines in the Napa and Sonoma valleys. Traveling back across the western Plains, we had fine roast beefs and sturdy pot roasts, breakfasts with hefty side orders of bacon, ham, grits, hash browns, and the inevitable orange slice. In a ski town in Pennsylvania, we warmed up with a white bean soup and, in New England, a pot of chowder made with quahog clams and topped with common crackers. Back in New York, we threw ourselves into every imaginable ethnic cuisine—from Czech to Greek, from Szechuan to Hunan, from Moroccan to Korean. And there were plenty of prime steaks, black on the outside, pink within, sided with crisp, golden onion rings and cottage fries. We were soon trying to make up our minds whether to buy a Jewish cheesecake on the Lower East Side or an Italian cheesecake in Little Italy.

In the years since then, Americans have become more interested in more kinds of food than anyone might have imagined two decades ago. Much of the writing on food and wine continued to praise the products and preparations of chefs in Lyon, Munich, Florence, and Hong Kong, but along with the growth of the delicacy or "gourmet" shops in American cities came a reevaluation of the conclaves of ethnic cooking in our immigrant cities, which in turn led to a reappreciation of regional American dishes. And although the new boomtowns like Houston and Atlanta made fast progress in installing deluxe French restaurants in their new hotels, there arose an attendant interest in American cookery. Trendy city magazines might review the new nouvelle cuisine dining room downtown, but they would also scour the countryside to find the best pizza, the best cheesecake, the best ice cream, the best chili, or the best hamburger in the state. Even Julia Child began demonstrating how to prepare American dishes on her TV show.

Ironically, the very critics who had argued that complexity meant excellence now began to see the virtues of simplicity in a well-grilled piece of fish or a beautifully roasted loin of pork with fresh applesauce. The idea of a clambake on a beach was taking on fashionable social overtones, and no one would argue that a Maine lobster, just boiled and served with butter, accompanied by a baked Idaho potato and a glass of California chardonnay could ever be improved upon by any chef in the world.

I thought about all this after that trip in 1977, and I was encouraged to write this book when I could find no gastronomic dictionary or encyclopedia that traced the origins, terminology, slang, and methods of American cookery, except as part of a larger international cuisine. I decided I needed such a book, and so I wrote it.

Since then, American gastronomy has gone through enormous changes, and it could be argued that the U.S. has become the world capital of cuisine, both as an exemplar of the most modern culinary styles and as an influence on world food culture. Not only has the intrusion (some would say invasion) of American fast-food eateries like McDonald's and KFC had enormous effect on the way young Europeans, South Americans, and Asians now eat, but the influence of American restaurants at the white tablecloth level has had an equal impact on the way fine dining is now perceived and carried out in cities from Berlin to Singapore.

So much has occurred in American gastronomy that this book has now entered its fifth edition in order to show the extraordinary evolution of the American table, both at home and in restaurants. The availability of new ingredients, the adaptation of new cooking techniques, the increased appetite for eating out among those who have little time left to cook at home, and the resiliency of an American food industry that must constantly create new foods and flavors designed for an international market have all required a more far-reaching look at what is now the subject of American gastronomy.

INTRODUCTION

TOWARD AN UNDERSTANDING
OF AMERICAN FOOD

IN 1947, EXPATRIATE American author Henry Miller wrote, "Americans can eat garbage, provided you sprinkle it liberally with ketchup, mustard, chili sauce, Tabasco sauce, cayenne pepper, or any other condiment which destroys the original flavor of the dish."

Miller might have gone on with such hyperbolic scorn by noting that the French will eat anything with a cream sauce, Italians anything with tomato and garlic, Indians anything with curry powder, and Chinese anything with soy sauce—all to cover up the original flavor of the dish.

None of these assertions holds true, but such facile and offhanded criticism of American food, wine, and drink has become almost a tradition; by now it is a gastronomic cliché to identify American food as hamburgers, hot dogs, Coca-Cola, and ice cream—a list that would not even adequately describe the offerings at a summer baseball game. More than once, back in 1982, the response of friends to the news that I was preparing the first edition of this book was "But what is American food? Fried chicken and pizza?"—as if to suggest that all American food is prepared at fast-food outlets and dispensed by young people wearing silly hats.

Others would argue that there *is* no such thing as American food (except, perhaps, whatever it was the Indians ate before the coming of the white man), because everything was brought over by Europeans, Africans, and Asians; or that, even if "created" here, an American dish is merely an adaptation of or variation on a foreign dish—as evidenced by America's distressing fondness for chop suey, spaghetti and meatballs, and French dressing. Jambalaya, these critics will assert, is little more than a Louisiana version of Spain's paella; New England clam chowder derives from French seafood soups cooked in a copper pot called a *chaudière*; even a quintessentially American cocktail like the Harvey Wallbanger depends for its effectiveness on Galliano, an Italian liqueur.

1

Such allegations completely and conveniently ignore how every culture in the world has borrowed, absorbed, and been changed by the food and drink of other cultures, whether through conquest, assimilation, or mere emulation. It has long been debated whether Marco Polo brought noodles back from the Orient, but we do know he returned with recipes for frozen milk desserts that may have been the first European sherbets. Had India not been dominated by the Persian Mughals, the cuisines of Punjab, Kashmir, and Uttar Pradesh would be utterly different from what they are, and Japan would not have its tempura dishes had Portuguese traders not introduced the idea there three hundred years ago. Italians will always be delighted to remind their French neighbors that Gallic cookery was forever transformed after Caterina de' Medici (who became Catherine de Médicis) brought her Italian chefs with her in 1547 when she set up her French court, even though there is no historical record to prove she did.

So, too, the influence of the American cornucopia on the rest of the world has been enormous, from the time the tomato was first introduced to Italy in the sixteenth century, through the era of triangular trade between the Caribbean, Africa, and New England, based on American cod and West Indies sugar, and up to the modern age, when American food-processing technology and agricultural surpluses have not only saved nations from starvation but altered the diets of their people. Even the American-inspired "Japanese steak house" has become popular in Tokyo, while the McDonald's hamburger stand on the Champs-Élysées is crowded with young Parisians who undoubtedly douse their burgers with ketchup, mustard, and the rest of the condiments Henry Miller deplored. Nor shall the *vignerons* of Bordeaux and Burgundy ever forget that it was roots from American vines that salvaged the French wine industry after the phylloxera blight of the nineteenth century.

The simple truth is that no nation's cuisine has ever sprung entirely and ingenuously from its own kitchens. Thus, the U.S.—a stewpot of cultures—has developed a gastronomy more varied, more distinctive, and more colloquially fascinating than that of any other country in the world, all based on an astounding bounty of meat, fruit, vegetables, grains, dairy products, and fish, as well as an incomparable system of transportation that makes finding Pacific salmon on a NYC dinner plate an unremarkable occurrence. In any major American city one will find restaurants representing a dozen national cuisines, including northern Italian trattorias, bourgeois French bistros, Portuguese seafood houses, Vietnamese and Thai eateries, Chinese dim sum parlors, Japanese sushi bars, and German rathskellers. Add to these an endless array of regional delicacies—Creole gumbo, Philadelphia scrapple, Texas chili, Maryland she-crab soup, the Detroit bullshot, Florida Key lime pie, Napa Valley zinfandel, North Carolina pork barbecue, New Mexican green chile stew, Rhode Island johnnycake, Long Island duckling, Boston scrod, the New Orleans Sazerac, Kentucky bourbon, Minnesota blue cheese, and thousands of others—and one must marvel at the diversity and breadth of American food and drink. And in the decades since this encyclopedia first appeared (as *The Dictionary of American Food and Drink*), the style and cuisine created by new generations of Americans have begun to affect the way gastronomy has developed around the world, from the appearance and popularity of fast-food outlets in Paris, Rome, Moscow, and Jerusalem to the look and taste of so-called California grill restaurants in London, Beijing, and Melbourne and Italian American restaurants in New Delhi and Tokyo.

"In nothing is there more evolution than the American mind," wrote Walt Whitman, and this is as true of an American's food as it is of his politics, his art, or his treasured mobility, which allowed him to maintain his immigrant heritage while assimilating a new one. The apple may have been brought to America by the Pilgrims, but it was a gentle Swedenborgian named John Chapman, better known as Johnny Appleseed, who extended the fruit into the western territories and helped turn the U.S. into the world's largest grower of apples. An ex-slave named George Washington Carver revived the depleted economy of the South through his experiments in and promotion of peanut farming. A movement of men and beasts from Texas to Kansas after the Civil War resulted in a cattle industry that determined the social, political, and even literary character of the Midwest. In 1840, a German American in Philadelphia named John Wagner produced a light lager that immediately became the dominant style of beer in America and led to the establishment of the great brewery families that shaped the destinies of cities like Milwaukee and Portland, Oregon.

For all this, however, American gastronomy has been chronically underrated, constantly satirized, and continuously characterized as unimaginative, unsophisticated, and irredeemably bland, depending more on portion size than preparation time for its effect. Such bias began early in our history, coming from both European and native gastronomes who found the American way of eating at odds with civilized behavior. It became fashionable for French travelers to shudder at the barbaric table manners and eating habits of Americans. Constantin-François de

Chasseboeuf, Count de Volney, showed his disdain for American palates in a report published in 1804 in London:

> *In the morning at breakfast they deluge their stomach with a quart of hot water, impregnated with tea, or so slightly with coffee that it is more colored water, and they swallow, almost without chewing, hot bread, half baked, toast soaked in butter, cheese of the fattest kind, slices of salt or hung beef, ham, etc., all of which is nearly insoluble. At dinner they have boiled pastes under the name of puddings, and their sauces, even for roast beef, are melted butter; their turnips and potatoes swim in hog's lard, butter, or fat; under the name of pie or pumpkin, their pastry is nothing but a greasy paste, never sufficiently baked. To digest these viscous substances they take tea almost instantly after dinner, making it so strong that it is absolutely bitter to the taste, in which state it affects the nerves so powerfully that even the English find it brings on more obstinate restlessness than coffee.*

Europeans gasped at the amount of salt pork, lard, oysters, and pastries Americans consumed, and in much of the criticism there is a strong hint of envy, for Americans, on the whole, ate far better than any other people on the face of the earth. After the initial years of starvation faced by the earliest settlers, the American land gave up its bounty, as the forests and lakes and seas had done immediately. There seems no exaggeration in the reports of the first Europeans on these shores about hundred-pound cod, forty-pound wild turkeys, six-foot lobsters, and game birds so numerous as to blacken the sky when they flew. In his first dispatch to England, in 1606, Captain John Smith asked, with a proud immigrant's exuberance, was it not wonderful to be in a land "where man, woman and childe, with a small hooke and line, by angling, may take divers sorts of excellent fish, at their pleasures? And is it not a pretty sport, to pull up two pence, six pence, and twelve pence, as fast as you can haule and were a line?" This was written at a time when the great majority of Europeans lived on nothing but bread or porridge, when they could get it at all.

Certainly deprivations persisted, but not for lack of abundance. The diets of African slaves on southern plantations were severely restricted by their owners, usually insufficient for good nutrition and rarely augmented by foraging in the fields and forests. The diet of the indentured servant was little, if at all, better. But for others the American larder was full and fully utilized.

Hogs, brought to the West Indies by Columbus and introduced to Jamestown by the English, proliferated so well that by the end of the seventeenth century Virginia and Maryland were exporting pork back to Europe. Corn, a native grain, became the most important crop in the States; molasses fueled the economies of several nations; and oysters were so plentiful that by the late eighteenth century they had become the staple of the urban poor's diet.

With the establishment of strong, well-governed colonies came wealth, and with wealth came refinement both in the arts and at the dinner table. For the most part, food remained plain— fried or roasted meats and game, boiled fish, cider to drink, and hot breads. Involved sauces were frowned upon as Gallic kickshaws and the food of fops. Yet there were large numbers of "cookery books" (most of them British until the publication, in 1796, of *American Cookery*, a forty-seven-page volume by "an American Orphan" named Amelia Simmons), which gave complicated, though less than detailed, recipes for stewed carp in a sauce of claret, anchovies, and shallots thickened with butter and egg yolks; ice creams and purees of fruits; and all manner of pastries. Few Americans of the eighteenth century ever made or even came across such dishes but, it must be stated forcefully, neither did most Europeans. The fallacy of European taste and elegance lies in its microcosmic scope; it involved no more than a small percentage of the population and focused on only two classes of people: the gentry and the nouveau riche. Nevertheless, tables set by Americans like Thomas Jefferson easily rivaled in gastronomic interest those presented at the finest dining salons of France or England.

Jefferson's passion for good food was merely an extension of his voracious appetite for knowledge in every form. His experiments in farming and gardening were directly involved with his experiments in cooking, and he was forever fascinated by foreign foods, methods of preparation, and botanical distinctions that affected the flavors of things. He even installed a French chef in the White House, then brought in two African American women to apprentice with the master and learn his techniques. Jefferson brought back a waffle iron from Holland, as well as a pasta machine from Italy, and imported all sorts of plants, fruits, and even olives from Europe. Though criticized by Patrick Henry for renouncing American victuals, Jefferson was not at all interested in turning Monticello into a Virginian Petit Trianon or in turning his back on American food; indeed, he was, in Evan Jones's words, "determined to surround the best of Virginia food with the best from European cuisine." As Jefferson told his friend Lafayette, if a man wishes to learn about French food, he must "ferret the people out of their hovels, as I have done, look into their kettles, eat their bread."

By the nineteenth century American cooking had developed quite naturally along regional lines and European traditions, always modified by the exigencies of the land. Foods that were major items in one region's diet may have been marginal in another's, but Americans did share a certain manner of cooking and eating by the middle of the nineteenth century. The cuisine of New Orleans was easily the most distinctive of all the gathered strains of American cookery, but there were dishes to be found in New England—Joe Froggers, Deacon Porter's hat, rum tum tiddy, Harvard beets, and Parker House tripe, to name a few—unlikely to be encountered in the South, while a South Carolinian spending a week in Vermont would be hard put to find a kitchen serving cooter stew, Lady Baltimore cake, mint juleps, hopping John, or benne brittle.

The farther west settlers trekked, the more culinary cohesion Americans took on, for although the Midwest was settled largely by people of German extraction, who continued making many dishes from the old country, the new territories and broad farms provided such a wealth of grain, fruits, vegetables, and livestock that the whole country began eating much the same diet, still buoyed by copious portions of meat. Barbecue grew out of the South and the Southwest, and there was considerable Mexican influence along the Rio Grande. The food of the pioneers was often horrifying, meant only to keep body and soul, though not appetite, together during the push across the wilderness. The stories of these settlers are harsh, full of tales of starvation and revulsion for a diet that never varied from St. Louis to Oregon. Mostly they ate preserved foods: salt pork, jerky, dried corn, and dried-apple pies. Trappers might make a "butter" from buffalo marrow, blood, and boiling water, while others survived on insects, vultures, and reptiles.

After the Civil War, beef asserted itself as a most desirable alternative to pork, and by the twentieth century "steak and potatoes" had become synonymous with the American diet; at the same time, the American sweet tooth developed with the drop in sugar prices. There were by the end of the nineteenth century lavish restaurants serving the most extravagant meals and bars serving all manner of beers and cocktails to a public that never lacked for ice, while everyone ate at chowder houses, delicatessens, coffeehouses, and tamale stands. Even as far west as Denver, in 1892 a hotel like the Brown Palace could put up a spread that included littleneck clams, consommé renaissance, trout ravigote, Maryland terrapin, German wines, and

French champagne. This was as nothing compared with the meals created in NYC's Delmonico's, Boston's Parker House, or Chicago's Sherman House, where ten-course meals were everyday suppers.

In fact, it was the virtue of such restaurants to bring America into gastronomic repute. They impressed even European visitors who previously had expected the kind of disastrous dining experiences noted by Charles Dickens, who described dinner, supper, and breakfast aboard a Pennsylvania canal boat as identical to one another—tea, coffee, bread, butter, salmon, shad, liver, steak, potatoes, pickles, ham, chops, black puddings, and sausages, all consumed by gentlemen who "thrust the broad-bladed knives and the two-pronged forks farther down their throats than I ever saw the same weapons go before except in the hands of a skillful juggler."

By the same token the opulent restaurants and grand hotels of the Gilded Age focused attention on the gluttonous nature of dining among the newly rich, which led quite naturally to a general criticism of all Americans' eating habits. And the menus of such establishments—fussed up with French dishes and French terminology for American dishes—scorned the food of the common man in an attempt to elevate the status and palate of the American trying desperately to appear civilized.

As a result, regional American cuisine became a subject of homely virtues, expressive of the gracious and genteel traditions of Victorian womanhood. Old recipes for local delicacies were not so much forgotten as ignored, so that the first edition, in 1896, of Fannie Merritt Farmer's extraordinarily successful *Boston Cooking-School Cook Book* contained sensible, well-tested recipes for *potage à la reine, maître d'hôtel* butter, *charlotte russe*, and cutlets *à la Maintenon* (along with hints on how to clean mirrors, remove wine stains, and sweep carpets) and had a three-page glossary composed almost entirely of French terms.

Nothing so relegates a culture to mediocrity as to be thought quaint, and by the beginning of the twentieth century American cookery had entered just such a phase, largely as a reaction to the ways in which the populace had come to enjoy its meals—at beer halls, ballparks, county fairs, on boardwalks, at roadside stands, soda fountains, at lunch counters, at pizzerias, at hash houses, at saloons, at spaghetti joints, and barbecue pits. Food was taken on the run, eaten on park benches, wolfed down at taverns, consumed at beach parties, and all of it was ingested too quickly. Concerns about the health of the population not only led to a reassessment of the nutritive values of foods but also resulted in federal regulations to combat corrupt and sickening practices in the meat and agriculture industries. These concerns ultimately led, with a strident moralism, to Prohibition, which radically altered the manner in which people cooked, ate, and dined out for more than a decade.

The so-called ladies' books had long imitated Victorian hesitancy when describing food in print—rice would be called "farinaceous dishes," and a meal was "a simple repast"—and this tradition continued well into the twentieth century. There was an attempt to ban the use of the term "hot dog" from all vendors' signs in Coney Island, lest people think their frankfurters really contained dog meat. And the vitality of lunch-counter speech—"cat's eyes" for tapioca, "baby" for a glass of milk, "jerk" for ice cream soda, and "Adam and Eve on a raft" for fried eggs on toast—had a raciness about it that many people sought to put an end to in the 1930s.

More profound than any other factor affecting the image of American cookery in the twentieth century was the pervasive influence of immigrants on the culture. The waves of new settlers driven to the American shore were inspired not by a belief that the streets were paved with gold but by sheer, basic hunger. What the Poles, Jews, Italians, Irish, Germans, Armenians, and others found in America was far more valuable than gold: it was a constantly available supply of fruits, fresh water, good grains, green vegetables, annual harvests of plenty, and safe, healthful milk.

The immigrants immediately set about adapting their native cookery to what was available in the American marketplace. Certain vegetables were not readily found here, and the water was different, as were the flour, the butter, the meat, and the wonderful cookstoves (and, by the 1930s, gas and electric stoves, too). These differences altered traditional cooking methods and changed the tastes and textures of their foods.

Lox, so closely associated with Jewish Americans, was unknown to European Jews; the Italian pizza, once a staple of the Neapolitan poor, became an American snack food; *gulyás*, in Hungary a dried meat carried by shepherds, became in America goulash, a kind of peppery stew; chop suey and chow mein came out of the makeshift kitchens of Chinese workers on the western railroads; and wines from native American grapes were labeled "green Hungarian," "Chianti," and "Sauterne."

The culture was immeasurably enriched by the influx of the immigrants, as was the language of our gastronomy: Americans spoke with evident familiarity about beerfests, wieners, bagels, tutti-frutti, hamburgers, Swedish meatballs, ravioli, smorgasbords, Danish pastries, liverwurst, vichyssoise, chow-chow, lager, curry, matzo ball soup, halvah, tortillas, paprika, baklava, moussaka, and sukiyaki, and they visited bodegas, delicatessens, trattorias, sushi bars, taco stands, Greek coffee shops, dim sum parlors, pizzerias, rathskellers, and bistros. All these foods and all these places were transformed into American institutions, for better or for worse. Add to these the extraordinary growth of the processed-food and confections industries, with items like Coca-Cola, Crisco, Sugar Daddy, Eskimo Pie, Cheerios, Grape-Nuts, Pork & Beans, Niblets, and thousands of others, and one begins to sense the dimensions of American gastronomy.

It is, of course, legitimate to suggest that many of these items fall far short of the culinary sublime, or that much of the "ethnic" food on this side of the Atlantic bears scant resemblance to that in the old countries. But such a criticism accepts three erroneous claims:

First, that people in France, Germany, Italy, or China at the turn of the century were eating splendid meals on a daily basis—that a citizen of Bordeaux sat down each evening to a fine coq au vin made with a bottle of excellent claret; that a Sicilian peasant each afternoon enjoyed a steaming plate of macaroni with a rich tomato-and-garlic sauce, followed by fresh mussels and a glass of marsala with dessert; or that a worker in Canton Province regaled his neighbors with a meal of lobster steamed with ground pork or chicken with wild mushrooms.

Second, that the transformation of a dish, especially by Americanized immigrants, is always inferior to the original. Yet, except for certain classic and mannered dishes in French and other gastronomies, there are really very few dishes in the world that have not been modified or radically altered by inventive cooks. In northern Italy, the cooks look down with dyspepsia on the olive-oil-and-garlic-rich cuisine of the South, while the people from one province to another regard the butter and wines of their direct neighbors with disdain. A French cassoulet will have as many variants as there are households in Toulouse, and every Moroccan will argue vociferously that her couscous is the only "authentic" one in her village. (This same form of debate rages among American cooks who consider the alteration of a single ingredient in a southern fried chicken recipe or the use of the wrong kind of cornmeal in a johnnycake tantamount to bona fide heresy and sacrilege.)

Third, that American cuisine is nothing more than the cookery of peasants, dispossessed people, and uneducated amateurs whose foods may taste wholesome, even delicious, but rarely sublime. Such a position is not only snobbish but misses the whole thrust of American cookery—

or any nation's cookery, for that matter. The cuisine of the royal courts, the gentry's manors, and the entrepreneur's town houses is never the cuisine of a country. Fabled dishes—from excesses like tournedos Rossini to glories like *poularde à la périgourdine*—are not to be found simmering in the kettles of French kitchens, but hearty choucroute, aromatic bouillabaisse, and oxtail stew are. For every Carême or Escoffier in France there are a million unheralded home cooks whose cuisine truly carries on the reputation of France over the centuries.

Yet French deluxe cuisine—meaning that prepared only in the greatest, most expensive, and most socially exclusive restaurants—continues as the measure of a country's culinary culture and sophistication, a criterion rigidly promoted by those who own, cook, and dine in such places. The notable restaurants of the nineteenth and early twentieth centuries in America were designed not for an appreciative mass of middle-class eaters—and certainly not for the new immigrant class—but for the wealthy, who did not expect to find on the menu homely dishes like peanut soup, barbecued spareribs, spoon bread, ham with redeye gravy, and fudge cake, much less Polish sausage, manicotti, and Irish soda bread. (To be fair, restaurants like Delmonico's, Rector's, and others offered a wide variety of American game, pies, and desserts, though they were usually described on the bill of fare as "*à la*" this or "*au*" that.) By the turn of the century, hotel restaurants like the Waldorf's Palm Garden had hired tyrannical maîtres d'hôtel like Oscar Tschirky, an ex-busboy who rose to near royalty in NYC society by decreeing who was and was not fashionable in his dining room, which served a menu rife with Gallicisms. A menu of 1904 served to William Howard Taft, then secretary of war, read as follows:

Cocktail aux Huitres, Consommé de Volaille, Printanière, Tortue Verte Claire, Radis Olives Céleri Amandes Salées, Coquilles de Bass à la Virchow, Concombres Marines, Couronne de Ris de Veau avec Champignons Frais, Mignons de Filet de Boeuf à la Cardinalice, Pommes de Terre Sautées en Quartiers, Petits Pois à la Française, Fond d'Artichauts Frais à la Dubarry, Sorbet de Fantasie, Pluviers d'Herbes Rôtis, Gelée de Groseilles Salade Chiffonade, Glaces à la Grenadine, Petits Fours, Fruits, Cigars, Café. [The wines were all French.]

Ironically, the Waldorf could turn out some very "American" meals—dishes like *colombine* of chicken California style, ruddy duck, and the famous Waldorf salad. Even in the French dishes, the chefs used excellent-quality American ingredients, a fact that should not be lost on those current-day practitioners of what is called the New American cuisine, which uses American ingredients and French techniques.

But reputations were not built on serving the kind of food that might just as easily be turned out by immigrant housewives or African American cooks. Interestingly enough, it was the African American cooks who maintained, even in restaurants, the great traditions of southern cuisine in cities like New Orleans, Charleston, Richmond, and Savannah and who kept up the strain of northern cookery in Boston, Philadelphia, and Chicago. None of these cooks, however, were known to anyone except steady customers, who might have called them by their first names. Professional American cooks were known only as "Jimmy" or "Thomas" or "Henry" to their public, and the fame of ethnic cooks in the northern cities was enshrined in the names of the restaurants themselves—Tony's, Haussner's, or O'Brien's, for example. Memoirs of the first half of this century speak of ethnic restaurants with believable affection, but rarely with high regard for the food, except to say that it was cheap, belly-filling, and honestly prepared.

It is significant that of the more than fifty volumes in the American Guide Series published under the Federal Writers' Project during the Depression, only a handful mention the food of a region, and fewer still mention restaurants at all. American cooking was simply not considered worthy of critical scrutiny, even though a work like Irma S. Rombauer's *Joy of Cooking*, which first appeared in 1931 and has gone through several revisions, remains a thorough and authoritative collection of American recipes and kitchen techniques.

American food was looked upon as rib-sticking, plain, sometimes wholesome, sometimes not, fun to eat, fast to eat, and never anything to be fussed with or over. Writers took true delight in exalting the lowliest of sandwiches, the greasiest of meats, the hottest of preparations, and the gloppiest of desserts with a kind of deliberate thumb-to-the-nose attitude that only hardened the opinions of gastronomic critics who believed all along that Americans reveled in bad taste. Or, as Henry Miller wrote, Americans would eat garbage if you put ketchup on it. We Americans prided ourselves on the number of hot dogs we could eat, the amount of candy we could consume, the heat of the peppers we could abide, and the time in which we could devour all of it. None of these achievements was likely to build a national reputation for gastronomic excellence.

At the same time, Americans were being taunted by one of the most unreasonable and baffling forms of temperance, which sprang not from a nutritional argument but, for the most part, from a religious one. We are the only people in the world who, possibly because of our abundance, have been made to feel guilty about our good fortune. In a mild form this self-recrimination is evident in the pangs of conscience a person feels when he goes off his diet and in the ridiculous way chocolate is described as "devil's food," especially considering that other cultures call chocolate the "food of the gods" (*Theobroma* in the Linnaean system), and rich desserts are described as "sinfully delicious." Clearly it was the duty of American religious crusaders to point out the sins of dissolution that result from too much wine, spirits, and extravagant food, but this was far more a position of the established English and German religions than of the new immigrant faiths.

Nevertheless, the passage of the Volstead Act in 1919 only ostensibly cut off most Americans from the enjoyment of wine and spirits (and actually led to more crime, corruption, and "sin") while severely crippling an already struggling wine industry in California, New York, and other states. To survive such a blow, vineyard owners turned to raisin production and selling grape juice for jams and jellies.

Prohibition also destroyed any possibility that American restaurants would develop a reputation for fine dining, much less a distinctive cuisine based on American fare. Even the first-class speakeasies of the era were not places one went to for great food. As Michael and Ariane Batterberry note in their book *On the Town in New York* (1973), "the depressing truth was that New Yorkers could not be enticed into a dry restaurant, no matter how superior the food; on the other hand, they seemed perfectly content to eat sawdust as long as it came with a drink."

The era of the grand banquets and twelve-course meals had vanished, too, as did Delmonico's and Louis Sherry, two of the outstanding restaurants of pre–World War I days. Ethnic restaurants—tellingly referred to as "joints"—provided the cities with considerable liveliness, and the speakeasies provided gossipmongers with a new "café society" to write about.

After Prohibition ended, in 1933, there was no scramble to restore the opulent dining of the past, though the enjoyment of good food was considerably more enjoyable now that wine and spirits were again available. Major cities began to nurture truly fine restaurants, like NYC's Le Pavillon, which opened in 1941, but again, most of these were French or described by a new word—*continental*. Continental restaurants aimed to please everyone's palate, serving up a mélange of dishes that ranged from filet mignon and clams casino to striped bass *à la meunière*, beef Wellington, and baked Alaska, usually with an emphasis on French and Italian items. This approach to menu planning was precisely what gourmets might have expected from inferior kitchens, and too often the results were as expected.

If a restaurant was not dishing out such international approximations of authentic classics, it was busy gearing everything, including the food and service, to a "theme," created so that people who felt uneasy about ordering a meal at a fancy, formal restaurant, where one had to dress and act in a certain way, could casually enter dining rooms that were decorated like pirates' coves, Wild West saloons, colonial taverns, or Roman temples, where all the waiters were dressed appropriately to the idea and where the food was described in the most expressive prose since *Euphues*. The most extravagant of such eateries were run by NYC's Restaurant Associates, which could certainly turn out good meals on occasion but did so according to a "concept." Thus, at the Forum of the Twelve Caesars, the menu was in Latin (with English subtitles), dishes were named after Cleopatra and Nero, and there were even barbaric puns on notable American dishes like Caesar salad ("The Noblest Caesar of Them All").

The theme concept was quickly adopted throughout the country, and one never quite knew what to expect when one walked through the swinging doors of a restaurant called the Auto Pub or Long John Silver's; certainly one's gustatory expectations were not very high.

Restaurants with a superb view of the city became faddish by the 1970s; some dining rooms even revolved atop bank buildings as customers wolfed down plates of "Mile-High Pie." Waiters themselves were encouraged to become so friendly as to announce their first name to customers, whether or not the customer wanted to know it. This practice expressed a democratic spirit of such insecurity that implicit in the act was the common understanding that having a swell time was more important than having a great meal. What did it matter if the fish had been frozen and cooked by microwave, or that the entire entrée had been packaged in a New Jersey processing plant and merely needed to be heated up in order to serve a customer a perfectly proportioned meal, complete with bright green beans and bright orange carrots and a rim of powdered mashed potatoes caressing the veal Parmesan?

The advent of frozen foods in the 1940s and 1950s made life easier and, to be sure, offered a new diversity of food items to a large number of people. The labor involved in cooking was reduced, and the guesswork and worry over a poorly wrought meal were removed. Another advance was "instant" foods—powdered puddings, potatoes, and cereals, prepackaged pancake batter, vegetables sealed in plastic pouches, and other less than delectable but wholly efficient preparations that seized the American imagination and made convenience a virtue far outweighing matters of taste and flavor.

Yet for all the criticism of such foods (and of an agricultural industry that propagated fewer varieties but hardier breeds of fruits and vegetables), the next phase of frozen, instant, and packaged foods was even worse: "gourmet dishes," such as fettuccine Alfredo, asparagus with hollandaise sauce, and "Oriental" vegetables. The final blow to American taste came with the plethora of diet foods, which were either traditional processed foods made with less sugar, oil, or syrup or smaller portions of the same old stuff. "Organic" and "natural" foods had no definitions or regulations by which to judge them, yet they sold at a higher price than other food. By the 1990s nutritional terrorists had begun haranguing Americans into believing that most of what they consume on an everyday basis is going to kill them—sooner or later.

It is no wonder, then, that American food deserved the hard knocks it took in the first half of the twentieth century. Indeed, Americans after World War II seemed proud of their so-called junk food, which at first meant snacks, candies, and other less than nutritious items but came to encompass "fast foods" sold at roadside stands usually run by nationwide chains. Several such operations have specialized in some of the more obvious items in the American kitchen—hamburgers, hot dogs, fried chicken, french-fried potatoes, apple pie, and ice cream—serving them lickety-split from assembly lines of griddles and deep fryers at the hands of patently chummy young people in standardized uniforms. Cheap, casual, and geared for ingestion of product rather than the pleasure of dining, these places reduced the flavor of such foods to the point where Henry Miller's comment about drowning the original taste with sweet-and-sour condiments began to make sense.

More disturbing was the fact that small, family-owned restaurants, where such food was traditionally made according to old recipes, were being nudged aside in favor of the fast-food eateries, so that even American institutions like the diner and the cafeteria, where excellent American fare could be had, found it difficult if not impossible to compete with the fast-food places' prices and "fun atmosphere."

The reaction to all this was the development of a culinary elitism that once again pronounced the excellence of French, Italian, and Asian cuisines and the horrid state of American gastronomy.

Even a charming Boston woman named Julia Child enjoyed a long run on public television showing Americans how to cook not turkey with stuffing, clam chowders, or scrod, but *rôti de porc poêlé*, *canard à l'orange*, and *choux de Bruxelles*. Credit must be given to such a television program and to Mrs. Child for relieving the inferiority complex American cooks had about French food and complex cooking processes in general. Her tone was typically Yankee and refreshingly reassuring, and she taught a generation how to care about excellent ingredients and attention to detail. And in her TV series in the 1980s, Child did feature American cooking and championed California wines.

There also appeared in the 1970s a number of works by authors who began seriously to restore traditional American fare to its proper perspective. James Beard, Craig Claiborne, James Villas, and Waverley Root spoke with authority and great affection of their childhood memories of catfish, Dungeness crab, pork barbecue, grits, blueberry bread, hot chilies, New England boiled dinner, Pacific oysters, potato salad, and scores of other delectables that many people had forgotten could be so very good when prepared with care and love and served with those same homely virtues.

At the same time, food magazines like *Gourmet*, *Cuisine*, and *Food & Wine* began devoting more space to American cookery, and even the Culinary Institute of America, a cooking school in Hyde Park, New York, long devoted to continental cuisine, opened a separate course of study on American food.

The publication, in 1970, of Time-Life's beautifully produced *Foods of the World* included seven volumes on regional American cookery, which gave the food a legitimacy of the kind afforded French, Italian, and Japanese cuisines. Well written, gorgeously illustrated, and full of well-tested, explicit recipes, these volumes on regional cooking—New England, Creole and Acadian, Northwest, Eastern Heartland, Southern Style, Great West, and the Melting Pot— showed just how diverse this nation's cookery is. They revealed the wealth of tradition and history behind each dish and a people's pride in every preparation.

Scores of other authoritative regional cookbooks began to appear in the 1980s, ranging from specific books on a single item like chili or cheesecake to thick volumes of recipes, some compiled by women's organizations throughout the U.S., others from historic recipe collections, in an attempt to puzzle out the culinary archetype of a dish. As a result, many excellent histories of American food and drink began to appear, at first fairly general and written by journalists, then highly specific and written by scholars. Indeed, the subject of American food, until then never a serious academic pursuit, exploded in interest by the end of the decade, first at colleges like Vassar, which collected thousands of cookbooks for its special collections, then throughout universities wherein culinary history became a major topic for Ph.D. dissertations and university presses.

Cookbooks came to dominate the self-help sections of newspapers' bestseller lists, and American novelists began filling their pages with anecdotal food stories. Julia Child not only became the subject of several biographies but was even the subject of a Hollywood romantic comedy.

So, too, wine—once an arcane subject among a tiny body of American connoisseurs—flared into prominence, so that every newspaper hired or syndicated a wine columnist, while publications like *Wine Advocate* and *Wine Spectator* gained amazing clout in the marketplace, helping to change Americans' former ignorance about wine into a form of gamesmanship and investment. Wine auctions boomed, even for American labels, which garnered international reputations, boosted by wine writers and recorded in narratives and encyclopedias with the same care and devotion to accuracy given the vineyards of Bordeaux and Burgundy. Things seemed to be on the right track again.

Since the first edition of this book appeared, in 1983, American restaurants have garnered worldwide bragging rights, the American marketplace has absorbed thousands of new foods from every corner of the globe, the American farmer is now raising everything from kiwifruit to foie gras, and the American consumer has become far more sophisticated and demanding about the quality, availability, and safety of his or her food. And finally, the FDA has put some meaning and muscle into monitoring and defining what goes into our processed foods.

As ever, but even more so now, American food is diversified, modified, substantial, complex, heterogeneous, subtle, humdrum, exciting, excessive, embracing, soul-warming and stomach-filling, hot, cold, prepared with honesty, concocted with audacity, promoted with passion, consumed with courage, debated with conviction, tossed in a pot, simmered in a kettle, fried in a skillet, chilled in a bowl, shaken in a canister, brewed in an urn, topped off, tossed out, shoved down, pushed aside, got through, held up, jiggled at the end of a pole, brought down with an arrow, skinned with a knife, tested with a finger, squeezed with a hand, sniffed at, cursed at, argued over, and beloved by a people who will try anything once.

What is American food?

It is this—

A GUIDE

TO THE ENCYCLOPEDIA

NO ONE EVER starts writing an encyclopedia of anything believing it will be a complete record of its subject. Even a compiler of known facts on Etruscan art hopes that tomorrow a new shard of pottery will be unearthed that will add to or alter his work in small but important ways. The subject of a country's food, more than most others, is as inexhaustible as language itself, for each generation renames, reworks, and reevaluates the culture that produced it, discarding some prejudices and reinforcing others. Two of the most American of American animals—the buffalo and the turkey—were misnamed from the start (the American buffalo is really a bison, and the turkey was confused with a guinea fowl brought from Turkey), yet we retain their appellations proudly. Other foods go through so many mutations that they bear scant resemblance to the original.

No county worth its salt has fewer than six different names for the same kind of regional fish, all of which differ from the next locality's names for the same creature. And what Yankees refer to as a "partridge" is really a ruffed grouse, while a southerner who points out a "partridge" is really indicating a quail. The American who calls a sweet potato a "yam" has never seen a true yam.

Language is consistent only in its mutability, as is the food and drink we eat, celebrate, and argue over. A Texan would never dream of letting a kidney bean near the chili, but a midwesterner couldn't imagine chili without a whole mess of beans. (A "mess," incidentally, may mean a lot of food sloppily thrown together, but an older usage denotes nothing more than an assemblage of people eating together or a portion of food.)

Etymologists will argue forever about the true origins of "martini" (indeed, the word "cocktail" itself is still under linguistic scrutiny), the exact derivation of "Harvard beets," the root of the name "calas" for the deep-fried rice cakes of New Orleans, and the way "doughboys" got their nickname. Who can say just when the old usage of "truck farm," meaning a fresh-produce market, took on the contemporary usage of the farm on which the produce sold at market is grown? Why and when did Americans show a preference for "hot dogs" over "weenies," or "bar" over "saloon"?

My aim in this encyclopedia is to demonstrate both the array of American food, wine, and drink and the way Americans speak of it, consume it, and have changed it over the centuries. In each case I have tried to answer the questions I myself would ask were I looking for information on an apple or a tamale, a brief history of Prohibition, or a slang term for a "bartender." I have endeavored to include as much as possible about American gastronomy, and, thanks to the input of so many readers of the first edition, this fifth edition is far more comprehensive.

More important than all-inclusiveness is accuracy, and I hope that my research has been fruitful enough to turn up the best information and the most reliable anecdote on a particular subject, although I have been quick to point out when this or that story is mere legend. Sometimes a story is so enjoyable it begs for inclusion, even with my strong reservations about its veracity.

While I regret any errors or omissions, I welcome corrections and addenda from the reader, and I fully expect to hear what I hope will be sympathetic words from people all over the country who can enlighten me as to the precise origin of a dish or the only correct way to mix a drink. It was a waitress in a NYC bar who called to tell me what seems the most reasonable explanation of the slang term "eighty-six" after etymologists for decades had failed to produce a satisfactory one.

This volume is not a history of gastronomy or of the American language, nor is it a cookbook. It assuredly is not a manual instructing the reader in how best to skin a rabbit or skim a broth. There are several books available on each of these subjects. This encyclopedia contains elements of all of them, gathered into a survey, from A to Z, of the origins, changes, and current status of food and drink items, terms of culinary interest, and slang.

Although my own background is academic and journalistic, my approach has been to inform the general reader in as readable and entertaining a way as possible. I have, therefore, kept abbreviations to a minimum and discarded footnotes in favor of giving full credit in the body of the text or in the Bibliographic Guide and the acknowledgments. While I hope every sentence makes a good point, I sometimes cannot resist an anecdote that I believe the reader will enjoy.

My dependence on the work of others who have labored for a lifetime in the fields of etymology and linguistics has been enormous, and I take scant credit for illuminating dark corners where others' lights have failed to find a convincing explanation. I merely suggest what seems to me plausible and then throw it open for discussion with the reader. I stand humbly in the shadow of H. L. Mencken, who wrote in the preface to his second supplement to *The American Language* (1948), "I am not trained in linguistic science, and can thus claim no profundity for my book. It represents gatherings, not of an expert in linguistics, but simply of a journalist interested in language, and if there appears in it any virtue at all it is with the homely virtue of diligence. Someone had to bring together the widely scattered field material and try to get some order and coherence into it, and I fell into the job."

Main Entries

Main entries are listed alphabetically, sometimes as a general heading for a type of food or drink. Under the more general topics—for example, **APPLE**, **BEER**, **PANCAKE**—there may very well be dozens of more specific terms, types, species, regional variants, slang phrases, or ancillary items within the body of the entry. The reader is urged to check the index for an item not found as a main entry. Within the main entries, a subitem may be printed in **boldface**, indicating that there is further information on that subject as a main entry.

Recipes

The recipes that follow a main entry's description of an item are chosen in most cases to be *representative* of a dish or item; the directions have deliberately been kept simple and brief. In some cases the source of a recipe is cited, especially if it is of historical importance or if it is the original source of the dish or drink. Recipes from an original source are always thus credited, as, for example, those for the Parker House roll and the Trader Vic's mai tai are. I have also included recipes from historical sources, either to give a sense of a food's original form or because such dishes are rarely, if ever, made anymore. Hartshorn jelly, for instance, was a well-known eighteenth-century confection, but as it is unlikely to be found today, I have provided an eighteenth-century recipe and noted the origin.

By a "representative" recipe I mean one that seems close to the way in which such a dish is usually made. I am well aware that there may be hundreds of variations on a "classic" recipe, but I have tried to choose the one that represents the principal ingredients and method of preparation that would be used by a wide range of cooks. I have not tried to choose the *best* recipe I've ever found for a specific dish, for the reason that it may very well *not* be representative of the way Americans cook. (Recipes for some of the finest desserts, pastries, and cookies I know come from several cookbooks written by Maida Heatter, but they often do not represent the way most American cooks would prepare an item; rather, they demonstrate the unique and imaginative talents of this singularly remarkable woman.)

Many readers may find the recipes stingy with details and not specific enough in comparison with many cookbooks that lead the reader by the apron strings, explaining everything from how to peel a carrot to how to beat an egg. I have assumed that the user of this book possesses a certain culinary acumen—as did his or her ancestors, who cooked by very simple directions— and I simply did not have the space to include instructions on how to whip an egg white to "soft, glistening peaks" every time such a preparation was called for. So, too, if a cooked-sugar recipe calls for bringing the caramel to a "hard-ball" or "soft-ball" stage, the reader is assumed to be familiar with such terms but is nevertheless provided with a temperature to test for on a candy thermometer. The details of making a dough and letting it rise in bulk are kept to a minimum, and often I will instruct the reader only to make a pastry crust, rather than tell again how to make one.

This is not a book on nutrition, and I have tried to keep clear of arguments for or against the "healthfulness" of this or that dish or spirit. Nor is this an industry manual meant to contain hints on how best to cut, package, and store meat, fish, or fowl.

One rule I do advise the reader to follow with these recipes is to pay attention to the order in which ingredients are listed, for the order indicates at what point they should be added to a preparation. Although in many cases the addition of several spices or seasonings at once is justified. I have attempted to indicate the moment at which the next ingredient should be added, and it is best to blend each new addition thoroughly before putting in the next one. Cooks more or less familiar with the routine of such matters will know when this is important or not.

As for the terminology of cooking, I have conservatively adhered to level teaspoons and standard measurements in ounces and pounds, and avoided old-fashioned instructions like "add a wineglass of" such and such. On the other hand, I see no reason to be stringently specific about what constitutes a dash or a pinch, long-honored terms that make sense to anyone who cooks regularly. (There is an apocryphal story about Fannie Merritt Farmer giving instructions on making a martini that go "To one cup gin, add...")

The recipes themselves come from a wide variety of sources from three centuries of American cookery, but the bulk come from cookbooks of the past thirty years, for it is impossible to gauge the success factor of a recipe from an era when flour, yeast, molasses, baking powder, wine, spirits, and even ovens were very different from what they have become in the past quarter century. (Baking powder, for example, came along only in the 1850s.) Despite the prejudice of those who believe that cookbooks of the eighteenth and nineteenth centuries represent American culinary arts at their highest, there is really no way to reproduce recipes that call for ingredients like isinglass, pearl ash, and sack. Others would shudder at the thought of my including recipes from "ladies' magazines," because such journals often try to oversimplify or change recipes to suit some imaginary housewife who has access only to processed and packaged foods. The point is well taken, especially since many of these magazines depend on the advertising of the very products they recommend in a recipe. But if one is to compile an encyclopedia of gastronomy that tells the reader how Americans actually do cook and eat, such recipes play an important part. I have, for the record, never recommended margarine where butter is preferred, but it may be argued that Americans cook with far more margarine and shortening than butter. So, too, have I avoided brand names of products, except where they seem an intrinsic part of a recipe—Tabasco sauce, for example.

I claim no originality in any of these recipes—that would defeat the whole point of the book—and I have tried to cull workable recipes from reliable sources and to stay clear of arguments as to the "correct" method of preparing a dish. "Correct" methods are usually those that an individual believes to be the best method or those derived from a recipe of antique interest. American cookery has very few "classic" recipes; even those that originated at a specific place and time have been changed, sometimes for the worse, often for the better. That is the role of a good cook, for absolute imitation is the drudgery of the slave or the pedant.

Biographies

This is the first edition of the *Encyclopedia* to include biographies of important figures in American food and drink. My basic criterion for inclusion was this question: if this person had never lived, or died tomorrow, would American gastronomic history be significantly different?

Certain figures were obvious choices—Fannie Merritt Farmer, James Beard, Julia Child, and many others. Others may be unfamiliar to the general reader but were of exceptional importance in the development of American food and drink, including Luther Burbank, George Washington Carver, and Konstantin Frank. I hope the reader will discover the reasons for their inclusion after reading their bios. In other cases, such as Ernest Hemingway, Upton Sinclair, and M. F. K. Fisher, all of whom wrote about food and wine as topics ancillary to other cultural concerns, their effect on the way we think, enjoy, and write about food are indelible.

Readers might argue about the exclusion of so many contemporary celebrity chefs (although several, like Emeril Lagasse, Rick Bayless, and Mario Batali are included) who appear constantly at food and wine festivals and on their own TV shows. If I have sinned on the side of including those individuals who I believe have made an impact during a long career over those who are often more media stars, however fleeting, than enduring contributors to American food culture, I simply propose that time will tell, and perhaps a future edition of this encyclopedia will reassess their contributions.

What Is and Is Not Included

As I have indicated, there is no workable definition of what constitutes American cuisine. Most American dishes are essentially variations or derivatives, which is true of almost every dish in the world. "The discovery of a new dish is more beneficial to humanity than the discovery of a new star," wrote Anthelme Brillat-Savarin (who rather liked American food when he visited here in 1794), but every new dish is really a variation on an old one. Anyone who has ever paged through Escoffier's *Le Guide Culinaire* will immediately be struck by the minor modifications of one dish that allow it to be called something entirely different. The same is true of *Larousse Gastronomique*, in which one finds that the addition of one standard sauce or another to poached chicken deserves a new appellation and brief cooking instructions.

Certain dishes and drinks indisputably originated in America: Key lime pie, corn bread, bourbon, fudge, and hundreds of others. Other dishes, like jambalaya, gumbo, beignets, and much of the cuisine of the Creoles and Cajuns, were derived from European, Caribbean, Indian, and African sources but were then turned into distinctive American foods. Beverages like shrubs, flips, grogs, and punches became popular in Great Britain and America at the same time, while turkey, buffalo, and numerous species of fish were exported to Europe, where they became delicacies.

I have been liberal in my choices of what to include, but I believe I have good reasons to keep many items out. While it may be true that the Bloody Mary cocktail was created in

Paris in the 1920s (when it was called the "Bucket of Blood"), the drink caught on here, not there, and has remained a standard American bar item since the 1930s. On the other hand, even though Americans drink more Scotch than any other people outside Britain, the fact is that by law Scotch is produced only in Scotland and has no business being in an encyclopedia of American gastronomy.

The real problem develops when one deals with the foods brought over by the immigrants of the late nineteenth and early twentieth centuries. (Fifty years from now, it will be interesting to see how many Korean, Vietnamese, and Thai dishes have become standard menu items here.) What is the rationale for including dishes like veal parmigiana or chili con carne or vichyssoise? These three are easily defensible: there is no dish in Italy by the name veal parmigiana (much less "veal Parmesan"); chili con carne is a Texas dish, frowned upon by most Mexicans; and vichyssoise was created at NYC's Ritz-Carlton hotel dining room by chef Louis Diat, who named it after a French spa. Such dishes are simply inspired by Italian, Mexican, or French notions.

Other ethnic foods have been so transformed over the years that they bear scant resemblance to their ancestral origins. Read, for example, the bewildering difference between the recipe given for *filets de sole Marguery* in *Larousse Gastronomique*, supposedly provided by the original chef, and that attributed to George Rector Jr., who brought the recipe back from France for the delectation of "Diamond Jim" Brady and, afterwards, for the approval of generations of American cooks. The original recipe for fettuccine Alfredo—ubiquitous here, rarely found in Italy by this name—contains no cream at all, which in America is the main ingredient. English muffins are never called by that name in England. And "french fries" refers not to potatoes as invented by some Frenchman, but to the way in which they are sliced, or "frenched."

My rule of thumb, then, with regard to such transformed dishes has been to include them if they have really been changed over the years by American cooks or if they have become so popular here as to be immediately identifiable by the majority of Americans. Certain items are so associated with the people of a region—such as Cornish pasties, with the miners of Michigan— that to exclude them would be to omit one of the dishes that help define a place's gastronomic character. The same would be true of many Pennsylvania Dutch or Moravian items, delicacies of New Orleans, or dishes of NYC's Jews.

By the same token, I cannot in good conscience include foreign dishes that may still be prepared in the traditional way for special feasts among a certain group of people. My wife, for instance, prepares traditional Russian foods at Easter, but none of them—such as the tall cake called *kulich* or the pot cheese dessert called *paskha*—has been Americanized, nor are they known outside of the Russian families that still make them in this country. So, too, Czech families in this country may still make *Brněnský řízek*, Greeks their *entrada*, Austrians their *haussulz*, and Japanese their *kyogashi*, but these foods are still uncommon, especially among second- or third-generation ethnic Americans.

As for drinks and cocktails, I have tried to list those that are well known today or that have some historic interest. These would include everything from Coca-Cola and Gatorade to the numerous slang terms for coffee and the various kinds of beer and alcoholic beverages enjoyed both regionally and nationally, such as mint juleps, screwdrivers, and Manhattans. I have avoided listing alcoholic concoctions that seem to have been invented and forgotten almost in the same night. As far as I have been able, I have traced the origins of these drinks and provided recipes according to current tastes, with notes on how such beverages might have changed through the decades.

Last, I have no intention of declaring my own fondness or antipathy for certain dishes or terms, nor do I ever want to get in between two southerners debating the right way to make hush puppies. Even though I will never understand all the fuss about chicken-fried steak or grits, I happily include them here. As someone who grew up on Bronx egg creams, I can understand others' astonishment that such a confection could have inspired so many New Yorkers to praise it.

If it's true—and it is—that we are what we eat, then what is included here is all about what we are.

Acronyms Used

ATF: Bureau of Alcohol, Tobacco, Firearms and Explosives

DARE: *Dictionary of American Regional English*

FDA: Food and Drug Administration

IACP: International Association of Culinary Professionals

NYC: New York City

OED: *Oxford English Dictionary*

USDA: United States Department of Agriculture

ABALONE (genus *Haliotis*). Any of a variety of univalve gastropods having an ear-shaped shell. The name is from the Spanish *abulón*, was introduced into English in 1850, and in 1883 appeared in George Brown Goode's *Fisheries and Fishery Industries of the United States*. There are about a hundred species of abalone in the world, eight of which inhabit the waters off the Pacific coast; they are pried from the rocks they attach themselves to and commercially harvested in California and to a lesser extent in Washington. All species are edible, but the flesh is rubbery and must be pounded. Abalone is usually dredged with flour and sautéed in butter. The main American species are "black abalone" (*Haliotis cracherodi*), "green abalone" (*H. fulgens*), "pink abalone" (*H. corrugata*), "red abalone" (*H. rufescens*), "white abalone" (*H. sorenseni*), "flat abalone" (*H. walallensis*), "threaded abalone" (*H. assimilis*), and "pinto abalone" (*H. kamtschatkana*).

Overfishing, illegal harvesting, and loss of habitat have led to commercial farming of abalone, principally in Southeast Asia, which constitutes the majority of abalone sold. Since 1993, only red abalone is allowed to be taken. After a heyday in the 1970s, when 2.5 million pounds of abalone were landed, the wild catch has declined greatly. The gastropod is also farmed in the U.S., in Hawaii, Alaska, and California, where abalone has been farmed since the 1850s.

ABERDEEN ANGUS. Also "angus" or "black angus." A breed of red beef cattle originally bred in Scotland (the name, first in print in 1839, comes from two counties in northeastern Scotland, Aberdeen and Angus), where they were called "doddies" or "humlies." Four of the steers were brought by George Grant to Victoria, Kansas, in 1873 and initially used only as a crossbreed, but the angus quickly replaced the longhorn as a beef steer. In 1978, the American Angus Association (founded in 1883) set up the Certified Angus Beef brand to promote the idea that such beef was of a very high quality, comparable to the best USDA-approved grades. To be eligible for the brand, cattle must meet ten criteria, including: the animal must be at least 51 percent black and exhibit Angus influence, have a modest or higher degree of marbling, and have medium or fine marbling texture.

ABSINTHE. A green cordial derived from wormwood (*Artemisia absinthium*). Absinthe is anise-flavored and rather bitter and has a proof of 136. It was originally promoted as a stomach tonic by French doctor Pierre Ordinaire in Neuchâtel, Switzerland, in 1792, and was popularized by Henri-Louis Pernod in about 1797. Its first appearance in English was in 1804. Its alcohol content by volume ranges from 90 to 148 **proof**.

The drink was reputed to have aphrodisiacal qualities and became extremely popular among bohemian artists in the late nineteenth century in Europe and in New Orleans, which came to be known as the absinthe capital of the world and where the liqueur was known under brand names such as Green Opal, Herbsaint, and Milky Way. It became a standard ingredient in many New Orleans **cocktails**, such as the **Sazerac**. One of the city's most famous restaurants was called the Old Absinthe House, opened by bartender Cayetano Ferrer in 1874.

Absinthe was usually diluted by dripping it through a perforated spoon containing a sugar cube and then dripping water, which turned the liqueur cloudy, through the absinthe.

At the turn of the century, wormwood was discovered to have harmful effects on people's health and to be habit-forming. Belgium banned the sale of absinthe in 1905, and after a celebrated trial in 1906 of a Swiss farmer, Jean Lanfray, who was said to have murdered his wife and children under the influence of absinthe, the Swiss legislature banned the drink in 1910. The U.S. followed with its own ban in 1912. Absinthe was replaced in cocktails by anise or other licorice-like flavors. But in the 1990s the liqueur had a revival in countries like Great Britain that had never banned it and in those, like Belgium and Switzerland, that had again made it legal; in France the ban was repealed in May 2011. The U.S. Alcohol and Tobacco Tax and Trade Bureau lifted the ban in 2007.

OLD ABSINTHE HOUSE FRAPPÉ

Mix 1 T. Herbsaint or Pernod with a dash of anisette and pour into a small, thin glass filled with crushed ice and water; let the mixture get very cold and serve. (The absinthe frappé may be served without the anisette. Some add the white of an egg.)

ABSINTHE SUISSESSE

Combine 1 ½ oz. Herbsaint or Pernod with 2 T. cream, 1 T. orgeat syrup, 1 egg white, and crushed ice and shake (or mix in an electric blender) until completely blended. Pour the unstrained liquid into a chilled glass.

ACHIOTE. The hard seed of the annatto tree (*Bixa orellana*), whose red berry is pounded into a powder or made into a paste for its mild, earthy flavor. It is also used as a coloring for butter. The word, first appearing in English in 1648, is from Spanish, derived from Nahuatl *achiotl*.

ACORN. A hard-shelled nut, the fruit of an oak tree, that in some varieties can be poisonous. The word is from Old English *aecern*.

Acorns are rarely eaten today, but they were once an important food of Native Americans. Of the sixty species of oak in America, twenty-seven yielded acorns that were eaten by about half the Indians in North America and that provided California Indians with a staple of their diet. Because of their bitter, sometimes poisonous character, the acorns were cracked with a hammer, ground up with a mortar and pestle, and then leached in a stream by rinsing with several changes of water. They were then often boiled or roasted.

ACORN SQUASH. A native American acorn-shaped **squash** weighing between one and two pounds, measuring four to seven inches in length, with a dark-green-and-orange-streaked fluted rind. Sometimes called a "Des Moines squash," this American winter fruit was long favored by Native Americans. The name first appeared in American print in 1924.

ADAM'S ALE. Slang for "water." A colloquialism, dating in print to 1643, based on the biblical assumption that the only drink Adam had was water; this term is often heard in soda fountains and as **lunch counter** slang.

ADAMS, LEON D. (1905–1995). Author. One of the earliest historians of the American wine industry, Leon D. Adams founded the trade organization the Wine Institute.

Born in Boston, Adams studied at the University of California at Berkeley and afterward wrote for newspapers in the Bay Area, including the *San Francisco Bulletin*. Adams believed that wine should be inexpensive and a civilizing beverage; he wrote *The Commonsense Book of Wine* (1958) for the general public.

His comprehensive survey of U.S. wine history, *The Wines of America* (1973), was widely hailed as the most important ever published on the subject, especially since it came at a time when California wineries in particular were gaining a justified reputation for quality. The book went through four editions; in its second edition (1978), Adams wrote, "When the wine revolution began a little over a decade ago, many considered it merely a fad because it resembled in many ways the fads of the past that swept across the nation and soon faded away. Today wine is being recognized as an integral, wholesome new part of the national diet. After four centuries during which Americans dined without wine, it is finally here to stay."

Throughout his life, Adams was a strong advocate for farm winery laws that would allow grape growers to run wineries and sell their wines at wholesale and retail, which was often restricted by local governments.

He founded the Society of Medical Friends of Wine, which helped promote wine's health benefits, and the Wine Advisory Board, funded by California's wineries to provide marketing research and advertising services for producers.

Adams died of heart failure at the age of ninety.

ADDITIVE. Any substance added either directly or indirectly to a food product. About twenty-eight hundred substances, ranging from vitamins to preservatives, are added directly, while more than ten thousand—including pesticides used on growing plants, drugs added to animals' diets, and chemicals from wrapping materials—enter indirectly.

Most of the time, the term refers to those substances added directly and intentionally for a wide variety of reasons that include: (1) Maintaining freshness by adding nitrites and sodium nitrates to protect cured foods from bacterial toxins such as botulin. Antioxidants such as butylated hydroxyanisole (BHA) help prevent discoloration; vitamin C keeps peaches from turning brown. (2) Maintaining or improving nutritional value by adding vitamins, iodine (to salt), and other minerals. Often this is done after processing has already removed many of the same nutrients from a food item like bread. (3) Making food more appealing to the eye by adding coloring agents. (4) Making food tastier by adding natural or synthetic flavors, enhancers such as **monosodium glutamate** (MSG), various sweetening agents such as **sugar**, **corn syrup**, and **saccharin**, or just plain **salt** and **pepper**. (5) Aiding processing and preparation by adding emulsifiers to give consistent texture, thickeners to prevent the formation of ice crystals.

In recent years there has been a great deal of concern about food additives, and **health food** zealots damn them all without considering the virtues of or necessity for some. Many harmless additives add immeasurably to the appearance, freshness, and edibility of food items, and the availability of certain foods year-round is due to the preserving additives that have revolutionized the marketplace throughout the world and made scarcity far less severe than it might be. The first governmental attempts to oversee food additives came with the 1906 Pure Food and Drug Act, followed by the Food, Drug, and Cosmetic Act of 1938, which helped remove some dangerous and poisonous elements from processed food. In 1958, the Food Additives Amendment established specific laws, bolstered two years later by the color-additive amendments, authorizing the **Food and Drug Administration** (FDA) to monitor and regulate additives for safety, although no power was given the FDA to limit the number of additives in a food or the reasons for their being added. Approval of a new additive comes after a long, thorough process of experimentation, and there is a "100-fold margin of safety" rule that dictates that only $1/100$ of the maximum amount of an additive that has been found *not* to produce any harmful effects in test animals may be used by a manufacturer of a food item. Under the Delaney Clause, no substance that has been shown to cause cancer in man or animal may be added to food in any amount.

Exempt from such tests are what are known as "generally recognized as safe" (GRAS) substances in use before the passage of the amendments, and "prior sanctioned substances" that had already been approved before 1958, although substances in both of these categories are under constant review. Currently, thirty-one color additives are fully approved.

ADOBE BREAD. A bread made by the Pueblo Indians in a beehive-shaped adobe oven called an *horno*. Often meat, vegetables, nuts, or seeds were mixed into the dough, and the bread was frequently shaped like animals indigenous to the Southwest.

ADOBE BREAD

In a small bowl dissolve 1 pkg. yeast in ½ c. warm water to proof. In a large bowl mix 1 c. flour, 2 T. shortening, 1 ½ c. hot water, 2 t. salt, and 2 t. sugar. Mix until well blended, then add the yeast mixture. Blend well, then add 3 c. more flour to make a dough. Knead well. On a pastry board spread out 1 c. flour, place dough on it, and incorporate the flour into the dough. Knead for 10 min. Place in a greased bowl, turn over to grease entire dough, and cover with a towel. Let rise until doubled in bulk. Divide into 2 portions and form into round loaves. Cover again and let rise until doubled in bulk. Bake in an adobe oven or at 350° for 1 hr.

AFRICAN AMERICAN FOOD. A general term for the food brought by African slaves to America as well as the food that African Americans widely cook and have developed since their arrival. Since the 1960s, many African American dishes like **chitterlings** and **collard greens** go by the term **soul food**, but while many foods brought from Africa, like peanuts, sesame seeds, yams, and cowpeas, are part of the general American diet, few soul food dishes are as yet very popular among non–African Americans.

The European and American slave trade that brought Africans to the Americas began soon after the discovery of the New World, drawing mainly from West African regions. Most slaves were used primarily to work on the large plantations in South America, the Caribbean, and the American South, but women and children were soon working as cooks for their owners. At Mount Vernon, George Washington had a slave named Hercules who cooked his master French dishes, and **Thomas Jefferson** promoted his slave cook James Hemings to top positions at Monticello. In Dutch communities, slaves often worked in grist mills and taverns. By the end of the seventeenth century, New York City had more blacks than any other city, and a century later it was second only to Charleston, South Carolina, in this measure. By the end of the colonial period, roughly one out of every five Americans was either an African immigrant or a descendant of one.

While the food provided to the slaves was meager, mostly corn and bacon, some were allowed to raise their own crops and to forage for food. Cravings for fat were barely satisfied by the scraps of poor cuts of meat provided to them, and many continued the custom of geophagy, **dirt** eating, to acquire needed minerals.

Since many of the plantations grew rice, many dishes served in the slave masters' "big houses" were based on that staple, including **hopping john**, made of beans and rice. In her popular cookbook *The Virginia Housewife* (1824), Mary Randolph used many ingredients like field peas, eggplant, and okra that had originated in Africa, as did most nineteenth-century cookbooks to follow.

Some freed slaves opened their own eateries, like Emmanuel "Manna" Bernoon, who opened an oyster-and-ale house in Providence, Rhode Island, as early as 1736. By the beginning of that century most African Americans had been liberated in the North, leading many of them to enter the food service, including one of the most well-regarded caterers of Philadelphia, Robert Bogle, who opened a catering store there in 1812 and whom W. E. B. DuBois called "the butler of the smart set, and his taste and eye for the palate set the fashion for the day." A freeman named Robert Roberts, who said he had been a butler in France and was to become one for the governor of Massachusetts, wrote a highly popular book, *The House Servant's Directory* (1827), based on English service principles.

Upon Lincoln's freeing the slaves with the 1863 Emancipation Proclamation, many African Americans migrated from the South; by 1925 one-fifth of the black population had moved north. In the West, some freemen became cooks for the wagon trains. Black street vendors roamed city streets, including New Orleans, where the sellers were called "Green Sass Men." Free blacks opened their own restaurants, although they catered primarily to the white upper classes, a condition that continued, usually by de facto law, well into the twentieth century. African American cookbooks began to appear after the Civil War, the first being *A Domestic Cook Book: Containing a Careful Selection of Useful Receipts for the Kitchen*, by Malinda Russell, published in 1866 in Paw Paw, Michigan, followed in 1881 by Abby Fisher's *What Mrs. Fisher Knows About Old Southern Cooking*.

Discrimination and segregation followed blacks everywhere, but big-city enclaves, like Harlem in NYC in the 1920s, became crucibles for African American cookery and restaurants, including Harlem nightclubs like the Cotton Club, the Ubangi Club, and Connie's Inn, which featured top black entertainers, semi-nude black dancers, and menus of fried chicken and barbecue, as well as an early-morning dish of chicken and waffles, always to an exclusively white clientele.

Beginning in 1936, the Tuskegee Institute published *Service*, a magazine devoted to the African American food-and-hospitality industry, this at a time when blacks were ubiquitous as waiters, especially on the dining cars of American railways. Caterer Lena Richard's 1939 *Lena Richard's Cook Book* garnered so much attention that it was published internationally a year later as *The New Orleans Cook Book*. By 1946 the African American general interest magazine *Ebony* had hired its first food editor, Freda DeKnight, who stressed nutrition in her columns and later wrote *A Date with a Dish* (1948), still in print as *The Ebony Cookbook*.

For African Americans, the 1950s and 1960s were driven by social protests for civil rights, nowhere more evident than in sit-ins at whites-only lunch counters, famously at a counter in Greensboro, North Carolina, on February 1, 1960, which led to similar sit-ins around the country. Within four years the U.S. would pass the Civil Rights Act, banning discrimination in public accommodations and forcing once segregated restaurants either to serve everyone or be shut down.

It was also at this time that the term **soul food** entered African American speech, referring to the soulful bond among blacks who ate foods like fried chicken, salmon croquettes, black-eyed peas, ham hocks, corn bread, pork chops, collard greens, and sweet potato pie as part of a post–Civil War urban tradition. In 1969, Bob Jeffries wrote in his *Soul Food Cookbook*, "While all soul food is southern food, not all southern food is soul." That same year, Leonard E. Roberts's *The Negro Chef Cookbook* became a bestseller, largely in black communities. Several black restaurateurs, like **Leah Chase**, of Dooky Chase in New Orleans, and Sylvia Woods, of Sylvia's in Harlem, were widely covered by the white food media, and regional African American books like **Edna Lewis**'s *The Taste of Country Cooking* (1976) won critical acclaim and broad readership.

In 1966, Ron "Maulana" Karenga promoted a seven-day feast of African American food culture in a New Year's feast called **Kwanzaa**, based on seven nights of ritual centered on African and American foods.

In the 1980s, a handful of African American cooks began to graduate to the more respected title of chef in top dining rooms, including Patrick Clark at NYC's Tavern on the Green, where he cooked more modern American cuisine; in New Orleans, Lazone Randolph kept the traditions of classic Creole cuisine alive at Brennan's. Ethiopian-born Marcus Samuelsson, adopted by a Swedish family, first achieved recognition for Scandinavian food at the restaurant Aquavit, in NYC, but in 2011 he opened a southern food restaurant called Red Rooster, in Harlem, to great success.

Today, while it has not achieved the popularity of Italian American, Mexican American, or Chinese American cooking, African American food and its culture have become more accepted in the U.S. than ever before, enriched as well by the contributions of black cooks from the Caribbean. As historian **Jessica B. Harris** has written in *High on the Hog: A Culinary Journey from Africa to America* (2011), "With the improvisational genius that gave the world jazz and salsa, as well as rumba, rap, and reggae, [African Americans] have cooked our way into the hearts, minds, and stomachs of a country."

AGAVE. Any of more than three hundred species of plants in the genus *Agave* (family Amaryllkidaceae), its chief species being the American aloe. It is also called "mescal" and "century plant," so named for its long life span (which in fact tops out at thirty or forty years). *Agave*, in New Latin, means "noble," because of the plant's tallness. Its first appearance in English print was in 1830.

Edible species of this fast-growing golden-flowered plant thrive in Arizona, New Mexico, southeastern California, southern Utah, and northern Mexico. The plant was extremely important to the Indians of the Southwest, especially the Mescalero Apache, who held to a lengthy ritual in cooking the agave. The crowns of the plant were carefully placed in a deep pit covered with bear grass and a thick layer of earth, then roasted for about two days, during which the tribe refrained from both drinking and sexual activity. When fully cooked, the centers of the crowns could be eaten immediately or dried in the sun. The leaves were consumed like artichokes or boiled into a syrup. Ground agave would be mixed into a drink.

The Chiricahua Apache referred to blooming agaves as "woman" plants and nonblooming ones as "man" plants.

The agave also makes an alcoholic drink known to both the Indians and the Mexicans, who call the drink *maguey*, *mexca*, or *mescal*. (*Mezcal* is also a name for a candy made from a piece of the barbecued leaf of the agave.)

The fermented pulp of the agave is made into a liquid called *aguamiel*, which is similar to, but not the same as, sotol and **tequila**, made from the "blue agave" (*A. Rigidae tequiliana weber*, var. *azul*), although "mescal" is a general term that covers tequila. In her book *American*

Indian Food and Lore (1974), Carolyn Niethammer wrote that the plant has a "pleasant, sweet flavor," but that it is poisonous if eaten raw. It is best baked or made into a nut butter or syrup.

AGUARDIENTE. A form of Spanish or Mexican brandy, though in the Southwest the term may refer to any strong alcoholic beverage. The word is from the Spanish for "brandy" and first appeared in English in 1818.

ĀHOLE (*Kuhlia sandvicensis*). A silvery large-eyed Hawaiian fish whose name derives from the Hawaiian for "to strip away," because the fish was used to drive away evil spirits. The young *āhole* is called "*āhole-hole*," which first saw print in 1926.

AIRLINE FOOD. The American airline industry has since its earliest days provided some form of food service for passengers. The first airplane to have an actual onboard galley was an American Airlines Douglas DC-3 in 1936. The service of alcohol beverages on board was inaugurated in October 1949 by Northwest Airlines. Most of the food is prepared and usually precooked in large airport kitchens or purchased in frozen form from food-service companies. In regular coach class, the food is usually prepackaged in plastic containers and heated in onboard ovens, although in first class the food may well be cooked and prepared on board. Service in first class can become quite lavish, with linen, fresh flowers, fresh cheeses, and premium wines.

Airlines also offer "special meals," which must be ordered prior to boarding, for vegetarians and others with particular religious dietary restrictions, as with Jews who keep **kosher**. The average amount spent by the airline for coach class food was $5.86 per passenger in 1992, but only $3.03 in 1997, with one airline spending only twenty cents per passenger on domestic travel. Average spending for food per passenger on overseas travel is generally higher.

By the beginning of the twenty-first century and after the 9/11 attack on New York and Washington, with profits dwindling, U.S. airlines largely stopped serving free food on board, though international flights still do. Light items like snacks, as in sandwiches or pastries, are sold on board.

Given the difficulties involved in such mass feeding, airline food has been the consistent butt of many jokes, and in a survey of one hundred thousand frequent fliers, food service was ranked eleventh out of fourteen concerns when people booked a flight. As a result, different airlines spend widely varying amounts of money on their food service.

AKU. Hawaiian name for the red-fleshed **skipjack** tuna (*Katsuwonus pelamis*), considered the region's most important commercial fish, dating in print to 1933.

AKULE (*Selar crumenophthalmus*). A food fish of Hawaii, known on the mainland as "bigeye scad." Hawaiians usually salt and dry the fish. The word first appeared in print in 1902.

ALABAMA SLAMMER. A cocktail popularized at the University of Alabama, made with sloe gin, amaretto, Southern Comfort, and orange juice.

ALBANY BEEF. A nineteenth-century slang term for sturgeon, so called because the specimens taken from the Hudson River near Albany, New York, could weigh up to two hundred pounds. The term was used at least as early as 1779.

ALBÓNDIGA. A meatball flavored with vegetables and served with a sauce. Albóndiga (the name is the same in Spanish) is a popular dish in the Southwest and comes from Mexico. The name dates in English print to a 1923 menu at the Sonora Cafe, in Los Angeles, as "Spanish meatball soup," and as "albondigas" at its offshoot, El Cholo, in 1927. It is almost always used in the plural, "albóndigas."

ALBÓNDIGAS

Combine ½ lb. each of ground pork, beef, and veal, add ½ c. bread crumbs, 1 chopped onion, ½ t. cumin, salt and pepper, and 1 beaten egg. Form into 1 ½-in. balls, roll in flour, and sauté in a skillet until browned. Remove from skillet. Puree 3 chile peppers with ½ c. warm water. In skillet, sauté 1 clove minced garlic, 1 chopped onion, and then the chile puree. Add 2 c. peeled, seeded, chopped tomatoes and sauté for 5 min. Add 1 c. beef stock, season with salt and pepper and ¼ t. sugar, simmer, add meatballs, cook for about 20 min. Serve with rice. Serves 6.

ALE SLIPPER. Also "ale boot" and "ale shoe." A boot-shaped vessel made of copper, cast iron, or tin, used in colonial times to hold heated beverages.

ALGIN. A thickening agent derived from seaweed and used in processed foods to maintain desired texture, first in print in 1883. Propylene glycol alginate thickens soda pop, ice cream, candy, and yogurt and stabilizes the foam in beer.

ALLIGATOR (*Alligator mississippiensis*). A large, lizard-like reptile that may grow up to nineteen feet in length. It is a dangerous denizen of the swamplands of Florida, Louisiana, and the other Gulf states and was introduced into the Rio Grande in Texas. The name is from the Spanish *el lagarto*, "lizard," and ultimately from the Latin *lacertus*. As "lagarto" the name appeared in English print first in 1568. The alligator, unique to American waters, along with the crocodile (from the Greek *krokodilus*, "worm of the pebbles," for its habit of lying on pebbles to absorb the sun's heat), has long been a favorite meat of Cajuns and is considered a delicacy by others. But, more for its hide than its meat, the alligator was brought dangerously close to extinction by the early 1960s, when state game officials began protection of the animal and restocking of nesting areas. By the late 1960s the alligator was once again abundant, and today it is more widely available as meat than ever before. Today about 300,000 pounds of alligator meat are sold annually. The tail of the alligator is particularly relished and usually cooked in a form of stew or fried in nuggets.

ALLIGATOR BREAD. A round loaf of bread with a bumpy top like an alligator's skin, first recorded in 1968.

ALLIGATOR CORN. Colloquial name for the edible seed of the American lotus known as "water chinquapin" (*Nelumbo lutea*), first in print in 1841.

ALMOND (*Prunus amygdalus*). A tree native to the Mediterranean and a member of the rose family whose nut is widely used in desserts, candy, and garnishes and as a **snack**. The name is from Old French *almande*, derived from the Greek *amygdalē*, and is first found in English print in 1398.

In the mid-1800s, almonds were introduced by Franciscan missionaries to California, which since the early 1900s has been the only state that produces them commercially, now providing 70 percent of the world's crop, about two billion pounds.

American almonds are often roasted and ground as a topping for ice cream or cakes, made into a marzipan paste, or coated with candy or chocolate. After peanuts, almonds are American's favorite nut, with per capita consumption of 1.4 pounds as of 2011.

ALPHABET SOUP. A soup, usually tomato- or chicken-based, containing pasta cut into the shapes of alphabet letters. The term saw print in 1907.

AMARETTO. A cordial with the flavor of almonds, though it may contain no almonds at all and is often made from apricot pits. The original formula, called Amaretto di Saronno, comes from the Italian town of Saronno. (*Amaretto* in Italian means "a little bitter.") A wholly unsubstantiated legend, promoted by the producer's American distributor, Glenmore Distilleries of Lexington, Kentucky, tells of how Renaissance artist Bernardino Luini came to the town of Saronno in 1525 to paint a fresco in the sanctuary of Santa Maria delle Grazie. One of his models was a widow who gave him the liqueur that came to be called amaretto.

The drink was imported into the U.S. in the 1960s, and by 1980 it had become the second-best-selling cordial here (after Kahlúa), causing several American producers to make their own amarettos in American distilleries.

Amaretto is sometimes used as a topping for ice cream desserts and as a flavoring for cakes and pies or coffee.

AMBROSIA. A **cocktail** reputedly first concocted at Arnaud's restaurant, in New Orleans, immediately following the end of **Prohibition**. The name, from the Greek *ambrotos*, "immortal," refers to the food of the Roman and Greek gods, thought to bestow immortality.

AMBROSIA COCKTAIL

Shake together the juice of 1 lemon, 1 oz. applejack, 1 oz. brandy, and ½ oz. Cointreau and top with champagne.

AMBROSIA. A dessert made from fruits, sugar, and grated coconut, most popular in the South, dating in print to 1932.

AMBROSIA DESSERT

Peel and slice 3 oranges into ¼-in. wedges and layer in a bowl. Sprinkle with confectioners' sugar and about 1 T. grated coconut. Make another layer the same way, and another, until the oranges are used up. Chill before serving. Serves 4.

AMERICAN VITICULTURAL AREAS. Grape-growing areas recognized by the federal Bureau of Alcohol, Tobacco, Firearms and Explosives. Such areas must meet the following guidelines: (1) That a named viticultural area is locally and/or nationally known as a grape-producing area. (2) That the geographical features of the region (climate, soil, elevation, physical features, etc.) are distinctly different from surrounding regions.

The currently approved Recognized Viticultural Regions are:

ARIZONA: Sonoita

ARKANSAS: Altus, Arkansas Mountain, Ozark Mountain

CALIFORNIA: Alexander Valley, Alta Mesa, Anderson Valley, Arroyo Grande Valley, Arroyo Seco, Atlas Peak, Ben Lomond Mountain, Benmore Valley, Bennett Valley, Borden Ranch, California Shenandoah Valley, Capay Valley, Carmel Valley, Central Coast, Chalk Hill, Chalone, Chiles Valley, Cienega Valley, Clarksburg, Clear Lake, Clement Hills, Cole Ranch, Cosumnes River, Covelo, Cucamonga Valley, Diablo Grande, Diamond Mountain District, Dos Rios, Dry Creek Valley, Dunnigan Hills, Edna Valley, El Dorado, Fair Play, Fiddletown, Guenoc Valley, Hames Valley, High Valley, Howell Mountain, Jahant, Knights Valley, Lime Kiln Valley, Livermore Valley, Lodi, Los Carneros, McDowell Valley, Madera, Malibu–Newton Canyon, Mendocino, Mendocino Ridge, Merritt Island, Mokelumne River, Monterey, Mt. Harlan, Mt. Veeder, Napa Valley, North Coast, Northern Sonoma, North Yuba, Oak Knoll District of Napa Valley, Oakville, Pacheco Pass, Paicines, Paso Robles, Potter Valley, Ramona Valley, Red Hills Lake County, Redwood Valley, River Junction, Rockpile, Russian River Valley, Rutherford, Saddle Rock Malibu, Saint Helena, Salado Creek, San Antonio, San Bernabe, San Benito, San Francisco Bay, San Lucas, San Pasqual Valley, San Ysidro District, Santa Clara Valley, Santa Cruz Mountains, Santa Lucia Highlands, Santa Maria Valley, Santa Rita Hills, Santa Ynez Valley, Seiad Valley, Sierra Foothills, Sloughhouse, Solano County Green Valley, Sonoma Coast, Sonoma County Green Valley, Sonoma Mountain, Sonoma Valley, South Coast, Spring Mountain District, Stags Leap District, Suisun Valley, Temecula Valley, Tracey Hills, Trinity Lakes, West Elks, Wild Horse Valley, Willow Creek, York Mountain, Yorkville Highlands, Yountville

COLORADO: Grand Valley

CONNECTICUT: Southeastern New England, Western Connecticut Highlands

IDAHO: Snake River Valley

ILLINOIS: Ohio River Valley

INDIANA: Ohio River Valley

KENTUCKY: Ohio River Valley

LOUISIANA: Mississippi Delta

MARYLAND: Catoctin, Cumberland Valley, Linganore

MASSACHUSETTS: Martha's Vineyard, Southeastern New England

MICHIGAN: Fennville, Lake Michigan Shore, Leelanau Peninsula, Old Mission Peninsula

MINNESOTA: Alexandria Lakes

MISSISSIPPI: Mississippi Delta

MISSOURI: Augusta, Hermann, Ozark Highlands, Ozark Mountain

NEW JERSEY: Central Delaware Valley, Outer Coastal Plains, Warren Hills

NEW MEXICO: Mesilla Valley, Middle Rio Grande Valley, Mimbres Valley

NEW YORK: Cayuga Lake, Finger Lakes, the Hamptons, Hudson River Region, Lake Erie, Long Island, Niagara Escarpment, North Fork of Long Island, Seneca Lake

NORTH CAROLINA: Yadkin Valley

OHIO: Grand River Valley, Isle St. George, Kanawha River Valley, Lake Erie, Loramie Creek, Ohio River Valley

OKLAHOMA: Ozark Mountain

OREGON: Applegate Valley, Chehalem Mountains, Columbia Valley, Dundee Hills, Eola Amity Hills, McMinnville, Red Hill Douglas County, Ribbon Ridge, Rogue Valley, Snake River Valley, Southern Oregon, Umpqua Valley, Walla Walla Valley, Willamette Valley, Yamhill-Carlton District

PENNSYLVANIA: Central Delaware Valley, Cumberland Valley, Lake Erie, Lancaster Valley, Lehigh Valley

RHODE ISLAND: Southeastern New England

TENNESSEE: Mississippi Delta

TEXAS: Bell Mountain, Escondido Valley, Fredericksburg in the Texas Hill Country, Mesilla Valley, Mississippi Delta, Texas Davis Mountains, Texas High Plains, Texas Hill Country, Texoma

VIRGINIA: Monticello, Northern Neck George Washington Birthplace, North Fork of Roanoke, Rocky Knob, Shenandoah Valley, Virginia's Eastern Shore

WASHINGTON: Columbia Gorge, Columbia Valley, Horse Heaven Hills, Puget Sound, Rattlesnake Hills, Wahluke Slope, Walla Walla Valley, Yakima Valley

WEST VIRGINIA: Kanawha River Valley, Ohio River Valley, Shenandoah Valley

WISCONSIN: Lake Wisconsin

AMERINE, MAYNARD (1911–1998). Plant physiologist and professor. A prolific author of scientific books and articles, Maynard Andrew Amerine was critical to the technical development of California viticulture in the twentieth century. He has been called "the Father of American Wine."

Born in San Jose, California, Amerine grew up on a farm in nearby Modesto. He earned his B.A. in plant science at the University of California at Davis in 1932 and his Ph.D. at Berkeley in 1936. At the end of Prohibition, at a time when America's vineyards were fallow, Berkeley began its Department of Viticulture and Enology to help restore California's wine industry, appointing Amerine as its first researcher in 1935. His work on climate's effects on grapes was the basis of vineyard improvements that led to better-quality wines. In 1938, he and collaborator Albert J. Winkler developed the system of classifying wine-growing regions by measuring heat summation, which allowed vineyard owners to maximize propagation by planting varietals best suited to their soils. Amerine became a full professor at Berkeley in 1952 and chaired the Department of Viticulture and Enology from 1957 to 1962. Before World War II, Amerine traveled widely through Europe's vineyard regions, then joined the Army's chemical warfare service in North Africa and India. After the war, he was instrumental in helping Algeria, Australia, Brazil, Chile, Japan, and New Zealand with development of their own wine industries. Clark Kerr, former president of the University of California, remarked that wherever he traveled, "in every wine country as soon as I mentioned that I came from California, people would ask me, 'Do you know Professor Maynard Amerine?'"

Amerine wrote more than four hundred scientific papers and sixteen books, including *Wine: An Introduction* (1965), with Vernon L. Singleton, and, with Edward Roessler, *Wines: Their Sensory Evaluation* (1976), both of which became instant classics in the field. Amerine's international awards were legion, including the Croix d'Officier of the Ordre National du Mérite, the Chevalier de Mérite Agricole, and the Merit Award and presidency of the American Society for Enology and Viticulture. The first endowed chair at the University of California was named after Amerine, an honor given to him by his old school friend **Ernest Gallo**.

Many of Amerine's students, including Robert Mondavi, went on to develop the California wine industry of the 1960s and 1970s. Amerine retired in 1974, donating his book collection to UC Davis's Shields Library. For sixteen years he was the science adviser to the Wine Institute. He continued to lecture and write until developing Alzheimer's disease. He died at eighty-six in St. Helena, California.

AMISH PREACHING SOUP. A thick bean soup served in large quantities before or after Amish church services, dating in print to circa 1965.

AMMONIA COOKIES. Any of a variety of cookies made with a leavening agent called ammonium carbonate, or baking ammonia. They are most commonly found in Scandinavian American communities. In their book *Farm Recipes and Food Secrets from the Norske Nook* (1993), Helen Myhre and Mona Vold wrote, "Talk about Old Faithful, this was one of those basic standbys every farm lady made."

ANADAMA BREAD. A bread made from cornmeal and molasses. The term dates in print to 1915 but is probably somewhat older. If it were not for the frequency of their citation, it would be difficult to believe the stories of how this New England bread got its name. The story most often cited is of a Gloucester, Massachusetts, fisherman's wife named Anna, who gave her husband nothing but cornmeal and molasses to eat every day. One night the fisherman got so angry, he tossed the ingredients in with some yeast and flour and made a bread in the oven while muttering to himself, "Anna, damn her!"

A more affectionate story has a New England sea captain referring to his wife with the same expletive as a phrase of endearment. This Anna was apparently adept at bread baking, and she became well known for her cornmeal-and-molasses loaf among the fishing crews who appreciated this long-lasting, hearty bread. There was, supposedly, a gravestone to this legendary woman that read, ANNA WAS A LOVELY BRIDE, BUT ANNA, DAMN 'ER, UP AND DIED.

One source contends that a commercial bakery called its product "Annadammer" or "Annadama" bread.

ANADAMA BREAD

Combine 3 c. all-purpose flour, 1 c. cornmeal, 2 pkgs. dry yeast, and 1 T. salt together in a bowl. In another bowl mix 2 c. hot water, 4 T. butter, and ½ c. molasses, then add to flour mixture. Beat and knead to form a stiff dough. Place in greased bowl and let rise until doubled. Punch down, shape into two balls, and place in greased 8-in. cake tins. Let rise until doubled. Bake at 375° for about 1 hr., until deep brown in color.

ANDRÉS, JOSÉ (1969–). Chef, restaurateur, educator, author, and innovator of modern cuisine, José Ramón Andrés brought to the American table a wider and deeper knowledge of Spanish food culture than anyone before him. Born in Asturias, Spain, Andrés attended the School of Restaurants and Hotels, in Barcelona, at the age of fifteen and trained at El Bulli under avant-garde chef Ferran Adrià. In 1993, Andrés moved to Washington, D.C., and ten years later he opened a small counter eatery named Minibar, where he served ever-changing menus based on avant-garde cuisine, earning him *Food & Wine* magazine's title "hero of the Spanish revolution [who] helped create the Spanish food boom in America." He also opened one of the country's first authentic tapas bars, Jaleo, after which he and friend and journalist Richard Wolffe published *Tapas: A Taste of Spain in America*, in 2005. Andrés then followed with Café Atlantico, a Mediterranean small-plates concept called Zaytinya, and a Mexican restaurant, Oyamel Cocina Mexicana. In 2006, Andrés and partner Rob Wilder founded ThinkFoodGroup, which won the 2010 Richard Melman Award from *Restaurant Hospitality* for the development of new restaurant concepts, and in 2011 he was named Outstanding Chef by the **James Beard Foundation**.

Andrés's most ambitious project to date has been the Bazaar by José Andrés, at the SLS Hotel Beverly Hills in 2009, which won *Esquire* magazine's Restaurant of the Year award for its dual menus of traditional and modern tapas and received a James Beard Award nomination for Best New Restaurant. In 2010 he went on to open a new Jaleo concept called China Poblano (Chinese-Mexican fare) and é by José Andrés, at the Cosmopolitan of Las Vegas.

In a unique collaboration with the National Archives, Andrés opened a temporary homage to American culinary history, America Eats Tavern, in Washington, D.C., in 2011. Andrés welcomed the second outpost of the Bazaar by José Andrés in Miami, at the SLS Hotel South Beach in the summer of 2012.

Andrés was host and executive producer of the PBS travel-food series *Made in Spain*, and author of the companion cookbook, *Made in Spain: Spanish Dishes for the American Kitchen*. In Spain, his TV show *Vamos a Cocinar* was the country's most popular cooking program.

In November 2010, Andrés became the first chef to be awarded Spain's Ministry of Culture Order of Arts and Letters medallion for his efforts to promote Spanish culture abroad. He became the dean of Spanish studies at the International Culinary Center, in New York and California, with the creation of the first professional culinary program dedicated to the gastronomy of Spain.

After visiting the devastation wrought by the 2010 earthquake in Haiti, Andrés launched World Central Kitchen to help feed people in humanitarian crises around the world and is the culinary ambassador of the Global Alliance for Clean Cookstoves, which aims to raise awareness of the harmful effects of inefficient and toxic cooking in the developing world and to promote new alternative technologies. He is also chairman emeritus

for DC Central Kitchen and teaches at the Harvard School of Engineering and Applied Sciences as part of the course Science and Cooking. In the fall of 2012, he joined the U.S. State Department Diplomatic Culinary Partnership, and he will participate in the American Chef Corps. *Time* named Andrés one of the 100 Most Influential People in the World in 2012.

ANCHOVY (family Engraulidae). A small, herringlike fish that travels in large schools. Anchovies are generally packed in oil and canned for the American market, even though there are sixteen species in U.S. waters and they are abundant on both coasts. The word is from the Spanish *anchova* and was first printed in English in Shakespeare's *Henry IV, Part One* (circa 1597). Anchovies are often used as an ingredient on pizza and as a part of several salad preparations. In 2010, U.S. landings for anchovies totaled 2.815 million pounds, most used for animal food, reduction, or bait.

ANDOUILLE. A highly seasoned smoked-pork sausage commonly made from neck and stomach meat. The word dates in English print to 1605. This specialty of **Cajun** cookery is traditionally made in only three parishes in Louisiana and takes its name from a French word meaning "sausage," ultimately derived from Latin *inductilia*, "to insert." It is commonly used to flavor **gumbos** and **jambalayas**, though it is eaten on its own. LaPlace, Louisiana, calls itself the Andouille Capital of the World and each year holds an Andouille Festival in October.

ANGEL FOOD CAKE. Also "angel cake." A very light, puffy cake, perhaps of Pennsylvania Dutch heritage, made without yeast and with several beaten egg whites. The egg whites give it a texture so airy that the confection supposedly has the sublimity of angels. Angel food cake was known by the 1870s in America (the word appeared in print in 1881) and served as a sensible usage of leftover egg whites.

ANDREWS, COLMAN (1945–). Author and editor. In the 1970s and 1980s, Colman Andrews became one of the first California-based food writers to monitor the emergence and evolution of the food scene in the state, and, as co-founder of *Saveur* magazine, he later brought a sophisticated, authoritative focus to the traditions of global and ethnic food with Falstaffian gusto.

Colman Robert Hardy Daniel Andrews was born in Santa Monica, California, and grew up in West L.A. and Ojai, California, where his father had distinguished himself as a newspaperman, novelist, and screenwriter; his mother, of French Canadian descent, was a screen actress. Andrews attended Loyola Marymount University, in L.A. but was dismissed for neglecting his studies. For the next year and a half he traveled in the U.S., returning to earn his B.A. in history and philosophy at UCLA.

His interest in food earned him the restaurant-reviewing job for *The Staff* newspaper, using the pen name "Mr. Food." He also worked in the publicity department of Atlantic Records, then became editor of the lifestyle magazine *Coast* through 1975, while also writing music criticism for various journals. He began freelancing as a restaurant reviewer and travel writer for the *Los Angeles Times*, and he later edited the newspaper's *Traveling in Style* magazine (1992–1994). He took on a wine column for *Los Angeles* magazine in 1978, under the pen name Van Delanay (a pun on *vin de l'année*), and was hired as an editor at *New West* magazine (1978), where he briefly became romantically involved with food writer Ruth Reichl. During this period, Andrews championed the emergence of what came to be called New California cuisine, then spearheaded by chefs like **Wolfgang Puck**, **Alice Waters**, **Michael McCarty**, **John Sedlar**, and others.

Andrews was hired by NYC editor Dorothy Kalins to write for *Apartment Life* (later *Metropolitan Home*), reporting from around the world. His authoritative first book, *Catalan Cuisine* (1988), was named by the *Observer* one of the 50 Best Cookbooks of All Time in 2011. He followed with a collection of essays under the title *Everything on the Table* (1992), *Flavors of the Riviera* (1996), *The Country Cooking of Ireland* (2009), and *The Country Cooking of Italy* (2011).

In 1994, Andrews moved to NYC to co-found *Saveur* with Dorothy Kalins and Christopher Hirsheimer. *Saveur* eschewed covering trends and new restaurants, focusing instead on regional and ethnic cuisines, home cooks, and gastronomic history.

Andrews also co-authored several *Saveur* cookbooks and during this time won many James Beard Journalism Awards. In his book *Flavors of the Riviera*, Andrews wrote of the issue of authenticity, "traditional cuisine isn't made from recipes; it is born out of necessity, availability, and intuition, and it is codified not in books but in individual recollections or in common wisdom."

Six years after the sale of *Saveur*, Andrews left in 2006 to write for *Gourmet* magazine, where Reichl was editor in chief, for three years. In 2011 he published a book on the life and cuisine of Spanish master chef Ferran Adrià, *Ferran: The Inside Story of El Bulli and the Man Who Reinvented Food*.

In 2010, Andrews became editorial director of the website *The Daily Meal*. Andrews was awarded the Creu de Sant Jordi by the government of Catalonia and was named to the IACP's Who's Who of Cooking in America.

ANGELLIQUOR. Also "angel liquor." An African American term (dating in print to 1942) for a wine made from the angelica plant.

ANGEL'S TIT. Also "King Alphonse." A cocktail made by floating heavy cream on crème de cacao and topping it with a cherry (1984).

ANTELOPE (*Antilocapra americana*). Also "pronghorn." A North American deerlike horned animal with a white rump and two white throat bands. They inhabit the plains and prairies of the U.S. The word derives from Middle English and dates to about 1430. Antelope are most commonly cut into steaks and then roasted, fried, or stewed.

ANTIFOGMATIC. A colonial-era term for a drink of alcohol taken in the morning to counteract the effects of dampness or fog, dating in print to 1789.

AOKI, HIROAKI "ROCKY" (1938–2008). Restaurateur. Starting in the mid-1960s, Hiroaki Aoki, who took the nickname "Rocky," brought the first teppanyaki restaurants to the U.S., all under the name Benihana of Tokyo, introducing many Americans to their first taste of Japanese food. He soon expanded his restaurants worldwide and inspired a myriad of imitators using the concept.

Born in Tokyo, Aoki came from a family in food service; his father, Yunosuke Aoki, ran a steakhouse named

Benihana (Japanese for "safflower"). The younger Aoki attended Keio University, competing in track and field. His wrestling acumen qualified him for the 1960 Summer Olympics, but he did not compete. After attending C.W. Post College, on Long Island, New York, on a scholarship, he became a champion wrestler in the flyweight class.

Aoki moved to NYC at the age of nineteen and studied restaurant management at New York City Community College. With money he saved from driving an ice cream truck and with a co-investment from his father, he opened his first Benihana on West Fifty-sixth Street, using the teppanyaki ("steel grill") to make American foods like steak, shrimp, and lobster with Japanese seasonings, accompanied by bean sprouts, zucchini, onions, and mushrooms, all prepared by a cook schooled in the dramatics of knife handling, flaming food, and joking with the customers seated at the surrounding counter. The menu, beginning with an onion soup, rarely varied, though sushi was later added. Benihana served "no slippery or slimy things," said Aoki. "The minute I forgot I was Japanese, success began."

The concept fared well, and Aoki opened one Benihana after another. By 1974 his business was worth $15 million. In 1982, his corporation went public and franchised, while Aoki retained several under his own name. All the restaurants were consolidated under Benihana Inc. in 1995. In 1998, Aoki was investigated for illegal insider trading, fined, and placed on probation. After a life of flamboyant sporting activities, including a powerboat accident that nearly killed him, and after several debilitating illnesses, Aoki died of pneumonia in 2008.

There are currently ninety-two company-owned Benihanas and sixteen franchises.

APEE. Also "apea" and, in the plural, "eepies." A spiced butter cookie or form of gingerbread. Legend has it that the word derives from the name of Ann Page, a Philadelphia cook who carved her initials into the tops of the confection. This was first noted in print in John F. Watson's *Annals of Philadelphia* (1830) to the effect that Ann Page, then still alive, "first made [the cookies] many years ago, under the common name of cakes." But William Woys Weaver, in *America Eats* (1989), wrote,

"The origin of the name is a bit confusing. Essentially, they were a form of *Anis Plätchen* (anise cookies) and stamped *A.P.* to distinguish them from cookies with caraway, which were known as 'seed cakes.' A great many bakers hawked apeas to children on the streets. One of those bakers in Philadelphia was Ann Page. The *A.P.* became associated with her, if only because *Anis Plätchen* were extremely popular."

APEES

Cream 1 c. butter with 1 t. vanilla and 1 ⅓ c. sugar until very smooth. Add 2 eggs. Sift 2 ⅓ c. flour, ¼ t. cream of tartar, and ¼ t. salt, then stir into mixture with ⅔ c. sour cream. Drop by spoonfuls onto buttered cookie sheet, bake for 10 min. at 375°. Cool on rack. Makes about 70 cookies.

APLET. A confection made with boiled-down apple juice, gelatin, and nuts. If made with apricots, it is called a "cotlet." The confection was first produced in 1920 by Armenian immigrants Armen Tertsagian and Mark Balaban, who based it on a Middle Eastern sweet called *rahat locum*, made with orange-blossom water or rosewater and nuts.

APPLE (genus *Malus*, family Rosaceae). A sweet fruit with a firm flesh and thin skin found in temperate regions. The apple is native to Europe and Asia, though the U.S. now produces about one-quarter of the world's crop. There are probably tens of thousands of apple varieties, but most apples sold at market come from no more than fifty varieties, and the consumer is unlikely to encounter more than a half-dozen of the most successfully propagated varieties.

About 2,500 varieties are now grown in the U.S., with more than one hundred varieties grown commercially. The most popular varieties are Red Delicious, Gala, Golden Delicious, Granny Smith, Fuji, McIntosh, and Rome.

The largest producing states are Washington, New York, Michigan, Pennsylvania, and California. The U.S. produces about 236 million bushels per year, for sales of $2.4 billion, and almost one in four apples are exported, with the top markets being Mexico, Canada, and Taiwan.

In 2011, Americans consumed 2.373 million tons of apples. Sixty-four percent are grown for fresh consumption, 36 percent for processing. During the months of March through July, the U.S. imports apples from Chile, New Zealand, Canada, Argentina, and Brazil. The apple (the word is from the Old English *aeppel*) has been a favorite fruit for millennia; it was known to the people of the Iron Age and cultivated four thousand years ago in Egypt. The Roman Pliny the Elder listed thirty-six varieties in the first century A.D., and the fruit has mythological associations in many civilizations.

There were no native American apples aside from crab apples when the first settlers arrived on these shores. (The "custard apple," *Annona reticulate*, of the American tropics and the "mayapple" or "mandrake," *Podophyllum peltatum*, of eastern North America are not true apples.) The first apple seeds were brought by the Pilgrims in 1620, and there were plantings in New Jersey as of 1632. Governor John Endecott of the Plymouth Colony traded five hundred three-year-old apple trees for two hundred acres of land in 1649, and in 1647 Governor Peter Stuyvesant brought to New Amsterdam a Dutch apple tree that flourished until it was accidentally knocked down in 1866.

The French brought the apple to Canada, and the fruit was grown up and down the thirteen colonies. In 1730, the first commercial apple nursery was opened on New York's Long Island, and by 1741 apples were being shipped to the West Indies.

The proliferation of the fruit into the western territories came by the hand of an eccentric but gentle man named **John Chapman**, affectionately known as "Johnny Appleseed." Born in Leominster, Massachusetts, in 1774, Chapman started nurseries over ten thousand square miles of American frontier. (He did not, as folklore would have it, merely toss apple seeds to the ground in the faith that they would grow true.) He got as far as Fort Wayne, Indiana, where he died at the age of seventy-one in 1845.

Apples were introduced in the Northwest by Captain Aemilius Simmons, who planted seeds at Fort Vancouver, in Washington, in 1824. His first tree grew but one apple, but the seeds of that single fruit bore future generations of hardier stock. Commercial growing of apples in the Northwest began with two Idahoans, Henderson Luelling and William Meek, who became the fathers of Washington's major crop and made the state the top producer of apples in the U.S.

Apples were among the most versatile and long-lasting of fruits for the early settlers, and they have long been stored for the winter in "dry houses" or made into **cider**. By the year 1800 there were a hundred American-bred varieties, and *Downing's Fruits and Fruit Trees in America* (1872) listed more than a thousand varieties of apples bred in America. By 1905 one chronicler listed seventeen thousand. Most of these have been forgotten or are grown only in "collectors' orchards," where varieties such as the Roxbury Russet, Golden Russet, Black Gillflower, Chenango, Black Esopus Spitzenburg, Sweet Bough, and Winter Banana are still sustained. But the majority of the most important varieties still marketed date from before 1850, and only one, the Cortland, is the result of experiments by a scientific plant breeder; the rest come from seedlings.

The early apple storage cellars, called "common storages," lasted well into the nineteenth century. One of the first commercial cold-storage plants for apples was established in 1870 in Niagara County, New York, but not until 1915 was a refrigerated storage facility possible. A method of slowing apple maturation by what is called "controlled atmosphere storage" (pioneered by Frenchman Jacques Bérard in the early 1800s) extended the life of apples so that they have become available year-round. Increasingly, this method is being used throughout the U.S. to preserve apples. "Apple harvest time" is a festive and social occasion in America, and "apple bees" used to be held to core apples to be dried for the winter. October is National Apple Month, and at Halloween children "bob for apples," that is, they attempt to pick up apples floating in a large tub of water with their teeth, a pastime that may derive from druidic or Roman harvest rites.

The following list includes the most popular and most important American apple varieties sold and cultivated. In addition to these common varieties, some newer apples that show promise for the future include Kendall (a cross between McIntosh and Zusoff); Spartan (McIntosh and Yellow Newtown); Idared (Jonathan and Wagener); and Jondel (Jonathan and Delicious). In recent years, small farmers have been planting heirloom varieties that have not been propagated for decades or more.

BALDWIN. Red-skinned; harvested in autumn. An all-purpose apple not easily found anymore except in New England and New York retail outlets in the autumn months. The Baldwin appeared around 1740 as a seedling on the farm of John Ball, in Wilmington, Massachusetts. For a long while the apple was called "Butter's apple," after the name of the next farmer to own the land. Butters himself called it "Woodpecker." The variety was publicized by Colonel Baldwin of Woburn, Massachusetts, who gave his name to the apple, and after 1850 it was introduced into New York, where it was the major variety for years. Since 1945, the Baldwin has declined in popularity, though it is still used by commercial processors.

CORTLAND. Red-skinned; September to April. An all-purpose apple that stores well. The only major variety that is the result of scientific breeding, the Cortland was first propagated at the New York State Agricultural Experiment Station at Geneva, New York, and introduced in 1915 as a cross between the McIntosh and the Ben Davis. The word dates to 1712 in print.

CRAB. Red-skinned. Used primarily in cooking, the crab apple is small and deep-hued. It is a wild species and goes by the names "American sweet," "garland" (*Malus coronaria*), and "prairie crab apple" (*Malus ioensis*).

DELICIOUS. Red-skinned; mid-September to August. A heart-shaped eating apple also called the Red Delicious, this variety is the largest apple crop in the U.S., with several sports, strains, and tree types. It was discovered by a farmer named Jesse Hiatt at Peru, Iowa, in 1872, near an old Yellow Bellflower apple tree. Hiatt cut it down twice because of its irregular growing pattern, but it grew back, and finally Hiatt named it the Hawkeye. In 1895, rights to the variety were bought by a commercial nursery, Stark Brothers, which renamed it the Delicious. Today the eastern variety of Red Delicious is often possessed of better flavor than the western variety of the same name.

FUJI. Red-skinned. A hybrid of Red Delicious and Ralls Genet, the Fuji was first propagated in the late 1930s in Fujisaki, Japan, but not marketed until 1962. It was first sold in the U.S. in the 1980s, eventually becoming the fourth-most-popular apple in the country. Grown in Washington and California, the Fuji is crisp and has a long shelf life without refrigeration.

GALA. Also "Royal Gala." Red-skinned. As the number-two-bestselling apple in the U.S., this small variety has a thick skin and a mild but sweet taste. It was originally a cross between a Golden Delicious and a Kidd's Orange Red, first planted in the 1930s in New Zealand, then obtaining a U.S. patent in 1974. Various sports of the Gala include the Galaxy, Treco Spur Red, Fulford, Obrogala, Applewaites, Alvnia, and Galaval.

GOLDEN DELICIOUS. Gold-skinned; late September to August. An eating apple with a long peak season, the Golden Delicious bruises less readily than other varieties. It was discovered in 1914 on the Anderson Mullins farm, in West Virginia, possibly from a Grimes Golden variety pollinated by the Golden Reinette. First called "Mullins' Yellow Seedlings," the variety was purchased by the Stark Brothers nursery as a companion to its Red Delicious and is now the second-largest apple crop in the U.S.

GRANNY SMITH. Green-skinned; August to November. An eating and cooking apple now gaining popularity in the U.S., it is widely grown in California. The apple was discovered in Ryde, Australia, in about 1850 by Maria Ann Smith, who lent the fruit her name, and within a decade it was widely propagated in Australia and New Zealand, not coming to the U.S. for a century. Commercial plantings in California's San Joaquin Valley began in the 1970s at H. P. Metzler and Sons Orchards.

GRAVENSTEIN. Yellow-skinned; early fall. An all-purpose apple of uncertain origins. Some authorities hold that the variety came from the eighteenth-century garden of the duke of Augustenberg, in Gravenstein, Germany, but others cite the Grafenstein Garden, in Shleswig, Germany. Still others trace the variety to Italy. No one knows who first introduced the breed to the U.S., but Russians had planted the variety in Bodega, north of San Francisco, by 1820, and the apple was apparently grown in New York prior to 1826. Today the Gravenstein is still better known as a California breed, where it is a major variety for applesauce.

JONATHAN. Red-skinned; mid-September to March. A highly aromatic, spicy apple, good for eating, pies, and applesauce. Discovered in 1800 in Woodstock, New York, where it was originally called the "Rick," after farmer Philip Rick, who found it among his trees, the variety was popularized by Jonathan Hasbrouk and Judge J. Buel of Albany and took the former's first name. The Jonathan may be a seedling of the Esopus Spitzenburg variety. The Jonathan grew better in Michigan and the Ohio Valley than in the East and became a major variety in the Midwest and as far west as Idaho and Colorado.

MCINTOSH. Red-skinned; mid-September to July. A round, all-purpose apple, the McIntosh is excellent for crossbreeding and has given us varieties such as the Cortland, Spartan, Melba, Macoun, Niagara, and Puritan. A plaque in Dundas County, Ontario, across the Lawrence River from Massena, New York, reads, "The Original Mcintosh Red Apple Tree stood 20 rods north of this spot. It was one of a number of seedlings taken from the border of the clearings and transplanted by John Mcintosh in the year 1796." John McIntosh took seedlings from the brush near his home, outside Dundela, Ontario, and planted them in his garden. By 1830 only one tree had survived, and this was the original tree that, with some grafting assistance given by an itinerant peddler five years later, resulted in a nursery of identical trees that gave excellent, sweet fruit. McIntosh's wife, Hannah, took care of the nursery, and neighbors took to calling

the apple "Granny's apple" after her, though a son, Allan, gave the family name to the variety, and other relatives began propagating it in New York and Vermont. It became the predominant variety of the Northeast (the original Ontario tree was burned in a fire and died in 1910), especially in New York State, where it is grown in the Hudson Valley, the Champlain Valley, and near Lake Ontario.

NEWTOWN PIPPIN. Greenish-yellow-skinned; mid-September to April. An all-purpose apple of uncertain origins, the Newtown Pippin is also called the "Albemarle." The original seedling may have come from Gershon Moore's estate, in Newtown, Long Island, though it is not certain whether the fruit of the original tree, which died in 1805, was yellow or green. Both varieties go by the name Newtown Pippin, with the yellow primarily grown in the West and in Virginia (where Albemarle County lent its name to the variety, brought from Philadelphia in 1755 by Dr. Thomas Walker). It was the first variety sent to England, in 1759, when Benjamin Franklin gave some to the royal court of England.

NORTHERN SPY. Red-skinned, with some blush; mid-October to February. A robust eating and cooking variety produced mainly in New York, Michigan, and Ontario, the Northern Spy is not widely available. It originated as a seedling in an orchard planted in 1800 by Herman Chapin in East Bloomfield, New York, from Salisbury, Connecticut, seeds. The origin of the name, however, is obscure. Some say it may derive from the fact that Bloomfield was a site of activity for the Underground Railroad, a secret system by which slaves were brought north to freedom. The original seedling died, but the first apple from the seedling's transplanted suckers came from the farm of Roswell Humphrey, and it became an important apple throughout the northern states. Owing to its tendency to appear only in alternate years, the variety has declined in popularity, but many people consider Northern Spy apples among the very best in America.

RHODE ISLAND GREENING. Yellow-green-skinned. A baking or cooking apple considered the best for apple pie, the Rhode Island Greening is produced mainly in New York and is commercially processed for applesauce and frozen pies and, therefore, rarely seen in the market. The variety began in Green's End, Rhode Island, in about 1748, through the efforts of a tavern keeper named Green. It was carried from Newport to Plymouth, Massachusetts, then to Ohio by 1796, where it was established in a nursery at Marietta.

ROME BEAUTY. Red-skinned; late September to July. An excellent baking apple, originally propagated by Alanson Gillett from a discarded tree given to him by his brother Joel, of Proctorville, Ohio, the variety was named by George Walton in about 1832 for the township of Rome, where the Gillett farm was located. The Rome Beauty has given us hybrids like Gallia Beauty, Monroe, and Ruby. The Rome Beauty is produced in all the apple-growing regions of the U.S.

STAYMAN. Red-skinned; early October to May. An eating apple grown throughout Appalachia, with some uses for cooking. The variety came from a winesap seedling, discovered in Leavenworth, Kansas, in 1866 by Dr. J. Stayman. It is sometimes called "Stayman's winesap" or "Stayman winesap." After 1900, extensive plantings took place in the East and Midwest.

WINESAP. Red-skinned; late October to June. A tart, crisp apple for eating, the winesap comes from obscure origins, possibly of New Jersey stock before 1800. Its long keeping time made it popular until controlled atmosphere storage made other varieties even more so. It is now produced mainly in Washington, Virginia, and West Virginia.

YORK IMPERIAL. Red-skinned; mid-September to May. A good baking apple, the York Imperial was first discovered near York, Pennsylvania, in about 1830 by a man named Johnson. He took it to nursery owner Jonathan Jessup, who in turn produced the variety and called it "Johnson's Fine Winter Apple" but had little success with it. Other farmers planted the discarded variety, and it took on its noble name from horticulturist Charles Downing, who in the mid-1800s promoted its long keeping qualities. It is now a processing apple.

APPLE ANNIE. A term for any vendor who sold apples on city street corners during the Great Depression of the 1930s. Most were very poor people with no other trade and no other wares to sell at regular markets. It was the name of a beggar character in the film *Pocketful of Miracles* (1961).

APPLE BROWN BETTY. A layered dessert of apples and buttered crumbs. The origin of the name is unknown, but the dish was first mentioned in print in 1864. It is also called "apple crisp" and "apple crust."

APPLE BROWN BETTY

Mix together 1 ½ c. dry bread crumbs with ¼ c. melted butter and place one third of the mixture in a buttered baking pan. Slice 4 pared and cored apples into ¼-in.-thick slices and place a layer on top of the crumbs. Cover with part of a mixture of 1 t. cinnamon, ¼ t. ground cloves, ¼ t. nutmeg, and 1 t. grated lemon rind. Repeat layers of bread crumbs, apples, and spice mixture, then sprinkle the top with a mixture of the juice of 1 lemon and ¼ c. water. Bake at 400° for 10 to 15 min. Serve with whipped cream or ice cream.

APPLE BUTTER. A Pennsylvania Dutch cooked fruit puree, dating to at least 1765, made by cooking and pureeing apples with cider.

APPLE CHARLOTTE. A dessert of French origins, made of cooked apples and bread slices. Apple charlotte is distinguished from **charlotte russe**, a creamy pudding placed in a deep mold lined with ladyfingers, a dessert generally credited to Frenchman Marie-Antonin Carême, who first called it *Charlotte parisienne*. But apple charlotte predated charlotte russe. In France it was called a "fruit charlotte" and, according to Andre Simon's *A Concise Encyclopedia of Gastronomy* (1952), named after Charlotte Buff, on whom the heroine of Johann Wolfgang von Goethe's *Die Leiden des Jungen Werthers* (1774), a tremendously popular epistolary novel of the time, was based. Apple charlotte became a fashionable dessert in America soon afterwards, as a rather fancy version of **apple brown betty**.

APPLE CHARLOTTE

Line the bottom and sides of a charlotte mold with thin bread slices (which may be cut into the shape of hearts) that have been soaked in melted butter. Slice up a dozen apples that have been peeled and cored, and place in a saucepan with 3 T. butter. Add 2 T. powdered sugar, ¼ t. cinnamon, ½ t. grated lemon rind, and ¼ t. vanilla extract. Cook until apples have broken down, then add 4 T. apricot jam. Stir and blend. Fill the mold, place buttered bread slices on top, trim, then cook in a 350° oven for 40 min. Let rest for a few minutes, then turn out on a plate. Serve with apricot sauce if desired.

APPLE DUMPLING. A baked dessert made of apples wrapped in pastry dough.

APPLE FRITTER. An apple slice that has been covered with a batter and fried in hot oil. Apple fritters have been popular since the middle of the eighteenth century.

APPLE FRITTER

Peel and core 4 apples and cut into ¼-in.-thick slices. Mix together 2 c. flour, 2 beaten eggs, 1 T. dark rum, ¼ t. salt, and 1 c. milk. Dip apple slices in batter, then deep-fry. Serve with powdered sugar and/or sour cream and maple syrup.

APPLEJACK. Also "jack." A hard apple **cider**, or a **brandy** made from apple cider. Apple brandy was particularly favored in early New England, where any household might have the means to make the spirit.

When produced in the U.S., applejack must spend at least two years in wooden casks, though most are aged much longer, and the proof is 100 or, if blended with neutral spirits, 80. As a term for cider, "applejack" dates back to at least 1816. Later in the century, it was also referred to as "apple john" (which in England is a term for a specific type of apple).

"Applejack" is also a term for sweet apple syrup, dating in print to 1968, or to an apple turnover, as of 1852.

APPLE KNOCKER. A club used to loosen fruit from trees, or a person who picks apples very fast (in use since at least 1919).

APPLE PANDOWDY. A dish of sliced apples covered with a crust, sometimes referred to as "apple grunt" or "apple Jonathan" in the Northeast. First mentioned in print in 1805, apple pandowdy seems to be specifically American by name, and Nathaniel Hawthorne mentions the dish in his *Blithedale Romance* (1852). The name's origins are obscure, but perhaps its homely simplicity connotes a "dowdy," i.e., unstylish, appearance.

APPLE PANDOWDY

Core, peel, and slice 4 apples and place in a buttered dish. Pour ½ c. cider over them, sprinkle with ½ t. cinnamon, ⅛ t. ground cloves, ⅛ t. nutmeg, ¾ c. light brown sugar, and ¼ c. maple syrup and dot with butter. Cover with a biscuit dough about ¼-in. thick, then slit the top to allow for the escape of steam. Bake in 350° oven until apples are tender. Serve with cream.

APPLE PIE. If something is said to be as "American as apple pie" (or cherry pie), it is credited with being as American as "The Star-Spangled Banner." In fact, **apples** were brought from Europe to America, and apple pies (1780) were very popular in Europe, especially in England, before they came to epitomize American food. But Americans popularized the apple pie as the country became the world's largest apple-producing nation. In 1971, singer-composer Don McLean had a bestselling record entitled "American Pie."

There are hundreds of apple pie recipes, from every region of the country, some with a top crust, some without, some with a bottom crust, some without, some with raisins or dates or nuts or cranberries, some with buttery crumbs on top. "Deep-dish apple pie" means it is baked in a pie pan at least 1 ½ inches deep.

See also **mock apple pie**.

APPLESAUCE. A puree of apples, sugar, and, sometimes, spices. The term dates in print to 1672. In New England it is often called "apple sass."

APPLE SNOW. Also "apple float." A dessert made from applesauce, sugar, and beaten egg whites, quite popular in the early twentieth century. It first appeared in print in 1939.

APPLE SNOW

Beat 3 egg whites, add ¼ c. sugar and 1 c. applesauce, and serve with whipped cream or custard sauce.

APRICOT (*Prunus armeniaca*). A tree native to western Asia and Africa that gives a yellow-orange fruit. The word is from Portuguese and Spanish, derived from the Latin *praecquum*, "early ripening," and first appeared in English print in 1551.

The apricot was cultivated in China five thousand years ago, reaching North America sometime in the eighteenth century when Spanish monks brought it to California, which now produces 95 percent of the American crop (with the rest from Oregon, Washington, Utah, and Idaho). The first commercial orchard was started in 1792 in California's Santa Clara Valley. About 56 percent of the crop is canned, 16 percent dried, 12 percent frozen, and only 16 percent sold fresh.

The major cultivated varieties include the Patterson, Blenheim, Tilton, Castlebrite, Modesto, and Katy.

Apricots are called "cots" for short. Americans eat about 1.5 pounds of apricots per person annually.

AQUACULTURE. Seafood cultivated in water. Aquaculture has long been part of man's history, though the term—from the Latin *aqua* (water) plus *culture*—dates in print only to 1867. "Hydroponics"—from Greek *hýdör* (water) and *geo* (earth) plus *pono* (work)—refers more specifically to the cultivation of plant life underwater and dates in print to 1937.

Hawaiians developed aquaculture at least a thousand years ago. The industry grew rapidly in the U.S. in the 1920s, especially in fisheries along the Columbia River after the Fish and Wildlife Coordination Act was passed in 1934 to protect species endangered by the Federal Power Act (1920), which built river dams for hydroelectricity.

Aquaculture grew rapidly in the 1980s, with advances in the cultivation of mussels, crayfish, trout, oysters, catfish, salmon, hybrid striped bass, and tilapia. Today more than four hundred species are cultivated worldwide. More than 3,400 farms in twenty-three states are raising approximately 15 percent of the U.S. seafood supply, with catfish, trout, crayfish, and salmon accounting for 80 percent of all domestic aquaculture products.

ARAB. Also "street Arab" and "arabber." A term used in Baltimore for a street peddler of fruits and vegetables. Often they drove through town on horse carts. The term first appeared in print in 1935 but dates back in usage to at least the turn of the century.

ARCTIC WINE. Also "ar'tic wine." Slang term for straight whiskey, dating in print to 1939.

ARKANSAS TRAVELER. Also "Arkansas wedding cake." A dish of sliced corn bread with roast beef and brown gravy, served with french-fried potatoes, pinto beans, and a slice of onion. It is a specialty of the Fort Worth, Texas, area. Also a name for a fast-growing plant like **kudzu**.

ARKANSAS WATER. Derogatory slang term for a nonalcoholic beverage served at a picnic, because of the connotation that people from Arkansas are crude and have common taste. The term first appeared in print in 1951.

ARMADILLO. Any of a variety of New World mammals of the family Dasypodidae having bony plates resembling armor, especially the "nine-banded armadillo" (*D. novemcinctus*). The name comes from the Spanish *armado*, "armed," and first appeared in English print in 1570. The armadillo is rarely eaten in the U.S. today, but some westerners consider it an unusual delicacy, usually to be stewed.

ARMY CHICKEN. World War II Army slang for frankfurters and beans, dating in print to 1942.

ARMOUR, PHILIP DANFORTH (1832–1901). Entrepreneur. Had Philip Danforth Armour only been a major pork producer in his day, he would have been considered a titan of the industry, but his adaptation of nineteenth-century transport and technology helped change the way food was preserved, shipped, and enjoyed by Americans.

Born in Stockbridge, New York, to a farm family of Anglo-Scottish settlers, Armour migrated at the age of nineteen to California to join the Gold Rush of 1849. Instead of mining, he turned to constructing sluices for the mines and made a small fortune of about $8,000. He then moved to Milwaukee to open a wholesale grocery business and, with Frederick Miles, a grain business in 1859; then he joined the meatpacking industry as co-founder, with John Plankinton, of Plankinton, Armour & Co.

During the Civil War, Armour capitalized on the changes in pork prices, selling bacon and barreled beef short at $40 and buying it back later at $18, profiting to the tune of between $500,000 and $1.5 million. With his brothers Herman and Joseph, he expanded his business throughout the Midwest, pioneering canned meat products and the assembly line. He constructed several meatpacking plants in the Menomonee River Valley and formed Armour and Co. in Chicago in 1867, making it the world's largest food-processing and chemical-manufacturing enterprise. In 1886 he hired the industry's first chemist, Dr. Herman B. Schmidt, to find ways to use the tremendous amount of wasted pork by reconstituting it as fertilizer, soap, and other products.

In 1883, Armour founded the Armour Refrigerator Line, which by 1900 had twelve thousand refrigerated railroad cars. By 1893 the company had sales of $110 million. In that year, when a run on the Chicago banks began, Armour shored them up, using his own money and purchasing $1 million in European gold.

As with many industrialists of the Gilded Age, Armour was a generous philanthropist. In 1893 he donated $1 million to found the Armour Institute of Technology, later known as the Illinois Institute of Technology, and founded an educational and health center called the Armour Mission. He was not, however, as generous toward his own workers, battling his plants' unions over better pay, encouraging the creation of militias to suppress them, disbanding unions, and blacklisting their leaders.

During the Spanish–American War of 1898, Armour was charged with selling 750 cases of tainted beef in what was called the "embalmed beef scandal"; this became the inspiration for Upton Sinclair's muckraking 1906 novel *The Jungle*.

By his death in 1901, from heart disease, Armour was believed to be worth $50 million.

After Armour's death, the company thrived, but during the Depression, family members sold their majority interest to financier Frederick H. Prince, who expanded the company during World War II, with sales of $1 billion, especially from its Dial deodorant soap product. After World War II, the company's meat business declined, and in 1959 Armour closed its Chicago slaughterhouse. Armour has been owned by the Blackstone Group since 2007.

ARELLANO, GUSTAVO (1979–). Author. As one of America's foremost authorities on Mexican food, Gustavo Arellano has since 2004 written the long-running syndicated weekly column ¡Ask a Mexican! for the *OC Weekly*, where he is an editor and food critic with a readership of more than two million people.

Born in Anaheim, California, to Mexican parents, Arellano grew up eating his family's traditional cooking, along with American fast food. While a film student at Chapman University, in Orange, he began writing for the *OC Weekly* and went on to earn his M.A. in Latin American studies at UCLA.

His newspaper reporting was often about abuses against and among the Mexican population in Orange Country. His ¡Ask a Mexican! column began as a spoof in answer to the question Why do Mexicans call Americans gringos? "Mexicans do not call gringos gringos," Arellano responded. "Only gringos call gringos gringos. Mexicans call gringos *gabachos*." In the column, he continues to answer questions about Mexican culture, and he has been accused by many of stereotyping and responding to readers in scurrilous ways. "The people who write in—they have this preconceived notion of what a Mexican is," he responds. "I answer their question, but in a way that's either going to flip the stereotype or going to explode it."

The column has won many awards, including the 2006 and 2008 Best Non-Political Column in a Large-Circulation Weekly from the Association of Alternative Newsweeklies, the 2007 President's Award from the Los Angeles Press Club, an Impact Award from the National Hispanic Media Coalition, and a 2008 Latino Spirit Award from the California Latino Legislative Caucus.

In 2012, Arellano published the first authoritative study of Mexican food culture in America, *Taco USA: How Mexican Food Conquered America*, with much material culled from his columns.

ARROZ CON POLLO. A Hispanic American dish whose name is Spanish for "rice with chicken." The term was first mentioned in print in 1938.

ARROZ CON POLLO

Brown cut-up pieces of 1 chicken in 4 T. olive oil until browned, add 6 chorizo sausages cut into chunks, and brown with the chicken. Add 2 c. cooked rice to the skillet. In another pan, sauté 2 chopped cloves of garlic, 1 chopped onion, and 1 chopped green bell pepper and add to the chicken and rice. Mix 1 ¼ t. crumbled saffron in 6 c. chicken stock and add to rice. Add 4 peeled and chopped tomatoes and 1 c. peas. Cover and bake at 350° for 1 ½ hr. Garnish with pimiento strips. Serves 8.

ARTICHOKE (*Cynara scolymus*). A tall plant native to the Mediterranean, bearing a large, globular flower head with scaly, thistlelike bracts. The artichoke is eaten as a vegetable, usually boiled and served with butter or stuffed with bread crumbs and other seasonings and baked.

The word is from the Italian dialect word *articiocco*, ultimately from the Arabic *al-khurshūf*, first mentioned in English print in 1531.

The Spanish introduced the artichoke to California, but it was almost unknown to most Americans until well into the twentieth century, when its cultivation in the South and, principally, in California (which now produces 100 percent of the U.S. commercial crop) gave the vegetable a popularity that today is equaled only in France and Italy. Sicilian importer and mobster Ciro Terranova of NYC cornered the California artichoke market after World War I, and by 1935 he was nicknamed "the Artichoke King."

The only commercial kind grown in the U.S. is the "common" or "globe" artichoke. See also **Jerusalem artichoke**.

ARUGULA. Also "rugola." An herb (*Eruca vesicaria sativa*), known in England as "rockets." The name is derived from Italian regional words for the herb, *rucola* or *ruccetta*, and first appeared in American print in 1960. The herb is native to Eurasia but was brought to America by the Italian immigrants of the late nineteenth century, and it is still very much localized in this country within cities with large Italian populations. It is eaten with salad dressing and often with tomatoes. It should not be confused with "rocket salad," an American winter cress.

ASCORBIC ACID. Vitamin C. Ascorbic acid can be used as an antioxidant or a nutrient and color stabilizer; it also prevents the formation of nitrosamines (cancer-causing chemicals).

ASEPTIC PACKAGING. A package of food or drink filled so that almost all the air is driven out, thus preserving the contents from bacteria and spoilage. The word "asceptic" has been in print since 1855, but the first aseptic plant, for milk production, was opened only in 1961, in Switzerland. Aseptic packages first appeared in U.S. supermarkets in the 1970s. Wines thus stored are commonly called "wine in a box" or "wine in a bag," terms used since the 1980s.

ASHER, GERALD (1932–). Author, wine merchant. As *Gourmet* magazine's wine editor and columnist for thirty years, Gerald Asher was considered one of the most knowledgeable and stylish writers on the subject.

Asher was born in London, and as a student he worked part-time in a wine shop, where he developed an avid interest in wine. He took classes at the Vintners' Company and, through scholarships, worked with vintners in Spain, Germany, and France, eventually starting his own mail-order wine business and writing about wine for its brochures.

In 1955, he founded Asher, Storey & Co. in London, then in 1971 moved to New York City to work as vice president at Austin, Nichols & Co. He was president of the Monterey Wine Co., in San Francisco, from 1974 to

1976; vice president of "21" Brands from 1976 to 1978; and president of the Mosswood Wine Co. from 1978 until his retirement from the trade in 1987.

As a writer, Asher wrote a monthly column in the British magazine *Wine & Spirits* for three years and contributed to *Decanter* and *The World of Fine Wine.* In 1972 he was asked by *Gourmet* to begin a wine column on whatever he liked. "You must have real knowledge about what you're writing about," said Asher. "You can't wing it....I've always been surprised at the sloppiness of writers about all topics—if you know even a little sometimes you can tell just how little the writer knows himself." He also insisted that wine writing "has to be entertaining. So you start your story, and you throw in a little digression here or there. The little digressions you give can relieve the whole thing, give some background and relief and humor....My fingertips curl when I read tasting notes. Boring stuff."

Such an approach gave Asher's writing authority and readability, buoyed by his in-depth knowledge of the industry for which he worked, a connection he was sometimes criticized for as a conflict of interest. His column at *Gourmet* ended in 2002.

In 1974, Asher was awarded France's Order of the Mérite Agricole, and in 2009 he was inducted into California's Vintners Hall of Fame. Asher's books include *On Wine* (1986), *Wine Journal* (1996), *Vineyard Tales* (1996), *The Pleasures of Wine* (2002), and *A Vineyard in My Glass* (2011).

ASHLEY BREAD. A southern batter bread, similar to **spoon bread**, made from rice flour. The name may commemorate Anthony Ashley Cooper, first earl of Shaftesbury (1621–1683), one of the first proprietors of the royal colony of Carolina, for which he had John Locke draw up the first constitution. The following recipe is from Panchita Heyward Grimball, of the Wappaoolah Plantation, Cooper River, South Carolina, as printed in *200 Years of Charleston Cooking* (1930).

ASHLEY BREAD

Mix and sift 1 c. rice flour, ½ t. salt, 1 ½ t. baking powder; beat 1 egg with 1 c. milk and add to the dry ingredients. Stir in 1 ½ t. melted butter and turn batter into a well-greased shallow pan. Bake at 350° for about 45 min. Makes 8 large pieces.

ASIAN AMERICAN FOOD. A general term for the various foods cooked and enjoyed by Asian immigrants as well as those adaptations of classic Asian cuisine that became part of American gastronomy.

While **Japanese** and **Chinese** immigrants began arriving in the U.S. in the nineteenth century, other Asians did not come in large numbers until the second half of the twentieth century. Although there had been some Korean immigrants on Hawaii at the beginning of the century, they did not arrive on the mainland in significant numbers until after the end of the Korean War, in 1953, with about thirty thousand immigrating annually in the 1990s. They quickly established themselves in big cities as green grocers, especially in New York City and Los Angeles, where there are large Koreatown neighborhoods, with populations of about 200,000 and 120,000, respectively.

Koreans brought with them a food culture largely based on rice and grains, green vegetables, and, since World War II, a good deal of beef, which became the centerpiece of Korean American restaurants, where the customer sits at a brazier and cooks his own raw beef, a dish called *bulgogi*, with dipping sauces and the hot fermented cabbage condiment kimchi.

In the past decade, more sophisticated Korean restaurants have opened in U.S. cities, featuring diverse menus of traditional and modern dishes.

Thai immigrants began arriving in America after 1965, increasing by the end of the Vietnam War, and they now account for more than 300,000 residents, with the largest settlements in Los Angeles and other California cities.

Thai cuisine has long drawn on Chinese and Vietnamese influences, but its principal signature ingredient is the intensely hot *phrik khi nu*, "bird's eye" chile pepper, added to many savory preparations, along with rice or noodles and pungent sauces like *nam chim* and the fermented fish sauce *nam pla*. Pad Thai, a dish of noodles and shrimp, has become a standard dish in Thai American restaurants, as has the crispy noodle dish *mi krop*. Thai curry paste, garlic, Thai basil, coriander, lemongrass, and kaffir lime leaves are frequent components.

Coconut milk is used in curries and combined with fruit in many desserts. Peanut sauces are widely used on skewered, grilled meats.

The cuisine has proven very popular with Americans, and there are several authoritative Thai cookbooks on the market, including David Thompson's *Thai Food* (2002).

Many Vietnamese fled their homeland after the Communist takeover of South Vietnam in 1975, and today there are more than one million residents in the U.S., most settled on the Pacific coast, especially California. In Houston, many entered the fishing industry. Even the former prime minister of Vietnam, Nguyen Cao Ky, escaped in 1975 to the U.S., where he ran a liquor store in Westminster, California.

Owing to Vietnam's being a longtime colony of France, which called the country Indochina, there is a good deal of French influence on the food. Vietnamese food is not as spicy as some other Asian cuisines and does not use as many of the fiery condiments found in Thai, Malaysian, and certain regional Chinese cuisines. Spring rolls made with rice paper are myriad in Vietnamese food culture, and the adaptation of French baguettes, called *bánh mì*, to a variety of sandwiches such as pork belly, sausages, and pork pâté is now called a "banh mi sandwich" in America. One of the first authoritative cookbooks in English on Vietnamese cuisine was Nicole Routhier's *The Foods of Vietnam* (1989).

Few Vietnamese chefs have achieved the reputation enjoyed by Japanese and Chinese chefs in America. Perhaps the most famous to live in America is Charles Phan, of Chinese descent but born in Da Lat, Vietnam. Phan came to the U.S. with his family in 1977, settling in San Francisco's Chinatown. After studying architecture at the University of California at Berkeley, he began cooking for his large family, then, along with them, opened the Slanted Door restaurant in 1995, in the city's then run-down Mission District, winning acclaim in the local and national press and elevating the image of Vietnamese restaurants. Today he is owner of seven restaurants in San Francisco, including two at the Academy of Sciences. He is the author of *Vietnamese Home Cooking* (2012).

Other Asians have made headway as immigrants in the past three decades—Malaysians, Indonesians, Filipinos—each bringing their own food culture to enrich America's. Given Americans' interest in Asian ethnic foods since the end of the Vietnam War, many of those immigrants have thrived by opening restaurants introducing dishes like Indonesian beef skewers called *satay*, Filipino spring rolls called *lumpia*, and Malaysian chili crab.

ASPARAGUS (genus *Asparagus*). Any of 150 species of a Eurasian plant with long branchlets, the shoot of which is a very popular vegetable and is usually boiled or steamed. The name is from the Greek *asparagos* and first appeared in English print around A.D. 1000. Though it is not known when the vegetable reached America, Swedish naturalist Peter Kalm reported finding them growing both wild and cultivated in New Jersey during his travels in 1740, and asparagus recipes appear in cookery books of the latter eighteenth century. By the 1850s it was being propagated in California, which still produces 70 percent of the national crop.

The common asparagus (*A. plumosus*) has flourished in the United States. A particularly hardy variety, the Mary Washington, was developed by the USDA. Most American asparagus is sold fresh.

ASPARTAME. An artificial sweetener of aspartic acid and phenylalanine created accidentally in 1965 by chemist James M. Schlatter of G. D. Searle & Co., in Skokie, Illinois. Aspartame, also known as NutraSweet, is two hundred times sweeter than sugar and is used in processed foods and as a substitute for sugar. The monopoly on the use of the name "aspartame" by the NutraSweet Co. in the U.S. market ended in 1992.

ATKINS, ROBERT (1930–2003). Physician and author of several books promoting a high fat, low carbohydrate diet. Dr. Atkins was famous enough to cause *Time* to name him one of the Ten Most Influential People in the World in 2002. Atkins was not the first to promote such diets—previous proponents date back to the eighteenth century, and in 1967 *Dr. Irwin Stillman's The Doctor's Quick Weight Loss Diet* proposed high protein and low carbohydrates but also low fat. But Atkins was by far the most successful at it.

Born in Columbus, Ohio, Robert Coleman Atkins moved to Dayton, where his family ran restaurants. He graduated from the University of Michigan in 1951 and received his M.D. from Cornell University Medical College in 1955, specializing in cardiology and internal medicine after residency, then opening his practice in NYC.

When his own weight rose to 224 pounds, Atkins went on a low-starch, low-sugar diet proposed by Dr. Alfred W. Pennington. After Atkins appeared on Johnny Carson's *Tonight Show* to promote his diet, *Vogue* published an article (1970) about it that came to be known as "The Vogue Diet," which led to his publishing the bestselling *Dr. Atkins' Diet Revolution* (1972). He then opened the holistic Atkins Center for Complementary Medicine to sell diet products and in 1998 founded his own nutrition and supplements company, Atkins Nutritionals. He followed this with *Dr. Atkins' New Diet Revolution* (1992), which sold more than fifteen million copies in the U.S. For many Americans, the idea of a high-protein diet rich in meat, eggs, and bacon was regarded as an appealing alternative to one that cut fats and promoted vegetables. The impact of the Atkins diet on the American public was enormous—it was calculated at one point in the late 1990s that one out of eleven people were on it—and its effect on the downturn in sales of carbohydrate food products like pasta was significant for a while.

While critics warned of the prospects of long-term cardiovascular health problems associated with the diet, Atkins insisted that his clinical research indicated this was not a problem, at least in the short term. Atkins suffered cardiac arrest in 2002, which he contended was due to a chronic infection. Other cardiologists agreed there was no connection to Atkins's diet.

On April 8, 2003, Atkins slipped on icy pavement, causing severe head trauma, and he died nine days later. After his death, without an avid spokesman for the regimen, the Atkins diet faded in popularity, and in 2005 Nutritionals filed for bankruptcy.

ATOLE. A southwestern drink made from **masa** or a form of cornmeal mush, often sweetened with honey and frequently served with **buñuelos**. The term is from Mexican Spanish and dates in English print to 1672.

AUTOMAT. An inexpensive and informal restaurant where food was displayed in small compartments whose windows opened when the required number of coins was deposited. The term comes from the Greek *automatos*, "self-acting." The first such establishment was Joseph Horn and Frank Hardart's Automat, which opened June 9, 1902, in Philadelphia and used German equipment based on a Swedish patent, but it was in New York City (where they opened their first Automat in Times Square on July 2, 1912) that the concept became an important part of city life, with forty establishments operating by 1939.

So linked to the idea of the Automat were its originators' names that Americans more often than not referred to such places as "Horn & Hardarts." These eateries became representative of Americans' love of economy coupled with a mock grandiosity that resulted in a period of lavish Automats full of white tile and Carrara marble. They were kept spotlessly clean, and it was quite normal to find everyone from unemployed drifters, lingering over a five-cent cup of coffee, to the brightest of Broadway's celebrities there. Silver-ornamented spigots dispensed coffee, tea, and hot chocolate. Stews, desserts, rolls, and sandwiches were offered in profusion.

Robert F. Byrnes wrote of the Horn & Hardart Co. in its heyday: "If you were the young man who had escaped from Easton, and you went to Horn & Hardart for Thanksgiving and for company, after you ate your fill you could walk back to your furnished room and write to your sister about the great meal. You could say you went in with a dollar in your pocket, and came out with 50 cents."

After World War II, **fast food** restaurants and hamburger stands ascended in popularity while the Automats declined; the last Automat closed its doors in New York City on April 10, 1991.

The facade of glass doors of an original Automat is displayed at the Smithsonian Institution's Museum of American History.

AVOCADO (*Persea gratissima* or *Persea americana*). Also "alligator pear." A tropical tree that bears a globular green fruit with a large seed and tough skin. The name is from the Nahuatl *ahuacatl*, "testicle" (because of its shape), and entered English via the Spanish, first appearing in print in the seventeenth century and in America in 1690.

The Aztecs ate avocados, as was noted by the early Spanish explorers, but the avocado was long considered a rather tasteless food, enjoyed only in Central and South America and in the Caribbean, where it acquired its alternative name "alligator pear," possibly because it grew where there were alligators, as in Florida, or because of its alligatorlike skin.

Horticulturist Henry Perrine planted the first avocados in Florida in 1833, but it was not until the turn of the century, after it was planted in California in the 1880s, that the plant took on commercial importance. In 1915, the California Avocado Society was founded, its members uniting under the name Calavo. The avocado was promoted as a healthy fruit and found its way into Mexican recipe books and restaurants in the 1920s. Even then the avocado was not particularly relished by most Americans, and only in California, Florida, and Hawaii, the major producing states, was it much appreciated until it became popular as a salad item in the 1950s. The El Torito restaurant chain popularized tableside preparation of guacamole.

The major varieties grown include the Hass, Fuerte, Bacon, Zutano, Rincón, Mexican, Guatemalan, Booth 8, Booth 7, Lula, and Waldin.

The avocado is the major ingredient in **guacamole**, which is consumed in such quantities on the National Football League's Super Bowl Sunday that 79 million tons of avocados are used, representing 5 percent of U.S. annual consumption of the fruit.

'AWA (*Piper methysticum*). The Hawaiian name for the kava shrub, with heart-shaped leaves, traditionally used by Hawaiians as a drink and a medicine. The word is Polynesian, dating in English print to 1930.

Awa also is a Hawaiian word for the milkfish (*Chanos chanos*), similar to a herring and at least three feet in length (1960). They are usually baked or steamed.

AWENDA BREAD. Also "Awaendaw." A Carolinas bread made from hominy grits and/or cornmeal, named after an Indian settlement near Charleston, South Carolina. The term dates in print to 1847.

AWENDA BREAD

Push ½ c. cooked hominy grits through a sieve, beat in 1 egg, ½ c. cornmeal, 1 t. sugar, 1 t. salt, 1 t. baking powder, and ¾ c. milk to make a thin batter. Grease a 1-qt. baking pan, pour in batter, and cook 40–50 min. at 350°. Serve with butter.

BABY BEEF. Western term used since the 1890s for young cattle killed for market. Today the term refers to a calf several months old and weaned from its mother. This is often sold as **veal**, though it is not considered of the highest quality because of its age.

BABY FOOD. A general term, dating in print to 1832, for any food served to infants, but also a food-industry term for those products developed for feeding infants. Until the twentieth century, infant food was a matter of individual families' choices, directed by conventional and inherited wisdom as well as published guidelines for good nutrition.

In 1867, Henri Nestlé of Switzerland created the first artificial baby food, which became an instant success in the U.S., Europe, and even Asia. Gail Borden promoted his condensed milk, created in 1856, as baby food, and Moores and Ross Milk Co. came out with Franklin Infant Food in 1924, changing its name to Similac three years later.

In 1927, Daniel F. Gerber began marketing a strained baby food under the name Gerber's (now based in Fremont, Michigan); a year later Gerber was issuing five varieties of baby food. In 1931, Beech-Nut Packing Co. introduced thirteen varieties of pureed baby food in glass jars. By 1935 more than sixty other companies had entered the baby-food market.

Beginning in the 1960s, there were consumer protests against putting additives like sugar and monosodium glutamate into baby food, at the same time that a new advocacy for breast-feeding arose, opposing the widespread use of bottled formula.

Today only 15 percent of American families make baby food at home.

BABY VEGETABLE. Also "miniature vegetable." A food marketing term that gained currency in the early 1980s to describe vegetables that are picked very young and small or for hybrids genetically grown to be of a small size. They are prized both for their sweetness and texture and for their appearance on a plate.

BACARDI COCKTAIL. A cocktail made with lime juice, sugar, grenadine, and Bacardi light rum. The name dates in print to at least 1934 and is directly associated with the firm Bacardi Imports Inc., of Miami. In 1936, a New York State Supreme Court ruled that, to be authentic, a "Bacardi cocktail" had to be made with Bacardi rum, since the name Bacardi was a registered trademark.

BACARDI COCKTAIL

Shake together with ice 2 t. lime juice, ½ t. sugar, 1 t. grenadine, and 1 ½ oz. Bacardi light rum. Strain into chilled cocktail glasses.

BACHELOR'S BUTTON. A cookie with a cherry set on top and made to resemble a button (1969). The cookie has nothing to do with the flower of the same name, except for its similar shape.

BACKDAAG. A Pennsylvania Dutch word for "Baking Day," which was Friday on Pennsylvania Dutch farms. One day was set aside for baking because occasional baking of one or two items could not satisfy the needs of the hardworking farmers.

BACK OF THE HOUSE. Restaurant workers' slang term meaning the kitchen or the kitchen staff itself.

BACON. Salted and/or smoked meat taken from the sides and back of a pig. Bacon is cut in slices and fried, usually as a breakfast item, or used as larding in certain dishes. It is customarily served with broiled or fried calf's liver. "Belly bacon" is taken from the belly of the animal.

The word *bacon* (circa 1330) derives from Middle English *bakoun*, though it was also a more general term for pork well into the sixteenth century. In America bacon has long been a staple of most households, largely because of a long history of pork consumption and hog butchering on farms. "Bacon pigs" are animals especially grown for their bacon, often from breeds like the Yorkshire and Tamworth.

Bacon may be cured at home with salt and some sugar, but factory bacon may be either "dry cured" with salt before cooking and smoking or "pickle cured" with brine before being smoked and cooked.

"Regular" bacon is sold at markets cut into slabs or slices. "Thin-sliced" (also known as "hotel" or "restaurant" bacon) is sliced approximately $^1/_{32}$ of an inch in thickness; "regular" is sliced $^1/_{16}$ of an inch; "thick-sliced" or "thick-cut" is cut about twice as thick as regular bacon. "Country style" bacon is usually a generously sliced, well-cured bacon. Canned bacon is usually precooked and used where there is little access to kitchen stoves and equipment. **Cracklings** are the fried pieces of fat left in the pan after the bacon is removed. In Mexican American regions, these are called *chicharrons* (from the Spanish). "Bacon bits" are preserved and dried (though there are also artificial bacon-flavored bits sold in jars), usually for tossing with a salad dressing.

"Canadian-style" bacon (called "back bacon" in Canada) is cut from the loin, strip, or sirloin muscles along the pig's back. It is a leaner, drier, fully cooked meat, usually sold in a packaged hunk. The reason for the name is not clear. "Flitch" is a term used in Pennsylvania for unsmoked "slab bacon," sometimes called "side bacon."

"Lower-salt bacon" has decreased levels of salt. "Salt pork" is a very fatty cured pork (also called "white bacon"), generally used as a cooking fat or flavoring for other dishes. "Beef bacon" is made from boneless beef short plates cured like regular bacon. "Turkey bacon" is made from turkey that is cured and then molded to look like regular bacon.

"Bac-Os," introduced in 1966 by General Mills, are bits of **soy protein** isolate flavored to taste like bacon.

In the U.S., 1.7 billion pounds of bacon are consumed each year, nearly 70 percent at breakfast.

BAGEL. A round yeast bun with a hole in the middle, which is cooked in boiling water and then baked. The bagel, once a staple of Jewish immigrants' Sunday breakfasts, has become a reasonable substitute for sandwich bread in many American cities where **delicatessens** exist. Traditionally the bagel is eaten with such delicacies as **lox** or Nova Scotia salmon and slices of white onions; the most classic match is cream cheese (an American creation) and lox. Bagels are sometimes toasted, and one will find them studded with onion flakes, sesame seeds, poppy seeds, or raisins or made from dark flours. Because of its heaviness, the bagel is sometimes referred to as a "cement doughnut."

The bagel was first mentioned in English print in 1892, as "beuglich," and in American print as "bagels" only in 1916. The first bagels sold in a supermarket were from Lender's Bagel Bakery (the nation's oldest frozen bagel maker), in New Haven, Connecticut, in 1955. The same company was the first to sell frozen bagels, as of 1962, which helped enormously to popularize the item nationally. Lender's also claims credit for the first green bagels, now a common variation baked each year for Saint Patrick's Day.

The origins of the bagel are lost. The word *bagel* derives from a Yiddish word, *beygl*, from the German *bügel*, for a round loaf of bread. There is a story that the word may also derive from the German word *böugel*, meaning "ring" and also "stirrup," referring to a legend that the bakers of Vienna commemorated John III's victory over the Turks in their city in 1683 by molding their bread into the shape of stirrups, because the liberated Austrians had clung to the king's stirrups as he rode by. But Leo Rosten in *The Joys of Yiddish* (1968) notes that the first printed mention of the word "bagel" is in the Community Regulations of Krakow for 1610, which stated that the item was given as a gift to women in childbirth. So associated with NYC folklore and food culture is the bagel that in 1951 the *New York Times* printed a story on its front page headlined BAGEL FAMINE THREATENS IN CITY/LABOR DISPUTE PUTS HOLE IN

SUPPLY. In 2012, the newspaper also included the bagel as part of "A History of New York in 50 Objects."

Bagel sales rose in the 1980s and had doubled by 1993 but began to drop at the beginning of the twenty-first century. Currently the top ten bagel suppliers in the U.S. have sales of about $600 million.

BAGEL DOG. Trademarked name for a hot dog boiled and then baked in a bagel dough topped with poppy seed. The item, similar to the cocktail-party item called "**pig in a blanket**," was created in 1980 by bakery owner Milan R. Burger of Durham, North Carolina.

BAGOONG. A fermented fish or shrimp condiment used in Hawaii to flavor meats and vegetable dishes. The word derives from the Tagalog and dates in English print to 1940. Bagoong is made by salting the fish or shrimp and allowing it to ferment for several days, after which the liquid is pressed out. The condiment is usually eaten raw.

BAKED ALASKA. A dessert made of sponge cake covered with ice cream and a meringue that is browned in the oven, with the ice cream remaining frozen (1905).

The idea of baking ice cream in some kind of crust so as to create a hot-cold blend of textures occurred to Thomas Jefferson, who in 1802 served minister Manasseh Cutler a puddinglike dish that included "ice cream very good, crust wholly dried, crumbled into thin flakes." And a report in the French journal *Liberté* for June 1866 indicates that the master cook of the Chinese mission in Paris imparted a technique for baking pastry over ice cream to the French chef Balzac of the Grand Hotel. But baked Alaska as we know it today may be traced to the experiments in heating and cooking conducted by Benjamin Thompson (1753–1814), born in Woburn, Massachusetts, who became a celebrated scientist both at home and in England, where he was awarded the title of Count Rumford for his work. (The name Rumford came from the town of Rumford—now Concord—New Hampshire, where his wife was born.) His studies of the resistance of egg whites to heat resulted in the browned topping that eventually became the crown for what came to be called baked Alaska. Patricia M. Tice, in *Ice Cream for All* (1990), asserted that Delmonico's chef Charles Ranhofer created "baked Alaska" in 1869

to commemorate the purchase of Alaska by the U.S., although in his own cookbook, *The Epicurean* (1893), Ranhofer calls the dish "Alaska, Florida." The term "baked Alaska" dates in print to at least 1905 and was used by Fannie Merritt Farmer in the 1909 edition of her cookbook.

BAKED ALASKA

Trim a sponge cake to a 1-in. thickness and cover with about 3 in. of ice cream. Freeze until very firm. Beat 5 egg whites until stiff with 1 t. vanilla, ½ t. cream of tartar, and ⅔ c. sugar. Remove the ice cream cake from freezer and spread the egg whites in swirls around the ice cream in the shape of a dome. Bake in a 500° oven until the top is golden brown, about 3 min. Serve immediately.

BAKE SALE. A neighborhood or school social event at which baked goods and confections are sold in order to raise money for a charitable purpose. The idea goes back to colonial America, when money would be raised to build a church, barn, or other building.

BAKING POWDER. A combination of sodium bicarbonate and acid salt that became popular in the 1850s as a leavening agent in baking what came to be called "quick bread," "lightnin' bread," or "aerated bread." By 1854 Americans had self-rising flour, which was baking powder mixed with flour. In 1867, James A. Church introduced Arm & Hammer "baking soda," a new term for the earlier used but less desirable potassium or sodium bicarbonate, also called "saleratus," an American variant of the Latin *sal* (salt) plus *aeratus* (aerated).

In 1889, William M. Wright developed a "double-acting" baking powder whose leavening action began in the dough and repeated in the oven. Wright and his partner, chemist George C. Rew, marketed the product under the name Calumet Baking Powder. (Calumet was the name the French gave the peace pipe that Indians offered to Father Jacques Marquette when he explored the territories around Chicago in the 1670s; for Wright the name symbolized "friendliness.")

BALD FACE. Nineteenth-century slang term for inferior whiskey (1836).

BALKENBRIJ. A pork loaf that is cooked and cut into slabs and usually served for breakfast. The word comes from the Dutch term for the rafter from which the meat was hung to cure, dating in English print to 1940.

BAMBOCHE. Also "bambache." A Cajun or Deep South term for a drinking spree, from the French, dating in English print to 1944.

BAMBOO COCKTAIL. A cocktail said to have been invented in about 1910 by bartender Charlie Mahoney of the Hoffman House, in NYC.

BAMBOO COCKTAIL

Combine 1 oz. sherry, 1 oz. dry vermouth, and a dash of orange bitters, stir with ice, strain, and serve in a wineglass with a lemon peel.

BANANA. Any of a variety of tropical or subtropical trees of the genus *Musa*, bearing clusters of long yellow or reddish fruits. The name is from Portuguese and Spanish, via a West African name, and was first printed in English in the seventeenth century.

The banana, which has been traced to southern Asia and India, may have been cultivated as long ago as 1000 B.C. in Assyria. The Arabs brought the fruit to Egypt in the seventh century, and Portuguese navigators found bananas in 1482 on Africa's west coast and thereafter transplanted them to the Canary Islands. The early Spanish explorers of the New World remarked on the "bananas" in the West Indies, but what they had actually seen was plantains (*Musa paradisiaca*). In 1516, on the island of Hispaniola, Fray Tomás de Berlanga planted the first banana trees in the West Indies, but propagation of the fruit was limited to the islands until well into the nineteenth century. The first bananas entered the U.S. only in 1804, when they were brought from Cuba to NYC by Captain John Chester on the schooner *Reynard*. But no further shipments arrived in the city, or anywhere else in North America, until 1830, when Captain John Pearsall brought in fifteen hundred stems on the schooner *Harriet Smith*. By the 1840s NYC markets were receiving frequent shipments of bananas, and in 1870 Captain Lorenzo D. Baker of the *Telegraph* brought a cargo of the fruit to Boston from Jamaica, leading to a partnership with a fruit broker named Andrew Pearson. Together they founded the Boston Fruit Co. and introduced the banana as an exotic fruit wrapped in foil and sold for a dime at the Philadelphia Centennial Exposition of 1876. The Boston Fruit Co. was merged by Samuel Zemurray and Minor Keith into the United Fruit Co. (later United Brands) in 1899, which, with the introduction of refrigerated cargo holds, began shipping bananas to new ports and markets in the U.S. The success of the banana after the turn of the century led to widespread involvement of American companies and the federal government in the affairs and politics of the Caribbean and Central and South America. Plantations were established in what came to be called "banana republics," run for the benefit and interests of the fruit companies in the U.S., often to the detriment of the inhabitants of those countries.

Although Hawaii had long grown bananas (discovered there by Captain James Cook in 1799), the state has never had a significant commercial banana industry. Most bananas eaten in the U.S.—between 70 million and 80 million bunches a year, making it Americans' most popular fruit—are shipped in from Costa Rica, Guatemala, and other countries, with the majority being the common banana (M. *sapientum*), of which the Gros Michel variety (from Jamaica) was the predominant variety until 1944, when the Valery, Lacatan, Williams, Grand Nain, and other varieties entered the marketplace.

The "red banana" and the plantain varieties are becoming more common in American markets.

Americans, who consume 28 pounds of bananas per capita each year, eat them raw, in salads, in various desserts, and as a flavoring for breads and other confections.

The "frozen banana" is a banana that has been frozen, then dipped into hot chocolate and usually coated with toppings of crushed nuts or sprinkles. According to a 2007 article in the *Daily Pilot*, the confection was created around 1940 by Don Philips (called the "frozen banana king") at a stand called the Original Frozen Banana on Balboa Island (part of Newport Beach, California).

BANANA BREAD. Also "banana cake." A loaf with a cakelike consistency made from flour and mashed bananas. Fannie Merritt Farmer's cookbook made reference in 1896 to a "banana cake," which was really a cake with sliced bananas on top. But in the 1960s and 1970s, a period of delight in hearty, fresh-made breads, banana bread took on a certain faddishness.

BANANAS FOSTER. A dessert made from sliced bananas cooked with butter, brown sugar, rum, and banana cordial and served with vanilla ice cream. The dish was created in the early 1950s by chef Paul Blange at Brennan's restaurant, in New Orleans, as part of a Breakfast at Brennan's promotion that has since become a city tradition. (The restaurant was opened in 1946.) It was named after a regular customer, Richard Foster, owner of the Foster Awning Co., in New Orleans. The recipe below is from Brennan's.

BANANAS FOSTER

Melt 4 T. butter in a flambé pan over an alcohol burner. Add 1 c. brown sugar, ½ t. cinnamon, and 4 T. banana cordial and mix well. Heat for a few minutes, then place 4 bananas that have been cut in half lengthwise and then halved widthwise in pan and sauté until soft. Add ¼ c. rum and allow to heat well, then tip pan so that flame from burner ignites alcohol. Allow to burn until flame dies out. Serve over vanilla ice cream by placing 4 pieces of banana on each portion, then spooning hot sauce from the pan onto the bananas and ice cream.

BANKET. A Dutch American rolled pastry filled with almond paste. It is commonly shaped into alphabet letters and called "banket letters." The word is from the Dutch, dating in print to 1969.

BANNOCK. Also "Indian bannock." A nineteenth-century New England cornmeal cake derived from a Scottish barley or wheat pancake of the same name, first in English print in 1483. Sometimes this was called "white Indian bannock," because of the use of white Indian cornmeal.

BAPTIST CAKE. A New England deep-fried dough-nut-like confection. Baptist cakes are risen dough balls that have been immersed in hot oil, like Baptists who are immersed in water at their baptism. The term

dates in print to 1931. In Connecticut they are called "holy pokes," in Maine "huff juffs," and in other parts "hustlers."

BAR. Also "bar room" or "barroom." A tavern or room where alcoholic beverages are served, or the long counter at which one stands or sits to drink such beverages. The word derives from the more general meaning of a long slab or block of wood or other material used to separate or support, and in this sense derives from Vulgar Latin *barra*. In its usage for a tavern, the word dates from the sixteenth century, when bars would be pulled across the counter at closing time. "Bar room" came into the language in the late eighteenth century, and in America "bartender" (one who tends the bar) was known by 1836; ten years later, "bar keep" was also used. "Bar-counter" was used by Dickens in his *American Notes* (1842), and by 1857 there were female hostesses called, with some condescension, "bargirls" (also "B-girls").

By the 1830s "saloon" (from the French *salon*, "room") was an alternative word for a bar, and there were many other, less savory terms, like "barrel-house," "watering hole," "gin mill," "rum hole," "whiskey joint," and, later, **juke** joint," to join the more refined, post-Prohibition "cocktail lounge." "Dram shop" first saw print in 1839. Today the word "bar" suggests an establishment where the principal business is the dispensing of alcoholic drinks, while "tavern" is somewhat quaint and "saloon" a bit dated, except when used as a deliberately nostalgic reference. The idea of the "corner saloon" began in NYC after an 1841 ordinance permitted the sale of meat and vegetables in shops removed from the marketplace. This eventually led to the sale of spirits in these same shops, many of which were located on corners. When the sale of spirits took precedence over the sale of food, a "corner saloon" or "corner bar" was the result.

"Bar and grill" conveys a bar that holds some culinary interest, while "lounge" refers more to a bar's booths-and-tables section than to its counter, which is usually flanked by "barstools" (first noted in Arthur Koestler's novel *Twilight Bar* in 1945) and a "bar rail," on which to rest one's foot.

A "smart bar" is a 1990s term denoting a bar (often set within a conventional bar) that serves nonalcoholic drinks. A "dive bar" is a particularly unsavory one, although the term "dive" has been more commonly applied to any unsavory place as dated back to 1867.

BARBECUE. Also "Bar-B-Q," "BBQ," "'cue," and other variations. A method of cooking meat, poultry, or fish over an open pit fire, often with the whole animal skewered on a spit, and almost always done out-of-doors. Barbecues are as much a social ritual in America as they are a means of cooking, for they are held as often for large parties, celebrations, and political rallies as for cooking a family's meal. Barbecuing methods go back to the earliest days, when man first used fire to cook his food, but the term "barbecue" comes from the Spanish and Haitian word *barbacoa* ("framework of sticks"), which referred first to a kind of latticework bench but soon after was adapted to mean the grill on which meat was roasted. The *Dictionary of American English* shows that the word was in use in America by at least 1655, when it first appeared in print, and by 1733 it had taken on the implications of a social gathering. By 1836 barbecues were popular in Texas, and in 1850, at a barbecue held in Kansas, the menu included six cattle, twenty hogs, fifty sheep, pigs, and lambs, a hundred hams, and hundreds of baked goods.

Regional distinctions and preferences for various styles of barbecue have long been part of folkloric debate in America, and barbecue contests have proliferated in recent years throughout the U.S. In the South, barbecue is akin to a religion, and from county to county, preferences for a certain ratio of tomato to vinegar or sugar to chile peppers are myriad. Even the condiments and side dishes are steeped in tradition. In eastern North Carolina, for instance, vinegar-based barbecue sauce is preferred with coleslaw colored with turmeric. In western North Carolina, recipes are more tomato-based, and pure white coleslaw is preferred.

Barbecue may be done over an open fire on a spit (as is most common in Texas and the West) or over a "barbecue pit," which may be constructed of anything from a simple outdoor grill to an iron smoker, and barbecue enthusiasts delight in inventing new contraptions in which to cook and smoke their barbecue. In Hawaii, **kalua pig** is wrapped in **ti** leaves and cooked in a pit dug in the ground.

The most basic distinction in barbecue is the meat used, with pork more commonly used east of the Mississippi River and beef preferred west of it, although both meats are common throughout the U.S. Sausage is also a very popular meat, and hamburgers, hot dogs, steaks, seafood, and vegetables are barbecued, too.

Pork barbecue takes two primary forms: as ribs or as meat that has been sliced, chopped, or shredded (called "pulled pork"), then served on a hamburger bun or sliced white bread. In St. Louis, deep-fried pig's noses, called "snoots," are a local **soul food** favorite.

Beef barbecue, especially in Texas and Kansas City, Missouri, is heavily smoked, usually made from the brisket, and served with white bread and pickles on the side.

Next comes the issue of sauce. Barbecue of various kinds has always been basted with herbs and marinades, but "barbecue sauce" as such is of rather recent vintage. The earliest reference to a sauce by this name was cited by Betty Fussell—in *I Hear America Cooking* (1986)—as a "French brown sauce, spiked with ketchup, onions, mustard, and Worcestershire sauce," that came from Louis De Gouy's *Chefs Cook Book* (1939).

In parts of the South (even within the same city), "wet barbecue" vies with "dry barbecue" for honors. The former is based on a sauce that commonly contains tomato, vinegar, chile, and other seasonings and sugar that is continuously basted on the meat. Dry barbecue is made by rubbing the meat with dry seasonings like chiles, cumin, black pepper, and herbs, then barbecueing it slowly.

A third main difference in barbecue styles is in the kind of wood used to smoke and cook the meat, usually dependent upon the wood available in the region. Hardwoods like oak, ash, apple, beech, butternut, chestnut, cherry, and walnut are popular in the South, while mesquite is preferred in the West, and grapevines are often used in viticultural areas.

Americans barbecue 2.3 times a week in summer (steak is the most popular item on the grill), with most of the cooking done by men. The most popular grill was for decades the saucer-shaped "Weber Kettle" grill, invented by George Stephen of Chicago in 1952 and now produced by Weber-Stephen Products Co. of Palatine, Illinois. Charcoal grills have given way to gas grills in popularity, with gas grills outselling charcoal by about 30 percent. Most people barbecue year-round. Small

Japanese-style "hibachis" are commonly used in small spaces. The use of store-bought charcoal and packaged "briquettes" of compressed charcoal is widespread. The two principal aromatic woods used to add flavor to barbecue are hickory and mesquite. "Water smoker" cookers utilize a water pan, usually containing wood chips for flavor, set above the coals to generate steam that slow-cooks the ingredients.

SPARERIB BARBECUE

Sauté 3 c. coarsely chopped onions and 1 ½ T. minced garlic in 4 T. oil until soft but not brown. Add one 1-lb. can drained, chopped tomatoes with liquid, 2 T. dry mustard, 2 T. sugar, 1 ½ T. vinegar, ¾ c. tomato paste, salt, pepper, and about 6 seeded chiles (or add chiles to taste). Bring to a boil and reduce till thickened. Correct seasoning and remove from heat. Skewer spareribs, baste lavishly with sauce, and grill over hot coals, basting often, for about 30 min. Serve with heated sauce on side. (This same sauce may be used for chicken barbecue.)

PORK BARBECUE

In a large kettle, brown 3 lb. pork shoulder in 3 T. fat. Mix together ½ c. ketchup, 1 t. chili powder or cayenne, ½ t. nutmeg, ¼ t. cinnamon, 1 t. celery seed, 1 t. sugar, ½ t. nutmeg, salt and pepper, ⅓ c. vinegar, and 1 c. water. Bring to a boil and cook for 10 min. Pour over pork, cover, and bake at 325°, basting often, for about 1 ½ hr. or more, until pork is very tender and comes away easily with knife and fork. Remove all meat from bone and chop into fine pieces or shreds, then add salt, pepper, and hot sauce to taste. Serve with coleslaw and corn bread.

BAR CHUM. Bartender slang for snack foods served at a bar, usually free with drinks. The term dates in print to 1991.

BARFLY. A term dating in print to 1906, for someone who stays too long at a saloon, or a drunkard. Harry MacElhone, owner of Harry's New York Bar in Paris, founded a less-than-serious organization called International Bar Fly (IBF) in 1924, which now supposedly has more than eighty thousand members.

BAR GLASSES. Any of the various types of glassware used at a bar. There are dozens of such glasses (*Grossman's Guide to Wines, Beers, and Spirits*, a 1977 book by Harold J. Grossman, revised by Harriet Lembeck, shows thirty-seven different types), but few bars or restaurants stock more than a few useful kinds, such as those listed below.

COCKTAIL GLASS. A 2 ½-ounce stemmed glass with a tapered bowl, used to serve cocktails. A larger 4 ½-ounce cocktail glass with a wider rim is preferred, especially for **martinis**, and this glass is usually called a "martini glass."

COLLINS GLASS. A cylindrical 12-ounce glass for long drinks like the **Tom Collins**.

HIGHBALL GLASS. A cylindrical 8-ounce glass for mixed drinks on the rocks.

JIGGER. A short, squat, thick glass used to hold 1 ½ ounces of spirits, it is often used as a measuring glass or shot glass.

OLD-FASHIONED GLASS. A short, cylindrical, sometimes stemmed 6-ounce glass with a thick bottom, used for serving short drinks on the rocks, like the **old-fashioned**.

PILSNER GLASS. A long, conical glass of at least 10 ounces, used to hold beer. Its design helps to maintain a foamy head on the beer.

PONY OR LIQUEUR GLASS. A 1-ounce glass that is stemmed and tubular in shape, used for **cordials**.

SAUCER GLASS OR CHAMPAGNE GLASS. Traditionally (though not recommended by connoisseurs) used for serving **champagne** and sparkling drinks, this stemmed 5-ounce glass has a flat, saucerlike bowl.

SHERRY GLASS. A slightly fluted 2-ounce glass used for sherry and cordials.

SHOT GLASS. A short, squat, thick-bottomed glass used to serve a "shot" of whiskey and other spirits. It is often called a "cheater," because the customer often does not receive a full ounce.

SOUR GLASS. A stemmed 6-ounce glass for serving **sours**.

WINEGLASS. According to the wine served, these glasses may be of various heights, shapes, and stems. The all-purpose wineglass holds between 6 ½ and 8 ½ ounces of liquid. White wines are customarily served in long-stemmed glasses with a medium-size bowl; Bordeaux and other red wines are served in glasses with a slightly larger bowl; Burgundy and other red wines are considered best served in a balloon glass with a large bowl; German wines customarily are served in a small-bowled glass with a long green stem; brandies are served in snifters, glasses with short stems and large-bottomed bowls.

BARLEY (*Hordeum vulgare*). A grain of the grass family that was brought to the U.S. by early settlers, who ground the seed for use as a cereal, in breads and cakes, and as "barley sugar." The word is from Old English *boerlic*. Today the U.S. is the second-largest producer of barley, after the Soviet Union. Most barley is used for livestock feed or for making beer, but it is still also used in cakes, breads, and mixed **cereals**. The total U.S. production of barley in 2011 was 168 million bushels.

BARRACUDA (genus *Sphyraena*). Any of various long, silvery tropical fishes with a row of sharp, long teeth. Barracuda are often poisonous to eat, though the Pacific barracuda has long been a delicacy in California, where it is sold fresh. The fish, which is voracious and feared, may be broiled, grilled, or smoked. The word is from the Spanish, and its first appearance in English was in 1678.

BASS. Any of a variety of salt- or freshwater fish, whose general name derives from Old English *baers* and has German roots that mean "bristle," which describes the spiny appearance of any number of fish of the perch and other families. *The American Heritage Dictionary* defines bass, first, as "any of several North American freshwater fishes of the family Centrarchidae" and, second, as "any of various marine fishes of the family Serranidae." U.S. commercial landings of sea bass totaled 1.8 million pounds in 2008, and recreational landings 1.6 million pounds. The **Chilean sea bass**, also known as the "Patagonian toothfish," is not a true bass.

Some sea **perch**, **grouper**, **jewfish**, **black bass**, **black sea bass**, **striped bass**, and others go by the name "bass," but the only fish in Europe by this specific name is what the French call *loup*.

BASTARD BREAD. Bread made with a mixture of white flour and cornmeal (1965).

BATALI, MARIO (1960–). American chef, restaurateur, cookbook author, and TV personality. Born in Seattle, Batali is of Italian American and French Canadian ancestry. After attending Rutgers University, where he majored in Spanish, theater, and economics, Batali attended London's Le Cordon Bleu cooking school, then worked in kitchens in London and Paris before returning to the U.S. to work as a chef at the Four Seasons hotel in Santa Barbara, California. In 1989, he moved to Borgo Capanne, Italy, to learn Italian cooking at La Volta restaurant, then returned to NYC to open his own restaurant, Pó, in 1993 (later sold to his partner). Batali than paired with restaurateur Joseph Bastianich to open a series of high-profile restaurants including Babbo Ristorante e Enoteca (1998), Lupa (1999), Esca (2000), Casa Mono (2004), Del Posto (2005), Pizzeria Mozza (2006) and Osteria Mozza (2007) in Los Angeles, two restaurants in Las Vegas, and one in Singapore.

Rotund, redheaded, with a ponytail, and always in his uniform of khaki shorts and orange clogs, Batali is known for his bravura cooking and for introducing a style of rich, lusty regional Italian cuisine at Babbo that often used offal and parts of animals not commonly seen on New York menus.

Batali became one of the first TV celebrity chefs when he appeared on his own cooking show, *Molto Mario*, from 1997 to 2005 and was one of the master chefs of the *Iron Chef* series, both on the **Food Network**. For the PBS network he did a series entitled *Spain…on*

BATH TOWEL—BATTERBERRY, MICHAEL AND ARIANE RUSKIN

the Road Again with actress Gwyneth Paltrow. He also appeared as a character in the film *Bitter Feast* (2010).

In 2011, Batali and investors opened a fifty-thousand-square-foot food market in NYC called Eataly, a branch of the original in Turin, Italy. In 2008 he established the Mario Batali Foundation to raise funds for children's disease research, hunger relief, and literacy programs.

Batali's cookbooks include *Simple Italian Food* (1998), *The Babbo Cookbook* (2002), *Molto Italiano: 327 Simple Italian Recipes* (2005), *Molto Gusto* (2010), and *Molto Batali: Simple Family Meals From My Home to Yours* (2011).

In 2010, *Esquire* magazine voted him into its Restaurant Hall of Fame.

BATH TOWEL. Meatpacker's slang for beef tripe.

BATHTUB GIN. Prohibition term for alcohol mixed with herbs for illicit sale (1930). The name derives from the fact that often the liquor was actually mixed in a bathtub.

BATTERBERRY, MICHAEL (1932–2010) and **ARIANE RUSKIN** (1935–). Authors, magazine editors, and founders of the magazines *Food & Wine* and *Food Arts*.

Ariane Ruskin was born and bred in Manhattan, while Michael Carver Batterberry was born in Newcastle upon Tyne, England, to American parents and moved to the U.S. at the outbreak of war. Ruskin graduated from Barnard College, in NYC, and received an M.A. from Cambridge University. Batterberry grew up in Cincinnati and attended Carnegie Institute of Technology, in Pittsburgh, then moved to Venezuela with his family, then to Rome, where he lived for four years to become a painter and learned to cook. In the early 1960s, he moved to NYC to freelance as a writer. The couple were married in 1968 and spent fifteen months in Paris, after which they became contributing editors at *Harper's Bazaar*.

According to Ariane, "I realized early that I had no talent for cooking. You know, you have it or you don't. My husband loves to cook, and he's so talented, and he can just put anything together and make it taste good." **James Beard** declared Michael the best cook in America outside a professional kitchen, and invited him to teach several classes at the James Beard Cooking School.

In 1973, they published their first book together, *On the Town in New York, from 1776 to the Present* (updated in 1998), and it was immediately hailed as a seminal work in its field, especially for its attention to the changes in food and entertainment after World War II. *New York Times* food editor **Craig Claiborne** called it "the best book ever written on the subject." Together and separately, they also wrote several volumes on art and fashion history.

Confident that there was a growing national interest in food and wine, the couple helped found *The International Review of Food and Wine* in 1978 (later shortened to *Food & Wine* magazine), intended as an antidote to the elitist food coverage then in *Gourmet* magazine and as an appeal to a growing interest in food and drink among men, who by 1980 formed half of *Food & Wine*'s readership. That same year American Express bought the publication.

Pioneers in electronic food publishing as well, the Batterberrys created the top-rated computerized "magazine" *Dining In* for Time Inc. in the early 1980s.

In 1988, the Batterberrys founded *Food Arts*, intended for professionals in the food industry. Unlike other industry magazines, *Food Arts* was gossipy, with travel articles and chef profiles along with coverage of new products and equipment, wine, and spirits. One year later, M. Shanken Communications acquired the magazine, which remained under the direction of the Batterberrys as editors and publishers.

Ariane Batterberry has written fifteen books, with and without Michael, who, with or without Ariane, wrote thirteen books on art, food, and social history. Michael was co-founder of the New American Farmer Initiative, dedicated to fostering restaurants supporting local farming and helping immigrant farmers, and served as chairman of the food education committee for "Food Culture USA" for the Smithsonian's 2005 Folklife Festival.

The couple received the **James Beard Foundation**'s Who's Who of Food & Beverage in America and received its Lifetime Achievement Award (2010). In 1998, Ariane was chosen as Woman of the Year by the Roundtable for Women in Foodservice. She was inducted into the DiRoNA Honorary Hall of Fame and has received the Culinary Institute of America Masters of Hospitality Award and the Madridfusión award, presented by the mayor of Madrid, for having propelled the course of the American food revolution.

Michael Batterberry died of cancer in 2010; Ariane continues as publisher and editor of *Food Arts*.

BATTER BREAD. A cornmeal bread often associated with Virginia and first mentioned in print in 1897. The following recipe by Houston Eldredge appeared in *Famous Old Receipts*, published in Philadelphia in 1908.

BATTER BREAD

Scald 1 c. cornmeal, cool, then beat in 1 c. clabber with 1 t. melted butter, 1 t. salt, and another 1 c. clabber. Dissolve ½ t. baking soda in ½ c. clabber, beat into mixture, place in buttered pudding dish, and bake at 425° for about 30 min.

BATTERY ACID. Slang term for poorly made or distasteful coffee (1941). In Army slang, "battery acid and armored cow" would be bad coffee with canned milk, but by 1945 servicemen used "battery acid" to describe lemonade and by 1946 canned grapefruit juice.

BAUM, JOE (1920–1998). Restaurateur. As one of the principals of the New York City–based Restaurant Associates in the 1950s, Joe Baum helped bring the restaurant business into a glamorous postwar period of innovative design and menu innovation.

Joseph Harold Baum was born in Saratoga Springs, New York. His parents owned and ran the seasonal Gross & Baum Family Hotel. Baum worked as a busboy and waiter, graduated from Cornell University's hotel administration program in 1943, then enlisted to serve as supply officer on a U.S. Navy destroyer-minelayer in the South Pacific for the duration of World War II.

Baum entered the hotel business in 1946 as manager of the Monte Carlo in Las Vegas, then moved on to the Florida-based Schine hotel chain, and after that the Rikers Restaurant Associates (which became Restaurant Associates, or RA), where he opened the Newarker, an innovative restaurant at Newark Airport that became a destination for people from New Jersey and New York. Rising to the top of RA, he hired young, enthusiastic professionals like George Lang, Tom Margittai, Paul

Kovi, and Stuart Levin to help open a dazzling array of theme restaurants, mostly in New York City, including the Romanesque Forum of the Twelve Caesars (with gladiators' helmets for ice buckets), the Italian Trattoria and a German sausage eatery called Zum Zum in the Pan Am Building, the Mexican La Fonda del Sol (with South American folk art), and the groundbreaking **Four Seasons** restaurant in the new Seagram Building, which has a lighted pool in the dining room.

After being deposed by RA in 1968, he and Michael Whiteman formed Baum Associates (now Baum + Whiteman LLC) in 1970, and they set out to create even more extravagant restaurants, including **Windows on the World** (1976), on the 107th floor of the World Trade Center, which they ran for three years. At the bottom of the building they installed one of the first food courts, the Big Kitchen. After the 1993 bombing of the Trade Center, the Port Authority hired Baum and Whiteman to reopen Windows on the World in 1996 (the restaurant was later destroyed in the 9/11 attack).

Baum Associates also acquired—and did a $25 million restoration of—the Rainbow Room (1987–1999) at Rockefeller Center, as well as the far more modest restaurant Aurora, in midtown Manhattan.

Money, of which just as much went to research and travel as to design and food, was rarely an object in these grand projects, created as much for tourists as for local traffic. Baum was known for his fiery demeanor and high standards, and Baum's legacy is of a visionary who sought to turn the sometimes sleazy image of restaurants into centers of glamour, entertainment, and sophistication, always based on a high quality of food and service more American in style than European. His quest for the best boiled down to his personal mantra: "What can I do? What's possible?"

BAYLESS, RICK (1953–). Chef, restaurateur, author, TV show host. As an acolyte of Mexican cooking authority **Diana Kennedy**, Rick Bayless was one of the first North Americans to bring modern regional Mexican cuisine to prominence in the U.S.

Born in Oklahoma City, Bayless grew up in a restaurant and grocers' family and graduated from the University of Oklahoma with a degree in Spanish language and Latin American culture.

After living in Mexico with his wife, Deann, for six years, Bayless published his first cookbook, *Authentic Mexican: Regional Cooking from the Heart of Mexico* (1987). That same year he moved to Cleveland Heights, Ohio, to be executive chef at the restaurant Lopez, then to Chicago to open both the upscale Mexican restaurant Topolobampo and, next door, the casual Frontera Grill. Beginning in 1980, Bayless hosted the PBS TV series *Cooking Mexican*, then *Mexico: One Plate at a Time*.

In 1995, he started selling a line of Mexican salsas and foods under the Frontera Foods label. In 2007, Bayless opened Frontera Fresco, a fast-food restaurant in Macy's department stores in Chicago and San Francisco, and in 2010 he was a consultant to the acclaimed Mexican restaurant Red O, in L.A. He also runs two Tortas Frontera sandwich shops in Chicago, one at the city's O'Hare International Airport.

Bayless is one of the founders of Chefs Collaborative, which supports sustainable, environmentally sound agricultural practices, and since 2002 he has headed the Frontera Farmer Foundation, to which he donated $100,000 that he won on the TV show *Top Chef* in 2009. His Frontera Scholarship foundation raises money to send first- and second-generation Mexican American students to Kendall College to study culinary arts. In 2012 he said, "I see that I have a role to play in our society and I can use it for good. So I take the stage that has been offered to me because it presents the opportunity to say things that a lot of people can hear. I want to use it to say that we can help improve the quality of our own lives and make this world a better place to live."

He was named Chef of the Year 1988 by *Food & Wine* magazine; Best American Chef: Midwest 1991, National Chef of the Year 1995, and Humanitarian of the Year 1998, all by the James Beard Foundation; and Chef of the Year 1995 by the International Association of Culinary Professionals; and he won the 2011 Golden Beet Award from the Illinois Stewardship Alliance, in the category of Community Food Projects. In 2012 Bayless was named to the Order of the Aztec Eagle, the highest distinction awarded to foreigners by the Mexican government, "for his important work in promoting and disseminating one of the most internationally recognized cultural expressions of our country: Mexican cooking in general, and Mexican haute cuisine in particular."

"I think it's quite remarkable how far we have come since I first opened Frontera twenty-five years ago," said Bayless in 2012. "The first customers would come in the door, see the menu, and walk out. They'd say, 'I don't know what you're going to do. This isn't Mexican food. You're going to go out of business in a few days.' I knew that once people started tasting the real food of Mexico, because I spent a lot of years learning how to cook it well, that they were going to find something really remarkable in it."

His books include *Authentic Mexican: Regional Cooking from the Heart of Mexico* (1987), *Rick Bayless's Mexican Kitchen* (1996), *Mexico: One Plate at a Time* (2000), *Mexican Everyday* (2005), and *Margaritas, Guacamoles and Snacks* (2012).

BAYOU BLUE. Prohibition term for inferior or illicit whiskey made in the bayou and backwoods country.

BEACH PLUM. A northeastern shrub, *Prunus maritima*, that grows along the seashore and has edible berries.

BEAN. Any of a variety of pods from plants in the genus *Phaseolus*, and, for culinary purposes, especially *P. vulgaris*, of which there are more than a thousand varieties. The word is from the Old English *bēan*.

The oldest domesticated beans in the Americas were found in the Ocampo Caves of Mexico, dating back to 4000 B.C. Beans were often planted in the same fields with corn and were carried to North America from Mexico.

The two main types of beans grown and eaten in the U.S. are "field" beans, including the pea or **navy bean**, the **black bean**, the **kidney bean**, and others raised in Michigan, California, Idaho, New York, Colorado, New Mexico, and elsewhere; and "garden" beans, including the **string bean**, the "butter" or **lima bean**, and the wax bean. **Soybeans** (*Glycine max*), whose seeds are called "soya" or "soyabean," are generally used for fodder, though some oil, soy sauce, and bean curd is made from them, too. "Edamame" is Japanese for immature salted soybeans, which are popularly steamed and eaten with the fingers in Asian restaurants.

BEAN EATER. Since 1881, a slang term for a Bostonian, because of the association with **Boston baked beans**. Also a slur word for Mexicans because of their fondness for beans. See also **cowboy slang**.

BEANERY. Also "bean wagon." A small, inexpensive eatery like a diner. The term dates in print to 1887.

BEAN-HOLE COOKERY. A method of baking, originally used by the Indians of the Northwest and adopted by lumberjacks, by which a hole in the ground is filled with very hot stones on which is placed an earthenware pot filled with beans. This is then covered with more hot stones, then earth, and left to bake for hours. The technique was first mentioned in print in 1907.

BEAN SUPPER. A New England social event, usually held by a local church to raise money. It dates in print only to 1968, but bean suppers have long been part of New England social life.

BEAR. Any of a variety of large, shaggy-furred mammals in the family Ursidae, especially, in North America, the "black bear" (*Ursus americanus*), also called the "cinnamon bear"; the "grizzly bear" (*U. horribilis*), also called a "brown bear" or a "silver tip"; and the "polar bear" (*U. maritimus*).

Omnivorous and ferocious, bears have been among the most sought-after game for their fur, their fat, and their meat, all of which the Native Americans used long before the arrival of the European trappers, who hunted the animal mainly for its coat and nearly drove the beast to extinction in the East. Because of bear's gaminess, young bear is the most desirable, and bear meat, needing to be marinated or covered with a strongly seasoned sauce to make it palatable to most tastes, was available in city markets of the nineteenth century.

BEARD, JAMES ANDREW (1903–1985). Cook, teacher, author. Called the "Dean of American Food" by the *New York Times*, James Beard was positioned to see much of the development of American gastronomy over eight decades and chronicled its history in several classic cookbooks.

Beard was born in Portland, Oregon, where his England-born mother, Elizabeth, ran the Gladstone Hotel. It was at the hotel that Beard learned his earliest lessons about American cookery, as prepared by his mother and a Chinese cook named Let.

He briefly attended Reed College, in Portland, but was expelled, and thereupon joined a theatrical troupe, hoping for a career as a singer or actor in theater and movies. For three years he traveled in Europe, returning in 1927 to try to break into show business, but after a decade with little success, he opened a catering business and food shop called Hors d'Oeuvre Inc., in 1937, which led three years later to the publication of *Hors d'Oeuvre & Canapés*, then *Cook It Outdoors* (1942).

During World War II, Beard served as a cryptographer, and with the United Seamen's Service he helped set up canteens in Puerto Rico, Rio de Janeiro, Marseilles, and Panama. Once out of the service, he moved to New York City and continued to write cookbooks that sold well. Beard became the first host of a TV cooking show, NBC's *I Love to Eat*, in 1946.

By then Beard was well known as one of America's eminent food authorities, and he was asked by restaurateurs and food companies to be a consultant. From 1955 and for the next three decades, Beard ran the James Beard Cooking School in New York City and Seaside, Oregon. By then he had become a brand name, one he would sell to endorse products like Green Giant and Heckers Flour.

In 1981, food writer **Gael Greene** enlisted Beard's aid to found Citymeals-on-Wheels, a charity that feeds the homebound elderly in New York City.

A very tall, very large man whose appetites were legendary, Beard died of heart failure at the age of eighty-one. In his honor, the **James Beard Foundation** was set up to provide culinary scholarships.

Beard's books, many of which have been revised or republished, include *Fowl and Game Cookery* (1944), *The Fireside Cook Book* (1949), *Paris Cuisine* (1952), *James Beard's Fish Cookery* (1954), *The James Beard Cookbook* (1959), *James Beard's American Cookery* (1972), *The New James Beard* (1981), and a memoir, *Delights & Prejudices* (1964).

BEEBE, LUCIUS MORRIS (1902–1966). Author and gourmand. As an author, journalist, and columnist on many subjects, including poetry and railroad history, Lucius Beebe was best known for his writings on gastronomy.

Born into wealth in Wakefield, Massachusetts, he attended but was expelled from both Yale and Harvard graduate school (he returned to earn an M.A.) for pranksterism. Beginning in 1929, Beebe became a journalist for various newspapers, including the New York *Herald Tribune*, the *San Francisco Examiner*, and the *Boston Telegram*, while writing magazine articles for *The New Yorker*, *Holiday*, *Town & Country*, and *Gourmet*. In his syndicated column This New York, in the *Herald Tribune*, from the 1930s through 1944, he wrote of the city's society and of what its members ate and drank. His column Along the Boulevard, in *Gourmet*, was erudite and worldly, written in a highfalutin American style.

In 1950, with his partner, photographer Charles Clegg, Beebe moved to Virginia City, Nevada, to restore the *Territorial Enterprise* newspaper (sold in 1961), for which he and Clegg wrote the "That Was the West" series. He later wrote the "This Wild West" series for the *San Francisco Chronicle*, on all topics that interested him. Known as a fashion plate, Beebe, who was six foot four, appeared on the cover of *Life* magazine in 1939 with the caption "Lucius Beebe Sets a Style." He once tipped a cabdriver with $25 worth of pâté de foie gras.

In 1992, he was voted into the Nevada Writers Hall of Fame. He died of a heart attack in 1966 in Hillsborough, California, and his ashes, supposedly with those of his two dogs, were returned to his hometown cemetery in Wakefield. He'd already written his own obituary, "His Own Life in His Own Words," which he kept updated, for the *Herald Tribune*.

Beebe summed up his self-image in the *San Francisco Chronicle*, writing, "I admire most of all The Renaissance Man, and if it can be said without pretentiousness, I like to think of myself as one, at least in some small measure. Not a Michelangelo, mark you, but perhaps a poor man's Cellini or a road company Cosimo de' Medici."

Beebe's books on food and restaurants include *The Awful Seeley Diner* (1932), *The Ritz Idea: The Story of a Great Hotel* (1936), *The Plaza: Fortieth Anniversary, 1907–1947* (1947), and *The Big Spenders* (1966).

BEEF. The meat of a full-grown steer, ox, cow, or bull. Beef, in preparations ranging from steak and stews to **hamburgers** and **barbecue**, is one of the most important meats in the American diet.

The word is from the Latin *bōs* (ox), which in Middle English became *beef*, from Old French *buef*.

Cattle for beef have been domesticated for millennia, all descended from the wild bulls of Europe called "aurochs" (*Bos primienius*). By 3500 B.C. cattle were being raised in Egypt, and the ox is constantly used as a symbolic animal of the Old and New testaments. By A.D. 500 the aurochs had been brought to England to be bred with the native "shorthorn," and most American breeds are descendants of English cattle, though the Spanish explorer Francisco Vásquez de Coronado brought cattle to the Southwest in 1540. Jamestown had cattle by 1611, but there was no commercial meatpacking in the colonies until William Pynchon set up a slaughterhouse in Boston in 1662. In 1690, cattle were brought to missions in Texas by the Spanish, and once the missions were abandoned, the cattle ran wild, eventually developing into what were called longhorns, the only cattle used for beef production in America for the next 160 years.

Pork was much preferred for meat until well into the nineteenth century, however, because pigs were easier to care for and feed. Still, while beef was not so common as pork, the early settlers had sufficient land on which to raise enough beef for their needs, and the word "beef-steak" was in use by the late seventeenth century. In 1711, a "Beef-Stake Club" was thriving in London and later was imitated in Philadelphia, where a similar organization under the same name met at Tun Tavern in 1749. In those days a "beef-steak" was a flattened piece of beef that was usually fried and served with gravy. The English liked it served very rare, so the American colonists followed suit. By the 1760s some cities had "beef steak houses." Nineteenth-century American cookbook authors insisted that beef should be cooked until very well done.

Most of the beef consumed, however, was salted or corned, and little meat was shipped over long distances. By 1767 the Franciscan friars of California had enlisted Mexicans and Indians to herd cattle, and the French in Louisiana initiated the first cattle drive in 1779, when they brought in cattle from the Spanish in San Antonio. Americans were involved in similar activities by the 1820s in Texas, where the longhorn steer became an important breed in the decades to follow. By the 1850s Chicago had already established itself as a meatpacking center, but again, the industry produced mainly salted or corned meat products. After the Civil War, the demand for beef increased with the rise in population and the decrease in forage land east of the Mississippi River, and on September 5, 1867, the first cattle were shipped by railroad car out of Abilene, Kansas, a town that livestock trader Joe McCoy bought for $4,250 as a central depot for cattle movements out of Texas. This began the era of the great cattle drives and the expansion of the West's mythos into romance and literature, with the cowboy as the central figure of America's seemingly unending destiny. According to Edwin C. McReynolds in *Oklahoma: A History of the Sooner State* (1954), the total number of cattle driven from Texas to Kansas City between 1866 and 1885 was six million head, with a peak of six hundred thousand in 1871. The main cattle drives were from Austin to Abilene (the Chisholm Trail), San Antonio to Baxter Springs, Kansas (the Shawnee Trail), and Bandera, Texas, to Ogallala, Nebraska (the Western Trail). But the cattle drives were short-lived, for several reasons. The introduction of barbed wire in 1875 and the intrusion of more farm families into the western territories meant an end to free access to land. Then, over the winter of 1886–1887, a bitter cold spell wiped out 90 percent of the herds, and the end came quickly.

Americans had developed a great appetite for beef by the turn of the century, and after Detroit meatpacker G. H. Hammond brought out the refrigerated railway car in 1871, chilled carcasses became readily available in the East, though fresh beef was still not common in the outer reaches of the western frontier. Still, by the 1880s beef was being shipped even to England, and "steak houses" were among the most popular restaurants in large American cities.

A hardy American breed of cattle called the Santa Gertrudis, developed from shorthorns and Brahmans at the King Ranch, in Texas, became an extremely adaptive steer for the beef market, though **Aberdeen angus**, Herefords, and Galloways were also important in the late nineteenth century.

Slaughterhouses of this era were primitive and generally unhygienic, leading to frequent campaigns to correct their abuses and to the passage in 1906 of the Pure Food and Drug Act, to a large extent the result of the impression made on the public by Upton Sinclair's accusatory novel about the meatpacking industry, *The Jungle* (1906).

In rural communities where there was little or no refrigeration, as in the South, "beef clubs" were formed by members who acquired shares by bringing in beef to be slaughtered and taking their portion.

By the 1920s beef had become a competitor with pork in terms of consumption, and Europeans began characterizing Americans as a "nation of beefeaters." To be sure, a meal of a two-inch-thick steak and a baked potato or french-fried potatoes became an icon of American gastronomy and remains so to this day, despite the fact that beef consumption has begun to decrease in recent years. In 1952, the average American ate 62 pounds of beef per year; by 1960, 99 pounds; by 1970, 114 pounds; today that number stands at about 60 pounds per person. The decrease is due both to Americans' desire to cut out excessive fat and cholesterol from their diet and to the high price of beef.

In recent years there have been attempts by meat producers to change the federal regulations on meat quality (based on marbling of intramuscular fat, color, and texture), but for the moment the standards are as follows: "prime," "choice," "good," "standard," "commercial," "utility," "cutter," and "canner." Prime, which has the heaviest marbling, constitutes only about 3 percent of all graded beef and is very expensive to produce because of additional special feed and the time needed to bring the animals to the proper weight and fat consistency. The lowest five grades are generally available only in processed or canned meats.

These standards are enforced by the Department of Agriculture and stamped on the outside of each carcass, but for producers this is a voluntary process and must be requested of the Department of Agriculture. "Grass-fed" must "receive a majority of their nutrients from grass throughout their life," but this "does not limit the use of antibiotics, hormones, or pesticides" in the animals' feed.

Heavily marbled and very expensive "Kobe" beef, sometimes called "*wagyu*," comes only from the Hyogo Prefecture of Japan. The name derives from Kobe, Hyogo's capital city. After banning it for years because of fears over foot-and-mouth-disease outbreaks, the USDA again allowed Kobe beef to be imported as of August 17, 2012.

The terminology of American butchering is often confusing, and many terms are used as synonyms for poorly defined standard cuts. The most commonly used terms are explained below.

PRIMAL BRISKET. The breast section of the animal, just under the first five ribs of the chuck. The brisket, which is usually braised or pot-roasted, is cut into two pieces, the flat half and the point half. See also **corned beef**.

PRIMAL CHUCK. The shoulder and part of the neck. Chuck is usually ground for hamburger or other meat dishes. The "cross-rib roast" (also called "English" or "Boston" cut) is usually pot-roasted, as is the next cut, the arm pot roast (also called "shoulder roast"). The "blade cut," which may be made into a roast or steak, is next. This may be further divided into the "chuck eye" (also called "market" or "Spencer" roast), the "chuck steak" (or "flat iron" steak), and the "mock tenderloin" (or "Scotch tender," "Jewish fillet," or "chuck eye").

PRIMAL FLANK. Meat from the belly section below the loin. It is usually braised or, if marinated, grilled for **London broil**.

PRIMAL PLATE. From the chest in front of the "flank steak," which Jewish Americans call **flanken**. It is cut into short ribs or braised without the bone. **Pastrami** is often made from this cut, as is the "skirt steak" (also called "Romanian steak"), a diaphragm muscle that is braised or ground. It is the basis for the **fajita**.

PRIMAL RIB. The meat between the primal chuck and the short loin, containing seven ribs. "Prime rib," often encountered on menus and considered the most desirable part of the animal, is from this section. A boned rib roast is often called a "Delmonico steak" (after Delmonico's restaurant, in NYC, where it was a popular cut of the nineteenth century). A "standing rib roast" includes the seven ribs of this section.

PRIMAL ROUND. Meat from the hind leg of the animal, from the end of the primal loin to the hock or ankle. This is divided into several other cuts: the "top round" (often sold as **London broil**), the "bottom round," the "eye of the round," the "sirloin tip," the "heel of the round," and the shin.

PRIMAL SHANK. Meat taken from the shin section of the front leg of the animal. Primal shank requires braising or grinding.

PRIMAL SHORT LOIN. Meat from the hindquarter between the pinbone of the primal sirloin and the small end of the rib. It is considered the best cut for steaks, which include the **porterhouse** (containing the top loin, the tenderloin, and the tail and retaining the "T-bone"); the "T-bone steak" (which first appeared as a term in 1916), composed of meat that is often the same as the "porterhouse"; the "club steak," sometimes called a "Delmonico steak," having no tenderloin or flank attached; the **tenderloin**, also called "filet mignon," "tournedos," and "chateaubriand" (though this last is also the name of a recipe for a porterhouse steak); and the "strip steak" or "strip roast," which contains the top loin muscle and bones and is called in some parts of the country "New York strip," in others "Kansas City strip," and "shell" in others.

PRIMAL SIRLOIN. The meat on the animal's hip, which may be cut into "pinhouse sirloin," "flat-bone sirloin," "round-bone sirloin," "wedge-bone sirloin," "cut-with-the-grain tenderloin," "top butt sirloin" (also called "boneless rump steaks" or "honeymoon steaks"), "cut-with-the-grain bottom sirloin," and "whole sirloin roast." See also **sirloin**.

The varieties of ground beef recognized by the USDA include the following:

GROUND BEEF. Meat from any part of the animal except "undesirable" parts, such as ears, snout, and innards.

GROUND SIRLOIN. Meat specifically from the primal sirloin section.

GROUND ROUND. Meat exclusively from the primal round section.

GROUND CHUCK. Meat exclusively from the primal chuck.

HAMBURGER MEAT. Meat that is intended for use in meat patties; however, this is an ambiguous term. See **hamburger**.

BEEF. Slang term for a restaurant check.

BEEF ON WECK. A Buffalo, New York, specialty, made of thin slices of roast beef topped with its own juices and served on a hard caraway-seeded roll called a "kummelweck" (1952), from German *Kümmel* (caraway) plus *Weck* (roll). The term "beef on weck" dates to 1969 but is certainly older. The sandwich is usually eaten with horseradish.

BEER. A low-alcohol beverage made from fermented barley and other grains and flavored with hops. Beer is easily the most popular of all alcoholic drinks enjoyed by Americans, with an annual per capita consumption of 20 gallons.

The word *beer* comes from the Middle English *ber* and, ultimately, from Latin *bibere*, "to drink." The beverage in various forms has been made for at least eight thousand years, evidence having been found in Babylonian records of beer being used in sacrificial rituals. Egypt, China, and India all made beer, as did the Inca in Peru. Beer was well known throughout Europe even before viticulture had developed to any significant degree, with evidence dating back five thousand years; the addition of hops (the dried flowers of vines of the genus *Humulus*), to give a characteristics bitterness, has been traced to at least as early as A.D. 768.

The first brewery in America was set up by the Dutch in New Amsterdam in 1612, and Governor Peter Minuit established the first public brewery in 1632. The Pilgrims, who had intended to settle in Virginia in 1620, instead landed at Plymouth Rock, Massachusetts, because, according to a chronicler, "we could not now take time for further search or consideration, our victuals being spent, especially our beer."

Early settlers in America made beer from all sorts of substances, including corn, pumpkins, and persimmons, sometimes flavored with sassafras or pine. Early colonial breweries generally reflected the preference for English-style beers, which were strong, lusty, and dark, over the lighter German styles. By 1629 there were breweries in Virginia, and eight years later the first licensed brew house was opened in Massachusetts. ("Brewery" entered the language a century later.) During the seventeenth century, beer was considered a light, everyday "small drink," consumed by men, women, and children throughout the day. Before that time, "ale" (from Old English *ealu*) was distinguished from beer because it contained no barley or hops. When brewers added both to ale in the seventeenth century, the two terms became synonymous, with Englishmen preferring to keep the name "ale" and Americans "beer." Both were "top-fermented," meaning that the spent yeast rose to the top of the barrel.

Beer was a perfectly respectable beverage among the founding fathers of the country. William Penn (1644–1718) set up Philadelphia's first brew house in 1685, and Jefferson, Madison, and Adams all had interests in such establishments, while George Washington maintained his own brew house at his Mount Vernon home.

Several kinds of beer were available to the Americans of those days. "Stout," a strong English beer or ale, was dark in color and bitter in taste; "porter," which originated in England in about 1722, was a blend of ale and beer. Its name derived from its popularity among the eighteenth-century porters who carried produce to London's Covent Garden. Porter was heavily malted and had a slightly sweet taste. In America it was purveyed at "porterhouses," and the proprietor of one such place, Martin Harrison, became known for his cut of beef, which after 1814 was called a "porterhouse steak." And then there was spruce beer, made with the tops of spruce trees, which became so popular during the Revolutionary War that the Continental Congress in 1775 decreed that the American troops should receive a choice of one quart of either cider or spruce beer daily.

After the turn of the century, the arrival of German immigrants in Philadelphia made that city a major brewing center, and German-style beers became increasingly available. Then, around 1840, John Wagner of Philadelphia began making a "lager" (from the German *Lagerbier*, storehouse beer) that used a different, "bottom-fermenting" yeast and was stored, or "lagered," at colder temperatures. These beers were lighter and somewhat weaker than top-fermented beers. Wagner's German contemporaries followed suit, building special facilities to keep the beer cool during fermentation and to age the product for two to three months. Although some immediately dismissed these light lagers (also called "pilsner" or "pilsener," from the Pilsner Urquell beer of Pilsen, Czechoslovakia, where quality beer had been made since 1292) as a "woman's drink," they caught on rapidly, at first in German communities, where beer halls and beer gardens flourished in midcentury, and afterwards in every major city in America. The first outdoor beer garden was opened in St. Louis in 1854, by Franz Josef Uhrig, who cooled the beer in a limestone cave called Uhrig's Cave.

"Beer halls"—some of which could hold up to twelve hundred people—became social centers for the lower and middle classes, and one moralist of the day wrote of their lavish and bawdy atmosphere: "The quantity [of lager] sold in a day is enormous. A four-horse team from the brewery…finds it difficult to keep up the supply."

Soon "lager" and "beer" were interchangeable terms, and the golden, effervescent beverage (sometimes called "a bucket of suds") surpassed cider and all others in popularity. The cities of the Midwest—Cincinnati, St. Louis, Chicago, and particularly Milwaukee—grew powerful as brewing centers, all following the lead of John Wagner's Philadelphia. One of the first in the new market, however, was a NYC family, Frederick and Maximilian Schaefer, who purchased the Sebastian Sommers Brewery in NYC in 1842 and began making lager there under their own name. Two years later, Jacob Best Sr. and his four sons opened a brewery on Chestnut Street Hill, in Milwaukee, that later came under the control of Frederick Pabst, who increased output to half a million barrels in 1889 and by 1902 had built the first plant in America equipped to carry the fresh beer from the brewery to a bottler. Before then all beer had been drawn from a spigot and referred to as "draft beer," later also called "schenk beer," from the German *schenken* (to pour out) *plus bier*.

The Joseph Schlitz Brewing Co., founded in 1858, advertised its product as "the Beer That Made Milwaukee Famous." By 1900 the brewery facilities of Anheuser-Busch covered sixty acres of St. Louis. The firm had forty-two branches in other cities and even operated its own railroad. Jacob Schmidt built another great brewery in Minneapolis–St. Paul, while Henry Weinhard and Arnold Blitz merged resources to make Portland, Oregon, a major beer producer. In San Francisco, where the shortage of ice in midcentury was a factor in making decent lager, there developed steam beer, so called because of the high amount of pressure built up in the barrel through a special process of fermentation (see more at **steam beer**). By 1870, however, American refrigeration techniques made it possible to produce beer year-round without regard to temperature. By 1876 there were more than four thousand breweries in the United States. **Prohibition** in America (which lasted from 1920 to 1933, with some states banning alcoholic beverages, that is, "going dry," as early as 1916) was a disaster for the beer industry, which survived by producing malt and yeast and by providing ice. The Volstead Act defined a forbidden beverage as one containing 0.5 percent alcohol (regular beer varies from 3.2 to 5 percent by weight), so a market developed for "near beer," which had been made since 1909 as a substitute for the real thing and contained 0.4 percent alcohol. If illegal spirits were added to near beer, it was called "needle beer" or "needled beer." On April 7, 1933, President Franklin D. Roosevelt signed the Cullen-Harrison Act, which raised the definition of an intoxicating beverage to 3.2 percent, and people started referring to such brews as "3.2 beer." Of course, illegal beer was made throughout Prohibition, often at home, where it was called "home brew." When Prohibition finally ended, in December 1933, only 750 breweries reopened, and though new ones opened and demand for beer grew rapidly through the 1930s and 1940s, competition drove many breweries into consolidation or out of business.

One of the greatest boons for the industry was the introduction in 1935, by the Gottfried Krueger Brewing Co. of Newark, New Jersey, and the Adolph Coors Co. of Golden, Colorado, of beer in cans. At first scoffed at by those used to bottles, canned beer acquired popularity during World War II, when GIs overseas got used to the idea. The aluminum beer can was introduced in 1958. The nonreturnable bottle became the norm in the early 1950s, further increasing the ease with which the consumer could enjoy his beer at home.

With this expansion of the market came increased competitiveness. Price-cutting among the largest breweries drove the small local breweries out of the market, so that today there are only about seventy full-scale breweries left in the U.S., while it is still the largest beer-producing country. (Germans are the largest beer drinkers per capita in the world; Americans rank twelfth worldwide on that measure.) There are, however, more than nineteen hundred breweries in operation today. The total revenue from beer sold in the U.S. is $196 billion, with the top three breweries being Anheuser-Busch Inc. of St. Louis, MillerCoors of Chicago, and Pabst Brewing Co., now based in Los Angeles.

In the 1980s, "microbreweries" or "craft breweries" (breweries making fifteen thousand or fewer barrels per year) proliferated, swelling from forty-five in 1986 to more than two thousand currently in the U.S. During this same period, "brewpubs," where beer was both made and served along with food, increased in popularity. There were 184 brewpubs in the U.S. in 1992, 1,910 in 1998, and 2,075 by 2012. In addition, there are "regional breweries" that have a production capacity of between fifteen thousand and two million barrels, and a subcategory of "regional specialty breweries" whose flagship brand is an all-malt or specialty beer. All these categories fall under the general term "craft breweries," which have sales of more than $3 billion annually and represent 12.4 percent of the U.S. market. The top-selling craft breweries are Boston Beer Co. (makers of Sam Adams) of Boston, Sierra Nevada Brewing Co. of Chico, California, and New Belgium Brewing Co. of Fort Collins, Colorado.

Making beer is a complex process, beginning with the malting of barley, which is combined with a cereal like corn that has been cooked. The two are mixed and mashed to convert starch to maltose and dextrin. This is called "wort" and is filtered through a "lauter tun," which separates wort from grain (the latter is used for cattle feed). Hops are added to the wort for flavor, and high heat is added until the wort is completely soluble (called the "hot break"), at which point it is run through a "hop strainer" or "hop jack," which removes the hops

and leaves "hot wort." This is cooled, yeast is added, and fermentation begins. Lager beer is usually fermented at between 37 and 49 degrees Fahrenheit, whereas ale, which uses a different type of yeast, ferments at temperatures between 50 and 70 degrees. Brewer's yeast is used in beer; in lagers, it settles to the bottom, whereas ale yeasts settle at the top. Lagers ferment for eight to eleven days, ales for five to six. Carbon dioxide is thrown off during fermentation or from a process called "krausening," by which a small amount of still-fermenting young beer is added to produce a short second fermentation.

The beer is then refrigerated, filtered, and, if intended for bottling or canning, usually pasteurized. (Beers put in strong aluminum or stainless-steel kegs are usually not pasteurized, because they are likely to be consumed faster and therefore would not undergo any further fermentation, which could cause additional carbon dioxide to burst cans or bottles.) Peak drinking time for canned beer is considered to be about four months; for bottles, six. Some bottled or canned beer that has not been pasteurized goes under the name "draft beer," but "draft-brewed" and "draft beer flavor" are phrases used on bottles and cans that may contain pasteurized beer, as long as the pasteurization is noted on the label.

Other beer terms include:

ALE. Once a term for a brew of malt and cereal without hops or barley. In the seventeenth century, hops and barley were added, and the distinction between ale and beer disappeared for a hundred years, until the lagers of the 1840s became synonymous with "beer," while ale continued to be made in an older, more flavorful style. Ales average 4.5 percent alcohol by weight, slightly higher than beer.

BOCK BEER. Also "bockbier." In Germany, bock beer was usually brewed in the spring and was a heavier, darker beer than most other lagers. In America, its style and taste are a matter of individual companies' definition and marketing.

DRY BEER. Beer made to have a somewhat less "sweet" flavor, accomplished by allowing the yeast to consume more of the sugar in the fermentation process. Dry beer was introduced in Japan in 1987 by Asahi Breweries, and in the U.S. in June 1988 by Kirin. Michelob Dry (owned by Anheuser-Busch of St. Louis) was the first American-made dry beer, introduced in 1988. Dry beer is also somewhat lower in calories than regular beer.

LIGHT BEER. Also "Lite." Beer that is lower in alcohol (averaging 3.1 percent alcohol by weight) and has fewer calories than regular beer. The first light beer sold in a bar was Miller Lite, in 1973. Light beer has become an enormously popular category among American beer drinkers. Five out of the six top-selling beers today are light, with Bud Light, made by Anheuser-Busch of St. Louis now the top-selling brand in America by far.

LOW-ALCOHOL BEER. Also called "L.A.," this beer has an alcohol content of less than 2 percent.

MALT LIQUOR. A malt beverage that is higher in alcohol than beer, up to 8 percent by weight in some states (1693).

NONALCOHOLIC BEER. A malt beverage containing no more than 0.5 percent alcohol. The term "nonalcoholic beer" is actually nonlegal under FDA regulations, which categorize beverages with less than one-half of one percent of alcohol as "near beers," "malt beverages," or "nonalcoholic brews." Beverages containing no alcohol whatsoever may include the word "alcohol-free" on their labels, but not the word "beer." Such brews make up less than 1 percent of all beer sales in the U.S. "California beer" is a slang term for nonalcoholic beer made from "beer seed," sugar, and water.

The taste of most beers in the U.S. has been mellow and, to some, lacking in distinction from one major brand to another, though brewpubs and microbreweries offer a much wider range of taste, color, and richness of flavors. There has been a great increase in the importation of stronger beers from other countries (currently about 10 percent of the American market). Nevertheless, the same brand of beer may taste different from state to state because the alcoholic content is regulated by each state's legislation. Federal law requires a minimum alcohol level for beer of 0.5 percent but sets no maximum.

Annual beer production worldwide is now more than fifty billion barrels, with China producing more than 25 percent of that total and the U.S. 11.7 percent.

BEER BLAST. Also "beer bust," "beer bash," and "kegger." Campus or young people's term for a party at which the primary beverage is beer, often served from a keg. It has been used since at least the 1950s but first appeared in print in 1963.

BEER UP. Colloquialism meaning to drink a good deal of beer.

BEET (*Beta vulgaris*). A dark reddish-purple fruit of a plant with leafy greens sometimes eaten as a vegetable on their own.

The name is from the Latin *bēta*, which in Middle English became *bete*. The vegetable is a native of the Mediterranean, but it was not of much gastronomic interest until the nineteenth century in France and, afterwards, in America, where most of the beet crop is canned or sometimes pickled. The most popular varieties are the Detroit Dark Red, Egyptian, and Eclipse. Swiss chard is also known as the "spinach beet."

BEGGAR'S PURSE. An appetizer of caviar and crème fraîche wrapped in a crepe and tied with thin strips of chives to resemble a little purse. The term was used by Barry and Susan Wine for such a dish served at their restaurant, the Quilted Giraffe, in NYC, in the 1980s, after having enjoyed the item at La Vieille Fontaine, in Maisons-Laffitte, outside Paris, where chef François Clerc called it *un aumonière* (an alms purse).

BEHIND THE STICK. Bartender slang for working the beer taps. The term first appeared in print in 1990.

BEIGNET. A puffy yeast pastry deep-fried and served with sugar (1835). The beignet, which is French for "fritter," is a traditional food item of New Orleans,.

In the French Market in New Orleans's Vieux Carré, beignets are served with **chicory** coffee for breakfast and as an afternoon snack.

BELL, GLEN (1923–2010). Restaurateur and entrepreneur. As founder of the fast-food chain Taco Bell, Glen William Bell Jr. helped spread the popularity of Mexican American food throughout the U.S.

Although Bell's maternal grandfather made a fortune in California real estate, Bell, born in Lynwood, California, came from a family of six children whose itinerant father left them in poverty. Bell joined the Marines in 1943, working as a waiter in mess halls in the Pacific during World War II. He moved back to San Bernardino, California, to open a drive-in called Bell's Hamburgers and Hot Dogs, in 1948, not far from the successful McDonald's hamburger eatery.

Convinced that non–Mexican Americans were developing a taste for Mexican food, in 1951 he introduced crispy tacos to the menu at his third hamburger unit. Three years later, he opened a Mexican stand named Taco Tia, promoted by his placing of hundreds of cheap sombreros around town with the Taco Tia name on them, a ploy that attracted hundreds of people to the opening. He sold Taco Tia in 1957 to open four El Tacos in Long Beach, California.

After several years of buying and selling various fast-food eateries, including a German-themed eatery named Wienerschnitzel, Bell sold his interest in El Taco and opened his first Taco Bell, in Downey, California, in 1962, adapting an adobe-style architecture that would later become the standard design of the chain. He also created a statue of a little Mexican boy in a sombrero (who resembled a Warner Bros. cartoon mouse named Speedy Gonzales) that became the chain's first logo. In 1965, Bell began franchising Taco Bell and by the end of the decade was opening two units every week. In 1978, Bell sold his 868-unit chain to PepsiCo for $125 million in stock, and PepsiCo in turn spun it off in 1997 to Tricon Global Restaurants (later Yum! Brands), which by 2012 had nearly six thousand Taco Bell units around the world.

Bell published his own biography, *Taco Titan: The Glen Bell Story*, by Debra Lee Baldwin (1999). On the cover Bell was shown wearing a Mexican sombrero.

BELT. Colloquialism for a swig of liquor (1922).

BEND AN ELBOW. To drink whiskey. The term dates to at least the 1830s.

BENDER. Slang term for a drunken spree. By 1728 the term meant a hard drinker, but by 1846 it referred also to a bout of drinking.

BENEDICTINE SANDWICH SPREAD. Caterer and Louisville *Courier-Journal* household editor Jennie C. Benedict of Louisville, Kentucky, invented this green sandwich spread made of cream cheese thinned with mayonnaise, flavored with grated onion and cucumber, and tinted green with spinach, parsley, and green food coloring. She published her recipe in the fourth edition of her *Blue Ribbon Cook Book* (1922). It was particularly popular on Derby Day in Louisville.

BENEDICTINE SANDWICH SPREAD

Peel and grate 1 cucumber and squeeze out the juice into a dish, discarding pulp. Repeat with 1 onion. With a fork, blend in 8 oz. softened cream cheese, 3 T. cucumber juice, 1 T. onion juice, 1 t. salt, a dash of cayenne pepper, and 2 drops green food coloring. Smooth onto sandwich bread.

BERGERON, VICTOR (1902–1984). Restaurateur, author. By capitalizing on his gimmicky ideas for a theme restaurant called Trader Vic's, which served pseudo-Polynesian fare, Victor Jules Bergeron Jr. not only popularized an entire genre of theme restaurant but invented several dishes and cocktails that included stylized versions of the typical Chinese American food of the time, adding Polynesian decor.

Bergeron was born in San Francisco to a French Canadian hotel waiter/grocer, who gave his son a taste for the business. Contrary to his story that he lost his left leg to a shark, Bergeron actually had lost the leg when he was six years old due to tuberculosis of the knee.

He attended Heald College, in San Francisco. After Bergeron sailed through Polynesia as a painter and sculptor and fell in love with the culture, he borrowed $500 to open a small saloon he called a "glorified beer parlor" named Hinky Dink's, in Oakland, California, in

1934. Two years later, this evolved into Trader Vic's, now with Polynesian decor, and the new restaurant thrived, particularly among servicemen on shore leave, for whom Bergeron smuggled liquor aboard supply ships bound for the South Pacific.

So popular was the place that Bergeron began franchising his restaurants in 1940, first in Seattle, then in Hawaii. In 1951 he opened a unit in San Francisco that became the chain's flagship.

His decor was the basis of what came to be known as Tiki culture, an invention of American designers and restaurateurs like Bergeron and Don the Beachcomber (Ernest Raymond Beaumont-Gantt), in L.A., who a decade earlier had transformed simplistic ideas of Maori bamboo furniture, woven palm leaves, sculpture, and totems into a version of populuxe design. So, too, Trader Vic's food, much of it cooked in specially crafted Chinese ovens, mimicked dishes based on Hawaiian, Chinese, and Malaysian food and ingredients, including creations like crab Rangoon, barbecued pork ribs, and coconut prawns. Rum cocktails like the mai tai, which Bergeron claims to have invented, were the drink specialties, some served in ceramic cups shaped like skulls.

Bergeron at one time had twenty-five worldwide franchises of Trader Vic's restaurants; after his death, the corporation that ran them faltered, but it rebounded in the twenty-first century, and as of 2012 there are again twenty-five locations, including units in Europe, the Middle East, and Asia. The corporate headquarters is now in Emeryville, California.

Bergeron wrote many cookbooks and cocktail books, including *Trader Vic's Book of Food and Drink* (1946), *Trader Vic's Pacific Island Cookbook* (1968), *Trader Vic's Bartenders Guide* (1972), *Trader Vic's Book of Mexican Cooking* (1973), and *Trader Vic's Helluva Man's Cookbook* (1976).

BERINGER, FREDERICK (1840–1901) and **JACOB** (1845–1915). Winemakers. The Beringer Brothers Winery was one of the first to open in California's Napa Valley and is now the longest continuously operating winery in the region. The Beringer brothers went on to set standards for wineries that followed.

With roots in Mainz, in Germany's Rhine Valley, Jacob emigrated first to New York City, in 1868, but,

hearing that Northern California had a climate similar to the Rhine Valley's, he moved to the Napa Valley and became cellar foreman for Charles Krug, one of the area's first commercial wineries. Eight years later, Jacob and his brother Frederick purchased a 215-acre parcel of land in St. Helena for $14,500 and set up Los Hermanos winery, producing an impressive forty thousand gallons of wine in their first vintage, 1876. The winery was later renamed Beringer Brothers.

The brothers expanded their vineyards and cellar space, and in 1887 their wines won awards of excellence at the Mechanics' Institute Exhibition, in San Francisco.

After their deaths, the winery survived selling sacramental wines, and though the winery and its quality declined during Prohibition, by the end of the war it was producing forty thousand cases annually. In 1967, the winery was declared a California historical landmark, and it is a major tourist stop in the valley.

Beringer Brothers has been sold several times, including to the Nestlé Co. and Foster's Wine Estates, of Australia. Beginning in 1971, Beringer's fifth winemaker, Myron Nightingale, and its sixth, Ed Sbragia (who later bought the winery), greatly improved the quality of the wines. In 2001, Beringer celebrated its 125th anniversary.

BETA CAROTENE. A coloring agent added to butter, margarine, and nondairy products used as shortening. The body converts beta carotene to vitamin A.

BETTY CROCKER. As a fictitious company icon of General Mills, Betty Crocker has provided recipes and culinary advice for American cooks for nearly a century, since her debut in 1921. That year, a Minneapolis milling company named the Washburn Crosby Co. (merged in 1928 into General Mills) sought a personalized way to answer consumers' baking questions. Taking the last name of a retired company executive, William Crocker, with the "warm and friendly" first name "Betty," home economist Marjorie Husted created the character, complete with a cordial signature, still used today for responses to queries. The figure was given a radio voice—actually thirteen different actresses' voices in different parts of the U.S.—and starred in the nation's first cooking show, *The Betty Crocker School of the Air*, which ran for twenty-four years. In 1930, the company began publishing a highly successful series of softbound cookbooks.

In 1936, the character was given a face by artist Neysa McMein, taken from various features of General Foods employees. The face of Betty Crocker was to change eight times over the decades to suit the era's style and taste. In 1945, a poll by *Fortune* magazine voted Betty Crocker the second most popular American woman, after First Lady Eleanor Roosevelt.

In 1949, the character (first played by actress Adelaide Hawley Cumming) appeared on the TV series *The Betty Crocker Search for the All-American Homemaker of Tomorrow*, which ran from 1954 to 1976, with various actresses playing the title role.

In 1950, the bestselling *Betty Crocker Cookbook*, by Agnes White Tizard, was published; now in its eleventh edition (2011), it has fifteen hundred recipes. More than two hundred different cookbooks have appeared under her name. General Mills has also marketed Betty Crocker brand food products, from baking mixes to microwavable desserts. The character now even has a Facebook page of her own.

BETWEEN THE SHEETS. A cocktail made from rum, triple sec, and lime juice. The name probably refers to the cocktail's supposed ability to send one to bed, but with a sexual innuendo of the same slang term for sexual activity in bed, as noted by Shakespeare in his comedy *Much Ado about Nothing* (1600). See also **three sheets in the wind**.

BETWEEN THE SHEETS

Shake with crushed ice 1 part triple sec, 2 parts lime juice, 3 parts brandy, and 3 parts gold rum. Serve with lemon twist.

BIALY. A Jewish American baked bread roll sprinkled with onion flakes. The name, first mentioned in print only in 1965 but certainly older, is Yiddish and comes from the Polish city of Bialystok. They are commonly eaten with butter, cream cheese, or halvah. Kossar's is the only remaining bialy store of many that were part of NYC food culture.

BIÈRE DOUCE. A Louisiana Creole beer made from the skin of the pineapple, sugar, rice, and water. The term is from the French for "sweet beer."

BILLI-BI. A soup made from mussels, cream, and seasonings. Under the name "mouclade," it is a well-known soup of Normandy, where the mussels are left in the final preparation; in a true billi-bi they are removed before straining the soup.

Billi-bi (sometimes spelled "Billy By") is a popular soup in American restaurants, but its origins are French. Some have claimed that the soup was created at Maxim's restaurant, in Paris, and named after William Bateman Leeds (1861–1908), president of the American Tin Plate Co. But Jean Mauduit, in his book *Maxim's, Soixante Ans de Plaisir et d'Histoire* (1958), wrote, "The recipe was created by chef [Louis] Barthe to please an old regular customer who nourished an exclusive passion for mussels; the success of the dish was so great that they named it, as an honor, with the diminutive and the initial of the customer's name, even though he was not really the creator" (my translation). Mauduit gives the man's name as William Brand. The management of Maxim's, however, says that Barthe created the dish for Brand ("an American client of Maxim's") in 1925, but at Ciro's restaurant, in Deauville, not at Maxim's.

BILLI-BI

Clean 2 lb. mussels, place in kettle with 2 chopped shallots, 2 chopped onions, 2 sprigs parsley, salt and pepper, ⅛ t. cayenne pepper, 1 c. white wine, 2 T. butter, 1 bay leaf, and ½ t. dry thyme. Cover, bring to a boil, lower to simmer, and cook for 10 min., until mussels have opened (discard those that do not). Strain soup through cheesecloth, reserve mussels for other use. Return soup to kettle, bring to boil, add 2 c. heavy cream, remove from heat, add 1 beaten egg yolk, and return to heat to thicken. Sprinkle with Parmesan cheese. Serves 6.

BILLY-GOAT DATE CAKE. Also "Kansas cookies." A cookie made with dates and nuts, dating in print to 1932. Betty Fussell, in *I Hear America Cooking* (1986), writes that the cookie is specific to the Pacific states, a result of the Deglet Noor date's being introduced from Arabia into the Coachella Valley, in California, in 1890, but it is better known as a midwestern confection. The reason for the cookie's name is not known.

BINDER. Also "extender." A food additive that binds meat and poultry products together and helps retain moisture. Binders are sometimes used as a supplement for nutrients in the meat or merely to add bulk. A non-meat binder would be **soy protein**.

BIRDSEYE, CLARENCE (1886–1956). Inventor, entrepreneur. By perfecting the process of freezing food safely and retaining its nourishment, Clarence Birdseye transformed the food industry and made food more available to more people than ever before.

Birdseye was born in Brooklyn, New York, and grew up as an outdoorsman. He attended but did not graduate from Amherst College, instead taking a job with the U.S. Agriculture Department in New Mexico and Arizona as an assistant naturalist, which involved the killing off of coyotes and the learning of taxidermy. From 1910 to 1911, he researched the cause of Rocky Mountain spotted fever by examining ticks there, then, from 1912 to 1915, while on assignment in Labrador, Birdseye began research on fast-freezing food, the rudiments of which he learned from the ice fishing of Inuit people. Freezing fish was already an established process to preserve fish in the wild, but Birdseye found that fast-freezing fish and other food better preserved it, by causing smaller ice crystals to form, thereby better maintaining the food's original texture.

Birdseye returned to the U.S. in 1917 and continued his experiments in 1922 at the Clothel Refrigerating Company, with a seven-dollar investment in an electric fan, brine, and ice. He then founded his own company, Birds Eye Seafoods Inc., which went bankrupt in 1924. By then, however, he had improved his process by freezing fish between two refrigerated surfaces under pressure. He thereupon established the General Seafoods Corp., in 1925, in Gloucester, Massachusetts. Two years later he expanded his operations to other foods and debuted his patented "Quick Freeze Machine." Two years after that, he sold both his company and his patents to Goldman Sachs Trading Corp. and the Postum Cereal Co. for $22 million, which, as the newly founded General Foods Corp., launched the highly successful Birds Eye Frozen Food Co. in Springfield, Massachusetts, in 1930, shipping products in refrigerated boxcars.

During his lifetime, Birdseye also raised foxes for their pelts, pioneered frozen-food grocery display cases, and held more than two hundred patents for lightbulbs, harpoons, and paper, made from sugarcane pulp. Birdseye died in New York City of a heart attack in 1956. According to the National Inventors Hall of Fame, "Clarence Birdseye improved the nation's diet and created a new industry based on his innovative food preservation processes."

BIRD'S NEST PUDDING. Also "crow's nest pudding." A very old New England fruit pudding (most commonly made with apples), usually with a crust and some kind of sauce. The finished dish somewhat resembles a bird's nest. It dates in print to 1833.

BISCUIT. A small leavened and shortened bread served with meals. The word, first mentioned in English in 1330, derives from the Latin words *bis* (twice) plus *coctus* (cooked). In England, a "biscuit" is what Americans usually call a **cracker** or **cookie**. The American meaning for "biscuit" was first noted by John Palmer in his *Journal of Travels in the United States of North America, and in Lower Canada* (1818), and by 1828 Webster defined the confection as "a composition of flour and butter, made and baked in private families." In general usage, such puffy leavened little breads were called "soda biscuits," "baking powder biscuits," or "baking soda biscuits," in contrast to the unleavened cracker type.

The most common form of biscuit is made from dough with baking soda and baking powder, rolled out to the thickness of one-quarter inch or so, cut into the form of a disk, then baked. "Dropped biscuits" are made by simply dropping biscuit dough onto a baking pan rather than cutting it into disks. "Funeral biscuits" were biscuits whose tops were impressed with ornate symbolic and religious designs from specially made molds or stamps and served at funerals.

Recipes for soda biscuits are found in every nineteenth-century cookbook, especially with reference to the cookery of the South, where biscuits with ham remain a specialty. The South is also home of the "beaten biscuit," which was first mentioned in 1853. This curious confection, known in Maryland as a "Maryland biscuit," is rarely made today but was once common in the South, where the sound of a mallet beating the biscuit dough was a nostalgic morning sound. This process made for a very hard, crisp biscuit that is the antithesis of the soft, puffy biscuits usually encountered. "Angel biscuits" are described by Betty Fussell in *I Hear America Cooking* (1986) as "a double-light biscuit because they use both yeast and baking powder to leaven the dough…[and] made of very moist buttermilk dough more easily shaped into biscuit blobs than rolled."

In 1930, General Mills began selling a packaged quick biscuit mix called "Bisquick" that was a great success and spawned many imitators.

Biscuits are usually broken open and buttered or served with slices of ham and gravy.

BISCUIT

Sift together 2 c. flour, 1 ½ t. salt, and 4 t. baking powder. Cut in 2 T. butter or lard with a fork till mix has the texture of coarse meal. Add ¾ c. milk and blend quickly. Knead for about 30 sec., then roll out to ½-in. thickness on floured board. Cut out in 2-in. circles, let stand, bake for 20 min. at 425°.

BEATEN BISCUITS

Combine ½ c. lard with 4 c. flour and 1 t. salt until the texture is like that of coarse meal. Add ½ c. milk and ice water mixed together, then add 1 beaten egg white. Beat with a mallet for 30 min. or more, until dough is blistered and smooth. Roll out on floured board to ½-in. thickness, cut in 2-in. circles, prick with fork, and bake for 25 min. at 350°.

BISHOP. A drink of mulled wine, sugar, spices, and citrus fruit. The name possibly derives from its red color, as in a bishop's robes. Jonathan Swift was the first to mention the drink in print, as of 1738, and James Boswell in his *Life of Johnson* (1791) says that it was a favorite drink of his subject, as it was in America throughout the eighteenth and nineteenth centuries. Often, as in the recipe below, the citrus fruit is first roasted. "Smoking bishop," mentioned by Charles Dickens in *A Christmas Carol* (1843), is a heated version of the beverage.

BISHOP

Insert about 1 doz. cloves into the rind of an orange and roast it for about 15 min. Cut into quarters, place in a saucepan with 1 qt. port or wine and 1 T. sugar, and simmer on a very low flame for about 30 min.

BISHOP'S BREAD. A sweet bread made with dried fruit. According to the *Better Homes and Gardens Heritage Cook Book* (1975), it is a bread of the American nineteenth-century frontier, where settlements would be visited by traveling clergymen. Legend has it that "one early Sunday morning a circuit-riding bishop in Kentucky dropped in on one family unexpectedly for breakfast. The resourceful hostess invented a quick fruit bread for the occasion [and] named it Bishop's Bread in honor of her guest."

There is, however, a similar bread traditionally made in Germany by this same name, *Bischofsbrot*.

BISMARCK. Also "Berliner" and "long john." An oblong cake, usually fried in oil, with a filling of jelly. In bakeries, bismarcks, dating in print to the 1930s, are commonly baked, not fried, and often sugared or topped with whipped cream. The item is particularly popular in the northern Midwest, and the name may refer to Bismarck, North Dakota, although it may refer in some way to Otto von Bismarck, first chancellor of the modern German Empire (1871–1890). Such cakes are also sometimes called "long johns."

As a beverage, a bismarck refers to a blend of champagne and stout, in print since 1910, also called a **black velvet**.

BITE-AND-STIR BOX. A box used by the New York Dutch, with two compartments—one containing sugar lumps that one may bite and chew and one holding granulated sugar to use in one's tea or coffee.

BITTERS. Aromatic, bitter blends of various spices, herbs, and alcohol (1705). Bitters are usually sold as a digestive or medicinal aid, but several bottlings of bitters are used specifically as seasonings in foods and alcoholic beverages. "Peychaud's bitters," introduced to New Orleans by pharmacist Antoine Peychaud in the 1790s, was an essential ingredient in many Louisiana cocktails, and many recipe books call for Angostura bitters as a matter of course. The herbs most often used would include gentian, orange, quinine, and ginger. Bitters have been spoken of in England since the early eighteenth century.

BLACK-AND-WHITE. A term used to describe several soda-fountain confections mixing chocolate and vanilla flavors, although it may also refer to black coffee with a container of cream on the side. In the East, "black-and-white" usually refers to a chocolate soda made with vanilla ice cream. Elsewhere, it may be a chocolate **milk shake** with vanilla ice cream blended in (a "black-and-white float" would have the vanilla ice cream floating on top of the milk shake) or even a sundae made with vanilla ice cream and chocolate sauce.

In and around NYC, "black-and-white" also refers to a circular yellow cookie about five inches wide, topped with contrasting frostings of vanilla and chocolate. They are commonly sold in pastry shops and at lunch counters. In 2012, the *New York Times* included the black-and-white cookie as part of "A History of New York in 50 Objects."

BLACK BASS (genus *Micropterus*). A member of the **sunfish** family, Centrarchidae, these freshwater fish of North America have been widely introduced throughout the U.S. Because of the difficulty in catching black bass, they became popular for consumption only during the nineteenth century, when they were shipped from eastern to western waters for sport fishermen. "Black bass" first saw print in 1815. Black bass are now found in forty-nine states of the union. The best black bass are those less than three pounds; they are prepared in all manner of ways—grilled, poached, fried, or broiled. The principal kinds of black bass for eating are "largemouth bass" (*M. salmoides*), "redeye bass" (*M. coosae*), "smallmouth bass" (*M. dolomieui*), and "spotted bass" (*M. punctulatus*).

BLACK BEAN (*Phaseolus vulgaris*). A bean usually cooked in a soup called "black bean soup." The legume, which is known to have been eaten in Mexico as early as seven thousand years ago, is used throughout the Caribbean. Venezuelans refer to the bean as *caviar criollo*, "creole caviar," and Brazilians make it part of their national dish, *feijoada*. In America, the black bean has

long been part of southern diets, and in Florida it is a favorite dish of the Cuban American communities. The following recipe is from the Coach House restaurant, in NYC, which popularized the dish in the 1970s.

BLACK BEAN SOUP

Brown 3 lb. beef bones, 1 lb. beef shin, and 3 lb. ham shank with rind in a 400° oven for about 20 min. Cut off meat and place in a kettle with 15 c. water, 3 cloves, 1 t. black peppercorns, and ¾ t. celery seed. Bring to a boil, simmer with lid ajar for 8–10 hr. Strain, remove meat for other purposes, and refrigerate stock. Soak 2 ½ c. black beans overnight in refrigerator. Remove congealed fat from stock, reserving 2 T. Melt fat in skillet and sauté 1 c. chopped onion and ½ c. chopped celery until soft. Drain beans and add to skillet. In a kettle, add beans and vegetables, 2 c. water, and 7 c. stock. Add 2 t. chopped garlic, simmer for 2 ½ hr., stirring occasionally. Coarsely puree the bean mixture through strainer or in blender. Reheat, add salt and pepper. Before serving, add a dash of dry sherry. Top with lemon slice and garnish, if desired, with chopped boiled egg.

BLACKBERRY. Any of a variety of plants in the genus *Rubus* that bear sweet black berries. The berry is often called a "bramble" because it grows on prickly shrubs. The word dates in print to about 1300.

Blackberries have long flourished in North America, where the majority of the crop is produced in Texas, Oklahoma, and Arkansas, with a great amount of wild blackberries growing throughout the Southwest. Americans have always cherished the blackberry, and Walt Whitman wrote in *Song of Myself* (1855) that "the running blackberry would adorn the parlors of heaven."

Two important hybrids of the blackberry were discovered by Americans: the "loganberry" (possibly a cross between the blackberry and the **raspberry**, found by Judge J. H. Logan of California, in 1881); and the "boysenberry" (a cross of the loganberry and the blackberry), developed by horticulturist Rudolph Boysen in 1923. The **dewberry** is another form of blackberry, particularly beloved in the South.

The most important cultivated varieties include the Marion, the Himalaya, the Lucretia, the Black Diamond, the Agawam, the Lawton, and the Snyder.

"Blackberry winter" is the period of cool weather in May when the blackberries are in bloom. The term dates in print to 1904, "blackberry summer" to 1906.

"Blackberry vinegar" is a drink of blackberries, sugar, and vinegar boiled together, strained, and cooled, dating in print to 1818 in the diary of explorer William Clark.

BLACK BETTY. A bottle of liquor that is passed among wedding guests. It dates in print to 1737.

BLACK BOTTOM. A term describing either of two confections: a sundae made with chocolate ice cream and chocolate syrup or a pie made with a chocolate custard topped with rum custard and whipped cream.

The term derives from what the *OED* describes as "a low-lying area inhabited by a coloured population," first mentioned in print as of 1915. The black-bottom pie probably derives its name from this usage, and, notes James Beard in his *American Cookery* (1972), recipes for the pie began appearing in cookbooks around the turn of the century, although the first printed reference known for the pie is not until 1951.

The "black-bottom sundae," on the other hand, probably gets its name from a popular dance of 1926 and subsequent years, called the "Black Bottom," which itself may have come out of African American culture.

〰〰〰〰〰〰〰〰〰〰〰〰〰〰〰〰〰〰〰
BLACK BOTTOM PIE
〰〰〰〰〰〰〰〰〰〰〰〰〰〰〰〰〰〰〰

Dissolve 1 T. unflavored gelatin in ¼ c. cold water. Scald 2 c. milk over low heat. Mix together ½ c. sugar, ¼ t. salt, 2 T. flour, and 4 beaten egg yolks. Pour in some of the hot milk until blended, then pour this mixture into the rest of the hot milk. Stir over low heat to thicken (about 15 min.), remove from heat, and remove 1 c. of custard. Add 2 oz. unsweetened chocolate and ½ t. vanilla, blend well, then cool. Add gelatin to remaining custard and blend well. Add 2 T. dark rum. Chill. Spread chocolate mixture into chilled baked graham-cracker crust and refrigerate. Beat 3 egg whites with ¼ t. cream of tartar and, gradually, add ⅓ c. sugar. Fold into gelatinized custard and spread over chocolate layer. Top with whipped cream and garnish with shaved chocolate.

BLACK CAKE. Also "black fruitcake," "dark fruitcake," "English fruitcake," and "Merry Christmas cake." A nineteenth-century cake made from molasses, spices, and fruit, dating in print to a recipe given in a letter by Emily Dickinson in 1883. The name derives from the dark color of the cake.

BLACK COW. Any of a variety of ice cream sodas made with a scoop of vanilla ice cream. Usually the soda itself is either chocolate, sarsaparilla, or root beer (called a "Boston cooler"), and the name refers to the mixture of dark soda with the white dairy item floating in it. If made with chocolate soda (that is, seltzer, milk, and chocolate syrup), it might be called a **black-and-white**, especially in the East. In the 1930s, plain root beer sometimes went by this term, as did chocolate milk as of 1918 in print, especially at lunch counters.

BLACK DRINK. A drink of the boiled leaves of *Ilex cassine* in water, used for thousands of years by the Gulf-states Indians as a ritual purification medicine. The drink sometimes induced a nervous state of mind and was drunk as part of a ritual, then vomited up. The Catawba Indians called it *yaupon*, the Creeks *ássi-lupupútski* ("small leaves"), and the English traders named it the black drink or "Carolina tea."

BLACKENED. A style of cooking fish or meat by searing seasoned food in a black skillet at a very high temperature. The term was first used by Cajun chef **Paul Prudhomme** to describe a dish of red **drum** (in Louisiana called "redfish") so cooked, and in the 1980s "blackened redfish" became an enormously popular dish, the recipe for which is contained in *Chef Paul Prudhomme's Louisiana Kitchen* (1984). Indeed, the dish became so popular that the species was in danger of being depleted, and a federal ban on commercial fishing of the species was put into effect in 1987.

Prudhomme said that the dish was created out of necessity at his New Orleans restaurant, K-Paul's Louisiana Kitchen, because he had no grill or salamander, so he used the black skillet to give his food its crisp texture.

BLACKJACK. A hard molasses candy with a pronounced burnt flavor. The name dates in print to 1851. The word also refers to rum sweetened with molasses, in print since 1863, as well as to a tankard of ale.

BLACK SEA BASS (*Centropristis striata*). Also "black-fish" (though different from the true blackfish or **tautog**), "Black Harry," "hannahill," "humpback," "tallywag," "rock bass," and "Black Will." A carnivorous fish that ranges from Maine to Florida, though most come from the coast between North Carolina and New York (1835). The black sea bass has always been a highly valued eating and sport fish, and, as A. J. McClane notes in *The Encyclopedia of Fish Cookery* (1977), in the early nineteenth century, "party boats already in vogue (the first record is of George Washington chartering a boat to fish the banks off Sandy Hook) became so popular that woodcut posters were distributed around New York depicting men carrying great strings of sea bass." Sea bass usually run between one and a half and five pounds at market, and they are a major fish in Chinese American recipes. See also **black bass**.

BLACKSTRAP. Also "blackstrap molasses." A mixture of rum and molasses originating in New England, dating in print to 1724. Also a very dark molasses often used to make cattle feed or industrial alcohol, dating in print to 1915. See also **molasses**.

BLACK VELVET. A cocktail made with equal parts champagne and Guinness Stout. The drink was supposedly concocted in 1861 by the steward of London's Brooks's club on hearing the news of Prince Albert's death, commemorating the event with a "black" champagne drink. See also **bismarck**.

BLENDED WHISKEY. A whiskey blended from at least 20 percent straight whiskey together with varying amounts of grain spirits, light whiskeys, or neutral spirits, dating in print to 1935. About half the American whiskey consumed in the U.S. is blended. It is sometimes erroneously called "rye," but a true rye must contain at least 51 percent of that grain.

BLIND TIGER. Also "blind pig." A term used to describe an illegal establishment serving alcoholic beverages. It may also mean a cheap or inferior whiskey, though the phrase is no longer used in either sense.

The *Dictionary of Americanisms* cites an 1857 account in a sportsmen's gazette called *Spirit of the Times* as the term's first appearance in print: "I sees a kinder pidgeon-hole cut in the side of the house, and over the hole [a sign,] 'Blind Tiger, ten cents a sight.' Says I to the feller inside, 'here's your ten cents. Walk out your wildcat.'…I'll be dod-busted if he didn't shove out a glass of whiskey. You see that 'blind tiger' was an arrangement to evade the law, which won't let 'em sell licker there, except by the gallon."

The alternate term "blind pig" appeared in print in 1872.

BLINTZ. A pancake or crepe stuffed with any of several fillings, such as cheese, jam, fish, fruit, or potatoes, and then folded. The word is from the Yiddish *blintseh*, via the Russian *blinyets*, and first appeared in English print in 1903. Blintzes are commonly served with sour cream.

BLINTZ

Make a batter from 3 beaten eggs, ¾ c. matzo meal, ½ t. salt, and 1 ½ c. water. Pour a very thin layer of batter into a frying pan brushed with fat and brown on one side. Continue to make pancakes until all batter is used. Mix 1 lb. cottage cheese with 2–3 T. sugar and 2 T. sour cream. Fill pancakes with mixture, fold over three sides, and roll into envelope shape, tucking in the flap to seal. These may be fried or baked. Serve with sour cream. Serves 6.

BLOODY MARY. Also "Bloody" for short. A cocktail made of tomato juice, vodka, and seasonings, most popular as a part of weekend **brunches**. Recipes for the Bloody Mary date in print to at least 1944.

Ernest Hemingway wrote in a letter in 1947 that he had introduced the Bloody Mary to Hong Kong in 1941, an act he said "did more than any other single factor except the Japanese Army to precipitate the Fall of that Crown Colony."

But the drink seems to have originated at Harry's New York Bar, in Paris, under another name. Bartender

Ferdinand "Pete" Petiot was experimenting with vodka, to which he'd been introduced in 1920, and a year later came up with the blend of tomato juice, vodka, and seasonings that American entertainer Roy Barton christened the "Bucket of Blood," after a nightclub in Chicago. The drink did not become popular in Paris, but in 1933 Petiot was brought to NYC by Vincent Astor to man the King Cole Bar, at the St. Regis Hotel, where the drink caught on—particularly as a supposed cure for hangovers—under the less sanguine name "Red Snapper."

Just when other bars around town began calling it the "Bloody Mary" (with reference to Mary Tudor, Mary I of England and Ireland, known for her bloody reign against Protestants) is vague, but in an ad campaign for Smirnoff vodka, entertainer George Jessel claimed to have named the drink after a friend, Mary Geraghty, first mentioned in print in the *New York Herald Tribune* in 1939.

Butch McGuire's bar, in Chicago, claims to have added the celery stick as a flavored stirrer, now a common ingredient in Bloody Marys.

Bloody Marys have been made with gin or rum, and replacing vodka with tequila and the lemon juice with lime gives one a Bloody Maria. When Japanese sake is used, the drink becomes a "Bloody Mary Quite Contrary," and when no alcohol at all is used, the drink becomes a "Virgin Mary," which some imbibers have called a "Bloody Shame." A "clam digger" is a version made with a canned tomato juice and clam juice beverage called Clamato.

BLOODY MARY

Shake with ice cubes 1 ½ oz. vodka, 2 oz. thick tomato juice, 1 dash lemon juice, 2 dashes salt, 1 dash black pepper, 2 dashes cayenne pepper, and 3 dashes Worcestershire sauce. The Bloody Mary is often served with a celery stick or a slice of lemon or lime.

BLOW FOAM. Slang expression meaning to drink beer, known in print since the 1890s.

BLUE, ANTHONY DIAS (1941–). Author, radio commentator, publisher. At a time in the 1970s when food-and-wine writing was still largely the purview of newspapers and a few ladies' magazines, Anthony Dias Blue was one of the first to make those interests into a full-time career as a writer, radio commentator, and publisher. Beginning in the mid-1970s, "Andy" Blue was among the most prolific young food-and-wine writers to chronicle a time when world gastronomy was changing rapidly.

Born in New York City, Blue grew up in Westchester County and graduated from Amherst College in 1962. At first he worked in the pop music industry, then, while living in New York City, began writing about food and wine for a variety of publications, including as wine columnist for *Diversion* magazine. He was food-and-travel commentator for WCBS Radio, with a segment that became nationally syndicated, "The Blue Lifestyle Minute" (winner of a James Beard Foundation Award for radio). In 1978, Blue and his family moved to San Francisco, where he wrote for the local media, and from 1981 to 2006 he was wine-and-spirits editor for *Bon Appétit* magazine.

Blue moved to L.A. in 1998. In 2007, he became owner and editor in chief of the beverage trade publication *The Tasting Panel*, which claims the highest circulation within the beverage industry. He has been executive director of the two largest beverage competitions, the San Francisco International Wine Competition and the San Francisco World Spirits Competition.

Blue's books include *California Wine* (1985; revised 1988), *America's Wine: A Comprehensive Guide* (1992), *The Complete Book of Spirits* (2004), and *The Buyers' Guide to Wine* (1992 and subsequent editions).

BLUEBERRY. Any of a variety of native North American shrubs of the genus *Vaccinium* bearing deep blue berries (1709), which give the fruit and shrub its name. Blueberries, first noted by Captain James Cook in the late eighteenth century, are often confused with **huckleberries**, for both grow wild. Blueberries are cultivated in Michigan, Maine, New Jersey, North Carolina, Washington, and elsewhere, with an annual commercial crop of about 280 million pounds; commercially grown varieties account for more of the crop than do the wild ones (98 percent of which are picked in Maine, largely by Mi'kmaq Indians and schoolchildren). The "blueberry rake," invented by Abijah Tabbutt of Columbia Falls, Maine, in 1822 is still used today for gathering wild berries.

The most important variety is the "highbush blueberry" (*V. corymbosum*), while the wild "lowbush berry"

(*V. angustifolium* or *V. pennsylvanicum*) is important as a crop in Maine. Other varieties include the "dryland blueberry" (*V. ashei*) of the South and the "evergreen blueberry" (*V. ovatum*) of the Northwest. Nurserywoman Elizabeth White and USDA plant breeder Dr. Frederick V. Coville of Oregon were the first to crossbreed wild blueberries commercially.

Blueberries are eaten raw, with cream, and baked in muffins or pies.

BLUE BLAZER. A cocktail made from Scotch sweetened with honey and dramatically ignited to form a blue flame that is passed back and forth from one mug to another. The drink was the creation of a famous bartender named "Professor" Jerry Thomas, author of *How to Mix Drinks* (1862) and other recipe books. The story goes that Thomas made the drink for a weary miner whose time away from civilization made him long for something out of the ordinary. Thomas came up with the blue blazer, cautioning the amateur mixer "to practice for some time with cold water." The name "blue blazer" refers to the blazing blue flame passed between mugs, but it has also come to share its meaning with the men's jacket with brass buttons named after the colorful jackets worn by the crew of the Lady Margaret Boat Club, of St. John's College, Cambridge.

BLUE BLAZER

In a silver mug dissolve 1 T. honey in 4 oz. boiling water. Put 4 oz. Scotch in another mug, ignite, and pour Scotch into the honey water, passing the liquid back and forth between the mugs until the flame dies out. Pour into a glass and garnish with lemon peel and grated nutmeg.

BLUEFISH (*Pomatomus saltatrix*). Also "snapper" (though no relation to the true **snapper**), "tailor," and other names. A warm-water fish found from Maine to the Gulf of Mexico (1615), the bluefish is ferocious and a great sport fish, nicknamed "bulldog of the ocean" for its tenacity. Early English settlers on Nantucket caught bluefish in abundance as of 1659, but a hundred years later the schools had vanished, and they did not reappear until 1800. They became abundant again around 1825, when bluefish sailing parties were organized for both men and women of Connecticut and New York.

Bluefish may have a strong flavor and must be dressed quickly. U.S. commercial landings of bluefish totaled 7.386 million pounds in 2010, valued at $976,000.

BLUE LAGOON. A cocktail made from blue curaçao, vodka, and lemon juice, created at Harry's New York Bar, in Paris, in about 1960, by Andrew MacElhone, son of the original owner, Harry MacElhone. The name refers to the blue coloring of the curaçao.

BLUE LAGOON

Shake together 1 part blue curaçao, 1 part vodka, and 1 part lemon juice, strain, and pour over an island of ice.

BLUE MEAT. Ranchers' term for the meat of an unweaned calf, dating in print to 1944.

BLUFF LETTUCE. Also "powdery liveforever" and "powdery dudleys." A succulent plant (*Dudleya farinosa*) in the stonecrop family, it is native to the Pacific coast, first mentioned in print in 1925.

BLUSH WINE. A trademark term used by Mill Creek Vineyards, in Healdsburg, California, for a white wine made from red grapes whose short skin contact imparts a rosy-pink "blush" of color to the wine. The name came about when winery co-owner Bill Kreck discussed the new wine with wine writer Jerry Mead, who commented, "You sure picked up one hell of a blush." The term was registered in 1981, though the trademark was retroactive to 1977, and other wineries must pay a fee to Mill Creek for use of the term on their labels.

BOARDINGHOUSE MEAT. Ranchers' term for the meat of an unweaned calf.

BOARDINGHOUSE POTATOES. A southern term for fried potatoes, probably because they were so common at boardinghouse tables, dating in print to 1966.

BOARDINGHOUSE REACH. A nineteenth-century colloquialism referring to the need to reach quickly and decisively across a boardinghouse common dinner table or risk not getting any food, dating in print to 1947. At such establishments, the social graces were usually not observed, and grabbing at food was more the norm.

BODEGA. A Hispanic American grocery store, but also, less commonly, a Hispanic American wine shop or wine warehouse. The word is American Spanish, derived from the Latin *apotheca*, "storehouse." The word dates in print to 1846, but gained currency in the U.S. only in the 1950s.

BOERENJONGENS. A Dutch American drink (from the Dutch for "peasant boy") made from whiskey and raisins, traditionally served at Christmastime, dating in print to 1940.

BOG. A dish made with rice and meat such as chicken ("chicken bog") or squirrel; the name dates in print to 1941.

BOILERMAKER. A shot of straight whiskey followed immediately with a beer, called a "chaser" or "helper." Sometimes the whiskey is poured right into a glass of beer or the glass of whiskey is dropped in, as with a **depth charge**. The name's origins are unknown. In the Montana mining camps of the early part of this century, a similar drink, called a "Sean O'Farrell" or "Sean O'," owing to the number of Irish immigrants who became miners there, was a popular after-work refresher. The *Oxford Encyclopedia of Food and Drink in America* suggests that "boilermaker" might refer to the nickname for boxer Jack Johnson, heavyweight from 1899 to 1905, or to the nickname of the Purdue University football team since 1891, both unlikely. "Boilermaker" was also slang for a prostitute by 1908, but the first mention of the word in print as a drink came in 1934, as a "boilermaker's delight," meaning cheap whiskey, with no mention of the beer chaser. Only in 1953 does the whiskey-and-beer description appear in print. As a "depth charge," dating in print to 1956, Adam Smith, in an April 1984 *Esquire* article about Johnstown, Pennsylvania, observed, "If you get three steelworkers at a bar, [drinking depth charges] can become a competitive sport."

"Imp 'n' Ahrn" is the term used for the drink, associated with Pittsburgh, made from Imperial Blended whiskey and Iron City beer.

BOLICHI ROAST. A beef roast stuffed with hard-boiled eggs. The term, dating in English print to 1939, is from Cuban Spanish *boliche*, for roasted round of beef.

BOLLO. A fritter made from black-eyed peas. The term, first cited in 1966, is from the Spanish for a small loaf.

BOLOGNA. Also "baloney" and "boloney." A smoked, seasoned **sausage** made from a variety of meats and popular as a sandwich meat or **cold cut**. The word derives from the Italian city of Bologna, where the sausage was supposedly first produced, an observation first made in print in 1555. In the U.S., bologna (pronounced "baloney") is usually made of pork and beef and sold in groceries as a sliced meat.

"Lebanon bologna" is a specialty of the Pennsylvania Dutch who live around Lebanon, Pennsylvania, where two versions—"regular" and "sweet"—are produced, mostly made from beef. Most of it is produced by two manufacturers, the Daniel Weaver Co. (which claims to be the oldest) and the Palmyra Bologna Co., both established in the late nineteenth century in Lebanon County.

"Bologna" is also a meatpacker's term for an inferior-quality animal whose meat is fit only for making sausages.

BOLTED MEAL. Corn that has not been home-ground.

BOMBO. Also "bumbo," which first appeared in print in 1848. A North Carolina term for a beverage made from equal parts rum, water, and New England molasses, possibly named after British admiral John Benbow (1653–1702).

BONEFISH (*Albula vulpes*). Also "banana fish," "ladyfish," and, in Hawaii, "*ō'io*." A silver fish with a piglike snout, found in the waters of Florida and the Caribbean. It is a popular game fish, though rarely caught for food. "Bonefish" dates in print to 1735.

BONGO BONGO SOUP. A soup made with oysters and spinach, created by Victor "Trader Vic" Bergeron, owner of the Trader Vic's restaurants. Bergeron contended that he had tasted the soup during World War II in New Zealand, where it was made with Toheroa clams (*paphies* *ventricosa*), for which he substituted oysters at his restaurant in San Francisco.

<hr>
BONGO BONGO SOUP
<hr>

In a saucepan, heat 2 ½ c. half-and-half to a simmer. Poach 10 oz. oysters, then puree them in a blender and add ¼ c. spinach puree, 2 T. melted butter, 1 ½ t. monosodium glutamate, 1 t. A.1. sauce, pepper and salt to taste, a dash of garlic salt, and a dash of cayenne. Place back in saucepan, bring to a simmer, add 2 T. cornstarch dissolved in 2 T. water. Simmer until thickened, top with whipped cream, and place under broiler until browned. Serves 8.

BONITO. Any fish of the species *Sarda*, especially the "Atlantic bonito" (*S. sarda*), also called the "skipjack" or "horse mackerel," and the "skipjack" (*Euthynnus pelamis*). The beauty of this steel-blue-striped fish gives it its Spanish name, *bonito*, which means "beautiful." The word "bonito" dates in English to 1599 and, with reference to *S. sarda*, to 1884 in American print. U.S. commercial landings of bonito totaled 104,000 pounds in 2010.

BOOTLEG. A term, dating in print to about 1885, for making illegal whiskey, derived from the attempt to conceal something in one's boot. A "bootlegger" is one who makes or sells illegal whiskey. The term was in wide usage during Prohibition.

BOOVA SHENKEL. Also "bova shankel" and other names. A Pennsylvania Dutch beef stew with potato dumplings. The name means "boys' legs," which may refer to the shape of the dumplings. A recipe appeared in the Pennsylvania Dutch chapter of the *United States Regional Cookbook* (Culinary Arts Institute of Chicago, 1947).

<hr>
BOOVA SHENKEL
<hr>

In a large kettle, cover with water 1 ½ lb. beef, 1 t. salt, and ⅛ t. pepper. Bring to a boil, lower to a simmer, and cook for 2 ½ hr. Boil 6 potatoes until tender, peel and rice, add 1 T. butter, 1 T. minced onion, and 1 beaten egg, and let stand. In a bowl, sift 1 ¼ c. flour, 1 t. baking powder, and ½ t. salt and cut in 2 T. butter to make a coarse, crumbly texture.

Add 3 T. water to make a dough. Roll into 10-in. circles and spread potato mixture on top. Fold in half-circles, press together, and place on top of the meat and broth in the kettle. Cover and boil for 25 min. When done, place on large platter and decorate with croutons. Serves 4.

BOOYA. A Minnesota and Wisconsin dish of meats like turtle, oxtail, beef, or chicken, with carrots, potatoes, and, commonly, rutabagas. Because the dish is usually cooked in enormous batches for large social gatherings and church suppers, "booya" has also come to refer to the outdoor feast itself. Most booyas are held in the fall when the harvest comes in. The origin of the word is unknown, perhaps from the French *bouillir* or the Canadian French *bouillon*, "broth," although it has been suggested that the dish is of Belgian or Bohemian origin. It appeared in print at least as early as the 1880s. According to Marcia Adams, in *Heartland* (1991), the Belgian immigrants in Wisconsin originally used turtle meat in the dish, but later chicken and other ingredients were substituted.

<hr>
BOOYA
<hr>

Soak 1 c. navy beans overnight. Cook in salted water for 1 hr. In a very large kettle place beans, a 4–5 lb. stewing chicken, and 2 lb. cut-up stewing beef. Add water to cover, bring to a boil, lower to a simmer, and cook, covered, for 2 hr. Remove meat, skim fat from surface of liquid, and remove skin from chicken. Separate the meat from the bones, chop coarsely, then add back into kettle. Add 1 lb. chopped carrots, 4 sliced celery ribs, 2 large minced onions, 1 minced garlic clove, ½ c. barley, one 16-oz. can of tomatoes, one 10-oz. pkg. of kernel corn, and 2 large peeled and diced potatoes. Add ⅓ oz. pickling spices wrapped in cheesecloth. Add salt, pepper, and allspice to taste. Cover and simmer for about 1 hr.

BOP. An old North Carolina confection—the name may describe the puffy appearance of the pastry.

<hr>
BOP
<hr>

Mix 2 c. milk, 3 beaten eggs, 1 T. butter, and 4 T. flour to make a batter, which is then baked in a pan at 450° until brown.

BORSCHT. Also "borsch." A beef-and-cabbage soup of Russian and Polish origins, borscht was particularly popular among Jews who immigrated from those countries, so much so that Abel Green, an editor at the showbusiness industry newspaper *Variety* in the 1930s, used "Borscht Belt" (also "Borscht Circuit") as a synonym for those resorts in New York's Catskill Mountains frequented by Jewish entertainers and patrons.

The Russian *borsch* (*borscht* is Yiddish) actually means "cow parsnips," which originally were the basis of the soup. The term dates in print to 1829.

The soup is traditionally served hot or cold, often with a dollop of sour cream on top.

BORSCHT

In a large kettle place 8 scraped, coarsely grated beets, 4 coarsely chopped onions, 2 cloves minced garlic, 1 c. peeled, seeded chopped tomatoes, and 2 lb. beef brisket. Pour in 2 qt. water and bring to a boil. Lower heat to a simmer and cook until meat is tender. Add about 2 T. sugar and lemon juice to taste. Add salt and pepper to taste.

BOSK. *Also "boos-ke-tan."* The so-called "green corn dance," an eight-day ritual of the Gulf-states Indians, during which they drank the **black drink**, which had the effect of altering their state of mind in ways they believed increased the spirituality of the feast.

BOSTON BAKED BEANS. A dish of navy beans made with molasses and salt pork or bacon. Some argue that baked beans were introduced to the colonists by the Indians, but novelist Kenneth Roberts, in an essay on "The Forgotten Marrowbones," printed in Marjorie Mosser's *Foods of Old New England* (1957), argues that baked beans had long been a traditional Sabbath dish among North African and Spanish Jews, who called the dish *"skanah."* Roberts also cites *Riley's Narrative* (1816), by James Riley, as a source and supposes that New England sea captains brought the idea home with them from Africa.

Nevertheless, the dish clearly became associated with Boston, whose Puritan settlers baked beans on Saturday, serving them that night for dinner, for Sunday breakfast with codfish cakes and **Boston brown bread**,

and again for Sunday lunch, because no other cooking was allowed during the Sabbath, which extended to Sunday evening. Sometimes the housewives would hand over their pots of uncooked beans to a community oven, often located within a tavern, to be baked.

Because of the association between Bostonians and beans, the city came to be called "Beantown." A recipe for baked beans of this type was printed in Lydia Maria Child's *The American Frugal Housewife* in 1832, though the term "Boston baked beans" dates to the 1850s. "Boston strawberries" was a restaurant slang term for the same beans in the late nineteenth century. Baked beans of this kind were first canned in 1875, by the Burnham & Morrill Co. of Portland, Maine, for local fishermen. The first canned beans with tomato sauce were sold by the Van Camp Packing Co. of Indianapolis in 1891.

BOSTON BAKED BEANS

Rinse 32 oz. of pea (navy) beans in cold water. Heat beans over high heat in large pot, add 4 t. salt, 8 c. boiling water, and boil for 2 min. Cover and let stand for 1 hr. Reboil beans, then turn heat to low and simmer for 1 hr. Mix together ¼ c. dark molasses, ¼ c. dark brown sugar, 1 t. pepper, 1 t. dry mustard, and stir into beans. Alternate layers of beans with slices of browned-salt-pork-and-molasses mixture, adding onion to the middle if desired. On top lay strips of salt pork or bacon, and bake in a covered pot at 250° for about 7 hr., adding more water if necessary to keep the beans moist. Serves 12.

BOSTON BROWN BREAD. Also "brown bread" and "Boston bread." A rye-flour bread made with molasses. Boston brown bread was well known among the Puritans, who served it on the Sabbath with **Boston baked beans**. It is often made with graham flour. "Brown bread" was first mentioned in print in 1831; "Boston bread" in 1889. It is sometimes baked in a coffee can and commercially packaged in a tin can.

BOSTON BROWN BREAD

Sift together ½ c. rye flour, ½ c. whole-wheat or graham flour, ½ t. baking soda, ½ t. baking powder, ½ c. cornmeal, and ½ t. salt. Mix in 1 ½ c. buttermilk and ½ c. dark molasses, then pour into 1-qt. buttered baking pan, tall pudding mold, or coffee can and cover tightly. Place in kettle of boiling water until mold is immersed halfway. Cover and steam in 300° oven for about 3 hr., then place bread, uncovered, in oven to dry for a few minutes. Serves 6.

BAKED BOSTON BROWN BREAD

Sift 4 ½ c. graham flour with ¾ c. sugar and ½ t. salt, then add 1 c. dark molasses, 2 beaten eggs, and 2 c. buttermilk in which 2 t. baking soda have been dissolved. Add 2 c. raisins if desired. Pour into greased pans and let rise for 1 hr. Bake at 300° for 1 hr.

BOSTON BUTT. Also "Boston shoulder." A late-nineteenth-century term for meat cut from the top of the shoulder of a California ham and consisting of about two-thirds lean and one-third fat. The term was first used in print in 1903.

BOSTON CRACKER. A large, thin, semisweet biscuit, similar to a **common cracker** and eaten with cheese or other savories. Boston crackers were first mentioned in print in 1818.

BOSTON CREAM PIE. A pie made of white cake and custard filling or topping. If chocolate icing is added, it is called "Parker House Chocolate Pie," after the Parker House Hotel, in Boston, where the embellishment was first contrived.

The pie goes back to early American history, when it was sometimes called "pudding-cake pie" or, when made with a raspberry jelly filling, "Mrs. Washington's pie." The first mention of the dessert as "Boston cream pie" was in the New York *Herald* in 1855.

BOSTON CREAM PIE

Mix together 1 c. cake flour, ¾ c. sugar, 6 T. softened butter, ⅓ c. milk, 1 ½ t. baking powder, 1 ½ t. vanilla, ¼ t. baking soda, a dash of salt, and 2 beaten eggs. Pour into greased pan and bake at 375° for 25 min., or until inserted knife comes out clean. Cool on cake rack. In a saucepan stir 2 c. milk, ¼ c. sugar, 3 T. cornstarch, ¼ t. salt, and 2 beaten egg yolks. Cook until thickened, boil for 1 min., stir

in 1 t. vanilla, and remove from heat to cool. Spread thickly onto cake and cool in refrigerator for 30 min.

BOTTLE BABY. Slang term for an alcoholic, dating in print to 1925.

BOTTLE CLUB. An after-hours social club where liquor may be legally sold. The term dates back to at least the 1940s.

BOTTLE SERVICE. The sale and service of whole bottles of liquor to a table at a nightclub, a practice begun in the 1990s by Mark Baker and Jeffrey Jah, promoters at the nighclub Tunnel in New York City. The exorbitant price of the bottle was usually based on the number of cocktails it could make.

BOTTLED WATER. Any water sealed in bottles and intended for drinking. This designation includes mineral water, which usually comes from a source of water containing various minerals, rather than water to which such minerals have been added.

Because of the relative purity of American drinking water in this century, bottled waters held little allure for most Americans, who never developed the habit of taking mineral waters as a medicinal aid, as Europeans did. There were, in the nineteenth century, spas and resorts where the waters were considered of healthful benefit, and in Saratoga, New York, "Saratoga Vichy" water (later "Saratoga Mineral Water") was bottled and had widespread popularity. Bottled waters took on a certain fashionability after an intensive advertising campaign by Perrier, a French water-bottling company, in 1977, which stressed its purity at a time when Americans had begun to doubt the merits of their own water-purification systems and started to regard mineral water as an alternative to high-calorie soft drinks.

As a result, the bottled-water business soared in the 1980s, and there are now more than 430 American bottling facilities and 700 brand labels in the market, in addition to more than 75 imported brands (most of which are carbonated mineral waters). Bottled water is now a $60 billion industry worldwide. The U.S. per capita consumption of bottled water was 29.2 gallons in 2011. More than 70 percent of all bottled water is sold in five states—California, Florida, Illinois, New York, and Texas.

Bottled waters are either "sparkling," with natural or added bubbles, or "nonsparkling" (also called "still"). The various categories of bottled waters are as follows.

DRINKING WATER. Bottled water obtained from an approved source that has undergone a minimum of treatment and filtration.

MINERAL WATER. Under 1993 FDA regulations, mineral water is defined as bottled water with at least 250 parts per million of total dissolved solids like calcium. Mineral water must also come from a protected underground water source.

NATURAL WATER. Bottled spring, mineral, or artesian-well or well water not derived from a municipal water supply.

PURIFIED WATER. Bottled water produced by distillation, deionization, reverse osmosis, or another suitable process that meets U.S. Pharmacopeia standards for purified water.

SPRING WATER. Bottled water derived from an underground formation from which water flows naturally to the earth's surface.

WELL WATER. Bottled water from a hole bored in the ground that taps the water of an aquifer.

BOTTOMS UP! A drinking toast, indicating that the entire contents of a glass or bottle should be drunk up quickly.

BOUDIN. A Louisiana sausage of two varieties: *boudin rouge* (French for "red pudding"), which is a blood sausage, and *boudin blanc* (French for "white pudding"), which is made with pork shoulder. Boudin (the name dates in print to 1805) is customarily made and served at hog-butchering parties called "boucheries," still held occasionally in the Cajun country during autumn or winter. *DARE*, however, gives a primary definition of "boudin" as "the intestines of buffalo esp[ecially] as prepared for food," citing an 1805 report from the journals of Lewis and Clark.

According to Bruce Aidells and Denis Kelly, in *Hot Links and Country Flavors* (1990), white boudin often contains rice and onions, and the sausage filling is usually pushed out of the casing after cooking and eaten without the casing.

BOULA. Also "boula boula." A green-pea-and-green-turtle soup, flavored with sherry and topped with whipped cream and cheese, dating in print to 1931. The dish is described in *The White House Cookbook* (1964) as "an old favorite which was served in President Martin van Buren's day. President and Mrs. John F. Kennedy served it at the White House and, as sports enthusiasts, renamed it for the old college song, 'Boola-Boola!'" It was very popular in NYC restaurants in the 1930s. Theodora FitzGibbon, in *The Food of the Western World* (1976), noted that the soup came originally from the Seychelles.

BOULA

Combine 1 can pea soup with 1 can green turtle soup, boil, season with ¾ c. sherry and a dash of ground pepper. Fill bowls and top with whipped cream and a sprinkle of Parmesan cheese. Place under broiler until lightly browned. Serves 4–6.

BOULEY, DAVID (1953–). Restaurateur, author. Since the opening, in 1987, of his namesake restaurant Bouley, in NYC's Tribeca neighborhood, David Bouley has been considered one of the most innovative chefs in America, fusing French classicism with American and global ideas that made his kitchen a form of graduate school for many of the finest contemporary American chefs.

Bouley was born in Storrs, Connecticut. As a teenager he worked as a dishwasher, then moved to Santa Fe, New Mexico, to work with French pastry chef Michel Richard at the La Fonda hotel, then moved with him to Los Angeles, where Richard opened his own restaurant.

Bouley then worked in France under master chefs like Gaston Lenôtre, Roger Vergé, Paul Bocuse, and Frédy Girardet before returning to the U.S. to do stints at New York City's Vienna '79 and Le Cirque. He met **Drew Nieporent**, who in 1985 hired him as chef for his new Tribeca restaurant Montrachet, which quickly earned three stars from the *New York Times*.

After some acrimony with Nieporent, Bouley left Montrachet in 1987 to open Bouley nearby, which became one of the city's most creative and celebrated restaurants, with four *Times* stars, known for Bouley's long tasting menus and his unstinting devotion to perfecting every dish. In 1994, *People* selected him as one of its 50 Most Beautiful People. Two years later, however, the restaurant closed, and Bouley began plans to develop a new restaurant named Bouley; an Austrian restaurant named Danube; Bouley Bakery, Café & Market (later reconfigured as Bouley); a Test Kitchen; and Bouley Market. He later closed Danube and reopened it as Secession, in 2008. In 2011, he opened a Japanese restaurant named Brushstroke, which enlisted chefs from the Tsuji Culinary Institute, in Osaka.

Along with Mario Lohninger and Melissa Clark, Bouley contributed to the cookbook *East of Paris: The New Cuisines of Austria and the Danube* (2003), and, with **Jean-Georges Vongerichten**, he contributed recipes for the volume on the *United States of America* (2005) in the World Cuisine series.

BOULUD, DANIEL (1955–). Chef, restaurateur, author. Trained in the classic traditions of French cuisine, Daniel Boulud was to distinguish himself in the U.S. by melding that tradition with **nouvelle cuisine** by applying it to American regional ingredients in his own sumptuous style, thereby changing the formerly staid image of French cuisine.

Born in Saint-Pierre-de-Chandieu, France, to a farming family, Boulud apprenticed with chef Gérard Nandron in Lyon, then worked in various Michelin star kitchens, including La Mère Blanc, Le Moulin de Mougins, Georges Blanc, and Michel Guèrard. He moved to Washington, D.C., in 1981 to become private chef to an ambassador of the European Commission. In 1982 in New York City, he was appointed chef at the Westbury Hotel and afterwards the Hôtel Plaza-Athénée's Le Régence. From 1986 to 1992 he was chef at Le Cirque, where he transformed the classic menu with his creative new ideas, like "scallops in black tie" (with black truffles) and sea bass with potato scales and a red wine reduction.

In 1993, Boulud opened his own haute cuisine restaurant, Daniel (relocated to East 65th Street in 1999), voted one of world's ten best restaurants by the *International Herald Tribune* and earning four stars from the *New York Times* and three from the Michelin Guide to New York City. His success led him to open a catering company named Feast & Fêtes (1994) and to partner with François Payard to run Payard Patîsserie & Bistro (1997), selling his interest in 2000.

Through Boulud's Dinex Group LLC (1997), many projects followed, including Café Boulud (1998) and a branch in Palm Beach, Florida (2003). His db Bistro Moderne (2001), in NYC, updated the traditions of French bistro cooking and added one of the first gourmet hamburgers, made with foie gras, short ribs, and truffles, selling for $55. DBGB (2009), on NYC's Bowery, featured a menu based around charcuterie, which was a novel idea at the time.

Having said he had no interest in joining colleagues in Las Vegas, he was finally coaxed to open Daniel Boulud Brasserie (since closed) at the Wynn Las Vegas Resort in 2005. Next was a still more casual NYC restaurant, Bar Boulud (2008), a Maison Boulud, in Beijing (2008), and both db Bistro Moderne and Lumière, in Vancouver, British Columbia, which he ran from 2008 to 2011; other branches of db Bistro Moderne opened in Miami (2010) and Singapore (2010). In 2011, he debuted Boulud Sud, specializing in the cuisine of the Mediterranean, and Épicèrie, both on New York City's Upper West Side. Another outpost of Bar Boulud was opened to great acclaim in London in 2012. In 2012, a Café Boulud opened in Toronto and a Maison Boulud in Montreal.

Boulud expanded his reputation as a co-founder of the Bocuse d'Or USA Foundation (2008), a nonprofit organization that selects, trains, and supports U.S. competitors for the international culinary competition held biennially in Lyon.

The James Beard Foundation named Boulud Best Chef of NYC in 1992, Outstanding Chef of the Year (1994), and Outstanding Restaurateur (2006). He received the Chevalier de la Légion d'honneur from the president of France in 2006, for his advancement of French culture, and the Culinary Humanitarian Award at the United Nations, from the Adopt-a-Mine Field Foundation (2007). The Culinary Institute of America honored Boulud with the Chef of the Year 2011 Augie Award, named in honor of Georges Auguste Escoffier. In 2012, Johnson & Wales University granted Boulud an honorary doctor of culinary arts degree.

Boulud's cookbooks include *Daniel Boulud's Café Boulud Cookbook* (1998), *Braise: A Journey through International Cuisine*, with Melissa Clark (2006), and a memoir, with Peter Kaminsky, *Letters to a Young Chef* (2003). His TV show *After Hours with Daniel* featured chefs cooking and eating after finishing service.

BOUNCE. A fermented beverage popular in colonial days, made by pouring spirits such as rum or brandy over fruit and adding sugar, citrus fruit, spices, and water. Bounce is similar to, and perhaps interchangeable with, "shrub," which is strained and sweetened with brown sugar. The former's name probably derived from its ability to give the imbiber a bounce, the latter's possibly from the Arabic *shrub*, "drink."

BOUNCE

Pour 1 qt. rum or brandy over 5 pt. pitted cherries or other fruit and let stand to ferment for a week. (For a shrub, strain the liquid and add brown sugar to taste.) Bottle and let stand another week.

BOUNCER. A person hired by a saloon or restaurant to "bounce" unwanted customers from the premises. The term dates to 1865 in print.

BOURBON. A spirit distilled from a fermented mash of grain, at least 51 percent of which must be corn. Bourbon is bottled between 80 and 125 proof (legal minimum is 60 proof) and must be aged at least two years in new, charred white oak barrels. Only limestone-filtered spring water may be used to lower alcoholic proof.

Bourbon is the only distinctly American spirit, although it was not until May 4, 1964, that the federal government recognized it as such and protected it under law. In the South it has been traditionally synonymous with **whiskey.** It is the essential ingredient of a Kentucky **mint julep** and finds its way into many sweet confections, such as "bourbon balls" and "bourbon cakes."

The name comes from Bourbon County, originally in Virginia but now part of Kentucky. (The Bourbons were a line of European monarchs whose subjects settled colonies in the Americas.) Corn spirits had been made as early as 1746 in America, and Evan Williams established

a distillery in Bourbon County as of 1783. But credit for creating the distinctive taste of bourbon goes to a Baptist minister, Reverend Elijah Craig, who began making spirits at Royal Spring, Virginia (presently Georgetown, Kentucky), in 1789. At first this was called merely "corn whiskey" or "corn," but by 1821 an ad had appeared in the *Western Citizen* selling a spirit specifically called "bourbon whiskey." By the middle of the nineteenth century the spirit was so associated with Bourbon County, Kentucky, that it was called, simply, "bourbon," and often "Kentucky bourbon." The first bottled bourbon was sold in 1870, all bourbon prior to that being shipped in barrels to taverns.

Most bourbon uses sour mash (introduced in 1823 by Dr. James C. Crow)—that is, a part of the spent beer, or distiller's beer (a residue from a previous mash run), allowed to sour overnight and then added to a new batch of mash. "Sour mash whiskey" or "sippin' whiskey" refers to whiskey made by such a process.

The law requires the use of new, charred white oak barrels to give the bourbon its character, part of a tradition whose origins are obscure. In *American Cooking: Southern Style* (1971), Eugene Walter gives three stories about how the distilling method came about:

> One story tells of a careless cooper who drowsed while some dampened staves were steaming by the fire. The staves burned but he made the barrels with them anyway, and a new flavor was imparted to the contents. Another tarrydiddle would have it that a thrifty cooper, intending to resell some barrels in which salted fish had been shipped, carefully burned out the interiors to get rid of every trace of fishiness. My own favorite explanation holds that a Kentucky farmer buried several barrels of whiskey under his barn to age. Lightning struck the barn, it burned down and a few years later, digging there, the farmer rediscovered the barrels, charred black but with the honey-red liquid unharmed, and noticeably better than any other whiskey he had made.

There are now thirteen operating distilleries in Kentucky making bourbon—78.6 percent of the world's supply—with the remaining 21.4 percent produced in Tennessee, Virginia, and Missouri. See also **Tennessee whiskey**.

"Single-barrel bourbon" is a 1990s marketing term for specially selected barrels of bourbon whose distinctive taste allows them to be sold at a premium price.

"Small-batch" bourbons are made in lots of fewer than one thousand gallons (about twenty barrels).

Bourbon is drunk **straight**, **on the rocks**, ideally with so-called **branch water**, or in **sours** and other mixed drinks. In 2011, total U.S. production of bourbon (including Tennessee whiskey) was 16 million nine-liter cases, with revenues of $2.1 billion.

In 2007, Senator Jim Bunning of Kentucky sponsored a bill that declared September officially Bourbon Heritage Month.

BOWFIN (*Amia calva*). Also "grindle," "jack grindle," "John A. Grindle," "mudfish," "mudjack," "prairie bass," "scaled ling," "speckled cat," "spot-tail," "lake lawyer," "choupique," "blackfish 5," "cypress trout," and "dogfish." A carnivorous ganoid freshwater fish of North America. "Bowfin" first saw print in about 1845, although "grindle" dates back to the beginning of the eighteenth century and derives from the German *Gründel*, "ground," because it inhabits sluggish waters. They are generally not considered good eating fish, but in Louisiana the roe of the fish (there called "*choupique*," a word that derives from French and in American print since 1763 as "*choupic*") is cultivated as a form of **caviar**.

BOZZI, PIO (1894–1942), and **JOHN (GIOVANNI) GANZI** (1894–1963). Restaurateurs. Starting out as saloonkeepers during Prohibition, Bozzi and Ganzi established the model for the New York City Italian steakhouse, which became a standard in the industry in postwar America.

The two men immigrated from Parma, Italy, and during **Prohibition** opened a saloon in 1926, on New York City's Second Avenue. If customers asked for something to eat, Ganzi ran to a butcher shop to buy steaks, then cooked them. When Bozzi and Ganzi sought to register their place as a restaurant, a NYC clerk who could not understand their accent issued the license under the name "Palm," which they retained.

Palm began serving a full menu of simple Italian dishes and their steaks, personally selected from prime carcasses in the Meat Market District, adding items like a tomato-and-onion salad, cottage fried potatoes, lobsters, and, for dessert, cheesecake. It was a menu not dissimilar to those served at other steakhouses in the immediate vicinity—an area called "Steakhouse Row"—like Christ Cella, Colombo's, and Bruno's Pen & Pencil (all now closed), but Palm became the best known, not least for the murals of cartoon caricatures of regular customers, a tradition that began when local artists paid for their meals by drawing cartoons. Later, some of New York City's finest cartoonists added their work to the walls.

For decades Palm was very much a male enclave, including many journalists from the nearby newspapers, and not until the 1970s was it a place where women would feel comfortable dining without a man to bring them there. In 1976, the *New York Times* gave Palm its highest rating of four stars.

After Bozzi and Ganzi's deaths, great-grandson Bruce Bozzi and Ganzi's son Walter Ganzi Sr. took over the operation. Until the 1970s, there was only the original Palm and an adjunct across the street. In the 1980s, however, the company began franchising, and as of 2013 has thirty-two units in the U.S. and abroad.

BRAMBLE JELLY. An eighteenth-century jelly made from crab apples and blackberries. It originated in England.

BRANCH WATER. Supposedly the clearest, purest water, from a small stream called a "branch." The term dates in print to 1835. "**Bourbon** and branch water" is a nostalgic request in the South, but one that can hardly be fulfilled unless the bartender has access to such a stream's water supply.

BRANDON PUFF. A South Carolina muffin of flour and cornmeal. The origin of the name may in some way refer to Charles Brandon, first duke of Suffolk (died 1545).

BRANDON PUFF

Combine 1 qt. flour, ¾ c. cooled melted butter, 4 beaten eggs, 1 yeast cake, and enough milk to make a muffin batter. Let rise overnight. Add 1 t. cornmeal, pour into muffin tins, and bake until brown at 425°, about 10–15 min.

BRANDY. A spirit obtained from distilled wine or the fermented mash of fruit. The word comes from *brandewijn*, a Dutch word meaning to "burn" or "distill." In America, most brandy (about 72 percent) is made in California, from grapes such as the **Thompson Seedless** and the Flame Tokay, although some is made from fruits such as apples (**applejack**), peaches, and others. About 20 percent of the distilleries use a "pot still" (or "alembic") by which the wine is heated in a pot, becomes vaporized, and condenses into a receptacle. The rest of the brandy is produced in a "continuous still," which allows brandy to be produced without pausing between batches and gives off a very clean product.

Brandies are aged in fifty-gallon white oak barrels that add flavor and slight color. By federal law, brandy must have a minimum proof of 60 (30 percent alcohol by volume).

BRANDY ALEXANDER. Also "Alexander." A cocktail made from brandy, cream, and a chocolate cordial. The origin of the name is unknown, as is its date of concoction, though it was first in print in 1925. A recipe appeared in 1939 in the *World Famous Chef's Cook Book*, by Ford Naylor, who calls it simply "Alexander." For a long time it was considered a "ladies' cocktail"—an alcoholic beverage for those who were not used to drinking strong liquors. If made with gin instead of brandy, the drink is called a "Panama," after the country in Central America.

"Brandy Alexander pie" is a cream pie that includes the same ingredients, in a graham cracker or cookie crust.

BRANDY ALEXANDER

Shake with ice cubes 1 ½ oz. brandy, 1 oz. chocolate cordial, and 1 oz. light or heavy cream. Strain into cocktail glass.

BRANDY SMASH. A cocktail of the mid-nineteenth century made from brandy, crushed ice, and mint.

BRANNIGAN. Archaic term for a drinking bout, dating in print to 1892.

BRASSERIE. In France, a small, inexpensive restaurant (usually with Alsatian roots) serving various types of beer, or an actual brewery. It dates in print to 1864, from French *brasser*, "to brew," although the term has also come to mean a restaurant serving simple neighborhood fare. In America, a brasserie more often approximates this second meaning, usually connoting a place serving inexpensive French food in informal surroundings, though in the later twentieth century the word was used liberally to describe many styles of restaurants just below those serving haute cuisine.

BRAT. A slang term for German pork bratwurst sausage, especially in the Midwest, dating in print to 1950. "Double brat" refers to two sausages on a hard roll, a food especially popular in Sheboygan, Wisconsin, which calls itself the "Bratwurst Capital of the World" or the "Wurst City of the World."

BREAD. One of the world's basic foods, made from flour and water, often with the addition of yeast, salt, and other ingredients. Shaped into loaves, rolls, flat cakes, or rings and then baked, bread is one of man's earliest foods, dating back more than ten thousand years, soon after man cultivated cereal grains and pounded them to make porridge (which may have been baked as the first breads). The word itself is from the Old English *brēad*.

The bread of the Native Americans was based on cornmeal and included a wide variety of preparations. Piki bread was very thin, often made from blue cornmeal batter on a hot stone. This was the bread of the Hopi; the Zuni call it *hewe*, the Tewa call it *mowa*, and those in San Ildefonso, New Mexico, call it *bowahejahui* ("Put it on, take it off"). As Carolyn Niethammer notes in *American Indian Food and Lore* (1974), "Piki making is an art and a ritual....Years ago a young woman was required to demonstrate that she had mastered the art of piki-baking before she was considered a suitable bride...but today the number of those who excel in this art is dwindling." The **tortilla**, still common in Mexican American restaurants, was originally a Native American cornmeal bread. Later, after Columbus brought wheat to the New World in 1493, tortillas were also made with wheat flour. Other breads were baked in adobe ovens or in a hole in the earth. Niethammer describes *kinaalda*, a bread measuring eight inches deep and five feet across, as "the traditional food for the Navajo girl's puberty ceremony."

The Native Americans of the East Coast also used corn exclusively for their bread, and as of the 1650s the European settlers called this "Indian bread," as an alternative to the earlier "pone" or "corn pone" (from the Algonquian word *apan*, "baked"). The colonists immediately adapted cornmeal as a flour and made their own "corn bread" (first mentioned in 1750) or combined rye, molasses, cornmeal, and yeast to make **rye 'n' Injun bread**.

Yeast was easily obtainable from beer brewers (the yeast-rich foam atop the beer was called "barm"), and there was also a whole range of steamed breads like **Boston brown bread**. **Biscuits** were found throughout the U.S., especially after the new leavenings like pearl ash, saleratus, **baking powder**, and baking soda came into use during the mid-nineteenth century, thereby creating a new variety of "quick" or "lightnin'" breads. Home baking was further helped along with a novelty of the 1850s, self-rising flour, and an increase in store-bought and bakery bread was spurred by the invention, in 1834, of the Swiss steel roller, which processed flour finely and uniformly. In the 1830s, temperance lecturer Sylvester Graham promoted the use of whole-wheat, unbolted flour to make bread, which took the name "Graham bread" by 1834, and he published the first book devoted solely to bread making, *Treatise on Bread and Bread-Making* (1837).

During the Gold Rush in California, in 1849, an old-fashioned form of bread was revived—**sourdough**—that has since been associated with San Francisco's history.

During a period of deprivation in the Civil War, a wing of the U.S. Senate in Washington was turned into an enormous oven to bake sixteen thousand loaves of bread a day for the Union troops.

After the Civil War, bakeries grew in number, especially in large cities with new immigrant populations, and there was a trend toward purer, whiter bread. Before this time, bakers were accused of adulterating their bread with lime. "Whole wheat" bread (also called "middling bread," which referred to the coarse particles of whole wheat in it) came to be considered a coarse, common type of bread, while white bread signified purity and a more refined product. But later in the twentieth century, nutritionists advocated whole-wheat bread as healthier and won the support of those in the **health food** movement.

Ready-made, packaged yeast was available for the homemaker by 1868, and for the rest of the century most bread was still made at home. By 1900, 95 percent of the flour produced was sold to home bakers. But in 1911, the National Association of Master Bakers quoted a study showing that the percentage had changed radically: 60 to 65 percent of the city families did not make their own bread any longer. (Today only 15 percent of the flour bought is used by home bakers.)

The twentieth century also brought innovations in technology that produced a loaf whiter but less nutritious than those previously baked. The whiteness represented purity to those brought up on dark, coarse breads (however full of nutrients they were), but the new loaves were made by extracting 28 to 30 percent of the wheat kernel's bulk, thereby eliminating the bran and wheat germ. In 1904, J. N. Alsop of St. Louis developed the Alsop Process, by which chlorine was used to bleach the flour white. Such processes resulted in a 1943 federal law requiring that such breads be "enriched" with thiamine, niacin, riboflavin, and iron, an action that seemed to placate nutritionists for two decades, until the **health food** movement pointed out the contradictory idea of removing nutrients only to replace them in another form.

Today some commercial breads are in fact jammed with vitamins and minerals ordinary breads do not have; but then, bleached-flour breads lack the other nutrients derived from the bran and wheat germ.

Packaged bread was made possible in 1911 by virtue of a wrapping machine. Sliced bread, also called a "sandwich loaf," was introduced in 1930 by the Continental Baking Co. under the name Wonder Bread (which had been around in an unsliced form since 1920) after Otto Frederick Rohwedder, of Battle Creek, Michigan, invented the bread-slicing machine in 1928. Most American bread is bought sliced.

There has been a trend in the past fifteen years to produce commercial breads of coarser textures and varied grains, ironically often sweetened with sugar, molasses, or honey. "Artisanal breads," suggesting bread made by small producers, can take many forms, much of it dependent on "identity-preserved" wheat composed of a single type of wheat. At the same time, there has been tremendous growth in packaged mixes for breads, rolls, muffins, and biscuits, as well as frozen breads and pastries or "heat-and-serve" (also "brown-and-serve") varieties that need no true baking, only warming.

Peak consumption of white bread in the U.S. was nine billion pounds in 1963. In 2010, bread sales in the U.S. totaled $196 billon.

"Italian bread" is a long, cylindrical bread with blunt-pointed tips. It is slightly fatter or wider than "French bread" (also "baguettes") as sold in American groceries. "Pita bread" (from the Greek *pitta*) is a flat Middle Eastern–style bread often called "pocket bread." "Raisin bread" is a popular sweet variety, while **rye** and **pumpernickel** are used for sandwiches. See also **Cornell bread**, **sourdough**, **Boston brown bread**, **monkey bread**, **anadama bread**.

"Bread and skip" is an archaic New England colloquialism for a scanty meal, while "bread and with it" refers to a meal of bread and some other foods.

BREAD LINE. A term first used in 1825 to describe the lines of poor, hungry people who received loaves of bread and other food from charitable institutions. Bread lines became a common sight in American cities during the Great Depression of the 1930s.

BREAKFAST. The first meal of the day. The word means "to break one's fast" and dates back to at least 1425. "Brekkie" is a modern colloquialism for "breakfast."

The Native American breakfast consisted of cornmeal mush and perhaps corn bread, both items the first European settlers adapted for their own breakfasts. The settlers also breakfasted on a quickly prepared porridge called "hasty pudding," made with cornmeal and molasses. Later, bread or toast and coffee or tea were the usual breakfast, while in the nineteenth century, affluence brought more variety to the diet and larger portions of meats, fish, cheese, bread, jams, and often a tot of rum or cider. Scotsman John Melish visited America in 1811 and reported in his *Travels in the United States of America* on "A Backwoods Breakfast," at which his humble hostess sought to wring the necks of two chickens.

I told her to stop, and she gave me a look of astonishment. "Have you any eggs?" said I. "Yes, plenty," replied she, still keeping in a stooping posture, with the chicken in her hand. "Well," said I, "just boil an egg,
and let me have it, with a little bread and tea, and that will save you and I a great deal of trouble." She seemed quite embarrassed, and said she never could set down a breakfast to me like that.... She detained me about half an hour, and at last placed upon the table a profusion of ham, eggs, fritters, bread, butter and some excellent tea....I mention the circumstance to show the kind of hospitality of the landlady, and the good living enjoyed by the backwoods people.

Also popular were **pancakes**, especially buckwheat pancakes, which were consumed in stacks with butter and molasses or maple syrup. Of these the English author of *Mrs. Beeton's Every-Day Cookery* (1909) wrote, "Hot cakes at breakfast are quite a national institution [in America]. These are made with soda and baking-powder, and must be regarded as somewhat beyond the capacities of average digestive organs."

In different parts of the U.S., different food items are served for breakfast, although a meal of eggs, bacon, toast, and coffee seems ubiquitous, with the addition in the South of **grits**, **ham**, or **biscuits**, of **chile** peppers in the West, of sausages and hash-brown potatoes in the Northeast, and, in urban restaurants, with preparations of **eggs Benedict**, finnan haddie, melon, **French toast**, **caviar**, **waffles**, **Danish pastry**, fruit, **English muffins**, and many other items. In Jewish communities, breakfast may consist of **bagels** and cream cheese.

The popularity of breakfast **cereals** began in the middle of the nineteenth century and has continued since then, especially as a children's breakfast item. Today annual sales of breakfast cereals is 2.7 billion boxes, with sales of $7.7 billion. The industry spends $762 million a year to broadcast 1.3 million TV commercials.

Americans have to a large extent curbed their hearty breakfasts in recent years because of dietary concerns (although the midmorning "coffee break" often serves to bolster an early light breakfast with a roll or muffin) and increasing numbers of women in the workforce, saving the tradition of a big breakfast for weekends or Sunday **brunch**. "Business breakfasts" held at hotel dining rooms are also popular, for, as **James Villas** contends, in *American Taste* (1982), "Show me the fool who finds something sensible and dignified about offering plastic cups of instant coffee and a puny piece of bread as an excuse for a business breakfast, and I can only hope that he collapses from lack of adrenaline before the meeting is finished."

The American food industry has marketed scores of breakfast foods designed to save time in the kitchen, including frozen waffles, packaged pancake batter, heat-and-serve eggs, powdered eggs, imitation **cream**, already cooked sausage, fake bacon, canned fruit, and tarts shaped to fit conveniently into the toaster. **Fast-food** restaurants also offer standard fare, such as scrambled eggs, sausage, pancakes, and coffee, and many restaurants, diners, and luncheonettes advertise the fact that "breakfast is served twenty-four hours a day." One out of four Americans eats breakfast in the car on the way to work, but only 44 percent of Americans eat breakfast every day of the week.

BREAKFAST CLUB. A business or social organization that holds regular meetings over breakfast, often with a featured speaker. Most clubs are either all male or all female and have between twenty and thirty members. The concept dates back to at least the 1940s.

BREAKFAST CREAM. A New Orleans term for light cream.

BREAKFAST DANCE. A term used to describe all-night parties held in nightclubs in Harlem, NYC, dating in print to 1934.

BRENNAN FAMILY. The Brennan family of New Orleans was critical in elevating the standards of Creole cuisine and service in that city, and brought a greater recognition of the region's food to the rest of America.

Owen Patrick Brennan (1886–1958) was born in New Orleans's "Irish Channel" neighborhood, where his wife, Nellie, later gave birth to six children: Owen Edward (1910–1955), Adelaide (1910–1983), John (1919–1998), Ella (1925–), Dick (1931–), and Dottie (1933–). The younger Owen became the primary support of the family early on, working as a liquor salesman and restaurant manager. In 1943, he bought the Old Absinthe House (opened 1798), on Bourbon Street, where he had a "Secret Room" with mannequins of pirate Jean Lafitte and Andrew Jackson.

In 1946, he and his father opened Owen Brennan's Vieux Carré. With his siblings Adelaide as bookkeeper and Ella (who had taken courses at a local business school) as kitchen supervisor, the dapper, ever ebullient Owen made the restaurant one of the most successful in the French Quarter, and it was said of him that he could hit someone over the head with his personality—"a blow from which few tourists, writers, movie celebrities or presidents ever completely recovered."

The Brennans moved the restaurant to 417 Royal Street (during the war a military rooming house) in 1955, where it was to be called, simply, Brennan's. But Owen died from a heart attack in November 1955, at the age of forty-five, shy of the opening of the new restaurant the following spring. His death made front-page news in the city's *Times-Picayune*. When the new, far more elegant Brennan's finally opened, the event was covered by *Life* magazine.

Owing to various financial considerations, the restaurant's interests were split among Owen's siblings and his three sons, Owen Jr., called Pip (1934–); Jimmy (1940–2010); and Ted (1948–). Under Ella's urging, the Brennan's name was expanded to restaurants in Biloxi, Mississippi, and Dallas, and in 1969 the family purchased the old Commander's Palace (opened by Émile Commander in 1880), in New Orleans's Garden District.

Difficulties in managing the empire and squabbles about how to run the core restaurants caused a bitter battle among the Brennans; after months of negotiation, the dispute was settled in November 1973, with Owen's widow, Maude, along with Pip, Jimmy, and Ted, assuming complete control of the flagship Brennan's, while Ella, Adelaide, Dick, John, and Dottie took over Commander's Palace and the other Brennan's restaurants (all closed), but they did open a successful Brennan's in Houston, run by Ella's son, Alex Brennan-Martin.

Under Pip, Jimmy, and Ted, Brennan's flourished, and "Breakfast at Brennan's" became a weekend ritual for locals and a requisite event for tourists, with a menu that included the flaming dessert **bananas Foster**, created by chef Paul Blange. The menu followed a traditional Creole style, with classic dishes like **oysters Rockefeller**, shrimp **rémoulade**, turtle soup, chicken Clemenceau, **eggs Sardou**, and crawfish **étouffée** always on the menu. The family was also very involved in the planning and operation of the Mardi Gras parades.

At Commander's Palace, Ella and Adelaide were joined by Ella's daughter Ti (1960–) and Lally (1953), daughter of John Brennan, whose other daughter, Cindy (1955–), and son Ralph (1951–) ran restaurants of their own, including Ralph's on the Park, Red Fish Grill, and Mr. B's Bistro. Their house in the Garden District became famous for its lavish entertaining, which drew celebrities from every segment of American society.

At Commander's Palace, the Brennans began to develop a style of modern "haute Creole" cooking along the lines of France's **nouvelle cuisine**. A traditional French or American dish at Commander's was said to be "Creolized." As explained by Ella and Dick in The Commander's Palace New Orleans Cookbook (1984), "In Old Creole style, everything was cooked for hours—vegetables and meats were cooked to death. Now everything is being cooked to order, à la minute, because we have better ingredients....Perhaps the most important innovation is in the reduction of stocks to intensify the flavor of our sauces....We are also inspired by the burgeoning of small local producers to take advantage of our local Louisiana resources." Dick Brennan came up with the idea of a Sunday jazz brunch.

The Brennans lifted the standards of service and hospitality to replace the entrenched, staid attitudes of restaurant workers in the past, when regular customers were overwhelmingly favored and newcomers often snubbed. Ruth Reichl, of Gourmet, wrote of her first visit to Commander's Palace in 1980, "It was the most extraordinary service I'd ever had in an American restaurant.... It was like we're here to make you have a good time.... You went to Commander's Palace and you understood what you'd been missing all along. 'Oh, this is what it's supposed to be like.'"

Ella, not a cook herself, did intense research on the history of Creole and French cuisine, butchering, wine, cocktail making, and service. With her children and siblings in tow, she traveled extensively around the U.S. and Europe to get a sense of how the world's best restaurants were run, an endeavor she called "restaurant chasing." When Ella visited **Danny Meyer**'s Union Square Cafe, in NYC, he remarked, "She was as close as I had seen to an American version of Queen Elizabeth walking into a restaurant. She stood proudly and looked around. And there was just something about her presence that made me stand at attention with deep respect."

Ella realized that after her star chefs—like **Paul Prudhomme**, **Emeril Lagasse**, and Frank Brigtsen—learned all they could about food and service at Commander's Palace, they would want to open their own places. "When you run a restaurant," she says, "if the people who work for you are any good at it, they want to leave and start their own. And you help them."

In 2005, Hurricane Katrina severely damaged Commander's Palace and Brennan's, but both reopened. Of Ella Brennan's contributions, NOLA.com, the Times-Picayune's website, wrote, "She used her kitchen at Commander's Palace as a kind of de facto New Orleans culinary academy, turning out dozens of the city's finest chefs and thereby enlivening the local food scene beyond measure. In a business known for its here-today-and-gone-tomorrow vagaries, as well as its chew-'em-up-and-spit-'em-out mercilessness, Brennan has maintained a place for her restaurant in the hearts and minds of generations of New Orleanians, as well as hordes of visitors. And in doing so, she has attained a place for herself in the culinary history of the nation."

Other members of the Brennan family involved in restaurants include Dick's son Dickie (1960–), who runs Palace Café, Dickie Brennan's Steakhouse, and Bourbon House; his daughter, Lauren Brennan-Brower (1959–); and Dottie's son Brad (1965–), with Commander's Palace, SoBou, and Reginelli's pizzerias.

Jimmy Brennan, who saw Brennan's vast 35,000-wine cellar destroyed by Hurricane Katrina (he restocked it later), died of cancer in 2010. His brother Pip retired at the same time. Brennan's closed in 2013.

Pip, Jimmy, and Ted Brennan published Breakfast at Brennan's and Dinner, Too (1994). Ella and Dick Brennan published The Commander's Palace New Orleans Cookbook (1984), and Carl Walker published Brennan's of Houston In Your Kitchen (2001). Ti Adelaide Martin published Commander's Kitchen (2000), with chef Jamie Shannon; Commander's Wild Side (2008), with chef Tory McPhail; and In the Land of Cocktails (2007), with Lally Brennan.

The awards won by all sides of the Brennan family are far too numerous to list here.

BRETT. Winemakers' term for wine that has been contaminated with the genus of the wild yeast *Brettanomyces*, first isolated in bottled wine in the 1950s. It can be controlled by the use of sulfur dioxide.

BREW. Also "brewski." As a slang term, a beer, dating in print to 1907.

BRICK CHEESE. A smooth cow's-milk cheese created in 1877 by John Jossi of Wisconsin. It is formed into bricks of about five pounds in weight, has small holes, and is aged about three months.

BRIDGE MIX. Also "bridge assortment." A mixture of snacks or candies customarily served at a social gathering like a bridge game. Many snacks or candies are packaged under this term, which dates to the 1950s.

BROCCOFLOWER. A registered trademark since 1990 of the Tanimura and Antle company of Spreckels, California, for a vegetable that is a genetic cross between **broccoli** and **cauliflower**. Originally grown in Holland, the vegetable was brought to the U.S. by Rick Antle in 1987 and is now grown exclusively at the company's farms in the Salinas Valley and elsewhere.

BROCCOLI (*Brassica oleracea* var. *botrytis*). A plant in the mustard family having a flowery green head and related to **cabbage** and **cauliflower**. The word is from the Italian *broccolo*, "cabbage sprout," and was first recorded in English in 1699 as a plant from Naples. The plant arrived in England in about 1720, and John Randolph of Williamsburg wrote, in *A Treatise on Gardening by a Citizen of Virginia* (1775), that "the stems will eat like Asparagus and the heads like Cauliflower." Nevertheless, broccoli virtually disappeared from American soil until its reintroduction in the twentieth century by Italian immigrant farmers. According to film producer Albert R. Broccoli, in a 1987 interview in *USA Today*, his uncle reintroduced the seeds in Long Island, New York, in the 1920s. The Italian variety of broccoli began to grow slowly in favor with the creation of a popular dish containing broccoli, called **Chicken Divan**, in the 1930s. In the U.S., the green sprouting varieties are most often grown. Broccoli is usually boiled or steamed and served with butter sauce.

"Broccoli rabe" (*B. rapa parachinensis*), also called by a variety of names and pronunciations like "broccoli di rabe," "broccoli rape," "broccoli di rape," "broccoli raab," and "rapini," is a winter vegetable with slightly indented leaves with small sprouts and a bitter taste. (It is sometimes called "bitter broccoli.") The word *rabe* or *raab* denotes its relation to the turnip family (Latin *rapa*). It is a widely grown and beloved vegetable of Italian Americans and Chinese, and is now cultivated in the U.S. in California, Arizona, Florida, and New Jersey. The vegetable was first planted by Stephen and Andrew D'Arrigo, from Messina, Sicily, who in 1964 officially named it "broccoli Rabe" under the Andy Boy label, holding four patents for growing the vegetable. Broccoli is usually boiled or steamed and served with butter sauce.

Owing to the promotion of broccoli as a very healthy vegetable, consumption had risen 900 percent by the end of the twentieth century, with per capita consumption by Americans going from 1.9 pounds in 1982 to eight pounds in 2012.

BROKEN VICTUALS. Leftovers, a colloquialism dating in print to 1861.

BRONX COCKTAIL. A cocktail made of gin, sweet and dry vermouths, and orange juice, concocted by bartender Johnnie Solon at the Waldorf-Astoria Hotel, in NYC, sometime between 1899 (when he joined the establishment) and 1906 (when the word first appeared in print). As Solon related the story, to Albert Stevens Crockett, author of *Old Waldorf Bar Days* (1931), Solon was challenged by a customer to come up with a new cocktail. The bartender thereupon mixed two jiggers of Gordon's gin with one jigger of orange juice, then a dash each of French and Italian vermouths. The success of the cocktail caused the Waldorf to use a case of oranges per day. According to Solon, he chose the name on the spur of the moment, because he had recently been to the Bronx Zoo and was reminded that some of his customers saw strange animals when they drank too much. The addition of an egg yolk to the following recipe makes the drink a "Silver Bronx," while the juice of a blood orange makes it a "Bloody Bronx."

~~~~~~~~~~~~~~~~~~~~~~~~~~~~~~~~~
BRONX COCKTAIL
~~~~~~~~~~~~~~~~~~~~~~~~~~~~~~~~~

Shake over ice cubes 1 ½ oz. gin, ½ oz. dry vermouth, ½ oz. sweet vermouth, and ½ oz. orange juice. Strain into cocktail glass and serve over ice cubes.

BROOKLYN CAKE. A nineteenth-century light cake whose name probably has nothing to do with the borough of NYC but rather with Brooklyn, Connecticut, or, perhaps, a misreading of Brookline, Massachusetts.

~~~~~~~~~~~~~~~~~~~~~~~~~~~~~~~~~
BROOKLYN CAKE
~~~~~~~~~~~~~~~~~~~~~~~~~~~~~~~~~

The recipe given in *The Pentucket Housewife* (1882) calls for a batter of 1 ½ c. sugar, 6 egg whites beaten with 1 t. cream of tartar folded into ½ c. creamed butter, ½ t. baking soda, ½ c. cornstarch, 1 ½ c. flour, and lemon juice.

BROTHER JONATHAN'S HAT. A suet pudding of nineteenth-century New England. The name derives from a derisive term used by the British and the Loyalists during the Revolutionary War for American rebels. Later the name was applied to any American citizen, and the *Dictionary of Americanisms* disputes the claim that it originally referred to Governor Jonathan Trumbull (1710–1785) of Connecticut. As a dish it seems to be synonymous with **Deacon Porter's hat** but may predate the latter.

BROWN BAG. A term used to describe a meal packed in a brown paper bag, usually for lunch consumed at work. Brown paper bags were first made in Pennsylvania in 1852, though not patented (by Luther C. Crowell of West Dennis, Massachusetts) until 1872, two years after Francis Wolle had patented a machine that fabricated the paper into a flat-bottomed, easily folded bag that became the standard of the food-service industry.

Today there are about sixty million Americans who eat lunch out of a brown bag, and the phrase "to brown-bag it," meaning to eat one's lunch in this manner, goes back to at least the 1950s, according to David Lyon, head of the Brown Bag Institute, in Connecticut.

In 1979, cheaper plastic grocery bags began to appear alongside the large paper bags in grocery stores and now account for half the bags used.

BROWN GOODS. Liquor-industry term for spirits that are usually brown in color, like Scotch, **bourbon**, and **blended whiskey**. "White goods" are spirits that are usually colorless, like **gin** and **vodka**.

BROWN, ELLEN (1947–). As food editor of *USA Today* from 1980 to 1986, Ellen Brown was one of the first to explore in depth the New American cuisine movement and continued to do so in more than thirty cookbooks on the subject.

Born in New York City, Brown graduated with a B.A. in art history from Mount Holyoke College, in South Hadley, Massachusetts, in 1969. In 1970 she moved to Cincinnati, where she became curator of education at the Contemporary Arts Center. In 1973, she was art critic and feature writer for the *Cincinnati Post*, then three years later moved to become senior feature editor for the *Cincinnati Enquirer*, where she would write about restaurants, food, art, interior design, and fashion. She also taught cooking at the University of Cincinnati.

In 1980, Brown moved to Washington, D.C., to become the first food editor at *USA Today*, whose national scope required her to travel extensively throughout the U.S. to report on the evolution of American gastronomy, whether it was to cover a barbecue championship or the emergence of a new style of cooking in NYC or Los Angeles. Her reports and interviews were among the first to define and provide focus to the burgeoning **New American cuisine** movement, which she showed was not confined only to East and West Coast cities.

Her award-winning book *Cooking with the New American Chefs* (1985) profiled the young chefs of the movement, including **Larry Forgione**, **Wolfgang Puck**, **Paul Prudhomme**, and **Barbara Tropp**, and featured many of their recipes. "The new American chefs have no sense of inferiority," Brown wrote in her preface. "When they draw from the American cookery of the past, it is because it is a component of their philosophies.... While it may be impossible to define American cuisine, it is quite easy to describe new American chefs: They are cooking creatively with a personal style. They are concocting dishes nightly bearing signatures as large as John Hancock's on the Declaration of Independence. And they are shaping the next chapter of American food."

In 1985, Brown was included in *Cook's* magazine's Who's Who of Cooking in America. She was adviser to the *Great Chefs* television series, which involved the selection of the more than two hundred chefs to appear on TV, and she adapted their recipes in a book series for the home kitchen, *The Great Chefs of Chicago* (1985), *Southwest Tastes* (1987), and *Great Chefs of the East* (1995); she also edited *Great Chefs Cook American* and *Great Chefs Cook Italian* (1995). In 1989, she authored *Gourmet Gazelle Cookbook*, one of the first to create nutritionally controlled recipes for their taste rather than their dietetic analysis. *Gourmet Gazelle* was on the *Cook's* magazine bestseller list for much of 1989, and her recipes also appear in the *Fresh Ways* series, published by Time-Life Books.

After leaving *USA Today*, Brown wrote for many publications, including the *Washington Post*, the *Los Angeles Times* syndicate, *Bon Appétit*, *Texas Monthly*, the *Baltimore Sun*, and the *San Francisco Chronicle*, and lectured frequently on New American cuisine and food trends at the annual meetings of the American Institute of Wine & Food (for which she was vice chair of the National Capital Area chapter) and the International Association of Culinary Professionals. She is a former board member of Les Dames d'Escoffier and the New England Culinary Institute.

In 1993, she co-founded Brown & Whiting, a boutique public relations agency specializing in food, wine, and hospitality, whose accounts included the Colonial Williamsburg Foundation, Time-Life Books, Procter & Gamble, and numerous independent restaurants.

Brown moved to Nantucket, Massachusetts, in 1997 to become CEO of Nantucket Cuisine and wrote the *Nantucket Cuisine Cookbook* and *All Wrapped Up* (1998), one of the first devoted to cooking wraps. She closed her agency in 2002. In 2003, she moved to Providence, Rhode Island, where she began a weekly recipe column for the *Providence Journal*. For five years she worked closely with Alpha Books as an author for a series on basic instruction, *The Complete Idiot's Guides to Cooking with Mixes* (2003); her other books are *Cover and Bake Meals* (2005), *Slow Cooker Cooking* (2007), *Smoothies* (2012), and others.

BROWNIE. A rich chocolate cake cut into squares and eaten as a dessert or snack. The name comes from the deep brown color of the confection, and it has been an American favorite since the nineteenth century, first appearing in 1906, in *The Boston Cooking-School Cook Book*. The word was first in print in 1883, referring to a bread sweetened with brown sugar and currants. A reference to "brownies" in the Sears, Roebuck catalog for 1897 was for mail-ordering chocolate candies named after cartoon elves created by author Palmer Cox, in a series that began with *The Brownies: Their Book* (1887), and the 1896 edition of the *Boston Cooking-School Cook Book* for a browned molasses confection containing no chocolate. Some brownies are quite moist at the center, while others are more cookielike. In the South, a brownielike cake made without chocolate, baked in two layers, and topped with butterscotch meringue is called a "mud hen," "mud hen cake," or "butterscotch brownie."

BROWNIE

Combine 2 c. sugar, ½ c. flour, and ½ c. cocoa. Add 4 beaten eggs, ½ lb. cooled melted butter, 2 t. vanilla, and 1 c. chopped pecans or walnuts. Pour into buttered pan and place in a larger pan half-full of hot water. Bake for 45 min. at 300°.

BROWNSTONE FRONT CAKE. A rich chocolate cake with a vanilla or caramel icing. According to culinary historian Meryle Evans, recipes for the cake date back to at least 1903, and though the origin of the name is unknown, it would seem to refer to the reddish-brown color of brownstone buildings' facades.

BRUISS. A dish of boiled bread and milk. The origin of the name is unknown, but the dish is mentioned in *The Pentucket Housewife* (1882), with the instructions to add milk to crusts of bread, boil slowly, and add salt and butter.

BRUNCH. A portmanteau word combining "breakfast" with "lunch," for a meal taken late in the morning or just around noon. According to the English magazine *Punch*, (August 1, 1896), brunch was "introduced…last year by Mr. Guy Beringer, in the now defunct *Hunter's Weekly*, and indicating a combined breakfast and lunch," probably one taken just after arriving home from hunting.

The practice of having brunch did not really take hold in the U.S. until the 1930s, but today it is part of many hotel and restaurant menus on weekends, as well as a popular form of social entertaining for weekend hosts. "There may be some perfectly nice people who use the word 'brunch,'" commented humorist Heywood Broun, "but I prefer not to know about them."

BRUNSWICK STEW. A stew made originally with squirrel, now made with chicken or other meats. There have been many claims as to the dish's origins, especially from the citizens of Brunswick County, North Carolina, but the most creditable one comes from Brunswick County, Virginia, where in 1828 Dr. Creed Haskins, of the Virginia state legislature, requested a special squirrel stew from "Uncle Jimmy" Matthews to feed those attending a political rally. This original Brunswick stew was said to have contained no vegetables except onions, but it soon went through several transformations before the squirrel itself was dropped from most recipes after the turn of the century. The first mention of the dish in print was in 1856. In *Cross Creek Cookery* (1942), Marjorie Kinnan Rawlings contended that the name might have originated in Braunschweig, Germany.

BRUSH ROAST. A North Carolina term for a dish of oysters cooked on a wire netting over a wood fire and served with butter, **chow-chow**, and corn bread, dating in print to 1939.

BRUSSELS SPROUT (*Brassica oleracea* var. *gemmifera*). A small cabbage of the mustard family, originally developed from primitive cabbage in fourteenth-century Brussels, Belgium. It is first mentioned in English print in 1796 but did not enter England until the mid-nineteenth century. In the U.S., brussels sprouts are grown predominantly in California and New York, with the most popular variety being the "Improved Long Island."

BUBBLE TEA. Also "pearl tea" and "boba tea." A beverage made by shaking tea and mik with ice, sometimes containing fruit or syrup and commonly served with large tapioca balls called "pearls." The beverage originated on Taiwan, where it is sold by street vendors, though it might have originated at the Chun Shui Tang teahouse, in Taichung, or the Hanlin teahouse, in Tainan City. sometime in the late 1980s, arriving in American Asian neighborhoods in the next decade.

BUCK. Originally a Prohibition-era drink made with gin (and called a "gin buck"), ginger ale, and the juice of a lemon whose shell was then added to the drink. It contains no sugar. Later bucks were made with other carbonated drinks and spirits. "Buck" is also a term for fermented mash used to make **moonshine** (1933).

BUCK

Over ice cubes, pour 1 ½ oz. gin, then squeeze the juice of half a lemon into the glass, add the lemon shell, and top with ginger ale.

BUCK AND BRECK. A cold pickle condiment like **chow-chow**. The origin of the name is unknown, but see **Buck and Breck cocktail**.

BUCK AND BRECK

To 1 gal. of vinegar add 1 lb. brown sugar, 1 c. salt, 2 oz. black pepper, 2 oz. ginger, 2 oz. white mustard seed, 2 oz. dry mustard, 2 oz. cloves, 2 oz. celery seed, 1 oz. turmeric, 1 c. grated horseradish, 2 oz. cloves, 2 chopped onions, 1 head of chopped cabbage, 2 lb. peeled and chopped tomatoes, 2 each of red and green peppers, mix, pour into bottles, seal, and, according to old advice, "let stand until Thanksgiving."

BUCK AND BRECK COCKTAIL. A drink made from champagne, sugar, bitters, absinthe, and brandy. Spirits writer David Wondrich contends that the cocktail dates to the 1860s in print, called "Breck and Brace" in *The American Bar-Tender* (1891). The name derives from the epithet given to the 1856 Democratic presidential ticket of James Buchanan and John C. Breckinridge.

BUCK AND BRECK COCKTAIL

Coat the inside of a flute glass with sugar, then fill with 1 ½ oz. rye, a dash of bitters, a dash of absinthe, a dash of lemon juice, and champagne.

BUCKET CANDY. According to the *DARE*, "The type of small candies packed and sold from a bucket," such as gumdrops, lozenges, and various bonbons. The term dates in print to 1950 and is associated with South Carolina.

BUCKET OF BLOOD. A western term for a very tough saloon or bar. Originally the term referred to the Bucket of Blood saloon, owned by Shorty Young, in Havre, Montana, the fame of which became the basis for describing any similar establishment by the same name by about 1880. One may also find such places referred to as "bucket shops." See also **Bloody Mary**.

BUCKEYE. A peanut-butter-and-chocolate candy made in little balls resembling buckeye nuts. The term dates in print to 1970. According to Marcia Adams, in *Heartland* (1991), "If Ohio were to declare a state candy, this recipe would be it.…Some cooks like to leave a bit of peanut butter ball exposed when dipping in the chocolate so it more closely resembles a real buckeye."

BUCKEYE

Mix together in a bowl 4 c. peanut butter, 1 c. softened butter, 6 c. confectioners' sugar, and 2 T. vanilla. Cover bowl, chill until firm, then pinch off pieces about 1 in. in diameter, place in waxed-paper-covered pans, and chill again until firm. In a double boiler melt 12 oz. semisweet chocolate morsels. Using a toothpick, dip the peanut balls into the chocolate, drain, then refrigerate until firm. Makes about 36 buckeyes.

BUCKLE. A kind of cake made with berries, most commonly blueberries. The use of the term is probably quite old, but its first record in print came only in 1959, in Elsie Masterton's *Blueberry Bill Cookbook*. Blueberries are tossed with flour and added to a cake batter that is sprinkled with more batter or a topping.

BUCKWHEAT. Any plant of the genus *Fagopyrum*, whose seeds are coarsely ground to make flour. The name is from the Middle Dutch *boecweite*, "beech wheat," so called because the seeds resemble the nuts of the beech tree. The word was first recorded in English in 1548. The plant is a native of Central Asia, but it was propagated in the New World for fodder and cereal, as is known through a reference by Adam Smith in 1776. "Buckwheat cakes," pancakes made with buckwheat flour and dating in print to 1772, were popular everywhere in the country in the nineteenth century. "It is hard for the American to rise from his winter breakfast without his buckwheat cakes," wrote English traveler George Makepeace Towle in *American Society* (1870). It was American painter James Abbott McNeill Whistler (1834–1903) who introduced buckwheat cakes to London society. "Slip go down" is a slang term for buckwheat pudding, as well as for a dumpling, also called "slick go down" and "slick."

There are two basic forms of buckwheat—unroasted and roasted. The latter is known by the Russian word *kasha*, which is also the word used for a cooked porridge made from the roasted buckwheat.

BUFFALO. An erroneous name for the American bison (*Bison bison*), a shaggy-maned, short-horned, hoofed mammal of the cattle family, with a large, low-slung head and massive hump, reaching a height of five feet, a length of nine feet, and a weight of 2,500 pounds. The word *buffalo* correctly applies to various species of Asian or African oxen, but Americans have called their native bison by this name ever since explorer Hernando de Soto spotted the animal in the New World in 1544 and called it by the Portuguese *búfalo*. The word *buffalo* in reference to *Bos bubalus*, native to India, goes back to 1588.

The buffalo population in this country once spread on both sides of the Mississippi River in thick waves, numbering more than sixty million at the beginning of the nineteenth century. Native Americans' respect for the buffalo was born out of their total dependence on its meat and hide for sustenance, clothing, tepee coverings, and rope, while other parts of the beast went into making utensils, medicines, even children's toys. The buffalo was deified by the Great Plains Indians for good reason.

By slicing the meat from the carcass and drying it in the sun or smoking it in their tepees, the Native

Americans produced a jerky they called **pemmican**, which they pounded and preserved in buffalo-skin pouches and often enriched with fat and wild berries.

Despite their respect for the buffalo, Native Americans engaged in wanton killing of the herds, sometimes driving them off a cliff into a ravine. But this was as nothing compared with the deliberate and wholesale slaughter of the herds brought on by the easterners who killed the buffalo for its hide and for sport. Buffalo hunters sent back tens of thousands of pelts to be made into coats. By 1800 the herds had largely disappeared east of the Mississippi. The Kansas Pacific Railway, desiring an efficient way to remove the herds from its westward path, arranged special hunting tours on which well-dressed easterners with long rifles shot from the moving train windows and cut down the animals, leaving them to rot where they fell. But the main reason for the deliberate destruction of the herds was to eliminate the life-sustaining animal as a resource for the Native Americans, who were the real object of the slaughter.

By the end of the century, fewer than a thousand remained on the whole continent. Only the interdiction of President Theodore Roosevelt, who in 1905 established in Kansas and Montana two protected reservations for the beast, saved the buffalo. Today herds have been restocked and expanded, mostly in private hands, so that the buffalo now numbers about 250,000 head, some of which are raised for sale as meat. The state of Kansas named the buffalo its state animal, and for a time this most American of cattle appeared on the nickel coin.

The buffalo has never been of much gastronomic interest to Americans, although today there is a certain exotic curiosity about the meat, which is occasionally found on menus. The early pioneers were forced to eat buffalo meat and Indian pemmican on the long trek westward, but later on, cattle breeders preferred the more passive longhorn steer to the ornery bison. A few attempts have been made to breed the buffalo with other cattle. One such crossbreed, by Charles Goodnight, between a bison and a Polled Angus steer, produced the "cattalo," and since 1973 there has been some interest in a hybrid called the "beefalo," a cross between the buffalo and a Hereford or Charolais. There is even an American Beefalo Association, with 950 members worldwide. The beefalo is said to be easier and faster to bring to full weight, and its meat leaner. Still, the beefalo has never fulfilled its early promise as the "meat of the future."

Buffalo meat itself tastes a good deal like beef and has no pronounced gamy flavor. Young bulls make for the best meat, especially if marinated.

"Buffalo cider" is a euphemism for the liquid in a buffalo's stomach, which a Great Plains hunter would drink if he was far from water.

BUFFALO CHICKEN WINGS. Deep-fried chicken wings served with a **hot sauce** and a blue cheese dressing. The dish originated at the Anchor Bar, in Buffalo, New York, on October 30, 1964, when owner Teressa Bellissimo, having just received an oversupply of chicken wings, was asked by her son Dominic and his friends for something to nibble on. The name first appeared in print in 1980. According to Dominic, in an interview for *Nation's Restaurant News* in 1991, "She cut off the doohickeys, fried them, drained them and swished them around in margarine. Then she improvised on the hot sauce and put blue cheese dressing—our house dressing—on the side." Being Catholics, the Bellissimos did not eat meat on Fridays, so they waited until midnight to serve the first wings.

The dish became an immediate sensation at the restaurant (which today sells seventy thousand pounds of chicken per month), and soon Buffalo wings (sometimes called "Western New York chicken wings") were being served all over the city. In 1977, the city of Buffalo declared July 29 "Chicken Wing Day."

Today the dish is a staple in restaurants and bars across the U.S.

BUFFALO CHICKEN WINGS

Separate the wing bone at the joints of 20 chicken wings, then cut off the tip of each wing. Deep-fry in peanut oil for about 10 min., until golden brown and cooked through. Melt 4 T. butter in a saucepan and add 4 T. bottled hot pepper sauce. Add salt and pepper to taste and a dash of cayenne pepper. For the dressing, blend 1 c. mayonnaise with 2 T. chopped onion, 1 t. minced garlic, ½ c. sour cream, 1 T. white vinegar, and ¼ c. blue cheese. Serve chicken wings with the sauce and the dressing. Serves 4.

BUFFET. A form of food service whereby diners move along the length of tables set with various cold and hot foods. The word, from the French and dating in print to 1718, also applies to the sideboard or cabinet on which food is placed. In euphemistic slang, "buffet" is also applied to a tavern or **speakeasy**.

BUG JUICE. Also "bugjuice." Cowboy slang for whiskey, in print since 1863. The *New Dictionary of American Slang* (1986) suggests it derives from the drink's "resemblance to the *juice* secreted by grasshoppers," but among schoolchildren the term has come to mean (since at least its first appearance, in 1889) any very sweet, usually non-carbonated soft drink and, commonly, the product Kool-Aid, in which case the tendency of the drink to draw bugs may better explain its usage.

BULL AND BEAR. A sandwich created at the Caucus Club restaurant, in Detroit, made with corned beef, chopped liver, lettuce, tomato, **coleslaw**, and **Russian** or **Thousand Island dressing**. The name has nothing to do with the ingredients, but instead with the traditional symbols of trends on the New York stock exchange, which provides much of the Caucus Club's clientele. The "bull and bear" is also a cocktail created at the Caucus Club.

BULL AND BEAR

Mix 1 ½ oz. vodka, ½ oz. clam juice, ½ oz. beef bouillon, a slice of lemon, and a dash each of celery salt, A.1. sauce, and Tabasco sauce.

BULL CHEESE. A western term of the nineteenth century for dried strips of buffalo meat. The Spanish words *carne seca* were also used for the same item.

BULLSHOT. An alcoholic drink made with vodka, beef bouillon, and seasonings. The drink originated at the Caucus Club restaurant, in Detroit, in the early 1960s, when then owner Lester Gruber and a representative of a national soup company created the cocktail together. The name, a play on the expletive "bullshit," derives from the blend of beef bouillon and a shot of vodka. A "Danish bowl" cocktail, also invented at the Caucus Club, substitutes aquavit for vodka in the recipe.

BULLSHOT

Mix 1 ½ oz. vodka with 3 oz. beef bouillon. Add dashes of Worcestershire sauce, A.1. sauce, Tabasco, and Angostura bitters. Stir, pour over ice, and garnish with slice of lemon and a sprinkling of celery salt.

BUMPER TO BUMPER. A New England cooking term for foods set in a pan so that their sides are touching. As cited by food writer Christopher Idone, in the *New York Times* in 1991, "bumper scallops [are] a dish of scallops moistened with a little clarified butter, lightly dusted with paprika and broiled in a pan into which they fit snugly side by side, or bumper to bumper, as Nantucket natives put it."

BUNDT CAKE. Any of a variety of cakes baked in a round, tubular Bundt pan, developed by H. David Dalquist of Nordic Products, in Minneapolis, in 1950 upon being asked by members of the local Hadassah chapter to make an aluminum version of the European cast-iron kugelhopf pan. The pan (now a registered trademark of Northland Aluminum Products Inc. of Minnesota) became very popular after it was featured in a pound cake recipe published in the *Good Housekeeping Cookbook* (1960). According to culinary historian Jean Anderson, in *The American Century Cookbook* (1997), the Bundt pan became ubiquitous in American kitchens after a "Tunnel of Fudge Cake" recipe was printed from the Pillsbury Bake-Off for 1966, followed by a Bundt Streusel Spice Cake in the same contest for 1972.

BUÑUELO. A round pastry, deep-fried and sprinkled with sugar, very popular in the Southwest. Buñuelos were brought from Mexico, where hot chocolate and buñuelos are part of the Christmas Eve meal.

BURBANK, LUTHER (1849–1926). Agronomist. Through his experiments in developing more than eight hundred plant varieties, Luther Burbank, "the Wizard of Horticulture," was in the forefront of American agricultural science.

Burbank was born and raised on a farm in Lancaster, Massachusetts, as one of fifteen children. Though he never attended high school, Burbank began his career as a nurseryman after his father died, leaving him with enough money to buy seventeen acres of land near

Lunenburg, Massachusetts, where, at the age of twenty-two, he developed the Burbank potato. He sold the rights for $150, using the money to move to Santa Rosa, California, in 1975. There, on a four-acre farm, using Charles Darwin's *The Variation of Animals and Plants under Domestication*, he bred his original Burbank potato into the Russet Burbank, still the most widely cultivated in the U.S.

He then moved to a larger farm, in Sebastopol, and with support from the Carnegie Institution continued his experiments in crossbreeding, hybrids, and grafting, cross-pollinating flowers of plants by hand and using the seeds to produce new hybrids. In 1893, he published the first of many bestselling plant catalogs, *New Creations in Fruits and Flowers* (1893), and followed with books (some co-authored) that included *How Plants Are Trained to Work for Man* (eight volumes, 1921), *Harvest of the Years*, with Wilbur Hall (1927), and *Partner of Nature* (1939).

Although criticized during his life as being unscientific in his methods—he stopped making notes of his crossbreeds by 1901, instead merely using those he believed worked best—Burbank was widely respected for his work, as detailed in the twelve-volume *Luther Burbank: His Methods and Discoveries and Their Practical Application* (1914), prepared with the help of the Luther Burbank Society from Burbank's original field notes and covering more than 100,000 experiments made during forty years devoted to plant improvement. Among his other creations were ten apples and eight peaches.

Reviewing his 1927 memoir *The Harvest of Years* and *The Early Life and Letters of Luther Burbank*, by Emma Burbank Beeson, the *New York Times* wrote, "No prominent man in all the history of this country, outside of those connected with public affairs, has so touched the imagination of the people and so enlisted their interest as Luther Burbank. Perhaps this is because he combined in his endowment and achievement two qualities to which they are always responsive, the vision of fine things and the practical ability to make them come true."

After Burbank's death, his work helped pass the 1930 Plant Patent Act, which made it possible to patent new varieties of plants. By then the Burbank potato alone was said to add $20 million to the annual productive wealth of the U.S.

Burbank was inducted into the National Inventors Hall of Fame in 1986, and the Luther Burbank Home and Gardens, in Santa Rosa, is designated a national historic landmark. His boyhood home was moved by Henry Ford to Dearborn, Michigan, as part of Greenfield Village.

In a speech given to the First Congregational Church of San Francisco in 1926, Burbank said:

> *I love humanity, which has been a constant delight to me during all my seventy-seven years of life; and I love flowers, trees, animals, and all the works of Nature as they pass before us in time and space. What a joy life is when you have made a close working partnership with Nature, helping her to produce for the benefit of mankind new forms, colors, and perfumes in flowers which were never known before; fruits in form, size, and flavor never before seen on this globe; and grains of enormously increased productiveness, whose fat kernels are filled with more and better nourishment, a veritable storehouse of perfect food—new food for all the world's untold millions for all time to come.*

BURBOT (*Lota lota*). Also "maria." A freshwater cod found on both coasts and throughout the Great Lakes states. The burbot has a slightly oilier flesh than the saltwater varieties. The name is from Middle English *borbot* and Old French *bourbeter*, "to burrow in mud," entering English circa 1475.

BURGOO. Also "burgou." A southern stew of various meats and vegetables. Burgoo is often associated with Kentucky and is frequently seen at political rallies in the South. The word was known to British sailors at least as early as 1700, as a kind of oatmeal porridge, making some etymologists suspect that it may derive from the Turkish wheat pilaf called *burgbul* (or *bulgur*), meaning "bruised grain." The word is used in that sense in its first appearance in American print, in 1830, and in subsequent citations.

But an 1853 citation from *Western Characters* associates "birgoo" with an impromptu barbecue, and an 1885 citation in the *Magazine of American History* calls it a feast with "everything, fish, flesh and fowl, being compounded into a vast stew." The first association, in 1941, with Kentucky cites "a Frenchman in John Morgan's cavalry who introduced the 'burgoo' which has become a culinary tradition in Kentucky. The Bluegrass dish was first made during Reconstruction days, and blackbirds, because of food scarcity, were the chief ingredient." If the French connection is true, "burgoo" or, as is sometimes seen, "burgou," might derive from either French "*à la bourgeois,*" a term for a hearty family meal of braised beef, or "*à la bourguignonne,*" (Burgundian style), as in *boeuf bourguignon,* a well-known stew of braised beef in red wine.

There is a highly suspect story about a Civil War soldier with a speech impediment who cooked up some blackbirds in a five-hundred-gallon copper kettle used for making gunpowder. When he called his fellow soldiers to dinner, the word came out not "bird stew," but "burgoo."

Whatever its origins, it was a very popular stew. In 1895, Gus Jaubert cooked up a batch for the Grand Army of the Republic that came to six thousand gallons, and the so-called Kentucky burgoo king, James T. Looney, was used to serving crowds of people numbering up to ten thousand. A recipe for a mere five thousand people was printed in the Louisville *Courier-Journal* not long ago, which called for 800 pounds of beef, 200 pounds of fowl, 168 gallons of tomatoes, 350 pounds of cabbage, six bushels of onions, 85 gallons of tomato puree, 24 gallons of carrots, 36 gallons of corn, 1,800 pounds of potatoes, two pounds of red pepper, half a pound of black pepper, 20 pounds of salt, eight ounces of Angostura bitters, one pint of Worcestershire sauce, half a pound of curry powder, three quarts of tomato ketchup, and two quarts of sherry.

A somewhat less gargantuan portion printed in the same journal goes as follows:

BURGOO

Place in a large kettle 2 lb. pork shank, 2 lb. veal shank, 2 lb. beef shank, 2 lb. breast of lamb, one 4-lb. hen, and 8 qt. water. Bring slowly to a boil and then simmer until meat falls from bones. Pare and dice 1 ½ lb. Irish potatoes and 1 ½ lb. onions. Remove and chop up the meat, discarding the bones. Return to stock with potatoes and onions, together with 1 bunch scraped, chopped carrots; 2 seeded, chopped green peppers; 2 c. chopped cabbage; 1 qt. tomato puree; 1 c. whole corn; 1 pod red pepper; 2 c. diced okra; 2 c. lima beans; 1 c. diced celery. Add salt, cayenne pepper, Tabasco, A.1. sauce, and Worcestershire sauce to taste. Cook about 10 hr., or until thick but still soupy. Stir frequently. Add chopped parsley.

BURRITO. A flour **tortilla** rolled and cooked on a griddle, then rolled around a variety of fillings. Burritos are a staple of Mexico's regions of Baja California and Sonora, dated by the *Diccionario de Mejicanimos* (1895) to the late 1800s as a food term in Guerrero. The word, from *burro,* Spanish for "little donkey," first saw print in America in 1934 and was used by Mexicans for a small meal. Ironically, Mexican immigrants considered the burrito an object of shame and poverty, but it was made popular among San Franciscans as cheap, filling fare at El Faro restaurant, in San Francisco's Mission District (which is why El Faro's burrito is sometimes called "Mission style"), opened in 1961. Three years later, the *Los Angeles Times* published its first burrito recipe.

The most famous burritos are those sold by the national chain Chipotle Mexican Grill, the first opened in Denver in 1993 by Steve Ells, who insisted on better meat, naturally raised pork, and fresher ingredients for his product. The company now has more than 1,200 stores in the U.S., Canada, Great Britain, and France.

If fried, the burrito becomes a **chimichanga**. The "kosher burrito" was a Los Angeles creation made with pastrami and cheddar cheese. A "Mexican **hamburger**" is a burrito stuffed with a hamburger patty and smothered in **chile**, a specialty of Denver, supposedly created at Joe's Buffet in the late 1960s, where it was named "Linda's Mexican Hamburger" after a waitress there. Breakfast burritos have also become very popular, filled with egg, chorizo, and other condiments.

BUSBOY. A restaurant worker who helps the waiter by clearing ("busing") and setting a table and by keeping water glasses filled. The term was first in print in 1913. A "busgirl" would be a female helper.

BUSCH, ADOLPHUS (1839–1913). Beer entrepreneur. As co-founder of Anheuser-Busch, Adolphus Busch pioneered new technologies in American beer that kept it fresh longer, allowing it to become a national beverage easily shipped across the country.

Born in Mainz-Kastel, Germany, Busch was the youngest of twenty-two children. His family was well-off, thanks to the success of his parents' vineyards. After attending the Collegiate Institute of Belgium, in Brussels, he emigrated to the U.S. in 1871 with three of his brothers—Johann, who founded a brewery in Washington, Michigan; Ulrich Jr., who married a daughter of Eberhard Anheuser, owner of the small brewery E. Anheuser, and settled in Chicago; and Anton, a hops dealer who later returned to Mainz-Kastel. Busch landed in New York City but settled in St. Louis, where he met and married another of Anheuser's daughters, Lily Anheuser.

Busch served in the Union army during the Civil War, earning the rank of colonel. He returned to St. Louis to buy a share in his father-in-law's brewery, then one of dozens in the city, and became a full partner in 1875. After Anheuser's death, in 1880, Busch changed the name to the Anheuser-Busch Co. In 1891 he bought the trademark and name Budweiser, named after the (then) Bohemian town Budweis. The Michelob brand was launched in 1896.

Although he preferred wine to beer, Busch saw the great potential in selling his brand nationally, calling the beer a "Bohemian style lager," and he created a chain of **icehouses** along railroad routes to ship pasteurized beer in bottles. By 1901 the company's sales surpassed one million barrels annually. His St. Louis brewery sprawled over 142 acres and employed 7,500 workers.

Busch was called "the king of brewers." and Budweiser "the King of Beers." He built and owned railroads, coal mines, and hotels, including the Adolphus, in Dallas, and became involved in political campaigns. Having made $60 million by 1914, he had become a generous philanthropist, including sending money back to charitable institutions in Germany before World War I broke out.

So well liked was Busch that on his fiftieth wedding anniversary, festivals were held throughout America, including a party at St. Louis's Coliseum where forty thousand bottles of free beer were consumed. Busch himself celebrated the event at his home in Pasadena, California. "I am an eternal optimist," said Busch in 1912, "[and] never lean in the least to the other side, and I am always coming out right." Busch and his wife traveled often to their Rhine castle in Prussia, Villa Lilly—named after her—where he died after a long bout with dropsy. His burial in St. Louis was attended by six thousand employees and a representative of the German kaiser. After Busch's death, his eldest son, August A. Busch, took over the company. During Prohibition, when Anheuser-Busch could not sell beer, the company instead promoted Bevo, a beer whose alcohol content fell below the legal definition. In 1946, August A. Busch Jr. became president of Anheuser-Busch.

Today Budweiser beer is sold in more than eighty markets worldwide, and its brands account for more than half the beer sold in the U.S. In 2008, the company sold a majority share of its stock to InBev, on whose board Augustus Busch IV serves. It is now the world's largest brewing company.

BUSINESS LUNCH. A lunch at a restaurant where business is discussed. The term has been in currency since at least the 1950s. A "businessman's lunch" is a restaurant term for a fixed-price lunch designed to attract businessmen, especially those on a short lunch hour. See also **power lunch**.

BUTTER. An emulsion of fat made from churned milk, usually whitish yellow to yellow in color and used as a cooking fat or as a spread on bread and other preparations. The word is from the Greek *boutyron*, "cow's cheese," becoming, in Middle English, *buter*.

Butter has been widely used for centuries as a cooking fat, at first by herdsmen, and it is mentioned several times in the Bible. It was not until the Middle Ages, however, that Europeans began to use butter extensively, although, because of its tendency to turn rancid quickly, it was not a preferred food until well into the eighteenth century. Even today, other oils are preferred for cooking in warm Mediterranean countries.

There is no evidence that Native Americans made butter, but the early European settlers made their own with whirling wooden blades inside a butter churn. The surplus was sold to neighbors and local stores, for there was no commercial creamery in the U.S. until the mid-nineteenth century; possibly the first was opened in 1856 in Orange County, New York, by R. S. Woodhull. In 1879, his factory produced 29 million pounds of butter;

by 1921, more than a billion pounds. Beatrice Creamery Co. was the first to package butter, in 1898. Only after 1900 was creamery butter widely available, first made into quarter-pound bars by a cooperative of creameries (later called Land O'Lakes) in Meeker County, Minnesota, in 1922. New processes in the 1930s that allowed continuous production boosted sales.

Pasteurized "sweet cream" butter, as opposed to "sour," which spoiled quickly, was promoted by the industry as of the 1920s. **Margarine**, used as a substitute in World War II, was much cheaper than butter and so increased its market share after the war; furthermore, concerns about butter's fat and cholesterol content drove more Americans to buy a substitute. From a high point in 1940 of 2.2 billion pounds of butter produced, sales have declined in the United States. In 1997, U.S. per capita consumption of butter was 4.2 pounds, and total U.S. production of butter was 1.5 billion pounds; by 2004, it was 1.35 billion, and 1.8 billion in 2011. Per capita consumption in 2010 was about 4.9 pounds.

Today, very little butter is made at home, and in fact, Americans now buy far more butter substitutes, such as margarine, than real butter. All American butter is made from cow's milk and is pasteurized, that is, heated to 163 degrees for thirty minutes or to 182 degrees for ten minutes (called "high temperature, short-time pasteurization"). It is then cooked and churned. FDA gradings of AA, A, B, and C are then assigned.

The U.S. and the Soviet Union are the world's leading producers. The leading butter-producing states are Minnesota, Wisconsin, and Iowa, with the butter industry as a whole using up 20 percent of all milk produced.

"Sweet butter," or "unsalted butter," contains no salt. "Sweet cream butter" has some salt added. "Whipped butter" is combined with air to give a more spreadable texture when cold. "Clarified butter" is made in the kitchen by melting butter and letting the casein and other nonfat ingredients drop out, thereby creating a clear liquid with a higher burning point but less flavor.

"Buttermilk" is the liquid left after butter granules have reached the breaking point on the milk's surface during the production process (see also **milk**). Today Americans per capita consume less than a gallon of buttermilk per year.

BUTTERFISH. Also "pumpkinseed" in New England. A fatty fish, *Peprilus triacantbus*, ranging from Nova Scotia to Cape Hatteras, that grows up to twelve inches and one and a half pounds. Butterfish are usually found fresh in summer in NYC and Boston markets. The name dates back to at least 1674 and is often applied to various other fish, such as the **pompano**.

BUTTERMILK PIE. A pie made from buttermilk, eggs, sugar, and vanilla, particularly popular in the South. For a description of buttermilk, see **butter** and **milk**.

BUTTERMILK PIE

Beat together 4 eggs and 1 ½ c. sugar until well blended, then mix in 1 T. flour, ¾ c. buttermilk, ½ t. vanilla, a dash of salt, and ½ c. cooled melted butter. Mix until a smooth butter is formed. Pour into pie shell and bake in a 300° oven until set. Serve warm.

BUTTERNUT. Also "white walnut" and "oil nut." A native tree of eastern America, in the walnut family, dating in print to 1741.

BUTTERSCOTCH. A confection made from butter, brown sugar, and lemon juice. The association with Scotland has never been satisfactorily explained. "Butterscotch sauce" or "butterscotch topping" is an American dessert sauce with the flavor of butterscotch candy and is served over ice cream (for a "butterscotch sundae"), on **pound cake**, and on other sweets. According to the *OED*, the word was first printed in 1855, earlier as "butterscot," though Wikipedia cites "Doncaster Butterscotch" in *The Liverpool Mercury* in 1848.

BUTTERSCOTCH

Combine ½ c. butter with 1 lb. brown sugar, heat to 290° (use a candy thermometer), and flavor with 1 T. lemon juice. Beat to make creamy in texture, then pour out on a marble slab and let cool.

BUTTERSCOTCH SAUCE

In a double boiler combine 2 c. brown sugar, ½ c. butter, ¼ pt. heavy cream, and 1 T. lemon juice. Cook for about 1 hr., stirring to thicken.

BUTTERY. A larder or pantry where provisions are stored, dating in print to 1654.

BUYBACK. Bartenders' term for a complimentary drink given a customer who has already paid for three or four others.

BX. Also "body shop." Abbreviation for "body exchange," a slang term from the 1960s to describe a bar where people go primarily to meet partners of the opposite sex.

BYOB. Slang abbreviation for "Bring your own bottle" or "bring your own booze," meaning a guest should bring his own liquor or beer to a party. As "BYOL" ("bring your own liquor") the phrase dates in print to 1928.

CABBAGE (*Brassica oleracea* var. *capitata*). A plant whose large head of tightly wrapped leaves is eaten in a variety of ways—boiled, stuffed, or raw, as in **coleslaw**. The word is from Vulgar Latin *bottia*, "bump," which in Middle English became *caboche*.

The term "cabbage" includes **broccoli**, **brussels sprouts**, **cauliflower**, **kale**, and **collard greens**, but it usually refers more specifically to the white and red cabbages, as well as the purple and green varieties, with their characteristic large heads and firmly packed leaves.

The "savoy cabbage" (not related to **salad savoy**), mostly grown in Europe, is considered among the finest, while "Chinese cabbage" (*B. pekinensis*), also called "celery cabbage" and "pe-tsai," is an oriental cabbage of a different species.

Cabbages were brought to the New World by the European settlers, and the plant grew well in temperate climates, particularly in the Middle Atlantic colonies. German immigrants especially valued the cabbage, which was a major vegetable in their diet, and the Dutch made coleslaw from it. After the Civil War, with the proliferation of railroads, cabbage became widely available to all Americans, and it remains a very popular garden plant. Nevertheless, cabbage became associated with poor European immigrants who could afford little else and were disparaged for the smell cooked cabbage produced.

CABERNET SAUVIGNON. A variety of vinifera grape that makes a rich, tannic red wine with a distinctive varietal character. The word was first printed in 1833 as "carbenet," by 1911 as "cabernet."

Cabernet sauvignon (also called just "cabernet" or "cab," for short, though distinguished from another varietal called "cabernet franc") is the predominant grape in the wines of Bordeaux and has, since the 1960s, become the leading red varietal planted in California, with 77,602 acres by 2010 and 446,136 tons crushed. Although increasingly the wine is a blend with varietals like merlot and cabernet franc, many examples may contain 100 percent cabernet sauvignon. Napa Valley has the greatest number of acres, with 19,000 planted in cabernet sauvignon.

Cabernet also flourishes in the Northwest, and some wine from this varietal is also made in Ohio, Texas, New Jersey, New York, Arkansas, and Virginia.

CABINET. A Rhode Island name for a soda-fountain confection of milk, syrup, and ice cream blended in a mixer. *DARE* cites 1957 as the first evidence in print, and another appearance from 1968, by a resident of Fall River, Massachusetts, named Dorothy Cahill, who contended that the drink's name was originated by a pharmacist in that town who kept the ice cream in a cabinet at the soda fountain. Elsewhere such a drink is called a **milk shake**.

CAB JOINT. Also "steer joint." An illicit bar and bordello of NYC's Prohibition era, dating in print to 1930. As described by Charles G. Shaw, in *Nightlife: Vanity Fair's Guide to New York After Dark* (1931), "'Cab' or 'steer' joints operate as 'clubs' and depend largely on taxi-drivers to corral their victims. The formula, nine times out of ten, is identical. 'Like to meet some pretty girls?' asks the affable cabbie. 'I'll show you a place with real hot mammas, good booze, and all you want.' A knowing wink, a sidelong leer, and fate arranges the rest. Either the joy-hunter falls for the bait (and enters) or wisely turns elsewhere." See also **speakeasy**.

CACTUS. Any of a variety of plants in the family *Cactaceae* whose branches have either spines or scales; in print since 1752, although the word was also applied by 1607 to the cardoon or artichoke. Cacti grow mainly in desert areas, where the branches are sometimes used in cooking, especially in the Southwest, where the edible pads are called **nopales**. They are especially part of **Mexican American** cuisine.

CAESAR SALAD. A salad of romaine lettuce, garlic, olive oil, croutons, Parmesan cheese, Worcestershire sauce, and, often, anchovies. It was created by Caesar Cardini, an Italian immigrant who opened a series of restaurants in Tijuana, Mexico, just across the border from San Diego. On Fourth of July weekend in 1924 at Caesar's Palace, Cardini concocted the salad as a main course, arranging the lettuce leaves on a plate with the intention that they would be eaten with the fingers. Later Cardini shredded the leaves into bite-size pieces. The salad became particularly popular with Hollywood movie people who visited Tijuana, and it became a featured dish at Chasen's and Romanoff's, in Los Angeles. Cardini was adamant in insisting that the salad be subtly flavored and argued against the inclusion of anchovies, whose faint flavor in his creation he believed might have come from the Worcestershire sauce. He also decreed that only Italian olive oil and imported Parmesan cheese be used. In 1948 he established a patent on the dressing, which is still packaged and sold as "Cardini's Original Caesar Dressing Mix," distributed by Caesar Cardini Foods, Culver City, California. Cardini died in 1956, and the business is now carried on by his daughter, Rosa Cardini.

The Caesar salad was once voted by the International Society of Epicures, in Paris, the "greatest recipe to originate from the Americas in fifty years."

The following recipe is the original and does not include anchovies.

CAESAR SALAD

Cut up white bread into ½-in. pieces to make about 2 c. Mash 2 cloves garlic in some olive oil. Dry out the croutons in the oven, basting them with the garlic and oil. Strip the leaves from 2 medium heads of romaine lettuce to provide 6 to 8 leaves per person. Wash gently, shake dry, and refrigerate in a plastic bag until ready to serve. Puree 2 cloves mashed garlic with ¼ t. salt and 3 T. olive oil, strain, and place in frying pan. Add croutons, heat briefly, and toss, then turn into serving bowl. Boil 2 eggs exactly 1 min. Grate ¼ c. Parmesan cheese. In a very large bowl pour 4 T. olive oil over the lettuce leaves and scoop in large motions to coat. Sprinkle lettuce with ¼ t. salt, 8 grinds of fresh black pepper, and 2 more t. oil, toss again, add juice of 1 lemon and 6 drops Worcestershire sauce, and break in eggs. Toss and add cheese. Toss and top with croutons. Serve on a chilled plate.

CAFÉ. A coffeehouse or other inexpensive, usually small, restaurant, although many cafés of the late nineteenth century in Eastern European neighborhoods in U.S. cities became quite large and grand. The term, first in English print in 1789, is from the French for "coffee."

CAFÉ AU LAIT. Creole term for hot, strong coffee served with an equal amount of hot milk. The term, first in print in English in 1763, means "coffee with milk" in French and was first advocated in the late seventeenth century by Dr. Monin, of Grenoble, France, as a healthful alternative to powdered coffees that were often adulterated with other substances like toasted bread, fava beans, and peas.

CAFÉ BRÛLOT. A dark coffee mixed with the flavors of citrus rind and brandy. The name of this traditional New Orleans coffee is a compound of the French *café* (coffee) and *brûlot* (burnt brandy). Although it is not mentioned in *The Picayune's Creole Cook Book* (1901), it is apparently an old recipe, since flameproof "brûlot bowls" made especially for the coffee were known before 1900.

CAFÉ BRÛLOT

In a fireproof brûlot bowl or saucepan place 2 sticks of cinnamon, 6 cloves, 1 ½ T. sugar, the rind of 1 lemon, and 3 oz. brandy. Heat to below boiling point, ignite with a match, and mix. Pour strong, hot coffee into bowl, then pour into small coffee cups.

CAFÉ SOCIETY. A term coined by New York *Journal-American* society columnist Maury Paul (who wrote under the name "Cholly Knickerbocker") in 1937 to describe a chic, young crowd that frequented saloons as well as fine dining rooms during and after Prohibition. "The newcomers of today are the Old Guard of tomorrow," wrote Paul.

CAFETERIA. A restaurant at which people move along a line and select the food and drinks they want, then carry them on trays to a table to eat their meals. The word is an American rendering of a Spanish word for "coffee shop," a meaning it had in print as of 1839.

The first self-service restaurant was the Exchange Buffet, in NYC, opened in 1885, which catered to an exclusively male clientele. Food was purchased at a counter, and patrons ate standing up. The word *cafeteria* was first used by John Kruger, who ran a self-service eatery at the 1893 World's Columbian Exposition in Chicago, although he also nicknamed them "conscience joints," because customers tallied their own bills.

The Childs brothers of NYC introduced the tray around 1898, and New Yorkers called such establishments "grab joints." In 1900 in NYC, Bernarr Adolphus Macfadden opened the first "penny restaurant," where every item cost a penny. The **Automat**, in which people chose their food from a wall of boxes covered with glass doors, was introduced in Philadelphia in 1902 by Joseph Horn and Frank Hardart.

The first cafeteria in the West was opened in 1905, by Helen Mosher in Los Angeles, and easterners called such western examples "California-style restaurants." The first cafeteria in the South—where the industry proliferated most and thrives today—was the 1918 Britling Cafeteria, in a department store in Birmingham, Alabama. Many current cafeteria chains also came out of the South—S&W Cafeteria, in Ashville, North Carolina; the Morrison's chain, in Mobile, Alabama; the Piccadilly chain, in Baton Rouge, Louisiana; Furr's, in Lubbock, Texas; Wyatt's, in Dallas; and Luby's, in San Antonio. In the face of competition from family-style and fast-food restaurants, many cafeterias have closed around the U.S., with few of the chains remaining.

Cafeterias are the most common form of eating room at American schools, so that "cafeteria" has become synonymous with such dining halls.

The suffix "-eria" has led to all manner of words meaning a kind of shop— "chocolateria," "meateria," "caviarteria," and others.

CAJUN. A descendant of the French Acadians who settled in Louisiana after the British deported them from Acadia, in Nova Scotia, and the other Maritime Provinces of Canada in 1755, for refusing to pledge allegiance to England. In Louisiana these people were soon called "'Cadians" and, by 1842, "Cagians." The spelling "Cajuns" first saw print in 1880.

Cajun cuisine, with its French, Spanish, African, and Indian influences, is distinctive, but Louisiana authorities and gastronomes have argued for decades about just what is and is not Cajun cookery. Few would refuse to list the following dishes in the Cajun canon: **jambalaya**, **étouffée**, coush-coush, **boudin**, **andouille**, **chaudin**, **gumbo**, and all manner of crab dishes and dishes requiring heavy doses of **hot sauce**.

Cajun festivals often revolve around food, including the Breaux Bridge Crawfish Festival, a yam festival, and "boucheries" (large-scale butchering parties), where Cajuns consume prodigious amounts of food and drink and everyone works hard to live by the Cajun motto *"Laissez le bon temps rouler"*—"Let the good times roll." In *American Cooking: Creole and Acadian* (1971), Peter S. Feibleman wrestled with the problem of defining Cajun cookery and finally realized there was no final word on the matter:

> *What, then, is the difference between the terms Creole and Acadian as applied to food? Most authorities will start with a simple answer: they will tell you that it is the difference between city French cooking and country French cooking. But then the reservations and qualifications begin. Both Creole and Acadian cooking are Louisiana French in style, of course—which (authorities will add) isn't French at all. Is that clear? No? Well, Acadian cooking is a little spicier than Creole—sometimes, not always. Acadians like a lot of rice—well, of course, the Creoles like a lot of rice, too. Acadian cooks are likely to put all the ingredients for a course into one big pot, while Creoles like these ingredients separate. Yes, that's true—at least, most Creoles like them separate. "Look [the authorities will finally say], maybe you'd better just taste it."*

Louisiana cooking authority Tom Fitzmorris, in *The New Orleans Eat Book* (1991), noted, "Unalloyed Cajun food is almost never found in restaurants, not even in Cajun country. I suspect the reason for this is that Cajun cooking, for all its glorious flavor, looks ugly (unless, of course, you grew up with it). Much of it is pot food from very big pots. Getting the polished look restaurant patrons require screws up the flavor." And, as Louisiana culinary authority JoAnn Clevenger has said, "Cajun food can only be corrupted, but Creole food must evolve."

Interest in a particular form of Cajun food was fueled by Cajun chef Paul Prudhomme, who began serving his own highly seasoned version of his family's recipes at his New Orleans restaurant, K-Paul's Louisiana Kitchen, which opened in 1979 and where he popularized nontraditional dishes like **blackened redfish** and "Cajun popcorn" (fried **crayfish** tails).

CAKE. A baked confection usually containing flour, butter, eggs, and sweetener, although some cakes do not contain flour. The word derives from Old Norse *kaka*, which in Middle English became *cake*.

Until the nineteenth century, cakes were usually very large, baked in pans shaped to resemble bread loaves, and were often studded with fruit. "Fine cakes" were iced, often with meringue, and several at once might be served at a dinner party. With the availability of the more modern bake ovens after 1870, it became possible to make much lighter cakes with the new baking sodas and powders. The "layer cake," composed of two or more layers of cake with various fillings between, started to become popular by the 1870s, especially for celebratory wedding and birthday cakes. The "ice cream cake" was a layer cake or cake roll filled with ice cream. "Cup cakes" or "measure cakes" were originally those whose measurements were by the cup, not the pound.

After the turn of the century, layer cakes were among the favorite of American confections, especially with the improvements in stoves and after the General Foods Corp. and the Pillsbury Co. brought out boxed cake mixes between 1947 and 1948, so that by the end of the 1950s more than half the cakes Americans baked were from such mixes.

"Cake flour" is a low protein white soft-wheat flour with a very fine texture. It is usually bleached.

A "cake social" is a social gathering at which cake is either served or sold to raise money for a charitable purpose. A "cakewalk" (dating in print to 1879) is a term used mainly by African Americans to describe a social entertainment wherein the participants dance or strut fancifully in order to win the prize of a cake.

CALA. A New Orleans Sunday-morning breakfast confection made of rice that is mixed with flour, spices, and sugar and then deep-fried. Sometimes it is made with ground black-eyed peas. The word, first printed in 1880, derives from one or more African words, such as the Nupe *kàrà*, "fried cake."

Calas (the term is used almost exclusively in the plural) were sold by African American street vendors in the city's French Quarter, and one would hear the cry *"Belles calas tout chauds!"*

"Cala" is also a term for a shoulder cut of **ham**, usually referred to as "shoulder bacon," "picnic ham," or "California ham."

CALAS

Mix 3 c. cooked rice, 3 beaten eggs, ¼ t. vanilla, ¼ t. nutmeg, ¼ t. cinnamon, and ¼ t. lemon rind. Sift ½ c. flour with ½ c. sugar, 3 ½ t. baking powder, and ½ t. salt. Stir into rice. Drop by spoon into deep, hot fat and fry for about 2 min. Sprinkle with confectioners' sugar. Makes about 2 dozen.

CALIFORNIA SPRAWL. A term describing a system of vine trellising used in California vineyards since the 1980s to prevent phylloxera damage. The system results in a vine whose canopy sprawls and provides shade.

CALLABASATE. A candied pumpkin, usually made at home. In print the word (from the Spanish *calabazate*) dates to 1967.

CALABASH. Also "calipash," "capapash," and other forms. This word refers to two plants, one an Old World vine, *Lagenaria siceraria*, the other a tropical American tree, *Crescentia cujete*, also called the "bottle gourd" for its large, round shape, dating in print to 1596. The word is from the Spanish *calabaza*, "gourd."

In South Carolina, "calabash" is also the name for a dish of turtle cooked in its shell, now served rarely.

In North Carolina, "calabash style" refers to fish that is breaded or coated with a batter and fried, the name deriving from the seacoast town of Calabash, where many restaurants specialize in this style of cooking.

CALCIUM (OR SODIUM) PROPIONATE. A preservative used to prevent the growth of mold in bread products.

CALCIUM (OR SODIUM) STEARYL LACTYLATE. An additive mixed with dough to strengthen its texture. It is also used in artificial whipped cream, cake fillings, and processed egg whites.

CALIBOUGAS. Also "calibogus" and other spellings. A beverage of rum, spruce beer, and molasses, known since the middle of the eighteenth century, but a word of unknown origins.

CALIFORNIA ROLL. Also "carifonia roll." A form of sushi made with avocados, crabmeat, cucumbers, and other ingredients wrapped in vinegared rice. There are two claims for the dish's invention: according to one, in the early 1960s, sushi chef Ichiro Mashita and his assistant Teruo Imaizumi created it at a Japanese restaurant in Los Angeles named Tokyo Kaikan; another credits Ken Seusa, sushi chef at Kin Jo, in L.A. The term first appeared in print in 1979, in an Ocala, Florida, newspaper. The dish, though disdained by many Japanese and food critics, eventually gained popularity in Japan, where it is called *kashu-maki*, a literal translation of "California roll." Variations followed, including the "Hawaiian roll" (avocado, tuna, pineapple), "Philadelphia roll" (smoked salmon, cream cheese), and "Cajun roll" (crawfish and cucumber). See also **Japanese American food.**

CALL LIQUOR. Bartenders' term for a brand-name liquor specified by a customer. "Well liquor" is an inexpensive liquor used by a bartender if the customer makes no specific request.

CALZONE. An **Italian American** pastry made from **pizza** dough that is stuffed with a variety of fillings like cheese, sausage, or ground meat and folded into a half-moon shape that resembles trousers, which in Italian are *calzoni*. The word entered English print in 1944.

"Calzone" is also applied to a sweet sugar cookie of Mexican origins.

CAMBRIC TEA. Also called "hot-water tea" and "kelly tea," cambric tea is merely hot water, milk, sugar, and perhaps a dash of tea, given to children to make them feel part of a social gathering. The term comes from cambric fabric, which is white and thin, like cambric tea; it is American slang, used since at least 1888.

CAMPER. Bartender slang for a customer who "camps out" in a bar for the entire evening, as cited in *Newsweek* magazine in 1991.

CANAIGRE (*Rumex hymenosepalus*). Also "wild rhubarb," "pie dock," "wild pie-plant," and "tanner's dock." Canaigre is a species of buckwheat found in Wyoming, Utah, western Texas, New Mexico, Arizona, and California, dating in print to 1878. It has long green leaves and a reddish stem. The Indians of the Southwest, including the Maricopa, Pima, Navajo, and Hopi, prepared it in various ways, and the plant was used for soothing sore throats and for tanning leather. The Maricopa used the seeds in a flatbread; the Navajo blended them into a mush.

CANAPÉ. A slice of thin toast or cracker spread with any of a variety of meats, vegetables, cheeses, or fish, or any of a variety of "finger foods" usually served on trays before the first course. The word is from the French for "couch."

According to the *World Famous Chefs' Cook Book* (1941), compiled by Ford Naylor, "It is correct to offer [canapés] to guests in the living room, just before dinner; or as a first course at luncheon or dinner; or at receptions and teas. When canapés or tidbits are served with relishes, the combination is known as an hors d'oeuvre."

The term first appeared in English print in 1890, as a reference to a tidbit served with anchovies, still a popular canapé. Other canapés might include minced hard-boiled eggs, sliced olives with pimiento, cheese puffs, ham, liver, or fish pâté, smoked salmon, pickles, small frankfurters wrapped in pastry (called "**pigs in a blanket**"), and oysters wrapped in bacon (an English canapé known as "angels on horseback"). "Devils on horseback" are an American canapé made with chicken livers wrapped in bacon.

"Canapés" are often synonymous in America with "hors d'oeuvres."

CANO, LARRY J. (1924–). Restaurateur. Capitalizing on the increased popularity of **Mexican American** food in the U.S. in the 1950s, Larry Cano made many innovations that helped elevate the image of the cuisine, including the preparation of **guacamole** tableside and the sizzling **fajita** platter.

Born in 1924 to Mexican immigrants in East Los Angeles, Cano attended UCLA but dropped out to join the Army Air Forces as a fighter pilot in World War II and Korea. He eventually graduated from USC with a business degree and in 1954 bought a restaurant named Bali Hai, in Encino, California. Cano saw a need for a good sit-down Mexican restaurant in the area, so he turned Bali Hai into El Torito, serving food based on his Mexican cooks' own recipes. Within two years he had two more units and drew many celebrities to the Hollywood branch, including John Wayne and Lana Turner. El Torito expanded, always to upscale neighborhoods, while creating new marketing ideas to push the brand, including the mariachi Sunday brunch. Cano also opened two gourmet Mexican restaurants: Cano's, in Newport Beach (1977), and Las Brisas, in Laguna Beach (1979). After establishing twenty-two El Torito units, Cano sold the chain to W.R. Grace & Co. in 1976 for $20 million, staying on as president.

In 1982, Cano was cited among "the Enchilada Millionaires" by *Time* magazine. At the age of sixty-four, he retired from El Torito, while retaining ownership of Cano's and Las Brisas, and in 1992 he opened an Italian–Mexican fusion restaurant called Pasta Mañana, which sold pizza fajitas. But owing to increased competition from Mexican restaurant chains, Cano was bankrupt by 1994, and El Torito's new owner, Real Mex, declared bankruptcy in 2011.

CANDY. Any of a wide variety of sweet morsels, bars, lozenges, figures, or other confections eaten on their own, as a snack or treat beyond the usual mealtime foods. Candy may take the form of fluffy marshmallow, chocolate-covered nuts, citrus rinds, spun sugar, bars with cream centers, tiny hard drops, gums, and many other shapes and types. Many are based on crystallized sugar, whose once high price made such sweet confections a delicacy indulged in only by the wealthy.

The ancient Egyptians preserved nuts and fruits with honey, and by the Middle Ages physicians had learned how to mask the bad taste of their medicines with sweetness, a practice still widespread. Boiled "sugar plums" were known in seventeenth-century England and soon appeared in the American colonies, where maple-syrup candy was popular in the North and benne-seed confections were just as tempting in the South. In New Amsterdam, one could enjoy "marchpane," or "marzipan," very old decorative candy made from almonds ground into a sweet paste.

While the British called such confections "sweetmeats," Americans came to call them "candy," from the Arabic *qandi*, "made of sugar," and from the French *sucre candi*, and is found in English as of 1475. Originally Americans used the word to mean a "toffee" (a hard candy made from sugar and butter), but by the nineteenth century "candy" was a general term for all kinds of sweet confections.

Caramels were known in the early eighteenth century, and **lollipops** by the 1780s, as were **pralines**— named after French diplomat César du Plessis-Praslin, later duc de Choiseul—a candy that became particularly well known in Louisiana.

"Hard candies" made from lemon or peppermint flavors were popular in the early nineteenth century, and Eliza Leslie, in her *Directions for Cookery* (1837), speaks of chocolate-covered nuts and "bonbons" (from French, meaning "good-good") wrapped in papers on which were printed lines of verse. "Peppermint sticks" were enjoyed by midcentury, as were **hoarhound candy** and other lozenges used as sore-throat remedies. Soft, chewy **taffy** was made at taffy pulls during this period, and people also delighted in peanut brittle and a candy so hard it was called a "jawbreaker." "Vinegar candy" was boosted by being continuously mentioned throughout the popular 1867–1869 series *Dotty Dimple Stories*, by Rebecca Sophia Clarke, whose pen name was Sophie May. By the 1860s there were "gumdrops."

A significant moment in candy history occurred at the 1851 Great Exhibition in London, where "French-style" candies with rich cream centers were first displayed. These caught on immediately in America, and within a few years there were more than 380 candy factories in the U.S., many turning out candy that cost one cent (called "penny candy"), a price that extended well into the twentieth century. Most of these candies were sold in batches or by the pound and displayed behind glass cases. Hard, clear candies, traditional at Christmas, were made at home in patterned molds, most of which were made by Thomas Mills & Brother, a Philadelphia company established in 1864.

Flavored gums from tree resins had been known throughout the nineteenth century, but chewing gum did not come along until the 1870s. "Bubble gum" appeared by the end of the century. "**Fudge**" originated at women's colleges in the late nineteenth century, "sourballs" appeared by the turn of the last decade, and "Cracker Jack" was the hit of Chicago's World's Columbian Exposition of 1893. "Jelly beans" came along in 1905.

But it was the discovery of milk chocolate in Switzerland in 1875 that made the American **candy bar** such a phenomenon of the late nineteenth century. The first such chocolate bar was produced in 1894, by Milton Snavely Hershey, and there soon followed an endless array of candy products containing peanuts, cream centers, fruit fillings, nougat, coconut, and many other sweet fillers with names like Milky Way, Snickers, 3 Musketeers, Mary Jane, Goo Goo Cluster, and hundreds of others.

In 1912, Americans began buying Life Savers, made by Clarence A. Crane of Cleveland. These were round white peppermints with distinctive holes in the middle (thus their resemblance to the life preserver on a boat); later, five more flavors were added. Crane sold his formula for $2,900 to New Yorkers Ed Noble and Roy Allen, who solved the problem of keeping the Life Savers fresh by "shrink-wrapping" them in aluminum foil—a first in the industry.

Nineteen twelve was also the year NECCO Wafers (an acronym for the New England Confectionary Co., which opened in 1847) appeared. These were previously called "Peerless Wafers" and had been carried to the Arctic and the South Pole by Donald MacMillan and Richard Byrd. (Byrd allegedly brought two and a half tons of them with him.) In 1920, the newest candies on the market were **Jujubes**, tiny morsels of colored candy, and Jujyfruits, shaped into fruit forms.

Americans went to the "candy shop" specifically to buy various kinds of candies, usually sold by the pound or produced in bars by the shop itself. "Candy stores" were small shops selling mostly commercially produced, packaged candies, as well as everything from newspapers and magazines to ice cream sodas and cigars, and, in fact, were more or less synonymous with "soda fountains" and "cigar stores" by the twentieth century. At such stores a child could purchase penny candy, which sometimes was merely icing in a little tin plate, or malted-milk balls, or strings of licorice, or sweet liquids inside small wax bottles. One favorite was hard pellets of candy stuck to long strips of paper.

Cotton candy, made by spinning colored sugar in a centrifuge, causing it to puff into cottonlike strands, came along in 1900 and was usually sold at carnivals, circuses, and state fairs, and rarely at candy stores.

Today Americans consume more than 24 pounds of candy per person each year, not including chewing gum, for sales of $29.4 billion in 2010. The American candy industry turns out more than two thousand different items. Chocolate represents about 60 percent of all confectionary sales. About 25 percent of confectionary sales are made around four holidays—Halloween, Easter, Christmas, and Valentine's Day.

BIT-O-HONEY (1924). A bar made of almond bits and honey-flavored taffy, produced by the Schutter-Johnson Co. of Chicago, now produced by the Chunky Corporation of NYC.

CHUCKLES (1921). A jellied candy coated with sugar crystals, created by Fred W. Amend of Chicago and now produced by Nabisco Confections Inc.

HERSHEY'S KISSES (1907). Small chocolate droplets wrapped in foil, with identifying paper plumes. Kisses are made by the Hershey Co., although the Wilbur Chocolate Co. of Lititz, Pennsylvania, had been making similar candies called "Wilbur Buds" since 1894.

JUNIOR MINTS (1949). These small morsels comprising a creamy mint center covered with chocolate were produced by the James O. Welch Co. (now part of Nabisco Confections Inc.). Welch himself named the candy after seeing a performance of a Broadway play entitled *Junior Miss*, based on *New Yorker* magazine short stories by Sally Benson.

M&M'S PLAIN CHOCOLATE CANDIES (1941). Usually called "M&M's," these chocolate morsels coated with variously colored sugar shells were produced by M&M Limited of Newark, New Jersey. In 1954, "M&M's Peanut Chocolate Candies" appeared, and both are known by the slogan "Melts in your mouth, not in your hand."

MARY JANE (1914). A molasses-and-peanut-butter candy made by the Charles N. Miller Co.

MILK DUDS (1926). Caramel-and-chocolate morsels, first made by the M. J. Holloway Co. of Chicago, now by Beatrice Foods Co.

REESE'S PEANUT BUTTER CUPS (1923). Produced by H. B. Reese in Hershey, Pennsylvania, these chocolate-and-peanut-butter candies came in waxed-paper cups. The candy is now made by the Hershey Co.

SKITTLES BITE SIZE CANDIES (1974). Hard-sugar-coated, fruit-flavored nuggets, first made in England and, since 1982, in the U.S. by the Wm. Wrigley Jr. Company.

STARBURST (1960). A chewy fruit-flavored candy in the shape of a cube. The brand was created in the UK under the name Opal Fruits in four flavors, and upon export to the U.S. changed to Starburst. In 1984, Starburst Strawberry Fruit Chews was launched, followed by Starburst Tropical Fruit Chews (1988), California Fruit Chews (1988), Starburst Sour Fruit (2002), and other flavors. It is now manufactured by the Wrigley Company.

TOOTSIE ROLL (1896). Leo Hirshfield of NYC named these chewy chocolate morsels after his daughter, Clara, whose nickname was Tootsie. In the 1930s he came up with Tootsie Pops, which are lollipops filled with the original chocolate product.

A **candy bar** is usually coated with or containing chocolate, and may include nuts, jellies, peanut butter, fruit, nougat, caramel, coconut, cookie wafers, and other fillings.

The first candy bars were made by François-Louis Cailler in Switzerland in 1819, and by 1842 Birmingham's Cadbury Limited (UK) offered eating chocolate for sale through its catalog. But the candy bar as we know it was the idea of Milton Snavely Hershey, who in 1894 manufactured the first American chocolate bars, the Hershey's Milk Chocolate and Milk Chocolate with Almonds bars, after seeing some German chocolate-making machines at the 1893 World's Columbian Exposition in Chicago. Hershey had before then made caramels at his Lancaster (Pennsylvania) caramel plant, which he sold in 1900. After a trip to Europe Hershey built a plant in Derry Church, Pennsylvania, and opened the Hershey Co. in 1904.

Before long the Bunte Brothers were making chocolate-coated bars, and in 1912 Howard H. Campbell of the Standard Candy Co. of Nashville, Tennessee, produced the first combination bar, called the "Goo Goo Cluster" (supposedly named after the sounds made by his infant son), which contained caramel, marshmallow, peanuts, and milk chocolate. The Goo Goo has long been advertised as "the South's Favorite Candy."

After World War I, the candy-bar craze swept the country, giving impetus to dozens of candy manufacturers, including the Curtiss Candy Co., the Fox-Cross Candy Co., Peter Paul Candy Co., the D. L. Clark Co., Mars Inc., and the Charles N. Miller Co. During the war, candy bars were given to servicemen for nourishment, to provide quick energy, and to build morale.

The first candy bars sold for ten cents, which at the time was too much for a public not hooked on such confections, especially when a pound of loose candy cost the same price. After World War I, a drop in the prices of sugar and chocolate helped lower the price of a candy bar to five cents, and a nickel was the prevailing price for most candy bars until the 1960s. By 1968 the average candy bar cost ten cents again, and by 1980 thirty-five cents was the usual tab for a bar that changed shape, size, and weight through competition and as the result of falling or rising sugar prices.

Although there have been a few attempts to make "health bars," containing honey instead of sugar, carob instead of chocolate, and vitamins instead of caramel, the American candy bar remains a persistent reminder of the American sweet tooth. Some of the most famous and popular candy bars over the years include:

3 MUSKETEERS (1932). Originally three bars of chocolate coating on fluffy chocolate, vanilla, and strawberry nougat, these were named after the 1844 novel by Alexandre Dumas, *The Three Musketeers*, and were created by Mars Inc. Today the item is all one bar, with chocolate nougat.

5TH AVENUE (1936). A peanut-butter-and-almond bar covered with milk chocolate, first produced by William H. Luden of Reading, Pennsylvania.

BABY RUTH (1920). A chocolate-covered bar with a caramel-and-peanut center (originally called "Kandy Kake"), produced by the Curtiss Candy Co. of Chicago. The company insists that the item was not named after New York Yankees baseball player George Herman "Babe" Ruth (1895–1948) but instead honored the daughter of former president Grover Cleveland, whose name was Ruth and who as a child had won the hearts of the nation.

CHARLESTON CHEW (1922). A chocolate-covered bar with a vanilla-nougat center, manufactured by the Fox-Cross Candy Co. of Emeryville, California. The current producer is Nabisco Confections Inc.

CHUNKY (mid-1930s). A square chunk of chocolate containing Brazil nuts, cashews, and raisins, created by NYC confectioner Philip Silverstein, who named the candy after his "chunky" little daughter. It is now manufactured by the Ward-Johnston Division of the Terson Co.

CLARK (1917). Usually referred to as the "Clark bar," it was made by the D. L. Clark Co. and contained roasted peanuts and a milk chocolate covering. The company is now merged with the M. J. Holloway Co., a division of the Beatrice Foods Co.

HEATH BAR (1932). Introduced as "Heath's English Toffee" in 1928, by L. S. Heath, this chocolate-covered toffee bar was considered a premium item because it was smaller than most other candy bars. People often referred to it as the "H and H Bar," because the two *H*'s in the word "Heath" were capitalized around lowercase letters.

KIT KAT (1937). A chocolate-covered biscuit bar, whose sections may be snapped off to eat individually. Probably named after London's Kit-Kat Club, the confection was originally a brand of a box of chocolates made by Rowntree's, based in the United Kingdom. The biscuit was first produced in 1935 as "Rowntree's Chocolate Crisp," then renamed "Kit Kat Chocolate Crisp" in 1937 and exported to Commonwealth countries in the 1940s and, by 1970, to the United States. Nestlé bought the brand in 1988 for worldwide distribution, while the Hershey Company acquired rights to make the candy in the U.S.

MILKY WAY (1923). Introduced by Frank C. Mars, this bar of chocolate nougat, caramel, and chocolate covering has been one of the most popular of all candy bars.

MR. GOODBAR (1925). A chocolate-and-peanut bar produced by the Hershey Co.

MOUNDS (1922). A double bar of dark chocolate covering and coconut center, manufactured by Peter Paul Halajian, of Naugatuck, Connecticut. In 1948, a similar bar using milk chocolate and almonds became another success for the company, which called the new candy Almond Joy.

OH HENRY! (1921). Made by the Williamson Candy Co. of Chicago, this milk-chocolate-and-peanut bar was not named after short-story writer William Sydney Porter, whose pen name was O. Henry. According to Ray Broekel in *The Great American Candy Bar Book* (1982):

Mr. Williamson was operating a combination retail and wholesale candy store, and every day about the same time, a young fellow named Henry would come into the store and kid around with the girls who were making candy. Before long, the girls got into the habit of asking Henry to do little odd jobs and favors for them…[and] you'd hear, "Oh, Henry, will you get me this?" Or, "Oh, Henry, will you get me that?"

Later in the year, when it came time to find a name for the nut roll that was being manufactured, Mr. Williamson's salesmen said, "All we hear around here is 'Oh, Henry,' so why not call the candy bar Oh Henry!"

SKY BAR (1937). A combination bar of chocolate segments containing centers of caramel, vanilla, peanut, or fudge, made by NECCO of Cambridge, Massachusetts.

SNICKERS (1930). A bar of peanut butter nougat, peanuts in caramel, and a milk chocolate coating. Snickers was produced by Frank C. Mars of Chicago and is the top-selling candy bar in the U.S.

CANDY APPLE. Also "candied apple." A confection made by immersing an apple in a red sugar syrup that forms a hard, candylike crust on the fruit. Candy apples are usually eaten on a stick and are a specialty of carnivals and county fairs.

CANDY STEW. Also "candy boiling." A party where candy is made by everyone. It dates in print to 1837.

CANE BEER. A kind of beer fermented from the skimmings of boiled sugarcane syrup. It is said to have a sweet-sour taste and dates in print to 1938.

CANE CORN. Slang term for corn whiskey made from corn and cane sugar.

CANOE RACE. A campus phrase for drinking beer in relay teams.

CANTALOUPE (*Cucumis melo reticulatus*). A musk melon, elsewhere called the "netted" or "nutmeg" melon, that is round or oval, weighs about two to four pounds, has orange flesh, and is known for its sweetness. The word is from the name of a papal villa near Rome, Cantalupo, where the fruit was supposedly first grown, but in Europe the cantaloupe is specifically *C. melo cantalupensis*. The melon is first mentioned in print in 1739. It might have first been brought to America by Columbus, before 1494, when the first European melons were planted. The crops are now primarily raised in California, Arizona, and Texas.

Americans often eat cantaloupe for breakfast, sometimes with cottage cheese.

CANTINA. A saloon in the Southwest; also "canteen," which has the additional meaning of a metal flask used to carry water. The word *cantina* is from the Italian (for "wine cellar") and the Spanish (for "wine cellar" or "storage room"); by extension it came to mean a place where one could buy a drink of wine or spirits. The word was first printed in 1844.

CANVASBACK DUCK (*Aythya valisineria* and *Fuligula valisneriana*). A wild North American duck found throughout the U.S. whose name derives from the light color of its neck and back. Thomas Jefferson first mentioned the bird by this name in 1782, and it has long been considered one of the tastiest of all American fowl, its flavor the result of its wild celery diet. The most preferred canvasbacks came from the Chesapeake Bay, Long Island Sound, and along the Delaware and Susquehanna rivers; for these, gastronomes paid a high price, and Europeans had the ducks imported. In the Chesapeake Bay region, the canvasback almost became extinct after the Army Ordnance Corps appropriated some of the fowl's feeding grounds in 1917.

CAPE COD TURKEY. Also "Cape Ann turkey." A slang euphemism for baked codfish since at least 1805. The term might have derived from the gratefulness of Cape Codders for nature's bounty of cod, their major industry in the eighteenth and nineteenth centuries. So, perhaps in the spirit of the Thanksgiving turkey, the people called the fish by this name. Others believe it may derive from Boston Catholics' attempt to make more palatable the thought of eating fish every Friday, when no meat was allowed for religious reasons.

~~~~~~
CAPE COD TURKEY
~~~~~~

Season a 3-lb. cod with salt and pepper, then fill its cavity with 3 c. bread crumbs, 1 chopped onion, 2 T. parsley, ⅓ c. dill pickle, salt, pepper, 3 beaten eggs, and 4 T. melted butter. Close cavity and bake for 45 min. at 350°. Serves 6.

CAPER (*Capparis spinosa*). Any of 150 species of shrub bearing a flowered bud pickled for use as a condiment. Capers might have originated in Asia Minor; the word is from the Greek *kapparis*. Capers are grown in the U.S. in Florida and California. It is first mentioned in print around 1382.

CAPPUCCINO. A dark coffee served with a foamy head of milk or cream. A traditional beverage of Italy, cappuccino is made by forcing steam through milk or cream to form a creamy topping for the coffee, though in America it may be served simply with whipped cream on top. The drink is supposedly named after a Capuchin monk in Brazil, in whose garden coffee was grown in 1774. Others say the name derives from the drink's resemblance to the tonsured heads of Capuchin monks. The word is first found in American print in 1948.

CARAMBOLA (*Averrhoa carambola*). Also "star fruit," "five-angled fruit," and "Chinese star fruit." An elongated, lantern-shaped yellow fruit that, when cut into slices, resembles a star shape. It is sweet, resembling a plum, and has Asian origins, though the name "carambola" came from India via the Portuguese and dates in print to 1598. The carambola is grown in Hawaii, especially the Arkin and Golden Star varieties.

CARAMEL. A confection made from sugar, cream, butter, and flavorings, or merely melted sugar used as a flavoring, topping, or coloring in soups, desserts, and spirits.

The term came into English from the French, via Old Spanish and, ultimately, the Greek *kalamos*. It first appeared in English print in 1725, referring to the melted-sugar variety. The candy caramel was first mentioned in 1884 by the *Philadelphia Times*. To "caramelize" sugar is to heat it to the melting stage, just before it begins to burn. Some recommend the addition of a small bit of water during the cooking of caramel.

CARBO-LOAD. A slang term, particularly popular among athletes in the 1980s, to describe eating large portions of foods rich in carbohydrates, such as potatoes, rice, and pasta, before strenuous activity or athletic competition.

CARIBBEAN AMERICAN FOOD. A general term for the various foods cooked and enjoyed by Caribbeans who have emigrated to the U.S., as well as those adaptations of Caribbean cuisine that have become part of American gastronomy.

Before the European conquest of the Caribbean, the natives of the West Indies, who arrived as early as 4000 B.C. cultivated **sweet potatoes**, manioc, **peanuts**, **chile peppers**, **guava**, and many other foods, which were usually boiled. Animal proteins included bats, rodents, **opossum**, agouti, **armadillo**, land crabs, dogs, small deer, and birds, usually roasted over an open fire. The Taino tribe domesticated Muscovy ducks. Seafood was abundant, especially **conch** and **turtle**.

From the moment **Christopher Columbus** set foot on the Caribbean islands, he was astonished at the "extremely verdant and fertile" land and the variety of foods he knew nothing of, leading to the Columbian Exchange, which changed the way the entire world ate. It also led to the colonization of the Caribbean by Europeans, who often enslaved the native populations and brought over slaves from Africa as part of the triangular trade routes, by which slaves were shipped to the Americas to work plantations that grew crops that would be shipped to Europe, where the profits were used to buy more slaves in Africa. This was particularly profitable in the rum trade, wherein sugar produced in the Caribbean would be shipped to New England to make rum, which was then sold in Europe for a large profit.

By the eighteenth century the British controlled many Caribbean islands as well as Florida, and the French, the Dutch, and the Spanish colonized others.

The food culture of the Caribbean, often called "Creole," developed after the end of the slave trade, in 1807, although slavery itself was still legal in certain territories. Not until well after the Civil War did Caribbeans begin to emigrate to the U.S., especially after the Spanish–American War ended, in 1898, with the U.S. acquiring Cuba and Puerto Rico.

Cuban specialties, all brought to the U.S. through immigration, include dishes like the **Cuban sandwich**, *mofongo* (mashed plantains and gravy), *bistec encebollado* (steak and onions), *moros y cristianos* (black beans and rice), and *tostones* (fried plantains). A large number of Cubans emigrated to the U.S. after the Cuban Revolution on the island, in 1960—200,000 between then and 1973, settling primarily in Miami. There, the Cuban American food culture developed rapidly in cafés and restaurants like Versailles, which opened in 1971 on Eighth Street, or "Calle Ocho," in what came to be called Little Havana, one of the city's first Cuban communities. Cuban cocktails include the **daiquiri** and the **mojito**.

Puerto Ricans, who were U.S. citizens, for the most part migrated not to nearby Florida but to New York City, which by 1980 had more Puerto Rican residents than San Juan did. They brought their own food culture, derived from native Indian and Spanish cooking, including dishes like *lechon asado* (roast pork), *arepas* (stuffed dumplings), **arroz con pollo** (chicken and rice), **empanadas** (meat-filled turnovers), *escabeche* (fried, pickled fish), *mofongo* (mashed, seasoned plantains), and *pasteles*, a holiday dish made from meat or fish wrapped in a banana or plantain leaf. Puerto Rican cocktails include the **piña colada**.

Jamaicans began emigrating to the U.S. in large numbers after 1960, when Caribbeans from the islands took advantage of the abolishment of severe immigration quotas. Jamaicans now form the largest group of American immigrants from the English-speaking Caribbean, with perhaps a million living in the U.S., largely in New York City, South Florida, and other eastern cities, where they have settled into "Little Jamaica" neighborhoods, entering food service and the grocery business, selling and serving native foods like jerk chicken and meats, rice and peas, cod fritters, coco bread, curry chicken, and curried goat.

Haitians first came as refugees fleeing from a series of corrupt dictatorships, largely to Miami and to a lesser extent to the big eastern cities like New York. After fifteen thousand arrived by boatlifts in the 1970s, the U.S. began stopping such refugees from landing. Those who have been successful in emigrating since 1980 have largely tended to settle in the poorest neighborhoods. With them they brought their food culture, called Manje Kreyòl, influenced by their colonial ties to France, so that many dishes have French names, like *bouillon* (meat-and-vegetable stew), *griot* (fried pork), and *legumes*, or *legim* (a vegetable stew). Other foods are indigenous, with African antecedents, like *lambi* (conch stew), *acra* (taro fritters), *tchak* (a hominy-beans-and-meat stew), and *tonmtonm* (steamed breadfruit), with many savory dishes spiced with a spicy sauce called *epis*, made from peppers, garlic, herbs, and spices.

CARIBOU (*Rangifer tarandus*). Also "cariboo," "carraboo," and other spellings. A large wild deer of the arctic and subarctic regions of North America, taxonomically the same as the reindeer but never domesticated. The domesticated reindeer, on the other hand, was introduced into Alaska, from Siberia, only in the 1890s and became an essential part of the Alaskan Eskimo's way of life.

The caribou has shaggy hair, grows to about eight feet in length and four feet in height at the shoulder, migrates in herds, and is highly prized by hunters. The name comes from French Canadian, in turn from Mi'kmaq *khalibu* or other Native American words meaning "pawing the snow," and has been traced to 1610. By 1672 it had other Indian names, such as *maccarib* and *Pohano*.

Caribou meat would typically be marinated and stewed. *Nipku* is a Canadian Eskimo trail food made by partially thawing chunks of the meat, slicing them very thin, and drying the slices on bushes.

CAROB. A chocolate substitute made from the pods of the carob tree (*Ceratonia siliqua*), native to the Mediterranean. The word is derived from Middle French *carobe* and dates in English print to 1548. It is cultivated in Hawaii and California.

CARP (*Cyprinus carpio*). A warm-water fish native to Asia and introduced to the U.S. from Germany in 1876, by the U.S. States Fish Commission. The fish proliferated so fast that 260,000 carp were distributed throughout 298 congressional districts in an effort to make fishermen out of the constituencies. It propagated so successfully that it invaded the habitats of trout and other fish, and efforts were made to eradicate the oversupply of carp. Despite its widespread distribution in muddy waters throughout the U.S., the carp has never been favored by Americans as an eating fish, although it has been a principal ingredient used by Jewish Americans to make **gefilte fish**.

The name of the fish dates back to Old French and other European languages and is first mentioned in English circa 1440.

CARPETBAG STEAK. A grilled steak of beef into which is cut a pocket enclosing a stuffing of oysters. The name derives from a handbag for travelers that was popular from about 1840 to 1870. The dish resembles the sacklike bag with its top closure. There does not seem to be any specific association with the American slang term "carpetbagger," for a hated post–Civil War opportunist who took advantage of both white and black southerners politically and economically. In fact, the carpetbag steak is much more popular in Australia and is mentioned for the first time in American print only in 1941, in Louis Diat's *Cooking à la Ritz*. Although there is no proof that the dish originated at Chasen's restaurant, in Los Angeles, which opened in 1936, it did become one of the restaurant's signature dishes.

CARRAGEENAN. Also "carrageen." A thickening and stabilizing agent obtained from Irish moss seaweed (*Chondrus crispus*), often added to ice cream, chocolate milk, and infant formula. It first appeared in print as "carrageen" in 1830.

CARROT (*Daucus carota*). A long orange root vegetable having fine leaves called "carrot tops." The carrot originated in the Middle East but is now propagated worldwide. The word is from the Greek *karōton* and first appeared in English print in 1538.

The carrot was not much appreciated in Europe until the sixteenth century, but the roots were brought to America by the early English settlers at Jamestown, Virginia, in 1609 and had appeared in Plymouth, Massachusetts, by 1629. With improved types developed in France around 1830, the vegetable took on commercial interest. Today carrots are grown in half the states in the union, especially Texas, California, Michigan, and Wisconsin.

Americans nibble on carrots raw, often cut into "carrot sticks" served as appetizers at parties. They are also boiled and buttered, sometimes made into puddings, and often shredded and baked into a cake, especially popular since the 1960s, topped with a cream cheese frosting.

CARVER, GEORGE WASHINGTON (c. 1864–1943). Agricultural scientist. Born a slave, George Washington Carver became one of the most noted agricultural scientists, for his work on the improvement and diversification of crops, as part of his mission to improve the economy of the South.

A week after his birth, in Diamond, Missouri, Carver and his mother were abducted and sold in Kentucky (he never saw his mother again) for a racehorse valued at $300. Carver returned to Missouri, to his original master, who freed the child and raised him as a son. As a child, Carver learned about farming, cooking, and food preservation at home but was unable to read or write till he was twenty years old, striking out on his own and putting himself through high school in Minneapolis, Kansas, and at the Iowa State College of Agriculture and Mechanic Arts, where he earned a B.S. and an M.A. in agriculture in 1894. He joined the faculty there in systemic biology, then, in 1896, transferred to the Tuskegee Institute, in Alabama, where he remained for the rest of his life, directing the Department of Agricultural Research.

There Carver began studies in soil depletion that resulted in thousands of improvements in plant biology, beginning with a sand-resistant crossbreed of cotton, officially called "Carver's Hybrid," that revolutionized cotton growing in the South. When the boll weevil devastated the South's cotton crop, Carver developed alternative crops, including the **peanut**, for which he found more than a hundred product uses, from flour and breakfast foods to face cream and medicinal peanut oil for the treatment of infantile paralysis. His 1916 booklet *How to Grow the Peanut and 105 Ways of Preparing It for*

Human Consumption was a standard text for many years, through many reprints.

From the sweet potato Carver developed molasses, a coffee substitute, and flour. In 1935 he worked closely with the U.S. Department of Agriculture's Bureau of Plant Industry.

For all his work, Carver sought little financial reward, turning down a highly lucrative offer from Thomas Edison to work with him in Orange, New Jersey. "My discoveries come like a direct revelation from God," he said.

Widely respected by both black and white colleagues, Carver was accorded a membership in the Royal Society of London in 1916. The National Association for the Advancement of Colored People awarded him the Spingarn Medal in 1923, for his work in changing the South's economy. In 1939, he received one of the first Roosevelt Medals, and the George Washington Carver Museum (later destroyed by fire) was installed at Tuskegee in 1941. During World War II, two Liberty ships were named after h im.

Carver donated his life savings to establish a creative chemistry department at Tuskegee, and before he died, in 1943, he agreed to take part in various food experiments at the Ford laboratories at Detroit.

In addition to his scientific work at Tuskegee, Carver taught a popular Bible study class, impersonating characters, and he once produced a form of manna like that described in the Book of Exodus.

Carver was elected to the Hall of Fame for Great Americans, in 1977, and inducted into the National Inventors Hall of Fame in 1990. Iowa State University awarded him a posthumous Doctor of Humane Letters degree in 1994, and in 2000 Carver was made a charter inductee in the USDA Hall of Heroes, as the Father of Chemurgy.

CASABA. A variety of winter melon (*Cucumis melo*) with a yellow skin and sweet white flesh (1885). The name comes from the Turkish town of Kasaba (now Turgutlu). The melon might have been brought to California by Turkish or Armenian immigrants, although, notes Waverley Root in *Food* (1980), "The first officially recorded import…seems to have been the Netted Gem variety, imported from France in 1881. This started commercial melon cultivation in the U.S., though not until 1895 did they develop reliable quality in this country, starting in Colorado."

The "Crenshaw" (also "Cranshaw") melon is similar to the casaba.

CASSABANANA (*Sicana odorifera*). An orange-crimson-colored squashlike fruit with a pronounced aromatic flavor. The term dates to 1911 in print. The cassabanana is grown to some extent in the Gulf states and is often cooked like a **sweet potato**.

CASSEROLE. A dish or stew pot made from a material such as glass, cast iron, aluminum, or earthenware in which food is baked and, often, served. The word, which may also refer to the food itself—as, for example, a "tuna casserole"—is from the French and was first printed in English in 1706.

Cooking in such dishes has always been part of most nations' gastronomy, but the idea of casserole cooking as a "one-dish meal" became popular in America in the twentieth century, especially in the 1950s, when new forms of lightweight metal and glassware appeared on the market. The virtues of easy-to-prepare meals were increasingly promoted in the women's magazines of the era, thereby supposedly freeing the housewife from the lengthy drudgery of the kitchen. Casserole cooking also coincided with the popularity, during this same era, of **buffets**, **brunches**, **potluck dinners**, patio parties, and other casual social meals at which guests could help themselves from a common dish. By the 1970s "casserole cookery" had taken on a less-than-sophisticated image, even though many such dishes were still served at formal dinners and casual meals without characterizing them by the name.

CATAWBA. An American labrusca grape originally found growing along the banks of the Catawba River in North Carolina in 1823 and popularized by John Adlum of Washington, D.C. It became a popular wine grape of Ohio in 1842, when Nicholas Longworth made the first American **champagne** from it. Catawba is still widely used in the East to make sweet red, white, and rosé wines, often blended with the **Delaware** grape.

CAT BEER. Army slang for milk (1941).

CATFISH (family Ictaluridae). Any of a wide range of spiny, scaleless fish with eight barbels (or "whiskers") on the snout, jaw, and chin. Catfish have bristlelike teeth, and some species contain a poison gland at the base of the pectoral spine. There are two thousand species of catfish, whose name, derived from its whiskered appearance, was first mentioned in print in 1612.

North America has twenty-eight species of catfish, about a dozen of which are eaten and three of which make up the most important edible species: the "channel catfish" (*Ictalurus punctatus*), also called the "black warrior," "blue catfish," "canal boater," "prairie trout," and many other names; the "white catfish" (*I. catus*); and the "blue catfish" (*I. furcatus*), also called the "Mississippi catfish." Smaller catfish, called "madtoms" (genus *Noturus*), are used mainly for bait.

Catfish are greatly enjoyed in the South, where they are usually dredged in cornmeal and fried. These are usually served with hush puppies and coleslaw on the side. "Catfish Friday" is a common term in the South for Good Friday, when tradition dictates that Christians consume fish. A "catfish row" is a slang term for a neighborhood where African Americans live, so called because of their supposed affinity for catfish.

In the southern states, catfish are produced on fish farms (90 percent in Mississippi) and sold fresh or frozen. Challenged by foreign imports and a glut of domestic supply, production of American farm-raised catfish, despite federal subsidies that purchase frozen catfish, has declined in the twenty-first century, with 20 percent of farming operations closed between 2010 and 2011.

U.S. landings totaled 7.173 million pounds in 2010, valued at $3.11 million. Per capita U.S. consumption is 0.8 pounds annually.

CAULIFLOWER (*Brassica oleracea* var. *botrytis*). A plant with a large head of crowded white flowers, related to the **cabbage** and the **broccoli**. The word is probably from Latin, "flowered cabbage," and was first recorded in English in 1597. Cauliflower originated in Asia Minor and did not reach America until the seventeenth century, when it was first grown on Long Island, New York, where it has been cultivated ever since. The most popular U.S. variety is the "snowball."

CAVIAR. Specifically, the eggs or roe of the **sturgeon**, but generally referring to the eggs of other fish as well, such as **tuna**, lumpfish, and **salmon**. Dating in print to 1560, the word *caviar* is of uncertain origins, found as the Turkish *khāvyār* and in Italian as *caviale* by the sixteenth century, and for most of man's history the eggs of the sturgeon were consumed as a matter of course throughout the Middle East and Eastern Europe.

Caviar is traditionally made by pushing the roe through a sieve in order to remove fatty tissue and membranes. It is then salted and packed into tins or jars.

It was hardly considered a delicacy in nineteenth-century America, when caviar was given away in saloons as part of the **free lunch** designed to build a thirst for beer. At the end of the nineteenth century, America was the largest supplier of caviar in the world. American caviar was obtained from "Atlantic sturgeon" (or "sea sturgeon"), which Henry Hudson had noted in abundance in 1609 and which were a mainstay of the Indians' diet but were not much prized as a food fish among the white settlers.

In 1873, German immigrant Henry Schacht set up a caviar business near Chester, Pennsylvania, catching his sturgeons in the Delaware River and shipping his product to European markets for a dollar per pound. Seven years later, another plant opened in Bay Side, New Jersey, and business boomed for the next quarter-century. So successful was the sturgeon industry in those years that it soon depleted its own product, so that by 1900 such fisheries found themselves without a source of supply. Sturgeon fisheries were also established along the Columbia River, in the Northwest, in 1888, and by 1892 six million pounds of the fish were caught. By 1900 these, too, were depleted almost to the point of extinction, although the state of Pennsylvania that year reported that 90 percent of so-called Russian caviar sold in Europe and the U.S. was coming out of the Delaware River.

During those boom years, America shipped much of its caviar supply to Europe and then imported it back again under the label "Russian caviar," for ever since the word *caviar*, the best examples were thought to come from Russian rivers. With the end of the American sturgeon industry, caviar prices jumped wildly, and true Russian and Iranian caviar needed to be imported.

Americans not willing to pay such prices were forced to switch to domestic fish roe. In the 1960s, the

Romanoff Caviar Co. (which began when German immigrant Ferdinand Hansen came to Penns Grove, New Jersey, in 1859 to supervise caviar production and which is now owned by Iroquois Foods) began marketing more affordable varieties made from the roe of salmon (called "red salmon caviar"), lumpfish, and, in 1982, whitefish (called "golden whitefish caviar").

FDA regulations forbid the use of the word *caviar* alone on a label unless it is truly from sturgeon roe; if other fish roe is used, the name of the fish must precede "caviar." During the 1970s, there was increased interest in the production of domestic sturgeon caviar because of an encouraging rise in the number of the fish in Arkansas, Oklahoma, and Oregon rivers. California also has sturgeons, but it is illegal to catch them for commercial purposes. The two main wild species are the "white" and "green" sturgeons, the former now farm-raised. The largest sturgeon farm in the world is Sierra Aqua Farms, begun in 1980 in Elverta, California, which produces about 100,000 pounds of white sturgeon per month.

Other companies market the roe of the Mississippi paddlefish (*Polyodon spathula*) as "American sturgeon caviar," because the paddlefish is similar to the sturgeon. In Louisiana, the roe of the local fish called "choupique" (see **bowfin**) is used as caviar.

After a temporary suspension of exports of caviar from the Caspian Sea, owing to dwindling supplies, in 2006 a global ban was put into effect indefinitely, which made farm-raised American caviar and fish roe far more appealing in the world market.

CAYENNE PEPPER. Also "cayenne." A seasoning of pulverized chile peppers and salt (1756). The word comes from the seasoning's association with the peppers of Cayenne Island, French Guiana, but the powdered peppers were produced elsewhere. Today the term "cayenne" connotes no particular type of ground chile or degree of heat, according to the American Spice Trade Association, which believes the term should be phased out of the market.

Eliza Leslie, in her *Directions for Cookery* (1837), gives the following instructions for mixing cayenne, advising one to "wear glasses to save your eyes from being incommoded by [the peppers]. Dry ripe chilis before a fire the day before. Trim the stalks, pound the pods in a mortar until powdered, add one-sixth their weight in salt."

CELEBRITY CHEF. A chef who, through his cookbooks, multi-unit restaurants, and TV appearances, becomes a media celebrity. Although **Julia Child** was a widely known figure in American food culture from the 1960s on, the first restaurant celebrity chefs were the innovators of France's **nouvelle cuisine**, such as Paul Bocuse, Roger Vergé, and Gaston Lenôtre, who were widely covered in the American media in the 1970s. These three, in fact, even became part owners of Les Chefs de France, a restaurant at Disney World's Epcot Center, in Lake Buena Vista, Florida, in 1981.

Beginning in the late 1970s, American chefs like **Wolfgang Puck** of Spago, in Los Angeles, and **Paul Prudhomme** of K-Paul's Louisiana Kitchen, in New Orleans, became the darlings of the food media, each signing lucrative cookbook contracts and appearing on their own TV shows, thereby gaining national recognition. With the debut of the TV Food Network (later **Food Network**), several young chefs were groomed for celebrity status, none more so than **Emeril Lagasse**, whose show *Emeril Live*, on the Food Network, catapulted him onto the covers of magazines—in 1999, *People* chose him as one of the "25 Most Intriguing People of the Year." He briefly had his own situation comedy TV show *Emeril*, on NBC.

Gaining such celebrity has opened doors for chefs to obtain lucrative licensing deals for cookware, kitchen, wine, and food products, and they have worked as consultants to airlines on their in-flight food service and hotels and for frozen food companies, as well as doing product endorsements, boosting their celebrity along with their income to heights previously reached by only the best-known movie stars and athletes. According to a 2012 *Forbes* article, Puck earned $20 million between 2011 and 2012; **Mario Batali** earned $13 million; Todd English, $11 million; and Nobu Matsuhisa, $10 million. Rachael Ray, who went from being a buyer for a gourmet food market in Albany, New York, to a local PBS host of the series *30 Minute Meals*, achieved extraordinary success on the Food Network. She eventually became a partner in her own magazine, *Every Day with Rachael Ray*, in 2005 and hosted her own namesake syndicated daytime talk show in 2006, with nearly two million viewers, earning her a net worth of $60 million.

Many have become judges on TV-show cooking competitions like *Top Chef* and *MasterChef*, whose winners often go on to their own celebrity.

Although many celebrity chefs have been criticized for no longer actually cooking in any of their restaurants, many in the media happily use them to promote sponsored food festivals in cities like Aspen and Miami Beach, where chefs' appearances can draw large attendance.

CELERY (*dulce*). A plant of the **carrot** family, related to the **parsnip** and **parsley**, used as a flavoring or vegetable in soup, salads, and sauces or eaten raw as an appetizer. The word derives from the Greek *sélinon* and first appeared in English print in 1664, thirty-two years after its first cultivation in France as a soup ingredient. Celery grows wild in Europe and Asia, and some wild varieties, which are believed to have escaped from cultivated varieties, are found in California. Florida and California grow most of the U.S. celery crop, and most of that is of the Pascal variety.

"Celery salt" was first advertised in the Sears, Roebuck catalog for 1897 and is still used as a milder flavoring.

CELLAR KITCHEN. A kitchen located in the basement. The term dates back in print to 1830 and usually referred to inferior housing conditions, especially in the northeastern cities, but in the twentieth century many immigrant families, especially Italians and Jews (who might keep a separate kosher kitchen) who were able to move up to a certain affluence and buy homes, would very often put in a cellar kitchen as a second kitchen where much of the everyday cooking took place.

CEREAL. Generally, any edible grain, such as wheat, oats, barley, or corn. In America, however, the word (from the Latin *cereālis*, "of grain") has since the end of the nineteenth century meant a breakfast food prepared from such grains. Such dishes are often called "breakfast cereals," such as oatmeal and cornflakes.

The first examples of American cooked cereals were the corn-mush porridges adapted from Native American cookery. Quaker Oats, made by a process of hulling oats

developed by Asmus J. Ehrrichsen, appeared in 1877. Cream of Wheat was created by flour miller Tom Avidon of Grand Rapids, Michigan, in 1894. But the interest in nutrition in the mid-nineteenth century, as promoted by Reverend Sylvester Graham, creator of graham flour, led to pronouncements on the value of grain in the diet. One of Graham's followers, Dr. James Caleb Jackson, of NYC, created the first packaged breakfast cereal, which was called Granula.

In the 1890s, another nutritionist, Dr. **John Harvey Kellogg** (1852–1943), head of the Battle Creek Sanitarium in Battle Creek, Michigan, doled out portions of "Battle Creek health foods" to his patients, who consumed great quantities of bran and **zwieback**. Kellogg developed packaged cereals at this time—the first named Granola, quickly changed to "Granose" to avoid conflict with Jackson's Granula, and a later product called Granose Flakes. Later, Kellogg's brother, **Will Keith Kellogg**, created one of the most popular and enduring of all American breakfast cereals, Kellogg's Toasted Corn Flakes, introduced in 1907.

One of Kellogg's patients, Charles William Post, founded the Postum Cereal Co. in 1896, marketing a coffee substitute made from cereal, called Postum Cereal Food Coffee, and, in 1898, a wheat-and-malted-barley cereal called Grape-Nuts (which contained neither grapes nor nuts; Post claimed grape sugar was formed in the baking process). Post's other contribution of that era was a cornflake cereal he originally called Elijah's Manna, in 1904, but, after being criticized for his use of a biblical name, he changed it to "Post Toasties" two years later.

In 1892, a Denver lawyer named Henry Perky traveled to Watertown, New York, to work with an airbrake designer named William Ford on a corn cereal, but discovered instead a process for pressing wheat into shreds that could be formed into biscuits. These he called Shredded Wheat, and he returned to Denver to open a bakery and restaurant and to sell the item door-to-door by wagon. He set up the Shredded Wheat Co. in Niagara Falls, New York, which was bought in 1928 by the National Biscuit Co. (today Nabisco Brands Inc.).

Maltex, a toasted-wheat-and-barley cereal made by the Standard Milling Co. of Kansas City, Missouri, appeared in 1899. Wheaties, a wheat-flake cereal, was accidentally created in 1921 when a Minneapolis health theorist named Mennenberg (or perhaps Minniberg) spilled some gruel on a hot stove, making a crisp wheat flake. The Washburn Crosby Co. (changed in 1928 to General Mills Inc. of Minneapolis) bought the rights to this cereal and introduced it in 1924. The same company's corn-puff cereal, Kix, was marketed in 1937, and its ring-shaped oat cereal, Cheerioats, appeared in 1941. (The name was changed in 1945 to Cheerios, marketed as "the first ready-to-eat oat cereal").

In 1935, the Ralston Purina Co. of St. Louis came out with Shredded Ralston, a cereal of small wheat squares in a waffle pattern. Later the name was changed to Wheat Chex, and Rice Chex (1950) and Corn Chex (1958) followed.

Because of criticism of breakfast cereals in the 1960s as being of little nutritional value on their own, many cereal manufacturers have since added vitamins and minerals to their products and cut down on the sugar content, which had become very high in cereals aimed at the children's market. Many of these were named after cartoon or movie characters like Dracula ("Count Chocula"), Frankenstein ("Frankenberry"), and others.

Also in the 1960s, there was a surge of interest in "natural grain" cereals that were supposedly unadulterated by sugar and additives, although many of these contained high amounts of honey, brown sugar, or raisins, as well as dried fruits. The most successful was granola, a new mixture of various cereal grains. Wheat germ was also promoted as an additive, giving a nutritional boost to packaged cereals.

Hot cereals made from grains include cream of wheat, farina, and oatmeal, which are all variations of basic porridge.

Today, annual sales of breakfast cereals are $7.7 billion, with 2.7 billion boxes sold. The industry spends $762 million a year to broadcast 1.3 million TV commercials.

CHALLA. Also "challeh" or "challah." A shaped loaf of white, slightly sweetened egg bread coated with an egg-white glaze. Challa is a traditional Jewish bread served on the Sabbath and assumes different shapes at different holiday feasts: for Shabbat it is braided; for Rosh Hashanah and Yom Kippur it is rounded and might be topped with a dove-wing or ladder pattern made from

the dough. By tradition, when the bread is baked, a small morsel is thrown into the oven as a sacrifice to commemorate the Hebrew term *challa*, "the priest's share," mentioned in the Bible (Numbers 15:20 and Ezekiel 44:30). It first appeared in English print circa 1782.

CHALLA

Dissolve 2 pkgs. yeast in ½ c. warm water. Add a pinch of saffron that has steeped in some hot water to 2 c. boiling water, 3 T. vegetable oil, 1 T. salt, and 1 T. sugar. Cool to lukewarm and add yeast. Add 2 beaten eggs and mix with 3 c. flour. Set aside for 10 min., add enough flour to make a dough, and knead. Shape into a ball, grease the surface, and cover to let rise until doubled. Knead again, then cut dough into two loaves. Cut each half into three long pieces, fasten the ends together, and braid. Place on greased sheet, let rise until doubled, brush with egg white in 1 T. water, bake at 400° for 15 min., reduce to 350°, and bake for 45 min.

CHALUPA. A tortilla formed in the shape of a "little boat" (the word's meaning in Mexican Spanish) and filled with various ingredients, such as shredded pork, beef, poultry, fish, tomatoes, onions, or cheese. The term dates in American print to 1895. Chalupas are often served as an appetizer and are a staple of Mexican American menus.

CHAMPAGNE. Also "bubbly." A sparkling wine. True champagne comes from the Champagne region of France, northeast of Paris, which is centered around the cities of Reims and Epernay. Sparkling wine (as opposed to the still wines produced in the same region) was produced in France as early as the sixteenth century, and experiments with sugar, to produce a secondary fermentation, were done by English scientist Christopher Merret in 1662. Much credit, some perhaps legendary, has been given to a Benedictine monk named Dom Pérignon, cellar master at the Abbey of Hautvillers until his death in 1715, for his work in stopping the bottles from exploding because of the excessive effervescence by using better corks and thicker bottles. Dom Pérignon is also credited with important work in the blending of champagnes.

Champagne became extremely popular at the French court, and soon afterwards it came to be considered a wine for special occasions and lavish dinners. It is still so used to celebrate weddings, anniversaries, births, holidays, and other feasts in America and the rest of the world.

Champagne is made by any of three methods. The first, called the "champagne process" (*méthode champenoise* in French), involves pressing the grapes and fermenting them for about three weeks. The wine is then chilled either by fresh winter air or in refrigerated tanks, and a small amount of sugar dissolved in old wine is added to initiate a second fermentation in the bottle. The yeasts and sugar create additional carbon dioxide and alcohol. Sediment in the bottle is positioned in the neck by a process called "riddling," or turning the bottles periodically to force the sediment down the neck. This process, traditionally done by hand, is now occasionally done by machine. The sediment is then disgorged from the bottle by freezing the neck and removing the cork with the sediment behind it. The wine lost in disgorging is replaced with more wine and with a concentration of sugar dissolved in mature wine. This last addition gives the wine its final degree of sweetness, which ranges from "brut" (very dry) to "extra dry" or "extra sec" (dry) to "dry" or "sec" (somewhat sweeter) to "demi-sec" (quite sweet) to "doux" (very sweet). The bottle is then recorked. About forty U.S. wineries use the *méthode champenoise*.

The second method is called the "Charmat" or "bulk process," invented by French enologist Eugène Charmat in 1907. Fermentation takes place in large tanks, and bottling is done under pressure, all in a continuous process. About 70 percent of American sparkling wines is made by the Charmat method.

The third method is a "transfer process," developed in Germany, in which a second fermentation does take place in the bottle but in which the bottles are not riddled. Instead the cork is removed after being chilled, the sediment is twice filtered out under pressure, and the wine is put into clean bottles.

The first American champagnes were made in 1842, by Nicholas Longworth, from Catawba grapes grown on twelve hundred acres of vineyards near Cincinnati, and these wines enjoyed great success and acclaim even in England, where a writer for the *Illustrated London News* reported that Longworth's sparkling wine "transcends the Champagne of France." There were other attempts after Longworth's, including those of **Ágoston Haraszthy** in California's Sonoma Valley in the 1860s, based on methods learned at France's Moët & Chandon cellars, but his efforts failed. In 1884, French-born **Paul Masson** brought champagne-making equipment to his employer Charles Lefranc in Santa Clara, California, and began making sparkling wine there after the phylloxera blight destroyed the French vineyards. In 1892, Masson founded his own Paul Masson Champagne Co., and his wines won awards both in America and abroad, including honorable mention at the Paris Exposition of 1900. Masson prospered and became known for his lavish parties, at one of which, in 1917, singer Anna Held took a notorious bath in Masson champagne. During Prohibition, Masson continued to make some champagne for "medicinal purposes," but federal agents raided his winery in 1929 and severely crippled the operations there.

Another name in California champagne making of that era is the Korbel brothers, whose winery dates to 1886 but whose first sparkling wines were not made until 1896, by winemaker Franz Hazek, from Prague. Both the Paul Masson Vineyards and Korbel Champagne Cellars thrive today.

New York State also produced champagne in the nineteenth century. In 1860, Charles Davenport Champlin opened the Pleasant Valley Winery in Hammondsport, in the Finger Lakes district. By 1865 Champlin had made the first New York champagne from Catawba grapes, and he won an honorable mention at the 1867 Paris Exposition. In 1870, the winery blended Catawba with Delaware grapes; on tasting it, horticulturist Colonel Marshall Wilder said, "Truly, this will be the great champagne of the West!" (meaning west of Europe), and soon afterwards the wine was called Great Western, which took a gold medal at the 1873 Vienna World Exposition. Great Western was an enormous success, and the company even built a railroad in 1872 to haul its product. It was called the Bath & Hammondsport Railroad but was nicknamed "the Champagne Trail."

Although the French rage at the practice of American wines being labeled "champagne," there is nothing in U.S. law to prevent it. (It is interesting to note that when the French champagne producer Moët

Hennessey built a winery in California's Napa Valley in 1973, the company labeled its product "sparkling wine," refusing to call it champagne.) Americans have also referred to their sparkling wines as "the bubbly" since the 1890s and, more colloquially, "gigglewater" by the 1920s. There are also American wines labeled "sparkling burgundy" or "sparkling moscato" that may or may not possess any of the characteristics associated with the true wines of Burgundy or Italy.

American champagnes have traditionally been fermented somewhat sweeter than their European counterparts, although this has changed in the past decade as drier wines have become more popular. The grapes used in the production of California champagne include the traditional **pinot noir** and **chardonnay** used in France, along with **French Colombard**, **chenin blanc**, Sémillon, Folle Blanche, and others. New York State champagnes are principally made from **Catawba** and Delaware varieties. In 2010, Americans consumed 15.4 million cases of sparkling wine, with 9.2 million produced in the U.S. and, of that, eight million produced in California.

CHAPMAN, JOHN (1774–c. 1845). Pioneer. Familiarly known as "Johnny Appleseed," John Chapman planted fenced-in nurseries throughout Pennsylvania and Ohio, helping settlers to begin and tend their own orchards.

Chapman was born in Leominster, Massachusetts, but facts about his life are nebulous. He may have become a nurseryman in Wilkes-Barres, Pennsylvania, then planted his first apple nursery at Brokenstraw Creek, Pennsylvania, and branched out from there to Ohio. Contrary to popular legend, Chapman did not merely throw or distribute seeds to settlers or plant orchards; rather, he established nurseries of sour apples, the type used to make cider.

As a missionary for the New Church, he also spread the teachings of Emanuel Swedenborg, at times converting Indians, writing of them, "I have traveled more than 4,000 miles about this country, and I have never met with one single insolent Native American."

As an itinerant, Chapman was shabbily dressed, wearing a multipurpose tin pot on his head, and, as a vegetarian ever kind to animals, he was said to douse his campfire if he thought it would disturb them.

The circumstances of his death are vague, reported in an 1845 obituary in the *Sentinel* of Fort Wayne, Indiana, where he is thought to be buried, his grave now consecrated in Johnny Appleseed Park, a national historic site. There is a Johnny Appleseed Museum at Urbana University, in Ohio. In 1948, the Walt Disney Studio made a cartoon about his life, "The Legend of Johnny Appleseed."

Chapman's most recent biographer, Howard Means, in *Johnny Appleseed: The Man, the Myth, the American Story* (2011), concluded that his subject was "almost certainly insane," yet he became one of the most beloved figures in American folkloric history.

CHARDONEL. A white hybrid grape made from a cross between **chardonnay** and **seyval blanc** grapes. It was cultivated in the Finger Lakes region of New York by Cornell University. The grape was first developed in 1953, with vine propagation begun in 1960. The technical name was "Geneva White 9" ("GW9"), and "chardonel" became the official name in 1991.

CHARDONNAY. A white vinifera grape that produces a well-balanced, fruity wine. It is the grape used in the finest whites of Burgundy and within the past twenty years has become the premium white grape of California and the Northwest. Some plantings are also found in the East. The label on American chardonnays may read "pinot chardonnay," but the grape is not now believed to be related to the pinot family. The word was first printed in 1911 in the *Encyclopedia Britannica*.

Chardonnay is the most popular wine in the U.S. by consumption.

CHARLIE TAYLOR. A mixture of sorghum or syrup and bacon grease, used by westerners as a substitute for butter, dating in print to 1933.

CHARLOTTE RUSSE. A French dessert, supposedly created by master chef Marie-Antonin Carème, made in a mold with ladyfingers and Bavarian cream. The term, first in print around 1845, is from the French for "Russian charlotte." (See also **apple charlotte**.)

While this confection is known and made in the U.S., a simple version consisting of a square of sponge cake topped with whipped cream (sometimes with chocolate sprinkles) and a maraschino cherry was also called a "charlotte russe," a variation of which appeared in **Lafcadio Hearn**'s *La Cuisine Créole* (1885). This was a standard item in eastern cities, particularly among urban Jewish Americans (some of whom pronounced the item "charley roose" or "charlotte roosh"), who made it at home or bought it at a pastry shop, where it was set on a frilled cardboard holder whose center could be pushed up so as to reveal more cake as the whipped cream was consumed.

CHASE, LEAH (1923–). Chef, author, TV host. Considered one of the finest exemplars of and inspiration for African American cooking, Leah Chase is the owner of the New Orleans restaurant Dooky Chase.

One of fourteen children, Chase was born in New Orleans but grew up in Madisonville, Louisiana, which had no high school for black children, so she moved to New Orleans at fourteen to attend St. Mary's Academy, which was run by black nuns. Hating New Orleans, she moved back home after graduation to work as a maid, but returned to the city to take menial jobs, including as a waitress in the French Quarter, making a dollar a day plus tips, a job she enjoyed.

In 1945, she married musician Edgar "Dooky" Chase II, whose parents owned Dooky Chase, a sandwich restaurant where she worked, first as hostess, then as chef, adding Creole recipes to the menu, including her famous **gumbo** z'herbes.

The restaurant became so popular that it expanded to take over the entire block in 1984, by which time she was known as the "Queen of Creole Cuisine." During the 1960s, black and white civil-rights activists met at the restaurant at a time when New Orleans was still highly segregated. She was also an early patron of African American artists and still serves on the board of the New Orleans Museum of Fine Arts.

In 2005, Hurricane Katrina shut down Dooky Chase, and the city's restaurant community vowed to help Chase, then eighty-two, reopen by holding a benefit that raised $40,000. The restaurant reopened for takeout in 2007.

Chase's honors include induction into the James Beard Foundation's Who's Who of Food & Beverage in America (2010); a lifetime achievement award from the Southern Foodways Alliance (2003); and several honorary university degrees. The Southern Food and Beverage Museum, in New Orleans, named a permanent gallery in Chase's honor in 2009.

Her books include *The Dooky Chase Cookbook* (1990) and *Down Home Healthy: Family Recipes of Black American Chefs* (1994).

CHASER. A drink imbibed immediately after swallowing another, different drink; for instance, a "beer chaser" would be a glass of **beer** drunk after one has had a jigger of spirits. The term has been in print since 1897.

CHAUDIN. A stuffed pig's stomach that is browned and then cooked in a kettle. It is a traditional Cajun dish, and the word is derived from the French *chaud*, "hot." The pig's stomach itself is called a "ponce" (from the French *panse*, "belly").

CHAURICE. Also "hot sausage." A Creole and Cajun hot pork sausage made with a good deal of chile powder and fresh vegetables. The name probably derives from the spicy, dry Spanish sausage called *chorizo*. It is most often pan-fried and served with beans.

CHAVEZ, CESAR (1927–1993). Called by Robert F. Kennedy "one of the heroic figures of our time," as a leading advocate of farm workers' rights in California, Chavez had an enormous effect on American labor and the way food is harvested, packed, and shipped.

Cesar Estrada Chavez was born in Yuma, Arizona, where early on his father was swindled out of farmland deeded to him. In 1938, the family moved to Oxnard, California, taking jobs as fruit and vegetable pickers, and after finishing eighth grade, Chavez, who said he went to sixty-five different schools throughout his childhood, dropped out to work full-time. He joined the U.S. Navy in 1944 but suffered discrimination as a Mexican American, being given menial jobs on board. Returning to California, he married Helen Favela and moved to San Jose, where he continued as a field laborer.

There, his activism on behalf of his fellow workers began in 1952, as organizer for the Community Service Organization (CSO), targeting police brutality and helping other Chicanos to register to vote. In 1958 he became CSO's national director, but he left because he felt the organization was dominated by non-Hispanic liberals. In 1962, he co-founded the National Farm Workers Association (NFWA), and for five years led a series of labor strikes for higher wages—called La Huelga ("the Strike")—in California, then Texas, Wisconsin, and Ohio. In 1966, the NFWA merged with the Filipino-led Agricultural Workers Organizing Committee to form the United Farm Workers union.

Chavez's most famous act began in 1965, when he organized a national boycott of grapes grown in the San Joaquin Valley until workers' contacts were signed, which the growers did two years later. Despite growing dissent among United Farm Workers members and the rival Teamsters Union, Chavez won passage of the California Agricultural Labor Relations Act, which gave collective bargaining rights to farm workers.

As head of the UFW, Chavez opposed unrestricted immigration, setting up a "wet line" along the U.S.–Mexico border in 1973 to prevent illegal aliens from entering. That year, the first four-year Mexican American college was founded, in Mount Angel, Oregon, named Colegio Cesar Chavez (closed in 1983).

During the 1980s, Chavez, by then taking a salary of only five dollars a week, led a boycott to protest the use of toxic pesticides on grapes. Also at this time, while promoting nonviolence, he began public fasting in protest of Arizona's forbidding of boycotts and strikes. He also became a vegan and voiced his support for animals' rights.

By the mid-1980s, the growers had regained much of their political clout as the union lost much of its power.

Once, when asked what had motivated his activism, Chavez said, "For many years I was a farm worker, a migratory worker, and, well, personally—and I'm being very frank—maybe it's just a matter of trying to even the score." At his funeral, in Delano, California, in 1993, forty thousand mourners followed his plain pine casket.

Both during his life and posthumously, Chavez won many awards, including the Pacem in Terris award (1992) and the Presidential Medal of Freedom, from President Bill Clinton (1993).

The National Chavez Center was opened in 2004 on the UFW campus in Keene, California.

In 2006, California governor Arnold Schwarzenegger inducted Chavez into the California Hall of Fame, located at the California Museum for History, Women and the Arts. There are also many buildings, schools, and streets named after him, and March 31 has been declared Cesar Chavez Day in California, Colorado, and Texas.

CHAYOTE (*Sechium edule*). Also "vegetable pear" and, in Louisiana, "mirliton" (because it resembles a small hornpipe like a kazoo). A squashlike, pear-shaped fruit with a taste similar to cucumber, often served as a vegetable, first in print in 1884. The name derives from the Spanish, from the Nahuatl *chayotli*. Chayote is pale green to dark green in color. It is raised throughout the Caribbean and Latin America as well as in small gardens of Louisiana, where stuffed mirlitons are served as a main dish.

CHEDDAR. A cow's-milk cheese produced in many states, ranging from mild to quite sharp in taste and from white to pumpkin orange in color (the deeper hues come from the American annatto vegetable dye). Americans consume about 9.6 pounds of cheddar annually, most in the form of processed cheese. The name was first used in print in 1661.

The name and the cheese derive from the village of Cheddar, a district of Somerset, England, where it has been made since at least the sixteenth century, but since there was never any legal protection of the name, it may be used by cheese makers anywhere. American cheddars are usually made in blocks, with a firm, not crumbly, texture, or they may be dipped in paraffin. The main varieties are:

COON. Very sharp, aged for more than a year and cured at high temperatures. Coon has a more crumbly texture than other cheddars.

GOAT'S-MILK CHEDDAR. Made in Iowa, this variety is not commonly found in other states. It is rich and has a slightly sweet flavor.

NEW YORK CHEDDAR. Some varieties are white and sharp, like Herkimer cheddar; mild and yellow, like Cooper cheddar; or smoked.

PINEAPPLE CHEDDAR. Made in Litchfield County, Connecticut, pineapple cheddar is now uncommon. Its name derives from its shape as it hangs in the netting during the curing process.

TILLAMOOK. A highly esteemed yellow Oregon cheddar that may be well aged but may also range from mild to sharp.

VERMONT CHEDDAR. A sharp cheese, light yellow in color and distinctive in taste—especially the Crowley variety, which may have a tangy taste after aging. Vermont sage cheddar is flavored with sage.

WISCONSIN CHEDDAR. Wisconsin produces the most cheddar cheeses in the country, ranging from Colby (after the town in Wisconsin where it was created) to longhorn, which is somewhat mild.

In the 1964 World's Fair, in NYC, a six-ton cheddar, made from Wisconsin and Canadian cheese, was exhibited; it was later served in a London restaurant. "Cheddar cheese soup" is said to have been created, or at least popularized, at Emily Shaw's Inn, in Pound Ridge, New York.

Cheddar cheese is often served in New England with a slice of apple pie and coffee.

CHEESE. A food made from the pressed curd of milk. The word is from the Latin *cāseus* and became *cese* in English around the year 1000. Medieval monks raised cheese making to a sophisticated and diverse craft.

Americans developed their own cheese-making talents mainly from English traditions, although German methods had a distinct effect on the production of nineteenth-century cheeses, and Scandinavians who settled in the Midwest brought their own talents to bear. American colonists in the North loved cheese and enjoyed it frequently; the Dutch of the Middle Atlantic colonies ate it twice a day, and it was certainly a staple of the Germans' diet in New Jersey and Pennsylvania. Most of the cheese eaten by English colonists was imported from the mother country, and after the Revolution high duties were placed on imported Cheshires and **cheddar**s.

In the South, where fresh milk quickly soured in the heat, cheese was brought in from the North. As in other countries, cheese was a delectable way to preserve milk in much of the U.S. The basic technique for cheese making begins with mixing milk with rennet, the stomach lining of a slaughtered calf. The rennet curdles the milk, leaving the whey on top to be drawn off. The curds are then pressed into a mold and eaten fresh or aged for flavor and texture. Cheese was used with other foods of the colonial period as barter for goods.

Good cheeses were considered something of a luxury, however, and served as part of celebrations. On New Year's Day 1802, President Thomas Jefferson was presented at the White House with a 1,235-pound Cheshire cheese from Cheshire, Massachusetts. A fourteen-hundred-pound cheese was delivered to President Andrew Jackson's last reception, in 1837—the ten thousand citizens who attended left the cheese and the White House in shambles. It is said that the smell of the cheese lingered in the carpets and furniture for a month afterwards.

The most popular cheese of the nineteenth century was **cheddar**. American varieties of this English cheese were sold in every New England grocery as "store cheese," largely as a result of improved techniques developed by Englishman Joseph Harding. Vermont and New York became famous for their cheddars. In Monterey, California, in the years following the Gold Rush of 1849, farmer David Jacks created a cheese called Monterey Jack that was similar to cheeses made by the Spanish friars. A Wisconsin farmer named Adam Blumer, recently arrived in the U.S. from Switzerland, began making imitation "Swiss cheese," complete with the identifying holes, in about 1850. Brick cheese was made first in Wisconsin, in about 1877; **Liederkranz** was the creation of Swiss-born Emil Frey of Monroe, New York, in 1892. Creditable Limburgers, first made in Belgium, were produced by German immigrants in upstate New York and became a standard item at beer halls, where the drinks were accompanied by large slabs of cheese and pumpernickel bread.

The best-known U.S. cheese is termed, simply, "American cheese" or "American cheddar," so named in the wake of the Revolutionary War, when proud dairy workers scorned English items. This factory-made cheese was further popularized when a Chicago grocery clerk named J. L. Kraft had the idea of wrapping individual portions of cheese in paper for his customers to buy and, as of 1903, of selling his cheese door-to-door by horse and wagon. But wrapping cheese slices in cellophane was perfected by Arnold N. Nawrocki of the Clearfield Cheese Co., in Curwensville, Pennsylvania, in the 1950s. In 1918, Wisconsin cheese maker Hubert Fassbender created a cheese that could be spread at room temperature and sealed it in a small ceramic pot he called a "cheese crock."

Several small commercial cheese producers, led by Laura Chenel of Santa Rosa, California, in the early 1980s, now make goat cheese, and in recent years there has been a growth in sales of mozzarella cheese (primarily used on pizza), low-fat **cottage cheese** (used in diets), and cream cheese, while imported cheeses have become readily available year-round.

Today the U.S. is the largest producer of cheese in the world—10.6 billion pounds in 2011—much of it bought by the federal government as part of a dairy price-support system. Still, the U.S. is only the fifteenth-largest consumer of cheese in the world. Cheese is made in thirty-seven states. Wisconsin, California, Minnesota, and New York are the country's largest cheese producers, making all sorts of traditional cheeses as well as process-cheese spread, pasteurized process-cheese food, and other dairy products.

In 2010, Americans ate 33.3 pounds of cheese per person. The following list details the main varieties of American-made cheeses.

AMERICAN. A form of **cheddar** (1795).

AMISH BABY SWISS. Produced by Ohio Amish farmers; sometimes smoked.

BAKER'S. Made from skim milk, for commercial use.

BANDON. An Oregon-produced cheddar.

BEL PAESE. An Italian cheese (the name means "beautiful country," the title of a children's book by Father Antonio Stoppani) created by Egidio Galbani of Lombardy in 1929, also produced in America.

BIERKÄSE. In Germany, this cheese is called Weisslacker. "Bierkäse," which is made in Wisconsin, means "beer cheese" and is associated with the strong-tasting cheeses, like Limburger, usually consumed with beer.

BLUE. A blue-veined cheese under various names. Originally made from goat's milk by the USDA and the California Experiment Station in 1918, using *Penicillium roqueforti*, American blue cheeses were later made with cow's milk after further successful experiments in universities in Washington and the Midwest.

BRICK. See main entry.

BRIE. A French cheese now made in small amounts by small dairies in the United States. Brie, whose name derives from the region of Brie, in northeastern France, is creamy inside and has a white rind.

CAMEMBERT. A soft-centered cheese originally made in France's Normandy (wherein lies the village of Camembert) but for some years made in the U.S. The best-known is Borden's Military Brand Camembert, made by the Borden Co. in Van Wert, Ohio.

CHEDDAR. See main entry.

CHEESE FOOD. Cheese that has been processed with cream, milk, skim milk, cheese whey, or whey albumin. Under FDA regulations, at least 51 percent of the product must be pure cheese.

COLBY. A granular cheese first made at the end of the nineteenth century by the Steinwand family in Colby, Wisconsin. Colby is now made outside the U.S. as well (1940). FDA standards require that it contain not less than 50 percent milk fat.

COON. A sharp American cheddar, usually aged a year or more.

CORNHUSKER. Developed by the Agricultural Experiment Station at the University of Nebraska (nicknamed the "Cornhusker State") in about 1940, this cheese is similar to colby.

COTTAGE CHEESE. See main entry.

COUGAR GOLD. A form of cheddar first made at the State University of Washington at Pullman.

CREAM CHEESE. See main entry.

CREOLE. A very rich and moist New Orleans cheese made from clabber and heavy cream.

CUP. A cheese made in Pennsylvania Dutch country, whose name derives from the white china cups in which it was carried to market. According to Evan Jones in *The World of Cheese* (1979), "Berks Cup Cheese is the result of baking curds in the oven, with new curds added each day for a week. The baked curds are poured into a heated pan and simmered slowly to a boil, without stirring; salt, cream, butter, and baking soda are added, and the mixture is boiled 15 minutes, during which time eggs are mixed into the curds. The cheese is cooled in cups."

COLD PACK. A cheese made from one or more varieties of cheddar. Flavorings, such as wine, are sometimes added to this unheated, tangy cheese, which may also be called "club cheese."

EDAM. Originally a cheese of Holland, Edam is formed into a ball and usually coated with a red covering of paraffin or other substances. It must contain not less than 40 percent milk fat.

FARMER. Also "farmer's." A general term applied to fresh cottage cheese, although there are regional farmer cheeses of firmer, drier textures (1945).

FETA. A crumbly white cheese made in the style of Greek goat's-milk cheese, although American varieties are more often made from cow's milk (1935). After curds are formed, the cheese is pickled in a brine solution. The *word* feta is from the Greek.

GOAT. Also "goat's." Called *chèvre* in France, this is a fresh, sourish cheese made from goat milk by about a hundred producers in states around the U.S., including California, Iowa, New Jersey, and Pennsylvania.

GOLD-N-RICH. A semisoft loaf developed from Port Salut cheese at Elgin, Illinois.

GORGONZOLA. A crumbly, blue-veined cheese of Italian origin (named after a town in Piedmont where the cheese was first produced), Gorgonzola is injected with *Penicillium glaucum*. The American version must contain at least 50 percent milk fat.

GOUDA. Named after a Dutch town, this is a firm cheese formed into a compressed sphere. It is similar to Edam and must contain not less than 46 percent fat solids.

HERKIMER. An American cheddar made in New York's Herkimer County.

LIEDERKRANZ. See main entry.

LIMBURGER. A strong cheese of Belgian origins (it is named for the town of Limburg), it was made popular by German cheese makers of the nineteenth century and served at beer halls with pumpernickel bread, onions, and drafts of beer (1810).

LONGHORN. An American cheddar.

MAYTAG BLUE. See main entry.

MINNESOTA SLIM. An orange, loose-textured cheese, good for melting, that was developed by the University of Minnesota. It was named at the Lund Market, in Minneapolis.

MONTEREY JACK. A mild cheese that originated in Monterey, California, it resembles the cheeses made by early Spanish friars in that territory and is named after David Jacks, who first made the cheese in 1849, just after the start of California's Gold Rush. It is widely used as a topping for Mexican American dishes.

MOSSHOLDER'S. First developed by Otto Mossholder in 1925 in Appleton, Wisconsin, this cow's-milk cheese has a pronounced flavor and a semisoft, creamy texture.

MOZZARELLA. Of Italian origins, first in English print as of 1911, this fresh white cow's-milk cheese comes in two forms: a mild, unsalted fresh cheese kept in water (commonly made in Italian American groceries) and a firmer, salted cheese, primarily made for pizza toppings. Both must contain at least 45 percent milk fat.

MUENSTER. Of Alsatian origins, this cheese was developed in monasteries by medieval monks (the word "Muenster" derives from the Latin *monasterium*). In the U.S. (where it is sometimes spelled "munster"), the cheese must contain not less than 50 percent milk fat. The first appearance in English was in 1858.

NUWORLD. A white-mold cheese developed by the universities of Wisconsin and Minnesota after World War II. It must contain at least 50 percent milk fat.

PARMESAN. This hard, well-aged cheese takes its name—first in print in 1519—from the Italian city of Parma. In Italy there are strict regulations as to region, quality, and aging of the cheese (which they call Parmigiano), whereas in the U.S., domestic Parmesan is used primarily for grating and must contain no less than 32 percent milk fat.

PECORINO. Although in Italy this cheese is made from sheep's milk (the name is from the Italian *pecora*, "sheep"), U.S. versions are made from cow's milk and are used primarily as grating cheeses that have a very sharp, tangy flavor.

PINEAPPLE. An extra-rich cheddar cheese made in a wooden mold so as to resemble the shape of a pineapple, this cheese originated in NYC, with its first mention in print in 1830, though similar cheeses had been produced in England earlier. In 1808, Lewis M. Norton of Goshen, Connecticut, received a patent for the cheese, and it was produced there until 1904. A relative named Eugene Norton bought rights to the company, however, and built a factory in Attica, New York, which closed in 1918 when Kraft Foods bought the patent. Another version of pineapple cheese was produced by O. A. Weatherly in Milford, New York, until 1945, when his company was sold to Dairylea, which produced the cheese for another decade, although the equipment was moved to Wisconsin, where a form of the cheese continued to be made.

PROCESS. Also "processed." A product made from melting various kinds of cheeses with emulsifiers, acids, flavorings, and colorings to produce a smooth consistency (1915). "Process-cheese food" contains less real cheese than "process-cheese spread," whereas the latter has more moisture and less butterfat than cheese.

RICOTTA. A fresh, moist white cheese originating in Italy, where its name means "recooked." Ricotta is similar to cottage cheese and most often used in Italian American cookery.

ROMANO. A hard grating cheese whose name derives from the Italian capital. American versions tend to be quite salty and are used mostly on pasta dishes (1905).

SWISS. A generic term for all imitations of the original Swiss Emmentaler (1815). The words "imported Swiss" on a label mean only that the cheese is of this type and not necessarily made in Switzerland. American Swiss cheese is aged about four months, has holes, and was created by Wisconsin's Adam Blumer in about 1850.

TELEME JACK. A melting cheese said to have originated around 1922, by makers of Monterey Jack who had immigrated from Greece. The cheese was named after a Romanian brine-cured cheese.

TILLAMOOK. An American cheddar made in Oregon's Tillamook County.

TRAPPIST. A generic term for cheeses made by the monks of the Trappist order. A form of this cheese is made by Trappists near Gethsemane, Kentucky.

CHEESECAKE. A dessert cake or pie made with cream cheese, cottage cheese, or ricotta. Various forms of cheesecake have been popular for centuries. The first mention in print of such a dessert dates to 1440, and recipes for such a dish can be found throughout the eighteenth and nineteenth centuries.

American cheesecakes are primarily of two varieties. "Jewish cheesecake" has a smooth cream cheese filling, commonly set on a graham cracker crust. Because of their association with NYC restaurants and bakeries, such items are commonly called "New York cheesecake," especially outside of NYC. Particularly light examples are sometimes called "French cheesecake." Such examples are sometimes topped with fruit, which itself may be glazed with jelly. Jewish cheesecakes have become a staple of American steakhouses. One of the most famous cheesecakes of this type is that associated with Lindy's restaurant, in NYC, now a trademarked name of Lindy's Food Products of New York. The supposed recipe for the original Lindy's cheesecake is given below.

The second basic variety is the "Italian cheesecake," usually made from ricotta cheese and set on a pastry crust and commonly containing bits of candied fruit.

LINDY'S CHEESECAKE

Combine 1 c. flour, ¼ c. sugar, 1 t. grated lemon rind, and 1 t. vanilla in a large bowl. Make a well in the center and add 1 egg yolk and ¼ lb. softened butter, adding water if necessary to make a pliable dough. Wrap in waxed paper and chill 1 hr. Meanwhile, with an electric mixer, combine 2 ½ lb. cream cheese, 1 ¾ c. sugar, 3 T. flour, and ½ t. each of grated orange and lemon rind. Add 5 whole eggs, 2 egg yolks, ¼ c. vanilla, and beat well. Add ¼ c. heavy cream and blend thoroughly. Butter the sides and bottom of a 9-in. springform pan. Roll out one third of the dough to ⅛-in. thickness and mold into the pan's bottom. Bake at 400° for 15 min. until lightly browned, then cool. Place the top of the pan over the base, roll the remaining dough to a ⅛-in. thickness, cut into strips, and press into the pan to line the sides completely. Pour in the cheese mixture, bake for 10 min. at 550°, reduce heat to 200°, and continue to bake for 1 hr.

ITALIAN CHEESECAKE

Combine 2 c. flour sifted with ½ t. salt, cut in 1 c. butter to make a coarse meal. Make a well in the center and add 2 beaten egg yolks and 1–2 T. cold water to make a soft, pliable dough. Roll to a thickness of ¼ in., place in a buttered pan, trim edges, and set aside. Beat 4 eggs until light in color, gradually adding 1 c. sugar. Combine 3 c. ricotta cheese, ¼ c. flour, 2 t. candied fruit, 2 T. each of grated lemon and orange rind, 1 T. vanilla, and ⅛ t. salt. Beat in egg mixture till smooth, pour into pastry, and bake for 1 hr. at 350°. Cool before serving. If desired, dust with confectioners' sugar.

CHENIN BLANC. A white vinifera grape that makes a slightly spicy wine that is sometimes slightly sweet. It is an important grape in France's Loire Valley and has been used by high-volume California wineries. Before Prohibition, California winemakers referred to the grape as "white zinfandel," and later as "white pinot." Then, in 1955, the Charles Krug winery began making the varietal under the name "chenin blanc," which has since been adapted as standard in the industry.

CHERIMOYA (*Annona cherimola*). A South American fruit with scalelike skin and soft flesh. The word is from American Spanish and dates in print to 1736. It is also called the "custard apple," although properly that fruit is *A. reticulata*. It is now being grown in California and eaten cold or made into a custard.

CHERRIES JUBILEE. A dessert made with black cherries flambéed with kirsch or brandy, then spooned over vanilla ice cream. The dish is a standard continental menu item, especially fashionable from the 1930s through the 1960s in deluxe restaurants, and also a popular dinner-party dish of the same period. The origins of the dish are unknown, but it has been credited to chef Georges Auguste Escoffier as a celebratory dish for Queen Victoria for either her Golden Jubilee, in 1887 or her Diamond Jubilee, in 1897. *Larousse Gastronomique* lists a dish of cherries called *cérises jubilées* cooked with a sugar syrup, then arranged in small ramekins and flamed with kirsch.

CHERRIES JUBILEE

Combine 1 c. sugar and 2 c. water in a saucepan and bring to a boil. Poach 1½ lb. pitted black cherries in the sugar syrup until tender. Drain the cherries and reserve 1 c. of the syrup. Add 1 T. cornstarch to the syrup, warm until somewhat thickened, add cherries. Warm ½ c. kirsch or brandy slightly in a saucepan, pour over cherries, and carefully ignite with a match. Serve over vanilla ice cream.

CHERRY. Any of a variety of trees in the genus *Prunus*, but especially *P. avium*, the "sweet cherry," bearing small red berries that are eaten raw, baked in pies, and used in relishes, ice creams, cordials, and brandies and as flavorings. The word *cherry* is from the Greek *kerásos*, which in Middle English became *chery*.

The cherry originated in Asia but was widely dispersed throughout Europe and North America in prehistoric times. European colonists found wild cherries in America and cultivated them, also crossbreeding them with European varieties.

Today the U.S. is the leading producer of cherries, with 85 percent of the country's crop grown in Michigan, California, Oregon, and Washington. The total crop is sold as follows: 44 percent canned, 35 percent fresh, 20 percent dried, 1 percent frozen. The leading variety is the "Bing" cherry, developed in 1875 by Seth Luelling in Milwaukie, Oregon, and named, according to Janie Hibler, in *Dungeness Crabs and Blackberry Cobblers* (1991), after Luelling's Manchurian foreman. Other principal varieties include the sweet cherry Lambert and the tart cherries Early Richmond, English Morello, and Montmorency. Sour cherries are called "pie cherries" because they are so suitable for pie making. See also **maraschino**.

CHERRYBARB. A drink of brandy and sugar.

CHERRY SOUP. A midwestern soup of Scandinavian and Eastern European origins. It is traditionally served cold in the summer but may be served hot or cold in the winter.

CHERVIL (*Anthriscus cerefolium*). An aromatic plant used in soups and salads. It originated in Russia, though the name is from the Greek *khaiéphullon*, and the herb is raised mostly in the northeastern U.S.

CHESS PIE. Also "chess-cake pie" and "chess tart." A simple egg-butter-and-sugar pie (commonly made with buttermilk), long associated with the South. Meringue is sometimes added as a topping. The origin of the name has eluded a definitive answer. Some believe it may be a derivation of "cheese pie," although traditional chess pies do not contain cheese of any kind. According to Sarah Belk, in *Around the Southern Table* (1991), old cookbooks often referred to "cheese" cakes and pies that did not actually contain cheese, using the term to describe the curdlike texture of the confection, and she cited a selection of cheeseless "cheese" pastries in *Housekeeping in Old Virginia* (1979) made with eggs, sugar, butter, milk, and lemon juice—ingredients often used in a chess pie. Belk also cited Elizabeth Hedgecock Sparks, author of *North Carolina and Old Salem Cookery* (1955), who said chess pie was "an old, old tart which may have obtained its name from the town of Chester, England." A recipe for "Old Virginia Chess Cakes," which are actually filled pies, is printed in the *World Famous Chefs' Cook Book* (1939), by Ford Naylor.

In *Southern Food* (1987) **John Egerton** offered two stories as to why the confection is called chess pie. The first involves a mutation of "chest pie," that is, a pie kept in a piece of furniture called a "pie chest" (or "pie safe"), which was a cupboard with perforated tin panels to allow air flow. The other, more folkloric story involves an unknown southern housewife who, when asked what kind of pie it was, answered, "It's jes' pie." The earliest printed reference to the pie was in a cookbook published by the Fort Worth Women's Club in 1928.

Belk noted that chess pies made with white sugar were called "sugar pies," those with brown sugar "brown-sugar pies," and those with raisins "Osgood" pies (an elision of "oh-so-good").

CHESS PIE

Beat 3 eggs for 1 min., gradually add 1 ½ c. sugar, 3 T. cooled melted butter, ⅓ c. buttermilk, ½ t. salt, and ½ t. vanilla extract. Mix well and pour into a 9-in. pie shell. Bake in 375° oven for 15 min., reduce heat to 250°, and bake 20 min., until set. Top with meringue and brown if desired.

CHESTNUT. Any of a variety of trees in the genus *Castanea* that bear a sweet bud eaten roasted, boiled, in a stuffing, or as a flavoring. The name is from the Greek *kastenea*, first in English print in 1519.

The first American colonists found the land covered with tall American chestnut trees (*C. dentata*) whose nuts were eaten by the Indians, but the Europeans also brought their own varieties with them. Far East varieties were planted in 1904 on Long Island, New York, which carried a blight (*Endothia parasitica*) that virtually wiped out the native chestnut trees over the next three decades, so that most chestnuts today are still imported from Europe, especially the "Spanish chestnut" (*C. sativa*) and the "Chinese chestnut" (*C. mollissima*), this last now grown in the United States. Efforts are currently being made in New York State to create a new fungus-resistant hybrid that is 99 percent American chestnut and 1 percent Chinese chestnut.

CHEWING GUM. A sweet, flavored chewable substance made from "chicle" (from the Nahuatl *chictli*), a gummy juice of the tropical evergreen, enjoyed as an idle snack. The word "gum" is from Middle English *gomme*. Its first appearance in English was in 1850.

Americans had long chewed gum resins from trees, as they had seen the Indians do. Spruce gum was particularly popular in the early eighteenth century and is mentioned in Mark Twain's 1876 novel *Tom Sawyer*, wherein Tom and Becky pass a single piece of "chewing gum" (a term that saw print as of 1755) back and forth. The first commercial gum was made around 1755, by John Curtis, who called it State of Maine Pure Spruce Gum. In the 1870s, a chewing gum was created from chicle by a Staten Island, New York, inventor named Thomas Adams, who had observed the exiled Mexican general Antonio Lopez de Santa Ana chewing the substance (which the general had hoped could be made into a rubber substitute).

Adams called his invention Adams' New York No. 1, which he persuaded a Hoboken, New Jersey, druggist to sell for a penny per piece. Adams's son, Thomas Jr., sold the product as far as the Mississippi, as "Adams' New York Gum—Snapping and Stretching," and introduced the first flavored gums—sassafras and licorice (which he called Black Jack).

In the 1880s, William White produced the first corn-syrup-based, peppermint-flavored, flat sticks of gum, called Yucatan, and by the turn of the century New Yorkers could buy chewing gum from the new **vending machines** on railroad platforms and in "gumball machines." A candy-coated gum named Chiclet was the creation of Henry Fleer, whose brother Frank made the first "bubble gum," in 1906, which could be blown into a bubble—though not until 1928 did an accountant named Walter Diemer come up with a formula, which he sold to Fleer, that wouldn't stick to the blower's face. The new gum was at first called Blibber-Blubber, then Dubble Bubble. The Topps Chewing Gum Co. produced another bubble gum in 1947, called Bazooka, so named because its tubular length resembled the World War II weapon.

The man who would become the world's largest maker of chewing gum was William Wrigley, whose brands were called Spearmint (introduced in 1892), Juicy Fruit, and Doublemint.

A "low-sugar gum" called Dentyne (a contraction of the words "dental hygiene") was invented in 1899 by drugstore manager Franklin V. Canning, and sugarless gum was first sold as of 1969.

One of the most popular pastimes of American children was collecting bubble-gum trading cards, which were packed inside the gum packages and which featured pictures of popular sports figures and movie and television heroes. Trading cards were first packed with cigarettes in 1879, but by the 1880s Old Judge Tobacco was printing up "baseball cards" with pictures of baseball players on them. In 1951, the Topps Chewing Gum Co. came out with a line of Bazooka gum packaged with a card series called "Freedom's War," depicting scenes from the Korean War; that same year, Topps also began issuing packages with baseball cards in them, and these now sell at a rate of 500 million each year. Baseball cards have since become a much sought-after collector's item that may sell for thousands of dollars apiece at auction.

Americans' per capita annual consumption of chewing gum is 1.8 pounds—three hundred sticks per year—with about 100,000 tons consumed, in an industry whose annual sales are $2 billion.

CHIANG, CECILIA (1920–). Restaurateur, chef. At Cecilia Chiang's San Francisco restaurant The Mandarin, she was one of the first to introduce authentic Chinese food to America.

Chiang was born near Shanghai to a wealthy family who enjoyed elaborate meals she was not allowed to see the cooks prepare. When Japan occupied the region in 1942, she and her sister escaped to Chongqing, where she married Chiang Liang and the two returned to Shanghai. There their two children were born, and for the remainder of the war, she worked as a spy for the U.S. Office of Strategic Services.

When the Chinese Communists came to power, Chiang fled to Tokyo (1949), while her parents and sister stayed behind, dying in squalor. Chiang then moved to San Francisco in 1958, where with her own money she secured a deposit for friends who wanted to open a restaurant in Chinatown but backed out of the deal, leaving Chiang to take over the business. There, she was discriminated against by merchants and suppliers because she was a woman. Chiang had little success with her northern Chinese menu, which listed two hundred dishes, at a time when **egg foo yung** and **chow mein** were staples in Chinatown restaurants. But powerful *San Francisco Chronicle* columnist Herb Caen raved about the restaurant, helping ensure its success.

She moved the restaurant in 1968, to the tourist-driven Ghirardelli Square, and The Mandarin became one of the city's most elegantly appointed dining spots, with three hundred seats, and Chiang monitoring every detail and attending to every guest. Here she introduced guests to new dishes like Szechuan kung pao chicken and twice-cooked pork, tea-smoked duck, and beggar's chicken, baked in clay.

Chiang sold the restaurant in 1991 (it closed in 2006) and retired to devote herself to charitable causes, especially the Chinese American International School. Her son Philip ran a branch of The Mandarin in Beverly Hills and went on to co-found the P.F. Chang's restaurant chain.

Of her own legacy, Chiang told the *Chronicle* in 2007 that the city's Chinatown restaurateurs never changed anything as long as they remained profitable: "I think they're getting worse, not better. It makes me sick inside....I think I changed what average people know about Chinese food. They didn't know China was such a big country."

In 1974, Chiang wrote a memoir titled *The Mandarin Way*, but later said she had omitted material about life in Communist China, because she still had family there. A second, more comprehensive memoir, *The Seventh Daughter*, written with Lisa Weiss, appeared in 2007.

See also **Chinese American food**.

CHICAGO. A slang term for pineapple or, as in "Chicago sundae," a sundae made with pineapple, so called because of the tendency of Chicago gangsters during Prohibition to use hand grenades called "pineapples." A jelly-filled doughnut is often called a "Chicago" in the Midwest.

CHICKEN (*Gallus domesticus*). A common name for the domestic fowl raised throughout the world as a food and cooked in every conceivable way, except as a dessert. The word is from the Old English *cícen*.

The domesticated chicken first appeared around 2000 B.C. in India, and was brought to America by Columbus in 1493. In Hawaii, European travelers found a domesticated fowl called the *moa*, a descendant of a wild jungle fowl probably brought from Malaysia. In 1826, however, the ship *Wellington* docked in Hawaii, dumping its old water into the harbor. This water contained a mosquito larva carrying a bird pox, called "bumblefoot," that immediately infected the island's birds and devastated the chicken population.

Early on in American history, chickens were brought to the colonies but were used not as everyday foods but as egg layers, although in the nineteenth century, poultry breeding resulted in some excellent stocks that increased yields. The "Plymouth Rock" breed was noted in 1849, and the "Wyandotte" received its name from a Mr. Houdette of Waltham, Massachusetts, in 1883. The state bird of Rhode Island, the "Rhode Island Red," was developed by William Tripp of Little Compton, Rhode Island, in 1902, by crossing a "Brown Leghorn" with a "Malay Hen," while the "Rhode Island White" was developed in 1926, at a time when factory production of chickens made it far more available and cheaper than ever before for American cooks, who had previously reserved it as a special Sunday dinner dish. Today Americans consume more than eighty pounds of chicken per capita each year.

The "Cornish game hen" was developed from a Plymouth Rock chicken and a "Cornish game cock" and weighs between one and two pounds. A "squab chicken" is not a true squab, but is instead a very small chicken weighing between three-quarters and one and a half pounds. "Chickalona" is a kind of chicken **bologna**, developed from chicken necks and backs by Cornell University's poultry department.

Federal law mandates the following standards for chickens: A "broiler," also known as a "fryer," is a bird two and a half to four pounds. A "roaster" weighs between five and seven pounds. A "capon" ranges up to ten pounds. A "hen," "stewing hen," or "boiling fowl" is above ten pounds and is a year and a half old. "Deedie" is a southern colloquialism for a young chicken.

The Department of Agriculture grades chickens "A" (the best and most readily found in markets), "B," and "C." They are sold "fresh-killed"—which may actually mean they have been shipped at about the standard 35-degree refrigerator temperature or in shaved ice—or "deep-chilled" at 30 degrees, as well as frozen, canned, and freeze-dried.

Over the past twenty years, there has been an increase in small producers raising "free range" chickens, which are not penned and fed processed feed but allowed to peck for their food outside. There has also been a decrease or elimination at such farms in the amount of antibiotics and unnatural chemicals used in raising the chickens.

Americans eat about 74.4 pounds per capita of chicken a year (and about 245 eggs), preparing the fowl in many ways, including such standard dishes as **southern fried chicken**, **chicken à la king**, **chicken Tetrazzini**, **chicken cacciatore**, **country captain**, and **barbecue chicken**.

CHICKEN À LA KING. A dish of chicken with a cream sauce, garnished with pimientos. Several theories as to the dish's origins date from the late nineteenth century. One credits NYC's Brighton Beach Hotel, where chef George Greenwald supposedly made it for the proprietors, Mr. and Mrs. E. Clark King III. Chef Charles Ranhofer of Delmonico's restaurant, in NYC, suggested that Foxhall P. Keene, son of Wall Street broker and sportsman James R. Keene, came up with the idea at Delmonico's in the 1880s. A third story credits James R. Keene himself as the namesake, and the place and time of origin as Claridge's restaurant, in London, after Keene's horse won the 1881 Grand Prix. However the dish got its name, first mentioned in print in 1911, it became a standard luncheon item in the decades that followed, often served from a chafing dish, with rice or on a pastry shell.

CHICKEN À LA KING

In a saucepan blend 4 T. flour with 4 T. butter and cook for about 2 min. Add 2 c. chicken broth and 2 c. light cream, thicken, and remove from heat. In a skillet sauté 1 T. minced onion, ¼ lb. sliced mushrooms, and 1 sweet green pepper cut into strips. Add ½ c. chopped pimiento and 3 c. diced cooked chicken. Season with salt and pepper. Spoon a little sauce into 2 beaten egg yolks, then stir eggs and the rest of the sauce into chicken mixture and cook over low heat for 1 min. Remove from heat and stir in ½ c. sherry and ½ c. blanched toasted almonds. Serve on toast, rice, or pastry shells. Serves 6.

CHICKEN BOG. North Carolina slang for a chicken **pilau** made with rice and sausage. The name may derive from the fact that a bog is a section of wet, soggy ground, and the chicken in this dish would be mixed with wet, soggy rice. Loris, South Carolina, holds a Great Loris Bog-Off Festival cooking competition each year.

CHICKENBURGER. A patty of ground chicken, broiled, grilled, or fried to resemble a beef **hamburger.** The chickenburger followed the latter sometime in the first quarter of this century.

CHICKEN CACCIATORE. Also "chicken alla cacciatore." A dish of chicken cooked with mushrooms and, often, tomato sauce. It is an **Italian American** specialty whose name means "chicken hunter's style," but there is no traditional dish by this name in Italy. Chicken cacciatore has appeared on Italian American menus since at least the 1930s.

CHICKEN CACCIATORE

Cut a chicken into several pieces, dredge in flour, and sauté in 3 T. olive oil. Add 1 lb. sliced mushrooms and cook together. Add 1 sliced onion, then 1 ½ c. seasoned tomato sauce and salt and pepper. Cook, covered, until chicken is tender.

CHICKEN DIVAN. A dish of sliced chicken breast poached in chicken broth and served on broccoli with a sherry-laced cream-and-cheese sauce. The chicken is placed in a casserole, layered with the broccoli spears, topped with the sauce, and set briefly under a broiler until browned. It was created in the 1930s at the Divan Parisien Restaurant, in NYC (also credited with introducing **broccoli** to the U.S.).

CHICKEN FIXINGS. Also "chicken fixins." A western colloquialism for a fancy chicken dinner, and, by extension, any fancy food. The term dates in print to 1838.

CHICKEN FRANCESE. An Italian American dish of sautéed chicken cutlets with a lemon-butter sauce. The word *francese* is Italian for "French style," although there is no specific dish by this name in either Italian or French cookery. It is also made as "**veal francese.**"

CHICKEN FRANCESE

In a shallow bowl beat together 2 eggs with ½ c. milk and 3 T. minced parsley. Dredge 2 lb. pounded, flattened chicken cutlets in flour, then dip into egg mixture. Sauté in hot oil until golden brown, turn, and sauté the other side the same way. Remove from pan and drain on paper. In another pan melt ⅓ c. butter, add ½ c. chicken broth, squeeze in 3 T. lemon juice, and add salt and pepper to taste. Add the chicken cutlets and cook until thoroughly heated through.

CHICKEN-FRIED STEAK. Also "chicken-fry steak." A beefsteak that has been tenderized by pounding, coated with flour or batter, and fried crisp. Usually a lesser cut of beef is used. The name refers to the style of cooking, which is much the same as for **southern fried chicken**. Chicken-fried steak has been a staple dish of the South, Southwest, and Midwest for decades, although it dates in print only to 1952.

CHICKEN-FRIED STEAK

Pound until thin and tender 4 slices of round steak. Dip in a mixture of 1 beaten egg and 1 c. milk, dredge in flour seasoned with salt and pepper, and fry in shortening or other oil until crisp and well done. Pour off the oil. Sprinkle 1 T. flour into skillet and cook with pan drippings until browned. Add 1 c. milk and bring to boil, then lower to simmer and cook until thickened. Pour gravy over steaks.

CHICKEN-IN-THE-SHELL. A dish of chicken in a creamed mushroom sauce served in a cockleshell; well known in San Francisco at the turn of the last century, it was first served at the Iron House, on Montgomery Street.

CHICKEN RAPHAEL WEILL. A dish of chicken parts sautéed in butter, then simmered in chicken broth and white wine and finished with a sauce of heavy cream, sherry, and egg yolks. The dish dates to the turn of the century in San Francisco and is named after its creator, Raphael Weill (1837–1920), owner of that city's White House department store, opened in 1870. Weill often cooked Sunday breakfast as a founding member of the Bohemian Club, for which he might well have created the dish. He might also have served it at the White House's tea room.

CHICKEN TETRAZZINI. A dish of chicken (though turkey is often substituted) in a cream sauce, served over spaghetti and browned in the oven with bread crumbs and Parmesan cheese. It is named after the Italian coloratura soprano opera singer Luisa Tetrazzini (1871–1940), who was extremely popular in the U.S. after 1908. It is not known when or where the dish was created, though some say it was in San Francisco (the dish was first mentioned in print in 1931), and Tetrazzini herself does not mention the dish in her autobiography, *My Life of Song* (1921). The rather stout singer did write of her eating habits, however: "I eat the plainest food always, and naturally, being Italian, I prefer the foods of my native land.…I allow the tempting pastry, the rich and over-spiced patty, to pass by untouched, consoling myself with fruit and fresh vegetables."

CHICKEN TETRAZZINI

In a saucepan make a roux of 4 T. flour and 4 T. butter, add 2 c. heavy cream and 1 c. chicken broth, stir, and cook until thickened. Remove from heat, blend in 3 c. cooked chicken meat cut into small pieces. In a buttered dish place ¾ lb. cooked buttered spaghetti, pour chicken mixture on top, spread with bread crumbs and Parmesan cheese, and brown in oven or under broiler. Serves 6.

CHICKEN VESUVIO. An Italian American dish of chicken sautéed with garlic, olive oil, oregano, lemon, and wine, piled with potato wedges. According to an article in *Nation's Restaurant News*, the dish was "created in Chicago by a Neapolitan cook shortly after World War II." It has become a staple item in Italian American restaurants in that city. Although it is obviously named after the volcano Mount Vesuvius, near Naples, Italy, there are several stories as to the reasons why. It has been speculated that the name derives from the amount of smoke produced in the cooking process when the wine is added to the hot pan. But, according to *The Italian Cookbook*, published by the Culinary Arts Institute of Chicago in 1954, "the rim of this casserole is topped with deep-fried potatoes and seems to be erupting flavorful fried chicken."

CHICKEN VESUVIO

In a large skillet brown a 2–3 lb. chicken cut up into pieces in ½ c. olive oil. Remove the chicken pieces from skillet and place in a single layer in a large casserole dish. Drain all but 2 T. olive oil from skillet, sauté 2 cloves of sliced garlic, and stir in ½ c. marsala wine, the juice of half a lemon, 1 t. oregano, and 1 t. chopped parsley. Reduce for 1 min. Pour over chicken and bake at 325° for 45 min., turning the chicken pieces once. When chicken is done, place fried potatoes around the rim of the baking dish to form the look of a volcano.

CHICKPEA (*Cicer arietinum*). The hard seed of a plant indigenous to the Mediterranean and central Asia. The chickpea is not actually a pea, though both are of the same subfamily, *Papilionoideae*. The name for the seed comes from the Latin, *cicer*, but in the U.S., where it was introduced by Hispanics, it is called a "garbanzo" (a word that worked its way from the Latin *ervum*, "bitter vetch," through Old Spanish *arvanço*, to Spanish *garbanzo*). The word was first printed in 1548, and first in American print in 1844. Chickpeas are usually soaked for several hours, roasted, and eaten as a snack or put into stews and salads.

CHICORY. American nomenclature is very confusing for this salad green, *Cichorium intybus*, with its curly leaves and bright blue flowers (it is sometimes called "blue sailors"). Chicory is quite bitter and is often mixed with other salad greens.

The same plant's roots are dried and ground into a granular powder, often referred to as "succory," that resembles coffee and is used as an additive to or substitute for real coffee in Creole and Cajun cooking, a legacy of the French influence on these cuisines.

The confusion begins with what Americans call "endive," which is a form of *C. intybus* cultivated to produce silky white leaves for salad and which is often referred to as "Belgian endive" or "witloof." The Belgians, however, call that *chicon*.

True endive is another variety, *C. endivia*, with curly, succulent leaves, more commonly known in America as "escarole" (from the Italian *scarola*), first in print in 1822.

CHICORY COFFEE. Also "chicken coffee." Adding chicory to coffee began in New Orleans during the food-scarce Civil War. Chicory adds a bitterness to coffee, which may be moderated with milk to make **café au lait**, although morning coffee tends to be black, café noir. In New Orleans, the coffee and chicory can be bought already blended into light or dark mixtures, and it is meant to be made by a drip method. Most of this chicory is imported from Spain. There is an old saying among Catholic Creoles in New Orleans to the effect that "good coffee and the Protestant religion can seldom if ever be found together." And the same people are fond of the description of chicory coffee as being "black as the devil, strong as death, sweet as love, hot as hell!"

CHIEF COOK AND BOTTLE WASHER. A slang phrase, dating back to 1840 in print, for a handyman or someone who can do many menial jobs well.

CHIFFON. A very light, sweet, fluffy filling for a pie, cake, or pudding. The word is from the French, meaning "rag," and ultimately from the Middle English word *chip*, as "chiffon" also refers to pieces of sheer, delicate ribbon or fabric for women's clothing.

Chiffon pie is first mentioned in American print in 1929, as a "chiffon pumpkin pie" in the *Beverly Hills Women's Club's Fashions in Foods*. The 1931 edition of Irma S. Rombauer's *Joy of Cooking* gave a recipe for lemon chiffon, and the *Better Homes and Gardens Heritage Cook Book* (1975) said that "chiffon cake was invented by a professional baker and introduced in May 1948. Made with cooking oil instead of solid shortening and beaten—not creamed—this light cake was the first new cake to have been developed in one hundred years of baking." Other authorities, however, credit an amateur baker with creating the confection in 1927. In the 1953 cookbook *250 Superb Pastries*, edited by Ruth Berolzheimer of the Culinary Arts Institute, forty chiffon recipes are given.

CHILD, JULIA (1912–2004). Author, cooking teacher, media personality. No one in American gastronomy has ever achieved the renown and respect of the public and her peers like Julia Carolyn McWilliams Child, whose work advancing the techniques of French cuisine—and later American cuisine—had indelible effects on both professional and home cooks.

Born in Pasadena, California—her father a land developer, her mother heiress to a paper company fortune—Julia grew up to be six feet two inches tall and athletic, attending Smith College, in Northampton, Massachusetts, as a history major, class of 1934. After graduation she moved to New York City, where she wrote ad copy for the W&J Sloane furnishings company, then returned to California to work at the company's branch in Los Angeles.

In 1941, she joined the Office of Strategic Services, first as a typist and then as a researcher in the Secret Intelligence division. In 1945, she was posted to Ceylon, then China, where she won the Emblem of Meritorious Civilian Service. In Ceylon she met her husband-to-be, Paul Child, also in the OSS. The couple married in 1946 and moved to Paris in 1948, where Paul was assigned to the U.S. Foreign Service.

There, Julia fell in thrall to French cuisine, attending Le Cordon Bleu cooking school and afterwards working with cooking teachers Simone Beck and Louisette Bertholle to compile a two-volume French cookbook for Americans. "My immediate plan was to develop enough foolproof recipes so that I could begin to teach classes of my own," she later wrote. She and her two colleagues set up such a school in Julia's home kitchen, calling it L'École des Troie Gourmandes. Of the venture, she said in 1952, "I have finally found a real and satisfying profession that will keep me busy well into the year 2000."

After extensive travels through Europe, the Childs moved back to the U.S., first to Washington, D.C., then to Cambridge, Massachusetts, in 1956. In 1961, Alfred A. Knopf published the book by the three women as a single volume, under the title *Mastering the Art of French Cooking*. It became a bestseller and led to Julia's developing a cooking show, *The French Chef*, on Boston's WGBH-TV channel, which debuted on February 11, 1963, and ran for ten years. The show won a Peabody Award (1964) and, beginning in 1966, five Emmy awards for Outstanding Service Show Host. In 1966, *Time* magazine dubbed her "Our Lady of the Ladle."

A good deal of the show's appeal was Julia's own quirky, irreverent personality, lilting voice, and homey approach to a subject that demanded rigorous detail over the 30-minute duration of each episode. Food writer Betty Fussell called her "a major television comic second only to Carol Burnett and Lucille Ball." Of her onscreen method, Child said, "Doing television you want amusing things, something fun and unusual. I think also on the television you want to do things loud; people love the whamming noises."

When the show ended, Julia went on to make seven more TV series, including *Julia Child & Company*, *Dinner at Julia's*, *Cooking with Master Chefs*, *In Julia's Kitchen with Master Chefs*, *Baking with Julia*, and *Julia Child & Jacques Pépin Cooking at Home*, whose contents went far beyond French cuisine. Child was one of the founders of the American Institute of Wine & Food, in 1981, and afterwards of COPIA: The American Center for Wine, Food and the Arts, in Napa, California. She also produced the comprehensive book and video series entitled *The Way to Cook* in 1989.

In 1993, she became the first woman inducted into the Culinary Institute Hall of Fame, and in 2000 she received France's highest award, the Légion d'honneur. So beloved was Julia's early kitchen set for her TV show, designed by Paul Child, that it is now part of the permanent collection of the National Museum of American History, in Washington, D.C. (She later used her own Cambridge home kitchen for the show.) Julia herself donated her house and office to Smith College.

In 1981, Julia moved to Santa Barbara, California, where she continued to write and do TV. After a long illness, Paul died in 1994. Julia died from kidney failure on August 13, 2004, two days before her ninety-second birthday. In an interview a year before, she said, "I still feel that French cooking is the most important in the world, one of the few that has rules. If you follow the rules, you can do pretty well."

A year after her death, her memoir *My Life in France* was published, with the help of her great-nephew Alex Prud'homme. In 2009, Child was portrayed by actress Meryl Streep in the movie *Julie & Julia*.

Child's books include *Mastering the Art of French Cooking* (two volumes, 1961 and 1983), *The Way to Cook* (1993), *In Julia's Kitchen with Master Chefs* (1996), *Julia and Jacques Cooking at Home* (1999), and, posthumously, a memoir, *My Life in France* (2005).

CHILE (*Capsicum annuum*). Also "chili," "chilli," "chile pepper," and "chili pepper." Although the American Spice Trade Association continues to use the spelling "chili" for such peppers, most authorities, including *Chile Pepper* magazine, generally prefer the spelling "chile" for the pepper and "chili" for the dish **chili con carne**. As "chille" it appeared in print in 1662.

Chile pepper is a very hot red, green, or yellow fruit of a New World plant, or the powder made from this fruit. There are more than three hundred varieties, originating in South America. The word is from the Nahuatl *chilli* and came into English in the mid-seventeenth century via the Spanish.

Christopher Columbus found that the Indians of the New World had cultivated the plant and used the fruit as a principal seasoning for their food. In fact, the Indians of Central and South America had done so from at least as early as 3300 B.C., and chiles were among their most beloved and revered foods, used as everything from a seasoning to a medicine and aphrodisiac. It was reported in 1529 by a Spanish missionary that the Aztecs put chile peppers in everything they ate, including chocolate.

The chile was brought back to Spain as early as 1514, but a German botanist named Leonhard Fuchs, believing Columbus had landed in India, called the chiles "Calcutta peppers," despite the fact that chiles were not related to the **pepper** family (nor did they reach India until 1611). Nevertheless, the English and Americans have continued to refer to the plant as the "chile pepper." Chiles might have first been brought into what is now the U.S. by General Juan de Oñate, who founded Santa Fe around 1609, although it is possible they were brought north much earlier by missionaries. By the early 1800s commercial seeds were for sale in North America; by 1888 the Burpee Seed Co. offered twenty pepper varieties, and by the beginning of the next century, 114 varieties (more than half of the bell variety) were counted by the USDA. In 1991, the Chile Institute was founded at New Mexico State University to study chile peppers.

Chiles are used both fresh and dried, some roasted over open fires or in ovens, others left to dry in braided strands called "ristras."

"Chili powder" was first made commercially by café owner William Gebhardt of New Braunfels, Texas, in 1894. In Texas, chile powder is commonly the basis of **chili con carne** and is a prime ingredient in **Tex-Mex** and **Mexican American** cuisine, including stuffed chiles called **chiles rellenos**.

Chiles' heat is measured by "Scoville units," originally developed in 1912 by pharmacologist Wilbur Scoville, based on human tasters' reaction to solutions of chile peppers in alcohol and sugar water. Today "high-performance liquid chromatography" has replaced the Scoville test, but chiles are still rated according to Scoville units, ranging from 0 for "sweet banana" chiles up to 300,000 for "habanero" and beyond. The major U.S. growing regions for chiles are New Mexico, California, Texas, and Arizona, where several hybrids have been created. Today there are about 125,000 acres of commercially cultivated peppers, of which about 40 percent are of the hot varieties. India, however, grows the largest acreage (2.23 million acres), with the U.S. seventh in production among the world's chile growers. Owing to increased competition from imported chile peppers, U.S. production has decreased since 2000, with about new 26,000 acres planted.

The main varieties of chiles used in the U.S. include:

ANAHEIM. A generic name for several long green chiles, it is a fairly mild chile. These chiles were originally New Mexican in origin and later grown in California, around Anaheim, although they are no longer a significant crop in that region. The preferred name, "New Mexico," is now used instead of "Anaheim." When dried, they are sometimes called "chile colorado."

ANCHO. Also "pasilla" and "mulato." A dark reddish-brown, slightly hot, dried poblano. Measures 1,000–1,500 Scoville units. The name is American Spanish for "wide chile." It appeared in English print in 1929.

BANANA PEPPER. Also "sweet banana" and "yellow wax pepper." Very mild, yellow, often pickled. Measures 0 Scoville units.

CAYENNE. See main entry. Measures 30,000–50,000 Scoville units.

CHILACA. Mildly hot to hot, this is often used in soups and sauces. When dried, it is called "pasilla" or "chile negro." Measures 1,000–1,500 Scoville units.

CHIPOTLE. A smoked jalapeño (see below), this is a very hot brown chile that may be dried or sold in cans. Also called "chile ahumado" or "chile meco." Measures 2,500–5,000 Scoville units. The word first appeared in print in 1950.

DE ARBOL. Extremely hot, measuring 15,000–30,000 Scoville units. The name in Spanish means "treelike." The chile de arbol is usually ground into a powder or used to season oils, soups, and sauces.

FRESNO. A mild chile, cone-shaped, mainly cultivated in the U.S. It goes under the more general name "New Mexico" and is often used in salsas.

GUAJILLO. Very hot, grown in Mexico and imported. When dried it is called "mirasol" or, erroneously, "dried Anaheim." Measures 2,500–5,000 Scoville units.

HABANERO. Extremely hot yellow-orange pepper. The name is Spanish for "from Havana," possibly referring to the chile's origins in Havana, Cuba. In Jamaica it is known as "Scotch bonnet" or "Scot's Bonnet," and "Bahamian" or "Bahamian Mama" in the Bahamas. It belongs to the *C. chinense* species. It is commonly used in sauces and barbecue recipes. Measures 200,000–300,000 Scoville Units. The word first appeared in print in 1845.

JALAPEÑO. Green, about two inches long, hot. The most widely consumed chile in the U.S. Smoked jalapeños are called "chipotles." Texas is the largest producer of jalapeños. Commercially, pickled jalapeños cut into slices are sometimes called "nacho slices" or "nacho rings," for use on **nachos**. Measures 2,500–5,000 Scoville units.

NEW MEXICO. Both green and red (fresh and dried), formerly called "Anaheim" but now descriptive of various strains originally grown in New Mexico. The main varieties include NuMex Big Jim, New Mexico No. 6-4, and Española Improved. New Mexico chiles make up 50 percent of all chiles grown in the United States. Measures 100–1,000 Scoville units. The word first appeared in print in 1949, in a Texas cookbook.

PASILLA. A wrinkled, dark brown chilaca chile whose Spanish name means "little raisin," first appearing in print in 1929. It is mildly hot, measuring 1,000–1,500 Scoville units, and is used mainly as a powder to flavor mole dishes. In California it is often (erroneously) called an "Anaheim."

PEQUIN. Also "piquin," "chiltepin," "bird pepper," "chile mesquito," and "chile bravo." Very hot dried pepper, usually canned. This small pepper probably takes its Spanish name from *pequeño*, "small." It is usually crushed and put into soups or sauces. Measures 50,000–100,000 Scoville units.

PIMIENTO. A sweet, quite mild pepper like the bell pepper. The word first appeared in print in 1662. It is used to stuff olives and in ground form can become paprika. Sometimes confused with "pimento" or "allspice," a berry from the *Pimenta* genus.

POBLANO. A fairly hot, large, dark green pepper, it is the fresh counterpart of the ancho. Measures 1,000–1,500 Scoville units. The word first appeared in print in 1950, in the *Spanish-Mexican Cookbook*.

SERRANO. Long, slim, very hot chile, sold green. The name is from the Spanish for "from the mountains," referring to their origins in the Mexican mountains of northern Puebla and Hidalgo. The main varieties include the Balin, the Tipico, and the Largo. The Hidalgo, bred in 1985 by the Texas Agricultural Experiment Station, has become very popular in the U.S. The serrano is most often used in fresh salsas. Measures 10,000–23,000 Scoville units. The word first appeared in print in 1952.

CHILEAN SEA BASS. Also "Patagonian toothfish." A deepwater fish (*Dissostichus eleginoides*) found along the length of Chile that grows to about twenty pounds. Its first printed reference was in 1984. It is not a true bass but took on the name for marketing purposes. Its high oil content made it an extremely popular fish in American restaurants as of the mid 1990s—so much so that it is now considered close to being an endangered species.

CHILES RELLENOS. Also "chilies rellenos." A Mexican dish of fried stuffed chile peppers (the term means "stuffed chiles"), served throughout the Southwest and in Mexican American restaurants (1890).

CHILES RELLENOS

Peel 12 charred chiles, leaving on the stems, and slit them open to remove seeds. Stuff the pockets with 8 oz. Monterey Jack cheese cut into thin strips. Sift together 1 c. flour, 1 t. baking powder, ½ t. salt, and ¼ c. cornmeal and add 1 c. milk blended with 2 beaten eggs. Dip the chiles in the batter and cook in hot oil until golden. Drain and serve with guacamole, onions, and other Mexican condiments. Serves 4.

CHILI CON CARNE. Also "chile con carne," or simply "chili." A dish of well-seasoned and well-cooked beef with chile peppers. Chili con carne is one of the most famous dishes of Texas, although wide variations are known throughout the U.S. In New Mexico, for instance, chili is sometimes made without meat at all and is more a stew of chile peppers and vegetables, and is called "green chile stew" or "chili verde." "Chili con carne" was first mentioned in print in the 1880s and later by author Stephen Crane, in his description of the food stands in San Antonio when he visited in 1895.

According to Dave DeWitt and Nancy Gerlach in *The Whole Chile Pepper Book* (1990), a dish that sounded identical to what came to be called chili was described by J. C. Clopper, who visited San Antonio in 1828 and commented on how poor people would cut the little meat they could afford "into a kind of hash with nearly as many peppers as there are pieces of meat—this is all stewed together." The first mention of the word *chile* was in a book by S. Compton Smith entitled *Chile Con Carne, or The Camp and the Field* (1857), and there was a "San Antonio Chili Stand" at the 1893 Chicago World's Columbian Exposition. As Waverley Root and Richard de Rochemont point out in *Eating in America* (1976), "One Mexican dictionary," Francisco J. Santamaria's *Diccionario de Mejicanismos* (1959), "even goes so far as to define chili con carne as 'a detestable food with a false Mexican title which is sold in the United States from Texas to New York.'"

Ironically, derogatory slang terms like "chili chaser" and "chili eater" are used by Americans to refer to low-class Mexicans, and Stephen Crane wrote, "Upon one of the plazas, Mexican vendors with open-air stands sell food that tastes exactly like pounded fire-brick from hades—chili con carne, tamales, enchiladas, chili verde, frijoles." A "chili joint" referred to a cheap restaurant, more often than not serving inferior-quality food.

Although chili most probably originated in Texas and has become a staple of **Tex-Mex** cooking, chili con carne (the preferred spelling among chile purists) is found throughout the U.S. in diverse forms. In 1889 a can of the food was displayed at the Paris Exposition. In 1902, a German immigrant in New Braunfels, Texas, created a "chili powder" that helped popularize the dish throughout the state and the Southwest. In Texas, cubed or shredded meat is preferred, while in other parts of the country ground beef is more common. In New Mexico, one may find pork or lamb used instead of beef. In the Old West, cowboys would often throw bull's eyeballs into their chili.

In chili's native state of Texas, there are several quasi organizations devoted to the glories of the dish, and every year there are several chili contests held. The most famous is the annual World's Championship Chili Cookoff, in Terlingua, sponsored by the Chili Appreciation Society International and begun in 1967 as a promotional aid for restaurateur Frank X. Tolbert's book, *A Bowl of Red: The Natural History of Chili with Recipes* (1953). ("A bowl of red" is a common term for chili in Texas.) The championship is held on the first Saturday of November, with participants from all over the world. Although the hotness of the chili is a virtue, it is the blend of flavors that ultimately decides a champion recipe.

Texas chili purists consider the addition of red kidney beans to their favorite dish (except perhaps as a side dish) tantamount to a criminal act. Yet chili both in and outside of Texas is commonly cooked or served with beans. Chili is traditionally served with rice and beer.

In many parts of the country, chili is served on top of a hamburger and called, for unknown reasons, "chili size."

"Cincinnati chili" was the creation of Macedonian immigrant Athanas "Tom" Kiradjieff, who settled in Cincinnati and opened a hot dog stand called the Empress (named after the Empress burlesque theater, in the same building), where in 1922 he concocted a layered chili (seasoned with Middle Eastern spices) that could be served in various "ways." "Five-way" chili was the most elaborate—a mound of spaghetti topped with chili, then chopped onions, then red kidney beans, then shredded yellow cheese, and served traditionally with oyster crackers and a side order of two hot dogs topped with shredded cheese. Kiradjieff later changed the name of his chain of eateries to Empress Chili, although the popularity of another restaurant chain's Cincinnati chili—Skyline Chili (opened in 1949 by Nicholas Lambrinides)—has for some made the term "Skyline Chili" synonymous with "Cincinnati chili."

Chili con carne has even become a partisan issue in the U.S. Senate. In 1974, Arizona senator Barry Goldwater challenged Texas senator John Tower on the floor of the Senate to a cooking contest with the words "A Texan does not know chili from the leavings in a corral." The following spring, a panel of five "experts" judged chilis made by the two legislators, and Goldwater's came out the best of the lot.

Today, chili con carne is still sold in restaurants called "chili parlors" or "chili joints." Chili is also widely available in cans. The Department of Agriculture stipulates that products labeled "chili con carne" must contain at least 40 percent meat; "chili con carne with beans," at least 25 percent meat; "chili hot dog with meat," 40 percent meat; "chili mac" (with macaroni and beans), at least 16 percent; and "chili sauce with meat," at least 6 percent.

CHILI CON CARNE

Cut up 4 lb. beef chuck into cubes and brown in hot oil, then remove and drain off excess grease. Brown in oil 1 ½ c. chopped onions with 6 green or red chile peppers, then add to meat and mix well. Add 3 T. cumin, 2 T. oregano, 1–2 bay leaves, ¾ c. hot paprika, 1 ½ T. chili powder, 3 T. chopped coriander (cilantro), 5 cloves chopped garlic, ¼ t. ground pepper, 1 t. salt, and 1 c. water. Simmer until meat is tender, add a little water if necessary, adjust salt, pepper, and hot seasonings to taste. Serves 10.

CINCINNATI FIVE-WAY CHILI

Brown 1 lb. ground beef with 2 chopped onions and 3 cloves minced garlic in a skillet with 3 T. vegetable oil. Add 1 c. tomato sauce, 1 c. water, 1 T. red wine vinegar, ¼ c. ketchup, 1 t. black pepper, salt to taste, 1–2 T. chili powder, ½ t. ground cumin, ½ t. marjoram, ½ t. turmeric,

½ t. nutmeg, ¾ t. cinnamon, ½ t. allspice, ¼ t. ground cloves, ¼ t. mace, ¼ t. cardamom, 1 crumbled bay leaf, and ½ t. unsweetened cocoa powder. Bring to a boil, lower heat to a simmer, and cook, covered, for about one hour. Boil ¾ lb. thick spaghetti until soft, drain, and divide into 4-6 portions on plates. Spoon some of the chili onto the spaghetti. Spoon some warmed red kidney beans onto chili. Spoon chopped onions on top of the beans. Grate yellow cheddar cheese on top of the dish. Serve with oyster crackers and cheese-topped hot dogs on the side. Serves 4-6.

CHILI CON QUESO. An appetizer dip made of chile peppers and cheese (the Spanish term means "chile pepper with cheese"), it is a staple of Tex-Mex and Mexican American menus.

CHILI CON QUESO

Melt 1 c. Monterey Jack cheese with ¾ c. sharp cheddar in a double boiler. Add ¼ c. heavy cream and blend with 1 chopped tomato, 1 chopped onion, 1 chopped charred chile pepper, and 1 clove minced garlic. Serve with corn chips.

CHILI QUEEN. A Texas slang term for a Mexican in the downtown section of San Antonio who sold tamales and **chile con carne** from quickly set-up stands, which started appearing in the municipal market in Military Plaza, as mentioned in *Scribner's* magazine as of 1882. By 1889 they were prohibited from the plaza, near the Alamo; by 1919, the writer O. Henry lamented that the chili queens he called "coquettish señoritas" were gone. In 1937, the stands were prohibited entirely, for sanitary reasons, by Mayor Charles Kennon Quin. According to Green Peyton, in his book *San Antonio: City in the Sun* (1946), "The singers still gather around your car and serenade you. But without the chili queens to exchange the anatomical insults with them in sonorous Spanish, they seem a bit lackadaisical and depressed."

CHILI SAUCE. Any of a variety of well-seasoned, chile-pepper-based condiments, most often used with Mexican American dishes (1880).

CHIMICHANGA. A deep-fried flour tortilla stuffed with minced beef, potatoes, and seasonings. The term was long considered a nonsense word—a Mexican version of "whatchamacallit" or "thingamajig"—reputedly coined in the 1950s in Tucson, Arizona, but first in print as of 1968. Diana Kennedy, in her *Cuisines of Mexico* (1972), reports that fried burritos in Mexico are called by a similar name, *chivichangas*. But in *The Food Lover's Handbook to the Southwest* (1992), Dave DeWitt and Mary Jane Wilan noted that Tucson writer Janet Mitchell found that *changa* means a female monkey in Spanish and *chimenea* a chimney or hearth. When put together this becomes, according to Jim Griffith of the University of Arizona's Southwest Folklore Center, a polite version of an "unmentionable Mexican expletive that mentions a monkey." According to DeWitt and Wilan,

> Investigator Mitchell heard tales about the first chimichanga being created when a burro was accidentally knocked into a deep-fat fryer, and the cook exclaimed, "Chimichanga!" She had also heard that a baked burro cooked in a bar in Nogales [Arizona] in the 1940s had been called a toasted monkey.
>
> The logical conclusion, then, was that the idiom chimichanga *means toasted monkey and is an allusion to the golden-brown color of the deep-fried burro.*

There have been various claims to authorship, including El Charro restaurant in Tucson, AZ, when, in 1922, owner Monica Flin accidentally dropped pastry into a deep fryer and cried out the name instead of a Mexican swear word.

CHIMICHANGA

Coarsely chop 2 lb. chuck steak, add 2 diced potatoes, 6 green or red chiles that have been charred, peeled, and deseeded, 1 onion, 3 cloves garlic, 1 t. oregano, salt, pepper, and enough water to cover. Boil, then lower heat and simmer for 1 hr., till meat is tender and texture is stew-like. Place the mixture in 12 flour tortillas and fold into a packet, then fry in hot oil until golden brown. Drain, serve with shredded lettuce, sour cream, guacamole, and chile sauce. Serves 6.

CHINESE AMERICAN FOOD. Along with **Italian American** and **Mexican American** food, Chinese American food has for much of the past century been one of the most popular ethnic cuisines in America, principally at restaurants and as **takeout** fare.

The first significant influx of Chinese came after the discovery of gold in California in 1848. By 1855 many Chinese from the Pearl River Delta, in Guangdong Province, emigrated to open dozens of fishing villages along the California coastline, with a thousand Chinese fishermen working in and around San Francisco Bay alone.

By 1849 there were already three Chinese restaurants in the city, serving up what one chronicler called "chow chow and curry." The earliest known was Hang Far Low (which lasted until 1960). The three-story Hong Heong banquet restaurant appealed mostly to tourists, though most white Americans' contact with Chinese food was at teahouses that served beverages, fruits, **chow-chow** pickle, and sweets. Chinese cooks were hired by white households, though the menus were usually all American. Those Chinese who did not settle in California were likely to become cooks for the railroads, while others settled in western towns and opened cafés—but, again, serving American food.

By 1860 the Chinese formed the largest immigrant group in San Francisco, settling in a Chinatown at the intersection of Stockton and Dupont streets. By 1882 about 300,000 Chinese had entered the U.S., but in that year, President Chester A. Arthur passed the Chinese Exclusion Act, suspending immigration, a fiat that lasted until 1943.

Beyond San Francisco, other cities had smaller Chinese populations, and by the end of the 1840s there were still only two Chinese restaurants in NYC, but by the 1870s, about five hundred Chinese lived in what developed into the city's own Chinatown, centered around Mott Street, where white New Yorkers would go to eat the exotic dishes made there. Bigotry toward the Chinese grew rapidly in the late nineteenth century as people accused them of taking white Americans' jobs. Part of the prejudice against the Chinese was against their food, which was said to contain dogs, cats, and rats, which were repulsive to European Americans, and this attitude persisted well into the twentieth century. Chinese restaurants were believed to be dens of white slavery. One of the defenders of the quality of Chinese cooking was Wong Ching Foo, editor of the city's first Chinese newspaper, *The Chinese American*, who in 1883 offered $500 to anyone who could prove that Chinese ate cats and rats, going on to describe dishes like wonton soup, dim sum dumplings, and "Chop soly," a stir-fry of pork, bacon, chicken, bamboo shoots, and vegetables, which he called China's "national dish." NYC Chinese restaurants called the dish "chow-chop-sui" or **chop suey**. By 1915 chop suey was being sold in cans, and in Detroit, Wally Smith and Ilhan New began canning bean sprouts under the La Choy label of Chinese foods. By the 1930s chop suey had become a staple item even in luncheonettes, diners, school cafeterias, and church suppers.

By 1920 New York City and San Francisco were home to 40 percent of the Chinese living in the U.S., but many new Chinatowns followed in other cities, and Chinese restaurants, all of them very cheap, became centers of bohemian life. By 1938 Los Angeles had two competing Chinese neighborhoods, New Chinatown and China City, which became tourist attractions. Lavish Chinese-styled nightclubs opened, sometimes called "chop suey jazz places," like Grand Star Chinese Restaurant, which had Chinese performers and food but mainly attracted non-Chinese patrons who loved stereotypes of Chinese culture as portrayed in Hollywood movies, like the Charlie Chan detective series.

Chinese emigration to Hawaii began in the 1850s. Many Chinese worked on the sugar plantations, and they established a Chinatown along Honolulu Harbor, with open-air markets and restaurants catering to both Chinese and white Americans; by 1890 they made up 20 percent of Hawaii's population. After World War II, other Asian immigrants enriched the food scene in Chinatown, leading to a style of fusion cuisine that combined Asian ingredients and techniques with American foods and tastes, called "New Hawaiian cuisine." Pioneers in this movement included Roy Yamaguchi, Alan Wong, Sam Choy, and several non-Asian Americans.

The first Chinese recipes for the non-Chinese cook appeared in *Good Housekeeping*, in an 1895 article called "Some Celestial Dishes," which included chop suey. The first cookbook appeared in 1912: *Chinese Cookery in the Home Kitchen*, by Jessie Louise Nolton of the

Chicago *Inter-Ocean* newspaper. A year later, *Harper's Bazaar* published an article on how to have a Chinese tea party at home. In 1941, the Chinese Committee of the Honolulu YWCA published *Chinese Home Cooking*, which had far more authentic Chinese recipes than had previously been published. In 1945, Buwei Yang Chao published *How to Cook and Eat in Chinese*, which went through three editions in the 1970s.

After the war, Chinese restaurants proliferated, with those in Chinatowns offering Chinese Americans extravagant banquet facilities and dim sum dining rooms, while non-Chinese Americans went to restaurants that overwhelmingly offered the same dishes, from chop suey and egg foo yung to wonton soup and chow mein. The combination dinner, by which a customer chose one dish from column A and one from column B, was ubiquitous.

A pseudo-Chinese menu had meanwhile been developed by two American restaurateurs, Ernest Raymond Beaumont-Gantt, who owned Don the Beachcomber, in Los Angeles, and **Victor Bergeron**, who opened Hinky Dink's tavern, in Oakland, California (later changing the restaurant's name to Trader Vic's, which became a worldwide chain). Both came up with what they said was Polynesian food, including the pupu platter of Chinese-style canapés, egg rolls, and almond chicken.

By the 1960s, Western interest in more authentic Chinese cuisine encouraged the opening of more authentic, classic restaurants, like the Mandarin, which was started in San Francisco in 1961 by immigrant **Cecilia Chiang**, who refused to serve dishes like chop suey and egg foo yung. Johnny Kan, who owned Kan's and Empress of China I San Francisco, is credited with introducing Peking duck to America. Around the U.S., regional Chinese restaurants debuted with menus featuring Mandarin, Szechuan, and Hunan cooking, some with chefs who had once worked in China's aristocratic kitchens and had fled Communist China after 1949. A New York City restaurant named Shun Lee Dynasty, opened in 1965 by chef Tsung Ting Wang, specialized in spicy, fiery Szechuan cuisine, receiving a top rating of four stars from the *New York Times*.

In 1965, a new immigration act made it easier for Chinese to enter the country, bringing a new vitality to Chinatowns across America. Much credit for the expansion of Chinese regional cuisine in America has been given to the opening of trade relations with China when President Richard Nixon, in 1972, attended a banquet in Beijing with Premier Zhou Enlai—a meal immediately featured as a promotion by Chinese restaurateurs back in the U.S. More important, large numbers of Chinese immigrants came to the U.S. after Nixon's trip. Szechuan and Hunan restaurants proliferated in suburban shopping malls, with names like Hunan Village and Szechuan Gardens, many serving dim sum brunch on weekends. By the same token, immigrants from the Fujian Province flooded into the U.S. and set up thousands of storefront eateries serving standard menus with scores of dishes like spareribs, spring rolls, **General Tso's chicken**, and beef with orange sauce, specializing in cheap takeout fare. Stir-fried dishes predominated at such eateries. One of the non-Chinese authorities on Chinese cuisine, Ed Schoenfeld, ran or consulted on many of the upscale Chinese restaurants of that period, including Uncle Tai's, David Keh, Pig Heaven (a Chinese barbecue restaurant), and Auntie Yuan, and helped introduce dishes like honeyed Hunan ham (on white bread), hot-and-sour soup, lobster *soong*, crispy honeyed walnuts, and cold noodles.

As of 1980, the availability of ingredients from China made the variety of cooking greater than could have been imagined; these included dried mushrooms, seaweed, bird's nests, soy sauces, fermented black beans, and hoisin sauce. So popular was Chinese food by the 1980s that operators like Manchu Wok and Panda Express (the largest, with more than fifteen hundred locations by 2011) began putting their counter eateries in airports around the U.S., while sit-down chains like P.F. Chang's China Bistros, now with more than two hundred branches worldwide, became enormous successes in large shopping malls. In 1987, Susanna Foo, who grew up in Outer Mongolia, opened a deluxe namesake Chinese restaurant in Philadelphia; *Food & Wine* magazine named her one of America's Best New Chefs.

One of the first Chinese chefs to have a successful TV show was Martin Yan, born in Guangzhou, who immigrated from Hong Kong to San Francisco, where he earned an M.A. in food science from the University of California at Davis in 1975. Afterwards, he began holding Chinese cooking classes, which led to the long-running PBS series *Yan Can Cook*, beginning in 1978, which won a **James Beard Foundation** Award. He went on to open restaurants in California, sold a line of kitchen knives, and wrote dozens of cookbooks, including *The Joy of Wokking* (1978), *Martin Yan's Chinatown Cooking* (2002), and *Martin Yan's Feast* (2003). Second-generation chefs like Ming Tsai, born in California and raised in Dayton, Ohio, had great success in refining Asian concepts, as Tsai did at his restaurant Blue Ginger (1998), in Wellesley, Massachusetts, which led to the TV series *East Meets West* (1998–2003) and *Simply Ming* (2009), as well as cookbooks and a line of kitchen knives.

Furthermore, Austrian-born Los Angeles chef **Wolfgang Puck** pioneered Asian "fusion" cooking at his restaurant Chinois on Main, and later at a more traditional Chinese restaurant named WP24.

Although non-Chinese Americans rarely cook much Chinese American food at home, packaged Chinese food is very popular, easily ranking with Italian American and Mexican American among favorite immigrant cuisines.

CHINESE CABBAGE (*Brassica rapa pekinensis*). Also "celery cabbage," "Chinese white cabbage," "Chinese mustard cabbage," and "white celery mustard." A long-stemmed, leafy cabbage used in salads and oriental cooking.

The term has been used in print since 1842. "Bok choy" (*Brassica rapa chinensis*) also goes by the name "Chinese cabbage" and is a similar plant.

CHINESE GRITS. A slang term for rice. See **grits**.

CHINO-LATINO. Caribbean adaptations of Chinese and Latino (often Peruvian) food-culture dishes, served side by side. The dishes originated in Cuba but thrived among Cuban immigrants who opened inexpensive, very casual eateries that began in the 1970s on New York City's West Side and in other Latino and Caribbean neighborhoods.

CHIPPED BEEF. Dried beef. The term derives from early English usage of the word *chip*, "to strip or pare away a crust." The dish has been known since at least 1819 in print.

Dried beef was a staple of the early American diet, and even much later, when more desirable forms of beef were readily available, chipped beef in a flour-based gravy—creamed chipped beef—continued to be

a popular luncheon or buffet item, called, in slang, **shit on a shingle**.

"Chipped ham" is a similar form of dried meat, especially popular in Pittsburgh, Pennsylvania.

CREAMED CHIPPED BEEF

Shred ½ lb. dried beef into strips. Melt ½ c. butter in pan and brown meat. Add salt and pepper and sprinkle with 6 T. flour. Add 2 pt. milk gradually, stirring constantly until blended, and cook until it boils. Lower heat and simmer until thickened. Serves 12.

CHITTERLINGS. Also "chitlins." A hog's innards, which are either fried or boiled, most popular in the South and as soul food in the northern cities. The term dates in print to the fifteenth century.

Chitterlings were rarely found in American cookbooks until recently, and sometimes disguised under the name "Kentucky oysters." Most African Americans pronounce the word "chitlins," but the origin of the word is the Middle English *chiterling*, "body organs." Chitterlings may also be called, euphemistically, "wrinkled steak" or "ruffles."

Salley, South Carolina, calls itself the "Chitlin Capital of the World," and has held a post-Thanksgiving "Chitlin Strut" each year since 1966.

CHITTERLINGS

Chitterlings should be well washed so as to remove any residue. For 5 lb. of chitterlings, add 1 large chopped onion, 1 t. salt, ¼ c. vinegar, and about ½ c. water, simmer for 2 hr., stirring occasionally, then cut into smaller pieces and continue cooking for two more hours. Correct seasoning and add water as necessary. To fry chitterlings, repeat steps above, but do not cut up into small pieces. Make a batter from ⅔ c. milk, 1 beaten egg, ⅔ c. flour, ½ t. baking powder, and ¼ t. salt and stir until smooth. Dip chitterlings in batter and fry in hot fat.

CHOC. An inferior beer originally made by the Choctaw Indians, dating in print to 1929. The term came to mean any such low-grade beer.

CHOCOHOLIC. A slang term for a person with a very strong appetite for chocolate. The term, a play on "alcoholic," gained currency in the 1980s.

CHOCOLATE. Both chocolate and cocoa come from the tropical bean known as *Theobroma cacao*. The use of chocolate in everything from hot and cold drinks (noted in English print by 1604) to **candy** to pastries and other confections makes it one of the world's most versatile flavorings. The word *chocolate* comes via the Spanish from the Aztec word *xocolatl*, meaning "bitter water." The Aztecs drank the pounded beans with spices but no sugar and believed that the bean was brought from the heavens by the gods (indeed, *Theobroma* means "food of the gods"). So valuable were these beans that a hundred of them were worth the price of a slave in Mexico, where they were used as currency. Recent scientific studies have indicated that the cacao bean cultivated today is more closely related to wild South American plants than to domesticated Mayan trees.

Some authorities say Columbus brought cocoa beans to Spain, but they were of little interest until Hernán Cortés returned with the beans and some Aztec hints on how to process them. Cortés first tasted chocolate at a ceremony with the Aztec king Montezuma II, who reputedly believed in the drink's aphrodisiac powers and consumed up to fifty large cups a day. The Aztecs also enjoyed chocolate with red peppers and chilled with snow. The Spanish found its bitterness off-putting, but, with the addition of sugar, a chocolate drink was prepared that immediately became popular throughout Europe. By 1657 a Frenchman had opened a "cocoa house" in London that sold prepared chocolate at the very high price of ten to fifteen shillings per pound.

Chocolate became the fashionable drink in Europe in the eighteenth century, and it was first manufactured in America in 1765, at Dorchester-Milton Lower Mills, Massachusetts, with beans from the West Indies. By 1780 John Hannan had opened the first chocolate factory, under the financing of Dr. James Baker, and the products sold from there were called "Baker's Chocolate." (There is still a Baker's Chocolate, made by the General Foods Corp.) Baker's also produced a sweet chocolate named "Baker's German Sweet Chocolate," after an English confectioner at the factory whose name was Samuel German,

which forms the basis of **German's sweet chocolate cake**. Cocoa powder was first produced in 1828.

But hard chocolate, of the consistency of candy, was still unknown at the beginning of the nineteenth century, while the liquid form was promoted mainly as a restorative. (Thomas Jefferson believed chocolate superior to tea or coffee in this regard.)

On the basis of a Mexican Indian's process of using sifted wood ashes to refine the raw cocoa into a more digestible form, Holland's C. J. Van Houten found a way to alkalize chocolate and make it darker through a process that came to be called "dutching," which also released cocoa butter. When combined with sugar and chocolate, the butter enabled processors to make a hardened candy bar, and by 1842 the Cadbury Co. of England was selling such confections; Americans were eating "chocolate creams" (candies with sugar-cream centers) by the 1860s.

In 1875, a Swiss chocolate manufacturer named Daniel Peter combined his product with sweetened condensed milk, recently discovered by Henri Nestlé, a Swiss chemist, thereby creating the first milk chocolate, which became extremely popular in Europe and the U.S. The Nestlé Food Co. opened facilities in NYC in 1905 to act as a sales agency for its products. But America's first mass-produced milk chocolate candy was the Hershey Bar, manufactured in 1894 by Milton Snavely Hershey of Lancaster, Pennsylvania.

In the twentieth century, chocolate took powerful hold of the candy and confections market, and "cocoa" or "hot chocolate"—a mixture of cocoa powder, sugar, and milk or water—became a popular wintertime beverage. Hershey's first manufactured such a cocoa in 1894. This was in time packaged with dried milk, which needed only water to turn it into a beverage.

After World War II, powdered and sugared chocolate were processed so that they would dissolve in cold milk, and "chocolate milk" became a household word. Chocolate is also made into syrups, sodas, milk shakes, **fudge**, **cookies**, **cakes**, and every imaginable kind of dessert. Its association with Valentine's Day (February 14)—represented by giving chocolate hearts or boxes of gift-wrapped chocolate candies filled with sweet sugar creams, fruits, liqueurs, or nuts—was well promoted by the 1890s. Chocolate Easter bunnies and Easter eggs have made that feast a rather sweet one, and one may well throw in chocolate Santas for Christmas. Commercial "chocolate kisses" (a large droplet of milk chocolate or other chocolate shaped something like an acorn cap), made by the Hershey Co. since 1907, were called "Wilbur Buds" when first introduced in 1893 by a manufacturer of that name (although there are recipes for kisses before then). "Chocolate babies" (once called "nigger babies" in less enlightened times), tiny figures of babies molded in chocolate, have been known since the 1890s.

Within the past decade, world consumption of cacao beans has averaged six hundred thousand tons annually, most of it coming from Africa. The "chocolate belt" of countries producing the bean extends around the middle of the tropical regions of the earth, from places like the Ivory Coast, Ghana, and Indonesia. The "Maracaibo" bean and the "Puerto Cabello," both from Venezuela, are highly prized and are blended in the more expensive chocolates.

The production of chocolate begins with the picking of the pods with a "cacao hook." Each pod on the tree contains between twenty and forty beans, which are removed from the pods by hand and then left in the open air before fermenting in "sweating boxes," boxes with perforated slats that allow the beans to drip their juices. The beans are then dried, washed, and put into sacks for shipping. At the chocolate plants, the beans are roasted in various ways to produce several different flavors that will be blended. The shells are removed by a machine, called a "cracker and fanner," that separates the nibs and shells and blows away the debris.

The beans are approximately 50 percent fat (called "cocoa butter") and 50 percent liquid (called "chocolate liquor"). The former is expressed as a gold liquid, while the latter becomes a thick paste that, unsweetened, is turned into baking or cooking chocolate. "Cocoa powder" is made by melting the chocolate liquor and pressing out more of the cocoa butter. The remaining hard mass is then ground into a fine powder and sold, either as a flavoring or for making cocoa and hot chocolate.

To make "sweet" chocolate for candy and other confections, sugar and a little vanilla are mixed with the chocolate liquor. It is then processed to a smooth texture in the form of a paste, to which cocoa butter is added before it is hardened by cooling. "Milk chocolate" is mixed from this sweetened chocolate and more cocoa butter, sugar, and milk, and then processed to remove moisture and to give smoothness. "Semisweet chocolate" has a lower quantity of sugar than sweet chocolate. Most American chocolate is made with large amounts of cocoa powder and some lecithin emulsifier to reduce the required amount of cocoa butter. Chocolate represents about 60 percent of all confectionary sales, with increasingly expensive artisanal varieties often sold in boutiques.

Americans consume about 11 pounds of chocolate per person per year—fourteenth on the list of nations, led by Germany, Switzerland, and the UK—but the U.S. represents 32 percent of the world market.

CHOCOLATE VELVET CAKE. A very rich, densely textured chocolate cake that originated at the Four Seasons restaurant, in NYC. It was the creation of pastry chef Albert Kumin in 1959. Since then, chocolate velvet cake has become synonymous with very rich, thick cake with a fudgelike consistency.

CHOPHOUSE. In its most basic form, a restaurant that specializes in serving beef, lamb, veal, and pork chops. In the nineteenth century, the term, which dates in print to 1699, usually referred to an inexpensive, very rudimentary eating establishment. But according to Charles G. Shaw in *Nightlife: Vanity Fair's Intimate Guide to New York After Dark* (1931), chophouses became far more elaborate establishments after the turn of the century, growing out of the older "dining saloons" or "oyster rooms" of the nineteenth century, and were originally based on English models:

> *The New York chophouse of to-day has acquired a true Yankee tang and in many cases has gone so far as to outstrip its London counterpart. Native, and even local dishes, will frequently be featured; elaborate dressings introduced; while in some instances a "ladies section" has been actually installed. On the whole, you will find the chophouse plain and I fear rather noisy. You may feel a certain primness in the dearth of brilliant color. For its aspect is seldom a gay one....On the other hand, the chophouse has a real solidity, a thorough, wholesome quality in everything from the furnishings to the cooking.*

Everyone talks at the top of his voice (to be heard above the din of jingling cutlery, rushing waiters, and orders from the kitchen), and if, perchance, the man at the table next to you bellows in your ear, do not be alarmed. It is all in the game, and the tenderness of the sirloin is the first consideration. For these are halls of honest worth and simple fare, where show and chi-chi are unknown and the vigor of grills and roasts triumph supreme.

CHOP SUEY. A **Chinese American** dish of widely varying ingredients, but usually containing bamboo shoots, water chestnuts, bean sprouts, celery, soy sauce, and either pork or chicken. Although there is no such dish by this name in China, there is a story that when the first Chinese statesman to visit the U.S., Viceroy Li Hongzhang, arrived in 1896, he was asked by American newspapermen what kind of food he ate. "Chop suey" was supposedly their transcription of the Mandarin words "*tsa tsui*," which means "a little of this and a little of that." Yet "chop suey" appeared in American print as early as 1888.

Chop suey is probably derived from the mixture of vegetables and meat concocted by the Chinese cooks who fed the workers on the Pacific railroad lines in the middle of the nineteenth century. When Chinese began opening restaurants in Chinatowns in NYC, San Francisco, and other cities in the late nineteenth century, they became known as "chop suey parlors."

Americanized Chinese dishes such as this and chow mein were served in Chinese restaurants to American customers, but rarely would a Chinese indulge in such a food. In his book *Bohemian San Francisco* (1914), Clarence E. Edwards noted that after the earthquake of 1906, "a number of places [in Chinatown] have been opened to cater to Americans, and on every hand one sees 'chop suey' signs and 'Chinese noodles.' It goes without saying that one seldom sees a Chinaman eating in the restaurants that are most attractive to Americans." And in the 1944 motion picture *Destination Tokyo*, a flight officer warns a B-24 bomber crew, "If you land in China, don't order chop suey. That's strictly an American dish."

"American chop suey" is a New England dish of ground beef, noodles, and tomato sauce.

CHOP SUEY

Slice 2 chicken breasts into thin strips, then sauté in 2 T. oil until lightly cooked. Add 1 c. sliced button mushrooms, 1 chopped green pepper, ½ c. sliced water chestnuts, 1 can Chinese vegetables, 1 chopped stalk of celery, 3 T. soy sauce, and ½ c. chicken broth. Bring to a boil, then simmer for 3 min. Blend 1 T. cornstarch into 4 T. cold water, mix, then add to simmering chicken. When thickened, remove from heat and serve over hot white rice.

CHORIZO. A spicy pork sausage found in Hispanic cooking from Spain to California. Called "chaurice" in Louisiana, chorizo is used in egg dishes and tortillas, as appetizers, or as part of a main dish. The word was first printed in 1846.

CHOW. A slang term, dating in print to 1856, especially popular with American servicemen, for food served to them by the cook. It also referred to mealtime, either as "chow" or "chow time." A "chowhound" was someone who was first in a "chow line" for food. These were well-known Army terms by World War I, but the word *chow* goes back to the era when Chinese laborers worked on the Pacific railroads during the 1850s. The word might have been picked up by sailors from pidgin English, which in turn got it from the Mandarin Chinese *ch'ao*, "to fry" or "cook."

CHOW-CHOW. A relish of pickles or other vegetables. The word may be from the Mandarin Chinese *cha*, "mixed," and dates in print to 1795, when Chinese laborers worked on the railroads of the American West.

CHOW-CHOW

Mix together 1 qt. small cucumbers, 1 qt. large cucumbers, 1 qt. sliced green tomatoes, 1 qt. sliced onions, 1 qt. small onions, 1 qt. chopped cauliflower, and 4 chopped peppers. Cover with 1 c. salt in 4 qt. water. Let stand for 24 hr., then heat until scalded. Drain. Mix 1 c. flour, 1 ½ c. sugar, 6 T. mustard, and 1 t. turmeric with 1 pt. vinegar. Pour into 2 pt. vinegar and heat in double boiler until thickened. Add to vegetables and pack into clean jars and seal.

CHOWDER. A seafood soup associated with New England, the most popular of which is clam chowder. The term may also describe a buttery, hearty soup made with corn, chicken, or other chunks or bits of food still evident in the blend.

The origins of the word *chowder* are somewhat obscure, but most authorities believe it derives from the French *chaudière*, for a large cauldron, into which Breton sailors threw their catch to make a communal stew, a custom carried to Newfoundland, Nova Scotia, and down to New England in the seventeenth and eighteenth centuries. But in *Down East Chowder* (1982), John Thorne contends that evidence for such a derivation is very tenuous, noting that "the phrase *'faire la chaudière'* seems no longer to exist in Brittany, while *chaudrée*, another touted source of origin, resembles chowder no more and no less than any fish soup resembles another. (The French word for cauldron, by the way, is *chaudron,* not *chaudière*—that latter word has more the meaning of a steam boiler.)"

Although the *OED* suggests *chaudière* as the etymological link, it also lists "chowdee" as a dialectical variation of an old Cornwall or Devonshire word, "jowter," for a fish peddler. Certainly fish stews existed in almost every seabound country in the world, and the distinction between these and the earliest chowders of New England are a matter of interpretation. New England chowders have been known since at least the 1730s and were first mentioned in print by a New England diarist in 1732, by which time salt pork seemed to have already attained the status of a prerequisite ingredient. The first printed recipe for chowder was a piece of doggerel published in the *Boston Evening-Post* for September 23, 1751, that called for fish, onions, salt pork, sweet marjoram, savory, thyme, and biscuit, to which was added a bottle of red wine. This and other early chowders were undoubtedly more like a pudding or thick stew than a soup, a perfect consistency for onboard consumption, especially since, as Thorne notes, "it uses a minimum of one of the most precious of shipboard supplies: water."

The first American cookbook to give a chowder recipe was the second edition of Amelia Simmons's *American Cookery* (1800). It called for bass, salt pork, crackers, and a side dish of potatoes. **Ketchup** and flour were suggested to thicken the dish in early-nineteenth-century recipes,

by which time New England chowders had become more like soups. Although by 1836 "clam chowder" was known in Boston, where its associations are still strong, throughout the century chowder was less commonly a dish of clams than of fish, usually cod or haddock, and by the 1840s potatoes had become a traditional ingredient.

Chowder was a staple dish of New Englanders, and for sailors merely another way to make a constant diet of fish palatable. In *Moby-Dick* (1851), Herman Melville wrote of the Try Pots, a chowder house in Nantucket, where one might have a choice of either cod or clam chowder. Melville's hero, Ishmael, ordered the latter: "Oh! sweet friends, hearken to me. It was made of small juicy clams, scarcely bigger than hazel nuts, mixed with pounded ship biscuits, and salted pork cut up into little flakes! the whole enriched with butter, and plentifully seasoned with pepper and salt." Melville went on to describe the menu at the Try Pots—"Chowder for breakfast, and chowder for dinner, and chowder for supper, till you began to look for fish-bones coming through your clothes."

By the end of the century, certain New England regions became known for their various interpretations of chowder—one might find cream in one spot, lobster in others, no potatoes elsewhere—but most were by then a creamy white soup brimming with chopped fish or clams, crackers, and butter. By the 1830s in Rhode Island, however, cooks often added tomatoes to their chowder, a practice that brought down unremitting scorn from chowder fanciers in Massachusetts and Maine, who associated such a concoction with New York, because the dish came to be called, for no discernible reason, "Manhattan clam chowder" sometime in the 1930s. By 1940, Eleanor Early in her *New England Sampler*, decried this "terrible pink mixture (with tomatoes in it, and herbs) called Manhattan Clam Chowder, that is only a vegetable soup, and not to be confused with New England Clam Chowder, nor spoken of in the same breath. Tomatoes and clams have no more affinity than ice cream and horseradish." In her 1954 *New England Cookbook*, she goes on to note that Rhode Islanders and Connecticut cooks believe Cape Cod milk chowder is fit "only for babies and sick people," to which Early replies, "Nonsense! Cape Cod is full of happy octogenarians." She nevertheless includes a recipe for tomato-laden Rhode Island clam chowder.

Just why tomato-based chowder is called "Manhattan" has never been satisfactorily explained. A note in the *New York Times* for January 24, 1990, cites a letter dated December 25, 1978, from Austin Phelps Winters, to the effect that his father, William H. Winters, and his uncle James ran a fish store at NYC's Fulton Fish Market where the two brothers made a chowder with tomatoes instead of milk, because milk "was too expensive," and called it "Manhattan clam chowder." There is no other corroboration of this report, however.

The issue of whether one should add tomato to chowder is merely a regional preference, for tomatoes fill the fish stews of many countries' kitchens, and neither Manhattanites nor Rhode Islanders are original or adamant on the matter.

Today chowders made with clams predominate, but fish chowders are also popular. Noting that in Oregon a "first-rate chowder is made with corn and fresh salmon," Thorne recommends cod, haddock, whiting, flounder, hake, and halibut. The best clams for a chowder are traditionally the large quahogs.

The term "to chowder" means to make a chowder.

CLAM CHOWDER

Shell 3 doz. clams, remove tips, and chop up coarsely. Peel and dice 5 potatoes. Fry ¼ lb. salt pork with 2 diced onions until soft. Add potatoes to 1 qt. boiling water, then add pork and onions. Cook until tender. Scald and strain 1 ½ c. clam liquid, then add to kettle. Add clams, bring to a boil, add 1 qt. milk, pepper to taste, and several common crackers. Serve when warm.

FISH CHOWDER

Cook 3 diced onions in 2 T. salt pork until soft. In 2 c. water, boil 4 diced potatoes until tender, add onions, 2 lb. cut-up fish, ½ lb. butter, salt, pepper, ¼ t. savory, 1 can evaporated milk, and 3 c. milk. Heat but do not boil. Serves 6.

MANHATTAN CLAM CHOWDER

Brown 2 oz. salt pork in a skillet, then remove and drain. In a large kettle place the salt pork, 1 pt. opened clams chopped fine, 1 ½ c. clam liquid, 2 peeled and diced potatoes, ½ c. water, 1 chopped onion, 1 stalk celery, 1 chopped carrot, 6 peeled, seeded, chopped tomatoes, 1 chopped green pepper, ⅓ c. tomato paste, 1 bay leaf, ½ t. thyme, salt, and pepper. Bring to a boil, reduce heat, and simmer for 2 hr.

CHOWDER BEER. A liquor made from boiled spruce mixed with molasses, first in print in 1732.

CHOW MEIN. A **Chinese American** dish made of stewed vegetables and meat with fried noodles. The term comes from Mandarin Chinese *ch'ao mien*, "fried flours," and probably was brought to the U.S. by Chinese cooks serving the workers on the western railroads in the 1850s. The word first appeared in print in 1900. Although most chow mein bears scant resemblance to true Mandarin cooking, it has become a staple in Chinese American restaurants. H. L. Mencken noted that at least one Chinese authority vouched for the Chinese origins of the dish, though in America it is "a bit flavored up for Western palates."

Owing to its inexpensive ingredients, chow mein has long been a lunch dish in American school cafeterias.

CHOW MEIN

Heat 3 T. oil in a saucepan over high heat and sauté 1 c. sliced beef or chicken until brown. Add 1 c. sliced celery, 1 c. diced onion, and 1 c. water. Stir and cook until tender, covered. Add 1 can of Chinese vegetables, 3 T. flour mixed with ½ c. water, 2 T. soy sauce, 1 t. salt, ½ t. paprika, and ¼ t. celery salt. Serve on rice and top with 1 can Chinese fried noodles.

CHRISTY GIRL. A cocktail that originated at the Carnival Room at NYC's Sherry-Netherland hotel. The drink was named after the famously daring illustrations by Howard Chandler Christy (1873–1952) of the American girl as a perky outdoorswoman.

CHRISTY GIRL

Shake together ½ jigger peach brandy, ½ jigger dry gin, a dash of grenadine, and the white of 1 egg with ice cubes. Strain into a cocktail glass and decorate with a maraschino cherry.

CHUCK. A western term for food of any kind, dating back to 1840 in print; also used as a verb, "to eat." A "chuck habit" is a fear of or obsession for a certain kind of food.

"Chuck" is also a butcher's term for a cut of **beef** extending from the neck to the ribs, including the shoulder blade. This cut is often used to make hamburgers or rib roast (or "blade roast"). One oval-shaped part of the chuck may be sliced into slabs to make **chicken-fried steak**, which is quickly grilled or pan-fried.

CHUCK WAGON. A converted farm wagon that served as a mobile kitchen and center of social activity in the West. The chuck wagon was manned by a cook who had to store utensils and food enough to feed the range cowboys three hot meals a day. Early Texans called it the "commissary," and other terms were "mess wagon" and "growler." A "chuck box" of shelves and storage space, attached to the rear of the wagon, swung down on hinges as a worktable. Underneath was a dishpan, called a "wreck pan," and under that a "cooney," a piece of dried cowhide slung to carry firewood and buffalo or cow chips. A good chuck wagon was one that could carry at least a month's provisions. The word was first printed in 1860; by the 1940s "chuck wagon" was also used for a roadside or neighborhood lunch counter. "Chuck-wagon chicken" was a cowboy term for fried bacon.

CHUG-A-LUG. Also "chug." A campus term, dating in print to the 1930s, that describes the sound of someone drinking a long draft of beer or spirits. Usually to "chug-a-lug" a drink means to swallow it down without pausing between gulps.

CHURCH KEY. Slang term for a bottle or can opener, dating in print to 1951.

CIDER. Pressed apple juice that is used to make both vinegar and an unfermented drink called "sweet cider" or a slightly fermented drink called "hard cider." The word, first in print circa 1315, derives from the Hebrew *shēkār*, which in Middle English became *cidre*. In America, "to cider"—that is, to make cider—is known in the Appalachians.

Cider was by far the most popular drink of colonial America. Everyone, including children, drank it, and it was bought very cheaply by the barrel, if not made at home. "Ciderkin" was a diluted form of cider made from a second pressing of the apple pulp residue and more water. "Cider royal" was a more pungent form that might be mixed with brandy or boiled down for strength. If mixed with rum, it became a drink called "stonewall." "Cider wine" is a mixture of cider and cider brandy.

There was not only variety but a great range of quality in ciders, and the French gastronome Anthelme Brillat-Savarin (1755–1826), who spent three years in America, pronounced the native product "so excellent that I could have gone on drinking it forever." President John Adams (1735–1826), who lived to be ninety-one, prided himself on drinking a pitcher of cider every morning.

The popularity of cider waned in the nineteenth century as beer predominated with the adult population, but hard cider is still extremely popular with Americans, especially in autumn, when the pressings take place. Sales among a handful of commercial cider producers, with names like Woodchuck and Strongbow, have risen in recent years to 5.7 million cases.

"Hard cider" ranges from 3 to 7 percent alcohol, while "sweet cider's" alcohol content must fall below 3 percent. Above 7 percent alcohol, the drink becomes wine or **applejack**. "Cider vinegar" is cider that has decayed beyond the vinous stage and become vinegar, widely used in cooking and salads. "Cider molasses" or "cider sauce" is cider cooked to a syrup and used as a sweetener.

In the eighteenth century, the word *cider* was occasionally applied to drinks made from the pressings of other fruits, like peaches and pears (see **peachy** and **perry**).

CILANTRO (*Coriandrum sativum*). Also "coriander," "Mexican parsley," and "Chinese parsley." A leafy herb of the parsley family whose dried seeds, more commonly called "coriander," are also used as a flavoring. Coriander (from the Middle English *coriandre*) has been enjoyed as a flavoring agent for millennia, though it was never much in favor in Europe, with the exception of Portugal (where it is called *coentros*), whose people may have brought it to America. The word *cilantro*, which entered print in 1903, comes from the Spanish, and Americans more commonly refer to it by this name because of its prevalence in Mexican food. Indeed, cilantro has achieved real popularity only in the past 20 years, because of the increased interest in Mexican and Asian food. Cilantro is now grown in California's Central Coast and the Coachella Valley, with more than four thousand acres under cultivation.

CINCI. Midwestern slang for a short glass of beer. The term, dating in print to 1981, refers in some way to Cincinnati and is often applied to a small glass.

CINCINNATI OYSTER. A slang term for pickled pig's feet, because Cincinnati was so associated with pork products, dating in print to 1877.

CINDERELLA. A muffin flavored with wine or sherry and nutmeg. The name comes from the heroine of the old fairy tale and may have something to do with the muffin's fancy appearance, just as Cinderella emerged as a grand, fancily dressed girl for the prince's ball. The recipe is from *Directions for Cookery* (1837), by Eliza Leslie, who notes that these muffins are also sometimes called "German puffs."

CINDERELLA

Beat 8 eggs until light in color, mix in 8 T. flour, 1 qt. milk, ½ lb. cooled melted butter, ¼ t. powdered nutmeg, and 1 t. cinnamon. Make a smooth batter. Fill buttered muffin tins and bake for 15 min. at 375°. Turn muffins out onto rack and sprinkle sugar over them. Serve hot with whipped cream flavored with sherry and nutmeg.

CIOPPINO. A fish stew cooked with tomatoes, wine, and spices and associated since at least the 1930s with San Francisco, where it is still a specialty in many restaurants, dating in print to 1935. The word is from Genoese Italian *ciuppin*, for a fish stew, and the dish seems to have originated with the Italian immigrants of San Francisco, who often used the crabmeat available in the city's markets.

CIOPPINO

In a large kettle with 4 T. olive oil, sauté 4 chopped onions, 8 chopped garlic cloves, 1 diced carrot, 1 diced leek, and 1 diced celery stalk, until limp. Add 1 c. tomato puree and ⅓ t. crumbled saffron. Add the meat from 2 or more crabs, 10 shrimp that have been peeled and deveined, 2 doz. clams, 2 doz. mussels, ½ lb. bay scallops, and 8 oz. each of two or more fish (such as snapper or sea bass) and stir to coat with oil and other ingredients. Add 2 c. white wine, 3 c. fish stock, 2 bay leaves, ½ t. oregano, ½ t. thyme, salt, pepper, and 4 peeled and seeded chopped tomatoes. Cover, bring to a boil, then simmer for 15 min. Remove fish and reduce stock for 15 min. Return fish to stock, bring to a boil, then serve. Serves 8.

CITRIC ACID. Abundant in citrus fruits, this is used as an additive (as an antioxidant and flavoring agent), imparting a tart flavor to processed food.

CLABBER. Also "clabbered." Sour, curdled milk, rarely seen now in the U.S. because most milk is pasteurized and will not naturally turn to curd before it goes bad. "To clabber" is to sour milk. In the South, clabber was often eaten with sugar, or even with black pepper and cream. *New York Times* food writer Craig Claiborne recalled that "it was a common dish of my Southern childhood. My father raised and milked cows. The milk was allowed to stand in churns and more often than not became clabber, a semifirm, very white liquid on the bottom and a semifirm layer of yellow cream on top. The clabber was a pure product, the result of a natural bacterial action. Clabber tends to 'break apart' when dipped into. It is quite sour but of a different texture and flavor than yogurt. When you 'churned' the clabber, you wound up with butter (from the top cream layer) and buttermilk." The word comes from the Irish *bainne clabair* ("thick milk") and dates in print to 1625.

A "clabber biscuit" is a **biscuit** made with clabber. "Clabber cheese" is a synonym for **cottage cheese.**

CLAIBORNE, CRAIG (1920–2000). Author, food critic. In 1957, at a time when food editors were largely women, Craig Claiborne assumed the title of food editor and restaurant critic for the *New York Times* and wrote with an independence and professional knowledge unusual for his day.

Claiborne was born in Sunflower, Mississippi, and raised in Indianola at his mother Kathleen's boardinghouse, where he acquired his love of home-cooked southern food. He graduated from the University of Missouri with a degree in journalism in 1942, then joined the U.S. Navy as a communications specialist in intelligence and, after training at the University of Notre Dame, became an officer on a subchaser.

Postwar, Claiborne worked in public relations in Chicago and NYC. As a bachelor (many years later he revealed that he was gay), he learned to cook for himself from the *Joy of Cooking*. He then moved to France, where his appreciation and knowledge of food grew fervid. Upon his return he rejoined the military during the Korean War while deciding what to do with his life.

After service, Claiborne entered the school of the Société Suisse des Hôteliers, near Lausanne, Switzerland, earning certificates in table and banquet service as well as classic French cuisine. He returned to New York City and took a receptionist's job at *Gourmet* magazine, where he rose to become an editor and writer. In 1957, he applied for and got the job of food editor at the *New York Times*, where his early pieces were simple capsule lists of four or five restaurants for the women's pages of "Food Fashions Family Furnishings."

As time went on, Claiborne began to write longer reviews of one or two restaurants per week, visiting them anonymously, at the newspaper's expense, two or three times before writing his critique. While his main focus was on the food, he would also write about the atmosphere, decor, and service, scolding a captain for having a pencil in his breast pocket and the owner of a French restaurant for not wearing a dinner jacket. If a restaurant was of poor quality, he would not review it at all.

But while his standards for expensive restaurants were high, he enjoyed just as much writing about Chinese restaurants in Harlem and the chain of Chock full o' Nuts coffee shops, giving them the same careful eye he did to the city's finest restaurants. In 1963, mimicking France's Michelin one-to-three-star rankings system, Claiborne began awarding one star to three (later four) for restaurants, a feature many U.S. food sections then adopted.

In 1961 Claiborne's *The New York Times Cook Book*, with more than 700 pages and 1,500 recipes, became one the best-selling cookbooks of its time, which he followed with several others using the *Times*'s name on the cover.

Nevertheless, by then Claiborne had become jaded by dining out, quitting the *Times* in 1971, saying, "At times I didn't give a damn if all the restaurants in Manhattan were shoved into the East River and perished"—this at a time when he was spiraling into alcoholism and depression. Unable to make a living outside the newspaper, with expenses mounting from a failing newsletter he founded, Claiborne returned to the paper solely as food editor, writing feature stories and recipes, often with fellow *Times* food writer Pierre Franey. Delighting in discovering new talent and approving of France's *nouvelle cuisine*, Claiborne was the first to bring national attention to chefs like **Paul Prudhomme** in New Orleans and home cooks like Marcella Hazan and **Diana Kennedy**, all of whom became famous as a result of his reviews.

Claiborne's most controversial article came in 1975, when, after winning a TV station auction sponsored by American Express for a dinner with no price limit, he wrote about a single meal with Franey at Chez Denis, in Paris, that cost $4,000 and was composed of thirty-one courses. The publication of the story caused outrage from *Times* readers as much for the gluttony of the experience as the gross expenditure of so much money.

Claiborne finally retired from the paper for good in 1986 but continued to author cookbooks and an 1982 autobiography, *A Feast Made for Laughter*. Claiborne's influence on restaurants and restaurant reviewing was considerable, but his approach to food and recipes was just as important. Chef and cookbook author Jacques Pépin contended that "Craig broke down the formality of cooking, like we had in France, and in the process made it accessible to all."

In his last years Claiborne fought alcoholism and various other diseases but continued to live a sybaritic life, and in 1995 his friends organized a trbute dinner for him called A Hug for Craig, attended by more than a hundred members of the food establishment.

Claiborne received countless awards and honors during a career buoyed by a number of bestselling cookbooks, including *Classic French Cooking* (1970), with Pierre Franey; *The New York Times International Cook Book* (1971); *The Chinese Cookbook* (1972), written with Virginia Lee; *Craig Claiborne's New York Times Cookbook* (1979); and *Craig Claiborne's Southern Cooking* (1987).

CLAM (class *Pelecypoda*). Any of a variety of bivalve mollusks that burrow in sand in both salt- and freshwater. The word derives from Old English *clamm*, meaning "bond" or "fetter," for its clamped shell. The mollusk has had this name in English since at least the end of the fourteenth century, although a Scot may mean a scallop when he says "clam."

Clams, of which there are more than two thousand species, exist in most regions of the world and have been consumed since prehistoric times. The earliest white settlers of North America found clams to their liking, and the Native Americans used the clamshell as money, or wampum. They also showed the New England colonists how to hold "clambakes"—social gatherings, often held at the beach after a fresh catch, that have endured to this day in that region.

The two main varieties of clams eaten on the East Coast are the "soft-shell" (*Mya arenaria*) and the "hard-shell" (*Mercenaria mercenaria*), better known as the "quahog" (from the Narragansett word *poquaûhock*) and as the "round clam." "Quahog" in English dates to at least 1753.

The soft-shell clam, also called the "long-necked clam," "piss clam," and, via Algonquin dialect, "maninose," found from the Arctic Ocean to Cape Hatteras and introduced to Pacific waters north of San Francisco, is used for making clam **chowder** and frying, though it is most commonly steamed. Soft-shell clams are often called "steamers" or "clam bellies."

The hard-shell clam is preferred raw and in chowders, its size often determining its use. The smallest quahogs, less than 2 ¼ inches, are called "littlenecks," after Little Neck Bay, on Long Island, New York—although William and Mary Morris, in their *Morris Dictionary of Word and Phrase Origins* (1971), give "Little Neck" as a clamming region of Ipswich, Massachusetts. The next size, up to three inches, is "cherrystone" (after Cherrystone Creek, Virginia); still larger quahogs are called "chowder clams" and used for that purpose. Sometimes clams of less than two inches are called "Philadelphia Nicks," while those larger than two inches are called "New York Nicks."

The "razor clam" or "jacknife clam" of the East (*Ensis directus*), so called because of its sharp shell, is not as popular, because it is difficult to catch. The "bar clam" (*Spisula solidissima*), also called the "beach clam," "Atlantic surf clam," "hen clam," "sea clam," and "skimmer clam," is used for chowders or deep-fried as "clam strips."

There are several clams of culinary interest on the West Coast. The "Pacific razor clam" (*Siliqua patula* and other species) is not related to the eastern variety named above; the "Pacific littleneck" (*Protothaca staminea* and others) is not related to the eastern variety, either, nor is the "Philippine littleneck" (*Tapes philippinarum*). The "California bean clam" (*Donax californicus*) is eaten in soups; the "geoduck" (*Panopea generosa*)—pronounced "gooey-duck"—is very large, up to eight inches in length and five pounds in weight (erroneously called "giant clam," which is actually another species, *Tridacna gigas*), and has a tough texture. Its name, first appearing in English in 1883, is most probably from the Nisqualli Indian for "digging deep." This last species is dug out of beds twenty to seventy feet deep, and most of the supply is shipped to Japan, where it is considered a great delicacy. Americans may find the clam on Pacific beaches during very low tides. The process of catching one is described by Lila Gault in *The Northwest Cookbook* (1978):

> *The digger must first find the neck of the geoduck, which is directly below the "mark," and then center a stovepipe over it. The stovepipe is then driven into the sand as deeply as possible and the fun truly begins. The neck is held with one hand and the other scoops sand away from it, making a large hole in the process. Unlike razor clams, geoduck do not move their bodies when disturbed. Once the neck is grabbed, if the diggers are persistent, they will always get their clam! When the body of the clam is reached, often two and sometimes as much as four feet below the surface, the geoduck can be lifted out of the hole. This chase and capture actually works better with two or three people at work—a single digger must be extremely agile and tenacious to get even one of these clams.*

The "Manila clam" (*Venerupis japonica* or *T. japonica*) was imported from the Orient after 1900 and became a dominant species harvested in the Northwest.

Clam farming was pioneered at the National Marine Fisheries at Milford, Connecticut, around 1930, with the first commercial hatcheries established on the East Coast in the 1960s. U.S. commercial landings of clams totaled 88.9 million pounds in 2010, with sales of $200.7 million. Per capita U.S. consumption annually is 0.34 pounds.

CLAMBAKE

Build a fire in a deep pit, place a layer of large, flat rocks on top of the burning wood, and repeat procedure with more wood and rocks twice more. Let burn until very hot. Rake the fire, retaining embers, and lay on top wet seaweed to a depth of about 6 in. Then place clams, mussels, lobsters, potatoes, corn, and onions on top. Cover with layers of wet canvas and cook about 1 ½ hr. Serve with butter.

CLAM FRITTER. A deep-fried clam in batter, supposedly first made by Lawrence Woodman at Woodman's Restaurant in Essex, Massachusetts, on July 3, 1916. Clam fritters are also called "fannie daddies" on Cape Cod and "boat steerers" in other parts of New England.

CLAM FRITTER

Beat 2 egg yolks, add ½ c. milk, 1 T. butter, 1 c. flour, salt, pepper, and 1 T. lemon juice. Beat in 2 stiffly beaten egg whites, mix in 1 pt. clams, and chill for several hours. Fry small amounts in hot oil till golden brown.

CLAMS CASINO. A dish of clams mixed with butter, paprika, and shallots, then baked with small strips or pieces of bacon on top. In his autobiography, *Inns and Outs* (1939), restaurateur Julius Keller described how, around 1917, society woman Mrs. Paran Stevens asked Keller, then maître d' at the Narragansett Pier Casino, in Newport, Rhode Island, to create a new dish for a luncheon she was holding for friends. Keller came up with a recipe for clams baked with bacon. When Stevens inquired as to the dish's name, Keller replied, "It has no name, Mrs. Stevens; but we shall call it clams casino in honor of this restaurant."

CLAMS CASINO

In a bowl combine 8 T. softened butter, ⅓ c. minced shallots, 1 minced pimiento, ⅓ c. minced green pepper, 3 T. minced parsley, salt and pepper to taste, ½ t. Worcestershire sauce, a dash of cayenne, and 2 T. lemon juice. Mix well, then spoon over 2 doz. opened clams on the half shell. Top each clam with half a slice of uncooked bacon. Place on a bed of rock salt on a baking sheet and cook in a 450° oven for 6-8 min., until bacon is crisp.

CLAMS POSILLIPO. An **Italian American** dish of clams cooked with garlic, red peppers, tomatoes, and seasonings. The dish is named after the cape of Posillipo, near Naples, Italy, but there is no specific, traditional dish by this name in Italy. Neither is there a "classic" Italian American recipe, but the following recipe is typical.

CLAMS POSILLIPO

Wash and drain 4 doz. clams (littlenecks or cherrystones). In ½ c. olive oil, sauté 1 ½ T. minced garlic and 2 seeded dried red peppers for about 1 min. Add ½ c. dry white wine, reduce by half, and add 3 c. canned tomatoes and 1 T. tomato paste. Add salt and pepper, 1 T. oregano, and ¼ c. chopped parsley. Cover, bring to a boil, then simmer for 15 min. Add clams, cover, and cook until clams open, about 8-10 min. Serves 4-5.

CLUB. A term for a bill or check for one's meal. It was first mentioned in print in 1793 but is now obsolete.

CLUB SANDWICH. A sandwich usually made with three slices of toast enclosing fillings of lettuce, mayonnaise, cooked chicken breast, tomato slices, cooked bacon strips, and a garnish. James Beard, in *American Cookery* (1972), insists, however, that the original club sandwiches were made with only two slices of toast (sometimes called a "junior club") and called the three-slice rendition "a horror." He and others have also cited the alternate name of "clubhouse sandwich," which suggests its origins were in the kitchens that prepared food for men's private social clubs.

A letter to the *New York Times* in 1983 cited an explanation of the sandwich's origins in a book entitled *New York, a Guide to the Empire State* (1962): "In 1894 Richard Canfield (1865–1914), the debonair patron of art, purchased the Saratoga Club [in Saratoga, New York] to make it a casino. Canfield Solitaire was originated in the casino's gambling rooms and the club sandwich in its kitchens."

The first appearance of the term "club sandwich" was on a menu of the steamer *Rhode Island* for October 17, 1899, and was mentioned in Ray L. McCardell's *Conversations of a Chorus Girl* in 1903, the same year the first recipe appeared in and recipes were printed in the *Good Housekeeping Everyday Cook Book*, by Isabel Gordon Curtis. At least three restaurants at the 1904 Louisiana Purchase Exposition, in St. Louis, listed a club sandwich on their menus, and Fannie Farmer's *Boston Cooking-School Cook Book* (1906) gave a recipe, which indicates the item had been popular for some time.

COBBLER. A cold drink made from wine, sherry, liquor, or other alcohol with citrus juice and sugar. The word's origins are obscure; one conjecture has it associated with a shortened form of "cobbler's punch," meaning that it had the effect of "patching up" the imbiber. Washington Irving's reference to a "sherry-cobbler" in his *History of New York…by Diedrich Knickerbocker* (1809) is the first printed appearance of the word in reference to a drink.

Another kind of cobbler is a deep-dish pie with a thick crust and a fruit filling. This dish is called **bird's nest pudding** or "crow's-nest pudding" in New England; it is served with a custard but no topping in Connecticut, with maple sugar in Massachusetts, and with a sour sauce in Vermont.

COBB SALAD. A chopped salad made with avocado, lettuce, celery, tomato, bacon, chicken, chives, hard-boiled egg, watercress, and Roquefort cheese. The dish was created at the Brown Derby, in Los Angeles, in 1937 by owner Bob Cobb, who invented it as a way to utilize leftovers in the refrigerator. According to food writer Merrill Shindler, "The name Cobb has become generic for every sort of chopped salad, even concoctions that are more shredded or julienned than chopped." The original recipe, from the *Brown Derby Cook Book*, is given below.

COBB SALAD

Cut ½ head lettuce, ½ bunch watercress, one small bunch chicory, and ½ head romaine into fine pieces and arrange in salad bowl. Cut 2 medium, peeled tomatoes in half,

remove seeds, dice finely, and arrange in strips across the salad. Dice 2 boiled chicken breasts and arrange over the greens and tomatoes. Finely chop 6 strips crisp bacon and sprinkle on salad. Cut 1 avocado into small pieces and arrange around the edge of the salad. Decorate by sprinkling the top with 3 chopped hard-boiled eggs, 2 T. chopped chives, and ½ c. grated Roquefort cheese. Just before serving, mix the salad with French dressing. Serves 4-6.

COBIA. Also "sergeant fish," "lemonfish," "black salmon," "crabeater" and other names. A warm-water fish (*Rachycentron canadum*) of the Mid-Atlantic coast, up to five feet long, with wide stripes and a spindle shape. The origin of the word is unknown, appearing first in 1879.

COCKTAIL. A beverage combining liquors with juices, sodas, or other ingredients. Examples include **martinis**, **manhattans**, **Sazeracs**, **screwdrivers**, and many others. The term does not usually refer to punches or any hot drinks and is usually associated with aperitifs.

The word *cocktail* has been a subject of some controversy among etymologists and historians. H. L. Mencken, in his first supplement to *The American Language* (1945), notes seven sources of origin for the term, including references to the British "cock ale," a seventeenth-century concoction of chicken broth and ale. The word has been traced in print to 1803, but it appears to be somewhat older than that. Stuart Berg Flexner, in *Listening to America* (1982), strongly supports the contention that the word derives from the French *coquetier*, for "egg cup," the container in which French apothecary Antoine Peychaud served his concoction of bitters and Sazerac-du-Forge brandy after his arrival in New Orleans, in about 1795. Other authorities have problems with this assertion, including Professor Arthur Schlesinger Jr., who wondered how the word could have so quickly found its way into a Hudson, New York, newspaper (the *Balance*) by 1806 if it had only recently been coined from the French word for "egg cup."

A "cocktail dress" would be a fancy dress worn by a woman to a "cocktail party," a social gathering that became popular in the 1920s, during Prohibition, when alcoholic drinks were hard to find outside the home, except illegally. A "cocktail table" is a low table, usually set between sofa and chairs, around which guests sit and enjoy cocktails. A "cocktail pianist" is an entertainer who plays while people sip cocktails. A "shrimp cocktail" is a variation on the "oyster cocktail," created around 1860 by a San Francisco miner who dipped his oysters in ketchup. A "cocktail finger" is a finger-shaped piece of crabmeat similarly served as an hors d'oeuvre. "Cocktail lounges," where one would go to enjoy cocktails, have been so called since the 1930s.

By the nineteenth century, any mixture of various whiskeys was called a cocktail. Since the 1870s, a mixture using champagne or a sparkling wine was called a "champagne cocktail." A "cocktail shaker," in which cocktails could be mixed with ice, had been created as of the 1860s.

The "cocktail hour" is a period in the late afternoon or early evening when people enjoy a cocktail before dinner. The term is said to have originated in NYC during Prohibition, when **speakeasies** had a tacit understanding with police officials not to open until 6:00 P.M. An establishment named Tony's restaurant at 42 East Fifty-third Street defied this agreement by opening at 4:00 P.M., and a press agent took to calling this period between 4:00 P.M. and 6:00 P.M. "the cocktail hour."

COCONUT. Also "cocoanut." The large pod fruit of the coconut palm (*Cocos nucifera*). The interior white meat of the fruit and its milky liquid are eaten fresh or dried as desserts or as a garnish, and its oil is used for cooking. The word is a combination of a Portuguese children's term *coco*, for the "goblin" shell of the fruit, and the English word "nut." The fruit was first mentioned in English print in 1555, and the first American reference was in 1834.

The origins of the coconut have never been fully understood, but some believe it is native to tropical America and was dispersed to Pacific islands by the drift of the pods through the ocean. Coconuts were known in Egypt by the sixth century, and Marco Polo noted them in India and elsewhere in the Far East. Certainly coconuts were encountered on the Pacific shores of South America and Hawaii, but coconut is not a major crop of the latter. Most of the coconut enjoyed by Americans is imported from Indonesia, the Philippines, and other Pacific countries. Half the coconuts used in the food industry actually come from noncultivated trees.

The dried meat of coconut, called "copra" (probably from the Hindi *khopra*, for "coconut"), is shredded or flaked, often sweetened, or processed to make coconut oil or coconut milk. Americans eat coconut fresh but most often use it in its dried form in desserts such as coconut cake, known since at least 1830. By 1909 coconut ices were enjoyed. Coconut cream, a viscous, sweet, homogenized liquid made with coconut, sugar, and various thickeners, was created in 1948 by Don Ramón Lopez-Irizarry, of Puerto Rico, who sold the item under the name Coco Lopez. It is principally used to make cocktails like the **piña colada**.

COD (family Gadidae). Also "codfish." Any of a variety of marine fishes in this family. Cod is one of the most important food fishes in the world, both fresh and, especially, salted and dried. The word is possibly related to the Middle English word *cod*, meaning a "bag," the shape of which resembles the hefty codfish. The first printed mention of the word as a fish was in 1387.

Cod is a fish inextricably linked to the history and fortunes of America; the fish's abundance in eastern waters was excitedly noted by Venetian navigator Giovanni Caboto (who sailed for England as "John Cabot") on his exploration of Newfoundland in 1497. An English adventurer, Bartholomew Gosnold, found so many of the fish when he sailed south of Nova Scotia in 1602 that he named the arm of land in those waters "Cape Cod," later a center of the New England fishing industry. In 1630, Francis Higginson wrote, "The abundance of Sea-Fish are almost beyond beleeving, and sure I would scarce have baleeved it except I had seene it with mine owne eyes." Ten years later Massachusetts, whose fishing industry had begun in Gloucester in 1623, sent three hundred thousand dried codfish to market. By 1640 the Massachusetts Bay Colony was shipping 300,000 cod to the world market.

The cod trade developed rapidly. American shipbuilders in 1713 created the New England schooner for fishing in the worst of weather, and the newly rich fishing families of the region were slightingly referred to as the "codfish aristocracy." So important was the cod to the livelihood of Massachusetts that the state's house of representatives voted in 1784 to hang a white pine carving of the "Sacred Cod" in its meeting room, where it is still displayed today.

Cod also had a role in maintaining the lucrative triangular trade between England, the North American and West Indian colonies, and Africa. Dried cod would be shipped to Europe, the boats would then pick up slaves in Africa, stop in the Caribbean to load on molasses and sugar, and sell the latter goods to New England–run distilleries, a continual journey of economic barbarism that lasted for more than eighty years.

The American Revolution's peace treaty included provisions for American boats to fish in English waters, thanks to Massachusetts's John Adams.

Young cod is called **scrod**, which is also the name of a dish of young cod baked with white wine and milk. Dried cod is sometimes called "dunfish" in New England.

Per capita U.S. consumption of cod is about one pound annually, with 557 million pounds landed in 2010, for sales of $175 million.

The principal types of cod found in American waters include:

ATLANTIC COD (*Gadus morhua*). This enormous cod dominates the industry, with nearly seven billion pounds caught annually around the world. It ranges the North Atlantic, rarely going as far south as Virginia. It is sometimes called "rock cod."

HADDOCK (*Melanogrammus aeglefinus*). Ranging throughout the North Atlantic as far south as New Jersey, the haddock usually weighs between two and five pounds and is preferred fresh rather than salted. "Finnan haddie" (from a Scottish port, Findhorn, and the Scottish word for haddock) is a smoked haddock popularized by John Ross Jr. in the nineteenth century. The word *haddock* is from Old French *hadot* and first appeared in English print circa 1307. Haddock landings peaked in the mid-1980s, started to make a comeback, then declined again; there were fewer than a million pounds landed by U.S. commercial fishing in 2011.

LING COD. Also "blue cod." A large Pacific-coastline fish (*Ophiodon elongatus*) with a greenish

hue to its skin, first in print in 1929. The **burbot** (*Lota maculosa*) also goes by this name (first in print as of 1946), as well as by "buffalo," "cultus cod," and "green." U.S. commercial and recreational landings of ling cod have soared since the 1990s, with the majority coming from the Pacific Northwest.

CODDES. Also "coddies" and "codfish ball." Salt-cod cakes mixed with mashed potatoes, coated with bread crumbs, deep-fried, and served at room temperature with mustard between two saltine crackers, either as a snack or a lunch item. They are a specialty of Baltimore, where they were commonly sold at drugstore soda fountains.

CODDLE. To cook in a liquid just below the boiling point, as with eggs. Coddled apples are made by cooking apple slices in a syrup of water and sugar in a ratio of 2 to 1. The term dates back to the sixteenth century in print.

COFFEE. Roasted, ground beans from the coffee plant (genus *Coffea*) or a beverage made from these beans. The main species, *C. arabica*, indigenous to Ethiopia, is now grown throughout the so-called coffee belt that rings the world between the latitudes of 25 degrees north and 30 degrees south. Arabica beans now constitute about 75 percent of the world's coffee-bean production. "Congo coffee" (*C. robusta*), with a more robust taste, makes up most of the rest of the world's production.

Coffee plants originated in Ethiopia, and the word's etymology derives either from its shipping point, Kaffa, in that country, or from the Arabic *guhiya* or the Turkish *kahveh*, which referred to a wine tonic that restored the appetite.

There are several legends as to who first brewed coffee. One involves a goatherd of Kaffa named Kaldi, whose goats were particularly sprightly after consuming the caffeine-rich coffee beans—an activity noticed by a local monk named Mullah, who brewed a beverage from the beans and spread word of its restorative virtues throughout the region. An Arab legend of the fifteenth century contends that the ninth-century mufti of Aden was the first to make the drink, after which it became a favorite of the Middle Eastern courts. The first mention of coffee in English is in 1598.

Coffee beans were brought to Italy by 1615, and by 1644 to France, where, thanks to the efforts of Turkish ambassador Suleiman Aga, it became a fashionable beverage in 1669 at the court of Louis XIV, who introduced a single coffee seedling to the Caribbean island of Martinique, thus beginning the spread of the plant throughout Central and South America, which eventually made Brazil the world's largest coffee producer. (The Dutch introduced the plant to Indonesia and Java, and "java" became an American slang term for all coffee as of the mid-nineteenth century.)

The first coffeehouse in London was opened in 1688 by Edward Lloyd (who later built the insurance company Lloyd's of London), and more sprouted quickly, as they did in America, where the Dutch had introduced coffee by 1670. The Merchants Coffee House, in NYC, had by the middle of the eighteenth century become known for entertaining several of the leading revolutionary dissenters of the day. In protest against the high taxes imposed by the British on tea, Americans turned to coffee, causing its sales to increase during the Revolutionary War by 600 percent. But coffee's own high price prevented it from becoming a truly popular drink for decades afterwards, and mock coffee made from rye (called "Boston coffee," although since the twentieth century this has referred to a cup of half coffee and half cream), peas ("Canadian coffee"), or burnt bread ("crumb coffee") was often substituted.

In the 1860s, tea importers George Huntington Hartford and George Gilman organized the American Coffee Corporation to buy beans directly from Brazil and Colombia, thereby making coffee less expensive for the American consumer—twenty-five cents per pound, as compared with the two dollars per pound Americans had paid before—and helping it to become America's favorite beverage.

Americans got the coffee percolator from the English, but "drip pot" was an American term by the end of the century. The "Neapolitan flip" (so called because it is of southern Italian origins) is a method of pouring boiling water over ground coffee placed in a paper filter inside a funnel inside a pouring pot.

"Iced coffee" was first served at the Philadelphia Centennial Exposition in 1876.

In 1878, James Sanborn and Caleb Chase produced the first ground coffee sealed in tin cans. The American taste in coffee was largely due to a blend developed by Joel Cheek of Nashville, Tennessee, served in the 1880s at the Maxwell House Hotel, in that city. It became extremely popular, especially after President Theodore Roosevelt, in 1907, pronounced the coffee "good to the last drop," which remains the motto of the brand Maxwell House to this day.

In New Orleans, the people were drinking **chicory** coffee, a more bitter brew than most American blends. In 1903, a caffeine-free coffee called "Sanka" (a coinage from the French *sans caféine*, "without caffeine") was developed by Dr. Ludwig Roselius of Bremen, Germany, but was not successful until it was promoted in the 1930s by the General Foods Corp. Decaffeinated coffee is made by various methods utilizing either water processing or chemical solvents like ethyl acetate. Today, decaffeinated coffee makes up nearly 22 percent of the American market.

Powdered coffees had been known as of the eighteenth century, but it was not until 1901 that "instant coffee" from powder first appeared, introduced by Satori Kato at the Buffalo Pan American Exposition (later marketed as Nescafé in 1939). Credit for instant coffee also goes to Belgian-born inventor George Washington, who in 1906, while living in Guatemala, discovered a practical process for condensing coffee so that it could be reconstituted merely by adding boiling water in a cup, calling his "soluble" product G. Washington's "Red E Coffee."

Today there are two basic methods for producing instant coffee: "Spray-dried" (or "regular") instant is sprayed through hot air after being brewed, thereby removing the water. "Freeze-dried" instant is made from brewed coffee frozen into slabs, then ground and passed through a vacuum and heat in order to remove the water. "Agglomeration" is a process by which spray-dried coffee powder is made into more appealing little nuggets.

Coffee is almost always a blend of beans from various sources. Brazil provides the beans for one-third of the world's consumption, Vietnam is the second-largest producer, Colombia third, and there are large plantations in Costa Rica, Mexico, India, Indonesia, Ethiopia, and various other African countries. Some of the best beans come from Jamaica, and Hawaii produces a coffee, known as "Kona," that is highly esteemed.

Americans have generally preferred a lighter, less robust coffee than the rest of the world, and instant coffee makes up a great share of the domestic market. The term "American coffee" has become useful to restaurants within the past decade to describe a blend that is percolated, as opposed to **espresso**, "café filtré," or Hispanic coffees, which are very hearty and rich and brewed by a drip method. An "American roast," also called a "regular roast," is somewhat heavier than a "light roast." A "heavy roast" (sometimes called "dark French") is extremely dark, while "Italian roast" (preferred for espresso) is glossy and dark brown. "Viennese roast" is a blend of one-third heavy and two-thirds regular, while "European roast" transposes the ratio. "Mocha" is either a coffee from Yemen (whose name is derived from the city of Mocha there) or a Yemeni coffee having a taste of chocolate. "Mocha" may also refer to a beverage made with coffee and cocoa mixed together with water or milk or to any flavor derived from these two beans. "Jamoke" (also "jamoca" or "jamocha") is an early-twentieth-century term for coffee in general, a combination of "java" and "mocha."

The popularity of darker coffees like espresso was fueled by a new interest in coffee shops with stylish decor, baked goods, and new, expensive variations on Italian and European coffees. This trend was started in 1987 by Howard Schultz, who bought Starbucks Coffee in Seattle that year and built two thousand locations; the company now has eighteen thousand coffeehouses in sixty-two countries. Today 34 percent of coffee drinkers get their beverages from premium stores. The specialty coffee market now takes in annual revenues of $18 billion.

Americans consume half the world's coffee supply, and 65 percent of Americans over the age of eighteen drink coffee—down from a high of 74.7 percent in 1962—consuming about 100 billion cups each year, which translates to 23.5 gallons per person. September 29 is National Coffee Day in the U.S.

The U.S. produces only about nine million pounds of coffee annually, with the rest imported. Thirty-five percent of America's 155 million coffee drinkers take their coffee black; 30 percent add cream or sugar. Americans drink coffee with breakfast, in the middle of the morning at a "coffee break" (so called since the mid-1940s), at lunch, with snacks (especially doughnuts), and with or after dinner. In many restaurants, the coffee cup and saucer will be placed on the table at the start of the meal. Coffee mugs are popular at inexpensive restaurants,

diners, and lunch counters, and takeout eateries offer Styrofoam or cardboard coffee cups. Americans take their coffee either "black" (with no sugar, milk, or cream), "light" (with a lot of milk or cream), or "regular" (which usually refers to coffee with some sugar and milk or cream, although regional differences may eliminate one or the other in usage).

COFFEE AND. A colloquial abbreviation for coffee served with doughnuts, pastries, cake, etc., at a social function. The phrase, dating in print to 1901, is most commonly used to describe the snacks served after a business meeting.

COFFEE FILTER. Cooks' slang for the tall, white paper hat they traditionally wear (formally called a "toque"), because it resembles a paper filter through which coffee is dripped, dating in print to 1999.

COFFEE KLATCH. An informal get-together over coffee. The term, which comes from a similar German term, *Kaffeeklatsch* ("coffee gossip"), first in English print in 1890, was especially popular during the 1950s and 1960s.

COFFEE MILK. A blend of a little coffee in a glass of sweetened milk. It is a specialty of Rhode Island, where the tradition dates back to 1905, when Daniel Ablesen began selling coffee milk in Pawtucket. In 1914, Eclipse Food Products began bottling a coffee syrup, using the slogan "You'll smack your lips when it's Eclipse." Today the drink can also be purchased in containers, already mixed. "Coffee milk" also refers to simple coffee with hot milk.

COFFIN. A pastry crust, a deep-dish pie, or the pan it is baked in; the name refers to a coffin in which a body is laid.

COLA CAKE. A cake made with marshmallows and Coca-Cola soda.

COLA CAKE

In a bowl sift 2 c. sugar with 2 c. flour. Add 1 ½ c. small marshmallows. In a saucepan mix 1 stick butter, ½ c. vegetable oil, 3 T. cocoa, and 1 c. Coca-Cola. Bring to a boil, pour into dry ingredients, blend well, and add ½ c. buttermilk, 1 t. baking soda, 2 eggs, and 1 t. vanilla extract. Mix well, pour into a greased 9-by-13-in. pan, bake in 350° oven for 45 min. Remove. Make frosting by combining 1 stick butter, 3 T. cocoa, and 6 T. Coca-Cola in a saucepan. Bring to a boil. In a bowl put 16 oz. confectioners' sugar. Pour frosting liquid over sugar, blend, and add 1 t. vanilla extract and 1 c. chopped pecans. Spread frosting onto cake.

COLA ROAST. A southern dish made by basting a roast beef with cola soda as it roasts.

COLCANNON. A dish of boiled cabbage and potatoes. The term dates in print to 1843 and comes from the Irish Gaelic *cál ceannan*.

COLD CUT. Usually meant to refer to a thin slice of meat served cold for lunch, either on a **sandwich** or with various salads, vegetables, mayonnaise, or mustard, or made into snacks. The most common meats are bologna, liverwurst, beef, turkey breast, ham, chicken, tongue, pastrami, and various salamis. The first printed reference to the term appeared in 1940.

COLD DUCK. A mixture of American sparkling red and white wines (1965), it is a semisweet, low-alcohol beverage that achieved widespread popularity in the 1970s and then faded by the beginning of the 1980s.

There are several versions of how cold duck got its name, though most authorities agree that it is a mistaken transformation of the German words *Kalte Ende*, "cold ending." Some assert that the drink originated in Bavaria, where hunters would begin the day with a glass of sparkling wine. The unused wine was then mixed together with other leftover wines and drunk cold at the end of the day.

Another story credits the court of German emperor and king of Prussia Wilhelm I (1797–1888) with the drink's origins, when General Alexander August Wilhelm von Pape, attending a dinner hosted by the emperor, remarked that he preferred a "cold ending" rather than coffee at the end of a meal and proceeded to mix *Sekt* and a Moselle wine with lemon juice. Enjoying a *Kalte Ende* became popular after that.

Somehow *Kalte Ende* was erroneously transformed, perhaps in dialect, into *Kalte Ente*, meaning "cold duck."

The drink came to America by way of a German immigrant named Harold Borgman, original owner of the Pontchartrain Wine Cellars, in Detroit, where, he contended, he first made the drink with champagne and still burgundy wine in 1935. It remained a local favorite until, in 1963, the general manager of an importing firm sampled the drink and talked one of his suppliers into bottling the concoction. A year later, the first commercially sold cold duck was produced, followed by examples from California and Michigan. American sparkling burgundy replaced the still burgundy originally used, and American champagne was used instead of *Sekt* or true French champagne. (Germany has bottled a lemon-flavored version of *Kalte Ente* since 1948 and a red variation called *Turkenblut*.) After 1971, cold duck was a semisweet aperitif with enormous sales in America, but the American palate soon grew tired of the soda-pop-like quality of the beverage, and sales had dropped precipitously by the end of the decade.

COLESLAW. Also "cabbage salad." Shredded cabbage, mayonnaise, and seasonings, usually served cold as a side dish. The word is from the Dutch *koolsla*, a combination of *kool* (cabbage) and *sla* (salad), a dish that was known in America in print by 1785. Because it is usually served cold, some call the dish "cold slaw," in contrast to "hot slaw," but there is no relation to the temperature in the etymology.

COLESLAW

In a large bowl stir together 1 c. mayonnaise, 1 T. lemon juice, 4 c. shredded cabbage, and 1 ½ c. shredded carrots. Add ½ c. raisins if desired. Makes about 5 c.

COLLARD GREENS. Also "collards." A variety of kale (*Brassica oleracea* var. *acephala*) with a rosette of green leaves. The word comes from "colewort" (a word that describes the *Brassica* family of cabbages) and dates in American print to 1745. This nutritious green vegetable is one of the staples of southern cooking, particularly among African Americans, who often refer to collards simply as "greens." They are usually boiled and seasoned with ham hocks, and they form the basis for **potlikker**.

COLLATION. A light meal or refreshment served to one's guests. It originally referred to a light repast taken by monks, first appearing in print circa 1305, derived from the end-of-the-day reading of the lives of the saints or scriptures.

COLUMBUS, CHRISTOPHER (1451–1506). Explorer, author. Indisputably, no one has had a more powerful effect on American food than Christopher Columbus, whose sailing westward from Europe to find a spice route to Asia actually resulted in a radical alteration of the world's gastronomy, from the introduction on both sides of the Atlantic and Pacific of new foods to the establishment of new empires built on trade. It is also wholly reasonable to claim that his setting foot on the island the natives called Guanahani was the single most transformative event in human history.

Born in the Republic of Genoa, Cristoforo Colombo became a sailor and adventurer early on, sailing as far as Iceland as of 1477. Although not formally well educated, he read widely in scholarly languages and combined what he learned with his own empirical observations of the world. The idea that the world was round, not flat, was long acknowledged, and Columbus developed plans to mount a discovery mission to the Orient.

His goal was to sail westward from Spain to find a spice route to the Orient (he estimated Japan to be about three thousand miles from the Canary Islands) and to bring back gold—this at a time when spices were nearly worth their weight in precious metals. As a reward, his Spanish benefactors, King Ferdinand and Queen Isabella, said Columbus would be entitled to 10 percent of all the revenues from the new lands in perpetuity and the option to buy a one-eighth interest in any commercial venture and receive one-eighth of the profits.

Driven by easterly winds for two and a half months, Columbus spotted a light at two o'clock in the morning of October 12 and upon landing found a tropical Eden, a place "extremely verdant and fertile, with the air agreeable, and probably containing many things of which I am ignorant, not inclining to stay here, but to visit other islands in search of gold."

Columbus made four voyages to the New World, exploring most of the Caribbean and reaching Central America on his last expedition.

In every sense, Columbus failed to find what he'd been sent to find, but within a decade that fertility he found was of far more importance. "The Columbian Exchange," a term coined in 1972 by historian Alfred W. Crosby, was a radical, headlong transformation of the world's food, land use, wealth, and geopolitics.

America gave scores of new foods to the rest of the world—corn, tomatoes, potatoes, chile peppers, agave, turkey, cocoa, pineapple, squash, vanilla, wild rice, and more. In exchange, Europeans brought to America cattle, chickens, honeybees, bananas, rice, barley, garlic, oats, rye, rice, and sugarcane.

On such an exchange were built colonies and empires, economies and fortunes, with slavery and war the by-products.

Columbus, who was jailed for committing atrocities against the native people, died in poverty in 1506, perceived by most, and by himself, as a failure. Yet, as the philosopher George Santayana wrote, "He gave the world another world."

COMBINATION PLATTER. Also "combo platter." Restaurant term for a dish composed of several items on the menu. It is especially associated with barbecue, Chinese, and Mexican restaurants.

COMFORT FOOD. Any food that a person considers to put him at ease, often as part of nostalgia for a favored childhood food. First in print in 1977. Often it is of a soft consistency, like mashed potatoes. In her book *Comfort Food* (1986), Sue Kreitzman wrote of her subject:

> [Comfort foods] don't take us back to the womb but to the period shortly thereafter when we were safely cradled and gently fed. Fragrant, gutsy stews, thick chunky soups, and bubbling gratins make us feel safe, warm, and well protected from the raging elements. Old-fashioned desserts that contain plenty of texture and temperature contrasts help us surrender to sensual pleasure and so forget the stresses of a sometimes cruel world.

COMMON CRACKER. Very crisp, hard, thick wheat-flour cracker that may be split and grilled with butter or cheddar cheese, ground into bread crumbs, or eaten in chowders; similar to **Boston cracker**. The term first appeared in print in 1939. One manufacturer claims common crackers were first baked by Charles Cross in about 1830 in his Montpelier, Vermont, bakery, and were called "Cross crackers" or "Montpelier crackers." But in her *New England Cookbook* (1954), Eleanor Early credits the cracker's invention to Artemus Kennedy of Menotomy, Massachusetts, almost two hundred years ago. Early wrote that "Artemus had a large family and it was said that the children learned to retrieve the crackers [that Artemus tossed on the floor of a big Dutch oven]… before they could walk. Baking was done three times a week, and Artemus rode about the countryside on his horse, selling them from his saddlebags."

Whatever their origins, common crackers are no longer easily found, and the news that a Rockingham, Vermont, citizen named Vrest Orton had bought the original Charles Cross machinery and begun to sell common crackers again in 1981 was greeted with considerable interest by those who remember the taste of dry, crisp morsels split opened and eaten with good Vermont cheddar. See also **Trenton cracker**.

COMMON CRACKER

A recipe from Louise Andrews Kent's *Mrs. Appleyard's Kitchen* (1942) gave the following recipe for "Puffed Montpelier Crackers": "Split each cracker in half….Put ice cubes into a large bowl of cold water. When the water is very cold, put in the split cracker halves….At the end of three minutes—or sooner, if they seem to be getting too soft—remove the crackers from the ice water….When they have drained about five minutes, put them into iron dripping pans and dot them thickly with soft butter. Dust them with paprika, if you wish. Heat the oven to 450° and bake them until they are puffed, crisp, and golden brown. They should be done in 25 to 35 minutes."

COMMON DOINGS. A frontier term dating in print to 1838, for any plain food.

COMMONS. A college or university dining hall, where the students are served a "common" meal. It may also refer to the food itself, a meaning dating to the sixteenth century in England.

CONCH (genus *Strombus*). A brightly colored gastropod mollusk eaten in the Caribbean and Florida. The word (which is pronounced "conk") is from the Latin *concha* and, as slang, has been applied since at least 1852 to the inhabitants of Key West, Florida, especially to those with a Bahamian ancestry of mixed cockney and African American blood, probably because of their fondness for the marine food. (Low-class white North Carolinians have also been called "conchs" for the same reason.)

Because of its popularity, conch was almost fished out in Florida waters, and commercial fishing of the mollusk has been banned for more than a decade. Most conch comes from Bahamian and other waters.

Conch meat is tough and must be pounded or finely chopped. It is often served in salads, as fritters, or in a chowder.

CONCORD. A dark red labrusca hybrid grape used to make wine and jelly, jam, and preserves, first in print in 1858 after being propagated in 1849 from a seedling grown in Concord, Massachusetts, by Ephraim Wales Bull, whose discovery enriched others but not himself: His gravestone reads, "he sowed, but others reaped."

Concord was especially successful in New York State, both as a wine grape and as an eating grape. Oversupply in the 1890s led to a bust, which in turn prompted two dentists named Welch to set up the world's first large grape-juice plant, at Westfield, New York. The Welch Grape Juice Co. prospered under Prohibition by selling unfermented wine and the juice to make jellies, jams, and preserves. Jacob Merrill "Jack" Kaplan bought the company in 1945 and began making a very sweet kosher wine from Concord grapes. He neglected to put the word "kosher" on the label, however, and thereby lost out to other kosher-wine producers like Manischewitz and Mogen David.

Today the majority of New York's Concord grapes go into making jams, jellies, and preserves, as well as grape juice and concentrates.

CONEY ISLAND. Also "coney." Principally this refers to a **hot dog** whose popularity was associated with Brooklyn's Coney Island amusement-park vendors, but it may also refer to a **hamburger**, **hero** sandwich, or, prior to World War I, fried clams. In Syracuse, New York, "coney" refers specifically to a white pork sausage much like a German *Weisswurst* served in a bun.

CONVENIENCE STORE. Also "C-store." A small market carrying an array of basic packaged foods, coffee, some **fast food**, and other nonfood goods intended for customers stopping quickly to pick up a few items. The term dates in print to 1960, but credit for the idea has gone to Joe C. Thompson, of Dallas, who in 1927 began selling bread, milk, and eggs at his **icehouse**, out of which grew the largest chain of convenience stores—the 7-Eleven stores, owned by the Southland Corporation. Indeed, according to a 1983 *Newsweek* article about a murder at a convenience store in Port Arthur, Texas, *"all convenience stores were called 7-Elevens in the language of the street."*

Many convenience stores are located within gas stations, and most stay open for long hours or twenty-four hours a day.

CONVERSATION HEART. Also "candy heart." A small, heart-shaped candy made from sugar paste, corn syrup, and dextrose and imprinted with a Valentine's Day message such as i love you or kiss me. They were created in 1902 by the New England Confectionary Co., better known as NECCO (which also produces NECCO Wafers candies from the same ingredients), of Cambridge, Massachusetts. They were originally called "Tiny Conversation Hearts." NECCO makes about eight billion pieces each year, although the candy is also produced by other companies.

COOKBOOK. A term for a book of recipes, dating in print to 1800. Before 1809, such volumes were referred to as "cookerie books," "recipe books," "receipt books," or "culinary reviews." The first American cookbooks were family collections of favorite recipes handed down from one generation to the next, as well as American editions of English volumes like *The Compleat Housewife* (1742), by **Eliza Smith**. But in June 1796, Amelia Simmons, who called herself "An American Orphan," published the forty-seven-page *American Cookery: Or, the Art of Dressing Viands, Fish, Poultry, and Vegetables. And the Best Modes of Making Puff Pastes, Pies, Tarts, Puddings, Custards and Preserves. And All Kinds of Cakes, from the Imperial Plumb to Plain Cake. Adapted to This Country and All Grades of Life*. It was the first published volume to include recipes for specifically American dishes such as cranberry sauce and pumpkin pie.

Cookbooks began appearing rapidly after Simmons's successful venture. Lydia Child's *The American Frugal Housewife* (1832), Mary Randolph's *Virginia Housewife* (1824), Eliza Leslie's *Directions for Cookery* (1837), Sallie Rutledge's *Carolina Housewife* (1847), Elizabeth H. Putnam's *Mrs. Putnam's Receipt Book* (1850), and others were very popular. Catharine Esther Beecher's *Treatise on Domestic Economy for the Use of Young Ladies at Home and at School* (1841) and *Miss Beecher's Domestic Receipt Book* (1846) were significant for their tips on food storage and the use of ovens and kitchen utensils.

In 1896, **Fannie Merritt Farmer** published *The Boston Cooking-School Cook Book*, which for the first time applied scientific terms and precise measurements to recipes. In it appeared the first American instructions to use a "level teaspoon" rather than the usual "dash" or "pinch" other writers decreed. Farmer's cookbook, originally published in a three-thousand-copy edition at her own expense, was an immediate and tremendous bestseller, and she became one of the most important women in America for changing the way women of the period cooked and managed their households.

In the twentieth century, cookbooks were often issued by food companies to promote their product, cooking institutes to promote their schools, and newspapers to promote their sales. The *Boston Post Cook Book*, for instance, which originated in *The Great Breakfast Table Paper of New England*, listed favorite dishes of famous American women, including Mrs. Calvin Coolidge, and pages of "household hints" ranging from the use of a corn popper to methods for removing tea stains. Various food-industry organizations—apple growers, meatpackers, cereal makers, and canned-product companies, for example—offered cookbooks to the public, and there is a long tradition of church groups, Junior Leagues, and women's clubs that publish their own, usually based on members' own recipes. Some of these grew into bestselling books, such as *The Joy of Cooking*, by Irma S. Rombauer and Marion Rombauer Becker, published in numerous editions since 1931 (the first commercial edition was published in 1936 by the Bobbs-Merrill Co.). Other popular cookbooks issued forth from the editorial departments of the so-called Seven Sisters women's magazines: *Woman's Day* (which began in 1931 as a menu sheet given away free at A&P supermarkets), *Better Homes and Gardens*, *McCall's*, *Good Housekeeping*, *Redbook*, *Family Circle*, and *Ladies' Home Journal*. **Betty Crocker**'s *Cookbook*, first issued in 1950, has since sold more than twenty-two million copies.

Ethnic foods formed but a small section of most of these books, and only after World War II did ethnic cookbooks begin to interest the American public, although the authors almost always "adapted" foreign recipes to an American palate that supposedly did not care for highly seasoned or spicy foods or for dishes that took much time to prepare and cook. Such modifications led to mistaken notions among many Americans about the true nature of ethnic foods, and foreign restaurateurs catered to the same conventions.

In the 1950s and 1960s, there appeared a number of very popular cookbooks that were sold on gimmickry, from an attempt to sympathize with the housewife who really did not much enjoy cooking (with titles such as Peg Bracken's *I Hate to Cook Book*) to small volumes, often enhanced by strong graphic design, that catered to a specific approach to cookery, such as patio, fondue, backyard, or hibachi cookbooks in which every recipe was adapted to the book's idea.

Also in the 1960s, however, came the first series of serious, specialized, and challenging cookbooks that demonstrated some of the more sophisticated and authentic techniques of preparing French, Italian, Chinese, and other ethnic cuisines, beginning with **Julia Child**'s *Mastering the Art of French Cooking*, first published in 1961 and keyed to a very well-received public-television show. Child abated the fears of some American cooks who regarded classic French cuisine as intimidating, and there quickly followed volumes by other authors on regional Italian cookery, authentic Cantonese and Szechuan cookery, and true Mexican cookery. Later came Vietnamese, Indian, and Thai cookbooks of great authority, as well as translations of the cookbooks of the French practitioners of **nouvelle cuisine**.

In the late 1960s and 1970s, there appeared a series of beautifully designed and thoroughly researched volumes by Time-Life Books, under the general editorship of Richard L. Williams, entitled *Foods of the World*. These books surveyed the cuisines of Japan, Russia, Italy, and other countries, along with several volumes on American cooking, from the South to the Northwest, including a volume gathering up the various ethnic influences on American food, entitled *The Melting Pot*.

There was increased interest in American food in the 1980s, resulting in large numbers of regional cookbooks that more often than not provided a good deal of information on the region's food culture and history. One of the most important was *Chef* **Paul Prudhomme**'s *Louisiana Kitchen* (1984), which sparked a national interest in Cajun cooking. **Celebrity chefs** who had cooking shows on television, like Jeff Smith (*The Frugal Gourmet*), or ran celebrated restaurants, like **Wolfgang Puck**, of Spago, in Los Angeles, and Jasper White, of Jasper's, in Boston, wrote cookbooks that expressed their own sense of style and personality as much as they did good taste. Two of the bestselling cookbooks of the 1980s were "lifestyle" books in which the mood created by the settings in which food was photographed was every bit as important as the food itself. These were **Martha Stewart**'s *Entertaining* (1982) and *Lee Bailey's Country Weekends* (1983), and their imitators grew numerous in the decade to follow. In the late 1980s, the genre turned more toward culinary memoirs and authoritative ethnic works on regional cookery of various parts of the world, especially Italy and France, such as *A Taste of Alsace*, by Sue Style (1990), *The Cooking of the Eastern Mediterranean*, by Paula Wolfert (1994), and *The Foods of Vietnam*, by Nicole Routhier (1989). Others included *The Food and Wine of Greece*, by Diane Kochilas (1990), *Memoirs of a Cuban Kitchen*, by Mary Urrutia Randelman and Joan Schwartz (1992), *Catalan Cuisine*, by **Colman Andrews** (1988), and *Naples at Table*, by Arthur Schwartz (1998). This period also saw a number of general cookbooks, such as Julia Child's *The Way to Cook* (1989) and Mark Bittman's *How to Cook Everything* (1998), that attempted to show how recipes go wrong and how dishes can best be made in the home.

At the turn of the twenty-first century, celebrity chefs published scores of cookbooks, especially TV show hosts who tied the books' recipes to their series, such as Rick Bayless's *Mexican Everyday* (2005), Ming Tsai's

Ming's Master Recipes (2005), Guy Fieri's *Guy Fieri Food* (2011), and Lidia Mattichio Bastianich's *Lidia's Little Italy in America* (2011). University publishers began to reissue historic cookbooks like *Madame Begué's Picayune Creole Cook Book* (first published in 1901, reissued in 2012).

COOKIE. A small, flat, sweet cake eaten as a snack or with other desserts. The word is from the Dutch *koekje*, "little cake," and first appeared in print in 1695. The term is little used in England, where "biscuit" is still preferred, as it was in America until the late twentieth century; in Scotland, "cookie" refers to a small bun. In America, the cookie has been a favorite snack food since the Dutch made cookies popular in their early settlements. A "filled cookie" is a form of cookie sandwich stuffed with a fruit filling, usually date or raisin, as in a Fig Newton.

One finds dozens of cookie recipes in eighteenth- and nineteenth-century cookbooks, but the most popular cookie in America today—the chocolate-chip or **Toll House cookie**, created by Mrs. Ruth Wakefield, who owned the Toll House Inn, in Whitman, Massachusetts—did not appear until after 1930. The next most popular cookies are oatmeal raisin, peanut butter, and oatmeal.

See also, **Moon Pie**, **Girl Scout Cookies**, **whoopie pies**, and **Oreo**.

COOKING WINE. Any wine primarily intended to be added to cooked foods for flavor. The alcohol in cooking wine is burned off in the cooking process, leaving a faint taste of the wine. Although gourmets recommend using a good wine for cooking, most wines used for this purpose are inexpensive and lack distinction. During Prohibition, many of these wines were salted so as to make them undrinkable.

COOTER. A southern-dialect word for a box **turtle**. From either a West African word, *kuta*, or a Kongo word, *nkuda*, it was first printed in English in 1832, though probably used for a long while before that on southern plantations. Cooter stew is still part of southern cookery.

COQUINA SOUP. A Florida soup of periwinkle clams. "Coquina" derives from the Spanish for "small clam"

and since the 1800s has referred to a buildup of marine shells bound by calcareous cement and used as a building material.

COQUINA SOUP

Rinse clams in water several times, cover with water, bring to a boil, and simmer 10 min. Pour through sieve and serve.

CORBITT, HELEN (1906–1978). American chef and cookbook author. Corbitt is considered one of the first modern food editors of the postwar era and had an effect on the nation's gastronomy through her rigorous recipe development and her sense of culinary style.

Born in New York City, Corbitt was a dietitian at Cornell Medical School before moving to Austin, Texas, in 1931 to manage the Tea House at the University of Texas, then went to Joske's department store, in Houston. She began her own catering business in Austin at the Driskill Hotel, then, in 1955, became director of food services at the Zodiac Room at the Neiman-Marcus department store in Dallas, which allowed her to travel extensively to collect recipes and write several cookbooks.

In 1969, the Texas Restaurant Association gave Corbitt the Outstanding Service Award. In 1975, the *Chicago Tribune* called her the "Balenciaga of food and the best cook in Texas," and in 2009 the *Los Angeles Times* called her "the Julia Child-esque cooking celebrity with a Texas twang."

She wrote columns for the *Arkansas Democrat* and the *Houston Chronicle*. Her books include *Helen Corbitt's Cookbook* (1957), *Helen Corbitt's Potluck* (1962), *Helen Corbitt Cooks for Company* (1974), *Helen Corbitt Cooks for Looks* (1967), and *Helen Corbitt's Greenhouse Cookbook*, published posthumously in 1978.

CORDIAL. A sweet, syrupy spirit, synonymous with "liqueur," which is the preferred term in England and France, though it is often heard in America. "Cordial" derives from the Medieval Latin *cordialis*, from the Latin *cor*, "heart," first appearing in print in 1637 in John Milton's *Comus*, to describe a "cordial julep."

Cordials once had medicinal uses, and the oldest-known example dates back to Hippocrates, who concocted one of cinnamon and wine-sweetened honey in about 420 B.C. The tradition was carried on by European monks, and many cordials now made commercially were first created by such men of the cloth.

Cordials are made by three processes: infusion (or maceration), in which the flavorings steep in alcohol; percolation, in which the alcohol percolates above the flavorings; and distillation, in which ingredients are distilled directly from their extracted flavors in copper stills, a method that results in clear, colorless liquids of varying proofs. A fruit-flavored brandy is a cordial made with a brandy base, but other spirits are used for other kinds of cordials.

Most American cordials are quite sweet, with up to 35 percent sugar, and are made from various fruits, beans, and herbs, ranging from cherry to chocolate to mint. Some are milk-based, with low alcohol. A "dry" cordial must have less than 10 percent sugar, but no cordial may have less than 2.5 percent sugar by weight.

CORN. Any of a variety of a cultivated cereal plant, *Zea mays*, yielding a sweet kernel that is made into oil, eaten fresh, or cooked in a wide variety of dishes. In Great Britain, the word generally refers to any major cereal crop and was applied to this new cereal they found in North America in 1608. But the word *maize* (from the Taino Indian *mahiz*) was more common in the New World. Because the cereal was so associated with the Native Americans, it was soon being called "Indian corn" by the white settlers, to distinguish it from their own cereals, such as barley and wheat.

Corn was not only a staple crop of the Native Americans; it was the staff of life for many tribes ranging from Canada to South America long before Columbus arrived in the West Indies. It was grown in Mexico in prehistoric times and reached the territory that is now the U.S. more than two millennia ago, where it became part of Native American rituals and religion. Many legends and deities were devoted to the cycle of raising corn. The Native Americans called the cereal "Sacred Mother" and "Giver of Life," and the Zuni dusted their doorways with cornmeal in the belief that its miraculous powers would prevent the marauding conquistadores from entering. According to Alfred Whiting, in *Ethnobotany of the Hopi* (1966), the Hopi of the Southwest had at least twenty different varieties of cultivated corn, in a rainbow of colors, each of which was symbolic in some way.

Native Americans roasted their corn and ground it into meal to make cakes, breads, and porridges. Tortillas were made with cornmeal before the Spanish introduced wheat, and **succotash** was a Native American vegetable stew that provided a great range of nutrients. When the Spanish landed in Cuba on November 5, 1492, they were treated to *mahiz* in at least two forms: baked and ground into flour.

When Captain John Smith explored the Virginia territory in 1607, he commented on "great heapes of corn" stored away by the Native Americans, and the colonists from the ship *Susan Constant* were met at Chesapeake Bay in April 1607 by friendly Native Americans led by Powhatan, who gave them a feast of corn bread, venison, and berries. When Miles Standish alighted from the *Mayflower* at Plymouth in 1620, he immediately came upon an Indian cache of corn and collected it for the winter ahead. By the following spring the Pilgrims were planting corn in the Native American method, by poking a hole in the ground and putting in the corn kernels with a dead fish that served to fertilize them. By the fall, twenty acres of corn were harvested—the European grains of barley and wheat having failed—and served at the first **Thanksgiving.** The Native Americans even brought a remarkable delicacy to the feast: **popcorn**. The new cereal was precious and helped the early settlers to survive those first harsh years. There is a record of a public whipping in the Plymouth Colony in 1622 of settlers who dared eat the new corn before it was fully ripe (although immature corn, called "green corn" or "roasting corn," was long a staple of southern cooking, until the 1920s).

Before long, uniquely American dishes were being developed on the basis of this new grain, including an Indian bread called "pone" or "corn pone" (from the Algonquian word *apan*, "baked"), made of cornmeal, salt, and water. This was later called "corn bread" and is a staple of American cooking to this day.

Hominy was, as of 1629, a term for a cornmeal porridge, though it referred specifically to dried, hulled corn kernels. Once the crops took hold throughout the colonies, cornmeal foods were everyday fare, and slaves on the southern plantations lived on a diet of corn bread and water, as did the poorest white settlers. "Slapper" is a kind of fritter, like a pancake, also called "Indian slappers." "Dodger" (or "**corn dodger**") was a fried corn cake (first mentioned in print in 1831), the meaning of which is obscure but may derive from a Scots word, *dadge*, for a **bannock**. Mature "sweet corn" (also called "sugar corn"), fit to be boiled and buttered, was first found along the banks of the Susquehanna River in an Indian village in 1779, but it was not until the 1820s that it garnered much attention among farmers and not until the 1840s that it became a ubiquitous item on American dinner tables. In fact, the term "corn on the cob" entered the language only in 1876.

Throughout the nineteenth century, the corn crop increased as settlers moved into the western territories, using it both for food and fodder. In the mid-1800s, a new hybrid called Reid's Yellow Dent (after the farmer who discovered it, Robert Reid of Tazewell County, Illinois), created by chance cross-pollination, began to be widely cultivated in the Midwest, and by 1882 people were referring to the great corn-producing states of the Midwest as the "Corn Belt." "Corncrackers," mills for grinding corn, were known by 1844, and "corn poppers" were marketed in the 1870s. A breakfast **cereal** called "cornflakes," developed by **Dr. John Harvey Kellogg** and his brother Will Keith Kellogg, of Battle Creek, Michigan, made its appearance on the market in 1907. "Corn roasts" were popular social events by 1899, and **corn syrup** was known by 1903.

From 1877 through 1920, American horticulturists developed many new hybrids that became standard on the country's farms, including "Golden Chaff," "Shoepeg," "Country Gentleman," and "Golden Bantam." In 1924, Henry A. Wallace, of Iowa (later vice president under Franklin D. Roosevelt), showcased a hearty hybrid called "Copper Cross" that survived the great windstorm of 1836 and was thereafter widely planted. In 1950, Dr. J. R. Laughnam, of the University of Illinois, discovered very sweet strains of corn, which, because their dried kernels looked shriveled, were called "shrunken two" or "SH2," and were called in the market "supersweet," "ultrasweet," or "extra sweet." Even sweeter corn was produced in the 1960s by Dr. A. M. Rhodes, also at the University of Illinois, and called "sugar-enhanced" or, in seed catalogs, "Everlasting Heritage."

The major varieties of corn include "dent" (*Z. mays indentata*), so called because the kernel becomes dented in shrinking but also called "field corn"; a very hearty strain called "flint" or "Indian" (*Z. mays indurata*); "flour" (preferred by the Indians), of which "blue corn" is a variety; "waxy" (introduced from China as a tapioca substitute in 1907); and "popcorn" (*Z. mays everta*), also called "rice" or "pearl corn."

Today corn accounts for more than 90 percent of the primary feed grain in the U.S. The U.S. corn crop, planted on 80 million acres of land, is equal to the combined crop of wheat, oats, barley, rice, rye, and sorghum. The principal corn-producing states are Ohio, Indiana, Illinois, Nebraska, South Dakota, and, the largest, Iowa. Depending upon climate conditions, about twelve to fifteen billion bushels are grown annually. Currently more than one-third of the U.S. crop is used to feed livestock; another 20 percent is exported (Japan buys the most); and another 40 percent used to produce ethanol.

Depending on the region of the country they live in, Americans often stand firmly on the merits of either white or yellow cornmeal in their recipes, white generally being preferred in the South and Midwest.

Americans enjoy corn in a wide variety of ways, especially in late summer, when the fresh corn on the cob is boiled and buttered. Corn on the cob is also available frozen, and shucked corn kernels are widely bought in cans. Creamed corn, sold canned, consists of whole or partially cut kernels packed in a creamy liquid from the kernels or other ingredients (including monosodium glutamate, starch, butter or margarine, and often pieces of green or red pepper). In the South, fried corn is common, and fried "corn fritters" (also called "corn oysters"), made with an egg batter, are popular throughout the U.S.

Aside from those recipes given below, many corn items and dishes will be found under main entries, including **hush puppies**, **crackling** bread, **spoon bread**, **Indian pudding**, **succotash**, **tortillas**, and *maque chou*.

CORN BREAD

Pour 2 T. butter or bacon fat into a skillet and place in 450° oven to heat up. Combine 2 c. cornmeal, 4 t. baking powder, and 1 ½ t. salt. Beat 1 egg in 1 ½ c. milk, combine with dry ingredients, pour into skillet, and bake for 20–25 min.

CORN CHOWDER

Brown ¼ lb. salt pork and add 1 chopped onion. Put in 4 c. peeled potatoes, 2 c. water, salt, and pepper, and simmer until potatoes are tender. Stir in 4 c. scalded milk and 2 c. kernel corn. Correct seasonings, serve with pat of butter. Serves 6.

CORN CHIP. A snack food made from ground cornmeal that is flattened by machine and cut into chips of various sizes. These are often flavored or seasoned and are a staple of Mexican restaurants, where they are called "tortilla chips" and usually served with a **salsa**. They are also the basis for **Frito pie**.

Mexicans have long made corn chips at home, but it was not until the invention, in 1932, of a special rolling machine by I. J. Filler and its subsequent adoption by Charles Elmer Doolin for producing the item in large bulk, that the corn chip became a commercial product. Doolin called his product Fritos Corn Chips.

CORN DOG. A hot dog covered with a cornmeal batter, deep-fried, and eaten on a stick. A U.S. patent filed in 1927 (granted in 1929) for a Combined Dipping, Cooking, and Article Holding Apparatus indicates that "wieners" and many other foods could be deep-fried in the invention, and there is a citation of a "Krusty Korn Dog Baker" machine featured in a 1929 Albert Pick-L. Barth wholesale catalog of hotel and restaurant supplies. But while there have been other, later claimants to its creation, the deep-fried item was apparently perfected in 1942 by vaudevillians Neil and Carl Fletcher of Dallas, who originally called it "Fletcher's Original State Fair Corny Dog," because they sold it from a stand at the State Fair of Texas. "We have heard some fellow had used a mold to put cornbread around a wiener, but that was too slow," Neil Fletcher told a *New York Times* reporter in 1983. "So we started experimenting in the kitchen and finally came up with a batter that would stay on. It tasted like hell. When we got one that tasted O.K. it wouldn't stay on the weenie. We must have tried about 60 times until we got one that was right."

CORN DOG

Fry ½ lb. mashed spicy sausage with 1 chopped onion, 1 t. cayenne, and 2 T. beef stock. Grease cornstick pans and heat in 375° oven. Mix together 1 c. cornmeal, 1 c. flour, 2 T. melted butter, 3 t. baking powder, ¼ t. salt, 2 beaten eggs, and ¾ c. milk. Fill cornstick pans, cover each stick with some of the sausage mixture, cover with more corn mixture, and bake at 375° for 25 min.

CORN DODGER. A kind of corn bread shaped by hand and fried or baked, first cited in print in 1839, though "dodger" (probably from Scots *dadge*) alone dates in print to 1831, referring to corn bread.

CORNED BEEF. Beef that has been cured in salt. Corned beef, dating in print to 1621, is served either as a main dish or as a sandwich in America, especially as part of the menu in Jewish delicatessens and Irish American restaurants and pubs (though it is not well known in Ireland).

The term has nothing to do with American corn but rather with an English term, "corn," for any small particle, such as a grain of salt. Beef brisket is the usual cut, although rump, eye round, bottom round, and tongue may also be used.

Saltpeter (sodium nitrate or potassium nitrate) is added to most of the corned beef sold in the U.S.

CORNELL BREAD. A bread made with soy flour, wheat germ, and nonfat dry milk. It was developed as a high-protein bread in the 1930s by Clive M. McKay, professor of animal nutrition at Cornell University, in Ithaca, New York. Originally created with the help of the Dry Milk Institute as a way of improving the diet of patients in mental hospitals, Cornell bread became popular during World War II at a time when meat was rationed or increasingly expensive, and a high-protein alternative was needed.

The formula called for adding to the bottom of each cup of white flour in a bread recipe one tablespoon soy flour, one tablespoon dry-milk solids, and one teaspoon wheat germ. The rest of the cup would then be filled with sifted unbleached white flour.

CORN SYRUP. A sweet, thick liquid derived from cornstarch treated with acids or enzymes, used to sweeten and thicken candy, syrups, and snack foods. By far the most popular and best-known corn syrup is Karo, introduced in 1902 by Corn Products Co. of Edgewater, New Jersey. The name Karo might have been chosen to honor of the inventor's wife, Caroline or, some say, derived from an earlier trademark for table syrup, "Kairomel." So common is the use of Karo in making pecan pie that the confection is often called "Karo pie" in the South. See also **sugar**.

CORN WHISKEY. Also "corn." Whiskey made from corn, dating in print to 1835. **Bourbon** is the primary example of American spirits made from corn. By the time of Prohibition, the term came to connote cheap moonshine whiskey.

CORTI, DARRELL (1942–). Grocer and author. Described by *Saveur* magazine as "the man who knows more about food than anyone else in the world," Darrell Corti has written a highly respected gourmet newsletter for the past thirty-eight years and was the first to import many rare food products and wines to America.

Corti's family grocery, Corti Brothers, was founded in Sacramento, California, in 1947 by his father Frank and uncle Gino Corti, who adopted his sister Illa's motto, "At Corti Brothers we just don't sell groceries, we talk food."

After Darrell joined the business in 1964, his increasing knowledge of food and wine, gained through extensive travel, fed the company's literature, brochures, and promotions, not least championing California and Italian wines. Strongly opinionated, Corti has inveighed against high-alcohol wines. He has also consulted with wineries in Amador County, California.

Corti was the first to bring Italian *aceto balsamico tradizionale*, or balsamic vinegar, to the U.S., as well as the "super-Tuscan" wines Tignanello and Sassicaia.

Inducted into the **James Beard Foundation**'s Who's Who of Food & Beverage in America (1989), Corti was also knighted Cavalierato al Merito della Repubblica Italiana by the Italian government for advancing Italian food-and-wine culture. Inducted into the **Culinary Institute of America**'s Vintners Hall of Fame (2008), he was called "a catalyst in the re-evaluation and renaissance of zinfandel, a leader in advocating wider use of Italian varieties or grapes in California, and has been integral to the rediscovery of the Sierra Foothills as a fine wine growing region. Corti is an internationally sought after member of wine and olive oil tasting panels and has mentored a generation of seminal food and wine professionals with his impeccable taste and articulate discourse."

Corti is a foreign corresponding member of the Accademia Italiana della Vite e del Vino (Siena) and chairman of the Los Angeles International Extra Virgin Olive Oil Competition, the oldest U.S. oil competition.

COTTAGE CHEESE. A moist, soft white cheese usually made from skim milk (1840). Cottage cheese may be eaten on its own, in a salad, or with melon, and is sometimes used as a substitute for ricotta in American lasagnas. It is consumed fresh, not aged. Cottage cheese sales in the U.S. in 1997 totaled 707 million pounds, with per capita consumption of 2.7 pounds.

After milk has soured, it solidifies into a wet mass called "clabbered milk," which leaves behind the curds as the liquid ("whey") drops away. Sometimes this process is hastened by the addition of rennet. Cottage cheese is the product of one of the first stages of the process.

In the early part of the nineteenth century, the name for such cheese was "pot cheese" (which today is almost synonymous with "cottage cheese," though sometimes the term suggested a cheese that has drained for a longer period and acquired a slightly sour taste) or "card cheese" (a variation of "curd cheese"). Finely textured cottage cheese is sometimes called "cream cheese" in the Southwest (but see main entry for **cream cheese**). By the 1820s, "smearcase" (from German, *Schmierkäse*, a spreading cheese) was also heard, particularly in Pennsylvania Dutch communities, and by midcentury the name "cottage cheese" had entered the language. Cottage cheese to which thick cream has been added was called "cheese butter."

Today cottage cheese may be bought in various forms. "Sweet-curd cottage cheese" is mild, because it has been washed to remove acid; "creamed cottage cheese" contains 4 to 8 percent cream; and "California-style" or "small-curd cottage cheese" has smaller curds than regular cottage cheese. "Medium-curd" and "large-curd" cottage cheese, also sometimes called "popcorn cheese," are also available.

COTTAGE-FRIED POTATOES. Also "cottage fries" and "country fries." Potatoes that are sliced into thin disks and deep-fried. The term dates in print to 1965 and is used predominantly in the North.

COTTAGE PUDDING. A plain cake that is smeared with a sweet sauce. It was listed in the original Fannie Farmer *Boston Cooking-School Cook Book* in 1896 and mentioned by O. Henry in 1909.

COTTON CANDY. A confection made by spinning sugar at high speed in a large tub so as to create what appears to be candy cotton spooled onto a cardboard stick. The item originated in 1900 at the Ringling Bros. and Barnum & Bailey circus, when snack vendor Thomas Patton began experimenting with the long-common process of boiling sugar to a caramelized state, then forming long threads of it with a fork waved in the air. Patton heated the sugar on a gas-fired hot plate that spun, creating a kind of cottony sugar floss. Patton sold his patent on the machine, which was refined by the Electric Candy Machine Co. of NYC and Nashville, Tennessee, selling the new confection—called "Fairy Floss Candy"—at the 1904 Louisiana Purchase Exposition, in St. Louis.

Cotton candy, which dates in print to 1926, continues to be a popular item at circuses, amusement parks, and fairs, with most cotton-candy machines now made by the Gold Medal Products Co. Cotton candy is now flavored and colored.

COUNTRY CAPTAIN. A curried-chicken dish often attributed to Georgian origins. Eliza Leslie, in her mid-nineteenth-century cookbooks, contended that the dish got its name from a British army officer who brought the recipe back from his station in India. The word first appeared in 1769, in reference to a captain stationed in the countryside in India who served "a specimen of the indian taste." Others believe the dish originated in Savannah, Georgia, a major shipping port for the spice trade.

COUNTRY CAPTAIN

Fry 4 bacon strips until crisp. Remove from pan, then sauté in 2 T. bacon fat, 1 chopped green pepper, 1 chopped onion, 2 minced garlic cloves, and ½ c. celery for about 5 min. Add 6 chopped tomatoes and 1 c. orange juice, sprinkle in 2 T. curry powder and ½ t. thyme. Bring to a boil, then simmer for 5 min. Add 8 slices chicken breast and cook 30 min. Garnish with chutney or sprinkle with dried currants, roasted almonds, and minced parsley.

COUNTRY PIE. A southern term for a liver pie.

COURT BOUILLON. In classic French cuisine, a poaching liquid composed of various vegetables, vinegar or white wine, herbs, salt, and pepper. The word, first printed in English in 1715, is from the French for "short broth." In Creole and Cajun cuisine, however, the term usually refers to a dish of redfish cooked with a seasoned tomato sauce, as mentioned in *Mme. Begué and Her Recipes: Old Creole Cookery* (1900), from which the following recipe is adapted.

COURT BOUILLON

Roll six slices of redfish in seasoned flour and brown in hot oil, but do not cook through. Set aside. In a skillet sauté 1 large onion, chopped, with 1 t. flour in 2 T. oil. When brown, stir in ½ c. red wine, 2 T. chopped garlic, 3 bay leaves, a little fresh thyme and parsley, a piece of chile pepper, and salt and pepper to taste. When slightly reduced, add fish and cook over low heat for about 45 min. Serve with toast.

COWBOY SLANG. The lingo of cowboys is a colorful language of the West and includes a great number of slang terms for various foods, cooks, and utensils used for cooking. Many of the following were first noted by Ramon F. Adams, in his *Western Words: A Dictionary of the American West* (1968).

ARBUCKLE'S. A brand name for coffee in the Old West. Arbuckle's coffee was so ubiquitous that recipes for coffee would read, "Take a pound of Arbuckle's…"

BALDFACE DISHES. Used since 1840 to describe real china plates and dishes, in contrast to the tin or granite dishes usually used on the trail.

BAR DOG. A bartender.

BASQUE BARBECUE. A barbecue made from lamb, so called because many nineteenth-century sheepmen were of Basque ancestry.

BEAN EATER. A Mexican or Chicano, because beans were a predominant ingredient in Hispanic cooking.

BEAR SIGN. A doughnut, probably because of its resemblance to a bear's excrement (1903).

BELLY-WASH. Weak coffee, whiskey, or soup (1889).

BIG ANTELOPE. An animal belonging to someone else and killed for food. Adams notes, in *Western Words*, "It was the custom in the old days for a ranchman never to kill his own cattle for food, and many an old-timer was accused of never knowing how his own beef tasted."

BISCUIT ROLLER. The cook on a ranch, used since the 1870s. Also called a "biscuit shooter," which was sometimes applied to a restaurant waitress as well.

CANNED COW. Canned or condensed milk (1925).

CÍBOLA. A southwestern cowboy term, from the Spanish for "buffalo." A "cíbolero" is a buffalo hunter.

COFFIN VARNISH. Cheap, inferior whiskey. The term first appeared in print in 1935.

COOKHOUSE. A ranch building where food is prepared and served (1785). Cookhouses were also called "feed bags" or "feed troughs" (referring to the bags and troughs from which horses fed on grain).

COOKIE. A nineteenth-century term used by ranchers or cowboys for a cook or by sailors for a cook's helper (1852). The ranch cook was responsible for three hot meals a day, and he had to possess a good deal of imagination to please his men with dishes that often had to be prepared from meager sources on the open range.

A "cook's louse" was a cook's helper, and a cowboy's cook might also be called a "coosie" (from the Spanish *cocinero*), as well as "bean master," "belly cheater," "belly robber," "boardinghouse man," "boiler," "dinero," "dough-belly," "doughboxer," "dough-puncher," "dough roller," "dough wrangler," "flunky," "grease ball," "grease burner," "grease belly," "grub-spoiler," "grub worm," "gut burglar," "gut robber," "hash-burner," "hash slinger," "kitchen mechanic," "lizard," "scorcher," "mess moll," "mulligan mixer," "old woman," "pothook," "pot rustler," "Sallie," "sizzler," "sop and 'taters," "sourdough," "star chief," "stew builder," "stomach robber," "swamper," and doubtless scores of other appellations.

COOKIE PUSHER. A restaurant waitress (1936).

COWBOY COCKTAIL. Straight whiskey.

COWBOY COFFEE. Black coffee without sugar, a term dating back to 1943 in print. Cowboys themselves called their coffee "Arbuckle's," "belly-wash," "black-jack," "black water," "brown coffee," "jamoka" (from the words *java* and *mocha*), "six-shooter coffee" (strong enough to float a six-shooter pistol), and "Indian coffee" (a weakened, reboiled coffee made from used grounds, considered unfit for cowboys but good enough for Indian visitors).

COWBOY TOAST. Biscuits baked with butter, sugar, and spices. According to *Western Kitchen Cook Book of Original Chuckwagon and Mexican Foods* (1937), by C. C. and Dudley Yaws, "This dish has been enjoyed in ranch homes and cow camps in the west for many years."

COWBOY TOAST

Break 6 cold biscuits in half, place in bread pan, and brown in hot oven. Sprinkle with sugar and replace in oven until sugar is browned. Cover with ½ c. milk, sprinkle with a dash of allspice, pour 1 T. melted butter over the dish, replace in oven, and let simmer for 10 min.

EATIN' IRON. A knife, fork, or spoon.

GUN-WADDING BREAD. A light bread eaten by cowboys (1919).

GUT-EATERS. Native Americans, so called because of some tribes' taste for the entrails of animals.

HOT ROCK. A biscuit.

IMMIGRANT BUTTER. Grease, flour, and water.

JOHN CHINAMAN. Boiled rice, so called because the Chinese in nineteenth-century America subsisted on the grain. It has been a slang term for Chinese immigrants since the 1820s.

KANSAS CITY FISH. Fried salt pork.

KNOW YOUR CANS. A cowboy game in which players had to recite from memory the exact ingredients listed on the labels of canned foodstuffs, with every punctuation mark in the right place.

LARRUP. Molasses, which was also called "long sweetenin'." The origin of the name (1938) is unknown, though the same word in dialectical English means a beating.

MAN AT THE POT! An expression directed at a colleague who went to refill his cup with coffee. On hearing this call, he was duty-bound to fill his companions' cups, too.

MEXICAN STRAWBERRIES. Dried beans, which were often red.

MORMON DIP. Gravy made from milk. The name refers to the Mormons, members of the Church of Jesus Christ of Latter-day Saints, who founded Salt Lake City in 1841.

NIGGERS IN A BLANKET. A dessert whose now offensive name derived from the dark raisins in the dough. A similar pastry made with blackberries goes by the same derogatory name in Louisiana.

PAIR OF OVERALLS. An order of two drinks served at once.

PIG'S VEST WITH BUTTONS. Salt pork or sow belly.

PILONCILLO. From the Spanish *pilón*, for a small loaf of unrefined sugar, often given as something for good measure. The term has been in print since 1844.

POOCH. A dish made from tomatoes, sugar, and bread.

POOR DOE. Tough venison.

PRAIRIE BEEVES. A buffalo.

PRAIRIE BITTERS. A popular Old West beverage, also considered medicinal, made from the gall of the buffalo and water.

SALT HOSS. Corned beef.

SEA PLUM. An oyster.

SKUNK EGG. An onion.

SNAKE-HEAD WHISKEY. A cheap whiskey known among cowboys. The name came from the assumption that the drink's potency was the result of adding snake heads in the distilling barrel.

SOURDOUGH BULLET. Disparaging term for a poorly made biscuit.

SPOTTED PUP. Dish made from cooked rice and raisins.

SWAMPER. A cook's helper.

SWAMP SEED. Rice.

WASP NEST. A light bread.

WHISTLE BERRIES. Beans, perhaps because of the flatulence they often cause.

WOOSHER. A hog.

COWCUMBERS. An early variant of "cucumber" dating to at least the seventeenth century, but also cowboy slang for pickles.

COW GREASE. Also "cow salve." Slang for butter.

COWPEA (*Vigna sinensis*). Also "black-eyed pea" (so called because of a black rim on the inner curve of the coat seam), "black-eyed bean," "black-eyed Susan," "blue-eyed bean," "bung belly," "chain gang pea" (presumably because it was such a staple of the southern prison diet), "China bean," "cream pea," "Jerusalem pea," "field pea," "whippoorwill pea," "marble pea," "Tonkin pea," "crowder pea," and "zipper." George Washington Carver listed the varieties Extra Early Black-Eye, New Era Lady Cuban Blackeye, Iron, Speckled, Groot, Clay, Red Ripper, Brabham, and White Crowder. The cowpea has been known by that name since at least 1776, but "black-eyed pea" is probably in wider usage, especially in the South, where the term dates in print to 1728.

The cowpea is a native Asian vine-bearing pod, also used in Africa as food and fodder and probably brought to the West Indies in 1674 during the slave trade. It is said that James Oglethorpe brought the cowpea to Georgia in 1734, after which it became an important crop in the South and one of the staples of the Negro diet. Today it is still a cherished ingredient of African American **soul food**. Cowpeas are a main ingredient in **hopping john** and—with green peppers, green onions, vinegar, and red peppers—in a dish called "Texas caviar."

COWPUNCHER'S SANDWICH. An onion sandwich favored by cowboys. According to food writer Craig Claiborne, "A cowpuncher's sandwich is quite simple to make. Slice red onions about one-quarter-inch thick. Put them in a bowl with a generous sprinkling of crumbled oregano. Add equal amounts of ice water and vinegar to cover and let stand overnight. Drain the onions, sprinkle with salt and pepper and use as a filling for two slices of buttered bread."

CRAB (order Decapoda). Any of a large variety of crustaceans, mostly inhabiting salt water, with a hard shell and five pairs of legs, the front ones having pincers. The word is Middle English in origin, from Old English *crabba*. There are more than 4,400 species, all edible, ranging from tiny pea crabs to giant thirty-pound Tasmanians. After shrimp, crab is the most popular crustacean on American dining tables. Scores of preparations have been created, region by region, for the shellfish, and there are more varieties in North America than anywhere in the world. Blue crabs from Maryland's Chesapeake Bay are particularly savored in the East, while the Pacific's "Dungeness" and "king" crabs are highly popular in the West. Southerners pride themselves on their many different crab recipes, from **crab cakes** to **gumbos**.

The most important crabs in American cookery are:

BLUE CRAB (*Callinectes sapidus*). With its blue-green shell and romantic taxonomic name, which means "savory swimmer," the blue crab is the most important species on the East Coast. The egg-carrying female is called by various names—"sponge," "ballie," "punk," "sook," and others. A mature male is called a "jimmy." A crab that is getting fat and ready to shed its shell is called a "corner." The shedding crab, called a "buster" or "peeler" (a "rank peeler" is a crab one to three days before it sheds its shell), is particularly valued for its culinary interest. These "soft-shell crabs" are harvested alive, just as the crab has molted his hard shell and is in the process of growing a new one, which at first is soft. If the shell begins to harden too much and turn brittle, it is first called a "paper shell," then a "buck" or "buckram," and, finally, a "buckler." They are shipped to market and sold alive or flash-frozen. The soft-shell crab industry was begun in the nineteenth century in Crisfield, Maryland.

Blue crabs are sold according to size, ranging from the smallest, called "mediums" (which run 3 ½ to 4 inches across the back) to "hotels" (4 to

4 ½ inches), "prime" (4 ½ to 5 inches), "jumbo" (5 to 5 ½ inches), and "whale" (5 ½ or more inches).

DUNGENESS CRAB. See main entry.

KING CRAB. (*Paralithodes camtschaticus*). A large Pacific crab, also called "Alaska King crab," "Alaskan king crab," "Japanese crab," and "Russian crab," which derives its name from its regal size, which can reach twenty-five pounds. The term "king crab" has been in print since the end of the seventeenth century.

Only about 25 percent of the crustacean is actually edible, and most Americans buy its legs and claws frozen. Only the male crab is harvested; it is thereupon cooked and frozen before sale. The meat of the claws and legs is marketed, usually in five-pound units, and it is particularly popular in salads.

LAND CRAB (*Cardisoma quanhumi*). Also "mulatto" or "white crab." Land crabs are found throughout the Gulf of Mexico and the Caribbean. A. J. McClane, in his *Encyclopedia of Fish Cookery* (1977), notes that "this species was so abundant in south Florida until the 1950s that our streets were often overrun at night with migrating crabs. Evidently their place has been usurped in a changing ecology."

ROCK CRAB (*Cancer irroratus*). An East Coast crab that lives among rocks and in deep water. The similar "Jonah crab" (*C. borealis*) and "spider crab" (*Libinia emarginata*) also go by this name and others, including "sand crab" and "white legger." With its spindly legs, which make it resemble a spider, this crab is given market names that would make a consumer less squeamish, such as "snow" (more specifically *Chionoecetes opilio*), "tanner," and "queen crab." Another so-called spider crab (*Stenocionops furcata*) of the Southeast also goes by the name "decorator crab," because it "decorates" itself with algae, grass, and other items. In Maine, the crab is called "peekytoe," a name seafood wholesaler Rod Mitchell, of the Browne

Trading Co., in Portland, Maine, began using to sell the product to chefs in New York in the mid-1990s, and the crab took on a new popularity by that name in upscale restaurants.

STONE CRAB. See main entry.

Much American crab is marketed as "crabmeat," either frozen or vacuum-packed, which constitutes the overwhelming majority of crab used in restaurants. Crabmeat may be labeled "lump" meat, "flake" (small pieces), or "flake and lump," mostly from blue crabs. "Back fin" meat is from the breast of the blue crab. The mature female crab with eggs is colloquially called a "bally," "lemon-belly," or "punk." U.S. commercial landings of crabs totaled 349.6 million pounds in 2010, for sales of $572.8 million. Per capita U.S. consumption annually is 0.57 pounds.

CRAB BUTTER. The white-yellow fat inside the back shell of a large crab. Crab butter is much prized as a delicacy and is often added to a dressing or sauce.

CRAB CAKE. A sautéed or fried patty of crabmeat. The term dates in print to 1929 and appeared in 1939 in Crosby Gaige's *New York World's Fair Cook Book*, where they are called "Baltimore crab cakes," suggesting they have long been known in the South. A "crabburger" is a crab cake eaten on a hamburger bun.

CRAB CAKE

In a bowl combine 1 lb. crabmeat, 1 ½ t. salt, 1 t. dry mustard, 2 t. Worcestershire sauce, 1 egg yolk, and 2 t. mayonnaise. Pat lightly into small cakes and dip in flour, then into beaten egg, and fry in butter or hot oil.

CRAB HOUSE. A place where crabs are cooked, processed, and packed for distribution. Also a restaurant that specializes in crab dishes.

CRAB LANTERN. A fried apple pastry. According to *DARE*, the name may derive from "crab apple" and "lantern," owing to "the ventilating slashes that expose the fruit filling." The term dates in print to about 1770.

CRAB LOUIS. Also "crab Louie." A crabmeat salad made with hard-boiled eggs. The dish has been credited to chefs at Solari's restaurant (where it was served at least as early as 1914) or the dining room of the St. Francis Hotel, both in San Francisco, while others say it was the creation of the chef at the Olympic Club, in Seattle, at the turn of the last century. In their book *Northwest Bounty* (1988) Schuyler Ingle and Sharon Kramis describe "Dungeness Crab Louie" as a "classic Northwest Salad." There are many versions of the dish.

CRAB LOUIS

On a salad plate, place a bed of shredded lettuce, add a mound of lump crabmeat, and top with claw meat. Chop 6 hard-boiled eggs and sprinkle on crabmeat, then decorate with chopped chives. Dress with a mixture of 1 c. mayonnaise, ¼ c. French dressing, ½ t. tarragon, ½ c. chili sauce, 2 T. chopped green olives, 1 t. horseradish, 1 t. Worcestershire sauce, salt and pepper to taste. Serves 6.

CRABMEAT À LA DEWEY. A crabmeat dish made with green pepper, mushrooms, and cream sauce. There are two stories as to the dish's origin. One claims it was created at the Gage & Tollner restaurant, in Brooklyn, and named after proprietor Seth Bradford Dewey. But, according to Ned and Pam Bradford, in *Boston's Locke-Ober Café* (1978), the dish was created by the chef at the Maryland Yacht Club in honor of Commodore George Dewey's victory over the Spanish fleet in Manila Bay on May 1, 1898.

CRABMEAT REMICK. A dish made from crabmeat, chili sauce, mayonnaise, and other seasonings. It was created in 1920 at the Plaza Hotel, in NYC, by chef Albert Leopold Lattard, in honor of William H. Remick, president of the New York Stock Exchange from 1919 to 1921.

CRABMEAT REMICK

Combine 1 c. chili sauce, 1 c. mayonnaise, ½ oz. dry mustard, 1 t. paprika, 1 t. celery salt, ½ t. Tabasco sauce, and ½ t. Worcestershire sauce. Blend half of this mixture with 1 lb. crabmeat. Spoon the crabmeat mixture into 2 doz. empty clam shells, pour the rest of the sauce mixture on top of shells, sprinkle with Parmesan cheese, and set in 350° oven until sauce bubbles.

CRAB NORFOLK. A dish of crabmeat baked and seasoned with vinegar, Tabasco, and Worcestershire sauce. The name supposedly derives from the city of Norfolk, Virginia, where the dish was made in what was called a "Norfolk aluminum pan," a small oval cooking pan in which the crabmeat was placed. According to **Craig Claiborne**, the dish was created by W. O. Snowden at the Snowden and Mason Restaurant in Norfolk, which opened in 1924.

CRAB NORFOLK

Combine 1 lb. crabmeat with 2 T. vinegar, ½ t. Tabasco sauce, ½ t. Worcestershire sauce, salt, and pepper. Place portions in small pans each containing 1 T. melted butter. Bake in 350° oven until well heated.

CRACKER. A thin, unsweetened wheat-flour wafer made from unleavened dough and usually eaten as a snack, as a canapé, with soups, and with dips. The word comes from the "cracking" sound it makes when broken. Since the eighteenth century Americans have spoken of these wafers by this term, first appearing in print in 1739, but it is still a word rarely used in England, where "biscuit" is preferred. (To Americans, a biscuit is a small yeast-dough form of bread.) In the 1830s, Americans called the wafers "soda crackers," and **common crackers** or "oyster crackers" (see **Trenton crackers**) were placed in New England chowders or split and buttered. Graham crackers are sweet and made with **graham flour**, while Saltines is a trademark of the National Biscuit Co. for a very popular cracker made with salt on top.

In the nineteenth century, crackers were sold at grocery stores from cracker barrels or packaged in cracker boxes or Boston tins. "Cracker pudding" is a New England dish made from crackers, milk, eggs, and raisins.

Animal Crackers are actually a brand of **cookie**, first produced as Christmas tree ornaments in 1902 by the National Biscuit Co. (now Nabisco). They are formed in the shapes of various circus animals and packed in a box decorated like a circus train. Nabisco currently produces about seven million Animal Cracker cookies per day.

CRACKER BARREL. A large barrel, found in turn-of-the-century groceries and general stores, for holding crackers that were to be sold in quantity. The term first appeared in print in 1875.

CRACKLING. Also "cracklins." A crispy morsel left over after most of the fat has been rendered by cooking pork, a meaning the word has had since the beginning of the eighteenth century. It was first seen in print in 1834. Cracklings may be added to a variety of dishes—beans and other vegetables, for instance—and a particular favorite in the South is "crackling bread," which appeared in print in 1842 and may also be called "scrap johnny-cake" or "goody-bread." In Cajun Louisiana, cracklings are called "grattons" or "gratons," from the French *cretons*. In Mexican American regions, cracklings are called *chicharrons*.

CRACKLING BREAD

To 1 qt. cornmeal, add enough boiling water to make a stiff dough. Add 1 c. cracklings, mix, and form into oblong cakes. Bake at 400° until inserted knife comes out clean and top is golden brown. (Modern-day recipes usually include eggs and butter.)

CRACK SEED. A snack in Hawaii, available in scores of varieties and eaten like candy. The term first appeared in print in about 1970. Crack seeds are made by smashing the seed of a fruit and preserving the pulp with salt; they have a salty-sweet pungency, with a faint taste of licorice. Some of the varieties sold in small packages include sweet *li hing mui* (plum), rock-salt plum, salted mango, wet lemon peel, and wet *li hing mui*.

CRAIG, ELIJAH (c. 1743–1808). Preacher and bourbon maker. Although a Baptist preacher in Virginia, Elijah Craig is often credited with being Kentucky's first bourbon distiller.

Craig was born in Spotsylvania (now Orange) County, Virginia, and ordained a Baptist preacher in 1771. After the American Revolution, he was an early advocate, with founding father James Madison, for religious freedom to be guaranteed in the Constitution. He eventually moved, in 1782, to the new territory of Kentucky, where he established a school and donated land for the founding of Georgetown College.

As an entrepreneur, he built Kentucky's first cotton mill, paper mill, rope mill, and lumber and grist mills. Around 1789, he founded a distillery. According to an account written in 1874, long after Craig's death, he was alleged to have been the first to distill corn spirits in charred oak to gave it a distinctive taste, at a time when corn-based whiskeys made in the region were named **bourbons**, after Bourbon County. There is, however, no corroboration of the claim that Craig was the first to do this. Nevertheless, he is considered one of the pioneers of bourbon production, whose name is on the label of a bourbon made today by Heaven Hill Distilleries.

CRANBERRY (*Vaccinium macrocarpon*). Also "bearberry," "Roman bean," and "pembina." A very tart red berry grown in bogs from low, trailing vines. Cranberries are used in sauces, jellies, and beverages and as a traditional accompaniment at **Thanksgiving** dinners (1640). There are several species of wild cranberry in the world, but the "American" or "large" cranberry is the only one in wide cultivation. This variety makes up a major crop of Massachusetts, New Jersey, Wisconsin, and Oregon. Cranberry bogs are sandy and often flooded, and some continue to be productive after a century. In New England, the bogs are picked between Labor Day (when the "Early Blacks" ripen) and the end of October (when the "Late Howes" are brought in).

The word appears to have been adopted from Low German by American settlers in New England, first in print as of 1672, where it is also called the "Bear Berry." Native Americans of New England, who called them *sassamanesh* or *ibimi*, long enjoyed cranberries, both raw or sweetened with maple sugar, and they often added them to their **pemmican**.

The first European settlers found the fruit similar to their lingonberry, but somewhat too tart unless sweetened or made into a condiment.

There is no hard evidence that the Pilgrims ate cranberries at the first Thanksgiving, held in fall of 1621, but it is a fair assumption that the Native Americans might have brought them to the feast, since it was the time when the cranberries were at their ripest in that region. The name "cranberry" was not English, however; the settlers probably called the berries "fenberries," after a fruit they knew at home. Years later, the Dutch introduced the word *kranbeere* (from the Low German *kraanbere*, "crane berry," because its stamen resembled a beak). Others referred to them as "bounce berries," because of their bouncy quality. There is a story that a New Jersey grower named John J. Webb ("Peg-Leg John") initiated the development of the first cranberry separator after he transferred the berries from his loft to the ground by allowing them to tumble down the stairs—the ripest, firmest berries bounced to the ground, while the bruised fruit remained on the steps. Commercial cranberry cultivation began after another accidental discovery, this time on Cape Cod in about 1816. Henry Hall noticed that bogs that had had sand blown over them produced a sturdy crop of cranberries, so he spread some sand on his own property and duplicated the results. There is a cherished legend on Cape Cod about how the cranberry bogs began there. It seems that a Native American medicine man cast a spell over the Reverend Richard Bourne and then mired him in quicksand. For the next fifteen days, the two men waged a battle of wits, during which the immobilized Reverend Bourne was sustained only by a white dove that fed him cranberries. Eventually the medicine man fell exhausted from the strain, and the spell was lifted from the minister. The story goes on to tell how one of the berries fell to the ground and became rooted forever in the Cape Cod soil, which is acknowledged to produce some of America's best cranberries.

The commercial production of cranberries grew so rapidly that supply far outpaced demand by the turn of the twentieth century. In 1912, Marcus L. Urann, of the Cape Cod Cranberry Co., began canning "cranberry sauce" for sale throughout the year, calling his product Ocean Spray Cape Cod Cranberry Sauce. Urann merged in 1930 with several other growers to form the "Ocean Spray growers cooperative," which today has nine hundred members, representing 70 percent of all American cranberry growers. In 1946, the growers began selling fresh bagged berries and in 1930 developed a cranberry juice "cocktail."

In 2011, 681 million pounds of cranberries were harvested. Americans consume 400 million pounds of cranberries annually, with about 80 million pounds eaten over Thanksgiving week.

CRAYFISH. Also "crawfish," "crawdad," "crawdaddy," and "Florida lobster." Any of various freshwater crustaceans of the genera *Cambarus* and *Astacus*.

Although considerably smaller, the crayfish is related to the **lobster**, and there are 250 species and subspecies found in North America alone. The name is from Middle English *crevise*, and, ultimately, from the Frankish *krabītja*, and dates in English print to 1509.

Crayfish formed a significant part of the diet of the Native Americans of the South and still hold their highest status among the Cajuns of Louisiana. Louisianans have an enormous passion and appetite for what they call "crawfish" (a name used by Captain John Smith as early as 1615), "mudbugs," "creekcrabs," "freshwater lobsters," "yabbies," *"cheval du diable"* (Creole French for "devil's horse"), and other names. The crayfish figures in Louisiana folklore, and the natives hold "crawfish boils" whenever the crustacean is in season. Breaux Bridge, Louisiana, calls itself the Crawfish Capital of the World and holds a yearly festival of eating and drinking to prove it, cooking up crayfish in pies, gumbos, stews, and every other way imaginable. Yet one would not have easily found crawfish on restaurant menus in Louisiana much before 1960, because they were considered a common food to be eaten at home.

Crayfish are commercially harvested in waters of the Mississippi basin, most of them of the Red Swamp and White River varieties, with the season running approximately from Thanksgiving Day to the Fourth of July. In 2010, about fourteen million pounds were landed, valued at $13.7 million, with Louisiana producing most of the crop.

Crayfish are eaten with the fingers, picking the white meat out of the body. "Squeezing the tip" refers to squeezing the meat from the tail. It is also considered a delicacy to "suck the head" to extract the fat in the animal's thorax.

"Cajun popcorn" is a dish of battered, deep-fried crayfish, popularized by Cajun chef **Paul Prudhomme** in the 1980s.

CRAWFISH ÉTOUFFÉE

Sauté 1 chopped onion, ½ c. chopped green pepper, 2 chopped shallots or scallions, and 2 chopped cloves of garlic in 6 T. butter for about 15 min. Add 3 lb. crayfish and continue cooking for another 15 min. Add salt and pepper to taste, ¼ t. cayenne, and enough water to moisten bottom of pan. Bring to boil and simmer for 5 min., basting crayfish. Serve over boiled rice.

CREAM. The fat-rich, unhomogenized part of the milk that rises to the surface. FDA standards of identity mandate that a product cannot be called "cream" unless it contains at least 18 percent butterfat. The word is from Middle English *creem* and Old French *cresme* and was first mentioned in print in 1332. The marketed derivatives of cream are as follows:

HALF-AND-HALF. A mixture of half cream and half whole milk.

HEAVY CREAM. Must contain not less than 36 percent butterfat; may contain emulsifiers, stabilizers, nutritive sweeteners, and flavoring ingredients.

LIGHT CREAM. Also called "coffee cream." Light cream must contain less than 30 percent, but not less than 18 percent, butterfat and may contain emulsifiers, stabilizers, nutritive sweeteners, and flavoring agents.

LIGHT WHIPPING CREAM. Must contain less than 36 percent, but not less than 30 percent, butterfat and may contain emulsifiers, stabilizers, nutritive sweeteners, and flavoring ingredients.

POURING CREAM. A nineteenth-century term for cream poured out of a pitcher.

SOUR CREAM. Cream that has been treated with lactic-acid-producing bacteria and containing not less than 18 percent butterfat (1815). Sour cream may contain optional ingredients such as rennet, salt, sodium citrate, and flavoring ingredients.

CREAM CHEESE. A cow's-milk cheese with a very smooth consistency and a mild, slightly tangy flavor (1575). Under FDA regulations, cream cheese must contain not less than 33 percent milkfat and not more than 55 percent moisture. The cheese is not aged, but gum arabic may be added to increase firmness and shelf life. Diluted cream cheese may be called "imitation cream cheese" (although this may also refer to a nondairy product).

Cream cheese became available to everyone after Isaac and Joseph Breakstone of Breakstone Brothers Inc. produced "Breakstone's Downsville Cream Cheese" (named after the New York community where it was made) in 1920. It immediately became popular among Jewish communities in NYC as a spread for **bagels**.

In 1872, a dairyman named Lawrence, in New York State, began mixing cream and milk to make a particularly savory form of cream cheese that was soon being manufactured by various dairies. A cheese distributor named Reynolds enlisted Lawrence and the nearby Empire Cheese Co., of South Edmeston, New York, to produce the cheese under the name Philadelphia Brand, which in 1928 became a trademark of Kraft Foods, of Glenview, Illinois.

CREAM TOAST. A dish of toast with a cream sauce on it.

CREDIT CARD. A card that identifies a person who seeks to purchase an item on credit. The term has been in use since 1885, and "charge accounts" have been part of American business since 1807, established at Cowperthwaite & Sons, in NYC. The first popular card for charging was made by Western Union in about 1914, and "charge plates," usually in the form of thin metal cards called "metal money," came in around the same time at hotels. But the most important innovation for food service came in 1950, after businessman Francis X. McNamara (who himself worked for a credit company in Manhattan) found himself unable to pay for a restaurant meal in NYC because he'd forgotten his money. This gave him the idea to create the "Diners Club," with the help of attorney Ralph Schneider. For a fee of three dollars per year, cardholders could charge their meals at any of twenty-seven participating restaurants in NYC. By the end of 1951, more than $1 million had been charged on the new cards, and McNamara sold out his share to Schneider in 1953 for $200,000. Diners Club later became a subsidiary of Citicorp.

CRÈME BRÛLÉE. Also "burnt cream." A dessert custard topped with a burnt-sugar crust. *The Random House Dictionary of the English Language* traces the first appearance in print of "crème brûlée" to 1885, from the French meaning "burnt cream," which it is often called in England. But the dish is probably not of French origins. Escoffier does not mention such a dish; *Larousse Gastronomique* refers to a similar dish under the name *crème anglaise au miroir* ("mirrorlike English cream"). As "burnt cream," the dish originated in England, where, according to English food authority Jane Grigson, recipes for the dish appeared in seventeenth-century cookbooks. By the turn of the twentieth century it had become a favorite dessert at Trinity College, Cambridge, and, according to Jane Garmey, in *Great British Cooking* (1981), it is often referred to as "Trinity cream."

Recipes for "burnt cream" have been included in Creole cookbooks since the nineteenth century, though *The Picayune Creole Cook Book* (1901) indicates that the confection is made merely by adding caramel to a custard base that is then reduced, strained, garnished with fruits, and served cool. In *The New Orleans Eat Book* (1991), Tom Fitzmorris says, "*Crème brûlée* is a variation on caramel custard in which the custard part is much richer, yet semi-liquid in texture. The caramel part is baked into a hard shell over the top." The classic American cookbook *Joy of Cooking* calls it "a rich French custard—famous for its hard, caramelized sugar glaze." There are recipes for a burnt-glaze custard under the name "creme brulee" in *The Cordon Bleu Cook Book* (1947), by Dione Lucas, and *The White House Cookbook* (1964), edited by Jane Halliday Ervin.

But the popularity of the dish in the U.S. soared after it was made fashionable when chef Alain Sailhac brought the idea back from a trip to Spain (where the dish is known as an old Catalan dessert called *crema quemada a la catalana*) in 1982 and began making it at the restaurant Le Cirque, in NYC. After that it became a standard dish in American fine-dining restaurants, as well as, ironically, France.

CREOLE MUSTARD. A hot, spicy mustard made from seeds marinated in vinegar. It is a specialty of Louisiana's German Creoles, who brought the mustard seeds from Austria and Holland.

CRISCO. The trademark of a shortening made from vegetable oils, principally soybean. By a process called "hydrogenation," the oils are suspended in fat solids so as to form a soft white mass that is packed in airtight tin cans.

The product is manufactured by the Procter & Gamble Co., which began marketing the new shortening in 1911. Its virtues over lard, butter, and other vegetable oils at that time were that it did not pick up odors or flavors from foods fried in it, it did not smoke when heated, and it could be kept for long periods without going rancid. (In the early 1960s, the product was altered to double the amount of polyunsaturates, considered by some scientists to be important to health.)

The name Crisco was the result of a contest held among Procter & Gamble employees. The two leading choices were "Krispo" and "Cryst," meant to suggest the hissing sound of the shortening in the pan, and these were combined into "Crisco."

From the beginning, the product was marketed with recipes attached, and the name became fairly synonymous with "shortening," especially "white shortening," and was used as an alternative to heavier fats such as lard. It has been particularly favored in the South, where, according to **James Villas**, in *American Taste* (1982), it is the essential ingredient in making good **southern fried chicken**.

Artificially flavored "Butter Flavor Crisco" was introduced nationally in 1983.

CROCKERY COOKER. A large, lidded kettle containing its own heat unit for cooking. The first example was the "Crock-pot," brought on the market by the Rival Manufacturing Co., of Kansas City, Missouri, in 1971. Foods are placed in the Crock-pot, the pot is turned on, and the food is slowly cooked through.

CRUMB BUN. A pastry topped with crumbs made of flour, fat, and powdered sugar, usually eaten as a breakfast item or snack.

CRUMMIN. A Texas dish of crumbled-up corn bread and sweet milk.

CRUST COFFEE. A coffee substitute made at home in New England. It was made by toasting bread until almost burned, pouring boiling water on it, straining the liquid, and drinking it with sugar and cream. The term dates in print to 1863.

CRUVINET. Trademark name for a system developed in France to preserve wines from oxidation in bottles that have been opened. The system, which puts nitrogen into the opened bottle, is most often used in restaurants that offer several wines by the glass. The first restaurant in the U.S. to use the Cruvinet was Lavin's, in NYC, in 1982, to celebrate the arrival of the Beaujolais nouveau wine from France.

CUBA LIBRE. A cocktail made from rum, cola, and lime juice. The name in Spanish means "free Cuba," but its origins are obscure, dating in print to 1898, during the Spanish–American War, when Cuba was liberated from Spanish rule, but that reference is only to a drink of "water and brown sugar." Coca-Cola did not reach Cuba until 1900. According to a deposition by Fausto Rodriguez on October 24, 1965, the cocktail was made in August 1900 by a "Mr. X," who worked in the office of the U.S. Signal Corps in Cuba. (Mr. Rodriguez was a messenger for the corps.) The drink first appeared in print in Ernest Hemingway's 1937 novel *To Have and Have Not*.

CUBA LIBRE

Combine 1 oz. light rum, ½ oz. 151-proof rum, ½ oz. Coca-Cola, 1 oz. lime juice, and ½ t. sugar. Serve over ice cubes and garnish with a lime peel.

CUBAN CHINESE FOOD. A mixture of Cuban and **Chinese American** food items sold at restaurants opened by Cuban Chinese who fled Cuba in the 1960s after Fidel Castro seized power. Many settled in NYC's Hispanic neighborhoods, where they opened such restaurants primarily to serve the Latino community.

CUCUMBER (*Cucumis sativus*). A long green vegetable in the gourd family that is generally eaten raw, as in a salad, or made into pickles.

The word is from the Latin *cucumis*, which in Middle English became *cucumber*, first in print in a 1382 Bible.

Though the cucumber was long believed to have originated in India, there is now evidence that it came from Thailand and was cultivated there ten thousand years before Christ. By the fourteenth century A.D. it was being cultivated in England. Spaniards brought the cucumber to America, and it was then readily cultivated by the Pueblo Indians. In 1998, the U.S. produced 615 million tons of cucumbers for processing, mostly for pickles.

CUITLACOCHE (*Ustilago maydis*). Also "huitlacoche." A gray-black fungus that grows on the ears of corn, used in cooking as one would wild mushrooms. The word is from the Nahuatl *cuitlatl* (excrement) and *cochi* (black) and is pronounced "weet-la-*ko*-chay." In *The Cuisines of Mexico* (1972; revised 1986), Diana Kennedy spelled the word *huitlacoche*, citing *cuitlacoche* as an alternative in her *Recipes from the Regional Cooks of Mexico* (1978), then gave the latter spelling in her 1989 book *The Art of Mexican Cooking*.

Almost all cuitlacoche used in cooking is imported from Mexico canned. The fungus does grow wild on American corn, but most farmers burn it as a crop nuisance called "smut." It also may grow wild in some American gardens and farms and has been cultivated in very small quantities in California and Georgia. Cuitlacoche is usually sautéed with garlic and oil. Though a regional specialty of Mexico City cookery, cuitlacoche began to be treated as a delicacy among American chefs, particularly in the Southwest, only in the 1980s.

CULINARY INSTITUTE OF AMERICA. Recognized as one of the world's finest culinary schools, the Culinary Institute of America, nicknamed the "CIA," has graduated more than 44,000 students since its inception.

The CIA began in 1946 as the New Haven Restaurant Institute, in New Haven, Connecticut. It was founded by Frances Roth and Katharine Angell to draw returning World War II servicemen in need of training for jobs. Beginning with just fifty students, the school had six hundred graduates by 1951, when it changed its name to the Culinary Institute of America. In 1965, Roth retired, naming Jacob Rosenthal president. With more than a thousand students, the CIA moved in 1970 to much larger quarters in a former Jesuit novitiate on the Hudson River in Hyde Park, New York, and in 1971 was granted by the New York State Board of Regents a charter to confer an associate of occupational studies degree.

While continuing to train students, the CIA's Epicurean Room (later the Escoffier Restaurant) garnered a reputation for being one of the finest French restaurants in America. CIA students worked as both chefs and waiters for the dining room.

In 1980, former chef **Ferdinand E. Metz** took over as president of the school, enlarging its classrooms and restaurants and making it possible for the school to administer the American Culinary Federation's Master Chefs exam, the highest professional certification in the country.

Metz also opened an American restaurant named American Bounty; a nutritional restaurant, St. Andrew's Café; and, with the help of the Gruppo Ristoratori Italiani, the Catherine de'Medici Italian restaurant. In 1988, the CIA opened the General Foods Nutrition Center. In 1993, the board of regents granted permission to award two bachelor of professional studies (B.P.S.) degrees, in culinary arts management and pastry arts management.

As interest in the culinary profession grew, the CIA launched a West Coast campus, in 1995, at Greystone, in the Napa Valley, including the Wine Spectator Greystone Restaurant. In 2001, chef Timothy Ryan took the reins as president, and the Colavita Center for Italian Food and Wine opened on the Hyde Park campus. Two years later, the Cornell University School of Hotel Administration began a dual-degree collaboration with the CIA for a bachelor of science program in hotel administration from Cornell and an associate in occupational studies (A.O.S.) degree in culinary arts from the CIA.

In 2006, the CIA at Greystone offered an associate degree program in culinary arts, and in 2008 a third campus was opened, in San Antonio, Texas, focusing on Latin American cuisines. In 2009, an A.O.S. degree program in baking and pastry arts was offered at Greystone, and a year later its fourth campus, in Singapore, opened in partnership with the Singapore Institute of Technology, offering a B.P.S. in culinary arts management on the campus of Temasek Polytechnic.

CULL. Fishermen's term for a lobster with only one claw, usually the result of a battle with another creature.

CURRANT. Any of a variety of prickly shrubs of the genus *Ribes*, bearing small, dark berries that are often dried and used as a flavoring. The word is from Anglo-French

Corauntz, referring to the city of Corinth, because the berries were called in Middle English *raysons of Coraunte*—that is, "raisins of Corinth," first in print in 1334.

Currants first began to appear in England in the seventeenth century and were brought to America soon afterwards, even though there were already native varieties in the New World, specifically the "American black currant" (*R. americanum*). Until the twentieth century, currants were cultivated in the U.S., but their growth has now been discouraged because currants carry the parasite *Cronartium ribicola*, which does not harm the plant itself but attacks precious white pines in its vicinity. Most currants on the American market are therefore dried and imported.

CUSH. A cornmeal pancake made in the South. The name, first recorded in about 1770, arrived in America with the African slaves brought to the Caribbean and the South; it derives from the Arabic *kuskus*, "to grind small," and the grain dish of Morocco called "couscous." In Louisiana, "coush-coush caille" is a dish of corn bread and clabber.

CUSHAW (*Cucurbita moschata*). An American crooknecked **squash**, popular among the Cajun people of Louisiana. The name comes from the Indian (probably the Algonquian of North Carolina and Virginia) *coscushaw* and first appeared in English in 1580.

CUT STRAW AND MOLASSES. Western slang term for inferior food, dating in print to 1857.

CYCLONE CANDY. A sweet confection mentioned by Marjorie Mosser in her *Foods of Old New England* (1957). The reasons for its name are unknown.

CYCLONE CANDY

Cook 1 c. sugar with 1 c. molasses, 3 T. vinegar, and 2 T. butter to the hard-ball stage. Add 1 t. vanilla and ¼ t. baking soda, stir, and pour into buttered pan. Cool and cut into candy-size pieces.

CZARNINA. Also "czarina." A Polish American soup made from duck's blood, from the Polish *czernina*. It is usually served on feast days.

DAGWOOD SANDWICH. A multilayered sandwich made with slices of bread enclosing various kinds of meats, lettuce, vegetables, and other condiments. The name derives from the character Dagwood Bumstead, created and drawn by Murat Bernard "Chic" Young for the comic strip *Blondie*—which began on September 6, 1930, as part of the King Features Syndicate.

The sandwich first appeared in the comic strip on April 16, 1936, and, according to Dean Young, son of Chic Young and now co-author of the strip with Bill Yates, it was not at first as colossal a sandwich as it eventually became through the years. The character and the sandwich became immediately linked, and Americans began referring to such overstuffed items as "dagwoods." The sandwich was also a regular feature in the series of twenty-eight *Blondie* motion pictures made from 1938 to 1950 and in two television series, in 1954 and 1968, of the same name.

DAGUIN, ARIANE (1958–). Entrepreneur. French-born Ariane Daguin became one of the leading suppliers of luxury foods to American markets, chefs, and cooks and is especially known for selling fresh **foie gras** made from American ducks rather than French geese.

Daguin was born in the Gascony region of France, where her father was owner-chef of Hôtel de France, in Auch. As a young girl, she learned the craft of making charcuterie. Daguin moved to the U.S. to attend Columbia University while working part-time for a New York State pâté producer, which inspired her to market fresh domestic foie gras made from ducks. In 1985, with George Faison, she opened her gourmet specialties company D'Artagnan (named after the legendary character in Alexandre Dumas's 1844 novel *The Three Musketeers*), with corporate headquarters in Newark, New Jersey.

Prior to D'Artagnan's opening, foie gras was available only canned. Daguin first sold her products to professional chefs, then to the general public. She was a pioneer of natural, sustainable, and humane organic food production of chickens and veal. She often gives cooking demonstrations and seminars, has published *D'Artagnan's Glorious Game Cookbook*, and once ran a restaurant named D'Artagnan the Rotisserie in NYC.

In 2005, Daguin bought out Faison's share of the company and became sole owner and CEO. Today D'Artagnan contracts thirty-six co-ops in the U.S., with fifteen hundred farmers contributing.

Daguin is the founding president of Les Nouvelles Mères Cuisinières and is active in Les Dames d'Escoffier, the American Institute of Wine & Food, Women Chefs and Restaurateurs, and Chaîne des Rôtisseurs. In 2005, she received the Lifetime Achievement Award from *Bon Appétit* and has been honored to receive the prestigious medal of the French Légion d'honneur.

DAIQUIRI. Sometimes "Daiquiri" with uppercase *D*. A cocktail made from rum, lime juice, and sugar. It is named after the town of Daiquiri, near Santiago, Cuba, where, after the Spanish–American War of 1898, Americans came to work the mines, retiring on weekends to the Hotel Venus to drink such a cocktail. Chief engineer Jennings S. Cox has been credited with naming the drink after the mines, in 1900. Some say he himself invented the cocktail. The drink was supposedly brought to the U.S. by Lucius W. Johnson, a medical officer on the USS *Minnesota*, who enjoyed the drink in Cuba in 1909 and introduced it to the Washington Army and Navy Club. The cocktail was first cited in print in F. Scott Fitzgerald's 1920 novel *This Side of Paradise*.

The "frozen daiquiri," for which crushed ice is added before blending, was supposedly created at the El Florida bar, known to customers in Ernest Hemingway's day as El Floridita, in Havana, Cuba. Hemingway himself concocted a variation he called the "Papa Doble" (good friends often called the author "Papa"), which was made without sugar. In his book *Papa Hemingway* (1955), A. E. Hotchner gives a recipe for the Papa Doble containing 6 drops of maraschino, the juice of half a grapefruit, the juice of two limes, and 4 ounces of rum.

DAIQUIRI

Combine 2 t. lime juice, ½ t. superfine sugar, and 2 oz. light rum over ice, shake, and strain into a chilled cocktail glass. Sometimes the rim of the glass is sugared. A "frozen daiquiri," often made with bananas, strawberries, or other fruit, is made by adding about 4 ice cubes to the mixture and pulverizing it in an electric blender. A "pink daiquiri" is made by adding 1 t. each of maraschino or grenadine.

DAISY. A cocktail made from citrus-fruit juice, a cordial or fruit syrup, and liquor. Daisies are generally synonymous with "fixes," which were originally based on pineapple syrup, while daisies were based on raspberry or grenadine, but these distinctions have blurred since the mid-nineteenth century, when both drinks were especially popular. The name probably derives from a slang term meaning "something excellent," rather than directly from the flower.

DANDELION (*Taraxacum officinale*). A native Eurasian plant that has become naturalized as a weed in North America. The word, first in print in 1513, is from the Medieval Latin *dens leonis*, "lion's tooth," via Middle French *dent de lion*. Its leaves are sometimes added to salads, and its flowers are used to produce a **honey**, especially in Colorado. It is also used to make "dandelion wine." See **Dutch salad**.

DANISH PASTRY. Also "Danish." A term encompassing a variety of yeast-dough pastries rolled and filled with cheese, prune, almond paste, fruit preserves, nuts, or other condiments. These pastries are a staple breakfast item, especially on the East Coast, where one orders a "Danish" prefixed by the filling desired. Although the pastries may have Danish origins, these flaky buns and rolls are more often associated with NYC Jewish delicatessens and bakeries. With this meaning the word first appeared in print in 1928. In California, Danish pastries are sometimes called "snails," because of their snaillike appearance.

DATE. The fruit of the date palm (*Phoenix dactylifera*), a tropical tree. The sweet fruit is especially popular in Asia and the Middle East. The name is from the Greek *daktulos*, finger, after the shape of the fruit. The word first appeared in print circa 1300. The date began to be cultivated in California around 1902, principally from the variety Deglet Noor (meaning "date of light"). Dates are classified as "soft," "semi-dry," and "dry." More than 99 percent of the dates marketed in the U.S. are grown in California. "Date shakes," blended with ice cream and milk, are popular in Southern California, supposedly having been created around 1928 by Russ Nichol at his fruit stand on Highway 111 near Palm Springs.

DATE FISH. Name of either of two mollusks, the "great piddock" (*Zirfaea crispata*) or the "chubby mya" (*Platyodon cancellatus*). The term was first mentioned in print in 1826, but Goode's *Fisheries* (1884) notes that both mollusks "are esteemed delicacies on the coast of California under the name of 'Date fish.'"

DEACON PORTER'S HAT. A suet pudding steamed in a long cylindrical mold. It is fairly similar to the pudding called **Brother Jonathan's hat**. According to Eleanor Early, in her *New England Cookbook* (1954), "When this pudding…made its first appearance at dinner one noon in 1837, a student [at] Mount Holyoke Female Seminary, cried, 'Oh, see the Deacon's hat!'" referring to Deacon Andrew W. Porter, a member of the school's first board of trustees, who wore a stovepipe hat every day. Early also notes that "there is said to have been a light-colored pudding, made in a similar mold, called the Deacon's Summer Hat, but that is only a legend."

DEAD SOLDIER. Also "dead marine." Bar slang for an empty beer bottle, dating in print to 1899.

DE LATOUR, GEORGES (1856–1940). Winemaker. In the early twentieth century, Georges De Latour helped revitalize the California wine industry by importing French vines grafted onto phylloxera-resistant rootstock.

An immigrant, as of 1833, from France's Périgord region, De Latour bought a four-acre farm in Rutherford, California, in 1900 for his wife, calling it Quel Beaulieu ("beautiful place"). It was there that he first grafted French vines onto California rootstock, which prevented the ravages of phylloxera infestation.

De Latour then bought a stone winery, which he called Beaulieu Vineyard, or BV, and his success allowed him to expand its size three times over the next decade, to produce a million gallons of wine each year. During Prohibition, De Latour made sacramental wines while also making and storing his BV wines, in the belief that the law would someday be repealed. When it was, in 1933, his was among the most modern facilities in California.

Selling his wines only in bottle, not in bulk, De Latour maintained an image of quality he sought to improve as of 1938 by hiring André Tchelistcheff, a Russian-born émigré from France's Institut National Agronomique Paris-Grignon. In 1936, De Latour had laid down a **cabernet sauvignon** as a private reserve under his own name, but he died before its release. The 1938 vintage was the first by Tchelistcheff.

De Latour died in 1940, and his wife succeeded him in running the winery until her own death, in 1951, passing ownership to her daughter, Marquise Helene de Pins, who in 1969 sold the winery to the beverage corporation Heublein, which in turn was sold to RJR Nabisco, then to Grand Metropolitan in 1987, which became Diageo.

Georges De Latour was inducted into the **Culinary Institute of America**'s Vintners Hall of Fame in 2007.

DELAWARE. An American red labrusca grape that makes wines that rarely need the sugaring that other eastern varieties require. It was introduced in the 1840s and is today used as a table grape as well as a champagne grape.

DELICATESSEN. Also "deli." A grocery store that usually sells cooked meats, prepared foods, and delicacies. The word is from the German *Delikatessen*, "delicacies,"

first appearing in print in 1877. In the 1880s, it referred to preserved foods. During the period of post–Civil War emigration to America, many Jews set up butcher shops called *schlact* stores, but as more foods were added to the shelves, the term "delicatessen shop," "delicatessen store," and "delicatessen" became common, though some preferred the non-German term "appetizing store." Later, "delicatessen" was shortened to "deli" or "delly," which sometimes also refers to the foods sold in such an establishment. The first NYC delicatessen is said to have opened in 1868.

Many delicatessens made their own products. In 1905, Frank Brunckhorst began making products for NYC groceries, and in 1933 he opened a plant in Brooklyn to make cooked hams and other products, delivered by horse carts to city delicatessens (though ham was almost never carried in Jewish stores). His Boar's Head Brand became a standard of consistent quality that made his products very popular in and beyond NYC delicatessens.

NYC is still the hub for deli culture and sets the standards for those elsewhere. The oldest still surviving is Katz's, on the Lower East Side, opened by the Iceland brothers in 1888 and famous for its World War II promotion "Send a Salami to Your Boy in the Army." Other well-known NYC delis include the Carnegie Deli (opened 1937), the Stage Deli (1937, closed 2012), and the 2nd Avenue Deli (1954), which published the *Second Ave Deli Cookbook: Recipes and Memories from Abe Lebewohl's Legendary New York Kitchen*, by Sharon Lebewohl and Rena Bulkin (1999). In 1985, Sue Kreitzman published *Deli: 101 New York-Style Deli Dishes, from Chopped Liver to Cheesecake*.

Many delicatessens keep **kosher** and will not serve meat and dairy together. Delicatessens specialize in serving **pastrami**, **corned beef**, potato salad, pickles, rye bread, liverwurst, blintzes, and many other items enjoyed by the Jews of the eastern cities. To call such a store a "Jewish delicatessen" is, therefore, something of a redundancy. But today, many other ethnic groups run their own delis, as in "Italian deli" or "Latin American deli."

DELMONICO POTATOES. Potato balls boiled and buttered and sprinkled with lemon juice, parsley, pepper, and salt. The dish was featured at NYC's Delmonico's restaurant in the nineteenth century.

DEMOCRAT. A sweet, baked buttermilk confection of the nineteenth century. The nature of the connection is obscure, but the dish somehow refers to the Democratic party.

DEMOCRAT

Combine 1 pt. buttermilk with 1 c. confectioners' sugar, 3 beaten egg yolks, ½ c. butter, 3 t. baking powder, and 1 qt. flour. Fold in 3 stiffly beaten egg whites. Bake in muffin tins, 1 T. of batter to a tin, for about 20 min. at 375°.

DEPTH CHARGE. A bar drink made by dropping a shot of whiskey into a glass of beer. The imbiber is supposed to drain the glass of beer and end up with the shot glass between his teeth. The name derives from the depth-charge explosives dropped in the water from a ship in an effort to destroy a submerged submarine. The term first appeared in print in 1957.

DERBY-PIE. Trademark name of Kern's Kitchen, in Louisville, Kentucky, for a very thick, rich chocolate-chip pecan pie. Its name derives from the tradition of serving it on Kentucky Derby Day, the first Saturday in May. Walter and Leaudra Kern owned the Melrose Inn, in Prospect, Kentucky, where the pie was created in 1950.

DESIGNATED DRIVER. A person who volunteers or is appointed not to consume alcoholic beverages while at a party or restaurant so that he may drive his friends home safely without fear of accident or of being arrested by police for driving while under the influence ("DUI") of alcohol or, the more serious charge, driving while intoxicated ("DWI"). The term was first in print in 1982.

DEVILED. Also "devilled." Any of a variety of dishes prepared with hot seasonings, such as cayenne or mustard. The word derives from its association with the demon who dwells in hell. In a culinary context, the word first appeared in print in 1786; by 1820 Washington Irving had used the word in his *Sketch Book* to describe a highly seasoned dish similar to a curry.

Deviled dishes were very popular throughout the nineteenth and into the twentieth century, especially for seafood preparations and some appetizers. The first U.S. food product to be granted a trademark (number 82) by the U.S. Patent Office (1870), to William Underwood & Co. of Boston, was for "deviled entremets," introduced in 1867.

DEVIL'S FOOD. A cake, muffin, or cookie made with dark chocolate, so called because it is supposedly so rich and delicious that it must be somewhat sinful, although the association is clearly made with humor. Its dark color contrasted with the snowy white of **angel food cake**, an earlier confection. The first devil's food recipe appeared in 1900, after which recipes and references became frequent in cookbooks. The "red devil's food cake," now usually called "red velvet" cake, is a post–World War II version of the standard devil's food cake, given a reddish-brown color by the mixture of cocoa and baking soda.

DEWBERRY (genus *Rubus*). Any of a variety of trailing forms of the **blackberry**, including the "nagoonberry" (*Rubus arcticus ssp. acaulis*) of Alaska (1914). In his *Soul Food Cookbook* (1969), Bob Jeffries refers to dewberries baked in pastry as "dubies." The word first appeared in print in 1578.

DEXTROSE. A sugar (also called "glucose" or "grape sugar") derived from the sap and juice of grapes and other plants (1866). Dextrose provides the major source of energy in animals and is used to thicken and sweeten caramel, soda pop, baked goods, and candy.

DICK SMITH. Also "Dick Smither." Colloquialism for a man who drinks liquor by himself or one who never buys drinks for anyone else at the bar. The term, which may also be used as a verb, dates in print to 1876.

DILL (*Anethum graveolens*). An herb, native to the Old World, used as a seasoning in sauces, soups, and salads. Its name derives from the West Germanic *dilja*, first appearing in print in the eighth century. Pickles are often flavored with dill, which in the U.S. is grown primarily in Ohio and the Midwest. In *Food* (1980), Waverley Root noted that "the Romans mixed aneth oil in their gladiators' food in the belief that it was a tonic, and it may have been for the same reason that dill seeds were given to American children a century or two back to chew in church, perhaps to keep them awake during long sermons, for which reason they were called 'meetin' seeds.'"

DIME-A-DIP DINNER. Also "ten-cents-a-dip." A meal held to benefit a charity or raise funds, at which all food items cost ten cents or some other specific amount of money. The term dates in print to 1976 and seems closely associated with Mormon communities.

DINER. An inexpensive **restaurant** originally made to look like a railroad dining car. In its Fall 1990 issue, *Roadside*, a journal for diner aficionados, defined a diner as "a prefabricated structure with counter service, hauled out to its site." Diners grew out of the concept of the lunch wagon, at first a pushcart wheeled into city streets where workers could get a quick bite to eat. In 1872 in Providence, Rhode Island, Walter Scott improved on the idea with his "Pioneer Lunch," a horse-drawn lunch wagon that was quickly copied in New England and led to elaborately decorated versions with complete working kitchens and stained-glass windows. Among the first was Thomas H. Buckley's New England Lunch Wagon Co., which also was the first to try out the idea of a stationary lunch stand, in Worcester, Massachusetts, though this was not a success.

But the proliferation of lunch wagons (sometimes called "dog wagons") in New England and their unsavory reputation as blue-collar hangouts caused many towns to force the owners to close down by 10:00 P.M. As a result, many lunch-wagon owners removed their horses and set down their wagons as immobile units, which were allowed to stay open day and night. Railway dining cars were sometimes called diners, dating in print to 1890, and, by renovating dilapidated electric trolley cars, lunch-wagon owners upgraded the image of their eateries. Led by men like Patrick J. "Pop" Tierney, of New Rochelle, New York, the roadside eateries grew in number, popularity, and design, usually copying the look, finish, and details of the railroad dining cars of the era. By the 1930s, streamlining had made such restaurants—by 1935 called "diners"—gleaming beacons by the road, known for their fast, efficient service and crisp, clean lines.

The industry grew rapidly and came to be dominated by **Greek Americans**, whose families might own several diners, many of which were designed around traditional Greek motifs and given Greek names like "Apollo" and "Pegasus."

By the late 1940s, at least thirteen manufacturers were involved in building diners at a rate of 250 a year, but, owing to the changing eating habits of Americans and the intrusion of **fast food** chain restaurants in every American town, the diner went into a slow decline after 1960. There has been a revival of nostalgic interest in diners since the mid-1980s, and several new ones have been built around the U.S. to evoke the design elements, atmosphere, and food of the 1930s, 1940s, and 1950s. Currently there are about two thousand diners in the U.S.

DINNER. The main meal of the day. Until the 1820s, this was commonly the midday meal, supper being a lighter meal at the end of the workday. Today, dinner is usually the evening meal.

The word "dinner," dating to the thirteenth century in England, derives from the French *dîner*. "Supper" is also found in English as of the thirteenth century, from the French *super*, itself possibly related to "soup," which was often the simple repast of the evening meal. In American usage, "dinner" dates in print to 1622.

In America, the tradition of eating the heaviest meal at midday was superseded in the 1820s by the demands of workers whose mealtime was often not paid for by their employers, thereby necessitating a quick, light meal before getting back to work. This became known as **lunch**, and the main meal of the day, "dinner," was now consumed after work ended. The tradition of eating the main meal in the afternoon was carried on as the "Sunday dinner," since Sunday was for most people the only day of the week off from work. Even after the five-day workweek became the norm, the Sunday dinner, held anywhere from noon onward, continued to be an American family gathering.

Today southerners still speak of "supper" as the evening meal, though it may be eaten somewhat earlier than in the rest of the country. In the North, the term "supper" may refer to a light meal served after an evening's entertainment, as in "after-theater supper." "Pre-theater dinner" is served before the eight o'clock curtain. "Din-din" is a childish expression for dinner.

DINNER HOUSE. Restaurant-industry term for a moderately priced, fairly casual, family-oriented restaurant, often connected with a chain or franchise.

DIP. A condiment, often made with mayonnaise or sour cream, into which one dips any of a variety of vegetables or snacks. Dips are usually served with party food. In the mid-nineteenth century, "dip" (circa 1825) referred to a sauce of pork fat served on fish. By the next century "dip" was a sauce for puddings, and "dipping" or "dippy" referred to both a gravy or sauce to dip meats into and a sweet sauce for desserts. In the 1950s, "party dips" were sauces in which guests dipped snack foods like potato chips. The most popular party dips were cream-cheese dip, onion dip, clam dip, and other creamy sauces. "Salsa" is a term used for a tomato-based dipping sauce for tortilla chips.

In 1952, the Lipton food company developed a dehydrated onion-soup mix that became even more popular as the base for an onion dip (two envelopes of soup mix plus one cup sour cream), which Lipton thereafter printed as a recipe called "California Dip" on the back of the package.

DIRT EATING. Known anthropologically as "geophagy," a word coined by Aristotle and dating in English print to 1821. Mentioned as a "diseased appetite" in parts of Alabama in 1859, the eating of dirt is common to nearly every culture on earth, especially during famine, as a way of absorbing minerals. In the U.S., it is specific to African Americans and poor rural whites (called "clay eaters" or "sand-lappers," which term dates in print to 1836) in the South. The custom apparently was carried to the New World by African slaves, whose masters sometimes masked their mouths to prevent the practice.

Even today, the eating of dirt is still indulged by some southerners, who tend to favor particular patches, especially "hill dirt" from slopes. In 1975, a study done by anthropologist Dennis A. Frate revealed that of fifty-six African American women in rural Mississippi, thirty-two admitted to eating dirt, especially during pregnancy. Others consumed cornstarch or baking soda, a possible cause of anemia. *The Cambridge World History of Food* cites one African American southerner who spoke of dirt eating as a "craving," and distinguishes between the qualities of clay from one region to another, noting that "I never heard of a man eating dirt."

DIRTY RICE. A Louisiana Cajun dish of rice cooked with chicken gizzards and livers, so called because the meat gives the rice a "dirty" appearance. The term dates in print to 1967.

DIRTY RICE

Boil 10 each of chicken gizzards, necks, livers, and hearts in 2 qt. water until tender. Remove and retain liquid. Fry 4 lb. hot sausage and retain fat. Sauté 2 minced onions, 1 minced bell pepper, and 4 stalks minced celery in 3 T. of the retained fat, then add 5 chopped scallions and cook for about 10 min. Add 1 c. chopped ham-and-chicken mixture, 8 T. melted butter, and 2 T. chopped parsley. Add water from kettle, salt, and pepper and let simmer for 15 min. Blend in 3 lb. cooked rice.

DISH NIGHT. A night when movie theaters gave away free dishware as a promotional gimmick. The practice began in the late 1920s and continued through the 1950s. Moviegoers would go to the theater on dish night (usually a weeknight) and receive a different dish—a cup, saucer, plate, gravy boat, or other item—thereby encouraging the moviegoer to return week after week to get a complete set.

DISHWATER. Slang for very weak or badly made coffee.

DIXIE CUP. Trademark name for one of the first paper cups. It was produced by the Individual Drinking Cup Co. of NYC in 1908.

DIXIE WINE. Slang term, used mostly by Mormons, for fermented grape juice with a pronounced rough taste. The term dates in print to 1873.

DOG (*Canis familiaris*). A domesticated carnivorous mammal of many breeds. In America, the dog has never been a food animal except among Native Americans and Hawaiians, although the first settlers from England who landed in Virginia in 1607 staved off starvation by boiling and eating their mastiffs.

In precolonial Hawaii, dogs, which were brought from Polynesia, were called *'ilio* and raised in large herds for food; they were actually preferred to pig in those days, and in 1830 the Reverend William Ellis reported that dogs were "mostly fed on vegetables; and we have sometimes seen them kept in yards, with small houses to sleep in. A part of the rent of every tenant who occupies land, is paid in dogs for his landlord's table." Ellis claimed to have seen two hundred dogs baked at one time for a feast and to have heard that when King Taumuarii of Tauai visited the governor of Hawaii, Kuakini, four hundred dogs were baked for the dinner.

DOGFISH. Any of several species of small sharks, especially *Mustelus canis*, called "smooth dogfish," "smooth dog," "dusky smooth-hound," and "grayfish," and *Squalus acanthias*, called "spiny dogfish," "spur dog," "piked dogfish," and "grayfish." The name probably refers to the small size and shape of the species, which resemble dogs or puppies. In print the term dates back to 1425.

DOGGIE BAG. Also "doggy bag." A bag in which a customer may carry home the edible remains of a restaurant meal to be eaten the next day, though its name suggests—in a rather too-cute manner—that the contents will be fed to one's pet. Although leftovers have long been packed up for customers, the term "doggie bag" dates in print to 1963. Two claims have been made for the idea under that name: Lawry's the Prime Rib, a Los Angeles restaurant that dates its usage back to the 1930s, and the Old Homestead Steakhouse, in NYC, whose owner, Harry Sherry, also began to use the term in the 1930s.

After Janice and Al Meister founded a package/container company named Bagcraft Papercon, in Chicago in 1947, they began printing five dogs' pictures and a famous ditty on their doggie bags:

> *Oh where, oh where have your leftovers gone?*
> *Of where, oh where can they be?*
> *If you've had all you can possibly eat,*
> *Please bring the rest home to me!*

DOG IN A BLANKET. A steamed pudding containing fruit preserves, dating in print to 1887.

DOLLY VARDEN (*Salvelinus malma*). Also "bull trout," "red-spotted trout," and "Oregon char." This char or **trout**, which grows up to three feet in length, is a multicolored spotted fish found from Alaska to Northern California in both salt and freshwater. Its beautiful markings have caused some Alaskans to call the fish "golden trout" or "golden-finned trout," but the more common name, "Dolly Varden," comes from a character in Charles Dickens's novel *Barnaby Rudge* (1841) who wore a tight-fitting dress with a flowered skirt over a brightly colored petticoat. The *Yreka Union* newspaper of California, on June 3, 1876, insisted that the fish were "first caught in McCloud River by white men—Messrs. Josiah Edson of Shasta Valley and Geo. Campbell of Soda Springs, and were given the name of Dolly Varden by Elda McCloud, a niece of Mr. Campbell." But Goode's *Fisheries* (1884) contends that "in the Sacramento the name 'Dolly Varden' was given to [the fish] by the landlady at the hotel, and this name it still retains in that region." "Dolly Varden" is also the name of a New England cake, mentioned in *The Pentucket Housewife* (1882).

DOLLY VARDEN CAKE

Beat 4 egg yolks separately from 4 egg whites. Fold the two together, add 1 c. creamed butter, 2 ½ c. sugar, 1 c. milk, 4 c. flour, ½ t. baking soda, and 1 t. cream of tartar. Divide the mixture in two. To each half of the mixture add 1 T. molasses, 1 t. spices, and some raisins and currants. Pour each mixture into separate loaf pans and bake in medium-hot oven.

DOLPHIN. Either of two varieties of marine fish, *Coryphaena hippurus* or *C. equisetis*, ranging in size from two pounds to fifty pounds or more and inhabiting both oceans of North America. Reference to the former species was first noted in 1862; to the latter, circa 1387. These food-fish dolphins (also called "dorado") are not in any way related to the mammals of the same name. The word comes from Greek *delphis*.

These varieties are better known in Hawaii as **mahimahi** (1926) and are there considered a delicacy. They are also sought in Florida, where the roe is eaten. U.S. commercial landings of dolphin totaled 2.25 million pounds in 2010, valued at $4.8 million.

DOPE. Slang term in the South for cola drinks, because the caffeine in some soda pop acts as a slight stimulant. Originally it applied to true narcotics, especially heated opium, which became a gloppy substance like the Dutch sauce called *doop*, from which the word derives.

"Dope" is also a slang term for **gravy** (1807) and for dessert topping or molasses (1904).

DOUGHNUT. A deep-fried yeast pastry that has a hole in the middle. Doughnuts are a favorite snack and confection throughout the U.S. and are known in other forms throughout Europe.

The first American doughnuts did not have holes at all; they were quite literally little "nuts" of dough. The Pilgrims, who had spent the years 1607–1620 in Holland, learned to make doughnuts there and brought them to New England; the most direct antecedent of the pastry seems to be of German origin, and these doughnuts came in all shapes and sizes. The first mention of the term in print was in Washington Irving's *History of New York…by Diedrich Knickerbocker* (1809), in which he describes the Dutch settlers of New Amsterdam in the seventeenth century: "[The table] was always sure to boast an enormous dish of balls of sweetened dough, fried in hog's fat, and called doughnuts or olykoeks [oil cakes]—a delicious kind of cake, at present scarce known in the city, excepting in genuine Dutch families."

Eliza Leslie's *New Cookery Book* (1857) refers to the German origins of the doughnut, which by then had become quite popular. The Pennsylvania Dutch traditionally served doughnuts called "fossnocks" or "fastnachts" on Shrove Tuesday (Fastnacht) as the last sweet before Lent; at other times of the year they were called "Fett Kucke" or "fat cake." On Fastnacht Day, these doughnuts are served at breakfast; the last person to arrive at the table is labeled a "lazy fastnacht" and served the last of the dough.

The Pennsylvania Dutch were probably the first to make doughnuts with holes in their centers, a perfect shape for "dunking" (Pennsylvania Dutch *tunke*; German *dunke*) in coffee, which has become a standard method of eating doughnuts for Americans. There seems little real evidence to support the story of a Rockport, Maine, sea captain named Hanson Crockett Gregory, who claimed to have poked out the soggy centers of his wife's doughnuts in 1847 so that he might slip them over the spokes of his ship's wheel, thereby being able to nibble while keeping an even keel. Nevertheless, in 1947 a centenary plaque commemorating Gregory's alleged culinary creation was placed on the house where he had lived.

By the middle of the nineteenth century the hole must have been widely accepted, and a housewares catalog of 1870 shows a doughnut cutter that included a corer, as does the 1897 Sears, Roebuck catalog, which priced the gadget at four cents. "Crullers" (Dutch *krullen*) were an early egg-dough pastry shaped by the New Amsterdam Dutch into "love knots" or "matrimony knots" or the elongated shape that became familiar throughout the country. Sometimes crullers were called "wonders" or, among the Creoles, "croque-cignole."

By the twentieth century, doughnuts, dusted with powdered sugar or cinnamon, iced, or stuffed with jelly (sometimes called a **Chicago**) or cream (sometimes called a "cream doughnut" or "cream stick") had become a great American favorite. Today more than ten billion doughnuts are made in the U.S., the glazed variety being by far the most popular. The doughnut industry is worth $3.6 billion.

It is improbable that American soldiers in France during World War I were called "doughboys" because of their affection for the confection, or, as Evan Jones asserts in *American Food* (1981), that the name "doughboy" appeared after a Salvation Army worker in France made a batch for the soldiers away from home, although the term "doughboy" as meaning a flour or cornmeal dumpling goes back to at least 1753 in print; as meaning a doughnut, to 1887. Elizabeth Custer (widow of General George Custer) believed the name to derive from the similarity of doughnuts' shape to the infantry's globular brass buttons. Other associations have been made: a pipe clay, called "dough," with which the infantry cleaned their white belts, and a slang term of southwestern Hispanics for American soldiers quartered in adobe structures. The term is found even in a British soldier's reference, in 1809, to Lord Wellington's retreat after the Battle of Talavera, in Spain. Wellington's soldiers made bread by grinding wheat flour with their hands and with stones—"from which wretched practice we christened the place Dough Boy Hill." "Doughboy" is also a Rhode Island term for deep-fried and sugared dough. "Doughgod" is a variant term, used in the Northeast and the West, for the same confection. People in the North and the Northwest commonly call an oblong doughnut "long john" or "**bismarck**," a term also used by northeasterners for a "jelly doughnut," though the origin of "bismarck" is not known. A "cake doughnut" is a doughnut made with baking powder or soda rather than yeast.

Doughnuts, often spelled "donuts," are as popular as ever, and shops specializing in them—sometimes called "doughnuteries"— have been around for decades. Although the majority of homemade doughnuts are still deep-fried in oil, there are on the market electric appliances for making doughnuts without having to deep-fry the dough. "Sinker," once a term applied to a pancake or roll, became by the 1920s a term for a very heavy doughnut.

"Doughnut holes," the dough ball supposedly from the center of the doughnut, have been sold separately since at least the 1960s.

In 1950, William Rosenberg, of Quincy, Massachusetts, founded Dunkin' Donuts, the most successful donut shop chain, now with more than ten thousand locations in thirty-two countries. By focusing on the quality of its coffee, Dunkin' Donuts capitalized on what had formerly been a localized industry.

The first National Donut Day was held as a fundraiser for the Salvation Army in 1938.

REGULAR DOUGHNUTS

Sift 2 c. flour, ½ c. sugar, 1 t. salt, and 3 t. baking powder. Beat 1 egg with ½ c. milk and 2 T. cooled melted butter. Mix with flour and knead the dough lightly. Roll on a board to ¼-in. thickness and cut with doughnut cutter. Deep-fry in a light oil heated to 360–375° and of a depth that allows doughnuts to float to the surface. Brown on one side, turn over, and brown other side. Drain on brown paper or crisp in warm oven.

RAISED DOUGHNUTS

Cream 1 c. butter with ½ c. sugar, then add 3 eggs, 1 t. salt, 1 cake yeast dissolved in lukewarm milk, and the grated rind of 1 lemon. Blend in 3 c. flour and knead into

an elastic dough. Cover and let rise overnight in a warm place until doubled. Roll into ¼-in. sheet, cut into rings, let stand again until doubled, then fry in deep oil. Drain and roll in powdered sugar.

DOWNHOME. Also "down home." A colloquialism, in print since 1966, used to describe anything, including food, that has a simple, folksy, often rural quality to it. It is most commonly used to refer to foods in the South, like fried **catfish**, **hush puppies**, **southern fried chicken**, **grits**, and many other items

DR. BROWN'S CEL-RAY SODA. Trademark name for a celery-flavored carbonated beverage first bottled in 1869 and now bottled by Canada Dry Bottling Co. of New York, in Queens. Its unique flavor, from celery seeds, was supposedly developed by a Brooklyn doctor named Brown, though this has never been verified. The trademark was long owned by the American Beverage Co.

Long popular with NYC's Jewish community, the beverage was originally called "Dr. Brown's Cel-Ray Tonic," and its label proudly proclaimed that it "contains vitamins G B D." But the federal government forced the makers to change the name to "Soda" because the original name implied the drink had medical or health benefits.

Today, Dr. Brown's Cel-Ray Soda sells in excess of a million cases a year.

DRESDEN DRESSING. A cold sauce, made with hard-boiled eggs, onion, mustard, and other seasonings, to accompany meats. The name derives from the German city of Dresden, and the sauce itself may be of German origin, though it first appeared under the name "Dresden dressing" in American cookery of the nineteenth century.

DRESSING. A general term, dating in print to 1504, referring to gravies, salad sauces, dessert sauces, cake frostings, and **stuffings**. Most common usage would denote a "salad dressing," e.g., vinegar and oil, **French dressing**, **Green Goddess** dressing, **Thousand Islands dressing**, **ranch**, and Italian dressing. "Boiled dressing" is particularly associated with the Midwest and the South, although the ingredients are not necessarily boiled.

BOILED DRESSING

Combine ½ c. water and ⅔ c. vinegar in a saucepan and bring to a boil. Mix together 2 T. flour, 2 T sugar, 1 t. salt, ⅛ t. pepper, and ¼ t. dry mustard. Stir in the liquid and then one beaten egg, stirring rapidly. Return to heat to thicken. Cool before using.

DRIED APPLE. A staple of early American tables and travelers' provisions. Apples left to dry over the winter were often made into pies on the trail westward, causing one passenger on the overland stagecoaches to remark that it was "apple pie from Genesis to Revelation along the Platte." A bit of doggerel from the same period goes: "Spit in my ears/And tell me lies, but give me no dried apple pies." See also **McGinty**.

DRINK BOX. A commercially made waxed or plasticized paper carton for beverages.

DRINKING STRAW. A paper or plastic straw used for sipping beverages. Before 1888, Americans sipped drinks through stalks of rye or other hollow stalks, but in that year Marvin Chester Stone, of Washington, D.C., took out a patent for drinking straws made from paraffin-coated manila paper. Today drinking straws are made of various materials, some constructed to bend according to the level of the glass.

DROPPED EGG. New Englander's term for a poached egg, dating in print to 1884.

DROWN THE MILLER. Slang phrase meaning to dilute liquor with too much water or to add excessive water to a dough. The phrase first saw print in 1899.

DRUM (family Sciaenidae). Any of a variety of fish that inhabit temperate and tropical marine waters, with species ranging from those weighing less than eight ounces to giant "totuava" that may reach 225 pounds or more. The name comes from a "drumming muscle" that makes a drumlike sound when expanded against the gas bladder. The fish was so called at least as early as 1676. Many species are called "croakers," because the sound also resembles croaking. Some of the more important drums for culinary purposes include the "Atlantic croaker" (*Micropogon undulatus*); "banded croaker" (*Larimus fasciatus*); "black drum" (*Pogonias cromis*); "freshwater drum" (*Aplodinotus grunniens*), also called "sheepshead," "crocus," "gaspergu," "jewelhead," and other names; "spot drum" (*Leiostomus xanthurus*), also called "Lafayette," after a visit to NYC by General Lafayette in 1824, a time when the fish was particularly numerous in the harbor; "white sea bass" (*Cynoscion nobilis*); and "yellowfin croaker" (*Umbrina roncador*). The "red drum" (*Sciaenops ocellata*), also called "channel bass," "puppy drum," and "redfish," took on amazing popularity in the 1980s after Cajun chef Paul Prudhomme popularized his recipe for **blackened redfish**—so much so that the federal government banned commercial fishing of the species in the Gulf of Mexico in 1987.

DRUNK. Intoxicated with liquor. This word is only the most easily identifiable among hundreds of others to indicate intoxication. As Stuart Berg Flexner writes in his appendix to the *Dictionary of American Slang* (second supplemented edition, 1975):

> *The concept having the most slang synonyms is drunk. This vast number of drunk words does not necessarily mean that Americans are obsessed with drinking, though we seem obsessed with talking about it. Many of these words are quite old.... Later immigrant groups brought their own words for drink and drunkenness, and it seems that some, during their first period of adjustment had a fair number of members who turned to whiskey as a compensation for the rejection they suffered as newcomers in a strange land. Most of the words for drunk, however, originated or became popular during Prohibition.*

Flexner's list included 353 terms ("and I didn't exhaust the subject," he wrote later). The term first appeared in print circa 1340, while the American penchant for "drunk" slang was first noted by Benjamin Franklin, in the *Pennsylvania Gazette* in 1737, when "have a glass eye," "loose in the hilt," "nimtopsical," "mooneyed," "top heavy," and "been to Barbados" were all used to describe drunkenness. Franklin listed 228 terms, ninety of which—as pointed out by Edward D. Seeber, in *American Speech* (February 1940)—were not listed in either the *OED* or the *English Dialect Dictionary*.

The following list gives only a small sampling of the more familiar terms for "drunk," with the dates of first appearance in print in parentheses: "soused" (sixteenth century), "blind" (seventeenth century), "oiled" (1737), "stewed" (1737), "bent" (1833), "stinking" (1837), "lushed" (1840), "tight" (1843), "pixillated" (1850s), "swizzled" (1850s), "D and D," an abbreviation for the legal phrase "drunk and disorderly" (1870), "paralyzed" (1888), "looped" (1890), "pickled" (1890s), "woozy" (1897), "tanked" (1905), "plastered" (1912), "hooted" (1915), "potted" (1922), "dead to the world" (1926), "bombed" (1940s), "shitfaced" (1940s), "feeling no pain" (1940s), "sloshed" (1950s), and "zonked" (1950s).

DUCK. Any of a variety of web-footed birds of the family Anatidae that may be either wild or domesticated and that inhabit open water, marshes, ponds, lakes, and rivers. The word is from Old English *dūce*, appearing in print as *"ducan"* in 967.

Ducks have been esteemed for their culinary value by most cultures of the world, and it is possible that the Indians in Central America domesticated the bird even before the Chinese did. The first European explorers were amazed at the numbers of ducks in American skies and soon commented on the delicious and distinctive flavor of the native **canvasback**, whose name figures in every cookbook of the nineteenth century to the extent that no banquet would be considered successful without serving the fowl.

On March 13, 1873, however, the arrival in NYC of a Yankee clipper ship with a tiny flock of white Pekin ducks—one drake and three females—signaled the beginning of a domestic industry of immense proportions. The birds were introduced to Connecticut and then to eastern Long Island, where they propagated at an encouraging rate. Domestic ducks were bought mostly by newly arrived immigrants, who bought them plucked, cooled, and packed in a barrel (called "New York dressed"). Only in the twentieth century did the fowl, by now called the "Long Island duckling," attain gastronomic respect; Long Island now produces half the ducks sold in America and exports some as well.

In the nineteenth century, wild ducks were usually eaten rare, but today domestic ducks are generally preferred cooked, with a very crisp skin, and served either roasted with applesauce or in the classic French manner, with orange sauce. France's **nouvelle cuisine** made rare duck breast (*magret de canard*) popular in high-end restaurants as of the 1970s. "Peking duck" now refers to a Chinese dish of specially prepared duck skin and meat detached and served in thin pancakes or buns with scallions and a sweet sauce.

The wild ducks of culinary importance to Americans include the canvasback (*Aythya valsineria*), also called the "bullneck," as well as the "redhead" (*Aythya americana*), the "mallard" (*Anas platyrhynchos*), the "black duck" (*Anas rubripes*), the "ring-necked duck" (*Aythya collaris*), and the "scoters" (*Melanitta fusca, M. perspicillata,* and *M. nigra*), also called "coots." The "mergansers"—any of a variety in the genus *Mergus*, which derives its name from the Latin *mergus* (diver) and *anser* (goose)—are not preferred and are often referred to by hunters as "trash ducks."

The "Muscovy duck" (*Cairina moschata*) was originally called the "musk duck" for its distinct musky smell. Its first printed mention, in 1774, notes that the name "Muscovy duck" had already been erroneously applied to the bird, which was native to South and Central America. Because of the bird's strong flavor, it has been domesticated and crossed with other breeds. It is sometimes called the "Barbary duck," because it was assumed to be an African bird. The Muscovy duck is available at American markets in the fall and winter. It is usually roasted.

The USDA grades ducks as it does chickens, "grade A" being the highest, "grade B" next, and "grade C" the lowest.

"Duck" is also African American slang for an alcoholic beverage.

DUFF. A steamed pudding containing fruit, as an "apple duff" or "plum duff." It was usually boiled in a bag. The word, which first appeared in print in 1816, is a nineteenth-century Scots or Northern England rendering of "dough," pronounced like "rough." In his novel *Two Years Before the Mast* (1840), Richard Henry Dana Jr., notes that on the Sabbath seamen would be "allowed on that day a pudding, or, as it is called, a 'duff.'"

DU JOUR. A French term meaning "of the day," which in America is usually attached to "soup," "fish," "dish," or other items, first appearing in English print in 1949, referring to a "cook du jour." The term refers to a special item on the menu for that particular day.

DULSE (*Rhodymenia palmata*). A coarse red seaweed that grows in profusion on the rocky coasts of the North Atlantic. The word derives from Gaelic *duileasg* and Welsh *delysg*, dating in print to 1547. It is dried and packaged, eaten raw, fried, and toasted and is a local specialty of New Brunswick.

DUMP CAKE. A cake made by "dumping" the ingredients directly into the baking pan, mixing them, and baking the batter. The Duncan Hines cake-mix company offers a recipe that uses a can of crushed pineapple, a can of cherry pie filling, a package of its Moist Deluxe Classic Yellow Cake Mix, a cup of chopped pecans or walnuts, and one stick of butter; it is made by dumping the pie filling on top of the pineapple, sprinkling on the cake mix, nuts, and butter, and baking for fifty minutes.

DUNGENESS CRAB (*Cancer magister*). A Pacific crab that is found from Alaska to Baja (1920). It is one of the rock crabs, colored pinkish green and yellow and weighing between one and three-quarters pounds and four pounds. It is named for a small town on the Olympic Peninsula, in Washington, where it was first commercially harvested. Only males at least six and a quarter inches long may be harvested, mainly during the winter months. Today the Dungeness is a major industry of the Northwest, and each season in San Francisco Bay, a Roman Catholic priest blesses the fishing fleet that will bring in the crabs.

U.S. landings totaled 65.3 million pounds in 2010, valued at $139.8 million. It is a very popular seaside delicacy sold by vendors who get "cracked crabs" fresh from the boat, scoop out the yellow-white fat, called **crab butter**, and serve them with mayonnaise.

In the Northwest, "crab feeds" are social gatherings (similar to New England clambakes or southern crab boils) where Dungeness crabs are featured.

DUSTY MILLER. An ice cream sundae made with powdered malted-milk topping. The term derives either from the auricula plant, which has fine powder on its leaves, or from a noctuid moth of the same name whose speckled wings resemble the dusty topping on the sundae. It probably dates from the 1920s.

DUTCH COURAGE. A slang term (dating back to at least 1809) for false courage induced by alcohol. Also an English term for gin imported from Holland.

DUTCH GROCERY. A slang term for a dirty grocery store. It was in use in the last quarter of the nineteenth century.

DUTCH LUNCH. A slang phrase usually referring to a buffet lunch consisting of cold meats, cheese, and beer, dating in print to 1904. It also refers to a shared lunch at which each person pays his own bill.

DUTCH OVEN. Also "Dutch bake oven." Usually a large, covered cast-iron kettle used for slow cooking. It may indeed have been of Pennsylvania Dutch heritage, though the word itself first appeared in print only in 1760. In colonial America, such kettles were often hung from a hook in the open fireplace, while at other times they were set on legs over the fire. In the West, the term referred to a thick, three-footed skillet used as an all-purpose cooking utensil that was placed over hot coals, with more coals placed on the lid in order to brown baked items like biscuits. In this century, a wall oven may also be called a "Dutch oven."

DUTCH SALAD. According to *DARE*, a Pennsylvania colloquialism for a dandelion salad, dating in print to 1960.

DYSPEPSIA COFFEE. A supposed aid for indigestion, made by mixing half coffee and half cornmeal moistened with molasses. This is browned in the oven and used as one would ground coffee. The term dates in print to 1940.

E

EARLY-BIRD SPECIAL. A restaurant meal served earlier and at a cheaper price than is usual at the regular dinner hours of 6:00 p.m. or later. It is popular with those on a budget and with senior citizens, and especially in resort areas like Florida. The term dates in American print to 1917, referring to a meal in effect at 9:15 a.m.

EAU SUCRÉE. This French-Creole term, which means "sugar water," refers to a glass of water in which has been dissolved one tablespoon of sugar. Eau sucrée is drunk after a heavy meal, supposedly to ease digestion, and, notes *The Picayune's Creole Cook Book* (1900), it "is used by all Creole mothers as a sedative for their little ones. Just before kissing her babes 'Good-night,' the Creole mother will give them a small glass of 'eau sucrée.' It is claimed that it insures easy digestion and perfect sleep."

Eau sucrée parties were frequent in old New Orleans, often held as a substitute for the more lavish parties of wealthier Creoles but no less enjoyed for their simple pleasures.

EDGE, JOHN T. (1962–). Author and media host. As director of the Southern Foodways Alliance, Edge coauthored *The Southern Foodways Alliance Community Cookbook* (2010) and has documented the diverse food cultures of the American South in numerous other publications.

Born in Clinton, Georgia, Edge earned an M.F.A. in creative nonfiction from Goucher College, in Baltimore, and an M.A. in southern studies from the University of Mississippi. He was the editor of the *Foodways* volume of *The New Encyclopedia of Southern Culture* and is general editor of the book series *Cornbread Nation: The Best of Southern Food Writing*. Edge has also served as culinary curator of National Public Radio's show *All Things Considered*.

His magazine and newspaper articles have run in the *New York Times*, the *Oxford American*, and *Gourmet*, including ten that have appeared in the annual *Best Food Writing* series. In 2009, he was inducted into the **James Beard Foundation**'s Who's Who of Food & Beverage in America. The *Miami Herald* once called Edge "the Faulkner of food writing."

"To me, what is interesting is to write about food that's relatively unheralded and people that are relatively unheralded," Edge has said. "To turn a camera or a mic on them and listen to their stories. That's a responsibility and it's also, for me, a real joy."

Edge's books include *Southern Belly: The Ultimate Food Lover's Guide to the South* (2002), *A Gracious Plenty: Recipes and Recollections from the American South* (2002), *Fried Chicken* (2004), *Apple Pie* (2004), *Hamburgers & Fries* (2005), and *Donuts* (2006).

EEL (*Anguilla rostrata*). A long, snakelike fish of the order Anguilliformes, found in eastern waters. The word is from Old English *ael*, first appearing circa 1000.

Long considered a delicacy by Europeans and Asians, eels have not been of much gastronomic interest to most Americans, but in colonial New England, "eel time," in autumn, was anticipated with the same enthusiasm that attended the run of the shad or the apple harvest. Later, Mediterranean immigrants—the Italians, Greeks, Portuguese, and others—kept their traditions of eating eel on certain holidays, especially Christmas, and the eel industry in America is still seasonal. Eels are prepared in diverse ways: boiled, steamed, stewed, grilled, or fried.

EGERTON, JOHN (1935–). Author. As a writer on Southern food and as co-founder of the Southern Foodways Alliance, in the Center for the Study of Southern Culture at the University of Mississippi, John Egerton was among the first to consider Southern cookery as a serious academic subject.

He was born in Atlanta and grew up in Cadiz, Kentucky. After service in the Army (1954–1956), Egerton earned his B.A. (1958) and M.A. (1960) at the University of Kentucky, where he worked in the public relations department. From 1960 to 1965 he was director of public information and publications at the University of South Florida, in Tampa, then began writing for *Southern Education Report* and *Race Relations Reporter* in Nashville, Tennessee. He was a contributing editor for *Saturday Review of Education* (1972–1973), *Southern Voices* (1974–1975) and the Southern Regional Council, in Atlanta (1973–1975), then journalist in residence at Virginia Polytechnic Institute and State University (1977–1978).

His food writing began in 1988, with a syndicated column for the *Atlanta Journal-Constitution*. His first food book was *Side Orders: Small Helpings of Southern Cookery and Culture*; in 1993, he co-authored a seminal work on Southern food culture, *Southern Food: At Home, on the Road, in History*. In 1996, he became a senior correspondent for the *Tennessean*, in Nashville. In 1997, he became a senior lecturer in American studies at the University of Texas at Austin, and two years later was one of the founders of the Southern Foodways Alliance, which, for his work, established the John Egerton Prize in his honor in 2007.

EGG. A shelled ovum of a bird, especially from domesticated fowl. The word is from Old Norse, first appearing in English around 1000.

Eggs are a staple food of the world's people, and although the eggs of wild fowl, turkeys, geese, doves, and other birds are eaten, it is the egg of the chicken that is most widely cultivated. Americans consume about 245 eggs per capita each year.

The Native Americans did not have chickens until the Europeans brought them to America, but wild fowl's eggs—quail, geese, turkey, and pigeon—were part of the Native Americans' diet, as were turtle and crocodile eggs in the territories near the Gulf of Mexico. Columbus brought chickens to the West Indies in 1493, and the Puritans and English settlers of Jamestown brought them to North America. Since chickens—and, therefore, eggs—were common but not abundant enough to provide everyday meals in the colonial era, they remained expensive items well into the nineteenth century, especially in the West, where domesticated fowl were rare. In fact, the dish called **Hangtown fry** was made in the California Gold Rush days from the two most expensive ingredients of the kitchen—eggs and oysters.

The egg industry was revolutionized in 1934 when John Kimber realized it was more efficient to breed chickens specifically for egg laying. Today, egg production is a finely mechanized science, overseen by both federal and state inspectors. The U.S. currently produces 63 billion eggs per year, in a $16.5 billion industry. Per capita, Americans consume about 250 eggs per year. Eggs are sized by weight, averaged by the dozen. "Jumbo" eggs must weigh thirty ounces or more, "extra large" between twenty-seven and thirty, "large" between twenty-four and twenty-seven, "medium" between twenty-one and twenty-four, "small" between eighteen and twenty-one, and "peewee" between fifteen and eighteen.

Eggs are also graded on the basis of physical condition, with the more viscous yolks scoring highest, from "grade AA" ("Fancy Fresh") to "A," "B," and "C." About 10 percent of the country's eggs go into egg products, such as frozen and dried eggs. "Egg substitutes," produced for those concerned about cholesterol in their diet, are made from egg whites alone, with added food coloring, although a process developed by Michael Foods, of Minneapolis, in 1992 cut cholesterol in real eggs by using centrifugal force to drive out the substance.

Indeed, concern over the supposed high cholesterol content of eggs (about 215 milligrams per egg) cut into Americans' egg consumption throughout the 1980s and 1990s, but recent studies, including a 1999 study by the Harvard School of Public Health, published in *The Journal of the American Medical Association*, found that healthy people eating up to seven eggs a week did not increase their risk of heart attack or stroke.

Americans eat their eggs poached (called "dropped eggs" in New England), boiled (or hard-boiled), as an omelet (or "omelette"), fried, or, since 1864, scrambled, that is, sautéed in butter by mixing the eggs around in a skillet. Americans also created the term "shirred eggs" as of 1883, for eggs cooked unshelled in molds. A well-known omelet, or egg sandwich, is the **western**," made with green pepper, chopped ham, and eggs on toast. A "Spanish omelet" is made with onions, peppers, tomatoes, and other seasonings. See also main entries for **egg foo yung**, **eggs Benedict**, **eggs Sardou**, **egg salad**, **deviled eggs**, **frittata**, **huevos rancheros**, and **eggnog**.

EGG BREAD. A corn bread without leavening, known since the middle of the nineteenth century. It was first mentioned as an American bread in 1854.

EGG BUTTER. A sweet spreading butter made with molasses. *The Buckeye Cookbook* (1883) gives the following recipe.

EGG BUTTER

Boil 1 pt. molasses slowly for 15–20 min., stirring frequently. Add 3 beaten eggs, stirred in quickly so as not to curdle. Boil a few minutes longer, partially cool, and add lemon juice to taste.

EGG COFFEE. Coffee to which an egg has been added, dating in print to 1896.

EGG COOK. Restaurant workers' slang term for the breakfast cook.

EGG CREAM. A NYC soda-fountain confection made from chocolate syrup, milk, and seltzer. The simplicity of the egg cream is deceptive, for its flavor and texture depend entirely on the correct preparation. There is no egg in an egg cream, but if the ingredients are mixed properly, a foamy, egg-white-like head tops off the drink.

Nevertheless, as David Shulman pointed out in *American Speech* (1987), there was a confection called an "egg cream" syrup listed in W. A. Bonham's *Modern Guide for Soda Dispensers* (1896) that was made with both eggs and cream but no chocolate. This was probably not the egg cream that gained legendary fame in eastern cities. Also, Lettice Bryan, in *The Kentucky Housewife*

(1839), gives a recipe for an orange-flavored custard dessert called "egg cream."

There seems no basis for believing the legend that Yiddish actor Boris Thomashefsky brought the idea for the egg cream back from Paris after having tasted a drink called *chocolat et crème*. Indeed, the unchallenged claim for the invention of the egg cream is that of Louis Auster, a Jewish immigrant who came to the U.S. in about 1890 and opened a candy store at Stanton and Cannon streets, in NYC, then another at Third Street and Avenue D. According to Auster's grandson, Stanley, the egg cream was a matter of happenstance: "[My grandfather] was fooling around, and he started mixing water and cocoa and sugar and so on, and somehow or other, eureka, he hit on something which seemed to be just perfect for him."

Auster's egg creams became famous (he'd sell three thousand on a hot day) and were based on a secret formula that has never been revealed, although the Schrafft's ice cream company supposedly offered him twenty thousand dollars for it. The chocolate syrup used was made in the rear of the store, and windows were blacked out for privacy. "The name of the egg cream was really a misnomer," recalled Stanley Auster. "People thought there was cream in it, and they would like to think there was egg in it because egg meant something that was really good and expensive. There never was any egg, and there never was any cream." Auster also insisted a glass, not a paper cup, and ice-cold milk were basic to the success of a good egg cream.

After Louis Auster died, in 1955, the candy store closed and the recipe passed to his family, with the last batch of the secret syrup made up by Stanley and his uncle Mendy around 1974. The first printed reference to the egg cream was in 1950.

Without access to Auster's syrup, other soda fountains and candy stores make the drink with Fox's U-bet Chocolate Flavor Syrup, created by Herman Fox sometime before 1920 in Brooklyn and now considered the most widely accepted ingredient in the mix.

EGG CREAM

In a tall soda-fountain glass, pour 1 ½ oz. chocolate syrup, add 1 ½ oz. ice-cold milk, stir to blend, then, while stirring, fill to the top with a fast jet of seltzer deflected off a spoon in order to create a foamy white head.

EGG FOO YUNG. A dish of scrambled eggs and Chinese vegetables. Egg foo yung is a Chinese American menu item not found in authentic Chinese cooking. The name may derive from a Guangdong word meaning "egg white."

EGG FOO YUNG

Beat 4 eggs lightly and combine with 1 c. bean sprouts, 1 T. chopped scallions, 1 T. bamboo shoots, 1 T. water chestnuts, and salt to taste. Add ¾ c. chopped seafood or cooked meat. Mix well. In a skillet or wok with 3 T. oil, drop ⅓ c. egg-and-vegetable mixture in small cakes and cook until browned. Pile cakes together and pour over them sauce made from 1 c. chicken broth, ¼ t. sugar, salt, 2 T. soy sauce, 2 T. monosodium glutamate, and 1 T. cold water in which 1 t. cornstarch has been dissolved.

EGGNOG. Also "egg nog" and "egg pop." A rich beverage made with eggs and spirits, traditionally served in America at Christmastime. The word *nog* is an Old English term for "ale," a meaning known since the late seventeenth century. In England, the drink was often made with red Spanish wine, but in America, where the first printing of the word was in 1765, rum and later other spirits were substituted.

According to FDA standards, commercially produced eggnog must contain at least 1 percent by weight egg-yolk solids and must be pasteurized; it may also be homogenized.

EGGNOG

Separate 6 eggs and beat the yolks with ½ c. sugar until light yellow. Add ½ c. bourbon or blended whiskey and ½ c. brandy and blend well. Chill in refrigerator for several hours. Beat egg whites until soft peaks are formed. Whip 1 ½ pt. heavy cream until slightly thickened, then fold into yolk mixture. Fold in egg whites, chill again. Serve with a sprinkling of grated nutmeg.

EGGPLANT (*Solanum melongena*). The plump deep purple fruit of a plant in the potato family, native to India. The name, derived simply from the egglike shape of the fruit, was first mentioned in English print in 1767. Thomas Jefferson has been credited with introducing the eggplant to America, though it has never achieved great popularity with most of the population. It is usually sautéed or baked, often as "eggplant parmigiana," an Italian American dish of breaded, sautéed eggplant baked with tomato sauce. Because of its association with Italian Americans, eggplant is sometimes called, in derogatory slang, "guinea squash."

"Eggplant caviar" is a snack dip made from roasted eggplant pureed with garlic, oil, and other seasonings.

EGGS BENEDICT. English muffins topped with a slice of ham or Canadian bacon, poached eggs, and a hollandaise sauce. It is a very popular **brunch** and breakfast item. The word first appeared in print in 1893.

The *Dictionary of Americanisms* and the *Morris Dictionary of Word and Phrase Origins* agree on the story of how the dish got its name, with *Morris* reporting: "The legendary Delmonico's Restaurant in NYC has been the birthplace of eggs Benedict. According to a well-founded report, two of the regular customers were Mr. and Mrs. LeGrand Benedict. One Saturday at lunch Mrs. Benedict complained that there was nothing new on the menu, so the maître d'hôtel asked what she might suggest. Out of their colloquy came the now internationally famous recipe." Another story attributes the dish's inspiration to Wall Street broker Lemuel Benedict, and food writer George Lang contends that Oscar Tschirky, the famous maître d'hôtel of the Waldorf-Astoria Restaurant and Hotel, in NYC, changed the recipe by adding truffles and a *glace de viande*, but *The Waldorf-Astoria Cookbook* (1981) follows the traditional form of earlier years.

EGGS BENEDICT

Split 2 English muffins and toast lightly. Spread with butter. Sauté in butter 4 slices baked ham or Canadian bacon and place one slice on each muffin half. Keep warm in slow oven. Boil water and add 1 T. vinegar and 1 t. salt. Lower heat to a simmer and poach 4 eggs for about 5 min. Remove and drain, then place over muffins. Pour over them a freshly made hollandaise sauce.

EGGS SARDOU. A dish of poached eggs with artichoke hearts, anchovies, chopped ham, truffle, and hollandaise sauce. Eggs Sardou is a specialty of New Orleans and, specifically, of Antoine's Restaurant, where it was created by first owner Antoine Alciatore (1824–1877) on the occasion of a dinner he hosted for French playwright Victorien Sardou (1831–1908), author of a satire on America entitled *L'Oncle Sam* (1873).

EGGS SARDOU

Place 2 cooked artichoke hearts on a serving dish, set 4 anchovy fillets and 2 poached eggs on top, and pour ⅓ c. hollandaise sauce over them. Sprinkle with 1 T. chopped ham and garnish with a slice of truffle. Serves 1. (Some recipes call for creamed spinach to be set under the artichoke hearts.)

ELECTION CAKE. A raised fruitcake of New England, first mentioned by Amelia Simmons in her *American Cookery* as early as 1796, although records show that such cakes have been baked to celebrate Election Days at least as far back as 1771 in Connecticut. Although this practice spread throughout the Midwest and the West in the nineteenth century, the cake is usually associated with Hartford, Connecticut, and by the 1830s was often called "Hartford election cake." There were also "election buns," which were doled out along similar party lines. Cookies, usually of gingerbread, served at such functions were often called "training cakes," because another name for Election Day was "Training Day."

ELECTION CAKE

Heat ½ c. dry sherry in a saucepan, add ½ c. raisins, and remove from heat. Let stand several hours until raisins soften and absorb sherry. Heat 1 ½ c. milk to lukewarm and remove from heat. Combine 1 ½ c. flour, ⅓ c. sugar, 1 pkg. yeast, and ½ t. salt. Add milk, blend, cover, and let rise until doubled. Punch dough down. Mix together ¾ c. butter, ½ c. brown sugar, 2 beaten eggs, and 3 ½ c. flour. Add 1 t. ground cinnamon, ½ t. ground nutmeg, ¼ t. ground cloves, 1 c. chopped pecans or walnuts, and ½ c. candied citron. Drain the raisins, but reserve the sherry. Add sherry to yeast flour, then add this into egg flour, blend well together, add raisins, and place batter in greased and floured 10-in. tube pan. Let rise again, then bake at 350°

for 1 hr., covered with aluminum foil for the last 15 min. Invert on rack and cool. Combine 2 c. confectioners' sugar, 1 t. vanilla, and 2 T. sweet sherry to make an icing. Frost cake and garnish with nuts and flower shapes of citron.

ELEVENER. Southern slang for a person who waits until midmorning before having his first drink of spirits.

EL PRESIDENTE. A cocktail whose name is Spanish for "the president," possibly named after (and perhaps concocted by) General Mario García Menocal y Deop, president of Cuba from 1913 to 1921. But *Esquire* magazine cocktail authority David Wondrich said the cocktail was created by bartender Eddie Woelke at the Jockey Club, in Havana, and named after President Gerardo Machado, in office from 1925 to 1933. According to Basil Woon, in his book *When It's Cocktail Time in Cuba* (1928), "It is the aristocrat of cocktails and is the one preferred by the better class of Cuban."

EL PRESIDENTE

Shake with ice 1 ½ oz. gold rum, ½ oz. dry vermouth, 1 t. dark rum, 1 t. curaçao, ¼ t. grenadine, and 2 t. lime juice. Serve in a chilled cocktail glass.

EMMALINE SAUCE. A nineteenth-century flavoring sauce, whose recipe was included by Sarah Tyson Rorer in *McIlhenny's Tabasco Sauce Recipes* (1913) and is given below. There is also a trademarked bottled **hot sauce** by this name, created by Emmaline Humphries (born 1893 in Columbia, Alabama), a caterer in Elba, Alabama, and, in the 1930s, in Hartford, Connecticut. Her granddaughter, Alice T. Crowe, trademarked the product Emmaline's All Natural Hot Sauce in 2004 and still runs the company, in Nyack, New York.

EMMALINE SAUCE

Pare and grate raw pumpkin, squash, or pawpaw to make 1 pt. Add 1 chopped Spanish onion, 4 mashed garlic cloves, 1 t. celery seed, 2 red peppers, 2 green peppers, 1 t. turmeric, and 1 bottle Tabasco. Add 1 pt. vinegar, stir, then bring to boil and simmer for several minutes. Bottle and seal. Use as a flavoring for soups or stews.

EMPANADA. A fried turnover pastry of Spanish origins thast became very popular in Central and South American restaurants and are now a staple of Mexican American restaurants. The word was first printed in English in 1920. *Empanar* in Spanish means "to bake in pastry."

EMPANADA

Dissolve 1 pkg. yeast in ½ c. lukewarm water. Cut 4 T. lard or butter into 4 c. flour, add 1 t. salt and 1 T. sugar. Pour in yeast and make a dough. Roll into a thin sheet and cut into rounds. Fill with mincemeat or fruit preserves, moisten edges of dough, and seal one round to another. Deep-fry in hot oil to a golden brown, drain, and dust with powdered sugar or cinnamon.

ENCHILADA. A corn **tortilla** stuffed with various fillings of meat, cheese, chorizo sausage, and other ingredients, then smothered in chile sauce and baked in the oven. It is an American Spanish term meaning "in chile" and was first printed in the U.S. in 1885. An article in *American Speech* in 1949 asserted that an enchilada was "a Mexican dish prepared more for *turista* than for local consumption." The dish has become a staple of **Mexican American** restaurants.

ENCHILADAS

In a blender, puree one 16-oz. can tomatoes, 2 red chile peppers, ½ t. salt, and ¼ t. pepper. Add 1 c. sour cream. Mix 2 c. chopped cooked chicken with ½ c. shredded Monterey Jack or cheddar cheese. Sauté briefly a dozen corn tortillas in 1 T. oil until golden on both sides. Drain tortillas and spread chicken on each, roll up, and place in greased baking dish. Pour tomato-and-chile mixture over them, cover with aluminum foil, and bake at 350° for 30 min. Remove foil, sprinkle with more cheese, and place under broiler until top melts and browns. Serves 6.

ENGLISH MONKEY. A cheese dish similar to Welsh rabbit, made with bread crumbs, milk, butter, and cheese poured over crackers, but with the addition of tomatoes. The term dates in print to 1896.

ENGLISH MUFFIN. A round, flat muffin made from white flour, yeast, malted barley, vinegar, and farina. English muffins are usually split and toasted, buttered, and spread with jam or preserves. Although tea muffins that were once popular in England resembled the American "English muffin," there is no single muffin in Britain by this specific name. In 1842, *The Great Western Magazine* did mention "that dream of farinaceous enjoyment, the English muffin." The American version of the food derives from those made famous by the S. B. Thomas Co. of NYC, whose founder, Samuel Bath Thomas, immigrated from England in 1875 with his mother's recipe and began making muffins at his Ninth Avenue bakery in 1880. A citation in 1896 in a *Receipt Book for Bakers* noted, "These are the genuine English Muffins that were introduced into Chicago during the World's Fair," which took place in 1893.

Recipes for English muffins generally do not contain many of the ingredients in the Thomas formula. For muffin rings, *Joy of Cooking* (1964), by Irma S. Rombauer and Marion Rombauer Becker, recommends using "small unlacquered fish cans and deviled meat cans [with the] tops and bottoms removed and the rims… thoroughly scrubbed."

"English muffin pizza" gained popularity in the early 1970s.

ENTRÉE. The main course of a meal or, occasionally, a dish served between two chief courses. The word is French for "entry," and in France the word formally has the second meaning, as it does in England, where it might also be called a "made dish." In America, menus usually list the entrée as the main course, although this has been its principal usage only over the past half century. Ford Naylor, in his *World Famous Chefs' Cook Book* (1941) noted, "It is only in the less expensive restaurants and lunchrooms, where the word 'entrée' has come to describe any main dish, including roasts." Often in America, the word is spelled without the accent mark, and first appeared in 1761.

ESKIMO ICE CREAM. An Eskimo confection, called *akutaq*, originally made as a mixture of salmonberries, seal oil, and snow. Today it is more commonly made with salmonberries, **Crisco**, sugar, and mashed potatoes. The term dates in print to 1913.

ESPOSITO, MARY ANN (1942–). Author, media personality. Mary Ann Saporito Esposito's PBS series *Ciao Italia!* is the longest-running cooking show on American television and was among the first to bring authentic Italian cooking to the American public.

Born and raised in Buffalo, New York, Esposito was the daughter of a dietitian, Louise Florence Saporito, and granddaughter of an immigrant from Sicily, Maria Assunta Saporito, who ran a butcher shop. Esposito learned to cook, can, and bake from her Neapolitan grandmother, Anna Cerullo Galasso, who ran a boardinghouse, but she had no interest in food as a profession and instead went to Daemen College, in Amherst, New York, to study education. After graduation, she taught in a high school.

While on a trip to Italy in 1980, with her husband, Guy Esposito, she took cooking classes and continued to do so on subsequent trips to different regions. She learned to speak Italian at the University of New Hampshire, then wrote a master's thesis on the cuisine of the Italian Renaissance while teaching cooking at its division of continuing education. She made a pilot in her home in Durham, New Hampshire, for a TV show for the state's PBS station, which went on the air as *Ciao Italia with Mary Ann Esposito* in 1989 and has been on ever since.

Esposito's aim has always been to show people how to make regional Italian food that is "doable, authentic, and good," always insisting on the importance of the family meal: "When we cook, we are empowered because we are in control of how our foods are selected and prepared. What is that kind of power worth to you? How could you measure its worth in terms of your and your family's health?"

Esposito oversees a scholarship fund in her name. She was honored with a Lifetime Achievement Award in the Culinary and Cultural Arts of Italy by the Order Sons of Italy in America, and was inducted into the Hall of Fame of the Italian Trade Commission. She holds an honorary doctorate from Saint Anselm College, in Manchester, New Hampshire.

Among her cookbooks are *Ciao Italia* (1991), *Celebrations Italian Style* (1995), *What You Knead* (1997), *Ciao Italia Pronto! 30-Minute Recipes from an Italian Kitchen* (2005), and *Ciao Italia Family Classics* (2011).

ESPRESSO. A very dark, bitter Italian coffee, often spelled "expresso." The name has nothing to do with the idea of a "quick cup" of coffee, but everything to do with the Italian meaning "pressed out," for in the preparation of this coffee, the essence of freshly ground beans (almost always the Arabica variety) is pushed out of a special espresso machine by steam and water, creating a very concentrated half-cup of brew.

The word "espresso" first appeared in English print in 1940, but in Italy it has been known since at least the turn of the twentieth century. Its invention has been traced to the Italian railway station in Milan, where those about to board a train wanted a quickly made cup of coffee, and some espresso makers contend that the term *espresso* may be associated with the "express trains" of those stations. The first espresso machine manufacturer was a company named Bezzera, in 1902.

In America, espresso often comes out as a full cup of less strong Italian coffee. Espresso may also be prepared in a drip pot. In the U.S., espresso will often be garnished with a sliver of lemon peel, and a generous restaurateur may offer a complimentary shot of anisette liqueur to be added to the cup, but this, too, is rarely seen in Italy.

ESTOMAC MULÂTRE. Louisiana gingerbread made with flour and cane syrup. The name is French for "mulatto stomach" and refers to the light brown color of the puffy little confections.

ÉTOUFFÉE. A cooking term, dating in print to the 1930s, connoting a kind of stewed dish served over white rice. The term is derived from French cuisine, meaning a braised dish. According to Cajun chef **Paul Prudhomme**, in *Chef Paul Prudhomme's Louisiana Kitchen* (1984), "in Louisiana cooking [étouffée] signifies covered with a liquid." For a recipe of "crawfish étouffée," see **crayfish**.

FAJITA. A **Tex-Mex** dish made from marinated, grilled skirt steak (the diaphragm from the rib cage of cattle) served in a flour tortilla. The word derives from the Spanish *faja*, for "girdle" or "strip," and describes the cut of meat itself. There has been much conjecture as to the fajita's origins, though none has been documented. Grilling skirt steak over mesquite coals has been characteristic of Texas cooking since the days when beef became a dominant meat in the American diet. But the word *fajita* did not appear in print until 1971, in the *Tex-Mex Cookbook*.

In 1984, Homero Recio, a lecturer on animal science at Texas A&M University, obtained a fellowship to study the origins of the item, coming to the conclusion two years later that, ironically, it was his grandfather, a butcher in Premont, Texas, who might have been the first to use the term "fajita" to describe the pieces of skirt steak cooked directly on mesquite coals for family dinners as far back as the 1930s. Recio also hypothesized that the first restaurant to serve fajitas—though under the name "*botanzas*" (appetizers)—was the Roundup, in McAllen, Texas. But Sonny "Fajita King" Falcon claimed to have opened the first "fajita stand," in Kyle, Texas, and in 1978 he opened a "Fajita King" stand in Austin (though he does not claim to have created the fajita itself). The popularity of the dish certainly grew after Ninfa Laurenza introduced a version of it on her menu at Ninfa's Restaurant, in Houston, on July 13, 1973, but that was under the name "*tacos al carbon*," and increased still further as a "fajita" after the item was featured at the Austin Hyatt Regency hotel, which by 1982 was selling thirteen thousand orders per month. Since then, the term "fajita" has been corrupted to mean any kind of meat or seafood served in a flour tortilla, as in "lobster fajita" or "chicken fajita." Usually these items are marinated and grilled, and have become known in chain Mexican restaurants for the novelty of being presented at the table on a **sizzling platter**.

FAJITA

Marinate a skirt steak in ½ c. lime juice, 1 T. crushed garlic or 1 t. garlic powder, ¼ c. vegetable oil, and ¼ c. vinegar. Grill meat over hot coals. Cut into smaller pieces and serve in a flour tortilla.

FAMILY RESTAURANT. A food-service establishment that specializes in offering menus and atmosphere particularly suited to families. Amenities usually include separate, limited-choice "children's menus," high chairs or booster seats, booths, counters, bright, colorful decor, and inexpensive food. Examples include national restaurant chains like Denny's, Applebee's, and Roy Rogers.

FARKLEBERRY. A native American shrub (*Vaccinium arboreum*) of the South with black, many-seeded berries, dating in print to 1755. The origin of the name is unknown. Farkleberries are used, though not commonly, in tarts and cookies. In Pittsburgh in 1971, the slogan "Star your heart, eat a farkleberry tart" was used to raise money for the local children's hospital.

FARMER, FANNIE MERRITT (1857–1915). Cooking teacher and cookbook author. Born in Boston, Fannie Merritt Farmer suffered from polio in high school, which ended her public education. She enrolled in the Boston Cooking School at the age of thirty-one and became principal in 1894. As one of the pioneers of "scientific cookery," she intended to make cooking healthier and easier for the home cook, as exemplified in her book *The Boston Cooking-School Cook Book* (1896), which was based on an 1884 cookbook by a former principal, Mary Johnson Bailey Lincoln. The book was published at Farmer's own expense, with an original print run of three thousand copies, but over time it went to eleven editions and sold more than four million copies, making Farmer a wealthy woman.

"It is my wish that [the cookbook] may not only be looked upon as a compilation of tried and tested recipes," she wrote in her preface, "but that it may awaken an interest through its condensed scientific knowledge which will lead to deeper thought and broader study of what to eat."

While the majority of her recipes might be found in any number of late-nineteenth-century cookbooks, Farmer's differed by virtue of its inclusion of fashionable restaurant dishes, chafing dish recipes, and, most important, specific, standardized measurements—she spent three pages on the subject—in contrast to the approximations of earlier cookbooks.

In 1902, she left the Boston Cooking School to open her own Miss Farmer's School of Cookery and also taught cooking for the infirm at the Harvard Medical School. Despite suffering two strokes, Farmer lectured from a wheelchair until ten days before she died. Her school continued on after her death, closing in 1944.

Farmer's monthly column in the *Woman's Home Companion* was widely read, as were all of her books: *Chafing Dish Possibilities* (1898), *Food and Cookery for the Sick and Convalescent* (1904), *What to Have for Dinner* (1905), *Catering for Special Occasions, with Menus and Recipes* (1911), and *A New Book of Cookery* (1912). On the centennial of its publication, a facsimile of the original *Boston Cooking-School Cook Book* was released.

FAST FOOD. Food that is cooked, dispensed, sold, and eaten quickly, first in print in 1960, usually at "fast food restaurants." The term took on currency in the 1960s after expansion of multi-unit chains like McDonald's, Pizza Hut, and Kentucky Fried Chicken (now KFC), but the term was used by writer George G. Foster in his *New York in Slices* (1848) to describe the frenetically paced "fast food" establishments in NYC's business district.

Most fast-food restaurants are places where one can buy a meal either inside the restaurant at a counter or from one's car.

Today the term "fast food" is often synonymous with **junk food**, which would also include store-bought items such as potato chips, candy, brownies, cakes, and cookies, items considered to have little nutritional value or to contain "empty calories." Today there are more than 160,000 fast-food restaurants in the U.S., with fifty million customers served daily and $110 billion in revenues. Forty-four percent of Americans eat fast food at least once a week, 28 percent never. Adults consume about 11 percent of their daily calories from fast food.

FENIGER, SUSAN (1953–) and **MARY SUE MILLIKEN** (1958–). Chefs, restaurateurs, authors. In 1983, these two American women opened City Café, in Los Angeles, which was among the first restaurants to showcase the concepts of modern California-Mexican cuisine.

Milliken graduated from Chicago's Washburne Culinary Institute, and in 1978 worked at the classic French restaurant Le Perroquet, in Chicago—where the owner at first offered her a job as hat-check girl. A few months later at Le Perroquet, she met Feniger, who had graduated from the **Culinary Institute of America**. Both were among the first female chefs to work in the kitchen of a fine-dining restaurant, then a notoriously male profession.

Feniger moved to L.A., to work at Ma Maison, and Milliken to Deerfield, Illinois, to open the Society Café. Separately, the two women apprenticed in France—Feniger at L'Oasis, in La Napoule, and Milliken at Restaurant d'Olympe, in Paris—before moving to L.A. There, in 1981, with only one week to prepare a menu, they opened City Café, where Mexican dishes shared the global menu with Thai, Indian, and French.

The café had evolved into the larger CITY restaurant by 1985. They also opened the first Border Grill, specializing in modern Mexican cuisine. Border Grill relocated to a larger space in Santa Monica in 1990, a sleek-looking taco eatery with an array of Mexican street food that got media attention, not just because it was run by two savvy women chefs but also because the taste of the food and the ingredients used were very different from most other Mexican food around the city.

A second Border Grill opened at Mandalay Bay Resort and Casino, in Las Vegas, in 1999. In 2009, Milliken and Feniger opened the Border Grill Truck, a gourmet taco truck on the cutting edge of the street-food scene in Los Angeles. That same year, Feniger opened STREET as a solo project, offering upscale global street food.

In 1995, they debuted the long-running TV series *Too Hot Tamales* on the Food Network and followed in 1997 with *Tamales World Tour*, canceled in 2001. In 1988, they were the first women ever to receive the Southern California Restaurant Writer's Chef of the Year award.

Both have been very active in charities and organizations. They are co-founders of Chefs Collaborative and actively advocate for sustainability in the food-service industry. Feniger became a founding board member of the Scleroderma Research Foundation in 1988 and has also championed gay and lesbian rights through the L.A. Gay & Lesbian Center. Milliken is a co-founder of Women Chefs and Restaurateurs, which fosters the careers of women in the food business. She is also passionate about children's causes and has championed No Kid Hungry as a long-standing board member of Share Our Strength, the leading hunger-fighting organization in the U.S.

Of their work together, Feniger, who is married with two children, said, "The rewards are all there, equal to what you send in emotion and anxiety and hard work—and the isolation from your personal or social life. All the sacrifices are worth it, because the rewards are there, too. We would never have done anything else."

Together they have written *City Cuisine* (1989), *Mesa Mexicana* (1994), *Cantina: The Best of Casual Mexican Cooking* (1996), *Cooking with Too Hot Tamales* (1997), and *Mexican Cooking for Dummies* (1999 and 2002). Feniger's *Street Food* appeared in 2012.

FENNEL. A plant in the parsley family (*Faeniculum vulgare*), with small yellow flowers and feathery leaves, used either as a flavoring or eaten as a vegetable in a salad or cooked as a side dish. The word is from Middle English *fenol*, first in English print around 700, and the plant was first grown in America from European seeds acquired by Thomas Jefferson at Monticello in 1824. Because of its anise-like flavor, it is sometimes confused with the latter, which is actually another member of the parsley family (*Pimpinella anisum*), whose seeds are used as a flavoring.

FERN BAR. A bar or restaurant with a bar whose stereotypical decor includes an abundance of hanging plants, especially ferns. Varnished oak, brass railings, and Tiffany-style glass are also common in such establishments, which tend to attract young adults interested in meeting people of the opposite sex. The term appeared in print in an article by Eric Pace in the *New York Times* in 1984, in which he cited it as "young adult slang, heard as far away as New Haven." See also **singles bar**.

FETTUCCINE ALFREDO. Also "fettuccine all'Alfredo." A dish of fettuccine egg noodles mixed with butter, Parmesan cheese, and cream. The dish has been a staple of **Italian American** restaurants since the mid-1960s. It was created in 1914 by Alfredo Di Lelio, who opened a restaurant in Rome, Italy, under his first name on the Via della Scrofa in 1914. The dish supposedly helped restore the appetite of his wife after she had given birth to their son. The original dish was made with a very rich triple butter Di Lelio made himself, three kinds of flour, and only the heart of the best Parmigiano-Reggiano cheese.

Fettuccine all'Alfredo became famous after Hollywood movie actors Douglas Fairbanks and Mary Pickford ate the dish at Alfredo's restaurant while on their honeymoon in 1927. They dined at Alfredo's daily and at the end of their stay presented the owner with a gold-plated spoon and fork with which to mix the pasta, inscribed "To Alfredo the King of the noodles July 1927." The international press picked up on this item and spread the fame of Alfredo's noodle dish around the world. Within a year a recipe had appeared in the U.S., printed in *The Rector Cook Book*, by George Rector (who in 1939 reported Di Lelio had donated the golden utensils to be melted down for Mussolini's war efforts).

After World War II, Di Lelio moved to the Piazza Augusto Imperatore, and in the 1950s his restaurant became a mecca for visiting Americans, most of whom came to sample fettuccine Alfredo. (The trademark for the name "Alfredo's the Original of Rome" was bought by Guido Bellanca to open a series of restaurants under that name in the U.S., with branches in New York and Lake Buena Vista, Florida.)

Because most American cooks could not reproduce the richness of the original butter, today the dish almost always contains heavy cream. (In Italy, this would be called *fettuccine alla panna* or *fettuccine alla crema*.)

FETTUCCINE ALFREDO

Boil in salted water 1 lb. fresh fettuccine until tender but firm. In a saucepan melt 7 T. butter with 7 T. Parmesan cheese and 1 c. heavy cream. Drain fettuccine, add to sauce, and toss. Serve with more grated Parmesan. Serves 4–6.

FIAMBRE. A Southwestern salad made with avocados, oranges, and beets. It is of South American origins and traditionally served on All Saints' Day and the Day of the Dead in Latino communities.

FIAMBRE

Mix together in a blender or food processor 1 clove crushed garlic, 3–4 sprigs parsley, 3 T. tarragon vinegar, ½ c. orange juice, 1 ½ t. salt, ¼ t. chile powder, and ⅔ c. vegetable oil. Slice in julienne strips 3 c. chicken and slice 4 hard-boiled eggs and 3 cooked beets. Slice 2 avocados into strips. Place several leaves of romaine lettuce on a plate and arrange chicken, eggs, and beets on top. Garnish with avocado and orange slices and pour on dressing. Garnish with diced scallions. Serves 6–8.

FIDDLEHEAD FERN (*Matteucia struthiopteris*, *Amsinckia intermedia*, and *Phacelia tanacetifolia*). Also "fiddleneck." Several ferns having tips shaped like a violin's scroll fall under this name, though the "cinnamon," the "brake," and, especially, the "ostrich fern" are the varieties most commonly referred to. Ostrich ferns from Maine are highly valued and are sometimes found canned or frozen. Because of their delicacy, fiddleheads should be eaten immediately after picking—boiled in saltwater and served with butter or in a salad. The earliest citation of a fern by this name (with reference to the cinnamon variety) was in 1892.

FIG (*Ficus carica*). A sweet, multi-seeded fruit of the fig tree or shrub, usually eaten dried. It originated in northern Asia Minor. The word is from the Latin *ficus*, first in English print around 1325.

Figs were introduced into America on the island of Hispaniola in 1520 by the Spaniards, and the Mission fig owes its name to the Spanish missions set up in the 1700s in California, where 100 percent of the fig crop is cultivated today, predominantly around Madera, Fresno, and Merced counties.

Today the most important varieties of figs cultivated are the Mission, Calimyrna, San Pedro, Kadota, Adriatic, and Brown Turkey.

Most of the fig crop goes into making a sweet filling for a cookie called the "Fig Newton," which was first produced after Philadelphian James Henry Mitchell developed a machine, in 1892, to combine a hollow cookie crust with a jam filling. He brought this machine to the Kennedy Biscuit Works, in Cambridgeport, Massachusetts, which tried it out, christening the resulting cookie "Newton's cakes," after the nearby Boston suburb of Newton. In 1898, the company combined with others to form the National Biscuit Co. (now Nabisco Brands, of East Hanover, New Jersey). The most frequently used jam in the cookie was fig, and soon the name became Fig Newton.

FILET MIGNON. A very tender center cut of beef, usually about one to one and a half inches thick. First used in American print on a menu for the Architectural League of New York in 1899, as "Filet Mignon Sauté à la Périgueux," the word is from the French *filet* (thick slice) and *mignon* (dainty).

Filet mignon is considered a very tender cut and is usually simply broiled or grilled, often served with a sauce of black pepper or cream and brandy. It may also be part of a shish kebab.

FILLING. A Pennsylvania Dutch side dish made of potatoes that are mashed, mixed with eggs, and baked.

"Filling" is also a synonym for a poultry stuffing or **dressing** in the East and for **icing** in the South and the West.

FINGER FOOD. Any food item that is picked up and eaten with the fingers, like snacks and canapés. The term has been in print since at least 1928.

FIRE. Used as a verb by restaurant workers, meaning to begin cooking a dish.

FIRE CAKE. A very simple cake made with flour and water and cooked before an open fire. The term dates in print to 1777.

FISH BOIL. A social gathering at which various kinds of fish are boiled in a large kettle and served with many side dishes, like potatoes, coleslaw, and bread. They are especially popular in the lake country of the upper Midwest, from which the fresh fish are taken and boiled in large outdoor kettles set over fires. Vegetables are often added to the boiling water, along with copious amounts of salt. In Wisconsin in the 1960s, restaurants began featuring fish boils for their customers.

FISH CAMP. Originally a term referring to a camp where people went to fish, but in the Carolinas, restaurants set on the grounds of such camps and specializing in fried-fish dinners were called fish camps. By extension, the term has also come to mean any roadside restaurant serving fish dishes. The original meaning dates in print to 1897.

FISHER, M. F. K. (1908–1992). Author. Through the elegance of her prose, Mary Frances Kennedy Fisher made writing about food a subject of the human heart and mind, and her work had a great influence on generations of food writers. Of her work, the British poet W. H. Auden said, "I do not know of any one in the United States who writes better prose."

She was born in Albion, Michigan, where her father, Rex Kennedy, was co-owner and editor of the local newspaper. In 1911, he sold his shares and moved to California, eventually buying a controlling interest in the *Whittier Daily News*, for which his daughter drafted stories.

Mary briefly attended Illinois College, then transferred to Occidental College, but dropped out to marry poet Alfred Fisher in 1929. They moved to Dijon, France, where Mary's love of food grew into a passion. While there, she attended painting and sculpture classes at the École des Beaux-Artes. Alfred received his Ph.D., and they traveled around France until they ran out of money, causing them to return to California in 1932,

where Mary began writing fiction for local magazines and food articles that became the basis of her first book, *Serve It Forth* (1937).

After further travels to Europe, the couple separated in 1937, and Mary moved to Europe with her lover, painter Dillwyn "Tim" Parrish, who developed a severe circulatory disease that forced them back to America. They settled on land in Hemet, California, that Fisher described as "90 acres of rocks and rattlesnakes." *Serve It Forth* was published to excellent reviews but poor sales. While tending Parrish, Fisher wrote three more books, the third a cookbook on oysters, titled *Consider the Oyster*.

In 1941, unable to bear the pain of his malady, Parrish shot himself to death. The next year, Fisher's *How to Cook a Wolf* appeared, in which she mixed humor with a serious intent to show how housewives could cook good food despite the limitations of wartime rationing. She added to her income by writing gags for Paramount Pictures stars Bob Hope, Bing Crosby, and Dorothy Lamour. Her next book was *The Gastronomical Me* (1943), published the same year her daughter Anne Kennedy Parrish was born.

On a trip to New York City in 1944, Mary met and married publisher Donald Friede, who helped her publish her next book, *Let Us Feast*, and gave her entrée to magazines like *Vogue*, *Town & Country*, *The Atlantic Monthly*, and *Gourmet*. The couple moved to California, where in 1946 Fisher's second daughter, Kennedy Mary Friede, was born.

Her literary reputation grew with her 1949 translation of Brillat-Savarin's *The Physiology of Taste*, but, under great stress at home, she suffered a nervous breakdown that year and was divorced from Friede a year later. Fisher eventually bought a house in St. Helena, but visited France whenever she could. "My life is simple," she said in an interview. "When I can't write, I read. When I can't read, I cook."

In 1966, Time-Life hired her to write *The Cooking of Provincial France*, a volume in its Foods of the World series, which required research in France, and there she met **Julia Child**. By then Fisher was writing regularly for *The New Yorker* magazine.

In 1971, Fisher returned to California for the last time, to live in a house she designed herself, built for her in a vineyard in Glen Ellen by her friend David Bouverie. After several more trips to France, she died at home from Parkinson's disease at the age of eighty-three.

Of her passion for food, Fisher wrote, "It seems to me that our three basic needs, for food and security and love, are so mixed and mingled and entwined that we cannot straightly think of one without the others. So it happens that when I write of hunger, I am really writing about love and the hunger for it, and warmth and the love of it and the hunger for it…and then the warmth and richness and fine reality of hunger satisfied…and it is all one."

In 1991, she was elected to the Academy of Arts and Sciences. Les Dames d'Escoffier gives an award for excellence under M. F. K. Fisher's name, to women writers. She was once photographed by the artist Man Ray.

She wrote more than thirty books, including *An Alphabet for Gourmets* (1949), *The Story of Wine in California* (1962), *A Map of Another Town: A Memoir of Provence* (1964), *With Bold Knife and Fork* (1969), *Long Ago in France: The Years in Dijon* (1991), *To Begin Again: Stories and Memoirs 1908–1929* (1992), and *A Life in Letters* (1998).

FISH HOUSE PUNCH. A **punch** made of lemon juice, brandy, and peach brandy. It was first created around 1732, at Philadelphia's Colony in Schuylkill (reorganized in the Revolutionary War as the State in Schuylkill) fishing club, also known as the Fish House, which was limited to thirty members, all of whom were expected to be good cooks. Each meeting is opened with a toast and a glass of Fish House punch and closed with a glass of Madeira and a toast to the memory of George Washington, who, legend has it, once dined at the club and for days afterwards left blank pages in his diary. There are many variations of Fish House punch, some made with brandy, some with rum or other whiskeys, though the "official" version, given below, was adopted in 1873.

FISH HOUSE PUNCH

Dissolve 5 lb. sugar in 1 qt. lemon juice, 1 qt. brandy, 2 qt. rum, and 4 ½ qt. water and ice.

FISH MUDDLE. A North Carolina term for a fish stew. "Muddle" refers to a jumble or something mixed up together. "Pine bark stew" is a fish muddle cooked in an iron pot over a pine-bark fire.

FISH MUDDLE

In a large pot sauté ⅓ c. diced salt pork in 1 T. oil for about 5 min. Add 1 chopped red or green pepper, 1 chopped onion, 1 chopped stalk of celery, and 1 chopped carrot and sauté for about 15 min. on low heat. Add 1 lb. peeled, quartered white potatoes, sauté briefly, then add 2 ½ c. fish stock, bring to a boil, lower to a simmer, cover, and cook for 15 min. Add 1 lb. or more of various seafood like cod, haddock, scallops, and clams and cook for about 5 min., until seafood is done. Add salt, pepper, and a pinch of mace. Add 1 t. or more hot sauce, stir, then add ¼ c. heavy or light cream. Blend well, cook for 1 min. Serves 6.

FISH STICK. Also "fish finger." A fillet of fish that has been sliced into sticks about one inch wide, battered or rolled in bread crumbs, and fried or baked. Frozen fish sticks were an outgrowth of frozen **crab cakes**, made and sold to grocers by Edward Piszek, of Philadelphia, in 1946. In 1952, Piszek introduced frozen fish sticks under the brand Mrs. Paul's Kitchens (named for one of his business partners), which became the leader in the field. *Time* magazine reported in 1953 the sale of frozen fish sticks made by the Birds Eye Co.

FLANKEN. A cut of beef similar to short ribs of flank steak, particularly popular in **Jewish American** communities. The term itself is Yiddish for "beef flanks" and dates in print to 1945.

FLANKER. Food-industry term for products made in "healthier" versions by removing some or all of the sugar and salt content, as in soft drinks.

FLATBREAD. An unleavened, very thin bread, usually applied to Scandinavian breads and derived from the Norwegian *flatbrød*. The term dates in print to 1762. Today the word more commonly refers to a kind of thin-crusted **pizza** with various toppings.

FLAT CAR. African American and hobo slang for pork chops (1936) or **pancakes** (1927). The term first saw print in 1936.

FLAUTA. A tortilla that is rolled with various fillings and then fried. Flautas, whose resemblance to a flute gives them their Mexican name, are made by heating a corn tortilla on a sheet-metal grill called a *comal*, then rolling a filling of meat or poultry in the center and frying the roll in hot oil. They are then drained and garnished with shredded lettuce and chile sauce.

FLETCHERISM. A fad of the early twentieth century, based on *The ABC of Nutrition* (1903), by Horace Fletcher (1849–1919), in which the author mandated that each mouthful of food be chewed exactly thirty-two times—once for each tooth in the mouth. To "fletcherize" meant to chew one's food thoroughly. The theory had the support of many prominent Americans, including John D. Rockefeller, William James, and Thomas Edison. After Fletcher's death, in 1919, his theories quickly lost their bite.

FLIP. A drink made with beer, sugar, molasses, dried pumpkin, and rum, all heated with a hot iron. A fireplace poker was called an "iron flip dog," hence the drink's name. A "yard of flannel" was flip with a beaten egg added, which gave it a flannel-like appearance on top. Flip is first mentioned in 1695 in England, and Herman Melville's hero Ishmael, in *Moby-Dick* (1851), expounded on the drink:

> *Flip? Did I say we had flip? Yes, and we flipped it at the rate of ten gallons the hour; and when the squall came (for its squally off there by Patagonia), and all hands—visitors and all—were called to reef topsails, we were so top heavy that we had to swing each other aloft in bowlines; and we ignorantly furled the skirts of our jackets into the sails, so that we hung there, reefed fast in the howling gale, a warning example to all drunken tars. However, the masts did not go overboard; and by and by we scrambled down, so sober, that we had to pass the flip again, though the savage salt spray bursting down the forecastle scuttle, rather too much diluted and pickled it for my taste.*

"Flip" is also a southern slang term for a pancake.

FLOATING ISLAND. A dessert made with fluffs of meringue set in a custard sauce (1630). The dish originated in France but became known in America by the late eighteenth century. The term is a translation of the French *île flottante*, and *Larousse Gastronomique* describes another version of the dessert made with sponge cake spread with jam, whipped cream, and nuts, set in a bowl of custard. Benjamin Franklin mentions eating a "custard with floating masses of whipped cream or white of eggs" in his *Letters* (1771), and Thomas Jefferson called the dessert "snow eggs," a translation of the French *oeufs à la neige*. By the nineteenth century the dish was well known and served at lavish dinners.

FLOUNDER. Any of a variety of flatfishes in the families Bothidae and Pleuronectidae, sometimes erroneously sold as **sole**. The name comes from Norman French *floundre*, first in English print in about 1450. The main American species of fish that fall under the name include: American plaice (*Hippoglossoides platessoides*), also called the "dab" or "sand dab" (*plaice* is from the Latin *platessa*, "flatfish"); "Atlantic **halibut**" (*H. hippoglossus*); "California halibut" (*Paralichthys californicus*); "Pacific halibut" (*H. stenolepsis*); "Pacific sand dab" (*Citharichthys sordidus*); "Southern flounder" (*P. lethostigma*); "starry flounder" (*Platichthys stellatus*); "fluke" (*P. dentatus*), also called "summer flounder"; "winter flounder" (*Pseudopleuronectes americanus*), also called "blueback flounder," "blackback flounder," and "lemon sole"; and "yellowtail flounder" (*Limanda ferruginea*), also called "rusty flounder."

FLOUR. A powdery substance made by grinding and sifting grains such as wheat, corn, rye, and others. The word is from Middle English.

Native Americans used corn flour almost exclusively for their breads, porridges, and other staple foods, and corn was the flour most readily available to the first settlers who came from Europe—their own grains, like wheat and barley, having failed in several instances. Cornmeal flour continued to be the most important variety until well into the nineteenth century, when wheat became a major crop in America. The production of wheat flour picked up after the invention, in 1834, of the Swiss steel roller, which ground the meal very finely, a process vastly improved in 1865 by French American Edmund LaCroix, who separated bran from granual middlings with a middling purifier and fan-driven air currents to clean the wheat as it moved through the mill. The first all-roller flour mill was displayed in the U.S. at the 1876 Philadelphia Centennial Exposition.

After 1900, American wheat flour was processed to appear white through bleaching and removal of the wheat germ and other flecks of grain, thereby lowering its nutritive value. Recently there has been a trend favoring unbleached and whole-wheat flours.

The peak for Americans' per capita annual consumption of wheat flour came in 1997, with 147 pounds, but it has steadily fallen since. In 2011, the figure was 133 pounds. The main types of flour are:

ALL-PURPOSE FLOUR. A blend of hard- and soft-wheat flours, suitable for general use in all baked goods. Now enriched with thiamine, niacin, iron, and riboflavin and available bleached or unbleached, this is the flour usually meant when no other is specified.

ARROWROOT FLOUR. A flour made from the arrowroot plant, used mainly as a starch for thickening sauces and gravies.

BARLEY MEAL. A coarse whole-kernel flour made from barley.

CAKE FLOUR. A flour made from soft wheats, although the term may also refer to a self-rising flour that contains baking powder and salt.

CORNSTARCH. Also called "corn flour." A flour made from corn and used as a thickener in gravies and sauces. The process was invented in 1842 by Thomas Kingsford, who eventually merged with the Argo Manufacturing Co. of Nebraska and others to form the United Starch Co.

FARINA. A flour made from hard, but not durum, wheat.

GLUTEN FLOUR. A starch-free flour made by washing the starch from a high-protein wheat flour.

HARD-WHEAT FLOUR. Milled from winter or spring wheat grown mainly in North and South Dakota, Montana, and Kansas. Hard-wheat flour has a higher gluten level than other flours and is excellent for bread making.

OAT FLOUR. A flour milled from oats, rarely used. But oatmeal, with a much coarser texture, is used for a porridge and in breads and cookies. Flaky rolled oats are used the same way.

PASTRY FLOUR. A finely milled, soft, low-gluten flour found in the South, where it is used to make pastries.

POTATO FLOUR. A flour made from potatoes, used primarily as a thickener in gravies and sauces or in sponge cakes.

RICE FLOUR. A flour made from milled rice, often combined with all-purpose flour in recipes.

RYE FLOUR. A coarse whole-kernel flour milled from rye.

SEMOLINA. A granular durum-wheat flour used to make macaroni, spaghetti, and other pastas. It is high in gluten.

SOFT-WHEAT FLOUR. Milled from winter wheat and grown mostly in Illinois and Indiana. Soft-wheat flour is used for biscuits and pastries.

STONE-GROUND FLOUR. A coarse flour milled with stone rather than steel rollers.

TAPIOCA FLOUR. A flour made from the cassava root, used primarily as a thickener in sauces and gravies.

WHOLE-WHEAT FLOUR. Also called **graham flour**. Whole-wheat flour is made from the entire wheat kernel, and for baking is usually combined with a white all-purpose flour.

FLUFFERNUTTER. A sandwich made with peanut butter and Marshmallow Fluff, a spreadable marshmallow product. The sandwich was named by Marshmallow Fluff's advertising agency, Durkee-Mower, in 1961, and is now a registered trademark of the company.

FLUMMERY. Also "furmenty." A very old term for a custard or fruit pudding or a gruel made from oats. The word dates to at least 1623 and derives from the Welsch *llymru*. In America it often connoted a pudding with fruit, and the name dates in print to 1615.

FOIE GRAS. Fowl liver that has been fattened through a process of overfeeding the animal. The term is from the French for "fattened liver," first in English print in 1818, and is specifically applied to goose liver and considered a great delicacy. The USDA, which inspects foreign slaughterhouses, approved the import of foie gras from France in 1989 after several European countries guaranteed that a poultry virus named Newcastle disease had been eradicated. Today, however, no French foie gras is imported, although Canadian foie gras is.

Only within the past two decades have American companies produced foie gras, in this case from the liver of a moulard duck, a crossbreed between a female Pekin and a male Muscovy. The first California producer of foie gras (from Muscovy ducks) was Marc Leinwand. In New York State there are two producers. Hudson Valley Foie Gras and Duck Products, in Ferndale, New York, was started by Michael A. Ginor and Izzy Yanay in 1989, using moulard ducks. Bella Bella Gourmet Foods, in Sullivan County, has been making foie gras since 1999. D'Artagnan, a food-products company founded by **Ariane Daguin** and George Faison in 1985, is now the nation's number-one supplier of domestic foie gras, purchased from the two New York suppliers as well as from a Canadian farmer.

Foie gras birds are raised cage-free, fed increasing amounts of corn for several weeks, then fed through a tube (a process called "gavage"), a process long opposed by animal rights groups, which contend it is inhumane. Their protests led to the city of Chicago banning foie gras

from 2006 to 2008, while in California, the state's single foie gras producer, Sonoma Foie Gras, spent seven years trying to respond to demands to develop a more humane method of fattening the livers, but this failed, forcing the company out of business.

American foie gras is usually graded "A," "B," or "C," depending on the size ("A" liver is about sixteen to twenty-two ounces, "B" twelve to sixteen ounces, and "C" less than twelve ounces), condition of the skin with regard to bruises or blood, shape, and color.

FOLSE, JOHN (1946–). Restaurateur, entrepreneur, author. Louisiana-born-and-bred John David Folse has been in the forefront of promoting Creole and Cajun food, both in his restaurants and retail food products and in his books on the subject.

Born in St. James, Louisiana, to a trapper's family, Folse hunted and fished in the bayous there. He graduated from Nicholls State University, in Thibodaux, Louisiana (1965–1970), with a B.A. in education and accounting, then was accountant for two years at the Howard Johnson hotel in Baton Rouge, while working at the Capital House Hotel, in that same city. He moved from management into the kitchen as sous-chef and banquet chef. In 1975, he opened the Tavern Restaurant across the street.

In 1978, he opened Lafitte's Landing Restaurant in an historic mansion in Donaldson, Louisiana, whose menus he introduced with dinners he cooked in Japan, Hong Kong, Beijing, Paris, and London, and in 1990 he was the first American chef to cook at a Vatican state dinner.

In 1998, Lafitte's Landing was destroyed by fire, but it reopened a year later as a bed-and-breakfast inn named Lafitte's Landing Restaurant at Bittersweet Plantation, which closed in 2005. In 2002, Folse opened Bittersweet Plantation Dairy. His catering company, White Oak Plantation, began in 1986; Chef John Folse & Co. Manufacturing was founded in 1991 and produces custom-manufactured foods for restaurants and retail. Chef John Folse & Co. Publishing began in 1989 and has issued ten cookbooks on Cajun and Creole cookery.

The Chef John Folse Culinary Institute, at Nicholls State University, opened in 1994, designed to preserve Louisiana's culinary heritage. In 2012, he opened his Home on the Range Restaurant Management Co., through which he launched his first restaurant in New Orleans, named Restaurant R'evolution.

Folse has been the host of the TV series *A Taste of Louisiana*, on Louisiana Public Broadcasting, since 1990, and the radio show *Stirrin' It Up* since 1997.

In 1987, the Louisiana Restaurant Association named him Louisiana Restaurateur of the Year, and in 1989 *Nation's Restaurant News* inducted Lafitte's Landing Restaurant into its Fine Dining Hall of Fame. In 1994, Folse became national president of the American Culinary Federation.

Folse has an honorary doctorate from both Johnson & Wales University (1992) and Baltimore International Culinary College (1995). *Food Arts* magazine awarded Folse the Silver Spoon Award for his contributions to the food-service industry. In 2007, he served as the American judge for the Bocuse d'Or World Cuisine Contest, in Lyon, France. He now serves as marketing specialist on the Louisiana Seafood Promotion & Marketing Board.

Folse's books include *The Evolution of Cajun & Creole Cuisine* (1990), *Chef John Folse's Plantation Celebrations* (1994), *The Encyclopedia of Cajun & Creole Cuisine* (2004), and *After the Hunt: Louisiana's Authoritative Collection of Wild Game & Game Fish Cookery* (2007).

FONDA. A hotel or restaurant in the West. The term dates back to at least 1844 and derives from the Spanish.

FONDANT. A sugar paste eaten as candy or as icing. The word is from the French, from the past participle of *fondre*, "to melt." The word first appeared in English in 1877. Candies made from fondant were called "ice cream candy" in print as of 1873.

FONDUE. A method of fast cooking by which bite-size pieces of meat, fruit, or bread are impaled on skewers and dipped into a bubbling liquid to be either quickly cooked or coated. Individual eaters insert their own skewers into the pot, and, because of the communal nature of the activity, fondue cooking has been very much a part of social gatherings and parties (1875).

Fondue originated in Switzerland, where it was part of peasant families' one-pot cooking methods and a means of using hardened cheese. The word comes from the French verb *fondre*, "to melt." The classic fondue, called *fondue neuchâteloise*, is made with Emmenthaler or Gruyère cheese and a Swiss white wine, intended to provide acidity. This mixture is placed in a flame-heated earthenware pot called a *caquelon* and melted; a cherry brandy such as kirsch is added, and skewered crusts of bread are dipped into the blend.

Although the French gastronome Brillat-Savarin referred to fondue in the nineteenth century, the dish actually remained a peasant meal of little interest until it was introduced in the U.S. in the 1950s. In 1952, chef-owner Konrad Egli, of NYC's Chalet Suisse restaurant, made a *fondue bourguignonne*, using beef cubes cooked in hot oil, that became an overnight sensation and spread rapidly to other restaurants. In the early 1960s, Egli, who noticed that many of his diet-conscious customers avoided his rich chocolate desserts, consulted with his public-relations agent, Beverly Allen, and came up with a chocolate fondue (introduced on July 4, 1964) into which one dipped pieces of cake, fruit, or cream-puff pastry—a variation completely unknown in Switzerland but one that has become popular even there within the past few years.

These various fondues were enormously popular as party food with Americans, particularly during winter and especially on skiing holidays. Fondue pots and skewers were a standard entertaining item in American homes throughout the 1960s, but the popularity of the dish has faded considerably since then.

CHOCOLATE FONDUE

Break 8-9 oz. of good Swiss chocolate (preferably Toblerone brand with honey and crushed almonds) into fondue pot, add ½ c. heavy cream and 2 T. kirsch or other brandy. Skewer morsels of any or all of the following—cake, fruit, cream-puff pastry—and dip in bubbling chocolate.

FOOD AND DRUG ADMINISTRATION (FDA). An agency of the Department of Health and Human Services (since 1979) whose purpose is to protect public health by monitoring standards of the food and drug industries.

The Pure Food and Drug Act of 1906 was the first instance of such monitoring, and in 1931 the FDA was formed. The Food, Drug, and Cosmetic Act of 1938 (amended in 1958 and 1962) increased the powers of the agency.

The FDA controls bureaus of food, product safety, drugs, and veterinary medicine, and its role in drawing up "standards of identity" has helped enormously in defining what American food products may or may not be or contain by law. For example, a product labeled "fruit jam" must contain forty-five parts fruit and fifty-five parts sugar or other sweetener, while "raisin bread" must have raisins equaling 50 percent of the weight of the flour. Skim milk is required to have two thousand international units of Vitamin A in each quart. "Standards of quality" set minimum specifications for such factors as tenderness, color, and freedom from defects in canned fruits and vegetables, limiting, for example, excessive peel in tomatoes, hardness in peas, or pits in pitted canned cherries. (These standards are not to be confused with the Department of Agriculture's voluntary "grades of meat." See **beef**.)

The FDA also monitors "fill-of-container standards," setting requirements as to the volume of food product that must be packaged in a container, sometimes specifying minimum weights of solid food that must remain after the drainable liquid has been poured off (referred to as "minimum drained weight"). Other items must have a minimum fill in terms of the total food as a percentage of the container.

In 1990, Congress passed the Nutrition Labeling and Education Act, which gave the FDA until May 8, 1993, to standardize food labels, at a time when twelve thousand new food items were appearing in the market annually, many with dubious health claims or questionable use of terms like "light," "cholesterol free," and "fat free." Regulations include definitions for serving sizes for some foods, nutritional information on calories, calories from total fat, total fat in grams, saturated fat in grams, cholesterol in milligrams, total carbohydrates in grams, complex carbohydrates in grams, sugars in grams, dietary fiber in grams, protein in grams, sodium in milligrams, vitamins A and C, calcium, and iron. Restaurants, roadside markets, grocers, and prepared foods made on the premises are currently exempt from these regulations. See also main entry for **light** foods.

The FDA may take the following actions against those who violate these standards: seizure of the product itself; prosecution of the packer or distributor, with possible fines or jail sentence; and court injunction to prohibit shipment of illegal goods.

FOOD COURT. A space within a building, usually in a shopping mall, featuring a range of fast-food eateries and a sit-down area (1980).

FOODIE. A slang term, first used by food writer Gael Greene in 1980 and in an article in *Harpers & Queen* magazine in 1982, entitled "Cuisine Poseur," to describe people who are intensely fascinated by food and talk about food. "A Foodie is a person who is very very interested in food," wrote Paul Levy (who edited the original article) and Ann Barr in their book *The Official Foodie Handbook* (1984). "Foodies are the ones talking about food in any gathering—salivating over restaurants, recipes, radicchio. They don't think they are being trivial—Foodies consider food to be an art, on a level with painting or drama."

Around 2008, the terms "foodie hipsters" or "hipster foodies" and "food dude" came to mean foodies who sought out new foods, ethnic eateries, and avant-garde chefs, as well as places that had the best hamburgers, pizza, and ethnic foods.

FOOD MAGAZINES. Food articles began to appear in the mid-nineteenth century, at first as part of women's magazines like *Godey's Lady's Book*, which in the 1840s had a circulation of seventy thousand, and *Ladies' Home Journal* and *Good Housekeeping*, which at different times both employed as food editor the nation's best-known cooking teacher, Sarah Tyson Rorer, who also edited *Table Talk*, appearing in 1889. **Fannie Farmer** began her *Boston Cooking-School* magazine in 1896, setting a new standard for cooking instructions by using measurements. The *National Food Magazine*, debuting in 1896, was the first to lobby for better monitoring of the nation's food-safety and sanitary conditions.

In the twentieth century, regional interest magazines like *Sunset*—"the Magazine of Western Living"—and *Southern Living* expanded food coverage. Many newspapers also developed food sections, which usually ran on Wednesdays. *Better Homes and Gardens*, appearing in 1924, devoted its attention to homegrown food, as well as articles on diet and allergies, under food editor Josephine Wylie.

The first magazine targeted to a sophisticated market for fine food was *Gourmet*, launched in 1941 by Ralph Warner Reinhold and Earle R. MacAusland. After the war, *Gourmet* drew the top food and travel writers of the day and featured articles on global cuisines, accompanied by on-location photography. The magazine was later bought by Condé Nast, which installed editor Ruth Reichl, who tried to update the style and focus of the magazine to reflect more modern concerns about food and cooking.

Other food magazines debuted in the 1970s and 1980s, including *Cuisine*, *Cooking Light*, and *Food & Wine*, the latter owned by American Express, used to promote expenditures through the Amex credit card. *Gourmet's* main competitor, however, was *Bon Appétit*, originally a liquor-store throwaway paper, begun in 1956 by M. Frank Jones, of Kansas City, Missouri, who merged the publication into the Pillsbury Co., which in turn sold it to Knapp Communications in 1970. *Bon Appétit* was intended for a more middle-class reader than *Gourmet*, though eventually it, too, featured travel stories and restaurant coverage. Knapp was purchased by Condé Nast, as was *Gourmet*, which, owing to a weak economy after 2008, was discontinued in 2009. *Bon Appétit* is still in print.

Saveur was co-founded by Dorothy Kalins, Michael Grossman, Christopher Hirsheimer, and Colman Andrews, who was editor in chief from 1996 to 2001. (It is now owned by World Publications, under the Bonnier Corporation.) *Saveur* was devoted to good writing about global food, as much in home kitchens in the developing world as at county fairs in the Midwest. Originally, the magazine did little restaurant coverage, but it later instituted an annual "Saveur 100" of "favorite restaurants, food, drink, people, places and things."

Cook's Illustrated, founded by editor Christopher Kimball, focused on "finding the best methods for preparing foolproof home-cooked meals. Unlike some glossy cooking magazines, our magazine is staffed with cooks and editors not food stylists," who would test and retest recipes up to thirty times. The staff also tested kitchen equipment. The magazine does not include any advertising and is wholly supported by subscriptions. *Cook's Illustrated*

also has its own PBS-TV series, "America's Test Kitchen," and a radio show, both of which are sponsored.

In 1988, **Ariane and Michael Batterberry** founded *Food Arts*, intended for professionals in the food industry; it is now owned by M. Shanken Communications.

Owing to the success of her Food Network and ABC Network series, Rachael Ray was offered a magazine in 2005 by the Reader's Digest Association, called *Every Day with Rachael Ray*. It was bought in 2011 by the Meredith Corp. The magazine reflects Ray's homey, casual style of cooking, and its demographic was more downscale than those of the other food magazines—a median income of $77,000, vs. *Bon Appétit's* $97,000—but its circulation of 1.8 million topped *Bon Appétit's* 1.3 million.

FOOD STAMP. A federally funded program designed to provide nutritional assistance to the poor in America by giving them coupons that may be exchanged at grocery stores for food products. During the Depression, the federal government alleviated both hunger and surplus farm products by allowing families to exchange money for stamps of equal value and additional stamps with which to buy food. Reduced surpluses during World War II canceled such federal programs, but in 1961, President John F. Kennedy directed the Agriculture Department to establish an experimental program, which in 1964 became a full-fledged program under the Food Stamp Act. By 1971 Congress had established uniform standards of eligibility. Since then, various changes in the regulations and funds available for food stamps have occurred under different administrations. By 2012, the number of Americans receiving food stamps was 46.5 million, more than one in seven people.

FOOD WINE. A phrase used by American wine producers to describe a wine that goes particularly well with different kinds of food, as opposed to a wine that may be drunk on its own. The phrase gained currency in the mid-1980s after being used in a 1983 article in *Wine Spectator*. "*No one admits to coining the term*," wrote Harvey Steiman in "What Is a 'Food Wine' Anyway?" in the same magazine in 1984, "but several winemakers suggested that it developed to counter an often-heard criticism of California wines—that they are too big and flavorful to make pleasant companions to food. Another possibility is that the term is a reaction to wines that are simply high in alcohol. Such wines stand out in tastings, but may not be the best choices with dinner."

FOO-FOO. Also "fufu." An African American term for dough made from boiled and pounded plantains, cassava, and yams. The word derives from West Africa, possibly Ghana, and dates in print to 1889.

FOOL. A dessert of cooked, pureed fruit served with cream. The word dates to 1590 in print, though the derivation of its usage is unknown.

FORGIONE, LARRY (1952–). Called the "Godfather of American Cuisine," Larry Forgione was among the first of the baby boomer chefs to create and promote the concepts of New American cuisine through his insistence on using the best American foods at a time when most restaurants used inferior ingredients.

Born on Long Island, New York, Forgione was the great-great-nephew of Catholic saint Francesco Forgione, called Padre Pio. A Golden Gloves boxer in high school and college, Forgione intended to become a physical education teacher, but a bout of pneumonia muffled that dream, forcing him to take a job in catering in Brooklyn, which caused him to consider going into cooking, switching from Concord University, in West Virginia, to the **Culinary Institute of America**, in Hyde Park, New York (1972–1974), where he was a member of the first graduating class.

In 1974, Forgione began working in a restaurant in Worcester, Massachusetts, then moved to London to work for chef Michel Bourdin at the Connaught hotel. In 1977, he returned to New York City to work at Regine's, under chef Michel Guérard. "It dawned on me when I was working in London," said Forgione, "all this beautiful produce and fresh butchered meats would come into the kitchens and it didn't make sense to me that in America it was reversed.…In America everybody was producing for the masses, and the chefs also had to use what was produced. So when I came back I thought that it was time that we started to reverse the wheel a little bit, and I started working with a lot of farmers and producers."

He moved to Brooklyn's River Café in 1979, where he followed through on his insistence to use seasonal American foods from local farmers. There he began buying eggs from microbiologist turned farmer Paul Keyser, who coined the term "free range chicken." In 1981, with forager Justin Rashid, he founded a food-products company named American Spoon Foods, based in Petoskey, Michigan, selling preserves and other food products at retail.

Under Forgione, the River Café became the first restaurant to print its producers' names on the menu. **James Beard** became a frequent guest, and informed Forgione of the best producers of American foods in the country.

In 1983, Forgione opened his own restaurant in Manhattan, called An American Place, named by Beard after a famous New York City gallery, The American Place, started by photographer Alfred Stieglitz. The restaurant was hailed as a new kind of American restaurant with modern ideas and an intense focus on ingredients available nowhere else in New York City at the time. "I want to give American food of the future an integrity by looking to the past, but I'm cooking in the present," he said. "My food must reflect the past, and I don't do slavish recreations of historic dishes, even those dishes with distinct roots in the past.…Some people have criticized me that my food is too pretty to be American, and it bothers me that they equate American food with slopping stuff on the plate."

In 1989, An American Place moved to larger quarters on Park Avenue, and Forgione expanded to open Beekman 1776 Tavern, in Rhinebeck, New York; Restaurant Above, in the Hilton Times Square; the Grill Room, at World Financial Center; and the Coach House, in the Avalon Hotel. In 1999, he moved An American Place to a third location, at Fiftieth Street and Lexington.

By 2003 all these had restaurants closed. Forgione then developed his Signature Café, at the Lord and Taylor department store on Fifth Avenue, where he increased food sales 100 percent, which led to his putting Signature Cafés in seven more branches. In 2005, he opened An American Place at the Statler Hotel, in St. Louis.

Forgione is the co-founder and culinary director of the Conservatory for American Food Studies (CAFS), located at the Greystone Campus of the **Culinary Institute of America**, in Napa Valley, California, promoting "the history, values and future of farm to table cooking in America." CAFS students will complete at least fifteen hours of work on farms, receive advanced studies in American regional cooking, and operate the CAFS's F2T restaurant, in St. Helena, California.

Forgione's two sons, Mark and Bryan, followed their father into the business, opening their own restaurants.

In 1993, Larry Forgione was named Chef of the Year by the **James Beard Foundation**. His *An American Place Cookbook* (1996) also won a Beard award. In 1996, *Life* magazine listed Forgione as one of the 50 Most Influential Baby Boomers.

FORTUNE COOKIE. A Chinese American cookie into which has been folded a printed message supposedly predicting one's fortune.

Fortune cookies are not known in Chinese food culture, but they have long been part of the hospitality of Chinese American restaurants, which traditionally serve them free of charge with tea after the meal. *The Random House Dictionary* dates the item in print only to 1960, though they have certainly been served for much longer than that. A 1987 article by food historian Meryle Evans in *Diversion* magazine provides several stories as to the possible origins of the fortune cookie. One story concerns Japanese landscape architect Makoto Hagiwara, who emigrated to San Francisco at the turn of the twentieth century and designed a teahouse where, sometime before World War I, he and his daughter Sada Yamamoto began serving fortune cookies to the patrons. Another suggests that just after World War I, a Los Angeles baker named David Jung handed out such cookies, containing words of encouragement to the poor and homeless people on the streets. He later started the Hong Kong Noodle Co. and did produce cookies with fortunes inside.

By the 1930s there were fortune-cookie factories, one of the first being William T. Leong's Key Key Fortune Cookie Co., in NYC.

Until the late 1960s, fortune cookies were always folded by hand. Then Edward Louie, owner of the Lotus Fortune Cookie Co., in San Francisco, invented a machine to do the job. Louie also pioneered giant fortune cookies up to six inches wide and was the first to insert bawdy fortunes into the confections.

FRANCONIA POTATOES. Boiled potatoes baked with butter. The name refers to the Franconia range of the White Mountains in New Hampshire. The recipe appeared in the 1918 edition of Fannie Farmer's *Boston Cooking-School Cook Book*.

FRANCONIA POTATOES

Boil potatoes in salted water, place on a buttered pan, pour melted butter over them, season with salt and pepper, and bake at 400° until browned.

FRANK, DR. KONSTANTIN (1899–1985). Viticulturist and winemaker. Dr. Konstantin Frank saw that the traditional winemaking techniques and use of native labrusca grapes in mass production had little future in New York State, and in the Finger Lakes region he began concentrating on European varietals like Riesling to compete with the best in Germany.

Frank was born in Odessa, Russia, where he earned his Ph.D. in viticulture at the Odessa Polytechnic Institute. He emigrated to the U.S. in 1951, obtaining a position at Cornell University's Geneva Experiment Station, where he became convinced that it was not the cold climate but the wrong *Vitis vinifera* rootstock then in use that produced bad results in the Finger Lakes region. In 1958, Frank bought land on Keuka Lake, and in 1962 he founded Vinifera Wine Cellars, where he first produced a sweet Trockenbeernauslese Johannisberg Riesling from grapes affected by the botrytis fungus, and afterwards an impressive array of drier Rieslings that compared with fine examples back in Europe.

After Frank's death, in 1985, his son Willy took over and produced sparkling wine at Chateau Frank, using champagne varietals made by the *méthode champenoise* process. Willy's son, Frederick Frank, took over leadership of the winery in 1993, producing a low-priced brand, Salmon Run.

In November 2001, Konstantin Frank was inducted into the Wine Spectator Hall of Fame for outstanding achievements in the field of viticulture.

FREE LUNCH. A midday meal offered free of charge to saloon customers in order to entice them to drink more beer or spirits. The word dates in print to 1835. In her book *The New Orleans Restaurant Cookbook* (1967), Deirdre Stanforth contends that the practice began in the New Orleans French Quarter, at the St. Louis Hotel, and was created for the business clientele who could not get home for lunch. So successful was the free lunch that the management sought to stop it, but by then it had become firmly entrenched and before long was practiced in other restaurants across the country, and especially in beer halls. In those days, the free lunch might consist of large platters of beef, ham, soup, potatoes, caviar, and oysters, all set on the bar, but as time went on, sliced meats, cheese, and bread became more the norm. By the middle of the twentieth century, the free lunch had deteriorated into a complimentary snack of pretzels, potato chips, or other cocktail nibbles, though one occasionally will still find a crock of cheddar cheese.

FREE RANGE. A restaurant-industry and butchers' term for animals, most commonly referring to chickens, that are allowed to forage on their own and are not penned in. The term gained currency in the 1980s among chefs engaged in the so-called **new American cooking**.

FRENCH AMERICAN FOOD. A general term for the various foods cooked and enjoyed by French immigrants, as well as those adaptations of classic French cuisine that have become part of American gastronomy.

Although the dominant immigrant group in Canada, people of French descent numbered only about 100,000 in the U.S. by 1790, with significant settlements in Louisiana, especially those Acadians ousted from Nova Scotia between 1755 and 1763. By 1860, New Orleans was home to 15,000 of French descent.

The respect among all Europeans for the cuisine of the French courts, whose master chefs, like Marie-Antoine Carême, had codified recipes for thousands of dishes by 1834, drove the banqueting and cooking of more affluent American homes. Thomas Jefferson, who had served as U.S. ambassador to France, developed a deep interest in French cuisine, educating his slave cook to learn how to make it and importing a French chef to

the White House during his tenancy, though there were as yet no true French restaurants in America.

The French had in fact invented the restaurant in the eighteenth century, which differed from taverns by virtue of having a menu from which to choose à la carte options. In 1794, French chef Jean Baptiste Gilbert Payplat ("Julien"), former cook for the archbishop of Bordeaux, opened a French-style restaurant in Boston, though the word *restaurant* does not appear in English print until 1806 or in American print until 1820.

The first true restaurant in America wholly in the French style was opened in 1831 in New York City, by John and Peter Delmonico, with a menu written in French, which became the standard in restaurants and hotel dining rooms to follow, not least in New Orleans, where Creole French culture had already transformed classic French cuisine by adopting Caribbean and American ingredients as a basis in dishes like **rémoulade**, fricassees, and **étouffées**. At the same time, French refugees from Nova Scotia, called Acadians there and **Cajuns** in Louisiana, adapted old French cookery to the backwoods, swamps, and bayous, blending in culinary influences from Spanish, African, and Choctaw food cultures, which led to dishes like **boudin**, **andouille**, *maque choux*, crawfish bisque, and *cochon de lait*, a suckling pig slaughtered and cooked at a boucherie party.

French service, by which large platters of food were placed in profusion on the table—one course for appetizers and soups, one for main courses (in the U.S., the word "entrée," which refers to a dish that in France precedes the main course, came to mean the main course)—was kept at affluent homes until **Russian service**, by which guests are offered individual dishes by a waiter, became popular, after the Civil War.

American cookbooks of the nineteenth century barely reflected regional American cuisine. French dishes still dominated menus. But with the onset of Prohibition, in 1920, fine dining rooms serving French cuisine and wines were crippled by a lack of business, while the new immigrant eateries—pizzerias, delicatessens, beer halls, tavernas, and chop suey parlors—proliferated, along with lunch counters, diners, roadhouses, and other low-end establishments serving American food. When Prohibition ended, in 1933, French restaurants bounded back in cities like New York, where many of the top restaurants, especially in hotels, had names like Gaston à la Bonne Soupe, Lafayette, Larré's, LaRue, and Voisin, all serving *sole à la meunière*, quail *à la veronique*, chicken *sauté chasseur*, and frogs' legs *à la provençale*—dishes that would endure on menus well into the twenty-first century.

French haute cuisine enjoyed a renaissance, however, during the 1939 New York World's Fair, where, among many national restaurants, Le Restaurant du Pavillon de France set a standard for food and service unmatched anywhere in the U.S. When war came, many of the staff of Le Restaurant remained in the U.S., and, after the fair closed in 1941, general manager Henri Soulé opened Le Pavillon as a free-standing restaurant in New York City, hiring most of his former staff. Until its closing in 1971, Le Pavillon was the template for fine dining in America, from its decor, with its red banquettes and pots of roses, to its layout, which included a section reserved for the most illustrious and well-heeled of Soulé's clientele, a form of exclusionism that became rife, even expected, in French restaurants. In New York City in particular, at restaurants like La Grenouille, Lutèce, La Côte Basque, and Le Périgord, classic French cuisine and hauteur were part of a very expensive evening out. In Philadelphia, chef Georges Perrier opened Le Bec Fin, which was also considered among the top restaurants in the U.S. Indeed, in 1980, when *Playboy* magazine did a survey of food critics, writers, and chefs, asking what the twenty-five best restaurants in America were, French restaurants took fifteen slots; four years later, the same poll had fourteen French restaurants among the top twenty-five.

The more egalitarian side of French cooking was expressed by a California-born woman named **Julia Child**, who, after attending Le Cordon Bleu cooking school, in Paris, joined cooking teachers Simone Beck and Louisette Bertholle to compile a two-volume French cookbook for Americans, *Mastering the Art of French Cooking*, published in 1961, which became a bestseller and led to Child's developing a cooking show on Boston's WGBH-TV, debuting on Feb. 11, 1963, and running for ten years. With her very American personality and casual approach to classic French technique, Child showed generations of American cooks that the basics of all good cooking were found in the basics of French home cooking. So influential was Child that in 2000 she received France's highest award, the Légion d'honneur.

Starting in the mid-1970s, the fashion for France's **nouvelle cuisine**, which bent the stultified rules of French classicism in favor of creativity and a somewhat lighter approach for better health, received tremendous media attention in the U.S., where a gourmet revolution of its own was just taking shape. Also of exceptional importance was **Alice Waters**, a former Montessori teacher and member of Berkeley, California's Free Speech Movement who opened a highly personalized bistro in Berkeley called Chez Panisse, where she and a staff of young Americans cooked Provençal-style French cuisine based on her demand for the very best ingredients California had to offer. This seemingly simple advance, at a time when most restaurants in the U.S. used little but canned and frozen products, had an impact that was to feed into what became the **New American cuisine** movement of the mid-1980s.

By the early 1980s, however, nouvelle cuisine was alive and well at restaurants like Dodin-Bouffant, the Quilted Giraffe, the Palace, Le Cirque, and Le Plaisir, in New York City, and L'Érmitage and L'Orangerie, in Los Angeles, while some of France's nouvelle stars, like Paul Bocuse and Roger Vergé, opened up satellite restaurants of their own in the U.S., including two at Disneyworld's Epcot Center, in Lake Buena Vista, Florida, in 1981.

By the end of the 1980s, the New American cuisine movement, based on French cooking principles but staunchly regional in flavor, was eclipsing French haute cuisine and its attendant snobbism. A signal exception was Le Bernardin, an ultra-sophisticated French seafood restaurant opened by chef **Gilbert Le Coze** and his sister Maguy in New York City in 1986, which brought a style of new, exacting cooking technique that afterwards transformed the way seafood was cooked, while at the same time graduating a great number of young cooks trained in that technique who would go on to open their own restaurants.

At Le Cirque, which opened in the early 1970s as a classic French restaurant in the Le Pavillon style, Italian-born owner **Sirio Maccioni** allowed young chefs like **Daniel Boulud**, Sylvain Portay, and Jacques Torres to take a more refined, modern approach to the cooking, and this kitchen acted as a crucible for a generation of cooks who trained there.

With the 1997 opening of Balthazar, a big, well-lighted brasserie in which British owner Keith McNally hoped to create the bonhomie of brasseries on Montparnasse, in Paris, the humbler bourgeois cooking of France caught on with young people, who had always loved steak frites, salade Niçoise, and *côte de boeuf* and tried new, unintimidating dishes like duck confit, *brandade de morue*, and sautéed *raie* while drinking wines from Provence and Alsace.

Nevertheless, new concerns in the 1990s about health and the richness of French cuisine, as well as a continuing belief in the restaurants' exclusionary attitudes and unaffordable prices, helped cause the demise of many of the French restaurants around the U.S. in favor of upscale versions of American and Italian restaurants. Today, many major American cities lack even one deluxe French restaurant.

With only about 5.3 percent of the American population of French background, the cuisine of France is no longer among the most popular, except at Franco-American homes. Nevertheless, many French dishes abound on American menus, cooked by chefs trained in French kitchens, and many of these, like onion soup gratinée, **lobster Thermidor**, tarte Tatin, mussels in white wine, quiche Lorraine, croissants, chocolate mousse, and crème brûlée, are now considered almost as American as they are French.

FRENCH COLOMBARD. A white vinifera grape used both in blending wines and as a varietal. In France the grape is known as the "Colombard" and by other names, but in California it was called "West's White Pacific" in the nineteenth century (when West & Sons of Stockton, California, brought it back from France) and "Winkler" (after viticulturist Dr. Albert J. Winkler) after the repeal of Prohibition. Later it was identified by enologist Harold P. Olmo of the University of California as French Colombard. The first varietal from this grape appeared in 1964 under the Parducci Wine Cellars label.

FRENCH CRULLER. A choux-batter fried pastry shaped like a doughnut but with a rippled, sugar-frosted top. The term was first mentioned in the *Philadelphia Cook Book*

(1886), simply referring to "German crullers...French crullers," suggesting that they were not of American origins.

FRENCH DIP SANDWICH. A sandwich made of sliced beef, lamb, or pork and hot mustard set on a sliced French loaf which is then dipped into the pan juices. Two restaurants claim its creation, both opened in 1908: Philippe's the Original and Cole's Pacific Electric Buffet, both in Los Angeles.

FRENCH DRESSING. A salad dressing made by mixing three parts oil to one part vinegar, though some other seasonings, like mustard or blue cheese, may be added. Dates in print to 1874.

FRENCH FRY. A method of cooking potatoes or other vegetables cut into narrow strips or rounds. "French fries" (also a "side of fries" or just "fries") are easily the most popular form of potato preparation in America and are a staple of **fast-food** restaurants. In France, where fried potatoes had appeared in cookbooks by the 1790s, they were only called *pommes frites*, a term not mentioned in French print as of 1858, and then, in 1868, as a low-class food item. In England they are known as "chips," first mentioned in a letter by Oscar Wilde, dated March 1876, wherein he writes, "My dear Bouncer, I am very glad to hear from Mark that you have come back safe out of the clutches of those barbarous Irish. I was afraid that the 'potato-chips' that we live on over there would have been too much for you."

The term "french fry" has nothing to do with the country of origin but instead refers to a method, called "frenching," of cutting the potatoes into narrow strips. The *OED*, which traces "French-fried potatoes" back to 1894, suggests that the usage is American in origin. "French fries" dates to 1902, "french frieds" to 1915. "French fried onion rings" appeared in print in 1939. "Shoestring potatoes," which are cut into very thin strips, dates in print to 1898.

Most commercial french-fried potatoes are precut, partially cooked, and frozen for delivery to groceries and restaurants. In fact, it is now uncommon to find freshly made french fries outside the home. At home, the potatoes may be fried in pure lard, but vegetable oil is the more common medium today. "Steak fries" and "Texas fries" are usually cut thicker than regular french-fried potatoes. Thickly cut potatoes cooked in a small amount of fat or oil are called "American fried potatoes," while thinly sliced potatoes done the same way are called "American raw fry." "Onion rings" are onion slices usually battered in flour, milk, and cornmeal before frying. See also **Saratoga potatoes**.

FRENCH 75. A cocktail made from gin, Cointreau, lemon juice, and champagne, though ingredients vary with different recipes. The drink is named after a French 75-millimeter gun, considered the finest fieldpiece of World War I, and appeared in print as of 1930.

"Count" Léon Bertrand Arnaud Cazenave, owner of Arnaud's restaurant, in New Orleans, which opened in 1918, claimed to have created the drink, but *Harry's ABC of Mixing Cocktails* (1919, revised 1939) refers to a "'75 Cocktail" made from one teaspoon absinthe plus two parts Calvados and one part gin as "the original 1915 recipe of the French '75 Cocktail," and gives another recipe for a French '75, calling for two ounces gin, the juice of a lemon, sugar, ice, and champagne, as having originated at Harry's New York Bar, in Paris, in 1925. David A. Embury, in his *Fine Art of Mixing Drinks* (1958), notes unpersuasively that "gin is sometimes used in place of cognac in [a French 75], but then, of course, it no longer should be called French." Embury's version calls for the juice of one lime or half a lemon, two teaspoons sugar syrup, and two ounces cognac.

Arnaud's recipe for a French 75, given in Deirdre Stanforth's *New Orleans Restaurant Cookbook* (1967), is as follows.

FRENCH 75

Shake with ice the juice of 1 lemon with 1 oz. gin and ½ oz. Cointreau, strain into a champagne glass, and top with champagne and a lemon twist.

FRENCH TOAST. A breakfast dish made from white bread dipped in an egg-and-milk mixture, then fried in butter and served with either syrup or powdered sugar. It is a very popular item both at home and in restaurants, and it is often accompanied by bacon, ham, or sausage.

The dish does have its origins in France, where it is known as *ameritte* or *pain perdu* ("lost bread"), a term

that has persisted, in Creole and Cajun cookery, and was first in American print in 1896. In Spain it is called *torriga*, and in England "Poor Knights of Windsor," which is the same name for the dish in Denmark (*arme riddere*) and Germany (*arme Ritter*). At one time or another in America it has been referred to as "Spanish," "German," or "nun's toast," and its first appearance in print as "French toast" was in 1871. In her 1893 cookbook, Mary Lincoln calls it "egg toast," as does *The Picayune's Creole Cook Book* (1900).

FRENCH TOAST

Dip a slice of white bread into a batter made from 1 beaten egg and ¼ c. milk or cream. Sauté in butter until brown on both sides. Serve immediately with maple syrup, cinnamon, powdered sugar, or honey.

FRESS. To eat greedily. The word is from the German *fressen*, "to devour," and is used primarily in Pennsylvania Dutch communities and among Jewish Americans. The word dates in print to 1916.

FRIED CHICKEN. A cowboy term for bacon that is rolled in flour and then fried. See also **southern fried chicken**.

FRITO PIE. Also "chili pie" and "corn chip chili pie." A Texas snack made with Fritos Corn Chips (a company trademark), **chili**, grated cheese, and onion. According to Texas food writer Alison Cook, "purists" demand that the chili, cheese, and onion be poured directly into a torn-open bag of Fritos, called "walk around corn chip chili pie." "THIS DISH MUST," wrote Cook, "REPEAT, MUST BE EATEN OUT OF THE SACK WITH A PLASTIC FORK OR SPOON, lest the whole effect be lost." The more "traditional" form of the pie is made in a baking dish. The Frito-Lay company, based in Dallas, has claimed that Daisy Dean Doolin, mother of the company's founder, Charles Elmer Doolin, may have invented the dish in the 1930s as a way of using leftovers. (Fritos Corn Chips themselves were first sold in San Antonio by Doolin as of 1932.) Cook, however, noted that a recipe for the dish appeared in 1946 in *The Fredericksburg Home Kitchen Cook Book*, as

"Chili-Frito Loaf," submitted by Viola Mae Schmidt. Another claim has been made for the wife of a Travis County, Texas, deputy sheriff's wife, who cooked up the pie for prisoners in the local jail.

FRITO PIE

In a 9-by-12-in. baking dish spread 2 c. Fritos Corn Chips evenly. Distribute 1 c. chopped onion and ½ c. grated cheddar cheese on top. Pour on enough chile to cover. Top with another cup of Fritos and ½ c. cheddar cheese. Bake in pre-heated 350° oven until bubbling, about 10–20 min. Serves 4–6.

FROGMORE STEW. A southern dish of boiled shrimp, crab, sausage, onions, and corn on the cob, traditionally served outdoors, similar to a New England clambake or Maryland crab boil. The name probably derives from a town on St. Helena Island, South Carolina (the town is now called St. Helena). One uncorroborated claim has been made by Richard Gay, of Gay Seafood Co., who says that while on National Guard duty in Beaufort in the 1960s, he made a cookout dish of leftovers and, upon returning home to Frogmore, printed up the recipe at his seafood market and sold the necessary ingredients. A similar dish is elsewhere called "Buford stew," possibly after Buford, Georgia.

FROGMORE STEW

Bring to a boil 3 qt. of water and add 2 T. seafood-boil seasonings. Add 1 lb. cooked hot smoked sausage, 1 whole onion, 1 t. hot red pepper flakes, and a wedge of lemon. Lower heat and simmer for 5 min. Add 6 ears of corn and cook for 2 min. Add 2 lb. unshelled shrimp and cook for 3–5 min. Serve with red beans and rice.

FROGS' LEGS. Any of various preparations using the legs of three U.S. species of frog: the green frog (*Rana clamitans*), the American bullfrog (*R. catesbeiana*), and the northern leopard frog (*R. pipiens*). The majority of these are caught in Florida and Louisiana, where they are a delicacy, either deep-fried or made with a spicy sauce.

DEEP-FRIED FROGS' LEGS

In a bowl with 1 c. vinegar, 1 sliced onion, and 3 chopped cloves of garlic marinate 2 doz. frogs' legs for about 3 hr. Make a batter of 1 beaten egg, 1 c. flour, ½ c. milk, ¼ t. cayenne pepper, and 1 t. salt. Drain frogs' legs, dip in batter, and fry in deep fat at 375° until golden brown.

FROM THE WELL. Bartender slang for the inexpensive house brands of liquor used for drinks when a customer does not specify a brand.

FROSTED. A half-frozen citrus-juice drink, made by freezing a fruit juice until almost firm, then whirling it through a blender. Frosteds may also be made by putting ice cubes made from one fruit juice, such as grapefruit, into a glass containing another fruit juice, like lemonade. Sometimes "**milk shake**" is used as a synonym for a frosted.

FRUIT COCKTAIL. A cup of various fruits served as an appetizer, usually containing pineapple slices, grapefruit slices, and, if canned, a sweetened liquid. (For the origins of **cocktail**, see main entry.) In the 1850s, recipe books called the item a "fruit salad." The term "fruit cocktail" was first used in print in *New York Hotel Review* magazine in 1922; "fruit cup" followed in print in 1931.

FRUIT SOUP. A Scandinavian American soup made with dried fruits and thickened with tapioca or sago. The term dates in print to 1950.

FRY BREAD. A bread of the Southwest Native Americans, particularly the Navajo and Hopi, that is deep-fried and sometimes served with honey and powdered sugar. Wheat flour was brought to the Americas by the Spanish, and this is one of the few Native American breads not based on corn flour. Fry breads are often featured at county fairs and Native American festivals throughout the Southwest, and a fry-bread contest, overseen by a Navajo woman named Hazel Yazza since 1946, is held annually at the Navajo Nation Fair and Rodeo, in Window Rock, Arizona, in September. See also **sopaipilla**.

FRY BREAD

Mix 2 c. flour with 2 T. baking powder and 1 t. salt. Add ½ c. warm water, or more, to achieve an elastic dough. Divide into 2-in. balls, roll out to a ¼-in. thickness, and fry in hot oil. Drain and serve with honey, cinnamon, or confectioners' sugar. (If Navajo bread is desired, punch a hole in the center of each flattened piece before frying, since the Navajo lower their bread into the oil with a stick, leaving a hole in the bread.)

FRYING-PAN BREAD. Cowboy bread made in a skillet from a thin batter of flour, water, and baking powder that was spread on a skillet placed over hot coals.

FUDGE. A semisoft candy made from butter, sugar, and various flavorings, the most usual being chocolate, vanilla, and maple. The candy was first made in New England women's colleges. The origins of the term are obscure. The *OED* suggests that it may be a variant of an older word, *fadge*, meaning "to fit pieces together." "Fudge" had been used to mean a hoax or cheat since about 1833, and by midcentury "Oh, fudge!" was a fairly innocuous expletive.

It has long been speculated that American college women, using candy making as an excuse to stay up late at night, applied the then-current meaning to the new candy, which was undoubtedly responsible for helping many students gain their "freshman fifteen," that is, fifteen pounds gained during the first year at college. In *Oh, Fudge!* (1990), Lee Edwards Benning cited a 1921 letter in the Vassar College archives, written by alumna Emelyn B. Hartridge, who contended that "fudge, as I knew it, was first made in Baltimore by a cousin of a schoolmate of mine…[and] sold in 1886 in a grocery store [at 279 Williams Street] for 40 cents a pound.… From my schoolmate, Nannie Hagner…I secured the recipe and in my first year at Vassar, I made it there—and in 1888 I made 30 pounds for the Senior Auction, its real introduction to the college, I think."

The word "fudge" as a candy first showed up in print in 1896, and by 1908 it was commonly associated with women's colleges, as in "Wellesley Fudge," "Smith College Fudge," and "Vassar Fudge." "Divinity fudge" (known since at least 1913), a light confection made with egg whites and, often, candied cherries, came along around 1910 and was especially popular during the holidays. The name probably referred to its "divine" flavor. "Fudge frosting" was being applied to cakes at the Wellesley Tea Room by 1898.

Most fudge is made from chocolate, though vanilla and maple are very popular, as is fudge riddled with walnuts or pecans. "Penoche" is fudge made mostly with brown sugar; the word is from American Spanish, first in American print in 1872. "Fudge brownies" are more cake-like than fudge but have a similar semisoft, moist texture.

CHOCOLATE FUDGE

Combine 2 c. sugar, 2 T. corn syrup, ⅔ c. evaporated milk, 2 oz. unsweetened chocolate, and 3 T. butter in saucepan, bring to a boil, and cook to 236° on a candy thermometer. Pour mixture onto marble slab and turn edges in with spatula until glossy sheen is gone. Add 1 t. vanilla and, if desired, chopped nuts.

FUMARIC ACID. An additive used to give a tartness to the flavor of processed foods like pie fillings, gelatin, and powdered drinks.

FUNERAL PIE. Also "raisin pie." A Pennsylvania Dutch pie traditionally baked before the imminent death of a family member, for the purpose of easing the grief of the mourners at the funeral. The pie is also sometimes called a "rosina" or "rosine" pie, because *Rosine* in German means "raisin." The term dates in print to 1949 but is certainly much older.

FUNERAL PIE

Soak 1 c. raisins in 2 c. warm water for 2 hr. In a double boiler combine 1 ½ c. sugar, 4 T. flour, 1 beaten egg, the juice of 1 lemon and the lemon rind, ¼ t. salt, then raisins and water. Cook for 15 min., pour into unbaked pie shell, top with a lattice of dough, and bake at 375° for 45 min.

FUNNEL CAKE. A deep-fried pastry made from batter dripped through a funnel. This Pennsylvania Dutch breakfast dish (which dates in print to 1950 but is certainly much older) is swirled in a spiral in hot fat and then served with sugar or maple syrup.

FUNNEL CAKE

Combine 1 c. flour, ¾ c. milk, 1 t. baking powder, ⅛ t. salt, and 1 egg to make a batter. Let stand for 10 min. Drip the batter through a funnel into very hot fat or oil, swirling to form a spiral design. Turn when browned and brown the other side. Drain and serve with powdered sugar or maple syrup.

FUNNY CAKE. As defined in its first printed reference, in the *Woman's Day Encyclopedia of Cookery* in 1965, this is a single-crust pie made with sugar, shortening, egg, milk, flour, baking powder, and vanilla, poured into a pan lined with a mixture of cocoa, vanilla, water, and sugar.

FUSION CUISINE. A term that gained currency in the late 1980s to describe a cuisine that draws on elements of many regional cookeries, especially by matching European and Asian ingredients and techniques.

FUZZY NAVEL. A cocktail made with peach schnapps and orange juice. "Fuzzy" refers to the effect of inebriation on the imbiber as well as to the fuzz on a peach; "navel" refers to the navel orange. A drink made with peach schnapps and grapefruit juice is called a "Fuzzy Pucker," because of the tartness of the grapefruit juice. Both became popular in the 1980s, when Doug Schuster, of Dublin, Ohio, was asked by his employer, National Distillers, to find uses for a new product called DeKuyper Peachtree schnapps. He mixed it with orange juice and called it a "Fuzzy Navel" after the marketing department's slogan, "You can taste the fuzz."

G

GALLEY QUEEN. Airline workers' slang for a lazy flight attendant who spends too much time loafing in the onboard galley, first mentioned in print in 1990.

GALLEY SLAVE. Slang term for a mess cook, referring to a slave who rowed in galley ships, dating in print to 1961.

GALLO, ERNEST (1909–2007) and **JULIO** (1910–1993). More than any other vintners, the Gallo brothers made wine an everyday beverage in America. Today E. & J. Gallo is the largest winery in the world.

Beginning in 1906, the Gallo brothers' father, Joseph, began selling wine from small wineries to bars in Oakland, California, under the name Gallo Wine Co. Their mother, born Assunta Bianco, also came from a family winery. In the 1920s, the Gallos began shipping wine grapes east on railroad cars, but the family fell into debt, driving Joseph to kill his wife and himself.

With an investment of $5,900, Ernest and Julio began their own winery, in Modesto in 1933, at a time when many people were converting their farms to wineries in an effort to cash in on the post-Prohibition sale of wine and spirits. (A third brother, Joseph, went into the cheese business and was later sued over his use of the Gallo name.)

In the 1930s, the Gallos committed themselves to a land management plan, by which every acre under cultivation was matched by one acre set aside as protected wildlife habitat. They also were leaders in minimizing the use of synthetic chemicals, fertilizers, and pesticides, and in recycling and reusing processed water. Eventually E. & J. Gallo Winery was recognized as the first winery in the U.S. to receive the International Standards Organization's ISO 14001 certification, created to assist companies in reducing negative impacts on the environment. They were also in the forefront of rotating the use of stainless-steel fermentation tanks, signed long-term grower contracts for varietal grapes, and funded major grape research programs.

With more than eight hundred post-Prohibition wineries operating in California, the Gallos' principal competitors, like Petri, Cribari, and Italian Swiss Colony, were far more successful, until the brothers launched a cheap citrus-flavored sweet wine that they named after a Ford sports car, Thunderbird, and sales of this wine reached thirty-two million gallons by 1958. During this same period, the Gallos were in the forefront of TV advertising of wines and the first vintners to establish significant foreign sales and marketing teams to export California wines overseas.

As California wineries like Robert Mondavi began making high-quality wines in the 1970s, the Gallos began improving their own products. Julio devoted himself more to the winemaking at Gallo, while Ernest took care of the business side. In 1993, having achieved renown for their efforts in the industry, Julio died in an auto accident. Today the company owns at least sixteen thousand acres of California vineyard land, with sales said to be in excess of a billion dollars a year. In 2006, *Forbes* listed Ernest Gallo at number 283 on its list of the 400 richest Americans. The company is now run by several members of the Gallo family.

Today, E. & J. Gallo Winery offers sixty brands, fourteen imported from abroad, and sells to ninety countries around the world. Their wines now include Gallo Family Vineyards, Barefoot Wine & Bubbly, Louis M. Martini Winery, William Hill Estate Winery, Mirassou Winery,

MacMurray Ranch, Rancho Zabaco, Ecco Domani, Frei Brothers Reserve, and Bridlewood Estate Winery.

In 2008, the Gallos were inducted into the **Culinary Institute of America**'s Vintners Hall of Fame. E. & J. Gallo Winery is the only American winery to be named "International Winery of the Year" three times (1998, 2001, and 2002).

GAP 'N' SWALLOW. Cornmeal mush. The term dates in print to 1939 and was described by Josephine H. Pierce, in *Coast to Coast Cookery* (1951), as "an emergency pudding made of cornmeal, much like Hasty Pudding. Also a plum pudding served with maple syrup." It is an old New England dish, whose name is a fanciful description of opening one's mouth and swallowing the dish with either relish or mere endurance.

GAR. Also "garr," "needlefish," and "alligator gar." Any of a variety of predatory fish in the species *Lepisosteidae*, of which five species occur in U.S. waters, principally in the southern and central states. The word *gar* is an American shortening of the English "garfish," which derives from the Middle English *geren*, dating in print to 1767. The gar was a basic food fish of the Florida Seminoles. The fish is often smoked.

GARBO. Also "garbo." An uncommon term for a toasted **English muffin**, probably not named after movie actress Greta Garbo.

GARDEN VEGETABLES. The American gardening tradition is basically derived from English roots. But the availability of fruits and vegetables at American markets has made a food-producing garden on one's own property more a hobby than a necessity. On southern plantations before the Civil War, slaves were often encouraged to keep their own gardens to add to their own diet; if there was a surplus, the food would be sold.

During World War I, Americans were urged to plant "liberty gardens" in vacant lots or their own backyards, in order to release other foodstuffs for shipment overseas to troops. This same practice came about again in 1942, when such plantings were called "victory gardens."

In the 1960s, gardening had a revival, owing to studies showing that many commercially grown fruits and vegetables were treated with pesticides and chemicals that rendered some items dangerous to consume. Many books appeared that encouraged Americans to raise some of their own food on their own land, while at the same time food raised without any chemical additives was pronounced natural or **organic**. Today more than half of all American households grow some or all of their own food. The Midwest has the most home gardeners, the South the least. The tomato, grown by 94 percent of home gardeners, is easily the most popular vegetable among such planters.

GARLIC (*Allium sativum*). An onionlike plant having a bulb that is highly aromatic and distinctly flavored. The word is from Old English *garleac*, "spear leek," dating in print to circa 1000. The plant is native to Central Asia and has long been enjoyed as a seasoning in Asia, Africa, and Europe, especially around the Mediterranean.

In America, there grew a wild garlic (*A. canadense*) eaten by pre-Columbian Indians, but the familiar market varieties (American, Creole, Mexican, Italian, and Tahitian) came via Europe and were appreciated as a seasoning only in those regions bordering the Gulf of Mexico, where the French, Spanish, African, and Caribbean influences were the strongest. In the rest of the country, garlic's usage was confined to ethnic neighborhoods in large cities until the middle of the last century. "Garlic has been the vehicle in the United States of a self-reversing snobbery," wrote Waverley Root in *Food* (1980). "Before I left America to live in Europe in 1927, you were looked down upon if you ate garlic, a food fit only for ditchdiggers; when I returned in 1940, you were looked down upon if you *didn't* eat it. It had become the hallmark of gastronomic sophistication, and I was overwhelmed by the meals offered by thoughtful friends, who catered to my supposedly acquired dashing Gallic tastes by including garlic in every dish except ice cream." It was hardly surprising, therefore, that lunch-counter slang terms for garlic in the 1920s and 1930s included "Bronx vanilla," "halitosis," and "Italian perfume."

Ninety percent of America's garlic is grown in California, which grows predominantly "Early" and "Late California" varieties. "Green garlic" is young garlic, picked in late winter or spring. "Elephant garlic," so called for its three-to-four-inch-diameter size, is technically not a garlic but related more closely to a leek. Two-thirds of the domestic garlic crop is dehydrated and processed into flakes or garlic salt, a milder-flavored seasoning that appeared in the 1930s; in the late 1940s, "garlic bread" was being served in Italian American restaurants as a standard item. In 1970, the per capita U.S. consumption of garlic was less than half a pound; by 1997 it had grown to 1.7 pounds.

GASTROPUB. A bar that puts emphasis on the quality of food served, which is often an upscale interpretation of traditional bar food. The word is a combination of "gastro" (stomach) and "pub," first in print as of 1996.

GATORADE. Trademark name for a sweet soft drink developed by Dr. Robert Cade at the University of Florida, in Gainesville, in 1965 to help athletes replenish fluids and minerals. It was so called because the university's football team was nicknamed the Gators. The beverage later became a very popular "performance drink" nationally, especially after it was adopted by the National Football League in 1967 as an official drink.

GAZPACHO. Also "gaspacho." A cold tomato-and-vegetable soup that is popular as summer fare and a staple of American restaurant menus, especially in the West. Another dish of the same name is "gazpacho salad," a layering of greens, sliced tomatoes, cucumbers, onions, bread crumbs, and French dressing. As such it was characterized by Mary Randolph in *The Virginia Housewife* (1824). As a soup, "gazpacho" has been in print since 1835.

Although antecedents of the soup are mentioned in the Bible and Greek and Roman literature (the word comes from the Arabic for "soaked bread"), gazpacho is more specifically an Andalusian dish, itself open to numerous interpretations—some thick, some hot, some cold—and often served with several garnishes, such as chopped eggs, bread cubes, peppers, onions, and scallions. In fact, *Cassell's Spanish Dictionary* defines gazpacho as an "Andalusian dish made of bread, oil, vinegar, onions and garlic; crumbs of bread in a pan" and makes no mention of the strained tomatoes that most identify gazpacho for Americans. Maite Manjón, in *The Gastronomy of Spain and Portugal* (1990), contended

that the original dish was a garlic soup called *ajo blanco* and was of Moorish origins. Tomatoes and peppers were added after the Spanish explorers brought those ingredients back from the Americas, and today there are many regional "gazpachos" throughout Andalusia.

Although long known in this country, gazpacho's popularity was for a great while confined to the South. Later, in the West, it took on a vogue that has made it one of the most often-found contemporary soups on a menu.

GAZPACHO

Peel and seed 2 tomatoes and chop together with 1 seeded sweet red pepper, 2 cloves garlic, and 2 T. seasonings, such as basil, tarragon, parsley, scallion, onions, and chives. Add ½ c. olive oil, 3 T. lime juice, and about 3 c. chicken broth. Puree in a food blender or food mill, add salt, pepper, and chopped cucumber, and chill for several hours. Serve with bread crumbs or bread cubes and white onions.

GEFILTE FISH. Also "gefulte fish." A small fish dumpling or quenelle seasoned with chopped eggs, onion, and pepper, which according to tradition should be made from several varieties of freshwater fish. The dish is frequently served at Jewish American homes on Friday night and at holiday dinners. The term is Yiddish, from the German *gefüllte Fisch* ("stuffed fish"), and first appeared in print in 1890.

GEFILTE FISH

Fillet 3 lb. whole fish of 2 or 3 varieties, such as whitefish, carp, or pickerel. Lightly salt the fillets and chill for several hours, then grind finely, adding 2 eggs, ½ c. water, 3 T. matzo meal, 2 t. salt, and ⅛ t. pepper. Chill for 10 min. and shape into loaves. Salt and chill the bones, skin, and head of the fish, rinse, and place in large pot with 2 chopped onions and 3 chopped carrots in a layer. Season with salt and pepper, cover with water, and bring to a boil. Cook for 5 min., then add fish mixture to broth and place sliced carrots on top. Cover, return to a boil, then simmer gently for 1 hr. Cool slightly before serving, garnishing with carrots, broth, horseradish, and dill pickles. Serves 6.

GELATIN. A thickening agent used in powdered desserts, yogurt, puddings, ice cream, cheese spreads, and other foods. Gelatin is a protein derived from animal bones, hooves, and other parts.

GEM. A muffin baked in a rectangular, sectioned pan with a round bottom. It is known mostly in the North and first saw print in 1875.

GERMAN AMERICAN FOOD. A general term for food enjoyed by German immigrants and their descendants, as well as those German foods that are enjoyed by all other Americans.

Although Germany was not a unified country until 1871, settlers from German regions came to America early in the seventeenth century, founding the first permanent settlement in Germantown, Pennsylvania, in 1683. Lutherans, Reformed, Mennonites, Amish, and other sects settled in the colonies, under the general name Pennsylvania Dutch. After the Civil War, Germans, including German Jews, formed the largest immigrant group for most of the nineteenth century, peaking in the 1880s, when 1,445,481 migrated. By 1870, about one in four were engaged in agriculture. Many became wealthy titans of industry, like fur trader and realtor John Jacob Astor and Midwest beer barons like **Adolphus Busch** and Frederick Pabst. Indeed, by 1876 there were more than four thousand breweries in the U.S., with the largest owned by German Americans with names like Yuengling, Best, Coors, Miller, Schlitz, Ehret's, and Ruppert.

Throughout the nineteenth century, German food culture was far more defined than any other immigrant cuisine, and common American speech is rife with German American food terms, including "wurst," "**frankfurter**," "**hamburger**," "**pretzel**," "sauerbraten," "**sauerkraut**," "schnitzel," "**pumpernickel**," and "lager." Pennsylvania Dutch cookery is well known to Americans in the East and the Midwest, especially dishes like **scrapple**, **Schnitz und Knepp**, chicken and dumplings, **rivel soup**, **sticky buns**, **shoofly pie**, and **funnel cake**. In Texas, homemade sausages and beef brisket barbecue were part of every German American community.

Before World War I, German American restaurants were very popular in America, led by rathskellers and beer halls in German American communities. In 1854, Franz Joseph Uhris brought the novelty of the outdoor restaurant to St. Louis, where he featured the newest Gilbert and Sullivan operettas. At Lueddemann's on the Lake, in Milwaukee, the nightly entertainment once featured a woman who set fire to herself and then dived forty feet into the river below. Pabst Park, in Milwaukee, grew into an eight-acre resort with the Katzenjammer Palace fun house and five-cent beers.

German fine dining restaurants abounded, like Schog's, Kau's, the Red Star Inn, Old Heidelberg, and the Berghoff, all in Chicago; Karl Ratzch's, in Milwaukee; Haussner's, in Baltimore; Grammer's, in Cincinnati; Jacoby's, in Detroit; Kolb's, in New Orleans; Pabst Café, in San Francisco; and New York City's famous Lüchow's, opened by August Guido Lüchow as a beer hall in 1882, whose theme song, "Down Where the Würzburger Flows," became a kind of anthem for all German restaurants around the country. New York City's Yorkville neighborhood in particular abounded with German American restaurants, many for the tourist trade. All of these restaurants served an amalgam of German, American, and foreign dishes, so that the huge menu of New York City's Hofbrau House for 1916 listed on its menu everything from *Kalbsnierenbraten* (roast veal) and *Riesen-Taube* (squab) to chicken à la king and chateaubriand with béarnaise, accompanied by Rhine wine and Liebfraumilch.

Anti-German feelings ran high during World War I, and German music, books, and foods were regarded as un-American. During Prohibition, German restaurants, whose profits were based so much on beer sales, suffered, and many closed. Beer gardens were shut down, as were the breweries that supplied them. World War II only reinforced anti-German sentiment, so that after the war there were few German restaurants left in the big cities, and those that remained became stereotypical. As one 1934 New York City guidebook said, "All waiters in these restaurants wear short corduroy pants, Alpine hats, socks that cover only the calves of their legs, and funny suspenders." Oompah music played, girls in pigtails and dirndls did singsong renditions of German songs, and the menus all featured the same dishes, from black bread and creamed herring to Wiener schnitzel and Black Forest cake. These restaurants, too, have largely disappeared, especially after nutritional concerns in the past thirty years have caused Americans to consider German food too heavy and rich with fat.

East Coast Jewish **delicatessens**, many owned by German Jews, prospered, with both Jewish and non-Jewish customers who came to eat beef frankfurters with sauerkraut, pickles, rye bread, liverwurst, and other foods derived from German culture, as well as many dishes from Eastern Europe and Russia.

The Pennsylvania Dutch managed to maintain the links to their food culture, albeit in stereotypical ways, at large restaurants in the farmlands, serving family-style meals at communal tables with bowls of chicken and dumplings, **Schnitz und Knepp**, and **shoofly pie**.

Today, with 17 percent of the population, German Americans are still the largest ethnic group in the U.S., but outside the Midwest, their food culture has little of the popularity that Italian, Mexican, or Asian American food does.

GERMAN'S SWEET CHOCOLATE CAKE. A cake made with Baker's German's Sweet Chocolate and topped with a coconut-pecan frosting. The original recipe, when first submitted by a reader to a Dallas newspaper in 1957, caused sales of Baker's German's Sweet Chocolate (a trademark name of the General Foods Corp.) to soar in Texas. A General Foods district manager brought the recipe to the attention of the company, and the recipe was perfected and promoted throughout the U.S.

The recipe has become so widespread over so many decades that it is often called "German chocolate cake," and many believe the cake is of German origins and, because of the inclusion of pecans and buttermilk, a specialty of Texas bakers. But in fact, the name of the chocolate derives from Dr. James Baker, who in 1780 financed the first chocolate factory in America. His descendant Walter Baker hired an employee named Samuel German, who developed a "sweet chocolate," which was added to the Baker's line under German's name.

A similar cake, apparently newer and adapted from German's Sweet Chocolate cake, is called a "Texas sheet cake" (also "Texas cake"), because it is baked in a large baking pan and not set in layers.

GERMAN'S SWEET CHOCOLATE CAKE

Melt one 4-oz. package of Baker's German's Sweet Chocolate in ½ c. boiling water, then remove from heat to cool. In a bowl mix 2 ¼ c. cake flour, 1 t. baking soda, and ½ t. salt. In another bowl cream 1 c. butter or margarine and beat in 4 egg yolks, one at a time. Blend in 1 t. vanilla extract and melted chocolate. Add flour mixture, alternating with 1 c. buttermilk. Beat until smooth. Beat 4 eggs whites until stiff and fold into batter. Pour batter into three 9-in. cake pans lined with waxed paper and bake 30 min. at 350° until set. Remove from oven and remove cakes from pans. Let cool on a rack. Make a frosting by combining 1 ½ c. evaporated milk, 1 ½ c. sugar, 4 beaten egg yolks, ¾ c. melted butter, and 1 ½ t. vanilla extract. Cook over medium heat, stirring until it turns a light brown color. Remove from heat and add 2 c. Baker's Angel Flake coconut and 1 ½ c. chopped pecans. Beat until cool and spreadable. Spread on each layer of the cakes, including the top.

GIBRALTAR. A hard candy associated with Salem, Massachusetts, and described in the book *Old Salem* (1886) as "a white and delicate candy, flavored with lemon or peppermint, soft as ice cream at one stage of its existence, but capable of hardening into a consistency so stony and so unutterably flinty-hearted that it is almost a libel on the rock whose name it bears. The Gibraltar is the aristocrat of Salem confectionery."

GIBSON. A **martini** cocktail garnished with a small white onion, dating in print to 1925. The drink was apparently named after the American illustrator Charles Dana Gibson (1867–1944), famous for his drawings of the turn-of-the-century "Gibson Girl." The story goes that Gibson ordered a martini—usually served with an olive—from bartender Charley Connolly, of the Players Club, in NYC. Connolly found himself out of olives and instead served the drink with two tiny white onions. The drink caught on, took the name of the more famous of the two men, and ever since has caused confirmed martini drinkers to shudder at the thought of drinking their favorite cocktail with such a garnish. The recipe, however, differs not at all from that of a dry martini. The *OED* dates the Gibson to 1930 in print, appearing in the British *Savoy Cocktail Book*, but that recipe calls for a measurement of half French vermouth and half gin, with lemon peel, not onions. However, *Harry's ABC of Mixing Cocktails* (1919), by London bartender Harry MacElhone, gives a recipe for nine-tenths gin, one-tenth dry vermouth, and a pearl onion.

There is another story as to the cocktail's creation years earlier, as reported in a 1968 article in the *San Francisco Chronicle*, which tells of how a customer at San Francisco's Bohemian Club named Walter D. K. Gibson invented the drink around 1898 after objecting to the way the bartender made martinis. Believing onions would prevent colds, Gibson asked for them in his martini. According to Gibson's grandson, an unnamed 1911 bar book shows a reference to the Gibson cocktail. A 2009 article by Eric Felten in the *Wall Street Journal* also cites this story, noting that Ward Thompson, another Bohemian Club member, mentioned the cocktail in print in 1898.

GIMLET. A drink of gin and lime juice. The word derives from a term for a boring tool (from Middle English and, ultimately, Middle Dutch *wimmelkijn*), which supposedly was used to puncture the kegs of lime juice shipped to the British colonies after 1795 as a preventive for scurvy. As a cocktail, the word first appeared in print in 1923.

Bartenders disagree as to the proportions for a gimlet, some adding carbonated water, as with a gin **rickey**, others not. In America, carbonated water is not usual. In his novel *The Long Goodbye* (1953), Raymond Chandler insists that "a real gimlet is half gin and half Rose's Lime Juice and nothing else."

GIMLET

Stir with ice 2 oz. gin and ½ oz. Rose's Lime juice (or fresh lime juice). Strain into sour glass.

GIN. A distilled spirit made from grain and flavored with juniper (*Juniperus communis*) and other aromatics. Gin was first made as a medicine in Holland, usually credited to one Franz de le Boë, also known as Doctor Sylvius, professor of medicine at the University of Leiden. But in his book *Gin* (2011), Richard Barnett contends that Sylvius was actually two people—a University of Leiden apothecary named Sylvius de Bouve and Leiden professor of medicine François dele Boë Sylvius—and that both probably worked on juniper distillation, which was

already well known in the Dutch Republic by the late sixteenth century. Called *genièvre* (French, from the Dutch *jenever*, "juniper berries," and first in English print in 1723), the spirit was also referred to as "Hollands" or "Schiedam" (after a gin-distillery center near Rotterdam).

The English imported gin, which they called "Dutch courage," but during Queen Anne's reign (1702–14) the spirit was produced locally and became the favorite—and least expensive—alcoholic drink sold throughout England, especially after George II's Gin Act of 1736 doubled excise taxes on foreign spirits and lowered them on domestic.

"London Dry Gin" used to mean a gin produced in or near that city, and such spirits differed in taste from the heavier Dutch gins. These lighter London-style gins became just as popular in the English colonies and have remained the preferred American variety ever since.

English gins run 80 to 97 proof, slightly lower than most American gins, and their taste has a bit more character than ours. (The English also make a rarely seen sweetened gin called "Old Tom," which purists insist is the correct spirit for a Tom Collins cocktail.) A "gin mill" is a slang term for a bar or saloon, known in print since 1865.

During Prohibition, those who opposed enforced temperance would often make liquor illegally at home, and so-called **bathtub gin**—that is, liquor mixed in one's bathtub—was the easiest spirit to produce. By obtaining a doctor's prescription for pure alcohol on some pretext of illness, one merely had to flavor the liquid with juniper berries (or their extract) and other botanicals, such as coriander, lemon peel, or angelica. Glycerin was often added to soften the home brew's rawness.

Commercially produced gin in America may be either distilled or made by combining distilled spirits with botanical oils, a process called "compounding." By law, all gins must have the flavor of juniper, though "sloe gin," which is really a cordial and not a gin, is allowed to carry the name by tradition. Minimum proof by federal law is 60 (30 percent alcohol by volume).

Gin is almost never aged, although there are some "golden gins" produced whose color comes from brief aging.

Gin is principally mixed with other spirits or citrus juices to make cocktails such as the **martini**, the **Gibson**, the **gimlet**, the **Ramos Gin Fizz**, and others. The U.S. is the biggest producer of gin, with about 8.7 million nine-liter cases produced, and imports more British gin than any other country.

GINGER (*Zingiber officinale*). This native plant of tropical and subtropical regions of Asia, especially Indomalaysia, is no longer extant in its wild form, but its cultivated root is valued for its pungent, aromatic spiciness and is a seasoning used throughout the world in everything from curries to desserts.

The name derives from the Sanskrit *srngaveram* ("horn root"), Greek *ziggiberis*, Latin *zinziberi*, and on to Middle English *gingivere*, dating in print to circa 1000. Ginger was well known to the ancient Romans, but it nearly disappeared in Europe after the fall of the Roman Empire. Marco Polo brought ginger back from the Orient, and afterwards the European appetite for spices made it once again a treasured and expensive condiment. Legend has it that Queen Elizabeth I of England invented the "gingerbread man," a cookie in the shape of a man, especially popular during Christmastime.

There was no ginger in the New World except a wild variety called "Indian ginger" (*Asarum canadense*), used in colonial times, but the English brought it to the American colonies early on, and ginger cookies were handed out to the Virginia voters to persuade them to elect certain candidates for the House of Burgesses. Ginger became a popular spice in Caribbean and Creole cookery, but in the rest of the country it was more often used in cakes, breads, and cookies. Virginian William Byrd remarked in 1711 that he "ate gingerbread all day long," and Amelia Simmons's *American Cookery* (1796) gives a recipe for molasses gingerbread. Eliza Leslie's 1828 volume, *Seventy-five Receipts*, listed both a common gingerbread and an enriched **Lafayette gingerbread** with lemon juice and brown sugar. **Fannie Merritt Farmer**, in her 1896 *Boston Cooking-School Cook Book*, speaks of three available grades of ginger—"Jamaica, best and strongest; Cochin [Indian], and African."

Today, fresh gingerroot is available in American markets, but Americans usually depend on dry, powdered ginger for use in cakes and cookies. Crystallized ginger is often found in specialty shops, and candied ginger was long served in the North as an after-dinner digestive. Ginger ice cream was a flavor popular in New England, though it is now rarely seen.

Booker T. Washington, founder of the Tuskegee Institute, in Alabama, recalled, in his autobiography *Up from Slavery* (1901), the childhood he spent as a slave and how he envied the white people's enjoyment of ginger cakes: "I remember that at one time I saw two of my young mistresses and some lady visitors eating ginger-cakes, in the yard. At that time those cakes seemed to me to be absolutely the most tempting and desirable things that I had ever seen; and I then and there resolved that, if I ever got free, the height of my ambition would be reached if I could get to the point where I could secure and eat ginger-cakes in the way I saw those ladies doing."

GINGERBREAD

Sift together 1 t. powdered ginger and 1 c. flour. Cream ½ c. butter with ½ c. brown sugar. Add flour mixture and blend well. Beat in ½ c. molasses and 1 well-beaten egg. Dissolve 1 t. baking soda in ½ c. boiling water and add to batter. Mix well, then bake in well-greased shallow pan at 350° for about 20 min. or until inserted knife comes out clean.

GINGER BEER. A nonalcoholic beverage flavored with fermented ginger, in print since 1800, first brewed in Great Britain. Ginger beer was popular in England at the beginning of the nineteenth century and later in America as a substitute for real beer. A **Moscow mule** is a cocktail made with ginger beer and vodka.

GINGER BEER

In a large earthenware vessel put 2 oz. pounded ginger-root, ¼ pt. lemon juice, 1 lb. sugar, and 1 gal. boiling water. Cool to 110°, then add 1 oz. yeast dissolved in a little water. Let ferment for 1 week. When fermentation ends, pour through strainer into bottles. Makes 1 gal.

GINGER CHAMPAGNE. A substitute cocktail without alcohol, made with ginger flavoring. The drink has been known by this name since at least 1842.

GINGERSNAP. A cookie made from ginger and molasses. "Snap" probably derives from an informal meaning for something easy, from German or Middle Dutch *snappen*, "to seize quickly." The word was first printed in 1795.

"Gingerbread men" are cookies cut in the form of human shapes and usually decorated with icing for eyes, mouth, and buttons.

GIRL SCOUT COOKIES. A trademark name for a series of cookies sold by the Girl Scouts of America to raise money for their organization. In 1917 the Mistletoe Troop, in Muskogee, Oklahoma, sold them for the first time, and by the 1920s the cookies were actually made by local Girl Scout units and peddled door-to-door each spring. Today the cookies are baked by two companies: ABC Bakers, of Richmond, Virginia (since 1936), and Little Brownie Bakers, of Louisville, Kentucky (since 1975), and still sold door-to-door by the Girl Scouts. About two hundred million boxes are sold annually, generating about $800 million in business, with 70 percent going to the Girl Scouts council within the local sales area. Girl Scouts of America receives a royalty for use of the licensed trademarks. The most popular cookie of the fourteen varieties is called Thin Mints (25 percent), followed by Samoas (19 percent).

GLYCERIN. Also "glycerol." An additive, derived from fat and oil molecules, for retaining the moisture of foods to which it is added, such as marshmallow, candy, and baked goods.

GOAT. Any of a variety of horned ruminants in the genus *Capra*, including the American mountain goat. The word is from Old English, dating in print to circa 1000. Goat's meat is not of much interest to most Americans, though it finds favor among some westerners and among certain immigrant groups, like the Italians, Greeks, and Spanish. In Mexican and Latin communities and in the Southwest, a suckling kid is often called by its Spanish name, *cabrito*. Slang terms for goat are "Adirondack steak" and "mountain lamb."

GOATFISH. Also "red mullet." Any of a variety of fish in the family Mullidae, usually golden or red, dating in print to 1634. In America, the name refers to several fish, especially the "red goatfish" (*Mullus auratus*), also known as the Hawaiian "kūmū" (1926), and the "moano,"

which means "pale red" in Hawaiian and refers to one of two species: *Parupeneus bifasciatus* or *P. multifasciatus*.

GOETTA. A specialty dish of Cincinnati made from ground meat and oatmeal boiled together, then molded, sliced, and fried, most commonly as a breakfast meat. It is similar to **scrapple**. The word is pronounced "getta" or "gheu-tuh" and must in some sense derive from German origins, although the exact reason for the name is not known. *DARE* notes that in a cookbook entitled *Cincinnati Recipe Treasury* (1983), "Martha Finke Oehler of Covington, Kentucky, claims that her ancestors 'invented' goetta (pronounced get-ta) back around the turn of the century.…The goetta became popular, and packages were transported across the Ohio River to Cincinnati markets, where the meat purveyors began selling their homemade versions in a German atmosphere."

GOETTA

In a large pot, boil 2 lb. pork cut into cubes and 1 onion cut in two for about 30 min. Remove from the liquid and grind into a fine mince. Into the liquid stir 2 ½ c. oatmeal and the pork and season with salt and pepper. Cook until liquid is absorbed, about 45 min., remove from pan, and cool. Pack into a loaf pan and chill well. Serve cut into slabs and fried in butter.

GOHAN. Cooked rice with vinegar and sugar, often used to make sushi. This is a term used in Japanese American communities and comes from the Japanese word for cooked rice, although *shari* is more commonly used when referring to the vinegared rice used to make sushi. "Gohan," which means, simply, rice in Japanese, dates in American print to 1958.

GOLDEN CADILLAC. A cocktail made from Galliano liqueur, white crème de cacao, and heavy cream. The name derives from the golden color of the drink and its richness, a characteristic associated with the American luxury car the Cadillac. In 1956, Columbia Pictures produced a motion picture entitled *The Solid Gold Cadillac*, and the cocktail may date from that period.

GOLDEN CADILLAC

In an electric blender mix with crushed ice 1 oz. Galliano, 2 oz. crème de cacao, and 2 oz. heavy cream. Pour into cocktail glass.

GOOEY BUTTER CAKE. A yeast-raised coffee cake whose butter-rich center gives it its "gooey" name. It is a specialty of St. Louis, but its creator is unknown. In an article in the *New York Times* in 1989, Ann Barry suggested it probably came out of South St. Louis, where many German bakers lived in the 1930s. According to the 1994 Junior League of St. Louis book *Saint Louis Days…Saint Louis Nights: A Culinary Tour of the Gateway City*, its creation might have been an accident, whereby a baker named John Hoffman added too much butter or other ingredients but, rather than waste expensive ingredients, served the cake anyway, much to customers' delight.

GOOEY BUTTER CAKE

In a bowl, cream 1 c. sugar, ⅓ c. vegetable shortening, 3 T. butter, 1 T. dried milk powder, 1 large egg, a few drops yellow food coloring, and a pinch of salt. Add ¼ c. bread flour, ¼ c. cake flour, ¼ t. vanilla extract, 1 T. light corn syrup, and 2 T. water. Mix briefly, just enough to blend ingredients. Take a 10-oz. Danish coffee cake and cut it to fit an 8-by-8-in. buttered pan, leaving a rim around the edge of the pan. Pour the butter mixture over the cake. Bake for 30 min. in a 375° oven. Sprinkle with confectioners' sugar. Makes 8–10 servings.

GOOSE. Any of a variety of wild or domesticated large birds of the family Anatidae, especially of the genera *Anser* and *Branta*. The word is from Old English *gōs*, first in English print circa 1000.

Geese were plentiful in the New World, but they have never been successfully mass-marketed and must be raised on small farms or taken in the wild, where the following species are found: "Canada goose" (*Branta canadensis*); "brant" (*B. bernicla*), a western subspecies of which is the "black brant"; "emperor goose" (*Philacte canagica*); "white-fronted goose" (*Anser albifrons*); "snow goose" (*Chen caerulescens*); and "Ross's goose" (*Chen rossii*).

Geese are almost always roasted but have never achieved much popularity with Americans.

GOOZLUM. Also "googlum." Slang term for a gravy, sauce, or other viscous food, like molasses or syrup. The etymology is unknown but possibly refers to the "oozing" quality of such a food. The term dates in print to 1911.

GORDOS. Also "gordas." A western trapper's term for wheat pancakes. But Blanche and Edna V. McNeil, in *First Foods of America* (1936), indicate that gordos were made from chiles, meat, frijoles, avocados, and corn-flour dough, while "gorditas" (Spanish for "little fat ones") are masa cakes made with cheese, chili, and avocados.

GORP. As a verb, to eat noisily or greedily, a meaning found in print since 1913. As a noun, "gorp" (also "trail mix" and "birdseed") refers to a mixture of dried fruit, seeds, nuts, and chocolate chips used as energy food by athletes, particularly hikers and mountain climbers, a meaning known in print since 1962. In his 1958 novel *The Dharma Bums*, Jack Kerouac writes of making such a mixture before setting out on a mountain climb: "Now as for food, I went down to Market Street…and bought my favorite cereal, bulghur, which is a kind of a Bulgarian cracked wheat and I'm going to stick pieces of bacon in it, little square chunks, that'll make a fine supper for all three of us…and in the bulghur too I'm going to throw in all kinds of dried diced vegetables…and for energy food this big bag of peanuts and raisins and another bag with dried apricot and dried prunes oughta fix us for the rest.'"

Hadley Fruit Orchard, which claims to have created trail mix, trademarked the name "Original Trail Mix" in 1968.

"Glop" and "goop" are similar terms used to describe such foods.

GOULASH. Also "Hungarian goulash." A Hungarian American stew of meat and vegetables seasoned with paprika. The Hungarian word is *gulyás*, which originally meant "shepherd," then was synonymous with the kind of stew. Its first printed reference in English was in 1866; as "Hungarian goulash," in 1915. It may be made with beef, veal, lamb, or chicken. The FDA requires canned or packaged goulash to contain at least 25 percent meat.

GOULASH

Brown 2 lb. beef in ¼ c. butter or lard. Add 2 chopped onions and sauté until golden. Add 1 c. beef stock, 1 t. salt, 1 t. paprika, and, if desired, 1 chopped green pepper. Cover and cook for about 1 hr., then add 6 small peeled potatoes. Continue cooking until meat and potatoes are tender. Serve with buttered egg noodles.

GO SOUTH. Restaurant cook's slang for food that is beginning to spoil.

GRAHAM FLOUR. An unsifted whole-wheat flour containing the bran of the wheat kernel (1825). It is named after Reverend Sylvester Graham (1794–1851), a tenacious advocate of temperance, healthy nutrition, and the virtues of home baking with this kind of flour. So influential was Graham's theory that he and his followers' appearance in Boston drew a protesting group of local bakers, who were routed only after Graham's people pelted the demonstrators with lime.

Graham set up "Graham hotels," serving strictly controlled meals quite in line with the belief of the temperance movement that food should not contain any stimulants or seasonings that might enflame the blood. Graham began his crusade in 1830, and within four years people were talking of "Graham bread." By 1882 a flat, slightly sweet cookie called a "Graham cracker" was well known, and the cookbooks of the nineteenth century always included recipes for such foods made with graham flour. He published the first book devoted solely to bread making, *Treatise on Bread and Bread-Making* (1837).

Graham's legacy survives today mostly in the form of the cookies named after him and graham-cracker crust, a pastry crust that is used often in lemon meringue pies, Key lime pies, cheesecakes, and other confections. Graham crackers made by Nabisco Brands Inc., of East Hanover, New Jersey, have long been one of America's most popular cookies.

GRAHM, RANDALL (1953–). While modern California wineries devoted their efforts and marketing toward **chardonnay** and **cabernet sauvignon** wines, Randall Grahm of Bonny Doon Vineyard, in Santa Cruz, devoted his to what he called "the ugly duckling varietals," in Rhône-style wines that won him great acclaim as a pioneer of what came to be known as the "Rhone Rangers," which he was dubbed by *Wine Spectator* in 1989. Grahm has also been an advocate of biodynamic viticulture, dry farming (that is, without irrigation), and the use of screw caps instead of cork closures.

He was educated at the University of California, at the Davis and Santa Cruz campuses.

Grahm founded his winery in 1983, at first focusing on pinot noir but changing to Rhône Valley varietals like grenache, mourvèdre, cinsault, and viognier. A year later, his first vintage, named Le Cigare Volant ("the flying cigar"), was hailed as a remarkable achievement. Later he planted Riesling, Italian, and Spanish varietals.

In 1994, his vineyards' vines were destroyed by Pierce's disease, forcing Grahm to buy grapes from other California, Oregon, and European vineyards. At Bonny Doon's height, in 2006, the winery sold more than five million bottles. Restless to make more distinctive wines, that same year Grahm debuted his Big House and Cardinal Zin labels and radically downsized the company. He later purchased land in the San Juan Bautista area, to focus on dry-farmed estate wines, with the intention of producing a true *vin de terroir*. He has also experimented with aging his red wines in glass rather than oak barrels.

In 2012, Grahm wrote on his blog, "My company, Bonny Doon Vineyard, is in some danger, perhaps some real danger if we are not careful, and by extension, so are my great and vivid dreams," referring to financial stress. "My fear is that some of the (tragic) elements of my own personality have become inculcated within the company culture."

As a man of many interests, Grahm became known for his unorthodox wine labels, with illustrations by artists like Ralph Steadman, Bascove, Grady McFerrin, and Gary Taxali. His 2009 book *Been Doon So Long: A Randall Grahm Vinthology*, was an erudite collection of essays, poems, arcana, and humor, including poems titled "The Love Song of J. Alfred Rootstock" and "Da Vino Commedia: The Vinferno." Wine writer and novelist Jay McInerney wrote, "If Donald Barthelme had studied philosophy and oenology he might have written like Randall Grahm. He's a provocateur, a punster, a philosopher, and jester."

In 2010, Grahm was inducted into the **Culinary Institute of America**'s Vintners Hall of Fame. In 2013, the Rhone Rangers organization recognized Grahm for "significant contributions made by an individual to the American Rhone wine movement" and created the Randall Grahm Lifetime Achievement Award in his name.

GRAPE. Any of a large number of species of fruit berries from vines in the genus *Vitis*, 90 percent of which are vinifera grapes, a species encompassing at least five thousand varieties. The word is from the Germanic, first in English print circa 1290.

The earliest colonists found America abundant with wild grapes. In fact, it has been estimated that North America has 50 percent of the world's wild grape species, including *V. labrusca*, with its characteristic "foxy" taste and aroma, and *V. rotundifolia*, the **muscadine** grape.

The settlers on the eastern coast immediately set to making **wine** from the native grapes, but found that their own European vinifera vines fared poorly. On the western coast, however, the Spanish missionaries successfully introduced vinifera varieties and made a great deal of wine from the 1780s onward. In the nineteenth century, many new varieties were imported to California, and these thrived until the phylloxera blight hit in the 1870s and devastated many vineyards, as it had in Europe before the vines were grafted onto resistant American roots.

In those same years, a grape industry had been building in New York and the West, providing table grapes, jellies, jams, preserves, juices, and raisins. The most popular table-grape varieties include the Thompson Seedless, Almeria, Calmeria, Cardinal, Emperor, Italia, Muscat of Alexandria, Ribler, and Tokay. Most grape juice, jellies, jams, and preserves are made with **Concord** grapes, a labrusca hybrid. Most raisins are made from either Thompson Seedless or Muscat of Alexandria.

Garden-variety grapes include the "mustang" or "winter" grape (*V. candicans*), the "post-oak" or "turkey grape" (*V. lincecumi*), the "little mountain" (*V. berlandieri*), the "sweet mountain" (*V. monticola*), the "frost" or "sour" grape (*V. cordifolia*), the "sweet winter" or "ashy" grape (*V. cinerea*), the "adobeland" or "dog ridge" grape (*V. champini*), the "Texas Panhandle" large grape (*V. doaniana*), the "solonis," "bush," or "gulch" grape (*V. longii*), the "sand bush," "sugar," or "rock" grape (*V. rupestris*), and the "riverside" or "riverbank" grape (*V. riparia*).

In 1869, a Methodist prohibitionist named Dr. Thomas B. Welch, of Vineland, New Jersey, developed a method of pasteurizing and bottling grape juice that would not ferment. For a long while he sold this beverage locally to church groups as Dr. Welch's Unfermented Wine, as a curative for all sorts of maladies. Then, after the onset of Prohibition, his son Charles promoted what he called "Welch's Grape Juice," with great success, and by 1923 his company was making grape jelly, which itself became an American bestselling product and the common basis for a peanut-butter-and-jelly sandwich. Today Welch Foods Inc. is owned by a cooperative of New York State grape growers and is headquartered in Concord, Massachusetts.

In 2011, the crop of fresh grapes was more than 850 million tons. Washington is the largest producer of grape juice, with about 44 percent of the total of 400,000 tons. Americans consume about eight pounds of fresh grapes per capita and four pounds of grape juice, which in 2011 totaled 1.193 million tons.

GRAPEFRUIT (*Citrus paradisi*). Also called "pomelo." A tropical tree bearing a yellow, globular fruit that grows in grapelike clusters that give it its name, first mentioned in print in 1805 in *Hortus Jamaicensis* by John Lunan, who also noted that the fruit had the flavor of a grape. The fruit was originally confused with the true pomelo (or pummelo), known taxonomically as *C. grandis*, which was also called the "shaddock," after an English captain named Shaddock brought seeds from Indonesia to Barbados in 1696. The grapefruit that Lunan described was not the pomelo, although it may have been a mutant of it.

The grapefruit was introduced to Tampa, Florida, in 1823, by a French count named Odette Philippe, but it achieved no gastronomic notice until well into the nineteenth century, when the first shipments of the fruit were made to northern markets. The first commercial plantings in Florida began in 1885, and by 1900 the grapefruit had taken on some interest as an alternative to oranges. With the introduction of the "Marsh Seedless" variety, it became all the more attractive as a breakfast fruit. In 1924, the pink-fleshed Thompson Seedless was marketed, followed five years later by a red variety named Red Blush. The Ruby Red, originally discovered as a bud mutation on a Thompson Pink tree, is one of the most popular of the pink-fleshed grapefruits and is the primary variety grown in Texas.

Today the U.S. produces between 75 percent and 90 percent of the world's crop, mostly in Florida, the rest in California, Arizona, and Texas. More than half of the crop is canned or made into fruit juice or frozen concentrate. Grapefruit is eaten fresh or, occasionally, broiled with sugar. In 2011, U.S. consumption reached 363,000 tons.

GRAPE PIE. A pie made from eastern grapes of the labrusca variety and its hybrids. This pie in some form was originally made by the Indians living along the vine-rich regions of Canandaigua Lake, in New York, and it is rarely made anywhere else in the U.S.

GRASSHOPPER PIE. A dessert pie made with green crème de menthe cordial, gelatin, and whipped cream. It derives its name from the green color of the cordial. The pie is popular in the South, where it is customarily served with a cookie crust, and probably dates from the 1950s.

GRASSHOPPER PIE

Crumble 1 ½ c. chocolate cookies very fine, combine with ¼ c. melted butter and ⅛ t. cinnamon. Press into buttered pie pan to create a thin crust. Sprinkle 1 ½ t. unflavored gelatin over ⅓ c. milk and mix. Stand bowl in double boiler and dissolve gelatin. Beat 4 egg yolks until thickened, beat in ¼ c. sugar and ¼ c. green crème de menthe, and blend completely. Stir in gelatin, chill mixture until quite thick, fold in 1 c. whipped cream, pour into pie crust, and chill overnight. Serve with a sprinkling of chocolate curls.

GRAVEYARD STEW. Slang for any soft, easily digested food, like milk toast, fed to sick people. The connotation is that such food is served to those near death. The term dates in print to 1911.

GRAVY. A sauce, usually flour-based, served with meat, poultry, and other foods. The word is from Middle English *gravé*, from Old French *grané*, which, according to the *American Heritage Dictionary*, is a misreading of *grane*, perhaps "(dish) seasoned with grains," from *grain*, "spice." The word entered English print circa 1390.

In America, "gravy" is a more common term than "sauce" or "sop" (which may indicate a basting sauce) and has been in print since the middle of the nineteenth century. By 1900 the word had metaphoric connotations of money obtained with little or no effort, so that to be on the "gravy train" was to acquire money gratuitously, often through political graft.

The FDA requires processed gravy to contain at least 25 percent meat stock or broth or at least 6 percent meat.

GRAYLING (*Thymallus arcticus*). Also "Arctic grayling." A cold-water fish found throughout the Arctic and northern U.S., where it has been widely introduced. The name of the fish, first used circa 1450, comes from its color. Although graylings are no longer marketed commercially, they were from 1860 to 1880 the mainstay of the diet of the lumberjacks in Michigan, when, according to A. J. McClane, in *The Encyclopedia of Fish Cookery* (1977), "enterprising merchants hauled them away by the wagonload to feed lumber camps, or down the Au Sable and Lake Huron in the live wells of houseboats to supply restaurants of Detroit and Chicago." Ecological and climatic changes have decreased the fish's population considerably, so that today the grayling is mainly a sport fish.

GRAZING. A synonym for snacking or eating small portions of many foods, at a market or restaurant, some of which were called "grazing restaurants." The activity may take place at various times throughout the day, instead of regular mealtimes. Grazing is also sometimes called "modular eating." The word dates in print to 1979.

GREASY SPOON. A cheap restaurant serving low-quality food. The connotation is that such a place has poor sanitation and uses a good deal of grease in the kitchen. The term dates in print to 1918.

GREEK AMERICAN FOOD. A general term for the food that Greek immigrants and their descendants eat, as well as those dishes non-Greeks in America enjoy.

The earliest Greek colonists in America arrived in 1768, when about 450 immigrants of various ethnic groups settled in New Smyrna Beach, Florida, but the colony died out. Not until 1850 was there another immigration, this time in New Orleans, in the 1850s, where they established the first Greek Orthodox church in the U.S. Larger-scale immigration of Greeks, mostly from Laconia and Arcadia, began at the end of the nineteenth century, especially after the Greek populace was devastated by Ottoman domination, with seventy thousand more arriving after World War I. From the end of World War II through 1982, about 211,000 Greeks emigrated to the U.S., mostly to the big cities, like NYC, Chicago, Detroit, Boston, and Baltimore, with a large contingent in Tarpon Springs, Florida, where many Greeks began in the sponge-diving business but transitioned to the tourism and restaurant business.

Like the Italians, Jews, and Mexicans, Greeks maintained their gastronomic traditions in America, and Greek restaurants serve menus based almost entirely on old-country staples. At home, eating with the family is extremely important, with traditional dishes celebrated. Greek cooks use a great deal of olive oil, mint, dill, oregano, garlic, olives, and feta cheese, with lamb the most favored meat and fish usually grilled or fried. Appetizers are called *mezethes*. Soups like avgolemono (lemon and egg), salads, and yogurt are usually on every table. *Taramasalata* is an appetizer made from mashed cod roe, lemon, and olive oil. *Saganaki* is a fried cheese appetizer. *Dolmathes* are rice-stuffed grape leaves. Moussaka, a layered dish of eggplant, meat, cheese, and béchamel sauce, is a standard, as are souvlaki (lamb shish kebab) and *keftedes* (meatballs). One of the specialties shared by Middle Eastern food cultures is a wide variety of layered phyllo pastry dishes for both savory and sweet items like the honeyed baklava. The "Greek salad" is made with lettuce or spinach, feta, tomatoes, onions, cucumbers, olives, oregano, and olive oil.

Greeks drink the anise-flavored ouzo as well as Greek wines, including the resinous retsina.

Greeks, with their historic coffee culture, came to dominate the coffee shop business in America and, for no traditional reason at all, the **diner** business, many of which are called by Hellenic names and decorated with Grecian motifs. Greek eateries also brought the **gyro**, a large cylinder of roasted beef or lamb sliced off to make a hero-like sandwich. More upscale Greek restaurants featured a full menu of Greek dishes, but imported

Mediterranean seafood became the focus of a new style of Greek restaurant in 1997, after Costas Spiliadis opened a branch of his Montreal restaurant, Estiatorio Milos, in New York City, featuring whole fish set on ice, from which the customer chooses his dinner.

Greek American chef Michael Psilakis took Greek food in America to a level of creative modernity rare even in Greece itself with the opening of the NYC restaurant Anthos (meaning "rebirth" or "blossoming"), and its influence lifted the whole genre of Mediterranean cuisine by applying thoroughly modern culinary techniques to transform the cooking, taste, and style of Greek food. For his efforts, Psilakis was named Best New Chef of the Year by *Esquire* magazine, *Food & Wine* magazine's Best New Chef, and *Bon Appétit's* Chef of the Year and went on to win a Michelin star—making his one of only two Greek restaurants in the world to hold that honor. In 2009 he published *How to Roast a Lamb*, which won the Gourmand World Cookbook Award that year.

There have been numerous Greek cookbooks published since the 1980s, eighteen of them by Greek American Diane Kochilas, including *The Food and Wine of Greece* (1993), *Glorious Foods of Greece* (2001), *Meze* (2003), and *Country Cooking of Greece* (2012). With her husband, Vassilis Stenos, she owns and runs Glorious Greek Kitchen, a recreational cooking school on the Greek island of Ikaria. She is also a columnist and restaurant critic for the Athens newspaper *Ta Nea*.

GREENE, GAEL (1933–). Author. As the self-titled "Insatiable Gourmet," Gael Greene brought a sensualist's appetite and journalistic style to food writing and restaurant reviewing, a career that had traditionally been dominated mostly by male bon vivants.

Born in Detroit, Greene graduated from the University. of Michigan, worked briefly for the UPI news syndicate, then moved to New York City and began writing for the *New York Post*. But it was at *New York* magazine, from 1968 to 2008, that she established her unique voice as a food writer, after editor in chief Clay Felker encouraged her to write not as a trained food authority but as a passionate eater. This led to stories like "Everything You Always Wanted to Know About Ice Cream but Were Too Fat to Ask," "The Mafia Guide to Dining Out," and "Nobody Knows the Truffles I've

Seen." She once wrote that "the two greatest discoveries of the 20th century were the Cuisinart and the clitoris."

A subsequent editor, James Brady, joked that in 1977 Greene's expense account at the magazine was "roughly that of Australia's gross national product." After being let go by *New York* in 2008 because the magazine was cutting costs, she wrote a weekly syndicated blog for *Crain's New York Business*, but this ended in 2012 for the same reason.

Greene was one of the first food critics to admit to loving **junk food** and being a **foodie**, both terms she is believed to have been the first to use.

More than once, Greene had romantic trysts with chefs whose food she reviewed, leading her to write "I Love Le Cirque, but Can I Be Trusted?" after she had a fling with the restaurant's chef. In a 2006 interview, Greene discussed the connection between food and sex, saying, "Obviously, the same senses transmit the pleasure of both food and sex: the taste buds, the mouth that registers texture, the eyes, the nose that responds to the scent of apple pie or sun on skin, the ears that hear crunch and kisses and moans. Many of the celebrated foodies I knew were as Rabelaisian in bed as at the table."

In 1981, she was co-founder, with **James Beard**, of Citymeals-on-Wheels, an organization set up to help feed NYC's homebound elderly, which is now the largest public/private partnership in the country, having raised more than $150 million since its inception and creating forty-five million meals by 2012. Her charity work earned her the Humanitarian of the Year award from the **James Beard Foundation** in 1992.

Greene has won the International Association of Culinary Professionals magazine writing award (2000) and a Silver Spoon from *Food Arts* magazine. Her books include *BITE: A New York Restaurant Strategy* (1972) and two novels, *Blue Skies, No Candy* (1976) and *Doctor Love* (1982). Greene's memoir *Insatiable: Tales from a Life of Delicious Excess* appeared in 2007. She also writes her own online newsletter, *Insatiable Critic*, and publishes a newsletter named *Fork Play*.

GREEN GODDESS. A salad dressing made from anchovies, mayonnaise, tarragon vinegar, and other seasonings. The salad of the same name was created by chef Philip Roemer, at San Francisco's Palace Hotel in the mid-1920s, at the request of actor George Arliss (1868–1946), who was appearing in town in William Archer's play *The Green Goddess* (which had opened in NYC in 1921 and was twice made into a motion picture starring Arliss, in 1923 and 1930). A recipe first appeared in the *Oakland Tribune* in 1933.

The following recipe is from the Sheraton-Palace.

GREEN GODDESS

Mince 8–10 anchovy fillets with 1 green onion. Add ¼ c. minced parsley, 2 T. minced tarragon, 3 c. mayonnaise, ¼ c. tarragon vinegar, and ½ c. cut chives. Chop romaine, escarole, and chicory and mix together dressing and greens in a bowl that has been rubbed with garlic. The salad may be topped with chicken, crab, or shrimp.

GREENINGS. Also "greens." The tops of leafy vegetables or the vegetables themselves, in print since 1940.

GREEN LAMB. Rancher term for a newborn lamb.

GREENLING (family Hexagrammidae). Also "sea trout." A fish of the Pacific that ranges from Baja California to the Aleutians, the two dominant species being the "kelp greenling" (*Hexagrammos decagrammus*) and the "painted greenling" (*Oxylebius pictus*). Greenlings are often made into steaks and broiled or grilled. The name dates in English print to 1440, from Middle English, but the American species dates in print to 1898.

GREEN MEAT. Rancher term for meat that has not been aged.

GRENADINE. A sweet syrup with a deep red color and the flavor of pomegranates, from which it takes its name (French *grenadier*). Grenadine may be bought with a small amount of alcohol (about 5 proof) or with no alcohol, and it is used both as a sweetener and coloring for cocktails. The first printed English reference was in 1896.

GRGICH, MIKE (1923–). Born Miljenko Grgić, the last of eleven children, in Desne, Croatia, Mike Grgich became one of California's most influential winemakers at many different wineries, including his own.

Grgich's family had been in the wine business for three generations, and he studied viticulture and enology at the University of Zagreb Faculty of Agriculture, but before graduating he emigrated in 1954 to West Germany on a United Nations fellowship, then to Canada, where he anglicized his name. In 1958 he moved to California, where he worked at a number of wineries, including Souverain Cellars (1958), Christian Brothers Cellars (1959), and Beaulieu Vineyard, where he met André Tchelistcheff and was appointed winemaker. In 1968, he worked for Robert Mondavi, then in 1972 went to Chateau Montelena, as winemaker and limited partner, where his 1973 **chardonnay** was selected to appear in what became a historic tasting: In 1976, wine merchant Steven Spurrier arranged a blind tasting in Paris of French and California wines, and Grgich's was ranked the best white wine overall—an event that showed that California wines were of the same quality as the best in France.

In 1977, with partner Austin Hills, of Hills Brothers Coffee, Grgich founded Grgich Hills Cellar (later Grgich Hills Estate) in Rutherford, California, whose first vintage beat out 221 international wines in the Great Chardonnay Showdown, in Chicago. Grgich also devoted his efforts toward making better **zinfandel** (a varietal that later proved to have originated as plavac mali in Croatia) made from old vines, and a highly regarded Yountville Selection cabernet sauvignon. In 1986, he was aided by his great-nephew from Zagreb, Ivo Jeramaz, who urged Grgich to make the estate wholly organic and biodynamic, using only solar energy.

In 1992, the University of California published *Miljenko Grgich: A Croatian-American Winemaker in the Napa Valley*.

In 1995, he returned to the University of Zagreb to receive his degree in viticulture and enology. A year later, in homage to his homeland, Grgich, whose motto was "You make wine with your heart," founded Grgić Vina, a three-thousand-case winery that specialized in plavac mali.

In 2004, the Society of Wine Educators gave Grgich its Grand Award and the Croatian Chamber of Commerce its highest honor, the Zlatna Kuna award. A scholarship fund was established in his name by the Culinary Institute of America, which inducted him into its Hall for Fame in 2008.

GRILLADE. A dish of veal or beef round braised with seasonings and served with grits. It is, in fact, usually referred to in Louisiana as "grillades and **grits**" and is a specialty of that region, especially for Sunday brunch. *Grillade* is a French term meaning "broiled meat," usually ham, but veal and beef are more usual in America. The term first appeared in print in circa 1656.

GRILLADE

Pound 2 lb. veal or beef that has been cut into pieces about 2–3 in. and brown in 2 T. oil, then remove. Brown 1 ⅓ T. flour in the same amount of hot oil to make a roux, add 1 T. oil, brown 1 chopped onion, ½ chopped green pepper, 1 chopped celery stalk, 2 cloves minced garlic, a pinch of thyme, 2 t. chopped parsley, and ⅛ t. cayenne pepper. Add 1 coarsely chopped tomato that has been peeled and seeded, stir in 1 ½ c. water, salt, and pepper, bring to a boil, then simmer for about 10 min. Add meat, cover, and simmer until meat is cooked through and tender. Serve with grits.

GRITS. Finely ground dried, hulled corn kernels that are prepared in a variety of ways as a side dish, pudding, soufflé, and breakfast food. Grits are a form of **hominy** and, especially when cooked, are often called "hominy grits." The word is from Old English *grytt*, for "bran," but the Old English word *greot* also meant something ground. Americans have used the word *grits* since at least the end of the eighteenth century.

Grits have been called an "institution" in the South, but they are rarely encountered in the North. Satisfying and filling, grits are a traditional southern breakfast food, but they are just as often served as a side dish. "**Grillades and grits**" is a Louisiana specialty of braised meat and buttered grits. "**Shrimp and grits**" is a Carolina dish.

Most grits consumed in the U.S. are packaged by large food companies like Quaker Oats, but in the 1990s, small artisan producers like Old Mill, of Guilford, North Carolina, Adam's Mill, in Dothan, Alabama, and Anson Mill, of Columbia, South Carolina, began producing a rougher grain of organic grits made from heirloom corn varieties, with names like John Haulk Yellow Dent and Bloody Butcher Red Dent.

~~~~
### BOILED GRITS
~~~~

Soak ½ c. grits in 1 c. cold water overnight. Add ½ t. salt and ½ c. cold water, heat, and stir until boiling, then lower heat to simmer and stir. Cover and let thicken, adding some more hot water to keep consistency from getting too thick. Serve with butter.

~~~~
### GRITS SOUFFLÉ
~~~~

Heat 1 ½ c. water with 1 c. milk, add ½ c. grits, add 4 beaten egg yolks, and stir until thickened. Cool, then add ¼ c. Parmesan cheese, Tabasco sauce, and salt and pepper to taste. Fold in 4 stiffly beaten egg whites, pour into buttered soufflé dish, and bake at 425° for about 30 min.

GROG. A mixture of hot water and rum, often with the addition of spices and citrus fruit, dating in print to 1770. The name supposedly derives from a British admiral named Edward Vernon (1684–1757), whose nickname was "Old Grog" and who tried to prevent scurvy among his crew by giving them a rum-and-water mixture, a concoction that did nothing for scurvy, but warmed the seamen's souls and gave the world "Old Grog's drink."

The U.S. Navy, following the Royal Navy's lead, included in the sailors' rations "one half pint of distilled spirits per day," and this was usually served from a "grog tub," kept locked away until seven bells, when the master's mate pumped the spirits and water into it.

On land, grog became a very popular stimulant among workers in the iron mills of the Northeast and was an ordinary drink for others. Americans usually sweetened the grog with molasses, which gave it the name "blackstripe," a variation on "blackstrap," a cold mixture of molasses and rum in New England.

"Grog blossoms" is a slang term, dating in print to 1791, for the broken blood vessels in the nose caused by too much alcohol.

~~~~
### GROG
~~~~

In a heated mug combine 1 oz. rum with 1 t. molasses and top with boiling water.

GROUPER (family Serranidae). A common name for a carnivorous member of the sea **bass** family, having more than four hundred species. Only two genera of true groupers, *Epinephelus* and *Mycteroperca*, which include about one hundred species, are of culinary interest. The name is from the Portuguese *garoupa*, its first printed mention in English being in 1671. In California, the "rockfish" (*Sebastichthys*) is also called a grouper.

The groupers of culinary importance in North America include the "black grouper" (*Mycteroperca bonaci*); **jewfish** (*Epinephelus itajara*); "Nassau grouper" (*E. striatus*); "red grouper" (*E. morio*); "spotted cabrilla" (*E. analogus*); and "yellowmouth grouper" (*M. interstitialis*), the most common market species of the South, especially popular in the Carolinas and Florida. In Hawaii, the deepwater *hāpu'u* (*E. quemus*) may also be called a sea bass.

GROWLER. A bucket or pitcher used to carry beer from a tavern to one's home. The term appeared in the last quarter of the nineteenth century. The vessels, suggests Stuart Berg Flexner, in *I Hear America Talking* (1976), were so called "perhaps because they made a growling, grating sound when they slid across the bar."

GRUB. A colloquial expression for any kind of food, often heard in the West among cowboys, ranchers, miners, and loggers. The term is quite old, however, deriving from Middle and Old English words meaning "to dig" and suggesting a person who had to dig for roots to eat. As a slang term for food, "grub" dates in print to 1659.

GRUNT. A very old colonial dessert made with berries and a dough steamed in a kettle. In New England, the term (which dates in print to 1896) is often synonymous with the more widely used term **slump**.

A grunt is also an American fish of the family Pomadasyidae, genus *Haemulon* and allied species, deriving its name from the grunting sound it makes. (It is not the same fish as the Dutch grunt, *Cyprinus gobio*.) The "pigfish" (*Orthopristis chrysopterus*) is a species of eastern American grunt, so called because of its piglike mouth. So, too, is the "sargo" (*Anisotremus davidsonii*), abundant in Pacific waters, a species of grunt. The "margate fish" (*H. album*), probably named after Margate, England, is found in Florida waters, although other species also take this name. The first mention of the grunt was in 1713, as the "Gray Grunt" in *Synopsis Piscium*.

"Grunt" is also a slang expression from the Old West meaning pork or ham, sometimes bacon. "Cluck and grunt" would be eggs and bacon, imitating the sounds made by the animals who provide them. Finally, "grunt" is a slang term from the late 1940s meaning a check or bill for a restaurant meal.

GRUNT

Cook 1 c. blackberries or blueberries in 1 c. water and ½ c. sugar for about 5 min., until soft, then place in a buttered mold. Sift 3 T. baking powder with 1 ½ c. flour and ¼ t. salt. Cut in 1 T. butter to make a coarse meal, then stir in ½ c. milk to form a dough. Place dough over berries, cover, and set in a kettle of boiling water to steam for about 1 hr. Serve with a hard or foamy sauce. Serves 6.

GUACAMOLE. A dip made from **avocados** and chile pepper, usually served with tortilla chips. Guacamole is a staple of Tex-Mex and **Mexican American** menus (the word is from Mexican Spanish, from Nahuatl *ahuacamolli*, "avocado sauce"). The first printed reference to the word in English was in 1915. The El Torito Mexican restaurant chain, founded in 1954 in Encino, California, made popular the tableside preparation of guacamole.

GUACAMOLE

Remove the pits from 2 avocados and mash the flesh with 2 t. lime juice, ½ t. salt, 2 chopped scallions, ½ chopped and seeded tomato, 1 minced garlic clove, 1 minced green chile or pickled jalapeño, and ½ t. coriander. Serve with tortilla chips or over lettuce leaves as a salad.

GUM. A variety of thickening agents and stabilizers, such as guar, locust bean, arabic, ghatti, karaya, tragacanth, and others, used in ice cream, beverages, puddings, salad dressings, candy, and other foods. See also **chewing gum**.

GUMBO. A Louisiana soup or stew, usually containing okra and any of a variety of meats, seafood, and vegetables. The dish reflects the influence of an amalgam of cultures, including those of the Indians of the region, the French and Spanish settlers, and the African slaves who gave it its name (from the Bantu *gombo*, akin to Umbundu *ochinggombo*, "okra"). The word *gumbo* first appeared in American print in 1795, and throughout the nineteenth century the dish was mentioned with affection and relish. "Gumbo" sometimes referred to okra itself (a usage cited in 1859), and by 1823 people also spoke of "gumbo file" (or "filé gumbo"), which was a gumbo thickened with filé powder (ground sassafras leaves), as used by the Choctaw Indians.

There are several forms of gumbo, incorporating meats and vegetables, or vegetables alone, or shrimp and crawfish, but usually containing okra pods. There is no such thing as an "authentic" gumbo, except that the tastes of such dishes seem to share a common heritage of heartiness. Even "gumbo z'herbes" (a corruption of the French *aux herbes*, "with herbs"), traditionally served on the meatless Maundy Thursday, is usually described as containing only vegetables, but the "Gumbo aux Herbes" recipe given in the esteemed volume *The Picayune's Creole Cook Book* (1900), contains veal brisket and ham. Gumbo z'herbes also traditionally contains seven greens, for good luck.

"Gumbo ya-ya" (dating in print to 1941) is a Creole expression meaning a group of women who are all talking at once or something that is all mixed up, a meaning that lends itself to various gumbo recipes.

The recipe that follows is from the Gumbo Shop restaurant, in New Orleans.

SEAFOOD GUMBO

Peel and devein 3 lb. shrimp and chill. Boil shrimp shells and 1 ham bone in 2 qt. water to make a stock. In a skillet sauté 1 qt. okra cut into small pieces in 1 T. oil for about 3 min. In a large kettle make a roux with ⅔ c. oil and ½ c. flour, add 2 chopped onions, 1 chopped bell pepper, 2 chopped celery stalks, 2 chopped garlic cloves, and ¼ c. chopped parsley and sauté until tender. Add one 16-oz. can stewed tomatoes, cook 15 min., then add sautéed okra, the ham-and-shrimp stock, 2 small boiled crabs broken into quarters, salt and pepper, 2 bay leaves, 2 T. Worcestershire sauce, and ½ t. cayenne pepper. Bring to a boil, then simmer for 2 hr., stirring occasionally. Add shrimp and continue cooking until done. Serve over steamed rice.

GUNDINGA. Also "gandinga." According to the *DARE*, this is a northeast Florida term for a pudding made with sausages and innards, dating in print to 1949. It is of Puerto Rican origins.

GYRO. A Greek American sandwich made from rotisserie-roasted, seasoned lamb that is sliced and served with onions in a pocket of pita bread. The word (which first appeared in print in 1970) is from the Greek *gyros*, meaning a "turn," and is pronounced "*jeer*-o." The dish is better known in America than in Greece and was possibly created in NYC, where gyros are sold at Greek lunch counters and by street vendors, although some say it originated in the Pláka neighborhood of Athens. It is not a dish found in classic Greek cookery or listed in Greek cookbooks. It also seems possible that the name "gyro" may have some association with the Italian American sandwich called the **hero**.

HAKE (genus *Urophycis*). With more than a dozen species, the hake is a member of the cod family and is found in both eastern and western waters. The name is from Middle English, dating in print to circa 1325. The two main species in the Atlantic are the "white hake" (*U. tenuis*); the "silver hake" (*M. bilinearis*), also called "whiting" and "New England hake"; and the "red hake" (*U. chuss*), also called "ling" and "squirrel hake," which, when washed ashore in winter, are picked up by people who live along the shore, who call them "frostfish." The Pacific hake (*Merluccius productus*) is abundant on the coast from Alaska to Baja California.

U.S. landings of hake in 2010 totaled 378.3 million pounds.

"Poor John" is a dried hake, first in American print in 1833.

HALIBUT. A term used for two large flounders—Hippoglossus hippoglossus, a North Atlantic fish, and H. stenolepis, a North Pacific fish—as well as other flatfish. The word is from Middle English and ultimately from the Danish helleflynder, a "holy flounder" eaten on holy days, dating in English print to circa 1430.

The Atlantic halibut is very large, reaching seven hundred pounds in weight, and is caught from Virginia to Greenland. It has firm white meat usually cut into fillets or steaks, and is sometimes smoked. The cheeks of the fish are particularly prized. The Pacific species swims in waters from central California to the Bering Sea, with most caught in Alaskan waters. The "California halibut" (*Paralichthys californicus*) is much smaller (up to sixty pounds) and generally cut into fillets. U.S. commercial landings of halibut in 2010 totaled 56.5 million pounds, for sales of $206.6 million.

HALVAH. Also "halva" and "halavah." A confection of mashed sesame seeds and honey. Halvah is of Turkish origin and was first sold in America at the turn of the century by Turkish, Syrian, and Armenian street vendors. (The word is originally Arabic, *halwā*, meaning "sweetmeat.") The candy soon became a favorite of the Jewish immigrants in NYC, and today halvah is still associated with Jewish delicatessens, even though one of the most popular commercial brands, Joyva—started in 1907 in Brooklyn by Russian immigrant Nathan Radutzky—still depicts a turbaned Turk on its wrapper. The word was first printed in 1840.

Halvah is often sold in oblong bars from which slabs may be sliced according to one's request or in smaller, cellophane-wrapped bars.

HAM. The smoked or cured dried thigh of the hind leg of the hog. The word is from Old English, dating in English print to circa 1000. See also **pork**.

Hams in America are cured in a variety of ways. Dry curing involves salting the meat heavily and allowing it to absorb the salt over time. Sweet-pickle curing involves immersing the meat in a sweet brine. Injection curing, which is today the most common practice, involves a sweet-pickle cure coupled with injections of brine into the meat's interior in order to speed the process. After curing, most hams are then smoked, the degree of smoking differing from region to region and ranging from a few hours to many weeks. The wood used for smoking is usually hickory or maple, though some large companies use sawdust or liquid-smoke flavorings. Most hams are then cooked, either partially or fully, and carry labels such as "fully cooked," "heat-and-serve," and "ready-to-eat," meaning they require no further cooking and may be eaten straight from the can or wrapper. "Sugar-cured ham" is a term that entered the language in the 1830s.

The most popular hams are sold "boneless. "Bone-in hams" are sold whole, as shanks and rumps and center slices. "Half sections" are called "butt halves" or "shank halves," while "portions" are halves with center slices removed. "Semiboneless hams" have the shank and aitch bones removed but leave the round leg bone in.

Most hams are prepared "urban style"—that is, made on a large scale—resulting in meat that is less expensive, because the processing is shorter and less complicated, and, usually, blander in taste. The first canned hams in the U.S. were made in 1926 by George A. Hormel & Co. "Country hams" (first recorded in 1949) are salt-cured; in Kentucky they are called "old ham." "Country-style" hams or "country-cured" hams (first recorded in 1944) go through more complex curings and smokings in rural sections of Virginia, Georgia, Tennessee, Kentucky, Vermont, and other states, though the term denotes a ham merely made in the "style" of a true country ham.

The famous "Smithfield ham" is coated with salt, sodium nitrate, and sugar, refrigerated for five days, salted again, refrigerated again for one day per pound of meat, washed, refrigerated for another two weeks, smoked for ten days, and then aged six to twelve months. In order to carry a Smithfield label, a ham must be prepared in this manner in the town of Smithfield, Virginia, though the hogs may come from the surrounding area. This ham is sometimes called the "Virginia ham," but that name is more generally applied to a specific method of roasting a smoked ham. In the South, ham steaks or ham slices are often served with **redeye gravy** made from the drippings.

"Scotch hams" once referred to hams produced in Scotland but now refer to uncooked, boneless, mildly cured hams sold in casings. **Prosciutto** is a dry-cured ham of Italian origin.

FDA regulations for ham labeling are as follows.

HAM. Contains no added water and at least 20.5 percent protein after removal of fat.

HAM WITH NATURAL JUICES. Contains at least 18.5 percent protein.

HAM, WATER ADDED. Contains up to 10 percent added water, but at least 17 percent protein.

HAM AND WATER PRODUCT. Contains any amount of water (amount must be listed).

HAMBURGER. Also "burger" and "beefburger." A grilled, fried, or broiled patty of ground beef, usually served on a "hamburger bun" and topped with ketchup, onions, or other condiments. Hamburgers, along with **hot dogs**, are considered the most identifiably American of food items, despite the German-sounding name. Certainly ground meat, served either raw or cooked, is not indigenous to America *or* Germany, but the name obviously derives from the German city of Hamburg, where some sort of pounded beefsteak was popular by the middle of the nineteenth century. *The Dictionary of American English* traces "Hamburg steak" to 1884, in an article in the *Boston Evening Journal*, but the term "hamburger" appeared on a menu from Delmonico's restaurant, in NYC, believed to be printed in 1834. Residents of Hamburg, New York, have long claimed that the item was created in the summer of 1885 at the Erie County Fair, when vendors Charles and Frank Menches ran out of pork with which to make sandwiches. (The brothers supposedly first wanted to name the new item after Erie County.)

By the 1890s, "Hamburg" (or "Hamburgh") steak specifically referred not to a ground-meat patty but to a piece of beef that had been pounded so as to tenderize the meat by breaking up the fibers. Both Oscar Tschirky, in *The Cook Book by "Oscar of the Waldorf"* (1896), and D. A. Mary Johnson (Bailey) Lincoln, in her *Boston Cook Book* (1896), refer to such a treatment, with fried onions enfolded by the edges of the meat, which was then broiled.

However, in one of the most widely used cookbooks of the day, *Mrs. [Sarah Tyson] Rorer's New Cook Book* (1902), Hamburg steak is described as beef put twice through a meat grinder and mixed with onion and pepper, which is close to the present concept of what a hamburger should be.

The first appearance in print of "hamburg" alone was in 1903, and according to **James Villas**, in *American Taste* (1982), a "hamburger steak" was featured at the

1904 Louisiana Purchase Exposition, in St. Louis. By 1912 the ground-meat patties we now call "hamburgers" were being served in a soft yeast bun having the approximate shape of the patty itself, and soon the suffix "-burger" was attached to all sorts of other foods, such as "lamb," "chicken," "clam," and the most famous and colloquially successful, "cheese" (known since at least 1938), which is a hamburger topped with a slice of American cheese that melts in the cooking process. *The Dictionary of American Slang* notes that the suffix came to mean "any hot sandwich served on a bun, often toasted, with many condiments....Occasionally a 'burger' is associated with a famous person, event, or historic spot," citing the "Ike-burger" as a popular item during the first presidential campaign of Dwight D. Eisenhower, in 1952. Still, the word "-steak" was used with "hamburger" well into the 1920s. In his novel *A Farewell to Arms* (1929), Ernest Hemingway makes such a reference to World War I versions of the dish.

"Hamburger stands" came along with the opening of a chain of roadside restaurants called White Castles (the first in Wichita, Kansas, in 1921), and the popularity of the hamburger grew rapidly with the increase in the number of Americans traveling the roads in automobiles. White Castle (and its imitators) steam-cooked their hamburgers, which were quite a bit smaller than other versions and were advertised with the slogan "Buy 'em by the Sack." Among White Castle's most devoted patrons, these hamburgers became known affectionately as "sliders," "belly bombs," and "gut grenades."

By the 1930s the hamburger—now loaded down with "the works," that is, onion, pickles, ketchup, and other condiments—was a standard item in inexpensive restaurants, and without its roll took on haughty pretensions at high-class restaurants, where it was called "chopped steak." Some Americans were calling hamburgers "Wimpy burgers"—inspired by an insatiable hamburger addict named J. Wellington Wimpy, from the Popeye comic strip drawn by Elzie Segar since 1919 and featured in movie cartoons after 1929. Even today "Wimpie" is a synonym for a hamburger in England, and there is a chain of Wimpy restaurants there and in the U.S. By the 1940s the hamburger was firmly entrenched as a quintessential American dish—beefy (though sometimes made with filler and usually with fat or gristle), easy to eat while on the move, and found almost everywhere in the country. In his annotations to H. L. Mencken's *The American Language* (1963), Raven I. McDavid Jr. noted that "the ultimate horror, *Trumanburger*"—after President Harry Truman (1945–53)—"coined during the dying days of the meat rationing in 1946, consisted of mashed baked beans."

A fresh leap of popularity came in the 1950s with the opening of the McDonald's chain of hamburger stands in Des Plaines, Illinois. The first McDonald's, however, was opened in San Bernardino, California, just before World War II. Modern, spanking clean, with an assembly-line efficiency and youthful atmosphere, these restaurants, immediately identifiable by their golden arches set outside the front-door parking lot, ushered in a new era of drive-in eating, featuring prepackaged hamburgers with the condiments already added. McDonald's spawned competitors like Burger King and Wendy's throughout the U.S., and although such places sold other items, a "burger and fries" (with french-fried potatoes) is still the most common order.

Today, hamburgers are just as likely to be made at home, year-round, from beef patties or ground meat purchased at a market and broiled, fried, or barbecued.

A "veggie burger" or "vegeburger" is a patty made from ground vegetables, then cooked like a hamburger and, usually, served on a bun. It dates to the 1970s and was particularly popular among vegetarians and **health food** adherents.

Americans eat three hamburgers per week per person—about thirty-eight billion annually—which accounts for 59 percent of all sandwiches consumed.

HAMILTON, DOROTHY CANN (1949–). As founder of the French Culinary Institute—now the International Culinary Center—in New York City, Dorothy Cann Hamilton has helped launch more than 22,000 careers, including those of many of America's most prominent chefs.

Born in Manhattan, Dorothy Cann graduated with a B.A. from the University of Newcastle-upon-Tyne, England, then spent three years in the Peace Corps in Thailand, where she first learned about Asian and French cuisine. Afterwards, she earned an M.B.A. from New York University.

After visiting European vocational schools, Hamilton founded the French Culinary Institute (FCI) in 1984, which developed into the International Culinary Center (ICC), with campuses in New York City, the San Francisco Bay Area, and Parma, Italy, where those students who attend the school's, spend a portion of their studies.

In addition to culinary studies, the ICC offers courses in restaurant management and sommelier training. In 2012, Hamilton announced Spanish master chef **José Andrés** would be dean of Spanish Studies, which—with author-editor **Colman Andrews**—is developing a curriculum in traditional and modern Spanish cuisine.

Hamilton conceived textbooks for the school—*The Fundamental Techniques of Classic Cuisine*, *The Fundamental Techniques of Pastry Arts*, and *The Fundamental Techniques of Classic Bread Baking*—and was creator and host of the PBS-TV series *Chef's Story* (2007) and author of the companion book. Her book on culinary careers, *Love What You Do: Building a Career in the Culinary Industry*, was published in 2009.

Hamilton has won many awards, including being inducted into the Who's Who of Food & Beverage in America by the **James Beard Foundation**; a Silver Spoon award from *Food Arts* magazine; the 2006, 2010, and 2012 IACP Award of Excellence for Vocational Cooking School; the Chevalier du Mérite Agricole from the French government; a knighting by the Association Internationale de Maîtres Conseil dans la Gastronomie Française; the Diplôme d'Honneur of the Vatel Club des Etats-Unis; and Dame de l'Année of the Académie Culinaire de France in 2006. In 2001, Hamilton also received the l'Ordre National du Mérite from the French government.

HANGTOWN FRY. A dish of oysters, eggs, and bacon, supposedly concocted during the California Gold Rush of 1849, when a recently lucky miner brought a sack of gold to the Cary House Restaurant, in Hangtown, and ordered the most expensive meal in the place. When the chef suggested oysters and eggs—very high-priced items at the time—the miner asked that bacon be added for good measure, and the dish gained local celebrity as the Hangtown fry. (Hangtown, which got its name from the notoriety of several public hangings, was by 1854 the third-largest city in California. It was renamed that year, becoming Placerville.)

HANGTOWN FRY

Dredge a dozen oysters in seasoned flour, then in a beaten egg, then in bread crumbs. Fry in butter, then add 8 beaten eggs and cook until firm. Season with salt and pepper. Turn and cook on the other side. Serve with bacon. Serves 4.

HAPPY HOUR. The period of one or two hours before dinner when people enjoy a cocktail or other beverage. It is very common that bars advertising a happy hour offer discounts on drinks in order to attract an after-work clientele. In April 1984, the Army chief of staff, General John A. Wickham Jr., ordered the end of happy hours at U.S. military base clubs and service-sponsored social events, citing such promotion of liquor as "not consistent with Army policies and programs to eliminate alcohol-related problems." Several states also banned happy hours in the 1980s.

The term "happy hour," which first saw print in 1961, refers back to the connotation (used as early as the 1920s) of "happy" as meaning slightly intoxicated.

HARASZTHY, ÁGOSTON (1812–1869). Called the "Father of American Wine," Ágoston Haraszthy de Mokcsa was responsible for bringing many European vinifera grape varieties to America and promoting winemaking during a life of legendary diversity.

Haraszthy was born into an aristocratic Hungarian family in Pest, where he studied law, was bodyguard for Emperor Ferdinand, and became chief executive officer of the state. In 1840, he emigrated to NYC and traveled widely, the basis of a book that he brought back to Hungary in 1842 and published under the title *Utazas Éjszakamerikában* ("Travels in North America"). Two years later, with $150,000, he brought his family back to live in a Wisconsin town he laid out himself, named Széptaj (later Sauk City), where Haraszthy built a mill, a bridge, and a Catholic school, ran a steamboat line, planted native American labrusca grapes, and dug a cellar (today the home of the Wollersheim Winery).

In 1849, he moved to California, where he was known by the honorific "Colonel," and began planting Mission-variety grapes in San Diego. After serving as sheriff of that city, he became a state legislator in 1852. He moved to San Francisco and planted vinifera grapes in Crystal Springs Canyon in 1853. A year later, he was appointed assayer of the new San Francisco branch of the U.S. Mint, but he was indicted (and acquitted) in 1857 for embezzlement of gold dust.

Haraszthy then moved to Sonoma County and bought property in 1856 that he called Buena Vista ("beautiful view"). He planted vinifera, including **zinfandel** (originally from Croatia), which became a major wine grape in the California wine industry. Buena Vista expanded to become the largest winery in the world at the time. His winemaker was **Charles Krug**, himself a pioneer in the industry. In 1859, Haraszthy published a "Report on Grapes and Wine of California," encouraging statewide plantings; he also wrote *Grape Culture, Wines, and Wine-making*, considered a seminal work in California wine history. In 1861, he toured Europe as the state's viticulture commissioner, bringing back more than 100,000 vine cuttings and introducing more than 350 varietals. The state refused to buy, so he sold them on his own. In 1862, he was elected president of the California State Agricultural Society, and a year later Haraszthy incorporated the Buena Vista Vinicultural Society.

In the mid-1860s, Haraszthy's vineyards were attacked by a phylloxera infestation, and in 1868 he was forced to sell Buena Vista and file for bankruptcy. With a partner, he gathered enough capital to open a sugar plantation for rum distillation in Corinto, Nicaragua, but after his wife died of yellow fever there, he returned to California. In 1869, he went back to Corinto, where, falling from a branch into a river, he was dragged underwater by an alligator and never seen again.

In 2007, Haraszthy was inducted into the **Culinary Institute of America**'s Vintners Hall of Fame.

HARD SAUCE. A dessert topping made with butter, confectioners' sugar, eggs, and vanilla, sometimes with the addition of rum or brandy, dating in print to 1880. The word "hard" seems to refer to the thickness of the sauce.

HARD SAUCE

Cream ¼ lb. butter with 1 lb. confectioners' sugar. Blend in 2 beaten eggs, then add 1 t. vanilla and, if desired, rum or brandy to taste. To make a "foamy sauce," cream the butter with ½ lb. confectioners' sugar and slowly add 1 beaten egg and ¼ c. hot water. Flavor with vanilla and, if desired, rum or brandy, and heat over hot water until thickened. Serve warm.

HARDTACK. Also "sea biscuit," "sea bread," "ship biscuit," and "pilot bread." A hard biscuit made with flour and water but no shortening or yeast. The word is a combination of "hard," for the firm consistency of the biscuit, and "tack," an English word meaning "food." The first mention of hardtack in print was in 1830, but in 1833 there was mention of "soft tack," referring to loaves of bread.

Hardtack was long part of the staple diet of English and American sailors, because of its ability to keep for lengthy periods of time at sea.

Other, more recent slang terms for hardtack include "hard Tommy," "artillery," "dog biscuits," "jawbreakers," and "pantile," the last being the name of a roofing tile. Hardtack and molasses is called "dandy funk."

HARRIS, JESSICA (1948–). Author, educator. For more than three decades, Jessica Harris has been considered the leading historian of African American food and culture. She is the author of twelve books documenting the foods and foodways of the African diaspora.

Born in New York City, Harris graduated from Bryn Mawr College, in Pennsylvania, Queens College, in New York, and Nancy-Université, in France. She has a doctorate in performance studies from New York University.

Harris joined the faculty as a professor of English at Queens College in 1969, and in 2007 she became the first scholar to hold the Ray Charles chair in African-American material culture at Dillard University, in New Orleans, where the next year she established an Institute for the Study of Culinary Cultures. In 2008, she was selected as scholar in residence for the International Association of Culinary Professionals' thirtieth annual conference. She also gave the keynote address for six years at the Caribbean Culinary Federation's annual Taste of the Caribbean.

While teaching, Harris also wrote for many newspapers and magazines, including *Essence*, where she was travel editor (1977–1980); *Travel Weekly*; *Gourmet*; *Food & Wine*; and *Saveur*. For six and a half years, she was a restaurant reviewer for *The Village Voice*, in NYC.

In her book *High on the Hog: A Culinary Journey from Africa to America* (2011), she wrote of African Americans' influence: "With the improvisational genius that gave the world jazz and salsa, as well as rumba, rap, and reggae, we have cooked our way into the hearts, minds, and stomachs of a country."

Harris has been a national board member of the American Institute of Wine and Food; a board member of the Caribbean Culinary Federation, the New York chapter of Les Dames d'Escoffier, the Ogden Museum of Southern Art, and the New Orleans Afrikan Film and Arts Festival; an advisory board member of the Southern Food and Beverage Museum and Edible Schoolyard New Orleans; and a founding member of the Southern Foodways Alliance. In 2012, Harris began a monthly online radio show called *My Welcome Table* for Heritage Food Radio.

In the corporate world, Harris has served as a consultant for Kraft Foods, Pillsbury Foods, Unilever, and Almond Resorts, and she is a member of Sterling Rice's culinary council.

Harris has been honored with scores of awards, including the Heritage Award from the Black Culinarian Alliance (1996); a lifetime achievement award from the Southern Foodways Alliance (2004); a Bert Greene Award for journalism, for her article "Open City," about a New Orleans Thanksgiving post–Hurricane Katrina (2009); and the **Lafcadio Hearn** Award from the John Folse Culinary Institute, in Louisiana, as a southern Louisiana food icon (2010). She was also inducted into the **James Beard** Foundation's Who's Who of Food & Beverage in America in 2010.

Among her books are *Sky Juice and Flying Fish Traditional Caribbean Cooking* (1991); *The Welcome Table: African-American Heritage Cooking* (1996); *A Kwanzaa Keepsake* (1998); *The Africa Cookbook* (1998); *Iron Pots and Wooden Spoons: Africa's Gifts to New World Cooking* (1999); and *Beyond Gumbo: Creole Fusion Food from the Atlantic Rim* (2003).

HARTSHORN. A source of ammonia used in baking cookies or, as "salt of hartshorn," as smelling salts. Once, the word meant literally the ground horn of a hart's (male deer's) antler, but ammonium carbonate was later used as a substitute, which also went by the name of "salt of hartshorn," dating in print to 1680. This is still available in American pharmacies and used occasionally in making cookies. "Hartshorn jelly" is a nutritive jelly once made from hartshorn and later from calves' bones.

HARVARD BEETS. A dish of beets cooked in vinegar, sugar, and cornstarch. The name probably comes from the deep crimson color of the cooked beets, similar to the color of the Harvard University football team's jerseys. The dish is more than fifty years old, but its origins are still unknown. A 1982 letter to the *New York Times* on the subject insisted that the dish was conceived at a seventeenth-century English tavern called Hardwood's, whose customers included a Russian émigré who, in 1846, opened up a restaurant in Boston under the same name. But the émigré kept pronouncing his establishment's name more like "Harvard," so the dish he brought from England became known as "Harvard beets."

"Yale beets," of even more obscure origins, are boiled beets prepared exactly as below, but with the substitution of ½ c. orange juice and 1 T. lemon juice for the vinegar.

HARVARD BEETS

Gently wash a dozen beets and simmer until tender, about 40 min. Drain and chop up or dice. Mix together ½ c. sugar, 2 t. cornstarch, and ½ c. vinegar and bring to a boil, then simmer for 5 min. Pour over the beets and reheat, then toss with 2 T. butter.

HARVARD COCKTAIL. A drink whose name derived from Harvard University, in Cambridge, Massachusetts, probably in the 1930s after Prohibition ended.

HARVARD COCKTAIL

Shake together with ice ¾ oz. brandy, ¾ oz. sweet vermouth, 1 dash sugar syrup, and 2 dashes orange bitters. Strain into chilled cocktail glass.

HARVEY HOUSE RESTAURANTS. Originally, eating houses opened at the Atchison, Topeka & Santa Fe Railway stations throughout the West by Englishman Frederick Henry Harvey, who came to the U.S. in 1850, at the age of fifteen, to work on the railroads. Appalled at the conditions under which the workers and travelers had to eat, he opened a clean dining room with good food and varied menus above the Topeka, Kansas, station in 1876, and convinced the railway to open a restaurant at each of its depot towns, every hundred miles along the route. The establishment of a Harvey House restaurant in a depot had a civilizing effect on these rudimentary towns, and the importation of well-groomed, well-mannered waitresses, called "Harvey Girls," had the further effect of bringing tens of thousands of prospective brides and mothers to the West, making the Harvey Girls part of American folklore, as exhibited in the 1946 Metro-Goldwyn-Mayer musical motion picture *The Harvey Girls*.

"Where the name Fred Harvey appears," wrote bohemian philosopher Elbert Hubbard in 1901, "the traveling public expects much. It may be on the desert of Arizona, a hundred miles from water, but if it is a Fred Harvey place, you get filtered spring water, ice, fresh fruit and every other good thing you can find at the same season in the best places in NYC or Chicago. How the miracle occurs, you do not know—it is a Fred Harvey concern—that is enough." Harvey has been credited with establishing standards of not only food and hygiene but of central planning of kitchens and distribution.

By the time of his death, in 1901, Harvey ran fifteen hotels, forty-seven lunch and dining rooms, and thirty dining cars. By 1928 there were "Harvey diners" and, by 1941, "Harvey House restaurants." By 1930 the company was serving fifteen million meals each year. But with the decline of the railroads after World War II, the Harvey restaurants declined, too, although their partnership with the Santa Fe Railroad lasted until 1968.

HARVEY WALLBANGER. A cocktail that supposedly originated at Pancho's Bar, in Manhattan Beach, California, and was named after a 1950s surfboard enthusiast named Harvey, who consoled himself after the loss of a tournament with several of these cocktails, which thereupon caused him to bang into the wall on his exit.

The name and drink are now a trademark of "21" Brands Inc., the importer of Galliano liqueur, which introduced the cocktail in 1970.

HARVEY WALLBANGER

Shake together with ice 2 oz. vodka, ½ T. Galliano, 4 oz. orange juice, and ½ t. sugar, pouring the mixture over ice cubes in a glass and floating some Galliano on top. Some prefer to omit the sugar.

HASH. A dish of chopped pork or beef combined with various chopped-up vegetables and seasonings. Hash is generally considered an odds-and-ends kind of dish and was thought of as such when the word first came into English in the mid-seventeenth century, from the Old French word *hacher*, "to chop," after which it was soon found in America to describe a form of **shepherd's pie** or another mélange of meat and vegetables. A recipe for "chicken hash" was printed in *Rector's Oyster House* in 1897.

By the middle of the nineteenth century, hash had become associated with cheap restaurants called "hash houses" or "hasheries" (an 1850 menu from the El Dorado Hotel, in Hangtown, California, lists "Low Grade Hash" for seventy-five cents and "18 Carets Hash" for a dollar), and the workers in such places were called "hash slingers." By the turn of the century, "corned beef hash" was being ordered, sometimes called "cornbeef Willie." By the 1930s the curious jargon of lunch counters and diners was referred to as "hash house Greek," owing to the large numbers of Greeks who owned such establishments.

HAUPIA. A Hawaiian dessert pudding made with coconut and sugar, dating in print to 1955. The name is from the Hawaiian. It is also a topping for cakes.

HAUPIA

In a saucepan combine 3 c. frozen coconut milk that has been thawed out (or 2 c. fresh coconut milk mixed with 1 c. water) and ½ c. sugar. Gradually add ½ c. cornstarch, blending carefully, then add 1 t. vanilla and a pinch of salt. Cook over medium heat, stirring constantly, until thickened. Pour into buttered cake pan and refrigerate overnight. Cut into squares and serve.

HAWAIIAN FOOD. The food of Hawaii is a diverse blend of all the island and mainland cuisines, especially those of Polynesia, Japan, China, and Korea, wed to Portuguese and American tastes. Hawaii was settled by Polynesians, who themselves originated in the Indomalayan region. Hawaii was inhabited as early as 300 B.C., and settlers depended largely on indigenous plants for food, although Polynesians brought other foods with them from other regions. Except for the bat (*ʻōpeʻapeʻa*), which was inedible, Hawaii had no indigenous animals, and all animals on the islands today were at one time or another brought to Hawaii. These included the **dog** (*ʻīlio*), which was bred for food, the pig (*puaʻa*), domesticated fowl (*moa*), and other animals.

Fish, which is a mainstay of the Hawaiian diet, was plentiful in the island waters, and every species was eaten, for no poisonous fish existed in the region. **Turtle** (*honu*), porpoise (*naiʻa, nuʻao*), sperm whale (*palaoa*), octopus (*heʻe*), squid (*mūheʻe*), **crayfish** (*ula*), **crabs** (*pāpaʻi*), **shrimp** (*ʻōpae*), yellowfin **tuna** (*ʻahi*), wahoo (*ono*), red **mullet** (*moana*), and pink **snapper** (*ōpakapaka*) were relished by the natives.

Wild plant foods were numerous and included the tree fern (*hāpuʻu*), the wild raspberry (*ʻakal*), lamb's-quarters (*ʻāweoweo*), and seaweed (**limu**), while other plants were introduced into the region, such as **coconut** (*niu*), breadfruit (*ʻulu*), **banana** (*maiʻa*), **taro** (*kalo*), **sweet potato** (*ʻuala, uwal*), yam (*uhi*), Polynesian arrowroot (*pia*), and sugarcane (*kō*).

Taro was easily the most important staple of the Hawaiian natives, and today it is still pounded into a thick, fermented paste called **poi**.

Although some Spanish explorers might have come upon the Hawaiian Islands, the first documented visit by a European was that of Captain James Cook in 1778, who named them the Sandwich Islands, after his patron, John Montagu, 4th Earl of Sandwich. Interest in Hawaii as a trading port brought various Europeans to chart the islands, and Protestant missionaries came in the early nineteenth century. In 1898, the islands were annexed by the U.S., and large-scale plantings and investment began, leading to coffee bean production, livestock, sugarcane, macadamia nuts, and, as a major crop, pineapple, the cultivation of which was begun by James Dole on Oahu in 1901. He later built a large plantation on Lanai, in 1922, and his Hawaiian Pineapple Co. became the world's largest. The total principal crop value in 2010 was $162,482,000.

The seafood industry grew based on Pacific species of tuna, much of it sold to Japan, as well as snapper, dolphin, and wahoo. The beef industry began when John Palmer Parker, of Newton, Massachusetts, came to Hawaii in 1809 to round up wild cattle there for King Kamehameha. Parker married the king's daughter, Kipikane, and was given a small plot of land, on which he began breeding cattle. Parker brought over Mexican cowboys, called by the Hawaiians "paniolos," to work his ranch in Waimea, which eventually grew to 225,000 acres. (*Paniolo* is a corruption of the Spanish word *espagnola*, "Spaniard," dating in print to 1875.) At one point, cattle raising was a major industry exporter, but after 1970 the Hawaiian beef industry shrank drastically.

The need for farmworkers brought influxes from Asia, including from Japan, China, and Korea, and also from Puerto Rico, each enriching the islands' food cultures, followed, after the end of the Vietnam War, by Southeast Asians, including Vietnamese, Thais, and Samoans. The first "eating house" in Honolulu was opened in 1849, by a Portuguese named Peter Fernandez, and in 1872 the Royal Hawaiian Hotel opened, which attracted a wealthy tourist clientele. As a U.S. Navy base, Hawaii developed a thriving restaurant business, especially after World War II, when the islands became a major tourist destination, further increased when Hawaii gained statehood in 1959.

In 1991, a group of twelve Hawaiian chefs (not all from a Polynesian background), including Sam Choy, Roy Tamaguchi, Alan Wong, George Mavrothalassitis, Peter Merriman, Philippe Padovani, Amy Ferguson Ota, Gary Strehl, Jean-Marie Josselin, Mark Ellman, Beverly Gannon, and Roger Dikon, created among themselves what they called "Hawaiian Regional Cuisine," at a time when New American cuisine had developed on the mainland. The association was devoted to using Pacific ingredients to create a new style of food that drew on all the cultures of the Pacific. In 1994, Janice Wald Henderson published *The New Cuisine of Hawaii*, which reflected this movement's ideas. The cuisine was also referred to as "Pacific Rim cuisine."

Hawaiian snacks are varied and include **crack seeds**, from dried fruit, *malasadas* (a Portuguese-inspired doughnut), and *manapua* (a stuffed yeast-dough bun). A traditional dessert of the state is **haupia**, a kind of gelatinous square pudding made from fresh coconut milk and cornstarch. **Spam**, first brought to the islands by military servicemen in their rations, is also one of the favorite foods of Hawaii, which, after Guam, has the highest per capita consumption in the world.

Hawaiians drink the same beverages as do mainlanders, with the addition of indigenous beverages that include an abundance of fruit juices, drinks made with coconut milk, and Kona coffee, made from plantation beans on the island of Hawaii. There is some wine produced in Hawaii, both from grapes and from pineapple.

The **luau** is a Hawaiian feast of some dimensions, and the featured dishes are often poi, **lomilomi salmon**, and **kalua pig**, cooked in a covered, smoky pit.

HAWAIIAN HAYSTACKS. A dish made of successive layers of rice, gravy, chow mein noodles, shredded cheese, tomatoes, onions, celery, coconut, mandarin oranges, and maraschino cherries, which together resembles a haystack; the coconut lends the Hawaiian association to the name. It is especially popular with young people.

"Haystack" is also a term for several multilayered dishes, desserts, and cookies, especially those made with coconut.

HAZELNUT. The nut of any of a variety of shrubs or trees of the genus *Corylus*, especially the "American hazelnut" (*C. americana*), the "beaked hazelnut" (*C. cornuta*), and the "California hazelnut" (*C. californica*). The name is from the Old English *haeselhnutu*, in English print circa 1050.

The hazelnut is sometimes called the "filbert," because it supposedly ripens on Saint Philbert's Day, August 22.

Until about 1940, most hazelnuts were imported to the U.S. from Sicily and Naples, but a native industry has since developed in Oregon, where the first trees were planted, in Scottsburg in 1858, and whose thousand growers produce 99 percent of the U.S. crop of between 20,000 and 39,000 tons annually from more than 3.6 million trees. The nuts are often ground or roasted to be used in pastries and desserts.

HEADCHEESE. A sausage made from a calf's or pig's head and molded in its own jelly and seasoned. Headcheese is

usually served as an appetizer or, according to C. Major's *Dictionary of Afro-American Slang* (1971), as a lunch meat in African American communities.

In England, headcheese is called "brawn," from a Germanic word referring to flesh or muscle. In French, however, the item goes by the name *fromage de tête de porc*, "cheese of the pig's head." Both the French and American usages refer to the crumbly, cheeselike texture of the meat, and its first appearance in American print was in 1841.

HEALTH FOOD. A vague term, first used in print in 1882, to describe food that is supposedly healthier than most of the processed, packaged, or prepared food sold in the market. Sometimes "health food" is a synonym for "**organic**" or "**natural**" foods," somewhat less vague terms that suggest foods grown or raised without any **additives**, pesticides, or special treatment whatsoever, but the term covers a wide range of food items, from fresh vegetables and fruits to herb teas and vitamin supplements.

One of the earliest promoters of a healthy diet was the Reverend Sylvester Graham (1794–1851), a Presbyterian minister who preached a vegetarian diet and developed graham flour. The American Vegetarian Society was founded NYC in 1850. Various health food movements were usually connected with a religious group like the Seventh-day Adventist Church, whose member Ellen G. White founded the *Health Reformer* magazine in 1865. In Battle Creek, Michigan, **John Harvey Kellogg** opened a vegetarian sanitarium, from which came the first popular dried cereal flakes.

After years of specious claims for various health foods and tonics by promoters and hucksters, in 1906 the Pure Food and Drug Act set rules for both sanitary conditions in food-processing plants and health claims that producers made about foods. After World War II, organic foods were popularized in large part by J. I. Rodale, publisher of *Organic Gardening and Farming* magazine, while the radio and television media proved fertile ground for health food promoters like Adelle Davis, whose 1954 book *Let's Eat Right to Keep Fit* became a bestseller, as did counterculture books of the 1960s and 1970s like **Frances Moore Lappé**'s *Diet for a Small Planet* (1971).

As "health food stores," a trend of the 1960s, 1970s, and 1980s, developed, their food counters were increasingly replaced by shelves full of vitamin and mineral supplements, literature on various diets, and expensive grain cereals.

One of the most successful health food books of the twenty-first century was Michael Pollan's *The Omnivore's Dilemma: A Natural History of Four Meals* (2007), followed by his *In Defense of Food: An Eater's Manifesto* (2009).

The Federal Trade Commission has taken no position on the term "health food," but it does monitor false claims for "healthfulness" and has proposed that "health food" be prohibited in advertising food products, because that claim may cost the consumer more than twice what a food item without the label would.

HEARN, LAFCADIO (1850–1904). Author. Though known primarily for his essays and sketches of exotic places he lived, especially Japan, Hearn wrote the first important books on the food culture of New Orleans.

Hearn was born in the Ionian Islands, of a Greek mother and an Irish father in the British Army, who sent him to France for his education. In 1869, he emigrated to the U.S. and began writing, to early good notices, while working for the *Cincinnati Enquirer*, from which he was fired after marrying a black woman. Hearn then joined the Cincinnati *Commercial* newspaper. Landing in New Orleans in 1877, he was sorely impoverished, but eventually found favor with Major William M. Robinson, editor of the *New Orleans Republican*. He then got a steady job writing pieces for *The Item* about life in New Orleans.

Though by no means well paid, Hearn saved two-thirds of his twenty-dollar-a-week salary to open an eatery with a hundred-dollar investment. It debuted on March 2, 1879, and intended to cater to the city's poor; it was first called the 5 Cent Restaurant, then he changed it with a sign reading, "The Hard Times, 160 Dryades, satisfies hunger for one nickel." By March 23 the restaurant had closed.

In 1881, Hearn wrote for the *Times-Democrat* of New Orleans, under editor Page Baker, from whom he received many recipes for his next project, a book of African American sayings in Gombo French and a Creole cookbook. Both books—*Gombo Zhèbes* and *La Cuisine Créole*—appeared in 1885. Intending the latter book for the housewife, Hearn contended, "Much domestic contentment depends upon the successful preparation of the meal; and as food rendered indigestible through ignorance in cooking often creates discord and unhappiness, it behooves the young housekeeper to learn the art of cooking."

The 268-page book was comprehensive in its recipes, from turtle soup and "gombo" to "mutton that will taste like venison" and sour orange wine. No cookbook on the subject would surpass it until the publication, in 1900, of *Mme. Begué and Her Recipes: Old Creole Cookery*. Still, Hearn's books did not sell well.

In 1887, Hearn traveled to the West Indies, then to New York, then settled for the rest of his life in Japan, where he married the daughter of a samurai warrior and became a Japanese citizen under the name Koizumi Yakumo. We went on to write twelve books about his adopted country and for nearly ten years was chairman of English Literature at the Imperial University of Tokyo.

He died of heart disease in Tokyo.

In 2009, the Library of America published a nine-hundred-page collection titled *Lafcadio Hearn: American Writings*.

HEART OF PALM. Also "palm heart." Also called "swamp cabbage." The edible shoot of the cabbage palm (*Sabal palmetto*), sometimes called the "palmetto," which flourishes in swampy land in Brazil and Florida. According to Howard Hillman, in *The Cook's Book* (1981), "Palm hearts are quite bland, but extravagant; they are sometimes made into 'millionaire's salad,' so called not only because of the price but also because the fledgling tree has to be chopped down to get at its heart." The palm heart is protected by Florida state law and is usually available only canned. It is usually boiled and eaten as a vegetable mixed in a salad.

HEAVENLY HASH. A name for several different foods, including a dessert made of vanilla wafers and whipped cream that is popular in the Midwest. Also a chocolate ice cream, also called "rocky road," made with marshmallow, nuts, and chocolate chips, and any cake or **brownie** made with similar ingredients, usually containing marshmallow and nuts.

HEAVENLY HASH

Beat 2 eggs with 1 c. confectioners' sugar and ½ c. butter, and mix with ½ pt. whipped cream and ¾ c. walnuts. Place a layer of vanilla wafer cookies in a pan and add the whipped cream.

HEINZ, HENRY JOHN (1844–1919). As founder of the food company H. J. Heinz, Henry John Heinz had a tremendous impact on the American diet through the development and sale of hundreds of processed, canned, and preserved food products.

Born in Pittsburgh, the son of German immigrants, Heinz learned gardening from his mother at their home in Sharpsburg, Pennsylvania. At the age of nine, Henry was bottling and selling horseradish sauce; by seventeen he was grossing $2,400 a year selling foods.

Heinz graduated from Duff's Business College and at the age of twenty-five began a small packing company. In 1869, he partnered with L. Clarence Noble to form Heinz, Noble & Co., moved the factory to Pittsburgh, and married Sarah Sloan Young. Six years later, a national depression bankrupted the company, but while paying back his creditors, Heinz joined with his brother John and cousin Frederick to found another packing company, called F. & J. Heinz; in 1888, Heinz bought his partners out and changed the name to the H. J. Heinz Co. At his new factory on the Allegheny River, Heinz ran his business according to Christian principles of fairness toward his employees.

Distressed by his wife's death, in 1894, from double pneumonia (he would become director of the Pittsburgh Tuberculosis Sanatorium), Heinz worked diligently to improve the reputation of the food business by supporting the passage of the 1906 Pure Food and Drug Act. He was also very active in the International Sabbath School Association, director of the Union National Bank and the Pittsburgh Chamber of Commerce, and chairman of the Flood Commission of Pittsburgh. He was also a member of the Catholic Interracial Council of Pittsburgh.

In 1896, Heinz introduced a slogan that would become famous worldwide—"57 varieties"—a number that had no actual significance, since the company produced far more products than that. In 1905, the company was incorporated.

The product most identified with Heinz is its ketchup, with a current market share of 50 percent.

Heinz passed away months shy of his company's fiftieth anniversary. By then the company had more than twenty processing plants, thirty thousand acres under cultivation, forty thousand harvesters, and international markets. Upon his death, the *New York Times* obituary read, "Pickle Manufacturer and Prominent Churchman Succumbs to Pneumonia at 74."

HEMINGWAY, ERNEST (1899–1961). Author. Considered one of the great stylists of American literature as a novelist, short story writer, and journalist, Ernest Miller Hemingway had a tremendous influence on food and travel writing and established a form of masculine gourmandism that included everything from how to cook **pancakes** in a forest to the correct way to make a **Bloody Mary**, which he said he introduced to Hong Kong in 1941.

Hemingway was born and raised in Oak Park, Illinois, where his father was a physician, his mother a musician. He began writing while in high school and afterwards worked as a reporter for the *Kansas City Star*. In 1918, he joined the Red Cross as an ambulance driver in Italy, a period he later wrote about in stories and the novel *A Farewell to Arms* (1929). After being wounded, he returned home to rest. Out of an autumn fishing trip to Michigan came the naturalistic stories he became famous for, including "Big Two-Hearted River," in which he described the details of catching and cooking trout in Crisco over an open fire.

In 1921, he married Hadley Richardson, and the couple moved to Paris, where he was a reporter for the *Toronto Star*. There Hemingway crafted his unique style of short, direct storytelling with as little embellishment as possible, which he applied to his appetite for food and drink at a time when, he wrote, "we were very poor and very happy."

While based in Paris, Hemingway wrote of his travels to other countries in articles like "Tuna Fishing in Spain," and in his novel *The Sun Also Rises* (1926) he described the meals, restaurants, and cafés of Pamplona.

Although he never thought of himself as a food writer, Hemingway often gave recipes in his fiction and nonfiction. He even sent one for fillet of lion to *Sports Illustrated*, writing, "First obtain your lion," and instructing that the tenderloins "should hang overnight in a tree out of reach of hyenas and should be wrapped in cheese-cloth to prevent them from being hit by blowflies."

His page-by-page descriptions of the meals, wines, and spirits he and his fictional characters consumed were so exquisitely crafted as to become quintessential moments readers ever after sought to evoke on the same exact spot, which he made famous, like the cafés in Pamplona, Harry's Bar, in Venice (in his 1950 novel *Across the River and Through the Trees*), the El Floridita bar, in Havana, and Sobrino de Botín, in Madrid. In fact, Hemingway put his stamp on so many restaurants in Spain that one restaurant in Madrid has a sign that reads "Ernest Hemingway Never Ate Here."

More than anywhere, Hemingway's spirit is still palpable in Paris, especially at the nexus of Boulevard Montparnasse and Boulevard Raspail, where brasseries and cafés like Le Dôme, Brasserie Lipp, La Coupole, Le Select, and La Rotonde are commemorated in Hemingway's memoir *A Moveable Feast* (1964).

In his description of a simple lunch at a Paris café, Hemingway evoked time and place linked to memory and feeling: "As I ate the oysters with their strong taste of the sea and their faint metallic taste that the cold white wine washed away, leaving only the sea taste and the succulent texture, and as I drank their cold liquid from each shell and washed it down with the crisp taste of the wine, I lost the empty feeling and began to be happy and to make plans."

Hemingway knew a great deal about liquor and wine, which he called "one of the most civilized things in the world and one of the natural things of the world that has been brought to the greatest perfection, and it offers a greater range for enjoyment and appreciation than, possibly, any other purely sensory thing which may be purchased." He had an amazing capacity for drinking without getting drunk, though he drank often, and he could describe with great exactitude drinks like the sugarless frozen **daiquiri** at the El Floridita bar in Havana: "The frappéd part of the drink was like the wake of a ship and the clear part was the way the water looked when the bow cut it when you were in shallow water over marl bottom. That was almost the exact color." He once wrote that absinthe "tastes exactly like remorse."

After physical disabilities suffered from a plane crash in Africa, bouts with alcoholism, and debilitating depression, Hemingway killed himself with a shotgun in 1961.

HERMAN. A midwestern colloquialism for a bread starter made with sugar or honey, often kept by families over decades. It is used to make sweet breads and coffee cakes. In *Real American Food* (1986), Jane and Michael Stern wrote, "Where did Herman come from and how did he get named? We have seen explanations that trace the first Herman starter back to Jesus and a certain Mount Herman in Israel; to Hermann, Missouri; and to a little girl in Richmond, Virginia, who simply wanted to give a silly name to her mommy's bubbly sourdough starter."

According to Harlene H. Watland and Dawn W. Johanson, editors of *The Herman Sourdough Herald* newsletter, published in Cambridge, Minnesota, from 1980 to 1983, the origins of Herman are obscure, but many of their subscribers told them that Herman starters had been in their families for generations.

HERMAN

In ½ c. tepid water dissolve 1 pkg. dry yeast. When foamy, blend in 2 t. honey or sugar, 2 ½ c. flour, and 2 c. water. Store in a large jar, cover with a damp cloth, and clasp with a rubber band. Let stand for 48 hr. Stir down bubbles, refrigerate, and stir each day for 5 days. Mix together 1 c. flour, 1 c. milk, and ½ c. sugar and add to the yeast mixture. On the tenth day remove 2 c. of starter for baking, add another flour-milk-sugar mixture, and keep going this way.

HERMIT. A cookie containing raisins, cloves, and nutmeg. They are made with either sugar or molasses. The first printed reference dates to 1896, and the name may refer to the brown, lumpy appearance of the cookie, like that of a hermit's robe. The cookies are sometimes called "Harwich hermits," suggesting they originated in Harwich, Massachusetts.

HERMIT COOKIES

Cream ⅓ c. butter with ⅔ c. sugar. Add 1 beaten egg, then 2 T. milk. Add ⅓ c. chopped raisins. Sift together 2 c. flour, 2 t. baking powder, ½ t. cinnamon, ¼ t. powdered cloves, ¼ t. mace, and ¼ t. nutmeg. Add to raisin mixture and blend. Mold into a ball, cover with waxed paper, and chill for 2 hr. Roll out to about ¼-in. thickness. Cut into cookie rounds and bake for 15 min. in a 325° oven.

HERO. Also "hero sandwich," "hero boy," and "Italian hero sandwich," but see below for other variations. A loaf of Italian or French bread sliced lengthwise and filled with a variety of meats and cheeses, spices, lettuce, peppers, and other items. A meatball hero would contain meatballs and tomato sauce; a veal parmigiana hero would contain a breaded, fried veal cutlet, mozzarella cheese, and tomato sauce.

In the 1930s, food writer **Clementine Paddleford** noted that the name derived from the hyperbole that one must be a hero to eat such a sandwich. In other parts of the country, however, the same item is known by other names. "Bombee" is heard in upper New York State. "Grinder" (first printed appearance in 1954), "Italian grinder," and "guinea grinder" ("guinea" is ethnic slur for an Italian) are used widely in New England and derive from the amount of chewing needed to "grind through" the sandwich. New Englanders also use "Italian sandwich," and in Boston it can be called a "spuky." Also common in New England is "submarine," dating in print to 1940, a term said to have been coined by grocer Benedetto Capaldo for the sandwich he made in Groton, Connecticut, which has long been a submarine base for the U.S. Navy. "Wedge" (for the shape of the sandwich, usually cut at an angle) is another common alternative for the hero, as is "hoagie," most often associated with Philadelphia and New Jersey. There are several versions of the hoagie's origins. One holds that it was named after the Hog Island shipyard, in Delaware County, Pennsylvania, during World War I, when many Italian immigrants worked there and ate such a sandwich at lunch. Another story credits Antoinette Iannelli, owner of Emil's restaurant in South Philadelphia, who said she created the first hoagie in 1936, for a policeman who'd had a fight with his wife and left the house without lunch. Before long she was making the sandwiches for policemen and shipyard workers at Hog Island. According to culinary historian William Woys Weaver, "hoagie" probably derives from "hokeypokey," which referred both to a cheap form of ice cream sold by street vendors and to the vendors themselves, "hokeypokey men." ("Hokeypokey" may be an American corruption of the Italian *O che poco*—"Oh, how little"—or a variant of hocus-pocus.) "Hoagie" dates in print to 1955.

In Chicago, an "Italian beef sandwich" is made with thinly sliced beef and warm, garlicky gravy served on Italian bread with sweet or hot peppers and, commonly, onions, carrots, and olives. In Northern Michigan "cudighi" is an Italian-style pork sausage, popular in Northern Michigan, where it is commonly served as a hot sandwich with onions, mozzarella and tomato sauce. The name may derive from the Italian *cotechino*, a spicy sausage.

In the South—especially in New Orleans—such an item is called a **po'boy** (since it is a relatively inexpensive item that yields a great deal of food) and made with thin slices of well-cooked meat such as shoulder roast, in a rich gravy, placed on a small, sliced French loaf with mayonnaise, tomatoes, and shredded lettuce. The most famous variant in that city is called the "peacemaker" or "*la médiatrice*," because in the nineteenth century husbands coming home late from the saloons would bring their wives a sandwich made with fried oysters and seasonings such as tartar sauce or cayenne.

A "Cuban sandwich" is a popular Cuban American version made with pork, smoked ham, Swiss cheese, mustard, mayonnaise, pickles, and other condiments, while a "medianoche" (Spanish for "midnight") is served on an egg roll. A Cuban sandwich made with turkey breast, creamed cheese, and strawberry preserves is called an "Elena Ruz," after a Cuban socialite.

Still another New Orleans version is the **muffuletta**, made on a round loaf of bread specially baked in the local bakeries and containing salami, provolone cheese, ham, minced garlic, and a mixture called "olive salad," made from chopped green olives, pimientos, chopped Greek olives, oregano, and parsley.

A "desert rider" or "camel rider," made with lunch meats and Italian dressing in a pita bread, commonly with tabbouleh served on the side and a cup of cherry limeade, is a specialty of Jacksonville, Florida, and so called because many Middle Eastern immigrants settled there after the 1890s. Credit for the sandwich has gone to Joe Assi, a baker who introduced it by that name in the early 1960s. In 1974, the *Florida Times-Union* called Assi's dish an "Arab club sandwich." Other Middle Eastern food vendors have disputed Assi's claim.

HERRING. Any of various fishes of the Clupeidae family, but especially *Clupea harengus*. The name "herring" is from Old English *haering*, dating in English print to circa 1300.

The herring is an important figure in European history; wars have been fought for control of its grounds, and there was even a Battle of the Herrings in 1429, near Rouvray, France, between the British and the French. The Hanseatic League dwindled in power with the decline of the herring in the Baltic, and by 1665 the Dutch had raided St. John's, Newfoundland, to halt the English herring industry that had developed there. In America, fishermen sought the fish both in the Atlantic and the Pacific, and in 1877 U.S. fleets paid England $5.5 million for the rights to fish the waters of the Gulf of St. Lawrence and Newfoundland. The agreement was not supported by Newfoundland sailors, who proceeded to cut the herring nets of the Americans, thus precipitating the Fortune Bay Riot.

Herring come in all sizes, but the two main species for American consumption are the "Atlantic herring" (*C. harengus*), also called "sea herring," and "Pacific herring" (*C. pallasi*), both ocean fish. The "alewife" or "spring herring" (*Alosa pseudoharengus*) of the Atlantic coast spawns in freshwater streams and is of some commercial interest when smoked or pickled. A Hawaiian species called the "makiawa" (*Etrumeus makiawa*) is about ten inches long, dating in print to 1926.

U.S. commercial landings of herring in 2010 totaled 253.4 million pounds. The following terminology for herring preparations are used in the U.S.

> **BISMARCK HERRING.** Cured with its skin on in strong vinegar, this herring, made from "schmaltz" fishes (see below), derives its name from a German process of the nineteenth century.
>
> **BLOATER.** A golden, hot-smoked, dry-salted herring whose name derives from its swollen appearance.
>
> **HARD-SALTED OR HARD-CURED HERRING.** A lean herring cured in salt alone.
>
> **KIPPER.** A brined, air-dried, cold-smoked fat herring; the name's etymology is unclear, but as

a cured fish it dates in print to 1326. The name "kippe" is also given to a male salmon; the female is called a "shedder."

> **PICKLED HERRING.** In the U.S., this term refers to a herring in vinegar and spices, but elsewhere it refers to a dry-salted herring cured in brine or blood pickle.
>
> **ROLLMOPS.** See main entry.
>
> **SCHMALTZ HERRING.** A herring containing at least 18 percent fat but usually more, filleted and traditionally served with sliced onions, boiled potatoes, and black bread. The word is from the German for "melted fat."

HIBACHI. A Japanese brazier using charcoal as its burning medium. The name is Japanese for "fire bowl." The hibachi became a faddish implement for cooking meats and fish in America in the 1960s. Ingredients are marinated in soy sauce and other seasonings and grilled over the open fire. The word *hibachi* dates in English to 1860.

HICKORY. Any of a variety of trees of the genus *Carya*, with seventeen species, thirteen of them native to North America. Of culinary importance is the native **pecan** (*C. illinoiensis*), but the word *hickory*," first in print in 1653 as "Pohickery," derives from a Virginia Indian name for a food made from crushed hickory nuts, *pawcohiccora*.

HIGDOM. A pickling brine made with green tomatoes, onions, cabbage, peppers, and other condiments and spices. According to William Woys Weaver, in *America Eats* (1989), "Higdom is one of those recipes, like Bordeaux pickle, that appears with great regularity in Victorian charitable cookbooks...[and] was once a popular feature of church suppers and picnics." The origins of the term are unknown.

HIGHBALL. A cocktail served in a tall glass, usually containing a carbonated beverage. The term's origin is obscure, though some have suggested it derives from the railroad semaphore signal having a large ball on top that means "Go ahead," which dates back to at least 1880, while the cocktail's name dates to 1898. The WPA guide *Missouri* (1941) attributes its creation to the Planter's Hotel, in St. Louis. By 1932 Americans were familiar with "highball glasses," and the Sears, Roebuck catalog for 1944 sold them by that name.

HIP FLASK. A slender container, usually made of metal, for holding liquor. Its shape made it easy to insert in one's hip pocket and keep out of sight during the days of Prohibition. The term first appeared in print in 1923.

HISTORICAL FLASK. A molded glass flask, used to hold liquor, decorated with American emblems, symbols, and nationally known figures, such as U.S. presidents. Historical flasks first appeared in the early nineteenth century and came in the colors light green, aquamarine, amber, and, occasionally, olive amber.

HOARHOUND CANDY. Also "horehound" and "slug." A candy, shaped in balls, drops, or squares made from hoarhound, an aromatic plant (*Marrubium vulgare*), and often used as a lozenge for sore throats.

HOARHOUND CANDY

To 3 c. hot water add 3 oz. hoarhound and simmer for 20 min. Strain, then add 3 ½ lb. brown sugar and cook until the syrup reaches the hard-ball stage (265° on a candy thermometer). Pour into a buttered pan and cool, then cut into small balls or squares. Makes about 5 doz.

HOBO EGG. Slang term for an egg dish made on camping trips by cutting a hole in a piece of toast, setting it on a griddle, and frying an egg inside the hole. The term dates in print to 1980.

HOBOKEN SPECIAL. Pineapple soda with a scoop of chocolate ice cream. The term refers to Hoboken, New Jersey, presumably for no other reason than that this 1920s drink was popular in that area.

HOCKEY PUCK. A slang term used to describe compact meats like hamburgers or filets mignons that have an overcooked, tough texture.

HOGFISH (*Lachnolaimus maximus* and other species). Also "hog snapper" and "Irish pompano." A fish of the wrasse family, with a hoglike snout, found from Brazil to North Carolina and particularly popular in Florida, dating in print to 1590. North Carolinians also refer to the "pigfish" (*Orthopristis chrysopterus*), so called because of its grunting sound, as "hogfish."

HOLISHKES. Used in the plural. A Jewish American dish of stuffed cabbage leaves, traditionally served at the holiday Sukkoth. The term, which dates in print to 1949, is from Yiddish.

HOME MEAL REPLACEMENT. A food-industry term for higher-quality take-home foods, usually prepared on the premises of a supermarket or gourmet food store, as opposed to frozen prepared meals.

HOMINY. Dried, hulled corn kernels cooked in a variety of ways in breads, puddings, and other preparations. It was one of the first foods European settlers readily accepted from the Native Americans, and the word, from one or another Algonquian words, such as *rocka-hominie* (parched corn) or *tackhummin* (hulled corn), was used as early as 1620. Different terms describe hominy that has been treated or ground in different ways. "Great hominy," also called "whole hominy," "pearl hominy" (from its pearly appearance), and "samp" (from the Narragansett *nasàump*, "corn mush"), is coarsely ground and prepared by scalding shelled corn in water and wood ash to separate the hulls, or "eyes." The corn is dried and then boiled until soft and porridgelike. Sometimes lye is used instead of wood ash, and this is often called "lye hominy." If the corn is ground more finely or ground twice, the result is called "hominy grits" or, as is usual in the South, just **grits**. Further grinding results in cornmeal.

"Hogs and hominy" is an old southern dish of hominy and fried pork.

HONEY. A sweet liquid produced by bees, from flower nectar. Honey, whose name comes from Old English *hunig*, was the first and most widespread sweetener used by man. About 80 percent of honey is sugar (mainly fructose and glucose). Worldwide, about a million tons of honey are produced each year, most of it gathered from various flowers rather than a single variety.

America has always had many species of honey-producing bees, and Waverley Root, in *Food* (1980), noted that the Spaniards found the Aztecs and Mayas consuming honey made by the species *Melipona beecheii*. But it was not until 1638 that honey was available to New England settlers, who had introduced the bee species *Apis mellifica* (possibly Italian or Dutch varieties), which the Indians called "English flies" or "white man's flies."

In *Food and Drink in America* (1981), Richard J. Hooker cited a chronicler's description of New York in 1670: "You shall scarce see a house, but the South side is begirt with Hives and Bees." By 1812 the honeybees had moved as far as Texas, where, in 1821, Stephen F. Austin found a bee tree that provided his party with a gallon and a half of honey. In 1852, the Reverend L. Langstroth had invented the "movable frame hive," which made the collection of honey far easier than it had been, and after the A. I. Root Company of Medina, Ohio, developed a roller press to make consistently thin wax foundation plates for the bees' hives, wide-scale honey production became feasible.

Today there are several hundred kinds of honey sold in the U.S. (one of the world's largest producers), in three basic forms: "comb," which comes straight from the hives; "chunk," which is bottled with bits of the honeycomb; and "extracted," which is usually pasteurized to prevent crystallization. Honey's flavor comes from the type of nectar used, and these may include, as James Trager lists in *The Enriched, Fortified, Concentrated, Country-Fresh, Lip Smacking, Finger-Licking, International, Unexpurgated Foodbook* (1970), "orange-blossom honey from Florida, raspberry honey and strong buckwheat honey from New Jersey, chewy dandelion honey from Colorado, tupelo honey from the swamps of Florida and Georgia, firewood honey (pale-gold and molasses-thick) from Oregon and Washington, river-willow honey from the banks of the Mississippi,...manzanita honey from California, sage-blossom honey from Arizona, gallberry honey from Georgia, hearts-ease honey from Illinois, tulip-tree honey from Maryland, linden honey from New York, anise-hyssop honey from Iowa, spearmint honey from Indiana, milky-white guajillo honey from Texas, and alergoba honey from Hawaii."

The U.S. is one of the world's largest producers of honey, with 125,000 beekeepers, the vast majority with fewer than twenty-five hives, tending nearly 2.49 million hives in all. In 2011, they produced 148 million pounds of honey, with North Dakota, California, and South Dakota the top producing states. Americans consume about 410 million pounds of honey annually, or 1.3 pounds per person. Approximately 60 percent of the supply is imported.

HONEYDEW. A variety of muskmelon, *Cucumis melo*, having a pale, yellowish skin and light green flesh. Its name comes from the fragrant, sticky sweetness of its flesh, dating in print to 1916. The honeydew is a winter melon, first brought to America around 1900 and originally called the French White Antibes.

HOOCH. Also "hootch." A cheap whiskey. The term, which became widespread during Prohibition, has been cited back to 1895. It was derived from the name of a Chinook Indian tribe, the Hoochinoo, that made a form of distilled spirits bought by U.S. soldiers who had recently occupied the new Alaskan territory and who had been forbidden liquor by their government. By 1877 the soldiers were using the term "hoochinoo," which, in the gold-rush era after 1896, was shortened to "hooch."

HOOSIER CAKE. Also "Hoosier bait." Either a kind of rough-textured gingerbread or a chocolate-and-buttermilk cake. The association with Indiana (the "Hoosier state") was explained in *Bartlett's Americanisms* (1859): "*Hoosier Cake*. A Western name for a sort of coarse gingerbread, which, say the Kentuckians, is the best bait to catch a hoosier with, the biped being fond of it."

HOPPING JOHN. Also "hoppin' John" and "happy John." A southern dish made of **cowpeas** and rice, served traditionally on New Year's Day to ensure good luck for the year. The origin of the name is obscure, but several stories abide. One ascribes the name to the custom of inviting guests to eat with the request to "hop in, John." Another suggests that it derives from an old ritual on New Year's Day in which the children in the house hopped once around the table before eating the dish. The first mention of the dish by name was in 1830.

In *Rice & Beans: The Itinerary of a Recipe* (1981), John Thorne suggests that the name is a corruption of *"pois à pigeon,"* a French term for "pigeon peas," which flourished in the Caribbean but not in the American South, resulting in an etymological dissolve into "hopping john." Whatever the origins of the name, the dish quite definitely was a staple of the African slaves who populated southern plantations, especially those of the Gullah country of South Carolina, and one will find similar dishes throughout the Caribbean. In Puerto Rico, for instance, such dishes are called *gandules*, while **red beans and rice** is a staple of Louisiana cookery, just as black beans and rice (or *moros y cristianos*, "Moors and Christians") is a famous Cuban dish. See also **limpin' suzan**.

HOPPING JOHN

Rinse 1 c. dry cowpeas in 8 c. water and boil for 2 min. Remove from heat and let stand for 1 hr., then drain, reserving 6 c. of the cooking water. In a skillet, sauté 6 pieces of bacon, 1 chopped onion, and 1 chopped clove of garlic, then stir in cowpea mixture. Season with salt and pepper and add cooking water. Stir in 1 c. rice, bring to a boil, then simmer for 1 hr., stirring occasionally. Serves 8.

HORSE (*Equus caballus*). A hoofed mammal up to five and a half feet at the shoulder and weighing up to eleven hundred pounds. The word is from Middle English, dating in print to circa 1275. Horses were brought to America by the Spanish, and wild horses, called "mustangs" in the West, are all descendants of these domesticated herds. Because of the horse's utility for both Europeans and Native Americans from the beginning of American history, it was never used for food, except in times of starvation, and Americans continue to respect the horse for its beauty, strength, and speed.

Horsemeat is a rarity in the U.S., though common in Europe and the Middle East, where American slaughterhouses send most of their available horsemeat. Although the slaughter of horses for meat was never officially banned, inspections of slaughterhouses by the USDA were, effectively precluding such a business, with the last one closing in Illinois in 2007. In 2011, Congress lifted the ban, and production was expected to resume in 2012.

HORSERADISH (*Armoracia lapathifolia* and *A. rusticana*). A perennial plant of the mustard family, cultivated for its roots, which produce a very pungent flavor and aroma when cut, shredded, or made into a paste. The word first appeared in print as of about 1590 and probably derives from its connotation of being strong as a horse.

Just when the root was brought to America is not known, although it was once called "German mustard." The three principal horseradish-raising regions in the U.S. are around Silver Lake, Wisconsin; St. Louis, Missouri; and Tule Lake, California.

HORSESHOE SANDWICH. An open-faced sandwich made with toast and ham, beef, or poultry, topped with French fried potatoes and a cheese sauce, similar to Welsh rarebit. The dish originated in 1928 at the Red Lion Room in the Leland Hotel in Springfield, Illinois, where it was created as a luncheon dish by Chef Joe Schweska, who, during Prohibition, made it with near beer. The shape of the cut of bone-in ham used in the dish gave it its name. The original contained sliced potato wedges. By the 1960s other cooks had replaced the potato wedges with French fries. A smaller version was called the "pony shoe."

The cheese sauce recipe below is said to be the original from the Leland Hotel.

In a large saucepan over medium heat melt ½ c. unsalted butter, then add ½ c. all-purpose flour and stir with a whisk to blend smoothly, about 2 mins. Whisk in 2 c. whole milk (room temperature), 1 tsp. salt, ¼ tsp. dry mustard, and ⅛ tsp. cayenne pepper. Bring to a simmer and stir until quite thick. Remove the saucepan from the heat and add 1 T. Worcestershire sauce and 8 oz. grated sharp cheddar cheese, stirring until completely melted. Whisk in ¾ c. beer (room temperature), and return the saucepan to the stove. Cook, stirring constantly, until the sauce comes to a bare simmer. Do not let it boil. Makes approximately 1 quart.

HORSE'S NECK. A strip of lemon or orange peel cut from the fruit in a continuous spiral and usually served as a garnish in a cocktail, dating in print to 1900. The term is also a euphemism for "horse's ass," but it had not been established when a drink by the name "horse's neck" first appeared. A nonalcoholic variety was made with just ginger ale and lemon peel, but there are recipes that add bourbon, blended whiskey, or gin.

HOT BALL. Also "red hot," "fireball," and "hot dollar." A cherry- or cinnamon-flavored candy with a strong, hot flavor. It is a common candy in the Mid-Atlantic states and dates in print to the 1960s.

HOT BIRD AND A COLD BOTTLE. A double entendre used to describe those late-night pleasures sought out by young men-about-town in NYC during the period just before World War I. The "hot bird" referred both to a warm dish and to a woman of easy virtue; the "cold bottle" would usually be champagne. "The Bottle and the Bird" is an 1889 poem by Eugene Field.

HOT BRICKS. A drink of whiskey, boiling water, and a ball of butter. Also called "stirrups," it was a drink of Louisville, Kentucky, now obsolete. "Hot bricks" was also a nineteenth-century term for something very dangerous.

HOT BROWN. A sandwich of turkey, bacon, or ham, with a Mornay cheese sauce, created at Louisville's Brown Hotel by chef Fred K. Schmidt in 1926 as a late-night dish after the dinner dances. The original recipe follows.

HOT BROWN

In a 2-qt. saucepan, melt 2 oz. butter and slowly whisk in 2 oz. flour until combined and a thick paste forms. Continue to cook roux for 2 min. over medium-low heat, stirring frequently. Whisk 16 oz. heavy cream into the roux and cook over medium heat until the cream begins to simmer, about 2–3 min. Remove sauce from heat and slowly whisk in ½ cup pecorino romano cheese until smooth. Add salt and pepper to taste. For each hot brown, place 1 slice of toast in an oven-safe dish and cover with 7 oz. sliced turkey. Take 2 halves of a Roma tomato and set them alongside the base of turkey and toast. Pour half of the Mornay sauce to completely cover the dish. Sprinkle with additional romano cheese. Place entire dish under a broiler until cheese begins to brown and bubble. Remove from broiler, cross two pieces of crispy bacon on top, sprinkle with paprika and parsley, and serve immediately.

HOT DOG. Also "frankfurter," "frank," "wiener," "weenie," "wienie," "dog," and "red hot." "Tube steak" is a servicemen's term for a hot dog, which is a pork or beef sausage, sometimes skinless, served on a soft yeast roll.

The hot dog is, with the **hamburger**, considered one of the quintessential American food items—inexpensive, easy and fast to cook, readily purchased all over the country, and ideal for eating while standing up. Most Americans eat hot dogs with combinations of mustard, pickle relish, and sauerkraut. Sometimes the hot dog is eaten without the roll but with beans, a dish called "franks and beans."

The hot dog is either boiled, grilled, or fried, and in Baltimore, some make split, deep-fried versions called "frizzled hot dogs." Today frankfurters are almost never made from scratch at home, though they are eaten in 95 percent of American homes, usually sold ready to eat but generally heated through by boiling or grilling in butter. Grilling hot dogs outside on a **barbecue** is a very popular method of cooking them, and American children enjoy inserting a stick through them and cooking them over an open fire.

"Corn dogs" are fried with a cornmeal batter. A "Kansas dog" is served with mustard and melted cheese, while a "Chicago-style dog" comes in a poppy seed bun with several relishes. In delicatessens, hot dogs are named for their sizes; "regulars" are about six inches in length. Small frankfurters wrapped in puff pastry are called "**pigs in a blanket**" and are served at cocktail parties or catered parties. "Lillies," short for "Lilliputians" (after the fictional city of Lilliput, in Jonathan Swift's *Gulliver's Travels*), are about half the size of one's thumb. An "Irish frank" is made from corned beef.

A great deal of etymological research has gone into the term "hot dog," dating in print to 1892, in the *Paterson Daily Press* of New Jersey, but there is still no certainty as to just who first used the words to describe the sausage, which in various forms had been a favorite of German Americans since the middle of the nineteenth century, when it was known as *Wienerwurst*, German for "Vienna sausage." German immigrants in NYC sometimes called smoked sausages *Hundewurst* ("dog sausage"), as of 1845 in print, and "Frankfort sausages" by 1877. By 1904 hot dogs were also called "wieners," and by the 1920s people were attending "wienie roasts," parties at which the attendees roasted their own hot dogs over an open fire. The "frankfurter" (from the German city of Frankfurt) is reputed to have been introduced in St. Louis in the 1880s, by a German immigrant named Antoine Feuchtwanger, who did popularize the roll the sausage came to be served in. But a crucial moment in the promotion of the item came in 1901, at NYC's Polo Grounds, where director of catering Harry Magely Stevens is reputed to have heated the roll, added the condiments, and exhorted his vendors to cry out, "Red hots! Get your red hots!" (Credit for the introduction of the heated roll in 1889 has also gone to Charles Feltman, owner of Feltman's restaurant and beer garden, in Brooklyn's Coney Island amusement park.) Stevens himself said the term "hot dog" was coined by Hearst sports cartoonist T. A. "Tad" Dorgan, who often caricatured German figures as dachshund dogs and who, by 1906, was drawing talking sausages in his newspaper's pages, playing off the suggestion that the cheap sausages sold at Coney Island and elsewhere contained dog meat. So accepted was this myth of the sausages' contents that the Coney Island Chamber of Commerce in 1913 banned the use of the term "hot dog" from all signs there.

The greatest promotion of the item was at Nathan Handwerker's frankfurter stand at Coney Island, called Nathan's Famous (today a franchise operation with many branches in the Northeast). The sausage became so associated with his concession that people began calling the item a "Coney Island" (a term reserved thirty years before for fried clams). By the 1920s "hot dog stands" were well known throughout the U.S., and the hot dog had become one of Americans' favorite foods, particularly at sporting events, county fairs, and carnivals.

Americans eat fourteen billion hot dogs per year, or thirty-seven million a day, and the average person consumes eighty hot dogs per year. Most are consumed at home, about 15 percent purchased from street vendors, and 9 percent at ballparks. Nearly 90 percent are eaten with mustard.

July has been "National Hot Dog Month" in the U.S. since 1957.

HOT FUDGE. A thick topping for ice cream sundaes, containing chocolate, butter, and sugar, kept hot so as to have a slight melting effect on the ice cream. John Schumacher, owner of an ice cream parlor in Los Angeles called C. C. Brown's, contends that hot fudge was invented by the original proprietor soon after opening the place in 1906. In the East, credit for one of the region's first hot-fudge recipes has been claimed for Sarah Dow, who bought Bailey's ice cream parlor, in Boston, in 1900 and started making the confection soon afterwards.

HOT FUDGE

In a double boiler, heat ½ c. milk, ¼ c. butter, and a dash of salt. Add 2 c. bittersweet chocolate and stir until smooth. Remove from heat, add 1 t. vanilla extract, and stir. Keep warm for serving.

HOT SAUCE. Any of a number of commercially bottled seasoning sauces made with chile peppers, salt, and perhaps vinegar. Bottled cayenne-based sauces were known in Massachusetts by 1807, and by 1849 Lea & Perrins Worcestershire Sauce was being imported from England to New York. The most famous hot sauce is **Tabasco** Pepper Sauce, made by the McIlhenny Co. as of 1859. One of the first was named after Maunsel White, a planter who brought slave-made hot sauce with him to the Gem Restaurant, in New Orleans, before the Civil War. Today hot sauces can have extravagant names, often based on the high degree of hotness or their origins, such as Hawaiian Passion, Texas Gunpowder, Cajun Power, Sweet Fire, Inner Beauty, and Jamaican Hellfire.

HOT SCOTCH. An alcoholic drink made with a little Scotch whisky and hot water, so called since at least 1882.

HOT WATER. A colonial-era term for distilled liquors.

HOUSE PIE. A pie of cooked crushed apples, including the peel and core. It dates back to the mid-eighteenth century.

HOUSKA. A sweet yeast bread shaped into a braid, often topped with poppy and caraway seeds. It is often baked as an Easter bread and is of Bohemian origins, the word deriving from the Czech, dating in print to 1952.

HUBBARD SQUASH (*Cucurbita maximus ohioensis*). Also "Ohio squash." A winter **squash** with a very thick, bumpy, green-to-orange skin and yellow-orange flesh, it was supposedly brought to America from the West Indies. The origin of the name was explained by James J. H. Gregory in a letter published in the December 1857 issue of the *Magazine of Horticulture*:

> Upwards of twenty years ago, a single specimen was brought into [Marblehead, Massachusetts], the seed from which was planted in the garden of a lady, now deceased; a specimen from this yield was given to Captain Knott Martin, of this town, who raised it for family use for a few years, when it was brought to our notice in the year 1842 or '43. We were first informed of its good qualities by Mrs. Elizabeth Hubbard, a very worthy lady, through whom we obtained seeds from Captain Martin. As the squash up to this time had no specific name to designate it from other varieties, my father termed it the "Hubbard Squash."

HUCKLEBERRY. Also "dangleberry." Any of a variety of deep blue native American berries of a tree in the genus *Gaylussacia*, often confused with the blueberry. The name may be a variation of "whortleberry." It entered English print in 1670.

Henry David Thoreau praised the huckleberry as among the finest fruits of the wild and cautioned interested eaters:

> If you would know the flavor of huckleberries, ask the cow-boy or the partridge. It is a vulgar error to suppose that you have tasted huckleberries who have never plucked them. A huckleberry never reaches Boston; they have not been known there since they grew on her three hills. The ambrosial and essential part of the fruit is lost with the bloom which is rubbed off in the market cart, and they become mere provender.

Those unfamiliar with the huckleberry and the blueberry may have difficulty telling them apart, the latter having a softer texture and many tiny seeds. On the West Coast, what is referred to as the "mountain huckleberry" is actually the "evergreen blueberry" (*Vaccinium ovatum*).

The "common huckleberry" (*G. resinosa*) is itself called the "black huckleberry," while the "bush huckleberry" (*G. dumosa*) is also called the "gopherberry." Like the blueberry, the huckleberry is most often eaten raw, in muffins, in breads, or in pies, this last called in slang "fly pie."

HUEVOS RANCHEROS. A Mexican dish of fried eggs set on tortillas and covered with a tomato-and-chile-pepper sauce. The dish has become a staple of Mexican American menus, especially as a brunch or luncheon item. The name is from the Spanish for "ranchers' eggs" and, as "eggs ranchera," dates in print to 1901.

HUEVOS RANCHEROS

Briefly sauté 2 tortillas on both sides, drain, and keep warm. Fry two eggs, place on the tortillas, and cover with a sauce of 1 tomato, 1 chopped clove of garlic, 1 chopped red or green chile pepper, 1 chopped onion, salt, and pepper blended together and cooked with 1 T. oil for about 5 min. Shredded Monterey Jack or cheddar cheese is often sprinkled on top.

HUKILAU. A Hawaiian word for a beach party. Originally the term was used as a verb meaning "to fish with a seine net" or "to pull rope." But it came to mean the party held on the beach when the fish nets were gathered in.

HUMBLE PIE. A pie made from the innards of deer (1640). There is a double pun in the name, for "umble" is a very old English word for the heart, liver, and gizzard of a deer, the kind of food eaten by servants and hunters while the lord of the house ate venison. And since certain British dialects pronounce "humble" with a silent *h*, "humble pie" would be pronounced "umble pie," connoting a dish for those of few pretensions.

The English brought the dish to America, and in Susannah Carter's *The Frugal Housewife*, published in Boston in the eighteenth century, from an English cookbook, a recipe for humble pie includes the entrails of the deer together with beef suet, apples, ½ pound sugar, salt, mace, cloves, nutmeg, and more than a pound of currants.

The dish is no longer found in America, except as a curiosity or as a version of the English steak-and-kidney pie.

HUMBOLDT DRESSING. A dressing of **crab butter**, mayonnaise, and seasonings to be mixed with a dish of crabs. One story of its origins is that it was created in the 1940s by a woman in Eureka, California, named Humboldt, who sold crabs from a stand there, but Eureka is actually located in Humboldt County. The dressing may, however, have been invented at the Casino and Boathouse in Humboldt Park, Chicago: An April 1, 1910, postcard from the casino has handwritten at the top, "Scene from the home of My Wifes Salad Dressing." On the back it reads, "Today saw my wifes Salad Dressing made. You know I have used it for years. Was delighted! everything was so clean and nice. You ought to use it, Its so good on meats, fish Etc and for making Salads so economical." It is signed, "Your grocer, Julie," giving a store in Moline, Illinois, that "carries it."

HUMBOLDT DRESSING

Mash crab butter from 2 crabs, stir in ½ c. mayonnaise, 1 t. Worcestershire sauce, 4 dashes hot pepper sauce, 1 c. diced celery, ½ c. chopped parsley, and 2 T. chopped scallion. Cover and chill for 30 min.

HUMBUG. A term used to describe a variety of very simple, plain foods of a kind often advocated by members of very strict religions. A printed reference dating to 1838 calls a peppermint-flavored molasses taffy by this name, and "humbug" is also used to describe fried-dough fritters sprinkled with cinnamon. A nineteenth-century pie made with a short crust, molasses, sugar, raisins, and bread or cracker crumbs is also called "humbug," because the simple ingredients of the pie were determined by Methodist prohibitions against luxury ingredients, especially festive Christmas puddings, which were often doused with spirits. The original meaning of "humbug" is "to deceive or delude" (the origins of the word are uncertain, but in this form it dates in print to the 1730s), so that such confections were made to "deceive" the palate of the person eating them.

HUMBUG PIE

In a bowl mix 1 c. molasses, 1 c. brown sugar, 1 c. chopped raisins, 1 c. cracker crumbs, ½ c. vinegar, 1 c. cold water, 2 T. melted butter, 1 ¼ t. mace, 1 t. allspice, 1 t. cinnamon, and 1 t. salt. Pour mixture into 10-in. pie shell, brush with cold water, and sprinkle with sugar. Bake for 10 min. at 400°, reduce heat to 350°, and bake for 35–40 min. more, until center is set.

HUMMER. A drink created at Detroit's Bayview Yacht Club using Kahlúa, light rum, and heavy cream. It was so called because after drinking two or three hummers, imbibers would start humming happily. Bartender Farouk El-Haje of Detroit's London Chop House, which made the drink its specialty, replaced the cream with vanilla ice cream.

HUMMER

In a blender mix 1 oz. Kahlúa, 1 oz. light rum, and 1 oz. heavy cream or vanilla ice cream. Serve in a stemmed old-fashioned glass.

HURRICANE. A cocktail made with passion-fruit flavoring, dark rum, and citrus juices. The drink was created in the mid-1940s, as a promotional cocktail that was featured at Pat O'Brien's French Quarter Bar, in New Orleans. There is even a tall "hurricane glass" in which the cocktail is served. O'Brien's has since given birth to similarly named cocktails, like the "cyclone," the "squall," and the "breeze."

HURRICANE

Fill a hurricane glass with crushed ice and add 2 oz. Jero's Red Passion Fruit Cocktail Mix, 2 oz. lemon juice, 4 oz. dark rum, 1 orange slice, and a maraschino cherry.

HUSH PUPPY. Also "wampus." A dumpling of cornmeal that is deep-fried, especially popular in the South. The term appeared in print for the first time in 1918. Although unconfirmed, the common assumption regarding the hush puppy's origin is that it dates from the period of scarcity following the Civil War, when cooks would toss scraps of corn batter to hungry dogs with the words "Hush, puppies!"

The *Morris Dictionary of Word and Phrase Origins* cites a southern reader's account that in the South, the aquatic amphibian called the salamander was often known as a "water dog" or "water puppy" (also "dwarf waterdog" and "mud-puppy"), because of its squat, stout legs. These were deep-fried with cornmeal dough and formed into sticks, and, so the account goes, they were called "hush puppies" because eating such lowly food was not something a southern wife would want known by her neighbors.

Hush puppies are the traditional accompaniment to fried catfish.

HUSH PUPPY

Sift together 1 ½ c. cornmeal with ½ c. flour, 2 t. baking powder, and ½ t. salt. Beat 1 egg in ¾ c. milk and add 1 grated onion. Mix with cornmeal and flour until well blended, then drop from a tablespoon into hot fat. Fry until golden brown, drain, and serve hot.

HYDRAULIC SANDWICH. Sailor's term for a liquid lunch, like beer. It was first cited as a buzzword of 1991 in *Newsweek* magazine.

HYDROLYZED VEGETABLE PROTEIN (HVP). A flavor enhancer used in processed foods like soup, frankfurters, and stews. It is vegetable protein (such as from the soybean) that has been chemically broken down to the amino acids.

I

ICE. Water that has been frozen solid. Ice has been long used as a preservative, as a substance with which to cool food and drinks, and as a solidifier for ice cream and sherbets. The word is from Old English, dating in English print to circa 1325.

Pits for ice storage have been found in the colonial ruins of Jamestown, Virginia. These were common in Europe and date back to the days of the ancient Romans.

Since the nineteenth century, Americans have enjoyed abundantly available ice in various forms. It was first used in icehouses or ice cellars, where food was kept right through spring and summer by being stored in structures filled with ice blocks cut in winter and well insulated with straw and sawdust. From 1806 until the 1850s, the ice-cutting industry was dominated by the "Ice King," Frederic Tudor, of Boston, who eventually shipped ice as far away as China. Tudor's business was increased considerably when Nathaniel Wyeth invented an ice cutter with parallel sawtooth runners, dragged through frozen ponds and lakes by horses. In 1802, Maryland farmer Thomas Moore designed an insulated "icebox" that was commonly used in homes by the 1830s. These insulated chests were supplied by "ice men," who brought hundred-pound blocks of ice on horse-drawn "ice wagons" (which first appeared on the streets of NYC around 1827). The delivery of ice was part of a standard of life enjoyed by most Americans well into the twentieth century, when electric refrigerators with freezers became affordable to everyone. The relative purity and accessibility of American water caused Charles Dickens, when visiting NYC, to remark on "gaining refreshment from the heat in the sight of the great blocks of clean ice which are carried into shops and bar rooms." In 1833, a Boston ship sailed for four months carrying 180 tons of ice to Calcutta, and as of 1830 American ice was bound for England for use on British fishing trawlers.

The first refrigeration unit to produce ice was made by Englishman Jacob Perkins, in 1834. The first U.S. patent for an ice-making machine went to Dr. John Gorrie, of the College of Physicians and Surgeons at Columbia University, in 1844; Gorrie used it as an air conditioner for fevered patients. Gorrie later moved to Apalachicola, Florida, where, in 1850, he saved the reputation of the local French consul by using the machine's ice blocks to cool down champagne for a Bastille Day celebration.

Artificial ice was soon being made by refrigeration in ice plants, the first of which was built in 1865 in New Orleans, and by 1875 restaurants had their own ice-making machines. Much later, around 1925, "dry ice" (solid carbon dioxide) became available for purchase in bulk, though it is almost never used at home.

Ice takes various forms in the preparation of food and drink. "Shaved" ice or "chipped" ice was once standard in bars and restaurants, where a bartender might actually chip his own from a large block. Ice crushers are mechanical or hand-cranked tools for making "crushed" ice, often used for blending or shaking cocktails. After World War II, ice cubes predominated in bars, as they have in home iceboxes.

"Aged ice" is commercially made ice that has been frozen very hard in order to retain the coldness. This form of ice is available in groceries or vending machines, and, through a process called "zone fractionalization," in which water is continually run over a cold surface, drives impurities to the center, resulting in a much clearer ice cube.

Many Europeans consider Americans' passion for ice a national characteristic. It is true that Americans drink few beverages aside from coffee and tea that are not served ice cold, whereas in Europe room temperature drinks are more usual.

The "ice bucket," known since at least 1919, is a bucket of ice in which one places wine bottles to chill.

ICEBOX PIE. A crusted, creamy pie that is frozen or chilled firm. It became a popular item in the 1920s, when Americans began buying refrigerators that made such confections easy to make. "Icebox cookies" were also popular.

ICEBOX PIE

Scald 2 c. milk with 1 ½ squares baking chocolate. Mix in ⅔ c. sugar, 3 T. cornstarch, ½ t. salt, and then stir in milk and cook in double boiler for 10 min. until thickened. Stir a small amount of the liquid into 3 beaten egg yolks, being careful not to curdle them, then add the rest of the liquid. Stir and cook for 2 min. Add 2 T. butter and 1 t. vanilla, then cool. Beat well and pour into pastry shell, top with whipped cream, and chill until quite firm.

ICE CREAM. A confection made from cream, sugar, and flavorings, chilled to a semisolid consistency and consumed as a dessert or snack food. The specific phrase "ice cream" dates in print to 1735, in a description by Virginian Thomas Black, who sampled some at Governor Thomas Bladen's mansion in Annapolis, Maryland.

Ice cream, in various forms, goes back at least as far as the ancient Greeks and Romans, who cooled their wine with mountain snow and ice. Marco Polo brought back from the Orient a recipe for a frozen dessert based on milk, and there is evidence that some form of ice cream was brought from Italy to France by Catherine de Médicis.

Around 1700, a pamphlet of ice cream and sherbet recipes was published, entitled *L'Art de Faire des Glaces*, and by then the major capitals of Europe were well familiar with the dish. The first known advertisement for ice cream in America appeared in 1777 in the *New York Gazette*, placed by confectioner Philip Lenzi, who said he offered ice cream "almost every day." And a 1786 advertisement in the *New York Post Boy* noted that the City Tavern served the confection every day.

Most ice cream of that period was made through an arduous method of beating cream in a pewter pot that was concurrently being shaken in a larger pot of salt and ice. But rudimentary ice cream machines were for sale by the 1780s; George Washington, who spent £51.6s.2d. (about two hundred dollars) for ice cream in the summer of 1790 alone, owned a "Cream Machine for Making Ice," and Thomas Jefferson, who wrote extensive notes on making the confection, has been credited with bringing "French-style" ice cream, made with egg yolks, to America. He also had an ice-cream-making machine he called a "*sorbetière*" at Monticello, where he followed a recipe that called for a stick of vanilla (which Jefferson brought back from Europe), two bottles of cream, and an egg-custard mixture, boiled, stirred, reheated, strained, and put in an "ice pail."

President James Madison's wife, Dolley, is said to have popularized ice cream by making it a frequent dessert at the White House between 1809 and 1817 (and she had also helped the bachelor Jefferson with his White House parties after 1801). But the dish had been making considerable headway on its own, both in recipe books of the eighteenth century and in confectioners' shops, very often run by Italians. Consequently, ice creams were often called "Italian ice creams" or "Neapolitan ice creams" throughout the nineteenth century, and the purveying of such confections became associated with Italian immigrants.

Philadelphia became renowned for its ice cream, and the phrase "Philadelphia ice cream," used since the early nineteenth century, came to mean a specifically American style of rich ice cream. One proud Philadelphia confectioner of the nineteenth century, James W. Parkinson, who also opened the grand Parkinson's Broadway Saloon, selling ice cream in NYC, wrote of the prejudicial distinctions made between American and French frozen desserts (as well as other foods): "The admission is well nigh universal that the French 'Made Us,' and that we are 'The Sheep' of French 'pastures.... So deeply rooted is this sentiment in the public mind... that when an American confectioner or caterer makes any invention in his craft, he feels that to secure its sales, and to establish its popularity, he must give it a French name." Parkinson had little reason to fear French competition, for he was enormously successful and claimed proudly to have created the first pistachio ice cream. He nevertheless played it safe occasionally by listing "biscuit glace" among his confections.

The availability of **ice** in America made ice creams and sherbets equally available to everyone, whereas they had continued to be expensive items in Europe. Even in hot climates, ice cream was offered on a year-round basis; by 1808 ice cream was available every day in New Orleans, where it was first sold at the Exchange Coffee-House. In 1835, English traveler Harriet Martineau reported "towers of ice cream" available daily in Kentucky. Two years later, Englishman Frederick Marryat marveled at seeing "common laborers" lapping up ice cream on their midday break.

A breakthrough in ice cream production came in 1846, when a small, compact ice cream freezer was invented by a New Jersey woman named Nancy Johnson, about whom little is known. The freezer was cranked by hand and made ice cream making a pastime (though still a chore) of American homelife. For some reason Johnson did not patent her invention, but in 1848 William G. Young did, calling it the "Johnson Patent Ice-Cream Freezer" (later known as the "Johnson-Young" ice cream maker).

By midcentury ice cream was no longer a novelty, and the editor of *Godey's Lady's Book* for 1850 noted that "a party without ice cream would be like breakfast without bread or a dinner without a roast." The confection had become relatively cheap to buy at the market, thanks to the efforts of Baltimore ice cream manufacturer Jacob Fussell, who began by using an oversupply of cream to make the confection and to undercut the confectioners' prices by more than half in 1851. He opened ice cream plants in several eastern cities, while his associate Perry Brazelton moved the industry into the Midwest. By the end of the century Americans were eating five million gallons of ice cream a year, prompted by technological improvements in mechanical ice cream makers.

By the 1870s Americans were going to "ice cream parlors" and stopping at "ice cream stands." They sat at "ice cream parlor chairs" made from bent wood or wire, mass-produced after 1870, and ate from "ice cream dishes" made from tinned steel. Many parlors were set in pharmacies, which had separate "ice cream fountains," which grew more and more ornate as the nineteenth century wore on. With marble counters and silver spigots, these ice cream saloons were among the most extravagant creations of the Victorian era in the U.S. The marble fountain at James Tufts's concession at the Philadelphia Centennial Exposition of 1876 was two stories tall. Elaborately decorated, molded ice cream became the fashion, and women who specialized in making such confections were called "fancy ladies."

Two claims have been made for the invention of the "ice cream soda." In 1868, Herr Harnisch, owner of the Harnisch & Baer Ice Cream Parlor, in San Antonio, Texas, introduced soda water to the city and, thereafter, placed a scoop of ice cream into the soda itself. Also, in 1874, an "ice cream soda" made with milk, a flavored syrup, and a scoop of ice cream was first featured by Robert M. Green at the Franklin Institute, in Philadelphia. By 1893 *The Critic* magazine could proclaim, "The ice cream soda is our national beverage." Americans also loved "milk sherbets" (from the Turkish *sherbet* and the Arabic *sharbah*, "drink"), which if made without milk were called "ices" or "Italian ices" (these last were scooped into pleated paper cups and licked).

Milk shakes, "malteds," and "frappés" came along toward the end of the nineteenth century, as did the "sundae" and the "ice cream cone." The origins of both items have been argued over the years. A 1913 reference to "sundae" noted that in New England the word was "now in established usage for college ices," a term that may have preceded "sundae" and hints at its origins at college soda fountains. But Paul Dickson, in his *Great American Ice Cream Book* (1972), cites two main contenders for the honor of creating the sundae, although he refers to several others with less credibility. The first claim concerns the Evanston, Illinois, civic moralists of the 1890s who inveighed against drinking soda water on the Sabbath, prompting confectioners to create a dish that would not corrupt public morals—scoops of ice cream with flavored syrups or toppings—called "Sundays." The other claim dates to the same period, when a man named George Hallauer, of Two Rivers, Wisconsin, ordered such a dish at Ed Berner's soda fountain. The ice-cream-and-syrup confection became so popular that other parlor owners had to serve it, and George Giffy, a fountain owner in Manitowoc, Wisconsin, began serving it only on Sundays as a loss leader. Although the original name was spelled with a *y* (the dish early on was called the "Soda-less Soda"), the -ae ending, contends Dickson, "came about when those who orated from the pulpit on the sinful soda went to work on the sacrilegious use of the name of the Sabbath for its stand-in." In any case, by 1900 soda-fountain suppliers were selling tulip-shaped sundae dishes.

The ice cream cone is equally as confusing when it comes to its origins. It seems clear that the cone (a wafer rolled to hold a scoop of ice cream) became popular at the 1904 Louisiana Purchase Exposition, in St. Louis, but there are several claims as to just who started hawking it there. Some authorities credit a Syrian immigrant named Ernest A. Hamwi with the invention, which was actually a Persian pastry, *zalabia*, that Hamwi rolled to hold ice cream when another concessionaire ran out of ice cream dishes. Another claim was made by David Avayou, owner of a Turkish ice cream parlor in New Jersey, who got the idea from seeing ice cream eaten in paper cones in France and who then purveyed the wafer cones at the St. Louis fair. Still another contender at that same exposition, Abe Doumar, claimed to have created the cone from waffles at a stand in the "Old City of Jerusalem" section of the fair; he called them "Cornucopias." (A 1905 version of Doumar's cone-making machine from Coney Island is still exhibited at Doumar's Cones and Barbecue Since 1904 restaurant, in Norfolk, Virginia.) There are other stories, too, but Dickson believes the most creditable claim is that of Italo Marchiony, an Italian immigrant who once offered documentary evidence that he took out a patent on an ice cream cone in December 1903 but had made them since 1896. It would appear, writes Dickson, "that the Marchiony patent wins for him the credit as American inventor of the ice cream cone, but since he never achieved any success or popularity with his invention the distinction of introducing it to a waiting America goes to a group of men—which one is not sure—at the St. Louis Fair of 1904," where there were at least fifty ice cream booths selling five thousand gallons a day. In 1910, Frederick A. Bruckmann, of Portland, Oregon, invented an ice cream cone machine that could produce three thousand cones each hour.

Today cones are made in a variety of shapes. The "sugar cone" has a cookie-like texture, while the "waffle cone" is lighter and more airy. Sometimes the latter is colored with food dyes.

A good deal of American ice cream was sold by street vendors in large cities. The slang term for their product as of the 1880s was "hokeypokey," which may derive from the Italian *O che poco* ("Oh, how little") or *occi-pocci* (mixed colors or flavors) because the "hokey-pokey man" who sold this cheap ice cream was often of Italian descent.

An advance in technique came when William A. Breyer, of Philadelphia began using brine instead of salt and ice to freeze his ice cream.

During World War I, ice cream was declared an "essential foodstuff," such that its ingredients were not rationed. By 1919 Americans were eating 230 million gallons of ice cream a year, and it became known as an "American typical food," like hamburgers and hot dogs. By 1940 the figure was up to 318 million gallons.

Americans would go to a soda fountain and order "hand-packed" ice cream (ice cream that was scooped from large containers behind the counter and packed into a cardboard container); otherwise the ice cream was packed at a factory and shipped, often with considerable lag time between its manufacture and its sale. "Ice cream cakes" were layer cakes filled with ice cream rather than icing, custard, or cream. "Banana splits," a dish of sliced bananas topped with scoops of ice cream, different syrups, ground nuts, and **maraschino** cherries, became popular after 1892, when the United Fruit Co. began bringing in large quantities of bananas to the U.S. The banana split was mentioned in the 1915 edition of *The Dispenser's Formulary, or Soda Water Guide* as the first "fancy fountain dessert [meaning a sundae with fruit] to win favor—and it still maintains its popularity."

The first chocolate-covered ice cream bar was invented by Christian K. Nelson in Onawa, Iowa, in 1920. Nelson, a Danish immigrant who became a schoolteacher and part-time candy-store owner, dubbed his confection the I-Scream Bar ("I scream, ice cream!" was recorded as a street vendor's cry in the New York *National Advertiser* as early as 1828), and in 1921 Nelson became partners with an Omaha, Nebraska, ice cream company superintendent named Russell Stover, who changed the item's name to Eskimo Pie, a reference to the Alaskan Eskimos' frigid climate. The promotion (and success) of the Eskimo Pie was largely based on its claims of purity at a time when problems of sanitation in the industry were of real public concern. The Eskimo Pie was wrapped in aluminum foil and advertised as "automatically frozen in silver-lined vessels, enrobed in chocolate, wrapped by machinery in a spotless, sun-lit factory and protected by zero temperature until served to you." By 1922 the company was selling two million ice cream bars a day. After a period of trouble defending their patent from imitators, Nelson and Stover sold their company to become a subsidiary of U.S. Foil, whose product was used to wrap the confection.

The sanitation problem was also addressed with the creation of the "ice cream sandwich" (slabs of ice cream sandwiched between cakelike cookies), which began appearing in the late 1890s on NYC street vendors' carts. In San Francisco, the **It's-It** ice cream bar was a similar item, made with oatmeal cookie layers, and in the 1980s considerable success was had with an ice cream sandwich using chocolate-chip cookies, called the Chipwich.

Credit for the first person to put ice cream on a stick goes to a Youngstown, Ohio, parlor owner named Harry Burt, who called his creation—a chocolate-covered ice cream bar set on a wooden stick—the Good Humor Ice Cream Sucker, which was sold by vendors driving clean white trucks. After Burt's death, in 1926, several Cleveland businessmen bought the company and began selling national franchises, which proliferated and made the "Good Humor Man" a summertime fixture in American communities.

In 1905, an eleven-year-old boy named Frank Epperson, of Oakland, California, accidentally left a mixing stick in a glass of juice on a windowsill while visiting friends in New Jersey. The juice froze with the stick in it, enabling the ice to be held in the hand and licked.

In 1922, Epperson introduced this new "ice lollipop" at a fireman's ball in Oakland and called it an "Epsicle," then later "Popsicle." (Frozen "juice bars" had been known in the nineteenth century, including one called the "Hokey Pokey," but none was marketed well until the Popsicle, in 1923.) In 1934, a Greek immigrant named Thomas Andreas Carvel, of Yonkers, New York, started selling a new form of soft ice cream he called "frozen custard," which was extruded from a machine he had invented. Carvel ice cream stores proliferated in the Northeast, while in the Midwest, Sherwood (Sherb) Noble opened similar soft ice cream stands under the name Dairy Queen, beginning with a store in Joliet, Illinois, in 1940.

Ice cream sales suffered during the Depression of the 1930s, but the small-town soda fountain survived, even as many of the large and opulent pharmacy fountains lost ground. Promoted as healthful and wholesome by the industry, ice cream took on a positively sanitary image in the 1940s, and Hollywood movies pictured ice cream soda fountains as oases of innocent Americana. During World War II, newspapers printed photos and stories of GIs and sailors who missed few things back home so much as ice cream. By 1946 Americans were consuming more than twenty quarts of ice cream per capita each year.

In the 1950s, Americans began buying more ice cream in groceries and in the new supermarkets than in soda fountains and drugstores, and the flavor and texture of American ice creams began to change as large companies cut costs by adding stabilizers, more air, and artificial ingredients. Supermarkets and large food corporations marketed their own brands nationally, at the same time that a number of smaller companies began, in the 1960s, to sell "premium ice creams"—many resembling the kinds made before the 1950s—with rich flavors of chocolate, vanilla, and other old favorites. Companies like Howard Johnson's, a restaurant chain begun in Wollaston, Massachusetts, in 1925, advertised "28 Flavors," and Baskin-Robbins, begun in Los Angeles in 1946, famously sold thirty-one. These premium and very high-priced ice creams and sherbets begat a new generation of small shops selling "homemade ice creams" that purported to be more "natural" and certainly more delicious than the supermarket varieties. In 1973, Steve Herrell, owner of Steve's Ice Cream, in Somerville, Massachusetts, began blending his customers' choice of cookie and/or candy morsels into his ice cream and called the item a "Mix-in," a copyrighted trademark he sold with the store in 1977. This idea, under other names (including "Smoosh-in," the new term used at Herrell's next shop, in Northampton, Massachusetts), became very popular in the 1980s in the new ice cream shops opening in towns and suburban shopping malls.

In 2011, America produced 1.53 billion gallons of frozen desserts (which includes frozen **yogurt**), with total revenues of $10 billion in 2010. Take-home ice cream sales represent the largest section of the market, generating revenues of $6.8 billion, or 67.7 percent of the market's overall value. The industry produced twenty quarts of frozen desserts per capita in 2010, which makes Americans the largest ice cream consumers in the world, followed by Australia and Sweden. The four most popular flavors of ice cream are vanilla, chocolate, strawberry, and butter pecan. The top five toppings for ice cream are **hot fudge**, chocolate syrup, **butterscotch**, **caramel**, and **strawberry**.

ICEHOUSE. While the term "icehouse" refers simply to a place where ice is made, stored, or sold, dating in print to 1830, it is also a southern term for a local beer bar (1988) or convenience store (1967). As Rebecca Trounson wrote in the *Houston Chronicle* in 1986, "Distinguished by their garage doors, their dank, dark interiors and their ice-cooled beer, *icehouses* are places men…can head straight from their jobs and not feel embarrassed to be in their uniforms or other work clothes." Icehouses usually have a few chairs out front for their regular customers. According to Texas historian Joe Frantz, icehouses first appeared along the Gulf Coast in the mid-1800s, when ice was first shipped in boats with straw insulation to Texas from New England. The ice was then stored in insulated buildings that before long began stocking beer and, later, a few other dry goods. Others, including historian Tom Denyer, contend that the icehouse as it came to be known in Texas started in San Antonio in the 1920s, and that by 1970 there were 287 in the city, though their numbers have dwindled drastically.

"Icehouse" is also the term used for a commercial ice-vending machine.

ICING. A term often interchangeable with "frosting" and preferred in America to describe the sugar-and-water mixture used to decorate and cover cakes. Icing may also contain other ingredients and flavorings, such as marshmallow, chocolate, nuts, and fruit.

"Frosting" actually precedes "icing" in print, the former appearing around 1610, the latter in 1760, with icing considered a somewhat lighter decorative glaze than frosting. But in America it became normal to use "icing" (and the verb "to ice") to describe either form of the confection.

ID. Bartender slang meaning to check a person's identification, such as a driver's license, to determine whether he or she is of legal drinking age. To "card" someone is to ask for similar identification. "Fake ID" is falsified identification used to gain access to drinking establishments.

IMITATION. Under FDA regulations, this term must be used on the labels of all products that are not as nutritious as the product that it resembles and for which it is a substitute.

IMPERIAL CRAB. Also "crab imperial." Either of two preparations of molded, baked crabmeat, one a variation of deviled crab made as a gratin, bound with cream or a cream sauce, the other bound with mayonnaise and topped with bread crumbs, first mentioned in print in 1932. In an article in *Washingtonian* magazine in 1990, Robert Shoffner traced the origins of the dish to Thompson's Sea Girt House, in Baltimore, in the late nineteenth century (a second Thompson's, opened in 1940, contends that it still serves the original recipe), where it was probably a mounded gratin containing mayonnaise, sautéed onions, bell peppers, pimientos, and egg yolks. Shoffner traces the second, later form of the dish to the Crisfield Restaurant, in Silver Spring, Maryland, where it was created by Lillian Landis in 1944. This version is traditionally served in a real or ceramic crab shell.

IMPERIAL CRAB

Combine 1 T. chopped onion with 2 T. chopped green pepper, 1 T. chopped pimiento, and 1 T. chopped celery. In 1 T. butter sauté vegetables until lightly browned. In a bowl blend together 1 beaten egg, ½ t. dry mustard, and 1 lb. lump crabmeat. Add vegetables and blend. Divide the mixture into four mounds or place in crab shells or shell-shaped ramekins. Dot the top of each portion with 1 T. mayonnaise, sprinkle with paprika, and bake for 15 min. at 350°. If preferred, the tops may also be sprinkled with bread crumbs.

IMU. A hole dug in the ground, in which heated lava stones are placed, then foods to be cooked, covered with earth or banana leaves. It is a Hawaiian cooking technique, very popular at outdoor parties called "luaus." Often a **kalua pig** is roasted this way.

INAMONA. A Hawaiian dish made from mashed roasted candlenuts and salt, used as a relish, dating in print to 1930.

INDIAN. Since colonial times, the word "Indian" has been applied to a wide variety of fruits, vegetables, grasses, foods, and drinks, most often to foods containing corn or cornmeal, as in **Indian bread** and **Indian pudding**, but also as a slur indicating something of inferior quality, as in **Indian whisky**.

INDIAN AMERICAN FOOD. A general term for the food that immigrants from India and their descendants cook and eat, as well as the food served at Indian restaurants in the U.S.

The first confirmed Indian immigrant did not arrive until 1900, and by 1944 there were only five thousand Indians in the U.S., but after 1980 their numbers grew, totaling 1.6 million immigrants by 2008. More than one in six live in the NYC area, with the largest total numbers residing in California and New Jersey.

Indian food culture is vast, varied, and ancient, influenced throughout the country's history by those who invaded or colonized its regions, including the Aryans, Greeks, and Persians, who brought the rich cuisine of the Mughals, as well as Europeans, including Portuguese, British, Dutch, and French. The British in particular influenced the food culture, while England's East India Company exported Indian spices back to Europe. The Tamil word *kari*, meaning a spiced sauce, was the basis for the English word "curry," first mentioned in print in 1598 and later an all-purpose word for a variety of spicy stews. The importation of chile peppers from America to India and their grinding with other spices into "curry powder" made that concoction requisite to curry, which was served in the British military dining rooms and hotels.

Indian food depends largely on cereals and pulses and a wide array of spices, especially ginger and garlic. Yogurt is used liberally in the cooking. Vegetarianism is a tenet of various religious beliefs common in India, being originally proposed in the ninth-century Upanishads and further evolved by Buddhism and Jainism as part of their nonviolence philosophies.

Before India gained its independence, in 1947, there was little restaurant tradition outside the European hotels, but many Punjabi cooks brought Mughal cuisine, including the tandoori oven, to England and the United States. A comprehensive 1939 NYC restaurant guide lists no Indian restaurants, but a 1949 guide lists several, including East India Curry Shop, Ceylon-India Inn, and Bengal Garden Restaurant, all located either below street level or on the second floor of a building. The guide also mentions that curries are served at any number of non-Indian restaurants, including the Pierre Grill at the Hotel Pierre. The menu at a restaurant called the Rajah included *badami* soup, *bhuja* fritters, *pappadum* wafers, *masoor dal* curried lentils, and rosewater-flavored *hulwa*.

By the 1960s a "Little India" section of New York City had grown up around Lexington Avenue south of midtown; in Astoria, Queens; and in Brooklyn, with stores selling a wide range of Indian goods and groceries, as well as small restaurants serving a Mughal-based cuisine that almost always lists mulligatawny soup, tandoori items, breads like *naan* and *paratha*, curries, and desserts like *kulfi* ice cream and *ras malai*, a milk-based pudding. Usually, a lunch buffet of many dishes is offered at a set price. Today, Indian American food reflects the lower-fat diet of the rest of the country, so that less *ghee* (a concentrated butter) is used now, in favor of vegetable oil.

It was the counterculture movement in America, largely on the West Coast, that boosted the popularity of ethnic foods from what were then called Third World countries. Cheap to prepare, with a distinct vegetarian component, Indian food appealed to the counterculture's antagonism toward the traditional American meat-and-potatoes diet. Indian food got a further boost when the Beatles went to Rishikesh, India, to study Transcendental Meditation with the Maharishi Mahesh Yogi, and although their stay was not long, the band inspired many of their fans to visit India, listen to Indian music, and eat Indian food. As a result, many new Indian restaurants opened in London and the U.S. in the 1970s, and the movement was helped by the publication of authoritative Indian cookbooks like *An Invitation to Indian Cooking* (1973), by actress Madhur Jaffrey (who later consulted for restaurants and opened her own, Dawat, in NYC), and *Classic Indian Cooking* (1980) by Julie Sahni.

One of the first upscale Indian restaurants in America was Nirvana, opened in 1971, perched in the penthouse of a building overlooking Central Park and elegantly decorated in the style of a *shamiana* tent of Indian fabrics. Others of distinction have since followed in major U.S. cities, but Americans continued to believe that Indian food, like most ethnic foods, should be inexpensive, so that while Indian restaurants proliferated, they were usually modest in decor and modestly priced. In 2009, a movie comedy entitled *Today's Special* depicted the difficulties of breaking entrenched menu traditions at an Indian restaurant in Queens, New York City.

A more modern, fusion-style Indian food was developed by both Floyd Cardoz, at New York's Tabla, in 1998 (he also wrote *One Spice, Two Spice* in 2006), and Suvir Saran, at Devi, also in NYC.

INDIAN BREAD. As described by Ramon F. Adams, in *Western Words*, "A tasty strip of fatty matter extending from the shoulder blade backward along the backbone of a buffalo. When seared in hot grease and then smoked, it became a tidbit the buffalo hunter used for bread. When eaten with lean or dried meat, it made an excellent sandwich." The term also referred to cornmeal bread.

INDIAN FRY BREAD. See **fry bread**.

INDIAN LEMONADE. Fragrant sumac (*Rhus canadensis*), first in print in 1898, as well as a beverage made from the berries.

INDIAN PUDDING. A cornmeal-pudding dessert made with milk and molasses. The name comes from the fact that corn was called "Indian corn" by the early English settlers, and anything containing corn or cornmeal might have the adjective "Indian" so applied. This dish was called *sagamite* by the Native Americans and, in the late seventeenth century, "hasty pudding" by the colonists.

"Indian pudding" was first printed in 1722 in the *New-England Courant*, where the dessert's color was described "to the great surprise of the whole family" as "Blood-red."

INDIAN PUDDING

Scald 4 c. milk in a double boiler, stir in ⅓ c. cornmeal, and cook, stirring, over boiling water for 15 min. Stir in ¼ c. dark molasses, cook for 5 min., and remove from heat. Stir in ¼ c. butter, ¾ t. salt, a pinch of ginger or cinnamon if desired, and 1 beaten egg. Pour into buttered baking dish and bake at 350° for about 2 hr., until set. Serve with whipped cream or vanilla ice cream.

INDIAN WHISKY. A very low-grade alcoholic spirit that white men sold to the Native Americans during the days of the Missouri River trade of the nineteenth century. One recipe, from E. C. Abbott and Helena Huntington Smith's *We Pointed North* (1939), suggests the horrifying nature of this brew:

> *Take one barrel of Missouri River water, and two gallons of alcohol. Then you add two ounces of strychnine to make them crazy—because strychnine is the greatest stimulant in the world—three bars of tobacco to make them sick—because an Indian wouldn't figure it was whisky unless it made him sick—five bars of soap to give it a head, and half-pound of red pepper, and then you put some sage brush and boil it until it's brown. Strain this into a barrel and you've got your Indian whisky.*

INGREDIENTS STATEMENT. A listing on a food product's label, mandated by the Federal Trade Commission, that must include the ingredients in order of predominance—that is, the most abundant ingredient must be listed first.

IN THE WEEDS. Restaurant workers' lingo for having too much work to do that night.

INVERT SUGAR. A sweetening additive blended from dextrose and fructose and used in candy, soft drinks, and other foods.

IRISH AMERICAN FOOD. A general term for the food of the Irish immigrants and their descendants, as well as those Irish foods enjoyed by all Americans.

Ireland's food culture was traditionally based largely on grains and vegetables, some seafood along the shores, and, when available, lamb and beef. Dairy products, which the Irish called *bánbhianna* ("white meats"), were a mainstay. But it was the introduction of the South American white potato by English settlers, in the sixteenth century, that came to seal the Irish peoples' fate in the nineteenth century, when an adult Irishman ate ten pounds of potatoes per day. In 1845, the potato crop upon which the Irish depended failed, causing a million to die from starvation and resulting in the emigration of a million Irish to the U.S. between 1846 and 1851, while the population of Ireland itself dwindled from 8.175 million to 6.552 million during the same period. Five million more left Ireland between 1852 and 1916, three-quarters of them settling in America.

The literature and songs of Ireland are filled with curses upon "the blighted potatoes" and laments over leaving the old country for the new, but America gave most of the immigrants a new life based on a decent diet that contained potatoes, of course, and cabbage, but with more meat, grains, and vegetables. There was not, however, as long a long cooking tradition among Irish immigrants as there was among German, Scandinavian, Italian, and Jewish immigrants. Simply fending off starvation was a higher concern for the Irish mother than providing a nutritious meal, and, in contrast to the literature and memoirs of other ethnic groups, the Irish rarely reflected on their home cooking. Irish girls were often criticized and lampooned for their lack of food-service skills as maids. Even women's-rights leader Elizabeth Cady Stanton warned that she might smash "the pate of some stupid Hibernian for burning my meat or pudding on some company occasion." Nor did those Irish who became well-to-do in America apparently expect much from their own people in the kitchen. Irish-run boardinghouses abounded in large American cities, but food was rarely a selling point. As some Irish grew affluent, like other immigrants they enjoyed lavish banquets at their benevolent and municipal organizations, though the food was not specifically Irish, with the exception of their bacon.

Before the Civil War, Irish entrepreneurs sold Irish foods, especially smoked meats, and during the immigrant period opening a grocery store was for the Irish, as for other ethnic groups, a fairly easy way to enter American enterprise, but again, those groceries did not sell Irish food as the Italians, Jews, and others sold theirs.

Like other immigrants, the Irish suffered from ethnic stereotyping, not least for their enjoyment of alcohol, and Irish women who achieved a higher social status in America led anti-alcohol programs. Among those of the lower class, alcohol was seen as the greatest scourge among families, whose husbands would squander their salaries on drink. Drinking feats and boasts became part of the characteristic spirit of the revelers. The Irish also ran liquor stores, both legally and illegally (a *shebeen* was their name for a household selling unlicensed alcohol). They also became well known as saloonkeepers, their saloons becoming gathering places for Irish Americans, and the non-Irish would refer to such an establishment as an "Irish bar." Unlike the German beer gardens or Italian street fairs, where the whole family was welcome, an Irish bar would find revelers at a feast such as St. Patrick's Day celebrating more with drink than with food. But by the first half of the twentieth century, a few dishes had come to be regarded as specifically Irish American, even if rarities in the old country.

Corned beef and cabbage has long been a staple, and Irish restaurants tend to set a menu that includes pub food like steak-and-kidney pie, Irish stew (either lamb or beef), fish and chips, and **shepherd's pie**. **Irish coffee** was introduced in 1952, in San Francisco, and made from coffee, Irish whiskey, and lightly whipped cream, which afterwards became a staple in just about every tavern and bar in America.

Irish oatmeal and Irish soda bread, with tea, are popular breakfast foods, and over the past decade an increasing number of imported Irish cheeses have become available in American supermarkets.

IRISH COFFEE. A blend of hot coffee, Irish whiskey, and whipped cream. According to a plaque outside the Buena Vista Bar, in San Francisco, "America's first Irish coffee was made here in 1952. It was inspirationally invented at Shannon Airport [Ireland] by [chef] Joe Sheridan. It was fortuitously introduced by [newspaper writer] Stan Delaplane. It was nurtured to a national institution by [the bar's owner] Jack Koeppler." Sheridan actually created the drink in 1942, at Foynes Dock, where flying boats docked in World War II. It was promoted as of 1947 at Shannon Airport as an official welcoming beverage.

In the nineteenth century, the term "Irish coffee" was slang for whiskey, entering print in 1875.

IRISH COFFEE

Rinse out an 8-oz. goblet with hot water, place 2 t. sugar in goblet, and pour in 1 ½ oz. Irish whiskey and 5 oz. strong hot coffee. Stir, then top with whipped cream.

IRISH MOSS. Also "carrageenan moss" and "sea moss." An edible moss (*Chondrus crispus*) of the North Atlantic coast, first in print in 1830, that is used as a stabilizer in milk-based puddings and to smooth out ice cream.

ISINGLASS. A transparent gelatin made from the air bladders of fishes, such as the **sturgeon**. Isinglass was used until the twentieth century to make jellies and clarify liquors. The name is from the obsolete Dutch *huizenblas*, and ultimately from German *hūsōn* (sturgeon) plus *blase* (bladder). Its first mention in English was in 1535.

ISLETA BREAD. A Pueblo Indian bread shaped like a bear's claw, hence the alternate names "bear claw" and "paw bread."

ITALIAN AMERICAN FOOD. A general term for the food of the Italian immigrants and their descendants, as well as those Italian foods enjoyed by other Americans.

While the food culture of Italy is based on more than two millennia of regional cuisines stretching from Sicily to Switzerland, Italian American food is primarily derived from the recipes of southern Italian immigrants, from regions like Campania, Calabria, and Sicily, from which, between 1880 and 1910, more than five million people came to the U.S., largely to the big cities of the Eastern Seaboard, like New York, Providence, and Boston, settling in what became known as "Little Italy" neighborhoods, where many entered the grocery business. By the 1930s there were eight pasta factories in Brooklyn and Queens, NYC, and 550 across the U.S.

By the end of the nineteenth century, 80 percent of California's immigrants were from northern Italy. Many got into the fishing business, while others became grocers and canners. One such company was Contadina, which by the mid-1930s was processing and shipping 200,000 tons of tomatoes across the U.S. In 1852, Domenico Ghirardelli founded the Ghirardelli Chocolate Co. in San Francisco, where the Italian coffeehouse proliferated.

Italian immigrants, most of them from very poor, feudal landlord systems, ate well in America, where foods once rare to their families, including macaroni, meat, and even bread, were now quite affordable. They began adapting the ingredients they found in America to their own tastes, so that tomato sauce—called "red sauce"—became an identifying characteristic of Italian American food, and many dishes, like meatballs and spaghetti, lasagna, chicken parmigiana, and pizza, utilized the tomato in their recipes. "Sunday gravy" referred to a meat sauce, traditionally served for the Sunday family meal.

The first pizzeria in America, G. Lombardi's, opened in 1905 in New York City. Pizza grew greatly in popularity after World War II, so that today 41 percent of Americans eat pizza at least once a week, with per capita consumption of twenty-three pounds. Pizzeria chains like Pizza Hut, Godfather's, Little Caesars, and Domino's, all begun in the Midwest, have became global brands. Groceries grew into small eateries and evolved into restaurants soon after the turn of the century, so that in 1906 the Theater District restaurant Barbetta was considered one of the finest in New York City, drawing musicians and opera and theater people as clientele. Most Italian restaurants, however, were far more modest, located largely in Little Italy neighborhoods like San Francisco's North Beach and Boston's South End. The menus were based largely on southern Italian home cooking, and pasta dishes appeared in myriad forms, from linguine with clam sauce and baked ziti to steak pizzaiola and Italian cheesecake. Many dishes were simply named after the immigrants' Old World towns, like **chicken Vesuvius**, seafood Golfo di Napoli, or eggplant Sorrentino, while others commemorated Italian American celebrities, like **chicken Tetrazzini** and **spaghetti alla Caruso**, after opera stars Luisa Tetrazzini and Enrico Caruso.

Italian American sandwiches, on loaves cut in half lengthwise and filled with everything from salamis and cheese to pickled vegetables and tomato sauce, are called "**heroes**" or, owing to their shape, "submarines." In 1965, an Italian American named Fred DeLuca, of Bridgeport, Connecticut, opened a submarine sandwich shop that he parlayed into a national chain named

Subway, which now has more than thirty thousand stores in more than ninety countries.

Italian Americans also ran steakhouses that served Italian food, especially in New York City, where restaurants like Palm, Christ Cella, and Pietro's set the mold for what came to be called either the "Italian steakhouse" or the "New York–style steakhouse," with standard menus based on shrimp cocktail, pasta, steaks and chops, lobsters, and cheesecake.

By the 1950s Italian Americans catered to non-Italians who expected the food to be cheap and generous in portion, usually made with inexpensive ingredients at a time when few imported ingredients were available. Immigrant Ettore "Hector" Boiardi had great success with a canned spaghetti dinner he called Chef Boy-Ar-Dee, which still sells millions of cans today. Similarly, Rice-a-Roni is a boxed packaged meal of seasoned rice, created by Vincent DeDomenico in 1958 in San Francisco.

Americans who visited Italy in the 1960s found the food there a great deal different from what was being served in Italian restaurants in the U.S., and the same was true for the wines. Few Americans had ever tasted anything but a cheap "pizza wine" like Chianti or "dago red," from American zinfandel. By the 1970s, however, imports of Italian food products, including better wines, flowed into the U.S., for the first time making it possible for Italian chefs, many of them immigrants who had worked on the elegant Italian cruise ships, to re-create food closer to regional Italian food. There was a conscious movement away from the ubiquitous "red sauce" in the 1970s as restaurants began serving cream and cheese sauces in pastas dishes like **fettuccine Alfredo** and **pasta primavera**.

Just as high-quality Italian wines became available in the U.S., young Italian American winemakers in California built on what their immigrant fathers and mothers had established before Prohibition. Names like Sbarboro, Rossi, Foppiano, Gallo, Martinelli, Bargetto, Delicato, Pedroncelli, Parducci, and Pellegrini dominated the California wine industry, and their children, like Peter and Robert Mondavi, improved the wines to a standard American wines had never before reached. By the end of the 1970s, wines like Mondavi, Pedroncelli, Louis Martini, and others were ranked among the best in the world.

So, too, Italian restaurants took on further refinement in the 1980s, owing to increased interest in "authentic" ethnic cuisine. This shift was largely spearheaded by young Italian American chefs who had studied in Italy and returned to pay homage to those who taught them. In the 1990s, Seattle-born **Mario Batali** opened Babbo to great acclaim, as a true representative of Italian cuisine. At the same time, the popular "Mediterranean diet" promoted a lifestyle close to that of Italians and other Mediterranean peoples, whose lower incidence of heart disease and longer life expectancy seemed to derive from their smaller portions of meat and fat and a greater reliance on seafood, grains, pasta, and olive oil. These data fit in perfectly with American baby boomers' concerns about good health, thereby boosting Italian food as a beneficial way to eat and drink.

Italian cookbooks proliferated in the 1990s and 2000s, so that when magazines like *Gourmet, Bon Appétit, Food & Wine,* and *Saveur* put Italian food on their covers, they sold far more copies than usual. An American edition of the Italian magazine *La Cucina Italiana* debuted in the U.S. in 1999.

Ironically, the once humble pizza became, by the middle of the first decade of the twenty-first century, even more popular after being researched and modified by young American chefs who competed in contests as to who made the best pizza in America.

ITALIAN BEEF. A **hero** sandwich made of sliced beef in a spicy gravy, commonly with pepper, garlic, and oregano, sweet and hot peppers, and sometimes provolone cheese. Italian beef is a specialty of the Midwest, especially Chicago. There is no such dish in Italy. According to Cecil Adams, in his Straight Dope Chicago column in 2009, the item was first sold to local factory workers by Al Ferreri, his sister and brother-in-law, Frances and Chris Pacelli Sr., in 1938. They opened a beef stand called Al's in 1940, and the eateries were imitated by many others around the Chicago area.

IT'S-IT. An ice cream sandwich made from vanilla ice cream between two oatmeal cookies, covered with chocolate and frozen hard. This confection originated in 1928 at the Playland-at-the-Beach amusement park in San Francisco, and credit for its creation is given to park owner George Whitney. San Franciscans still remember a "trip to the It stand," and today the confection is available in food stores and supermarkets under its original name, made by the It's-It Ice Cream Co., in that city.

IZER COOKIE. A cookie baked on a long wafer iron that is impressed with figures of designs that then appear on the cookie. The term derives from the Dutch word *izer* (or *yser*), meaning "iron," and the cookies were made by Dutch immigrants in NYC and elsewhere in the colonies. Often a date was stamped on the cookie. If split and buttered, they were called "split cakes."

J

JACK (genus *Caranx*). Any of a variety of ocean fish that includes the **pompano**, most of which are not significant food fishes in the U.S. The origin of the name is obscure, the first mention being in 1587. The principal eating fishes of this type include the "amberjack" (*Seriola dumerili*); the "bar jack" (*C. ruber*); the "blue runner" (*C. crysos*); the "crevalle" (*C. hippos*), also called "jack crevalle" or "crevalle jack"; the "jack mackerel" (*Trachurus symmetricus*), also called the "horse mackerel," though it is not a true mackerel; the "rainbow runner" (*Elagatis bipinnulatus*); the "yellow jack" (*C. bartholomaei*); and the yellowtail (*S. dorsalis*). U.S. landings of jack mackerel in 2010 totaled 684,000 pounds, almost all from California.

JACK ROSE. A cocktail made from apple brandy, lime or lemon juice, and grenadine. The name seems to be based on the drink's color, which resembles that of a rose named after French general Jean-François Jacqueminot (1787–1865), though it may refer to a pre–World War I gangster named "Bald" Jack Rose. The drink is first mentioned in print in Ernest Hemingway's 1926 novel *The Sun Also Rises*.

JACK ROSE

Shake together with ice 8 parts apple brandy, 2 parts lemon or lime juice, and 1 part grenadine. Strain into cocktail glass and add lemon twist.

JACOBSON, MICHAEL (1943–). Publisher, consumer advocate. As founder and executive director of the Washington, D.C.–based Center for Science in the Public Interest (CSPI), Michael Jacobson has been a watchdog of the healthy and unhealthy practices in American gastronomy and food production. He once said that he was "proud about finding something wrong with practically everything."

After receiving his Ph.D. in microbiology from Massachusetts Institute of Technology and working with consumer advocate Ralph Nader, Jacobson in 1971 co-founded CSPI, which is largely supported by sales of its *Nutrition Action Healthletter* (circulation 850,000).

CSPI's missions include getting **junk food** out of U.S. schools; reducing sodium in processed and restaurant foods; improving food-safety laws; ensuring accurate and honest labeling on food packages; obtaining federal funding for alcohol-abuse prevention policies; and reducing consumption of sugary drinks.

Despite these goals, Jacobson has been widely criticized for sensationalizing his subjects in the press, calling **fettuccine Alfredo** "heart attack on a plate" and claiming that "excess sodium" in food has benefited only funeral directors and coffin makers. He insisted that additives like caramel coloring and ascorbic acid (vitamin C) added to beers were toxins. On a TV show, Jacobson took a hammer and chisel to a block of vegetable shortening.

Lacking any laboratories for original research, his health claims based on others' studies have often been called into question, including his contention, despite clinical evidence, that acrylamide, a chemical found in potato chips and French fries, causes "tens of thousands" of incidents of cancer among Canadians.

Still, Jacobson has had significant impact in showing, if not proving, that there are "good" and "bad" foods that should be assessed for their roles in the healthfulness of the American diet.

Jacobson's works include *Eater's Digest: The Consumer's Fact-Book of Food Additives* (1972); *What Are We Feeding Our Kids?* (1994); *Restaurant Confidential* (2002); and *Salt: The Forgotten Killer* (2005).

JAKE. An alcoholic beverage made from a Jamaican ginger extract, with 70 percent alcohol by volume. Marketed for medicinal use, it was often sold at drugstore counters. In 1930, during Prohibition, the manufacturers added triorthocresyl phosphate to water down jake, though the ingredient turned out to be highly toxic, so that addicted victims, called "jakeheads," could be paralyzed, leading to the slang word "jake walk" and "jake-leg," first in print in 1925, also meaning the delirium tremens.

JAMBALAYA. A main dish of rice, pork, ham, sausage, shrimp, crayfish, and seasonings—or any combination of the above. Jambalaya is one of the most famous Cajun-Creole creations, with as many versions—and incorporating as wide a variety of ingredients—as any dish in American gastronomy. Most etymologists believe the name came from the Spanish word for ham, *jamón*, a prime ingredient in the first jambalayas of the eighteenth century, but others prefer the beloved story of a gentleman who stopped by a New Orleans inn late one night to find nothing left for himself to dine upon. The owner thereupon told the cook, whose name was Jean, to "mix some things together"—*balayez*, in the dialect of Louisiana—so the grateful guest pronounced the dish of odds-and-ends wonderful and named it "Jean Balayez."

The word first appeared in print only in 1872, in the *New Orleans Times*, and *The Picayune's Creole Cook Book* (1900) calls it a "Spanish-Creole dish." Missouri Creoles call it "jambolail." Today it is a great favorite and synonymous with Louisiana cuisine.

Jambalaya may be made with beef, pork, chicken, shrimp, oysters, crayfish, or any number of other ingredients, and none is more authentic than the next. Most will use the local sausage called **chaurice** (or **chorizo**), and green pepper and chile or cayenne pepper are fairly standard. Louisianans are passionate about jambalaya and even hold an annual jambalaya cook-off in the old Cajun town of Gonzales, the self-proclaimed Jambalaya Capital of the World.

JAMBALAYA

Sauté ½ lb. sliced smoked sausage and ½ lb. cubed ham in ¼ c. hot oil until browned. Remove from saucepan and then sauté 1 c. chopped onions, 1 c. chopped bell pepper, 1 c. chopped celery, 1 c. chopped scallion, and 2 cloves minced garlic in meat drippings until soft. Add one 16-oz. can drained tomatoes, 1 t. thyme, 1 t. black pepper, ¼ t. cayenne, and 1 t. salt and cook for 5 min. Stir in 1 c. converted rice. Mix together liquid from tomatoes, 1 ½ c. chicken stock or water, and 1 ½ T. Worcestershire sauce to equal 2 ½ c. Bring to boil, reduce to simmer, add 2 lb. raw, peeled shrimp and the ham and sausage and cook uncovered for about 30 min.

JAMES BEARD FOUNDATION. Named in honor of author and cooking teacher **James Beard** and founded in 1988, the foundation was started in order to raise funds for culinary scholarships and has, since 2001, awarded more than $2 million in aid.

After James Beard died, in 1985, his friend **Julia Child** and cooking-school owner Peter Kump sought to preserve Beard's townhouse at 167 West Twelfth Street in NYC as a working monument where chefs invited from around the world would cook in the original kitchen for eighty guests, several times a week, which brought further funds to the foundation.

The foundation's reputation was severely damaged in 2004, however, when it was discovered that its president, Leonard F. Pickell Jr., had squandered more than $1 million in cash for personal use and nearly bankrupted the foundation. Pickell pleaded guilty to second-degree larceny and was sentenced to one to three years in prison. He died in 2007. The board of trustees also resigned over the affair. Susan Ungaro was named the new head of the board, and she has gradually reduced the foundation's debt and continues to pay off the mortgage on the house.

Funds are also raised by the annual James Beard Foundation Awards, given to journalists, authors, TV and radio media, designers, wine-and-spirits professionals, and chefs at a gala ceremony held in New York City on the first Monday in May.

JANSSON'S TEMPTATION. A dish made from potatoes, onions, anchovies, and cream, baked in a pan and usually served as part of a *julbord* dinner at Christmas. Although the dish is associated with Sweden, where it is called *Janssons frestelse* (in Finland, *Janssonin kiusaus*), it is believed to have American origins. In the September 1989 number of *Food & Wine* magazine, Sharon Kapnick wrote of the dish:

> *In 1846, Erik Jansson, a Swedish religious reformer fleeing persecution, came to America with his followers. They settled in northwestern Illinois, where Jansson founded the village of Bishop Hill, named after his hometown of Biskopskulla. Jansson advocated strict asceticism, calling for a meager diet barely sufficient for survival. As the legend goes, an ardent follower discovered Jansson surreptitiously devouring a steaming casserole of potatoes and anchovies enriched with milk, onions, and butter. He was gorging so passionately that his reputation was forever ruined, and the dish was thereafter called Jansson's Temptation.*

More contemporary stories involve reference to opera singer Pelle Janzon (1844–1889) and, according to Gunnar Stigmark, in an article in the magazine *Gastronomisk Kalender*, to a recipe adapted by his mother from the title of the 1928 film *Janssons Frestelse*.

JANSSON'S TEMPTATION

Cut 2 lb. of peeled potatoes into ¼-in. strips and place half of them in a buttered baking dish. Layer on top 2 c. sliced onions and enough canned anchovies to cover. Cover with another layer of potatoes, add salt and pepper to taste, then pour on 1 ½ c. of light cream. Dot with butter and bake at 375° for about 45–50 min.

JAPANESE AMERICAN FOOD. A general term for the foods eaten by immigrants from Japan as part of their culture, as well as those dishes adapted to the American taste, including teriyaki, sukiyaki, and tempura.

The first Japanese migrant workers, called *dekasegi*, went to Hawaii as of 1880 to replace Chinese farmworkers denied immigration by the Exclusion Act of 1882. By 1895 there were thirty thousand Japanese in Hawaii. Like the Chinese, the first generation suffered abiding prejudice wherever they settled; many in the second generation, called *nisei*, began to assimilate, maintaining their own food culture, with dishes like *dango jiru* dumpling soup, while also adapting to American diets with dishes like the *"shoyu* dog," a hot dog seasoned with brown sugar and soy sauce. They developed the Hawaiians' taste for **Spam**, served with rice and nori wrapper, called "Spam *musubi*." They also ran small eateries and food trucks that served a wide range of American, Chinese, Portuguese, and Japanese items.

At the turn of the century, the California Fish Company, on Terminal Island in San Pedro, California, began hiring Japanese fishermen for their skill in catching albacore tuna. Canneries built housing for them and loaned them money to buy their own boats. In 1909, the San Pedro Japanese Fishermen's Association was founded. By 1917, one fishery expert reported that "half of the tuna fishermen are Japanese and this one-half catches 85 per cent of the fish," three years later accounting for twelve million pounds of tuna.

But anti-Asian "Yellow Peril" hatred flared as Japan's power in the Pacific grew, leading to the 1907 executive order barring Japanese immigration to the mainland, a law with a loophole allowing Japanese women to immigrate. In 1924, the Immigration Act banned all immigration but exempted Hawaii, where many Japanese had entered the fishing industry. Before World War II, Japanese restaurants were a great rarity outside of Hawaii and some West Coast cities—Los Angeles had a Little Tokyo District and San Francisco had a Japantown. A comprehensive 1939 New York City restaurant guide listed no Japanese restaurants. At the 1939 New York World's Fair, the Japan Pavilion had only a Formosan Tea Terrace, serving "the delicately-flavored black tea of Formosa, as well as delicacies representative of Japan." After the war, a few small Japanese restaurants made some headway. A 1949 restaurant guide, *Knife and Fork in New York*, lists Miyako on West Fifty-sixth Street, saying it had "many, many years of popularity behind it" and was located in an "orientalized substantial mansion," where the specialties were tempura and sukiyaki.

In 1964, Japanese immigrant **Rocky Aoki** opened the first of many teppanyaki griddle restaurants, under the name Benihana of Tokyo, where customers sat at counters in front of the griddle and watched a cook schooled in the dramatics of *honcho* knife handling, flaming of food, and joking with the customers seated at the surrounding counter. The menu rarely varied, though sushi was later added. The concept fared well, and Aoki opened up one Benihana after another. By 1974 his business was worth $15 million, and his teppanyaki concept and menu were replicated by other restaurateurs under many different names all around the U.S. There are currently ninety-two company-owned Benihanas and sixteen franchises.

Sashimi and sushi took a lot longer to make headway in the U.S. Raw fish had been served to Japanese customers in Japanese neighborhoods even before the war, and Kawafuku restaurant, in Los Angeles's Little Tokyo, listed the delicacy on the menu as of 1950, adding a small sushi bar in 1964. After the passage of the Immigration Act of 1965, more Japanese were allowed into the U.S. and more sushi bars followed, including one of the first to appeal to an American clientele: Nippon restaurant, in New York City, which created the beef dish called **negi-maki**. In 1975, Matao Uwate published *Sushi*, the first book on the subject in the U.S.

The **California roll**, a form of sushi made with avocados, crabmeat, cucumbers, and other ingredients wrapped in vinegared rice, first appeared in Los Angeles in the 1960s and became very popular with Americans. Between 1988 and 1998, sushi restaurants quintupled in the U.S. By the 1990s sushi was being sold in supermarkets, usually with a sushi chef working at a station before customers.

Today Japanese restaurants abound throughout the U.S., including sushi bars; noodle shops serving soba, ramen and udon; and *yakiniku* restaurants, where meat is cooked on a grill at the center of the table. Chef **Nobuyuki Matsuhisa**, who had spent years cooking in Peru, combined South American spices with sushi, which he first featured in 1993, at Matsuhisa restaurant in Beverly Hills, California. His acclaim led to the opening of a larger restaurant called Nobu, in NYC, with a more expansive menu that had wide influence around the world. Matsuhisa and his company went on to open restaurants under the Nobu brand in Athens, London, Melbourne, and other international cities.

Japanese food products are now readily available as a separate category on shelves in every supermarket. One of the most successful Japanese food companies in the U.S. and around the world is Kikkoman, which began in San Francisco in 1930, specializing in soy sauce products.

JAWBREAKER. Also "jawbone breaker." Very hard, round candies in various colors, so called because they are very difficult to bite into.

JEFF DAVIS. A northern slur first used during the Civil War for the kinds of inferior and substitute foods southerners were forced to consume because of the deprivations caused by the conflict. The name derives from American statesman Jefferson Davis, who, as president of the Confederacy during the war, was an object of northern scorn. Thus, "Jeff Davis coffee" was a substitute made from wheat grain rather than coffee beans, and to call someone a "Jeff Davis" was to label him a southern ignoramus. The term is not found in southern cookbooks of the nineteenth century, but "Jeff Davis pie" and "Jeff Davis pudding" have since lost all condescending connotations.

In an article in *Food & Wine* in 1989, Sharon Kapnick asserted that "Jefferson Davis pie" was actually created by a former slave named Mary Ann, cook for a Missouri merchant named George B. Warren, for Sunday dinners during the Civil War and so named because of Warren's admiration for the Confederacy's president.

The following recipe, from a Washington, D.C., woman named Florence Berryman, printed in the *D.A.R. Cookbook* (1949), is said to have gone back three generations in her family, suggesting that Jeff Davis pie was well known during Davis's own lifetime (1808–1889). A similar pie or tart in the South, based on English recipes known also in New England, was called "**chess pie**." Another very similar confection was called "Osgood pie." Some recipes call for more spices and raisins and nuts to be added to the batter.

JEFF DAVIS

Cream 1 c. butter with 2 c. sugar. Mix 3 beaten egg yolks with ½ c. milk, 2 T. flour, and the juice of 1 lemon. Add to creamed butter. Pour into pie plate with bottom crust and bake at 300° until set. Make a meringue and cover the pie, then brown in oven.

JEFFERSON, THOMAS (1743–1826). Founding father and third president of the U.S., Jefferson was a Renaissance man for whom all subjects of human inquiry were of interest, including agriculture, gastronomy, and wine. Throughout his life, Jefferson kept a Garden Book, imported plants from around the world, collected hundreds of recipes, and had his own four-hundred-acre orchard and vineyard, planting cuttings of *Vitis vinifera* vines from Europe to supplant native varietals.

Born to a Virginia planter family, Jefferson was well schooled in agriculture, and his home at Monticello, built in 1768, allowed him to indulge his interests in all forms of husbandry and cookery. His education about wine came from an Italian surgeon and horticulturist named Philip Mazzei, who found the four hundred best acres on Jefferson's land for grapevine plantings. Jefferson, with other investors, became a partner in Mazzei's "Wine Company," which eventually failed.

As minister to France from 1784 to 1789, Jefferson grew to appreciate the pleasures of the Parisian table, made notes on wines he tasted—commenting on the quality of various champagne vintages—and stored 680 bottles for export back to Virginia. Upon leaving France, he filled eighty-six crates with kitchen utensils, including a pasta-making machine from Italy.

On his return he adapted French principles of cuisine and service to his dinner parties, installing his slave, James Hemmings, whom Jefferson had trained in French cooking, as chef. (Hemmings later negotiated his freedom, in 1796, but only after training his brother Peter for the chef's position.)

A typical fine dinner at Monticello with James Madison and Alexander Hamilton—as re-created by historian Charles A. Cerami in his book *Dinner at Mr. Jefferson's: Three Men, Five Great Wines, and the Evening That Changed America* (2008)—would be service of a green salad with wine jelly; capon stuffed with artichokes and chestnut puree; Virginia ham with calvados sauce; *boeuf à la mode*; confections; and a dessert of vanilla ice cream inside warm puff pastry, all with accompanying wines.

Still, Jefferson was never a glutton. "I have lived temperately," he told his doctor in 1819, "eating little animal food, and that not as an ailment, so much as a condiment for the vegetables which constitute my principal diet." His favorite meal was a plate of English peas.

JELL-O. A trademark name for a gelatin dessert made from sugar, gelatin, adipic acid, disodium phosphate, fumaric acid, artificial color, natural flavor with BHA, and artificial flavor. A patent for a "gelatin dessert" was taken out in 1865 by Peter Cooper, and Charles B. Knox packaged unflavored instant powdered gelatin for making aspic in the 1890s. In 1897, Pearl Bixby Wait, of LeRoy, New York, came up with a flavored gelatin his wife, May Davis Wait, called "Jell-O," whose rights were sold for $450 to Orator Francis Woodward of the Genesee Pure Food Co., which he renamed the "Jell-O Company." The rights for the product were purchased in 1925 by the Postum Cereal Co., but today the product is made by Kraft Foods, which sells more than 450 million packages each year.

Some slang terms for gelatin desserts of this type include "shivering Liz," "shimmy," and "nervous pudding." The numerous gelatin desserts to be found in so many Junior League cookbooks of the South and the Midwest are somewhat explained by the fact that refrigerators and iceboxes required to make the dessert were owned only by families who could afford their high prices.

A "Jell-O shot," supposedly created in New Orleans in the 1980s, is a small paper cup of Jell-O mixed with vodka, schnapps, or other spirits.

JELLY. A sweet, semisolid, translucent condiment made by boiling fruit juice and sugar with pectin or gelatin. Jelly is used as a spread on toast or as a dessert filling. Sometimes it is added to sauces or gravies, and mint jelly is customarily served with roast lamb or lamb chops.

The word *jelly*, dating in print to the fifteenth century, derives from Middle English *geli*, and ultimately from the Latin *gelare*, "to freeze."

FDA standards require that commercial jelly must contain not less than forty-five parts by weight of fruit ingredients to fifty-five parts sweetening.

"Jam" differs from jelly in that it is made with fresh or dried fruit rather than juice and has a thicker texture. The word may derive from the sense of the verb "jam," to force something to congeal together.

"Preserves" differ from jams and jellies in that they contain pieces of the fruit, although jams and preserves are treated under the same heading in the FDA's *Code of Federal Regulations, Title 21.*

Commercial jellies, jams, and preserves are usually made by adding pectins rather than relying on the natural pectins of the fruit. Grape jelly, made with Concord grapes, is the most popular of commercial jellies.

JELLY BEAN. An egg-shaped candy with a chewy texture made by boiling sugar with a flavoring like fruit juice and setting it with gelatin or pectin. Jelly beans were first advertised for sale in the July 5, 1905, edition of the *Chicago Daily News*, at nine cents a pound.

JELLY ROLL. A dessert of sponge cake rolled around a jelly filling, with currant or raspberry traditionally used in the preparation. "Jelly cakes" have been known since at least the 1860s, but jelly rolls were not cited in print until 1895.

JERKY. Beef that has been cut thin and dried in the sun. The word comes from the Spanish *charqui*, which itself came from a Peruvian (Quechua) word, *ch'arki*. It first appeared in English in 1700 as a verb, *jerk*, then as a noun in 1890.

Jerky, in the form of **pemmican**, was a staple food among the Native Americans on the Plains. It is very rich in protein and may be cooked in a soup or smoked, but more commonly it is sold as a "meat snack" in the form of a thin stick sold at convenience stores and bars. The Wisconsin State Beef Council and Chase's Calendar of Events mark June 12 as National Jerky Day.

In Hawaii, jerky is referred to as "pipi kaula." According to Catherine Kekoa Enomoto, in a 1997 article in the *Honolulu Star-Bulletin*, the term means "beef string" and "once referred to two beef strips tied together with a piece of string, then slung over a clothesline to dry." In *E Ho'olako Mau: All Hawaiian Cook Book*, volume II (1990), Tamar Luke Pane'e wrote that the meat is sprinkled with sea salt or brined before drying, then fried or charcoal-broiled and eaten with **poi** or steamed **rice**.

JERUSALEM ARTICHOKE (*Helianthus tuberosus*). Also "ground artichoke." A tuber with lumpy branches, reddish-brown skin, and a slightly sweet flavor. The tuber is not a true **artichoke** and has nothing to do with Jerusalem, for it is a native American sunflower, which in Italian is *girasole*, the name given the plant when it was introduced to the garden of Cardinal Farnese, in Rome, around 1617. In 1620, the Italian word was transformed into the English "Artichocks of Jerusalem" and, thereafter, "Jerusalem artichokes."

The plant had been noted by Samuel de Champlain in 1605 as a garden vegetable of the Indians on Cape Cod, but the settlers who came after him developed little interest in the tuber. Very few Americans are familiar with the food at all, though some commercial growers have tried to market it under the less foreign-sounding name of "sunchoke."

Jerusalem artichokes are usually chopped up raw and used in salads, or they may be boiled or steamed and served with butter.

JEWFISH (*Epinephelus itajara*). Also "giant sea **bass**." A large, grayish-brown **grouper** that may weigh up to seven hundred pounds, found near Florida and in the Gulf of Mexico. The first mention of the name in print was in 1697, when William Dampier, in his *Voyages and Descriptions: A Voyage to New Holland*, wrote, "The Jew-Fish is a very good Fish, and I judge so called by the English, because it hath Scales and Fins, therefore a clean Fish, according to the Levitical Law." (See main entry for **kosher**, for Jewish dietary rules.)

JEWISH AMERICAN FOOD. A general term for the various foods cooked and enjoyed by Jewish immigrants as well as those adaptations of Jewish cuisine that became part of American gastronomy.

While Jews are originally a Middle Eastern people, those who emigrated to America were overwhelmingly from Eastern European countries. There were some Jews in America as early as 1654; by 1880 there were more than 250,000 Jewish people in the U.S.

Significant Jewish populations settled in the big eastern cities, especially NYC—nearly half the number of Jews in the U.S.—many from German, Russian and Polish territories. There they preserved many of the food traditions from Eastern Europe, but many kept kosher laws that forbade certain foods and certain mixing of foods. Still, most of the meats to be found at a German or Polish butcher's shop could be found in a Jewish one, and there were dairy stores, pickle stores, and pastry shops owned by Jews, which featured foods like **pastrami**, bagels, **bialys**, **rugelach**, **kreplach**, **matzo**, **knishes**, and others. **Delicatessens** were almost entirely owned by Jews, who sold dried and smoked fish, **latkes** (potato pancakes), borscht (beet soup), liverwurst, beef brisket, and much more.

These foods were enjoyed in Jewish homes, especially at religious holidays, when certain traditional dishes foods were prepared, including matzo ball soup, potato kugel, and brisket at Passover; kreplach and hamantaschen pastries at Purim; and **challah** for Yom Kippur.

Most non-Jewish Americans' only familiarity with Jewish American food would be through delicatessens, which have dwindled in the past twenty years. But Jewish cookbooks, like **Joan Nathan**'s *Jewish Cooking in America* (1994; revised 1998) remain popular, and many U.S. newspapers publish Jewish recipes during the religious holidays in their food sections.

JEWISH PENICILLIN. A slang term for chicken soup, because of its supposed curative powers, dating in print to 1968. In 1987, a mock court called the Court of Historical Review and Appeals, in San Francisco, awarded chicken soup the "official" title of "Jewish penicillin."

JIBARITO. A sandwich of fried plantains (instead of bread), sliced steak, cheese, mayonniase, lettuce, tomato, onion and fried garlic. It is a popular dish among Puerto Ricans living in Chicago, invented around 1996 by Juan Figueroa, owner of Borinquen restaurant.

JICAMA (*Pachyrhizus erosus*). Pronounced "hee-ka-mah," this tropical American tuber is a legume eaten as a vegetable. The name is from the Nahuatl *xicama*, appearing first in English print, as "Xiquima," in 1604. The tuber gained popularity first in the West and the South in the 1980s, although most jicama is imported from Mexico.

JIM HILL MUSTARD. Also "tall tumble mustard" and "tall rocket mustard." A northwestern term for a wild mustard (*Sisymbrium altissimum*) discovered in the 1890s, although a native of Europe, first in print in 1923, when James Jerome Hill (1838–1916) built the Great Northern Railway to Seattle.

JIMMIES. Also "sprinkles." Very small pellets or rods of colored candy or chocolate, used as a topping for ice cream. Associated with New England, the word was first in print in 1963 but goes back much further. Various theories have been advanced as to jimmies' origins, which seem to have been in Boston. A 2003 article in the *Boston Globe* cited a 1986 remark on National Public Radio by the Boston poet John Ciardi, who claimed in about 1922 that he enjoyed jimmies on his ice cream, saying, "no ice cream cone was worth having unless it was liberally sprinkled with jimmies." In 1935, the Just Born candy company of Brooklyn, New York, moved to Bethlehem, Pennsylvania, and acquired the Maillard Corp., which made hand-decorated chocolates, crystallized fruits, Venetian mints, and jellies. Sometime in that decade, Just Born made a topping called "chocolate grains," which afterwards, according to Ross Born, current CEO and grandson of the company's founder, Sam Born, were named jimmies, after Jimmy Bartholomew, who worked the machine. They soon registered the name "jimmies" but discontinued the product (and the trademark expired) in the mid-1960s. Under the name "sprinkles," QA Products, of Chicago, is now the world's largest maker of the confection.

JOE FROGGER. A thick New England cookie spiced with ginger, nutmeg, cloves, and other spices. The origins of the name are unknown, though the most often cited story concerns an old man named "Uncle Joe" who lived near a frog pond in Marblehead, Massachusetts. He loved rum and always put it into his cookies, which resembled the frogs in the pond. The cookies are a traditional Sunday-night snack in New England.

JOE FROGGER

In a bowl combine ¼ c. molasses, 4 T. melted butter, ½ c. honey, 2 T. hot water, 3 T. rum, ½ t. baking soda, 2 c. flour, ½ t. ground ginger ¼ t. ground cloves, ¼ t. nutmeg, and ⅛ t. allspice. Blend well to form a dough. Chill for 1 hr. Pinch off a ball of dough about the size of a walnut, flatten to about ¼-in. thickness, place on buttered cookie sheet, and bake for 10 min. at 375°. Cool on rack. Makes 10 cookies.

JOHANNISBERG RIESLING. A white vinifera grape, properly called the White Riesling, that goes into some of Germany's finest white wines. It has been increasingly planted as a wine grape in the U.S., especially in California, where it is vinified either as a dry, spicy wine or as a **late-harvest** sweet dessert wine.

JOHNNYCAKE. Also "johnny cake," "johnnycake," and "jonny cake." A form of **pancake** traditionally made with Rhode Island ground flint ("Indian") corn. The name was in print at least as early as 1739, as "Rhode Island johnnycake" since 1895, but its derivation is very much clouded by speculation. Some authorities believe it may derive from an Indian word for flat cornmeal cakes, *joniken*. Others think it a derivative of "Shawnee cake," after the tribe of the Tennessee Valley. It is also possible that *johnnycake* is a form of the Dutch *pannekoeken*, for a *j* could be easily replaced by a *p*, and the word is often spelled "jonnycake," without the *h*. An 1831 sailing chronicle describes "johnny cake," a West Indian sort of tea bread. An 1835 Southern political cartoon by James Akin calls johnnycake "the stamina of the south."

Most Rhode Island aficionados of the johnnycake—especially those who belong to the Society for the Propagation of the Jonnycake Tradition—insist that the word is from "journey cake" (1754), because it might be carried on a long trip, and the word *journey* is commonly pronounced "jonny" in that part of New England. Given the traditional thinness and brittleness of johnnycakes, however, they seem hardly substantial or durable enough to pack in saddlebags for a long trek through the New England wilderness.

The society also states that a true johnnycake must be made with an obsolete strain of Indian corn called "whitecap flint corn," which is cultivated in very small quantities because of its low yield (twelve tons to an acre, as opposed to twenty tons for dent corn). In 1940, the Rhode Island legislature again considered the johnnycake question by deciding that only those made with flint corn could be labeled "Rhode Island johnnycakes." (Johnnycake mixes are sold in packages.) Flint cornmeal is still made by Gray's Grist Mill, in Adamsville, Carpenter's Gristmill, in Perryville, and Kenyon's Gristmill, in Usquepaugh, Rhode Island.

In Newport County, Rhode Island, johnnycakes are commonly made with cornmeal, salt, and cold milk; in South County, they are made with cornmeal, salt, and boiling water, resulting in smaller, thicker johnnycakes than those in the north.

The johnnycake became part of New England folklore with the publication of a series of articles in 1879–1880 in the *Providence Journal* entitled *The Jonny-Cake Papers of "Shepherd Tom"* by Thomas Robinson Hazard. As might be expected, Rhode Island holds a Johnnycake Festival annually, in the last week of October, and the item is common to "May Breakfasts."

JOHNNYCAKES, NEWPORT COUNTY STYLE

Mix 1 c. stone-ground white cornmeal, ½ t. salt, 1 ½ c. cold milk, and 2 T. melted butter. Mixture will be thin. Spoon onto buttered griddle in 5-in. rounds and fry until golden.

JOHNNY MARZETTI. Also "Johnny Mazetti." A baked dish of ground meat, tomato, and macaroni. It was created at Marzetti's restaurant, in Columbus, Ohio, in the 1920s and named after the owner's brother, Johnny.

JOHNNY MARZETTI

Brown 1 ½ lb. ground beef with 1 chopped onion, add 1 can tomatoes, 1 can mushrooms, 1 can tomato paste, and ¼ lb. cheddar or mozzarella cheese. Cook until tender and well blended, place on top of 8 oz. boiled noodles, sprinkle with cheese and bread crumbs, and bake at 300° for about 40 min. Serves 8.

JOJOBA. A shrub (*Simmondsia chinensis*) and its nut, which is considered better used in a beverage than in other forms of food. It dates in print, in *California Fruits*, to 1900.

JOLLY BOY. A nineteenth-century New England fried cake. Jolly boys were sometimes split in half, buttered, and served with maple syrup.

JOLLY BOY

Stir ½ t. baking soda into 1 c. sour milk, then add 1 beaten egg and ½ c. molasses. Mix in 2 ½ c. cornmeal or rye meal to form a biscuit dough. Drop balls of dough into hot oil and fry until golden brown. Makes about 25.

JONES, JUDITH B. (1924–). Publisher, editor, and author. As an editor of many of the most popular and authoritative cookbooks of postwar America, Judith Jones helped instill in Americans the idea that cooking could be an opportunity for learning about food culture as well as an enjoyable pastime. Her authors include **Julia Child**, **James Beard**, Marion Cunningham, Marcella Hazan, Madhur Jaffrey, Irene Kuo, **Edna Lewis**, **Joan Nathan**, Claudia Roden, Nina Simonds, and Lidia Bastianich.

Jones first worked for Doubleday, in both New York City and Paris, where in 1948 she met her future husband, author Evan Jones. There, in 1950, she discovered *The Diary of Anne Frank* in a rejection pile. In 1957, she went to Knopf, where at first she translated works by French authors Albert Camus and Jean-Paul Sartre, then went on to edit prominent American authors like John Updike, John Hersey, and Anne Tyler, while signing on the emerging food writers of the 1960s, including Julia Child, whose *Mastering the Art of French Cooking* appeared in 1961. She was also the force behind the eighteen-volume series *Knopf Cooks American*.

She and her husband (who died in 1996) wrote *The Book of Bread* (1981); *The L.L. Bean Game and Fish Cookbook*, with Angus Cameron (1983), and *The L.L. Bean Book of New New England Cookery* (1987). In 2007, Jones published her memoir *The Tenth Muse: My Life in Food*, which was followed by *The Pleasures of Cooking for One*, in 2009.

In 2006, the **James Beard Foundation** gave her the Lifetime Achievement Award.

JOOK. A rice gruel sold in inexpensive Chinese American "jook house" restaurants in San Francisco's Chinatown. Such places became popular just after World War II. See also **juke**.

JUJUBE (*Ziziphus jujuba*). Also "Chinese date." The fruit of an Old World tree having dark red skin and yellowish flowers. The term, which comes from French *jujube* and Latin *jujuba* and dates in English to about 1400, also applies to several varieties of candies that are fruit-flavored and chewy, though not necessarily similar in taste to the jujube fruit.

A commercially produced candy called "Jujubes" (which probably took its name from the ju-ju gum that gave the tiny morsels their chewy texture) came on the American market sometime before 1920 and was followed by "Jujyfruits," which were shaped like candy berries, in 1920. Both candies are produced by the Heide Candy Co. of New Jersey.

JUKE. Also "jook" or "juke house." A roadside saloon, usually of a very low grade and long associated with prostitution in the South, where most jukes were operated. Many of the jukes were frequented by African Americans, and the word, which found its way into print only in 1934, derives from the African Wolof *dzug*, "to lead a disorderly life."

By the 1940s "to juke" meant to go around to various bars and taverns, often in search of prostitutes. The word survives today in "jukebox," an automatic record player operated by dropping a coin in a slot and pushing buttons that indicate a listed song.

The food in such places usually included barbecued ribs and sandwiches, aside from liquor and beer, and jukes became known for their bold and intimidating signs, such as YOU CAN DRINK IN HERE, BUT YOU GO OUTSIDE TO GET DRUNK, printed outside a Florida juke, or WHAT THE HELL ARE YOU LOOKING UP HERE FOR?, printed on the ceiling of an Alabama juke.

JULEKAKE. Also "julekage" and "julicokki." A Christmas cake of dried fruits and nuts, served traditionally in Scandinavian American homes. The term, which means "Yule cake," dates in print to 1940.

JUMBLE. Also "jumbal." A simple spiced butter cookie, usually with nuts "jumbled" up in the dough (1827). Jumbles, among the first American cookies, came in various shapes, sometimes dropped on a baking sheet, sometimes cut with a cookie cutter. The first printed recipe appeared in Lettice Bryan's *The Kentucky Housewife* (1839), where they are called "common jumbles" and made into rings; they do not contain nuts.

JUMBLE

Blend ¼ c. butter with 2 c. flour. Blend in 2 beaten eggs, ½ c. grated coconut, ½ t. rosewater, and ¾ c. walnuts. Make a stiff dough. Drop by teaspoon onto a buttered baking sheet and bake for 10 min. at 450°.

JUNK FOOD. Inexpensive food with little nutritional value, often eaten as **snacks** or bought at **fast-food** establishments. Junk food might include potato chips, pretzels, tortilla chips, sodas, french-fried potatoes, sugared cereals, candy, and ice cream. The first appearance of the term in print was in a 1971 article by food writer **Gael Greene**, called "Confessions of a Sensualist," in *New York* magazine, in which she wrote, "My respect for the glories of French cuisine are unsurpassed, but I am a fool for junk food."

KAISER ROLL. Also "Vienna roll" and "hard roll." A crisp, puffy, light roll used to make sandwiches in delicatessens or eaten as a breakfast roll. The name is from the German *Kaisesemmel*, "emperor roll," and refers to the crownlike appearance of the roll. The word first appeared in English in 1968, as "Kaiser buns."

The kaiser roll originated in Vienna. Some say it was named after Franz Josef (1830–1916), emperor of Austria from 1848 to 1916, and was brought to America by German and Jewish immigrants. Today the confection is usually called simply a "hard roll" and is often topped with poppy seeds.

KALUA PIG. A Hawaiian form of barbecue in which a whole pig is baked in a pit dug in the ground, called an **imu**. The pit is lined with wood, rocks are added, and a fire lighted. Once the fire is burning well, the wood is removed and the pit is lined with ti or banana leaves. The pig is also wrapped in leaves and placed in the pit, which is then covered with more leaves. The pig is usually seasoned beforehand. It is commonly accompanied by servings of roasted bananas, sweet potatoes, or taro. See **Hawaiian food**.

KAMIKAZE. A cocktail made with citrus juices, Cointreau, and vodka. The name derives from the Japanese term meaning "divine wind," for the Japanese pilots of the last years of World War II who would commit suicide by crashing their planes into American ships; metaphorically, drinking such a cocktail would be a suicidal act.

The drink might have once had less dramatic associations. Bartender Tony Lauriano claimed he created the drink at Les Pyrénées restaurant, in NYC, in 1972, to honor the Broadway show *Jesus Christ Superstar*, after which the cocktail was originally named. Later, the same ingredients came to be mixed into what was called the "kamikaze," but the person who coined that name is unknown.

KAMIKAZE

Shake with ice the juice of 1 lemon and 1 lime, 1 ½ oz. Cointreau, and 1 ½ oz. vodka. Garnish with sprig of mint.

KATZEN, MOLLIE (1950–). Author and food advocate. Mollie Katzen was among the first postwar food advocates for a healthier diet, as exemplified in her seminal vegetarian cookbook *The Moosewood Cookbook* (1977). *Health* magazine in 1999 called her one of the five Women Who Changed the Way We Eat.

Katzen was born in Rochester, New York, attending the Eastman School of Music and Cornell. While studying, she worked at local restaurants, thus developing an interest in growing vegetables. She graduated with a B.A. in fine arts from the San Francisco Art Institute. After graduation, Katzen and friends formed a cooperative in Ithaca, New York, called the Moosewood Restaurant, whose menu was primarily vegetable-based. This spawned the recipes for *The Moosewood Cookbook*, which went on to become one of the ten bestselling cookbooks of all time (it was revised in 1998).

In 1995 Katzen, published *Vegetable Heaven* and the children's cookbook *Honest Pretzels: And 64 Other Amazing Recipes for Cooks Ages 8 & Up*.

Despite her reputation as a brilliant vegetable cook, Katzen herself has never been a vegetarian, instead insisting that an animal protein should play a minor, rather than major, part of a well-balanced dish. "Just because one loves vegetables doesn't mean one is against meat," she said. "I don't like the word *vegetarian*, and I don't identify with it. It too often means 'anything but meat,' rather than lots of fruits and vegetables." She also has insisted that "low-fat" is a misguided concept: "Some fat is very good for you and you should go out of your way to eat it…Lumping all fat together is meaningless, as fat calories do not make you fatter than carb calories. Calories are calories."

Katzen hosted the PBS series *Mollie Katzen's Vegetable Heaven, Mollie Katzen's Vegetarian Cooking*, and *Mollie Katzen's Cooking Show II: Vegetable Heaven*.

Katzen was a founding member of the Harvard School of Public Health Leadership Council, with a charter seat at the Harvard School of Public Health's Nutrition Roundtable. She was inducted to the Natural Health Hall of Fame.

Her other books include *The Enchanted Broccoli Forest* (1982); *Still Life with Menu* (1988); *Vegetable Heaven and Sunlight Cafe* (1997); *Eat, Drink and Weigh Less*, co-authored with Dr. Walter Willett (2003); and *Get Cooking* (2009).

KAUKAU. Hawaiian pidgin slang for "food" or, as a verb, "to eat or drink," dating in print to 1820, derived from pidgin Chinese *chowchow* or perhaps the Hawaiian word for table, *pākaukau*. (The Hawaiian word for food is *'ai*.)

KEDGEREE. An East Indian dish brought to America by seamen that was originally composed of rice, lentils, eggs, and spices. New Englanders had added cod or other fish by the eighteenth century. The word comes from the Hindi *khichrī*, from the Sanskrit *khiccā*, and first appeared in English in 1662 as "Kitsery."

KEDGEREE

In a double boiler combine 2 c. cooked rice, 2 c. cooked cod, 4 chopped hard-boiled eggs, 2 T. minced parsley, ½ c. heavy cream, 1 t. salt, and ⅛ t. pepper. Heat thoroughly. Serves 6.

KEECH CAKE. Also "keeling." A Pennsylvania German small cake made with cornmeal but without yeast, and fried in fat. The name derives from the German *Küchlein*.

KELLER, THOMAS (1955–). Chef, restaurateur, author. With the opening of his restaurant the French Laundry, in California's Napa Valley, Thomas Keller created a style of intensely personalized tasting menus that had wide influence on chefs throughout the world.

Keller was born in Oceanside, California, his father a Marine drill instructor, his mother a restaurateur. After their divorce, Keller moved with his mother to Palm Beach, Florida, and attended junior college. He spent summers as a teenager in Rhode Island, moving up to a cook's position at the Dunes Club, in Narragansett, Rhode Island, where he learned classic French cooking from chef Roland Henin. Keller cooked in various places in Florida, then became chef de cuisine at La Rive, in Catskill, New York, where his talent came to the attention of Serge Raoul, owner of Raoul's, in New York City's Soho neighborhood, who hired him as chef. In 1983, Keller moved to France to hone his skills under master chefs at Taillevant, Guy Savoy, and Le Pré Catalan, returning in 1987 to NYC to open Rakel, along with Raoul, which won high praise in the press for its daring nouvelle cuisine.

After parting with Raoul over finances and the direction of Rakel, Keller moved to Los Angeles to become chef at Checker Hotel, which was sold soon afterwards. He then began making California olive oil while acquiring funds to open his own restaurant. Two years later, in 2004, he opened the French Laundry, in Yountville, California. There he won a reputation for a commitment and perfectionism that gave the restaurant a reputation among the finest in the U.S., eventually earning three Michelin stars.

The French Laundry has been a training ground for many chefs who left to make their own mark on American gastronomy, including Corey Lee, Jonathan Benno, and Richard Blais. Keller next opened a French bistro called Bouchon in Yountville in 1998, then in 2004 opened the New York City haute cuisine restaurant Per Se (so called because it would not be a copy of the French Laundry), which also won every major accolade possible in the U.S. and abroad.

In 2006, Keller opened Ad Hoc in Yountville, where he serves American comfort food like fried chicken. He also opened Bouchon and Bouchon Bakery, in Beverly Hills, California, in 2009, as well as a branch in Tokyo.

There are now twelve restaurants under Keller's ownership. He now markets a signature line of Limoges porcelain dinnerware by Raynaud, called Hommage Point (named after French chef Fernand Point), as well as a collection of silver hollowware by Christofle, and knives manufactured by MAC.

Keller is the president and recruiter of the Bocuse d'Or U.S. team. His awards are numerous, including the Top 50 Restaurants in the World by *Restaurant* magazine; Outstanding Chef in America from the **James Beard Foundation** (1997); Chef of the Year, *Bon Appétit* (1998); America's Best Chef, *Time* (2001); and Chevalier in the French Légion d'honneur (2011).

His books include *The French Laundry Cookbook* (1999); *The Bouchon Cookbook* (2004); and *Ad Hoc at Home* (2009).

KELLOGG, JOHN HARVEY (1852–1943) and **WILL KEITH** (1860–1951). The name Kellogg is nearly synonymous with American breakfast cereal, which, although not created by the Kellogg brothers, became a staple of the breakfast table with their invention of Kellogg's Toasted Corn Flakes.

Born in Tyrone, Michigan, John Harvey Kellogg and his brother Will Keith grew up in Battle Creek, where their father owned a broom factory. John Kellogg attended the local schools, then graduated from the Michigan State Normal School and in 1875 earned a medical degree from New York University.

Will Kellogg was a businessman who helped his brother run the Battle Creek Sanitarium, owned by the Seventh-day Adventist Church, of which both brothers were members. John became chief medical officer there and developed controversial regimens of vegetarianism, exercise, and abstinence from tobacco, alcohol, and sex. Among his famous patients at the sanitarium were William Howard Taft, Amelia Earhart, George Bernard Shaw, Henry Ford, Thomas Edison, and actress Sarah Bernhardt.

John advocated a diet rich in fiber, which, as of 1894, inspired them to create grain cereals. In 1902, a cereal called Kellogg's Toasted Corn Flakes was produced. This was not a wholly novel idea—Dr. James Caleb Jackson, of NYC, had already produced the first packaged grain cereal, which he called Granula—but Will saw its potential in the open market. But the brothers broke over making the recipe so public after one guest, Charles William Post, allegedly used their recipes to begin his own cereal company, called the Postum Cereal Co. (later General Foods). In 1906, Will left the sanitarium to begin the Battle Creek Toasted Corn Flake Co., which eventually became the Kellogg Co., while Will founded the Battle Creek Food Co. to develop soy bean products.

John continued to run the sanitarium but had to sell it during the Depression. He then opened a new facility in Florida, continuing to publish his unorthodox views on health, sex, and hygiene in a series of books under the title *Plain Facts for Old and Young*.

Meanwhile, Will became a multimillionaire by selling his corn flakes and other new cereals like All-Bran and Raisin Bran nationwide. He was the first to put children's prizes in the cereal boxes, the first being "The Funny Jungleland Moving Pictures Book."

Known as a generous philanthropist and caretaker of his employees, Will kept his plants running at full capacity during the Depression and, in 1930, with a $66 million donation, founded the W.K. Kellogg Foundation. Kellogg hoped to groom his son, John Jr., to take over the company, but the young man committed suicide in 1938; Kellogg stepped down as the head of the company a year later.

After Will's death, in 1951, the company kept expanding, sometimes contracting, eventually buying the Eggo Waffle Company and Keebler Foods. In 1964, Kellogg's introduced Pop Tarts and in 1989 Smart Start Cereal Bars, later called Nutri-Grain.

KENNEDY, DIANA (1923–). Author and teacher. In the 1970s, with the help of *New York Times* food editor Craig Claiborne, Diana Southwood Kennedy emerged as one of the most important champions of regional Mexican cuisine.

Born in the UK, Kennedy emigrated to Canada in 1953, then to Mexico City in 1957 to join her future husband, *Times* bureau chief Paul P. Kennedy. There she learned to cook Mexican food from her maids and would serve Mexican dishes to visiting dignitaries, including Claiborne, who saw in her work the prospects of elevating the image of Mexican food and exploring its regional character.

In 1966, the couple moved to NYC, where, after Paul's death, a year later, Kennedy began offering cooking classes in 1969. Again with Claiborne's urging, she co-authored *The Cuisines of Mexico* with Fran McCollugh in 1972 (revised 1986), which Claiborne praised as "the definitive book in English on that most edible art." This and Kennedy's following books, *The Tortilla Book* (1975; revised 1991), *Recipes from the Regional Cooks of Mexico* (1978), and *The Art of Mexican Cooking* (1989), established her reputation among the foremost American writers on the subject. Her *Oaxaca al Gusto: An Infinite Gastronomy* (2010) divided the cuisine of Oaxaca into eleven regions.

The *Washington Post* called Kennedy, known for her feistiness, an "obsessive pop anthropologist." "All anthropologists and botanists, they ought to learn to cook," she told the *Post*. "I am suggesting that all the syllabi for would-be biologists include classes in cooking, or they will miss the whole point, of how the culture and plants and food come together."

Over the years, Mexican food authorities accused Kennedy of appropriating recipes from people who would never share in her royalties; nor did she gain any friends among the Mexican American food media when, in a 1985 interview in *Texas Monthly* magazine, she called Tex-Mex food "over-seasoned, loaded with all those false spices like onion salt, garlic salt, MSG and chili powder." In 1981, the Mexican government awarded her the highest honor for foreigners, the Order of the Aztec Eagle. Queen Elizabeth II also appointed Kennedy a Member of the Order of the British Empire for her work strengthening Mexican and UK relations and her work with the environment.

KENTUCKY BREAKFAST. A colloquial slur defined as "three cocktails and a chaw of terbacker" (1882).

KERR, GRAHAM (1934–). TV show host, author. As the flamboyant and irreverent host of one of the first TV cooking shows, *The Galloping Gourmet*, Graham Kerr showed Americans that even haute cuisine might be accomplished at home in simple steps while having a highly entertaining time in the kitchen. Kerr has written twenty-nine books, with total sales of fourteen million copies.

Born in London to a family of hoteliers, Kerr attended Brighton College and got his first job at the Roebuck Hotel, in East Sussex, before joining the British Army as catering adviser. After leaving the service, he became general manager of England's Royal Ascot Hotel, then moved to New Zealand in 1958 as catering adviser for the Royal New Zealand Air Force.

There he began publishing recipes in the local media and published his first book, *Entertaining with Kerr*. His appearance on New Zealand TV and a 1967 book, written with Len Evans, titled *The Galloping Gourmets*, led to the TV show *The Galloping Gourmet* (1969–71), in which Kerr developed his onscreen persona, literally galloping through his TV set kitchen, dressed in an ascot and suspenders as if he were welcoming good friends to his home for dinner. With dry British wit and considerable winking, Kerr balanced bonhomie with mild raciness as he prepared rich classic French cuisine, slurping wine as he did so, ending by bringing an audience member to the table to eat with him what he had just cooked.

A serious car accident in 1971 crippled Kerr in the spine and arm. When Kerr returned to TV in 1974, it was in a daily five-minute syndicated series called *Take Kerr*, by which time his onscreen manner was considerably subdued by his experiences and subsequent conversion to Christianity. After his wife, Treena, suffered a heart attack, Kerr further changed his style of cooking, developing "Minimax" recipes with less fat and cholesterol, which he debuted on his next production, *The Graham Kerr Show* (1990–1991). He followed with a series of cookbooks based on healthy eating—*Graham Kerr's Smart Cooking*, Graham *Kerr's Minimax Cookbook*, and *Graham Kerr's Creative Choices*, in connection with a syndicated series on PBS. From 1996 through 2000, Kerr was an editor at large for *Cooking Light* magazine.

By the time he published *Swiftly Seasoned* (1996), built around an idea he called a "Moulded Ethnic Vegetable," Kerr had moved closer to vegetarian cooking, and his subsequent media appearances have had an increasing component of healthy cooking, including his radio series for the National Cancer Institute's 5 a Day program, titled *Do Yourself a Flavor*. Kerr served on the American Dietetic Association Foundation/ConAgra Foundation Home Food Safety Expert Panel. In 2001, he published *Growing at the Speed of Life*. Among his awards have been an honorary doctorate in "culinary nutrition" from Johnson & Wales University (2003), induction into the American Culinary Federation Hall of Fame (1999), and inclusion in the James Beard Foundation's Who's Who of Food & Beverage in America (1997).

KETCHUP. Also "catsup" and "catchup." A variety of condiments, the most common of which contains pickle and tomato. The word derives from Chinese Amoy dialect, *kê-tsiap*, "pickled fish" or perhaps Malay *kēchap*, which was picked up by English sailors in the seventeenth century and first mentioned in print as of 1711. Since in America most ketchups were made with tomato (bottled tomato ketchups were sold as of 1876 by the F. & J. Heinz Co. of Pennsylvania), "tomato ketchup" as a description was little used after the end of the nineteenth century. Few Americans make their own ketchup any longer, though the bottled variety has come to be thought of as a necessary condiment with hamburgers, and much facile criticism of American food is aimed at the frequency with which Americans pour ketchup on their food, even though it is a traditional item both here and in England.

Worldwide, thirty-five million tons of ketchup are consumed annually.

"Tomato soy" is a nineteenth-century form of ketchup.

The following recipe is from Jacqueline Harrison Smith's *Famous Old Receipts* (1908).

KETCHUP

Peel 4 qt. tomatoes and place in a kettle with 2 qt. vinegar, 6 chopped red peppers, 4 T. salt, black pepper, 2 T. dry mustard, and 3 T. allspice. Boil for 4 hr., until thickened. Bottle, seal, and serve as a condiment for meat and fish.

KETTLE MEAT. Offal and meat from the head of an animal (1968).

KICKAPOO INDIAN MEDICINE. A trademark name for a beverage produced by John Healy and Charles Bigelow, of New Haven, Connecticut. It was promoted as a tonic for neuralgia and "impure blood" and derived its name from a band of Native Americans from various tribes whom the two hucksters called "full-blooded Kickapoo Indians" (an actual branch of the Algonquian tribe, originally from the Midwest). It was featured as of 1881 in a series of traveling Wild West–type shows throughout New England. The name of the drink was later adapted by cartoonist Al Capp as "Kickapoo Joy Juice" in his hillbilly comic strip *L'il Abner*.

KIDNEY BEAN (*Phaseolus vulgaris*). A species of kidney-shaped bean, the most familiar being reddish brown in color. The word was first printed in 1548.

KIELBASA. Also "kolbasy" and other spellings, or "Polish sausage." A pork sausage (sometimes containing beef or veal) seasoned with garlic. Kielbasa is sold in long links and is usually smoked and precooked, then eaten in smaller chunks. The word is from the Polish for the same sausage. *Kolbasa* is a Russian alternative. The term was first printed in English in 1950 and was also mentioned in American print in Saul Bellow's 1953 novel *The Adventures of Augie March*: "Just catch the picture of this lousy classroom, and all these poor punks full of sauerkraut and bread with pig's-feet, with immigrant blood and washday smells and kielbasa and homebrew beer."

KILLER BAR. A bar whose liberal policy toward customers' alcohol limit results in many accidents traced to inebriation. According to an article in the *New York Times* in 1987, the state of Massachusetts began in 1982 to ask intoxicated offenders where they'd had their last drink, in an effort to find bars that were habitually serving customers already intoxicated. In local parlance these establishments were called "multiple offender bars" or "killer bars."

KING CAKE. A brioche-style cake made during the Louisiana carnival season, beginning in January and ending at Mardi Gras, during which time bakeries produce about 250,000 such cakes and many "king cake parties" are held (1889). By tradition, the cake contains a red bean (sometimes covered in gold or silver leaf) or a figurine of the baby Jesus. It is sold widely throughout Louisiana during the weeks prior to Mardi Gras, and the person who finds the bean or figurine is promised good luck.

There are various stories as to the origins of the cake, though most in some way derive from the legend of the Three Kings visiting the infant Jesus in Bethlehem, as described in the New Testament. In the first half of the sixteenth century, France commemorated Kings' Day—the twelfth day after Christmas—with a "Twelfth Night cake." A century later, King Louis XIV took part in such a feast, at which a *gâteau des rois* ("kings' cake") contained a hidden bean or ceramic figure, as it does to this day.

Before the Civil War, American king cakes often contained gold, diamonds, or valuables instead of beans; after the war, with the end of gala Creole balls in Louisiana, peas, beans, pecans, and coins were used, and in 1871 the tradition of choosing the queen of the Mardi Gras was determined by who drew the prize in the cake. Then, in 1952, Donald and Gerald Entringer, owner of a New Orleans bakery called McKenzie's, began baking china dolls (late plastic) into the cake, which is the predominant tradition today.

The colors of purple (for justice), green (for faith), and gold (for power) that traditionally tint the cake's icing first appeared in 1872, after the Rex Krewe, a Mardi Gras parade organization, chose those colors to celebrate that year's festival.

KING CAKE

Proof 2 envelopes yeast with a little sugar in 1 c. warm water. In a saucepan melt 1 stick butter, 1 c. evaporated milk, ½ c. sugar, and 2 t. salt. In another bowl beat 4 eggs until light, then add to the yeast mixture. Add milk mixture and blend well. Gradually add 5 c. flour and knead for 8–10 min. Place in a greased bowl, turn to grease all sides, cover the bowl with a cloth, and let the dough double in bulk, about 2 hr. Punch dough down and roll out to about 18 in. by 36 in. Brush with melted butter. Sprinkle with a mixture of 1 c. sugar, ½ c. brown sugar, and 2 T. ground cinnamon. Cut dough into three strips, roll each one up, braid, insert a bean or figurine somewhere in the dough, then cover with damp cloth and let rise again until doubled.

Bake at 350° for 20–30 min. Glaze with icings colored green, yellow, and purple.

KINGFISH. Also "black mullet," "hogfish," "whiting," "sea mink," **opah**, and other names. Either of two saltwater fish, *Menticirrhus americanus* or *M. saxitilis* (1743), although the name is also applied to the Spanish

mackerel (*Scomberomorus cavalla* or *S. regalis*) and other fishes.

KING RANCH CHICKEN. Also "King Ranch casserole." A layered casserole dish made with cut-up poached chicken, cream of mushroom soup, chiles, chicken soup, grated cheese, corn tortillas, and tomatoes (most often Ro-Tel brand). The dish is very commonly served at Texas clubwomen's buffets. For unknown reasons, the name, which dates in cookbooks to at least the 1950s, refers to the King Ranch, in Kingsville, Texas, but there is no evidence that the dish was created there.

KISHKA. Also "kishke." A Jewish American baked sausage made with beef, flour, and spices. The word, from the Russian for "intestines," was first printed in English in 1936.

KIWIFRUIT (*Actinida chinensis*). Also known as the "Chinese gooseberry," this round green fruit with black seeds originated in the Yangtze Valley of China, where it was called *yang tao*. Plants were brought to the U.S. in 1904 and seeds to New Zealand in 1906. But agricultural testing of the berries did not begin until 1935 in the U.S., and the first commercial cultivation in America came in 1960, by John Heinke, who had nine vines in Paradise, California. The first New Zealand–raised fruit was served a year later at Trader Vic's restaurant, in San Francisco.

In 1962, a request for the fruit by a customer in a Los Angeles Safeway supermarket led the manager to contact Frieda Caplan of Frieda's Finest/Produce Specialties Inc. (now called Frieda's Inc.), of Los Angeles, who began importing the fruit from New Zealand. A year later, customs broker Norman Sondag, of Ziel Growers, suggested to Caplan that the name might be more appealing to Americans if changed to "**kiwifruit**" (because of its association with New Zealand and its resemblance to the fuzzy little kiwi bird), which the New Zealand growers thereupon did. The name kiwifruit first appeared in print in 1966.

Caplan went on to buy the entire harvest of Heinke and other American growers in the late 1960s, and the kiwifruit gained enormous popularity as part of the **nouvelle cuisine** movement of the 1970s and 1980s, when it was used in everything from desserts to sauces and garnishes.

Today, 95 percent of the U.S. crop is grown in California, on about 9,300 acres, by 650 growers, primarily in the San Joaquin Valley. The overwhelmingly predominant variety is the Hayward, developed by New Zealand horticulturist Hayward Wright.

KLATCH. Also "coffee klatch" or "kaffeeklatsch." An informal get-together, usually with the service of coffee and sweet confections (1888). From the German *Klatsch*, "gossip."

KNISH. A Jewish American pastry stuffed with mashed potato, cheese, buckwheat groats, or chopped liver. Usually knishes are baked, though sometimes they are fried.

Knish is a Yiddish word, first in English print in 1916, that comes from the Russian *knysh* or the Polish *knyz*. The ubiquity of the knish in NYC's Jewish community led to the lower section of Second Avenue being nicknamed "Knish Alley." Abe Gross's *The Kibitzer's Dictionary* (1930) humorously defines knishes as "dyspepsia."

~~~~~~
KNISH
~~~~~~

Mix 1 c. mashed potatoes with 1 beaten egg, 1 T. chicken fat, ½ t. salt, a pinch of pepper, 1 T. minced onion, and enough flour to make a dough that is stiff enough to be shaped into oval patties about 4 ½-in. long. Make a depression in the center of each patty, fill with cooked chopped chicken liver, mashed potato, cheese, or buckwheat groats, and enclose filling with folds of dough. Brush the dough with egg yolk and bake on a greased sheet at 350° for about 20 min. Makes about 6.

KNOCKWURST. Also "knackwurst." A smoked beef and/or pork sausage, first in American English in 1939, from the same German word (spelled *Knackwurst*), whose name refers to the crackling sound the skin of the sausage makes when bitten into. The sausage also goes by the name *Regensburger Wurst* in Germany. Knockwurst may be boiled, grilled, or steamed and are often eaten with sauerkraut. A "special" is a NYC term for a beef knockwurst eaten like a **hot dog** and sold at **delicatessens**.

KOLACH. Also "kolacky." A sweet pastry bun filled with cheese, poppy seeds, sausage, or, more commonly, jam or fruits like cherry, apricot, peach, pineapple, or prune, first mentioned in print in Willa Cather's novel *My Ántonia* (1918). It is of Czech origins and derives from the Czech word *koláč*, "wheel."

Kolaches are most popular in West Texas, where Czech immigrants settled in 1852.

KOSHER. A Yiddish term for food prepared according to strict Jewish dietary laws. The word is from the Hebrew *kāshēr*, "proper," and has taken on colloquial meanings in America to mean "correct" or "honest" or "acceptable." The word first appeared in English print with reference to meat in 1851, and in 1892 with reference to butter and cheese. In 1935, Abraham Goldstein founded Organized Kashrut Laboratories (OK Labs) to oversee American Jewish kosher food products. Today there are more than fifty kosher-certifying organizations in the U.S. The OK Kosher Certification utilizes TRACK, a proprietary computer program, to maintain a database of over 140,000 kosher ingredients.

According to kosher laws, meat and milk may not be eaten together, a prohibition that even necessitates separate cooking utensils and dishes both in the home and at food-processing plants. There are also "clean" and "unclean" animals that are listed in Leviticus and Deuteronomy, kosher animals being those that have a cloven hoof and chew their cud. A non-kosher (*trayf*) animal chews its cud but is not cloven-hoofed *or* is cloven-hoofed but does not chew its cud. Fish with scales and fins are kosher; birds of prey are not.

Slaughter of animals must be done according to a ritual by a *schochet*, who slashes the throat, and the meat must then be stamped by a supervisor, the *mashgiach*.

These laws are biblical in origin, and, Leo Rosten notes in *The Joys of Yiddish* (1968):

> *Eating and drinking, to the ancient Jews, involved grave religious obligations, and strongly reinforced the idea of the Jews as a people "set apart," chosen by the Lord as "Mine…" "holy unto Me" (Leviticus). The strict observance of dietary rules was believed to strengthen the dedication of a Jew to his role as one of God's instruments for the redemption of mankind.*

There are ninety-seven kosher-certifying organizations in the U.S., with 23,590 U.S. food products certified kosher as of 1993.

Some American Jews have modified adherence to kosher rules over the years, especially in food stores or restaurants catering to a non-Jewish clientele. When the first NYC non-kosher **delicatessens** opened at the turn of century, store owners often used the term *wurshtgesheft* ("sausage shop") in their windows rather than the Hebrew letters for "kosher," but a group of rabbis forced the city to ban its usage in favor of "kosher-style."

KOSSUTH CAKE. A sponge cake filled with whipped cream or ice cream, covered with icing, and set in individual paper cups. According to tradition, the cake was created in 1851 by an East Baltimore confectioner to honor the arrival in that city of Lajos Kossuth (1802–94), a Hungarian revolutionary leader who sought funds from the Marylanders. (Legend has it that he collected only twenty-five dollars.)

KREPLACH. A dumpling containing chopped meat or cheese, often served in soup. The word is Yiddish, from the German *Kräppel*. Kreplachs are by tradition served on Purim, Rosh Hashanah, and the day before Yom Kippur. In its use as a Jewish dish, the word was first mentioned in print in 1892.

KREPLACH

Mix together 1 beaten egg, 1 c. flour, and ¼ t. salt and knead into an elastic dough. Roll out very thin and cut into 3-in. squares. Mix together 1 c. chopped cooked beef, 2 T. minced onion, 2 T. chicken fat, and ½ t. salt, place some in each half of the squares, then fold them to form triangles. Secure edges with a fork and boil in salted water for 20 min. Serve in soup or fry in hot fat. Makes 24.

KRINGLE. A lemon-flavored Christmas cookie (1950). The name derives from the German *Christkindlein*, "gifts of the Christ Child," which in American became "Kris Kringle" (also an early name for Saint Nicholas or Santa Claus).

"Kringle" is also the name for a multilayered pastry with a variety of fruit or nut fillings. It is a specialty of the Wisconsin city of Racine, whose nickname is Kringleville because of its large Danish immigrant population, who called cookies and tea cakes made with butter "kringle." According to Jane and Michael Stern, in *A Taste of America* (1988), Racine's kringle refers to a "broad cake wider than a dinner plate…less than an inch high, a lightweight sheaf of several dozen near-microscopic layers of dough and butter—like an enormous croissant but flakier—glazed with brown sugar and cinnamon, then filled with pecan, apple, date, prune, or cheese, and finally iced with a clear sugar frosting. One kringle serves about a dozen people."

KRINGLE COOKIES

Cream 8 T. unsalted butter with ½ c. sugar. Beat 6 egg yolks and 2 whole eggs until creamy and add to butter-and-sugar mixture. Add grated zest of 1 lemon and 1 t. lemon extract. Sift 3 ½ c. flour into the batter to make a soft dough. Roll out to ¼-in. thickness, cut into ring shapes, and set on greased cookie sheets. Bake at 375° for 10 min. Cool on racks.

KROC, RAY (1902–1984). Entrepreneur and restaurateur. With his purchase of the franchise rights to the McDonald's hamburger chain, Raymond Albert Kroc became one of the most successful fast-food entrepreneurs in the world, earning him a place on *Time* magazine's Time 100: The Most Important People of the Century.

Kroc was born in Oak Park, Illinois, to a family of Czech immigrants. During World War I, he was a Red Cross ambulance driver, afterwards taking a series of jobs that included paper-cup salesman and radio disc jockey. Eventually he became a salesman for Prince Castle Multi-Mixer, used primarily to make milk shakes and, after visiting a McDonald's hamburger store in San Bernardino, California, offered to be the owners' franchising agent. In 1961, he bought the McDonald's company for $2.7 million. Kroc opened his first McDonald's in Des Plaines, Illinois, on April 15, 1955.

Although drive-in restaurants were not new, Kroc capitalized on his restaurants' speed of service and the low price of the McDonald's hamburgers, which he achieved by getting rid of servers, silverware, glassware, and salt and pepper shakers and forcing customers out of their cars and into the store, where their orders were taken and dispatched in less than five minutes. Kroc worked hard to ensure that the product would taste exactly the same anywhere a unit was installed throughout the world. The architecture of the units maintained a specific design that always included a huge yellow *M* as the logo, which came to be known as the "golden arches." He prohibited cigarette machines and jukeboxes in his stores, which were all done in bright colors of red and yellow.

Kroc also created a TV clown character called Ronald McDonald, who first appeared at the 1966 Macy's Thanksgiving Day Parade, in New York City. He added new food items like the Filet-O-Fish (1964), the Big Mac (1968), the Quarter Pounder (1971), the Egg McMuffin (1973), and Chicken McNuggets (1982). In 1965, with 738 stores that, until then, had sold one billion burgers, Kroc took the company public, established an international division, and opened a "Hamburger University" in Elk Grove, Illinois, graduating students as of 1975 with a "Bachelor of Hamburgerology with a minor in French fries." He also, for a time, owned the San Diego Padres baseball team.

As both a perfectionist and a relentless promoter, Kroc drove himself hard. He suffered from alcoholism and diabetes, and in 1978 he suffered a stroke, entering alcohol rehab soon afterwards. He died of heart failure in 1984. The title of his autobiography, *Grinding It Out: The Making of McDonald's* (1977), says much about Kroc's drive to succeed.

During his life, Kroc was a generous philanthropist, donating millions to support research in alcoholism and other diseases, and he established the Ronald McDonald House foundation to provide safety and advocacy for families with critically ill children. The foundation now has chapters in fifty-two countries.

KRUG, CHARLES (1825–1892). Winemaker. As one of the first wine producers in California's Napa Valley, Charles Krug was a pioneer of the industry and sought to protect the provenance of California wine through his efforts with the Napa Valley Wine Co.

Born in Prussia, Krug traveled to the U.S. in 1847 to teach at a freethinkers' school in Philadelphia for a year, then returned to Germany, where he was imprisoned as a political reactionary. Once freed, he sailed

for California in 1858, to edit a German newspaper in Oakland, tried his hand at farming, then apprenticed himself to **Ágoston Haraszthy** at Buena Vista Winery, in Sonoma County, before building his own. He moved to St. Helena, in the Napa Valley, and in 1861, with a dowry of 520 acres of land from his marriage to Carolina Bale, he opened one of the first wineries in the valley. He named his winery Krug and over the next twenty years earned the title "Wine King of Napa Valley." Over the years to follow, Krug was a viticultural innovator, experimenting with various rootstocks and terroirs and using a cider press to crush his grapes.

He helped found the St. Helena Viticultural Society, the Board of State Viticultural Commissioners, and the Napa Valley Wine Company, which helped its members brand, market, and protect the provenance of California wines.

The phylloxera devastation, caused by root-eating aphids that began in the valley in the 1880s, ruined Krug's vineyards, putting him in debt until his death. His nephew tried to resuscitate the vineyards but failed, and the winery was taken over by banker James Moffitt Sr., who shut it down in 1894 but leased the property. In 1943, Cesare and Rosa Mondavi purchased the estate for $75,000 and ran it under the Krug name with their two sons, Peter and Robert, until the latter struck off on his own to open a winery under his own name.

In 2007, Krug was inducted into the **Culinary Institute of America**'s Vintners Hall of Fame.

KUGEL. A noodle or potato pudding served on the Jewish Sabbath. The word is from the Yiddish for "ball," derived from German. If made with noodles, the more frequently prepared of the two varieties, the dish is called *lukshen kugel*. Raisins are sometimes added to sweeten the dish. It is also commonly served with applesauce. "Kugel" first appeared in English print in 1846.

KUGEL

Cook ½ lb. noodles in boiling water and drain. Beat 3 egg yolks with 2 T. chicken fat, 2 T. sugar, and ½ t. salt, then fold into noodles. Beat 3 egg whites until stiff and fold into noodle mixture. Pour into greased pan, bake in 350° oven for about 30 min., then brown under flame. Serves 6.

KŪLOLO. Hawaiian word for a steamed pudding made with taro and coconut (1938), once wrapped in ti leaves and cooked in an **imu** oven.

KUMISS. Also "koumyss," "koumiss," and other variants. A beverage of fermented milk, possibly originating with the Mongols, having an acrid flavor and a small bit of alcohol present. Kumiss was thought to have some digestive benefits. The word comes from the Russian *kumys* and was first printed in English in 1598. "Laban" is a similar item.

KUMISS

Dissolve 4 oz. sugar in 1 gallon skim milk, pour into 1-qt. bottles, add 2 oz. dry yeast to each bottle, and seal tightly. Set bottles in warm place to ferment, then in cool cellar, set on their sides. Fermentation takes about 3 days.

KWANZAA. A Swahili term meaning "first fruits of the harvest," which in the U.S. has become the name of an African American festival that runs from December 26 to New Year's Day. Kwanzaa was created by activist Ron Maulana Karenga, of California State University at Long Beach, in 1966 as a way to encourage African Americans to commemorate their African heritage, which is marked on the last day of the festival with a feast called Kwanzaa Karamu, featuring the foods of Africa, South America, and the Caribbean. Karenga based Kwanzaa on what he called the Swahili Nguzo Saba, "Seven Principles of Sharing and Sustaining the World": unity, self-determination, collective work and responsibility, cooperative economics, purpose, creativity, and faith.

In 1991 Eric V. Copage published the first cookbook about the festival, entitled *Kwanzaa: An African-American Celebration of Culture and Cooking*.

L

LACTIC ACID. A spoilage inhibitor, added to cheese, desserts, carbonated drinks, and Spanish olives, that imparts a tart flavor to foods.

LA CUITE. Cooked sugar syrup in the last stage before it blackens and becomes bitter. The term is used among Louisiana Cajun cooks and derives from the French word for "cooking."

LADIES' NIGHT. A bar promotion offering women lower prices on drinks on a certain night of the week. The term dates to 1828. The idea is to attract more women and therefore more men to the bar. In 1972, the New York State Division of Human Rights prohibited ladies'-night promotions at Yankee Stadium because they discriminated against men, and in 1986 the Connecticut Commission on Human Rights ruled that ladies' nights be prohibited in all public bars for the same reason.

LADY BALTIMORE CAKE. A white cake filled with nuts and raisins and covered with a vanilla-and-egg-white frosting.

There are several stories about how the cake was named, but the most accepted version concerns a cake by this name baked by a Charleston, South Carolina, belle named Alicia Rhett Mayberry for novelist Owen Wister, who not only described the confection in his next book but named the novel itself *Lady Baltimore* (1906). In *American Food* (1974), Evan Jones noted that "it may also be true that the 'original' recipe became the property of the Misses Florence and Nina Ottolengui, who managed Charleston's Lady Baltimore Tea Room for a quarter of a century and annually baked and shipped to Owen Wister one of the very American cakes his novel had helped to make famous." Blanche S. Rhett, in *200 Years of Charleston Cooking* (1930), says the recipe came from the Woman's Exchange when Wister wrote his novel.

LADY BALTIMORE CAKE

Cream ½ c. butter and 1 ½ c. sugar, gradually adding 1 c. water, then 3 c. flour and 2 t. baking powder. Fold in 4 stiffly beaten egg whites and 1 t. vanilla. Bake in 3 buttered cake pans in a 375° oven. Boil 1 ½ c. sugar and ½ c. water in a double boiler until syrup forms a thread. Beat well and pour slowly over 2 stiffly beaten egg white with 1 t. vanilla. Beat until mixture can be spread on the cakes. Sprinkle on ½ c. raisins, 5 diced figs, ½ c. chopped pecans, and ⅓ c. candied cherries. Spread completely over layered cake.

LADYFINGER. A light sponge-cake biscuit. The name comes from the usual shape of the confection, which is long and narrow, light and delicate. (**Okra** is sometimes called "lady's fingers," too.) The word often appears in the possessive—"lady's finger" or "ladies' fingers"—and was first mentioned by John Keats, in an 1818 letter and again in his poem *The Cap and Bells* (1820). Ladyfingers have long been a popular confection in America, where some recipes call for the pastry to be pushed through a pastry tube.

"Lady finger" also applies in America to a variety of potato, dating in print to 1827.

LADYFINGER

Beat 1 egg white with a pinch of salt until foamy, add 1 ½ T. sugar, and beat until stiff. Beat 1 egg yolk with ½ t. vanilla and 1 ½ T. sugar until light. Fold in white and yolk together, then fold in ¼ c. flour. Spoon long, finger-shaped portions onto ungreased paper set on a cookie sheet and bake about 10 min. at 350°. Cool, then dust with confectioners' sugar. Makes 12.

LADY LOCK. A spiral-shaped pastry filled with whipped cream or marshmallow cream and shaped to resemble a lock of hair, first in print in 1920.

LAFAYETTE GINGERBREAD. Also called "Mary Ball Washington's ginger bread." A cakelike ginger-and-spice bread made by George Washington's mother when General Lafayette paid her a visit at her Fredericksburg, Virginia, home in 1784.

LAFAYETTE GINGERBREAD

Cream ½ c. butter, 1 c. brown sugar, and 1 c. molasses with ½ c. warm milk, 2 T. powdered ginger, 1 ½ t. cinnamon, 1 ½ t. mace, 1 ½ t. ground nutmeg, and ¼ c. brandy. Sift 3 c. flour with 1 t. cream of tartar and 3 beaten eggs and add to butter mixture. Add the juice of 1 orange and its grated rind, 1 t. baking soda in 2 T. water, and 1 c. raisins. Blend thoroughly. Bake in a buttered 12-by-9-in. pan at 350° for about 45 min. Serves 15.

LAGASSE, EMERIL (1959–). Chef, restaurateur, author, TV host, entrepreneur. In the 1980s, Emeril Lagasse emerged as one of the most exciting young chefs of modern Creole cuisine, and in the 1990s was the first professional chef to become a television and media star; he helped make food and cooking into subjects of major interest with the American public.

Of French Canadian and Portuguese background, Lagasse was born in Fall River, Massachusetts. He took culinary classes at Diman Vocational High School there and at Johnson & Wales University, in Providence, Rhode Island, then trained further in France. He returned to the U.S. to work in various restaurants in the Northeast, then, in 1982, was offered the chef's position by the Brennan family at Commander's Palace, in New Orleans, where he continued to develop their commitment to a modern form of Creole cooking.

Having garnered attention as a young chef to watch, Lagasse was able to open his own restaurant, Emeril's,

in 1990, and it was named by *Esquire* magazine the Best New Restaurant of the Year. His menu featured food from the various cultures that influenced Creole cuisine, such as French, Spanish, African, and Native American. The restaurant itself, in the Warehouse District, was a distinct departure in decor from the traditional look of New Orleans restaurants at the time.

Two years later, he opened a more casual restaurant called NOLA (an acronym for "New Orleans, Louisiana"), and the following year his first book, *Emeril's New New Orleans Cooking*, written with Jessie Tirsch, won wide acclaim, leading to Lagasse's being hired by the Food Network to do a cooking show.

Initially, Lagasse's wooden demeanor on camera caused little stir, but he was groomed to act in a more spirited manner, and in his 1994 series, *Essence of Emeril*, for which he was paid $50 per show, he adopted catchphrases like "Bam!," "Oh yeah, babe!," and "Let's kick the flavor up a notch!" The new on-air personality won him a wide audience as much for his entertainment value as his teaching skills. "I used to think when I started, 'I'm a chef, so I have to act like Alain Ducasse on TV,'" he said. "Doesn't work. Bores people." In 1976, *Time* magazine called the show one of the ten best shows on television. *People* magazine called him one of the 25 Most Intriguing People of the Year.

His next show, *Emeril Live*, filmed before a live audience, with a small band on the set, made Lagasse a media star, taking the idea of the celebrity chef much further than it had gone in the 1980s. In May 2003, Lagasse signed a five-year, multi-million-dollar deal for ninety new episodes on the Food Network, for which he was nominated (but never won) eight times for a daytime Emmy award. In the same period, he also opened new restaurants around the country, in Las Vegas, Atlanta, Miami, Charlotte, and other cities (not all succeeded), which led to criticisms that he was spreading himself too thin, especially after his TV sitcom show of 2001 was canceled within one season. Today Lagasse has thirteen restaurants.

In order to maintain quality control at his restaurants, Lagasse employed an outside firm to dine at his units each month and grade them, with half of the restaurant manager's bonus that year dependent on the score he received. "Inside all of this whatever-this-is, there's a serious chef in my body," he said in 2005. "That's what I am, that's what I know, that's where I came from, and everything revolves around that. And without that, I'm nothing."

Emeril Live was canceled at the end of 2007, but Lagasse went on to host a weekly variety show, *The Emeril Lagasse Show*, on Ion Television, beginning in 2010. *Emeril's Table* airs on the Hallmark Channel.

In addition to everything else, Lagasse had branded a number of products, including his signature Essence spice blend, canned pasta, wine, kitchen knives, and cookware. In 2008, **Martha Stewart** Living Omnimedia acquired the rights to all of Lagasse's TV shows and products (but not his restaurants) for $50 million.

Lagasse's books include *Louisiana Real and Rustic* (1996), *Emeril's Creole Christmas* (1997), *Emeril's TV Dinners* (1998), *From Emeril's Kitchens: Favorite Recipes from Emeril's Restaurants* (2003), *Emeril's Potluck: Comfort Food with a Kicked-Up Attitude* (2004), and *Emeril at the Grill: A Grilling Book for All Seasons* (2009).

Among the awards Lagasse has won are GQ Man of the Year, from *GQ* magazine; Best Southeast Regional Chef, from the **James Beard Foundation**; induction into the MenuMasters Hall of Fame by *Wine Spectator*; and the Silver Spoon Award, from *Food Arts*.

LAGNIAPPE. A Creole term for a small extra gift or bonus, such as a free roll given when one buys a dozen. It has been used in Louisiana since at least 1840 and is taken from the Spanish *la ñapa*, "the gift," by way of the Peruvian Quechua word *yápa*, "addition." In *Life on the Mississippi* (1883), Mark Twain wrote:

> We picked up one excellent word—a word worth traveling to New Orleans to get; a nice, limber, expressive, handy word—"Lagniappe." They pronounce it lannyyap….It is the equivalent of the thirteenth roll in a "baker's dozen." It is something thrown in, gratis, for good measure. The custom originated in the Spanish quarter of the city. When a child or a servant buys something in a shop—or even the mayor or the governor, for aught I know—he finishes the operation by saying: "Give me something for lagniappe."
>
> The shopman always responds; gives the child a bit of licorice-root, gives the servant a cheap cigar or a spool of thread, gives the governor—I don't know what be gives the governor, support, likely.
>
> When you are invited to drink—and this does occur now and then in New Orleans—and you say, "What, again?—no I've had enough," the other party says, "But just this one more time—this is for lagniappe."…If the waiter in the restaurant stumbles and spills a gill of coffee down the back of your neck he says, "F'r lagniappe, sah," and gets you another cup without extra charge.

LALLA ROOKH. A nineteenth-century dessert made with eggs, spirits, and whipped cream, although there are many variations. A 1910 cookbook by San Francisco chef Victor Hitzler, of the Hotel St. Francis, listed Lalla Rookh as nothing more than a crème de menthe cordial poured over ice in a sherbet glass, to be served as a digestive between courses.

The name comes from a long poem about a beautiful princess of India, *Lalla Rookh* (1817), by Thomas Moore. The poem, praised for its "barbaric splendors" and exotic details, was a great success in both England and America, and this rich dessert was named after the poem's heroine.

LALLA ROOKH

In a saucepan beat 5 egg yolks with 1 c. sugar, stirring until thickened. Cool, then add ¾ c. brandy and ¼ c. rum. Fold in 1 qt. whipped cream and 5 stiffly beaten egg whites. Mix in a pinch of nutmeg, pack in ice and salt, and freeze.

LAMB. A sheep (*Ovis aries*) less than a year old, usually slaughtered between four and twelve months for its meat. The word is derived from the Proto-Germanic *lambaz*. The meat of the lamb is considered one of the most desirable foods by many people, but it has never been among the more popular meats in the U.S., where beef and pork are preferred. Americans have also tended to slaughter their lambs somewhat later than Europeans and Asians, so that the taste is not as delicate as it is in other countries. Also, the social divisiveness and bloodshed caused by the introduction of sheep herds into the cattle country of the western territories in the late nineteenth century gave lamb a bad reputation for much of the twentieth century. In fact, Americans now eat only 0.9 pounds per person, as compared with sixty pounds of beef and forty-eight pounds of pork. When lamb is eaten, it is usually in the form of a roast or in lamb chops, much of it shipped in frozen from New Zealand.

There are three categories of lamb recognized in the U.S.: "baby" or "hothouse lamb," which is milk-fed and usually slaughtered at under six weeks of age; "spring lamb," milk-fed and slaughtered at under four months; and "lamb," weaned on grass and slaughtered at under one year; after one year, the animal's meat is termed "mutton," which is not very popular in America. Most U.S. lamb is sold as spring lamb, which federal regulations require be slaughtered between the beginning of March and the first week in October. A very small amount of baby lamb comes from Pennsylvania and New Jersey.

Lamb is customarily served with mint jelly in the U.S., and it is most popular at the Easter meal.

LAMB'S LETTUCE. Also "Pawnee lettuce," "fetticus," "corn salad," and "mâche." A salad green (*Valerianella locusta*) that grows into the fall and is usually eaten fresh, dating in print to 1817.

LAMB'S-QUARTERS (*Chenopodium album*). Also "lambs' quarters" or "quarter." A species of a wild plant, called "pigweed," "goosefoot," and "wild spinach," that originated in Europe and spread throughout the American West. The name, first in American print as of 1804, derives from "Lammas quarter," an ancient English festival at which a similar plant (*Atripex patula*) played a role. The Hopi packed the leaves around foods to be baked in order to keep in moisture, but others used them in stews or in salads. They may also be cooked like spinach, and the black seeds of the plant were used for breads. In the Southwest, the plant is sometimes called by its Spanish Mexican names, *quelites* and *epazote*.

LANE CAKE. A layer cake with a fluffy frosting and containing coconut, chopped fruits, and nuts in the filling. The cake was named after Emma Rylander Lane, of Clayton, Alabama, who published the original recipe under the name "Prize Cake" in her cookbook *Some Good Things to Eat* (1898). But according to Cecily Brownstone, author of the *Associated Press Cookbook* (1972) and friend of Mrs. Lane's granddaughter, the original recipe is very imprecise. In various forms it has become popular throughout the South.

According to Mrs. Lane, the cake "is much better… made a day or two before using."

LANE CAKE

Beat 2 c. sugar, 1 ¾ c. butter, and 2 t. vanilla until light. Combine 3 ½ c. flour, 4 ½ t. baking powder, and 1 ½ t. salt and add to butter mixture, alternating with 1 ½ c. milk until smooth. Fold in 8 stiffly beaten egg whites. Divide batter and pour into 3 buttered and floured cake pans. Bake for 20 min. at 375°, then cool. Melt ½ c. butter with 1 c. sugar, ⅓ c. bourbon, and ⅓ c. water, bring to boil, dissolve ingredients together, and stir half the mixture into 9 lightly beaten egg yolks. Return to saucepan and cook until thickened. Remove from heat, then stir in 1 c. chopped raisins, ¼ c. chopped pecans, ½ c. chopped maraschino cherries, ½ c. flaked coconut, and ¾ t. vanilla. Cool to room temperature, then spread over cake layers and on top. Combine 1 c. sugar, ⅓ c. water, ¼ t. cream of tartar, and a dash of salt in a saucepan and bring to a boil, stirring until sugar is dissolved. Add 1 t. vanilla, then pour mixture very slowly into 2 beaten egg whites. Frost the cake with this icing.

LANG, GEORGE (1924–2011). Restaurateur, author. After emigrating to the U.S. from Hungary, George Lang became one of the most creative young restaurateurs of the postwar period, helping to transform the image of the business from an often unsavory, second-class endeavor to a modern expression of high-class American food culture.

Born György Deutsch to a Jewish family in Székesfehérvár, Hungary, he later adapted his mother's maiden name, Lang, because *Deutsch* meant "German." His talent for the violin allowed him to attend the Franz Liszt Academy of Music until, at nineteen, his family was sent by the Germans to a forced-labor camp in Komárom, from which he escaped to Budapest. (His parents would die at Auschwitz.)

Lang helped fellow Jews into hiding, but he was captured and tortured by the occupying Soviets, who one day forced him at gunpoint to play the violin for eight hours. Put on trial but acquitted of fascist activities, Lang escaped in a coffin to Austria and in 1946 traveled to NYC, where he earned a summer scholarship to Tanglewood and a place as violinist in the Dallas Symphony Orchestra. But he gave up on the idea of being a professional musician after seeing a concert by Jascha Heifetz and realizing he could never play like that.

Lang returned to New York City to work at the Waldorf-Astoria Hotel and in the catering business—"a wedding factory," he called it—then was hired by the Brass Rail company to open a modern restaurant at NYC's Idlewild Airport (later renamed John F. Kennedy), where in 1960 he came to the attention of **Joe Baum**, of Restaurant Associates, who hired Lang to open the Tower Suite, atop the Time-Life Building. He went on to develop more than a dozen restaurant operations at the 1964 New York World's Fair, including the international-pavilion food services, employee cafeterias, a private dining room for Henry Ford, and a first-class restaurant named Festival 64/65, with glass walls overlooking a reflecting pool, outdoor tables of unbreakable glass, and updated American classic dishes.

In 1967, Lang was director of the Four Seasons restaurant, in NYC, where he made the menu grander and more international while cosseting a higher-class clientele.

In 1970, Lang left Restaurant Associates to found his own restaurant consulting business. In his essay "A Sure-Fire Recipe for an American Bistro," he listed, with his usual irony, the main ingredients: "Several sackfuls of money, preferably not yours and without strings attached. 1 seasoned chef…preferably one whose ego has to be fed only once a day. The combined leadership qualities of de Gaulle and Genghis Khan. The optimism of a person who is getting married for the seventh time." (Lang himself was married thrice.)

During this time he also wrote the authoritative *Cuisine of Hungary* (1971).

In 1975, David Garth, a board member of New York's Hôtel des Artistes, asked Lang to run the famous but by then decrepit Café des Artistes, famous for its murals of nude women painted by former Hôtel resident Howard Chandler Christy. Lang restored the paintings and premises in the style of "an elegant bistro." He updated the menus, with some dishes, like his mother's

Ilona torte, culled from his childhood. In 1984, he published *The Café des Artistes Cookbook*.

In 1991, under prompting from Hungarian American philanthropist and art collector Ronald S. Lauder, Lang restored and co-owned Gündel, a famous Budapest restaurant then in severe decline, bringing back the sumptuous cooking of Budapest's glorious past.

Through the 1990s, the Café des Artistes, run by Lang's wife, Jenifer, was a continuing success with artists and musicians from Lincoln Center, across the street, but eventually labor-union problems forced the Langs to close the restaurant in 2009. (It reopened in 2011 as the Leopard.) Lang suffered through ten months of decline from Alzheimer's disease, from which he died in 2011.

Lang's memoir was entitled *Nobody Knows the Truffles I've Seen* (1998), in which he wrote of his childhood, "Clearly I was precocious; I already knew what foods were worth consuming. And I was just as impatient then as I have been for the rest of my life—my daily prayer being 'Please, God, give it to me, and *now*!'"

LAPPÉ, FRANCES MOORE (1944–). Author and advocate. With the publication of her 1971 book *Diet for a Small Planet* (three million copies sold), Frances Moore Lappé became a forceful advocate for change in the American way of eating. In it she wrote that she had "discovered the incredible level of protein waste built into the American meat-centered diet," concluding that "feeding the earth's people is more profoundly a political and economic problem which you and I must help to solve."

Born in Pendleton, Oregon, and raised in Fort Worth, Texas, Frances Moore graduated from Earlham College, in Indiana (1966), and soon after married toxicologist and environmentalist Dr. Marc Lappé. (They divorced in 1977.) While in graduate studies in social work at the University of California at Berkeley, she concluded that much of the malnutrition in poor countries was due to an inadequate means of distributing the world's abundance of food, an idea introduced in *Diet for a Small Planet*, which became a seminal work in its field, not least for its advocacy of the importance of vegetables over animal protein.

In 1975, Lappé helped launch the Institute for Food and Development Policy, the Center for Living

Democracy (1990), and its American News Service (1995–2000) to promote her ideas in the media. In 2002, with her daughter Anna, she established the Small Planet Institute, based in Cambridge, Massachusetts, for research and popular education. The Small Planet Fund raises resources for democratic social movements worldwide.

Lappé is an adviser to the Calgary Centre for Global Community and to Corporate Accountability International's Value the Meal campaign. She is also a member of the International Commission on the Future of Food and Agriculture and the National Advisory Board of the Union of Concerned Scientists.

Along with seventeen honorary doctorates, Lappé has taught at the Institute for the Study of Social Change, at the University of California at Berkeley (1984–1985), and the Massachusetts Institute of Technology (2000–2001). In 2006 and 2008, Lappé was a visiting professor at Suffolk University, in Boston.

Her list of awards is extensive, including the Right Livelihood Award (1987); the Rachel Carson Award, from the National Nutritional Foods Association (2003); and the **James Beard Foundation** Humanitarian of the Year award (2008).

The Women's National Book Association chose *Diet for a Small Planet* as one of "75 Books by Women Whose Words Have Changed the World." In 2008, *Gourmet* named her among twenty-five people whose work has changed the way America eats.

Lappé's books have been translated into fifteen languages, including *Food First: Beyond the Myth of Scarcity* (1977) and *World Hunger: Twelve Myths* (1986, revised 1998), both with Joseph Collins; *Rediscovering America's Values* (1989); *Hope's Edge: The Next Diet for a Small Planet*, with Anna Lappé (2002); and *EcoMind: Changing the Way We Think to Create the World We Want* (2011).

LAP LUNCH. A meal eaten on a plate set on one's lap at a casual party, dating in print, as "laptea," to 1867.

LAST CALL. A bartender's announcement to customers just before closing time that last orders for drinks must be put in immediately.

LATE HARVEST. A term used by American winemakers to indicate a wine made from grapes picked late in the fall, after they have been attacked by the mold *Botrytis cinerea*. The mold allows moisture to escape and concentrates the sugars in the grapes, resulting in a very sweet, almost syrupy wine having high alcohol content. In California, late-harvest wines are often made from the **Johannisberg Riesling** grape.

LATH-OPEN BREAD. Appalachian biscuit-dough bread made into thin cakes so that when broken with the fingers, they break into flakes that resemble lath, dating in print to 1913.

LATKE. A Jewish pancake, usually made from potatoes, traditionally served at Hanukkah, dating in print to 1927. The word is Yiddish, from the Russian *làtka*, for "pastry." The dish commemorates the biblical story of the Jewish Maccabees' defeat of the Syrians in 165 b.c. (1 Macc 3:57). They found in the Temple of Jerusalem only enough oil to burn for one night, but the oil miraculously burned for eight nights. The oil used for frying the latkes symbolizes this miracle.

This tradition developed among the Ashkenazi Jews of Northern and Eastern Europe, many of whom came to America in the late nineteenth century and who carried the tradition with them. The potato latke has been made for more than two hundred years, ever since the potato, brought from America in the sixteenth century, was accepted by Europeans as an edible food.

LATKE

Wash 6 potatoes and dice. Dry them, then grate, retaining some of the juice. Grate 1 small onion, add ½ t. salt and 1 egg. Blend well. Mix in 3 t. matzo meal with ½ t. baking powder and blend into potatoes. Drop spoonfuls of the mixture into hot fat and cook until browned on all sides. Drain. Serve with applesauce or sour cream. Serves 4.

LAULAU. Hawaiian word for food cooked in ti leaves, usually steamed or baked in the **imu** pit, dating in print to 1938. Traditionally filled with fish, laulau may now be stuffed with pork, beef, or chicken.

LEATHER. An early American confection made from dried-fruit "butters" or purees baked slowly and cut into long strips resembling strips of leather, dating in print to 1849. Today it is commonly marketed as "fruit leather."

LEATHER

Cook 1 lb. of fruit, such as peach or apricot, in simmering water until tender. Run through a sieve or food mill, add 1 part brown sugar or honey to 4 parts fruit puree, then simmer for 5 min. Spread in thin sheets over a buttered baking pan and let dry out thoroughly in a slow, 250° oven for 2 hr. Cool, sprinkle with confectioners' sugar, and, if desired, roll up. Serves 4.

LEATHER OR FEATHER. Airline workers' slang for the choice between the beef and chicken entrées offered as part of in-flight service. The term was first in print in 1989.

LEBKUCHEN. A Pennsylvania Dutch spiced drop cake made especially at Christmastime. The term is from German, appearing in English print as of 1850.

LEBKUCHEN

Boil 1 qt. honey in a pan, then mix with ¾ lb. sugar with ¼ lb. citron, ½ lb. ground almonds, ¼ lb. orange peel, 1 oz. cinnamon, 1 pkg. yeast, 3 T. cherry brandy, some nutmeg, and 2 ¼ lb. flour. Knead for 15 min. Let stand overnight. Roll out and cut into 2-in. squares. Bake in a tin dish.

LECITHIN. An emulsifier and antioxidant found in animal and plant tissues and used in baked goods, chocolate, ice cream, and other foods. Lecithin also keeps oil and water from separating.

LE COZE, MAGUY (1943–) and **GILBERT** (1945–1994). Restaurateurs, cookbook authors, and chef. Upon opening Le Bernardin restaurant, in New York City, in 1986, sister and brother Maguy and Gilbert Le Coze set a new standard and style for seafood cookery in America, demanding the best product, almost entirely from American waters, and preparing it with exquisite simplicity in dishes widely copied by other chefs.

The Le Cozes were born in Port Navalo, Brittany, France, where Gilbert learned about fishing from his grandfather and about cooking from his father, who ran the Hôtel du Rhuys, where, from the ages of twelve and thirteen, Gilbert and Maguy worked.

After Gilbert finished his military service, with Maguy set on a modeling career, the two moved to Paris in 1966, where she worked in restaurants and he as a bartender. Borrowing money from relatives, friends, and the bank, they opened a thirty-five-seat bistro on the Left Bank in 1972, naming it Le Bernardin, after the folksong "Les Moines de St. Bernardin." After initial harsh reviews, the restaurant garnered its first Michelin star in 1976. Eight years later, the Le Cozes moved to a larger space, near the Arc de Triomphe, and earned their second star.

In 1986, they were invited by Ben Holloway, head of the Equitable Life Insurance Co., to open a branch of Le Bernardin in its new New York City headquarters, on West Fifty-first Street. Within months of opening, it earned four stars from the *New York Times*.

The elegant Maguy, dressed in Chanel, with a bobbed haircut to match, managed the dining room while Gilbert, who spoke no English, ran the kitchen and created innovative ideas like his black bass in extra virgin olive oil and a French style of raw fish that evoked Japanese sashimi, at a time when much of the fish served in restaurants was inferior or frozen. Gilbert was famous for visiting the Fulton Fish Market at 3 a.m. to pick out the finest catch of the day and was resolute in paying the highest price for it.

Owing to the great success of the New York City Le Bernardin, and after learning from the Michelin Guide that they would never get a third star because they served only seafood, the Le Cozes closed the Paris restaurant and concentrated on NYC, where some meat dishes were added to the menu. They also opened brasseries in Coconut Grove, Florida, and Atlanta, but later closed both.

In July 1994, Gilbert died of a heart attack while working out at a health club. Maguy carried on operating Le Bernardin with executive chef Eric Ripert, who eventually became her partner in the business and co-authored *Le Bernardin Cookbook: Four-Star Simplicity* (1998) with her, as well as writing other books on his own.

As a master chef in his own right, Ripert maintained Le Bernardin's style of cuisine, maintaining its four stars from the *Times* and three from the Michelin Guide.

After Gilbert's death, Maguy wrote of their relationship as "two halves of a whole who made a life together. Gilbert was the most important person in my life, and I in his. We had a bond that for some was incomprehensible and more than blood. For us, it was always natural. We came into the world separately, first me, then Gilbert, but we were barely a beat apart."

LEE CAKE. Also "Robert E. Lee cake." A white cake flavored with citrus rind and juice, supposedly based on recipes of cooks for General Robert E. Lee (1807–1870), commander of the Confederate Army in the Civil War. In *The Robert E. Lee Family Cooking and Housekeeping Book* (1997), Anne Carter Zimmer suggests that a recipe for such a citrus layer cake was well known in the Lee family but never written down. The first recipe dates to 1879, in *Housekeeping in Old Virginia: Contributions from Two Hundred and Fifty of Virginia's Noted Housewives, Distinguished for Their Skill in the Culinary Art and Other Branches of Domestic Economy*, edited by Marion Cabell Tyree.

LEE CAKE

Beat 10 eggs until light in color and add 1 lb. sugar and 1 lb. flour, alternating the two ingredients. Grate in the rind of 1 lemon and add its juice, mix well, pour batter into cake pans, and bake at 350° until inserted knife comes out clean. Make icing of 1 lb. powdered sugar, 2 beaten egg whites, and the juice and rind of 1 orange. Coat layers of cake, sides, and top.

LEEK (*Allium porrum*). An onionlike plant of the lily family, having green leaves and a white bulbous stalk. It is eaten as a vegetable, usually boiled, but has had little popularity in the U.S. until recently. Wild leek (*A. tricoccum*) is found in eastern North America. The word in Old English is *lēac*.

LEFSE. Norwegian American thin, flat bread made from potatoes, first in print in 1902, from the Norwegian. It is a Thanksgiving and Christmas holiday bread. The Norsland Lefse bakery, in Rushford, Minnesota, makes about 500,000 lefses annually. In 1983, to celebrate its centennial, Starbuck, Minnesota, claimed to have made the world's largest lefse, at seventy pounds and ten feet in diameter.

LEMON (*Citrus limon*). A yellow-skinned, tangy citrus fruit native to Asia. Its juice, pulp, and rind are used in a wide variety of dishes, desserts, drinks, and **cocktails**. The word is from the Persian *līmūn* and first appeared in print around 1400. "Lemonade" is sweetened juice and water.

Lemons have been cultivated around the eastern Mediterranean for at least 2,500 years, and after the Crusades they became a desirable fruit in Europe, where they began to be grown in Sicily, Spain, and other Mediterranean countries. Legend has it that Columbus brought lemon seeds to Florida, and Spanish friars grew the fruit in California, where it flourished in the middle of the nineteenth century—especially the Eureka (possibly first cultivated in California or brought from Sicily) and the Lisbon (brought from Australia). In 1874, James W. Parkinson, writing of American dishes at the Philadelphia Centennial Exposition, noted that "citron" (*C. medica*), a lemon-like fruit, had "lately been transplanted in California, and promise[s] in the near future to equal the best."

In 1934, Irvin Swartzberg, of Chicago, began selling gallon bottles of fresh lemon juice to bars and restaurants and, after perfecting a method of concentrating the juice with water, sold the product in the market under the name Puritan-ReaLemon.

"Lemon meringue pie," made with lemon curd and topped with meringue, has been a favorite American dessert since the nineteenth century. "Shaker lemon pie," made from sliced lemons, was beloved by the Shakers because lemons were one of the foods they themselves did not produce and valued highly.

Today, California produces most of the American lemon crop, with Florida and Texas also contributing. The common or "acid" lemon is the variety most used in the food industry and at home. In 2011, Americans consumed 855,000 tons of lemons.

LEMON MERINGUE PIE

Combine ⅓ c. cornstarch, ⅛ t. salt, and ⅔ c. sugar, stir in 1 ½ c. water, and cook over medium heat until mixture thickens and comes to a boil for 1 min. Remove from heat. Beat 4 egg yolks, stir in 2 T. of cornstarch mixture, then stir eggs into the rest of the cornstarch, being careful to stir out lumps. Add juice of 2 lemons and grated rind of 1 lemon. Cook in saucepan until thickened, but do not boil. Pour into pie crust and cool 10 min. Beat ½ c. sugar into 4 egg whites until stiff, mold on top of pie, and bake in 400° oven until top is lightly browned. Cool.

LESLIE, ELIZA (1787–1858). Author. With her cookbook *Receipts for Pastry, Cakes, and Sweetmeats*, by "a Lady of Philadelphia," in 1828, Eliza Leslie was among the first American cookbook writers and the most popular of the nineteenth century.

Born in Philadelphia, Leslie grew up mostly in London with her father, a watchmaker turned exporter. He returned with his family to the U.S. in 1800, where he went bankrupt, forcing his wife and daughter to open a boardinghouse. Eliza was educated in women's crafts of the day, mainly sewing and cooking, and attended Mrs. William Goodfellow's cooking school. But she had a literary bent, saying, "the dream of my childhood [was] one day seeing my name in print." At the age of forty, having collected recipes from Goodfellow's, she published *Seventy-five Receipts for Pastry, Cakes, and Sweetmeats* (1827), one of the first cookbooks by an American.

Still, her heart was in fiction, at first children's stories, and she found acceptance in the women's magazines of the day, including the annual gift book *The Gift*, which she edited. At a time when women did not write under their own names, she published the *American Girl's Book* in 1831 as "Miss Leslie," following with *Miss Leslie's Behavior Book* (1834), *Miss Leslie's Lady's New Receipt-Book* (1850), *Miss Leslie's Directions for Cookery* (1851), *Miss Leslie's New Receipts for Cooking* (1854), and, in 1857, the book that brought her the greatest recognition, *Miss Leslie's New Cookery Book*. In her cookbooks, Leslie often used British and French recipes but favored American dishes using indigenous ingredients, including catfish and okra. She recommended measurements, which, although she was not always strict about them, were enough to give an untutored cook confidence to obtain good results.

In a new nation with a growing middle class both in and beyond cities, Leslie's cookbooks provided easy recipes for housewives and home cooks to follow.

She also wrote a novel of manners, *Amelia: Or, A Young Lady's Vicissitudes* (1848). Leslie never married, living her later life at the U.S. Hotel, in Philadelphia, but she died in Gloucester, New Jersey, in 1858.

LETTUCE. Any of a variety of plants in the genus *Lactuca*, especially *L. sativa*, cultivated for its leaves, which are used in salads. The word is from the Latin *lactūca*, which in Middle English became *letuse*.

England had cultivated lettuce as of the fifteenth century, but Christopher Columbus may have been the first to bring it to America. Lettuce was grown only in home gardens until the twentieth century, when Americans' new appetite for salad made commercial production profitable. Today lettuce is raised in twenty of the states, cultivated in three main botanical varieties:

HEAD LETTUCE. Also "cabbage lettuce" (*L. s. capitata*). This variety includes the "butterhead," the principal horticultural varieties of which are the "Boston" and the "Bibb" (supposedly named after amateur breeder John B. Bibb, of Frankfort, Kentucky, although the variety was introduced in 1890 as "Half Century"); and the "crisp head," which includes the "Imperial" and "iceberg" varieties, this last having been introduced by W. Atlee Burpee & Co. in 1894, becoming the most popular lettuce in America by the 1930s.

LEAF LETTUCE (*L. s. crispa*). This variety includes the "oak leaf" and "salad bowl" lettuces.

ROMAINE OR COS LETTUCE (*L. s. longifolia*). "Romaine" derives from Old French for the city of Rome, whereas "cos" refers to the Greek island of Cos, or Kos, from which it may have originated.

LEWIS, EDNA (1916–2006). Author, teacher, chef. As both a cookbook author and teacher of generations of Americans, Edna Lewis was a leading caretaker and living repository of African American culinary traditions and lore.

Lewis was born into a family of eight children in Freetown, Virginia, on a farm granted to her grandfather after he was freed from slavery. She learned to cook from her aunt Jenny on a wood-fired stove. Upon her father's death, Lewis left home at sixteen for Washington, D.C., then New York City, where she worked as a seamstress while becoming politically active, including working for the Communist newspaper the *Daily Worker*. She married retired merchant seaman and fellow Communist Steve Kingston.

In 1949, an antiques dealer named Johnny Nicholson hired her as a cook for his restaurant Café Nicholson, which drew clientele from the fashion, arts, and literary worlds. After five years there, Lewis left and tried her hand at pheasant farming and other ventures while continuing to cook at home. She began compiling a cookbook while convalescing with a broken leg, and published *The Edna Lewis Cookbook* in 1972. This was followed by the far more successful *Taste of Country Cooking* (1976), which contained as much information about southern and African American food culture as it did recipes.

When her husband passed away, Lewis returned to the restaurant business, making her mark at places like the Fearrington House, in Pittsboro, North Carolina; Middleton Place, in Charleston, South Carolina; U.S. Steak House, in New York; and the historic landmark Gage & Tollner, in Brooklyn. She retired as a chef in 1992.

Lewis founded the Society for the Revival and Preservation of Southern Food, telling the *New York Times* in 1989, "As a child in Virginia, I thought all food tasted delicious. After growing up, I didn't think food tasted the same, so it has been my lifelong effort to try and recapture those good flavors of the past." Her next books were *In Pursuit of Flavor* (1988) and *The Gift of Southern Cooking* (2003), which she co-wrote with Scott Peacock, whom she befriended after meeting him while he was a cook at the Virginia governor's mansion. Peacock later became Lewis's caretaker, until she died in her sleep at the age of eighty-nine, in Decatur, Georgia.

Tall and regal-looking, the woman known to everyone as "Miss Edna" garnered many honors, receiving the first lifetime achievement award from the Southern Foodways Alliance and being named a Grande Dame by Les Dames d'Escoffier, both in 1999.

In July 2004, the U.S. State Department's *U.S. Society & Values* journal, in its issue on "Americans at the Table," includes Lewis as one of seven "Taste Setters," writing, "No one has done more than Edna Lewis to acquaint the general public with traditional Southern cooking, and to bring it the recognition and respect that it deserves."

LIBERTY CABBAGE. A euphemism created during World War I as a patriotic substitute for the German "sauerkraut." The term, H. L. Mencken noted, was "a complete failure." In a similar vein, Representatives Robert W. Ney of Ohio and Walter B. Jones Jr. of North Carolina, in March 2003, declared that House of Representatives cafeteria menus would list "freedom fries" and "freedom toast" in place of "French fries" and "French toast," in an effort to be "patriotic and supportive of President George W. Bush" during the invasion of Iraq that spring, which was opposed by France. By 2005 the names had been changed back.

LIEDERKRANZ. Trademark name for a strong-smelling cow's-milk cheese of distinctly American origins. The story of Liederkranz began in 1889, when NYC delicatessen owner Adolphe Tode, who also owned the Monroe Cheese Co. in Monroe, New York, asked his cheese makers to try to duplicate the flavor of an imported German soft-ripened brick cheese known as *Bismarck Schlosskäse* ("Bismarck castle cheese"), which was popular among German Americans. Swiss immigrant cheese maker Emil Frey took up the challenge and failed, but he managed to come up with a similar but distinctly different cheese that he sent to Tode, who ordered more. Unfortunately, Frey was unable to duplicate the cheese until 1892, when Tode introduced it to a popular singing group called the Liederkranz Society (whose members included Theodore Roosevelt). The word means "wreath of song" in German.

Liederkranz was an instant success, listed on a menu at the Liederkranz Halle, in NYC, for May 19, 1892, and its popularity caused the Monroe Cheese Co. to expand production where there was more milk available, in Van Wert, Ohio. At first, Tode could not reproduce the cheese, but he did so after bringing in his old factory's equipment and allowing the bacteria to fill the air at his new plant.

In 1929, the Monroe Cheese Co. was bought by the Borden Co., which, after a fire at its Van Wert plant in 1981, discontinued its natural cheeses, selling that division the next year to General Foods, which stopped making the cheese altogether. The Van Wert plant was bought by the Fisher Cheese Co., which began making Liederkranz again, but bacterial contamination of a batch in 1985 forced the cheese from the market, with the bacteria culture sold to Beatrice Foods and the New Zealand Dairy Board, which discontinued the cheese. Based on surviving cultures, however, the cheese was finally reintroduced in 2010 by DCI Cheese Co. of Richfield, Wisconsin, and trademarked.

LIGHT. Also "lite," "lighter," and "lower fat." A food-industry term implying a fat content lower than that in similar products. "Light beer" (which makes up 18 percent of the domestic market) may contain only one-third the calories of regular beer.

According to the Nutrition Labeling and Education Act of 1990, whose regulations were adopted in May 1993, a product labeled "light" may mean two things: (1) that a nutritionally altered product contains one-third fewer calories or half the fat of the reference food (if the food derives 50 percent or more of its calories from fat, the reduction must be 50 percent of the fat); or (2) that the sodium content of a low-calorie, low-fat food has been reduced by 50 percent. "Light in sodium" refers to a food in which sodium content has been reduced by at least 50 percent. The term "light" may continue to be used to describe properties such as texture and color if the label describes the intent, as in "light brown sugar" or "light and fluffy."

Meat, poultry, seafood, and game products labeled "lean" must have fewer than ten grams of fat, fewer than four grams of saturated fat, and fewer than ninety-six milligrams of cholesterol per serving and per one hundred grams. "Extra lean" products must contain fewer than five grams of fat, fewer than two grams of saturated fat, and fewer than ninety-five milligrams of cholesterol.

"Reduced" means that a nutritionally altered product contains 25 percent less of a nutrient or of calories than the regular product (unless the regular product

already meets the requirement). The rule for any food, altered or not, using the word "less" is the same.

"Low" (also "little," "few," or "low source of") may be used on foods that could be eaten frequently without exceeding dietary guidelines for one or more of these components: fat, saturated fat, cholesterol, sodium, and calories. "Low fat" indicates three grams or less per serving; "low saturated fat," one gram or less; "low sodium," fewer than 140 milligrams per serving; "very low sodium," fewer than thirty-five milligrams; "low cholesterol," fewer than twenty milligrams per serving; "low calorie," forty calories or fewer per serving.

"Free" means that a product contains no amount of, or only physiologically inconsequential amounts of, one or more of the following: fat, saturated fat, cholesterol, sodium, sugars, and calories.

Under these regulations, nutrition labeling is required on most foods (voluntary for many raw foods, many fresh fruits and vegetables, and raw fish).

LIMA BEAN (*Phaseolus limensis*). A green flat bean, called the "butter bean" in the South. The lima bean takes its name from the city of Lima, Peru, where it was cultivated very early. The bean was introduced to North America, where it was enjoyed by the Native Americans long before the arrival of the European settlers; it is the principal ingredient of **succotash**.

The lima bean is first mentioned in print in 1756.

Lima beans are eaten fresh but are more often boiled and buttered. California produces most of the U.S. lima bean crop.

LIME (*Citrus aurantifolia*). A tangy green citrus fruit similar to the lemon. Its name derives from the Arabic *līmah* and was first mentioned in English in 1615. Indigenous to Southeast Asia, the lime was introduced to Europe through Italy. In *Fading Feast* (1981), Raymond Sokolov writes, "Whether Columbus brought seeds of *C. aurantifolia* with him to Haiti in 1493 is a matter of conjecture, but it seems probable, since limes were flourishing on that island in 1520. Limes then spread gradually across the West Indies, westward to Mexico and northward to the Florida Keys." Lime trees were established in the Keys by Dr. Henry Perrine in 1835, and these so-called Key limes (called "Mexican" in the Southwest) became a major commercial crop after 1906. But a hurricane in 1926 destroyed many of the groves. The groves were replanted with a more practical crossbreed called the "Tahiti" lime (particularly the Persian, Bearss, Idemore, and Pond varieties), which had been grown in California since the 1850s and in Florida since 1883.

Today, almost all limes grown in America are of the Tahiti variety, while true Key limes are a rarity grown only on private, noncommercial plots in the Florida Keys.

Americans use limes as a flavoring for desserts and cocktails and to enhance the flavor of fish and salads. The most famous confection made with limes is "Key lime pie," a tangy pie made with condensed milk and piled high with meringue or whipped cream. Because of the unavailability of true Key limes outside the Florida Keys, Key lime pies are almost never made with anything but Tahiti limes.

Key lime pies were first made in the Keys in the 1850s. Jeanne A. Voltz, in *The Flavor of the South* (1977), explains that the recipe developed with the advent of sweetened condensed milk, in 1856. Since there were few cows on the Keys, the new canned milk was welcomed by the residents and introduced into a pie made with lime juice.

The original pies were made with a pastry crust, but a crust made from graham crackers later became popular. Today it is a matter of preference, as is the choice between whipped cream and meringue toppings. There are three recipes for Key lime pie in *The Key West Cook Book* (1949), only one of which refers to a graham cracker crust, and two of which do not require the pie to be baked. One has no topping, one whipped cream, and one meringue.

KEY LIME PIE

In a bowl combine ¼ c. graham cracker crumbs, ⅓ c. sifted confectioners' sugar, and 6 T. unsalted butter, melted and cooled. Press the mixture into a pie plate to form a crust, bake in a 350° oven for 10 min. until lightly browned, then cool on rack. Beat 4 egg yolks until light in color, stir in one 14-oz. can sweetened condensed milk, ¼ c. lime juice, ½ t. cream of tartar, then another ¼ c. lime juice. Spoon into shell and bake at 325° until it sets, about 10-15 min. Freeze for at least 3 hr. Beat 4 egg whites with ¼ c. sugar

until stiff, spread over pie, and bake in 450° oven until meringue is golden.

LIMPA. Swedish American rye bread made with molasses, dating in print to 1948. From the Swedish.

LIMPIN' SUZAN. Also "limping Susan." A southern dish of red beans and okra or rice, dating in print to 1952, a corollary to the more familiar **hopping john**.

LIMPIN' SUZAN

Cover 1 lb. red beans with water and let soak for several hours. Drain and add 1 chopped onion, ¼ lb. salt pork, and water to cover. Cook until tender. Remove ½ c. of the beans and 2 T. of the liquid and mash into a puree. Add pepper and salt and 3-4 c. cooked rice. Cook through until heated and top with the rest of the beans. Serves 6-8.

LIMU. Hawaiian word for edible seaweeds or algae. In primitive Hawaiian culture, women gathered and prepared seaweeds and made them a staple of their diet. Today Hawaiians eat about fifteen species, both fresh and salted, but not usually dried. Some of the more popular limu include *wawae'iole*, *ogo*, and *manauea*. While many seaweeds are connected with legends and rituals, *limu kala* is specifically eaten at family gatherings called *ho'oponopono*, where grievances are aired and arguments settled peacefully. The word *kala* means "to forgive."

LINGUINE. Also "linguini." A flat pasta about one-eighth of an inch wide. Linguine, a staple of Italian American restaurants, is commonly served with a red or white clam sauce. The word, from the Italian for "little tongues", was first printed in English in 1945.

LIQUOR. A distilled spirit. The word, originally from the Latin, derives from Middle English *liccur* and dates in English as a spirit to 1340. Liquor is a general term for spirits that includes **whiskey**, **brandy**, **rum**, **vodka**, **gin**, and **cordials**. "Malt liquor" is brewed like **beer** from malt but has a higher alcohol content than beer, though it is usually nowhere close to the proof of most liquors.

American slang for liquor constitutes a freewheeling, sometimes hilarious compendium of imaginative speech, with entries running into the hundreds for general terms and into the thousands for specific cocktails (most of which have not worn well or become part of the bartender's repertoire). For specific cocktail names, look under main entries—**martini**, **manhattan**, **piña colada**, and others. The following list includes general terms for spirits, followed by dates indicating when they came into use or were first recorded in print: "Jersey lightning" (1780), "**antifogmatic**" (1789), "phlegm cutter" (1806), "firewater" (1817), "rotgut" (1819), "red eye" (1819), "coffin varnish" (1845), "tanglefoot" (1859), "tarantula juice" (1861), "sheep dip" (1865), "pick me up" (1867), "**shot**" (1906), "belt" (1921), and "panther sweat" (1929).

LIQUOR SOCK. A knitted sock used in dry counties in the Midwest to carry liquor bottles to bring to restaurants forbidden to sell alcohol.

LITTLE JOE'S. A dish made of ground meat and spinach, with various seasonings according to taste. It would seem to be a variation on the kind of thrown-together dish elsewhere called **sloppy joe** or **Johnny Marzetti**, but John Thorne, in his *Simple Cooking* newsletter (1982), states, "Little Joe's is a popular San Francisco dish, named after the restaurant where, as legend has it, the meal was tossed together from left-overs in the kitchen late one night for a hungry customer."

LITTLE JOE'S

In 2 T. oil sauté 1 chopped onion until soft. Add 1 lb. ground beef and break up, cooking until gray. Add 1 c. cooked spinach, salt, and pepper and cook until spinach is wilted. Beat 2 eggs with a dash of Tabasco sauce, add to beef, and cook until eggs have set. Sprinkle with Parmesan cheese if desired, then spoon onto crisp rolls. Serves 4.

LITTLE RONCADOR. Also "roncador," "shiner," "tomcod," and other names. A fish (*Genyonemus lineatus*) of the California coastline. The name derives from the Spanish *roncar*, "to grunt," because of the grunting sound the fish makes by inflating a bladder. The word dates in print to 1867. "Ronco" is a **grunt** in the genus *Haemulon*, found in West Indian waters.

LIVERWURST. Also "liver pudding" and "liver sausage." A sausage made with chopped liver that has a very smooth texture and is usually sliced into slabs. The word is derived from the German *Leberwurst*, "liver sausage," and was first printed in English in 1852. Originally it was called "Braunschweiger," because it came from Germany's Brunswick region (Braunschweig); it has long been associated with German immigrants.

Liverwurst is seasoned with onions, pistachios, and other spices, smoked, and packaged, usually to be spread on a sandwich or served as a canapé or cold cut. Occasionally it is sold fresh.

LOBSCOUSE. Also "labskaus." A beef-and-potato stew, described by Marjorie Mosser in her *Foods of Old New England* (1957) as "one of the most frequently used dishes in the galleys of New England sailing ships," first in print in 1707. The dish seems to have originated in Hamburg, where it is still popular and called either *Labskaus* or *Lapskaus*.

LOBSCOUSE

Cut up 2 lb. bottom-round beef, 1 qt. potatoes, ½ lb. salt pork, and 4 onions, cover with water, and boil for 1 hr. Add 4 c. chopped corned beef and cook an additional ½ hr. Serves 6.

LOBSTER. Any of a variety of crustaceans of the genus *Homarus*, having five pairs of legs, including two large front claws. The name comes from the Old English *loppestre* and Latin *locusta*, dating in print to circa 1000.

The American lobster (*Homarus americanus*) is today one of the more expensive food items on the market, owing to the difficulty of obtaining sufficient quantities to meet the demand. But when the first Europeans came to America, the lobster was one of the most commonly found crustaceans. They sometimes washed up on the beaches of Plymouth, Massachusetts, in piles two feet high. These settlers approached the creatures with less than gustatory enthusiasm, but the lobsters' abundance made them fit for the tables of the poor. (One observer remarked that "the very multitude of them cloys us.") In 1622, Governor William Bradford of the Plymouth Plantation apologized to a new arrival of settlers that the only dish he "could presente their friends with was a lobster…without bread or anything else but a cupp of fair water."

Lobsters in those days grew to tremendous size, sometimes forty or more pounds. (A record-holding forty-two-pounder was taken in Virginia in 1935 and now hangs in Boston's Museum of Science.) New Englanders could easily pick them off the beach for their tables, and ships carried them to other ports. When ships in New York Harbor were bombarded during the Revolution, the lobsters went to other waters, only to return at the cessation of hostilities.

The taste for lobster developed rapidly in the nineteenth century, and commercial fisheries specializing in the crustacean were begun in Maine in the 1840s, thereby giving rise to the fame of the "Maine lobster," which was being shipped around the world a decade later. In 1842, the first lobster shipments reached Chicago, and Americans enjoyed them both at home and in the cities' new "lobster palaces," the first of which was built in NYC by the Shanley brothers. Here men made the consumption of several lobsters at one sitting a mark of one's affluence and joy in the good things of life.

Diamond Jim Brady thought nothing of downing a half-dozen, in addition to several other full courses. The March 1982 issue of *Yankee* magazine listed professional wrestler André the Giant as the all-time lobster-eating champion after he put away forty of the crustaceans at Custy's restaurant, in North Kingstown, Rhode Island. The news elicited a response from Tom Shovan, of Woodlands, California, who claimed he had, at the same restaurant, once eaten sixty-one lobsters at a sitting. Shovan demanded from the magazine a "correction to this gross misstatement that would lead the naive to believe that a mere 40 lobsters are enough to satisfy a truly voracious appetite!"

By 1885 the American lobster industry was providing 130 million pounds of lobster per year. Soon afterwards, the population of the lobster beds decreased rapidly, and by 1918 only 33 million pounds were taken. Today, thanks to conservation efforts, the production is again above 83 million pounds, while millions of pounds of other lobsters come from South Africa, South America, Mexico, Australia, and elsewhere, usually in the form of "spiny lobsters" and sometimes called "crawfish," but distinct from the true native freshwater **crayfish**.

The so-called Maine lobster does not come only from Maine anymore, either, but from beds in Canada as well. The average American lobster weighs between one and two pounds (in New England, these are called "chicken lobsters," supposedly for their tenderness), although many eastern steak and lobster houses carry them at five or more pounds. Frozen lobster tails, usually broiled and served with clarified butter, are brought in great quantities from South Africa and, now, from North Atlantic waters. Other preparations of lobster range from simple boiling or steaming to elaborate dishes like "**lobster Newburg**" and "lobster thermidor," which require the removal of the meat from the tail and claws (Americans usually do not eat the innards) and combining it with cream, seasonings, sherry, and other ingredients.

Besides the American lobster, the following also figure in culinary preparations in the U.S., when available:

LOBSTERETTE (family Nephropidae). Lobsterettes are smaller members of the lobster family, ten species of which are found in the Atlantic and the Caribbean, including the "Caribbean lobsterette" (*Metanephrops binghami*), the "Florida lobsterette" (*Nephrops aculeata*), and the "red lobsterette" (*Metanephrops rubellus*). In Europe these are called the "*langoustine*," "*scampo*," "Dublin Bay prawn," and other names.

SPANISH LOBSTER (*Scyllarides aequinoctialis*). Also "shovel-nosed lobster," "sand lobster," "slipper lobster," "buccaneer crab," "gollipop," and other names. Rare in the U.S., this lobster is usually brought in frozen from Southeast Asian waters.

SPINY LOBSTER (*Panulirus argus*). A favorite Floridian species, the spiny lobster ranges from the Carolinas to the Caribbean and is related to a Californian species, *P. interruptus*. At market, spiny lobsters are often called "rock lobsters."

U.S. lobster landings in 2010 totaled 115.4 million pounds, valued at $396.8 million.

LOBSTER À L'AMÉRICAINE. A dish of lobster prepared with a sauce of tomatoes, brandy, white wine, cayenne pepper, and seasonings. It is certainly of French, not American, origins and in France is called *homard à l'américaine*. Some gastronomes insist that it is actually a dish of Breton or Armorican origins, and that *à l'américaine* is an incorrect transcription of *à l'armoricaine*. Robert Courtine, however, in his book *The Hundred Glories of French Cooking* (1973), shows that the error was probably the other way around, pointing out that "no menu from any important restaurant, either in Paris or elsewhere, has ever been found with *armoricaine* antedating *américaine*. No, the latter has always preceded the former."

Courtine goes on to repeat the story told by Maurice-Edmond Sailland (better known as Curnonsky) of how the dish was in fact created. Chef Pierre Fraisse had begun his cooking career in the U.S., where he often prepared lobsters. Fraisse, known by the more American name "Peters," opened his own restaurant in Paris around 1860. One evening, a group of Americans came in late, and Fraisse, having little left to work with, prepared a dish with lobsters that he called, in deference to his guests, *"homard a l'américaine." Sauce a l'américaine* is often used with other fish dishes.

LOBSTER À L'AMÉRICAINE

Cut the claws off a lobster and cut the tail into even rings. In 4 T. oil sauté the meat with salt and pepper until the shell has turned red. Remove from pan. To pan with oil add 1 finely chopped onion, 2 chopped shallots, and ¼ clove crushed garlic and sauté until limp. Pour off the oil, add ½ c. white wine, ½ c. water, and 2 T. brandy, and burn off the alcohol. Add 2 peeled, seeded tomatoes, 3 sprigs of tarragon, and ⅛ t. cayenne. Place the lobster pieces on top, cover, and cook for 20 min. Remove lobster and place on serving platter. Remove tarragon. Over high heat, reduce sauce in pan by half. Mash the lobster roe (called "coral") and green tomalley with 2 t. butter, a pinch of chervil, and a pinch of tarragon. Add to sauce in pan and stir to bind. Bring to boil, add 2 T. butter and 2 T. brandy, and pour over lobster. Garnish with chopped parsley and serve with rice.

LOBSTER FRA DIAVOLO. An Italian American dish whose name translates as "lobster brother devil," made with lobster cooked in a spicy, peppery tomato sauce. It was a creation of southern Italian immigrants and not known in the old country, since American lobsters were not available there. (In Italy, dishes termed *"alla diavolo"* indicate one made with a good deal of coarsely ground black pepper.) It had become a popular dish in Italian American restaurants in NYC by the 1940s.

LOBSTER NEWBURG. Also "lobster à la Newburg" and "lobster Newberg." A rich dish of lobster meat, sherry, egg yolks, cream, and cayenne pepper. The dish was made famous at Delmonico's restaurant, in NYC, in 1876, when the recipe was brought to chef Charles Ranhofer by a West Indies sea captain named Ben Wenberg. It was an immediate hit, especially for after-theater suppers, and owner Charles Delmonico honored the captain by naming the dish "lobster à la Wenberg." But later Wenberg and Delmonico had a falling-out, and the restaurateur took the dish off the menu, restoring it only by popular demand and renaming it "lobster a la Newberg," reversing the first three letters of the captain's name. Chef Ranhofer also called it "lobster à la Delmonico," but the appellation "Newberg" (by 1897 it was better known under the spelling "Newburg") stuck, and the dish became a standard in hotel dining rooms in the U.S. It is still quite popular and is found in French cookbooks, where it is sometimes referred to as *"homard sauté à la crème."*

The sauce itself is used with other shellfish, and such a preparation retains the name "à la Newburg." In some recipes the lobster is not sautéed in butter but only boiled. The first printed recipe appeared in 1895.

LOBSTER NEWBURG

Cook 2 lobsters in salted water until tender. Cool, then cut up meat into slices and sauté with 6 T. butter. Salt to taste and add a dash of Tabasco or ¼ t. cayenne pepper. Pour in 1 c. heavy cream and 2 T. sherry and boil, reducing to half. Remove from heat and add 3 beaten egg yolks to thicken the sauce. Reheat, finishing it with a little more butter.

LOBSTER ROLL. A sandwich made with lobster meat mixed with mayonnaise and seasonings on a hot dog roll, first mentioned in print by the *New York Times*, as a Cape Ann, Massachusetts, "quick lunch delicacy" in 1937. Around 1966 or 1967, Fred Terry, owner of the Lobster

Roll Restaurant (a.k.a. "Lunch"), in Amagansett, New York, produced a recipe containing mayonnaise, celery, and seasonings mixed with fresh lobster meat, placed on a heated hot dog roll. It has come to be known as the "Long Island lobster roll," and this version has become very popular elsewhere, although a similar item was known in print in New England as of 1966. According to Carolyn Wyman, in the *New Haven Register* in 1996, lobster meat drenched in butter and served on a hamburger or hot dog roll has long been available at seaside eateries in Connecticut and may well have originated at a restaurant named Perry's, in Milford, where owner Harry Perry concocted it for a regular customer named Ted Haley sometime in the 1920s. Furthermore, Perry's was said to have a sign from 1927 to 1977 reading "Home of the Famous Lobster Roll."

LOBSTER SHACK. A roadside restaurant that specializes in selling freshly cooked lobsters. They are a fixture in New England and particularly in Maine.

LOCAVORE. A person who tries to cook and eat food from small farms as close as possible, no more than a hundred miles away, believing it to be both healthier and more sustainable. The word was coined in 2005 during World Environment Day in San Francisco, by Jessica Prentice, Jen Maiser, Sage Van Wing, and DeDe Sampson, who used it to describe themselves. Van Wing said, "Our food now travels an average of fifteen hundred miles before ending up on our tables," a process that imperils "our environment, our health, our communities, and our taste buds." On their website, the locavores contend, "Our goal is to eat from within a 100 mile radius of San Francisco of our homes. Failing that, we will attempt to eat foods that come from within our State, or are purchased directly from small scale farmers elsewhere in the world. Some of us will interpret these guidelines more strictly than others, but the main goal is to pay attention to where the food that we eat comes from."

The idea was further popularized by author Barbara Kingsolver in her 2007 book *Animal, Vegetable, Miracle*, and caught on with professional chefs, restaurateurs, and public relations people to describe similar ideas, like community gardens and farmers' markets. The term farm-to-table is synonymous with locavore food.

LOCO MOCO. A Hawaiian dish made with a scoop of steamed white rice topped with a grilled hamburger patty, a fried egg, and meat gravy. It is believed to have been created in 1949, as an after-school snack at the Lincoln Grill, in Hilo, Hawaii, opened by Richard and Nancy Inouye. The dish is said to be named after a local football player, "loco" being local slang for "crazy."

LOGGER SLANG. American loggers and lumberjacks have long had their own lingo for food and culinary terms, as indicated by the following:

BAIT CAN. A lunch pail used by loggers.

BELLY WASH. A soft drink.

BLACK MIKE. Stew made from meat and vegetables.

BOARDINGHOUSE MAN. The cook at camp.

BOILER. A cook.

CACKLEBERRY. An egg. The cackle refers to the sound made by chickens, and in prison lingo, eggs are referred to as "cacklers" (or "shells").

CRIB. A loggers' term for lunch, derived from the crib-shaped boxes in which lumber was sorted.

FORBIDDEN FRUIT. Pork.

FORTY-FIVE-NINETY. According to *DARE*, loggers' slang for a large sausage, so called after a large-caliber rifle cartridge.

LUMBERJACK PIE. A pie made with various vegetables and deer meat. The term is used by New England loggers.

MULLIGAN CAR. A railroad car set in the woods, from which the workers would take their lunch.

SPUD WITH THE BARK ON. An unpeeled potato.

LOLLIPOP. A hard candy attached to a stick usually made of rolled paper. It is a favorite children's snack and has been so since it was introduced in England in the 1780s. The name comes from an English dialect word, *lolly*, meaning "tongue," and the "pop" is probably associated with the sound made when the candy is withdrawn from the mouth. The word entered print in 1784.

The "Tootsie Pop," a lollipop with a soft chocolate candy center, is a trademark of Tootsie Roll Industries Inc., of Chicago.

LOMILOMI SALMON. Also "lomi salmon." A salted salmon dish of Hawaii, often served at large feasts called "**luaus**." *Lomi* means "mashed with fingers" in Hawaiian and also refers to a shampooing. A recipe for the dish dates in print to 1928.

LOMILOMI SALMON

Soak 1 lb. salted salmon in water and refrigerate overnight. Remove the skin, drain the fish, and cut up into small pieces. Add 5 large chopped, peeled, seeded tomatoes, 1 finely chopped Maui onion, and 2 finely chopped scallions. Squeeze all these ingredients through fingers until well blended. Serve ice cold. Serves 6.

LONDON BROIL. Flank steak that is broiled and cut into slices, though the term may also refer to another cut of beef appropriate for cooking in this manner. The name obviously derives from the city of London, though the term is not used in England. It seems more specifically American in origin and dates in print to at least 1931, appearing in Charles G. Shaw's *Nightlife: Vanity Fair's Intimate Guide to New York After Dark* as a recommended dish at Keens Chophouse, in NYC.

LONG ISLAND ICED TEA. A cocktail composed of various clear spirits, including vodka, gin, and tequila, with Coca-Cola and lemon. The drink is said to have been concocted by bartender Robert C. "Rosebud" Butt in 1976, at the Oak Beach Inn, in Hampton Bays, Long Island, New York. "I was fooling around with some drinks," said Butt, "and I'm a tequila drinker, so I put together one shot each of tequila, light rum, vodka, gin, a dash of triple sec, a splash of sour mix, and topped it off with Coca-Cola and a slice of lemon, served it on the rocks in a Collins glass, and the thing tasted just like iced tea. I started serving them to the public about a year later."

Many other cocktails took similar names, like California iced tea (with orange juice and 7-Up soda), Pittsburgh iced tea (with bourbon), and Texas iced tea (with tequila).

LONGNECK. A beer bottle or liquor bottle with a long neck, long known in the Southwest and particularly popular in Texas, dating in print to 1907. Beer drinkers carry the bottle around by the neck with considerable swagger and do not drink from a glass.

LONG SAUCE. Root vegetables with long roots, such as carrots, parsnips, and beets, dating in print to 1809; also a dish made from such vegetables. "Short sauce" refers to vegetables that grow aboveground, such as peas, beans, and tomatoes.

LOOSE MEAT. Midwestern term for seasoned ground meat cooked loosely in a skillet and served with gravy or in a sandwich, dating in print to 1986. Common in the Midwest.

LOUISBURG PIE. A pie made with chicken fricassee, potato balls, sliced mushrooms, and sausages. It may derive from the region around Louisburg, North Carolina.

LOVE AND TANGLE. A deep-fried doughnut that has been twisted and entwined, with reference to a western vine called "love-entangle."

LOVE APPLE. A romantic colloquialism for tomatoes, so called because of a mistranslation of the Italian *pomo dei Moro*—"Moor's apple" (because tomatoes came to Italy from Morocco)—into the French *pomme d'amour*, meaning "love apple." Certain aphrodisiacal attributes thereby accrued to tomatoes with no justification. The term also applies to eggplant, first in print in 1578.

LOW MULL. A meat-and-vegetable stew whose ingredients vary according to the person preparing it. The origin of the word may derive from the colloquial verb "to mull"—"to make a muddle or mess" of something—used since at least 1821. Or the name may be a shortened form of **mulligan stew**.

LOX. A Jewish American version of smoked **salmon**. The word is from the Yiddish *laks*, from Middle High German *lahs*, "salmon." According to Leo Rosten, in *The Joys of Yiddish* (1968), "the luxurious practice of eating lox, thought to be so typical of East European Jews, actually began for them in NYC. Lox was entirely unknown among European Jews and is rare to this day there—and in Israel." The word first appeared in English in 1940.

Lox is sliced very thin and usually served on a bagel with butter and cream cheese. The preferred variety is the Pacific salmon cured in saturated salt brine.

"Pickled lox" has been a specialty of the Concord Hotel, in the Catskill Mountains of New York, since 1939. The original recipe, given below, was refined by Frank Stubitz in 1949 and first printed in the *New York Times* in 1985.

PICKLED LOX

Place 3 lb. filleted, skinless brined salmon in a glass or stainless-steel dish, cover with cold water, cover with plastic wrap, and let stand in refrigerator for 48–60 hr., changing water frequently. Drain fish and trim away cartilage. In a saucepan combine 4 c. white vinegar. 1 c. water, 1 ½ T. pickling spices (without cinnamon), and 1 c. sugar and bring to a boil. Lower heat and simmer for 20 min. Allow to cool. Cut fish into ½-in.-thick slices and layer the slices with 2 sliced Bermuda onions in a glass dish. Strain the marinade liquid and pour over fish. Cover with plastic wrap and refrigerate for 24–36 hr. In a bowl whisk 4 c. sour cream, 1 t. sugar, and 1 T. fish marinade. Drain salmon and onions, then layer with the sour cream mixture. Serves 12.

LUAU. Hawaiian-style feast, usually held in the outdoors, often at the beach, first in print in 1853 and featuring pig cooked in an **imu**. The word, which in Hawaiian means "young taro tops," may also refer to the edible taro leaf or a dish made from taro leaves, dating in print to 1843.

LUCAS, DIONE (1909–1971). Teacher, author, TV host. After opening a branch of France's Le Cordon Bleu cooking school in New York City, Dione Lucas went on to host *To the Queen's Taste* from 1948 to 1949, of which Ann Cooper, in *A Woman's Place Is in the Kitchen: The Evolution of American Chefs* (1998), wrote, "This show, certainly one of the first to showcase instructional cooking, was the precursor to the TV Food Network almost fifty years later."

Born and raised in England, Lucas lived part of her youth in Venice and Paris, where she studied cello at the Conservatoire. Her English mother taught her cooking, and she enrolled at Paris's Le Cordon Bleu cooking school, then exclusively male. "I cried for 48 hours," she said of her first classes there, "and then I cried no more." Lucas became the school's first female graduate. "Whatever talents I had were best expressed in the alchemy of the kitchen," she wrote. "Transforming new ingredients into a finished product, knowing that my fingers and my skill were responsible for this creation, gave me a tremendous sense of satisfaction. I always imagine this is much the same feeling the leader of an orchestra experiences when he succeeds in drawing exquisite music from each instrument he directs, translating all these sounds into one harmonious composition."

After graduation, Lucas opened a branch of Le Cordon Bleu in London with her friend Rosemary Hume. In 1937, they opened Au Petit Cordon Bleu restaurant there. Before the war, Lucas also worked as a hotel chef in Hamburg, where she served squab to regular patron Adolf Hitler, later saying, "Let us not hold that against a fine recipe though."

In 1940, Lucas closed the London school and moved to Ottawa, Canada, then to the U.S., where her first job was cutting mushrooms at Longchamps restaurant, in New York City. She then moved to a ranch near Cody, Wyoming, where she cooked French food for local cowboys. Returned to New York City, she opened a Cordon Bleu restaurant and school in 1942, which gained recognition for having Hollywood movie stars Brian Aherne, Harold Lloyd, and Joan Fontaine as students.

In 1947, Lucas published the bestselling *Cordon Bleu Cook Book*, which was voted into the **James Beard** Foundation's Cookbook Hall of Fame. A year later, her cooking show *To the Queen's Taste* was broadcast from her restaurant on CBS-TV. On one segment, Salvador Dalí came on the set with his pets. When that show ended after a year, she produced the WPIX series

The Dione Lucas Cooking Show, which was syndicated in sixty cities. In 1953, she prepared the luncheon for Queen Elizabeth II's coronation.

In 1956, she opened the Egg Basket Restaurant and the Gourmet Cooking School, both in NYC. She also opened Potters Yard Brasserie, in Bennington, Vermont, and the Heritage Village Restaurant, in Southbury, Connecticut. In 1956, Lucas opened the Ginger Man restaurant (named after the 1955 novel by J. P. Donleavy), in New York City, where it is said she introduced Americans to the French omelet. She kept on cooking until 1970. After serious surgery that year, she moved back to London, where she died the following year.

While Lucas introduced America to many classic French dishes, she considered American food at its best to be the best in the world, insisting that Americans suffer from a shortage of the ingredient that makes a meal truly epicurean: time.

Lucas's books include *The Dione Lucas Meat and Poultry Cook Book*, with Anne Roe Robbins (1955), *The Gourmet Cooking School Cookbook* (1964), and *The Dione Lucas Book of Natural French Cooking*, with Marion and Felipe Alba (1977).

LUKINS, SHEILA (1942–2009), and **JULEE ROSSO** (1944–). As trendsetters in a new, well-seasoned European style of cooking at their gourmet store the Silver Palate and in an affiliated series of cookbooks, Sheila Lukins and Julee Rosso had widespread influence on the way Americans cooked at home after 1980.

Sheila Gail Block was born in Philadelphia and grew up in Norwalk and Westport, Connecticut, earning a B.A. degree in fine arts at New York University and a degree in arts education from the School of Visual Arts, in New York City, in 1970. She then studied at London's Le Cordon Bleu school and went on to France to apprentice to restaurants there.

Julee Rosso was born in Mt. Clemens, Michigan, grew up in Kalamazoo, and graduated from Michigan State University.

The two women met in New York City, where Rosso had been working in fashion and advertising. Together they opened the Other Woman Catering Company as a hobby out of a New York City apartment, aiming at a new generation of working women who had little time to cook at home. The food was far from the usual standard fare of the time, with more emphasis on Provençal and Mediterranean flavors. In 1977, they opened a small, eleven-by-fourteen-foot store on Columbus Avenue and Seventy-third Street, which they called the Silver Palate, featuring much the same food. They soon garnered local attention from the NYC media for the adventurous style of their dishes, like ratatouille and asparagus salad, and their use of ingredients like raspberry vinegar, zucchini pickles, French cheeses, and tomato vinaigrette. In canning and bottling such products, Rosso said, "People are dying for foods that look like what their grandmother used to make."

In some ways, Silver Palate foods were a response to the ethnic health food movement of the 1970s but at the same time explored new global flavors that had never much been represented in standard American cooking. Their food was a break from the stultifying menus of catered affairs where cold beef, casseroles, and canned vegetables ruled and women were urged to improve their culinary skills along the lines of French women cooks. "There was no pizzazz in the kitchen [back then]," said Lukins, "no pizzazz enticing people to say, 'Oh Wow! This is great. This is fun. This is new.'"

The popularity of the Silver Palate store led to its products being sold at Saks Fifth Avenue in Manhattan and in other markets. Beginning in 1982, Lukins and Rosso began to write a series of immensely successful cookbooks (eventually selling seven million copies). The first, with Michael McLaughlan, was entitled *The Silver Palate Cookbook*, which alone sold hundreds of thousands of copies. Said Rosso, "I think one of the reasons that our book hit a nerve was that it conveyed our enthusiasm, and our passion for what we were doing, which we were just making up as we went along, every day. I think people got that."

The original Silver Palate was sold in 1988 (closed in 1993), and Lukins and Rosso separated as business partners, with Rosso returning to Michigan to buy the Wickwood Inn, in Saugatuck, while publishing cookbooks and lecturing. In 1991, the two women became involved in a public feud; both continued to publish their own books but reunited to do a twenty-fifth-anniversary edition of *The Silver Palate Cookbook* in 2007.

Lukins took over Julia Child's food column in *Parade* magazine and wrote it for twenty-three years. In 1991, she was paralyzed by a cerebral hemorrhage that caused her to slow her activities. She died of brain cancer.

Together, the two women wrote *The Silver Palate Cookbook* (1982), which was inducted into the James Beard Foundation's Cookbook Hall of Fame; *The Silver Palate Good Times Cookbook* (1985); *The New Basics Cookbook* (1989); and *Silver Palate Desserts* (1995). Alone, Lukins wrote *Sheila Lukins' All Round the World Cookbook* (1994), *USA Cookbook* (1997), *Celebrate!* (2003), and *Ten: All the Foods We Love and Ten Perfect Recipes for Each* (2008). Rosso has written *Great Great Food* (1993), *Fresh Start* (1996), and *Less Is More* (1998). She conducts cooking classes and lectures at universities and symposiums, including Stanford University Business School, the Women's Economic Development Association, NYU, the Smithsonian Institution, and the Wharton School of Business. She is also a business consultant and has sat on boards of the National Association for the Specialty Food Trade, the Culinary Institute of America, and the American Institute of Wine and Food.

LUNCH. The midday meal. The word originally referred to a chunk or lump of something, including perhaps a slice of food, and in its first appearance in print (1591) it was related to the Spanish *lonja*, for "slice." By the seventeenth century it was often used to designate a piece of food or a light meal, but when the word *lunch* first appeared in print, as an abbreviation of *luncheon* in 1812, it was considered something of a fashionable colloquialism. Americans picked up the word quickly, however, and used it as a synonym for the midday meal taken quickly, as a worker might on the job. Before the 1820s, the midday meal was called "**dinner**" and the evening meal "supper." Today, "luncheon" connotes a more formal lunch, usually given for friends or associates.

The midday meal at home was generally the heaviest meal of the day, but workers found neither the time nor the stomach for lengthy dinners while on the job, and so the custom of eating a sandwich or going to a lunchroom or **cafeteria** became common, although more affluent businesspeople of the nineteenth century would indulge in lavish midday dinners at city restaurants, where six or more courses were not unusual.

Workers would carry their lunches, usually consisting of a sandwich and a snack. to work in "lunch pails," and children would take theirs to school in "**lunch boxes**." For most Americans today, lunch is a fairly light meal, with the largest meal of the day saved for the evening. The partially tax-deductible "business lunch" has become an American institution (see also **power lunch**), and opponents of lengthy, lavish restaurant lunches at taxpayers' expense have called such exemptions unfair to the average wage earner, who may not deduct the cost of his lunch. Such business lunches have been characterized as "three-**martini** lunches" since the 1960s, sarcastically referring to the number of cocktails imbibed.

LUNCH BOX. Also "lunchbox" and "lunch pail." A portable container for one's lunch. Originally, workers carried their lunches in "dinner pails" or "dinner buckets"—first cited in print, respectively, in 1856 and 1901—which were designed to keep food warm. "Lunch boxes," cited in print in 1850, held cold food. Schoolchildren of the nineteenth century would often use their fathers' tobacco tins to carry their lunch, but by the twentieth century manufacturers made lunch boxes especially for carrying to school.

The first licensed "character lunch box" appeared in 1935 with a picture of Mickey Mouse, from the Walt Disney cartoons, but the boom in lunch boxes began in 1950 when Aladdin Industries, of Nashville, Tennessee, sold 500,000 lunch boxes with TV cowboy hero Hopalong Cassidy on them. Since then, most lunch boxes have been made with pictures of children's favorite characters (the most popular ever was the "Disney School Bus," which sold more than two million units between 1961 and 1973). Today, about seven million lunch boxes are produced each year, all manufactured by two companies, Aladdin and the King-Seeley Thermos Co., of Freeport, Illinois.

LUNCH COUNTER. An inexpensive, casual restaurant serving simple food at a counter, although most lunch counters also have tables or booths. The term, first recorded in 1865, has many synonyms—"lunch stand," "hash house," "short-order restaurant," "snack bar," "lunchroom," and "lunch," superseded in the 1930s by "luncheonette." The term may also be used to refer to a

diner, which is a lunch counter originally made to look like a railroad dining car.

Lunch counters have provided etymologists and linguists with one of the richest stores of American slang, cant, and jargon, usually based on a form of verbal shorthand bandied back and forth between waiters and cooks. Some terms have entered the familiar language of most Americans—"BLT" (a bacon, lettuce, and tomato sandwich), "stack" (an order of pancakes), "mayo" (mayonnaise), and others—but most remain part of a bewildering and colorful language specific to workers in such establishments. The following list is culled from various sources, including Supplement Two of *The American Language* (1948), by H. L. Mencken, who wrote, "The queer lingo used in transmitting orders from table to kitchen was noted by a writer in the *Detroit Free Press* so long ago as Jan. 7, 1852, *e.g.*, *fried bedpost, mashed tambourine* and *roasted stirrups*. In 1876 J. G. Holland, then editor of *Scribner's*, discussed it in his *Everyday Topics*, p. 386. It was richly developed by the colored waiters who flourished in the 1870s and 80s, but is now pretty well confined to the waitresses and countermen who glorify third-rate eating-houses."

Many of these terms are shared by workers in soda fountains or ice cream stores.

AC. A sandwich made with American cheese.

ADAM AND EVE ON A RAFT. Two poached or fried eggs on toast (1909).

ADAM'S ALE. Plain water.

ALIVE. Raw (said of oysters).

ALL THE WAY. A sandwich made with lettuce, mayonnaise, onion, and butter (1957); also a chocolate cake with chocolate ice cream.

…AND. Preceded by a food item, "and" indicates another food that invariably goes with the first, as in, "ham and" for "ham and eggs" or "burger and" for "hamburger and french fries."

ANGEL FOOD CAKE AND WINE. Also "Lord's Supper." Bread and water (1942).

A-PIE. Apple pie.

ARIZONA. Buttermilk, so called, according to Robert Shafer in "The Language of West Coast Culinary Workers," *American Speech* (April 1946), because "a waitress thinks any man drinking buttermilk ought to be in Arizona for his health."

AXLE GREASE. Also "skid grease." Butter or margarine (1883).

BABY. Also "moo juice," "Sweet Alice," and "cow juice." Milk.

BELCH WATER. Seltzer or soda water.

BIRDSEED. Cereal (1919).

BLACK STICK. A chocolate ice cream cone.

BLONDE. Coffee with cream. "Blonde and sweet" is coffee with cream and sugar.

BLUE-BOTTLE. Bromo-Seltzer, a trademark for a digestive aid of bicarbonated soda that comes in a blue bottle.

BLUE-PLATE SPECIAL. A dish of meat, potato, and vegetable served on a plate (usually blue) sectioned in three parts.

BOSSY IN A BOWL. Beef stew, so called because Bossy was a common name for a cow.

BOTTOM. Ice cream added to a drink.

BOWL OF RED. A bowl of chili con carne, so called for its deep red color (1900).

BOWWOW. A hot dog.

BREAK IT AND SHAKE IT. Also "make it cackle." To put a raw egg in a drink, especially a milk shake.

BREATH. An onion.

BRIDGE. Also "bridge party." Four of anything, so called from the card-game hand of bridge.

BUCKET OF HAIL. A small glass of ice.

BULLETS. Also "whistleberries" or "Saturday nights." Baked beans, so called because of the supposed flatulence they cause (1893).

BUN PUP. A hot dog.

BURN IT AND LET IT SWIM. A float, made with chocolate syrup and ice cream floated on top.

BURN ONE. Put a hamburger on the grill; or add chocolate.

BURN ONE ALL THE WAY. A chocolate milk shake with chocolate ice cream.

BURN THE BRITISH. A toasted English muffin.

CANARY ISLAND SPECIAL. Vanilla soda with chocolate ice cream.

CARFARE. Also "subway." A worker's tip or percentage of the check as a gratuity. The meaning referred to the money to provide transportation home.

CAT'S EYES. Tapioca.

CB. A cheeseburger.

CHINA. Rice pudding.

CHOPPER. A table knife.

CITY JUICE. Water.

CJ. A cream-cheese-and-jelly sandwich.

CLEAN UP THE KITCHEN. Hash or hamburger.

C.O. HIGHBALL. Castor oil. See **highball**.

COKE PIE. Coconut pie.

COLD SPOT. A glass of iced tea.

CONEY ISLAND CHICKEN. Also "Coney Island." A hot dog, so called because hot dogs were popularly associated with the Coney Island stands at which they were sold.

COWBOY. A western omelet or sandwich.

COW FEED. A salad.

CREEP. Draft beer.

CROWD. Three of anything. Possibly from the old saying "Two's company, three's a crowd."

DEADEYE. Poached egg.

DOG AND MAGGOT. Cracker and cheese.

DOG BISCUIT. Cracker (1908).

DOG'S BODY. A pudding of pea soup and flour or hardtack.

DOUGH WELL DONE WITH COW TO COVER. Buttered toast.

DRAW ONE. Coffee (1896).

ECHO. Repeat the order.

EIGHTY-ONE. A glass of water.

EIGHTY-SIX. "Do not sell to that customer" (1943) or "The kitchen is out of the item ordered." The term dates in print to 1936, perhaps from the practice at Chumley's restaurant (once a speakeasy), in NYC, of throwing rowdy customers out the back door, which is No. 86 Bedford Street.

EVE WITH A LID ON. Apple pie, referring to the biblical Eve's tempting apple and to the crust that covers it (1923).

FIFTY-FIVE. A glass of root beer.

FIFTY-ONE. Hot chocolate.

FILET. Served with ice cream.

FIRST LADY. Spareribs. A pun on Eve's being made from Adam's spare rib.

FIVE. A large glass of milk.

FLY CAKE. Also "roach cake." A raisin cake or huckleberry pie.

FORTY-ONE. Lemonade.

FRENCHMAN'S DELIGHT. Pea soup.

GAC. Grilled American cheese sandwich. This was also called "Jack" (from the pronunciation of "GAC"); a "Jack Benny" (after a radio comedian) was cheese with bacon.

GENTLEMAN WILL TAKE A CHANCE. Hash.

GEORGE EDDY. A customer who leaves no tip.

GO FOR A WALK. An order to be packed and taken out.

GRAVEL TRAIN. Sugar bowl (1935).

GRAVEYARD STEW. Milk toast (1911).

GROUNDHOG. Hot dog (1911).

HAMLETTE. An omelet made with ham.

HARLEM. Also "Harlem soda." A soda made with chocolate, named after the section of NYC known for its predominantly black population. A "Harlem midget" was a small chocolate soda.

HEMORRHAGE. Ketchup.

HIGH AND DRY. A plain sandwich without butter, mayonnaise, or lettuce.

HIGH, YELLOW, BLACK AND WHITE. A chocolate soda with vanilla ice cream.

HOLD THE HAIL. No ice.

HOPS. Malted-milk powder.

HOT CHA. Hot chocolate.

HOT SPOT. Tea.

HOUSEBOAT. A banana split, made with ice cream and sliced bananas.

ICE THE RICE. Add ice cream to rice pudding.

IN THE ALLEY. Serve as a side dish.

IN THE HAY. A strawberry milkshake, punning on *hay* as straw.

IRISH TURKEY. Corned beef and cabbage.

JAVA. Coffee.

JERK. An ice cream soda, referring to the jerking motion of a seltzer spigot.

JOE. Coffee.

L.A. Serve an item with ice cream.

LOOSENERS. Prunes, so called because of their supposed laxative effect.

LUMBER. A toothpick.

MAIDEN'S DELIGHT. Cherries, so called because "cherry" is a slang term for the maidenhead.

MAKE IT VIRTUE. Add cherry syrup to a cola soda.

MAMA. Marmalade.

M.D. Dr Pepper, a commercially produced soda.

MIKE AND IKE. Also "the twins." Salt and pepper shakers.

MONKEY BOWL. Plate used for a side dish.

MUD. Also "Omurk." Black coffee or chocolate ice cream.

MURPHY. Potatoes, so called because of their association with the Irish diet of potatoes, Murphy being a common Irish name.

NATURAL. A commercially produced soda called 7UP, from the combination of 5 and 2, called a "natural" in the dice game craps.

NOAH'S BOY. A slice of ham, because Ham was Noah's second son.

NO COW. Without milk.

O.J. Also "Oh gee." Orange juice.

ON THE HOOF. Meat done rare.

ON WHEELS. An order to be packed and taken out.

OVER EASY. ALSO, "EASY OVER." Eggs turned over and cooked briefly.

PAIR OF DRAWERS. Two cups of coffee.

PITTSBURGH. Something burning, such as toast, so called because of the smokestacks evident in Pittsburgh, a coal-producing and steel-mill city. In meat cookery, this refers to a piece of meat charred on the outside while still red within.

PT. A pot of tea.

PUT OUT THE LIGHTS AND CRY. Liver and onions.

RADIO. A tuna-fish-salad sandwich on toast, punning on "tuna down," which sounds like "turn it down," as one would the radio knob.

SAND. Sugar.

SEABOARD. Item wrapped for takeout, referring to "cardboard."

SEA DUST. Salt.

SHOOT IT YELLOW. Add lemon syrup or a slice of lemon to a cola soda.

SHOOT ONE FROM THE SOUTH. Make an especially strong cola soda.

SINKERS AND SUDS. Doughnuts and coffee.

SQUEEZE ONE. Orange juice.

STRETCH ONE. A cola soda.

THROUGH GEORGIA. Add chocolate syrup; supposedly because of Georgia's large black population, though possibly referring to General William Tecumseh Sherman's infamous "scorched-earth policy" of the Civil War, when he marched his army through Georgia, burning everything in his wake.

TO THE LEFT. Lemon syrup, customarily set to the left of the cola-syrup pump.

TO THE RIGHT. Cherry syrup, customarily set to the right of the cola-syrup pump.

TWENTY-ONE. Limeade.

VERMONT. Maple syrup, because maple syrup comes primarily from Vermont.

WARTS. Olives.

WREATH. Cabbage.

YUM-YUM. Sugar.

ZEPPELINS IN A FOG. Sausages in mashed potatoes.

LUTEFISK. A Scandinavian dish made from dried cod preserved in lye and soda. The word is from Norwegian (also Swedish *lutfisk*, "lye fish"), first in print in English in 1924. It is traditionally served at Christmastime and is considered a delicacy among Scandinavian Americans, especially in the Midwest. Madison, Minnesota, even calls itself the "Lutefisk Capital of the USA." Lutefisk is rarely made at home and is usually bought at specialty stores. It is softened by simmering in salted water for about ten minutes and served with a white sauce and potatoes on the side. It may also be made into a pudding.

MACADAMIA NUT. Also "Queensland nut." The seed of two tropical trees, *Macadamia intergrifolia* and *M. tetraphylla*, originally native to Australia but now forming the third-largest crop of Hawaii. The tree is named after chemist John Macadam (1827–1865), who promoted the plant's cultivation in Australia. The name "macadamia" was first used in print in 1858. The alternate name, "Queensland nut," derives from Australia's second-largest state.

According to S. A. Clark, in *All the Best in Hawaii* (1949), the nut was brought to Honolulu from Tasmania in about 1890, by E. W. Jordan. Originally the tree was used merely as an ornamental shrub, but researchers at the Hawaiian Agricultural College forty years later discovered the nuts' culinary value, leading to widespread planting for commercial harvesting.

Today macadamia nuts are usually roasted and salted, eaten as snacks, or used in salads or fish or meat preparations.

MACARONI. A form of dried pasta that is usually tubular or shaped in some way, in contrast to the long, thin shape of spaghetti. The word is of Italian origins (from *maccherone*, "mixture of elements," but the word serves as a name for the pasta, too) and dates in English print to 1661. (The reference to "macaroni" in the famous eighteenth-century American song "Yankee Doodle Dandy"—"stuck a feather in his hat and called it macaroni"—refers not to the pasta itself but to a slang term of the period for a fop or dandy, after London's Macaroni Club.) Thomas Jefferson sent his emissary, William Short, to Naples for a macaroni machine (though Short returned with a spaghetti machine instead).

Macaroni is eaten in America in the traditional Italian manner—that is, with various sauces (most often tomato)—but a specifically American dish is macaroni and cheese, which is made by placing a layer of boiled macaroni in a buttered baking dish and grating over it American, cheddar, or Swiss cheese, then baking it until the cheese has melted. This dish was first made in the nineteenth century but took on great popularity when Kraft Foods in 1937 introduced the Kraft Dinner, a macaroni-and-cheese meal that today sells 300 million boxes per year.

Macaroni salad is a dish of cold macaroni to which is added mayonnaise, along with various vegetables and seasonings, like celery, onions, peppers, tomatoes, chives, and pimiento.

MACCIONI, SIRIO (1932–). Restaurateur. Though a proud Tuscan, Sirio Maccioni rose through the service ranks of deluxe French restaurants in Europe and New York to become one of the most influential restaurateurs in America, at his New York City flagship, Le Cirque.

Born in Montecatini Terme, Italy, during the war, in which his father was killed, Maccioni escaped poverty in his own country to take jobs in French restaurants in Europe and on the Home Lines cruise ship *Atlantic*, which brought him to ports such as Nassau, Port-au-Prince, Havana, and New York City, where he disembarked in 1956, penniless, to pursue his career in America. There he eventually rose to become maître d' at NYC's high-society restaurant the Colony, where he acquired the knowledge and trust of its moneyed clientele, many of whom became his regulars when he opened his own restaurant, Le Cirque, in 1973, with partner Jean Vergnes and a $100,000 loan undersigned by real estate titan William Zeckendorf Jr.

At the time, Maccioni regarded the New York City French restaurants of the day as places "for masochists willing to submit to the French culinary act," but maintained that he wouldn't dare serve the kind of simple Italian food he truly loved. "Right or wrong," he later said, "the way of restaurants in America was French. I love the trattorias of Italy, but America was not ready for this kind of cooking." Le Cirque quickly became known as much for its cuisine as for its clientele, who were constantly being photographed entering or exiting the restaurant for magazines like *Town & Country*, *Vogue*, *New York*, and *W*.

In contrast to the staid, formal, cookie-cutter decor of the French restaurants of the era, Le Cirque was more frivolous, with an orangerie motif and images of cavorting monkeys. Food editor **Michael Batterberry** explained Maccioni's methodology by saying, "He dares to have fun. He is the quintessential dashing Italian. But behind all the bravura, he's in a perpetual state of high hysteria. And all of his best customers are a part of it. He involves you in some kind of ancient Italian agony that is far beyond the dashing maître d'."

Despite Chef Vergnes' refusal to serve any Italian dishes at Le Cirque, Maccioni came up with one of the most popular spaghetti dishes of the century—**pasta primavera**—which became an international sensation.

After most of the old-line New York City French restaurants closed in the 1980s and 1990s, Le Cirque thrived and became a showcase for many of the finest chefs in America, including Alain Sailhac, **Daniel Boulud**, and Sottha Kuhn, and a kind of graduate school for many chefs who afterwards became famous in their own right, including **David Bouley**, Alfred Portale, Terrance Brennan, Jacques Torres, Michael Lomonaco, Alain Allegretti, Bill Telepan, Alex Stratta, and Geoffrey Zakarian.

Maccioni moved Le Cirque twice—in 1997, to the Palace Hotel, at Fiftieth Street and Madison Avenue, and in 2006, to the Bloomberg Tower, on East Fifty-eighth Street. With the help of his wife, Egidiana ("Egi"), he finally realized his dream of bringing Tuscan food to New York City with the opening of Osteria del Circo in 1996, with a branch to follow at Bellagio Hotel, in Las Vegas. He also opened a Sirio Ristorante, in the Aria Resort & Casino, in Las Vegas, with another of the same name following in NYC in 2012. By the 1990s, Maccioni's three sons, Mario, Marco, and Mauro, were working in their father's restaurants, helping to expand the Maccioni brand to other cities, including branches of Le Cirque in Mexico City (now closed), the Dominican Republic, and New Delhi.

In 2004, Maccioni (with writer Peter Elliot) published his memoir, *Sirio: The Story of My Life and Le Cirque*. In 2003, Egi Maccioni published *The Maccioni Family Cookbook*. The family was the subject of an HBO-TV documentary called *A Table in Heaven* (2007).

Maccioni's awards include the **Joe Baum** Lifetime Achievement Award, from the Food Allergy Initiative (2000), and the Fine Dining Legend award, from *Nation's Restaurant News* (2003).

MACKEREL. Any of a wide variety of fishes in the family Scombridae. As a food fish, the Atlantic mackerel (*Scomber scombrus*), also called "Boston mackerel," is the most important mackerel in the U.S. It travels in large schools, ranging from Labrador to Cape Hatteras, and is known for its swiftness. The name "mackerel" derives from Old French *maquerel* and has been found in print in English since 1300.

Most American mackerel used to be salted. Much of the salting was done in Boston; hence, salted mackerel was called "Boston mackerel." It was not until ships stocked ice in their holds that the mackerel was sold fresh. In 1885, a fishery at Eastport, Maine, brought in 100 million pounds. As with other fish of this era, overworking the sea resulted in a decline in population, with the result that the mackerel has gone through cycles of scarcity and proliferation.

The most important species for the table include the "cero" (*Scomberomorus regalis*), also called "painted mackerel"; "chub mackerel" (*S. japonicus*), also called "hardhead"; "king mackerel" (*S. cavalla*), also called "kingfish" and "cero"; "Spanish mackerel" (*S. maculatus*); and "wahoo" (*Acanthocybium solandri*), whose etymological roots are unknown and which in Hawaii is known as **ono** ("sweet"). U.S. commercial landings of Atlantic mackerel in 2010 totaled 21.8 million pounds, with sales of $4.4 million. Chub mackerel landings totaled 4.7 million pounds, valued at $447,000.

MADEIRA NUT. The English walnut (*Juglans regia*), now widely planted in California (1821). The name derives from the island of Madeira. It was first mentioned in print by **Thomas Jefferson**, in 1791.

MADEMOISELLE (*Bairdiella chrysura*). Also "corvina," "maomao" (in Hawaii), and "croaker." A small fish of the Gulf and Atlantic coasts, dating in print to 1882. It was nicknamed "lafayette" by New York fisherman when the fish arrived in large numbers at the same time the Marquis de Lafayette arrived in 1824 as "the nation's guest." They are usually pan-fried.

MADISON, DEBORAH (1945–). Restaurateur, author, educator. Although not a vegetarian herself, Deborah Madison brought both attention and respect to vegetable cookery in America at a time when vegetables and fruits were being produced by agribusiness for their shelf life rather than their flavor. Her restaurant Greens, opened in 1979 in San Francisco, was one of the first to offer gourmet vegetarian cuisine in America.

Madison was born in Hartford, Connecticut, grew up in California, and graduated from the University of California at Santa Cruz in 1968 with a degree in sociology and city planning. "Growing up in a California walnut orchard and having a dad who grew a great garden meant that farms and food were in my sights from the start," she said. "I first put that awareness into motion at the San Francisco Zen Center where I was a student for eighteen years." While at the center, Madison held a host of cooking positions, then she joined the staff at **Alice Waters**'s Chez Panisse, in Berkeley, California, and in 1978 opened Greens at Fort Mason, in San Francisco, which won international praise as a standard of vegetarian cuisine done with imagination and flair but without the polemicism in the dining room. After a year of cooking as a private chef to the director at the American Academy in Rome (1984–1985), she returned to California to co-author, with Edward Espe Brown, *The Greens Cookbook* (1986). Since then she has written a number of other books, including *Vegetarian Cooking for Everyone* (1997), which won the **Julia Child** Cookbook of the Year award (IACP); *Local Flavors, Cooking and Eating from Americas Farmers' Markets* (2002), based on visits to more than one hundred U.S. farmers' markets, which won a **James Beard Foundation** Award; *What We Eat When We Eat Alone* (2009), illustrated by her husband, Patrick McFarlin; *Seasonal Fruit Desserts from Orchard, Farm and Market* (2010); and *Vegetable Literacy: 11 Plant Families in Our Kitchens* (2013).

"Connecting people to the food they eat, its source and its history has long been my work," Madison has said, "and writing is one way to reveal the deeper culture of food, whether through recipes or through profiles of farmers and ranchers, producers and cooks, and even a humorous book on eaters, called *What We Eat When We Eat Alone*. My interests lay with issues of biodiversity, seasonal and local eating, farmers markets, and small and mid-scale farming."

Her journalistic writing has ranged from a column in the *New York Times* to articles in *Gourmet, Food & Wine, Organic Gardening, Garden Design*, and *Saveur*.

In 1990, she and her husband moved to Santa Fe, New Mexico, where she ran Café Escalera and managed the Santa Fe Farmers Market. Madison was a board member of the Seed Savers Exchange and co-director of the Edible Kitchen Garden at Monte del Sol charter school. She has also been a chef or consultant for Cal Dining at the University of California at Berkeley and for Procter and Gamble and was a spokesperson for California Artichokes. She has taught courses or classes at many schools and colleges, including Warren Wilson College, Davidson College, the Culinary Institute of America, the Napa Valley Culinary School, Peter Kump's School of Cooking, Santa Fe School of Cooking, Scottsdale Culinary Institute, Tante Marie's Cooking School, and Western Reserve School of Cooking. Madison was keynote speaker at the Ecotrust Farmer-Chef Connection, in Seattle in 2006, and the International Exchange Forum on Children, Obesity, Food Choice and the Environment, in France in 2007.

Among her many honors are induction into the James Beard Hall of Fame (2006) and Who's Who of Food & Beverage in America (2005).

MAID OF HONOR. A custard tart made with damson plums or other fruits. This popular early-American dish came from England, where the tarts were named after the maids of honor at the court of Elizabeth I (1558–1603) and are associated with the palace at Richmond, Surrey, dating in English print to 1769.

~~~~~~
MAID OF HONOR
~~~~~~

Roll out pastry for a 2-crust pie and line 10 tart shells about 3 ½-in. in diameter. Beat 2 eggs with ½ c. sugar.

Soften ½ c. almond paste with 2 T. dry sherry, 2 T. butter, and 1 T. lemon juice and add to egg batter. Mix in 2 T. flour. Drop 1 t. fruit jam or preserves into each shell, pour batter over each, and bake for 45 min, at 350°.

MAI TAI. A cocktail made from lime, curaçao, and rum, created in 1944 by **Victor "Trader Vic" Bergeron**, then owner of an Oakland, California, restaurant called Hinky Dink's, which later became Trader Vic's. In his book *Trader Vic's Bartender's Guide* (revised, 1972), Bergeron told how the drink came about:

> I was at the service bar in my Oakland restaurant. I took down a bottle of seventeen-year-old rum. It was J. Wray Nephew from Jamaica—surprisingly golden in color, medium bodied, but with the rich pungent flavor particular to the Jamaican blends. The flavor of this great rum wasn't meant to be overpowered with heavy additions of fruit juices and flavorings. I took a fresh lime, added some orange curaçao from Holland, a dash of rock candy syrup, and a dollop of French orgeat for its subtle almond flavor. I added a generous amount of shaved ice and shook it vigorously by hand to produce the marriage I was after. Half the lime shell went into each drink for color, and I stuck in a branch of fresh mint. I gave the first two of them to Ham and Carrie Guild, friends from Tahiti who were there that night.
>
> Carrie took one sip and said, "Mai Tai—Roa Aé." In Tahitian this means "Out of this world—the best." Well, that was that. I named the drink "Mai Tai...."
>
> Anybody who says I didn't create this drink is a dirty stinker.

There is, however, no evidence that the term means what Bergeron said it does in Tahitian.

~~~~~~
MAI TAI
~~~~~~

Squeeze juice of 1 lime into an old-fashioned glass, add ½ oz. orange curaçao, ¼ oz. rock-candy syrup, ¼ oz. orgeat syrup, 1 oz. dark Jamaican rum, and 1 oz. Martinique rum. Shake with shaved ice. Decorate with lime shell, fresh mint, and fruit stick.

MAÎTRE D'HÔTEL BUTTER. A classic preparation of butter mixed with pepper, salt, lemon juice, chopped parsley, and occasionally chives. It is used as a garnish for grilled meats and fish. The term derives from the French for "master of the house," referring to a headwaiter who usually takes reservations and assigns seating, and dates in print to 1861.

MAKOOLA. Home-brewed liquor. The word's earliest citation in print (1882) says the name comes from a "Russian brewer," while the *Dictionary of Alaskan English* (1991) suggests it may be derived from Russian *muka*, "flour."

MALASADA. Also "malassado." A puffy pastry made from an egg batter that is deep-fried and rolled in sugar, dating in print to 1967. It is based on similar pastries brought by the Portuguese immigrants, and each year the Portuguese Society of Hawaii holds a contest to decide the best version. The term is from two Portuguese words, *mal* (bad) and *assado* (baked), and may have originated when scraps of Portuguese sweet-bread dough were hastily thrown into hot fat, thereby making a "badly baked" bread.

~~~~~~
MALASADA
~~~~~~

Dissolve 2 pkgs. dry yeast in 1 c. warm water with 1 T. sugar and 1 T. flour. Let stand until proofed. In a large bowl combine 5 lb. flour, 3 c. sugar, and 1 t. salt. Beat 1 doz. eggs, add 1 c. milk, add to flour mixture, and blend. Add ½ lb. melted butter. Knead well, then let dough rise until doubled in size. Remove from bowl, pinch off pieces of dough the size of a walnut, deep-fry in oil, drain, and roll in sugar.

MALTED MILK. Originally created in 1887 as an easily digestible infant's food made from an extract of wheat and malted barley combined with milk. The resulting powder, called "diastoid," was made by James and William Horlick, of Racine, Wisconsin, and sold under the name Horlicks Malted Milk. It was featured by the Walgreen drugstore chain as part of a chocolate milk shake, which itself became known as a "malted" and became one of the most popular soda-fountain drinks.

MANAPUA. A dough bun, filled with pork, bean paste, and other stuffings, that is steamed and usually sold from roadside stands in Hawaii (1938). The word derives from the Hawaiian *mea* (thing) plus *ono* (delicious) plus *pua'a* (pig), possibly once referring to various Chinese dishes such as *char sia bao*.

MANGO (*Mangifera indica*). An oblong tropical fruit known for its sweetness. They are commonly used in salads, side dishes, and many desserts, as well as a puree added to cocktails. "Mango" entered English print in 1575, derived from Portuguese *manga* and, earlier, possibly from the Malayalam *māna*.

Only about 15 to 20 percent of the mangoes in the American market are grown here—mostly in Florida—with the rest coming from Haiti, Mexico, Belize, and Brazil. Among the most popular varieties are the Tommy Atkins and the Keitt.

In the Midwest (especially the Ohio Valley), a sweet pepper is called a "mango."

MANHATTAN. Also "Manhattan cocktail." An alcoholic drink of bourbon or blended whiskey with sweet vermouth and bitters. The word, which refers to the NYC borough of Manhattan, dates in print to 1882. The drink is said to have been created for a banquet given by Winston Churchill's American mother, Jennie, at NYC's Manhattan Club in 1874, to celebrate Samuel Tilden's election as New York governor.

Modern versions of the Manhattan tend to be drier than recipes from the early twentieth century. A "perfect Manhattan" uses ¼ ounce sweet vermouth and ¼ ounce dry vermouth with the whiskey, while a "dry Manhattan" substitutes dry French vermouth entirely for the sweet vermouth. A "sweet Manhattan" is synonymous with a regular Manhattan, except, perhaps, for the amount of sweet vermouth added. A "Scotch Manhattan," more often called a **Rob Roy**, is made with Scotch instead of bourbon or blended whiskey. **James Villas** gives the following recipe as the original.

MANHATTAN

Combine 2 oz. rye, blended, or bourbon whiskey with 1 oz. sweet Italian vermouth and a dash of Angostura bitters in a pitcher. Add 2-3 ice cubes, stir quickly until well chilled, and strain into a cocktail glass. Garnish with a maraschino cherry.

MANINI. In Hawaiian waters, a surgeonfish (*Acanthurus sandvicensis*), in print since 1926, as well as a kind of green-and-white-striped banana, usually cooked (1948).

MANNITOL. A sweetener used in chewing gum and low-calorie foods.

MAPLE SYRUP. A sweet syrup or sugar made from the sugar maple tree (*Acer saccharum*), also called the "hard maple" or "rock maple." The word is from Old English *mapel*. Although Europeans were familiar with various species of maple trees in their own countries, they were unaware of the American sugar maple's virtues as an agent for such a delicious sweetener as the northeastern Native Americans obtained merely by slashing the bark and letting the sap drip out. This technique was learned by the early colonists, who found maple syrup and maple sugar a fine substitute for the expensive cane sugar imported from the West Indies. By the 1720s the settlers were doing a good deal of "sugaring" of maple trees, waiting for the sudden thaw of late winter, when the sap would begin flowing through the trees. The colonists would gash the tree trunks, guide the sap into troughs, and boil it over fires.

Maple sweeteners became even more popular after the passage of the 1764 Sugar Act, which imposed high duties on imported sugar. "Maple syrup" first appeared in American print in 1792. After the Revolution, New England maple production boomed, providing products like maple candy, beer, wine, and molasses. Abolitionists urged their fellow citizens to eat more maple sugar than West Indian sugar, in order to "reduce by that much the lashings the Negroes have to endure to grow cane sugar to satisfy our gluttony." In New Hampshire, people called maple syrup "humbo," from an Indian word.

Maple products remained principal forms of sweetening well into the nineteenth century, especially after tin cans became available in which to pack the syrup. Before then, most maple was turned into sugar loaves. Today, most of the maple sugar and syrup produced comes from Vermont, though a good deal of the syrup used on American foods like pancakes is no longer maple syrup at all. In 1887, P. J. Towle, of St. Paul, Minnesota, produced a blend of maple and sugarcane syrup that was less expensive than pure maple syrup. He packed it in a tin can shaped like a log cabin of the kind his childhood hero, Abraham Lincoln, had grown up in, and called it Log Cabin Syrup. Since then, many syrups have been produced from other sweeteners, and these by law must be labeled "pancake syrups."

The sugaring of maple trees has long been a New England social ritual. Both professional and amateur sugarers will head for a grove of maple trees, called a "sugar bush," to collect the sap, return to a "sugarhouse" to boil it down, and hope for a "sugar snow"—that is, a late snowfall that prolongs the running of the sap in the trees. It takes about thirty-five gallons of boiling sap to produce one gallon of syrup. Often a late-season "sugar in the snow" party is held, during which maple syrup is poured on fresh snow and eaten like an ice.

Maple syrup is graded "fancy" (the finest), "grade A," "grade B," and "unclassified," a dark syrup used in commercially produced maple and blended syrups.

Maple sweeteners are used on breakfast dishes like pancakes, waffles, French toast, bacon, and sausage and in candies, cakes, ice cream, and many other confections. Vermont and New York produce more than two-thirds of the country's maple syrup. In 1998, total U.S. production of maple syrup was 1.159 million gallons.

MAPLE SUGAR

Boil 1 pt. maple syrup, then reduce heat to a simmer and stir for about 10 min., until candy thermometer registers 240°. Cool by stirring over a pot of cold water until it thickens to light taffy stage. Return to medium heat to liquefy again, pour into candy or other molds, cool for 15 min., and turn out.

MAQUE CHOU. Also "macque choux," "maquechoux" and other variants. A Cajun dish made with corn, onions, peppers, and milk (1931). The meaning of the term, which is Cajun French, is not clear. According to the anonymous author of *New Orleans Cuisine*, published in the 1930s:

One of the most popular traditional dishes of south Louisiana is Mocquechou; *also one of the most controversial as to origin. Some natives believe that this succulent stew was brought to Louisiana by the Spanish, and that the name originated with the Spanish name "machica" which was a dish of toasted corn meal sweetened with sugar and spices. Others think the name came from the word "maigrichou" which means "a thin child" as this dish was originally more soup than stew. The "Cajuns" of Louisiana have their own interpretation, making it a dish soaked with cabbage and calling it "moque-chou" or "mock cabbage."*

The original dish was made of fresh scraped corn and tomatoes, simmered with water and butter. Maque chou is often added to chicken or other meats.

MAQUE CHOU

In a saucepan melt 2 T. butter, add 3 T. chopped onions, and 2 T. chopped bell pepper. Cook on low heat for about 3 min. Cut off the kernels from 8 ears of corn and add to the saucepan. Cook for 3 more min., then add ½ c. milk, a pinch of cayenne, and salt and pepper to taste. Cook for about 15 min., until creamy.

MARASCHINO. A cordial made from the fermented juice of the Dalmatian marasca cherry or a maraschino-flavored preserved cherry. The cordial runs 60 to 78 proof. The cherry is used as a garnish in cocktails like the **old-fashioned** and the **Manhattan**, as well as a flavoring for some cakes and cookies.

The word comes from the Italian *marasca*, referring to the wild cherry tree from which the drink is made, dating to 1770 in English print. The drink was originally made along the Adriatic coast, from cherries and honey allowed to ferment, then distilled into a liqueur. The cherries themselves were often marinated in the liqueur and enjoyed on their own. The French flavored and colored their own local cherries bright red and called them maraschinos, a process used by American manufacturers around the turn of the last century in Ohio and Illinois and modified for use with any kind of cherry in the 1920s by food scientist E. H. Wiegand, of Oregon State University. The cherries are put into a brining liquid of sodium metabisulfate, calcium chloride, and citric acid, then soaked in corn syrup and fructose solution, then artificially flavored and colored either red or green.

MARGARINE. Also "oleomargarine." A blend of animal and vegetable oils and fats mixed with milk and salt to form a semisolid that is often used as a substitute for **butter**.

The word, dating in English to 1871, comes from the French *margarine*, referring to margaric acid, a fatty substance, and its pearly color (from Greek *margaron*, "pearl"). Oleo derives from the French *oléo*, "oil." The product was originally called in French *oleomargarine*, first made by French chemist Hippolyte Mège-Mouriès in the 1860s, for a contest sponsored by Napoleon III to find a substitute for butter. By 1867 a French patent had been filed, by 1869 a British one, and by 1873 an American one. Dairymen in the U.S. fought the use of margarine as a substitute, but it was widely manufactured by the end of the century, first in 1881, by Community Manufacturing Co. of NYC. In 1886, Congress passed the Oleomargarine Act to regulate and tax the manufacture and sale of the product.

American margarine is usually made from corn, cottonseed, or soybean oil that is refined, deodorized, hydrogenated, homogenized, chilled, and reworked with salt, then often enriched with vitamins A and D. Although regular margarine is of about the same caloric count as butter, diet margarines are sold.

Once believed to be a healthier fat than butter, margarine saw its sales surpass those of butter after World War II, hitting a high of 5.5 pounds per person annually in 1985, but in the 1990s, when margarine was shown not to be healthier than butter, its sales decreased, falling to 3.6 pounds by 2010, with butter at 4.9 pounds.

MARGARITA. A cocktail made from tequila, triple sec or Cointreau, and lime juice. According to *The Tequila Book* (1976), by Marion Gorman and Felipe de Alba, there are several claims as to the creation of the drink. One story traces the margarita to the bar at the Agua Caliente Racetrack, in Tijuana, Mexico, in about 1930. Another credits Doña Bertha, owner of Bertita's Bar in Taxco, Mexico, as having made the drink about 1930.

Former Los Angeles bartender Daniel Negrete claimed to have originated the cocktail at the Hotel Garci-Crespo, in Puebla, Mexico, in 1936 and named it after a girlfriend named Margarita. Still another story gives the credit to a San Antonio, Texas, woman named Margarita Sames, who made the drink for houseguests in 1948 while living in Acapulco. Yet another claim pinpoints the drink's birthplace as the Tail o' the Cock restaurant, in Los Angeles, in about 1955 and says it was named after a Hollywood starlet.

A 1974 article in *GQ* magazine credited Pancho Morales, a bartender at Tommy's Place, in Ciudad Juárez, Mexico, with the invention of the drink in 1942. Others say it was concocted at Dallas's El Charro Bar by Mariano Martinez, whose son, Mariano Jr., supposedly made the first "frozen margarita" with crushed ice in 1971.

Whatever its origins, the margarita was the cocktail that increased American interest in tequila in the 1960s, particularly among college students in the West. The first appearance of the word in print was in 1963.

MARGARITA

Chill a stemmed cocktail glass and dip the rim in salt. In a metal shaker, put a scoop of chopped ice, 1½ oz. tequila, ½ oz. triple sec or Cointreau, and 1 oz. lime juice. Shake gently a few times, strain into glass, and garnish with lime peel, if desired.

MARINARA. A spicy, quickly cooked tomato sauce of Italian origins, but far more popular in American restaurants featuring southern Italian cuisines than in most of Italy. There is a 1905 printed reference to "eggs alla marinara" (*alla* in Italian means "in the style of") in an Italian recipe book, but the term was probably widely known by the 1920s, by which time Italian American restaurants had proliferated. As a sauce for spaghetti, "marinara" is mentioned in the 1930 film *Rain or Shine*.

Marinara sauce is often called "red sauce," although that may also refer to a meat-and-tomato sauce.

The name means "mariner's " and is perhaps associated with the custom of plopping the fresh catch of the day into steaming cauldrons of tomato, onion, and spices for the evening meal.

MARLBOROUGH PIE—MARSHMALLOW

MARINARA

In a large skillet heat ½ c. olive oil. Add and brown 4 mashed cloves of garlic. Put through a sieve 3 ½ c. Italian canned tomatoes and add to skillet. Add 1 ¼ t. salt, 1 t. oregano, ¼ t. chopped parsley, and ⅛ t. pepper. Cook uncovered on medium heat for about 15–20 min., until tomatoes have broken down and thickened.

MARLBOROUGH PIE. An apple-and-cream pie, sometimes called "Marlborough pudding" or "Marlborough tart," since there is no top crust, dating in print to 1869. The pie is a Massachusetts specialty, often served at Thanksgiving dinners, although the origin of the name is obscure. There is a town of Marlborough in Connecticut, while Massachusetts, New Jersey, New Hampshire, and New York all have towns named Marlboro.

MARLBOROUGH PIE

Combine 1 c. applesauce with 3 T. lemon juice, 1 c. sugar, 4 beaten eggs, 2 T. butter, ½ t. nutmeg, 1 c. cream, and ¼ c. sweet sherry. Pour into a 9-in. pie crust and bake at 400° for about 10 min., then at 325° for about 45 min. more. Cool until the filling gels.

MARLIN. Any of a variety of fish in the genera *Makaira* and *Tetrapterus*, with a long, swordlike jaw, dating in print to 1915. The "striped marlin" (*T. audax*), in Hawaii called either "nairagi" or "a'u," is a great game fish that ranges from California to Chile. Also in Hawaii, the shortbill spearfish (*T. angustirostris*) is called "hebi," usually used in stews and soups. The "blue marlin" (*M. nigricans*) swims in the north Atlantic, while the "white marlin" (*T. algidus*) can be found in warmer waters of the Atlantic.

MARMALADE. A form of thick jam that contains pieces of the fruit used. The name comes from the Portuguese *marmelada*, meaning "quince jam," and first appeared in English print in 1480.

Early marmalades were in fact made with quince and served as dessert in the form of a bar, but by the eighteenth century Seville orange had become the preferred flavor, and it remains so today.

MARSHMALLOW. A pasty, sweet confection made from corn syrup, gelatin, and sugar. It was once made from the root of the marshmallow plant (*Althaea officinalis*), from which the word derives its name, originally Old English *merscmealwe*, from *mersc* (marsh) and *mealwe* (mallow). As a confection, marshmallow dates in print to 1857. In America, marshmallows, like chocolates, were once made by the "cast" method, in molds. They became a favorite to roast over an open fire, especially after bite-size Campfire-brand marshmallows were created, in 1917, by the Imperial Candy Co./Redel Candy Corp., of Milwaukee. In 1939, Mildred Day and Malitta Jensen, of the Campfire Girls of America's Michigan Council, used Campfire marshmallows to create the first Rice Krispies marshmallow treat, which are squares of Rice Krispies cereal mixed with heated marshmallows. The treats became a national favorite soon afterwards. Campfire has since been owned by the Angelus Co., Borden Inc., International Home Foods, ConAgra, and, since 2003, Doumak Inc., of Bensenville, Illinois.

In 1954 in Los Angeles, Alex Doumak engineered a method of extruding marshmallow slurry through tubes, allowing it to be cut into bite-size pieces. Kraft Foods began using the method by decade's end, and in 1963 the Borden Co., which then owned Campfire marshmallows, introduced "miniature marshmallows," which became popular as a salad ingredient.

Marshmallow Fluff is a product (originally called "Toot Sweet") introduced in 1920 by H. Allen Durkee and Fred L. Mower, of Lynn, Massachusetts. Used as a topping for ice cream and desserts, it also became an ingredient in a peanut butter–and–Marshmallow Fluff sandwich on white bread, called the "Fluffernutter." "Peeps" are variously colored marshmallow Easter candies in the shape of small chicks or bunnies, originally made by Rodda Candy, in Lancaster, Pennsylvania. Now a registered trademark of the Just Born company of Bethlehem, Pennsylvania, Peeps are now the bestselling non-chocolate Easter candy.

MARSHMALLOW

Soak 1 envelope gelatin in ½ c. cold water for 5 min. Bring ¾ c. water and 2 c. sugar to a boil until liquid forms a thread when dropped from a spoon. Add gelatin and let stand away from heat until cooled. Add a dash of salt and 1 t. vanilla extract. Beat until white and thickened, and pour into pans dusted with powdered sugar to a depth of about 1 in. Let cool, then turn onto greased marble, cut into cubes, and roll in powdered sugar.

RICE KRISPIES TREATS

Melt ¼ c. butter or margarine in a saucepan over low heat. Add one 10-oz. pkg. of marshmallows and blend well. Remove from heat, then add 6 c. Kellogg's Rice Krispies cereal and stir until coated with marshmallow. Press mixture into a buttered square cake pan, 13 by 9 by 2 in., then cut into 2-in. squares.

MARTINEZ, ZARELA (1947–). Restaurateur, author. Upon opening her New York City restaurant Zarela, in 1987, Zarela Martinez became an arbiter of authentic regional Mexican food, a subject she further explored in her cookbooks.

Born in Agua Prieta, Mexico, Martinez began cooking professionally in El Paso, Texas, in the late 1970s. Encouraged in 1981 by New Orleans chef **Paul Prudhomme** and *New York Times* food editor **Craig Claiborne**, who published several of her recipes in the newspaper, she was invited in 1983 to represent Mexican food at the first regional American buffet for seven heads of state, at the G7 Summit in Williamsburg, Virginia, hosted by President Ronald Reagan.

Martinez moved to New York City in 1983, first as a menu designer, then as executive chef of Cafe Marimba. In 1987, she opened her own restaurant, Zarela, which quickly became known for the regionality of her recipes. (The restaurant closed in 2011.)

Martinez later launched a program for the Mexican Cultural Institute called Food Is Arte, and she is active in organizations such as Mano a Mano, the MexEd Foundation, Latino Nutrition Coalition, Citymeals-on-Wheels, and the Hispanic Children and Families Fund.

Martinez has been honored for her accomplishments by *Hispanic* magazine, the Women's Leadership Exchange, and the Women's Venture Fund. Her family (her son Aarón Sanchez is also a chef/restaurateur) received the Coalition for Hispanic Family Services' Orgullo de la Comunidad Award in 2006.

Her cookbooks include *Food from My Heart* (1992); *The Food and Life of Oaxaca* (1997); and *Zarela's Veracruz* (2001), the companion book to her PBS-TV series *Zarela! La Cocina Veracruzana* (2001). In July 2004, the U.S. State Department's *U.S. Society & Values* journal, in its issue on "Americans at the Table," named Martinez one of seven "taste setters," noting, "Today, with the help of skilled professionals such as Martínez, Mexican cuisine is fully appreciated in all its delicious diversity and authenticity [having] redefined the American culinary landscape since the last half of the twentieth century."

MARTINI. A cocktail made from gin and dry vermouth and served with a twist of lemon peel. The origins of the martini have never been satisfactorily explained, despite numerous claims for the drink's invention and the exhaustive research of Lowell Edmunds in *The Silver Bullet: The Martini in American Civilization* (1981), wherein he cites the first appearance of a drink called the "Martinez" in O. H. Byron's *The Modern Bartender* (1884), which contained curaçao, bitters, gin, and Italian vermouth. This is similar to a recipe for a "Gin Cocktail" in *The Bon-Vivant's Companion, or How to Mix Drinks* (1862), by "Professor" Jerry Thomas, a bartender at San Francisco's Occidental Hotel who has been credited with the invention of the drink in that year. Legend had it that the drink was named after a bone-chilled traveler on his way to Martinez, California, although others have claimed that the Martinez (and the weary traveler) first appeared at Julio's Bar, in Martinez, California, where it was concocted by bartender Julio Richelieu.

Thomas first gives the name for the cocktail as the "Martinez" in the 1887 edition of his book, while "martini" appeared in the *Brooklyn Daily Eagle* in 1887, and "Martine" in Harry Johnson's *New and Improved Bartender's Manual or How to Mix Drinks for the Present Style* in 1888. As Edmunds pointed out, this confusing nomenclature seemed to describe pretty much the same drink, but the term "martini" came to be the preferred form by the turn of the century. Most probably the name is somehow connected to the Italian vermouth producer Martini, Sola & Co. (later Martini & Rossi), which had been making vermouth since 1829 and is said to have exported it since 1843. (Little credence is given to the association of the name with a Swiss breechblock single-shot rifle, used by the British Army as of 1871, named after its inventor, Friedrich von Martini; the drink was said to have the "kick of a Martini.")

Early forms of the martini had a definite sweetness to them. But by the 1920s sweet ingredients had pretty much been eliminated. "Dryness" came to be associated with the ratio of gin to vermouth. A pre-Prohibition recipe calls for two parts gin, one part dry vermouth, and a dash of orange bitters, and before World War I the gin had reached four parts to each part vermouth. H. L. Mencken said the martini was "the only American invention as perfect as a sonnet."

After World War II, the bitters vanished in the cocktail, and the vermouth was reduced to a shadow of its former self, with gin-to-vermouth ratios of five, six, or seven to one becoming standard. There is one drink, called the "Montgomery," that has a ratio of fifteen to one; it is so called after England's World War II field marshal Bernard Law Montgomery's preference for having fifteen troops for every German troop in battle. Another, called the "naked martini," is no more than gin on the rocks with a lemon twist. This mania for dryness has led to joke recipes that direct the bartender to pour in some vermouth, swirl it around, toss it out, and pour in the gin, or the command for the bartender merely to look at the bottle of vermouth.

Martini fans will argue over the merits of their drink having a lemon twist or an olive as a garnish, but there is general agreement that the addition of a white sour cocktail onion makes the drink a **Gibson**. The "martini sandwich," devised by John Kepke, of Brooklyn, consists of a martini between two glasses of draft beer. A "martini glass" is a stemmed cocktail glass with a flared bowl.

The vodka martini became very popular in the 1960s, following the success of a series of books and movies based on the exploits of fictional British spy James Bond in novels and stories by Ian Fleming. Bond's first instance of ordering a vodka martini (made with "three measures of Gordon's [gin], one of vodka, half a measure of Kina Lillet [an aperitif wine]," shaken, not stirred, and garnished with lemon peel) was in the book *Casino Royale* (1953). Nikita Khrushchev, first secretary of the Communist Party of the USSR between 1953 and 1964, once called the martini "America's most lethal weapon."

MARTINI, LOUIS (1918–1998). Through his innovations in the wine industry after Prohibition, Louis Peter Martini was one of the most respected vintners of his era, pioneering the planting of pinot noir and merlot grapes, the use of wind machines to battle frost in the vineyards, and mechanical harvesters.

He was born in Livermore, California. His father, Louis Michael Martini, had immigrated from Pietra Ligure, Italy, in 1900 to join his father in his San Francisco shellfish business. In 1922, Louis Michael turned his family's winery into the L.M. Martini Grape Products Co. in Kingsburg, California, moving to Napa Valley in 1933, where, with the end of Prohibition, he changed the company's name to the Louis M. Martini Winery.

His son, Louis Peter, who grew to be six feet four inches, studied enology and graduated from the University of California at Berkeley in 1941, then spent four years in the Army Air Forces during the war. He returned to the winery to become vice president in 1946 and winemaker in 1954. (His father died in 1974.)

During the 1950s and 1960s, Martini worked to improve every aspect of viticulture, especially by identifying superior grape clones in the Carneros, where he made that district's first pinot noir as of 1952 and, from 1968 to 1970, the first varietal merlot wine in the U.S. As a great believer in blending wines from different districts, Martini said, "The most important thing on a label is the brand name, the name of the winery.

From 1968 to 1985, Martini was president and general manager of the winery. He was a founder and chairman of the Wine Institute and a charter member of the American Society for Enology and Viticulture, though he kept his distance from what he saw as a troubling commercialism among his colleagues that attracted nouveau riche amateurs to Napa Valley to produce heavily marketed, expensive trophy wines.

"Martini was a member of that generation of California vintners who brought the Golden State's wine industry back to life after Prohibition," *Wine Spectator* wrote of him. "He wasn't a promoter, or even a marketer, for that matter, but a quiet and patient man who sought to make wines that could be enjoyed by people like himself. Alas, in this sense, Martini was also a member of the last generation to live in a simpler and much more rural California."

In 2008, Louis P. Martini was inducted into the **Culinary Institute of America**'s Vintners Hall of Fame.

MARYLAND STUFFED HAM. A dish of boiled ham with slits in the meat, into which are stuffed cabbage, onions, mustard, hot pepper, and other seasonings. It is available only in southern Maryland and, more specifically, will be found in St. Mary's County. Traditionally served at Easter, the dish may date from the time of Maryland's founder, George Calvert, 1st Lord Baltimore (c. 1580–1632), who reportedly enjoyed stuffed ham as a boy in Yorkshire, England. In a 1982 article in the New York Times, Mary Z. Gray noted that "Stuffed Chine," calling for a ham cut to the bone to be slit and stuffed with herbs before being boiled, was a familiar recipe in Elizabethan England. She also records a story suggesting that Maryland stuffed ham might have originated in the early eighteenth century, "when a slave at St. Inigoe's Manor House dished it up as a special Easter treat for the Jesuit Fathers emerging from their Lenten fast."

Preparation of the dish is time-consuming, requiring that a whole corned ham be cut with ten or so deep slits, into which a mixture of cabbage, kale, onions, mustard seed, celery seed, crushed hot pepper, and various other seasonings is stuffed by hand. More of the mixture is packed around the ham, which is then placed in a cloth bag, covered with water, and simmered for several hours. After the ham cools, the bag is cut away and the ham is refrigerated overnight, then served, usually cold, the next day.

MASA. A finely ground, parched corn that has been treated with lime or a dough made from corn flour. The word *masa* comes from the Spanish for "dough," dating in American print to 1914. In 1958, the Quaker Oats Co. registered the name Masa Harina for its cornmeal flour, which has since become a staple flour among Hispanic Americans and is traditionally used in the making of southwestern breads, tortillas, and tamales.

MASHU. Also "masru." A sweet vetch (*Hedysarum alpinum*), sometimes referred to as the "Indian potato" or "Eskimo potato," because it tastes something like potato when cooked and is a staple of Eskimos. The word derives from the Inupiaq *masu*.

MASON JAR. A glass jar with a removable threaded top and rubber gasket that keep the contents airtight to prevent spoilage. The jar was invented in 1858 by John Landis Mason, of Brooklyn, New York. A year later, paraffin was used as a sealer. When Mason's patent ran out, in 1878, the jar was further refined by the Ball brothers of Buffalo, New York, the Hero Fruit Jar Co., and the Consolidated Fruit Jar Co., although the Ball jar became the most popular with American consumers.

MASSON, PAUL (1859–1940). As one of the early promoters of California sparkling wine, Paul Masson came to run one of the largest wine companies in America.

Masson was an immigrant from France's Burgundy wine region, arriving in California in 1878 to study science at the University of the Pacific, then working for fellow Frenchman Charles Lefranc, who had planted vineyards in the Santa Clara Valley. In 1884, Masson went to France to buy sparkling-wine-making equipment and began producing sparkling wine for Lefranc, whose daughter he married in 1888. The company changed its name to Lefranc & Masson, then in 1892 Masson bought out Lefranc's son and formed the Paul Masson Champagne Co.

In 1905, he moved the winery to the Santa Cruz Mountains near Saratoga, where he opened the Paul Masson Mountain Winery—at two thousand feet above the valley, it was called the "vineyard in the sky"—a Romanesque mansion that grew to be one of the largest and most visited wineries in the world. There he courted celebrities in the entertainment business and received considerable notoriety for giving singer Anna Held a bath in his sparkling wine. The winery is now on the National Park Service's National Register of Historic Places and is used for arts events and banqueting.

Masson would eventually earn many awards and the nickname "Champagne King of California," but he was proudest of having received an honorable mention for his sparkling wine at the Paris Exposition of 1900.

During the first years of Prohibition, Masson obtained a federal license to make medicinal sparkling wine, but after repeal, he sold out his interests and retired, dying four years later.

Masson also held proprietary interest in the wine he called Emerald Dry (from Riesling grapes) and other wines.

After changing hands many times, today the Paul Masson Winery is now owned by Wine Group LLC, in San Francisco.

MATSUHISA, NOBUYUKI (1949–). As a classically trained sushi chef, Nobuyuki Matsuhisa—better known as Nobu—combined global ingredients and techniques that had enormous influence on Japanese cuisine in America and, afterwards, the world.

Born in Saitama, Japan, Matsuhisa apprenticed for seven years at Matsue Sushi, in Shinjuku, Tokyo, before being asked by a Peruvian entrepreneur to open a sushi bar in Lima in 1973, where, unable to obtain the Japanese ingredients he needed to make classic sushi, he developed his own "Nobu style" by incorporating Peruvian ingredients into traditional sushi making.

Matsuhisa moved to Argentina, then back to Japan, then to Alaska, and finally, in 1977, to Los Angeles, where he worked at various Japanese restaurants before opening his own, Matsuhisa, in Beverly Hills, in 1987. There he quickly distinguished himself as among the city's finest chefs and won national acclaim, being named one of the top ten restaurant destinations in the world by the *New York Times* in 1993.

In 1994, with restaurateur **Drew Nieporent** and actor Robert De Niro, Matsuhisa opened the first of many Nobu restaurants, of which the *Times* wrote, "This is sushi as it has not been served before in New York City," citing dishes like his monkfish liver pâté with caviar floating in sweet mustard sauce and a dish of raw sea bass drizzled with hot pepper sauce and cilantro.

In 1989, *Food & Wine* magazine named him among America's Ten Best New Chefs, and he was inducted into the **James Beard Foundation**'s Who's Who of Food & Beverage in America in 2002.

Of his approach to food, Matsuhisa has said, "For me, cooking is most about giving my customers little surprises that will lead them to make discoveries about their own latent tastes. It's about communicating my *kokoro* ["heart"] through every single dish I make."

Matsuhisa is currently associated with nineteen restaurants around the world that carry his name, including ones in Athens, Dubai, London, Melbourne, Mexico City, Beijing, and Milan, as well as at his namesake Nobu Hotel Caesar's Palace, in Las Vegas.

MATZO. Also "matzah," "matzoh," and other spellings. Unleavened bread made in thin sheets that are perforated for easily breaking apart. Matzo is the traditional bread of the Jewish Passover, a holiday commemorating the flight from Egypt of the Israelites, who had no time to wait for their bread to rise. The tradition has been passed on, as commanded in Exodus 12:15: "For seven days you shall eat unleavened bread." The word is from the Hebrew, first appearing in English print in 1650.

Today matzo is enjoyed year-round by Jews and non-Jews as a snack or cracker, with all commercially produced matzo made by just two companies, Streit's, in NYC, and B. Manischewitz, in Jersey City, New Jersey, whose combined production totals twenty million pounds annually.

"Matzo brei" is a breakfast dish made with broken, moistened pieces of matzo, eggs, and black pepper, sautéed in butter. It is often accompanied by cottage cheese.

MAWMOUTH. Either of two freshwater fish of the American South—the warmouth (*Lupomus gulosus*), first in print in 1839, or the calico bass (*Pomoxys sparoides*), in print in 1890.

MAY, TONY (1937–). Restaurateur. Born Antonio Magliulo, Tony May both championed and taught Americans authentic regional Italian cuisine, at a series of restaurants he opened in NYC and in the formation of the Gruppo Ristoratori Italiani to educate American chefs and public.

May came from a family of eight children, born in Torre del Greco, near Naples, Italy. He began his work in restaurants as a dishwasher in Argentina, but by the age of twenty he had become a maître d' in a restaurant in Australia. To learn English, he moved to England and worked at the Dorchester hotel. In 1960, he signed on to work in the restaurant of the *Italia* cruise ship.

"In those days, fine dining meant 'international cuisine,'" he recalled. "It was hotel cooking, based on making everything with a demiglace and *sauce espagnole*. Everything was cooked with butter and cream."

May settled in New York City in 1963, taking a job at a society restaurant named the Colony, serving continental cuisine. Of the Italian restaurants in the city, he remembers, "They spoke a language I didn't understand and served a food I'd never eaten. I'd open a menu and not recognize anything on it. The tomato sauces were cooked and cooked for hours, with too much garlic and oregano. The pastas were boiled for twenty minutes in advance."

From the Colony May went on to take over the Rainbow Room, atop Rockefeller Center (1968–1986), where he introduced a series of "Italian Fortnights," bringing over some of the best chefs working in Italy at the time to show off how Italian cuisine had gone far beyond the clichés of Italian American food.

In 1979, May was a founder and president of the Gruppo Ristoratori Italiani (GRI), which had a goal of fostering "authentic Italian cuisine and enhancing its image through education" by providing "a constant flow of information about Italian cuisine to member restaurants, U.S. press, culinary schools, importers, distributors and general consumers with the intent to achieve a better understanding of Italian food and wine in North America." In 1983, May also brought together an array of Italian and American food writers to a three-day GRI convention in NYC, entitled "The Presence of Italian Cuisine in the World Today, Particularly in the United States."

Building on the efforts of GRI in the 1980s, which had been awarding Americans scholarships to study in Italy, May helped found the Caterina de' Medici restaurant and teaching program at the **Culinary Institute of America** in 1984, which eventually used May's compilation of recipes in the cookbook *Italian Cuisine* (1990).

After leaving the Rainbow Room, in 1986, May ran, with chef Sandro Fioriti, a Roman trattoria named Sandro's. In 1986, the principals of the Equitable Life Insurance Company approached May to open a lavish Italian restaurant named Palio in their New York City headquarters, where, with chef Andrea Hellrigl, from Merano, Italy, he promoted the most modern concepts of Italian cuisine, along with the finest Italian decor and amenities, including a four-wall mural of Siena's annual Palio horse race by artist Sandro Chia.

May left Palio in 1988 to open San Domenico, based on the cuisine of a restaurant of the same name in Imola, Italy, where chef Valentino Marcattilii featured a lighter style of Italian cooking called *alta cucina* (an Italian version of French haute cuisine). San Domenico NY was one of only twenty-four restaurants in the world to receive the first Insegna del Ristorante Italiano from the president of the republic of Italy, recognizing the finest Italian restaurants outside Italy.

After two decades, May closed San Domenico and, with his daughter Marisa, opened SD26, where, in keeping with changes in American gastronomy, he served small-plate options in a more casual, less expensive atmosphere.

May also opened two restaurants in the World Trade Center: Gemelli (the name is Italian for "twins," a pun on the twin towers) and Pasta Break. After they were destroyed by the terrorist attack of September 11, 2001, May managed to feed rescue workers at the scene.

In 1991, May founded the Italian Culinary Institute for Foreigners, in Costigliole d'Asti, Italy. He is currently chairman of GRI and president of the Italian Culinary Foundation.

Among May's honors are the Firenze a Tavola Caterina de Medici International Award (1985), the IWFI Outstanding Achievement Award (1986), Who's Who of Cooking in America (1989), and the Silver Spoon, from *Food Arts* (1992). He was invested as a Cavaliere and subsequently as Commendatore dell'Ordine al Merito della Repubblica Italiana, for his efforts on behalf of his native country's gastronomy (1996), received the Boys Town of Italy Humanitarian Award (2005), and was named a Fine Dining Hall of Fame Legend by *Nation's Restaurant News* (2005).

MAYFISH. A killfish of the Atlantic coast (*Fundulus majalis*), first in print in America in 1778.

MAYHAW. Also "mayhull" and "May hawthorn." Either of two hawthorn trees or their fruit, *Crataegus aestivalis* (1868) or *C. opaca* (1960), native to the South and often made into jellies. The word dates in print to 1840.

MAYONNAISE. Also "mayo." A mixture of egg yolks, oil, lemon juice or vinegar, and other seasonings. Mayonnaise is used as a salad dressing, in sandwiches, on canapés, in dips, and in some sauces and desserts. The name is French, but its origins are obscure. Marie-Antonin Carême, in his *Le Cuisinier Parisien* (1833–1834) insisted the name should really be "*magnonaise*," from the word *manier*, "to stir." *Larousse Gastronomique*, however, believes the word is a popular corruption of *moyeunaise*, itself derived from an old French word, *moyeu*, "egg yolk." *The OED* lists the origins as "uncertain," while the *American Heritage Dictionary* mentions that the dressing is "possibly named in commemoration of the capture in 1756 of the city of Mahon, capital of Minorca, by the Duke of Richelieu." The first appearance of the word in English print was in 1823.

In France, there are several classic mayonnaise dressings, but in the United States most people think of bottled mayonnaise, the first important example of which was marketed by NYC delicatessen owner Richard Hellmann in 1912 (although he actually created the formula in 1903). The Hellmann's name and facilities were later acquired by Best Foods Inc., of California, and are now owned by CPC International, which produces a "real mayonnaise" sold east of the Rocky Mountains under the label "Hellmann's" and west of the Rockies as "Best Foods." The two brands account for almost half of the bottled mayonnaise sold in the U.S. In 1937, Hellmann's developed a chocolate-cake recipe using mayonnaise that became an American favorite.

The FDA standards of identity require that mayonnaise have not less than 65 percent vegetable oil, whereas "mayonnaise-type salad dressings" (sometimes called "spoonable salad dressings") must contain not less than 30 percent vegetable oil.

MAYONNAISE

Beat 3 egg yolks until thickened and light yellow. Add 1 ½ t. dry mustard, a dash of cayenne, and ¾ t. salt. Beat in ¼ c. vinegar or lemon juice, then gradually add 1 ½ c. olive oil mixed with 1 ½ c. salad oil. Beat in another ¼ c. vinegar.

MAYTAG, FRITZ (1937–). As the owner of Anchor Brewing Co., in San Francisco, Frederick Louis "Fritz" Maytag III is considered one of the pioneers of modern American microbrewing.

Maytag was born in Newton, Iowa, the great-grandson of the founder of the Maytag Washing Machine Company and son of the founder of Maytag Dairy Farms (see **Maytag Blue**). He graduated in 1959 from Stanford University, in Stanford, California, and in 1965 bought 51 percent of the rights to the defunct brewery Steam Beer Brewing Co., which had opened in 1896, closed during Prohibition, reopened, and again come to the brink of closing. There he changed the recipes and the brewing process for Anchor Steam Beer, by which he blended pale and caramel malts, fermented them with lager yeast at warmer ale temperatures in shallow open-air fermenters, and used gentle carbonation through the process called krausening. The term "steam" dated to nineteenth-century West Coast brewers who fermented their beer on the city's rooftops, where the night fog naturally cooled the fermenting beer, creating steam off the warm, open pans. The name Steam is now trademarked by Maytag's company.

Maytag bought total control of the company in 1968, for what he said was the cost of a used car, and within four years the brewery was unable to keep up with demand, so he relocated it to larger facilities near Potrero Hill, where he produced America's first wheat beer since Prohibition and a beer based on a four-thousand-year-old recipe called Ninkasi. By 1975 Maytag was also producing Anchor Porter, Liberty Ale, Old Foghorn Barleywine Style Ale, and Christmas Ale. After the brewery survived the city's 1989 earthquake, Maytag produced an Earthquake Beer.

Maytag insisted Anchor would never "become a giant company—not on my watch." Throughout his years at Anchor, he was tireless in promoting small American breweries and helped colleagues and competitors begin what became known as "microbreweries." Their growth and competition helped keep Maytag's capacity at a level he desired. "It's not any fun when you can't produce enough to satisfy people," he said. "What if you had a pizza store with 100 customers outside waiting in line, getting angry, fighting, threatening? In business school they say, 'Raise your prices.' Not in the real world. You get a backlash if you raise prices too much. You lose your validity. Luckily, we didn't have to go through that again."

Maytag had expanded into a distillery by 1993, making Old Potrero rye whiskey and a pot-distilled gin called Junipero.

In 2010, Maytag sold the Anchor Brewing Co. to Keith Greggor and Tony Foglio.

Maytag continues as chairman of the board of Maytag Dairy Farms, in Newton, Iowa, and is owner of York Creek Vineyards, in St. Helena, California.

In 2005, *Inc.* magazine named Maytag one of the nation's 26 Most Fascinating Entrepreneurs; in 2008 he won the **James Beard Foundation**'s Lifetime Achievement award.

MAYTAG BLUE. A blue-veined, tangy, smooth-textured cheese from Iowa, made from the milk of Holstein-Friesian cows. The cheese was first made on October 11, 1941, by Robert and Frederick Maytag II, in cooperation with Iowa State University.

MCCARTY, MICHAEL (1953–). Restaurateur, author. Though born on the East Coast, Michael McCarty became one of the progenitors of what became known as California cuisine in the 1980s, based on rigorous French models done with a casual Southern Californian style.

McCarty was born in Mount Kisco, New York, and raised in Briarcliff Manor, New York, and Rockford, Illinois, where he learned from his parents an appreciation for entertaining and good food. He attended the Hill School, in Pottstown, Pennsylvania, then lived in Rennes, France, for a year as part of the Andover-Exeter School Year Abroad program, during which, he says, he "discovered the artistry and quality, and joie de vivre of French dining." He studied cooking, wines, and hotel and restaurant management, earning diplomas from the École Hôtelière de Paris, Le Cordon Bleu, and the Académie du Vin. In 1974, he returned to the U.S. to attend Cornell University's hotel-management summer program and earned a B.A. in the business and art of gastronomy from the University of Colorado in Boulder.

In 1979, at the age of twenty-five, he opened Michael's, in Santa Monica, California, where his goal was "to take the foundations of classic French cuisine, combine them with the simplicity and freshness of the **nouvelle cuisine** revolution, and add a contemporary, youthful, open-minded California sensibility…As Californians we're very susceptible to new ideas, and very eager, almost pioneers, to try anything and just be fascinated by the new ingredients we were able to bring

in." Even though his food was inspired by French nouvelle cuisine, he proudly insisted, "It's American food because *I'm* American."

Decorated with modern art by David Hockney, Frank Stella, Jasper Johns, Jim Dine, and McCarty's wife, Kim, the restaurant had the look of an art gallery, brightly lighted, with an outdoor patio whose tables were set under white umbrellas. Waiters were dressed not in tuxedos and bow ties but in khaki pants, pink button-down shirts, and colorful knit ties.

McCarty also owned a duck farm, where he produced the first American foie gras. In his kitchen he hired many young American chefs later to be stars in their own right, including Jonathan Waxman, Mark Peel, and Ken Frank. Ten years after opening in Santa Monica, McCarty debuted a branch of Michael's in midtown Manhattan, which attracted a power breakfast and **power lunch** crowd from the publishing and media industries. In 1989, he published *Michael's Cookbook*, with recipes from the restaurant.

In 1985, the McCartys planted a vineyard around their home in Malibu, California, the first in the region, releasing their debut vintage in 1989. The vineyard and the McCartys' home burned down in the Great Malibu Fire of 1993; the next vintage was three years later. New acreage has been added since.

In 2012, McCarty was honored by the Careers through Culinary Arts Program.

MCGEE, HAROLD (1951–). Author. Harold McGee brought food into the science lab, by investigating how the farming, preparation, and cooking of food actually works.

Born in Cambridge, Massachusetts, McGee attended the California Institute of Technology and Yale University. After graduating, he taught literature and writing at Yale, then decided to write a book about the science of everyday life, which evolved into *On Food & Cooking: The Science & Lore of the Kitchen* (1984; revised and updated 2004). "My timing was lucky," he said. "America and Britain were awakening to the pleasures of good food and to the diversity of world cuisines, and *On Food & Cooking* helped satisfy the growing hunger for information about ingredients and techniques."

The book created a stir both because McGee shattered a number of old culinary myths (like the belief that searing meat keeps the juices in) and because, as an outsider from the American food media, he brought to the subject a new level of objectivity through a presentation of the chemical structures ingredients undergo during cooking. The book would become a standard reference for chefs and food media.

He followed with *The Curious Cook: More Kitchen Science and Lore* (1990) and a practical kitchen handbook, *Keys to Good Cooking: A Guide to Making the Best of Foods and Recipes* (2010). McGee has written for magazines as disparate as *Food & Wine* and *Physics Today*, lectured at the Oxford Symposium on Food, the American Association for the Advancement of Science, and the American Chemical Society, and taught the Harold McGee Lecture Series at the French Culinary Institute, in NYC. His column The Curious Cook ran for five years in the *New York Times*.

MCGINTY. A pie made in Oregon from dried apples. The recipe below is from Mrs. John James Burton and dates back to the 1870s. The name probably derives from a common name for Irish loggers and miners in the Northwest in those days.

MCGINTY

Wash, core, and skin 1 lb. dried apples, then soak overnight. Stew in water to cover, puree or push through a sieve, then add enough brown sugar to make a rich, thickened puree. Cool, add 1 ½ T. cinnamon. Line a pie pan with a pastry crust, place fruit mixture in crust, cover with top crust, make gashes in top crust, and press edges together. Cook in hot oven for over 15 min., then reduce heat. Serve hot with cream.

MCNALLY, KEITH (1951–). Restaurateur. Dubbed by the *New York Times* "The Restaurateur Who Invented Downtown," Keith McNally reinvigorated the dynamic of casual dining and celebrity-rich environments that differed from the staid old moneyed clientele of the past that had always favored uptown Manhattan restaurants.

McNally was born into a working-class family in London, and he didn't eat in a restaurant until he was seventeen years old. He took a job as a bellhop at the London Hilton, where a film producer discovered him

and cast him in a movie, *The Life and Times of Charles Dickens*, after which he decided to become an actor. In 1975, he moved to New York City, intending to direct plays, but could only get jobs as a waiter, including at One Fifth, where he met many of the TV and fashion celebrities who dined there.

In 1980, he opened a French bistro called Odeon, in Tribeca, then an area with few places of any kind to eat. Odeon was a huge success, at first with actors and models who found downtown New York City a retreat from the formality of uptown restaurants. McNally would capitalize on his sense of which sections of the city were ripe for gentrification, opening Café Luxembourg on the Upper West Side (1983), Nell's in the Meatpacking District (1986), Lucky Strike in Soho (1989), Pravda in Nolita (1996), and his biggest success, Balthazar, in Soho (1997). Of McNally's prowess as a restaurateur, the *New York Times* wrote that he "combine[s] the restaurant equivalent of big box office with serious **foodie** followings."

McNally has opened several more restaurants, including Schiller's Liquor Bar (2003), Morandi (2007), Minetta Tavern (2009), and Pulino's Bar & Pizzeria (2010), always swearing that his latest would be his last. He never replicated any of his restaurants until 2013, when he opened a branch of Balthazar in London. He has also always been adamant that he does not seek out a celebrity clientele and knows very few of them. Yet, through his choice of out-of-the-way neighborhoods, a recurrence of bistro-like designs, and menus of French and Italian comfort foods, McNally's restaurants have always been able to attract a powerful mix of celebrities, fashion editors, artists, and media, who are duly reported on in newspaper and magazines' gossip columns.

MEADOW TEA. A Pennsylvania Dutch beverage made from meadow herbs like peppermint and spearmint steeped in hot water to make a form of **tea**.

MEAT. According to the USDA, "meat comes from the muscles of cattle, sheep, swine, and goats." "Skeletal meat" refers to the muscular cuts of tissue that had been attached to the animal's bone structure. A "meat food product" or "meat product" is "any food suitable for human consumption made from cattle, sheep, swine, or goats containing more than 3 percent meat." The word is from Old English and dates in English print to the fifteenth century.

"Meat loaf" is a baked loaf of chopped meat and bread, first in print in 1899.

MEAT BY-PRODUCT. Also known as "variety meat." The edible and wholesome parts of cattle, swine, sheep, and goats, other than skeletal meat. The USDA requires that meat by-products be listed on labels.

MEETING SEEDS. A Puritan term for fennel seeds, which were chewed at Sunday church meetings, probably to mask the smell of alcohol on one's breath.

MELBA TOAST. Also "Melba toast." A very thin, crisp, dry toast, first made in 1897 by chef Georges Auguste Escoffier, of London's Savoy Hotel, for Australian opera singer Nellie Melba (1861–1931), after whom Madame M. L. Ritz, wife of the hotel's owner, César Ritz, named the item. The toast became a standard item served with salads or on a restaurant's bread dish. In the U.S., a flat version of melba toast was first mass-produced and packaged by Marjorie Weil, owner of the Devon Bakery, in NYC, in 1932, who introduced round versions of the square toast in 1940 and gave her company a more English-sounding name—the Devonsheer Melba Co.

Curiously, Nellie Melba does not mention the famous toast in her autobiography, *Melodies and Memories* (1925), nor does Escoffier in his recipe book, *Le Guide Culinaire* (1921).

MELBA TOAST

Slice stale bread very thin, dry in a warming oven, then toast in a slow oven or under a grill.

MELMAN, RICHARD (1942–). Restaurateur, entrepreneur. Since 1971, Rich Melman has been a restaurant concept innovator, with more than ninety establishments under his Lettuce Entertain You Enterprises Inc. (LEYE).

Melman was born in Chicago. His father had been in the restaurant business, buying his own in 1950. Melman wanted to join his father's business but was rebuffed, so, with a partner in real estate, Jerry A. Orzoff, he founded LEYE (whose full name was a play on a song from the musical *Gypsy*). With a $17,000 investment, they created an offbeat eatery called R.J. Grunts in 1971 in Chicago's Lincoln Park area, where he employed a young, attractive staff and a menu designed to appeal to his own age group, with hamburgers, sandwiches, milk shakes, macrobiotic and vegetarian dishes, and rock music playing in the background. It was here that Melman created the first "salad bar" concept, whereby guests could make their own salads from a wide selection of ingredients.

The roaring success of R.J. Grunts led Melman to pursue the same eclectic, energetic, witty styles in several more Chicago-area restaurants, at a time when the counterculture in America was still a significant part of the zeitgeist. In 1973, LEYE debuted Fritz That's It! followed by the Great Gritzbe's Flying Food Show (1974), Jonathan Livingston Seafood (1975), whose name punned on a popular novel of the day about a seagull, and Lawrence of Oregano (1976), punning on British hero Lawrence of Arabia. Cafe Ba-Ba-Reeba! (1986) was one of America's first Spanish tapas restaurants. Papagus was Greek. In 1989, Melman partnered with TV host Oprah Winfrey to open Eccentric, which closed after two years, replaced by a chophouse called Wildfire. When he opened Ed Debevic's, Melman completely changed the seedy image of the American diner to one of good, clean fun, evocative of the 1950s, with rock-and-roll music, singing waiters, and several flavors of Jell-O.

As his successes grew (Orzoff died in 1981), Melman put his efforts into fine dining restaurants, taking over the old Pump Room, in Chicago's Ambassador East Hotel, in 1986, and opening a nouvelle French restaurant named Ambria; a fine Italian restaurant, Avanzare; a New American cuisine restaurant, Tru, in 1999; and, in 2008, a French haute cuisine seafood restaurant called L2o.

In 1993, in Water Tower Place, he opened the booth Foodlife, with thirteen food kiosks, the Mity Nice Bar & Grill, which evoked 1940s style, and other concepts. At first Melman did not want to repeat concepts, but, urged by his partners to do so, opened branches of Wildfire and subsequent restaurants like Big Bowl, Wow Bao, and the French brasserie Mon Ami Gabi in other cities.

While Melman re-concepted or added to his existing restaurants (M Burger took part of Tru, Brasserie

Jo became Paris Club, and Ben Pao became RPM), he never sold off any of his properties.

"We've had the ability to give people what they want almost before they know they want it," said Melman. "You can call it trendsetting. I prefer to call it the ability to listen to people."

Melman is currently founder and chairman of the board of LEYE. His three children, R. J., Jerrod, and Molly, are all involved in the restaurant business.

MENUDO. Tripe soup or stew, common in the Southwest. The word is derived from the Spanish for "entrails," dating in American print to 1904.

MERITAGE. A trademark name (pronounced like "heritage") and symbol for an association of California wineries making wines from a blend of grapes traditionally used in Bordeaux winemaking. In 1988, a group of vintners formed "the Association in Search of a Name" for their organization, and the name Meritage was submitted by Neil Edgar, of Newark, California, who combined the words *merit* and *heritage*. The association sought to develop wines that had more complexity than traditional California varietals (which may contain 100 percent of a single grape variety), which they achieved by blending in classic Bordeaux varieties. A year later the term was in American print.

To obtain the right to use the Meritage trademark, a wine must meet the following criteria:

1. It must be a blend of the traditional Bordeaux grape varieties: Cabernet Sauvignon, Merlot, Cabernet Franc, Petit Verdot, Malbec, Gros Verdot, and Carminère for red; Sauvignon Blanc (Sauvignon Musque), Sémillon, and Muscadelle for white.

2. It must be the winery's best wine of its type.

3. It must be produced and bottled by a U.S. winery from grapes that carry a U.S. appellation of origin.

4. It must be limited in production to no more than twenty-five thousand cases from each vintage by a single winery.

Association members' blended wines may carry the word Meritage on their labels, although member wineries may instead carry only their own proprietary names. In 1993, the Meritage Association petitioned the ATF to recognize Meritage as a "designation of varietal significance." As of 2013, the ATF had yet to do so.

MERITFISH. Also "green smelt." A silversides fish (*Menidia menidia*) of the New England coast (1884).

MESS. Although a "mess" of food may connote a sloppily presented meal of indiscriminate quality, the term "mess," used in print since 1570, actually goes back to the Latin *missus*, a portion or course of food. Later, in England, "mess" referred to a group of people eating together, and in America a "mess house" (1865), "mess hall," or "mess tent" is a group dining space, often makeshift; at a serviceman's eating area, a "mess sergeant" and "mess crew" prepare the food.

METATE. A stone used by Native Americans, Mexicans, and frontiersmen to grind cornmeal. The word is from Spanish, derived from Nahuatl *metatl*, first printed in English in 1625.

METZ, FERDINAND (1941–). Educator. Upon taking over as president of the **Culinary Institute of America** in 1980, Ferdinand Metz transformed the cooking school into the most respected and expansive in the country, graduating hundreds of students who went on to become some of the best-recognized chefs in America.

Metz was born in Munich and grew up in Germany, where his father owned a hotel, butcher shop, and restaurant. At fifteen, he began apprenticeships in both cooking and pastry at Trade College (1959). He moved to New York City and worked at the Preakness Hills Country Club (1961–1962), as chef tournant at Le Pavillon (1962–1964), then as banquet chef at the Plaza Hotel (1964–1965), but he was dismayed by the entrenched poor techniques, work ethic, and the cutting of corners on display in professional kitchens at that time. "When I went to work at a New York hotel years ago," he said then, "I saw the banquet kitchen placing hot food in the warmers at 2 in the afternoon. I asked, 'What is this for, late luncheon?' The chef said, 'No, it's for dinner.'"

Metz received his M.B.A. from the University of Pittsburgh (1965), then became senior R&D Manager at H.J. Heinz Co. (1965–1980), while working for twenty years with the U.S. Culinary Olympic Team, for which he oversaw four cookbooks, leading it to three consecutive world championships and one World Cup. Metz served for four years as president of the American Culinary Federation and was the first-ever certified Master Chef to receive an M.B.A.

From 1976 to 1980, Metz owned the Café Cappuccino and Gourmet Cooking School, in Pittsburgh, and in 1980 became president of the Culinary Institute of America, serving in that position for twenty-one years, during which time he greatly expanded its facilities and renown as the nation's most prestigious culinary school, overseeing the graduation of more than thirty thousand students. In 2010, Metz became executive dean and chairman of Le Cordon Bleu's National Advisory Board, for which he has worked to reduce the cost of culinary training by half. "The average associate of occupational studies degree costs more than $40,000," he said in 2011. "There's a great deal of imbalance between the cost of education and the earning capacity of graduates just coming out." His innovations were to focus on a twelve-to-fourteen-month program, then afterwards to have the students take online courses to get their AOS or baccalaureate degrees.

Metz now runs two consulting companies, Ferdinand Metz Culinary Innovations (since 2002) and Master Chefs Institute (since 2003), and serves as president emeritus of the Culinary Institute of America, as chairman of the National Restaurant Association Educational Foundation, and as president of the World Association of Chefs Societies.

Among his scores of awards, Metz has received from the **James Beard Foundation** a Lifetime Achievement Award and induction into the Who's Who of Food & Beverage in America; Taste Masters, from the American Academy of Chefs; the Medal of the French republic and Maître d'Honneur from Chaîne des Rôtisseurs; the Caterina de Medici Award; the Grand Prize for Culinary Arts from the German government; Man of the Year from the Escoffier Society; a Silver Spoon Award from *Food Arts* magazine; induction into the Hall of Fame by the American Academy of Chefs; inclusion in the Top 50 Most Influential People in Foodservice by *Nation's Restaurant News*; National Culinarian of the Year from the American Culinary Federation; and Educator of the Year from the American Culinary Federation.

METZEL SOUP. A Pennsylvania Dutch sausage given as a gift by the person who slaughtered the animal (1872). The word is from the German *Metzelsuppe*, "sausage soup."

MEXICAN AMERICAN FOOD. A general term for food and drink cooked and consumed by Mexican American immigrants as well as such foods enjoyed by non–Mexican Americans.

Archaeologists and anthropologists estimate that the first people came to the Americas from across the Bering Strait at least 23,000 years ago. Pre-Columbian Mexicans depended heavily on maize (which they called "our mother"), squash, and beans in their diet, and the Aztecs had advanced systems of trellising, irrigation, and fertilizing and built artificial islands called chinampas that could yield four harvests per year. By A.D. 200, corn (maize) had reached North America, as had beans by 1100. The Mayas and Aztecs who occupied Mexico for millennia depended on those foods that helped spark the Columbian Exchange, with **corn**, **cocoa**, **tomatoes**, **potatoes**, **chile peppers**, **agave**, **squash**, **vanilla**, and more. In exchange, Europeans brought to America cattle, chickens, honeybees, bananas, rice, garlic, wheat, and sugarcane. Indeed, many of the foods that came to exemplify Mexican cuisine, like carnitas, tortas, **tacos**, **tamales**, and **burritos**, were nonexistent before the arrival of Europeans, who also introduced frying techniques to the New World.

The Spanish settlers maintained their links to their own food culture, but even as they decimated and drove out the indigenous people, the regional food of Mexico endured.

Until Mexico lost its western territories to the U.S. with the Mexican–American War (1846–1848), Mexican food had little visibility in North America outside of Texas. Largely based on corn, Mexican food culture was rich in beans and legumes, seafood along the coasts, and, when affordable, pork and chicken. By the 1800s cattle ranchers in Texas (then called Tejas) used more beef than pork, turning some into dried meats, or *"carne seca."* Chile peppers were a dominant seasoning in Mexican food but were rarely used elsewhere in the U.S. until the twentieth century. **Chili con carne** is a Mexican-Texan creation that developed north of the Rio Grande around the 1870s, especially in San Antonio, where it was sold by **chili queens** in the plaza.

America's acquisition of the western territories resulted in unimaginable expansion and need for workers, but deep-seated bigotry toward Mexicans kept their food from becoming a significant part of the American diet, even in the West. Mexican-owned restaurants in cities like Los Angeles and San Diego were usually called "Spanish" restaurants, even though the menus listed traditional Mexican dishes like **tamales**, **tostadas**, and **enchiladas**, which came mostly from the border states of Sonora and Chihuahua. Chili was the one dish that proliferated in the U.S. after World War I, when it was offered in non-Mexican eateries like diners and even high-class Hollywood restaurants like Chasen's, which was famous for its chili, and the NYC nightclub La Conga. By the 1930s Arthur Whizin had one of the first fast-food chains in Southern California, named Chili Bowl, where "size" was a name for a steak topped with chili, along with tamales and "Spaghetti Texas Beans." *Good Housekeeping* magazine printed the first **tamale** recipe in America, in 1894, calling it a San Francisco street item, and by 1901 more than a hundred tamale wagons rolled through the streets of Los Angeles.

The popularity of **tacos** also began in California, especially after the opening of the Mexican American business district on Olvera Street, in Los Angeles, which became a tourist attraction in the 1930s. One of the taco pioneers was not of Mexican ancestry at all: **Glen Bell** ran hamburger eateries in San Bernardino in the 1950s, to which he added Mexican food, eventually opening a chain of enormously successful Taco Bell **fast-food** restaurants, now with six thousand units worldwide. Fish tacos were first popularized in San Diego, by restaurateur Ralph Rubio in 1983.

By the 1960s, Mexican American restaurants and their counterparts, Tex-Mex restaurants, were casual, cheap, and more often a chain-operated roadside stand than a full-scale restaurant. Larry Cano's El Torito chain popularized the margarita cocktail and the making of guacamole tableside, which brought up the level of such sit-down restaurants.

Inclusion of Mexican dishes in cookbooks dates back to the 1870s, including dispatches from western newspaper columnist **Charles Fletcher Lummis**, who wrote for the *Los Angeles Daily Times* and *The Land of Sunshine* magazine in the 1880s and 1890s. In 1902, the newspaper published seventy Mexican recipes in a popular series. *The California Mexican-Spanish Cook Book*, by Bertha Haffner-Ginger, appeared in 1914, containing the first recorded taco recipe, with illustration. In the midst of World War II, Elena Zelayeta's *Elena's Famous Mexican and Spanish Recipes* (1944) sold briskly. Only in the 1970s, however, did Mexican food receive true recognition, when the *New York Times'* food critic championed the Mexican cooking of Diana Kennedy, whose 1972 *The Cuisines of Mexico* was the first attempt to distinguish authentic regional Mexican cuisine from the staples of Mexican American and Tex-Mex fare. Concomitant to these new expressions, large food companies specializing in Mexican American prepared and packaged food, like Ortega and Old El Paso, pushed recognition into American home kitchens.

As New American cuisine developed as a movement among both ethnic and non-ethnic young American chefs, the focus shifted to regional Mexican food at places like **Mary Sue Milliken and Susan Feniger**'s Border Grill, opened in Santa Monica, California, in 1985. As a separate genre of New American cuisine, the term "New Southwestern cuisine" was promoted by western chefs like **John Rivera Sedlar**, of Abiquiu, in Los Angeles, and Mark Miller, of the Coyote Café, in Santa Fe, while Dean Fearing, at the Mansion on Turtle Creek, and Stephen Pyles, of Routh Street Café, both in Dallas, along with Robert Del Grande, at Café Annie, in Houston, and others, launched "New Texas cuisine" in their stylish, upscale, expensive restaurants. Chefs like **Zarela Martinez**, of Zarela's, in New York City, and **Rick Bayless**, of Topolobampo, in Chicago, improved public perception of regional Mexican fare, which now included more of the Yucatán, Oaxaca, and Mexico City styles.

Tex-Mex, meanwhile, continued to be the dominant menu style throughout most of the U.S., with "combo platters" of **enchiladas**, tacos, **burritos**, **chimichangas**, **refried beans**, and rice as staples. Defenders of this kind of cookery, dependent on cheap ingredients, large portions, and low prices, insisted that Tex-Mex was a cuisine all its own, with its own historic traditions. The same was true of the less well-known cuisine of New Mexico, which derives more from Native American cookery and has its own green chile stews, posole, sopapillas, and heavy use of blue corn.

Much was made of the moment when, in 2000, Mexican **salsa** sales surpassed ketchup for the first time.

MEXICAN BREAKFAST. Southern term, intending a regional slur, for a cigarette and a glass of water, usually prescribed for hangover victims (1954).

MEYER, DANNY (1958–). Restaurateur, entrepreneur, and author. Widely credited with changing American restaurant hospitality to encourage more interaction between service staff and guests, Meyer is owner of several restaurants in New York City, as well as a chain of Shake Shack hamburger eateries.

Born in St. Louis, Meyer is of German-Jewish descent. He graduated from Trinity College in Hartford, Connecticut, with a political science degree and in summers worked as a tour guide in Rome, Italy. After giving up his fantasy of playing professional baseball, Meyer went into politics before heading to New York City to learn the restaurant business as an assistant manager at an Italian seafood restaurant named Pesca, following up with formal culinary training in Rome and Bordeaux. Upon his return to New York City, in 1985, at the age of twenty-seven, he took over a vegetarian restaurant at Union Square and turned it into the Union Square Cafe, hiring chef Michael Romano to do a predominantly Italian menu, using ingredients sourced from the Union Square Greenmarket.

It was at Union Square Cafe (nicknamed "USC") that Meyer developed a new style of service and hospitality, focusing on the idea that an evening at a restaurant should be enjoyable not just for the food but for a warm, egalitarian relationship between guests and service staff, made up of young, attractive men and women for whom the restaurant business was a career rather than just a part-time job. Buoyed by his own midwestern upbringing, Meyer eschewed the kind of urban restaurant service that either fawned over regulars or provided guests with only token service by waiters whose jobs were considered low-end.

So distinctly different was Meyer's approach, by which the guest was attended to from the moment he made a reservation through the payment of his check, that USC became noted as much for its hospitality as for its cuisine. "I'm watching the staff," Meyer told *Wine Spectator* in 2012. "Are they having fun with each other? Helping each other out? If they are having fun, the customers will have fun." With Romano, he wrote *The Union Square Cafe Cookbook* (1994) and *Second Helpings from Union Square Cafe* (2001).

With his restaurant booming, Meyer founded and became CEO of the Union Square Hospitality Group (USHG) and began opening a wide range of restaurants across the economic spectrum, all in New York City. First was Gramercy Tavern (1994), with chef Tom Colicchio, where the idea was to serve fine modern American food and wine in a casual, tavern-like atmosphere with a bar up front where guests could eat as well. In 1998, he opened two restaurants in one building: Eleven Madison Park (fine dining) and an upscale Indian restaurant called Tabla, with chef Floyd Cardoz. In 2002 he opened a barbecue restaurant, Blue Smoke (with later another in Battery Park City), and a music venue, Jazz Standard, again in one building.

Meyer branched out to midtown NYC in 2005 with a fine dining restaurant and café called the Modern, designed by architects Bentel & Bentel, adjacent to the new Museum of Modern Art's Abby Aldrich Rockefeller Sculpture Garden on West Fifty-third Street. In 2001, the Madison Square Park Conservancy contracted Meyer to run a hot dog cart, which three years later he turned into a permanent kiosk called Shake Shack, serving hamburgers, french fries, and milk shakes. He has since opened several more Shake Shacks, in New York City, Washington, D.C., and all across the East Coast, and as far abroad as Dubai.

In 2008, USHG began operating food concessions at the New York Mets' new baseball stadium, Citi Field. Meyer's affection for the kind of trattoria he loved in Rome led to his opening, in 2009, Maialino, whose name ("little pig" in Italian) was a pun on his own name given him in Rome. In 2011, the Whitney Museum of American Art provided space on its lower level for USHG for a café called Untitled. That same year, he closed Tabla and sold Eleven Madison Park to his chef Daniel Humm and general manager Will Guidara. A year later, USHG opened North End Grill in Manhattan's Financial District.

In 2006, Meyer published the bestselling book *Setting the Table: The Transforming Power of Hospitality in Business*, in which he wrote, "For us, the ongoing challenge has been to combine the best elements of fine dining with accessibility—in other words, with open arms. This was once a radical concept in my business, where excellent cuisine was almost always paired with stiff arm's-length service."

A documentary was made about Meyer's career, entitled *The Restaurateur* (2011). He is the recipient of Restaurateur of the Year (2005) and Humanitarian of the Year (1996) awards from the James Beard Foundation, among twenty-five awards for his chefs and restaurants. In 1999, *Bon Appétit* magazine honored Meyer as Best Restaurateur in America.

MIAMI GRILL. A dish of veal chops, lamb chops, orange slices, bananas, and tomatoes, all grilled or broiled together. It is associated with Miami, Florida, and probably dates from the 1930s.

MIAMI GRILL

On a greased rack place 4 veal chops, 4 lamb chops, 4 salted tomatoes, 8 pitted orange slices, and 4 peeled and buttered bananas. Broil for 10-12 min., turning once.

MICKEY. A potato roasted over an open fire. Mickeys were sold by street vendors during the first half of this century, and the name derives from the potato's association with the Irish immigrants, who collectively had been referred to as "micks" since the nineteenth century. The word's usage in print, in reference to the potato, dates back only to 1943, but it is probably much older.

MICKEY FINN. Also "Mickey." A bartender's term for a secretly concocted beverage designed to induce diarrhea in an unwanted customer. It is also a term for "knockout drops," a drink that will induce unconsciousness.

The origins of the drink are usually associated with San Francisco's Barbary Coast in the 1870s,

when, according to Herb Caen, in *Don't Call It Frisco* (1953), a discredited Scottish chemist turned bartender named Michael Finn helped shanghai sailors by serving them such potions. Sometimes these drinks contained Glauber's salt, a horse laxative, or potassium tartrate, an emetic. There was even an infamous "Mickey Finn Case" involving the poisoning of an orchestra playing at a club on Fisherman's Wharf, in San Francisco. But the *OED* cites two 1903 entries that refer to the proprietor Mickey Finn of the Lone Star Saloon, in Chicago.

By the 1920s, Mickey Finn in some quarters referred to a "double," or two servings of liquor at once.

MICROWAVE OVEN. An electric oven that uses high-frequency electromagnetic waves to generate heat within foods by vibrating their molecules.

The microwave oven was developed by microwave researcher Percy Le Baron Spencer, of the Raytheon Co., in 1946, after noticing that a piece of chocolate in his pocket had melted as he stood next to a magnetron, a device that drives radar equipment. By 1953 Raytheon had patented a very large, 750-pound "high frequency dielectric heating apparatus," which it marketed to restaurants as a "Radar Range." In 1964, Japan developed an improved electron tube that in 1967 was adapted for use in microwave ovens sold by Amana Refrigeration Inc. (purchased by Raytheon two years before). In 1971, the federal government set safety standards for microwave ovens, and today a majority of American homes use them.

MIDDLE EASTERN AMERICAN FOOD. A general term for food and drink cooked and consumed by Middle Eastern American immigrants as well as such foods enjoyed by non–Middle Eastern Americans.

As with people of so many other nations, Middle Easterners began their emigration to America in the second half of the nineteenth century, including the Greeks, who by then considered themselves closer to Europeans than to Asians. (See **Greek American food**.) Both before and after World War I, territories in the Middle East changed hands and names several times, so that immigrants from the Levant—Syrians and Lebanese—came on the same ships crowded with Christian Arabs from the dismembered Ottoman Empire. Between the late 1880s and 1924, when immigration was closed off, 100,000 Armenians took refuge in America, especially after the genocidal massacres of Armenians at the hands of the Turks during World War I.

The majority became peddlers when they settled in the U.S., mainly in New York City and Detroit, and as Middle Eastern immigrants moved slowly into American life, many found easy access via food stores specializing in selling dried fruits and nuts, and small restaurants that catered to their own people living in poor neighborhoods. Yet, despite significant differences in culture, religion, and language, the diets of Middle Eastern Americans was very similar, sharing a love of an array of *meze* appetizers, stuffed pastries, lamb dishes in every form, fried seafood, kebabs, *kofta* meatballs, sour cream, dill, bulgur salads, and pita bread, all of which might as easily be found on a Turkish American dinner table as on a Lebanese or Armenian one.

The most common dishes include *manti*, small, lamb-stuffed ravioli with sour cream; *borek*, a pastry stuffed with feta cheese or other fillings; *kibbeh*, meat or pumpkin fritters; *merguez*, a spicy lamb sausage; and desserts that are often made with phyllo pastry, butter, nuts, and honey. All these are eaten at Middle Eastern American homes as well as at restaurants run by the people of this region.

MIGAS. A Mexican American breakfast of scrambled eggs and corn tortillas with salsa. The word is from the Spanish for "crumbs" and refers to crumbled-up tortillas.

MILE-HIGH CAKE. Generally a tall cake of several layers, or a cake designed for baking at high altitudes. Mile-High Ice-Cream Pie was created at New Orleans's Pontchartrain Hotel.

MILK. The white liquid produced by the mammary glands of cows, goats, sheep, and other animals, although in the U.S. almost all milk comes from cows. The word is from Old English *milc*.

Although milk has been drunk by most of the world's people, especially infants and children, it was not known to pre-Columbian Indians, for the simple reason that they had no milk animals, which were brought to the New World by the Spaniards and English. In 1611, the first milk cows were brought to Jamestown, Virginia. At first the Europeans drank mostly goat's milk, but, notes Richard J. Hooker, in *Food and Drink in America* (1981), "by 1634 all the 'better' plantations of Virginia were said to have plenty of milk, butter, and cheese, and throughout New England milk was drunk, made into cheese, or eaten with samp, suppawn, fruits, and baked pumpkins."

Until the nineteenth century, however, milk was still treated with caution, especially in the South, where the heat quickly spoiled fresh milk. Plantation slaves drank skim milk, while their masters drank the first milk of the morning. In the North, where it was cooler, Dutch and German settlers enjoyed their milk, especially when made into cheese. Still, milk was frequently contaminated, especially in the cities, where dairies were often run by breweries that fed the cows on fermented mash and adulterated the milk with water, chalk, and other ingredients, leading to a pronouncement in *Frank Leslie's Illustrated Newspaper* in 1858 that such actions constituted "milk murder." Indeed, even in the country, people risked illness, even death, from a disease called "the milksick," "the milk evil," "milk poison," "the slows," and "the trembles" (from which Abraham Lincoln's mother died). Nevertheless, nutritionists and temperance leaders promoted the virtues of sanitary milk for their followers, and "milkmen" delivered their product from "milk ranches" (later "dairy farms") by "milk wagon," pouring it into customers' "milk cans."

A safer form of milk was developed by Gail Borden of Wolcottville, Connecticut, who had experimented with attar of meat and other concentrated foods but who made his fortune by creating condensed milk in 1853, after witnessing the deprivations of immigrant babies on a transatlantic crossing because the cows on board had milk sickness. Condensed milk was flavored with sugar and cooked under vacuum to remove 60 percent of the water, and it became standard issue among Civil War troops.

It was also during this period that French chemist Louis Pasteur (1822–1895) developed a process for killing off harmful microbes in milk. This became known as "pasteurization" and was widely adopted in the U.S. by the 1890s, so that European visitors marveled at the amount of milk consumed here. State laws were soon instituted to regulate sanitary conditions in dairies—for example, inspections were mandatory in Newark, New

Jersey, as of 1882. By 1908, 25 percent of NYC's milk and 33 percent of Boston's was being pasteurized. The first known "milk bottle" dates to at least 1866, though the first patented bottle, a milk jar by Louis P. Whiteman, was not patented until 1880. The store-bought paperboard milk carton was created by Pure-Pak, of Detroit, in the 1930s.

Milk was wholesome, nutritious, and available to everyone; it was sold fresh or canned, condensed, or, as of the 1920s, "evaporated," which was not sweetened like condensed milk. In 1927, Borden marketed the first homogenized milk. "Powdered milk" or "dry milk" was pioneered by David Peebles in 1953 and first marketed by the Carnation Co. the following year.

By 1950 Americans were drinking six hundred glasses of milk per person per year, but in the years that followed, consumption decreased, owing to concerns over too much fat and cholesterol in the American diet. When low-fat milk, containing between 0.5 percent and 2 percent milkfat (whole milk contains about 3.8 percent) came on the market in the 1960s, milk consumption rose again. Skim milk (or "skimmed milk"), dating to Shakespeare's 1598 play *Henry V, Part 1*, has nearly all the fat removed. In the South, this is colloquially called "blue john." "Evaporated milk" is milk that has had 60 percent of its water removed and been heat-sterilized, then canned (1870).

In 2011 the U.S. produced 196.2 billion pounds of milk. Americans consume about 200 pounds of fluid milk items per capita, 5.1 pounds of butter, 33 pounds of cheese, 2.4 pounds of cottage cheese, 7.1 pounds of evaporated or condensed milk, and 22.4 pounds of frozen dairy.

The top-producing states are California, Wisconsin, Idaho, New York, Pennsylvania, Texas, Minnesota, and Michigan.

Most American milk is homogenized, and some is treated with a relatively new process called "ultra-pasteurization," by which the milk is heated for two seconds at 280 degrees Fahrenheit, which has the effect of killing some organisms but not affecting the taste. This process produces "long-life milk," able to be kept on a market shelf without souring for up to six months. "Dried milk," "powdered milk," and "dehydrated milk" are made from either whole or skim milk.

"Buttermilk" is made from the sour liquid, containing some butterfat, that is left after the making of butter. Markets also sell a cultured buttermilk, made with a lactic-acid bacteria added to skim or partially skimmed milk. "Acidophilus milk" (or "LBA culture") is cultured with acidophilus bacteria and fortified with vitamins A and D. It is more easily digested by people who cannot tolerate whole milk.

See also **cream**.

MILK PUNCH. Any low-proof drink made of liquor, sugar, and milk, usually served for brunches. The term dates in print to 1792. Milk punches became in America a streamlined version of **eggnog** and include drinks with names like the "Milky Way" (half ounce of brandy, half ounce of rum, half ounce of bourbon, six ounces of milk, and a dash of vanilla, shaken with ice).

MILK SHAKE. A drink made with milk, a flavored syrup, and ice cream blended to a thick consistency. It is a favorite soda-fountain item, only occasionally made at home.

When the term first appeared in print in 1885, milk shakes might have contained whiskey of some kind, but by the turn of the century they were considered wholesome drinks made with chocolate, strawberry, or vanilla syrups. In different parts of the country the item went by different names. One might order a "frappé" (from the French past participle of *frapper*, to "strike" or "chill"), which in the nineteenth century referred to a frozen sherbet-like mixture of fruit juice and ice. "Frappé" is still used in this sense to some extent today but is usually synonymous with "milk shake" and often pronounced "frapp." One may also hear "frosted," "thick shake," and, in Rhode Island, "**cabinet**." A "malted" is made with **malted milk** powder—invented in 1887 by William Horlick of Racine, Wisconsin, and made from dried milk, malted barley, and wheat flour—promoted at first as a drink for invalids and children. By the 1930s a "malt shop" was a soda fountain not attached to a pharmacy. "Date shakes" are popular in Southern California.

MINCEMEAT. Also "mince." A mixture of chopped fruits, spices, suet, and sometimes meat that is usually baked in a pie crust. The word comes from *mince*, "to chop finely," whose own origins are in the Latin *minuere*, "to diminish," and "mincemeat" once referred specifically to meat that had been minced up, a meaning it has had since 1630 in print. By the nineteenth century, however, the word referred to a pie of fruit, spices, and suet, only occasionally containing any meat at all. In colonial America, these pies were made in the fall and sometimes frozen throughout the winter.

MILLIKEN, MARY SUE. See **Feniger, Susan**.

MING-MANG. Ozarks colloquialism for a mixture of either butter and molasses or butter and gravy, dating in print to 1936, akin to the term "mishmash" for "a mixture of things."

MINNEHAHA. A term for a variety of cakes, breads, or puddings that share little in common except the simplicity of their ingredients and preparation. The name commemorates the Native American heroine of Henry Wadsworth Longfellow's epic poem *Hiawatha*, published in 1855, after which the Minnehaha foods appeared in recipe books. There is scant mention of Minnehaha's culinary talents in the poem, only a reference to the "Yellow cakes of the Mondamin" served at the wedding feast of Hiawatha and Minnehaha.

MINT. Any of a variety of plants in the genus *Mentha* that bear aromatic leaves used for flavoring desserts, candy, gum, and other foods. The name is from the Greek *minthe*.

The two most popular varieties of mint, "peppermint" (*M. piperita*) and "spearmint" (*M. spicata*), are not native to America but were brought over early by the European colonists, and the species proliferated without much need of cultivation.

"Mint jelly" is a customary accompaniment to lamb dishes in America, and peppermint sticks are a favorite hard candy, often crushed to make "peppermint-stick ice cream," served with hot fudge sauce.

MINT JULEP. A **cocktail** made from bourbon, sugar, and mint. It is a classic drink of Kentucky and is traditionally served at the running of the Kentucky Derby, on the first Saturday of May. The word first appeared printed in John Davis's *Travels of Four Years and a Half in the United States of America* (1803), as a "dram of spirituous liquor that has mint in it, taken by Virginians in the morning."

The origin of the word "julep" is the Persian *gulāb*, "rosewater," which is not an ingredient in the Kentucky cocktail but indicates a very sweet concoction known since the fifteenth century. Mint juleps were known in the United States by the end of the eighteenth century, long before bourbon became the ingredient most associated with the drink, and one will find mint juleps made with whiskeys other than bourbon, though this would be heresy in the state of Kentucky, where there is also great debate as to whether the mint leaves should be crushed in the traditional silver mug. Frances Parkinson Keyes once observed that "like a woman's heart, mint gives its sweetest aroma when bruised. I have heard it said that the last instructions which a Virginia gentleman murmurs on his deathbed are, 'Never insult a decent woman, never bring a horse in the house, and never crush the mint in a julep!'"

By tradition, a mint julep is served in a frosted silver-plated cup.

MINT JULEP

Chill a silver mug (made in the South especially for juleps). Dissolve 1 ½ t. confectioners' sugar in 1 T. water. Fill mug with crushed ice, pour in enough bourbon to cover, then stir in the sugar syrup. Garnish with sprigs of mint.

MIRACLE. A nineteenth-century New England fried cookie.

MIRACLE COOKIES

Beat 3 eggs with 3 T. melted butter, 2 c. flour, and a dash of salt. Roll dough very thin, sprinkle with sugar, and cut into even, large squares. Fold in two, cut into long strips about 1 in. wide, and twist together to form a link. Fry in hot oil until golden brown.

MISSION BELL. A stevedore's term for a drinker of cheap wine, so called because of the widespread use of Mission grapes in such wines, especially in California.

MISSISSIPPI MUD PIE. A very dense chocolate pie that takes its name from the thick mud along the banks of the Mississippi River. According to Nathalie Dupree, in *New Southern Cooking* (1986), the top of what she calls "Mississippi Mud Cake" should also be "cracked and dry-looking like Mississippi mud in the hot, dry summer." It does, however, seem to be of fairly recent origin; according to Mississippi-born food authority **Craig Claiborne**, writing in 1987, "I never heard of a Mississippi mud pie or Mississippi mud cake until I moved North."

MISSISSIPPI MUD PIE

In a saucepan melt 3 squares of bittersweet chocolate and 1 stick butter. In a bowl beat 3 eggs with 1 ¼ c. sugar, 2 T. corn syrup, and 1 t. vanilla extract, then pour slowly and blend into the chocolate mixture. Pour the batter into a pie crust (graham cracker or chocolate cookie crust is often used) and bake at 350° for about 35 minutes, until set. The top should be fairly dry and crisp, the interior soft.

MIXED GRILL. A dish composed of various grilled meats such as beef, pork, sausage, chicken, lamb, and venison. The term dates in print to about 1910. See **Miami grill**.

MOCK APPLE PIE. A pie made with Ritz crackers (introduced by the National Biscuit Co. in 1933) and spices to resemble the taste of apple pie. The recipe first appeared during the Depression, when apples became a costly item.

MOCKTAIL. A colloquialism from the 1980s to describe a cocktail made without alcohol. See also **Shirley Temple**.

MOCK TURTLE SOUP. A soup made from calves' brains to resemble true turtle soup. It is of English origins, dating in print to 1783, made famous by the character of the Mock Turtle (with the shell of a turtle and the head of a calf) in Lewis Carroll's *Alice's Adventures in Wonderland* (1865). This recipe is from Mrs. James T. Halsey, of Philadelphia, as published in *Famous Old Receipts* (1908).

MOCK TURTLE SOUP

Boil the brains of a calf in 3 gal. water and reduce to 3 qt. Add a bunch of parsley, thyme, onions, 1 t. allspice, 1 t. cloves, 1 t. mace, 1 t. nutmeg, black and red pepper, and 1 t. salt. Cook for about 40 min. at a simmer. Remove meat, cool, then mince the meat. Return to pot with ½ pt. sherry, ½ c. walnuts, and ½ c. tomato ketchup. Make a roux of flour, 1 T. butter, and 1 T. vinegar and add to pot. Reheat, serve garnished with brain fritters, 6 hard-boiled eggs, parsley, and pepper.

MODERNIST CUISINE. A term used by billionaire inventor Dr. Nathan Myhrvold, founder of the Cooking Lab, for the title of his six-volume book *Modernist Cuisine: The Art and Science of Cooking* (2011), to describe a scientific approach to cooking techniques, using mostly untraditional machines like centrifuges, homogenizers, ultrasonic baths, and a one-hundred-ton hydraulic press, as well as liquid nitrogen, gelling agents, and sous-vide. The book's initial print run was six thousand copies, but another twenty-five thousand were soon printed after media touted it as both a challenging novelty and a landmark attempt to transform cooking in a radical way. It won the Book of the Year award from the **James Beard Foundation**.

Owing to the difficulty, expense, and length of cooking processes demanded by Myhrvold's techniques, in 2012 he published *Modernist Cuisine at Home* (with chef Maxime Bilet), with 150 recipes, including roast chicken, cheeseburgers, pizza, and milk shakes, calling for less expensive kitchen equipment than in the original book. Nevertheless, a recipe for scrambled eggs, cooked sous-vide, requires forty-five minutes to make. See also **molecular cuisine**.

MOI. Hawaiian name for a threadfish (*Polydactylus sexfilis*) that is caught along the shoreline (1926). It is usually baked or steamed.

MOJITO. A cocktail made with rum, lime juice, mint, sugar, and soda water. The mojito originated in Cuba, and the name is derived from the Spanish *mojo*, "wet." While the word *mojito* first appeared in English print in 1934, the origin of the cocktail has been disputed. One claim is that it was invented at La Bodeguita del Medio bar, in Havana, Cuba, in the 1960s.

The mojito was a favorite drink of author Ernest Hemingway, who made La Bodeguita del Medio famous as one of its regulars, writing, "My mojito in La Bodeguita, My daiquiri in El Floridita." This expression can still be read on the wall of the bar today, in his handwriting. A "Mexican mojito" uses the Mexican native tequila instead of rum as a primary alcohol, and simple syrup instead of sugar for a sweetener. To simplify production, some restaurants will add mint leaves and peppermint extract to premade margaritas for Mexican mojitos. A mojito without alcohol is called a "virgin mojito" or a "nojito."

MOJITO

In a cocktail shaker, muddle 1 sprig of fresh mint with 2 t. sugar. Add 2 oz. white rum, shake together, pour into tall glass, and top off with soda water.

MOLASSES. A sweetener made from refined sugar, including cane sugar, sugar beets, and even sweet potatoes. The word is from the Portuguese *melaço*, derived from the Latin *mel*, for honey. The first use of the word in print was in Nicholas Lichefield's 1582 translation of Lopez de Castanheda's *First Booke of the Historie of the Discoverie and Conquest of the East Indias*, which described "Melasus" as "a certeine kinde of Sugar made of Palmes or Date trees."

Molasses became the most common American sweetener in the eighteenth century, because it was much cheaper than sugar and was part of the triangular trade route that brought molasses to New England to be made into rum, which was then shipped to West Africa to be traded for slaves, who were in turn traded for molasses in the West Indies. When France forbade her West Indies colonies to export molasses to the mother country (where the French feared it would ruin the French brandy industry), the colonists began shipping molasses to America, and before long it was the principal sweetener of the British colonies. The Molasses Act of 1733 placed high duties on the substance, but widespread evasion of the tariff resulted in the tariff being lowered in 1764. Nevertheless, John Adams said that molasses was "an essential ingredient in American independence," because of England's attempts to tax the colonists in this manner.

Molasses remained Americans' most popular sweetener in the next century; it was used in drinks and confections and with meats, especially pork, causing English traveler Frederick Marryat to write in his *Diary of America* (1839) that, although the English "laugh at the notion of pork and molasses…it eats uncommonly well….After all, why should we eat currant jelly with venison and not allow the Americans the humble imitation of pork and molasses?" A sweetener like molasses was especially needed with salt pork, in order to temper the strong taste of the meat.

By the 1830s, new brides measured their popularity by the number of layers of the molasses cake (or "stack cake") the guests brought, and molasses cookies and candy were very popular.

One of the stranger events in food history occurred on January 15, 1919, when an enormous vat of molasses exploded at the Purity Distilling Co., in Boston, sending more than two million gallons into the streets and killing twenty-one people in what became known as the "Great Molasses Flood."

By the end of the century, molasses vied with **maple** syrup and sugar as the sweetener of choice, but when sugar prices dropped after World War I, both molasses and maple fell in popularity, and today both are used as sweeteners in confections and other foods only when their specific taste is desirable, as in **Boston baked beans**.

In the production of molasses, the sugarcane is crushed and the juice concentrated by boiling; after crystallization, the residue that remains is molasses, the residue of the first boiling being the best grade for table use. The top grades of molasses include "fancy" or "all natural," which would include the first "strike" (also "centrifugal") made from the first extraction of sugar crystals. "Second strike" molasses is the residue from a second crystallization. Both first and second strikes are then bleached with sulfur dioxide gas and termed "sulfured." The "third strike" is a very dark and thick molasses called **blackstrap** (also "mother liquor"), which may sometimes be found in health food stores but is generally distilled into animal feed or industrial alcohol. Molasses used to be called "long sweetening," while a darker, less-refined variety was called "short sweetening."

MOLECULAR CUISINE. Also "**modernist cuisine**" and "avant-garde cuisine." A culinary style of the beginning of the twenty-first century by which chefs inspired by the work of Spanish chef Ferran Adrià's highly experimental cuisine at his restaurant El Bulli, in Roses, Spain. Adrià sought to dazzle the eye as much as the palate, in wholly novel ways that transformed ingredients into new forms, using nontraditional techniques like centrifuges and liquid nitrogen to achieve various effects, which sometimes included serving a bowl containing only the scent of food. He created a fad for foamed sauces that he later abandoned.

In the U.S., the first molecular cuisine restaurant was WD-50, in NYC, opened in 2003 and headed by chef Wylie Dufresne, who served dishes like foie gras terrine with cocoa-dusted anchovies. A few other restaurants followed, most in Chicago, including Alinea, opened by chef Grant Achatz, who serves guests twenty-seven-course meals that might include a single peeled Thompson Seedless grape dipped in peanut butter and wrapped in a bread bite, and corned bison with a sauce of freeze-dried blueberries, to be consumed as the guest sniffs the aroma of burning cinnamon sticks. Said Achatz, "Sometimes, quite honestly, we want diners to feel confronted, if that makes their heart beat faster, if that helps them take note of the moment....I don't think we want to make people...fearful. But there can be levels of intimidation, surprise, excitement, intrigue, mystique."

An antecedent of molecular cuisine was the proposals of an eccentric Italian writer named Filippo Tommaso Marinetti (born Emilio Angelo Carlo Marinetti), author of, among countless poems, plays, and diatribes, a manifesto on cookery called *La Cucina Futurista* (1932), in which he wanted to replace the Italian diet's staple of pasta with decadent combinations of foods, like pineapple with sardines and salami with cologne, and "Alaska salmon baked in the rays of the sun with a Martian sauce." He would spray perfumes into a dark dining room and have diners stroke velvet, red silk, and sandpaper with their left hand while listening to the recorded sound of a loud airplane engine. He challenged cooks to make "sculpted food," like that created by Futurist painter Luigi Colombo—a rissole with minced veal, stuffed and roasted with eleven kinds of cooked vegetables, then placed on the plate and crowned with thick honey and supported at its base with a ring of sausage set on three spherical pieces of browned chicken. Marinetti urged the chemical industry to come up with pills, powders, albumen compounds, synthetic fats, and vitamins to replace food. Kitchens were to be equipped with ozonizers, ultraviolet lamps, electrolyzers, colloid blenders, and distillers.

Also of relevance here is the Experimental Cuisine Collective, founded in 2001 as a collaboration by Kent Kirshenbaum and Amy Bentley—from, respectively, the chemistry department at New York University and its nutrition, food studies, and public health department—with chef Will Goldfarb. The collective, as described on its website, is "a working group that assembles scholars, scientists, chefs, writers, journalists, performance artists, and food enthusiasts [whose] "overall aim is to develop a broad-based and rigorous academic approach that employs techniques and approaches from both the humanities and sciences to examine the properties, boundaries, and conventions of food."

MOM-AND-POP. Most often used with "grocery," "store," or "restaurant," this refers to a small, homey grocery or eatery typically run by a family. The term has been in print since the 1950s.

MONGOLE SOUP. A soup made from creamed split peas and tomatoes, usually from canned soups. It was especially popular during the 1930s, though its origins are uncertain. Food historian Jean Anderson has traced a recipe to 1935 under the name "Purée Mongole," for a soup using three bean purees, tomato, onion, and consommé, in *Those Rich and Great Ones*, by Henri Charpentier, whose restaurant in Lynnbrook, New York, featured the soup as a signature dish. The 1943 edition of *Joy of Cooking* contained a recipe for Mongole soup made with pea and tomato soups.

MONKEY BREAD. A sweet yeast bread, sometimes mixed with currants, formed from balls of dough, laid next to one another, which combine during baking. The origin of the name is unknown, though it has been suggested that the bread resembles the monkey puzzle tree (*Araucaria araucana*), whose prickly branches make it difficult to climb. There is also a fruit called "monkey bread," from the baobab tree (*Adansonia digitata*) of

Africa, dating in print to 1789, but there is no evidence of any connection between it and the baked bread. It is probable that the name comes from the appearance of the baked bread itself, which resembles a pack of monkeys jumbled together. The bread was a staple at the Mariposa restaurant, at Neiman Marcus department store in Houston, which opened in 1967, the recipe having been developed by Neiman Marcus food services director **Helen Corbitt**.

First Lady Nancy Reagan made monkey bread a traditional dish of the White House Christmas celebration; she claims that the bread is so called "because when you make it, you have to monkey around with it." The following recipe is from the former first lady.

MONKEY BREAD

Dissolve 1 pkg. dry yeast in ¼ c. milk. Add 2 eggs, beat, then mix in 3 T. sugar, 1 T. salt, 3 ½ c. flour, and 1 c. milk, and blend thoroughly. Cut in 6 oz. butter, knead well, and let rise to double. Knead again, let rise again for 40 min. Roll dough onto floured board, shape into a log, and cut into 28 pieces. Shape each piece of dough into a ball and roll in ½ lb. melted butter. Butter and flour two 9-in. ring molds, place 7 balls of dough in each mold, place remaining balls of dough on top, and let rise again. Brush tops with 1 beaten egg and bake for 15 min. at 375°.

MONKEY FOOD. Southern slang for snack food, dating in print to 1940.

MONKEY GLAND. A cocktail made with orange juice, grenadine, gin, and an anise cordial. It became popular in the 1920s, when Dr. Serge Voronoff (1866–1951), a Russian émigré to Paris and director of experimental surgery at the Laboratory of Physiology of the Collège de France, was promoting the benefits of transplanting the sex glands of monkeys into human beings in order to restore vitality and prolong life. His book *Life* appeared in 1920, but by the mid-1920s his theories had generally been discredited.

The cocktail, which facetiously promised similar restorative powers, may have been invented at Harry's New York Bar, in Paris, by owner Harry MacElhone.

MONKEY GLAND

Shake together with ice a dash of anise cordial, 2 dashes grenadine, and equal parts gin and orange juice. Strain into cocktail glass.

MONKEY RUM. A spirit distilled from the syrup of sorghum. The first mention of this drink, which is produced in North Carolina, was in 1941.

MONKFISH (*Lophius americanus*). Also "anglerfish," "goosefish," "fishing frog," and "allmouth." An Atlantic flatfish that usually dwells at the ocean bottom. Its European counterpart is *Lophius piscatorius*. The name "monkfish" has been used in print since 1582 and is said to refer to either the species's remoteness of habitat, like a monk's removing himself from the outside world, or the resemblance of its head to that of a cowled monk.

Although long a favorite in European gastronomy, the fish was never a popular species in the U.S. because of its ugliness and its unappetizing name, "goosefish." It also mysteriously disappeared from American waters at the end of the nineteenth century. But the frequent use of the fish in French **nouvelle cuisine** in the 1970s, under the name "lotte," and the adoption by American chefs of the name "monkfish" or "anglerfish" led, in the 1980s, to an increased appetite for the species. The tail is the only part of the monkfish that is eaten, and it may be broiled, sautéed, poached, or baked. Its meat is white and quite firm, often cut into medallions. U.S. commercial landings of monkfish totaled 15.985 millions pounds in 2010, valued at $18.989 million.

MONOGLYCERIDES. Emulsifiers that prevent spoilage in bread and baked goods and prevent the separation of oil in peanut butter.

MONOSODIUM GLUTAMATE (MSG). An amino-acid flavor enhancer used in seafood, cheese, sauces, and other foods, both at home and in processing. The substance was first produced commercially in the U.S. in 1934. Monosodium glutamate is often found in Chinese food, giving rise to "Chinese restaurant syndrome," meaning the sensations of dizziness, tightness of the chest, and burning some people feel when they eat food with MSG in it.

MONTE CRISTO. A sandwich composed of ham, chicken, and Swiss cheese enclosed in bread that is dipped in beaten egg and fried until golden brown, very similar to the French croque-monsieur, which, according to *Larousse Gastronomique*, was first served in 1910 "in a Parisian Café on the Boulevard des Capucines." The origin of the name Monte Cristo is not known, unless it is in some way a reference to the character of the wealthy Count of Monte Cristo in Alexandre Dumas's novel of the same name (1844–1845). The name Monte Cristo had become idiomatically associated with a very rich person, as is the sandwich itself. There was also a Monte Cristo Gold Mine in California's San Gabriel Mountains, which was in operation until 1979. The Brown Derby restaurant, in Hollywood, California, published the recipe (reproduced verbatim below) in its 1949 cookbook, and the sandwich became popular in the 1950s.

MONTE CRISTO

Take three slices of white bread. Butter the first and cover with lean baked ham and chicken. Butter the middle slice on both sides, place on meat, and cover with thinly sliced Swiss cheese. Butter the third slice and place, butter down, over cheese. Trim crusts; cut sandwich in two; secure with toothpicks; dip in light egg batter; fry in butter on all sides until golden brown. Remove toothpicks and serve with currant jelly, strawberry jam, or cranberry sauce.

MOONEYE. Also "gizzard shad," "toothed herring," "goldeye," and other names. A midwestern fish of the genus *Hiodon*, dating in print to 1842, so called because the retina of the fish's eyes reflects light.

MOONFISH. Any of several American fish, including the spadefish (*Ephippus gigas*), that range from New England to the Gulf Coast (1842); a variety of fish in the genus *Selene*, including the "dollarfish," "horsehead," "humpbacked butterfish," and others (1878); the harvest fish (*Peprilus alepidotus*), first in print in 1911; and the Hawaiian fish **opah** (*Lampris luna* and *L. regius*), first noted in print in 1896.

MOONPIE. Trademark name for a cookie made by the Chattanooga Bakery, in Chattanooga, Tennessee, consisting of two cookies with a marshmallow filling and chocolate icing. The MoonPie is one of the most beloved confections in the American South. "It was the basis of the ten-cent lunch," southern cultural historian William Ferris told the *New York Times* in 1986. "A nickel for the Moon Pie and a nickel for an RC Cola."

The cookie supposedly originated in 1917 at the bakery, when, around the turn of the century, a traveling salesman recommended creating just such a confection, whose size would be "as big as the moon." The MoonPie was trademarked in 1919. In 1969, the bakery introduced a "Double Decker" version with three cookies and two layers of marshmallow. The company now produces 300,000 MoonPies per day.

MOONSHINE. Illegally distilled **whiskey**, especially that made with corn. The term—which refers to the time of day when the cover of darkness hid the activities of "moonshiners," those engaged in such illicit whiskey making—dates back to at least 1782 in print and was later sometimes shortened to "shine" or "moon." The number of moonshiners, not surprisingly, increased during the Prohibition era. Moonshine is very potent, very raw, and often composed of dangerous elements, including battery acid, oil, and other ingredients used to speed up fermentation in order to reduce the risk of being discovered. This unhealthy brew was called "scared whiskey." Moonshine filtered through charcoal was called "coal juice." Federal revenue agents were called "revenooers" by the hill people of Appalachia and the Ozarks, where most moonshine was produced, and a great deal of folklore grew up around the people and object of this cat-and-mouse game, depicted in comic strips like Al Capp's *Li'l Abner* and Billy DeBeck's *Barney Google*.

Southerners commonly call such spirits "white lightning"; white southerners sometimes use the term "black thunder."

"Moonshine" is also the name of a dessert of egg whites and fruit preserves, the name—dating in print to around 1558—having nothing to do with the illicit whiskey of the same name. It may be named after the silvery white flower called "everlasting" (*Anaphalis margaritacea*), which in the mid-nineteenth century was called "moonshine."

MOONSHINE

Beat 6 egg whites, add 6 T. confectioners' sugar, then fold in 1 c. peaches or 1 c. jelly or preserves. In a saucer, pour cream flavored with vanilla and sugar and place egg-white mixture on top. Serves 6.

MOOSE (*Alces alces* or *Alces americana*). A large, antlered, deerlike animal, standing up to seven and a half feet high at the shoulder and up to ten feet in length, that ranges from the coastal tundra of Alaska down to northwestern Colorado. Its name, according to the *American Heritage Dictionary*, is from the Natick *moos*, from Proto-Algonquian *mooswa*, while Stuart Berg Flexner, in *I Hear America Talking*, cites Passamaquoddy *moosu*, "he trims smoothly," referring to the manner in which the animal strips bark from trees. In 1603, the first printed reference to the animal was made; by 1637 it was called "Mose," and by 1672 "Moose Deer."

Although the Native Americans hunted moose for their meat, early white settlers showed little interest in the animal as food. Even so, the moose's numbers dwindled in subsequent centuries, and the government finally had to step in to stave off extermination of the animal.

Today moose is rarely eaten, except as an exotic specialty in game restaurants. The meat is usually marinated and prepared as one would venison, or dredged in flour and pan-fried.

MORAVIAN CHRISTMAS COOKIE. A traditional Moravian spice cookie served at Christmastime.

MORAVIAN CHRISTMAS COOKIES

Sift 2 ½ c. flour, ¼ t. ground cloves, ½ t. cinnamon ¼ t. nutmeg, and ¼ t. salt. Cream 1 c. butter and add 1 ½ c. sugar. Beat well, then add 2 beaten eggs and 1 T. brandy. Beat in the flour and chill for several hours. Roll out very thin and cut with cookie cutter. Place on buttered baking sheets and bake at 375° for about 8 min.

MOSCOW MULE. A cocktail made from vodka and ginger beer. Its name refers to vodka's Russian heritage and ginger beer's zest, which combine to give the drink the kick of a mule.

The drink was created in 1947 by Jack Morgan, owner of a restaurant in West Hollywood, California, called the Cock'n Bull, together with Jack Martin and Rudy Kunett of Heublein, a spirits distributor then trying to promote Smirnoff vodka. The drink helped spur the popularity of vodka drinks in the United States soon afterwards. But during the Korean War, the cocktail was used as an object of scorn when NYC bartenders marched with banners proclaiming WE CAN DO WITHOUT THE MOSCOW MULE, to which Smirnoff answered that their company had long ago disassociated themselves from the Communists and had long been making the vodka in New England—a perennial stronghold of American patriotism.

MOSCOW MULE

In a copper mug with ice cubes stir 3 oz. vodka, the juice of ½ lemon, a twist of lime peel, and a twist of cucumber peel. Fill with ginger beer. (Sometimes ginger ale is substituted.)

MOUNTAIN DEW. Illicit liquor, especially from the mountains of Kentucky and Tennessee, though the term originated in the whisky-producing Highlands of Scotland. The first American printed reference to the word was in 1850.

There is also a trademarked commercial soft drink, which is slightly lemony and carbonated, called Mountain Dew, created in 1948 by Tennessee bottler Barney and Ally Hartman, with a revised formula in 1958 by Bill Bridgforth. The company was acquired by Pepsi-Cola in 1964.

MOUNTAIN OYSTERS. The testicles of a bull, pig, or lamb, dating in print to 1890. Sometimes called "Rocky Mountain oysters" or "calf fries," they are usually breaded and fried in the West. The name derives from the general appearance of the final product and not a little euphemism. It is a term used both by cowboys and meat-packinghouse workers. A "pig oyster" is a pig testicle, first in American print in 1991.

MOUNTAIN OYSTER

Wash 2 lb. lamb testicles and place in large pot with 1 on-ion and 1 T. salt. Cover with water, bring to a boil, lower to a simmer, and cook for 30 min. until tender, skimming top of water as necessary.

MOUNTAIN TEA. A wintergreen plant (*Gaultheria procumbens*) or a tea brewed from it, first in print in 1785.

MOXIE. Trademark for a fairly tart or bitter soft drink, concocted by Dr. Augustin Thompson in Union, Maine, in 1884, and originally sold as a "Moxie Nerve Food" to help remedy "paralysis, softening of the brain, and mental imbecility."

The drink's name was speciously pronounced by Thompson to have been in honor of a "Lieutenant Moxie," who was said to have been a classmate of Thompson's at West Point and the discoverer of a mysterious plant food in South America that became the basis of the beverage. The problem was, Thompson was never enrolled at West Point, and the officer was said to have died in California shortly before Thompson secured the trademark for Moxie. It is possible that the name derived instead from a wintergreen vine (*Gaultheria hispidula*) that was called moxie (1894), itself possibly derived from the Algonquian base *maski-*, "medicine."

The beverage became a very popular soft drink, and *moxie* itself entered the lexicon, having the meaning of courage, nerve, or shrewdness by 1890, when a line in a play entitled *Men and Women*, by H. C. De Mille, read, "Young man, you've got nerve enough to start a Moxie factory." In 1930, Damon Runyon wrote in *Collier's* magazine, "Personally, I always figure Louie a petty-larceny kind of guy, with no more moxie than a canary bird."

In 1966, the brand was sold to Monarch Beverage Co., of Atlanta, and in 2007 to Cornucopia Beverages Inc., of Bedford, New Hampshire.

Moxie was declared the official state drink of Maine in 2005.

MUCKAMUCK. An Alaskan Chinook Indian word for "food." When coupled with their word *hiu*, meaning "plenty," it means "plenty to eat." By extension, in American slang, a "high muckamuck" was not only someone who ate well but also, since at least 1840, a very powerful politician. Today it also means any powerful person.

MUDDLE. A fish stew or the gathering at which such a dish is made and served, dating in print to 1833.

MUDDLER. A stick with a nubby end used to mash sugar or other ingredients at the bottom of a glass, when making a cocktail or other drink, dating in print to 1855 as a utensil for sale at Hollister's Fancy Bazaar, in Chicago. The word is from *muddle*, "to mix something up."

MUFFIN. A small cake usually sweetened with a bit of sugar. In England, muffins were once called "tea cakes," while in America muffins are served primarily for breakfast or as an accompaniment to dinner. Americans make plain muffins from flour, yeast or baking powder, and sugar, but often add nuts and berries. Cornmeal muffins, blueberry muffins, and **English muffins** are particularly popular. Muffins are usually buttered.

The origins of the word are obscure, but it might come from Low German *muffe*, "cake." The term was first printed in English in 1703, and Hannah Glasse, in her 1747 cookbook, gives a recipe for making muffins. "Mush muffins" (called "slipperdowns" in New England) were a colonial muffin made with hominy on a hanging griddle.

"Gems" were a popular muffin of the nineteenth century, made with Gem commercial baking powder.

MUFFIN

Combine 1 beaten egg, 1 c. milk, and ¼ c. cooled melted butter. In another bowl mix together 2 c. flour, 2 T. sugar, 1 pkg. yeast, and a pinch of salt. Add milk mixture and stir lightly. Add berries or nuts if desired. Bake for 25 min. at 400°, until lightly browned. Makes 1 doz.

MUFFULETTA. Also "muffaletta." A **hero**-type sandwich on a large, round Italian bread loaf, stuffed with ham, Genoa and mortadella salami, cheeses, and pickled olives. It is a specialty of New Orleans, where it was created at the Central Grocery in 1906 by Salvatore Lupo, based on a Sicilian sandwich, although the word itself, according to the *OED*, did not appear in print until 1967.

Muffuletta is a Sicilian dialect word for a round loaf of bread baked so that the center is hollow, allowing it to be stuffed, usually with ricotta cheese.

The recipe below is purported to be the original Central Grocery muffuletta.

MUFFULETTA

Slice a 7-in. muffuletta bun or round Italian loaf with sesame seeds in half. Brush one half with olive oil. Layer fillings of 2 oz. sliced domestic ham, 2 oz. sliced Genoa salami, 2 oz. sliced Provolone or Swiss cheese, and 2 oz. sliced mortadella, and add an olive vegetable condiment made with pimientos, olive oil, garlic, vinegar, green and Greek olives, oregano, parsley, cauliflower, celery, and other vegetables on top. Cover with the other half of the bread and cut in half or into pie-shaped wedges.

MULACOLONG. A stewed chicken dish of obscure southern origins. The syllable "mul" may relate to the regional colloquialism "mull," for stew. A recipe is given in Sarah Rutledge's *The Carolina Housewife by a Lady of Charleston* (1847). In *200 Years of Charleston Cooking*, edited by Lettie Gay (1930), this dish is described thus: "The marching rhythm of this name is entrancing. Its origin is as mysterious as the flavor of the dish itself.

"A bird which has reached the age politely spoken of as 'uncertain' may serve as the pièce de résistance of any dinner and reflect glory on the hostess if it is prepared in this manner." The following recipe is from Gay's book.

MULACOLONG

Cut 1 fowl in pieces and fry until it is well browned. Then add 1 large chopped onion to the fat and allow this to brown also. Add 3 pt. veal stock, which should be very strong, and 1 t. turmeric mixed with 1 T. lemon juice. Season with salt and pepper and cook until the chicken is tender. The stock should cook down so that it forms a rich gravy, which should be served over the chicken.

MULBERRY. Any of a variety of trees in the genus *Morus*, especially the American red mulberry (*M. rubra*), which bears sweet berries used in making jellies, cordials, and pastries. The word is probably from Old High German *mūlberi*, via the Latin *mōrum*, first in English print circa 1382.

Other varieties include the "Mexican" or "Texas mulberry" (*M. microphylla*) and the "black mulberry" (*M. nigra*).

MULLET. Any of a variety of fish in the family Mugilidae, having more than a hundred species worldwide. The name is from Latin *mullus*, for the "red mullet" or "goatfish" (*Mullus surmuletus* and *M. barbatus*), dating in English print to 1393. In Hawaii the fish is known as *kūmū*. In the U.S., two species are important: the "striped mullet" (*Muqil cephalus*), also called "black mullet" in Florida and "gray mullet" in other parts of the world, and the "white mullet" (*M. curema*). Both are usually pan-fried or baked and in the South are often served as a breakfast fish. U.S. commercial landings of mullet totaled 19.6 million pounds in 1997.

MULLIGAN STEW. Hobo slang for a stew made from any food one can find, but usually containing meat, potatoes, and vegetables. The term has been in print since 1898 and may be commemorative of some real or fictional cook of the hobo camps, or simply a typical Irish surname. It has been suggested, too, that it comes from "mulligatawny" (from the Indian Tamil word *milagutannir*, "pepper water"), an Indian curry soup still widely enjoyed. But the association with a typical Irish name like Mulligan seems true to an earlier meat-and-potatoes concoction of the nineteenth century called "Irish stew."

A "mulligan-mixer" is a cook in a hobo camp (or jungle). "Mulligan" was also a word for a bottle of hot pepper seeds and water once used in saloons to intensify the flavor of beer—a use of the term that may well refer back to the Indian Tamil word noted above.

MUNCHIES. A colloquial term for a craving for something to eat, especially snack foods like potato chips, pretzels, and popcorn, dating in print to 1917. It may also refer to the snack food itself. "To get the munchies" was a phrase first heard in the 1960s, largely among marijuana smokers, whose appetites would increase under the influence of the drug, a meaning first noted in print circa 1971.

MUSCADINE (*Vitis rotundifolia*). A native American grapevine that proliferates in the Southeast, dating in print, as muscadine wine, to 1541. There are several species, including the **scuppernong**, sometimes called the "bullace grape." The word is a variant of "muscatel" or "muscat grape," from Latin *muscus*, "musk."

Muscadine grapes were the first to be vinified in America, and as early as the 1560s the French Huguenots who settled in Florida were making wine from them. The grapes grow in bunches and are usually not picked but rather knocked to the ground with sticks.

Although muscadine grapes and wines have always been made in the South and elsewhere, their greatest propagation in the nineteenth century was in North Carolina, where Captain Paul Garrett built a very successful wine business selling Virginia Dare Scuppernong wine. During Prohibition, the propagation of muscadine fell, and only after 1965, with the help of the North Carolina state legislature and the state university at Raleigh, has the grape again been grown significantly. Many new varieties have been developed, including the Mish, the Hunt, the Creek, the Higgins, the Tarheel, and others, most now marketed as wine under the general name of "Scuppernong."

MUSH. A porridge or cereal grain ground into a mushy consistency, dating in print to 1883.

MUSHROOM. Any of a large variety of fungi of the phylum Basidiomycota. The word is from the Gallo-Roman *mussiro*, which became *musseroun* in Middle English, dating in English print to around 1400.

When the first European settlers arrived in America, they found the woods filled with wild mushrooms of thousands of varieties, but the fear of eating poisonous mushrooms has prevented most Americans from developing any interest in them, relying only on the cultivated white or brown *Agaricus bisporus* for almost the entire mushroom crop offered at market. This variety was first cultivated in France at the beginning of the eighteenth century, probably by Louis XIV's agronomist, Olivier de Serres, near Paris. For this reason, the mushroom was called *champignon de Paris* or, outside France, the "Parisian mushroom." The English got hold of this fungus by the end of the nineteenth century and exported it to the U.S., where some mushroom cultivation was undertaken after the Civil War. Before the 1940s, the most available mushroom in the market was the "Italian brown" (*A. brunnescens*), also known as the "cremini" or "crimini." The "portobello" is merely a large cremini, but because of its rich, meaty texture and woodsy taste, it has taken on enormous popularity since the 1990s, with 32.7 million pounds shipped to market in 1997. Then, in 1926, Lewis Downing of Downingtown, Pennsylvania, discovered pure white spores growing among his mushrooms. He propagated these new types and spawned an industry that has made Pennsylvania the leading producer of mushrooms in the country, especially in Butler and Armstrong counties. California is the second-largest producer.

These were the only cultivated mushrooms in the United States until recent decades, and considerable success has been achieved in the growing of the "shiitake" or "Black Forest" mushroom (*Lentinus edodesi*); the "enoki" or "enoke" (*Flammulina velutipes*), originally imported from Japan; "oyster" (*Pleurotus ostreatus*); and the "wood ear" (*Auricularia polyticha*), also called "tree-ear," "cloud-ear," and "black tree fungus." There has even been some reported success with experiments in growing **truffles** in California, Texas, and Oregon, though American wild truffles also exist. Also found wild in the United States is the "morel" (*Morchella esculenta* and *M. elata*), also called "dog pecker," "dryland fish," "honeycomb," "moocher," and "pine cone," first cultivated in 1990 by Morel Mountain Mushroom Co., of Mason, Michigan; "cèpes" (*Boletus edulis*), sometimes called "porcini," "King Boletus," "red caps," and other names; "chanterelle" (*Cantharellus cibarius*), also called "egg mushroom"; "gyromitra" (*Gyromitra esculenta*) or "false morels"; "chicken mushrooms" (*Laetiporus sulphureus*), also called "chicken of the woods" or "hen of the woods" (though this name is also applied to *Grifola frondosa*); "man-on-a-horse" (*Tricholoma flavovirens*), possibly so called because of the elegant appearance of the mushrooms (1980); and "milk cap" (*Lactarius deliciosus*). The per capita U.S. consumption of commercially produced mushrooms in 1997 was two pounds. The U.S. now exports an enormous amount of wild mushrooms to Europe.

Americans eat mushrooms in salads, soups, and sauces, and stuffed with a forcemeat of various ingredients and seasonings.

MUSIC HALL INFLUENCE. A series of lavish restaurant/nightclubs begun the day after Prohibition took effect (January 16, 1920) by entrepreneur Billy Rose, whose Casino de Paris featured two orchestras, dancing, and a naked girl swimming in a fishbowl. The term was invented by press agent Bob Reud.

MUSSEL. Any of a variety of both salt- and freshwater bivalve mollusks having a blue-black shell. The name derives from the Latin *mūsculus*, meaning "little mouse," and in Old English the spelling was *mucxle*, dating in English print to 1298.

Mussels have not been a major American food item except in communities with Mediterranean heritage. The most common mussel used in cooking is the "blue" or "edible mussel" (*Mytilus edulis*), which ranges from the Arctic Ocean to South Carolina and has been successfully introduced on the Pacific coast, where it joined the indigenous "California mussel" (*M. californianus*). U.S. commercial landings of blue mussels totaled 6.9 million pounds in 2010.

Mussels are usually eaten steamed or cooked in a stew. They are the main ingredient of the soup **billi-bi**.

MUSTARD. A condiment, in either paste or powdered form, made from the seeds of any of a variety of plants in the genus *Brassica*, especially the "black mustard" (*B. Nigra*), the "white mustard" (*Sinapis alba*), and "brown mustard" (*B. juncea*), also called "Indian mustard." Mustard as a powder dates in print to 1289.

The word in Middle English was *mustarde*, derived from the Latin *mustum*, meaning the "must" of new wine, which was usually blended with early forms of mustard paste.

"English mustards" have long been popular in America, the first of note having been blended with various spices by a Mrs. Clements of Durham, England, in 1729, and another prepared in the nineteenth century by Jeremiah Colman of Norwich, England. In 1904, George T. French, of Rochester's R. T. French Company, introduced a mild yellow mustard called French's Cream Salad Mustard, which became the world's bestseller and the standard for most American mustards.

American mustards fall into two categories: "brown mustard," which has some pungency, and "yellow mustard," which is flavored with sugar, vinegar, turmeric, and white wine. Yellow mustard (also called "ballpark mustard" because of its prevalence in sports stadiums' food stands) is a fairly mild mustard that comes from the species *B. hirta* or *alba*, whose seeds were possibly brought to America by African slaves.

There is a National Mustard Museum, established in 1992 by Barry Levenson in Mt. Horeb, Wisconsin, and later relocated to Middleton, Wisconsin, where National Mustard Day is celebrated on the first Saturday of August.

Annual sales of mustard in the U.S. are $300 million, with per capita consumption of about twelve ounces. The bestselling mustard is Kraft's Grey Poupon, with a 15 percent share of the market.

"Mustard greens" are the leaves of the mustard plant, and in America the brown mustard plant, sometimes called "leaf mustard," is used in cooking by southerners and in **soul food**.

MUKTUK. An Eskimo dish made using the skin and fat of the bowhead whale.

MYSTERY MEAT. A term for cheap, unsavory chopped-meat dishes unidentifiable as beef or other meat. The term, as "mystery," has been used in print since 1877, and since 1968 as "mystery meat," to describe bad dining-hall meat. The term is commonly used among schoolchildren for their cafeteria food.

NAB. Slang abbreviation for "no-alcohol beer," a **beer** from which almost all the alcohol has been removed. The term has been used since the 1980s, as has its corollary, "LAB," for "low-alcohol beer." The beer trade itself lumps the two categories together as "NABLABs."

NACHO. A small **tortilla** chip topped with cheese and chile peppers or chile sauce. The word may come from the Spanish *nacho*, which means "flat-nosed," or from the nickname for "Ignacio."

The origins of nachos have been traced to Mexico in the 1940s, dating in print to 1948. They might have been created by Ignacio "Nacho" Ayala, a chef at Club Victoria, in Piedras Negras, Mexico, across the border from Eagle Pass, Texas. Having run low on certain food items one day, Anaya threw together the snack so that a group of Texas women having lunch at the club could have something to nibble on, calling the item "Nacho's Especial." This story seems to be confirmed by an advertisement for Club Victoria, calling itself the birthplace of "Nacho Specials" that appeared in the *St. Anne's Cookbook*, published in 1954 by the Church of the Redeemer in Eagle Pass.

Another claim was made by Connie Alvarez King, who said she created the item in 1943 at her restaurant in Harlingen, Texas, naming the snack after her best worker, Ignacio, whose nickname was "Nacho."

The popularity of "ballpark nachos"—covered with pickled jalapeño peppers and a melted liquid cheese, served at sports stadiums—has been credited to Sal Manriquez, who began serving such an item under the name "Margarita's State Fair Nachos," because that was what he called them when he first started serving them in 1964, at the State Fair of Dallas. Manriquez claims that he and his wife, Margarita, took broken, leftover pieces of tortillas, added beans and hot sauce, and began selling them, later substituting jalapeños and cheese. In 1975, Manriquez requested a permit to sell his nachos at Arlington Stadium but was turned down, only to find out later that the stadium was selling its own nachos with cheese, which became known as "ballpark nachos." The item is now said to be the third-best-selling concession food in the U.S., after popcorn and soda.

'NANA 'N' COOKIE PUDDING. According to Eric V. Copage, in *Kwanzaa* (1991), this is an African American dessert made from bananas, vanilla wafer cookies, and either meringue or whipped cream.

'NANA 'N' COOKIE PUDDING

In a double boiler combine 1 ⅓ c. sugar, ¼ c. flour, and 3 egg yolks. Blend with a whisk, then whisk in gradually 3 c. hot milk. Continue to cook, stirring until the liquid thickens to a thin custard (180° on a kitchen thermometer). Remove from heat and stir in 1 t. vanilla. Spread one layer of a buttered 7-by-11-in. baking dish with about one-third of a 12-oz. box of vanilla wafer cookies. Pour half the custard over the wafers, then arrange 6 peeled bananas cut into rounds over the mixture. Top with the remaining wafers, top with more custard and bananas, and put on another layer of wafers. Top with meringue if desired, place on a baking sheet, and bake in a 350° oven for 5–10 min. Cool and refrigerate before serving.

NAPLES BISCUIT. A light dessert or tea biscuit similar to a **ladyfinger**. Its name comes from the Italian city of Naples, suggesting this was the sort of biscuit found there, dating in English print to 1650. It was known in America soon after, appearing in several nineteenth-century cookbooks.

NATHAN, JOAN (1943–). Author, TV series host. As author of ten cookbooks, Joan Nathan has specialized in Jewish food culture, particularly that of immigrants who had to adapt their traditional food to incorporate the ingredients available in the United States.

Nathan was born in Providence, Rhode Island, and graduated from the University of Michigan with an M.A. in French literature, then got an M.A. in public administration from Harvard University. In the early 1970s, she moved to Israel to work for Jerusalem's mayor, Teddy Kollek, then moved to New York City in 1974 to work for Mayor Abe Beame.

Nathan founded NYC's Ninth Avenue International Food Festival and began an eight-year series of food columns for the *Washington Post*. Her first cookbook, *The Flavors of Jerusalem* (1975), was followed by *The Jewish Holiday Kitchen* (1979), *An American Folklife Cookbook* (1984), and her magnum opus, *Jewish Cooking in America* (1994; revised 1998), which won both a James Beard Cookbook of the Year award and the IACP Julia Child Cookbook the Year award and led to a PBS series, *Jewish Cooking in America with Joan Nathan*. In 2005, Nathan was guest curator of Food Culture at the Smithsonian Folklife Festival, tied to her book the *New American Cooking*, which was named the best American cookbook of 2005 by both the **James Beard Foundation** and the IACP. Her book *Quiches, Kugels, and Couscous: My Search for Jewish Cooking in France* was named one of the best of 2010 by *Food & Wine* and *Bon Appétit*. Many of her articles have appeared in the *New York Times* and *Food Arts*.

Nathan has said of her work:

> It is often the members of later generations who want to return to their roots and who question elderly relatives or track down cookbooks in seeking out the original recipes. This explains the transformation of Jewish food in the 1990s with baaleim tshuvah, returnees to the faith. These Jews, often from nonobservant homes, are studying Orthodoxy and are creating a new kosher cuisine mindful of health guidelines. It also explains

> why I myself, passionately interested in studying the roots of Jewish cuisine, am trying, through cooking, to provide a link to the past.

NATIVE AMERICAN FOOD. A general term for the food and drink of Native Americans, also called American Indian food, as well as those Native American dishes enjoyed by the rest of Americans.

The gastronomy of Native Americans is as broad as the regional tribes of peoples whom the Europeans called Indians upon their discovery and exploration of the Americas, when it is estimated there were perhaps twenty million people on the continents. The tribes of the Northeast and the Atlantic coast, which were principally gatherers and hunters, differed significantly from those of the Great Plains and the Southwest, where the tribes were often nomadic or lived in pueblos. Then, too, the fishing skills of the Gulf Coast people and the Pacific people, including those in Hawaii and Alaska, were formidable and guided their diet more than grains and cereals did elsewhere.

Corn, however, was of enormous importance to farming tribes, who depended on it as a staple (there was no wheat in America until Europeans brought it, as part of the Columbian Exchange), and it was revered by the Indians of Central America and the Southwest as a manifestation of the divine and matriarchal life force. (Oddly enough, some Southwest tribes were actually taught corn farming by the Spanish.) In Minnesota, the Indians depended largely on wild rice for nourishment, while in California, acorns were a staple and in Nova Scotia the Mi'kmaq planted tobacco but no edible crops, preferring to hunt and gather their food. Once the Plains Indians, including the Sioux, Cheyenne, Comanche, and Apache, learned to ride horses (introduced by the Spaniards), the hunting of buffalo became central to their diet and, ultimately, their survival, such that when the buffalo were nearly wiped out in the nineteenth century, the Plains Indians became wholly subjugated and largely dependent on the white man for their food.

Native Americans depended on seasonal hunting and rotating crops, preserving what they could for winter through methods of drying and smoking everything from venison to fruits, in what was called **pemmican**. Europeans taught Native Americans how to propagate crops, including those brought from the Old World, like apples, apricots, bananas, beets, cabbage, lettuce, oats, peas, rice, rye, soybean, and watermelons, as well as raising domesticated cows, chickens, goats, pigs, and sheep. In return, Native Americans exported bell peppers, chile peppers, cocoa, guava, jicama, papaya, peanuts, pumpkins, potatoes, tomatoes, yucca, and zucchini to the Old World. By the 1660s the Algonquian Mohegans of Connecticut were herding pigs and cattle, and the Iroquois had become adept at crop planting in that century.

The Europeans also brought diseases that decimated Indian populations throughout the New World. Large-scale trapping and hunting by the settlers wiped out whole species, like the passenger pigeon, and nearly all the buffalo, moose, and caribou. Incursions into Native American lands and the sheer slaughter of many tribes eventually, by federal fiat, drove them onto reservations, where they were allowed to farm on largely unproductive land.

By then the native forests of the East had already been so compromised by colonization that the traditional hunter-gatherer food culture of those regional tribes had passed into history.

Adapting to European foods also meant consuming European alcohol beverages, which became a scourge of Indian populations, as did obesity, with some tribes, like the Canadian Cree and Ojibwa, showing female obesity rates of 90 percent. Poverty led to diabetes because of an overdependence on carbohydrates, and many Indians were lactose intolerant and were made sick by dairy products.

Today, most Native Americans eat the same foods as other Americans, although there are groups and organizations that try to maintain the historical foods of various tribes out of a sense of preserving that history. In Central and South America, there is a far more complex food culture both among surviving Indian tribes and among regional peoples for whom foods like the tortillas, beans, and corn are still staples. Within the United States, only the native Alaskans still maintain a strong reliance on an ancient diet, rich in animal fats from whales, seals, walrus, fish, and, in season, berries, wild greens, kelp, and algae, as well as inland fish, like salmon and sturgeon, and also wild game. But their food resources, too, were compromised in the nineteenth century by the trapping, fishing, and logging industries of the Pacific Northwest, to the point that in the next century whales had to be federally protected as an endangered species, acts that were protested by the Inuit as depriving them of their basic food. When the Gold Rush of 1897–1920 hit Alaska, many Indians joined it and lost touch with their ancestral food culture, growing sedentary at the same time. The Inuit's adoption of the dogsled and, later, of gas-powered vehicles made hunting easier and more prolonged through the season but also depleted game faster. By the turn of the twentieth century, the native people of Alaska had come to depend on trade goods and store-bought food. By the 1930s, some tribes had adapted to spending the summer in fishing camps and the winter at trapping and hunting camps.

Today the maintenance of old food customs still endures among Northwest Coast tribes at the ceremonial feasts called potlatches, especially ones that mark funerals, when entire villages will gather and bring an abundance of traditional foods like salmon, duck, whitefish, beaver, and the highly valued moose.

Americans as a whole know little about and rarely encounter traditional Native American foods, except perhaps when visiting tourist attractions set on reservations. At the same time, however, many of the **Mexican American** foods loved by Americans have pre-Columbian antecedents—for example, tortillas, corn and bean dishes, chiles, tomatoes, and potatoes—and these remain very much a part of Native American food culture.

See also **Hawaiian food**.

NATIVE BEEF. Moose or deer harvested out of season, in print since 1979, colloquially called "some of the governor's meat."

NATURAL FOOD. A term, first appearing in 1671, that purports to describe unadulterated or unprocessed foods or foods that have been grown without the aid of pesticides or artificial fertilizers. There is, however, no consensus as to just what a "natural food" is. The U.S. Department of Agriculture defines the term, with reference to meat and poultry, as meaning the product is "minimally processed and contains no artificial colors or preservatives."

Because of the vagueness of the term, many manufacturers decide for themselves what they may or may not add. As a result, many "natural" foods may contain sugar, guar and carob gum, carrageenan, vitamin C, monosodium glutamate, artificial colors, and a long list of other substances.

To some people the term is synonymous with "**health food**."

Surveys have shown that Americans are willing to spend, on average, 10 percent more money on foods they consider "natural."

NAVY BEAN. Also called "pea bean" or "beautiful bean." The navy bean is one of several varieties of **kidney bean** (*Phaseolus vulgaris*). The name comes from the fact that it has been a standard food of the U.S. Navy since at least 1856, despite an old popular song that claims that "the Navy gets the gravy, but the Army gets the beans."

NED. A nineteenth-century slang term for pork. An 1833 account says the term was used in Tennessee for bacon, and by the 1840s, when the U.S. Cavalry entered the western Native American territories, soldiers were called "Neddies," because of the preponderance of pork in their diet.

NEEDLEFISH. Also "gar," "guardfish," "houndfish," "sea pike," "snipe," and other names, first cited in print in 1601. A fish of the family Belonidae, primarily in the genus *Strongylura*. *S. exilis* is a Pacific variety; *S. marina* lives in the Atlantic. The name comes from the fish's long body and long, sharp-toothed jaws. They are usually taken accidentally in nets designed to harvest other fish.

NEGATIVE RESERVATION. A restaurant term to describe a reservation taken for a table only when a regular customer calls to relinquish his usual reservation. The phrase has been in currency since the 1970s.

NEGIMAKI. A dish of thinly sliced beef wrapped around scallions and broiled with a soy-based sauce. The word is from the Japanese *negi* (onion) plus *maki* (roll). The dish, which has become very popular in Japanese restaurants in the U.S., was created at NYC's Nippon Restaurant in 1963 by owner Nobuyoshi Kuaoka, under the prompting of *New York Times* restaurant critic **Craig Claiborne**, who thought the restaurant should have more interesting beef dishes for the American customer. Kuaoka originally called the dish "negimayaki."

Negimaki is prepared by wrapping very thin slices of beef around several scallion stalks, broiling them with a soy-based teriyaki sauce, cutting them as with traditional Japanese *maki-zushi*, and serving them with another, thicker soy-based sauce.

NEGRO COFFEE. Also "mogdad coffee" and "senna coffee." The senna plant (either *Cassia occidentalis* or *C. Chamaecrista*) or a coffee-like beverage brewed from its roasted seeds, dating in print to 1889, so called because it was favored by southern black people.

NEGUS. A sweet alcoholic beverage made from port and citrus flavors. It is said to have been named after Colonel Francis Negus (died 1732), who is said to have invented the drink, and was so called in print by 1743. Legend has it that Negus averted a political free-for-all by diluting a dwindling bottle of wine that, in the words of the *Dictionary of National Biography*, was "passing rather more rapidly than good fellowship seemed to warrant over a political discussion" between Whigs and Tories.

NEGUS

Heat 1 qt. port and pour into warmed pitcher. Add 1 sliced lemon, 1 ½ oz. brandy, 1 T. sugar, a pinch of nutmeg, and 1 qt. boiling water.

NENE (*Nesochen sandvicensis*). A large Hawaiian goose, eaten there in precolonial times (1902).

NEW AMERICAN CUISINE. A phrase that developed in the early 1980s to describe foods made by American cooks with American ingredients but according to the principles of preparation, cooking, and presentation promulgated by the practitioners of France's **nouvelle cuisine**, a trend of the late 1960s and 1970s according to which lightness, expensive ingredients, untraditional marriages of foods, and less cooking time transformed classical French technique.

In America, many nouvelle cuisine chefs opened establishments featuring similar methods in the 1970s and 1980s, while hard on their heels came young American cooks who adapted such techniques and philosophies to the American larder. Their development of menus based on regional American cooking and traditions led to the coinage of regional terms like "California cuisine," "New New England cuisine," "New Southern cooking," "New Texas cuisine," and others.

The most influential of these was California cuisine, which itself was a development of two styles of cooking in the north and south of the state. In the north, especially around San Francisco and Berkeley, young chefs like **Alice Waters** of Chez Panisse in the 1970s were already searching out local ingredients and supporting local farmers to create a kind of cooking based on the freshest, best ingredients from California's cornucopia and the Pacific Ocean.

In the south, particularly in Los Angeles, this style of cooking became more eclectic, being sometimes deliberately dazzling in presentation, other times extremely simple and low in calories. Grilling and smoking were the favored techniques, baby vegetables were hallmarks of the style, and salads were featured as main courses. Regional wines from the Napa and Sonoma valleys were also exhibited as being particularly suited to this kind of cuisine.

The progenitors of New California cuisine, few of them from professional cooking backgrounds or training, included several who came out of Chez Panisse's kitchen, like Jeremiah Tower, a Harvard University–educated student of underwater architecture, who both washed dishes and cooked at Chez Panisse before becoming chef de cuisine there, next joining the Balboa Cafe and opening his own posh and glamorous Stars, where his menus teemed with the finest California ingredients, from baby lamb to Sonoma County goat cheese. Mark Miller, an Asian culture scholar, joined Chez Panisse in 1975, leaving four years later to open the Fourth Street Grill and the Santa Fe Bar and Grill in San Francisco, which led him to become one of the early innovators of New Southwestern cuisine at Coyote Café in Santa Fe, New Mexico; Judy Rogers was lunch chef at Chez Panisse, then opened Zuni Café (1987), in San Francisco, serving food with a southwestern flair; Joyce Goldstein, who had an M.F.A. from Yale University, worked at Chez Panisse for three years before opening her Mediterranean restaurant, Square One, in San Francisco in 1984, and publishing *The Mediterranean Kitchen*, in 1989.

Barbara Tropp, an Asian culture scholar, took a different turn, breaking down the traditional wall between kitchen and dining room at China Moon Cafe (1985), in San Francisco, which she defined as "food is entertainment, with the cooks and staff the actors and the exposed kitchen the center stage. Our plot and centerpiece is the food." Bradley Ogden, from Traverse City, Michigan, became chef at Campton Place Hotel, in San Francisco, where he showcased a modern style of traditional American food like apple ham pâté and poached lobster with blue corn cakes. Annie Somerville joined Greens in San Francisco's Zen Center in 1981, where, with **Deborah Madison**, she translated vegetarian food into a modern idiom.

In Southern California, the new cuisine was more firmly based on nouvelle cuisine at Los Angeles's fashionable Ma Maison, where Austrian-born chef **Wolfgang Puck** did lavishly rich French food, before shifting to open his own place, Spago, featuring grilled meats, California greens, and smoked salmon pizza. Puck also styled a new form of pan-Asian cuisine at Chinois on Main, in Santa Monica, California. Michael Roberts, at Trumps, in L.A., aimed for a more downhome style with European accents, like fried plantains with caviar and corn cakes with duck breast in pinot noir sauce. Meanwhile, **Susan Feniger** and **Mary Sue Milliken** brought an American sensibility to Mexican street food at the Border Grill, in Santa Monica. Ken Frank, of La Toque, used French technique to cook Pacific sand dabs and salmon with cabernet sauvignon. And while the menu seemed wholly French at first, the food at Michael's, in Santa Monica, California, was **Michael McCarty**'s brilliant synthesis of Southern California style and Provençal cuisine. At Saint Estèphe, in L.A., **John Sedlar** gave his nouvelle dishes a Latino twist, as in a soufflé of blue corn and chile pepper.

New Midwestern cuisine innovators included Richard Perry, of Richard Perry Restaurant, in St. Louis, who used seasonal midwestern ingredients like gooseberry and rhubarb in his menu and making his own charcuterie and breads. Jimmy Schmidt, of Detroit's London Chop House, where he served "a mess of perch" and a "heap of frogs' legs," afterwards opened his own Rattlesnake Club there, using pickerel, perch, and whitefish from local lakes and wild mushrooms from Michigan. In Chicago, Jackie Etcheber fused oriental techniques with midwestern ingredients at Jackie's (1982), while Michael Foley's Printer's Row showcased midwestern generosity in dishes like smoked chicken with curry mayonnaise, crepes with corn and goat's cheese, and apple crumb tart. At the minimalist Z Contemporary Cuisine, in Cleveland, Zach Bruell focused on American nouvelle color and presentation, and in Kansas City, Missouri, the American Restaurant, which had a succession of young, highly creative chefs who included Brad Ogden and Debbie Gold, was a bellwether of modern American cuisine, focused on Middle American ingredients and cooking traditions in a contemporary style, and wine in a stunning dining room overlooking the city.

New Texas cuisine pioneers included Amy Ferguson, of Charley's 517, who, though trained as a cook in France, returned to Houston in 1975 as a vegetarian and used mesquite, pecan, and hickory firewood for her cooking, while Anne Greer, of Nana Grill, proudly featured updated versions of western and Texas foods like black-eyed pea salad, red chile pasta salad, and salmon with tomatillo butter sauce.

Three figures in the New Texas cuisine movement have been particularly important. Dean Fearing, who worked for twenty-five years as chef at Dallas's Mansion on Turtle Creek, opened his own restaurant, Fearing's, becoming famous for his tortilla soup and roast pepper soup with serrano chiles. Robert Del Grande, a former biochemist, opened Cafe Annie, in Houston, which was wholly dedicated to the local provender in signature dishes like his Texas quail with corn and huitlacoche sauce; he followed it with his RDG + Bar Annie, where he evolved dishes with a strong Mexican influence, like Bar Annie nachos with red chile beef and crème fraîche, rabbit enchiladas with mole sauce, and cinnamon roasted pheasant. At first more nouvelle, with dishes like catfish mousse on the menu at Routh Street Café, in Dallas, chef Stephan Pyles shifted his focus more to Texas smoke-cooking tradition at his subsequent restaurants, including his namesake restaurant Stephan Pyles, where the menu featured red snapper with smoked corn and chile pop rocks, wood-fired fish with vanilla-roasted fennel,

and bone-in ribeye with red chile onion rings and pinto-and-wild-mushroom ragout. Similar ideas were incorporated into New Southwestern cuisine by chefs like Janos Wilder, of Janos, in Tucson, Arizona, and RoxSand Scocos, at RoxSand (1988), in Phoenix, especially in game dishes like antelope, bison, and venison.

New Pacific Northwest cuisine evolved slowly, with casual restaurants like Cafe Sport, in Seattle, where chef Tom Douglas featured Northwest ingredients like Idaho trout and Pacific ling cod on their menus. At Le Gourmand, also in Seattle, chefs Robin Sanders and Bruce Naftaly drew on seasonal ingredients for dishes like scallops steamed in Riesling, terrine of rabbit livers, and goat cheese from Vashon Island. At the city's Other Place, Robert Rosellini began with French nouvelle but quickly took advantage of its surrounding waters and forests for items like poached sablefish, wild boar and venison, and Oregon scallops with ginger. Seattle's best-known chef, Tom Douglas, opened his first restaurant, Dahlia Lounge, to showcase the broad ethnic reach of the Pacific Rim, utilizing Polynesian, Japanese, Chinese, and other Asian foods and techniques.

In the South, Commander's Palace, a very old New Orleans restaurant, was taken over by the **Brennan family** and turned out brilliant new Creole cuisine; one of its chefs who became widely known in the mid-1980s was actually very much a traditionalist, **Paul Prudhomme**. He served his own style of Cajun farm and bayou food at K-Paul's Louisiana Kitchen, in New Orleans, which included blackened redfish, red beans and rice, andouille and boudin sausage, and filé gumbo. Elizabeth Terry, of Elizabeth on 37th (1981), in Savannah, Georgia, won praise as one of the new faces of southern cuisine by updating traditional recipes with modern techniques and ingredients. A graduate of Chez Panisse, Frank Stitt III, moved back to his native Birmingham, Alabama, where he became one of the country's most highly praised chefs for marrying French ideas with southern ingredients. In Charleston and Pawleys Island, South Carolina, Louis Osteen was very much a traditionalist but always imbued his southern food with the precision of classic technique in dishes like hush puppies, shrimp and grits, and pecan pie. (For New Floridian cuisine, see **Nuevo Latino** food.)

In NYC, there were several important figures in the New American cuisine movement, foremost **Lawrence**

Forgione, whose restaurant An American Place was inspired by the work of **James Beard**. Ex-lawyer Barry Wine opened a highly eclectic nouvelle cuisine restaurant named the Quilted Giraffe, where he served beggar's purses filled with caviar, yellowtail with spaghetti squash, and kiwi sorbet. Wine once said, "We're an American restaurant because we're American, the rest of the staff is American, and the menus are printed in English. And like this country we draw influences into our food from the melting pot of ethnic groups."

Brendan Walsh, born in the Bronx, New York, did novel turns on southwestern food at Arizona 206, and at Jams, Jonathan Waxman, a former jazz saxophonist and graduate of Chez Panisse, brought New California cuisine to Manhattan.

The New New England cuisine was fueled by chefs like Jasper White of Jasper's Restaurant (1983), in Boston, where he championed Northern Atlantic seafood and American desserts like Seckel pears in a late-harvest Riesling wine. Boston-born Lydia Shire opened Seasons and, later, BIBA (1989) and other restaurants, utilizing the bounty of the New England land and sea with dishes like Cape Cod scallops with garlic and herbs, clam-and-oyster bisque, and cream biscuits. In Providence, Rhode Island, Johanne Killeen and George Germon garnered praise for their grilled pizzas at Al Forno (1980). Jim Burke, of Boston's Allegro, combined Italian American food with French sauce reductions.

Most of the elements forged by these chefs became part of a more general style of modern American cooking, with some of them abandoning the term "New American cuisine" in the 1990s.

NEW BEDFORD PUDDING. A pudding made from cornmeal, flour, eggs, and molasses. The name commemorates the town of New Bedford, Massachusetts. The recipe below is from Elizabeth H. Putnam's *Mrs. Putnam's Receipt Book and Young Housekeeper's Assistant*, published in Boston in 1850.

NEW BEDFORD PUDDING

Combine 4 T. flour, 4 T. cornmeal, 4 beaten eggs, 1 qt. boiling water, a pinch of salt, and 1 c. molasses. Bake for 3 hr. at a low temperature, about 300°.

NEW ENGLAND BOILED DINNER. A very hearty dish of various meats and vegetables that was originally made with salt beef but may also contain poultry. It was traditionally served at noontime, but begun early in the morning, when the meat would be boiled with cabbage in a kettle over an open fire. Later the other vegetables would go in, and, notes Evan Jones in *American Food* (1974), "Some Yankees call for a sprinkling of cider vinegar, but the most common accents are homemade horseradish sauce or strong mustard."

Boiled meals have long been part of many countries' culinary heritages: In France such a meal is called *pot-au-feu*, in Italy *bollito misto*, and New England boiled dinners derive from English versions of the dish. The term "boiled dinner" was in print as of 1882, and "New England boiled dinner" as of 1888.

NEW ENGLAND BOILED DINNER

In a large kettle place a 4–5 lb. corned beef, 2 cloves garlic, ½ t. black peppercorns, and enough water to cover. Bring to a boil, reduce to a simmer, and cook about 3 hr. Taste for desired degree of saltiness; if too strong, remove some of the simmering liquid and add fresh water. Add 1 chopped rutabaga, 10 red potatoes, 5 chopped carrots, and 1 chopped head of cabbage. Cook until vegetables are tender. Serves 8–10.

NEW ENGLAND HARDSCRAPPLE. A New England bread-pudding dish, dating in print to 1939. See **scrapple**.

NEW JERSEY TEA. Also "redroot." A ceanothus tree, either *Ceanothus americanus*, also called "redhank," "spangles," and "wild pepper," or *C. herbaceus* (1785), whose leaves were brewed into an astringent beverage. It was a substitute for tea among Whigs during the Revolutionary War.

NEW YORK SYSTEM. A term used in Rhode Island to describe an establishment that sells pork-and-veal **hot dogs** dressed with beef-based chili sauce, chopped onions, and celery salt. The New York System originated in 1927 when Gust Pappas opened a wiener stand on Smith Street in Providence, and today all the New York

Systems are run by members of the Pappas family. The term "system" refers to the cooking and preparation of the food, and the White Castle hamburger chain used the term in the 1930s. According to Elaine Chaika, of the University of Rhode Island:

> The wienies look as if they have been cut from a longer sausage at both ends. They are about four inches long, and are covered with a meat sauce.... At true New York systems the man at the grill—and it's always a man—wearing a white dirty apron, takes the order, then puts the required number of hot dog rolls (not "buns" here) on his arm, puts the wienies in the roll and then ladies on the sauce.... Those places that sell these things always have "New York System" in their names, such as "Olneyville New York System," "Mary's New York System," "Joe's New York System."

NIC-NAC. A form of simple shortbread cookie. The term is a variation of "nicknack" or "knickknack," meaning a simple trinket or toy. They were a favorite children's Christmas cookie in the nineteenth century.

NIEBAUM, GUSTAVE (1842–1908). Winemaker. As a Finnish immigrant, Gustave Ferdinand Niebaum became one of California's wine pioneers with the opening of his Inglenook Winery in the Napa Valley.

Niebaum (originally Nybom) was born in Oulu, Finland, and trained to be a sea captain at the maritime school in Helsinki. He would achieve a high reputation for mapping the California coastline. In 1867 he became consul of Russia in the U.S., helping to ratify the Alaska Purchase.

Niebaum made his fortune founding the Alaskan Commercial Co., in San Francisco, dealing in the fur trade there. In 1879, he bought the Inglenook Winery, in Rutherford, California, building a three-story Gothic stone chateau where he sought to make wines along the Bordeaux models, using cabernet sauvignon and other vinifera grapes. Within three years Niebaum was producing eighty thousand gallons of wine. His motto was "Quality not quantity," and in 1889 his wines won gold medals at the Paris Exposition.

Already wealthy, Niebaum never cared about making a profit from his wines, and after a revenue agent offended him during an inspection of his brandy distillery, Niebaum tore it down the next day.

Niebaum died in 1908, eleven years before the onset of Prohibition closed Inglenook. After repeal, in 1933, a great-nephew of Niebaum's wife, John Daniel Jr., restored the estate, selling it in 1964 to Allied Vintners. It was then was owned by Heublein Inc., from which film director Francis Ford Coppola purchased it in 1975, with profits from his *Godfather* movies.

In 2007, Niebaum was inducted into the **Culinary Institute of America**'s Vintners Hall of Fame.

NIEPORENT, DREW (1955–). Restaurateur. In the 1980s, Drew Nieporent helped change the image of fine dining with the opening of his restaurant Montrachet, while at the same time showing how a restaurant could bring vitality to a downtrodden neighborhood. His bringing Japanese master chef Nobuyuki Matsuhisa to NYC gave the genre of sushi a glamorous new perspective and range that Nieporent's Myriad Restaurant Group helped spread worldwide.

Born in NYC, Nieporent graduated in 1977 from Cornell University, in Ithaca, New York, with a degree from the School of Hotel Administration. While there, he worked as a waiter on the deluxe cruise ships *Vistafjord* and *Sagafjord*, then in 1978 joined restaurateur Warner LeRoy as manager of the restaurant Tavern on the Green, in NYC, which employed more than two hundred employees. By the time Nieporent left, revenues had gone from $10 million to $24 million.

Nieporent then worked at a succession of deluxe French restaurants in NYC—Le Périgord, La Grenouille, and Le Régence. In 1985, he opened Montrachet, in downtown's Tribeca neighborhood, where, with chef David Bouley, he did away with the formality of French haute cuisine and dining. "In our own way, we created the casual elegant restaurant in NYC," he said. "We broke down the barriers that said you had to be French to be elegant." He also worked to improve restaurant morale by eliminating the entrenched divide between kitchen and dining-room staff.

Montrachet's success brought more restaurants to the area, and light onto the once dark streets. Nearby, in 1990, his Myriad Restaurant Group opened Tribeca Grill, with actors Robert De Niro, Sean Penn, Lou

Diamond Phillips, Christopher Walken, Bill Murray, and Ed Harris, ballet dancer Mikhail Baryshnikov, rapper Russell Simmons, and Miramax Films as partners, whose occasional presence brought star power to the American-style restaurant. In 2000, *The Tribeca Grill Cookbook*, by chef Don Pintabona, was published.

In 1994, again with De Niro, Myriad opened Nobu, named after Japanese sushi master Nobuyuki Matsuhisa, who brought NYC a new style of sushi inflected with Peruvian spices and seasonings. Two more Nobu restaurants followed in NYC, then around the U.S. and in London.

That year, Nieporent, with De Niro, actor Robin Williams, and film director Francis Ford Coppola, opened a wine-driven restaurant called Rubicon (named after one of Coppola's wines) in San Francisco, to great acclaim. (De Niro and Nieporent later ended their business relationships and the various Nobu restaurants were split between them.)

Over the past three decades, Myriad has opened twenty-six restaurants around the world, including in Seattle, Louisville, Moscow, and NYC's Citi Field, home of the New York Mets baseball team.

Nieporent has long been active in charities, including Madison Square Garden's Garden of Dreams Foundation, Citymeals-on-Wheels, the City Harvest Food Council, and Share Our Strength. He has been honored by the Careers Through Culinary Arts Program (2009), the American Heart Association (1999), the Tourette Syndrome Association (2000), and others.

Among Nieporent's honors are Restaurateur of the Year from *Bon Appétit* and *Nation's Restaurant News* as well as Humanitarian of the Year and Restaurateur of the Year from the James Beard Foundation, which lists him in its Who's Who of Food & Beverage in America.

NIGHTCAP. A drink, usually one containing alcohol, taken just before bedtime or as the last drink of the night, dating in print to 1814.

NĪOI. A **Hawaiian** "chile water," made with chile peppers, water, and salt, that serves as a seasoning for various dishes.

NOCAKE. Corn that is parched in ashes and ground into a meal, which is afterwards mixed with water to make a paste. The word is from the Narragansett *nokehick*, dating in English print to 1634.

NOODLE. Any of a variety of thin strips of paste made from flour, water, and sometimes egg. The word is from the German *Nudel* and was first recorded in English in 1779. It may refer to German or Pennsylvania Dutch egg noodles or to Italian pasta as well as to Chinese, Japanese, and other Asian examples. "Spaghetti" (Italian for "little strings") did not enter the English language until the nineteenth century. American slang for "noodle" includes "apron string."

EGG NOODLES

Combine 1 beaten egg, 2 T. milk, and ½ t. salt. Pour into a bowl of 1 c. flour in which a well has been made, mix to make a firm dough, and roll out very thin on a floured board. Let rest for 30 min., then cut into strips about 1 ¼-in. wide.

NOONING. A lunch break between New England church services. "Nooning sheds" were sheds, often where horses were held, where these meals were taken. The word *nooning* is, in fact, very old, dating back to Middle English, in English print since about 1500.

NOPAL. Any of several cacti in the genus *Nopalea* that resemble the **prickly pear**, although sometimes the pads of the prickly pear itself are called "*nopales*," entering print in 1578, from Nahuatl *nohpalli*. In Mexican communities, they are called *nopales* or *nopalitos*, and these cacti have become popular in the American Southwest in the past two decades. The flavor is similar to that of a green pepper or okra, and they may be eaten raw, boiled, or sautéed. They are often added to the fillings of tortillas or salads.

NOSH. A Yiddish word meaning "to munch on one's food." Used as a noun, the word refers to a snack of some kind. A "nosher" is a habitual snacker. The word is from the German *naschen*, "to nibble," and first appeared as a verb (as *nash*) in American print in 1892. A British reference to a "Nosh restaurant" appeared in 1917.

NOUGAT. A confection made from sugar or honey with ground almonds (sometimes walnuts or pistachios). Nougat takes either of two forms: the first is white nougat, prepared from boiled sugar, egg whites, nuts, and sometimes dried cherries; the other is a caramel-based almond nougat molded into shapes. Either may be used in making candies.

The name originates in French, and ultimately the Latin *nux*, for "nut," dating in English print to 1827, in a recipe book on Italian cookery.

There is no truth to the old tale that a woman of the French town of Montélimar (known for its white nougat) created the confection in the eighteenth century, to the approval of her friends, who complimented her with the words, *"Tu nous gâtes"* ("You spoil us"). The confection probably goes back to the Middle Ages, when it might have been introduced to Europe by the Arabs via Spain. In the U.S., nougat is principally used as a filling for commercially produced candies.

NOUVELLE CUISINE. French for "new cooking." A style of cooking that developed in France in the 1960s and 1970s, by which young chefs like Paul Bocuse, Roger Vergé, Jean and Pierre Troisgros, and Michel Guérard broke from the entrenched traditions of classic French cuisine in order to develop their own methods, techniques, and new dishes. The phrase itself had been used prior to that period, first in English print in 1774, to describe any new cuisine.

The new style was formally christened *"la nouvelle cuisine"* by French food writers Henri Gault and Christian Millau, in the October 1973 issue of their *Gault-Millau* magazine, wherein they pronounced what they called the ten commandments of this modern cookery to be:

1. Avoid unnecessary complications.

2. Shorten cooking times.

3. Shop regularly at the market.

4. Shorten the menu.

5. Don't hang or marinate game.

6. Avoid too rich sauces.

7. Return to regional cooking.

8. Investigate the latest techniques.

9. Consider diet and health.

10. Invent constantly.

Many believed that nouvelle cuisine was much lighter and less caloric than classical French cooking because of the attention given Guérard's diet menu, called *"cuisine minceur,"* offered at his spa, Les Près d'Eugénie at Le Couvent des Herbes, in Eugénie-les-Bains, France. In fact, much nouvelle cooking was based on white butter sauces (*beurre blanc*) and required extremely rich and expensive ingredients in its preparation, like foie gras, truffles, and smoked salmon.

The first nouvelle cuisine restaurants in the U.S. were opened by young American chefs and entrepreneurs like Robert and Karen Pritsker, of Dodin-Bouffant, in Boston; Steven Spector and Peter Josten, of Le Plaisir, in NYC; Jean Bertranou, of L'Ermitage, in Los Angeles; and Jean Banchet, of Le Français, in Wheeling, Illinois; all of which opened in the late 1970s or early 1980s. The interest in such food and restaurants had a great effect on the development of what came to be called the **New American cuisine**, in which young American chefs applied nouvelle principles to regional American menus.

As the nouvelle cuisine movement evolved in both France and the U.S. exaggerated culinary effects, extravagant plate presentation, and exotic matches of ingredients became hallmarks of the style, so that by the mid-1980s to call something "nouvelle" connoted a dish that was overly stylized, preciously presented, and very expensive. As a result, many chefs avoided the term, preferring other terms, like "cuisine moderne."

NUEVO LATINO CUISINE. "New Latin," referring to modern Latin American cooking, a movement by young Latino and many other American chefs to incorporate traditional Central and South American and Caribbean ingredients and cooking techniques into a contemporary style and context. The term gained currency in the 1990s. See also **fusion cuisine** and **Mexican American food**.

Nuevo Latino cuisine began in the early 1990s, at first in restaurants in Miami, then in many major cities around the U.S. Among the first chefs to create Nuevo Latino dishes was Douglas Rodriguez, born to Cuban immigrants in Miami, where he opened the stylish Yuca (slang for "young, upwardly mobile Cuban Americans"), then opened three restaurants in NYC—Patria (1994), a Peruvian ceviche bar named Chicama, and the tapas bar Pipa—before returning to Miami to open OLA, in 2004. Rodriguez was selected by *Newsweek* as "one of the 100 Americans who will influence the 21st century." He published several cookbooks, including *Nuevo Latino* (1995) and *Latin Flavors on the Grill* (2000). Their cooking incorporated ingredients like yucca, hearts of palm, and plantains into modern dishes with great color and flair, in contrast to the traditionally unadorned look of Cuban and Caribbean food.

Rodriguez was one of a group of Florida chefs that included Norman Van Aken, Mark Militello, Robin Haas, and Alan Susser, who sought actively to design and promote a new style of cooking from Florida and the Caribbean that went by various terms, including "New World cuisine," "New Caribbean," "New Floridian," and "Floribbean," focusing on the ingredients and food cultures of the region, like mangoes, avocados, chiles, boniato, conch, grouper, yellowtail, and other fish.

Contemporary with those chefs, all originally in Miami, were Carmen González and Michelle Bernstein, also in Miami; Richard Sandoval, in NYC; and Randy Zweiban, in Chicago; followed by the modern Spanish master **José Andrés**, in Washington, D.C., where he introduced elements of **molecular cuisine** to the United States. Bernstein, of Jewish and Latin ancestry and a former ballerina, first created a very high-end style of Nuevo Latino cuisine mixed with Asian ingredients and techniques at Azul (2001), in Miami, then with simpler, home-style food at Sra. Martinez (2008). In nearby Coral Gables, Cindy Hutson and Delius Shirley opened a contemporary Jamaican restaurant named Ortanique on the Mile (1997).

Norman Van Aken, born in Key West, Florida, opened several restaurants under his name and published *Feast of Sunlight* (1988), *Norman's New World Cuisine* (1997), and *New World Kitchen* (2003). In 2006, he was honored as one of the "Founders of the New American Cuisine" at Spain's Madridfusión International Gastronomy Summit.

Other chefs who have figured prominently in the Nuevo Latino cuisine movement include Dean James Max, Johnny Vinczencz, and Clay Conley, in Florida; Anthony Lamas, of Louisville, Kentucky; Luis Bollo, in NYC; and Guillermo Pernot and José Garces, in Philadelphia.

NUTRITION LABELING. A listing of substances in a food product that is printed on the label. Such a list is now mandated by Federal Trade Commission rules. The listing must include: serving size and servings per can; the amount of calories, protein, carbohydrates, and fat per serving; and the percentage per serving of the Recommended Daily Intake (RDI) for protein, vitamins A and C, thiamine, riboflavin, niacin, and the minerals calcium and iron, although other nutrients may be listed, too, along with the cholesterol level per serving.

O

OAT. Usually used in the plural. Any of a variety of grasses in the genus *Avena*, especially the common cultivated variety, *A. sativa*, developed from the common wild oat, *A. fatua*. The word is from Old English *àte*.

While 93 percent of the U.S. oat crop is used to feed animals, more than forty million bushels—out of a total U.S. crop of 966 million bushels in 2012—was made into breakfast cereals, especially the porridge called "oatmeal," made from rolled oats—that is, oats with the husks ground off, which are then steamed and rolled flat to maintain their freshness longer. The largest and best-known oatmeal producer is the Quaker Oats Co. of Chicago, which was officially formed in 1901 but had made the first trademarked American **cereal**—Quaker Oats—in 1877. The company also introduced a quick-cooking oatmeal in 1921.

The U.S. is the world's leading producer of oats, grown primarily in Iowa, Minnesota, Illinois, Wisconsin, and South Dakota.

OCTOPUS. Any of a variety of marine cephalopod mollusks of the genus *Octopus*, having a sacklike head and eight tentacles with rows of suckers. The name is from the Greek *oktopous*, meaning "eight legs," dating in English print to 1759.

The "Atlantic octopus" (*Octopus vulgaris*) and the "common Pacific octopus" (*O. dolfleini*) are the two North American species. They are sometimes called "devilfish" because of their strange appearance.

Except in Hawaii, where they are called *puloa* and *he'e*, octopuses are not consumed by most Americans to any great extent, although Mediterranean and Caribbean immigrants enjoy them, usually in a stew or salad. Increasingly, grilled octopus shows up on contemporary restaurant menus.

OD GRAVY. A rural slang term of the South and the Midwest, dating in print to 1919, that is short for "ox dung gravy" or "olive drab" gravy, in reference to brown gravy. "OD coffee" is Army coffee, dating in print to 1919.

OGEECHEE LIME. Also "Ogeechee tupelo" and "gopher plum." A southern tupelo (*Nyssa ogeche*) used to prepare a summer beverage or preserves, dating in print to 1775. The name derives from the Ogeechee River, in Georgia.

ŌHELO. Also "Hawaiian huckleberry." A Hawaiian plant of the genus *Vaccinium*, especially *V. reticulatum*, dating in English print to 1825, which is added to foods to give them a sour flavor. The word is from the Hawaiian for "berry." "Ohelokai" is a native Hawaiian red wolfberry (*Lyceum sandwicense*) with a salty pulp. The Hawaiian word means "berry near the sea," dating in print to 1911.

ŌHI'A. Also "Malay apple." A native Hawaiian apple, *'ōhi'a* (*Eugenia malaccensis*), with a peach-like stone. The Hawaiian word means "edible (fruit)," dating in print to 1815.

OHIO PUDDING. A pudding of sweet potatoes, carrots, and brown sugar, popular in Ohio.

OHIO PUDDING

Combine 4 eggs with ¼ c. brown sugar, ½ c. cooked mashed sweet potatoes, ½ c. carrots, ½ c. squash, 1 t. salt, ¼ t. pepper, 1 c. bread crumbs, 1 qt. light cream, and 1 t. vanilla extract. Pour into buttered pan and bake 1 ¼ hr. at 350°. Serve with a sauce made from ¼ lb. butter beaten with 1 ½ c. confectioners' sugar, ½ c. heavy cream, and 1 T. lemon juice. Serves 6.

ŌKOLEHAO. Also "oke." A **Hawaiian** spirit, made illegally, from cooked ti roots (*Cordyline australis*). The Hawaiian word means "iron buttocks," referring to an iron pot still, and dates in print to 1924. Originally it was a liqueur made by an Australian, William Stevenson, around 1790, but today it is legally produced on Maui by Haleakala Distillers. Okolehao is not aged, and has a proof of 60 to 100. It may be drunk straight, on the rocks, or in various Hawaiian-inspired cocktails.

OKRA (*Hibiscus esculentus*). Also "lady's finger." A tropical or semitropical tree bearing finger-shaped green pods. The word, derived from the West African Twi *nkruma*, was in use in America by the 1780s. Okra was brought to America by African slaves, who used it in stews or soups and cut it up as a vegetable. The most famous use for okra is in Louisiana **gumbo**. Okra is particularly popular in African American **soul food**.

OLD-FASHIONED COCKTAIL. A **cocktail** made with **whiskey**, sugar, and **bitters**. The term dates in print to 1878 in a Wisconsin newspaper but may simply refer to a cocktail of an earlier period. In 1880, the *Chicago Tribune* referred to "old-fashioned cocktails," but by 1893 the same newspaper wrote, "The old-fashioned cocktail affected by Southern men differs in its composition in various cities." By 1895 the drink was included in *Modern American Drinks*, as the "old-fashioned whiskey cocktail." According to an unsigned article in the *International Review of Food and Wine* (November 1978), the birth date of the old-fashioned cocktail

> could be no earlier than 1881, the year in which Louisville's aristocratic Pendennis Club first opened its doors to its members, one of whom was the then-reigning patriarch of fine Kentucky Bourbon, Colonel James E. Pepper. The Colonel's grandfather, Elijah, had claimed twin birthdays for his distillery and the nation, and for generations his "Old 1776" brand of Bourbon would continue to be flogged under the proud slogan, "Born with the Republic." One might therefore surmise that the Old-Fashioned, created at the bar of the Pendennis and introduced in the East at the original Waldorf bar to honor Colonel Pepper some time in the 1890s, got its inspiration in part from Elijah's label.

Most aficionados of the old-fashioned insist a sugar cube be placed at the bottom of the glass (which is squat and holds about six ounces), but others prefer to use sugar syrup.

OLD-FASHIONED COCKTAIL

In an old-fashioned glass place 1 sugar cube in 2 T. water, then add a dash of bitters and 1 ½ oz. whiskey (usually bourbon or rye). Add ice cubes and a slice of orange. Many prefer the drink topped off with club soda and a maraschino cherry, although some like the addition of a small amount of an orange cordial.

OLD MAID. Southern and midwestern colloquialism for a kernel of popcorn that failed to pop, dating in print to 1947.

OLD NED. Salt pork or home-cured bacon, especially in the South, first noted in 1833 as a Tennessee colloquialism. An article in the *Overland Monthly* in 1896 noted that the name may be "an allusion to the famous Negro song, [and] was termed 'Old Ned' from its sable appearance."

OLESTRA. A synthetic food oil that is not absorbed into the human body, dating in print to 1995. Used for weight control, the word derives from the Latin *oleum* (oil) plus *polyester*.

OLIVE (*Olea europaea*). An Old World evergreen tree bearing a small fruit that is eaten on its own or pressed to make **olive oil**. The word is from the Latin *olíva*, first appearing in English in about 1225. (The "American olive" or "devil wood," *Olea Americana*, and the "California olive," *Oreodaphne californica*, are of no real culinary interest.)

The olive has long been cultivated throughout the Mediterranean, where it is a major food of the people's diet. It was first mentioned in records of seventeenth-century B.C. Egypt. The Spaniards introduced three olive saplings to Lima, Peru, in 1560, which became the ancestors of all olives in America, and introduced them to California's Mission San Diego de Alcalá circa 1769.

The English planted olives in South Carolina in 1670, so that by the eighteenth century Charleston's streets were lined with olive trees. In 1733, James Oglethorpe brought olive plantings to Georgia. Neither was ultimately successful. Thomas Jefferson planted olives at Monticello in 1774, calling the vine "the worthiest plant to be introduced to America," but these efforts, and subsequent plantings in South Carolina in 1791, came to naught, for the plants all died.

Nevertheless, the imported olive trees flourished in California, where technology has bred a tree that matures in fifteen to twenty years, rather than the usual thirty required in the Old World. By 1919 more than a million trees bore fruit, mainly used for olive oil. But because the product was cheaper to produce in Europe and had been so adulterated with cottonseed oil from the American South, the olive-oil industry languished in California.

In 1895, Mrs. Freda Ehmann, of Marysville, California,, produced a bumper crop of olives that she pickled (with the help of Dr. E. W. Hilgard, of the University of California) and sold in groceries and restaurants with great success, earning her the title "Mother of the Olive Industry." Around the same time, Professor Frederic T. Bioletti of the University of California invented a method of canning olives (called "green ripe") with an alkaline solution and brine so that they were available year-round.

Although Italy and Spain are the largest producers of olives in the world, California does produce a substantial crop (180,000 tons in 2012), mainly in the San Fernando and San Joaquin valleys. There, in contrast to European methods of leaving green olives to ripen to black on the vine, olives are picked in the fall at varying shades of green, given a lye cure, and, if marketed black (called "ripe"), are oxidized in a ferrous gluconate solution. California green olives thus treated with lye are called "Spanish-style olives." The predominant olives used in California are the large Sevillano, the Manzanilla, the Mission (used mostly for olive oil), the Barondis, and the Ascolanos. Olives are often sold with the pits removed, sometimes stuffed with pimiento slices.

Olives are sized, with some hyperbole, as "small" (3.2 to 3.3 grams), "medium," "large," "extra large," "jumbo," "colossal," and "supercolossal" (14.2 to 16.2 grams).

OLIVE OIL. An oil that is pressed from olives. It is a ubiquitous cooking ingredient around the Mediterranean, and much of it is imported by the U.S. from Italy, Spain (the world's largest producer), Morocco, Tunisia, Greece, and other countries (in 2011, about 292 tons, with 65 percent of virgin grade). Olive oil is monounsaturated and has a distinctive taste of the olive. In Europe, the grades of quality range from "extra virgin" (the finest, with 1 percent acid) to "fine" (1.5 percent), while others have more than 3.3 percent acid. "Pure olive oil" is extracted by solvent and refined, while "blended oils" may contain only 10 percent olive oil. None of this nomenclature is recognized by the FDA standards of identity.

In the late nineteenth century, California had a thriving olive oil industry, but after World War II, cheaper European olive oils nearly destroyed domestic production. It has since rebounded, and California currently produces about a million gallons of olive oil (now more than that produced by France), with 41 percent of consumption in the Northeast.

ONION. Any of a variety of pungent vegetables in the genus *Allium*, having a white, yellow, or red bulbous head. The word is from dialectical Latin *uniō*, which in Middle English became *unyon*.

Grown and eaten around the world, onions are a universal seasoning. Under the term "onion" fall **garlic**, **leek**, **scallion**, and **shallot**, but in all, there are about seventy species of onion native to North America. Hernán Cortés found onions in Mexico in the sixteenth century. Father Jacques Marquette, who explored the southern shore of Lake Michigan in 1624, survived for a time by eating a wild onion the Native Americans called "chicago," better known as the "tree onion" or "Egyptian onion" (*A. canadense*). Although the Native Americans and the pioneers certainly savored a wide variety of native onions, commercial production in the U.S. has largely been limited to one variety, the "common" or "seed" onion (*A. cepa*), brought from Europe in colonial times and now principally grown in California,

Texas, and Oregon. Some of the other onion varieties in the American market include the "pearl" or "button onion," the "red Italian" onion, the "Prizetaker" onion, the "Spanish onion," and the "Bermuda onion," though these last two names are often applied to a number of varieties. The "Vidalia onion" is a yellow hybrid Granex variety that has achieved popularity because of its sweetness, and the name Vidalia is protected under Georgia law, which specifies that, to be called by that name, the onion must be grown in any part of thirteen specified counties or in portions of six other specified counties in southeast Georgia.

Americans chop up onions for soups, stews, and sauces, boil them, roast them, sauté them, and use them in salads and as condiments. French-fried onion rings are very popular with meat dishes. "Tobacco onions" are deep-fried thin onion slices seasoned with chile power and so called because they resemble dried tobacco shreds. The U.S. produces more than 220 million tons of onions annually; the per capita U.S. consumption of onions is about twenty pounds per year.

ONION FISH. Also "rat fish." A grenadier fish, especially *Macrourus berglax* and *M. rupestris*, abundant along the Atlantic coast, dating in print to 1854 and so called because its eyes resemble onions.

ONO. A Hawaiian wahoo fish (*Acanthocybium solandri*) with a long, dark blue, purple-striped body, dating in print to 1898. Its Hawaiian name means "to have a sweet taste," and it is often used for sashimi.

ON SCHOLARSHIP. Bartender slang for a bartender who spends too much time talking with the customers, thereby forcing his colleague to do most of the work, dating in print to 1991.

ON THE ROCKS. A term to describe a beverage served with ice cubes. The phrase has become common usage in the post–World War II era, dating in print to 1949.

OOPU. Any of five species of Hawaiian freshwater fish, four of them gobies, from the Hawaiian word *'o'opu*, dating in print to 1960.

OPAH. Also "glance fish," "kingfish," "Jerusalem haddock," "moonfish," and "mariposa." A deepwater fish (*Lampris gutattus* and *L. regius*), first noted in print in 1752, from the African Ibo language.

ŌPAKAPAKA. Also "jobfish." Hawaiian name for a saltwater pink **snapper** of the family Lutjanidae, especially *Pristipomoides microlepsis*. The word dates in print to 1905.

OPALEYE. Also "greenfish" and "bluefish" (though it is not the **bluefish** species *Pomatus saltatrix*). A footlong marine fish (*Girella nigricans*) that swims off the coast of California, first noted in print in 1933.

ŌPELU. A Hawaiian mackerel scad (*Decapterus pinnulatus* and *D. maruadsi*), which dates in print to 1926.

OPEN DATING. A system of dating products that outlines the various dates at which an item was packaged and should be discarded and past which it is no longer fit for consumption. The "pack date" tells when the food item was packaged; the "pull date" or "sell date" indicates the last date on which the product should be sold, although some storage time in the home refrigerator is allowed for; the "expiration date" indicates the last date on which the food should be eaten or used; and the "freshness date" is similar to the expiration date but may allow for home storage. The "shelf life" of a product is the manufacturer's or grocer's indication of how long a product will last.

'OPIHI. A Hawaiian limpet of the family Patellidae, especially of the genus *Cellana*, dating in print to 1875.

OPOSSUM. Also "possum." A nocturnal marsupial of the family Didelphidiae that is fifteen to twenty inches long, weighs six to eight pounds, has gray fur, and inhabits the woodlands of much of the U.S. The only species in North America is the "Virginia opossum" (*Didelphus virginiana*), found mostly in the Southeast and in California and the Northwest, west of the Cascades and the Sierra Nevada (where it was introduced in the 1920s). Its name is from the Algonquian for "white animal" and was in print by 1610. The opossum is no longer widely used as a food animal, though it is still occasionally eaten in the South, either stewed or roasted.

ORANGE. Any of a variety of trees in the genus *Citrus* bearing round, yellow-red fruit that is eaten fresh, made into juice, and used as a flavoring. The name is from the Sanskrit *nāranga*, dating in English print to about 1400.

The orange is one of the most important fruits in the world and one of the oldest cultivated. Originating in the Orient, the fruit was cultivated in China as early as 2400 B.C. These were "bitter oranges" (*C. aurantium*), later brought to Spain, where they became known as the "Seville orange." The "sweet orange" (*C. sinensis*) also originated in China and was also brought to Spain, possibly by the Moors in the eighth century.

Christopher Columbus brought Canary Islands orange seeds to Hispaniola in 1493, and plantings by the Spanish and Portuguese soon followed throughout the Caribbean, Mexico, and South America. Some believe that Ponce de León brought orange seeds to Florida, but the first recorded evidence of the fruit on North American soil credits Hernando de Soto with bringing the orange in 1539 to St. Augustine, Florida, where the trees flourished until Sir Francis Drake sacked the city in 1586 and destroyed them. These grew back quickly, but commercial plantings were of only minor importance for more than two centuries. In the West, meanwhile, Spanish missionaries brought oranges from Mexico into California and Arizona, but there, too, they were not at first developed into a commercial crop.

In Florida, only one significant orange grower was to be found in the eighteenth century. His name was Jesse Fish, and in 1776 he shipped sixty-five thousand oranges and two casks of orange juice to England.

It was not until the U.S. acquired Florida, in 1821, that orange growing became a profitable business for Americans. Before long, the territory around St. Augustine and Jacksonville's St. Johns River supported a thriving crop of orange trees, and by the 1830s the major eastern cities enjoyed relatively dependable shipments of the fruit, although much of the supply came from the Caribbean, especially from Cuba, until the 1880s. It became the custom in the period before the Civil War to give children a fresh orange in their Christmas stockings, and it remains a tradition to this day in some regions of the South.

The Florida groves increased in size until 1835, when a February freeze struck the orchards, wiping out all but one hardy variety—the "Indian River"—raised by Douglas Dummett, from whose orchard the entire Florida stock was begun again (and still again, in the winter of 1894–1895, when the Dummet grove was the sole survivor of another frost). The Parson Brown orange, developed by the Reverend Nathan L. Brown, of Webster, Florida, became extremely popular as an early-season variety.

By the 1880s, orange production was growing rapidly, owing to the development of refrigerated ships that could carry the fruit from California and to the building of railroads into the heart of Florida. Also, a new orange, the "navel" (so called because of the bump on the skin of the fruit, which prompted people to call it the "belly-button orange"), entered California in 1873 from Bahia, Brazil, by way of Washington, D.C. (it is in fact also known as the "Washington navel"). By the 1890s, the navel orange had become commercially important to the developing California orange industry—at a time when Florida was already shipping more than a billion oranges per year. By the 1920s, nutritionists were promoting the benefits of orange juice, a juice especially high in vitamin C, and the drink became as ubiquitous as coffee on American breakfast tables, to such an extent that the industry's motto—"A day without orange juice is like a day without sunshine"—carried both figurative and scientific truth. A concentrate of orange juice was formulated by John Fox, of the National Research Corporation of Florida, in 1946, under the Minute Maid label. After World War II, orange juice became so popular that the sale of fresh oranges dropped 75 percent. Today most oranges grown are processed into juice, which more often than not reaches the consumer as a frozen concentrate or reconstituted and sold in bottles or cartons. In 1993, orange juice made up 56 percent of all juices sold in the U.S. The "blood orange" (also called the "pigmented orange") was brought to the U.S. by Spanish and Italian immigrants and flourished in the 1930s, but it did not become a productive commercial crop. Today the Ruby Blood and Moro varieties are raised in California and Florida.

The U.S. produces about 15 percent of the world's orange crop today, with Florida contributing about three-quarters of this, and California, Arizona, Texas, and other states the rest, for a 2011 total consumption of 1.615 million tons. Ninety-three percent of the Florida crop goes into orange juice concentrate. Before 1950, California produced most of the juice-orange crop, and Florida most of the eating oranges, but this has now been reversed.

Of all the oranges produced, the sweet orange is by far the most important; the bitter variety is used primarily in marmalade. The most common sweet oranges grown include the Hamlin, the Pineapple, the Valencia, and the navel, but hybrids such as the King, Temple, Orlando, Mineola, Robinson, Osceoloa, Lee, Nova, and Page are also well established.

The "mandarin orange" (*C. reticulata*), of which the principal U.S. varieties are the Dancy, the Clementine, the Murcott, and the Ponkan, is also called the "tangerine" (because it was first imported to Europe from Tangier, Morocco, the earliest recorded shipment being in 1841). The "tangelo" (also called the "red tangelo" or "honeybell")—developed by the Department of Agriculture in Mineola, Florida, in 1931—is a cross between a "Dancy tangerine," a "Bowen" grapefruit, and an "Orchid Island" grapefruit.

The USDA grades oranges "U.S. Fancy" and "U.S. No. 1," though these are not mandatory gradings and do not appear on most oranges.

The most popular culinary uses for oranges in the U.S. are in fruit salads, sherbets and ices, and sodas and as a flavoring for many desserts, cakes, cookies, and candies. There are also several orange-flavored substitutes for the real thing, some in powdered form.

ORANGE BLOSSOM. A drink made with orange juice and gin. The orange blossom was created during the Prohibition era to cut the taste of the gin and was sometimes called the "Adirondack Special" or "Florida," the first probably because illicit spirits could be had in the Adirondack Mountains and the latter because of Florida's great orange crop.

ORANGE JULIUS. Trademark name for a drink made with orange juice, crushed ice, sugar syrup, and a vanilla powder. The beverage was developed in 1926 by real estate broker Willard Hamlin, at the request of Julius Fried, who wanted to set up an orange juice stand in Los Angeles. Since the citric acid of orange juice upset his and others' stomachs, Hamlin modified the raw juice to create a drink named after the entrepreneur. At the time of his death, in 1987, there were more than seven hundred Orange Julius stands around the world.

ORANGE ROUGHY. A species of fish in the family Trachichthydiae that is harvested mainly around New Zealand, frozen, and sold at market. The name dates in print to 1979, and the species became an important frozen fish in U.S. markets as of the 1980s.

OREGANO (*Origanum vulgare*). Also "pot marjoram" and "wild marjoram." A strongly flavored herb, common in Europe and North America, that is used in Italy and the U.S. as a seasoning in tomato sauces, stews, and other preparations. It is similar to "sweet marjoram" (*Majorana hortensis*), which is milder and sometimes used as a substitute.

The word *oregano*, in American print as of 1889, is from the Italian *origano* and the Spanish *orégano*. As a seasoning, it was not popular in the U.S. until after World War II, when returning soldiers brought back a taste for the spicy food of southern Italy, requiring oregano for reproduction.

OREGON TEA. A brew made from boiling water and the shrub yerba buena, dating in print to 1891.

OREILLES DE COCHON, LES. Cajun confection of fried dough that is dusted with confectioners' sugar or syrup and chopped nuts. The term is French for "pig's ears" (which the item is sometimes called), because the flattened-out dough resembles the shape of a pig's ears. In the Midwest, these are called "elephant ears," and in the South Carolina Lowcountry similar pastries are called "marvels."

ORANGE BLOSSOM

Combine 8 oz. gin, 4 oz. orange juice, and ½ oz. sugar syrup over ice.

LES OREILLES DE COCHON

In a bowl beat together 2 eggs, 2 T. water, 2 T. melted butter, and a pinch of salt. Work in about 2 c. flour to make a smooth, slightly firm dough. Separate into pieces about the size of a walnut and roll each out into thin, flat circles about 4 in. in diameter. Place the tines of a fork on one end to grip the dough and give it a quarter-turn so that it resembles the crimp in a pig's ear. Drop the dough into hot oil and fry until brown and crisp. Drain on paper towels. In a saucepan heat 2 c. corn syrup and pour over the twists. Sprinkle with chopped pecans and confectioners' sugar.

OREO. A trademark name of Nabisco Brands Inc. for a cookie composed of two thin chocolate cookies enclosing a white cream filling. The name (originally "Oreo Biscuit") was apparently made up by the company. It has been suggested that the name may derive from the French word for "gold," *or*, because the original package had the product name in gold. Another guess is that the word is from the Greek for "mountain," the shape of which early test batches of Oreos resembled. The first Oreos were sold to a grocer named S. C. Thuesen on March 6, 1912; in 1921 the name was changed to "Oreo Sandwich," then "Oreo Creme Sandwich" in 1948, and "Oreo Chocolate Sandwich" in 1974. Oreos were not, however, the first cookie of this type: "Hydrox cookies" had been on the market since January 1, 1910, but Oreos have been far more successful. Oreos now sell more than 7.5 billion cookies each year, with nine out of ten American households purchasing them.

ORGANIC. With regard to food, the word *organic* refers to any food grown without using chemical fertilizer, pesticides, or other synthetic substances. In this context, the term gained currency in the 1970s and was allied to the **health food** movement in the U.S. Currently the USDA states that "organic is a labeling term that indicates that the food or other agricultural product has been produced through approved methods that integrate cultural, biological, and mechanical practices that foster cycling of resources, promote ecological balance, and conserve biodiversity. Synthetic fertilizers, sewage sludge, irradiation, and genetic engineering may not be used." The "USDA Organic" seal may be placed on any product whose content is "95 percent or more organic." In 1999, the USDA allowed farmers who raise meat and poultry without pesticide-treated feed, growth hormones, or antibiotics to label their products "certified organic." The USDA found that organic foods may cost up to double what other food does.

A 2010 Nielsen study found that 76 percent of Americans bought organics believing they are healthier, 53 percent to avoid pesticides and other toxins, 51 percent because they are more nutritious, and 49 percent because organic farming is better for the environment. Currently 75 percent of American consumers purchase organics, and one-third buy organic products monthly, up from 22 percent in 2000. Only 26 percent, however, buy them regularly. Certified organic acreage in the U.S. is now close to five million acres.

Total revenue for the organic market in 2011 was $28.6 billion, with organic produce food sales accounting for $12.4 billion (about 12 percent of the produce market) and organic meat sales $538 million. Yet in 2012, a four-year study by Stanford University concluded that organic products have no significant nutritional advantage over conventional foods, even though consumers can pay more for them, and that both organic and conventional foods were at similar risk for bacterial contamination.

There are now more than fourteen thousand U.S. certified-organic farms in the U.S., but today large food corporations like Coca-Cola, Cargill, ConAgra, General Mills, Kraft, and M&M Mars actually provide most of the organic food sold in the U.S.

See also **natural food**.

ORGEAT. An almond flavoring used in cocktails and food. The word is from the French, originally from Latin *hordeum*, dating in English print to about 1500. In the eighteenth century, when it became known in England, the syrup was made with barley, but later it was sweetened and used as a **punch**. Orgeat may be bought commercially.

ORGEAT

Crush together 1 stick cinnamon with ¼ lb. almonds. Add 3 c. milk, 1 c. cream, and 1 T. rosewater or orange flower water. Sweeten to taste, bring to a boil, strain, and serve in punch cups.

ORTOLAN. Also "sora" and "rail." A small native American bird (*Porzana carolina*), which first appeared in print in 1666, but not the true ortolan of Europe (*Emberiza hortulana*), which dates in print to circa 1667. It is a game bird caught in the fall and is considered a great delicacy, to be roasted and eaten whole. The name, from Middle French, is sometimes also applied to the bobolink (*Dolichoniz oryzivorus*), dated in print to 1907, also called "reedbird," "ricebird," and "Maybird." It is usually stewed.

OSTKAKA. A type of Norwegian American cheese pudding, dating in print to 1940, or milk-and-rennet custard, in print in 1967. The word is from the Norwegian *ostekake*, for cheesecake.

OSWEGO TEA. A horsemint (*Monardia didyma* or *M. fistulosa*) made into tea, dating in print to 1752.

OTW. An abbreviation for "on the way," used by restaurant maîtres d'hôtel to note that a party is late but has indicated it is in transit to the restaurant.

OXFORD JOHN. A simmered sliced mutton dish named after Englishman John Farley, who compiled *The London Art of Cookery* in the eighteenth century. It dates in print by that name to 1784, in Hannah Glasse's *The Art of Cookery*. It became a very popular dish in Virginia during those years.

OYSTER (genera *Ostrea* and *Crassostrea*). Any of several edible mollusks found in brackish waters, marshes, inland waters, and even on the roots of submerged trees and coral reefs. The name derives from the Greek *óstreon*.

Oysters have long been considered a delicacy and have been cultivated for at least two thousand years. The American Indians of the coastal regions enjoyed them as a staple part of their diet, and the earliest European explorers marveled at oysters that were up to a foot in length. Cultivation began soon afterwards, and Virginia and Maryland have waged "oyster wars" over offshore beds since 1632. Although the oyster might have been an expensive delicacy in Europe, it was a common item on everyone's table in America. By the eighteenth century the urban poor were sustained by little more than bread and oysters. Colonial citizens dined regularly on chicken and oysters, and the mollusk was an economical

ingredient for stuffing fowl and other meats. By the middle of the next century, English traveler Charles Mackay could write in his book *Life and Liberty in America* (1859) that "the rich consume oysters and Champagne; the poorer classes consume oysters and lager bier, and that is one of the principal social differences between the two sections of the community."

Americans were oyster mad in the nineteenth century, and as people moved and settled westward, the demand for the bivalves in the interior regions grew accordingly. This demand was met by shipping oysters by stagecoach on the "Oyster Line" from Baltimore to Ohio, followed, after the opening of the Erie Canal, in 1825, by canal boats laden with oysters. Canned or pickled varieties were available as far west as St. Louis by 1856.

An American who sat down to a dish of oysters was not satisfied by a mere half-dozen. Indeed, a man who could not put away a dozen or more was not considered much of an eater, and soup recipes of the nineteenth century call for oysters by the quart. Eliza Leslie's *Directions for Cookery* (1837) required two hundred of the mollusks for a stew, and there are records of prodigious feats of oyster consumption—not the least of which was the capacity of James "Diamond Jim" Brady (1856–1917), a wealthy financier who thought nothing of downing three or four dozen a day, in addition to soup, fowl, game, vegetables, desserts, chocolates, and gallons of his favorite drink, orange juice. (Lest anyone think the days of the great oyster trenchermen are over, consider that in 1972, Bobby Melancon ate 188 oysters in one hour at the Oyster Festival, in Galliano, Louisiana.)

Every coastal city had its oyster vendors on the streets, and "oyster saloons," "cellars," or "houses" were part of urban life. In NYC, where $6 million worth of oysters were sold in 1850, one looked for red-and-white-striped muslin balloons lighted by candles and set above basement restaurants where oysters were shucked day and night, in quarters that might be remarkably ornate or rather sleazy. The city's "Canal Street Plan," named after a street in lower Manhattan, was an invitation to consume all the oysters a customer desired for the fixed price of six cents. By 1877, NYC's Fulton Fish Market was selling fifty thousand oysters per day.

Charles E. Rector, of Chicago's Rector's Oyster House, which opened in 1884, wrote:

The real Oyster House is a specialized restaurant, the specialties of which are, in general, seafood, game, salads, certain delicatessen, and the choicest of wines, brandies and ales. In greater detail, it is a place where, in their season, the finest and freshest oysters of a dozen different varieties are to be found; where lobsters, and every variety of edible sea-food, from the hard-shell crab or the delicate soft-shell to the fragile, almost transparent shrimp are daily served.

Such places were frequented not only by men on the town but also by families, who ate to the rear, away from the bar. A few more refined spots, like Downing's, on Broad Street, catered to a high-class clientele with dishes like oyster pie, scalloped oysters, and poached turkey with oysters.

On the West Coast, oysters, including the indigenous Olympia variety, were just as popular. The dish called the **Hangtown fry** was created at the Cary House, in Hangtown, California (now Placerville), in 1849, from what were then the two most expensive items of those Gold Rush days: eggs and oysters. A San Francisco miner accidentally created the "oyster cocktail" about 1860 (and by extension the "shrimp cocktail") by dipping the bivalve in ketchup.

Most oysters in those days were simply roasted, grilled, made into a stew, or eaten raw, with side dishes of lemon juice, mustard, horseradish, and other condiments. The "oyster cracker" did not come along until about 1873.

Throughout the middle of the century, oysters remained plentiful. Even when other foodstuffs were scarce in the Civil War, Union soldiers in Savannah sated their hunger with bucketfuls of oysters brought to them by the slaves they had liberated. In 1869, more than eighteen thousand pounds of oysters were sold during the racing season by one Saratoga, New York, hotel.

Nowhere was the oyster more appreciated than in New Orleans, where several classic oyster recipes, like **oysters Bienville** and **oysters Rockefeller**, were created. The *Picayune's Creole Cook Book* (1900) lists nearly forty recipes for the mollusk, including the famous city specialty the oyster loaf, or *"la médiatrice"* (French for "peacemaker"), so called because a husband who had

stayed out too late would bring one home to his patient wife as an offering of peace.

The demand for oysters was so high that by the 1880s, the eastern beds had begun to be depleted. The Chesapeake Bay then produced fifteen billion bushels of oysters a year, but by the end of the century many cultivators had gone out of business for lack of product, and new sources in the South were tapped to placate the American appetite. Also, the increase in water pollution in cities became so bad as to cause real concern that typhus might be spread by shellfish that had been soaked in local water after delivery and before serving. "The great century of the oyster was over," wrote Richard J. Hooker, in *Food and Drink in America* (1981). "The joyous and uninhibited eating of oysters by rich and poor, Easterner and Westerner, Northerner and Southerner, had ended."

Americans harvested 28.1 million pounds of oysters in 2010, valued at $117.6 million. While many species of oyster are now brought in to the American market, five species are of widespread gastronomic interest. The "Virginia oyster" (*Crassostrea virginica*) ranges from the Gulf of St. Lawrence to the West Indies, is two to six inches long, has a gray, coarse shell, and is widely cultivated. It goes by a wide variety of names: Apalachicola (from Apalachicola Bay, Florida), Alabama Gulf or Black Bay (from Louisiana), Blue Point (originally from Blue Point, New York, but now a widespread Atlantic oyster), Bristol (South Bristol, Maine), Cape Cod (Cape Cod, Massachusetts), Chincoteague (Chincoteague Bay, Maryland), Cotuit (Cotuit Harbor, Cape Cod), Emerald Point (Emerald Point Bay, Mississippi), Florida Gulf (Horseshoe Beach and Wakulla Bay, Florida), Indian River (Cape Canaveral, Florida), James River (James River, Virginia), Kent Island (Kent Island, Maryland), Louisiana Gulf or Lynnhaven (Lynnhaven River, Virginia), Malpeque (Prince Edward Island, Canada), Nelson Bay (Nelson Bay, Alabama), Rhode Island Select, Texas Gulf (Galveston Bay and Corpus Christi), Wellfleet (Cape Cod), and many others.

The "coon" or "raccoon" oyster (*Lopha frons*) ranges from Florida to Brazil, has an oval, ridged shell, and attaches itself to coral in shallow waters and also to trees—a phenomenon Sir Walter Raleigh described to Queen Elizabeth's court, to the courtiers' disbelief. (The name, which dates in print to 1869, comes from their main predator, the raccoon.)

The "California oyster" (*Ostrea lurida*), native to the West Coast, is purplish black or brown in color, has various shapes, and ranges from Alaska to Baja California. This species is more commonly called the "Olympia oyster" (from the Olympia Peninsula, in the state of Washington) and is greatly valued for its flavor. Once very abundant, the species declined during the twentieth century, owing to pollution, but efforts to clean up Puget Sound have resulted in higher yields.

The "Japanese oyster" (*C. gigas*) is larger than the California variety, long in the shell, and gray with purplish streaks. It is also known as the Pacific, Golden mantle, and Portuguese (Vancouver, British Columbia), giant oyster, Hog Island Sweetwater, Tomales Bay, and Preston Point (Tomales Bay, California), Kumamoto (Kumamoto, Japan), Quilcene (Quilcene Bay, Washington), Rock Point (Dabob Bay, Washington), Skokomish (Hood River, Washington), Westcott Bay (Westcott Bay and Tiger Bay, Washington), Willapa Bay (Willapa Bay, Washington), and Yaquina Bay (Yaquina Bay, Oregon). It ranges from British Columbia to Morro Bay, California, and was introduced from Japan in 1902.

The "belon" (*O. edulis*), which derives its name from the famous oysters of France's Brittany region, grows in the Northwest and Maine. It is also known as a "European oyster" or "European flat." They were first cultivated in Maine in 1975 by the York Harbor Export Co., whose first crop was available in 1978.

OYSTER STEW

Shuck 1 pt. oysters, retaining liquid. In large kettle, simmer oysters in liquid for 3 min. Add 1 c. heavy cream and 3 c. milk. Heat until bubbles form at edge, add 1 t. salt, 1 T. Worcestershire sauce, and cayenne pepper to taste. Remove from heat, add 2 T. butter, and garnish with chopped parsley. Serves 4.

OYSTER SHOOTER. A raw oyster placed in a shot glass or jigger and gulped down. It is commonly doused with vodka or another clear spirit and perhaps some cocktail sauce before being consumed.

OYSTERS BIENVILLE. A New Orleans dish of oysters with a béchamel sauce of green pepper, onion, cheese, and bread crumbs. Named after the founder of the city, Jean-Baptiste Le Moyne, Sieur de Bienville (1680–1767), the dish was created in the 1930s or early 1940s by Roy Alciatore, owner of Antoine's Restaurant, in New Orleans, and chef Pete Michel. The following recipe, taken from Roy F. Guste Jr.'s *Antoine's Restaurant Since 1840 Cookbook* (1979), differs considerably from other New Orleans versions that contain cayenne pepper, bacon, shrimp, and other ingredients.

OYSTERS BIENVILLE

Melt 4 T. butter in a skillet. Sauté 1 ½ c. minced bell pepper, 1 c. minced scallions, and 2 cloves minced garlic until limp. Add ½ c. dry white wine and bring to a boil. Then add ½ c. chopped pimiento, 2 c. béchamel sauce, ⅔ c. ground American cheese, ½ c. bread crumbs, and salt and pepper to taste. Simmer for about 20 min., until very thick. Place 6 raw oysters on the half shell on each of six pie pans filled with rock salt. Cover oysters with sauce, bake in 400° oven for 10 min., until they begin to brown on top. Serve as an appetizer.

OYSTERS KIRKPATRICK. A dish of baked oysters, green pepper, and bacon. The creation of this dish is credited to chef Ernest Arbogast of the Palm Court (later the Garden Court), at San Francisco's Palace Hotel. Named after Colonel John C. Kirkpatrick, who managed the hotel from 1894 to 1914, the dish was already well known by the end of his tenure, when Clarence E. Edwards wrote in *Bohemian San Francisco* (1914) that the dish was merely a variation on the "oyster salt roast" served at Mannings Restaurant, on the corner of Pine and Webb streets. The following recipe is supposedly the original.

OYSTERS KIRKPATRICK

Combine 1 c. ketchup, 1 c. chili sauce, 1 t. Worcestershire sauce, ½ t. A.1. sauce, 1 t. chopped parsley, and half a small chopped green pepper. Cut bacon slices into thirds and cook halfway. Shuck oysters, dip them into sauce, and place them in shells. Place oysters on a bed of rock salt, cover with bacon, and sprinkle on Parmesan cheese. Bake at 400° until bacon is crisp.

OYSTERS ROCKEFELLER. A dish of oysters cooked with watercress, scallions, celery, anise, and other seasonings. It is a specialty created in 1899 by Jules Alciatore, of Antoine's Restaurant, in New Orleans. Roy F. Guste Jr., great-grandson of Alciatore, writes in *Antoine's Restaurant Since 1840 Cookbook* (1979):

> *[In 1899] there was a shortage of snails coming in from Europe to the United States and Jules was looking for a replacement. [He wanted it] to be local in order to avoid any difficulty in procuring the product. He chose oysters. Jules was a pioneer in the art of cooked oysters, as they were rarely cooked before this time. He created a sauce with available green vegetable products, producing such a richness that he named it after one of the wealthiest men in the United States, John D. Rockefeller. Rockefeller (1839–1937) was indeed one of the country's richest men, having built a fortune in the oil, steel, railroad, and banking industries.*

The original recipe for oysters Rockefeller has never been revealed; while many renditions include chopped **spinach**, Guste insisted that spinach was not an ingredient of the original recipe. There does appear a recipe, however, in a 1941 compilation by Ford Naylor, called the *World Famous Chefs' Cook Book*, in which the author contends, "Every recipe in this book, with few exceptions, is a secret recipe which has been jealously guarded. In many cases, its ingredients, proportions and blending have been concealed from the world for generations. Now, with as little change as possible in the directions of the chefs who produced them, these cherished recipes have been adapted for the use of the modern homemaker." The recipe for "Oysters à la Rockefeller" is given above the name "Antoine's Restaurant, New Orleans," and, allowing Naylor room for hyperbole and ambiguity of detail, it is possible that the following may be close to the original recipe, although Guste has denied that it is.

OYSTERS ROCKEFELLER

Select Louisiana oysters, open them and leave them on the half shell. Place the shells containing the oysters on a bed of rock salt in a pie pan…Use the tail end tips of special onions [scallions], some celery, chervil, tarragon leaves, crumbs of stale bread, Tabasco sauce, and the best butter obtainable. Pound all these into a mixture in a mortar, so that all of the fragrant flavorings are blended. Add a few drops of absinthe [substitute anise cordial] and a little white wine. Then force the mixture through a sieve. Place one spoonful on each oyster as it rests on its own shell, and in its own juice on the crushed rock salt, the purpose of which is to keep the oyster piping hot. Then place the oysters in an oven with overhead heat and cook until brown. Serve immediately.

PACK. A liquor made from molasses. It is most familiar in the region around New Orleans, though rarely seen now. The name comes from English major general Sir Edward Michael Pakenham (1778–1815), who was killed in January 1815, at the Battle of New Orleans, the final battle of the War of 1812.

PACKAGE-GOODS STORE. Also "package store" and "packie." A store selling liquor in packages, as opposed to a bar, where liquor is dispensed by the glass. The term came into use after the repeal of Prohibition, in 1933, at a time when words like "saloon" and "barroom" still made some state legislators skittish. In many states, such stores may also carry groceries and other items.

PĄCZKI. A Polish American yeast donut, traditionally eaten on Shrove Tuesday. The word is Polish, first in American print circa 1965.

PADDLEFORD, CLEMENTINE (1898–1967). Author. At a time when most newspaper food coverage was driven by food companies seeking to get their products into print, Clementine Haskin Paddleford was an independent voice who served for more than thirty years as food editor for the *New York Herald Tribune*, doing her own research and recipes on regional American cuisine and reaching a readership of twelve million by the end of her career.

Paddleford was born on a farm in Stockdale, Kansas, where she had a habit of rising at four or five A.M. that would stay with her for her entire life and where she learned her mother's cooking, memorialized in her book *A Flower for My Mother* (1958). By the time she was fifteen, she was writing social notes for *The Daily Chronicle*.

Paddleford graduated from Kansas State College in 1921, then moved to NYC to study journalism at NYU while working as a waitress at Union Theological Seminary.

In 1923, Paddleford took a job writing ads for Montgomery Ward & Co. in Chicago. After a failed marriage, she returned to NYC a year later to write for *Farm and Fireside* magazine.

She joined the *Herald Tribune* in 1936 and began a column called How America Eats for *This Week* magazine. She later wrote the column Food Flashes for *Gourmet* magazine (1941–1953). The *Herald Tribune's* managing editor, Richard C. Wald, spoke of her as "a regal presence in the newsroom, a woman of enormous clout." Logging fifty thousand miles a year traveling across the country for her articles and recipes, Paddleford had tremendous access to American food culture for more than four decades, insisting in an interview in 1949, "We all have hometown appetites. Every person is a bundle of longing for the simplicities of good taste once enjoyed on the farm or in the home town they left behind."

Paddleford's writing was rich in sensuous description, as when she wrote,

Apples flame the land. Tens of millions of fruit to touch with the hand, to snap from the twig gently, tenderly. Scent of apples down orchard lanes. A drowsy winy scent permeating the country cellar, spreading across the market place. A glowing apple in the hand, cool, hard-skinned. The teeth crack into the brittle flesh, a winy flavor floods the mouth—the soul of the apple blossom distilled.

She wrote of everything from Hungarian stuffed cabbage in Cleveland to **cioppino** in San Francisco; she even sailed on the submarine *Skipjack* to find out what the seamen ate. Her book *How America Eats*, based on twelve years of research and two thousand interviews, was published in 1961, followed by *Clementine Paddleford's Cook Young Cookbook* five years later. Still, she did not test her recipes, saving that job for the *Herald Tribune's* test kitchen. At her peak, she was earning $250,000 a year.

Paddleford died of cancer in 1967. She donated her books and papers to Kansas State University.

PAIL CANDY. Also "bucket candy." Candy sold in quantity from a pail or bin, first in American print in 1867.

PAIUTE CABBAGE. Either a wild cabbage (*Caulantas inflatus*) favored raw by the Paiute Indians, or a prince's-plume (*Stanleya elata*), first in American print in 1938.

PALACE COURT SALAD. A salad of lettuce, tomato, and artichoke with a dressing of mayonnaise and crabmeat. The salad was created at the Palm Court restaurant, in the Palace Hotel, in San Francisco, sometime around 1940; in 1942, the restaurant name was changed to the Garden Court. The recipe below is used at the hotel.

PALACE COURT SALAD

Prepare a bed of shredded lettuce ½-in. deep. On the center place a thick slice of tomato and a marinated artichoke bottom. Mix 1 oz. chopped celery with 5 oz. crabmeat, and fold in just enough mayonnaise to hold the mixture together. Season with salt, pepper, and lemon juice. Form the salad into a tower-shaped mound and place an artichoke bottom on top. Garnish with a crab claw or pimiento strip. Border the lettuce with chopped egg and garnish the plate with an asparagus spear, black olive, and lemon wedge.

PANADA. Bread boiled to be soft enough for an invalid to chew and digest. The word derives from French *pain*, first in English print in 1598.

PANCAKE. A flat cake cooked on a greased griddle and browned on both sides. The word dates in print to about 1400. Pancakes have long been a staple of the American breakfast table, and their history is as old as that of the Native Americans who shaped a soft batter in their hands and called it, in the Narragansett, *nokechick* ("it is soft"), transmuted by early white settlers into "no cake." Cornmeal pancakes were called "Indian cakes" as early as 1607. The Dutch in America made similar cakes from buckwheat, *pannekoeken*, which by 1740 were called "buckwheat cakes." English settlers brought with them the feast of Pancake Tuesday, an old name for Shrove Tuesday, the day before the Lenten fast begins. (In New Orleans this holiday was Mardi Gras.) Eating such rich, buttered cakes on this day was the last gasp of gourmandism before forty days of self-denial.

By 1745 Americans were also referring to "hoe cakes," perhaps because they were cooked on a flat hoe blade, and there were "rice cakes," "batter cakes," and "slapjacks" by the end of the eighteenth century. One of the most beloved versions of this simple cake is the **johnnycake**, specifically associated with Rhode Island but well known throughout New England.

Meanwhile, the rest of the country has gone on naming and renaming flat, griddle-fried cakes in all manner of ways. Thomas Jefferson served them at Monticello, and Benjamin Franklin called the Rhode Island variety "better than a Yorkshire muffin." By the nineteenth century northerners were referring to "flapjacks" and "griddle cakes," which by the 1830s and 1840s were being made with white flour rather than cornmeal. American versions of French crepes sought refinement through names like "quire-of-paper pancakes," a thin Virginia variety made with a little white wine. Another Virginia example, made with the coloring of beet juices and slathered with fruit preserves, was called "pink-colored pancakes."

The word *pancake* itself was not in general usage until the 1870s, but afterwards became the predominant American term for these traditional favorites. In mining camps and logging camps, they were called either "flannel cakes" (perhaps because they had the texture of the flannel shirts the workers wore), "a string of flats," or "flatcars" (after the flat, open cars used by the railroads to ship lumber). Still another name used by lumberjacks was "sweatpads," possibly after the round, perspiration-absorbent pads women wore under their dresses. Southerners called cornmeal cakes "Crispus Attucks," after the African American patriot killed in the Boston Massacre, in 1770.

Whatever they were called, pancakes became an American passion, and, as one English traveler wrote, "It is hard for an American to rise from his winter breakfast without his buckwheat cakes." American novelist James Fenimore Cooper made buckwheat cakes for Parisians in the 1820s. Buckwheat cakes are also called "ployes" among Acadians.

In 1889, Chris L. Rutt and Charles G. Underwood, of St. Joseph, Missouri, introduced the first ready-mixed commercial food product at the New Era Exposition, in St. Joseph, when they began marketing "Self-Rising Pancake Flour," later renamed "Aunt Jemima," after a minstrel-show song.

So popular are they today that nationwide chains of restaurants specialize in pancakes in any number of forms, including "silver dollar" pancakes (small enough to be served in portions of six to a dozen), pancakes mixed with fruit (especially blueberries) or nuts, and pancakes topped with preserves, whipped cream, and often eggs. The first such restaurant was the International House of Pancakes ("IHOP" for short), opened in North Hollywood, California, in 1958.

The classic accompaniment to a "stack" of three or four pancakes (a "short stack" would be one or two) is either crisply fried bacon or link sausage. **Maple** syrup is poured over the top, and one is also likely to find hash-brown potatoes nearby or, in the South, a side order of **grits**. Sometimes a garnish of orange slice is set on the plate.

PANCAKES

Sift together 1 ½ c. flour, ½ t. salt, and 2 ½ t. baking powder. In another bowl mix 1 well-beaten egg with 1 c. milk and 3 T. butter, then pour into flour mixture and stir just to moisten. Batter will be lumpy. Spoon out batter onto a hot buttered griddle in 4-in. rounds. When bubbles begin to show through top, flip over and cook until both sides are golden. Serve with butter and syrup.

FLANNEL CAKES

Cream ½ c. sugar with 1 T. butter, then add 2 c. milk with ½ cake of yeast dissolved into it. Add 1 beaten egg and enough flour (about 1 ½ c.) to make a stiff, pancake-like batter. Let stand overnight. Batter will thicken still more. Stir and cook on buttered griddle, or, preferably, bake in muffin tins at 400° until brown.

PAN DRIPPINGS. The browned bits of fat and meat left in a pan after roasting or frying. Pan drippings are usually mixed with flour or cornstarch, water, and seasonings to make a **gravy**.

PAN DULCE. Any of a variety of Mexican sweet breads or pastries. The word is from American Spanish and first appeared in print in 1922. "Pão doce" is a Portuguese variant.

PAPAYA (*Carica papaya*). Also "papaw" and "tree melon." A tropical American tree bearing a sweet yellow fruit. The word, which is from Carib *abadai*, was first recorded in English circa 1598. The papaya is sometimes called "pawpaw," but it is not the true **pawpaw**.

The papaya was first noted by Christopher Columbus as a staple fruit of the West Indian diet, and other travelers soon brought its seeds to the Far East, including the Philippines and Nepal. In the U.S., it has been grown successfully only in Florida, Texas, and, predominantly, Hawaii (where papayas have been cultivated since 1919). The main market varieties are the Kapoho Solo and the Sunrise. Usually eaten fresh as a fruit, papaya may also be boiled and served as a form of vegetable. Papaya's enzyme, "papain," is widely used in granular form as a tenderizer for meats and as a digestive aid.

New York City has a particular affinity for hot dogs and a drink made from the papaya, a combination said to have been started by Greek immigrant Constantine Poulos in 1928, when, having tasted papaya juice in Cuba, he began serving it at his hot dog stand on Eighty-sixth Street and Third Avenue. The stand was later christened Papaya King, and soon similarly named competitors appeared around Manhattan.

PARFAIT. A frozen dessert made from cream, eggs, sugar, and flavorings, or, as is more usual today, an ice cream sundae of several different ice creams garnished with various syrups or crushed fruits. The word comes from the French, meaning "perfect," and first saw English print in 1884.

PARKER HOUSE ROLL. A puffy yeast roll with a creased center, created at the Parker House Hotel, in Boston, by the kitchen's German baker, whose name was Ward, soon after its opening, in 1855. One story holds that Ward, in a fit of pique over a guest's belligerence, merely threw some unfinished rolls into the oven and came up with the little bun that made his employer, Harvey Parker, famous. Such light, puffy rolls, sometimes called "pocketbook rolls" because of their purse-like appearance, were a novelty in their day and became a standard item in American dining rooms and tables. The name was first in print as of 1873.

The following recipe is from the Parker House kitchen and makes four dozen rolls.

PARKER HOUSE ROLL

Mix 2 ½ lb. flour with ¼ lb. shortening, 2 ½ oz. milk powder, ¼ lb. sugar, and ½ oz. salt. Melt ½ oz. dry yeast in ¾ qt. warm water, then add slowly to flour mixture. Beat until smooth. Let the dough rest for 1 ½ hr., then knead it. Cut dough into 1-in.-sq. pieces, stretch each piece, and fold over. Arrange on a greased baking pan, let rise for 45 min., then bake in a 400° oven for 10 min., until golden brown. Brush with melted butter and serve.

PARKER, ROBERT (1947–). Author. Since beginning his *Wine Advocate* newsletter, in 1978, Robert M. Parker Jr. has helped stoke Americans' appetite and taste for quality wines by introducing a ratings system that grades wines with scores from 50 to 100 points. He has been called by the *New York Times* "the most influential wine writer in the world" and the person most responsible for making the reputations of various wineries.

Parker was born in Baltimore, graduated as a history major, then earned a law degree at the University of Maryland (1973). Upon graduating, he became an attorney for the Farm Credit Bank of Baltimore. In 1975, he began writing about wine as a consumer advocate, and three years later started publishing a newsletter, *The Baltimore-Washington Wine Advocate*, renamed *The Wine Advocate* in 1979, for which he initially had only a few hundred subscribers. Twenty years later, the newsletter has fifty thousand subscribers, with worldwide readership. His nose is now insured for $1 million.

Parker introduced his rating system to wine tasting, though rarely was any wine rated below 85 (a standard that was also adopted by *Wine Spectator*).

By the end of the 1990s, Parker's opinions—based on what he claims are tastings of ten thousand wines a year, often tasted as barrel samples—became so important that wine shops would list his ratings numbers and quote him in order to sell wines. He became the first non-French wine critic for the Paris newspaper *L'Express*.

Parker's power readily caused ripples throughout the established wine media, whose members he had criticized as being too intimate with the industry itself. His critics asserted that Parker's tastes ran to high-alcohol, low-acid, oaked wines with intense fruit flavors, which actually caused many winemakers to make wines that would meet those criteria. Parker himself denies this, but this phenomenon came to be called "Parkerization" in the wine world, and is sometimes referred to as the "International Style" of homogenizing of wines that taste much alike from country to country.

Parker has always insisted he is free from industry influence, though he has fired several of his associates at *The Wine Advocate* for perceived conflicts of interest.

In December 2012, Parker stepped away from editor-in-chief duties and, with the help of Singapore investors, shifted the publication to that Asian city. By the end of 2013 the publication was to be available only online.

Parker's awards include: Chevalier de l'Ordre National du Mérite (1993); **James Beard Foundation** Wine and Spirits Professional (1997); Commendatore dell'Ordine al Merito della Repubblica Italiana (2002); and the Wine Media Guild Hall of Fame (2008).

Among Parker's books are: *The Wines of the Rhône Valley and Provence* (1987); *Burgundy* (1990); *Bordeaux* (fourth edition, 2003); and *Parker's Wine Buyer's Guide* (seventh edition, 2008).

PARSLEY (*Petroselinum crispum*). A green herb with a grassy taste. It is usually sprinkled on dishes as a garnish, though its flavor enhances stocks and sauces. The word is from the Greek *petrosélinon* "rock parsley," which in Middle English became *persely*.

Waverley Root, in *Food* (1980), notes that Giovanni da Verrazano reported seeing parsley when he landed in what is now Massachusetts in 1524, adding, *vigilant writers since have insisted that this could not have been true, since parsley is an Old World plant. The rectifiers were perhaps wrong. There were Norsemen not far from Massachusetts, if not actually there, five hundred years before Verrazano, to say nothing of the Basque fishermen who came from parsley country to the Grand Banks off Newfoundland before Columbus…where perhaps they let drop a seed or two [that] could easily have migrated from Newfoundland to Massachusetts in a couple of centuries.*

Root goes on to say, however, that no written record of parsley's presence in America occurs before 1806. Today two main varieties, the "Italian" (*P. c. neapolitanum*) and "Hamburg" or "turnip-rooted parsley" (*P. c. tuberoseum*), are grown in the U.S. The latter is the most readily available nationwide; the former, grown in southern Louisiana, is essential to Creole and Cajun cookery.

PARSNIP (*Pastinaca sativa*). A plant having a white root that is boiled and eaten as a vegetable. The word is from the Latin *pastinaca*, which became in Middle English *pasnepe*.

The origins of the parsnip probably lie in northeastern Europe, though there is a wild parsnip found in the American West called "Indian celery" (*Hercaleum lanatum*). Europeans brought parsnips to North America in the seventeenth century, first to Virginia in 1608, where the Indians soon learned to enjoy them.

The vegetable has never been very popular with Americans, but a particularly hardy and early-maturing variety that was developed here is called the "All-American." Parsnips are usually boiled and buttered.

PARSON FOOD. A midwestern slang term for food served to a visiting parson after Sunday service.

PARTRIDGE. America has no true partridge (any of a variety of Old World game birds in the genera *Perdix* and *Alectoris*), but many birds are called by this name in America. The terminology is further confused by the use of other names, such as "quail" or "pheasant," for the same birds. The bobwhite (*Colinus virginianus*), a name first recorded in 1837, was erroneously called a "partridge" in print as of 1587. The "ruffed grouse" (*Bonasa*

umbellus), so called as of 1752, was also termed a "partridge" in print as of 1630. (The ruffed grouse has also been called on occasion a **pheasant** or "mountain pheasant.") The "gray partridge" (*P. perdix*), which is a true partridge, was introduced from Eurasia into the northern U.S., but, as noted in *Harper & Row's Complete Field Guide to North American Wildlife* (1981), has "generally [been] unsuccessful in becoming established."

PASCHA. Also "paska." A sweetened fresh cheese pudding traditional to Russian American Easter, first in American print in 1957.

PASSION FRUIT. Also "passionfruit." Any of a variety of fruit of the genus *Passiflora*. The word dates in print to 1752. The fruit was discovered in South America in the sixteenth century by Jesuit missionaries who gave it its name because the flower's parts appeared symbolic of the elements of the passion of Christ, such as the crown of thorns, the nails, and the whip.

Passion fruit was introduced to Florida at the beginning of the twentieth century. The shell is usually coarse, the shape oval, and it has a pronounced tropical aroma. The "purple passion fruit" (*P. edulis*), called "lilikoi" in Hawaii, and "yellow passion fruit" (*P. edulis forma flavicarpa*) are among the most popular varieties.

PASTA. A general term, from the Italian and in English print since 1827, for any spaghetti, macaroni, noodles, or other flour-and-water (sometimes with egg) preparations that are rolled and cut into myriad shapes and sizes. Pasta is made from either fresh or dried dough, sometimes stuffed (as in Italian "manicotti," "ravioli," and "tortellini"), commonly boiled, and sometimes baked (as in Italian *lasagne*, often spelled "lasagna" in American English).

While many of the world's cultures have long eaten various forms of boiled dough, it is most associated with the Italians and has become an Italian American staple. The English brought recipes for macaroni to America. The first commercial pasta plant in the U.S. was set up in Brooklyn, New York, in 1848, by Frenchman Antoine Zerega. By the Civil War pasta was well known and commonly available, usually baked with cheese. Italian immigrants made fresh pasta, but, as was common in the south of Italy, whence came most of the immigrants, dried pasta (preferably imported) made with hard durum wheat, which was not grown in the U.S. until the twentieth century, was preferred. Canned macaroni was first produced in the 1890s, by the Franco-American Co. In 1904, a group of Pittsburgh pasta makers formed the National Macaroni Manufacturers Association (since 1981 called the National Pasta Association). By 1929 there were 550 pasta factories in the U.S., second only to Italy itself, and they were exporting more pasta than the U.S. was importing.

The halt of pasta imports caused by World War I prompted the opening of hundreds of American pasta factories, and by the 1920s macaroni and spaghetti were promoted as highly nutritious items.

The word *pasta* gained currency in the U.S. only in the 1960s, with the popularity of Italian food. Prior to that, pasta varieties were referred to by their specific names, like "spaghetti," "macaroni," or "egg noodles."

Americans eat about twenty pounds of pasta per person annually (six billion pounds total), with 8.9 percent imported. The favorite shapes and preparations, in order of popularity, are spaghetti, macaroni (and cheese), fettuccine, linguine, elbow macaroni, pasta salad, and angel-hair. Ironically, Italian pasta makers now import more than 165 million pounds of American durum wheat for grinding into semolina flour.

PASTA FAZOOL. An Italian American colloquialism for the dish *pasta e fagioli* (Italian for "pasta and beans"), a bowl of pasta and white or red beans made into a thick soup. The term dates in print to 1940.

PASTA PRIMAVERA. A dish of noodles, macaroni, or spaghetti, made with a sauce of quickly cooked vegetables. *Primavera* in Italian means "springtime," but there is no traditional or specific dish in Italian cuisine by this name. Pasta with vegetables in Italy would be referred to as *pasta al verdure* or, as is more usual, according to the specific vegetables used—for example, *fettuccine con funghi e piselli* (fettuccine with mushrooms and peas). Pasta primavera became a very popular dish in America in the 1970s and 1980s, and although there are other claimants for the invention of the dish, the version that gave it its name and spurred its popularity was created

by **Sirio Maccioni**, owner of Le Cirque Restaurant, in NYC, who, while on a visit to Canada on October 2, 1975, made the dish from several vegetables he tossed together. Maccioni was encouraged by food writers to add it to his menu in NYC, and the newly christened dish became an immediate favorite, spawning instant imitators.

PASTA PRIMAVERA

Steam 1 c. sliced zucchini, 1 c. sliced broccoli, 1 ½ c. snow peas, 1 c. baby peas, 6 sliced asparagus stalks, and 10 sliced mushrooms. Rinse under cold water. Sauté in 1 T. olive oil 2 coarsely chopped tomatoes, ¼ c. parsley, salt, and pepper for a few min. In another pan, sauté ⅓ c. pine nuts and 2 t. minced garlic. Add to pan with garlic oil all the vegetables except tomatoes. Simmer, then add 1 lb. cooked spaghetti, ½ c. Parmesan cheese, ⅓ c. butter, 1 c. heavy cream, and ⅓ c. fresh basil. Toss, then pour tomatoes on top. Serves 6.

PASTELLES CALIENTES. A Puerto Rican meat pie wrapped in plantains. The term, which means "hot pies" in Spanish, appeared in print in 1953.

PASTRAMI. Beef that has been cured in a brine of salt and other preservatives for one to three weeks, smoked over hardwood sawdust for two to twelve hours, then cooked by steaming for one to three hours. The word dates in print to 1831.

Pastrami is traditionally made from a forequarter cut of meat called the "deckle" or "plate," is usually served on sandwiches, and is a Jewish American delicatessen item. Its name is derived from the Romanian word *pāstra*, "to preserve."

"Pastrami dip" is a sandwich made with pastrami on a French roll, dipped in gravy. It originated in Los Angeles in the 1940s or 1950s, at hot-dog stands that dipped the pastrami in gravy as a way of keeping the meat from drying out.

PASTY. Also "Cornish pasty." A pastry turnover that may contain a variety of meats and fillings. Pronounced *"pass-tee,"* the dish has been known in England since the Middle Ages, first entered print in 1296, and is mentioned in Shakespeare's *The Merry Wives of Windsor* (circa 1598). It has its variants in Scandinavian and Russian cookery.

Pasties became a staple midday meal for the Cornish miners who settled in Michigan's Upper Peninsula in the middle of the nineteenth century, and there have been attempts to have the pasty declared the state's official food. May 24 has been declared "Michigan Pasty Day," and people of the region will argue over every item that must go into a perfect pasty.

Cornish miners would wrap the hot pasty in a napkin, then in newspaper, and place it in their metal lunch pails so that by midday the pasty would still be warm. It was sometimes reheated on a shovel set over a miner's candle. There is some argument as to whether the pastry itself should be made with lard or suet. In *Heartland* (1991), Marcia Adams notes that "because the pasty was a portable meal, the dough was not known for its tender flakiness. It was said that a really good pasty should be tough enough to withstand being dropped down a mine shaft."

PASTY

Blend 3 c. flour with 1 c. suet and ¼ c. lard. Add 1 t. salt and about 7 T. cold water to make a dough. Divide into four pieces and roll into 9-in. circles. Stir together ¾ lb. coarsely ground beef chuck, ½ lb. coarsely chopped pork, 1 lb. diced peeled potatoes, 2 diced turnips, 1 chopped onion, 2 diced carrots, salt, pepper, and 2 t. butter. Spread on circles and fold the pastry together, crimping the top ridge. Bake at 350° on an ungreased sheet for about 45–50 min., until browned.

PAWPAW (*Asimina triloba*). Also "papaw" and "dog apple." A tree native to northern Central America, bearing a soft, fleshy fruit. The name, which is probably derived from the Spanish *papaya*, is often mistaken for the true **papaya**, and the first recordings in English of the fruit are variations of "papaya." The word first appeared in print in 1624.

The pawpaw, with a taste that has been described as a cross between a banana and a pear, grows on stream banks from temperate regions of New York down to Florida and into the Midwest, where it is sometimes called the "Michigan banana" or "custard apple."

PEA (*Pisum sativum*). A climbing plant having edible seeds enclosed in long pods. The word is from the Greek *pison*, which in Middle English became *pese* in the plural. There are many variant names for this species, including "field pea."

The pea is one of the oldest cultivated plants in the world. Peas were supposedly brought to the West Indies by Christopher Columbus in 1493 and planted at La Isabela, on the island of Hispaniola. By 1614 they were being cultivated at Jamestown, Virginia, and New England's first peas were planted by Captain Bartholomew Gosnold, on the island of Cuttyhunk in 1602.

The most popular variety is the "garden pea," also called the "English pea," the most popular forms being "Layton's Progress," the "Dwarf Telephone," "Gradus," and "Mammoth Melting Sugar," with the Great Lakes, Washington, and Oregon the highest producers. The "sugar pea" includes all edible pea pods, such as "snow peas," or "Chinese snow peas," and "sugar snap peas," developed as a crossbreed by Calvin Lamborn in 1979. "*Petit pois*" (French for "little peas") are merely small greenhouse varieties, and "pea shoots" are the tendrils of pea plants, used as texture and garnish in highly stylized restaurant cooking, while the **cowpea**, "sweet pea," and **chickpea** are not peas at all but plants in other genera.

"Split peas" are peas that have been dried so that the seeds split in two. They are customarily used to make split-pea soup. Whole peas, fresh or frozen or canned, are boiled or heated and served with butter, onion, or other seasonings.

PEACH (*Prunus persica*). A tree native to China that bears a sweet fruit with yellow flesh and a yellow-red, slightly fuzzy skin. The word is from the Latin plural of *Persicum mālum*, "Persian apple," which in Middle English became *pêche*.

The Romans imported the peach from the Persians, who got it from China and India. It was a popular, though rare, fruit in France and England through the seventeenth century. After the Spanish brought it to the New World, in the sixteenth century, the peach thrived among the southern Indian tribes (the Natchez even named one of the months of the year after the fruit) and became just as popular with the northern tribes when they began planting it. In 1661, Philadelphia's William Penn told a friend that peaches proliferated in Pennsylvania—"not an Indian plantation without them"—and Thomas Jefferson planted French varieties at Monticello in 1802.

Commercial plantings began in Virginia in the nineteenth century, led first by Maryland and Delaware, then by Georgia. "Peach brandy" was a specialty of the Ohio Valley. Today peaches, second only to the apple among American fruit crops, are produced in California, New Jersey, Pennsylvania, Virginia, North and South Carolina, Georgia, Alabama, Michigan, Arkansas, and Colorado.

Most peaches are eaten fresh or canned, often in a sweet syrup, and peach bread and peach pie are both long-standing southern specialties. The two main varieties of peaches are the "clingstone" (so called because the fruit's firm flesh clings to the pit) and the "freestone" (which has a softer flesh). The most popular yellow varieties include Muir, Lovell, Rochester, Blake, Late Crawford, Crosby, and the largest variety, the Elberta. The most popular white peaches include the Mountain Rose, Alexander, Champion, Heath Cling, Cling, Old-mixon, Summer Snow, Iron Mountain, and Belle of Georgia. Rareripe is an eastern freestone peach. The most successful crossbreeds include the Golden Jubilee, Halehaven, Redhaven, Dixieland, Dixi Gem, Southland, and Goldeneats.

"Nectarines," raised mostly in California and Oregon, are a variety of peach having a firmer flesh and a smooth skin.

In 2011, U.S. consumption of peaches and nectarines was 693,000 tons.

PEACH MELBA. A dessert of peaches poached in vanilla syrup and served with vanilla ice cream and raspberry sauce. The dish was created by chef Georges Auguste Escoffier (1846–1935) and named after Australian opera singer Nellie Melba (born Helen Mitchell, 1861–1931), but it is not clear exactly when or where. It was first in print 1906 on an Indiana menu, suggesting it was already well known. Many stories printed during the principals' lifetimes only served to obscure the truth. André L. Simon and Robin Howe, in *A Dictionary of Gastronomy* (1978), state unequivocally that Escoffier served poached peaches with vanilla ice cream at a party given at the London Savoy Hotel to honor Melba on her Covent Garden opening in *Lohengrin*. The authors

add that Escoffier later "improved [the dish] by adding a puree of fresh raspberries and a sprinkling of shredded green almonds," which appeared "on a menu of the Carlton Hotel on its first opening in London on July 15, 1899." In *Melba* (1909), the singer's biographer, A. G. Murphy, spoke of her 1898–1899 tour and noted that "by this time innumerable soaps and sauces, ribbons and ruffles, had been named after her." But Escoffier himself contended that the dish had not been created for Melba's *Lohengrin* debut, but instead that he put it on the menu merely because she so often demanded peaches and ice cream for dessert. Escoffier says the dish was created at the Ritz-Carlton Hotel in London and that the peaches were from the Montreal suburb of Paris, while the raspberry puree was merely a rendition of sauce cardinal with kirsch added. To make matters more confusing, Melba herself treats the subject of the dessert in her autobiography, *Melodies and Memories* (1925), in a chapter devoted to her activities during the years 1904–1905, insisting that Escoffier made the dish for her at the Savoy Hotel, which Escoffier had left in 1898.

By 1905, however, the dessert must already have been fairly well known, for American author Edith Wharton mentioned the dish in her novel of that year, *The House of Mirth*. By 1906 the dish, called in French *pêches melba*, was on Escoffier's menus and given as a recipe, which appears below, a year later in his *Le Guide Culinaire*. (The version mentioned by Simon and Howe as the one appearing on the menu in 1899 is listed in Escoffier's book as "*pêches cardinal*.") The dish became a favorite in American hotel dining rooms, and an already mixed "melba sauce" was being bottled by 1951.

PEACH MELBA

Poach the skinned peaches in vanilla-flavored syrup. When very cold, arrange them in a timbale on a bed of vanilla ice cream and coat with raspberry sauce.

PEACH SCHNAPPS. A cordial liqueur with a peach flavor, originally developed in the early 1980s by flavor scientist Earl LaRoe of National Distillers and sold as Peachtree schnapps. The rights were later obtained by DeKuyper Liqueurs. Peach schnapps is most often used in the cocktail called the **Fuzzy Navel**.

PEACHY. A **cider** made from peaches. It is quite possibly an American creation, since its first appearance in print was in *S. Peter's History of Connecticut* in 1781.

PEANUT. An edible, nutlike seed of the vine *Arachis hypogaea*, native to South America. Peanuts are widely enjoyed as a snack, in a sandwich spread called "peanut butter," and as an ingredient in candy. Peanut oil is often used in frying.

In *Food* (1980), Waverley Root points out that the seeds were found in Peruvian mummy tombs and pictured on Chimu pottery, but other authorities believe that the seeds came originally from Brazil. The Inca may have been the first to cultivate the plant. The Spaniard Hernán Cortés saw peanuts in Mexico; Columbus found them in Haiti. The Spanish and Portuguese took peanuts to other parts of the world, including the Malay Peninsula, China, and Africa. In West Africa, the Portuguese propagated the plant to feed the slaves bound for the New World, and the American colloquialisms "goober" and "pinder" (or "pindal") are derived from African words, brought by the slaves, either for the peanut itself or for an African underground species, *Voandgeia subterranea*, and other plants. These words soon appeared in print in America, the former in 1833, the latter first in Jamaica in 1707 and in South Carolina in 1848. Other names for the peanut include "monkey-nut," found in England and, to a certain extent, in America; and "groundnut," first recorded in 1602, or "ground-pea," in 1769. Root says that Thomas Jefferson was propagating peanuts in the 1790s. The first appearance of the word *peanut* in print was in 1802.

Before the arrival of Europeans, there were no peanuts on the North American continent. It was a locally propagated crop in the South, with Wilmington, North Carolina, the largest commercial market for the product. "Peanut boilings" were neighborhood get-togethers in the South. The peanut did not become a national food until after the Civil War, when Northern troops, having gotten used to the nut while fighting in the South, returned to the North, where they weren't to be found. Virginia filled the void, and by 1869 more than six hundred thousand bushels were being produced. By the turn of the century, vendors were selling peanuts on the streets of most major cities.

In the 1890s, **George Washington Carver**, of Alabama's Tuskegee Institute, promoted the peanut as a replacement for the cotton crop, which had been destroyed by the boll weevil, and by 1903 he had begun to develop hundreds of uses for the peanut, demonstrating its high nutritive value in dozens of recipes for appetizers, main dishes, soups, and desserts. His list of the most popular peanut varieties includes the "Spanish," "Georgia," "Tennessee Red," and "Virginia Running," this last referred to as the typical "American peanut."

At the beginning of the twentieth century, Italian immigrant Amedeo Obici developed a process for commercially roasting shelled peanuts in oil, and, with Mario Peruzzi, began packaging peanuts in airtight bags, under the "Planters" label. Meanwhile, Russian immigrant Sam Fisher patented a "salted-in-the-shell" peanut cooker that made the snack much more widely available. In 1890, an unknown St. Louis physician created "peanut butter" as a protein substitute for those with poor teeth. A local food-products manufacturer, George A. Bayle Jr., mechanized the process, and in 1903 a patent was issued to Ambrose W. Straub for a peanut butter machine. A year later peanut butter was being promoted as a health food at the Louisiana Purchase Exposition, in St. Louis, by concessionaire C. H. Sumner. In 1922, J. L. Rosefield of the Rosefield Packing Co., of Alameda, California, developed a process to prevent oil separation and spoilage in peanut butter, and in 1932 he began marketing his product under the name Skippy as "churned" peanut butter. It soon became a favorite sandwich spread among American schoolchildren, usually layered with grape jelly, and today more than half of the American peanut crop goes into the making of peanut butter. The earliest reference to such a sandwich is in the November 1901 edition of *The Boston Cooking-School Magazine of Culinary Science*, made with currant or crabapple jelly. The so-called PB&J sandwich became extremely popular after the invention of sliced bread in 1928, and in the late 1930s, the sandwich was served as part of school free lunch programs via the Works Progress Administration.

In the South, peanut soup is very common, as is "peanut cream gravy." Peanuts are boiled or eaten roasted, out of their shells, salted or unsalted. They are mixed into stuffings, salads, cakes, cookies, puddings, pies, and candies and are a versatile ingredient in many of the most popular commercial candy bars. "Peanut brittle" came along at the turn of the last century; "peanut stands" were known as early as the 1860s, and vendors selling peanuts in paper bags have been a fixture in sporting arenas and circus tents in America for decades. The "peanut gallery" referred to the cheapest, highest-up seats at the circus, from which patrons could toss peanuts down, or the first seats in movie theaters, from which viewers threw peanuts at the screen.

More than 50 percent of peanuts grown worldwide are crushed to make oil. By law, any product labeled "peanut butter" must contain at least 90 percent peanuts, with the remaining 10 percent restricted to salt, sweeteners, and stabilizers. The majority of peanut butter is now imported. The U.S. currently produces about 1.9 million tons annually, producing $4 billion in sales. Americans consume more than 1.5 billion pounds of peanut products annually, with peanut butter accounting for half the edible use of the product. annually, more than six pounds per capita each year.

The four principal peanut varieties raised commercially are the Virginia, the Runner, the Spanish, and the Valencia.

"Peanut" is also the name of a freshwater clam, *Tritigonia verrucosa*, first in American print in 1992.

PEANUT PIE

Beat 3 eggs with ½ c. sugar. Add 1 c. white corn syrup, 1 t. vanilla, 1 t. butter, a pinch of salt, and 2 T. peanut butter and mix for 5 min. Pour into a 9-in. pie shell, sprinkle top with ¾ c. toasted peanuts, and bake for 45 min. at 300°.

PEANUT SOUP

(Also known as "Tuskegee soup," for its creator, George Washington Carver, of the Tuskegee Institute.) Chop 5 scallions and sauté in 3 T. butter. Make a roux by blending in 3 T. flour, then add ½ c. peanut butter and 2 c. chicken stock and stir until smooth. Add ½ c. cream and the juice from 1 qt. shucked oysters. Add salt, cayenne pepper, and savory to taste, then finish with a dash of sherry, parsley, and the shucked oysters.

PEAR (*Pyrus communis*). A tree bearing a fruit with a spherical bottom and tapered top. The word is from the Latin *pirum*. In Middle English it appeared as *pere*.

The pear originated in Asia, possibly China, and has been cultivated since at least 2000 B.C., with more than fifteen thousand species having since been developed, from either the "Chinese pear" (*P. sinensis*) or the "European pear" (*P. communis*). Most American varieties have been developed from the latter, which was brought to the colonies in the seventeenth century by Jesuit missionaries, English settlers in Massachusetts, and the Dutch in New Amsterdam. In the West, the pear was introduced by Spanish missionaries.

By far the most widely cultivated variety in the U.S. is the "Bartlett," first mentioned in print in 1831. In Europe, the Bartlett was called the "Williams's Bon Chrétien," because the fruit was supposedly brought to France in the fifteenth century by Saint Francis of Paola (*bon chrétien* in French means "good Christian") and was perhaps propagated in England and on the Continent by a horticulturist named Williams. Neither of these stories has been proven, but the pear acquired its American name thanks to Enoch Bartlett, of Dorchester, Massachusetts, who promoted the variety in the U.S. The Bartlett now accounts for three-quarters of U.S. pear production. In 2011, U.S. consumption of pears totaled 456,000 tons.

Other important varieties include the Seckel, the Cornice, the Bosc, the Anjou, and the Kieffer. Americans eat pears fresh or canned in syrup, with ice cream, and cooked in cream and sugar. The leading pear-producing states are California, Washington, Oregon, New York, Michigan, Illinois, Pennsylvania, and New Jersey.

In Charleston, South Carolina, preserves of chopped pears (also pumpkins) are known as "chips," because the pears are "chipped" into pieces.

PEAR CHIPS

In a saucepan, bring to a boil 4 c. sugar with 1 qt. water and cook for about 5 min. Add 4 lb. peeled, seeded, and chopped pears and 2 thinly sliced, seeded lemons. Cook until the pears are tender, then serve with the syrup over ice cream or store in vacuum jars.

PECAN (*Carya illinoensis*). The nut of the tall hickory tree, native to America, ranging from Illinois down to Mexico. After the peanut, the pecan is the most popular nut grown in this country, with an annual production of about 228 million pounds, led by Georgia, and is used in pies, pralines, candies, and ice cream. The name comes from various Indian words (Algonquian *paccan*, Cree *pakan*, and others) and was first mentioned in print in 1712 as "Pacanes." Thomas Jefferson introduced the tree to the eastern shores of Virginia, and he gave some to George Washington for planting at Mount Vernon. A Louisiana slave named Antoine was the first to successfully graft and cultivate pecan trees, in 1846. "Pecan pie" is sometimes called "Karo pie," after Karo brand corn syrup (introduced in 1902 by Corn Products Co., of Edgewater, New Jersey), so often used in its preparation. The recipe below is adapted from *The Karo Cook Book* (1981).

The "pecan ball"—a dessert made by rolling a scoop of ice cream in chopped pecans and topping it with chocolate syrup—is a specialty of Pitsburg, Ohio.

PECAN PIE

Beat 3 eggs until light in color. Beat in 1 c. Karo light or dark corn syrup, 1 c. sugar, 2 T. melted margarine, 1 t. vanilla, and ⅛ t. salt. Stir in 1 c. pecans and pour mixture into pastry shell. Bake at 350° for 55–65 min. or until inserted knife comes out clean. Serves 8.

PEMMICAN. A Native American food made from buffalo meat or venison dried and compressed into small cakes, also containing some form of melted fat, berries, and sometimes bone marrow. This highly nutritious food, which kept well on long journeys, was introduced to the early pioneers, though they did not take to it with any particular relish. The pioneers' version often did not contain the meat.

The word comes from Cree Indian *pimihka·n*, from *pimiy*, "grease," and was first used in print in 1743. A struggle between the hunters and traders of the two major fur companies—the North West Co. and the Hudson Bay Co.—which lasted from 1812 to 1821, was referred to as the "Pemmican War," fought over the rights of the Metis (a culture of Indians who intermarried with French and Scots) to hunt buffalo and preserve the meat as pemmican.

PÉPIN, JACQUES (1935–). Chef, author, educator, TV host. Jacques Pépin is ranked among the finest contemporary cooking teachers in America, both for his seminal books *La Technique* and *La Méthode* and for his long-running TV cooking shows. Pépin was born in Bourg-en-Bresse, France, where he worked with his parents at their restaurant Le Pelican. From there he went to Paris to study with Lucien Diat, of the Plaza-Athenée Hotel, and for two years (1956–1958) was personal chef to President Charles de Gaulle. A year later Pépin moved to the U.S. to work at NYC's finest French restaurant, Le Pavillon, then, in a surprising move for a classically trained chef, he was hired by the family-restaurant chain owner Howard Johnson, a regular Le Pavillon patron, to develop the company's menu. It was at Howard Johnson's, Pépin later said, that he learned about mass production, marketing, and Americans' eating habits.

"I have an immigrant story," he said. "Most people come here for economic reasons, or religious reasons, or racial reasons, or gender reasons, or one of those things. I had a good job in Paris, but America was, and still is, the golden fleece. And I've done very well!"

While working for Howard Johnson, Pépin also earned an M.A. in French literature from Columbia University. In 1975, his first book, *Jacques Pépin: A French Chef Cooks at Home*, was published, followed by two of the most important cookbooks of the burgeoning gourmet revolution of the 1970s—*La Technique* (1976) and *La Méthode* (1979), in which he very clearly demonstrated how classic French cuisine could be made in the American kitchen. He followed with more than two dozen more books, including *Cuisine Économique* (1992), *The French Culinary Institute's Salute to Healthy Cooking*, with chefs Alain Sailhac, Andre Soltner, and Jacques Torres (1998), and *Fast Food My Way* (2004), as well as a memoir, *The Apprentice: My Life in the Kitchen* (2003).

Several of Pépin's books were tied to his award-winning PBS series, which began with *The Complete Pépin* (1997) and later the 1999 Emmy-winning show *Julia and Jacques Cooking at Home*, with Julia Child, who called Pépin "the best chef in America."

Pépin currently serves as dean of special programs at the French Culinary Institute and teaches an online class on French food culture for Boston University. He has won dozens of awards, including a Chevalier de l'Ordre des Arts et des Lettres (1997) and a Chevalier de l'Ordre du Mérite Agricole (1992); and the Légion d'honneur. He received an honorary doctorate of humane letters from Boston University in 2011.

PEPITA. A word for a pumpkinseed, borrowed from the Spanish. Pepitas are usually sold raw or toasted or fried and salted as a snack in the Southwest. Ground up, they are added to sauces for texture and flavor.

PEPPER. This word refers primarily to the peppercorn of the vine of the family Piperaceae, first domesticated in India and now used around the world as a seasoning, especially the peppercorn of the *Piper nigrum*, from which both black and white pepper are made. The word *pepper*, dating in English print to about 1300, is from the Greek *peperi*, ultimately from the Sanskrit *pippali*, "berry."

The distribution of pepper throughout the world was once fought over by several European countries that tried to monopolize the trade. For a while in the early nineteenth century, Salem, Massachusetts, was a dominant pepper-trading port of the Western Hemisphere, to which peppercorns from Sumatra were brought in the fast clipper ships developed in New England.

"Black pepper" is made from "peppercorn" berries that are picked prematurely, then dried. The major varieties of black pepper in the American market are Malabar (from the Malabar Coast), once called Alleppey, after a major shipping port; Tellicherry (Malabar); Lampong (Indonesia); Sarawak (Malaysia); Brazilian; and Ceylon.

"White pepper" is produced from mature peppercorns by removing the dark skin and using only the cores, which are then dried. "Decorticated" black pepper or decorticated white pepper is a form of white pepper made by removing the skin from dried black pepper. The major varieties of white pepper are Muntok (from Bangka, Indonesia), Brazilian, and Sarawak.

"Green peppercorns" are ripe peppercorns, mostly from Madagascar, used whole in cooking and in sauces, rather than ground.

The term "pepper" is also, erroneously, applied to a wide range of fruits from the plants of the *Capsicum* genus, including the **chile**, **cayenne**, **pimiento**, "sweet" red pepper (*C. frutescens*), and bell pepper (*C. grossum*). These last two are far milder than the rest and are often eaten as a vegetable because they have a sweet, rather than hot, flavor. In fact, the first mention of the "green pepper" in American print was as the "sweet pepper plant," in 1834. "Bell peppers," so called because of their bell-like shape, also have a sweet flavor and grow well in the southeastern U.S., and in the Midwest are called mangoes. Bell peppers have commonly come in red and green varieties, but the "golden bell pepper" was brought into the U.S. in 1981, by Moore Farming Inc., of Salinas, CA.

PEPPER POT. Also "Philadelphia pepper pot." A dish of tripe, pepper, and seasonings from the West Indies, dating in print to 1698. The dish is often associated with the severe winter deprivations of George Washington's ragged army in 1777–1778, when all the cook had to work with was tripe and pepper, later sold in the streets of Philadelphia by black women crying, "Peppery pot! Nice and hot! Makes backs strong, makes lives long!" As "Philadelphia pepper pot," the soup entered American print in 1932.

PHILADELPHIA PEPPER POT

Wash 3 lb. tripe thoroughly and bring to a boil in 4 qt. water. Cook on low heat for 6 hr., until tripe is soft, then allow to cool. Cut into small pieces. In another kettle place 1 ½ lb. veal knuckle, 3 sliced carrots, ½ c. chopped celery, 2 T. chopped parsley, 1 chopped onion, 1 t. each marjoram, bay leaf, summer savory, and basil, ½ t. thyme, ¾ t. whole black peppercorns, and 3 cloves. Cover with water and simmer for about 2 hr., until very tender. Strain, discard vegetables, cool, and skim fat from broth. Add tripe and 2 chopped potatoes. Simmer until potatoes are tender. Serves 6.

PEPPER STEAK. A dish of beef slices made with a sauce of onions, tomatoes, and green or red peppers. The French version, made with a peppercorn cream sauce, is called *steak au poivre*.

PEPPER STEAK

Dip 4 slices of chuck or pot roast beef in flour and sauté in 2 T. oil until browned. Add 2 T. oil, add 1 sliced onion, and cook with meat for 4 min. Add 4 chopped, peeled, and seeded tomatoes, 1 T. parsley, and salt and pepper to taste. In a separate pan in 2 T. oil, sauté 4 chopped green or red sweet peppers for 2 min. Add to meat pan. Toss and serve.

PERCH. Any of a variety of fish in the family Percidae. Perch are freshwater inhabitants, although their name is also applied offhandedly to some marine fish of the families Percichthyidae and Scorpaenidae. The name, dating in English print to 1381, goes back to the Greek *perké*. The main varieties of culinary interest in the U.S. are "yellow perch" (*Perca flavescens*); "white perch" (*Morone americana*), which is a temperate bass; and "ocean perch" (*Sebastes marinus*). U.S. commercial landings of ocean perch totaled 75.201 million pounds in 2010, valued at $13 million.

PERIWINKLE. Any of a variety of marine gastropod mollusks, like snails, first in American print in 1881.

PERRY. A pear **cider** made both still and sparkling. It is an ancient beverage in England, mentioned in print as of 1330, and was very popular throughout the thirteen colonies in America.

PERSIMMON (*Diospyros virginiana, D. texana*, and *D. kaki*). Also called "date plum." A tree chiefly of the tropics, bearing a late-ripening orange-red fruit. The word is from the Algonquian, akin to the Cree word for dried fruit, *pasiminan*, first appearing in print as "putchamin" in 1606, then in its present form in 1709. *D. texana*, which grows in Texas, is called the "black persimmon," "chapote," "Mexican persimmon," "mustang persimmon," and "possum plum."

The earliest explorers and colonists of the New World were fascinated by the persimmon. Hernando de Soto, in about 1540, compared it with the Spanish red plum and preferred the persimmon. John Smith, in Virginia at the beginning of the seventeenth century, called it "one of the most palatable fruits of this land," something like an apricot. Not every settler agreed, for before the fruit is wholly ripe, it is acidic and astringent to the taste; it achieves its succulent ripeness only late in the fall. The Native Americans made it into beer, which the colonists soon adapted, and bread, which in Missouri was called "stanica." In the November 1981 issue of *Cuisine* magazine, Meryle Evans wrote,

> *In 1863 Logan Martin, an enterprising young southern Indiana farmer, took a gallon bucket of native persimmons to market in nearby Louisville, Kentucky, where they sold so quickly that he decided on the spot to raise the fruit commercially. Every autumn, for over forty years, "Persimmon" Martin (as he came to be known) harvested and packed up over two thousand gallons for shipment by railroad from his hometown of Borden to city markets as far away as New York.*

Today, near Martin's hometown, the people of Indiana hold an annual persimmon festival the last week of September.

The native "American persimmon" was eventually pushed aside as a commercial crop in favor of the "Japanese persimmon" (*D. kaki*), which may have been introduced to the U.S. in 1855 by Commodore Matthew C. Perry. There are now about two hundred species of persimmon. Almost the entire crop comes from California.

In the South, persimmon seeds are ground to be used as a coffee substitute, and throughout the Southeast and the Midwest persimmon pudding is a Thanksgiving tradition. "Locust beer" is made from persimmons and locust pods.

PETITE SIRAH. Also "petite syrah." A red vinifera grape planted in California, first mentioned in print in 1872. The true identity of this grape has not yet been discovered, though some believe it derives from the Durif variety of the Rhône Valley, in southern France. Used both in blending wines and as a varietal, the petite sirah has an intense, spicy aroma and a range of colors from light to deep red.

Increased interest in the varietal began in the 1980s, and it is now principally grown in Paso Robles, Napa Valley, Lodi, and Dry Creek Valley, California.

PETTICOAT TAILS. A shortbread cookie of Louisiana brought to America by Scottish immigrants. The term dates from the French-influenced court of Mary Stuart (1542–1587), where the cookies were known as *petits gâtels* or *qâstels*, which later became *petits gâteaux*, "little cakes." The Scottish dialect transformed that sound into "petticoat tails," and the cookie is now made with scalloped edges that seem to resemble petticoat edges.

PFEFFERNUSS. A Pennsylvania Dutch small, hard spice cookie. The word in German means "peppernut," first in American print in 1920.

PHEASANT. Any of a variety of game birds in the family Phasianidae, with characteristic long tails and colored plumage. Pheasants are native to the Old World, and there is some confusion in American terminology for the birds. The common term, "pheasant," is from the Greek *phasianos*, referring to the bird of the Phasis River, in the Caucasus, and is dated circa 1299. In America, however, "pheasant" was applied by the early colonists to wholly different species, first in print as of 1625, especially the "ruffed grouse" (*Bonasa umbellus*), in print as of 1758. The Old World pheasant, specifically the "ring-necked pheasant" (*Phasianus colchicus*), also called the "English pheasant," was introduced from Europe and Asia, perhaps in the eighteenth century, but definitely by the nineteenth. L. Patrick Coyle Jr., in *The World Encyclopedia of Food* (1982), writes that "George Washington imported pheasants from Europe in 1789 to stock his Mt. Vernon estate…[and] by the 1830s it was common enough to figure in cookbooks of the period." Waverley Root, in *Food* (1980), noted that Thomas Jefferson once proposed to raise French pheasants in Virginia, but it is not known whether he succeeded. The usual date given for the introduction of the pheasant to America is 1881, when an American consul brought Shanghai pheasants home to his Oregon farm. Whenever the pheasant arrived in the U.S., it proliferated so successfully that now it is found in more than thirty states.

The bird is usually roasted, and it can be bought frozen.

PHILADELPHIA EGGS. A dish described by Oscar Tschirky, in *The Cook Book by "Oscar of the Waldorf"* (1896), as two split muffins topped with cooked white chicken meat, poached eggs, and hollandaise sauce.

PHILADELPHIA STICKY BUN. A yeast bun flavored with cinnamon and brown sugar. In Philadelphia these sweet rolls are called "cinnamon buns." "Sticky bun" alone first appeared in print in 1909. See **sticky bun** for recipe.

PHILLY CHEESESTEAK. Also "Philadelphia cheesesteak." A sandwich made with thin slices of beef topped with liquid cheese and other condiments and served on a crisp Italian-style roll. It is a specialty of Philadelphia. Its origins have never been satisfactorily explained, although Pat and Harry Olivieri, of Pat's King of Steaks, claim to have created the item in 1930 (although Pat Olivieri said he added the cheese only in 1948). An order for "cheese with" means the dish should be made with sautéed onions. The cheese is usually, though not always, American, sometimes squirted from a plastic canister, usually Cheez Whiz.

PHILADELPHIA CHEESESTEAK

Slice several pieces of rare beef very thin and sauté quickly on a griddle. Place thin slices of cheese on top of meat to melt, place on Italian-style roll, and add ketchup, if desired.

PHILPY. A South Carolina rice bread. The name is of obscure origins.

PHILPY

To ½ c. flour add ½ c. milk and ½ t. salt. Mash ¾ c. cooked rice and add to flour mixture with 2 t. melted butter and 1 beaten egg. Pour into buttered 8-in. layer pan and bake for 45 min. at 450°. Cut into 6 wedges.

PHOSPHORIC ACID. An acidifier and flavor enhancer used in soft drinks.

PICADILLO. A mincemeat stew of Latin America whose name is taken from the Spanish word for "hash." The word dates in print to 1877.

PICADILLO

Cook ½ lb. ground beef and ½ lb. ground pork, 1 minced onion, 1 c. canned tomatoes, 2 minced cloves of garlic, 1 T. vinegar, salt, pepper, 1 t. ground cinnamon cloves, ¼ t. ground cumin, 1 bay leaf, ½ c. seedless raisins, and ½ c. almonds. Add water if necessary to give a stew-like texture.

PICKLE. A food that has been preserved in a brine solution that has been flavored with herbs and seasonings. First mentioned in print in 1440, as a spicy sauce, in America the word most often refers specifically to a cucumber preserved in this way, though fish and many other foods may be pickled. Vinegar is most often the ingredient that defines the flavor of such items.

The word may derive from a Dutch fisherman named William Beukelz (died 1437), who is credited with inventing the pickling process. It was used in England as early as 1440 (*pekille* in Middle English), and by the eighteenth century any preserved food item could be called a "pickle." In America, pickled food became the product most associated with Henry J. Heinz, who put up fifty-seven varieties for sale to groceries around Sharpsburg, Pennsylvania, beginning in 1869. Breaded, fried dill-pickle slices are a Mississippi specialty.

There are numerous varieties of cucumber pickles, including these main varieties in the U.S.: "dill pickles," flavored with dill leaves and seed heads; "kosher pickles," flavored with garlic; "overnight pickles," fermented for only two or three days; "sour pickles," fermented in a sour brine; "sour mixed pickles," cut into chunks and mixed with other vegetables like onion, cauliflower, carrots, and peppers; "sour relish pickles," also called "piccalilli," made by finely chopping sour pickles with other vegetables; **chow-chow**; "sweet pickles," sugared as well as soaked in brine; "sweet mixed pickles," with other vegetables; "gherkins," miniature pickles used mainly as a garnish; "candied dills," sticks, chips, or strips of dill pickles packed in an extra-sweet solution; and "sliced sweet pickles" (also called "cross-cuts"), cut crosswise in chips, which include "bread and butter pickles." "Ice-water pickles" or "cold water pickles" are initially treated with ice water.

"Fresh-packed pickles" are not cured by fermentation, but pasteurized and sealed in containers, although some cured pickles are also processed this way.

Americans eat about nine pounds of pickles per person annually.

"Pickled peppers" are made with **chile** peppers much the same way as cucumber pickles. The most popular pickled peppers include jalapeños, cherry peppers, and banana peppers. Piccalilli is a pickle condiment of chopped vegetables and spices. The word, as "Paco-Lilla," dates in print to 1758.

PICCALILLI

Chop 4 qt. green tomatoes, add salt to cover, and drain. Chop ¼ head of cabbage, 3 medium onions, and 3 green peppers and blend. Add 1 t. turmeric, 1 oz. mustard seed, 5 stalks celery, 1 c. brown sugar, and ½ oz. allspice. Cover with cider vinegar and cook for about 30 min. Put up in jars and seal.

PICKLED PORK. Also "sweet pickled pork." A Louisiana specialty made from pork shoulder marinated in brine. It used to be made at home by a lengthy, arduous process extending over two weeks, but today it is prepackaged and sold in markets. It is considered an important ingredient in making red beans and rice. The following recipe is from John Thorne's booklet *Rice & Beans: The Itinerary of a Recipe* (1981).

PICKLED PORK

Combine ½ c. mustard seeds, 1 T. celery, 1 dried hot pepper (or 2 T. chile caribe powder or 2 T. Tabasco sauce), 1 qt. distilled white vinegar, 1 bay leaf, 1 T. kosher salt, 12 peppercorns, and 6 cloves garlic that have been peeled and flattened but left whole. Boil for 3 min. Let cool. Place ½ lb. boneless pork butt cut into 2-in. cubes (or 2 ½–3 lb. country-style spareribs individually cut) into pickling solution, stirring to remove all air bubbles. Completely submerge meat and refrigerate for 3 days, stirring occasionally.

PICNIC. A meal taken out of doors and away from home, often without benefit of tables, chairs, or other amenities. The word is borrowed from the French *piquenique*, meaning much the same thing, and entered the English language in about 1748. In America, picnickers usually pack a basket or hamper of cold foods, **sandwiches**, and cans or thermos bottles of beverages. Some people go to picnic areas specifically set up with outdoor tables in rural settings. A "**tailgate picnic**" refers to a party held at a sports event, usually in the parking lot, where foods are served from the drop-down rear door of a station wagon or van. "Picnic" can also refer to a large bottle of beer, suitable for bringing on a picnic, first in American print in 1969.

PICNIC HAM. Also called "California ham." A shoulder cut of **ham**, so called in print since 1890. The meat is sometimes also referred to as "**cala**."

PIE. Any of a wide variety of desserts or savories baked in a pastry crust. The word is from Middle English and dates in print to 1301. Pie fillings are made from fruits, vegetables, custards, fish, and meats. Some of the most popular American fruit pies include apple, blueberry, peach, and cherry. Common custard varieties include "custard pie," "banana cream pie," "**chess pie**," and "buttermilk pie." "Pumpkin pie" is particularly popular in autumn and winter, especially at Halloween and Thanksgiving. "Key lime pie" (see **lime**) is a Florida specialty, and "**Mississippi mud pie**" is best known in the South. "**Mock apple pie**" is actually made with **Ritz** crackers.

American meat pies are better known as **potpies** (first in print about 1785), the most popular being filled with chicken or beef and vegetables. "Hartley's Pork Pie" is a specialty of Fall River, Massachusetts, created by Thomas Hartley. According to an article in *Yankee* magazine in 1988, the pork pies of that region were sometimes called "jickey wedding cakes" ("jickey" being a slur against lower-class English immigrants), but Hartley's became locally famous. According to Hartley's grandson Harold, the original recipe was sold to Don Setters, who owned a pastry shop in Somerset, Massachusetts.

PIE CARD. A union card used since the turn of the twentieth century by loggers to obtain lodging or a meal.

PIEROGI. Also "pirogue." A boiled or baked stuffed dumpling. Of Eastern European origins, the word is Polish, first in American print in 1848. Polish versions are usually boiled.

PIE WASHER. Bakers' term for the worker who paints the top crust of pastry with a wash of water, milk, or egg to give the finished baked item a glossy look.

PIGEON. Any of a wide variety of birds in the family Columbidae. The word is from Latin *pipion*, entering English print in 1375. There are at least three hundred species, a half-dozen of which are found in North American skies, including the "mourning dove" (*Zenaida macroura*), also called the "turtledove," and the "common ground dove" (*Columbina passerina*), but none is of much culinary interest to most Americans, who regard pigeons as anything from a pet to an urban nuisance. At one time, however, the native "passenger pigeon" (*Ectopistes migratorius*) was highly esteemed as a game bird, and it might have been the most numerous bird on earth, with an estimated population of nine billion at its height. Almost immediately upon their arrival in the New World, European colonists hunted the passenger pigeon enthusiastically, and wholesale slaughter of the flocks continued unabated until well into the nineteenth century, when a shotgun could bring down a hundred of the birds in one burst. By 1900, however, only one wild bird was found, and the last passenger pigeon died in a Cincinnati zoo in 1914.

Today, only young pigeons less than four weeks old, called "squabs," are of much culinary interest. They are raised on farms, mostly for consumption in restaurants.

PIG IN A BLANKET. A small frankfurter wrapped in pastry, usually served as a canapé, first in American print in the 1960s. The term also refers to a Pennsylvania Dutch dish of boiled potatoes wrapped in dough and boiled in a broth, first in American print in 1935. See also **corn dog**.

PIG OUT. As a verb, a slang term from the 1970s meaning "overeat," usually without much discrimination. A "pig-out" refers to a binge of eating.

PIGS' EARS. Although this term may refer to a dish of pigs' ears, rarely served in the U.S., it is more often used to describe a fried pastry popular in Louisiana, called by the French name **les oreilles de cochons**, especially by Cajun cooks.

PIGS' EARS

Combine 2 c. flour, 1 t. baking powder, and ½ t. salt. Beat ½ c. cooled melted butter into 2 beaten eggs, stir into flour mixture, divide into 2 doz. balls, and roll out to 6-in. diameter. Deep-fry in hot oil. When the pastry rises to the surface of the oil, pierce center with a fork and turn pastry. Fry until golden brown, drain. Cook 1 ½ c. cane syrup to 230° on a candy thermometer, drizzle over pastries, and sprinkle with chopped pecans. Makes 24.

PIKE. Any of a variety of freshwater fish in the genus *Esox*, five species of which are found in North America. The name is from Middle English, possibly referring to the spiked appearance of the fish, dating in print to 1314. The pike has never been a popular eating fish in America, although it is highly praised by gastronomes as a fine food fish and is traditionally made into quenelles in French kitchens.

The main species in America include the "northern pike" (*E. lucius*) and the "muskellunge" (*E. masquinongy*), whose name derives from the Algonquian *maskinonge*, "big pike," and is often called "muskie" for short.

PIKI BREAD. Also "paper bread." A very thin **Native American** cornmeal bread baked on a griddle and rolled up. It is of Hopi origins but has been adapted by various pueblos and goes by other names such as *hewe* (Zuni) and *mowa* (Tewa). Blue cornmeal and ash can give the bread a purple-gray color. Often piki is flavored or colored. According to Carolyn Niethammer, in *American Indian Food and Lore* (1974), piki-bread making was considered an art and a ritual, now fading, but "years ago a young woman was required to demonstrate that she had mastered the art of piki-baking before she was considered a suitable bride."

Piki bread is made on a "piki stone" heated by a fire from cedar or juniper wood. Piki is made with a little ash left over from the burning of green plants such as bean vines, corncobs, or juniper.

PIKI BREAD

In a bowl mix 3 T. ash (or 1 T. baking soda) with about ½ c. cold water. In another bowl mix 4 c. blue cornmeal with 4 c. boiling water until well blended. Add 4 more c. boiling water and blend to make a thick dough. Strain the ash water through cheesecloth and blend into dough. Knead for a few minutes, then set aside to rest for about 10 min. Gradually add 4 c. cold water to make a creamlike batter. Grease a griddle, then brush on batter to make a thin film on the griddle. Cook for about 1 min., remove from griddle, and set aside. Spread another film of batter on the griddle. When it is dry, fold the first piki in thirds, and then roll into a cylinder. Continue to use all the batter this way to make about 50 piki.

PILAU. Also "plaw," "pilaw," "pilaf," "pilaff," and "purloo." Any of a variety of steamed-rice dishes made of meat, chicken, fish, or vegetables in a broth.

The word comes from Persian *pilāw* and dates in English print to 1609. The dish is known in numerous versions throughout the Middle East: The Greeks made *pilafi* with tomatoes, the Iraqis make a lentil version called *mejedrah*, the Iranians an apricot version called *geisi pelo*, the Poles cook *pilaw turecki*, and the dish found its way to France under the name *pilaff de crevettes*, made with shrimp.

By the eighteenth century it seems to have taken hold in Britain, especially after the empire spread through the Middle East and into India. In America the dish became popular in the South because of the influence of the spice trade and the rice crop, and in Louisiana the French culinary influence was felt so strongly as to make *pilou français* or *pilaff de volaille* local delectables. Greek Americans adapted their native dish to *pilafi tou fournou*, baked in an oven. Most pilaus use a touch of curry powder, though the Louisiana versions more often do not. Marjorie Kinnan Rawlings, in *Cross Creek Cookery* (1942), called pilau "almost a sacred Florida dish....A Florida church supper is unheard of without it." The word *pilau* is pronounced in a variety of ways, as in "*per*-to," "*pee*-laf," or per-*lo*."

PILAU

In a Dutch oven, cover 2 ½ lb. chicken with water, add salt and pepper, bring to a boil, and simmer, covered, for ½ hr. Remove, cool, and cut chicken meat into strips about 3 in. long. To 3 c. of the cooking liquid add 1 t. curry powder,

½ t. parsley, 2 T. butter, and 1 c. raw rice. Bring to a boil, lower heat, cook 10 min., add chicken, and cook 10 min. more.

PILCHER. Also "menhaden," "pogy," and many other names. An Atlantic fish, *Brevoortia tyrannus*, first in American print in 1637.

PILGRIM. Also "Puritan" and "gobble." A New England sandwich made with roast turkey, cranberry sauce and stuffing on a roll with gravy, although cheese and other ingredients are also used. The name commemorates the Pilgrim (or Puritan) settlers who came to Massachusetts in 1620 and the Thanksgiving holiday they helped initiate. The contents of the sandwich, particularly the stuffing from a turkey, suggest it was made from Thanksgiving dinner leftovers, but it is now served year round in New England eateries.

PILOT PELLETS. Airline workers' slang for the peanuts served on board, so called because pilots eat so many of them. The term first appeared in print in 1990.

PIÑA COLADA. A cocktail made from light rum, coconut cream, and pineapple juice. It is especially popular during warm weather with boating enthusiasts and at southern resort areas. The term is Spanish for "strained pineapple." The term "piña colado" was first printed in 1920, apparently referring to some kind of pineapple cocktail, but the cocktail made with coconut cream seems to have originated at the Caribe Hilton Hotel, in San Juan, Puerto Rico. Back in 1952, bartender Ramón Monchito Marrero Pérez was introduced to a new product called Coco López cream of coconut (containing coconut, sugar, water, polysorbate 60, sorbitan monostearate, salt, propylene glycol alginate, mono- and diglycerides, citric acid, guar gum, and locust-bean gum). On August 15, 1954, after three months of trying out various liquors with the product, Marrero mixed pineapple juice and light rum with it, blended the mixture with crushed ice, and came up with a sweet, creamy drink that did not really catch on until later in 1954, when it was served to a group of government officials at a convention there.

Another Puerto Rican claimed to have invented the piña colada in 1963, at the bar called La Barrachina,

in San Juan's Old City, where there still hangs a plaque that announces "The House Where in 1963 THE PIÑA COLADA Was Created by Don Ramón Portas Mingot." But Mr. Marrero's 1952 claim seems clearly more authoritative, so the recipe that follows is his original.

PIÑA COLADA

Pour 2 oz. Bacardi light rum, 1 oz. coconut cream, 1 oz. heavy cream, and 6 oz. unsweetened pineapple juice into a blender with a cup of crushed ice. Blend for about 15 sec. and serve in a large glass with a garnish of pineapple stick and maraschino cherry. (An almost identical drink, the Bahia, invented at Trader Vic's restaurant, in San Francisco, substitutes 1 oz. white Jamaican rum and 1 oz. light Puerto Rican rum for the Bacardi in this recipe.)

PINEAPPLE (*Ananas comosus*). A tropical plant bearing a large, ovular fruit with spiny skin and swordlike leaves. The word derives from its appearance, which resembles a pinecone, and its first appearance in print, circa 1390, actually referred to a real pinecone. Not until 1624 did the fruit known by this name enter the printed language.

The pineapple is native to America and was first discovered by Christopher Columbus on the island of Guadeloupe in 1493 and called by him *"piña de Indes,"* "pine of the Indians." Indians of Paraguay and Brazil, especially the Guarani tribe, had domesticated the plant and called it *naná* ("excellent fruit"), from which the Latin term for the pineapple derived.

In 1519, Ferdinand Magellan found the pineapple in Brazil, and by 1555 the fruit was being exported from that country to England. It was also widely dispersed throughout Asia's tropics, growing in abundance in India by 1583, and the Spanish might have planted it in Hawaii by 1827. The fruit proliferated in the West Indies, where, in Barbados in 1751, George Washington tasted and preferred it to any other tropical fruit.

The pineapple was introduced to Hawaii by Captain James Cook in 1790, but it was not commercially cultivated there at first, because of the difficulty of shipping between the islands and the mainland. In 1794, a Spanish horticulturist named Francisco de Paula Marín became an adviser to King Kamehameha I and began experiments with pineapple cultivation in the early

1800s. Throughout the nineteenth century the fruit was a rarity for most Americans, even though it was grown in Florida. In the 1880s, however, widespread cultivation was encouraged in Hawaii with the onset of the steamship trade in the Pacific, and Captain John Kidwell began crop development trials in 1885 on Oahu. In 1900, James Drummond purchased sixty-one acres in Wahiawa, on Oahu, incorporating the Hawaiian Pineapple Co. for commercial production and earning the nickname "Pineapple King." He also bought the island of Lanai in 1922, to build what became the largest pineapple plantation in the world, with twenty thousand pineapple-producing acres and more than a thousand pineapple workers and their families.

By the middle of the twentieth century there were eight pineapple companies in Hawaii, employing more than three thousand people, making it Hawaii's second-largest industry, after sugarcane. By 1990 tourism was far more profitable than pineapple farming, and by the twenty-first century, Hawaii's world market share had shrunk to just 2 percent. In 2008, Del Monte Foods Co. ceased growing pineapple in Hawaii. The top producer is Thailand, with 13 percent of the market.

Pineapple also comes into the U.S. from Honduras, Mexico, the Dominican Republic, and Costa Rica. The most popular variety there is the "Smooth Cayenne," followed by the "Red Spanish." Americans eat pineapple fresh, as part of a salad or fruit cocktail, in sherbets, ice cream, and ices, in gelatin, in cocktails, and as a flavoring, including in cordials. Canned varieties include sliced rings, chunks, and crushed pieces. Pineapple juice is extremely popular and often used in mixed drinks like the **mai tai** and the **piña colada**. Dishes made with pineapple are often called "Hawaiian style."

PINE NUT. Also "piñon," "pignoli," "pignotia," and "piñolos." Any of several pine tree nuts of the Southwest, especially *Pinus monophylla*, *P. edulis*, and *P. cembroides*. Pine nuts constitute the largest uncultivated crop in North America, harvested solely from wild trees. About three to five million pounds are harvested each year in the Southwest and Mexico. The word appeared in Middle English in the mid-fifteenth century.

Pine nuts are eaten raw or toasted, and used in soups, sauces, salads, and even candies.

PINK LADY. A cocktail, probably dating from the Prohibition era, dating in print to 1929, with a recipe given in *The Savoy Cocktail Book* (1930), made by mixing one part grenadine, two parts lemon or lime juice, two parts apple brandy, four parts gin, and one egg white. Some recipes add cream.

PINK SAUCE. A pink-colored sauce served with shrimp and dating probably from the 1950s.

PINK SAUCE

Blend ¾ c. mayonnaise, 1 c. ketchup, 1 t. horseradish, ¼ t. salt, 1 chopped onion, ¼ t. garlic, ¼ t. confectioners' sugar, ½ t. Worcestershire sauce, ¼ t. Tabasco, ½ t. paprika, and pepper to taste.

PINOLE. Dried, ground, spiced, and sweetened corn used in the Southwest, sometimes pronounced "panola." The term is Spanish American, from Nahuatl *pinolli*, and has been used north of Mexico, in print since 1648.

PINOT NOIR. A red vinifera grape that makes an intense, rich, tannic **wine** and is also used to make champagne. The word is from French, "black vine," dating in English print to 1854. It is the principal grape used in France's burgundies and in recent years has become an important grape in premium wines of California and the Northwest.

The first documented evidence of pinot noir planting in California was in the 1960s, around the Russian River, by Charles Bacigalupi and Joseph Rochioli. In 1965, Charles Coury and David Lett planted pinot noir in Oregon's Willamette Valley, where it is now the state's most widely planted varietal. Interest in and sales of pinot noir jumped 18 percent in less than a year after the success of a film entitled *Sideways* (2004), whose main character searches Santa Barbara County for the best examples of the wine. Today there are about twenty thousand pinot noir acres planted in California, with 147,732 tons of grapes crushed in 2010. There are more than ten thousand more acres planted across the U.S., including in New York's Finger Lakes region.

PINWHEEL. Any of a wide variety of snacks or canapés cut from a stuffed or layered roll of bread or pastry into thick rounds whose centers form a pinwheel shape.

PIPIKAULA. A Hawaiian dish made of beef jerky and soy sauce. The word is Hawaiian for "beef strong," because the meat was once dried in the sun by tying it with string and hanging it on a clothesline. Today, after curing with ingredients like honey, garlic, and kimchi, it is dried in the oven.

PISTACHIO (*Pistacia vera*). A tree, native to Asia Minor, that bears green nuts within a pod that is often dyed a bright pinkish red for commercial purposes. The first commercial crop in California was grown in 1976 in the San Joaquin Valley, and today the U.S. is the second-largest producer of pistachios in the world. Pistachios are eaten as a snack or, very often, used as a flavoring for ice cream, the first example of which was created by confectioner James W. Parkinson, of Philadelphia, in about 1840.

English use of the word, dating back to Latin *pistacium*, was in print circa 1440.

The dyeing of pistachios is not a Middle Eastern tradition but is said to have originated with a Brooklyn street vendor named Zaloom, who colored his pistachios red to distinguish them from his competitors'. The idea caught on—especially in the East—to the extent that most pistachios used to be dyed red. This is no longer true, with only about 15 percent of those sold today so colored.

PITA. A round, flat bread easily slit open to form a pocket that may hold everything from chicken salad to chili con carne to bean sprouts to cheese. The term possibly derives from medieval Greek, dating in English print to 1936. Its origins are in the Middle East, and it was first served in America in Greek, Turkish, Armenian, and other small restaurants. Pita became popular in the 1960s and 1970s as an ethnic bread, especially in the Greek sandwich called a **gyro**, whereas today it is easily found in groceries throughout the country.

PIZZA. Also "pizza pie" and "tomato pie." A flat pie made from a yeast dough topped with various cheeses, vegetables, meats, seasonings, and other ingredients. It is one of the most popular of all American meals and snacks, and it is made in restaurants called "pizzerias," sold frozen in groceries, or, occasionally, made at home.

Contrary to some assertions, the pizza is not an American creation, but its acceptance in this country has made it a far more widespread food item here than in its country of origin, Italy. The American promotion of pizza has resulted in its becoming an international favorite, from Tuscaloosa to Tokyo.

The word *pizza* is clouded in some ambiguity, but some believe it derives from an Old Italian word meaning "a point," which in turn led to the Italian word *pizzicare*, meaning "to pinch" or "pluck" from the oven. The word showed up for the first time in a Neapolitan dialect word—*picea* or *piza*—in about A.D. 1000, referring perhaps to the manner in which the hot pie is plucked from the oven, and by 1531 as *pizza*. In English, the word dates in print to 1598, as a "kind of cake or simnell or wafer."

Pizza has obvious analogues in Middle Eastern pita breads, and flat, seasoned yeast breads are known in many parts of the world (for example, Indian *naan*, Moroccan *khboz bishemar*, and Armenian *lahma bi ajeen*), but it is useless to argue direct linkage to any such breads, because pizza is merely an elaboration of all these variants. The fact is that the pizza as we know it today could not have existed before the sixteenth century, when the tomato was brought to Italy from South America. Although the tomato was held in low esteem by most Europeans, the poor people of Naples, subsisting quite literally on their daily bread, added the new ingredient to their yeast dough and thus created the first simple pizza, which by the seventeenth century had achieved a local notoriety among visitors, who would go to the poor section to taste this peasant dish made by men called *pizzaioli*. By the next century pizza was known only as a curiosity outside of Naples (whose first pizzeria opened in 1830), and it was not until the nineteenth century that mozzarella cheese (usually made from buffalo milk) became a standard ingredient. Legend has it that Neapolitan *pizzaiolo* Raffaele Esposito, of the Pizzeria di Pietro, was the first to make a pie with tomato, basil, and mozzarella (the colors of the Italian flag), to honor the visit of Queen Margherita, consort of King Umberto I, to Naples in 1889. This was thereafter called *pizza alla Margherita* and became very popular in that city.

But the pizza remained a local delicacy until the concept crossed the Atlantic in the memories of immigrants from Naples who settled in the cities along the Eastern Seaboard, especially in NYC. The ingredients these immigrants found in their new country differed from those in the old: In New York there was no buffalo-milk mozzarella, so cow's-milk mozzarella was used; oregano, a staple southern Italian herb, was replaced in America by sweet marjoram; and American tomatoes, flour, even water, were different. Here the pizza evolved into a large, wheel-like pie, perhaps eighteen inches or more in diameter, reflecting the abundance of the new country.

These first American pizzas may have been made at home, but the baker's brick oven, preferably fueled with wood or coal, was (and still is) essential to making a true pizza, with its crispy crust, soft, breadlike middle, quickly seared topping, and bubbling cheese. The first record of a pizzeria in NYC was Lombardi's, opened by Gennaro Lombardi in 1905 on Spring Street, but others quickly followed in the Italian communities around the city. Still, pizza and pizzerias and, later, "pizza parlors" were little known outside the large cities of the East until after World War II, when returning American GI's brought back a taste for the pizzas they had had in Naples along with the assumption that pizza, like spaghetti and meatballs, was a typical Italian dish, instead of a regional one.

Cookbooks of the early twentieth century containing recipes for Italian dishes do not list pizza, but by the 1950s the dish could be found in American collections as popular as *Ford's Treasury of Favorite Recipes from Famous Eating Places* (1954). In non-Italian communities in eastern states, pizza is often referred to as a "tomato pie," while the colloquial abbreviation "za" is particularly common among young people throughout the U.S.

Along with hamburger and hot dog stands, the pizzeria became a fixture in many American cities and, later, part of commercial chains that expanded throughout the country in the 1960s and 1970s. National pizzeria chains became most prevalent in the Midwest: Pizza Hut (1958), which started in Wichita, Kansas; Domino's (1960), in Ypsilanti, Michigan; Little Caesars (1959), in Garden City, Michigan; and Godfather's Pizza (1973), in Omaha, Nebraska, all opened by non-Italian Americans.

The first frozen pizza was marketed by the Celentano Brothers in 1957. "Deep-dish pizza" or "Chicago-style pizza," created in 1943 by Ike Sewell and Ric Riccardo, at the Pizzeria Uno in that city, is made with an inch-thick crust and cooked in a heavy skillet or pan; also called "pan pizza" and "thick crust pizza," it now accounts for 22 percent of total pizza orders. The claim for the invention, in January 1974, of the tartlike "stuffed pizza," with fillings of cheese, meats, vegetables, or other combinations of ingredients, topped with an extra crust, is made by Nancy's Pizza, of Chicago, whose owners, Nancy and Rocco Palese, based the idea on an Italian Easter cake called *scarciedda*. "Sicilian-style" pizza is usually cut into rectangles and has a thicker crust than standard, thin-crusted pizza, which is often called "Neapolitan-style." This standard pizza, cut into six or eight wedges, is usually made for more than one person and may be topped with ingredients as various as cheese and herbs, anchovies, onions, mushrooms, sausage, pepperoni, small meatballs, mussels, and many others, in any combination. A "plain" or "cheese pie" is the standard mozzarella-and-tomato-sauce pizza. A "white pizza" is topped with mozzarella (sometimes with broccoli underneath) and not sauced. "Grilled pizzas," cooked directly over an open grill, were developed by Johanne Killeen and George Germon, owners of Al Forno restaurant, in Providence, Rhode Island, in 1981, after seeing such a technique in Italy. "Designer" or "gourmet" pizzas were developed in California (they are sometimes called "California pizzas"), with unusual and exotic toppings that might include goat's cheese, lamb sausage, smoked salmon, or even caviar. A "bar pie" is a thin-crusted pizza, a name legally registered in 1992 by Joseph DiVittorio, of Eddie's Pizza, in New Hyde Park, New York.

The first commercial pizza-pie mix was produced in 1948 in Worcester, Massachusetts, by Frank A. Fiorello, who called it "Roman Pizza Mix." Often pizza is ordered by the slice, which may be folded in half and held in the hand or cut up with a knife and fork on a plate. (In Italy, pizza is usually served on a plate as an individual portion to be eaten with knife and fork.) By 2012 pizza accounted for 10 percent of all food sales. Today there are seventy thousand pizzerias in the U.S., most independently owned, about 80 percent of them offering delivery. The company Domino's Pizza is the world leader in delivery, with $1 billion in sales.

Today 41 percent of Americans eat pizza at least once a week, 94 percent regularly. Americans' per capita consumption of pizza is twenty-three pounds—about ten pizzas or forty-six slices per year. Of all toppings besides cheese, 36 percent are with pepperoni, followed by sausage and mushrooms. The U.S. pizza industry takes in annual revenues of $32 billion, selling three billion pizzas. The biggest pizza-consuming day is Super Bowl Sunday, in February. October is National Pizza Month.

The world's largest pizza was cooked by Lorenzo Amato, owner of Café di Lorenzo, in Tallahassee, Florida, in 1991; it was ten thousand square feet.

In 2012, a pizza museum opened on the premises of Pizza Brain restaurant, in Philadelphia.

PIZZA

Dissolve 1 pkg. yeast in ⅓ c. lukewarm water and let stand for 10 min. In a bowl mix 3 c. flour with 1 t. salt. Add the yeast mixture, blend, then add ⅔ c. lukewarm water to make a pliable, elastic dough. Form into a ball, cover with a clean cloth, and let rise until doubled in a warm place. Meanwhile, fry 2 cloves of garlic in 3 T. olive oil, add 1 ½ cans of Italian tomatoes, 1 t. salt, ¼ t. pepper, and ¼ t. oregano. Cook for about 20 min., until tomatoes have broken down and thickened. Roll out the dough onto a flat pan, spread tomato sauce over the top, then add 1 lb. chopped mozzarella cheese. Bake at 450° for about 20 min., until crust is crisp and cheese is melted. To brown cheese, quickly place pizza under broiler flame.

PIZZA STRIP. A strip of thick dough topped with tomato sauce and Parmesan cheese. Pizza strips are usually bought in Italian bakeries in New England, especially Rhode Island, and are eaten hot or cold.

PLACEBO BOTTLE. Bartender's slang for liquor bottles filled with water and consumed by the bartender when someone insists on buying him a drink. The word *placebo* (from Latin) refers to the medical use of a pill or other substance given to a patient to satisfy a supposed need for medication. The slang term first saw print in 1991.

PLANTAIN. A variety of banana plant (*Musa paradisiaca*), especially popular among Latin Americans. It is starchier and firmer than the banana enjoyed in North America, and must be ripened and then cooked. The word, dating in English print to 1582, is from Spanish *plantano*.

PLATE LUNCH. In Hawaii, a plate lunch usually consists of two scoops of rice, a macaroni-and-potato salad, and various kinds of meat or fish cooked in an Asian style, such as Korean barbecued ribs, *shoyu* chicken, or beef *teriyaki*, as well as Filipino-style *adobo*. It is commonly sold from lunch wagons parked at the beach or near office buildings.

PLUM. Any of a variety of shrubs or trees in the genus *Prunus*, bearing a smooth-skinned red, yellow, or purple fruit with a soft, pulpy flesh. The word is from Old English *plume*, ultimately from Latin *prunum*. The word in Latin once probably referred specifically to the fruit, but later, many varieties in the genus were differentiated by various names, of which "plum" was one. The word dates in print to about 1425. There are hundreds of varieties of plum today, but those of culinary interest in the U.S. include the "European plum" (*P. domestica*), brought to America in colonial times; the "native American plum" (*P. americana*); the "damson" (*P. damascena*), originally imported by the Romans from Damascus in about the first century A.D.; and the "Japanese" (*P. salicina* or *triflora*), brought to the U.S. in 1870. Other varieties introduced from other countries include the "sloe" or "blackthorn" (*P. spinosa*), the "bullace" (*P. instituta*), the "gage" (*P. italica*), and the "cherry" (*P. cerasifera*). Other main species native to North America include the "Canada" (*P. nigra*), the "Chickasaw" (*P. angustifolia*), the "Allegheny" or "American sloe" (*P. alleghaniensis*), and the "beach plum" (*P. maritima*), this last being found in New England and most often made into jams and jellies.

Principal hybrids include the "Italian prune," "Stanley," "Burbank," "Underwood," "Monitor," and many others.

Plums are usually eaten fresh. The traditional Anglo-American plum pudding (see **pudding**) contains no plums.

A "prune" is a plum that has been dried either in the sun or by artificial heat. The word *prune* comes from the Greek *proumnon*, which became in Middle English *prouynen*.

PO'BOY. Also "poor boy." A sandwich made from French bread loaves split in half and filled with a variety of ingredients like ham, beef, cheese, oysters, tomatoes, and gravy. Similar to a **hero**, they are a specialty of New Orleans, where they were originally called "push" sandwiches because the meat was pushed along the length of bread to save the best part for last. The po'boy was created in the 1920s by Benny and Clovis Martin, owners of Martin Brothers Grocery, who served the sandwich to striking streetcar workers free of charge (other sources say for fifteen cents) until the strike ended. They used up more than a thousand loaves of bread in one day. Another story says that the term is related to the French for a gratuity, *"pourboire."* Nonetheless, the term "poor boy" for a sandwich goes back to 1875. An "oyster loaf" (1893) is a form of po'boy made with oysters. "Poor-boy sandwich" dates to 1931.

POCKET SOUP. Also "cake soup." A soup that was boiled down into a jellylike mass that could be put in a pouch and later reconstituted with hot water. A recipe in the *Lady's Companion* of 1753 calls for boiling a leg of veal until the liquid in the pot thickens to a jellied stage when cooled. This is strained and poured into cups, which are then placed in a pan of boiling water until jellied. The gel is then cooled and turned onto a piece of "new flannel," in order to absorb the moisture. The result was a very concentrated, strong jelly that was turned back into soup by the addition of hot water and salt.

POI. A pasty preparation of taro, breadfruit, sweet potato, or banana, dating in print to 1798. This staple of the Hawaiian diet, often referred to there as the "staff of life," serves as the first solid food for infants and is recommended for everything from longevity to bee stings. The word is Hawaiian, possibly from Tahitian *po'e*, for a sweet pudding.

Today most poi is made with taro root, commercially produced and packaged in cellophane bags. In Hawaii's early days, taro was washed and cooked (cooked taro was called *'aipa'a*), then peeled, scraped, and pounded laboriously into a paste by the men of the tribe, who sat with taro on one side and water on the other, mashing the root into a firm mass called *pa'i'ai*. Poi was made by adding water to this mass and by kneading, usually followed by a period of a few days' fermentation, which imparted a sour taste to the paste.

Before World War II, Hawaiians could purchase poi in white cotton bags, which had to be strained free of its fiber in a "poi strainer" hung on a clothesline. Today packaged poi has a more pliable texture, and it is scraped in a bowl with some water to achieve a consistency referred to as a thin "one-finger poi," a thicker "two-finger poi," or a still thicker "three-finger poi." As these names indicate, poi is eaten by dipping one's fingers into the paste and is served as a condiment with main dishes of meat or fish or as a breakfast food or dip for **canapés**. The longer the fermentation of the poi—"one-day," "two-day," and "three-day" poi—the more sour it becomes.

Breadfruit poi is called *poi 'ulu*; sweet-potato poi, *poi 'uala*; and banana poi, *poi mai'a*.

POKE. A Hawaiian dish of diced fish marinated in various sauces. Hawaiian-style poke comes with chopped seaweed, "Korean-style" with chile, and "onion-style" with Maui onions. It is also a Hawaiian dish made with ogo seaweed, Maui onions, scallions, and raw fish.

"Poke" is also short for the salad herb "pokeweed" (*Phytolacca americana*), which dates in print to 1687, from the Algonquian *puccoon*. It is a wild field green and rarely planted. Some southerners even make wine from it.

"Pokeberries" are berries from the pokeweed.

POKE SUPPER. A community event at which bags (pokes) of food are auctioned off for charity, first in American print in 1912.

POLISH AMERICAN FOOD. A general term for food and drink cooked and consumed by Polish American immigrants as well as such foods enjoyed by non-Polish Americans.

There were Poles in the Virginia colony as of 1608, but the true wave came between the Civil War and 1900, when a million Poles emigrated to the U.S. (Today there are ten million Americans of Polish descent, about 3.2

percent of the population.) They settled, like most of the new arrivals, in the eastern cities, especially Baltimore, Cleveland, and Chicago, where Polish neighborhoods were large and Polish American social organizations provided support. There those foods that were a meager part of their culture in Europe became a daily diet in the U.S., one rich in sausages like kielbasa, meat stews, cabbage, sauerkraut, mustard, potatoes, cured hams, and dark bread. On festive occasions, *barszcz* (borsht), carp in aspic, stuffed mushrooms, pierogi, and herring in cream would be served. Desserts would include **pączki** doughnuts filled with preserves, a sweet poppy-seed cake called *makowiec*, and *sernik* cheesecake.

Except for kielbasa, pierogis, sauerkraut, and imported Polish canned hams, few non-Polish Americans eat much Polish-derived food. Also, outside of those cities where the Poles settled in the U.S., few Polish restaurants remain. A 1993 Chicago restaurant guide of two hundred restaurants listed none at all. Sokolowski's opened in 1923 in Cleveland but now serves few Polish dishes. Babushka's Kitchen opened in Cleveland in 2004 and now has three locations serving kielbasa dinners, *gołąbki* stuffed cabbage, and *kolachky* stuffed pastries.

POLISH SANDWICH. A sandwich of Polish-style sausage (such as **kielbasa**) in a soft roll. It is particularly popular in and around Baltimore.

POLLACK (*Pollachius virens*). Also "Boston bluefish" and "quoddy salmon." A very widespread North Atlantic fish of the cod family that ranges from the North Atlantic south to the Chesapeake Bay. The name is from the Scottish *podlok* and first appeared in English print as *poullok* circa 1427. The "walleye pollack" (*Theragra chalcogramma*), also called "Alaska pollack," ranges from Japan to central California, "walleye" referring to its whitish-gray eyes. This variety is usually sold salted rather than fresh and is the predominant fish used in the making of **surimi**.

U.S. landings of pollack totaled 1.9 billion pounds in 2010, the most of any species, but per capita U.S. consumption of pollack is only about one pound.

POLLY-IN-A-BAG. A dish of spiced meat cooked in an animal's stomach, first in American print in 1998.

POLYNESIAN FOOD. In American restaurants, this term refers not to any specific foods or dishes of Polynesia but to a number of dishes and cocktails concocted to sound and taste as if they were of Polynesian origins. Many of the cocktails, like the "**Zombie**" and the "Vicious Virgin," were created at a restaurant called Don the Beachcomber, in Los Angeles, while many others, like the "**mai tai**" and the "Samoan Fog Cutter," were created by "Trader" Victor Bergeron, who began the Trader Vic's chain in San Francisco in 1937, where he used Pacific decor to create an atmosphere that, in his words, made people think of beaches and "moonlight and pretty girls without any clothes on." Bergeron based his Polynesian concoctions on food he had eaten in the South Pacific. Some of those items he made popular included "**bongo bongo soup**," "**pupu** platters," "barbecued spareribs," and "Indonesian lamb roast." Many such dishes have also become standards of **Chinese American** restaurants, as have Polynesian cocktails, which are commonly served in ceramic mugs and glasses molded into fanciful shapes like skulls, rum kegs, and pineapples and garnished with chunks of pineapple, maraschino cherries, and small paper umbrellas. See also **Hawaiian food**.

POLYSORBATE 60. An emulsifier used in baked goods and other processed desserts to prevent spoilage. It also prevents oil and water from separating.

POMEGRANATE (*Punica granatum*). Also "Chinese apple." A tree native to Asia bearing a red, tough-skinned fruit containing many seeds and a pulpy, sour-sweet flesh. The name derives from the Old French *pome* ("apple") plus *grenate* ("many-seeded"), dating in print to circa 1330.

The fruit has been highly esteemed since biblical times, when its many seeds symbolized fertility to the Jews. The pomegranate was brought to America by the Spanish and was quickly dispersed into the wild. It was found growing in Frederica, Georgia, in 1773 and earlier in California. Today California is the only state with significant production (160,000 trees bearing about seventeen million pounds annually), with 80 percent of the crop from the "Wonderful" variety; the rest are "Granada," "Early Foothill," and "Early Wonderful."

POMFRET. Any of various fish of the family Bramidae, especially the Pacific "bigscale" or "sickle pomfret" (*Taractichthys steindachneri*), known in Hawaii as "monchong." The word is from Portuguese *pampo*, appearing in English print in 1703.

POMMES DE TERRE SOUFFLÉES. Also "*pommes soufflées*" or "puffed potatoes." Potatoes that are sliced thin and deep-fried twice so as to give them a puffy, crisp texture. The term is French, and there are two stories as to the dish's origins.

Larousse Gastronomique attributes the dish to an unnamed chef at a restaurant in Saint-Germain-en-Laye, near Paris, where in 1837 a new railway was being inaugurated. While waiting for the train to arrive for the meal ordered by the railway company, the chef prepared some fried potatoes, only to remove them from the hot oil upon the news that the train was having difficulty getting up the hill. When the party finally arrived, the chef put the now cold potatoes back into the hot oil and, to his delight, watched them puff up. "The famous analytical chemist Chevreul," *Larousse* explains, "who was informed of this phenomenon, studied it experimentally and established the conditions under which it occurred and could be reproduced at will."

But the man who brought these potatoes to America, Antoine Alciatore, owner of Antoine's Restaurant, in New Orleans, told of how he came by the recipe from the man who created it, the chef Collinet, under whom Alciatore apprenticed at the Hôtel de Noailles, in Marseille. Collinet had waited for the train at Saint-German-en-Laye for the arrival of King Louis Philippe I (1773–1850). Having cooked Louis Philippe's favorite potatoes, Collinet discovered that the king had been taken off the train as a precautionary measure and put on a carriage that would arrive late. When the king finally did arrive, the chef fried the cold potatoes again and produced the puffy crisps that instantly became popular.

~~~~~~
POMMES DE TERRE SOUFFLÉES
~~~~~~

Wash and peel 2 lb. potatoes, cut lengthwise into 1 ¼-in. slices about ⅛-in. thick. Soak in cold water, drain, and dry. Place a layer of potatoes in oil heated to 275°, moving the slices around until they begin to puff up. Remove potatoes, drain, and let cool for a few minutes. Replace the potatoes in 400° oil until puffed up and crispy. Remove, drain, salt, and serve.

POMPANO (*Trachinotus carolinus* and *Alectis crinitus*). A saltwater fish of the jack family (Carangidae). The pompano is esteemed as one of the favorite catches of the Gulf Coast and Florida, although it may be found as far north as Massachusetts. Most are taken at about four to five pounds. About 450,000 pompano, mostly from Florida waters, are landed each year.

The African pompano (*Alectis*) is also called the "threadfin" or "threadfish," but the "Florida pompano," sometimes known as the "Irish pompano," is more easily found at market. A similar fish, the "permit" (*T. falcatus*), which may run up to fifty pounds, is not a pompano and is rarely treated with the same culinary respect. The poppy fish (*Palometa simillima*) is sometimes called the "California pompano."

The name comes from the Spanish *pompano* and has been in English print since 1598. Mark Twain called the fish "delicious as the less criminal forms of sin." In New Orleans, the fish is sometimes called "sole."

The most notable way to prepare the fish is as "pompano *en papillote*," created by Jules Alciatore, owner of Antoine's Restaurant, in New Orleans, to honor Brazilian balloonist Alberto Santos-Dumont (1873–1932). According to Deirdre Stanforth, in *The New Orleans Restaurant Cookbook* (1967), the dish was a version of one Alciatore's father, Antoine, had made in honor of the brothers Joseph-Michel (1740–1810) and Jacques-Étienne Montgolfier (1745–99), who invented the hot-air balloon by inflating a linen bag with hot air in 1783. The dish was called "Pompano Montgolfier," and the later incarnation became a specialty of Antoine's and, soon afterwards, other restaurants in New Orleans and America. Movie director Cecil B. DeMille enjoyed the dish so much while filming *The Buccaneer* in New Orleans, in 1937, that he had it written into the script, even though the story took place long before Antoine's opened in 1840.

~~~~~~
POMPANO EN PAPILLOTE
~~~~~~

In 3 T. butter sauté 1 c. scallions until wilted, add 1 c. raw, peeled shrimp and 1 c. white wine, and bring to boil. Mix in 1 c. crabmeat and 2 c. fish velouté sauce, salt and pepper, and a dash of cayenne. Simmer for 10 min. and allow to cool. Poach 6 pompano fillets with water to cover, 1 sliced onion, 2 t. salt, 5 whole peppercorns, 1 ½ c. wine, 2 bay leaves, and the juice of 1 lemon. Cut 6 heart-shaped pieces of white parchment paper about 10 in. high and 14 in. wide. Spoon some sauce into the center of one half of a paper heart, top with a fillet, fold over the other half of the paper, and seal edges. Place on greased baking pan and bake for 15 min. at 400°, until paper begins to brown. Before serving, cut open top of paper. Serves 6.

POMPEY'S HEAD. A roll of ground meat with a sauce of tomatoes and green pepper. In *The White House Cookbook* (1964), the dish is described as having been "popular before automatic ovens were invented because it could cook unattended for hours." The name apparently refers to the broad head of Roman statesman and general Gnaeus Pompeius Magnus, known as "Pompey the Great" (106–48 B.C.), or perhaps to a typical slave name, first appearing in print in 1890.

POMPEY'S HEAD

Mix 1 lb. sausage meat with 1 lb. ground beef, season with salt and pepper, and form into a roll. Dust with flour and brown in a 450° oven. Add 2 c. chopped tomatoes, 1 c. chopped celery, 1 T. chopped onion, and half of a green pepper to pan and bake, covered, for 1 ½ hr. at 350°, basting occasionally. Serve with vegetables poured over it.

PONY. A short bar glass, shaped like a small sherry or brandy glass, that is often used for cordials or for measuring one ounce of liquid. The term may also refer simply to a small drink of straight liquor, a meaning that dates back to at least 1849. The word *pony* seems to refer to a short item like a horse pony.

POOCH. A western stew of canned tomatoes, sugar, bread, and vegetables, first in American print in 1885.

POOR-MAN DISHES. A very vague term for a wide variety of stews, pies, soups, desserts, and other foods, possibly because they are made with simple, inexpensive ingredients.

POPCORN. Also "popped corn." Corn kernels heated in oil until they burst open into white, fluffy, textured balls. An 1819 American memoir calls the kernels "poss corn," but as "pop corn" the word first appeared in American print in 1838.

Varieties of popping corn were known to Native Americans in both North and South America. The oldest ears of popcorn, dating back 5,600 years, were first discovered in 1948 in the Bat Cave of west central New Mexico. Native Americans believed that in the corn lived an angry demon who exploded when exposed to heat. In 1519 Spanish explorer Hernán Cortés found the Aztecs of Mexico eating popcorn, which was also used for decorative purposes.

Popcorn was brought to the first Thanksgiving, in 1621, by Chief Massasoit's brother, Quadequina. At first called by the early colonists "popped corn," "parching corn," or "rice corn," it became commonly known after 1820 as "popcorn" and was a popular treat for Americans, who not only ate it as a snack but strung it to hang on Christmas trees. By the 1870s people were adding molasses to make crunchy "popcorn balls," and in 1896 the firm of F. W. Rueckheim and Brother, of Chicago, came up with a combination of popcorn, molasses, and peanuts that they named Cracker Jack (the confection had been sold without that name at Chicago's 1893 Columbian Exposition), which came from a contemporary slang term for anything considered excellent. Before long Cracker Jack was a staple food item at baseball games throughout America, and the cry "Getcha peanuts, popcorn, and Cracker Jack" is still heard at circuses, sporting events, and carnivals throughout the land. Since 1912, the confection has come with a little "prize" in every box.

In 1914, C. H. Smith, of Sioux City, Iowa, developed a shelled popcorn whose kernels were guaranteed to pop every time. Before that, only about two-thirds of the kernels would typically pop.

Popcorn machines, patented by C. Cretors & Co., of Chicago, which opened in 1885, were soon fixtures on street corners and, particularly, in movie theaters, where popcorn became an absolute requisite for an enjoyable evening. By 1918 the Butter-Kist popcorn machine, which coated the popcorn with melted butter, was also common. In the 1920s, Purdue University pioneered research into popcorn hybridization in order to improve taste and consistency of popping, and several popcorn varieties were specially developed by Orville Redenbacher as of 1941. In 1945, James V. Blevins, of the Blevins Popcorn Co., in Nashville, Tennessee, developed a very fluffy, high-volume popcorn that proved highly successful in movie theaters, which he later introduced to baseball stadiums in Japan. In 1946, electronics engineer Percy Spencer developed the first microwavable popcorn after he casually paused in front of a magnetron power tube at Raytheon Laboratories and found that the chocolate bar in his pocket began to melt. He then placed popcorn kernels next to the magnetron and found that the kernels popped. From this experiment the microwave oven was developed. One of the first packaged microwavable popcorn was sold by Jim Watkins Golden Valley Foods in 1971, and by the 1980s many brands produced microwavable popcorn,

Today popcorn is often made at home with nothing more than corn kernels and a pot, though electric popcorn poppers and cellophane packages of popcorn are sold too. Americans eat about 16.5 billion quarts of popcorn per year, or sixty-five quarts per person. Seventy percent is eaten at home, with 90 percent of that made from unpopped corn.

POPE'S NOSE. Also "parson's nose." The rump of a cooked fowl, in print since 1740. The phrase is a demeaning term for both parts of the anatomy, for it was originally meant as a slur against Catholics during the reign of James II of England, although "parson's nose" seems to predate it. In America, "parson's nose" (called by New England poet Henry Wadsworth Longfellow an "epicurean morsel") was the more common slang term.

POP-OUT. A prepackaged frozen meal sold to many commercial airlines for use on their flights. The food pops out of the package and is then arranged on a tray, to be heated aboard the aircraft.

POPOVER. A light, hollow muffin made from an egg batter similar to that used in making **Yorkshire pudding**. The name comes from the fact that the batter rises and swells over the muffin tin while baking. The first appearance of the word in print was in 1850.

In *American Food* (1974), Evan Jones wrote: "Settlers from Maine who founded Portland, Oregon,

Americanized the pudding from Yorkshire by cooking the batter in custard cups lubricated with drippings from the roasting beef (or sometimes pork); another modification was the use of garlic, and, frequently, herbs. The result is called Portland popover pudding, individual balloons of crusty meat-flavored pastry."

Most popovers, however, are not flavored but merely set in buttered muffin tins. They are served at breakfast or with meats at lunch and dinner.

POPOVER

Combine 1 c. sifted flour and ¼ t. salt. Beat until very smooth 2 eggs and 1 c. milk, then blend well with flour. Pour into buttered muffin tins and bake in 450° oven for about 20 min. Reduce heat to 350° and bake 10–15 min., until puffy and brown.

POP-UP RESTAURANT. A restaurant that is opened and intended to stay in one location temporarily. The marketing concept became popular after 2005, and is distinguished from traditional lunch wagons in that it serves a varied menu for several weeks or months, then closes.

POP WINE. A term of recent years used to describe a sweet, fruit-flavored wine that is usually quite inexpensive.

PORGY. Any of a variety of marine fishes of the family Sparidae. Porgies are small-mouthed, have strong teeth, and inhabit sandy bottoms both inshore and offshore. The name, according to the *American Heritage Dictionary*, derives from the Spanish *pargo*, which goes back to the Greek *phágros*, "sea bream," the name by which the porgy is known outside the United States. A. J. McClane, however, in his *Encyclopedia of Fish Cookery* (1977), asserts that the name is "strictly American, derived from the Narragansett Indian word *mishcuppauog. Pauog* meant fertilizer, for which the fish was widely used." But the first instances of the word in English print were in 1671, and in Sir Hans Sloane's 1725 book *A Voyage to the Islands Madera, Barbados, Nieves, S. Christophers, and Jamaica, with the Natural History…of the Last.* Since the Narragansett were a tribe of North America, and specifically of what is now Rhode Island, the appearance of the word in a text on the Caribbean throws McClane's contention into doubt. The fish has always been enjoyed in the South, with more than twenty million pounds marketed annually along the Atlantic coast, and in the nineteenth century it was hawked on the streets of southern cities like Charleston, South Carolina, the setting for the American opera *Porgy and Bess* (1935), about a crippled black man named Porgy.

The main species of culinary interest in the U.S. include the "scup" (*Stenotomus chrysops*), whose name derives from the Narragansett word *mishcup*; "jolthead porgy" (*Calamus bajonado*); "Pacific porgy" (*C. brachysomus*); and "sheepshead" (*Archosargus probatocephalus*).

PORK. The edible flesh of a pig (*Sus scrofa domesticus*) or hog The word derives from Latin *porcus* and dates in English print circa 1300.

Pork is the most widely eaten meat in the world, and from the time the first settlers came to the New World, it was the predominant meat in the American diet. Pigs have been domesticated since the Stone Age. The wild peccary (*Tayassu tajacu* or *T. peccari*), also called "javelinas" and "skunk pig," is not a true pig but comes from the same suborder, *Suina*. It may have crossed the Bering Strait from Russia to disperse throughout North and South America. Hernán Cortés (1485–1547) found pigs in Mexico, but the first domesticated pigs were a herd of thirteen brought from Spain to Tampa, Florida, in 1539 by Hernando de Soto (c. 1496–1542), and from these all North American domesticated pigs are descended. Some of these Spanish pigs escaped into the forests and turned wild. They are called **razorbacks** and are not related to the peccaries.

English, French, and all other colonists found pigs easy to raise, for they foraged on their own and lived off scraps. By 1640 Massachusetts had already built a small salt-pork trade. Salting and smoking was the standard method of treating a butchered hog, and salt pork became the dominant meat in the colonial diet; it was used for its oil, and its meat for bacon, in stews, as flavoring, in pies, roasted, boiled, barbecued, and in all manner of preparations. The **hams** of Virginia became famous for their succulent flavor, especially those of Smithfield, where the pigs forage in the peanut fields.

Southerners ate every part of the hog, saving some pieces for special dishes like **red beans and rice**, a Louisiana delicacy traditionally made on Monday with the ham bone left over from Sunday's dinner. Families had pork barrels in their cellars, and the term "pork-barrel legislation" came to mean laws passed by a region's congressman designed specifically to help his local constituency. To be living "high on the hog" meant that one was eating the best meat on the pig, while others had to subsist on belly **bacon** meat.

Thomas Jefferson, with his usual curiosity, experimented with new breeds by crossing Virginia hogs with Calcutta varieties, soon cornering the local market and overcharging his neighbors, who began calling him the "Hog Governor" and in defiance hung his Monticello fence with pig entrails.

By the 1830s the streets of major cities were crisscrossed with hog tracks, for they were allowed to feed on the garbage, and English traveler Francis Marryat noted one Fourth of July in NYC that the three-mile-long stretch of Broadway was lined on both sides of the street with booths selling roast pig. During the same era, Cincinnati became the major pork-packing center, earning it the nickname "Porkopolis." Pork itself was sometimes called in slang "Cincinnati olive."

The demand for pork increased during the Civil War, when hog production doubled to provide meat for the Union troops while soldiers of the Confederacy starved for lack of it. After the war, a new industry arose in meatpacking, led by Gustavus Franklin Swift and Philip Danforth Armour, who independently set up companies in Chicago in 1875. Chicago soon became the center of the industry for the entire U.S., which was provided with pork in abundance, thanks to the newly developed refrigerated railroad cars. (Long into the twentieth century, "Chicago" was a slang term for pork.) Still, those pioneers who set out for California after the Civil War always packed a full load of salt pork, which they usually cursed for its monotonous appearance in their diet as they crossed the Great Plains.

The introduction of pigs (many of which ran wild) to Hawaii made this one of the favorite meats of the populace, especially pit-roasted or barbecued pork and **kalua pig**, which is roasted in ti leaves.

With the increase in available beef in the late nineteenth century, pork began to recede in popularity, tied as it was to a coarse and boring diet of the poor. By the twentieth century beef had begun to compete favorably in price and was preferred at the table, so that Americans ate less and less pork as the decades wore on. Today, though pork consumption is again on the rise, 40 percent of Americans, including kosher observant Jews and conservative Muslims, eat little or no pork at all. Americans consume about forty-eight pounds per person per year, compared with sixty-six pounds of beef.

In order to counter American dietary fears about excessive fat, the pork industry now produces hogs 50 percent leaner than they were in the 1950s.

Iowa leads the U.S. in pork production, followed by North Carolina, Minnesota, Illinois, and Indiana.

October is National Pork Month.

Today pork is served in a wide variety of ways: as roast pork or ham, as spareribs, chopped up in a southern-style **barbecue**, in sausages, in stews, as chops, and in a wide range of ethnic foods. Roast suckling pig in Louisiana is called *"cochon de lait,"* from the French for "suckling pig." The innards, especially the intestines, called **chitterlings**, are an important part of **soul food**. Pork rinds are popular snack foods, which Latin Americans called *chiccarónes*. The Department of Agriculture grades pork "no. 1," "no. 2," and "no. 3." The various cuts of pork are listed below.

PRIMAL BOSTON (OR SHOULDER) BUTT.
This section comprises the Boston butt and the picnic ham.

PRIMAL LEG. From this section is cut the meat to make fresh ham—that is, pork roasted as is—and the ham that is to be cured and smoked, which is cut into the butt end and shank end.

PRIMAL LOIN. This cut runs along the pig's back and is the preferred meat. It includes the sections from which come Canadian bacon and the best spareribs, as well as the tenderloin, sirloin, center loin, blade (or rib) loin, and the finest chops. The chops from this section are often called "country style."

PRIMAL PICNIC SHOULDER. A cut from the foreleg that is usually sold cured and smoked, though some of the meat is sold as an arm roast.

PRIMAL SIDE PORK. Also called "pork belly." This section provides bacon.

PRIMAL SPARERIBS. These lie under the primal side pork. A slab of between two and five pounds is cut into spareribs.

For information on **ham**, see main entry.

PORT. A fortified wine, usually made in America with **zinfandel** and other grape varieties. The name comes from the city of Oporto, Portugal, where the original port was made, dating in English print to circa 1626.

In the U.S., Portuguese ports are labeled "Porto" to distinguish them from American bottlings. Port wines began to be fortified with brandy in the eighteenth century, after which their distribution became dominated by the British shipping trade.

American ports generally contain between 18 and 20 percent alcohol and 5 to 10 percent residual sugar. Most are produced in California, and some, since the 1970s, are marketed as vintage ports.

Port is traditionally served with the cheese course or after dinner, although some light ports are enjoyed as aperitifs.

PORTERHOUSE. Also "porterhouse steak." A beefsteak cut from the thick end of the short loin, containing a T-bone and part of the tenderloin. The name derives from the taverns or alehouses of the eighteenth century that were called "porterhouses" (because porters in London's Covent Garden market drank ale in such places). The steak itself was popularized around 1814 by a NYC porterhouse keeper named Martin Morrison. It soon became the most popular form and cut of steak in America. The name dates in print to 1854.

PORTUGUESE SWEET BREAD. A white loaf of bread sweetened with sugar and sometimes baked with slices of sausage. The Portuguese, who call it *pao doce*, brought it to American communities on the East Coast, where it is called *massa suvada*, as well as to the Hawaiian Islands in the nineteenth century.

~~~~~~~~~~~~~~~~~~~~~~~~~~~~~~~~
PORTUGUESE SWEET BREAD
~~~~~~~~~~~~~~~~~~~~~~~~~~~~~~~~

Combine ⅓ c. sugar, 1 t. salt, 2 pkgs. yeast, and 1 c. flour. In saucepan over very low heat combine ¼ c. butter in ⅔ c. milk until warm, then gradually beat into flour mixture, increasing speed of mixer. Beat in 6 eggs and 1 ½ c. more flour to make a thick batter, then stir in about 2 ½ c. more flour to make a soft dough. Turn onto floured surface and knead until elastic, about 10 min., using more flour as necessary. Shape into ball, turn into greased bowl, cover, and let double. Punch down dough, cut in half, shape into 2 loaves, and place on buttered cookie sheet. Let double again, brush tops with milk, and bake 35 min. at 350°. Cool.

PORTY REEK LONG-LICK. A New England sailor's slang term for molasses, dating in print to 1924. "Porty Reek" refers to Puerto Rico, where sugar was produced. "Long-lick" probably referred to its dense, viscous texture and was also used by westerners. "Long-tailed sugar" was a variant of the phrase.

POSSET. A drink of sweetened hot milk, wine, or ale, similar to **syllabub**. The word is from Middle English *poshet* or *possot*, dating in English print to about 1425. It was a popular drink in the fifteenth century and continued to be well into the nineteenth, though it is rarely seen today. Sometimes posset contains egg, in which case it is called an "egg posset."

POTATO (*Solanum tuberosum*). A native South American plant having a rough-skinned, starchy tuber that is widely propagated and eaten in a great variety of ways as a vegetable. The word comes from the Spanish *patata*, which derives from the Taino word *batata*, first in English print in 1565, but this is only the beginning of the many confusions surrounding the potato and its history.

When Christopher Columbus explored the West Indies, he found a tuber, which is now called the **sweet potato** (*Ipomoea batatas*), known in the Taino language as *batata*. This tuber was immediately transported back to Spain and propagated there. The confusion arose when John Gerard's *Herball* (1597) listed the white potato as a North American plant, and for a good while afterwards it was assumed that there were white potatoes in North America. This, however, was not the case. The white potato is native to South America and was cultivated perhaps five thousand years ago in Peru. It was this plant that the Spanish, in 1537, found being cultivated by the Inca, who called it *papa* (the Quechua language has more than a thousand names for the potato), in the Andean village of Sorocota; the conquistadores believed it was a form of truffle thought to be an aphrodisiac that might cause both syphilis and leprosy. Potatoes were very important to the Indian diet, and the Inca even measured time by how long it took to cook potatoes.

Potatoes were sent back to Spain from Ecuador in the 1530s, may have reached France around 1540, and were mentioned in print in 1553 by Pedro de Cieza León in his *Crónica del Perú*.

Legend has it that Sir Walter Raleigh's men brought the white potato back from Virginia in 1586, but there is no evidence of the white potato's existence in North America at that time. Waverley Root, in *Food* (1980), suggests a plausible explanation of the legend by noting that Sir Francis Drake picked up Raleigh's disgruntled colonists in 1586, on his way back from Cartagena, Colombia, from where he had taken some white potatoes. These were of considerable interest to Thomas Harriot, one of Raleigh's men, and it was Harriot who gave the tubers to John Gerard, who thereupon planted them in his own garden and ten years later reported that this white potato had come from Virginia.

Whatever happened in Virginia and England, Raleigh has been credited with planting the first white potatoes in Ireland soon afterwards, where they were grown to prevent famine, as they were in Germany and elsewhere.

The white potato finally entered North America at least as early as the middle of the seventeenth century, for the first printed reference to its being planted is in 1685, clearly distinguished from the sweet potato. By 1762 it was a field crop in Salem, Massachusetts, and by 1770 it was grown for commercial sale back in England. It was not even eaten in Spain until the middle of the eighteenth century. By then Americans had learned to distinguish the white potato from the orange tuber that originally took its name. The latter variety was by the 1740s called the sweet potato.

Still, the white potato had few admirers well into the nineteenth century. Although praised by Shakespeare's

Falstaff and Byron's Don Juan as an aphrodisiac, the tuber was considered poisonous and a cause of everything from leprosy to birth defects. In Sicily, some believed you could cause someone's untimely death merely by writing the person's name on a paper pinned to a potato. The potato was considered fit only for the poor and largely associated with the Irish, who in their own country had staved off starvation with the potato in 1740 and continued to live on it almost to the exclusion of every other food. In fact, the potato was so closely associated with the Irish that the slang term for the tuber became the same as the slur word for an Irishman—"mickey." When the Irish Potato Famine hit in 1845, owing to a failure of the crop, the only solution for the poor was to emigrate to America, and more than a million did so in the decades to follow.

By the mid-nineteenth century the potato was no longer feared for its poisonous properties; they had been widely promoted by French agriculturist Antoine-Augustin Parmentier as of the 1770s, and cookbooks began carrying a few recipes for potatoes as vegetables. Even fried potatoes were called, by Sarah J. Hale, in the 1857 *Mrs. Hale's New Cook Book*, "an admirable way of dressing potatoes," and fried potato slices, called **Saratoga potatoes**, had become popular in that same decade. **French-fried potatoes** came along near the end of the century, by which time Americans consumed great quantities of the tuber—two hundred pounds per person per year by 1900. Cookbooks listed scores of ways to prepare them—boiled, baked in their skins, cooked in the fat of a roast beef, and sliced up to be baked in cream, called "scalloped potatoes." "Mashed potatoes" (first in print in 1896) are boiled and mashed, usually with butter and milk. In large eastern cities, street vendors would roast potatoes over coals, and children would cook them on a stick over an open fire. They were boiled and made part of hot ("German") or cold "**potato salad**," and Swiss *rösti* became Americanized as "hash browns" or "hashed browns"—potatoes that are shredded or chopped and cooked with butter, bacon, and onion in a skillet. Hash browns go by several other names, including "haystack potatoes" in the Midwest. "Home-fried potatoes" (in restaurants called "house-fried" or "cottage-fried") are similar—first boiled, then chopped or sliced and cooked in fat in a skillet. "Potato skins" are a dish of baked or fried potatoes whose insides have been scooped out

and the skins refilled with other ingredients like butter, cheese, and seasonings. They were supposedly first sold by the Prime Rib restaurant, in Baltimore, in about 1965. Frozen potato skins were first marketed in 1978 by Frederic D. Starret Jr., of the Penobscot Frozen Food Co., in Belfast, Maine. "Twice-baked potatoes" have the insides scooped out then mixed with other ingredients and replaced in the skins, then baked.

During World War II, dehydrated potatoes became a staple part of the serviceman's diet. Later these were a commercial success in the grocery. After the war, frozen french-fried potatoes supplanted freshly made french fries in most homes and restaurants, especially at **fast-food** stands, where thinly cut shoestring potatoes are generally sold. Today Americans eat forty-six pounds of potatoes per person, but only about one-third of that amount is made fresh. Potatoes are served in some form at 60 percent of the main meals of the day.

The main varieties produced in the U.S. may be broken into four groups: "round white," which includes the Kennebec (usually used for potato chips and for baking and boiling), Katahdin (used mostly for boiling and canning), Superior, Norchip, Irish Cobbler, Monona, Sebago, Ontario, and Chippewa; "russet" (mostly long), which includes the Russet Burbank and the Norgold Russet; "round red," which includes the Norland, Red Pontiac, Red La Soda, La Rouge, and Red McClure; and "long white," mainly the White Rose. The buttery-tasting "Yukon gold" variety, first marketed in America by Michigan farmer Jim Huston as of 1996, became very popular, especially in restaurants.

Most potatoes are harvested from September to November and then stored, although potatoes harvested and shipped directly to the market are called "early" or "new" potatoes.

The most important potato-producing states are Idaho, Washington, Maine, California, North Dakota, Oregon, Minnesota, Wisconsin, Michigan, Colorado, and New York. Despite its popularity, the so-called Idaho potato is actually a Russet Burbank that is grown in Idaho.

POTATO SALAD. A cold or hot side dish made with potatoes, mayonnaise, and seasonings. It became very popular in the second half of the nineteenth century and is a staple of both home and grocery-store kitchens. Hot potato salad, usually made with bacon, onion, and vinegar dressing, was associated with German immigrants and therefore often called "German potato salad."

COLD POTATO SALAD

In a bowl stir together ½ c. mayonnaise, 2 T. milk, ½ t. salt, ¼ t. pepper, 2 ½ c. cooked cubed potatoes, and ½ c. chopped celery and mix thoroughly. Chill for 2 hr. Makes 3 c.

HOT POTATO SALAD

Cook 6 potatoes in salted boiling water, peel, and slice. In a large skillet sauté 4 strips bacon, ¼ c. chopped celery, and ⅓ c. chopped onion until browned. In a saucepan heat to boiling ¼ c. chicken stock, ½ c. vinegar, ⅓ t. sugar, salt and pepper, and ⅛ t. sweet paprika. Pour into skillet, add potatoes, and stir thoroughly. Cook until well blended and slightly thickened. Serve with chopped parsley. Serves 6.

POTATO SNOW. Described by Eliza Leslie, in *Directions for Cookery* (1837), as potatoes that have been boiled, thoroughly dried, then pushed through a sieve but afterwards not mixed in any way.

POTICIA. Also "potica." A jelly- and walnut-filled coffee cake popular in Minnesota. The word is from Slovene, dating in American print to 1927, and the confection derives from Slovenian and other Yugoslavian immigrants. "It could not be a Slovenian wedding without poticia (pronounced po-TEET-tsa) and cabbage rolls," wrote Marcia Adams in *Heartland* (1991).

POTLIKKER. Southerners, particularly African Americans, call the liquid left over from a meal of greens, black-eyed peas, pork, or other items "potlikker," in print since 1742 as "pot liquor." Often served on its own as a vitamin-rich broth, potlikker was a staple among the field hands of the South and is now an essential ingredient of modern **soul food**.

A passion for potlikker (familiarity with the term is a prerequisite for political office in the South, for, as Marjorie Kinnan Rawlings observed, "a man addicted to the combination [of potlikker and corn bread could]

claim himself a man of the people." Governor Huey Long of Louisiana, in an all-night filibuster on the subject of authentically made potlikker, once claimed that fried corn pone must be dunked into the broth for the best results, although opponents countered that the corn pone should be crumbled into the potlikker. Franklin D. Roosevelt jokingly suggested that the issue be referred to the Platform Committee at the 1932 Democratic National Convention.

As for the spelling of the word, Lieutenant Governor Zell Miller of Georgia corrected a 1982 article in the *New York Times* with the following blast:

> *I always thought The New York Times knew everything, but obviously your editor knows as little about spelling as he or she does about Appalachian cooking and soul food. Only a culinarily-illiterate damnyankee (one word) who can't tell the difference between beans and greens would call the liquid left in the pot after cooking greens "pot liquor" (two words) instead of "potlikker" (one word) as yours did. And don't cite Webster as a defense because he didn't know any better either.*

POTLUCK. Also "pitch-in dinner" and "scramble dinner." A meal composed of whatever is available or a meal (also called a "carry-in" or "covered dish meal") whereby different people bring different dishes to a social gathering. In the West, "potluck" meant food brought by a cowboy guest to put in the communal pot. The term dates in print to 1867.

POTPIE. Also "pot pie." A crusted pie made with poultry or meat and, usually, chopped vegetables. The term, which first appeared in print in 1702, probably refers to the deep pie pans or pots used to bake the pies in, and it has remained primarily an Americanism. The most popular potpies have been chicken, beef, and pork. The first frozen potpie was made with chicken, in 1951, by the C. A. Swanson & Sons Co.

CHICKEN POT PIE

In a kettle cook 1 quartered chicken in 2 c. chicken broth for 30 min. Cool, reserve broth. In another pot cook 1 doz.

small onions in 1 c. chicken broth for 10 min., then add 4 chopped carrots, 1 c. peas, and ½ c. chopped celery. Cook 20 min., then remove from heat. In a saucepan make a roux of 6 T. butter with 6 T. flour, stirring about 1 min. Stir in reserved chicken broth, season with salt and pepper, cook 7–10 min., until thickened, and remove from heat. Remove chicken meat from bones, place in vegetable mixture, and blend in roux. Pour into pastry-lined deep-dish pan, cover with top crust, slit air vents for steam to escape, and bake 10 min. at 450°, then lower heat to 350° and cook another 20 min., until crust is golden brown.

POT ROAST. A meat that is browned and cooked with vegetables and gravy in a deep pot or saucepan, usually covered. The term dates in print to 1880, as a verb to 1893. Pot roast was once an appetizing way to cook beef from beasts that had been work animals rather than food animals, or other inferior cuts of meat. Today the availability of good beef makes pot roast a delicious, hearty dish, though lesser cuts of meat are still used for the cooking. Beef brisket, bottom and top round, and chuck are the usual choices.

POULTRY. Defined by the USDA as "all domesticated birds (chickens, turkeys, ducks, geese, guineas)." The word derives from Latin *pulletaria* and first appeared in English print circa 1387.

POULTRY BY-PRODUCT. Any edible part of a domesticated bird other than the sex glands and **poultry meat**.

POULTRY FOOD PRODUCT. Also called "poultry product." Any food suitable for human consumption made from any domesticated bird and containing more than 2 percent poultry meat.

POULTRY MEAT. The white- and dark-meat portions of deboned poultry, excluding fat, skin, and other edible poultry parts.

POUND CAKE. A plain white-cake loaf whose name derives from the traditional weight of the ingredients— one pound of flour, one pound of butter, one pound of sugar, and one pound of eggs—although these measurements are generally not followed in most modern recipes.

Its first printed mention was in 1743, and it has remained a popular and simple cake to this day.

POUND CAKE

Cream ½ c. butter with 1 c. sugar until light and fluffy. Add 1 ¾ c. flour, 3 egg yolks, a pinch of salt, and 1 t. vanilla extract. Pour into loaf pan and bake at 350° for about 45 min.

POUSSE-CAFÉ. A drink made by pouring successive layers of cordials on top of one another, creating a rainbow effect of color. The term is French, meaning "push down the coffee," and in France a pousse-café is merely a cordial, brandy, or other digestive alcohol. In America, however, it is a bibulous tour de force, its success depending upon the specific densities of the cordials, with the heaviest going on the bottom and the lighter ones toward the top. A tall, slender cordial glass (or special pousse-café glass) is needed, and care must be taken in pouring each cordial so as not to disturb the one under it. A typical pousse-café might be layered in the following order: kirsch, grenadine, orange curaçao, green crème de menthe, purple crème de cassis, and yellow crème de bananes. The word was first printed in English in 1862.

POWER LUNCH. A business lunch attended by the most powerful people within an industry. The term was coined in a 1979 *Esquire* magazine article by Lee Eisenberg, entitled "America's Most Powerful Lunch," to describe the number of powerful business people who dined at the Four Seasons restaurant, in NYC.

The "power breakfast" was begun unofficially (and not under that name) in March 1976, at NYC's 540 Park Restaurant, at the Regency Hotel, by Preston Robert Tisch, president of the Loews Corporation, which owns the hotel, as a way for businesspeople to fit in an early meeting before the regular business day began. ("Power breakfast" was being used by the end of 1980.) The idea had evolved out of breakfast meetings held by various Manhattan power brokers who had been meeting since the early 1970s to discuss ways to improve their city's image and fortunes. Currently the average price for a breakfast of juice, muffins, and coffee at that restaurant is between $25 and $30. "But you can't really complain about the price," said one habitué, "because it's cheaper than office space."

PRAIRIE CHICKEN. The "greater prairie chicken" (*Tympanuchus cupido*) and the "lesser prairie chicken" (*T. pallidicinctus*) are grouse of the open plains of the West. The birds were so named as early as 1685, and the Lewis and Clark expedition of 1804 referred to them as "prairie hen" or "prairie fowl." Later they were also called "prairie grouse." They are roasted, fried, or stewed.

PRAIRIE OYSTER. Also "prairie cocktail." A cocktail made by dropping 1 unbroken egg yolk into a tumbler, adding 2 t. Worcestershire sauce, 2 dashes Tabasco sauce, a pinch of salt and pepper, and 1 t. malt vinegar. It is considered by bartenders to be a good cure for the hiccups. The term has been part of western lingo since at least its first printing, in 1879.

PRALINE. A confection made from almonds or pecans and caramel. It is a great favorite in the South, especially in New Orleans, and derives from the French preparation of *praline*, which involves caramelized almonds or hazelnuts and sugar pounded into a fine, crumblike texture. Both terms come from the name of French diplomat César, comte du Plessis-Praslin, later duc de Choiseul (1598–1675), whose cook suggested that almonds and sugar aided digestion. The American Creoles substituted pecans for the almonds.

The confection was first mentioned in print in 1715, and was part of Louisiana food culture as early as 1762. The term had various meanings by 1809, when one chronicler told of pralines made from corn and sugar.

PRALINE

Combine 3 c. light brown sugar with ¼ c. water and 1 T. butter. Heat to a temperature of 238° on a candy thermometer, add 1 c. pecan meats, remove from heat, and stir until mixture loses glossiness. Drop in spoonfuls on waxed paper.

PRAWN (*Macrobrachium acanthurus*). A crustacean similar to a **shrimp** but with a more slender body and longer legs. The name is from German *Porr*, dating in

English print to 1336. At market, the term "prawn" is often used to describe a wide variety of shrimp that are not prawns at all. The only native American species is found in the South, ranging from North Carolina to Texas. Prawns are cultivated in Hawaii.

PRESSURE COOKER. A saucepan with a locking lid that creates intense steam heat within, to cook foods in a shorter time than in a conventional saucepan. The term dates in print to 1910. The commercial pressure cooker was introduced in the U.S. at the 1939 New York World's Fair by National Presto Industries.

PRETZEL. A crisp, salted biscuit usually twisted into a loose knot, though often made in sticks. The word is from German *Bretzel*, and some believe it refers to the Latin words *pretium* ("reward") or *brachiatus* ("cake"), dating in English print to about 1824.

Pretzels can be traced back to Roman times, and they have long been traditional in Alsace and Germany. Legend has it that a monk of France or northern Italy first twisted a piece of dough into this unusual shape around A.D. 610, in order to imitate the folded arms of someone praying. The Dutch probably brought the pretzel to America, and there is a story that in 1652 a settler named Jochem Wessels was arrested for using good flour to make pretzels to sell to the Indians at a time when his white neighbors were eating bran flour. The first mention of the word *pretzel* in American print was around 1824, and the first commercial pretzel bakery in the U.S. was set up in 1861, by Julius Sturgis and Ambrose Rauch, in Lititz, Pennsylvania. Most pretzels are twisted by machine, the first of which was introduced in 1933.

Today pretzels come in a variety of shapes and sizes, from sticks, called "thins," to rings and hard, thick, saltless teething pretzels called "Bavarians" or "Baldies" (because there is no surface salt), a registered trademark of the Anderson Bakery Co. (the world's largest pretzel producer) in Lancaster, Pennsylvania. Especially popular in NYC and other eastern cities are soft, puffy yeast pretzels sold by street vendors and at candy stores. In Philadelphia these same pretzels are usually eaten with a squirt of yellow mustard or slathered with melted butter. So famous are Philadelphia's pretzels that the city is nicknamed the "Big Pretzel," and Pennsylvania manufactures more than half the 400 million pounds of pretzels made in the U.S. annually.

PRICKLY PEAR. Also called "prickly cactus." "pencil cholla," and "pencil cactus." Any of a variety of cacti in the genus *Opuntia* bearing an ovular fruit with a spiny skin—hence its name, first recorded in print in 1605. It is native to the New World tropics and is grown in the southwestern U.S., where its leaves, or pads, are eaten in salads and its fruit made into jams, jellies, and pickles. Mexican Americans call the plant "*tuna*," and refer to the pads as **nopales**, while Hawaiians call it "*pānini*."

PROGRESSIVE DINNER. A meal in which each different course is eaten at a different neighbor's house. The practice became popular in the 1950s with the expansion of suburban housing developments.

PROHIBITION. The era lasting from 1920 to 1933, during which the U.S. government forbade the manufacture, sale, or transportation of intoxicating liquors. Prohibition began with passage of the Eighteenth Amendment to the federal Constitution, on January 16, 1919, which went into effect one year later and was repealed by the Twenty-first Amendment, on December 5, 1933.

The Prohibition era—which President Herbert Hoover (1874–1964; in office 1929–1933) called the "Noble Experiment"—was the result of intense pressure by temperance groups across the country, especially the Women's Christian Temperance Union, founded in 1874 in Cleveland, along with a Washington, D.C., lobbying organization called the Anti-Saloon League, founded in 1893, and the Prohibition Party, founded in 1869, which ran candidates in several presidential elections but failed ever to receive a large percentage of the popular vote.

The temperance advocates, whose main argument was against the deleterious effects of alcohol on the drinker and, by extension, on the family, the society, and the nation itself, sought to turn America "dry." Maine had already gone dry as of 1851, and Oklahoma followed in 1880, followed by most of the South and, by World War I, most of the Midwest, which argued that precious grain be reserved for the war effort rather than for distilleries. There was also a deliberate anti-German sentiment against the brewery owners, most of whom had German

backgrounds. Finally, bowing to temperance pressures or drawing support from temperance funds, the House of Representatives and the Senate passed a joint resolution on December 5, 1917, to propose ratification of the Eighteenth Amendment by at least thirty-six states. On January 16, 1919, the amendment was ratified, and it was put into effect one year later (after Congress had overridden President Woodrow Wilson's veto), with additional legislation under the Volstead Act—named after its sponsor, Minnesota representative Andrew J. Volstead (1860–1947)—to enforce it.

The law was stringent: An intoxicating liquor was defined as "any beverage containing ½ of 1% alcohol," which effectively put an end to the legal manufacture and sale of beer and wine as well as hard liquor. This aspect of the law crippled the hopes of building a great wine industry in America just when it seemed possible to do so. California and New York grape growers shifted to selling their fruit to home winemakers (originally allowed under the law, to placate Virginia apple farmers who sold their fruit to make cider), leading to an enormous two-thirds increase in wine consumption. Beer consumption, however, declined drastically, to three-tenths of what it had been before Prohibition.

Alcohol could still be sold for medicinal purposes under the Act Supplemental of 1921. But the Treasury Department issued only ten special permits for the storage and transport of whiskey to wholesale druggists. And many people found sympathetic pharmacists who were willing to sell alcohol or alcohol-based tonics to those who sought to drink them for more convivial purposes. The use of sacramental wine was also allowed in Catholic and Jewish services, and a good deal of New York State's wine production shifted to reaching this market.

The sale of illegal spirits soared, and the sale of bad spirits kept pace, causing 11,700 deaths in 1927 alone. The bootlegger, a smuggler of whiskey, became a kind of folk hero to those who found evasion of an unpopular law to be in the tradition of American individuality and resourcefulness. A most fashionable spot in the major cities was the **speakeasy**, which sold illicit liquor, often to prominent people in society and politics who publicly denounced the abuses of alcohol. In NYC alone, there were thirty-two thousand speakeasies, many of them horrid places, others clubbish and genteel, where "café society" congregated. It has been estimated that Americans drank $32 billion worth of illicit liquor during the Prohibition era.

The same law that kept such speakeasies thriving throughout the 1920s drove many legitimate restaurants out of business, including some of the famous opulent dining establishments of the pre-Prohibition era, such as Delmonico's. The development of fine cuisine suffered accordingly, with the lack of fine wines to accompany it.

Prohibition led immediately to opposition, mostly in the form of gangsters who controlled the importation of illegal spirits and the manufacture of the same. By also controlling distribution and many of the establishments that sold these spirits, the criminal underworld was able to coerce public officials, police, and the common people into maintaining a vicious circle of lawlessness, bloodshed, and corruption at every level of society.

Clearly the Noble Experiment had been a failure, and small concessions—such as allowing the public to buy beer and wine containing 3.2 percent alcohol, as of 1932 (called "McAdoo wine" after the bill's sponsor, Senator William Gibbs McAdoo of California)— did nothing to modify the wrongs that Prohibition had unwittingly wrought. Finally, on December 5, 1933, the Twenty-first Amendment repealed the Eighteenth and the Volstead Act, although it was not until 1966 that all statewide prohibition laws were finally repealed. Today there are still many counties, particularly in the South and the Midwest, that are dry.

PROLE FOOD. Short for "proletarian food," meaning food enjoyed by the working class. The abbreviation "prole" has been in use since at least the last quarter of the nineteenth century but seems to have been applied to food in America only in the 1960s. It was used as the title of an article in *Esquire* magazine in July 1968.

PROOF. A term, used in print since 1691, that describes the alcoholic strength of a spirit. The word originates in its meaning "to pass a test," as described in *Grossman's Guide to Wines, Beers, and Spirits*, by Harold J. Grossman, revised by Harriet Lembeck (1977):

Before making distilled spirits became a science, the primitive distillers had a very simple method for determining the potable strength of the distillate. Equal quantities of spirit and gunpowder were mixed and a flame applied. If the gunpowder failed to burn, the spirit was too weak; if it burned too brightly, it was too strong. But if the mixture burned evenly, with a blue flame, it was said to have been proved.

In America, approximately one-half the proof listed on the label of a spirit indicates its alcoholic content at a temperature of 60 degrees Fahrenheit. One proof gallon equals one measured wine gallon at 100 proof. Since each degree of proof equals one-half percent alcohol, an 80-proof spirit would contain 40 percent alcohol.

PROPYL GALLATE. An antioxidant used in vegetable oils, meat products, chewing gum, and other foods.

PROSCIUTTO. An air-cured or dry-cured ham that originated in Italy (1935). Prosciutto is sliced paper-thin and eaten raw, usually with ripe melon. Since an embargo prohibited the importation of Italian prosciutto until 1989, American companies have manufactured a similar product under the name "prosciutto," which is made according to the same method. The word is Italian, derived from the Latin *prae-* (pre-) plus *asciutto* (dried out), and first appeared in print circa 1777.

PROTOSE STEAK. A steak substitute made from vegetable protein. It was eaten by Jewish Americans prohibited by kosher dietary laws from eating meat at certain times.

PRUDHOMME, PAUL (1940–). Chef, entrepreneur, author. Before Paul Prudhomme opened his restaurant K-Paul's Louisiana Kitchen, Cajun food had little recognition as an independent regional cuisine distinct from those of the greater South and New Orleans. Prudhomme brought his own style of Cajun cooking and a taste for high spicing into the American mainstream.

The youngest of thirteen children, Prudhomme was born in Opelousas, Louisiana, where he learned to cook from his mother and relatives who had worked in restaurants in Baton Rouge. He then opened his own eatery, a hamburger stand called Big Daddy-O's Patio, which failed. He thereupon began traveling around the U.S. to explore American gastronomy in many forms, and by 1971 he had settled in New Orleans, where he was hired by the **Brennan** family as a cook at their Commander's Palace restaurant, where he became executive chef, helping to forge a new, lighter style of Creole cuisine.

Prudhomme left Commander's Palace in 1979 to open his own small eatery in the French Quarter, naming it K-Paul's Louisiana Kitchen (the "K" was in honor of his wife, Kay Hinrichs), where he crafted a new, highly spiced version of his childhood Cajun cooking. "Cajun is country food by farmers and fisherman that arrived in Louisiana from Acadiana, Canada," he said. "Creole is New Orleans city food. Communities were created by the people who wanted to stay and not go back to Spain or France." He insisted that his goal was to "make dishes taste round, so people get the sense of sweet and spicy in alternative bites." At a time when most Americans shied away from very hot, spicy food, Prudhomme popularized it. He was also one of the young American chefs of the decade who exhorted cooks to use the best, freshest local ingredients in their cooking.

Since New Orleans's culinary heritage is distinctly Creole, many in the city at first regarded Prudhomme as a Cajun interloper, especially after *New York Times* food editor Craig Claiborne brought national attention to him in 1984, which led to Prudhomme's becoming one of the first star chefs of the 1980s. In 1984, K-Paul's was voted one of the twenty-five best restaurants in America in a survey by *Playboy* magazine. Prudhomme's rich cooking, heavy with butter, initiated a new fascination with Cajun cookery. One of his signature dishes, blackened redfish, became one of the most copied dishes of its era, and was so popular on American menus that the Louisiana State Wildlife and Fisheries Commission issued quotas for commercial fishing of the species.

Prudhomme signed lucrative deals to bottle his Chef Paul Prudhomme's Magic Seasoning Blends and to produce his own seasoned **andouille** sausage and **tasso** ham for sale. His first cookbook, *Chef Paul Prudhomme's Louisiana Kitchen* (1984), had tremendous success, and he followed with *The Prudhomme Family Cookbook* (1987), *Chef Paul Prudhomme's Fork in the Road* (1993), and others, some matched to his PBS TV shows and videos, including *Fork in the Road* (1995), *Louisiana Kitchen* (1998), and *Always Cooking* (2007).

Prudhomme had battled his weight ever since childhood, eventually ballooning to more than five hundred pounds, and this prevented him from cooking in his own restaurant and caused him to need an electric wheelchair for mobility. Through dieting and change of eating habits, he lost 130 pounds and was able to stand and cook in his kitchen again.

In 2002, a TV documentary of Prudhomme's life was made for A&E's *Biography* series. His honors and awards include Restaurateur of the Year from the Louisiana State Restaurant Association (1983), the College of Diplomates Award (1993), a 1994 Louisiana Public Broadcasting Legend Award, induction into the *Nation's Restaurant News* MenuMasters Hall of Fame, and *Bon Appétit*'s Humanitarian Award (2006), for his work with charities, including Meals on Wheels, Easter Seals, the March of Dimes, Big Brothers Big Sisters, and the Alzheimer's Association.

PRUNE. A **plum** that dries without spoiling, resulting in a very sweet fruit eaten as a snack or used in desserts and other dishes. The word is from Latin *prūnum*, dating in Middle English print to circa 1398. Most prunes—about 200,000 tons—are grown in California, where the predominant variety is made from the "La Petite d'Agen" plum, brought from France in 1856 by French horticulturist Louis Pellier.

Americans consume about three-quarters of a pound of prunes per capita annually, 70 percent of them at breakfast.

PTARMIGAN. A bird of the genus *Lagopus* that inhabits the arctic and subarctic regions, first mentioned in print in 1599. The name is originally from the Scottish Gaelic *tarmachan*, which was transformed into a specious Greek form derived from *pteron*, "wing." The bird is hunted and roasted by Alaskans.

PUCHKI. Also "pusky," "pootschky," and other names. Either of two edible Alaskan plants—angela (*Angelica lucida*) and cow parsnip (*Heracleum lanatum*)—whose stems are similar to celery, first in American print in 1945.

PUCK, WOLFGANG (1949–). Chef, author, TV host, entrepreneur. Though born in Austria, Wolfgang Puck became a seminal figure in what was called the New California cuisine of the 1980s, upon opening his restaurant Spago, in L.A. He became a new kind of global chef, defined by his worldwide expansion into every form of food service, from frozen food to airport cafés.

Wolfgang Johannes Topfschnig (his stepfather, Josef Puck, gave him the last name Puck) was born in St. Veit, Austria, where his mother was a chef. At fourteen he apprenticed, then worked in several notable restaurants in France, including Maxim's, in Paris, the Hôtel de Paris, in Monaco, and L'Oustau de Baumanière, in Le Baux-de-Provence. At the age of twenty-four, Puck emigrated to the U.S. to work, first as executive chef at the restaurant La Tour, in Indianapolis.

A year later he moved to L.A., where he distinguished himself as chef (later partner, in 1975) at a glamorous restaurant called Ma Maison by combining the style of **nouvelle cuisine** with California ingredients. In 1982, he opened his own restaurant called Spago, decorated with modern art by Puck's first wife, Barbara Lazaroff. Puck at first intended to serve simple pizzas and grilled items, but his creativity elevated those dishes: pizzas were topped with smoked salmon and caviar, an idea he created for actress Joan Collins; Sonoma baby lamb was cooked over hardwoods and served with braised greens and rosemary. Most of Spago's food was cooked in a wood-burning pizza oven at an open kitchen, a concept he helped promote.

Despite its modest location, off Sunset Boulevard, Spago quickly became the most sought-out restaurant in L.A., its clientele rich with Hollywood movie people who often had Puck cater their events and weddings. As a result, Puck was spoken of as the first celebrity chef, not least because he was creating whole new cuisines, aligned with Southern California styles.

His next project was a stylized Asian fusion restaurant named Chinois on Main (1983), then Postrio, in the Prescott Hotel, in San Francisco (1989), a Northern California version of Spago. Some of his new restaurants foundered, including one built around sausages, and a Spago in Chicago. In 1997, he moved the L.A. Spago to fashionable Canon Drive, in Beverly Hills, where he added some of his childhood favorites, like Wiener schnitzel, to the menu. In 2006, Puck opened Cut, a new stylization of the American steakhouse, featuring a wider menu and various cuts of meats and offal, all within the modern decor of the Beverly Wilshire Hotel. *Esquire* named Cut the Best New Restaurant of the Year.

In 1991, Wolfgang launched a chain of fast-casual restaurants, now called Wolfgang Puck Express. With easy access to new investors, Puck had already branched out to Las Vegas, opening Spago in the Forum Shops at Caesars in 1992, then Postrio Bar & Grill at the Venetian (1999), Lupo in the Mandalay Bay Resort and Casino (1999), and restaurants in Atlantic City, New Jersey, Maui, Washington, D.C., Detroit, Dallas, and Singapore. In 2011, a branch of Cut was a huge success in London, and in 2012 Puck took over the food service and restaurant at the Hotel Bel-Air, in Los Angeles.

In 1998, he and partners formed Wolfgang Puck Catering (WPC), which has since served events like the annual Governors Ball, where Puck has become official chef for the post–Academy Awards celebrity party banquet, as well as for the Grammy Awards celebration, the ESPY Awards, the American Music Awards, and presidential galas and fundraisers.

WPC partnered with Compass Group and Restaurant Associates to form Wolfgang Puck Worldwide Inc., a privately held corporation that franchises locations of casual Wolfgang Puck Bistro restaurants, as well as consumer products that include branded packaged foods, his pizzas among them. He has also ventured into book publishing and other licensing and merchandising projects.

Puck has written six cookbooks, writes the syndicated column Wolfgang Puck's Kitchen in thirty newspapers, and produced a *Spago Cooking with Wolfgang Puck* video. His TV series *Wolfgang Puck* debuted on the Food Network in 2000 and aired for five seasons. In 2001, the A&E network's *Biography* series profiled the life of Puck.

He has long been actively involved in philanthropic endeavors and charitable organizations, including the American Cancer Society, the Alzheimer's Association, the Animal Foundation, the Special Olympics, and the Cystic Fibrosis Society.

Over the years, Puck has won numerous honors, including the James Beard Foundation Award for Outstanding Chef of the Year—twice, in 1991 and 1998.

Puck's cookbooks include *Modern French Cooking for the American Kitchen* (1980), *The Wolfgang Puck Cookbook* (1986), *Adventures in the Kitchen with Wolfgang Puck* (1991), and *Pizza, Pasta, and More* (2000).

PUDDING. A term describing several different desserts, usually cooked, including cakelike confections such as plum pudding; a dish of suet crust containing fruits and sugar; a spongy steamed dish; a pastry crust filled with chopped meats, like kidney; **Yorkshire pudding**, a crisp, breadlike side dish made from a flour-and-egg batter cooked in pan drippings; or, as is most common in contemporary usage, a milk-based dessert made with flavorings like chocolate or vanilla, cooked with a starch until thickened and then cooled until well set. The word is probably from Anglo-Norman *bodeyn* and dates in English print to about 1300.

Eighteenth- and nineteenth-century cookbooks refer to any and all of these as puddings. The word seems to derive from the Old French *boudin*, "sausage," and ultimately from the Latin *botelinus*, for many puddings were a form of encased meat or innards. The earliest examples of the word in English refer to such dishes. Dr. Johnson's *Dictionary* (1755) defines the word as "a kind of food very variously compounded, but generally made of meal, milk, and eggs." One of the earliest American desserts was a quickly thrown-together mixture of cornmeal, milk, and molasses called "cornmeal mush" or "hasty pudding," known since at least 1691. (Harvard's literary society has been called the Hasty Pudding Club since 1795.) "Plum pudding" did not contain plums ("plum" in the seventeenth century referred to raisins or other fruits).

Powdered mixes for making custard-style puddings appeared in 1837 in England, while in 1918 the My-T-Fine Co. produced the first boxed pudding mixes, first chocolate, then lemon, vanilla, butterscotch, and other flavors. In the 1950s, the company (now owned by the Jel Sert Co.) created "instant pudding" mixes that required no cooking.

"Tapioca pudding" (or "tapioca," from the Tupi word *tipioca*, "residue") is made with a starch from the cassava root. A Hawaiian pudding called **haupia** is made with coconut milk. "Indian pudding" is an old colonial dessert based on cornmeal, which used to be called "Indian meal." "Noodle pudding" is particularly savored by Jewish Americans, and "sweet potato pudding" is beloved in the South. Bread pudding is made from stale bread soaked with an egg custard and spices, then baked.

BREAD PUDDING

Combine 4 eggs, 2 c. sugar, and ¾ c. vanilla extract until light in color. Melt ¾ lb. butter in 1 ½ qt. milk, beat in egg mixture, and pour over 4 c. cubed stale bread. Add ¾ c. raisins and let soak for ½ hr. Pour into buttered dish, place in hot-water bath, and bake for 1 hr. at 350°. Serve with custard sauce or whipped cream.

INDIAN PUDDING

Scald 5 c. milk and pour slowly over ⅓ c. cornmeal. Cook in double boiler until slightly thickened, then add 1 t. salt, ½ c. molasses, and a pinch of grated nutmeg. Pour into buttered dish and bake at 300° for about 2 hr. or until set. Serve with whipped cream or ice cream.

PUDDING TIME. Colloquial term for dinnertime, dating in print to 1834.

PUEBLO BREAD. A white flour bread made by Native Americans of the Southwest, specifically the Pueblo of New Mexico. The dough, made with flour, salt, yeast, and water (and sometimes eggs), is allowed to rise overnight in a metal washtub or large basin. The loaves are shaped by the women of the tribe into various forms of animals or sunbursts. The bread is baked for about an hour in an adobe oven preheated with burning pine branches, the embers of which are removed.

PUFFARDS. Also "puffertjes." Dutch New York cookies baked in a pan called a "pullet-pan" and eaten hot with powdered cinnamon and sugar. The name suggests they would puff up in the baking.

PULLMAN CAR. A dining car on a railroad train, named and invented by George Mortimer Pullman of Palmyra, New York, in 1868. The first, rudimentary railroad dining cars had been put in service in 1863 on the Philadelphia,

Wilmington & Baltimore Railroad, with only stand-up buffets for food service. Pullman constructed elaborate dining cars with full-service signature china and silverware, and impeccable service. The first Pullman car was named the Delmonico, after the fashionable NYC restaurant.

PULLMAN LOAF. A square loaf of bread served on the **Pullman cars**.

PULLY BONE. The wishbone of a fowl, dating in print to 1877.

PULQUE. A fermented beverage from Mexico made from the agave plant. The word is Mexican Spanish, dating in print to 1877. See **tequila**.

PUMP. A mound of potatoes, turnips, corn, and other vegetables, covered with bark, mulch, earth, or metal, used for winter storage of food. The word is of uncertain origins, dating in print to 1953.

PUMPERNICKEL. A dark bread made from rye flour. Pumpernickel was originally made in Westphalia, Germany, and in that country is called *Schwarzbrot*, "black bread." It is firm, slightly acidic in flavor, and of varying densities and textures.

The term is of somewhat obscure etymology. The *American Heritage Dictionary* cites "German *Pumpernickel:* early New High German *Pumpern*, a fart (imitative) plus *Nickel*, 'devil,' general pejorative; so named from being hard to digest." The *Morris Dictionary of Word and Phrase Origins* states the word was a combination of *Pumper*, the sound "made by a person falling," and *Nickel*, a "dwarf" or "goblin." A "pumpernickel," therefore, was a dolt or fool. Theodora FitzGibbon, in her *Food of the Western World*, cited a story that the word is a corruption of the phrase *"pain pour Nicole"* ("bread for Nicole"), after Napoleon's horse Nicole's fondness for black bread. The word first appeared in English print in 1738.

Pumpernickel was brought by German immigrants to America and is now found in most supermarkets, though the best is usually found in German or Jewish neighborhood bakeries.

PUMPKIN (*Cucurbita pepo*). A trailing vine and its fruit, having a yellow-orange rind and flesh. The name is from the Greek *pepōn*, for a large melon. An English word for the pumpkin, *pompion* or *pumpion*, had been in use since at least 1545, whereas in America "pumpkin" did not make an appearance in print until 1640.

Pumpkins were among many squashes eaten by the Indians and introduced early on to the European settlers. In fact, pumpkin pie, still one of the country's favorite desserts, was served at the Pilgrims' second Thanksgiving, in 1623, and has become a traditional Thanksgiving food. The colonists made pumpkin beer, and pumpkin soup was also popular. Pumpkin seeds are roasted and eaten as a snack. Indeed, it was such a frequent and important item in the early American diet that a seventeenth-century rhyme went, "We have pumpkin at morning and pumpkin at noon. If it were not for pumpkin, we should be undoon."

Pumpkins may be cooked like other squashes, roasted with butter and brown sugar, or boiled as a side dish. Most Americans today use canned pumpkin filling for their pies.

The sugar pumpkin is also used as a Halloween jack-o'-lantern.

PUMPKIN PIE

Combine 2 c. cooked pumpkin with ⅔ c. sugar, 1 ½ t. cinnamon, ½ t. nutmeg, ¼ t. ground cloves, and ½ t. salt. Blend 3 eggs with ½ c. heavy cream and ½ c. milk, then mix in pumpkin. Pour into pastry crust and bake for about 45 min. at 400°, until inserted knife comes out clean. Serve with whipped cream.

PUNCH. An alcoholic beverage mixture of various ingredients, first appearing in print in 1600. Today the term usually refers to a bowl of citrus- or fruit-based party drink containing any number of liquors, sparkling wine, or champagne.

The word originally came from the Hindi *panch*, meaning "five," in reference to the five original ingredients used—lime, sugar, spices, water, and a fermented sap called "arrack." British sailors had picked up the drink and spoken of punch as of the early seventeenth century. It soon became a popular beverage in the West Indies and North American colonies, where it might be mixed with wine, milk, hot water, and, most often, rum. At the large Caribbean plantations, enormous bowls of punch—described by one onlooker as big enough "for a goose to swim in"—were served at lavish social gatherings, and people of the day already were arguing as to what made a perfect punch. An advertisement in the *Salem Gazette* for 1741 by a West Indies trader proclaimed that his orange juice was preferred by many punch enthusiasts to lemon. Few would agree on the exact proportions of "Planter's punch," which was created at Planter's Hotel, in St. Louis, in the 1840s.

Fish House punch, created at the State in Schuylkill fishing club, founded in 1732, is another punch whose original ingredients are hotly debated. Many other punches became associated with specific regiments, Navy crews, and Ivy League universities. "Sangaree" (from the French *sang*, "blood"), was a colonial punch made with red wine and fruits (sometimes ale), an early version of Spanish **sangria**, which became popular in the 1960s as a party punch. In the 1920s, many colleges lent their names to punches, such as "Yale punch," "Harvard punch" and "Columbia punch."

"Pisco punch," created in the 1870s by Duncan Nicol, of the Bank Exchange bar, in San Francisco, is made with pisco muscat brandy from Pisco, Peru.

Nonalcoholic punches, usually made with club soda or ginger ale and various fruits, are still popular at children's parties in America.

NAVY PUNCH

Mix 6 oz. lime juice, 2 parts liquid sugar, and 3 parts dark rum and blend over an ice chunk. Garnish with fruit and a sprinkle of nutmeg.

PUPU. Also "pu pu." A Hawaiian term for various appetizers or relishes, such as macadamia nuts, barbecued meats, coconut chips, and wontons, first appearing in American print in 1967. In Chinese American or Polynesian American restaurants, a "pupu platter" is usually a plate of appetizers spread around a lighted burner, into which one sticks the morsels for heating.

PURSLANE. A plant in the Genus *Portulaca*, used as a salad vegetable, first in print circa 1400, from French.

PX. Restaurant guest-list abbreviation for "person exceptional," meaning a special guest who needs to be well taken care of.

Q

QUAIL. Any of a variety of New World game birds—none of which are related to the Old World quail, such as *Coturnix coturnix*, though all are in the order Galliformes and the family Phasianidae. The common name "quail" derives from the Gallo-Roman *coacula*, probably from the sound made by the bird. In Middle English, the word was written, as of 1381, as *quaille*.

There is some confusion in American terminology for quail, especially since the most familiar variety, the "bobwhite" (*Colinus virginianus*), is called "quail" in the North and "partridge" in the South. (For further information, see **partridge**.) "Quail" was first applied to this fowl in print in 1625; "bobwhite" is first recorded in 1837, and "bobwhite quail" in 1920. The term "bobwhite" derives from the sound the bird makes, as Americans perceive it. This same bird has also been called the "blue quail" in the Southwest.

Other American quail include the "mountain quail" (*Oreortyx pictus*), "Montezuma quail" (*Cyrtonyx montezumae*), "Gambel's quail" (*Lophortyx gambelii*), also called "redhead," "California quail" (*L. californicus*), and "scaled quail" (*Callipepla squamata*).

Other varieties of quail are raised on farms in the U.S., primarily the "Pharaoh," "Egyptian," or "Japanese" quail, most of which are grown now for food rather than as game birds. Quail are usually roasted or grilled and are often served with wild rice.

QUAKER STEW. Also "stewed Quaker." A nonalcoholic cough syrup made with vinegar and a sweetener, dating in print to 1857.

QUAKING CUSTARD. A cream custard of New England, around which beaten egg whites are placed. The name refers to the quivering texture of the dish.

QUICHE. A pie or tart having an egg filling and a variety of other ingredients. The word is French, probably from the German dialect word *Kuchen*, "cake." Quiche is certainly a dish of French origins, especially of Lorraine, and "quiche Lorraine," made with onion and bacon, is the first mention of the dish in American print as of 1925. It became the most popular version in the 1960s, as a luncheon, brunch, or appetizer dish in the U.S. Since then, quiches have been adapted to contain all manner of ingredients, from peppers and cheese to vegetables, sausage, and other meats. There are even retail stores specializing in a variety of quiches, which may be cooked as a large tart or as individual tarts.

QUICK BREAD. A bread, biscuit, muffin, or other baked good without yeast or too much sweetness. The term was first in American print in 1882.

QUICKIE. A quickly consumed alcoholic beverage, as in "Let's have a quickie," dating in print to 1940.

QUINOA (*Chenopodium quinoa*). Also "quinua." Pronounced "*keen*-wah," this grain was central to the Incas' diet (they called it "the mother grain") but not raised in the U.S. until recently (first in Colorado). The word was first mentioned in print in 1598, derived from South American Spanish. There are about eighteen hundred varieties of quinoa in many different colors, and it has been termed the "supergrain" because of its nutritional benefits. It is used as a cereal, stuffing, and bread grain, and in salads.

RABBIT. A herbivorous, long-eared mammal of the Leporidae family that is found both wild and domesticated in America. Wild rabbits are up to sixteen inches long and weigh two to three pounds. The New World genus *Sylvilagus* includes the "cottontail," the "marsh," and the "swamp rabbit." The "Idaho pygmy rabbit" (*S. idahoensis*) is found in the Great Basin of the U.S. The "jackrabbit" and "snowshoe rabbit" are actually hares, though of the same family. The word in Middle English was *rabet*, dating in print to about 1398.

The rabbit was in America long before Europeans arrived, and the Aztecs worshiped a rabbit god; the North American Indians certainly ate them. Although Americans have always eaten rabbits, their association in the present century with pets and anthropomorphic images such as the Easter Bunny and the Bugs Bunny cartoon character have made many people squeamish about cooking such beloved animals. Nevertheless, they are still hunted and valued for their meat, which should be taken young. The best domesticated rabbits for eating are about two months old and can be roasted whole, sautéed, fried, or broiled. Mature rabbits should be stewed and are best marinated before cooking. Americans consume about fifty million pounds of rabbit meat each year.

RABBIT STEW

Disjoint a young rabbit and season inside and outside with salt and pepper. Melt 1 T. butter in pan and brown rabbit meat. Add 1 T. flour and simmer for 2 min. Add ½ c. red wine and ½ qt. chicken stock to cover the rabbit. Boil, then add 2 cloves of garlic, 2 cloves, 1 bay leaf, and a pinch of thyme. Cover and bake at 350° for 45 min. Add white onions and ½ c. mushrooms and return to oven for 15 min. Serves 4.

RABBITFISH. Also "puffer." A fleshy whitefish, *Lagocephalus laevigatus*, dating in print to 1787.

RABBIT FOOD. A slang term to describe meager vegetables or vegetarian diets, so called because it is the kind of food eaten by rabbits, a usage dating in Australian print to 1991 as "the only diet for many in the bikini capital wanting to lose weight."

RACCOON (*Procyon lotor*). Also "coon" and "racoon." A grayish-brown furred mammal with black, masklike markings, found throughout North America. The name comes from the Virginian Algonquian Indian *aroughcun* and is first noted in English as early as 1608, as "Rahaughcums." Raccoons also go by the very old name "chaoui," derived from Choctaw or Mobilian *shaui*.

Raccoon was once enjoyed by the early colonial settlers of the East and the South as a matter of course and continued to be enjoyed regularly by westerners. Today it is still a food animal among hunters and is almost never found commercially. Louisiana African Americans used to call a dish of raccoon sprinkled with gin and served with mashed potatoes "drunk coon."

RADICCHIO (*Cichorium intybus*). A bitter salad vegetable, with favored varieties having a deep-red-and-white coloring. *Radicchio* is the Italian word for the vegetable, mentioned in American print as of 1887, but it was first cultivated in the U.S. in 1981, by Moore Farming Inc., of Salinas Valley, California, and is now grown in New Jersey as well.

RADISH. Any of a variety of plants in the genus *Raphanus*, especially *R. sativus*, bearing pungent roots usually eaten raw in salads. The word is from the Latin *radix*, "root," dating in Middle English to about 1440.

The "wild radish" (*R. raphanistrum*) is common in both Europe and North America, but the origins of the cultivated species, *R. sativus*, is unknown. An oriental radish, the "daikon," is now seen at market.

RAG BREAD. Pieces and scraps of dough combined and cut into strips, then buttered, rolled into cylinders, and baked, dating in print to 1996.

RAG MUFFIN. A jelly roll pastry, dating in print to 1905.

RAICHLEN, STEVEN (1953–). Author, educator, TV host. In the 1990s, Steven Raichlen emerged as America's leading authority on barbecuing and grilling, with an increasing emphasis on global variations after 2000. His books have won five **James Beard Foundation** awards and been translated into seventeen languages. *USA Today* wrote of him, "Where there's smoke, there's Steven Raichlen."

Raichlen was born in Nagoya, Japan, and grew up in Baltimore. He received his B.A. in French literature from Reed College, in Portland, Oregon, and in 1975 won a Watson Fellowship to Paris to study medieval cooking. While there, he trained at Le Cordon Bleu and La Varenne cooking schools. He returned to the U.S. to settle in Boston, with the intention of becoming a novelist, and began reviewing restaurants for *Boston* magazine.

Raichlen moved to Miami to marry Barbara Seldin; there he wrote *Miami Spice* (1993), one of the first cookbooks on "New Florida cuisine" (see **Nuevo Latino cuisine**). His second book was *Steven Raichlen's High-Flavor, Low-Fat Vegetarian Cooking* (1997). Living in Florida and cooking outside led him to focus on barbecue and to write *The Barbecue! Bible* (1998), the result of a four-year odyssey to document outdoor grilling around the world, which won him the first of three IACP/**Julia Child** book awards.

In 2000, Raichlen wrote *How to Grill*. He produced the TV show *Barbecue University* for PBS and founded Barbecue University, at the Broadmoor resort, in Colorado Springs, Colorado. He also designed two lines of grilling accessories, Best of Barbecue and Planet Barbecue, and a French-language TV show entitled *Le Maître du Grill*.

Raichlen has lectured on the history and culture of barbecue at the Smithsonian Institution, the Library of Congress, the National Press Club, and Harvard University.

Author of twenty-nine books, his works include *Beer-Can Chicken* (2002), *BBQ USA* (2003) *Planet Barbecue!* (2010), and *Best Ribs Ever* (2012). His novel *Island Apart* was published in 2012.

RAILROAD COOKIE. A cookie swirled on the inside with cinnamon and brown sugar. The origin of the name may derive from the dark tracks of filling that look like railroad tracks. The cookies were mentioned in a Missouri recipe book as early as 1875.

RAILROAD COOKIE

Cream 1 c. butter with 2 c. brown sugar. Beat in 2 eggs, 1 t. baking soda, ¼ t. salt, 1 t. cinnamon, and 2 c. flour. Add 2 more c. flour (dough will be stiff), divide dough, roll out to ⅓-in. thickness, spread with date filling, roll up, and slice to ¼-in. thickness. Bake 15 min. at 350°.

RAISIN. A sweet, dried grape. Raisins are eaten plain, mixed with nuts, cooked in cakes, pastries, breads, and puddings, and mixed with cereals, especially bran flakes, as a breakfast dish.

The word comes from the Latin *racémus*, which became *raisin* in Middle English.

California produces more raisins than any other region in the world, mostly from **Thompson Seedless** and Muscat of Alexandria grapes. The industry began there in September 1873, when a heat wave dried out much of the grape harvest, causing one San Francisco grocer to market the shriveled grapes as "Peruvian Delicacies."

Raisins are sun-dried in the vineyards, then graded, cleaned, and packed, sometimes lightened in color with sulfur dioxide.

RAMOS GIN FIZZ. A cocktail made from cream, gin, lemon juice, orange-flower water, and egg whites. It was first made by Henry C. Ramos, a New Orleans bar owner who had purchased the Imperial Cabinet soon after he arrived in the city in 1888. The drink became famous for its preparation at the hands of the Imperial's squad of bartenders, who during Mardi Gras of 1915 numbered thirty-five. Rima and Richard Collin, in *The New Orleans Cookbook* (1975) cite Meyer's Restaurant as the place where Ramos actually concocted the drink, although since 1935 the Roosevelt Hotel, now the Fairmont Hotel, has held the trademark for the name Ramos Gin Fizz.

Most authorities on the cocktail recommend a long shaking time for the ingredients to achieve the proper texture.

RAMOS GIN FIZZ

Shake with crushed ice 1 T. confectioners' sugar, the juice of half a lemon, the juice of half a lime, 1 egg white, ½ oz. heavy cream, 1 ½ oz. gin, a dash of vanilla extract, a dash of seltzer, and 3 drops of orange-flower water. Continue shaking until foamy and of a consistent texture—about 5 min. Pour into a highball glass. (The ingredients may be mixed in an electric blender for 1 ½ min.)

RAMP (*Allium tricoccum*, *A. cernuum*, and *A. ursinum*). Wild onions native to North America with a long green leaf and slender white bulbs, resembling the **scallion**. The word, referring to *Arum macultaum*, is an Elizabethan dialect rendering of the wild garlic, *rams* or *ramson*, and is first mentioned in English print around 1500, though it was used earlier by the English immigrants of America's southern Appalachian Mountains. By 1828, "ramp" was in American print.

Ramps grow from South Carolina to Canada. "To many West Virginians," according to Kemp Miles Minifie, in an article in *Gourmet* magazine in 1983, "ramps are the harbingers of spring. The first appearance of the flat green leaves of this wild leek jutting through the snow signals the beginning of feasts and festivals where bushels of the pungent stalks are consumed, both raw and cooked, along with quantities of ham, eggs, and potatoes."

Ramps have a somewhat stronger flavor than scallions but are eaten raw, as well as in preparations where onions, scallions, or shallots would be called for.

RANCH DRESSING. A dressing made with mayonnaise, onion, garlic, buttermilk, and various seasonings. There are two claims as to the origin of the term "ranch dressing." Todds Foods, of Glendale, Arizona, claims that part-owner David Bears, of Todds, created the dressing for Bobby McGee's Restaurants in 1980 as a dipping sauce for breaded, fried zucchini. But the term dates in American print, in the *Edwardsville* (Illinois) *Intelligencer*, to 1962. According to the Clorox Co., of Oakland, California, however, "ranch-style dressing" was originated by the Henson family, owners of Hidden Valley Ranch, near Santa Barbara, California, who began marketing a packaged dry mix after World War II. In October 1972, Clorox purchased the trademark rights from the Henson family for "Hidden Valley Ranch Original Ranch" salad dressing, which is sold as a dry mix in two flavors, one made with buttermilk, the other with regular milk.

RANKINS. A nineteenth-century cheese pudding.

RANKINS

Combine 1 c. buttermilk, 6 T. grated cheese, 3 T. bread crumbs, 3 T. butter, ⅓ t. salt, ⅓ t. dry mustard, a pinch of cayenne pepper, and a pinch of ground pepper. Bring to a boil, cool, then add 2 beaten egg yolks and fold in two stiffly beaten egg whites. Bake 15 min. in a 375° oven.

RASPBERRY. Any of a variety of plants in the genus *Rubus* bearing fleshy dark-purple or red berries. The name derives from an earlier word, *raspis*, and was first recorded, as "Rasberies," in 1602.

America offered a wide variety of wild raspberries to the early colonists, who nevertheless imported their European variety, *R. idaeus*, for cultivation. The "American red raspberry" (*R. i. strigosus*) was known in Massachusetts and first listed as of 1621 among the region's wild fruits. The "black raspberry" (*R. occidentalis* in the East and *R. leucodermis* in the West) is the other major variety grown in the U.S., chiefly in Michigan, Oregon, New York, and Washington.

Americans eat raspberries fresh or frozen, in pies, ice cream, sherbets, and ices, and make them into sweet dessert sauces, such as "melba sauce" (see **peach melba**).

RATAFIA. A sweet cordial made from the infusion of fruit kernels in alcohol. The word is from the French, via West Indian Creole, and in France *ratafia* more specifically refers to sweetened aperitifs made from wines such as burgundy and champagne. It first appeared in print in English in 1670. By 1845 there was also a "ratafia biscuit" in print, to be eaten with the cordial.

Ratafia was a popular nineteenth-century home-made cordial but it is now rarely seen. There have been some efforts in California wineries to produce a French-style ratafia aperitif.

RAT CHEESE. Particularly smelly cheddar cheese, dating in print to 1910.

RATION. Generally a fixed allotment of food, but more commonly referring to the food served to the armed forces in the field. Long a subject of griping and jokes among military personnel, rations have played a great part in the success of various campaigns, for as Napoleon Bonaparte is said to have observed, "An army marches on its stomach." (The quote is also attributed to Frederick the Great.)

The set rations of the American Revolutionary War were established in 1775, with daily provisions including one pound of beef or one-quarter pound of pork or one pound of salt fish, one pound of bread or flour, three pints of peas or beans, one pint of milk, one-half pint of rice or one pint of cornmeal, and one quart of spruce beer or cider. Nine gallons of molasses was provided for a company of one hundred men per week. When providing these was not possible, soldiers had to live off a diet of **hardtack** and **jerky**, especially in the Navy, where fresh food was difficult to preserve.

By the time of the Civil War, soldiers also carried coffee, tea, potatoes, and seasonings (the cost of rations then was about fifteen cents per day per man), and strides in preserving foods through canning and vacuum packing, and in heating, gave the Union Army a pronounced advantage over Confederate forces that often went hungry for lack of set rations.

By World War I, one pound of hard bread and one pound of canned meat, along with coffee, sugar, and a cube of condensed soup, were provided. There were basically four types of ration: "garrison ration" (perishable food); "reserve ration" (nonperishable canned food); "emergency ration" (dried compressed meat and cereal bar); and "trench ration" (designed to protect against gas-chemical-attack contamination, these were rations placed in large steel cans for about twenty-five troops).

In the mid-1930s, the Quartermaster Corps began researching rations more scientifically and developed a wide range of products for use in the field and at home base. By 1940 the term "trench ration" had been done away with, "garrison ration" was called "A" ration, "reserve ration" became "B" ration, then "C" ration, and "emergency" ration was called "D" ration.

"C" ration (or "combat ration") was the most commonly used, consisting of six cans weighing 4.3 pounds and containing three different meals. Three cans were called "M units," for "meat units." "M-1" was meat and beans, "M-2" was meat-and-vegetable hash, and "M-3" was meat-and-vegetable stew. "B units" ("bread unit") contained bread, coffee, a sugar packet, soluble coffee, and sundry items. "C" rations cost about sixty cents per piece.

A big breakthrough came in 1940 with the "K" ration, a light, sealed ration for easy portability on paratroopers and other light infantry. Developed at the University of Minnesota by Ancel Keys (and possibly deriving its name from the first letter of his last name), this was originally called a "para-ration," until General George Patton asked for the name change because he wanted it used by his tank troops.

The "Logan bar" was a chocolate-and-oat-flour bar developed by Captain Paul P. Logan and made by the Hershey Chocolate Co., containing six hundred calories to provide quick energy.

A few enhancements of the World War II products were made during the war in Vietnam, around 1965. "Long-range patrol packets" were developed, to be carried in soft packets that wouldn't tear. Some further developments were made for the NASA astronaut programs, and experiments were done with irradiated foods in the early 1980s.

By the 1980s the goal was to provide personnel with two hot meals a day when possible. These fell under "group" rations and "individual" rations. The former included "B" rations designed for use in organized dining facilities, and "T" rations, which stands for "Tray Pack," intended to be boiled and served to twelve to eighteen people. These had a three-year shelf life. "Individual" rations have been where the most strides have been made in recent years. In 1975, the "MRE ration" (short for "Meal, Ready-to-Eat") was developed—a range of meals packed entirely in pouches and containing a complete thirteen-hundred-calorie meal that includes an eight-ounce entrée and items like cake, peanut butter, hot sauce, and candy. They are designed to be eaten cold, but MREs usually include a "flameless ration heater," a water-activated exothermic chemical heating pad containing magnesium iron and polyethylene powder, and salt. The food is placed in the bag, then in the soldier's pocket. After twelve minutes of walking, the food is heated to 100° Fahrenheit. MREs may also contain "pouch bread"—fresh bread sealed in a soft pouch and having a three-year shelf life. Responding to troops' complaints about the quality and variety of MREs served during the first Gulf War in Iraq, the Pentagon introduced a new array of twenty-four different MREs that included Jamaican-spiced pork chops, vegetable pasta with cream sauce, beef teriyaki, chili and macaroni, and a number of brand-name items like M&M's candy and bottles of **Tabasco** sauce.

In addition to MREs, the military now uses "MORE rations" (for "Meal, Operational, Ready-to-Eat"), which come packed on plastic trays as ready-to-eat meals and often contain many commercial items favored by personnel off-base.

RATTLESNAKE (genera *Sistrurus* and *Crotalus*). Any of a number of venomous snakes found in North America whose tails have interlocking links that make a rattling sound when shaken by disturbed vipers. The word dates in print to 1620. Rattlesnakes are found throughout the country and include such species as the "massasauga," "timber," "pygmy," "eastern and western diamondback," "red diamond," "sidewinder," "rock," "speckled," "black-tailed," "twin-spotted," "tiger," "Mojave," and "western" rattlesnake.

Although they have never been particularly relished as food by most Americans, rattlesnakes have held a certain gastronomic interest among hunters, woodsmen, trappers, and cowboys, who usually put them in a stewpot or grill them.

In Mooresfield, West Virginia, the people hold an annual Hardy County Rattlesnake Hunters' Rattlesnake Feed featuring a variety of rattlesnake recipes.

BARBECUED RATTLESNAKE

Remove head and skin snake, cut into 2-in. pieces, and parboil for ½ hr. in a broth seasoned with salt, pepper, and herbs. Combine juice of 1 lemon, ½ c. honey, 2 T. Worcestershire sauce, 2 T. red wine vinegar, 1 chopped chile pepper, 1 clove chopped garlic, salt, and pepper. Baste snake with mixture and cook on grill.

RAVIGOTE. The word, from the French for "to refresh," applies to both a spicy sauce of butter cooked with flour, wine, and white stock, and a cold sauce made with vinegar, oil, capers, parsley, tarragon, chervil, and onion. As the former, it is widely used in Louisiana Creole cooking, especially with crabmeat. The word was first recorded in 1733.

CRABMEAT RAVIGOTE

In a sauté pan melt 1 stick butter and sauté 1 c. chopped bell peppers, ½ c. chopped pimientos, ½ c. sliced mushrooms, ½ c. chopped scallions, ⅛ c. chopped parsley, ⅛ c. chopped chervil, 2 T. capers, ⅛ t. cayenne pepper, and salt and pepper to taste. Mix well, add 1 lb. lump crabmeat, and cook for about 10 min. Place equal portions into individual buttered ramekins, sprinkle with bread crumbs and melted butter, and brown under a broiler. Serves 4.

RAW BAR. A food stand or bar serving uncooked shellfish. They are quite often attached to a somewhat more formal restaurant, especially those specializing in seafood. The word dates in American print to 1914.

RAZORBACK. A wild hog of the southern U.S. that is descended from domesticated hogs brought over by the Spanish in 1539. The razorback was again domesticated by the American pioneers, who made bacon from its meat. It is not the same animal as the "peccary" or "javelina" (family Tayassuidae) of the Southwest. "Razorback" was first printed in 1845.

RED BEANS AND RICE. A Louisiana dish of kidney beans and rice flavored with a ham bone and traditionally served on Monday, after a Sunday dinner of ham. The dish originated with Louisiana's African American cooks, who call it "red and white," but it has also became associated with the Creoles and can be found in numerous New Orleans restaurants and homes on Mondays. As John Thorne notes in *Rice & Beans: The Itinerary of a Recipe* (1981), "Although red kidney beans are often used in making red beans and rice, strict purists aver that they have too strong a flavor for the dish, and that the small South Louisiana red bean is preferred." Similarly, purists insist on using Louisiana **pickled pork** (or sweet pickled pork), a packaged seasoning made from pork shoulder marinated in brine. There is also considerable debate as to whether the beans and rice should be cooked together or separately. The *Picayune's Creole Cook Book* (1900), from which the following recipe is taken, prefers the latter method.

RED BEANS AND RICE

Wash 1 qt. dried red beans and soak overnight in cold water. Drain off water, place beans in a pot, cover with at least 2 qt. fresh water, and heat slowly. Add 1 lb. ham or salt pork, 1 chopped carrot, 1 minced onion, 1 bay leaf, salt, and pepper and boil for at least 2 hr. When tender, mash beans, place meat and vegetables on top, and serve on a bed of white boiled rice. May be served as an entrée or side dish.

RED BEET EGG. A hard-boiled egg pickled with beets so that it has a red color, dating in print to 1916.

REDEYE GRAVY. Also "red-eye gravy," "red ham gravy," "slingshot gravy," "frog-eye gravy," "raised gravy," and other terms. A gravy made from ham drippings, often flavored with coffee. It is a traditional southern gravy served with ham, biscuits, and grits and takes its name from the appearance of a "red eye" in the middle of the reduced gravy. It has been popular since at least the 1930s, dating in American print to 1945.

REDEYE GRAVY

Remove ham steak from skillet in which it has been fried and add ½ c. water (some insist on ice water) or ½ c. strong black coffee. Scrape up ham drippings and cook about 3 min., stirring constantly. Pour over ham, biscuits, or grits.

RED FLANNEL HASH. A **hash**, usually with corned beef and beets that color it red, dating in print to 1907.

REDHORSE (genus *Moxostoma*). Any of a variety of reddish-brown fishes of which eighteen species inhabit the eastern rivers, including the "river redhorse" (*M. carinatum*), "silver redhorse" (*M. anisurum*), "shorthead redhorse" (*M. macrolepidotum*), "torrent sucker" (*M. rhothoecum*), "rustyside sucker" (*M. hamiltoni*), "golden redhorse" (*M. erythrurum*), and "black redhorse" (*M. duquesnei*). It is a popular food fish, and South Carolinians make a "redhorse bread" with cornmeal and redhorse. "Redhorse" first saw print in 1796.

RED HOT. A small, red cinnamon-and-pepper-flavored ball of candy, dating in print to 1877. It has since become a trademark name-brand candy. The word, usually used in the plural, is also a synonym for frankfurters, dating in print to 1890.

RED INK. Slang term used to describe the Italian American wine sold at delicatessens in NYC during Prohibition. The term appeared in print in 1906. Also called "dago red."

RED ONION. Slang term for an illicit bar or a cheap boarding or eating house, dating in print to 1930. See **speakeasy**.

RED RICE. Also "Spanish rice." A southern seasoned rice dish made with tomato to give it color. It is often served with shrimp.

RED SAUCE. This term may refer either to an Italian-style tomato sauce or to a tomato-flavored clam sauce, also a standard item in **Italian American** cookery. Both terms have become common since the end of the nineteenth century. A 1702 English citation refers generally to a "red Sauce," but by 1912 in American English, a reference in the *Syracuse* (New York) *Herald* is clearly to an Italian American tomato sauce: "Detective Patsy

Bennett dropped into Giuseppi's emporium for a platter of spaghetti with red sauce and grated cheese." See also **white sauce**.

RED SNAPPER VERACRUZ. Red snapper cooked with chile peppers, tomatoes, and other seasonings. In Mexico, this dish is called *huachinango a la veracruzana*, but it has also become a popular item in Mexican American restaurants across the country.

RED SNAPPER VERACRUZ

Salt and pepper 4 red snapper fillets and sauté in 3 T. olive oil. Remove from pan and keep warm. Add 1 T. olive oil to pan and sauté 1 chopped onion, 2 chopped garlic cloves, 4 peeled, seeded, and chopped tomatoes, the juice of 1 lime, a pinch of oregano, and 2 red or green chile peppers that have been seeded. Cook for 10 min., return fish to pan, and simmer, covered, for 10 min. Serve with rice. Serves 4.

REFERENCE DAILY INTAKE. Also "Recommended Daily Intake." Originally called Recognized Daily Allowance" when adapted by the restaurant industry as of 1941, the term referred to federal regulations laid down in 1945 for the minimum amount of nutrients needed by people over the age of four. It is usually included on food labels as a list of nutrients like vitamins and minerals. The "Recommended Dietary Allowance" (RDA) refers to the estimated amount of various nutrients needed each day to maintain good health, which varies slightly depending on age and sex. In 1997 the name was changed to Reference Daily Intake designed to meet sufficient nutritional requirements for Americans.

REFRIED BEANS. A Mexican American dish of mashed cooked pinto beans, usually served as a side dish or as a filling for various tortilla preparations. The term dates in American print to 1897. "Refried beans" is actually a mistranslation of the Spanish *frijoles refritos*, which means "well-fried beans," a distinction first mentioned in Erna Fergusson's *Mexican Cookbook* (1934), but "refried" has remained in common parlance with regard to this dish.

REFRIED BEANS

Cook 4 c. pinto beans in water to cover until tender, and place in a skillet with 4 T. lard or bacon fat. Mash down the beans, adding a little of the bean liquid. Add 2 minced garlic cloves, salt, and pepper. Cook over medium heat for about 30 min., until edges are crispy. Turn out onto a warm plate. Serves 6.

RELISH. Any of a variety of spicy, often **pickle**-based condiments served as a side dish or spread on a food item. The word, which first appeared in English in 1530, is from the Middle English for a "taste" and is derived from Old French *reles*, "something remaining." As Theodora FitzGibbon noted in *The Food of the Western World* (1976), "In Britain ["relish"] usually means a thin pickle or sauce with a vinegar base. In the U.S. the term also embraces finely chopped fruits or vegetables with a dressing of sugar, salt, and vinegar; this is not only served as an adjunct to a main course, but may also constitute the first course of a meal, as apple relish, garden relish, and salad relish."

American relishes include **chow-chow**, **piccalilli**, **ketchup**, watermelon rind, chutneys, and the many pickle-based bottled varieties that are customarily spread on hot dogs and hamburgers.

RÉMOULADE. Also "remoulade" and "rémolade." A mayonnaise dressing or sauce of French origin, flavored with mustard and other seasonings. The word, dating in English print to 1733, is from French, from the Picard dialect word *ramolas*, "horseradish." In New Orleans cookery, the sauce is made spicier than the French version and often contains hard-boiled eggs. If chopped parsley is added, it may be called a "green rémoulade" or "*rémoulade verte*." Different versions will include different ingredients.

RÉMOULADE

Mix 2 c. mayonnaise with ¼ c. hot mustard, ¼ c. horseradish, ½ t. cayenne, 2 chopped shallots, and 2 T. Worcestershire sauce. Chill and serve over fish, meat, or shrimp.

RESTAURANT. A dining room or other eatery where one pays for a meal. The concept of a public place selling full meals is of rather recent origins, for although inns and taverns of one form or another have long histories, the main business of such places was either as a dispenser of spirits or as a travelers' way-stop that sold food only incidentally. The word *restaurant* is French, from the verb *restaurer*, "to restore," first appearing in French around 1750, in reference to a chicken or beef broth prepared by cookshops called *traiteurs*. It was asserted that in 1787 a Parisian *traiteur* named Beauvilliers began serving guests at separate tables, and the term *restaurant* came to describe such establishments. But Rebecca L. Spang contends, in her book *The Invention of the Restaurant* (2000), that a Parisian financier and entrepreneur named Mathurin Roze de Chantoiseau—who called himself the "Author" of the restaurant—has a stronger claim to being the first restaurateur: In 1766, he opened an establishment near the Palais Royal where patrons could eat when and what they wished; because his restaurant was geared to his patrons' health, even women were allowed to dine there. Soon afterwards, restaurants in Paris proliferated.

The first appearance of the word in English print was in 1806, in American print in 1820; there is an early reference in the novel *The Prairie* (1827), by James Fenimore Cooper, to "the most renowned of Parisian restaurants."

The taverns and inns of England and America had, since the sixteenth century, served food, usually one set meal each day, called the "ordinary," which also came to mean the establishments themselves. These were common in colonial America, too, as were the coffeehouses and men's clubs first set up in London in the seventeenth and eighteenth centuries. The White Horse Tavern, in Newport, Rhode Island, established in 1673, claims to be the oldest continuously operating tavern in America. Hotel dining rooms began to improve after 1800, and the opening of the Tremont House, in Boston in 1829, was heralded for its two-hundred-seat dining room and its use of the new four-tined forks.

After the Revolution in France, many chefs once attached to the homes of the aristocrats opened public restaurants there, and before long the concept caught on in the U.S., where in 1794 French chef Jean Baptiste Gilbert Payplat ("Julien"), former cook for the archbishop of Bordeaux, opened a French-style restaurant in Boston where one might sit at a separate table, order from a menu, and pay one's bill for what was consumed. But the idea of a public restaurant not attached to a hotel was given its true impetus by John and Peter Delmonico, two Swiss brothers, the first a former sea captain, the second a pastry-shop manager, who in 1827 opened up a small, six-table coffee-and-pastry shop called Delmonico's on William Street, in NYC. In 1831 the brothers opened a full-fledged restaurant with a French chef and a number of then-exotic dishes that included salad and green vegetables served in the French manner.

Delmonico's became the beacon of good taste and lavish meals, and the brothers' success begat ten more restaurants under their family name, each one more grandiose than the last, usually run by a relative imported for the purpose of maintaining tradition.

Everyone of importance went to Delmonico's, where the finest wines and the greatest array of game were offered on a daily basis. The menu (a term first recorded in America in 1830) went on for several pages, with nearly thirty poultry dishes, eleven beef dishes, and sixteen pastries listed. The influence of French cooking on the Delmonico's menus set a mold for American deluxe dining rooms that has been maintained ever since. Delmonico's lent its name to many dishes, like "**Delmonico potatoes**," "Delmonico bombe," and "Delmonico steak."

Delmonico's had its imitators in NYC, like Rector's, Lüchow's, and Louis Sherry, and other cities followed suit, especially New Orleans, whose own French heritage enabled Antoine Alciatore to succeed immediately when he opened Antoine's in that city in 1840. Elsewhere the best restaurants were those opened in hotels, like Boston's Parker House; Niagara, New York's International Hotel (where waiters served to the sound of a full band); Denver's Brown Palace; and many others around the country. In such establishments the food was served course by course, and with military efficiency.

In lesser public dining rooms, meals were served at a furious pace and with all courses set on the table at once. English traveler Basil Hall noted that at one NYC lunchroom in 1827, two complete dinners were served to two sets of customers within twenty minutes. Crucial to the development of American hotel dining-room service was the concept of the "American plan," initiated around 1830, by which guests at hotels had to pay for their meals whether they ate them in the hotel or not. Guests on such a plan enjoyed four large meals a day at set hours, served by waiters tottering under huge platters of food, in cavernous dining halls that were often segregated by sex. Little of the food was prepared with much sophistication, and it was consumed by the hundreds of guests present with amazing speed.

The "European plan," introduced at NYC's Tammany Hall Hotel in the 1830s, allowed guests to dine at whatever hour they pleased and to choose what they wanted from the menu—an idea that at the time was regarded as something unacceptably aristocratic.

Eating out in America was an exercise of one's capacity to consume enormous amounts of food, whether it was at a restaurant like Delmonico's (where twelve-course meals were rather ordinary affairs) or at the "lobster palaces" and "beer halls" of the post–Civil War era, where customers ate and drank their fill very cheaply. Dickens once commented on the American passion for shellfish, saying he saw "at every supper at least two mighty bowls of hot stewed oysters, in any one of which a half-grown Duke of Clarence might be smothered easily." Game was equally relished by the gastronomes of the day, and a typically lavish meal, like the one served to President Ulysses S. Grant at Chicago's Parker House, might include young bear, Maryland coon, leg of elk, and loin of buffalo.

Women were not admitted to all dining rooms, and until the 1870s separate rooms were provided for them to take their meals at eastern hotels. All-male establishments like saloons and barrooms often gave away a "**free lunch**" in order to attract customers, and the fare might have included anything from crackers and cheese to caviar (then a very inexpensive item).

Cheap, low-class establishments went by slang terms like "hole in the wall," "mulligan joint," "slop joint," "slop chute," and "hash house."

"Coffee shops" were prevalent as early as the 1830s, and "**lunch counters**" as of the 1820s. "Snack bars" arrived in about 1895, while "**cafeterias**" began in the Midwest around the same time. The first "**Automat**" was opened in Philadelphia in 1902.

Americans have always prided themselves on their mobile eateries, from the chuck wagons used on the range to the urban lunch wagons and food-purveying street vendors of the post–Civil War period. Steamboats were especially lavish in their dining-room decor and offered extensive menus of fashionable foods. The first dining cars on American trains were known as of 1838, but the truly lavish and impeccably appointed dining car (later called the "club car") was the creation, in 1868, of George Pullman, who named his first mobile restaurant after Delmonico's. "**Diners**" were modeled after the design of railroad dining cars, though rarely adapted from an actual car. These stationary lunchrooms became representative symbols of American roadside hospitality after the automobile became part of most people's lives and traveling the highways part of the national destiny. In the East, diners were often bought and run by Greek immigrants who had previously run inexpensive hash houses or coffee shops, and some of the lunch-counter slang and jargon was once referred to as "hash-house Greek."

Mining towns like Denver and San Francisco grew rich overnight, and saloons and taverns were immediately followed by elegant restaurants to serve a newly affluent clientele who wanted to spend their wealth on the finest foods, wines, and amenities they could afford. Much more important to the establishing of culinary standards, however, were the contributions of Englishman Frederick Henry Harvey, who in 1876 in Topeka, Kansas, set up the first of hundreds of "**Harvey House restaurants**" along the route of the Atchison, Topeka & Santa Fe Railway. Harvey not only brought cleanliness, good food, changing menus, and reasonable prices to small towns in the West, but he also brought out more than a hundred thousand young women from the East to become waitresses in his restaurants, the effect of which was to bring a modicum of civilization to some rough-and-tumble new townships as well as providing prospective brides to an overwhelmingly male population in the West.

Immigrant food culture both influenced and was adapted to American gastronomy in remarkably diverse ways. Immigrants found that opening up food-service establishments—from Jewish "**delicatessens**" to Italian "pizzerias," from German "rathskellers" to "**Japanese steakhouses**"—was a relatively easy way to make money and to draw Americans into their neighborhoods, like Little Italy and Chinatown. In most cases, these immigrant restaurant owners had to adapt their traditional recipes to American products and to the American palate, so that dishes and foods like **lox**, **chicken Tetrazzini**, **Liederkranz**, **chop suey**, **egg foo yung**, **negimaki**, **London broil**, **Swedish meatballs**, and **Jansson's temptation** were actually American immigrant creations rather than traditional old-country foods. These foods and restaurants greatly enriched American food culture, so that dishes like pizza, bagels, and tacos now rank with hot dogs, steaks, and turkey as some of Americans' favorite foods.

Prohibition effectively put a brake on the evolution of fine dining at restaurants in America, and many of the old-fashioned establishments of the Gilded Age were forced to close, including Delmonico's itself, which went out of business in 1923. Speakeasies took up the slack, ranging from terrible "dives" to society saloons like NYC's "21" Club, which after Prohibition went on to become a serious restaurant.

But throughout the U.S., roadside eateries and "**fast food**" restaurants proliferated during Prohibition and afterwards. The cheap, fast restaurant in America might well be understood by the straightforward emblem (often in neon lights) reading EATS, which was set on many such establishments. This might apply to "chili stands," "taco stands," "night-owl" restaurants (places open late at night), or "burger joints." The idea of serving customers in their cars, using "carhops" who jumped up on the running board of cars to take customers' orders, was begun at the first "drive-in"—the Pig Stand barbecue stand, set up by J. G. Kirby in September 1921 on the Dallas–Fort Worth Highway. The drive-in flourished along the public highways and was widespread throughout the U.S. by the 1930s, when one would go to a drive-in for hamburgers, hot dogs, milk shakes, and other quickly prepared dishes, called "fast food" by the 1960s. The Pig Stand also pioneered the "drive-through," whereby the customer drives up to a window where a worker takes the order and money and hands the meal to the customer.

The possibilities for expansion rose to a new level when Howard Deering Johnson, of Wollaston, Massachusetts, began franchising his Howard Johnson's restaurants to other entrepreneurs as of 1935. The hamburger stand itself took on a new allure when franchised chains like White Castle—opened in 1921 in Wichita, Kansas, by Walter Anderson and Edgar Waldo "Billy" Ingram—began selling a standardized product. Another concept for rushed customers was the "one-arm lunchroom" (started in about 1912), at which the eater sat at a chair with armrests on which the food was placed.

In the 1930s, restaurants again started to acquire an affluent clientele, although the tastes of such people were either basic or informed only by the amount of money something on a menu cost. At the other end of the scale were the cheap immigrant restaurants that catered to Americans' ideas of what Italian, Greek, Chinese, German, and other cuisines were, resulting in standard dishes like chow mein, spaghetti and meatballs, and goulash, that had little to do with the traditions of the cooking of the countries from which these dishes were supposedly "imported."

New York City still dominated the rest of the country for its sheer number and variety of restaurants, although New Orleans had developed its own Creole-Cajun-French cuisine and restaurants that resembled few that could be found elsewhere. San Francisco, which had enjoyed something of a gastronomic reputation before the 1906 earthquake, slowly built up its renown for good American food after that disaster. It was not until the 1970s that Los Angeles began to diverge from its self-perpetuated image as the capital of **fast food**.

The 1939 World's Fair in NYC had an enormous effect on American restaurants, for it brought in excellent chefs from all over the world who served imaginative cuisine to a public generally ignorant of authentic European dishes. The manager of the restaurant in the French Pavilion, **Henri Soulé**, opened his own restaurant in NYC called Le Pavillon, which became the bellwether of classic French dining rooms for the entire country, although the restaurant's influence was not significant outside NYC until the 1960s.

In that same decade, a new gimmick became popular—"theme restaurants," in which the style, design, decor, and food itself were all made to coalesce around a central idea, such as the Wild West, a Roman garden, or a pirate's cove. A company called Restaurant Associates, begun in 1945 by Abraham F. Wechsler, opened sleek, well-thought-out dining rooms with names like the Forum of the Twelve Caesars, the Trattoria, and the Four Seasons, all wed to motifs that were carried through from menu items to ashtrays. Such restaurants were widely imitated around the country, often by franchise chains. The "singles bar" also became a genre of its own during this period, with NYC's T.G.I. Friday's, which opened in 1965, the first example of a place where the postwar "baby boomers" could congregate for a good meal and fellowship.

Concomitant with the growth of such mainstream and glamorous restaurants was a growing counterculture food movement spurred by the dissension over civil rights and the Vietnam War in the 1960s and 1970s. As a reaction against the fat-rich, excessive diet of traditional American restaurants, counterculturists showed a new interest in "ethnic restaurants"—Indian, Thai, Korean, Mexican, and a variety of Chinese restaurants featuring regional cuisines—as well as "health food restaurants" specializing in salads, vegetables, and, often, amateur cooks. One of these, Alice Waters, of Berkeley, California, came out of the protest movement of the 1960s to open a little restaurant called Chez Panisse in 1971, based on her love of French country food and organic produce, which she gathered from local California farmers. The success of Chez Panisse helped focus the iconoclasm of the counterculture into a far more productive, positive approach to food and cooking in America, so that virtues like freshness, local ingredients, and careful cooking techniques were exalted and became the basis of the "California cuisine movement"—itself, ironically, an extrapolation of the very fussy, very elaborate new French style of cooking called **nouvelle cuisine**, which was a deliberate reaction against the staid clichés of the classic menu as interpreted by kitchens in French and American hotel dining rooms for decades. This, in turn, led to a so-called **New American cuisine**, promoted by young American chefs and glossy magazines as using American ingredients in new, often startling combinations and with French techniques.

By the 1980s, new restaurants of every stripe—from the deluxe to the fast-food chains—were soaring in the U.S., driven by a heated economy that helped make gourmandism into another form of social climbing. Cities that previously had little in the way of fine dining suddenly had a slew of new, expensive establishments to cater to an affluent new clientele who demanded the very best in ingredients, wine, and decor. The recession of the 1990s restricted this growth and led to a good deal of "downscaling" of restaurants, so that instead of more posh dining rooms serving caviar and truffles with abandon, restaurateurs opened more bistros, trattorias, and cafés serving a wider range of less expensive foods from around the world. When the recession ended in the mid-1990s, the subsequent boom economy fueled new restaurant growth, and there was greater interest in more and newer ethnic foods, like Vietnamese, Japanese, Malaysian, Filipino, Caribbean, and South American. The "Mediterranean diet" also encouraged people to eat more healthful food in restaurants, leading to more vegetarian and vegan restaurants.

A deep recession that began in 2008 forced many chefs and restaurateurs to move out of city centers to cheaper neighborhoods, fueling expansion of modern restaurants in places like Brooklyn, New York; Cambridge, Massachusetts; Uptown New Orleans; and Chicago's Lincoln Park. Also, young chefs trained in highly regarded kitchens moved to open smaller, very personalized restaurants, some following trends and fads like **molecular cuisine** and **modernist cuisine**, in some cases serving a set, fixed-price, lengthy menu with no options, in spaces built around counters over which the chef might interract with patrons. Far more casual than traditional restaurants, many of these new-style examples removed tablecloths, used industrial materials in decor, and played the music list chosen by the chef or owner.

Despite the recession, industry sales grew to a record $632 billion in 2012—48 percent of the total U.S. food dollar—with 970,000 restaurants, of every kind, and 12.9 million employees. Seven out of ten restaurants are single-unit locations. One-half of all adults have worked in the restaurant industry at some point in their lives, and one-third got their first job experience in a restaurant.

Today the average American eats out about five times a week. Sixty-five percent say they favor Italian cuisine, 62 percent Mexican, 59 percent Chinese, and 58 percent pizza.

RESTAURANT ROW. A street, sometimes comprising several blocks, known for its extensive number of restaurants. The term originally referred to the block of Forty-sixth Street between Eighth and Ninth avenues in NYC, where many Theater District restaurants are located.

REUBEN SANDWICH. Also "Reuben." A sandwich made with corned beef, Swiss cheese, and sauerkraut on rye bread that is then fried like a grilled-cheese sandwich. Although there have been various claims as to the creation of the Reuben, the most probable is that of Arnold Reuben (1883–1970), owner of Reuben's Restaurant, at 6 East Fifty-eighth Street in NYC. According to *Craig Claiborne's The New York Times Food Encyclopedia* (1985), Reuben's daughter, Patricia R. Taylor, contended that the sandwich had been created in 1914 by her father for an actress named Annette Seelos. Arnold had a habit of naming dishes and sandwiches after the show-business celebrities who ate at his restaurant, but in this case he instead gave it his own name—the "Reuben Special." G. Selmer Foughner, in his book *Dining in New York* (1939), made reference to a dish at Reuben's called the "Reubenola" but did not describe its contents.

It has also been asserted that Reuben Kolakofsky, a grocer, invented the sandwich in 1922 during a poker game with friends at the Blackstone Hotel in Omaha, Nebraska. The recipe was later submitted by Fern Snider (a waitress at the Blackstone) and won first prize at the National Sandwich Idea Contest, held by the Wheat Flour Institute in 1956 and later revived by Pepperidge Farm.

RHUBARB. Any of a variety of plants with long stalks in the genus *Rheum*, although the leaf stem of *Rheum rhaponticum* is the species of culinary interest. The etymology of the word goes back to the Greek *rha*, which probably derived from the former name for the Volga River, Rha, where rhubarb was grown. In Middle English, *rha* became *rubarbe*, possibly through an alteration of the Latin term *rha barbarum*, meaning "barbarian rhubarb." The word entered English print in 1525.

Rhubarb is of Asian origins, and although it had been cultivated at monasteries for its medicinal values, Europeans showed little culinary interest in the plant. It was not until the nineteenth century that it began showing up in London markets. At that time in the U.S., its pouch of unopened flowers, which the Alaskan Eskimos customarily ate raw, was of some gastronomic interest. Rhubarb pie, first mentioned in print in 1855, was to become one of the two most popular preparations of the food; the other was stewed, sweetened rhubarb served as a dessert. So popular was rhubarb pie that the plant is often called the "pie plant." It has been particularly relished by the Pennsylvania Dutch.

In the U.S., rhubarb is grown either as a hothouse or field variety, the latter more flavorful and more deeply pink in color. A pie made with rhubarb, strawberries, and angelica is a traditional American dish.

RHUBARB PIE

Combine 4 c. chopped rhubarb, 1 ⅓ c. honey, 7 T. flour, 4 T. angelica, and ½ t. salt. Pour into pastry crust, dot with butter, cover with another crust, and bake at 450° for 10 min. Reduce to 350° and bake another 50 min.

RICE (*Oryza sativa*). A cultivated cereal grass that is one of the most important foods of the world, especially in Asia, where it forms a large part of the diet. The word is from the Greek *óruzon*, which in Middle English appears as *rys*.

Although rice was a popular food in Italy, Spain, and France by the Renaissance, it did not cause much of a stir in England, which nevertheless encouraged experiments to grow the crop in its American colonies, the first in 1622. In 1647, William Berkeley sowed half a bushel of rice in Virginia and reaped thirty times that amount in his first harvest. But the crop eventually failed. South Carolina is generally credited as the birthplace of the rice industry in America, based on a legend concerning the arrival at Charleston, in 1685, of a Captain John Thurber, who had been blown off course. Thurber gave some Madagascar rice to one of the city's foremost citizens, Henry Woodward, who planted it in his garden. Some stories tell of the rice dying, others of it flourishing. Another tale credits a Dutch captain with bringing the grain to Charleston in 1694, while still another gives the honor to Anthony Ashley Cooper, first earl of Shaftesbury, who planted one hundred pounds of seed in South Carolina and sent back sixty tons to England in 1698.

However rice got to South Carolina, the state remained the leading rice-producing region for two hundred years, exporting almost five thousand tons annually as of 1726. During the American Revolution, the British captured Charleston and shipped the entire rice crop home, leaving no seed behind. Thomas Jefferson smuggled some Italian rice seed out of Europe in 1787 and brought it back to the Carolinas. The industry eventually revived, and a favorable trade was established with England in the early nineteenth century, during which time every southern state east of the Mississippi began growing rice, the exception being Louisiana, which did not produce a rice crop until 1889, although it had been introduced there as early as 1718. California also grew rice as early as 1760, although it did not produce its first commercial crop of short-grain rice until 1912, and the territory between the Pacific and the Mississippi took on the crop slowly: Texas was not cultivating the grain until 1850, and ten years later referred to the crop as "providence rice," because low-lying regions depended wholly on collected rainwater for irrigation.

By 1905 Arkansas was growing rice, and the industry took off quickly in the Sacramento Valley, in California. Missouri followed in 1920 and Mississippi in 1949. Today very little rice is grown in the original delta lands of the southern Atlantic states, with Arkansas, California, Louisiana, and Mississippi the major producing states. South Carolina, ironically, is no longer a major producer, having picked its last commercial crop in 1927. The U.S. produces 20 billion pounds of rice and is today the world's fourth leading exporter of rice.

In the 1940s, Texan Gordon Harwell, using a British process of treating rice with pressurized steam to drive minerals and vitamins into the kernel and out of the discarded bran layer, marketed "converted rice" under the brand Uncle Ben's, the name being based on a renowned African American rice farmer in Houston known for the high quality of his rice.

"Minute Rice" was a precooked product developed by Ataullah Ozai-Durrani and sold to General Foods that could be cooked at home in only ten minutes. It was introduced in 1949.

Americans' consumption of rice has more than doubled in the past twenty years, and the U.S. is now the twelfth-largest consumer of the grain in the world. Americans of the South and Southwest eat the most rice in the U.S., for it is a staple food of Hispanic American, Creole, and Delta cookeries, although Hawaiians consume the most of all. In Charleston, South Carolina, rice is part of a long tradition. Samuel Gaillard Stoney,

in *Charleston: Azaleas and Old Bricks* (1937), records that "on every proper Charleston dinner table [there is] a spoon that is peculiar to the town. Of massive silver, about fifteen inches long and broad in proportions, it is laid on the cloth with something of the reverential distinction that surrounds the mace in the House of Commons at Westminster....If you take away the rice-spoon from the Charleston dinner table, the meal that follows is not really a meal."

Rice is combined into seafood and meat preparations, made into pancakes called "rice cakes" (see **cala**), used in breads, puddings, breakfast cereals, and dumplings, or served simply boiled and buttered. It is the basis of many American dishes, like **dirty rice**, **pilau**, **jambalaya**, and **red beans and rice**, and is used in the making of beer.

So-called Carolina rice is a long-grain variety, which accounts for nearly 69 percent of American rice. Medium-grain totals about 27 percent, and short-grain, also called "pearl white rice," about 4 percent. "Brown rice" (3 percent) is the unpolished grain of rice containing the wheat germ and outer layer of bran, which gives the seed a brownish coloring. **Wild rice**, which is not rice at all, is discussed under its main entry. "Rough" or "paddy" rice is rice as it comes straight from the field, with hull intact. "Brewers' rice" is taken from the smallest size of broken rice fragments and used in brewing and in pet foods.

"Converted," "conditioned," or "parboiled" rice is precooked (a process going back to ancient India), which improves nutritional value and inhibits rancidity. "Precooked," "quick-cooking," or "instant" rice has been cooked then dehydrated to cut down on cooking time. "Sticky," "sweet," "waxy," "*mochigome*," or "glutinous" rice has a sticky texture and is used primarily in Asian cooking.

"Arborio" rice is a plump, starchy rice used in the making of the Italian dish "risotto," with the most favored varieties coming from around the Po Valley, in Italy.

Various "aromatic" rices like "basmati," from India and Pakistan, and "Thai jasmine" (or "Thai fragrant"), from Thailand, are imported, although there is an American "basmati-type" rice that came to the U.S. at the turn of the century, and recently some American "jasmine-type" rices have been grown.

"Puffed rice" is a cereal introduced at the 1904 Louisiana Purchase Exposition, in St. Louis, by Dr. Alexander P. Anderson, who shot the product from a type of gun he invented.

RICE PUDDING

Combine 2 T. cooked rice with 1 T. raisins and place in buttered pudding pan. Beat 2 egg yolks, add ½ c. sugar, 2 c. milk, and 1 t. vanilla. Pour over rice and bake for 40 min. at 325°. When done, sprinkle with cinnamon.

RICKEY. A drink whose basic ingredients are lime juice and soda water, first in American print in 1889. In its nonalcoholic form, a sweet syrup is usually added. In its alcoholic form, sugar is traditionally forbidden, and a spirit is added, usually gin, though bourbon, blended whiskey, and applejack are sometimes used. Adding sugar would make the drink a **Tom Collins**.

In his abridged edition of Mencken's *American Language* (1963), Raven I. McDavid Jr. notes that "authorities agree that the drink was named after a distinguished Washington guzzler of the period, but his identity is disputed, as is the original form of the rickey." One attribution is to a "Colonel" Rickey from Kentucky, with no further information on the subject; another names him "Joe Rickey."

The "lime rickey" is a Boston soda-fountain drink made with a sweet lime syrup, the juice of a lime, the crushed lime skin, and seltzer.

RICKEY

In an old-fashioned glass, mix with 1 ice cube 2 oz. gin, 1 oz. fresh lime juice, club soda, and a twist of lime.

LIME RICKEY

Place in a tall glass 1 ½ T. lime juice, 1 T. bar sugar, and ice cubes. Fill with club soda or seltzer and garnish with a slice of lime.

RIVEL. A small dumpling, like spaetzle, added to soups. Betty Groff, in *Betty Groff's Pennsylvania Dutch Cookbook* (1990), wrote that "chowders and soups may be considered the main course when rivels are added." Rivels are usually considered to be a Pennsylvania Dutch dish, as is the word itself, dating in American print to 1907. *The Random House Dictionary*, however, says the item is "Chiefly Western Canadian" and lists the origins as "uncertain."

RIVEL

Combine 2 c. sifted flour with ½ t. salt and 1 beaten egg. Rub the mixture between your fingers to create very small droplets of dough. Drop into boiling water or broth and cook for 3 min.

RIZ. A Southern baker's term for biscuits or other confections made with yeast and therefore "riz'd," i.e., risen.

ROACH COACH. Slang for mobile catering trucks.

ROADHOUSE. An inexpensive restaurant, saloon, nightclub, or inn located along a highway. The term dates in print to 1806.

ROB ROY. Also "Scotch Manhattan." A cocktail made with Scotch, sweet vermouth, and bitters. According to William Grimes, in *Straight Up or On the Rocks* (1993), the cocktail was named after the Broadway operetta *Rob Roy*, about the legendary Robert MacGregor (1671–1734), hero of a Sir Walter Scott novel of the same name (1817), but the drink's name was first printed in 1865.

ROB ROY

Shake ¾ oz. Scotch whisky, ¾ oz. sweet vermouth, and 2 dashes bitters with cracked ice. Strain and pour into chilled glass. In a dry Rob Roy, dry vermouth is substituted for sweet.

ROCK AND RYE. A liqueur with a blended-whiskey base, having a proof of 60 to 70, to which is added rock-candy syrup and sometimes fruits, dating in print to 1875. It was used in the nineteenth century as a digestive aid.

ROCK CANDY. A hard candy made by cooling a concentrated sugar syrup, dating in print to 1620. It is often sold crystallized around a piece of string or a stick and is sometimes used to make **rock and rye** liqueur.

Dryden & Palmer, of Norwalk, Connecticut, has manufactured rock candy since 1880 and claims to be the only company still doing so.

ROCKFISH (genus *Sebastes*, family Scorpaenide). A family of fish that inhabit rocky regions of the sea and go by many names. The name dates in print to 1605. In his book *Seafood: A Connoisseur's Guide and Cookbook* (1989), Alan Davidson describes the confusion over the various species that fall under the name "rockfish," noting that in California more than fifty species of "rock cod" fall under the general group known as "rockfish." Among the most popular rockfish are the "bolina" (*S. auriculatus*) and the "goldeneye rockfish" (*S. ruberrimus*), the "cowfish" or "cowcod" (*S. levis*), and the "chili pepper" (*S. goodei*). Members of the genus *Scorpaena* are also called "rockfish," though they are more commonly known as "scorpionfish" or "sea scorpion" because of their venomous dorsal fins. *DARE* lists more than thirty regional names for rockfish, including "grouper," "striped bass," "chucklehead," "rasher," "Spanish flag," and "treefish."

ROCKY ROAD. A confection of milk chocolate or dark chocolate mixed with marshmallows and nuts. Its name derives from the texture of the finished product. Its first appearance in American print was in 1934 in the *Fresno (California) Bee*. Culinary historian Jean Anderson has found a recipe for the candy dating to *Young American's Cookbook* (1938). It is also the familiar name of a similarly flavored ice cream.

ROCKY ROAD

In a saucepan mix 2 c. milk chocolate or dark chocolate morsels, one 14-oz. can sweetened condensed milk, and 2 T. butter. Heat until chocolate is melted. Remove from heat. Combine 5 ½ c. small marshmallows with 1 ½ c. unsalted roasted peanuts or chopped almonds, then fold into chocolate mixture. Spread into a pan lined with waxed paper and chill for about 2 hr., until firm. Remove from pan, peel off waxed paper, and cut into squares. Makes 8 doz.

RODALE, JEROME IRVING (1898–1971). Publisher, health food advocate. As one of its leading exponents, J. I. Rodale has been called "the father of American organic farming." He and his son Robert (1930–1990) published a wide range of books and magazines on gardening, health, and fitness.

Jerome Rodale (born Cohen) was born in NYC, where his father was a grocer. He took up bodybuilding as a teenager and was known in his Jewish neighborhood as the "13-year-old cantor." Trained as an accountant, he worked for the IRS in Washington, D.C., then ran an electrical manufacturing business in NYC with his brother Joseph. Inspired by British agronomist Sir Albert Howard's studies on organic farming by, Rodale moved his family to Emmaus, Pennsylvania, where he set up his own farm. In 1930, he founded Rodale Inc. and, ten years later, the Rodale Organic Gardening Experimental Farm.

In 1942, he founded Rodale Press to promote his ideas, first through the magazine *Organic Gardening and Farming* (later called *Organic Farmer*), which lost money until the late 1950s.

In 1950, he started *Prevention* magazine, devoted to disease prevention and what became known as "alternative health," which promoted a diet rich in whole grains, herbal medicines, and breastfeeding. He produced a line of dietary supplements and disapproved of the consumption of sugar and milk by adults. *Prevention*'s popularity increased with the burgeoning of the counterculture **health food** movement of the 1960s. The magazine currently claims a readership of ten million.

Eventually Rodale Press made Rodale a multimillionaire, which enabled him to promote his ideas in NYC theater productions, but none succeeded. Controversial for many of his views, he was often criticized for advocating questionable science and in 1954 was cited by the Federal Trade Commission for false and deceptive advertising, though Rodale won the case. "In the old days, I used to get such a clobbering and insulting, you know," he said in 1971, "and if I wasn't so well nourished, it would have affected me, but I stood up under it, because I had plenty of Vitamin B, which is the nerve vitamin."

His son Robert graduated from Lehigh University, in Bethlehem, Pennsylvania, majoring in English and journalism, and in 1949 joined his father's publishing company, becoming president two years later. The company branched out into fitness and sports magazines, including *Runner's World*, *Backpacker*, *Bicycling*, *Men's Health*, and *American Woodworker*, using the tagline "You can do it!" throughout its publications. Robert himself competed in the Olympics in rifle shooting and was elected to the U.S. Bicycling Hall of Fame in 1991.

Upon his father's death, in 1971, from a heart attack (while appearing on a TV talk show), Robert became chairman of the board and CEO of Rodale Press. In 1990 he was killed in an auto accident while in Moscow on business to establish a Russian-language version of *The New Farmer*. Upon his death, his wife, Ardie, became CEO of the company, and she was later appointed "chief inspiration officer" until her death, in 2009; in 2007, Maria Rodale (Robert's daughter) was elected chairman of the board, and she became CEO in 2009.

Rodale Press has also published many books, including the *South Beach Diet* series and Vice President Al Gore's *An Inconvenient Truth*. The company currently claims more than twenty-seven million active customers in its database.

ROFFIGNAC. A cocktail made with whiskey, grenadine or raspberry syrup, and soda water. It is a New Orleans beverage named after an early mayor of that city, Louis Philippe Joseph de Roffignac.

An oyster dish made with mushrooms, red wine, shrimp, and scallions also goes by this name.

ROLLICHE. Also "roll-cheese" and other names. A Dutch New York dish of beef wrapped in tripe, boiled, pickled, and cut into rounds. The word is from Dutch *rolletje*, dating in American print to 1830.

ROLLMOPS. A marinated herring fillet that is stuffed and rolled and served as an hors d'oeuvre, dating in print to 1901. The name comes from Germany, a reference to a pug dog (*mops*), perhaps because of its stubby appearance.

ROLLMOPS

Spread individual herring fillets with mustard, then place chopped onion, a slice of pickle, and some capers on top. Roll into snug packages and tie with a string or secure with a toothpick. Marinate the rollmops in a boiled solution of 1 c. vinegar, 1 c. water, 1 t. sugar, 2 bay leaves, and 1 T. pickling spices.

ROLY-POLY. A rectangular pastry filled with fruit or preserves that is steamed, baked, or boiled. The term refers to the process of rolling the dough, dating in print to 1895.

ROMANO. A cow's-milk cheese that originated in Italy but is made in several American dairy states. The name derives from the city of Rome, and there are several varieties, including "Pecorino Romano" (which is quite sharp and salty) and a Wisconsin-made flattened ball of cheese called "Piccolo Romano" ("Little Roman"). Romano is fairly firm and is usually used as a grating cheese for pasta, salads, and other dishes. The word's first appearance in American print, in 1897, describes it as "the principal Italian cheese imported."

ROMBAUER, IRMA (1877–1962). Author. Few cookbooks have shared the popularity of Irma Rombauer's *Joy of Cooking*, which has been in continuous print since 1936 as a comprehensive compilation of American cooking, with tens of millions of copies sold worldwide.

Born in St. Louis, Irma von Starkloff was raised in Germany but returned to St. Louis in 1894, where she attended Washington University and met lawyer Edgar Rombauer, who married her in 1899 and taught her the rudiments of cooking.

The death of her first child the following year and Edgar's suffering a nervous breakdown in 1902 devastated Irma, but the birth of a daughter, Marion, and a son, Edgar, raised her spirits. Soon she became socially active in the St. Louis community, and by 1929 she had become president of the Women's Committee of the St. Louis Symphony Orchestra Board of Directors. But her husband's chronic mental breakdowns drove him to commit suicide in 1930, forcing Irma to become the sole income source for her family.

By taking local cooking classes, Rombauer improved her own cooking skills to the point where she became regarded as a cooking teacher in St. Louis. Inspired by a book for wealthy socialites, entitled *Choice Menus for Luncheons and Dinners*, by Gladys Taussig

Lang, Rombauer began collecting recipes for her own cookbook, which she self-published and marketed, with $6,000 from her husband's legacy, printing three thousand copies of *The Joy of Cooking: A Compilation of Reliable Recipes with a Casual Culinary Chat*. Its personal, conversational tone aimed at middle-class home cooks and was something novel among cookbooks of that era. It contained five hundred tested recipes from which, Rombauer wrote, "inexperienced cooks cannot fail to make successful soufflés, pies, cakes, soups, gravies, etc., if they follow the clear instructions given on these subjects." At the time, only two cookbooks in the country, neither of them recently updated, had widespread popularity: *The White House Cookbook* (1887) and **Fannie Farmer**'s *Boston Cooking-School Cook Book* (1896).

Rombauer's book had modest success, and in 1936 Bobbs-Merrill published a revised edition, with directions presented chronologically and with the required ingredients in bold type. In her introduction Rombauer wrote:

> Although I have been modernized by life and my children, my roots are Victorian. This book reflects my life. It was once merely a private record of what the family wanted, of what friends recommended and of dishes made familiar by foreign travel and given an acceptable Americanization. In the course of time there have been added to the rather weighty stand-bye of my youth the ever-increasing lighter culinary touches of the day. So the record, which to begin with was a collection such as every kitchen-minded woman possesses, has grown in breadth and bulk until it now covers a wide range.

Sales were slow at first but, by the mid-1940s *The Joy of Cooking* was a major success, not least for its frugal recipes. Rombauer followed up with *A Cookbook for Girls and Boys* (1946), written with her daughter, Marion Rombauer Becker (who had done the illustrations for the first edition), though Marion was not acknowledged as co-author until the 1951 edition.

In 1955, Irma suffered the first of a series of debilitating strokes, causing Marion eventually to take over all editorial and publishing duties. In 1962, a paralyzing stroke forced the amputation of Irma's left leg, which caused an infection that killed her in October of that year.

After her mother's death, Marion Rombauer Becker oversaw updates and revisions to *The Joy of Cooking* until the mid-1970s. A controversial 1997 edition, published by Simon and Schuster and edited by Maria Guarnaschelli, with the supervision of Marion's son Ethan Becker, deviated from the original format and style and added scores of modern recipes. A year later, Simon and Schuster published a facsimile of the original 1931 edition. Then, in 2006, a seventy-fifth-anniversary edition, with 4,500 recipes, restored many of the original recipes and reverted to Rombauer's more conversational tone.

Asked if she would write an autobiography, Irma Rombauer responded, "No. Why should I?" But Marion Rombauer Becker wrote a memoir of their book's publishing history, *Little Acorn: Joy of Cooking: The First Fifty Years, 1931–1981*. In 1996, Anne Mendelson published a biography of the Rombauer women, *Stand Facing the Stove: The Story of the Women Who Gave America the Joy of Cooking*.

In 1998, Irma Rombauer was inducted into the St. Louis Walk of Fame.

ROMMEGROT. A Scandinavian American cream porridge or pudding. The word is from Norwegian, dating in English print to 1951.

RONCADOR. Also "black croaker." A Pacific fish, *Roncador stearnsi*, whose Spanish name means "snorer" because of the sound the fish makes, dating in print to 1882.

ROOSTER-SPUR PEPPER (*Capsicum frutescens fasciculatum*). A hot red **chile** pepper, sometimes called the "bird pepper," whose name derives from its resemblance to the spur of a rooster's claw. These peppers are not commercially grown but raised in home gardens in the South. The name entered American print in the late 1960s.

The rooster-spur pepper took on some political clout in 1978, when Attorney General Griffin Bell snuck some sausages seasoned with the pepper past Secret Service officers and into the White House, to the delight of President Jimmy Carter (born 1924; held office 1977–1981), who asked Bell for more. As a result, the Justice Department was deluged with requests for the recipe, which came from a farmer named H. S. Williams, in Haralson, Georgia.

Sending rooster-spur condiments to politicians has been something of a small tradition in the South, maintained in Mississippi for half a century by J. C. Luter Sr., of Walthall County, whose pepper sauce was famous as of the 1920s.

ROOSTER-SPUR PEPPER SAUCE

Clip several rooster-spur peppers from a bush, leaving short stems. Wash, drain, and pack tightly in bottles. Pour boiling water into the bottles and let stand until scalded. Drain water, add a pinch of sugar and salt, then pour hot vinegar over peppers to fill the bottles. Seal tightly.

ROOT, WAVERLEY (1903–1982). Author. As a journalist who covered the world for American newspapers, Waverley Lewis Root used his enormous depth of experience and knowledge to write several of the most authoritative books of the twentieth century and hundreds of articles on food and wine.

Born in Providence, Rhode Island, and raised in Fall River, Massachusetts, Root graduated from Tufts College, then moved to NYC. In 1927 he moved to Paris, becoming the local correspondent for the *Chicago Tribune* and then, from 1957 to 1969, for the *Washington Post*, during which time he became a gourmand who was able to travel widely and, using a reporter's skills, to delve deeply into the food cultures of Europe. Erudite and voracious, he wrote books on topics ranging from *The Truth About Wagner* (1928) to *Winter Sports in Europe* (1956), and, a year after World War II ended, he published *The Secret History of the War* (1946).

It was his later food writings that made his reputation, first *The Food of France* (1958) and later *The Food of Italy* (1971), both encyclopedic in their scope. Root wrote *Eating in America: A History* (1976) with Richard de Rochemont, and followed in 1980 with his magnum opus, the scholarly *Food: An Authoritative and Visual History and Dictionary of the Foods of the World*. Root lent greater authority to his subjects by giving his own highly experienced opinion on them, adding personal anecdotes to the story that made him seem a jovial companion to the reader.

On the subject of partridge, Root wrote, "As a New Englander, when I learned that the bird which I trustingly called a partridge to the end of my adolescence was an imposter whose real name was the 'ruffled grouse,' the disillusionment was comparable to that of a child when he discovers there is no Santa Claus."

ROQUEFORT DRESSING. A salad dressing made with French Roquefort or blue cheese, entering English print in 1910.

ROQUEFORT DRESSING

Combine 1 lb. Roquefort, 2 T. lemon juice, ½ c. heavy cream or sour cream, 1 T. chopped chives, Worcestershire sauce and Tabasco sauce to taste, and a dash of garlic salt.

ROSETTE. A Scandinavian American pastry made by dipping a battered rose-shaped timbale iron into hot fat to create a crisp cookie in the shape of a rose, dating in print to 1950.

ROSSO, JULEE. See **Lukins, Sheila**.

ROTGUT. Also "ratgut." Cheap, inferior whiskey that, colloquially, drinkers said would rot out their insides, dating in print to 1857.

ROUX. A mixture of a starch (flour, cornstarch, or arrowroot) and a fat that is browned in a saucepan until thickened and that serves as the base of a sauce or gravy. The word is French, from Latin *russus*, "red," dating in English print to 1632.

Roux has a particular fascination for Louisiana cooks, who contend it is the ingredient that distinguishes their finest preparations. Creole roux are made with butter or bacon fat and are cooked far longer than most French roux, achieving a deep honey color (although there is also a white roux, which is pale in color because it is cooked quickly and not allowed to brown).

Cajun roux are made with vegetable oil or lard and cooked to a caramel color, although Cajuns also use lighter roux.

~~~~~~~~~~~~~~~~~~~~~~~~~~~~~~~~~~~~
ROUX
~~~~~~~~~~~~~~~~~~~~~~~~~~~~~~~~~~~~

Combine 4 T. butter or lard with 4 T. flour in a skillet and cook, stirring constantly, over a very low flame until it is a rich brown color throughout. This may take 20–45 min.

RUBBER-CHICKEN DINNER. A slang term for the kind of unsavory, mass-produced food commonly served at a banquet dinner. It is most often associated with political fundraisers. The "rubber-chicken circuit," dating in American print to 1941, is a series of such dinners a speaker or political candidate is often forced to attend. "Rubber chicken," dating back to at least the 1950s, is a reference to the rubbery meat served at such functions but, more specifically, to an actual rubber-chicken gag item sold at novelty stores.

RUBY CABERNET. A red vinifera grape used to make a medium-bodied red wine. It was developed in 1946 by Harold Paul Olmo at the University of California at Davis by crossing **cabernet sauvignon** and Carignane. Most ruby cabernet wine is produced in California's Central Valley.

RUGELACH. Also "rugalach" and "rogelach." Jewish American cookies, usually made with a cream cheese dough and stuffed with nuts, fruits, and raisins. The word is Yiddish, dating in print to 1941. According to **Joan Nathan**, in her *Jewish Cooking in America* (1994), "The American addition to *rugelach* was cream cheese and the myriad of fillings used today," suggesting that the cream cheese dough may have been developed by the Philadelphia Cream Cheese Co. One of the earliest references to such dough was in *The Perfect Hostess* (1950), by Mildred Knopf, who said the recipe came from Nela Rubinstein, wife of pianist Arthur Rubinstein. Nathan also contended that it was a rugelach recipe by Florida dessert expert Maida Heatter that "put *rugelach* on the culinary map…and is the *rugelach* recipe most often found in upscale bakeries nationwide."

RULLEPØLSE. A Danish meat dish that is rolled, pressed, boiled, then cut into rounds, from the Danish for "rolled sausage," dating in American print to 1952. A Norwegian version is called Ribberull.

RUM. A spirit distilled from fermented sugarcane, principally molasses. There are several types of rum, ranging from light to full-bodied, most produced in the islands of the Caribbean but also on Java, in Indonesia (where it's called "Batavia arrack"), and in Guyana along the Demerara River. Although some heavy rums may be distilled at up to 190 proof, federal regulations require a minimum of 80 proof.

Rum was first made in the Caribbean, possibly in Barbados, around 1600, after Christopher Columbus brought sugarcane to the West Indies from the Azores. These first rums were made by the Spanish, but the rum trade was quickly picked up by various Europeans. By 1639 the spirit was called "kill-devil." The word *rum* is of somewhat obscure origins. Some believe it may derive from the Latin *saccharum*, sugar. The *OED* suggests "rumbustion" and "rumbullion" are earlier forms. The first use of the word was in 1645, long before the date of another story sometimes cited to explain the origin of the name, the legend that in 1745 British admiral Edward Vernon (also credited with providing the word *grog*) tried to cure his crew's scurvy by switching their beer ration to the molasses-based spirit. The grateful seamen nicknamed their captain "Old Rummy," for "rum" was then a slang term for "the best."

The rum trade was exceptionally important in the colonial era, and by 1657 rum was even being produced in New England. The spirit was shipped to Europe and sold or traded in Africa for slaves to work the American plantations, which produced the molasses to make more rum.

Until gin replaced it as a cheap drink in the eighteenth century, rum was the predominant alcohol of the poor and a subject of frequent jeremiads from the pulpit. It was often drunk at breakfast or mixed with other ingredients to make early forms of **cocktails**, such as shrub, **flip**, **punch**, and **grog**. "Bombo" (possibly named after British admiral John Benbow, 1653–1702), made from rum, hot water, and molasses, was popular in North Carolina, while "blackstrap," a mixture of rum and molasses, was favored in New England, where pungent rums were called "stink-a-bus." "Samson," referring to the most powerful of biblical heroes, was rum mixed with cider.

Rum was given out at political rallies; in fact, George Washington gave out seventy-five gallons to voters during his successful campaign in 1758 for representative in the Virginia House of Burgesses. By 1775 Americans were drinking four gallons of rum per person per year, but this was soon to change. The British had passed the Molasses Act in 1733, which imposed high duties on the colonists; this was followed by the Sugar Act, in 1764, which cut the duties on molasses but made the importation of sugar, wine, and coffee very expensive. Both acts were strictly enforced against smugglers. These laws had a crippling effect on the New England distilleries and further hastened the general dissent that led to revolution in the next decade. One story has it that Paul Revere fortified himself with two drafts of Medford rum at Isaac Hall's distillery before beginning his famous ride to warn the colonists of a British invasion on the night of April 18, 1775.

After the war, America's favorable trade relations with the British West Indies were disrupted, and the price of rum rose. Also, a strong temperance movement was building in the new country that effectively prevented the recovery of the New England distilleries. Domestic production was further impaired by war between France and England and America's own War of 1812 with England. The abolition of the slave trade in 1808 destroyed any possibility for economic viability in U.S. rum production, although a low-grade drink made from molasses, called "tafia," was produced in New Orleans during the nineteenth century.

Rum continued to be very popular, however, and after the reestablishment of the U.S. Navy in 1794, an act of Congress decreed that every sailor's ration should include "one half pint of distilled spirits per day, or in lieu thereof, one quart of beer per day." Rum was preferred, usually drunk in the form of grog and mixed with water. The Navy Department tried to substitute whiskey for rum as an economic measure, but it was years before the latter spirit was accepted by most sailors. The grog ration was reduced throughout the nineteenth century, after a panel of surgeons in 1829 found it inexpedient and demoralizing. Finally, after urging from Assistant Secretary of the Navy Gustavus V. Fox, Congress resolved on July 14, 1862, that the "spirit ration shall forever cease and thereafter no distilled spiritous liquor shall be admitted onboard vessels of war, except as medicine." The grog ration ended when President Abraham Lincoln signed the resolution on September 1, 1862, though the

Confederate navy kept up the ration throughout the Civil War. (The British Admiralty did not abolish the ration until August 1, 1970.)

Today Americans obtain most of their rum from the Caribbean, where it has been made since the repeal of Prohibition, in 1933. Seventy percent of the rum comes, however, from Puerto Rico, which makes light "white" or "silver" rums and more flavorful "amber" or "gold" rums, all hovering around 80 proof, and "liqueur rums," which are dry and robust. There is still some rum made in Massachusetts, but the Bureau of Alcohol, Tobacco, and Firearms of the U.S. Treasury dropped the appellation "New England rum" from the U.S. standards-of-identity list in 1968. Nevertheless, New Englanders continue to consume more rum than any other Americans. In 2011, U.S. rum sales totaled 4.1 million nine-liter cases, with revenues of $2.3 billion.

Today rum is usually mixed with other ingredients to make cocktails like the "**daiquiri**," the "**piña colada**," "**El Presidente**," and the "**Cuba Libre**." "Rum and Coke" (rum mixed with Coca-Cola) is particularly popular among young Americans, and "hot buttered rum" is consumed in winter. In Kenneth Robert's novel, *Northwest Passage* (1937), a character says of this old New England favorite:

> *And it ain't a temporary drink….No matter how much you drink of anything else, it'll wear off in a day or so, but you take enough hot buttered rum and it'll last you pretty near as long as a coonskin cap….After a man's had two-three drinks of hot buttered rum, he don't shoot a catamount; all he's got to do is walk up to him, kiss him just once; then put him in his bag, all limp.*

Robert's recipe is found below.

Total rum production in the U.S. (including Puerto Rico and the Virgin Islands) in 1997 was 11.5 million nine-liter cases. August 16 has been called, unofficially, National Rum Day.

HOT BUTTERED RUM

Heat a tumbler, add ½ in. hot water, and dissolve 1 t. sugar in it. Add a jigger of New England rum, ½ t. cinnamon, a pat of butter, and more hot water.

RUMROUSAL. A New England milk punch made by combining one quart Jamaican rum, three quarts milk, one and a half cups honey, and half a pint of bourbon. The origin of the name is unknown but possibly indicates that the rum will arouse the imbiber's spirits.

RUMAKI. A canapé or appetizer made by wrapping bacon slices around around chestnuts and chicken livers that have been marinated with soy sauce and Chinese spices. The item became popular in so-called Polynesian restaurants like Trader Vic's, in San Francisco, whose owner said rumaki was of Chinese origin but with a Japanese name. Etymologists suggest the word may derive from the Japanese *harumaki*, a kind of spring roll. It first appeared in print on a California menu, in 1941, at a restaurant owned by Don the Beachcomber.

RINKTUM TIDDY. Also "rum-tum-tiddy." A New England dish of cheese, tomatoes, eggs, onion, and pepper served over toast. The term, dating in print to 1911, is probably just a nonsense word, sometimes found in folk songs.

RINKTUM TIDDY

To 2 c. of tomato soup add ½ lb. sharp cheddar cheese and cook in a double boiler until cheese is melted. Add ¼ t. dry mustard and 1 beaten egg. Stir briefly, then serve on buttered toast.

RUNZA. Also "runsa." A bread or pastry pocket usually stuffed with cabbage, chopped meat, pepper, and garlic powder. It is now a trademark name for a Nebraska drive-in restaurant chain's oblong bun filled with ground meat, cabbage, and onions. Similar to a **pasty**, it was at first called a "kraut runsa" and was first made after World War II by Sally Everett of Lincoln, Nebraska, as a picnic item. By changing the *s* to a *z*, she was able to trademark the name Runza, which in the 1960s her son Don expanded into a chain of drive-ins, later adding an "Italian-style Runza" to the menu.

RUSSIAN AMERICAN FOOD. A general term for the various foods cooked and enjoyed by Russian immigrants, as well as those adaptations of classic Russian cuisine that became part of American gastronomy.

The first Russians to emigrate to the U.S. were Jews escaping the pogroms of 1881–1884 and 1903–1906. Generally poor, they continued to eat the peasant foods of Russia, which included cured and salted food for preservation, black bread, kasha, cabbage, and potatoes.

Following World War I and the Russian Revolution of 1917, a new generation of refugees of a higher class came to the U.S., many of whom had fought in the White Russian army. These immigrants were largely well educated, wealthy or middle-class, and brought with them a food culture largely unknown to the vast majority of Russians. Some émigrés opened restaurants in big eastern cities. NYC's Russian Tea Room, opened on West Fifty-seventh Street in 1927, was expanded in 1932 by Alexander Maeff, who gave the place the ambience of a grand Russian banquet, serving blini crepes with caviar; skewered, flaming *shashlik* kebabs; smoked salmon; coulibiac; **borscht**; chicken Kiev; beef Stroganoff; and other delicacies, accompanied by champagne and vodka, which was just then entering the American market. Waiters dressed in Czarist-period satin tunics, violinists played Russian music, and many dishes were dramatically flamed at the table. The Russian Tea Room became famous as a magnet for musicians, composers, opera singers, and artists of every kind.

After World War II, those Russians who could escape totalitarian rule emigrated to the eastern cities in America, establishing neighborhoods in places like Brooklyn, New York, where some built vast restaurants and catering halls serving lavish, fixed-price banquet-style meals, which included entertainment and featured not only the traditional czarist-era dishes but more common fare like *pirozhki* pastry dumplings, *pelmeny* stuffed pasta, *shchi* cabbage soup, *syrnicki* fried cheese fritters, and *kotlety* meat patties. One such place, the National, was opened in 1978 by three Ukrainian immigrants, with four hundred seats, performances by Russian musicians, dancing, and a live stage show. The menu is printed in Russian and English.

Owing to antagonism toward Communist Russia during the Cold War, Russian cuisine has not become well known or popular in the U.S., and Russian restaurants are few and far between. At home, Russian Americans maintain their food culture, especially at Easter, when, after midnight Mass, they return home to a spread of cold foods that include baked ham, several salads, and for dessert a tall, domed cake called *kulich* and the molded sweet cheese pudding called *syrni pashka*, accompanied by many vodka toasts.

RUSSIAN DRESSING. A salad dressing made from mayonnaise, pimiento, chili sauce, green pepper, and chives. It is so called possibly because the mixture was thought to resemble those found in Russian salads, but it is American in origin, first found in print in 1900.

RUSSIAN DRESSING

Combine ½ c. mayonnaise with ¼ c. chili sauce, 1 T. chopped pimiento, 1 T. chopped green pepper, and 1 t. chopped chives.

RUSSIAN SERVICE. Also *"service à la russe."* A style of table service in which prepared dishes are brought to the table by servers who, moving counterclockwise around the table, serve food from the guest's left and removes dishes from the right. It differs from **French service**, wherein all dishes within a course are placed on platters in the center of the table at once and hosts and guests serve themselves. Dishes were changed for different courses. Russian service was slowly adapted to American manners as of the mid-nineteenth century. It might include ten or more courses, with side dishes and, at the end of the meal, cookies and candies set on the table.

RUTABAGA. A turnip-like root, *Brassica napus*, from Swedish *rotabagge*, dating in English print as "Roota Baga" to 1789.

RYE. A food grain from the plant *Secale cereale*, more common in Central Europe than America, dating in print to circa 1325, from Old English. Americans use rye mostly in bread and to make **rye whiskey**.

RYE 'N' INJUN BREAD. Also "Rhineinjun bread." A New York Dutch bread made from one quart unbolted Rhode Island rye meal and two quarts Narragansett cornmeal. According to Alice Morse Earle's *Colonial Days in Old New York* (1926), the bread was cooked in a fireplace and covered with hot ashes. Its first mention in print was in 1840.

RYE WHISKEY. One of the first whiskeys made in America, rye must be made from at least 51 percent rye grain, which can be mixed with corn and barley and must be aged in barrels for at least a year. The word *rye* for the grain is from Old English and was first printed in Middle English in 1325, and for a whiskey it dates to 1808. The term is often casually used to describe blended whiskeys that do not have the legal 51 percent rye grain, but to print such an appellation on the label would be forbidden by law.

The first distilleries to make rye whiskey were set up in the eighteenth century by Scots and Irish settlers in western Pennsylvania. The first appearance of the term in print was in 1775.

After several decades of sinking sales, rye began to show strength in the twenty-first century, especially from newer brands made by smaller producers. In 2011, rye sales totaled 25.1 million nine-liter cases, with revenues of $2.3 billion.

SABLEFISH (*Anoplopoma fimbria*). A rich, oily North Pacific fish. The name, first in print in 1918, derives from its blackish skin, and the fish is commonly called "black cod." It is usually sold frozen or smoked, and market size is usually about two feet long and ten pounds. U.S. commercial landings of sablefish totaled 40.3 million pounds in 2010, for sales of $124.3 million.

SACCHARIN. An artificial sweetener that is 350 times sweeter than sugar. Saccharin is used in processed foods and as a substitute for sugar.

Saccharin was first isolated in 1880 by a French chemist named Eugène-Melchior Péligot, but NYC chemistry student Constantine Fahlberg obtained a patent for "new and useful Improvements in Saccharin Compounds" in 1885. Saccharine is now manufactured by the Sherwin-Williams Company and currently accounts for about 70 percent of the artificial-sweetener market in America, packaged in familiar pink packets under the name Sweet'N Low that are ubiquitous on restaurant tables. The chemical makeup of saccharin is $C_7H_5NO_3S$, and the name derives from Latin, Greek, Pali, and Sanskrit root words meaning "sugar."

SAD CAKE. A term for a cake or bread so called because it sinks in the middle after baking and has a "sad" look to it, in print since 1688. The recipe below, for a pecan-coconut-raisin cake of the South, is adapted from one printed in 1984 in the Louisville *Courier-Journal*.

SAD CAKE

Mix 1 lb. brown sugar with 4 beaten eggs. Add ½ c. vegetable oil, 2 c. packaged biscuit mix, 1 t. vanilla, 1 c. chopped pecans, 7 oz. flaked coconut, and ½ c. raisins. Bake in an ungreased 9-by-13-in. pan at 325° for 45 mins. The middle should fall when almost done. Cut into squares.

SAGO. A starch from the sago palm (the genera *Metroxylon*, *Arenga*, and *Caryota*) used as a thickener for puddings and other desserts (1545). The word is from the Malay *sāgū* and first appeared in English print in 1555 for the tree, in 1589 for the starch.

SAI-MIN. A Chinese American noodle soup, probably from Cantonese, dating in American print to 1972.

SALAD. A dish of leafy vegetables dressed with various seasonings, sauces, and other vegetables or fruits. The word is from the Latin *sāl*, "salt," because the first salads of Rome were dressed with little more than simple salt. In Middle English, the word became "salade" by the end of the fifteenth century, and throughout the nineteenth century "salat" was often used in American cookbooks. In England, a salad composed of lettuce or another leafy vegetable on its own is called a "green salad" and is served as an accompaniment to cooked meats or poultry, whereas a "green salad" in America has, since at least 1891, meant a separate salad course, usually served before the main course, with a simple dressing of oil and vinegar. In France and elsewhere in Europe, salads are customarily served after the main course and before the cheese.

Americans had very little interest in salad for most of their history, and more often than not after the Civil War a salad was largely composed of poultry or seafood and vegetables surrounded by only a few lettuce leaves. The wealthy, however, began enjoying European-style salads in the new restaurants opening in the large cities, especially in NYC, where Delmonico's restaurant specialized in novel salad dressings and the **Waldorf salad** of the Waldorf-Astoria Hotel was an instant sensation.

"Molded" or "congealed" salads, made with gelatin or aspic and sugar or sweet fruits, were common in the late nineteenth century. The Shakers had long made "fruit salads," which might not have had any greens at all, and these became a popular luncheon dish in place of a first course. The Germans brought "**potato salad**," and the Italians made tomatoes the most popular ingredient of all in twentieth-century salads, especially with the availability of excellent fruit and vegetables from California then entering the market. California was also the inspiration for a great number of famous salads, such as the "**Green Goddess**," the "**Palace Court**," and (via Tijuana, Mexico) the "**Caesar salad**." So pervasive was the California influence that the "chef's salad," which includes ham and hard-boiled eggs, has become a common main-course item in itself, on many menus as well as at many hosts' tables.

In 1971, Chicago restaurateurs **Richard Melman** and Jerry Orzoff opened a place called R.J. Grunts, which featured a "salad bar," a long counter of greens, seasonings, vegetables, and condiments at which the customer arranges his own salad; this became a fixture of medium-priced and family restaurants throughout the U.S.

Some sandwich fillings made with mayonnaise are also called salads, as, for example, "tuna salad," "chicken salad," and "egg salad." In the 1970s and 1980s, cold "pasta salads," particularly those made with tortellini, mayonnaise, and dill, became fashionable.

Dressings have ranged from the very simple oil and vinegar, called **French dressing** since 1900, to elaborate sauces that might contain orange slices and marshmallows. Only in the recent past have endive, escarole, arugula, and other European greens become popular.

SALAD SAVOY. Trademark name for a vegetable in the Cruciferae family with a flavor resembling cauliflower, broccoli, and cabbage. The leafy heads have either white or violet centers. Salad Savoy was created by John Moore, of Moore Farming Inc., in Salinas, California, in 1983 and began production a year later, when the trademark took effect.

SALAMI. A well-seasoned, often smoked sausage of various kinds, most often used as a cold cut or sandwich meat. The name is from the Italian *salame*, "salted pork," and Vulgar Latin *salāre*, "to salt," dating in English print to at least 1852. Since foreign sausages are not allowed into the U.S. for health reasons, many varieties of Italian salami have been reproduced here, although usually somewhat less spicy. Most are made from a combination of pork and beef, the best known being "Genoa salami," which derives its name from the kind of sausage made in Genoa, Italy. "Mortadella" is a **bologna**-style sausage that is larded with pork fat. The name is from the Latin *murtātum*, a sausage made with myrtle and berries, first appearing in English in 1613.

SALERATUS. An early-nineteenth-century form of **baking powder**, dating in print to 1837. Used as a leavening agent, it was an improvement over pearl ash (used in the eighteenth century) and predated baking soda, which came along in the 1870s. Saleratus (which in Latin means "aerated salt") was first made from potassium bicarbonate, then sodium bicarbonate, and it imparted an undesirable bitterness. One may still hear of old-fashioned saleratus bread and biscuits, although one will no longer find saleratus in a grocery store.

SALISBURY STEAK. A patty made of ground beef and seasonings that is usually broiled. The dish was named after Dr. James Henry Salisbury, who devised a "meat cure" for Civil War soldiers suffering from "camp diarrhea." Salisbury insisted they be fed a diet of chopped beef patties cut from disease-free animals' muscle fibers, with no connective tissue, fat, or cartilage. He went on to advocate this same diet for all Americans, advising them to eat beef three times a day for health benefits. The term dates in print to 1897. The Salisbury steak is often cited as an early example of what was soon to become the **hamburger**.

SALISBURY STEAK

Combine 1 lb. chopped beef with 1 minced onion, 1 T. chopped parsley, salt, and pepper. Shape into ovals about

1 ¼ in. thick and broil on one side. Press in fried bacon bits on the other, and then broil that side until bacon is crisp and the inside is cooked as desired. May be served with a pan gravy. Serves 2.

SALLY LUNN

SALLY LUNN. Also "Sally Lunn bread." A tea bread, made from flour, yeast, eggs, and sugar, of English origins and usually associated with the city of Bath, where a woman named Sally Lunn is supposed to have sold these tea cakes in the eighteenth century. Others suggest the name derives from the French *soleil* and *lune* ("sun" and "moon") or *soleil* and *une* ("sun" and "one"), because of their golden bright, puffy appearance. The first appearance of the name in English print was in 1780. In 1827, William Hone's *Everyday Book* remarked that Sally Lunn was a Bath woman who sold the bread "about thirty years ago" on the streets and whose business was bought by a local banker and musician who made up a song about her.

Sally Lunn bread recipes are found throughout American cookbooks of the nineteenth century.

SALLY LUNN

Scald 1 c. milk, cool until warm, dissolve 1 pkg. yeast in the milk, and set aside. Cream ½ c. butter with ⅓ c. sugar until light. Beat 3 eggs into butter and add 4 c. sifted flour and 1 t. salt, alternating with the milk mixture. Cover and let rise until doubled. Beat again and pour into a 10-in. tube pan. Let rise to double again, then bake at 350° for 45 min.

SALMAGUNDI. Also "salmagundy." A dish of chopped meat, eggs, anchovies, onions, and vinegar, served on lettuce. The word is from the French *salmigondis*, for a "hodgepodge," and first appeared in English print in 1674. Salmagundi was a popular English and American colonial dish. An American reference in 1848 refers to it as a "Dutch dish common in New York."

SALMAGUNDI

In boiling water, cook 12 white onions until tender. Drain and cool. Mix together 3 c. cooked chicken cut into strips, 4 chopped hard-boiled eggs, 8 anchovies, 1 T. chopped parsley, ½ c. salad oil, ¼ c. white wine vinegar, salt, and pepper. Add white onions and mix together well, then pour over lettuce leaves. Serves 6.

SALMON. Any of a variety of fish of the genera *Salmo* and *Oncorhynchus* having six species in U.S. waters. The name is from Latin *salmō*, which became the Middle English *samoun*, first appearing in print circa 1387.

As with many of America's fishes, the salmon was noted for its size and abundance by the first white settlers, only to be fished out or driven out by pollution and the destruction of its habitat by dam building.

The salmon was extremely important to the Native American diet, and as Waverley Root pointed out in *Food* (1980), "in several of the Indian languages the word for 'salmon' was also the word for 'fish.'" The great majority of the fish consumed by the Northwest Native Americans was salmon, cooked in scores of ways, including planking the fish on driftwood or alderwood and allowing the embers of a fire to cook the flesh. Salmon was also dried and smoked, then stored in seal bladders, a preparation white settlers called "Siwash cheese."

The superstitions about salmon that abounded among the Chinook were based on the fear that if the salmon disappeared, the tribes would starve to death. They removed the heart and burned it, lest it be eaten by dogs, who would defile the fish's spirit; menstruating women and girls could not eat salmon. In *American Cooking: The Northwest* (1970), Dale Brown wrote that "the Chinook Indians believed…that anyone involved in preparing a corpse for burial could drive the fish away, and to avert this danger went so far as to bury the infirm alive."

Viking seafarer Eric the Red was amazed at the size of the Atlantic salmon he found when he sailed American waters in the tenth century, and early European settlers bemoaned the constant diet of salmon they endured, even to the point of having a clause written into indentured servants' contracts that forbade the serving of salmon more than once a week.

The waters of the East and West swarmed with salmon. When Lewis and Clark made their way down the Columbia River in Oregon Country, they found their boats blocked by thousands of enormous salmon that died spawning. In New England, it was not considered a true celebration of the Fourth of July if steamed salmon was not part of the feast. In Hawaii, **lomilomi** salmon is equally beloved. By 1840 salmon was being canned in New England and shipped across the country, and then the Californians reversed the transport around 1864. By the end of the nineteenth century, salting plants had proliferated on the Columbia River. "Alaskan turkey" is a slang term for salmon.

By 1889 the Maine coast salmon catch totaled 150,000 pounds, but by the First World War I overfishing and pollution had reduced the Northeast's salmon fisheries so severely that in NYC one might find only cod and trout sold fresh at market. The salmon became fewer in number in the East and began to dwindle in the West, too, so that by 1950 only about a thousand pounds—about eighty-two fish—were taken in Maine. In 1964, fishermen discovered a large salmon feeding ground off Greenland. This revived hopes of a resurgence, but domestic fisheries do not produce nearly enough salmon for the market, with only about seventeen million pounds landed in the Columbia River in recent years. Ttoday all Atlantic salmon comes from Canada or Europe. The country's domestic fisheries do not produce nearly enough salmon for the market.

The main species of salmon in American waters include the "Atlantic" (*Salmo salar*); "Chinook" (*Oncorhynchus tshawytscha*), also called "spring," "king," and "quinnat"; the "pink (*O. gorbuscha*), which is the smallest salmon; the "chum" (*O. keta*), also called "silver brite," "quisutsch," "keta" and "dog," because the Athabascan Indians of the Yukon fed it to their dogs (the word *chum* derives from Chinook jargon *cam*, "mixed colors"); "coho" (*O. kisutch*), also called "silver," "coho salmon," "blue jack," and "cohoe" (the word *coho* possibly derives from a Halkomelem word for the fish); and "sockeye" (*O. nerka*), also called blueback or red (the word *sockeye* is from dialectical Salish *suk-kegh*).

Domestic smoked salmon comes from the Pacific and is often labeled "Nova," "Novy," or "Novie," in imitation of true Nova Scotia salmon, which is rarely seen in U.S. markets. The Pacific fish is wet-cured, that is, it is placed in a salt brine, while the Atlantic, which is almost never encountered at market anymore (except if the salmon is from Canadian or European waters), is dry-cured with salt and sugar. "Indian cure" or Indian hard cure is a process of brining and cold-smoking Pacific salmon once used by the Northwest Native Americans. "Kippered salmon" is mildly brined and hot-smoked. "Squaw candy" is a colloquial term for strips of Pacific salmon salt-brined and hot-smoked. "Kennebec salmon" (the name derives from the Kennebec River, in Maine) merely refers to a preparation of poached salmon steaks.

U.S. salmon landings in 2010 totaled 787.74 million pounds, for sales of $554.8 million. Per capita U.S. consumption is just under two pounds annually.

In New England, poached salmon with egg sauce and a side dish of steamed peas is traditionally served on Independence Day. "Salmon burgers" were created in 1985 by the Alaska Seafood Marketing Institute's test kitchens, made from canned salmon, mayonnaise, bread crumbs, and Parmesan cheese, served on a buttered bun.

See also **lox**.

SALOON. A place where alcoholic drinks are sold by the glass and drunk either at a bar or a table. The term comes from the French *salon*, "room," and in England for a long while it meant just that, especially a large, public room, dating in English print to 1728. But in America the term had come to mean a bar or tavern by 1828, and "saloon keeper" was an acceptable term by 1860. Following the Civil War, NYC saw the opening of scores of "concert saloons," which were somewhat more savory than ordinary saloons and employed "waitergirls." Concert saloons had pretty much vanished by 1905. By the time of Prohibition the word *saloon* had taken on a particularly unsavory connotation, so that after the repeal of Prohibition, in 1933, Americans continued to use other terms, like "bar," "tavern," and "lounge." By the 1960s "saloon" had a distinctly antique ring to it, and establishments that used the word in their names often were trying to lend a certain "turn-of-the-century" connotation to the barroom.

SALSA. A general term for seasoned sauces, usually made with chile pepper and tomatoes, in Mexican American and Tex-Mex cookery. Salsa is used for dipping or as a condiment to main courses. The word is Spanish, dating in English print to 1846, referring to a Spanish version. By 1895 the condiment was well enough known in the American West for one California fan to write,

"I'm so sorry for ye, too. Life without love is like eatin' bull-beef jerky without *salsa*!"

Though it is traditionally associated with Hispanic food culture, by 1991 salsa sales had surpassed those of ketchup in the U.S.

SALSA

Chop up 1 tomato with 1 onion, 4 green or red chiles, and 2 cloves garlic. Add salt to taste and let marinate for ½ hr.

SALSIFY (*Tragopogon porrifolius*). Also "vegetable oyster" or "oyster plant." A native European plant with an edible taproot. The name (pronounced "sol-suh-fee" or "sol-suh-fie") is derived from the French *salsifis* and Italian *salsifica*, dating in English print to 1699. Some believe the root has a faint oysterlike flavor (nineteenth-century cookbook author Mrs. Sarah Tyson Rorer wrote that vegetarians would make a mock-oyster soup from it), and it was once very popular as a vegetable. Recently there has been a resurgence of interest in the plant.

SALT. Sodium chloride, widely used as a seasoning, a curing medium for meat and fish, and the basis for pickling brine. Salt appears in a wide range of foods, from cheese to applesauce, and in many foods where one would not expect to find it, such as in sweet desserts. The food-processing industry in America adds salt indiscriminately to food items that home cooks would rarely salt. As a result, one-fourth to one-half of Americans' salt intake comes from processed food; only one-third is added directly at home in cooking or serving. The rest is ingested through some foods and some drinking water in which salt is naturally found. Americans consume an average of about two teaspoons per day, or eight and a half pounds per year, an amount that has raised some concern among health officials and led some food makers in recent years to reduce the salt added to their products.

Salt (Old English *sealt*, from Latin *sāl*) is an ancient seasoning and a valued one, having at certain times in history been used as money and barter. It is obtained from the evaporation of seawater (in which case it is called "sea salt") and is also dug out of the earth in crystalline form, commonly called "rock salt" and, in Hawaii, *limu*.

The early settlers in America brought salt with them, as well as salted meat and pork, called "salt horse." Importing salt from England, France, Spain, the Canary Islands, and the West Indies was preferred to early attempts at domestic salt making. "Bay salt," another name for the type that comes from seawater, was preferred for curing meat and fish, while the salt used for seasoning at home was generally referred to as "table salt." Later, salt was obtained from the Great Salt Lake, in Utah. During the Civil War, the seizure by Northern troops of the saltworks in the Great Kanawha and Holston valleys cut off the South's supply, causing widespread spoilage of meats and other foods for the Confederacy and forcing some Southerners to scrape the floors of smokehouses for the residue dripped from ham and bacon cured with the substance.

In 1912, the Morton Salt Co. added magnesium carbonate to its salt, allowing it to pour freely rather than stick together.

A "saltcellar" not only was a treasured repository kept on the American dinner table of the eighteenth and nineteenth centuries, but also functioned as a centerpiece and social "borderline," with honored guests sitting above it with the host, and lesser guests positioned below it.

A "salt lick" is a natural deposit of salt licked by animals in the wild.

"Salt rising bread" is a bread of the 1830s and 1840s made from flour, water or milk, and salt, which had a leavening effect.

Salt is packaged and sold in a variety of ways. Seasoned salts are those flavored by onion, garlic, celery, pepper, monosodium glutamate, and other substances. "Kosher salt" is a large-grained, coarsely crushed salt used by Orthodox Jews, according to **kosher** food laws. "Iodized salt" contains cuprous iodide or potassium iodide, added as a public-health measure to prevent goiter due to insufficient iodine in the American diet.

SALTEUR LIQUOR. Diluted spirits given to the Native Americans by early fur traders.

SALT POTATO. A small new potato that has been soaked or boiled in a brine solution. It is a specialty of Syracuse, New York, once a great salt-producing center. The term dates in American print to 1986. Originally the potatoes were soaked in the residue of the brine used in the production of sodium carbonate (washing soda) by the Solvay process. Today the potatoes may be boiled in heavily salted water at home or purchased already packaged at a grocery.

SAMPHIRE. A glasswort or plant in the genera *Arthrocnemum* and *Sarcocornia* that grows in salt marshes and is used for pickles, dating in American print to 1794, though the European species, *Crithmum maritimum*, dates to 1542.

SANDBAKKELS. A Scandinavian American butter cookie baked in a flat fluted tin, from the Norwegian for "sand cookie," dating in American print to 1966.

SAND DAB (*Citharichthys sordidus*, *Hippoglosoides platessoides*, and *Scopthalmus aquuosus*). Also "Pacific sand dab." A flounderlike flatfish found from the Bering Sea to Cape San Lucas, Baja California. It is a delicacy of the Pacific, usually dredged in flour, salt, and pepper, sautéed in butter, and served with a dip of vinegar, parsley, and garlic or merely sprinkled with lemon. The word *dab* (etymology unknown) first appeared in print in 1577, as "sand dab" in 1839.

SANDERS, HARLAND (1890–1980). Restaurateur. As the founder of the franchise company Kentucky Fried Chicken, Harland Sanders made southern fried chicken among the most popular staples of the American table.

Sanders was born to a poor farm family outside Henryville, Indiana. After his father died when Harland was only five, he became the family cook while his mother worked in a tomato canning factory. He dropped out of school in the seventh grade and at fifteen joined the Army as a mule handler in Cuba. Afterwards, for the next twenty-five years of his life, he worked in a number of jobs, including as a farmhand, streetcar conductor, blacksmith's helper, railyard fireman, insurance salesman, tire salesman, and service station operator for Standard Oil.

In 1930, he opened Sanders Court & Cafe, a small eatery in the front room of a gas station he ran in Corbin, Kentucky. The café did well enough to earn him an honorary Kentucky colonel appellation in 1936 from the governor, Ruby Laffoon, in recognition of Sanders's contributions to the state's food culture. A year later, he opened a motel and restaurant called the Sanders Court & Cafe, destroyed in a fire but rebuilt in 1939, where he introduced the idea of frying chicken in a pressure cooker, which was faster and kept the meat juicier than the conventional pan-fried technique.

In 1940, Sanders came up with a batter recipe of eleven herbs and spices for his fried chicken, which gained local popularity. By 1952 he had decided to franchise his business by traveling from town to town and cooking batches of chicken for restaurant owners and employees. The first franchise, now called Colonel Sanders' Kentucky Fried Chicken, was in Salt Lake City, Utah, which paid Sanders five cents for every chicken sold.

In 1955, an interstate highway was built that bypassed Corbin, effectively killing Sanders's local business just as he reached retirement age. Nearly broke, living on a monthly $105 Social Security check, Sanders went back on the road to sell his Original Recipe and launch new franchises. Selling his chicken by the bucket, he developed more than six hundred units in the U.S. and Canada, plus one in England, by 1964. That year he sold his interest in the U.S. company for $2 million and a lifetime salary to a group of investors headed by John Y. Brown Jr. The corporation went public in 1966. In 1971, with more than 3,500 franchise units, the company was bought by Heublein Inc. Sanders agreed to be an avid spokesman for the fried chicken subsidiary, which would later change its name to KFC Corporation (based in Louisville) but continue to use Sanders's image in its logo, always dressed in his signature white suit and string tie (appended in 2008 with a red apron). Traveling for the company until he died, Sanders would often drop in at units unannounced to voice his criticisms of the way they were run. After he pronounced the company's gravy "wallpaper paste," Heublein unsuccessfully sued Sanders for libel in 1973. By 1976 he was said to be the world's second-most-recognizable celebrity.

Sanders devoted himself to numerous philanthropies, including the creation of the Colonel Harland Sanders Trust and Colonel Harland Sanders Charitable Organization. In 1965, he received the Horatio Alger Award from the American Schools and Colleges Association.

When Sanders died, of leukemia in 1980, flags throughout Kentucky were flown at half-staff, and his body lay in state in the capital rotunda. He was buried in his white suit and string tie at Cave Hill Cemetery, in Louisville.

In 1982, Kentucky Fried Chicken became a subsidiary of R. J. Reynolds Industries Inc. (now RJR Nabisco Inc.), then was bought in 1986 by PepsiCo Inc. Today the company is a subsidiary of Yum! Brands Inc., in Louisville. There are more than seventeen thousand KFC franchises in more than 115 countries and territories around the world. Each week, more than thirteen million people visit a KFC restaurant in the U.S.

In 2012, KFC's Facebook page gave access to *Colonel Harland Sanders: The Autobiography of the Original Celebrity Chef*, from a discovered manuscript written by Sanders in 1966.

SANDWICH. A dish of sliced bread and any variety of meats, cheese, relishes, jellies, vegetables, lettuce, and condiments. It is primarily a **lunch** item for most Americans and is far more popular here than in its country of origin, England, where it was named after a notorious gambler in the court of George III named John Montagu ("Jemmy Twitcher"), 4th Earl of Sandwich (1718–1792), who during a twenty-four-hour betting marathon in 1762 ordered bread-and-meat dishes that he could eat while continuing to gamble. The combination came to be named after him, and in her 1837 book *Directions for Cookery*, **Eliza Leslie** listed ham sandwiches as a supper dish, but it was not until much later in the century, when soft white bread loaves became a staple of the American diet, that the sandwich became extremely popular and serviceable. By the 1920s white loaf bread was referred to as "sandwich bread" or "sandwich loaf."

Most American sandwiches are made with this type of presliced bread, sometimes toasted, sometimes trimmed of its crusts to make "tea sandwiches" for afternoon teas. There are also toasted sandwiches, often made with melted cheese, and "open-faced" sandwiches, usually made with one slice of toast, slices of meat or poultry, and a gravy (these are also called "hot sandwiches"). "Brain sandwiches" are a delicacy specific to St. Louis saloons, made with fried calf's brains (either in slices or chopped up), commonly served with pickles and onions on rye bread. They originated in the Depression, when poor people ate all parts of the animal. Sandwiches are usually made on buttered bread. The most popular sandwich among Americans is the ham sandwich, followed by bacon, lettuce, and tomato ("BLT" for short), corned beef, and **pastrami**. Among schoolchildren, one of the most popular is the "peanut butter and jelly" (sometimes known by the abbreviation "PBJ"), as is the tuna-fish sandwich, invariably made from canned tuna and mayonnaise.

See also **canapé**, **club sandwich**, **cowpuncher's sandwich**, **dagwood sandwich**, **French dip sandwich**, **hero**, **Monte Cristo sandwich**, **Philly cheesesteak**, **Polish sandwich**, **Reuben sandwich**, **sloppy joe**, **St. Paul sandwich**, and **stromboli**. Fifty-nine percent of all sandwiches eaten in the U.S. are **hamburgers**.

SANGRIA. A drink made from red wine, fruits, and sometimes brandy (1960). The word is Spanish for "bleeding" and refers to the drink's blood-red color. Sangria originated in Spain, where it is made in batches and often served in a pitcher, a practice that has become just as popular in the U.S. It dates in English print to 1961.

The drink took on a certain faddishness after being introduced by Alberto Heras, supervisor of the Spanish Pavilion at the 1964 New York World's Fair (his recipe is given below). It was a very popular party drink throughout the 1960s and 1970s.

SANGRIA

Empty bottle of red Spanish wine into a pitcher, add 2 t. sugar, and mix until dissolved. Add 1 lemon cut in slices, ½ orange cut in slices, 1 ½ oz. Cointreau, 1 ½ oz. Spanish brandy, ice, and one 12-oz. bottle of club soda. Stir, then let chill for 15 min. Pour sangria into wineglasses without the fruit.

SAPSIS. A porridge flavored with beans. It was made by Native Americans on the East Coast of North America and may still be found in the New England states.

SARATOGA POTATOES. Also "Saratoga chips." Thinly sliced deep-fried potatoes. "Potato chips" have been known since the 1840s, but they were sliced fairly thick in those days. According to most authorities, the thin potato chip was created in 1853 at the Moon's Lake House, in Saratoga, New York (another story places it at the Montgomery Hall Hotel in the same town), when chef George Crum supposedly sliced his potatoes as thin as possible to placate the request of a particularly stubborn customer for thinner potatoes. (Legend has it that the customer was transportation tycoon Cornelius Vanderbilt, whose great-great-grandson's wife, Marylou Whitney, went so far as to write *The Potato Chip Cookbook*.) The next day the chips were given out free in paper cones to customers, and a sign was put on the bar reading HELP YOURSELF. They became very popular across the country (especially after automatic potato peelers were introduced, in 1925), and after a while the term "potato chip" meant a very thin, fried potato, usually served cold as a snack and most often purchased at a food store, usually from a large barrel or display case. (In England, french-fried potatoes are called "potato chips," a usage first referred to in a letter of Oscar Wilde, dated March 1876.)

In 1926, a potato-chip maker named Laura Scudder, of Monterey Park, California, had women workers iron sheets of waxed paper into bags that were thereupon filled with chips and sealed to maintain freshness. This was refined by the Dixie Wax Paper Co., of Dallas, in 1933, whose "preprint" waxed glassine bags allowed companies to print their names on them and shop them more easily.

Except at restaurants, potato chips are rarely prepared fresh. Potato chips grew into a major **snack** business in the twentieth century, with about three hundred potato-chip factories currently producing the item. The largest, Frito-Lay, begun by Herman Lay and Elmer Doolin in 1945 (though not called by that corporate name until 1961), uses 4.2 percent of all potatoes produced in the U.S.

Potato chips are made from specially grown varieties of potatoes called "chipping potatoes," with 25 percent coming from the Red River Valley of Minnesota and North Dakota.

Today potato chips come in a wide variety of styles and thicknesses, some with the skin still attached, others flavored with cheese, chile pepper, and other condiments.

The first flavored potato chips were "barbecue-flavored," introduced in the late 1940s. Sour-cream-flavored potato chips came out soon after. One popular form is the ridged potato chip. Some potato chips are made not from sliced potatoes but from mashed-up potatoes that are molded into uniform shapes.

SARDINE. Any of a variety of small species of fish in the **herring** family. The name derives from the Greek *sardinos*, which became the Middle English *sardeyn*, dating in print to about 1430.

Canning of the fish began on the island of Sardinia. Today sardines are air-dried and coated with oil, then canned, occasionally with other seasonings such as mustard or chile.

Most American sardines now come from Maine, after a long period during which the industry was dominated by Pacific companies, the "Pacific sardine" (*Sardinops sagax*) population having declined significantly since the 1930s. U.S. landings totaled 148.323 million pounds in 2010, valued at $12.615 million.

SARGO. Any of twenty species, in America referring to the Pacific coast grunt (*Pristipoma Davidsoni*) and other fish, dating in American print to 1873. The word is Spanish, from Latin.

SARSAPARILLA. Also "sarsparilla," "sassparilla," "rabbit's-root," and "rabbit's foot." A plant of the order Smilaceae, indigenous to tropical America, first appearing in print in 1577. The dried roots are used as a spice and tonic and were once used in the treatment of syphilis. A carbonated sarsaparilla beverage first appeared in print in 1844, made from the *Smilax regii* plant or ginger flavors. The name comes from the Spanish words for a bramble (*zarza*) and a small vine (*parrilla*). The soft drink is still found today, though it is not as popular as it once was.

SASSAFRAS (*Sassafras albidum*). An aromatic tree of the laurel family, native to North America. The bark of the root is dried and used as a flavoring for root beer and as a brew called "sass tea" (also "grub hyson," from the words *grub* and Chinese *hyson*, a type of green tea). The leaves were pounded by the Choctaw Native Americans to make filé powder, an essential ingredient in the Creole stew called "filé gumbo."

The tree was given the name *sasafrás* by the Spaniards, who may have taken it from a Native American word or confused it with the *Saxifrage* genus of plant. By 1577 it had taken on its English spelling in print.

The Food and Drug Administration banned the sale of sassafras tea when it was found to have carcinogenic properties, and the leaves may no longer be used as a flavoring for root beer or other beverages, although extracts of the plant are considered safe.

SAUCE PIQUANTE. A spicy Louisiana tomato-based sauce customarily cooked with shellfish, turtle, or frogs' legs. The term is from the French *piquante*, "sharp" or "tart," with a recipe given in Escoffier's *Le Guide Culinaire* in 1903, dating in English print to 1934.

SAUCE PIQUANTE

In 2 T. oil sauté 2 chopped onions, 2 chopped cloves garlic, and 1 chopped bell pepper. Then add 1 stalk chopped celery, 1 can tomato paste, 2 chopped scallions, salt and pepper, and ¼ c. vinegar. Bring to a boil, then lower to a simmer. Add meat from shellfish, turtle, or frogs' legs and enough water to cover meat. Cook until meat is tender and sauce is reduced. Serve over rice.

SAUERKRAUT. Also "sourcrout." A chopped cabbage that is salted and then fermented in its own juice. The word, which in German means "sour cabbage," was first mentioned in American English in 1776 (though it dates in English print to 1633), and the dish was long associated with German communities in the U.S. It is still widely enjoyed, especially with pork dishes and as a condiment on hot dogs. It is usually bought in groceries rather than made at home. Americans consume about 359 million pounds of sauerkraut per year, or 1.5 pounds per person.

SAUSAGE. Any of a wide variety of chopped or ground meat blended with herbs and spices and molded into a casing, usually made from animal intestines. The word is from Middle English *sausige*, dating in print to the fifteenth century.

Sausages have been common throughout the world for millennia, and the idea was brought to America by European settlers who used it as a way to preserve meat, especially the lesser cuts.

Sausages are divided into six major categories:

FRESH SAUSAGE. Made from meats that are neither cured nor smoked. They must be cooked before serving.

COOKED SAUSAGE. Made from uncured meats that are cooked but not smoked.

COOKED, SMOKED SAUSAGE. Made from cured meats that are lightly smoked, then cooked. They do not require further cooking. These include **bologna** and **hot dogs**.

UNCOOKED, SMOKED SAUSAGE. Either cooked or cured meats that are smoked and then later cooked before serving.

DRY SAUSAGE. Also called "summer sausage" (because it can be kept in warm weather without refrigeration) and "seminary sausage" (because it is associated with the type of sausages made at monasteries), made from cured sausage that is air-dried under controlled time/temperature/humidity conditions. They may or may not be smoked. Lebanon bologna, salami, **kosher** sausage, and Spanish chorizo are examples of such sausages.

SPECIALTY MEATS. A wide range of products made from cured or noncured chopped or comminuted meats, usually baked or cooked rather than smoked, and formed into loaves to be sliced and served cold in salads or sandwiches or as a breakfast meat, like **scrapple**.

The U.S. is home to twenty-one thousand sausage processors that produce more than 6.3 billion pounds of sausage each year and more than two hundred different varieties.

SAUVIGNON BLANC. Also "Fumé Blanc." A white vinifera grape that makes a fruity, spicy wine (1940). It is used extensively in the white wines of Graves, in Bordeaux, and in the Loire Valley. In California it has achieved great success in the past ten years, especially after the Robert Mondavi Winery of the Napa Valley introduced the name "Fumé Blanc" for a somewhat drier version in the late 1960s, in order to make it sound more attractive to American ears.

SAXIFRAGE. Also "pussyfoot." Any of a variety of plants in the genus *Saxifraga* bearing a leafy, lettuce-like green. The word is from the Latin *saxifragus*, "rock-breaking," because the plant grows in the crevices of rocks, dating in Middle English print to circa 1440. The main North American variety is the "mountain lettuce" (*S. micranthidifolia*), also called "branch lettuce" and "deer-tongue." Two other varieties, *S. virginiensis* and *S. pennsylvanica*, proliferate along the East Coast.

Saxifrage is cooked as a vegetable and added to soups. In the South it is often fried with bacon and onions.

SAZERAC. Trademark name for a cocktail made with whiskey, sugar, bitters, and an anise-flavored cordial. It is a famous drink of New Orleans and took its name from a French brandy made by the firm Sazerac-de-Forge et Fils, which was imported to the city by John Schiller, who opened his Sazerac Coffee House in 1859 at No. 13 Exchange Alley, in the French Quarter. In 1870, Schiller's bookkeeper, Thomas Handy, bought the establishment and changed the name to the Sazerac House. Around the same time, Handy changed the original recipe for the cocktail to include a slight taste of **absinthe** and a dash of red Peychaud **bitters** (introduced to New Orleans by pharmacist A. A. Peychaud in the 1790s), and, ironically, replaced the Sazerac brandy with American blended whiskey. (Leon Lamothe, another importer, has been mentioned as the man who added the absinthe back in 1857, but this seems rather early.)

The recipe was further changed when absinthe was banned from sale in the U.S. in 1912 because of its harmful effects on the body and anise-flavored liqueurs like Spanish Ojén and Louisiana Herbsaint were substituted. Some bartenders made the drink with bourbon instead of blended whiskey, and it is rarely made with brandy anymore.

The name Sazerac, dating in American print to 1941, became a trademark of the Sazerac Co., and the "original" recipe is still served at the Sazerac Bar, in the Roosevelt Hotel (formerly the Fairmont). Following is a substitute recipe.

SAZERAC

Combine 1 ½ oz. rye or bourbon, 4 t. bar sugar, ½ t. Peychaud bitters, and ice cubes. Pour 3 dashes of Herbsaint into a chilled old-fashioned glass, coat the sides, then pour out. Pour the mixed ingredients into the glass and garnish with a lemon twist.

SCALLION. A general term for any of a variety of onions, including the spring onion, the shallot, the leek, and the white onion. The name comes from the Latin *ascalonia*, referring to Ascalon, where a certain onion was grown. The word, in reference to a leek, shows up in Middle English in *Piers Plowman* (1393).

In the U.S., the word *scallion*, dating in print to 1790, usually refers to *Allium fistolosum*, a bulbless onion also called the "spring onion," "bunch onion," or "green onion." In Creole and Cajun cookery, however, the word is used to describe a young shallot, as explained in the recipe book *American Cooking: Creole and Acadian* (1971), by Peter S. Feibleman:

> *In Louisiana, which produces about 90 percent of the shallots grown in the United States, the shallot crop is sold and used in its green form. For this reason, perhaps, a special problem of terminology has developed there. Since the green shallot is the most readily available form of scallion in Louisiana, the term scallion is usually restricted to that vegetable in Creole and Acadian cooking. Elsewhere in the United States, the term scallion usually refers to a green or bunching onion, while a shallot is the mature vegetable, usually reddish brown, clove-shaped, and dried.*

SCALLOP. Any of a variety of marine mollusks of the family Pectinidae. Scallops are usually sold in American markets dead and without their coral (roe).

The name derives from Old French *escalope*, "shell," which refers to the shell in which the mollusk lives, dating in English to about 1440.

In the eastern U.S., there are four species: the "deep-sea scallop" (*Placopecten magellanicus*), the "lion's paw" (*Nodipecten nodosus*), the "calico scallop" (*Argopecten gibbus*), and the "bay scallop" (*A. irradians*). The first and last in this group are the most often encountered at market in the East, with the latter generally preferred for its delicacy of taste.

In the western U.S., one finds the "pink scallop" (*Chlamys herica* or *C. rubida*), the "Hinds' scallop" (*C. rubida*), the "Iceland scallop" (*C. islandica*), the "speckled scallop" (*A. circularis aequisulcatus*), the "kelp-weed scallop" (*Leptopecten latiauratus*), and the "giant rock scallop" (*Hinnites giganteus*), which may measure up to six inches.

In American kitchens, scallops are either breaded and deep-fried or cooked according to French recipes such as *coquilles Saint-Jacques*, with cream and seasonings. U.S. commercial landings of scallops totaled 57.6 million pounds of meats in 2010, valued at $456.6 million.

SCANDINAVIAN AMERICAN FOOD. A general term for the various foods cooked and enjoyed by Scandinavian immigrants, as well as those adaptations of Scandinavian cuisine that became part of American gastronomy.

As in most of Europe in the nineteenth century, poverty and a future with little promise of improvement drove Scandinavians to America. Before the Civil War, about 125,000 immigrants arrived in the U.S. More than half were Swedes, a third Norwegians, a seventh Danes. Crop failures in Sweden in the 1860s drove two million Scandinavians west, overwhelmingly to the U.S., where the passage of the Homestead Act of 1862 encouraged them to settle in the northern territories, with a guarantee of land. The Swedes spread themselves throughout the territory, the Norwegians favored Minnesota, Wisconsin, and North Dakota, Danes came to Minnesota, Wisconsin, Iowa, Illinois, and Kansas, and Finns settled in the upper Midwest, especially Michigan, and farther out in California.

In their home countries, Scandinavians lived in tightly knit, traditional societies, cemented by social clubs like the Swedish Vasa Order, the Finnish Knights of Kaleva, the Sons of Norway, and the Danish Brotherhood, which helped new arrivals adapt to America and maintain their languages and food culture.

Scandinavian food was hearty, based on a farmworker's dietary needs or the lunch-pail foods brought from home by miners, which included the pasty, an enclosed-crust pie of meats and vegetables. When the Scandinavians celebrated, it was with a lavish smorgasbord table set with hot and cold foods, breads, and pastries, including **Swedish meatballs** and **lutefisk**—dried cod once consumed by the poor but reclaimed as a Christmas food in their American communities. Around 1911, a popular bilingual cookbook on Finnish cooking was published, *Suomalais-Amerikalainen Keittokirja*, by Mina Walli, containing recipes for eel soup, Danish eggs, herring mousse, meat pies, Finnish pancakes, and "Jenny Lind soup," named after a famous opera star of the period, Johanna Maria Lind (1820–1887), known as the "Swedish Nightingale."

In Scandinavian American communities, bakeries and restaurants proliferated, though not as much in eastern, southern, or western cities. NYC had several in the 1930s, with names like Castleholm Restaurant, Restaurant Drottningholm, and Gripsholm, all offering a smorgasbord, as well as *krafter* (crayfish), Swedish *pannekaker* pancakes, Swedish meatballs, gravlax (cured salmon), and even reindeer. A revolving smorgasbord was the attraction at the Three Crowns, an offshoot of the New York World's Fair of 1939. In the 1960s, Scandia, owned by Ken Hansen, in Hollywood, California, was considered one of the finest restaurants in America. Not until 1987, however, did a thoroughly modern and highly stylized Scandinavian restaurant open—Aquavit, in NYC, opened by Håkan Swahn, which was inducted into the *Esquire* Restaurant Hall of Fame in 2000. Swahn also opened a branch in Minneapolis in 1999, but it closed in 2003.

Beginning in 2010, when a Copenhagen-based restaurant named Noma won international acclaim for its Modern Scandinavian cuisine, largely based on foraged foods, there was interest in establishing similar restaurants in the U.S., including Atera in NYC.

Except for **Danish pastry**, found throughout the U.S., the traditions of Scandinavian food are still most vital in cities with sizable Scandinavian populations, like Minneapolis, with restaurants and bakeries such as the

Finnish Bistro, Kaffe Stuga, the Bachelor Farmer, and Scandia Bake Shop, a Fika café in the American-Swedish Institute, opened in 2012.

SCAMPI. A Venetian term, dating in English print to 1920, that in America refers to shrimp cooked in garlic, butter, lemon juice, and white wine, commonly listed on menus as "shrimp scampi." The true *scampo* (*scampi* is the plural) of Italy is a small lobster or prawn, of the family Nephropidae, which in America is called a "lobsterette." These shellfish are available in U.S. waters, first introduced in 1962 by deepwater shrimp fishermen of Florida, but are not generally found in markets. The term "scampi," then, has come to mean any shrimp—usually of medium size—cooked in butter, to which is added finely chopped garlic and a dash of dry white wine. It is a staple feature of Italian American restaurants.

SCHICHTKUCHE. A Pennsylvania Dutch layer cake, typical examples of which are the king's cake and the queen's cake. The word *Schichte* in German means "layer." It is not to be confused with **king cake**.

KING'S CAKE

Add 16 egg yolks and 1 lb. sugar to 1 lb. whipped cream. Stir for 1 hr., then add 1 lb. fine flour and stir for ½ hr. Add 1 lb. Sultana raisins, 1 lb. dried currants, and 3 oz. finely cut citron shell. Add 9 stiffly beaten egg whites. Bake 1 hr.

QUEEN'S CAKE

Mix together 1 lb. sugar, 1 lb. flour, 1 lb. butter, and 8 eggs that have been separated and beaten separately, the whites until they are of a thick consistency that holds to the whisk. Add ½ lb. currants, 1 ground nutmeg, and an equal amount cinnamon and bake.

SCHLOSSER, ERIC (1959–). Author. In his book *Fast Food Nation: The Dark Side of the All-American Meal* (2002), Eric Schlosser exposed the poor sanitary conditions and manipulative corporate marketing of America's fast-food companies and facilities, including McDonald's, ConAgra, and Iowa Beef Packers. Along with the 1906 novel *The Jungle*, by **Upton Sinclair**, it is considered a seminal work on the subject of the food industry.

Born in NYC, Schlosser grew up in Los Angeles and attended Princeton University as an American history major. He received a graduate degree from Oxford University in British imperial history. After a period as a playwright, Schlosser wrote investigative reports for *The Atlantic Monthly*, winning a Peabody Award in 1994 for his series "Reefer Madness" and "Marijuana and the Law." His articles also appeared in *Rolling Stone*, which published "Fast Food Nation" as a two-part story that Schlosser turned into a 2002 bestselling book, which was adapted for a film of the same name, which he co-wrote and produced. The book was honored by *Fortune* magazine as the Best Business Book of the Year. Schlosser said of *Fast Food Nation*, "I've written this book out of a belief that people should know what lies behind the shiny, happy surfaces of every fast-food transaction. They should know what really lurks between those sesame-seed buns. As the old saying goes: You are what you eat."

Schlosser also wrote *Chew on This* (2006), an adaptation of *Fast Food Nation* for younger readers.

SCHMALTZ. A Yiddish American term for both herring and rendered fat, most often from chicken, first printed in 1935. The word is of German origin.

SCHMEAR. A Yiddish term for a daub or smear of a condiment, like cream cheese spread on a bagel or sandwich, dating in print to 1960. It is also used as a verb. See **smear**.

SCHNECKE. A type of German American or Jewish cinnamon roll. The word derives from the German word for "snail," dating in print to 1920.

SCHNITZ UND KNEPPE. Also "*schnitz un knepp*" and "*Schnitz-und-Gnepp*." A Pennsylvania Dutch dish made from the butt of an Easter ham, with dried apples and dumplings. "*Schnitz*" (often spelled "*snitz*"), dating in American print to 1848, refers to "slices" of dried apples, while "*knepp*" refers to the small dumplings pinched off from a mass of dough, derived from the Dutch *kneep*, meaning a "pinch." According to William Woys Weaver, in *America Eats* (1989), the dish is a descendant of another Pennsylvania Dutch dish called "*gumbis*" (derived from the Latin *compositum*, "compositions"), which also included cabbage and meat along with various fruits.

SCHNITZ UND KNEPP

Soak 1 qt. dried apples overnight in water, then drain and set aside. Place a 3-lb. ham butt in a large casserole and pour in enough water to cover the ham. Bring to a boil, reduce to a simmer, and cook for about 2 hours, or more, until tender. Pour off the water, remove the ham from the casserole, and cut into small cubes. Return the ham to the casserole, add the apples, 2 T. brown sugar, and about 6 c. chicken stock. Bring to a boil and cook for 20 minutes. Meanwhile, make a dumpling batter by sifting together 2 c. flour, 4 t. baking powder, 1 t. salt, and ½ t. ground black pepper. Add 1 beaten egg and 1 ½ c. milk. Blend well, then add 3 T. melted butter and blend completely. Drop the batter by spoonfuls into the boiling ham liquid, cover, and cook for about 15 minutes. Serve hot on a large platter.

SCHOOL LUNCH PROGRAM. Formally, the National School Lunch Program. A federally sponsored program (begun in 1946) of the USDA in 1990 that provides free lunches to 24.4 million schoolchildren at 91,400 schools each day. The federal school breakfast program, begun in 1969, provides breakfast to 4.5 million children in 47,627 schools.

In 1994, the Department of Agriculture was instructed to set limits on the fat, cholesterol, and sodium content of school lunches.

SCHOONER. A drinking glass popular in the last half of the nineteenth century, dating in American print to 1705. It held a pint or more of beer. The word probably derives from the large size of the ship that goes by the same name.

SCHOONMAKER, FRANK (1905–1976). Wine importer, author. At a time when American wine had a very poor reputation for quality, Frank Musselman Schoonmaker championed the emerging wineries of California in the 1930s, which eventually led to the wine revolution of the 1970s.

Schoonmaker was born in Spearfish, South Dakota. His father was a classics professor at Columbia University, his mother a feminist advocate. While at Princeton University (1923–1924), Schoonmaker edited a humor magazine called *The Hue and Cry*. He toured Europe, writing *Through Europe on $2 a Day*. He then worked for travel writer and publisher Lowell Thomas, producing a series of city guides, and then moved to *The New Yorker*, for which he wrote a ten-part series on European wines that became *The Complete Book of Wine* (1934), in which he brought good California wines to the attention of the public. He also traveled widely in France with Raymond Baudoin, editor of *La Revue du Vin de France*, in Paris. Both were responsible for having Burgundian winemakers switch from selling their wines in casks to bottling them under estate labels. When Prohibition ended in the U.S., Schoonmaker incorporated his import business, in partnership with Alexis Lichine. During World War II, he worked for the Office of Strategic Services in France and, underground, in Spain. In Burgundy he was nicknamed "Le Colonel."

After the war, Schoonmaker returned to the U.S. to write *American Wines* (1941), *The Wines of Germany* (1956), and *Frank Schoonmaker's Encyclopedia of Wine* (1964, revised 1974). He also became an importer in 1935. His wine labels carried the words "Frank Schoonmaker Selections," which lent luster to the wines, and he consulted for many wineries, including Almaden (for which he became general sales manager), Wente Bros., Louis Martini, and Widmer Winery. He encouraged them to label their wines as varietals rather than generics. In 1972, he sold his business to Souverain Cellars.

In 2007, Schoonmaker was inducted into the Wine Media Guild's Wine Writers' Hall of Fame. The **Culinary Institute of America** at Greystone inducted Schoonmaker into its 2013 Vintners Hall of Fame.

SCOFFLAW COCKTAIL. A drink made of Canadian whiskey, dry vermouth, and grenadine. According to the *Chicago Tribune* for January 27, 1924, "Hardly has Boston added to the gaiety of nations by adding to Webster's Dictionary the opprobrious term of 'scoff-law,' when Jock, the genial manager of Harry's Bar in Paris, yesterday invented the Scoff-Law Cocktail, and it has already become exceedingly popular among American prohibition dodgers."

SCOFFLAW COCKTAIL

Shake together with ice 1 dash orange bitters with a mixture made up of ⅓ Canadian whisky, ⅓ dry vermouth, ⅙ lemon juice, and ⅙ grenadine. Strain and pour into cocktail glass.

SCRAPPLE. Also "Philadelphia scrapple." A porridge-and-pork breakfast or brunch dish that is chilled and served in slices, dating in print to 1855. It is an old Pennsylvania Dutch dish often served with apple slices and brown sugar, the name being a diminutive of "scrap." The Pennsylvania Dutch also called it "pawnhaus" (finely chopped food) and, later, "poor-do," since it was often made from leftovers. It was introduced at least as early as 1817 to the city of Philadelphia, where it became an immediate favorite, especially among the upper-class gentry. In the Midwest, a similar dish made by German immigrants was called "gritz" (also "grits wurst," "breakfast grits," and "knipp"). In the Cincinnati area, a similar dish is called **goetta.**

SCRAPPLE

Cover 1 ½ lb. boneless pork with water, bring to boil, and simmer for 2 hr. Remove and slice and then mince meat. To 3 c. of the cooking liquid add ½ t. pepper, 1 t. sage, and ½ t. salt. Return meat to broth. Mix 1 ½ c. cornmeal with 1 c. water, stir into meat mixture, and cook on low heat until thickened, then 10 min. more. Rinse a 9-by-5-in. loaf pan with cold water, put in meat mixture, and chill. Unmold and slice. Brown in bacon fat. Serves 6-8.

SCREWDRIVER. A drink made with vodka and orange juice. It has been popular since the 1950s, but its origins are obscure. According to one story, the name came about when an orange juice salesman in Bakersfield, California, asked a bartender to mix orange juice with vodka and to serve the drink to six customers, five of whom liked the concoction but one of whom tasted it and said, "I'd just as soon swallow a screwdriver."

A more frequently cited story—though with no more evidence to back it up—contends the drink was created by American oil-rig workers in the Middle East who mixed vodka with orange juice packed in cans that they opened with screwdrivers, which were also used to stir the drink's ingredients. The word dates in American print to a 1956 *House & Garden* article calling it "the most popular drink the West Coast has seen in years."

SCREWDRIVER

In a glass with ice cubes pour 1 ½ oz. vodka and 3 oz. orange juice. Stir.

SCRIPTURE CAKE. A cake made with ingredients as listed in certain verses of the Bible. Though known throughout the American colonies, it was a traditional confection among the Baptists, dating in print, with recipe, to 1906. The recipe below is from a Pennsylvania woman, as published in *Famous Old Receipts* (1908). It is interesting to note, in light of the fact that baking powder was invented only in the 1850s, that the corresponding Corinthians verse says, "Your boasting is unseemly. Do you not know that a little leaven ferments the whole lump?"

SCRIPTURE CAKE

Combine 1 c. butter (Judg. 5:25), 3 ½ c. flour (1 Kings 4:22), 3 c. sugar (Jer. 6:20), 2 c. raisins (1 Sam. 30:12), 2 c. figs (1 Sam. 30:12), 1 c. water (Gen. 24:17), 1 c. almonds (Gen. 43:11), 6 eggs (Isa. 10:14), 1 T. honey (Gen. 43:11), a pinch of salt (Lev. 16:13), spices to taste (1 Kings 10:10), and 2 T. baking powder (1 Cor. 5:6).

SCROD. Also "scrode." A young **cod** or a young haddock, specifically one that has been split and prepared for cooking. The word may derive from obsolete Dutch *schrood*, "slice" or "shred," but the sometimes encountered variant *escrod* is more obscure. The Parker House Hotel, in Boston, famous for its simple preparation of the dish (see recipe below), calls it "schrod." There seems no evidence to support the contention that "scrod" is an acronym for "serving catch reeled on the day."

Although cod was a staple fish of old New England, this term for a young specimen seems to be of rather recent origins, appearing in print, according to the *Dictionary of Americanisms*, for the first time in 1835. Today it is still a specialty of New England.

~~~~~~~~~~~~~~~~~~~~~~~~~~~~~~~
SCROD
~~~~~~~~~~~~~~~~~~~~~~~~~~~~~~~

Marinate a 12-oz. fillet of cod (or haddock) in ½ pt. milk, 1 t. lemon, ½ t. Worcestershire sauce, salt, and pepper for about 1 hr. Mix 3 T. vegetable oil with ½ t. paprika and dip the fish into this mixture and then in ½ c. bread crumbs. Place in a baking dish with a little white wine and 2 T. butter. Bake for about 12 min.

SCUPPERNONG. A species of Muscadine grape, *Vitis rotundifolia*, used to make wines and jellies, or the wine made from such a grape, dating in print to 1811. The Scuppernong is grown throughout the South, particularly in North Carolina, where the name covers almost all wines made from various Muscadine grapes.

The origins of the word "Scuppernong" are given in Leon D. Adams's *Wines of America* (second edition, revised, 1978):

> Scuppernong was named for a town, which was named for a river, which was named for a tree. Ascopo was the Algonquian, meaning place of the Ascopo, appeared on old maps of North Carolina as the name of the river in Washington County, near Albermarle Sound. Later maps spelled it Cuscopung, then Cuscopung, next Scuponing and by 1800 the spelling of the river had become Scuppernong. The grape, however, was merely called the White Grape until James Blount of the town of Scuppernong took the census of Washington County in 1810 and reported 1,368 gallons of wine made there in "this small but very interesting branch of our infant manufactures." An article in the Raleigh (North Carolina) Star for January 11, 1811, commenting on Blount's report, was the first to call it "The Scuppernong Grape."

Wine has been made from the Scuppernong since the 1560s, when the French Huguenots who settled in Florida fermented the grapes, which were exceptionally abundant and needed only to be knocked to the ground from the high, prolific vines. Sir Walter Raleigh's men discovered the vine growing on Virginia's Roanoke Island in 1584 and introduced it elsewhere. (Supposedly, the original vine Raleigh's men propagated still exists on Roanoke and is called the "Mother" or "Raleigh" vine.)

The fame of the Scuppernong wines was fostered by a North Carolinian named Captain Paul Garrett (1863–1940), who, after working as a salesman for his uncle Charles Garrett's winery, established his own winery, Garrett & Co., in 1900. By 1903 he had four more and was becoming rich selling Scuppernong, which he first called "Escapernog," then "Minnehaha" and "Pocahontas," and, finally, "Virginia Dare," after the first child born of English parents in America. (Dare, born in 1587 of Ananias and Elenor Dare, vanished with the rest of Raleigh's settlers on Roanoke after four years of deprivation.) Garrett's wines became the most popular in the country until certain states, and then the country, went dry with Prohibition. Garrett had plantings of Scuppernong in other states, but after Prohibition the grapes were scarce in the East, and Virginia Dare no longer tasted the same. By 1966 propagation of the Scuppernong had fallen to a few hundred acres in North Carolina. Since then, with the help of the state legislature and the state university in Raleigh, there has been renewed interest in the Scuppernong, in addition to several other Muscadine varieties that now go under the name Scuppernong.

The original Scuppernong is a greenish-bronze grape, grown in bunches, that produces a distinctive, amber-colored wine that is most often sweetened. If blended with other labrusca grapes, it tends to mute the foxy taste of the finished wine.

SEA FOAM. Any of a variety of desserts or sweet confections whose texture or appearance resembles sea foam, dating in American print to 1905. They are usually made with some form of beaten egg whites.

SEA PIE. A stew of pork, veal, or fowl mixed with sweet dried apples, molasses, and dumplings. The dish is served in New England and so called, according to Josephine H. Pierce, in *Coast to Coast Cookery* (1951), "because a sea captain told how to make it." A recipe may be found in Mary Randolph's *Virginia Housewife, or Methodical Cook* (1836).

SEA URCHIN. Any of a variety of marine echinoderms of the class Echinoidea having a soft flesh encased in a spiny shell. The name derives from its resemblance to a hedgehog, which in Middle English was *(h)irchon*, and in Latin *(h)ēricius*, dating in English print to 1605.

Though sea urchins have become a gourmet item in the U.S., they are unappreciated by most Americans, and in fact are called "whore's eggs" by fishermen whose bait they steal and swimmers who brush up against the animal's sharp, painful thorns. But Mediterranean immigrants buy most of the catch at market, and Maine ships more than ten million pounds (especially the "green sea urchin," *Strongylocentrotus droebachiensis*) to Japan. The reproductive organs (called the "roe") of the animal are considered great delicacies in Japan.

The "giant red urchin" (*S. franciscanus*) of California is considered one of the best for eating. Other main species of sea urchin for consumption include: "purple sea urchin" (*Arbacia punctulata*), "keyhole urchin" (*Mellita quinquiesper forata*), "purple sea urchin" (*S. purpuratus*, a Pacific species different from the eastern variety above), "white sea urchin" (*Lytechinus vari egatus*), and "heart urchin" (*Moira atropos*). U.S. commercial landings of sea urchins total about 5,000 metric tons today.

SEDLAR, JOHN RIVERA (1954–). Chef and author. John Sedlar was among those California chefs of the 1980s who created a style of New Southwestern cuisine using their classical culinary training to bring discipline, color, and style to the food and the plate.

Growing up in Santa Fe, Sedlar had a long acquaintance with New Mexican cookery. He furthered his culinary knowledge by spending three years in Seville and Zaragoza, Spain. In 1973, he honed his skills by working at the classical French restaurant L'Ermitage, in L.A. Drawing on all he had learned, Sedlar opened Saint Estèphe, in a mall in Manhattan Beach, California, in 1980. In an interview with the *Los Angeles Times*, he said it was "a nice French restaurant" with the menu all in French, but he knew "it needed a bit of a spark," so, after a visit home to New Mexico, he returned to L.A. with fifteen cases of red Chimayó chiles and "integrated them in every item on the menu. Ice cream, pickles, chutneys, sauces, apps, entrees, all courses of the menu," creating dishes like salmon mousse tamale, duck liver mousse with pickled chiles in aspic, and posole consommé with foie gras and truffle. He eventually called his food "Modern Southwestern Cuisine." Of the movement, Sedlar said, "It taught people that you could offer what they thought was peasant food in an upscale environment, " he told

Gustavo Arellano, "challenge them with new dishes or interpretations of the classics." Sedlar's next effort, Bikini (1991), was more global in scope, and Abiquiu (1994), in Santa Monica, was a more stylish, higher-end restaurant.

After the 1994 Los Angeles earthquake, Sedlar lost heart for the restaurants, closed Abiquiu, did some restaurant consulting, and focused on a southwestern-food company, Abiquiu Foods LLC, for home consumption. Fifteen years passed before Sedlar began to feel his former chef colleagues "were having all the fun," so he returned to open a stylish downtown restaurant named Rivera (2010), where he went further in refining Mexican and southwestern flavors. The following year he opened a more casual restaurant, Playa, which featured a small-plates menu of what he called "Urban Latin Cuisine." Both restaurants won *Esquire*'s Best New Restaurants awards, and in 2011 Sedlar was also honored by the magazine as Chef of the Year for his contributions to American gastronomy.

Sedlar is the author of *Modern Southwest Cuisine* (1986, revised 1994) and *The Great Chile Relleno Cookbook* (2000) and co-author of *Tamales* (1997, reissued 2002). He is also the creator of the first Latino food museum in the U.S., Museo 26.

He is a member of Who's Who of Cooking in America and listed on *Food & Wine* magazine's Honor Roll of American Chefs.

SEED CAKE. A cake made from caraway seeds, dating in English print to 1570. The following recipe dates from *Mrs. Winslow's Domestic Receipt Book*, from 1865.

SEED CAKE

Combine 4 c. flour, 1 ½ c. cream, ½ c. butter, 3 eggs, ½ c. caraway seeds, 1 t. baking soda, and 1 t. rosewater and make a dough. Cut with biscuit cutter and bake at 350° for about 20 min.

SELTZER. A naturally or man-made carbonated water with no taste of its own, drunk plain or as a mixer in everything from soda-fountain confections to alcoholic drinks.

Carbonated waters have been known for hundreds of years. The word *seltzer* comes from a bottled mineral water called *Selterser Wasser*, made from the waters of the Prussian town Niederselters. The word was first printed in English in 1744.

Man-made carbonated water was created by Joseph Priestley in 1767, and Swedish chemist Torbern Bergman produced commercial quantities of carbonic gas in 1770. By 1807, such man-made sodas were sold around NYC by Yale University professor Benjamin Silliman, and in 1832 an English immigrant to NYC named John Matthews crafted a practical small machine to carbonate water for use in pharmacies. It was called a "soda fountain," and its use in drugstores was evidence of the era's belief in seltzer's medicinal and curative value. By the end of the century, soda fountains ranged from elaborate marble-and-silver salons that served as significant social gathering spots to small, unadorned neighborhood stores with counters (often part of a "candy store") in large cities. In NYC's predominantly Jewish Lower East Side, there were no fewer than seventy-three soda fountains located within a one-third-square-mile area.

Flavors were soon added to seltzers, and such mixtures were called "soda pop" by the 1840s, but the word *seltzer* has continued to mean an unflavored carbonated water to this day. Seltzer was served both at fountains and in siphon bottles that became standard items at the home bar, a practice that has all but disappeared. Today seltzer is distinguished from club soda by having less or no salt added. The terms "club soda" and "sparkling water" came into use after the repeal of Prohibition, in 1933, when elegant supper clubs and private clubs deliberately sought to remove the drink's medicinal connotations.

In NYC, seltzer was sometimes humorously called "Jewish champagne" because of its popularity among Jews, who in Yiddish called it *grepsvasser*, "belch water," and who drank it to help the digestion of their fatty diet and to adhere to kosher rules against mixing meats with milk. In the early part of this century in NYC, one would go to a candy store and order "for-two-cents-plain," a glass of seltzer for two pennies.

See also **soda**.

SEMMEL. A Pennsylvania Dutch crisp-crusted yeast roll, whose name is borrowed from the German for "roll," dating in American print to 1932.

SEMMEL

Mix ½ pkg. yeast in ¼ c. warm water. Add to ½ c. cooled, cooked mashed potatoes and stir in ½ c. sugar. Let stand 4 hr. Add ½ c. butter to 2 c. scalded milk. Cool, add 2 beaten eggs, ½ c. sugar, and ½ t. salt. Beat into yeast mixture, add 6 c. flour, cover, and let rise 8 hr. Roll dough into a square ¼ in. thick. Brush with melted butter and cut into 2-in. squares, then turn up corners. Place on buttered baking sheet and let rise to double. Bake at 450° for 20 min. Brush with butter and sprinkle with confectioners' sugar and cinnamon. Makes about 30.

SENATE BEAN SOUP. A white-bean soup served in the U.S. Senate restaurant, which is operated for the senators and their guests. Credit for the soup's creation has gone to Senator Fred T. Dubois of Idaho in the 1890s, but its association with the Senate restaurant began in 1907, when Senator Knute Nelson of Minnesota, chairman of the Senate Committee on Rules, decreed that the soup must be served every day in the dining room. Speaker of the House Joe Cannon of Illinois later ruled that it should also be served in the House of Representatives' dining room, while Representative Bob Traxler of Michigan further decreed that the soup must be made only with Michigan white navy beans.

SENATE BEAN SOUP

Wash 2 c. dried white navy beans, then (according to Senate directions) "run them through hot water until they are white again." Drain, place in a large pot with 3 qt. water and 1 lb. smoked ham hocks. Bring to a boil and lower to a simmer for 2 hr. until beans are tender. Add 3 cooked mashed potatoes, 3 chopped onions, 2 chopped garlic cloves, and 3 chopped stalks of celery. Cover, simmer for 1 hr., remove ham bone, and scrape off meat into soup. Stir in ¼ c. parsley. Serves 12.

SERRA, JUNÍPERO (1713–1784). Missionary. As one of the Spanish missionaries to the new territories of California, Father Junípero Serra was instrumental in both building a chain of missions and planting the first vineyards in the West.

Born Miguel José Serra in Petra, Majorca, Spain, he entered the Alcantarine Franciscan order in 1830, where he took the name Junípero. He became a respected lecturer on theology and philosophy, but in 1749 he sailed for North America, landing first in Mexico City, where he taught, before moving to the Sierra Gorda Indian Missions, north of Santiago de Querétaro.

Afterwards, Serra helped establish ten missions in Mexico, and in 1769 he opened the first of twenty-one in California, San Diego de Alcalá. Serra is believed to have been the first to bring vine cuttings of the Mission grape (also called Criolla) to California, in 1773, although the Jesuits are believed to have much earlier planted the varietal first in Baja California. The grapes proliferated and were used to make wines in all the Franciscan missions, for the priests' use. For the next eight decades these were the only wines made in California.

On August 28, 1784, Serra died at Mission San Carlos Borromeo, in Carmel, California.

SESAME (*Sesamum indicum*). A tropical Asian plant whose small, flat seeds are used to make oil and cookies and as a garnish for some breads and rolls. The name is from the Greek, dating in English print to circa 1440. In the South, the seeds are called *benne*, from an African word, and are much used in **soul food**. Benne cookies or cakes are sometimes called "good luck cookies" in South Carolina.

BENNE COOKIES

Combine 2 c. flour, 1 ½ t. baking powder, ¼ t. salt, and ¼ t. nutmeg. Cream ½ c. butter with ¼ c. sugar until light, then add the grated rind of 1 orange or lemon. Beat 1 egg with ⅓ c. milk and blend into butter and flour mixtures. Place by tablespoons on a greased cookie sheet and bake for 10 min. at 350°. Combine in a saucepan ½ c. honey, 1 T. butter, and 2 T. sesame seeds and cook until the mixture reaches 290° on a candy thermometer. Dip cookies in glaze or brush glaze over tops of cookies. Makes about 3 doz.

SEVEN SWEETS AND SEVEN SOURS. Side dishes of sweet, spiced fruits and sour pickles served as accompaniments to main dishes in Pennsylvania Dutch meals. They do not strictly have to be seven in number; more is better, and less is quite all right, as long as there are several from which to pick and choose, such as spiced apples, cantaloupe, **chow-chow**, peppers, and **coleslaw**.

SEX ON THE BEACH. A cocktail made by mixing vodka, peach schnapps, cranberry juice, and orange juice. It is a drink from the 1980s, dating in print to 1986, and its name suggests its association with college students, who annually take their spring vacation in warm climates.

SEYVAL BLANC. A white French hybrid grape officially named "Seyve-Villard 5-276," after its creator, Bertille Seyve Jr. (1895–1959), whose father owned a nursery with Victor Villard, whose daughter married the younger Seyve. It has become a notable wine grape in New York's Hudson Valley and elsewhere.

SHAD. Any of a variety of fishes of the herring family in the genus *Alosa*. The name is from the Old English *sceadd*. The "American shad" (*A. sapidissima*) is the most important shad from a culinary standpoint, although early in this country's history, the common availability of the fish was such that settlers considered it a fish of last resort, and it is thought that the Native Americans used it for fertilizer. But by the time of the American Revolution, shad was much appreciated, and Washington's troops had the fish as part of their rations in 1776.

Parties were held by the Native Americans to celebrate shad time, which occurred in spring. The Indians dried the shad and may have planked it on wood to cook it slowly. But specific credit for this method of cooking has been given to the State in Schuylkill, a fishing-and-cooking society formed in 1732. The fish fillets are seasoned and wrapped with bacon, then nailed to greased hardwood planks set at an angle near a hot ash fire made from charcoals. Shad roe, traditionally served with lemon, sorrel, and boiled potatoes, is particularly appreciated by gourmets, who cook it in a variety of ways.

By the nineteenth century, shad was a popular fish, and after several attempts, the American shad was successfully introduced in 1871 to the Sacramento and Columbia rivers by aquaculturist Seth Green. So plentiful were shad in the Connecticut River that they were colloquially referred to as "Connecticut River Pork" in the nineteenth century. By 1889, 4.5 million pounds of shad were taken, although some observers, like Henry David Thoreau, noticed a decline in the quality of the fish in certain waters. The pollution caused by industries on the rivers drove out or killed the large fish, but, as Thoreau wrote, "Perchance, after a few thousands of years, if the fishes will be patient and pass their summers elsewhere meanwhile, Nature will have leveled the Billerica dam and the Lowell factories, and the Grassground River run clear again, to be explored by new migratory shoals."

The shad have rebounded since their nadir at the beginning of the twentieth century and are now found in eastern markets, though often they are imported from western fisheries. Boned, filleted shad was introduced in 1922 to NYC's Fulton Fish Market after Peter Andreotti sold deboned shad to the J. P. Morgan Co. restaurant at $1.50 per fish. U.S. commercial landings of shad totaled 791,000 pounds in 2010, valued at $561 million.

SHAD ROE WITH BACON

Boil 4 shad roe for 5 min., remove and drain. Brush roe with melted butter and broil until golden brown. Serve on toast with strips of bacon.

SHAKE-UP WHISKEY. Prohibition slang for corn or rye whiskey sold in speakeasies. According to an interview with Naomi Washington, in *You Must Remember This: An Oral History of Manhattan from the 1890s to World War II*, compiled by Jeff Kisseloff (1989), "If you want to go to a house [i.e., a speakeasy], never mind everybody's drinking. You want a drink? Take that bottle. Shake it up. If it don't hold a head, pass it up. You don't need it. That was called shakeup whiskey. If it had good bubbles after you shook it, it was good."

SHALLOT (*Allium ascalonicum*). An onionlike plant of the lily family used to flavor a wide variety of dishes and having a more delicate flavor than onion. The word shares the same Latin root as "scallion"—*ascalonia*—referring to a kind of onion grown in Ascalon. The herb was first mentioned in English print in 1655, then called "Spanish garlick."

The shallot is a native of Central Asia, possibly introduced to England in the thirteenth century, though long known to the Romans. It is now widely planted in the U.S. and is an essential part of most European immigrant cookeries.

In Creole and Cajun cookery, however, the term "**scallion**" is often applied to the green shallot, that is, the shoots of the shallot before it matures.

Most of the mature shallots found in the American market are grown in New Jersey and New York, with others imported from Mexico and France.

SHANKEN, MARVIN (1943–). Publisher and entrepreneur. As owner and publisher of *Wine Spectator* magazine, Marvin Ray Shanken helped make wine a major topic of American journalism and culture.

Shanken grew up in New Haven, Connecticut, graduating from the University of Miami with a business degree and from American University with an M.B.A., followed by stints in real estate and investment banking.

In 1973, he bought a wine-and-spirits newsletter called *Market Watch*, which monitored and analyzed industry data, for $5,000. In 1979, he bought a failing tabloid published out of San Diego, California, called *Wine Spectator*, which he expanded into a glossy magazine that covered not only the burgeoning California wine industry but the global wine industry as well.

The magazine's writers and editors ranked wines on a 100-point scale, and those receiving 90 points and above usually found their reputations and sales soaring. *Wine Spectator*, which published its own line of wine books and gave awards to restaurants with good wine lists, also branched into travel and food coverage, as did *Cigar Aficionado* magazine, which he founded in 1992 after a trip to Cuba. Shanken also owns the food-industry magazine *Food Arts*, the wine-and-spirits-industry magazine *Market Watch*, and the Internet site *Shanken News Daily*.

Today he is CEO and chairman of M. Shanken Communications, based in NYC, which runs the Wine Spectator Scholarship Foundation. Shanken also operates the annual Wine Experience event of tastings and seminars in NYC.

In 2012, Shanken was inducted into the James Beard Foundation's Who's Who of Food & Beverage in America, honored for "helping to bring wine and the good life into mainstream American culture."

SHARK. Any of a variety of voracious marine fishes under the orders Squaliformes and Selachii. The origin of the name is obscure. Feared for their legendary attacks on man (which in truth are exceptionally rare), the shark has not garnered much attention as a food fish in America, although the U.S. government in 1916 tried to promote the "dogfish shark" (*Squalus acanthias* and *Somniosus microcephalus*) as a nourishing fish having large amounts of protein. After World War I, this momentary infatuation with the shark died out, although another peak of favor was reached just before World War II, when the liver of the shark was especially sought for its nutrients. Some fishermen have tried to pass off meat from the "mako" (*Isurus oxyrhynchus*) and "blue shark" (*Prionace glauca*) as "**swordfish**" steaks, and "soupfin shark" (*Galeorhinus zyopterus*) is often used to make the Chinese dish "shark's fin soup." Many other sharks are poor eating and may in fact cause sickness. U.S. commercial landings of sharks totaled 61.2 million pounds in 1997.

SHARPE, PATRICIA (1943–). Author. As the longtime food editor and restaurant reviewer for *Texas Monthly*, Patricia Sharpe both chronicled and defined Texas cuisine as it developed from the 1970s onward, always with distinctive wit and abiding affection for her subject.

Born in Lisbon, Portugal, Sharpe grew up in Austin, Texas, and graduated with an M.A. in English from the University of Texas at Austin. After graduating, she taught English and Spanish and wrote for the Texas Historical Commission. In 1974, she joined *Texas Monthly* as editor of cultural and restaurant listings, eventually focusing on food stories, including "War Fare," her account of eating military MREs for forty-eight hours.

Sharpe traveled the state for her column Eat My Words, visiting as many fine dining restaurants as she did barbecue, hamburger, and taco stands. She defended Tex-Mex food's image, writing that "Tex-Mex cooking, frequently maligned for its yellow cheese and chili gravy, is actually a legitimate regional cuisine of Mexico."

Her 2005 memoir of her three decades of reviewing, "Confessions of a Skinny Bitch," published in *Texas Monthly*, won a James Beard Foundation award for magazine food writing.

SHE-CRAB SOUP. A soup made from blue crabs, crab roe, sherry, and vegetables. It is a specialty of Charleston, South Carolina, and Savannah, Georgia, both of which claim credit for the dish's creation, probably at the beginning of the nineteenth century, though the earliest citation in American print is not until 1966 or 1967. The female crab's roe gives the soup a slightly sour, tangy flavor that marks it as distinct from other crab soups. State law, however, forbids taking she-crabs with mature eggs, so cooks often use male crabs and immature females and then add eggs from unfertilized females (which are allowed to be caught). Crumbled egg yolk is sometimes used to give the traditional orange color of the roe to the soup.

SHE-CRAB SOUP

In a saucepan cook 1 grated onion, ½ t. mace, 2 grated celery stalks, salt, and pepper in 2 T. butter. Add 1 c. crabmeat and heat through thoroughly. Heat 2 c. milk and add to crab mixture. Stir and add ½ c. cream, 2 T. Worcestershire sauce, and 2 T. flour dissolved in water. Add 3 T. sherry and cook for 30 min. Serves 4.

SHEENY DESTROYER. Slang for "pork," derived from the derogatory word for Jews, "sheeny" (or "sheenie"), possibly from the German *schin*, for a "cheat" or "miser." Since Jews are not allowed under religious law to eat pork, serving them such a dish would "destroy" them. The term probably dates from the period 1910 to 1930. In a similar vein, an order of two pork chops was sometimes called "a couple of Hebrew enemies."

SHELF-STABLE. Food that has been cooked at high temperatures so as to kill bacteria, thereby rendering it less likely to spoil, over a longer period of time, than foods not so treated. This period during which the product remains safe to eat is called its "shelf life," first used in print in about 1925.

SHEPHERD'S PIE. A savory potpie of meat and vegetables, topped with mashed potatoes, dating in English print to 1877, described as a Scottish dish. It is now a staple in pubs in England and Ireland, as it is in American pubs, especially Irish bars.

SHERATON, MIMI (1926–). Author. As the powerful restaurant critic of the *New York Times* for eight years, Mimi Sheraton brought to the job a rigorous, highly personalized, comprehensive commitment that changed the way restaurant criticism was written.

Born Miriam Solomon in Brooklyn, New York, Sheraton attended the NYU School of Commerce. She was hired by *Good Housekeeping* while studying to become a professional decorator at the New York School of Interior Design, but after developing an avid interest in food, she joined *Seventeen* magazine as food editor, a position she next held at *House Beautiful*. She also consulted and did research for **Restaurant Associates** and NYU.

Sheraton was appointed food critic for the *New York Times* in 1976 and quickly distanced herself from her predecessors' more casual, bon vivant writing styles, instead acting more as a consumer reporter. Sheraton would go multiple times to a restaurant—in the case of her review of Le Cirque, twelve—to eat everything and to assess service and attention to details. For *New York* magazine, her story "I Tasted Everything in Bloomingdale's Food Department" was based on eleven months of sampling 1,196 products. She was a champion of ethnic foods, especially those of Eastern European origins, like bialys and chicken soup, both of which she wrote books about.

Sheraton tried to remain anonymous in restaurant visits, donning wigs and glasses, and her attitude toward her fellow food critics could be brutal if they did not live up to her own personal standards.

Known for her obesity, she insisted that her weight made her feel "powerful." (She later lost a great deal of weight, telling the *Times*, "What finally prompted me to lose weight was a view of myself in a hairdresser's full-length mirror when I was seated and wearing one of the salon's floral print robes and realized that I looked like a slipcovered club chair.")

After leaving the *Times*, in 1983, Sheraton reported on food for *Time* and *Condé Nast Traveler* and wrote her own newsletter.

Sheraton's books include *The German Cookbook* (1965), *From My Mother's Kitchen* (1991), *Mimi Sheraton's Favorite New York Restaurants* (1991), *The Bialy Eaters* (2000), and her memoir *Eating My Words* (2004).

SHERRY. A fortified wine originally made in Spain and now produced in the U.S., most often by a process of "baking" that gives the drink its characteristic burnt flavor.

Sherry, dating in English print to 1608, was first made in and around the town of Jerez, in Spain's Andalusia, and the word *sherry* is an anglicized rendition of the town's name, for the British were major shippers of Spanish wines. By the sixteenth century the wine was called "sherris-sack," the word *sack* perhaps having been derived from Old French *sec*, "dry." H. Warner Allen, in *A History of Wine* (1961), however, suggests that it comes from the Spanish *sacar*, meaning "to take out" or "export," an opinion shared by Pauline and Sheldon Wasserman in their *Guide to Fortified Wines* (1982). Sack was the wine beloved by Shakespeare's Falstaff, who attributed his own "excellent wit" to the wine's powers. But by the beginning of the seventeenth century sherry was fast replacing sack (which is today a registered trademark of sherry shippers William & Humbert) as a drink.

Americans of the colonial era much preferred Madeira and port to sherry, and the sherries that later became favored were the sweeter Spanish varieties, like *olorosos*, and "creams," whose high alcohol content also coincided with Americans' tastes after the end of Prohibition, in 1933. American sherries are made by three basic methods. The most frequently used is the baker's method, by which dry or sweet white wine is fortified with brandy and then heated to between 120 and 140 degrees Fahrenheit for 45 to 120 days. (A variation on this method, called "weathering," exposes the wine and brandy to outdoor weather conditions.) The second process is the traditional Spanish "solera" system, by which the wines are constantly blended with other, older wines in a complex tier system involving stacked barrels, with the newest and freshest wines on top. The third method is the "submerged flor" process, by which new wine is continuously pumped over the yeast (*flor* in Spanish) that develops on the top of the wine, thereby giving the sherry a yeasty, tangy flavor without the benefits of aging.

American sherries are made from a variety of grapes, including Mission, Malaga, Palomino, and Concord, while traditional Spanish sherries are made with Palomino Blanco and Pedro Ximénez varieties, with some producers using Mantuo Castellano and others to a lesser degree.

Americans usually drink sweet sherries, either as an aperitif, on the rocks, or after dinner as a cordial.

SHIP STUFF. Inferior, cheap wheat flour, of a kind that would be part of a ship's provisions, dating in print to 1771, in George Washington's *Diaries*.

SHIRLEY TEMPLE. A nonalcoholic beverage usually made for children who enjoy the idea of drinking an "adult" cocktail before dinner. It is named after child actor Shirley Temple, who began making movies in 1932 and three years later had attained the position of number-one box-office star in the U.S. Her curly-haired image was world famous, and hundreds of products, from dolls to clothes, appeared with her name or face on them. She was held up to children as a model of good behavior, and thus a cocktail called a Shirley Temple was considered the very essence of innocence. The drink was invented in the 1930s at the Brown Derby restaurant, in Hollywood, but its first appearance in print came in 1966, when it was said to be "Served to children at Sardi's Restaurant in New York in lieu of a champagne cocktail."

In 1988, Shirley Temple herself sued to have her name dropped from two bottled soft drinks called "Shirley T Sparkling Soda" and "Original Shirley Temple Soft Drink."

A non-alcoholic cocktail made with cola instead of lemon-lime soda was sometimes called a "Roy Rogers," after an equally wholesome cowboy actor of the 1930s and 1940s.

Occasionally one will hear such nonalcoholic cocktails referred to as "pussyfoots." A term of some derision, meaning an indecisive or weak person, this word may have been coined by President Theodore Roosevelt (1858–1919), appearing in print for the first time in 1893 as a verb and later, in 1934, as a noun. One of the greatest enforcers of temperance laws in the 1890s, William Eugene Johnson, was called "Pussyfoot" for his zeal in sending offenders to jail, especially in Oklahoma.

SHIRLEY TEMPLE

In a cocktail or champagne glass pour ½ oz. grenadine syrup, fill with lemon-lime soda, and garnish with a maraschino cherry.

SHIT ON A SHINGLE. Also "S.O.S." A GI term for creamed **chipped beef**. Civilians often refer specifically to **Salisbury steak** by this term. In its first appearance in American print, it is described as "a rubbery piece of toast covered with a thick gravy composed of the leavings of yesterday's dinner." See also **Spam**.

SHOOFLY PIE. Also "shoo-fly pie" and "Montgomery pie." A pie made of molasses and brown sugar, so called supposedly because one had to "shoo away the flies" from this sweet dessert. It is of Pennsylvania Dutch origins but was not mentioned in American print until 1908. Shoofly pies are made with either a "wet bottom" (soft filling and crumb topping) or "dry bottom" (with crumb topping mixed into the filling), which is commonly served for breakfast.

SHOOFLY PIE

Line a pie plate with a pastry crust. Combine 1 ½ c. sifted flour, 1 c. brown sugar, ⅛ t. salt, and ¼ c. cold butter to make a crumbly blend. Dissolve ½ t. baking soda in ½ c. molasses, then add ¾ of the crumb mixture. Pour into pie pan, top with the rest of the crumbs, and bake in a 350° oven for about 30 min., until firm.

SHORE DINNER. A large meal based mostly on fresh, locally caught seafood. The term, in print since 1872, is most readily associated with the East Coast cities from New York to Maine, where restaurants featured lavish spreads of steamed clams in clam broth, mussels, lobsters, and corn on the cob. In NYC, the offerings might include shrimp or crabmeat cocktail and broiled fish as well.

SHORTNIN' BREAD. Also "shortening bread" and "crackling bread." A southern quick bread made with a shortening like butter or lard, dating in print to 1898 and made famous in the song "Shortnin' Bread," by Johnny Mercer and the Ink Spots.

SHORTNIN' BREAD

Mix 2 c. flour with ½ c. brown sugar and blend until crumbly. Work in ¼ lb. butter until dough is smooth. Divide, pat into a circle ½ in. thick, prick the top, and cook in an ungreased pan at 350° for about 30 min.

SHOT. A jigger of alcohol, about one to one and a half ounces. It is served in a "shot glass."

SHOT-AND-A-BEER. Bartender's term for a quick drink of alcohol followed by a glass of beer. A "shots-and-beer" bar is one that caters to patrons who do not order mixed drinks or wine. By extension, a "shot-and-a-beer town" is a slang term for a blue-collar industrial town like Pittsburgh, Ohio. A "shot house" is a bar that sells alcohol by the drink.

SHRAPNEL. Bartender's slang for a tip consisting of loose change. The word refers to the fragments of bullet or cannon shells in a bursting charge thrown in all directions, a weapon designed by English army officer Henry Shrapnel and dating in print to 1800, although the slang term only dates to 1991.

SHRIMP. Any of a wide variety of ten-legged crustaceans of the suborder Natantia. It is the most popular shellfish in the U.S., whose annual consumption is about 850 million pounds.

The word *shrimp* derives from Middle English *shrimpe*, meaning "pygmy" or the crustacean itself.

Shrimp harvesting was known as early as the seventeenth century in Louisiana, whose bayou inhabitants used seine nets up to two thousand feet in circumference. Only after 1917 did mechanized boats utilize trawl nets to catch shrimp. Americans have always eaten shrimp, but its tendency to spoil quickly has for most of our history confined its availability to regions having access to the sea or rivers. Fresh shrimp are available in the South, but almost all the shrimp Americans buy at market or in restaurants has been frozen for transport. Only in the twentieth century, with advances in refrigeration aboard trawlers (which began plying the waters for lengthy voyages only in 1917), did shrimp become readily available in American markets, with NYC consuming the lion's share of the catch—about a million and a half pounds a week.

Most shrimp come from Atlantic waters, though there are some from Alaska and from the rivers of the South. The main species for culinary use include seven species in the Atlantic—the "edible shrimp" (*Penaeus aztecus, P. set-iferus*, and *P. duorarum*), also called, respectively, "brown," "pink," and "white" shrimp; the "Caribbean shrimp" (*P. schmitti*); the "sea bob" (*Xiphopenaeus kroyeri*); the "royal red shrimp" (*Hymenopenaeus robustus*); and the "rock shrimp" (*Sicyonia brevirostris*)—and four in the Pacific: the "side-stripe shrimp" (*Pandalopsus dispar*); the "pink shrimp" (*P. borealis* and *P. jordoni*); the "coon-stripe shrimp" (*P. danae*); and the spot shrimp" (*P. platyceros*).

Shrimp are graded by size or "count," which indicates the number of shrimp likely to be in a pound, so that the smaller the number in the count, the larger the shrimp. A pound of "small" would therefore number 50-plus shrimp; "medium," 43–50; medium large," 36–42; "large," 31–35; "extra large," 26–30; "jumbo," 21–25; "extra jumbo," 16–20; "colossal," 10–15; "extra colossal," fewer than 10.

U.S. landings of shrimp in 2010 totaled 258.972 million pounds, for sales of $414 million. Per capita U.S. consumption of shrimp is four pounds per year. Americans eat shrimp boiled and served plain or with "cocktail sauce," a ketchup sauce seasoned with hot sauce and horseradish (called a "shrimp cocktail"), deep-fried, grilled, baked in various sauces, and in many other forms. In New Orleans, shrimp **rémoulade** is a traditional dish, and "shrimp boils" are popular social affairs. "Barbecued shrimp" is also a specialty of New Orleans, having originated at Pascal's Manale restaurant in 1952, although the shrimp are not actually barbecued but baked with butter and seasoning.

Many preparations originally made with lobsters are adapted for shrimp. Shrimp **scampi**, rarely made with true scampi, is a dish of shrimp sautéed in garlic and oil or butter.

BARBECUED SHRIMP

In a blender mix 2 peeled, sliced onions, 2 cloves garlic, ½ t. oregano, ½ t. marjoram, ½ t. salt, ¼ t. black pepper, 3 T. white vinegar, 1 T. cayenne pepper, and 2 t. lemon juice. In a casserole dish, melt 2 sticks butter and blend in other seasonings. Coat 2 lb. of peeled shrimp with the sauce and bake in a 375° oven for about 15 min. Serves 4.

SHRIMP CREOLE

In a sauté pan pour 3 T. vegetable oil. Sauté ½ c. chopped celery, ½ c. chopped onion, and 2 cloves chopped garlic for 2–3 min., then add 1 lb. peeled tomatoes and 8 oz. tomato sauce. Add 2 t. salt, ¾ t. pepper, ½ t. cayenne pepper, 1 t. sugar, 1 T. Worcestershire sauce, and a dash of bottled hot sauce. Cook over low heat for about 40 min. Mix 1 t. cornstarch with 2 t. water and add to mixture to thicken. Add 1 lb. peeled shrimp and ½ c. chopped bell pepper. Cook just until shrimp are tender and pink. Serves 4.

SHRIMP AND GRITS. A South Carolina Lowcountry dish made with sautéed shrimp served with **grits**. Because it is commonly served for breakfast during the shrimp season, the dish is sometimes called "breakfast shrimp." Often seasonings and bell peppers are added, as in the recipe below.

SHRIMP AND GRITS

In a skillet heat 3 T. butter and sauté 1 chopped onion and ½ chopped green bell pepper for about 10 min. Sprinkle vegetables with 2 T. flour and brown slightly. Add 1 lb. peeled shrimp, season with salt and a pinch of cayenne, and add 1 c. chicken or shrimp stock. Cook for about 3 min., add the juice of one lemon, and cook until sauce reduces. Serve over freshly made grits.

SHRIMPER'S SAUCE. A tomato sauce made by the shrimp fishermen of the South. The following recipe is given in the Federal Writers' Project American Guide volume on the *Mississippi Gulf Coast* (1939).

SHRIMPER'S SAUCE

Fry 1 c. chopped salt pork in 1 c. oil, add 3 French onions, 1 can tomato sauce, 3 c. boiling water, 1 t. chili powder, 2 cloves minced garlic, 1 sprig of thyme, 1 t. celery salt, salt, and pepper, and cook about 30 min.

SHRIMPS DE JONGHE. A dish of baked shrimp topped with seasoned bread crumbs. It originated around 1900 at Chicago's De Jonghe's Hotel and Restaurant, run by Belgian immigrant Henri de Jonghe. It is not known whether the dish was created by de Jonghe or by his chef, Emil Zehr.

SHRIMPS DE JONGHE

Cream ¾ c. butter with 1 t. salt, 1 mashed clove of garlic, 1 c. bread crumbs, ¼ c. parsley, ½ c. sherry, and a dash of cayenne and paprika. Shell and devein 3 lb. shrimp, then boil until half-cooked. In 8 small cooking tins place some of the bread-crumb mixture, top with the shrimp, layer on more of the bread crumbs, and bake at 375° for 20–25 min.

SHRIMP WIGGLE. A dish of creamed shrimp especially popular in New England and the Midwest. The reason for the name is not known, though it may refer to the ease and quickness with which the dish is made. It dates in print to at least 1949. In *American Cookery* (1972), James Beard comments, "For many years this was in the repertoire of every coed with a chafing dish and every girl who had a beau to cook for."

SHRIMP WIGGLE

Combine 1 T. butter, 1 T. chopped onion, 1 c. boiled rice, and ½ can tomato soup in a double boiler. Add a dash of red pepper, salt and pepper to taste, 1 c. cream, 2 c. shelled, deveined shrimp, and 2 c. peas. Heat through and serve on crackers, on toast, or in pastry shells.

SIBERIA. A section of a restaurant dining room that is considered either socially inferior or merely poor seating. While not all American restaurants have such undesirable sections or tables, much fuss is made over those that do, and some people would rather not sit down at all than to be escorted to Siberia.

The term is said to have originated in the 1930s, when a society woman named Peggy Hopkins Joyce entered the class-conscious El Morocco nightclub, in NYC, and found herself being led to a less-than-desirable table. "Where are you taking me," she asked the maître d'hôtel, "Siberia?"

In most society restaurants, the most treasured tables are usually situated along the banquettes that line the room as one enters, though in other restaurants a good table, called an "A" table, may be a corner table or one that is regularly occupied by a person of some celebrity.

An alternate term for Siberia is the "doghouse," used by those who frequented NYC's Colony Restaurant, opened in 1926, to describe the least desirable of its three rooms.

SIDECAR. A cocktail made from brandy, orange-flavored liqueur, and lemon juice. The drink seems to have originated at Harry's New York Bar. in Paris, but the date and inspiration of the invention are uncertain. The bar's owner, Harry MacElhone, claimed the drink was concocted in 1931 for a customer who always arrived in a motorcycle sidecar. But the sidecar appears in several places in Carl Van Vechten's 1931 short-story collection *Parties*. And David A. Embury, in *The Fine Art of Mixing Drinks* (3rd American ed., 1958), says it was invented by a friend of his during World War I and was "named after the motorcycle sidecar in which the good captain customarily was driven to and from the little bistro where the drink was born and christened." The drink was apparently well known by 1934, however, when a recipe for it was printed in *Dining in New York, an Intimate Guide*, by Rian James.

Embury recommends a blend of one part Cointreau or triple sec, two parts lemon juice, and eight parts cognac or Armagnac. But the more usual mix is as follows.

SIDECAR

Shake together with ice 1 part orange liqueur, 1 part cognac, and 1 part lemon juice. Strain and serve in cocktail glass.

SIL SALAD. A Scandinavian herring salad, from Norwegian *sildesalat*, dating in American print to 1951.

SINCLAIR, UPTON (1878–1968). Author and politician. Upton Sinclair's muckraking novel *The Jungle*, which exposed the unsanitary conditions of America's meatpacking industry, played a critical part in the federal government's passage, in 1906, of two pieces of landmark legislation: the Meat Inspection Act and the Pure Food and Drug Act.

Upton Beall Sinclair was born into poverty in Baltimore, paying his way through the College of the City of New York by writing dime novels. He went on to write several novels, including *Manassas* (1904), set in the Civil War. For the socialist newspaper *Appeal to Reason*, Sinclair wrote a series of articles in 1905 exposing the conditions in the Chicago Stock Yards. A year later, the series came out as a novel, called *The Jungle*, which author Jack London called "the *Uncle Tom's Cabin* of wage slavery." The revelations in the book were so horrifying that consumption of meat fell and the federal government came up with stringent regulations for sanitation and health in the meatpacking industry.

The book was a great success, and Sinclair invested his earnings in the Helicon Home Colony cooperative, in Englewood, New Jersey, and later in California, where he became involved in state politics, losing in a run for governor. As an outspoken socialist, most of his novels thereafter tackled themes of American schools, Prohibition, finance, motion pictures, and the auto industry. In 1956, he wrote *The Cup of Fury*, detailing the tragic ends to which many American writers he knew had come from the ravages of alcoholism, including O. Henry, Jack London, and Edna St. Vincent Millay.

His autobiography was entitled *American Outpost* (1932).

SINGAPORE SLING. A cocktail of gin, cherry brandy, Cointreau, Benedictine, and citrus juices. It was supposedly created by bartender Ngiam Tong Boon at the Long Bar in Singapore's Raffles Hotel in 1915 and is sometimes called the "Singapore Raffles gin sling" or the "Raffles bar gin sling." There are many variants; the first in English print was in the *Savoy Cocktail Book* (1930). One admirer of the drink has said the original was topped off with club soda, but the official Raffles version, given below, is without any such additive.

SINGAPORE SLING

Into a shaker with 4 ice cubes put 1 oz. gin, ¾ oz. cherry brandy, a "few drops" Cointreau, the juice of ½ a medium-size lemon, 2 oz. fresh pineapple juice, 1 or 2 drops bitters, and 1 dash grenadine. Cover and shake for 10 sec. and pour into a 10-oz. glass with 2 ice cubes. Garnish with a wedge of pineapple and a maraschino cherry.

SINGLES BAR. A bar or lounge dispensing alcoholic beverages and frequented by single—that is, unmarried—people who go to such places specifically to meet other single people of the opposite sex. The term has been used since the mid-1960s. Although bars have long been social centers, it was not until the 1960s that working women in large cities began to visit such establishments without worrying about public opinion. By the 1970s, however, the term "singles bar" had taken on a pejorative connotation. The first singles bar was T.G.I. Friday's (short for "Thank God it's Friday"), opened by Alan Stillman in NYC in 1965.

SINGLINGS. An Appalachian moonshiner's term for the crude first distillation, dating in print to 1808.

SIRLOIN. A cut of beef from the upper part of the loin between the rump and the porterhouse. Between six and eight one-inch-thick sirloins may be taken from the hip, though many Americans prefer a two-inch steak. If aged correctly, sirloin is one of the best steak cuts for tenderness and flavor.

Depending on the way a butcher cuts the meat, different kinds of sirloin may be produced. When cut across the grain, the steaks will be called "pinbone," "flat bone," "round bone," and "wedge bone," from the shape of the hipbone they contain. By cutting with the grain, the butcher produces boneless roasts called "tenderloin," "top sirloin," and "bottom sirloin." A whole, uncut sirloin is called a "king-sized roast," weighing between twelve and twenty pounds.

Sirloins are usually broiled or grilled, though they can be pan-fried.

The origin of the word is from Old French *surlonge*, from *sur* ("above") plus *longe* ("loin"). A cherished but wholly inaccurate legend attached to the name has to do with an English king who knighted a piece of beef "Sir Loin." Thomas Fuller's *Church History* (1655) maintained that the monarch in question was Henry VIII, but Jonathan Swift vouched for James I.

There are references to the word sirloin as far back as 1515. In many parts of the U.S., a sirloin is called a "New York cut."

SIX-PACK. Slang term for six bottles or cans of beer or other beverage sold in a package. The term has been in print since 1949.

SIZZLER. A logging-camp or construction-camp cook, as in one who sizzles food in a skillet, dating in print to 1925.

SIZZLING PLATTER. A service of meats on a heated platter so as to create an audible sizzle when brought to the table. The idea was introduced in NYC at the Longchamps restaurant chain in the 1930s. A "sizzle platter" is a shallow, aluminum platter set into a removable wooden or plastic tray.

SKATE. Also "ray" and "ray fish." Any of a variety of fishes in the family Rajidae, especially the genus *Raia*, whose radiating pectoral fins give it a flat, diamond shape. The word is from Middle English and first appeared in English print circa 1340.

In eastern waters of the U.S., the "smooth butterfly ray" (*Gymnura micrura*) and "winter skate" (*Raja ocellata*) are popular edible species, whose flesh was once cut into circles and sold dishonestly as scallops. Western species of culinary interest include the "California skate" (*R. inorata*), "big skate" (*R. binoculata*), and "longnose skate" (*R. rhina*). Skate is best when poached before any preparation, and its most popular culinary form is to serve it with a French *beurre noir* sauce. U.S. commercial landings of skate totaled 61.819 million pounds in 2010, valued at $12.617 million.

SKILLIGALEE. Gruel or stew thickened with bread. The name is a nonsense word, dating in print to 1819.

SKIPJACK. Any of a variety of species of fish (mostly tuna and mackerel) whose members "skip" out of the water. The term dates in print to 1554. The species *Katsuwonus pelamis* (also called "oceanic bonito" and "striped bonito") and *Sarda sarda* (also called "Atlantic bonito") are commonly called "skipjack." U.S. landings in 2010 totaled 423.9 million pounds, for sales of $382.8 million.

SKIRT. Ice cream maker's term for the rim of ice cream created when a scoop is pushed down onto an ice cream cone.

SKULLY-JO. Also "skulljoe." A dish made by the Portuguese settlers in Provincetown, Massachusetts, from dried cod or haddock cured in the sun until, in the opinion of one observer, "it's hard enough to bend lead pipe around." The children of the region would chew it instead of candy. It is rarely made anymore. The nonsense word dates in print to 1884.

SLANG-JANG. A spicy stew of oysters, peppers, pickles, and other condiments, best known in Texas and in print since 1894. The name is a made-up colloquialism.

SLINGER. A southerner's term for someone who takes a drink of spirits upon awakening in the morning.

SLING PANS. To allow a household employee to take leftovers home, dating in print to 2003, based on a 1965 reference.

SLIP-GO-DOWN. A northeastern name for cornmeal mush, dating in print to 1855. See **gap 'n' swallow**.

SLIPPERY JIM. Also "slippery jack." A soft sweet pickle relish, dating in print to 1941.

SLOPPY JOE. A dish of ground beef, onions, green peppers, and ketchup made in a skillet and often served on a hamburger roll. It is sometimes called a "skilletburger" or "Spanish hamburger."

The origins of this dish are unknown, dating in print to 1940, on an Ohio restaurant ad.

Its rather messy appearance and tendency to drip off the plate or roll make "sloppy" an adequate description, and while there is probably no Joe after whom it is named, Joe is an American name of proletarian character and unassailable genuineness. There are many individual and regional variations on the dish. In Sioux City, Iowa, a dish of this type is called a "loosemeat sandwich," created in 1934 at Ye Olde Tavern Inn by Abraham and Bertha Kaled. In an article on the website *Lunch Counter* as to what is called the "New Jersey sloppy joe, said to have originated in north New Jersey **delicatessens**," a respondent wrote, "The NJ version is not ground beef in a sauce on a bun. It's a double decker on rye with a combination of deli meats, cole slaw, Russian dressing and, sometimes, cheese. It's always cut into multiple sections, not just into 2 halves.

Usually you see them on a big platter at parties, carved into squares about 3" X 3" X 3" with a toothpick holding each section together."

SLOPPY JOE

Cook 1 lb. ground beef in a skillet with 2 T. butter. Mix in ¼ c. flour, 1 T. chopped onion, ¼ c. chopped green pepper, 1 c. chopped celery, ¼ c. ketchup (or canned tomato soup), 2 t. salt, ½ t. pepper, and 3 c. water. Boil together until tender and well blended.

SLUMGULLION. Also "slum." A slang term from the California Gold Rush days, used by miners for any disgusting or makeshift food or drink. It first appeared in print in 1851, in Herman Melville's novel *Moby-Dick*, and in *Roughing It* (1872), Mark Twain wrote of being offered a drink of slumgullion by a station keeper in Nebraska who said it was like tea. But, Twain remarked, "there was too much dish rag, and sand, and old bacon-rind in it to deceive the intelligent traveller." Nevertheless, Twain admired whoever it was who named it.

SLUMP. A dish of cooked fruit and raised dough, known since the middle of the eighteenth century and probably so called because it is a somewhat misshapen dish that "slumps" on the plate, dating in American print to 1831. Louisa May Alcott, author of *Little Women*, named her Concord, Massachusetts, home "Apple Slump" and recorded the recipe below.

SLUMP

Pare, core, and slice 6 apples and combine with 1 c. sugar, 1 t. cinnamon, and ½ c. water in a saucepan. Cover and heat to boiling point. Meanwhile sift together 1 ½ c. flour, 1 ¼ t. salt, and 1 ½ t. baking powder and add ½ c. milk to make a soft dough. Drop pieces of the dough from a tablespoon onto apple mixture, cover, and cook over low heat for 30 min. Serve with cream.

SMALL BEER. A beer of low alcoholic content. The term is more widely used in England, where it first saw print in 1560, than in the U.S.

SMEAR. Slang for "butter," dating in American print to 1891. "Smearcase" is a German American term for cottage cheese. See **schmear**.

SMELT (family Osmeridae). A small, slender silvery fish found in North American oceans, rivers, and lakes. The name is from the Anglo-Saxon *smoelt*, meaning "smooth" or "shining." U.S. commercial landings of smelt totaled 381,000 pounds in 2010, valued at $265,000.

In the Great Lake region, spring is marked by the arrival of smelt, which are cause for many nighttime fishing parties. Although the fish is not native to the Great Lakes, it was introduced there in the early 1900s. Smelts are a very perishable fish and are often sold frozen. They are best coated with seasoned flour and beaten egg and pan-fried in butter or oil. It requires about a dozen to make a pound. The main North American species are:

EULACHON (*Thaleichythys pacificus*). Also "candlefish" (because its oiliness made it a good candle when dried; Native Americans would insert a bark wick through the fish for this purpose). Found from the Bering Sea to central California, at lengths up to twelve inches, the eulachon is often marketed as "Columbia River smelt" in the Northwest. The name "eulachon" is from a Chinook Indian dialect word for the fish, *vlâkân*, and one encounters renderings such as "ulchen" and the colloquial American "hooligan" (which itself is a word for a ruffian). Because of their fattiness, eulachon are sometimes dried out in a warm oven after being fried.

RAINBOW SMELT (*Osmerus mordax*). Also "ice fish." A smelt found along the Atlantic coast, measuring about seven to eight inches long and having a silver band. It was introduced to the Great Lakes drainage in 1912, where it has proliferated.

SURF SMELT (*Hypomesus pretiosus*). Also "silver smelt." Found from Alaska to Southern California, the surf smelt grows to about ten inches and is netted on sandy beaches of the outer coast.

Other, less well-known smelts include: "night smelt" (*Sprinchus starski*), found from Alaska to central California; "delta smelt" (*Hypomesus transpacificus*), in the San Joaquin and Sacramento river systems; "longfin smelt" (*S. thaleichthys*), similar to the night smelt; "Pacific smoothtongue" (*Leuroglossus stilbius*), a Pacific species; "whitebait smelt" (*Allosmerus elongatus*); and "pond smelt" (*Hypomesus olidus*), found in Alaska and Canada. The "top smelt" and the "Jack smelt" are "Pacific silversides" of the family Atheriniclae, of a different order from other smelts, and "deep-sea smelts" are of the family Bathylagidae, but closely related to true smelts.

SMOOTHIE. A drink with a thick, smooth consistency made from pureeing fruit with yogurt, ice cream, or milk. The term dates in print to 1977.

S'MORES. A confection made from graham crackers, marshmallow, and chocolate, heated until the contents melt. The word "s'mores"—always used in the plural—is short for "some mores," referring to one's appetite for more than just one, and first appeared in print in 1934. It is a cookie said to be particularly popular at Girl Scouts' campfire cookouts. According to Jane and Michael Stern, in *Square Meals* (1984), s'mores are also known as "Princess Pats," "Perfection Crisps," and "Slapsticks."

S'MORES

Toast 1 large marshmallow and place on a graham cracker. Add a layer of chocolate-bar candy and place another graham cracker on top. S'mores may also be made by making a sandwich of graham crackers, chocolate bar, and marshmallow heated in an oven or microwave oven.

SMORGASBORD. A buffet meal of Swedish origins that in the twentieth century became a very popular party spread. The word comes from the Swedish *smörgåsbord*, which means a "bread and butter table," and first appeared in American print in 1893. The idea soon caught on, so that by 1941 the *West Hartford Ladies Aid Society Swedish American Cook Book* listed several suggestions for a smorgasbord, including the following items: butter balls, Swedish rye bread, **pumpernickel**, **hardtack**, pickled herring, baked ham, smoked tongue, lingonberries, radish roses, omelets, *rulle pulse* (rolled pressed lamb), *leverpastej* (liver pâté), jellied veal, **headcheese**, hot **Swedish meatballs**, Swedish pork sausage, brown beans, Swedish fish pudding, smoked salmon, stuffed eggs, **potato salad**, "sill salad" (herring salad), meat-and-potato sausage, fruit salad, Swedish apple cake, and coffee with cream.

Today smorgasbords may still contain many of these same items, as well as dishes from other countries.

SMOTHERED. A word used to describe any of a variety of dishes in which the meat, poultry, or fish is "smothered" with a gravy and/or vegetables while baked, braised, or cooked in a covered skillet, dating in print to 1942. To "smother-fry" is to fry food, especially potatoes, with a lid on the pan, dating in print to 1954.

SMOTHERED CHICKEN

Cut a 3-lb. chicken into pieces and dredge in a mixture of ¾ c. flour, 1 ½ t. salt, and ¼ t. pepper. Brown chicken in 4 T. butter, add ½ c. water, cover, and simmer for about 1 hr., until very tender. During the last 20 min. of cooking, add 1 c. green peas, 2 T. pimiento strips, and ½ c. onions. Reduce sauce and spoon over chicken. Serves 4.

SNACK. A meal or food item eaten hurriedly or casually, which might include anything from a candy bar to a hamburger. The word, also used as a verb, "to snack," derives from the Dutch *snacken*, "to bite," and in English print dates to 1402 as a noun. "Snack bars," where one bought a snack, were known as of 1895, though this term was more popular in England than in America until well into the twentieth century.

Americans buy about 4.3 billion pounds of snack food annually (a $13.4 billion market) and consume more than seventeen pounds per person. The most popular snack food among Americans is potato chips (6.1 pounds per person), followed by tortilla chips (3.9), snack nuts (1.6), pretzels (1.4), microwave popcorn (1.3), and corn chips (0.9).

SNAKE SOUP. A food left unfinished and later added to with more ingredients so that, according to *DARE*'s 1968 explanation, "it is snake soup because it is endless."

SNAPPER. A bony fish of the Lutjanidae family. There are 250 species in the world, of which fifteen are found in U.S. waters from North Carolina to the Gulf of Mexico. Snappers are usually pan-fried. The most popular American species for eating are:

GRAY SNAPPER (*Lutjanus griseus*). Also called "mangrove snapper." Found in southern U.S. waters, the gray snapper may weigh from under a pound up to ten pounds.

MUTTON SNAPPER (*L. analis*). Also "muttonfish." The mutton snapper, found from South Florida to the tropical Atlantic, is olive green and has range-red sides and brick-red fins. Though it is rarely seen in American markets, it is good baked.

RED SNAPPER (*L. campechanus*). By far the most popular of the species in America, the red snapper is found from North Carolina down through the Gulf of Mexico, and although it can grow to thirty-five pounds, the typical specimens found in markets weigh between four and six pounds. This beautiful red-pink fish takes well to most forms of cooking. It is quite similar to the "silk snapper" (*L. vivanus*), which is often called "red snapper" at market. The "Creole rouget" is red snapper, not kin to the "rouget" (family Mullidae), which is a "red mullet." In Hawaii, the "onaga" (*Etelis coruscans*) is a fish often called "red snapper," while the "uku" (*Aprion virescens*), also called a "jobfish," is a pale pink color, considered excellent for making sashimi. U.S. landings totaled 1.978 million pounds in 2010, valued at $5.683 million.

RED SNAPPER

A red-snapper recipe popular in Florida calls for the fillets to be marinated in a baking dish with ½ c. chopped onions, ¼ c. fresh orange juice, 2 t. grated orange peel, and 1 t. salt for about 30 min. Sprinkle a pinch of nutmeg and black pepper on the fish, then bake for about 10 min. in a 400° oven.

YELLOWTAIL SNAPPER (*Ocyurus chrysurus*). This yellow-striped, shallow-water snapper is usually about one and a half pounds in size and rarely weighs more than five pounds. Its main popularity has traditionally been around Key West, where it was long considered a breakfast fish because it was sold early in the morning, after the catch. It is excellent pan-fried with a squeeze of Key lime over it. The yellowtail snapper is not to be confused with a form of **tilefish**, found in American waters further north, that goes by the name "yellow snapper."

KALIKALI. Hawaiian name for a species of snapper (either *Pristipomoides sieboldii* or *Rooseveltia brighami*) of the Pacific (1926).

"Snapper" is also applied to various species of "snapping turtle," dating in print to 1792, which is the basis for "snapper soup."

SNEAKY PETE. A cheap wine or alcoholic beverage, dating in print to 1943. There is no specific person named Pete to whom the term refers.

SNICKERDOODLE. A New England cookie made with flour, nuts, and dried fruits. The name is simply a nineteenth-century nonsense word for a quickly made confection, dating in print to 1889.

SNICKERDOODLE

Sift 3 ½ c. flour with ½ t. salt, 1 t. baking soda, 1 t. cinnamon, and ⅛ t. nutmeg. Cream 1 c. butter, slowly add 1 ¼ c. sugar, beat in 3 beaten eggs, stir in flour, then add 1 c. chopped nuts, ½ c. currants, and ½ c. raisins. Drop in spoonfuls onto buttered cookie sheet and bake at 350° for 12–15 min. Makes about 10 doz.

SNOW BALL. Also "sno' ball" and "snow cone." A scoop of vanilla or other flavor of ice cream rolled in shredded, sweetened coconut, then chilled and served with a topping of chocolate syrup. The name "snow cone," or "sno-cone," can also refer to a ball of shaved ice with fruit syrup, though "snowball" is sometimes used, particularly in New Orleans. "Snow ball" dates in print to 1895. A snow cone is often a confection of crushed ice or freshly fallen snow drizzled with maple or fruit syrup and usually served in a paper cone. It is a traditional treat of summer, especially among Hispanic Americans, who call them *raspas*, from the Spanish *raspar*, "to scrape."

"Snow ball" also refers to a pastry-wrapped apple topped with a white icing to resemble snow.

SNOW CREAM. A southern confection especially popular with African Americans, snow cream is nothing more than freshly fallen snow that is scooped up and mixed with a variety of flavorings like vanilla, sugar, and cinnamon. The term dates in print to 1849. Some devotees claim that only the first snow of the season should be used, though some aver that it is the third snow of the season that is the purest.

In New England, children pour cooked maple syrup over snow and let it harden. This is called "sugar-in-snow." See **snow ball**.

SOBER SIDE OF THE BAR. The bartender's side.

SODA. Also "soda water," "soda pop," and "soft drink." Carbonated water or a flavored juice drink, usually flavored and colored. The word derives from the sodium or sodium bicarbonate, originally added to water as a digestive, and dates in print, as "soda-water," to 1834 ("soda" alone did not appear until 1898). The first carbonated waters were from natural sources and sold at the end of the eighteenth century as "soda water" at "soda fountains." By 1809 the drink was being sweetened and flavored to make items like "ginger pop," also called "ginger beer" (which once had a slight alcoholic content), and, later, "ginger champagne" or "ginger ale" (which does not). Belfast Style Ginger Ale was produced by Toronto pharmacist John J. McLaughlin in 1890, though in 1907 he changed the name to Canada Dry Pale Ginger Ale, which he began producing in New York City in 1922. (See main entry on **seltzer**.)

In 1812, English author Robert Southey commented on the new word *pop* as deriving its meaning from the sound made when the cork is drawn from the bottle.

By 1819 a patent had been issued for "carbonated mead," and in 1824 one for **sarsaparilla.** In the 1830s, the first man-made carbonated waters became available, and lemon, strawberry, vanilla, and other flavors were popular. By 1854 "cream soda" was vanilla-flavored. In 1889, a cream soda was cited as comprising ice cream in soda water—"a favorite drink of American women." "Birch beer" came along in the 1880s, to compete with Philadelphian druggist Charles E. Hires's "herb tea," later changed to "root beer" (a previously common term for a soda flavored with various roots and herbs). Hires had first made the beverage in 1875, advertised it as "the National Temperance Drink," and first served it at the 1876 Philadelphia Centennial Exposition.

In 1881, there appeared an Imperial Inca Coca, made from extracts of the cola (or kola) nut and the leaf of the coca plant. Five years later, in May 1886, an Atlanta pharmacist named John Stith Pemberton made a cola syrup that he brought to Jacobs' Pharmacy, where it was mixed with carbonated water to make the first cola drink. Pemberton's bookkeeper, Frank M. Robinson, named the drink Coca-Cola, which was registered as a trademark in 1893. Atlanta businessman Asa G. Candler bought total rights to the soda syrup in 1891, for $2,300, and immediately began promoting the drink as a refreshment, whereas it had previously been sold as a medicinal aid to cure hangovers and headaches.

Early batches of Coca-Cola (since 1909 called "Coke" for short) may once have contained trace elements of cocaine, but these were removed at the turn of the century. The formula for Coca-Cola has been one of the most closely guarded in American food. But in 2013, Mark Pendergast gave a formula in his book *For God, Country, and Coca-Cola* that he contended was the original formula from handwritten notes by Robinson, which had been handed down by his descendants who provided Pendergast with the notes. The formula contained sugar, water, lime juice, citric acid, caffeine, flavorings of alcohol, nutmeg, vanilla extract, lemon oil, cinnamon, coriander, neroli oil, food coloring, and coca. The company declares that coca is at least one of the ingredients no longer included in their product.

Today Coca-Cola has sales of $60 billion worldwide and is sold in every country except Cuba and North Korea.

"Cherry Coke" is a cherry-flavored version of Coca-Cola sold in cans, though it was once customarily mixed by **soda jerks**.

Another pharmacist, Caleb Bradham of New Bern, North Carolina, came up with a similar concoction in 1896, which he sold as "Brad's Drink" to his local customers. He changed the name in 1903 to "Pepsi-Cola" and began bottling the beverage in 1904; three years later, the Pepsi-Cola Co. had forty franchises, and the drink, usually sold by horse-drawn cart, began to be purveyed by motor vehicles. Auto racer Barney Oldfield was enlisted as a spokesman for the drink.

Coca-Cola and Pepsi-Cola went on to become great American success stories after World War I, thanks to a developing taste for such drinks and a drop in the price of sugar (although Pepsi-Cola had several difficult years because Bradham had overbought sugar when it was at its most expensive). Both companies also used advertising and marketing with amazing results. Pepsi-Cola was the first company to broadcast a jingle on radio, and every American was soon able to sing along with the words:

Pepsi-Cola hits the spot.
Twelve full ounces,
That's a lot.
Twice as much for a nickel, too,
Pepsi-Cola is the drink for you.

The lyrics indicated that Pepsi, as it was called for short, sold twelve ounces for the same price Coca-Cola charged for six ounces, then the standard of the industry.

Another soda that became a national favorite was created in 1885 by pharmacist Charles C. Alderton, at Wade B. Morrison's Old Corner Drug Store, in Waco, Texas. The drink was named "Dr Pepper" after Dr. Charles K. Pepper, of Rural Retreat, Virginia, whose daughter Morrison had once fallen in love with (but never married). Demand for the beverage caused Morrison to form the Artesian Manufacturing and Bottling Co. (where there is now a Dr Pepper Museum) with Robert S. Lazenby, and by 1991 Sam Houston Prim was bottling Dr Pepper in a plant in Dublin, Texas. In 1986, the company merged with Seven Up Inc., then was bought by Cadbury Schweppes in 1995.

The original formula for Dr Pepper, using sugar rather than corn syrup, is made at only one bottling plant in Dublin, owned by W. P. "Bill" Kloster, who refused to modify the formula when the national Dr Pepper Co.

(based in Dallas) changed to corn syrup. A popular way to drink Dr Pepper among Texas schoolchildren is to pour peanuts into the drink, drink the soda, and eat the peanuts.

Other significant soda drinks in the American market include: "7UP," a lemon-lime-flavored drink originally marketed in St. Louis by Charles L. Grigg, in 1929, under the name Bib-Label Lithiated Lemon-Lime Soda. The reason for the name 7UP was never divulged by Grigg, but Stuart Berg Flexner, in *I Hear America Talking* (1976), noted that a card game by that name was known after the 1820s. Others have suggested the number referred to the seven-ounce bottle size. But in *I'm a Spam Fan: The Stories Behind America's Favorite Foods* (1992), Carolyn Wyman wrote that

> recent 7-Up scholarship reveals the name had more to do with Grigg's long admiration for cattle brands as a simple and clear method of identification. Reading a newspaper article about several cattle brands, Griggs saw a reference to one that consisted of the numeral 7 with an adjacent letter u. So cattle were the real inspiration for the 7-Up name.

In New York City, a coffee-flavored soda called Passaro's Famous Manhattan Special was created in 1895 by Dr. Teresa Cimino.

The first sugar-free soda was sold in March 1953, by Morris Kirsch of Kirsch Beverages in Brooklyn, New York, who, with Dr. S. S. Epstein, came up with "No-Cal Soda" (short for "no calories") for diabetics, although it was soon marketed for those trying to cut calories from their diet. In 1964, Pepsi-Cola introduced one of the first diet sodas, "Diet Pepsi." Other diet drinks, including "Tab" (later "Diet Coke"), "Diet 7UP," and "Fresca," were developed, and they now represent about 13 percent of the $25 billion soda industry business. In the 1970s, led by Pepsi-Cola, plastic bottles (invented by Nathaniel C. Wyeth, of the DuPont chemical company) began to replace the traditional glass ones.

By 1984 Americans were actually drinking more soft drinks (11.5 billion gallons) than bottled water (11.2 billion), and soda still represents nearly 25 percent of the U.S. beverage market. In the past decade, however, sales and consumption of soda and soft drinks have been dropping. Current U.S. per capita consumption of carbonated soft drinks is 42.4 gallons, with 9.7 billion cases sold in 2011.

SODA BEER. A nineteenth-century substitute for real beer.

SODA BEER

For 5 min. boil together 2 oz. cream of tartar, 2 lb. sugar, the juice of ½ lemon, and 3 pt. water. Cool and add 3 stiffly beaten egg whites and ½ c. flour, ½ oz. wintergreen essence, and ½ oz. lemon essence. Stir to blend and bottle. Use 1 T. of soda beer for each glass of water or soda.

SODA JERK. Also "soda jerker." A person who prepares sodas and other confections behind the counter at a soda fountain. The word dates back in print to 1922 and comes from the jerking motion the hand had to make on the soda spigots then in use in order to fill glasses.

SODIUM NITRITE (NANO2). A preservative used in bacon and other cured meats. It is made by the transformation of sodium nitrate ($NaNO_3$) by sodium carbonate. Questions raised about nitrites that can combine with secondary amines to form compounds known as "nitrosamines" (which can cause certain types of cancer in laboratory animals) in some bacon as a result of severe frying caused a reassessment of the necessity of sodium nitrite in curing meats. In May 1978, the USDA announced regulations requiring bacon to be made using 120 parts per million of sodium nitrite or the equivalent amount of potassium nitrite plus 550 parts per million sodium ascorbate or sodium erythorbate, and that cooked bacon may not contain nitrosamines.

SOFKEE. A gruel or soup made from boiled corn, from Muskogee *safki*, dating in print to 1796.

SOFT PIE. A pie with a soft filling but no upper crust, dating in print to 1974.

SOLE. Any of a variety of flatfish of the family Soleidae. Some confusion has been created by the use of the name "sole" for other species, and restaurant terminology does not always adhere strictly to the rigors of taxonomic nomenclature. The word comes from Old French *sole*, referring to the shape of the foot, which the fish's flat form resembles. In English the word dates to 1347.

The true soles of American waters—four species—are rarely sold as food fish, while American flounders of various species are often called "sole." These include "butter sole" (*Isopsetta isolepsis*); "English sole," also called "lemon sole" (*Parophrys vetulus*); "petrale sole" (*Eopsetta jordani*); "rex sole" (*Glyptocephalus zachirus*); "sand sole" (*Psettichthys melanostictus*); and the best known, "Dover sole" (*Microstomus pacificus*), which is a common name for the major fish of the sole market but it is not the true "Dover sole" (*Solea vulgaris*) of Europe.

Americans enjoy sole sautéed or grilled with butter, sometimes breaded, and very often prepared according to classic French recipes, such as "sole Marguery," "*sole à la meunière*" (with butter and fines herbes), and "sole amandine" (with slivers of blanched almonds).

SOLE MARGUERY. Also "filets de sole Marguery." Fillets of sole served in a sauce made with egg yolks, butter, and white wine and cooked with mussels and shrimp.

Although it is decidedly a French creation—by chef M. Mangin of the Café de Marguery, in Paris—and is listed in Escoffier's *Le Guide Culinaire* and in *Larousse Gastronomique*, sole Marguery is far more popular in the U.S. than in France, and much of its celebrity derives from the story of how it came to these shores.

Diamond Jim Brady, one of the most flamboyant American gourmands at the turn of the century, returned from Paris to his favorite NYC restaurant, Rector's, with the news that he had enjoyed a remarkable dish called "filets de sole Marguery." George Rector thereupon withdrew his son from Cornell Law School and sent him off to Paris to get the recipe by working in the kitchens of the Café de Marguery, where he labored for more than a year before he was able to "get the hang of the famous sauce." The young Rector worked fifteen hours a day until he produced a version of the dish that seven master chefs pronounced perfect. He immediately quit his Parisian post, sailed for America, and was greeted in New York Harbor by Earl Fuller's Rector Novelty Orchestra, his father, and Brady, whose first words were "Have you got the sauce?" Rector made the sauce that night at a fabulous banquet, and Brady pronounced the dish "so good I could eat it on a Turkish towel," proceeding to down nine portions.

The dish immediately became a sensation and a standard item on American deluxe restaurants' menus.

Ironically, the recipe given by the originator, M. Mangin, to *Larousse Gastronomique* differs from that published by George Rector Jr. in his book *The Girl from Rector's* (1927). Following are both men's recipes, reproduced in their entirety.

MANGIN'S SOLE MARGUERY

Fillet two fine soles. Use the bones and trimmings to make a white wine fumet, flavored with a little chopped onion, a sprig of thyme, quarter of a bay leaf and a little parsley. Season with salt and pepper. Simmer for 15 minutes. Add to this fumet, which should be strained and concentrated, the strained cooking liquor of a quart of mussels cooked in the usual way (using white wine). Place the fillets of sole, seasoned and lightly flattened, on a buttered baking dish. Sprinkle over a few tablespoons of the aforesaid fumet. Cover with buttered grease-proof paper and poach gently. Drain the fillets well. Set them in an oval dish and surround with a double row of shelled mussels and shrimps. Keep hot, If covered, while the sauce is prepared.

The sauce. Strain the fumet to which will have been added the cooking juices of the soles. Boil down by two-thirds. Remove from heat, allow the sauce to cool a little, then add 6 egg yolks. Whisk the sauce over a gentle heat, like a hollandaise, incorporating about ¾ pound of the finest butter, slightly melted. Season the sauce and strain. Coat with it the fillets and garnish. Glaze in a hot oven.

RECTOR'S SOLE MARGUERY

Cut the fillet with a very sharp knife. There are four fillets to a fish. Take the rest of the fish and put them into a big boiler with plenty of leeks, onions, carrots, turnips, lettuce, romaine, parsley, and similar vegetables. The whole mass is reduced by boiling from eight to twelve hours. This leaves a very small quantity of a jellylike substance, which is the essence of the fish. If properly prepared, only a handful of jelly will be obtained from two hundred fish.

In another pan we place the yolks of four dozen eggs. Work a gallon of melted butter into this, stopping every ten minutes to pour in a pint of dry white wine of good Bordeaux quality. Add from time to time a spoonful of the essence of fish. This is stirred in and cooked in a double boiler in the same way as you would make a hollandaise sauce.

Strain the sauce through a very fine sieve. Season with a dash of cayenne salt. At no time in the preparation of the sauce should it be allowed to come to a boil.

Now we take the fillets, which should be kept on ice to retain their freshness until the sauce is ready. Place them in a pan with just sufficient water to float them a little. About half an inch of water should be sufficient to cover them. After they simmer for ten minutes or less, remove and place on a silver platter. Garnish the dish on one end with small shrimp and on the other with imported mussels from northern France.

Pour a liberal amount of the sauce over the whole platter. Sprinkle with chopped parsley and place under the grill for the purpose of allowing it to glaze to a golden brown. Then serve.

SON-OF-A-BITCH STEW. Also "son-of-a-gun stew" and "cowboy stew." A slang term, in print since 1941, among cowboys, loggers, miners, and other westerners, for a stew made pretty much from whatever was available at the moment or from kitchen scraps. Larry Ross, in *Nanny's Texas Table* (1987), contends that "'Son of a Gun Stew' can mean just about anything in the Lone Star State, and it doesn't always relate to food. 'Rich as…' or 'More full of…'…the possibilities are just as varied and equally questionable. Some say it's a stew of heart, lungs, and other organs, you name it. Others claim it's what the cowboys called what the cook couldn't identify."

SOP. Gravy or the piece of bread used to soak up the gravy, in print since the early eleventh century. Also a colloquialism of the West, "sop" may also refer to a habitual drunkard.

SOPAIPILLA. Also "sopapilla." A deep-fried pastry usually served with honey, dating in American print to 1927. Sopaipillas, derived from Spanish, are a staple of Mexican American menus. Yet in Jane Butel's *Tex-Mex Cookbook* (1980), the author notes that "history reveals they originated in Old Town, Albuquerque [New Mexico], about

300 years ago." Diana Kennedy, in her *Recipes from the Regional Cooks of Mexico* (1978), writes, "For years I have been denying to aficionados of the sopaipillas of New Mexico that they have a Mexican counterpart. I have now discovered that they can be found, though rarely, in the state of Chihuahua.…I have yet to see them on any restaurant menus in the north." A good sopaipilla is supposed to resemble a puffed-up pillow; they can be stuffed with meats or beans as a main course but are more common as a dessert, torn apart with honey drizzled into it. "Sopaipilla" was first found in American print circa 1940. See also **fry bread**.

SOPAIPILLA

Mix 2 c. flour, 1 T. baking powder, and ½ t. salt. Cut in 1 T. lard until of a crumbly texture, then gradually add ⅔ c. lukewarm water. Knead into a smooth ball and let rest for 10 min. Divide in two, then roll into thin sheets. Cut into 2 ½-in. squares and fry in hot oil until golden brown. Drain and serve with honey, cinnamon, or powdered sugar. Makes about 3 doz.

SORBIC ACID. A preservative that prevents the growth of mold. Taken from the berries of the mountain- ash tree, sorbic acid is used often in cheese, syrup, wine, and dried fruits.

SORBITAN MONOSTEARATE. An emulsifier that prevents water and oil from separating and prevents discoloration in heated chocolate. It is found in many dessert products.

SORBITOL. A sweetener and thickener added to diet drinks, candy, chewing gum, and other foods, dating in print to 1890.

SORGHUM. Any of a variety of Old World grasses in the genus *Sorghum* that are grown both for animal forage and for a sweet syrup. The word is from Vulgar Latin *Syricum granum*, "Syrian grain," although the grain may have originated in Africa. It is first mentioned in English print in 1597.

Sorghum might have been brought to the U.S. from Africa, probably around 1700, but it was not an important crop until settlers moved west of the Mississippi, where forage for cattle and sheep was needed in the Great Plains. Sweet sorghum (*S. vulgare saccharatum*), also called "sorgos," was made into "sorghum molasses," first recorded in print as of 1860. This was an important sweetener throughout the nineteenth century, but it decreased in popularity as refined cane sugar became cheaper and more available after World War I. The grain is still grown in the southeastern U.S. to some degree. The variety known as "Chinese sugar" (*S. v. drummondii*) is in the South called "chicken corn."

SORREL. Any of a variety of plants in the genus *Rumex*, especially the French sorrel (*R. scutatus*), whose leaves are used in salads and as a seasoning for soups, sauces, and other preparations.

The word is from Old French *surele*, from *sur*, "sour," because of its tangy taste, and in Middle English appeared in print as "sorel" circa 1440. Wild sorrel in the U.S. is rare, but the plant is widely cultivated in many states, often as a pasture fodder.

SOULÉ, HENRI (1903–1966). Restaurateur. Born in Saubrigues, France, the son of a building contractor, Henri Soulé took his first job as a busboy in the Continental Hotel, in Biarritz. He rose quickly to become, at twenty-three, the youngest restaurant captain in Paris, at Claridge's, on the Champs-Élysée, where he learned to cater to the wealthiest and most powerful people in the world, an education that stood him in good stead to become manager at the 350-seat Le Restaurant du Pavillon de France, which opened at the 1939 New York World's Fair.

With sixty kitchen workers and thirty front-room staff, Le Restaurant served thousands of visitors for whom its high style of French cuisine and service was of a standard never before seen in America. But when war broke out and France capitulated to Germany, in 1940, the restaurant staff was stranded in the U.S. This they remedied by crossing over to Canada, then returning to America as refugees, and many of them were then drafted.

Soulé, by then a stout man of thirty-two, was too old for the draft. He scraped together $14,000 and managed to open a restaurant at 5 East Fifty-fifth Street, in New York, in October 1941, calling it Le Pavillon. Despite the privations of the war, it grossed $263,714 its first year. Soulé became a U.S. citizen in 1946.

Soulé immediately set the standards for French haute cuisine and decor in the U.S. Le Pavillon's red banquettes, roses, tableside carving, and menu (in French) were copied by most other French restaurants in New York, whose chefs and owners were likely to have worked at Le Pavillon. Dishes like *terrine de canard*, *sole à la meunière*, and *mousse au chocolat* became ubiquitous clichés in French restaurants, along with a snobbishness that Soulé used to maintain his own ideas of class and to dismiss those he thought beneath them. "Henri Soulé did not invent the tyranny of the fine French restaurant," wrote food critic **Gael Greene**. "But he was a virtuoso of the tyrannical style."

After refusing to give a good table to his landlord, Columbia Pictures studio head Sam Cohn, Soulé was forced in 1957 to move Le Pavillon to 111 East Fifty-seventh Street, at Park Avenue. He then opened a slightly less formal restaurant, La Côte Basque, on Le Pavillon's original site in 1958. He also owned the Hedges restaurant in East Hampton, Long Island.

Soulé had few interests outside the restaurant, commenting that his only hobby was "paying the bills promptly." After his death, in 1966, Le Pavillon was taken over by new owners but closed finally in 1971. Still, the menus of Le Pavillon were entrenched in French restaurants throughout the U.S. until the next decade, and served as a springboard for chefs and restaurateurs who achieved great success in their own right, including **Jacques Pépin** and **Sirio Maccioni**.

SOUL FOOD. Although this term applies to traditional foods eaten by African Americans, especially in the South, it is of rather recent vintage, first in print in 1960, when it became associated with the growth of ethnic pride in African American culture, of which food was a significant part. The term dates in print to 1964 and comes from the fraternal spirit among African Americans that their culture, heritage, and cooking give them an essential "soulfulness" that helps define the African American experience.

Soul food dishes include **chitterlings**, black-eyed peas, **collard greens**, **hominy**, **grits**, ham hocks, and more. As Bob Jeffries, in his *Soul Food Cookbook* (1969), notes, "While all soul food is southern food, not all southern food is soul."

SOUP-EN-FAMILLE. A vegetable-and-beef-brisket soup served in Louisiana. The term is from the French for "family soup."

SOUP KITCHEN. Originally an Army term for a **mess** kitchen, used in print since 1839. During the Great Depression it was used to describe a charitable organization's kitchen, where free soup and bread were served to the poor and unemployed. Today soup kitchens are officially called "emergency food programs."

SOUR. A drink made with liquor, sugar, and citrus juice and usually shaken with cracked ice. Sours first became popular in the middle of the nineteenth century, at first made with brandy and by the end of the century with whiskey, dating in print as "brandy sour" to 1862. The bar at the "21" Club, in NYC, began mixing sours with bourbon and honey in the 1950s, in homage to society woman Patricia "Honeychile" Wilder. A sour glass is a squat bar glass that holds six ounces.

WHISKEY SOUR

Over cracked ice, shake together ¾ oz. lemon or lime juice, 1 t. powdered sugar, and 1 ½ oz. bourbon or blended whiskey. Strain into sour glass and add cocktail cherry and slice of orange. Scotch, gin, brandy, rum, vodka, or other spirits may be used instead of bourbon or blended whiskey.

SOURDOUGH. A white bread made with a sour starter composed of flour, water, and sugar, in print since 1301. The use of a sour starter is a method of bread baking that goes back at least six thousand years, for yeast had to be sustained from bread batch to bread batch. Legend has it that Columbus brought a starter with him to America, and the technique was certainly a standard method of baking in the early days of this country. With the advent of commercially available yeast and baking powder in the nineteenth century, the use of such starters was confined to those pioneers who moved farther and farther from settlements. These included the gold prospectors of Northern California in the 1850s and the Yukon in the 1890s. The first sourdough purveyor in San Francisco, called the French Bakery, opened the year the Gold Rush began—1849—and it was because of the bread's popularity among miners that "sourdough" became a slang term for the prospectors themselves and, later, by extension, all Alaskans.

Because many of these prospectors set out by boat from San Francisco, sourdough bread is often associated with that city to this day, and it is still a San Francisco specialty.

Although sourdough starter can be purchased, it can also be made by mixing together one cup flour, one cup water (Alaskans often use potato water), and one tablespoon sugar and letting it stand in a warm place for two or three days. It will begin to ferment and have a sour smell. This starter can be continued and preserved by adding a bit more flour and water to the mixture each week and storing it in the refrigerator.

Sourdough starter may also be made by combining a package of dry yeast with a cup of lukewarm water. Stir to dissolve completely, then blend in one cup flour and one tablespoon sugar. Cover and let stand for two to three days in a warm place. A sourdough yeast made from apples or pumpkins is called a "ferment," a term that dates back to seventeenth-century Long Island, New York.

In the West, some starters are said to have been handed down from one generation to the next. In the Midwest, a popular starter is called **Herman**.

SOURDOUGH BREAD

Mix 1 ½ c. starter with 1 c. warm milk, 1 ½ T. sugar, 2 t. salt, and 3 T. butter or shortening. Knead well with 4 ½ c. flour. Place in greased bowl and let rise in a warm place until doubled in bulk. Punch down and let rise again for 45 min. more. Shape into two loaves and bake on greased pan at 375° for about 45 min.

SOUSE MEAT. Headcheese, using the feet, ears, and noses of hogs. The word derives from Old French and dates in English print to 1391.

SOUTHERN COMFORT. A trademark for a cordial made from freshly pitted peeled peaches and bourbon, which is bottled at 100 proof. It was supposedly made and named by Louis Herron, a bartender at the Planter's Hotel, in St. Louis, in about 1875, when it was originally called "Cuff and Buttons," then a phrase that meant the equivalent of "white tie and tails," or formal dress.

SOUTHERN FRIED CHICKEN. Chicken parts that are floured or battered and then fried in hot fat. The term "southern fried" first appeared in print in 1877, although it refers to cooking lettuce; "southern fried chicken" appeared in print in 1920.

This description does little justice to what is perhaps the best-known and best-loved southern dish of all. There are hundreds of recipes for southern fried chicken, which may deviate in any and every variable, from the seasoning to the skillet to the fat to the cooking time, and significant debates can be heard in the South (where it may be called "country fried chicken," as noted in **Lafcadio Hearn**'s 1885 *La Cuisine Créole*) over the best accompaniment for this simple but delectable dish. Some will use Tabasco or lemon or garlic in the seasonings; some swear by lard, others by shortening; some insist gravy should never be served with the chicken, while others wouldn't serve the dish without it; some will swear it is best eaten hot from the skillet, while others prefer it cold the next day; some will argue that the best fried chicken is not fried at all, but battered or breadcrumbed and then baked in an oven.

Southerners were not the first people in the world to fry chickens, of course. Almost every country has its own version, from Vietnam's *gà xaò* to Italy's *pollo fritto* and Austria's *Wiener Backhendl*, and numerous fricassees fill the cookbooks of Europe. And fried chicken did not become particularly popular in the northern U.S. until well into the nineteenth century: Miss Leslie did not mention it in her 1857 Philadelphia cookbook, and Fannie Merritt Farmer's 1896 cookbook refers only to "Fried Chicken" as a fricassee served with "Brown Sauce" or as oven-baked "Maryland Chicken." But by the first quarter of the twentieth century, southern fried chicken was well known and appreciated throughout the country, as Lettie Gay, editor of *200 Years of Charleston Cooking* (1930), bears witness: "If you say the words 'south' and

'chicken' to most northerners they think of fried chicken. But in Charleston chicken is cooked in many ways."

The Scottish, who enjoyed frying their chickens rather than boiling or baking them, as the English did, might have brought the method with them when they settled in the South. The efficient and simple cooking process was very well adapted to the plantation life of the slaves, who were often allowed to raise their own chickens. Louisiana African Americans called a breakfast of fried chicken and grits a "Sunday breakdown."

The idea of making a sauce to go with fried chicken must have occurred early on, at least in Maryland, where such a match came to be known as "Maryland fried chicken." By 1878 a dish by this name was listed on the menu of the Grand Union Hotel, in Saratoga Springs, New York, and, Richard J. Hooker notes, "In B. C. Howard, *Fifty Years in a Maryland Kitchen* (Baltimore, 1873), p. 52, the only fried chicken recipe calls for a sauce made of butter, cream, parsley, salt and pepper." Except for the sauce, Marylanders make their fried chicken in as many different ways as do the rest of the cooks in the South—dusted with flour, rolled in cornmeal, patted with bread crumbs, or even dipped in an egg batter. This last method was harshly criticized by Virginia novelist William Styron, who wrote, "There is a school, developed mainly in the State of Maryland, which holds that, before cooking, the chicken parts should be immersed in some sort of 'batter.' This is absolute rubbish. Southern fried chicken should have after cooking a firm, well-developed crust—this is one of its glories—but the 'batter' principle simply won't hold up after pragmatic examination."

The cooking oil itself is of significance in such debates, with most authorities supporting the idea that a certain amount of bacon fat is advisable to give the chicken a full flavor. Some, like Styron, demand undiluted bacon fat, while others, like **James Villas**, suggest a few tablespoons mixed in with some Crisco shortening. Peanut and other vegetable oils are also popular.

Most southerners would argue that southern fried chicken is never "deep-fried," but rather fried in just enough oil to reach halfway up the sides of the chicken parts. Some suggest frequent turning, while others advise one side be completely cooked at a time. Some prefer to cover the skillet in order to keep in the moistness, while others believe this will make the chicken steamy. Almost everyone agrees the frying pan itself should be a black, well-seasoned iron skillet.

However southern fried chicken is cooked, it is always eaten with the fingers—a habit that is obviously practical but that probably kept the dish out of the more delicate ladies' cookbooks of the nineteenth century. It is to southern fried chicken that the colloquial phrase "finger-lickin' good" (adopted by one commercial fried-chicken company as its slogan) is most often applied.

Once a recipe has been decided upon, next comes the matter of what southern fried chicken demands as an accompaniment. Coleslaw is often cited, as is corn on the cob in season. There is one sect that likes it with rice, but most southerners would feel more comfortable with mashed potatoes and gravy made from the giblets and pan drippings of the chicken.

Southern fried chicken has been known to get dipped into honey as well, and biscuits are often found within reach.

After all this debate, one would think it is a difficult dish to prepare well, and many Americans have avoided the problem (and the mess of frying) by buying their fried chicken in groceries, where it is most often found frozen, or at restaurant chains that specialize in cooking the dish.

SOUTHERN FRIED CHICKEN

In a paper bag put 1 c. flour, grind a generous amount of black pepper, and add 2 t. salt. Cut a tender chicken into pieces and soak in cold milk for ½ hr. Place the chicken pieces in the paper bag and shake until they are all coated. In a skillet of hot oil, fry the chicken pieces on one side until golden brown. Turn and brown the other side. Drain on paper bags and serve hot.

SOUTHERN STYLE. A colloquial expression used in reference to chicken cut into uniform pieces for eating with the fingers.

SOUTHSIDE. A cocktail made by shaking over crushed ice the juice of 1 lemon, 2 t. sugar syrup, and 2 oz. Jamaican rum. A "Northside" substitutes orange juice for the lemon juice. The drink might have originated in Chicago, possibly in the 1950s.

SOYBEAN (*Glycine max*). Also "soya bean" and "soy-pea." Any of more than one thousand varieties of beans that come in a wide range of colors, though the yellow and black soybeans are the best known in the U.S., where, until World War II, they were used mainly for fodder and soil improvement. The soybean, dating in English print to 1795, yields a variety of "soy" products, a word (first in print circa 1670) derived from the Japanese *shoyu*, "fermented bean oil." The soybean has for millennia been part of oriental cookery, but it did not make its way to Europe until the seventeenth century. Today the soybean, in the form of condiments like "soy sauce" and "miso," is popular in Asian dishes as well as an ingredient in many processed foods for its high nutritive value. "Tofu" (from the Japanese) is a creamy cheese-like food made from "soybean milk" that has been curdled. It is eaten on its own and in a variety of dishes, including as "Tofutti," an ice cream substitute first sold in NYC in 1982, by David Mintz, who created the product as a kosher substitute for dairy products.

SOY PROTEIN. A substance made from soybeans that is often used as a binder or extender in meat and poultry products like sausages, luncheon meats, soups, sauces, and gravies. According to the USDA, "Soybeans are processed into three basic soy protein products: soy flour, soy protein concentrate, and isolated soy protein, each of which may be converted to textured vegetable protein. Whenever soy protein is added to a meat or poultry product, its presence is noted in the ingredients statement on the label." The word dates in American print to 1974.

SPACER. Bartender's term for a drink of nonalcoholic brew served between regular beers or other alcoholic beverages as a way to space out the intake of alcohol over an evening. Brewer Brooks Firestone reported, in November 1989, that he first heard the term in an English pub: "A friend of mine asked the publican to give him a 'spacer' and the man automatically gave him a nonalcoholic beer instead of the regular beer he'd been drinking."

SPA CUISINE. Trademark name for dishes served at the Four Seasons restaurant, in NYC, created to be lower in calories, fat, cholesterol, and sodium than most other dishes on the menu. It was developed by chef Seppi Renggli in concert with Dr. Myron Winnick of the Institute for Human Nutrition at Columbia University's College of Physicians and Surgeons. Although introduced in 1983, the term was registered as a trademark in 1985.

SPAGHETTI ALLA CARUSO. Also "spaghetti Caruso." An Italian American dish of spaghetti with chicken livers and tomato. The dish was named after opera singer Enrico Caruso, but there are several versions as to the dish's origins. One newspaper account, reprinted in the book *Spaghetti Dinner* (1955), by Giuseppe Prezzolini, contended that the dish was actually created for a reporter by Caruso himself while living at the York Hotel, in NYC. The sauce for this dish was made without chicken livers, using instead tomatoes, basil, parsley, red pepper, garlic, and olive oil, then "dusted with Parmesan cheese and decorated with coins of fried zucchini squash."

In Craig Claiborne's *The New York Times Food Encyclopedia* (1985), the author noted that a recipe for "Spaghetti alla Caruso" appeared in Louis P. De Gouy's *The Gold Cook Book* (no date given), with the remark "Original recipe as prepared by this writer." Claiborne also cited a book entitled *The 60 Minute Chef* (no date given), by Lillian Bueno McCue and Carol Truax, which contended that Caruso would visit Truax's house, where he once "slapped on a high chef's cap and created an enormous platter of his own very special spaghetti, with chicken livers." The earliest recipes date to 1939, including in Diana Ashley's *Where to Dine in '39*, where it is attributed to chef Antonio With of the Caruso chain of NYC restaurants.

SPAM. Trademark name for a canned ground-pork-shoulder-and-ground-ham product seasoned with salt, sugar, water, and sodium nitrite. It was introduced in 1937 by the Geo. A. Hormel Co. and was a staple of Army **rations** during World War II, when soldiers sometimes referred to it as S.O.S.—short for "**shit on a shingle**" (a term also applied to creamed chipped beef). Spam has been tremendously popular as a breakfast item and sandwich meat, with Hawaii consuming the most per capita, twelve cans per household per year. In Hawaii, Japanese

Americans enjoy a dish called Spam *musubi*, made with sautéed Spam, rice, and *nori* seaweed, which became popular when American servicemen were stationed in Hawaii.

SPANFERKEL. Suckling pig, or a feast where it is served, specifically in German American communities. The word is German, dating in print to 1909.

SPEAKEASY. Also "speak." A term popular during **Prohibition**, to describe an establishment illegally selling alcoholic beverages. In order to gain entrance, you had to speak in a low voice through a small opening in the back door and tell the attendant inside who it was who sent you to the place.

The term itself, which dates in print to 1889, may derive from the English "speak-softly shop," an underworld term for a smuggler's house where one might get liquor cheaply, its usage in this sense having been traced back to 1823. But with the onset of Prohibition in America, speakeasies sprang up overnight, sometimes in shabby sections of town, but often in the best neighborhoods, and many of these establishments were actually fine restaurants in their own right. NYC's "21" Club was a speakeasy during this period and had two bars, a dance floor, an orchestra, and dining rooms on two floors. French diplomat Paul Morand, visiting NYC for the first time in 1925, reported his experience at a speakeasy:

> *There is a truly New York atmosphere of humbug in the whole thing. The interior is that of a criminal house; shutters are closed in full daylight, and one is caught in the smell of a cremation furnace. Italians with a too familiar manner, or plump, blue jowled pseudo-butlers, carrying bunches of monastic keys, guide you through the deserted rooms of the abandoned house. Facetious inscriptions grimace from the walls. There are a few very flushed diners. At one table some habitués are asleep, their heads sunk on their arms; behind a screen somebody is trying to restore a young woman who has had an attack of hysteria.... The food is almost always poor, the service deplorable.*

Designed to shut down all saloons, the Volstead Act instead spurred more illicit ones to open, so that, thanks to a thoroughly entrenched system of graft and police corruption, NYC had more than thirty-two thousand speakeasies within its boroughs—twice the number of saloons that had closed.

SPIEDIE. A sandwich of Italian bread enclosing grilled, skewered cubes of marinated beef or lamb; a specialty of Binghamton, New York. The name—pronounced "speedy"—derives from the Italian word *spiedo*, "kitchen spit." Credit for the introduction of the item to the Binghamton area has gone to Augustino Iacovelli, who opened Augie's Restaurant in 1939 in nearby Endicott, New York, and began selling skewered meats reminiscent of those he'd enjoyed in his native Abruzzi section of Italy. The word dates in American print to 1942.

SPINACH (*Spinacia oleracea*). A dark green plant with rippling leaves, eaten raw in a salad or boiled as a vegetable. The plant is native to Asia, and the name derives from the Arabic *isfānākh*, appearing in English print in 1530.

Of the two main groups of spinach, the prickly-seeded and the smooth-seeded, the former is the most widely cultivated in the U.S., with about half the production coming from California. The Spanish brought spinach to the New World.

"New Zealand spinach" (*Tetragonia implexicoma*) is not a true spinach and is grown only to a small extent on the West Coast of the U.S.

The bitter taste of spinach has made the plant particularly anathema to American children, who have long been coaxed into eating it as a vegetable with the admonition that the cartoon character Popeye, created by Elzie Crisler Segar in 1919, derived his extraordinary strength from spinach. Nevertheless, Americans still eat only half a pound of spinach per capita each year.

SPLIT. A bottle half the size of a regular bottle of soda or liquor, a usage dating in print to 1884.

SPLO. African American slang for liquor, especially illegal cheap spirits, so called because it will cause a "splo" (explosion) inside you when drunk, dating in print to 1940.

SPOON BREAD. Also "spoonbread" or "spoon corn bread." A soft, custardlike dish usually made with cornmeal. The term may come from a Native American word for porridge, *suppawn*, but more probably from the simple fact that the dish is usually eaten with a spoon. Its first mention in print was in 1847.

SPOON BREAD

Sift together 1 c. cornmeal, ½ c. flour, 2 T. sugar, 1 ½ t. salt, and 2 t. baking powder, then mix in 2 beaten eggs and 2 c. milk. Blend well. In a baking pan melt 4 T. butter and pour in the cornmeal batter. Pour 1 c. milk over top, then bake for 45 min. at 375°.

SPOON MEAT. The meat of an immature coconut, dating in print to 2000.

SPORTS BAR. A bar where people congregate to watch televised sporting events, or a bar owned by a celebrity sports figure. Although there is a long tradition of sports figures owning such establishments, the term "sports bar" itself dates in print to 1975. A true sports bar is a place where sports is the principal topic of conversation. One of the common features at such a place is a large-screen TV, or several of them, broadcasting sporting events.

SPOT (*Leiostomus xanthurus*). Also "spot fish," "red drum," "Lafayette," and "Cape May goody." An eastern freshwater fish that ranges from Maine to Texas. Its black spot behind the gill cover gives it its name, which has been in print since 1873. Spot is a favorite fish in Virginia and the South. U.S. commercial landings of spots totaled 3.692 millions pounds in 2010, valued at $2.845 million.

SPOTTED PUP. A pudding made with raisins, dating in print to 1944. It is most commonly used in the West.

SPOTTED SEA TROUT (*Cynoscion nebulosus*). A variety of **weakfish** found in southern waters. It is not a true **trout**, but its black spots give it a similar appearance, and it is sometimes marketed as "gray trout." U.S. landings totaled 329,000 pounds in 2010, valued at $623,000.

SPRINGFIELD HORSESHOE. A sandwich made of various fillings topped with a cheddar-cheese sauce. According to food writer Susan Costner, in *Susan Costner's Great Sandwiches* (1990):

> Created by Steve Tomko and Joseph Schweska at the Leland Hotel in Springfield, Illinois, in 1928, this regional specialty starts with a slice of toast and can have a filling of ham, egg, hamburger, and chicken, just chicken, just ham, just egg, bacon, shrimp, or turkey and corned beef—but the sauce is the star of the show. This should be of sharp, creamy, slightly spicy cheddar cheese; a classic Welsh rabbit sauce is a good choice. When the filling has been doused with sauce, the horseshoe is topped with a second slice of toast. The name "horseshoe" was derived from the shape of the cut of ham used on the hotel's original sandwich. So far this local gem has gained no wider acceptance, but to Springfield residents it clearly ranks as that city's foremost contribution to gastronomy.

SPRINGHOUSE. A house built over a cold spring to keep dairy foods cool, the term dating back in print to 1755.

SPRING ROLL. An Asian American appetizer made of crisp dough wrapped around a filling of various ingredients such as vegetables, meat, shrimp, and seasonings. Sometimes synonymous with the "egg roll," it is considered somewhat more "authentic" and delicate than the latter. The name, which dates in English print to 1943, comes from the Chinese tradition of serving them on the first day of the Chinese New Year, which is also the first day of the lunar year's spring.

SPRINKLE THE INFIELD. A Chicago bar-goer's colloquialism meaning "to order another round of drinks."

SPRITZER. Originally a drink made with Rhine wine and club soda or seltzer, although today a spritzer may be made with almost any dry white wine. The name comes from the German, for a "squirt," and dates in print to 1940, but the drink became very popular in America in the 1960s, at a time when many people were just being introduced to wine. Often it is ordered as a "wine spritzer."

SPUD. A colloquial name for a potato. The word comes from a Middle English word for a short knife and, later, a spade with which to dig up a tuber such as the potato. The term as used in England in the nineteenth century was a slur against Irishmen, as it was later in America, because of Ireland's dependence on the potato for food. Americans also called a person who picked potatoes a "spud-glommer," especially in Idaho, one of the biggest potato-producing states.

There is no truth to the story that the term comes from a nineteenth-century organization formed to discourage the growing and eating of potatoes, the Society for the Prevention of an Unwholesome Diet, or "SPUD."

SQUASH. Any of a variety of plants of the genus *Cucurbita* and their fruits. This term includes the native American "summer" and "winter" squashes, as well as **pumpkins**, gourds, and **zucchini**. The name is from the Narragansett *asquatasquash*, meaning "eaten raw, green," and refers specifically to the summer varieties (*C. pepo*). The word *squash* first appeared in print in 1643.

The European settlers were introduced to squashes by the Indians, and John Smith, who traveled through Virginia in 1607, commented that the fruits, called by the Native Americans there *macocks*, were similar to English muskmelons.

Squashes were a staple of the Native American diet throughout the continent. The oldest evidence of their being used as food, dating back to between 7000 and 5500 B.C., was found at the Ocampo Caves, in Mexico, whence they were carried to North America, where evidence of squash has been found in the burial mounds of Ohio, Kentucky, and Virginia from two thousand years ago.

Early botanists disagreed on or confused the terminology of squashes, so that one may find some varieties described with various overlapping Latin names for three basic species: *C. Pepo*, *C. maxima*, and *C. moschata*. The English, meanwhile, call them "vegetable marrow." In America, squashes are generally separated at market into winter and summer varieties, as noted below.

"Summer squashes" include the "yellow" or "orange crookneck," "turban squash," "**zucchini**," "spaghetti squash" (so called because its fibers look like strands of spaghetti), and "pattypan" (also called "cymling" and "scalloped squash"). The "winter squashes" include the

"**Hubbard squash**," "winter crookneck," "butternut," "buttercup," "**acorn squash**," and "sugar pumpkin."

SQUAW BREAD. Quickly made fried breads, especially from corn, dating in print to 1879. The Narragansett word *squaw* means "woman."

SQUAW CANDY. Also "Eskimo ice cream." Strips of salmon smoked until hard, dating in print to 1943. The word *squaw* refers to a female American Indian, from Narragansett.

SQUEAKY CHEESE. Fresh cheese chunks, dating in print to 1950.

SQUID. Any of a variety of marine cephalopod mollusks of the genera *Loligo*, *Rossia*, and others, which is similar to the **octopus** but has instead ten legs. The origin of the word is unknown, but was first in print in 1613. In Hawaiian, the squid is called *muheʻe*. Most Americans know squid better by its Italian name, *calamari*. In the U.S., squid consumption is largely confined to ethnic restaurants and Mediterranean immigrants' homes, although breaded "fried calamari" rings are a popular appetizer. The most important food species is the "common Pacific squid" (*L. opalescens*), found in California waters. The best-known Atlantic species are the "long-finned squid" (*L. pealei*), also called "white squid" and "winter squid," and the "short-finned squid" (*Illex illecebrosus*), also known as "red squid" and "summer squid." Most Americans know squid better by their Italian name, *calamari*. U.S. commercial landings of squid were 337,223 pounds in 2010, valued at $97.8 million.

SQUIN. The edible viscera of an animal, etymology unknown, dating in print to 1890.

SQUIRT. A drink of liquor or wine, fresh fruit or fruit syrup, and seltzer or club soda, made deliberately sweet.

WHISKEY SQUIRT

Crush half a peach with 1 T. sugar syrup, 1 t. curaçao, and 1 ½ oz. bourbon or blended whiskey. Shake with crushed ice and fill glass with seltzer or club soda.

STACK CAKE. A six-layer (sometimes more) ginger cake filled with a cooked paste of apples. It is a specialty of Appalachia. A "stack pie" is a pie of alternating layers of filling and crust, covered in caramel, in print since 1903.

STATE DOIN'S. Trappers' term for "food."

STATES' EGGS. In the early days of the western frontier, eggs had to be shipped from eastern states to those cow-country territories not then part of the union.

STEAM BEER. A beverage produced on the West Coast in the mid-nineteenth century, by a process that circumvented the shortage of ice needed to make lagers, dating in print to 1857. In *The Great American Beer Book* (1978), James D. Robertson describes the process:

> *Fermentation proceeds at a relatively high temperature (60°–68°F.) and barley malt is used exclusively. Within twelve to eighteen hours after the yeast has been added to the wort in the fermenting tubs, the beer comes into "krausening," where it is kept from six to eight hours. It is then run into the clarifier for two to three days…for completion of fermentation. If fermentation has been proper, at the end of this stage the beer shall have undergone a reduction of fifty to sixty percent and be quite clear in appearance. From the clarifier, the beer is racked directly into barrels, where it receives an addition of about twenty percent of krausen, together with some fining. In four to six days the beer has raised a sufficient amount of "steam" in the barrels (some fifty pounds per square inch), and some bleeding of pressure must be done. In olden days these barrels were shipped to saloons, rested a few days, and then tapped for the trade. Steam beer is made today by only one West Coast firm [the Anchor Brewing Company of San Francisco, begun in 1896] and the product is bottled.… Steam beer has a golden brown color, sharp hoppy taste, full body, and a lingering malt finish.*

STEPMOTHER SLICE. A thick slice of bread, dating in print to 1906.

STERN, JANE and **MICHAEL** (both 1946–). Authors. As chroniclers of American food as found in diners, barbecues, cafeterias, and other eateries, Jane and Michael Stern were among the first to show that such foods and places were the true repository of and living testaments to the country's culinary heritage, at a time when most food writing was about high-end restaurants and recipes provided by large food companies to food editors.

Jane Grossman was born in NYC, Michael Stern in Chicago. She graduated from Pratt Institute, in New York, he from the University of Michigan. They met as graduate art students at Yale University and married in 1970; Michael went on to Columbia University to earn an M.F.A. in film studies.

After work in TV documentaries, they received a contract to travel around the U.S. for a book called *Roadfood: The Coast-to-Coast Guide to 700 of the Best Barbecue Joints, Lobster Shacks, Ice Cream Parlors, Highway Diners, and Much, Much More* (1977), which has had several subsequent editions through 2011; the most recent lists eight hundred eateries in the lower forty-eight states. On the road, they would eat up to twelve meals a day, writing of them with the affection and respect that food writers usually reserved for haute cuisine, while profiling many of the dedicated, often eccentric owners of bakeries, pizzerias, doughnut shops, and taverns. Describing the sauce at Arthur Bryant's barbecue, in Kansas City, Missouri, the Sterns wrote, "It is beautiful—a gritty, red-orange blend of spice and sorcery that is not at all sweet like most barbecue sauces. It packs a hot paprika wallop and tastes like a strange soul-food curry, a nice complement to any meat. Once you've tasted it, you'll understand why this old Grease House is a foodie legend."

Together the Sterns have written about American pop culture in more than thirty books, including *Amazing America* (1978), *Elvis World* (1987), *The Encyclopedia of Bad Taste* (1990), and *The Lexicon of Real American Food* (2011). They were longtime contributors to *Gourmet* magazine, have won several James Beard awards, and in 1992 were inducted into the Who's Who of Food & Beverage in America.

On her own, Jane Stern wrote *Ambulance Girl: How I Saved Myself by Becoming an EMT* (2003), a study of her bout with depression, which was made into a TV movie of the same name in 2005. In 2006 the Sterns wrote the memoir *Two for the Road: Our Love Affair with American Food*.

The couple divorced in 2008 but continue to work and write together.

STEWART, MARTHA (1941–). Entrepreneur, publisher, author. More than anyone else of her generation, Martha Stewart influenced Middle America's style in food and entertaining through her books, magazines, TV shows, and products.

Born Martha Kostyra in Jersey City, New Jersey, to a Polish American family, Stewart was raised in Nutley, New Jersey. She worked as a model before attending Barnard College, where she earned a B.A. in European and architectural history (1962) and met Yale law student Andrew Stewart, whom she married in 1961. After the birth of a daughter, Alexis, Stewart worked as a stockbroker on Wall Street until 1972. (The couple would divorce in 1990.)

The Stewarts moved to an 1805 farmhouse in Westport, Connecticut, where she devoted herself to cooking and restoration, and in 1976 she started a catering business in her basement, later buying out her partner and growing it into a $1 million business. Alan Mirken, head of Crown Publishing Group, asked her to write a cookbook based on recipes and photos from her catered events, resulting in her first book, *Entertaining* (1982), for which she hired Elizabeth Hawes to write the text. The book showcased Stewart's casually elegant country style, which would become her highly recognizable signature. "[*Entertaining*] is not intended only for the culinary elite, who are working to refine their cuisine," she wrote in the introduction, "but especially for all those people who regard cooking as 'preparing meals,' its drudgery or duty—and entertaining as an even greater worry. For them, I hope that there are many ways of entertaining and that each ultimately depends not on pomp or show of elaborate technique, but on thought, effort, and caring—much like friendship itself."

That book was followed by *Martha Stewart's Quick Cook* (1983), *Martha Stewart's Hors d'Oeuvres* (1984), *Martha Stewart's Pies & Tarts* (1985), *Weddings* (1987), *The Wedding Planner* (1988), *Martha Stewart's Quick Cook Menus* (1988), and *Martha Stewart's Christmas* (1989).

She became editor in chief of *Martha Stewart Living* magazine in 1990, for Time Publishing Ventures, and expanded her name into other fields. In 1997, she and investors secured funding to buy all of her television, print, and merchandising ventures under the Martha Stewart brand and consolidate them under Martha Stewart Living Omnimedia, for which she would serve as chairwoman, president, and CEO. At that time, she began a catalog business called Martha by Mail. All these endeavors were bringing in $763 million in annual retail sales by the end of the 1990s, when the company went through a highly successful public offering. She was invited to join the New York Stock Exchange board of directors. In May 1995, a cover story in *New York* magazine declared Stewart "the definitive American woman of our time."

Criticized by some for trying to transform everything in sight to conform to her vision, Stewart was not above self-satire, as when she did a commercial for American Express in which she was shown tiling her pool with cut-up credit cards.

In 2002, Stewart came under investigation by the federal government for securities fraud, obstruction of justice, conspiracy, and making false statements to prosecutors and the FBI; in February 2004, she was found guilty of conspiracy, obstruction of justice, and two counts of making false statements. Stewart was sentenced to five months in prison in Alderson, West Virginia, and a $30,000 fine.

Upon her release, Stewart immediately began two new TV shows, including *Martha*, which she hosted, and began publication of *Everyday Food*. She expanded her Martha Stewart Everyday line of home furnishings at Kmart and sold her line of wall paints in Sears stores.

In 2005, Stewart published a book on business management, *The Martha Rules*, followed by *Martha Stewart's Baking Handbook*. In 2007, she launched a housewares line for Macy's and a wine produced by E. & J. Gallo; a year later, her company began designing and building houses under her name.

In 2012, she again became chairperson of the corporation, for which she had always been majority shareholder.

Stewart is the recipient of many awards, including induction into the New Jersey Hall of Fame.

STEW THE DISHRAG. A slang term meaning to make an extravagant meal for guests, dating in print to 1893.

STICKY. A sweet molasses pastry popular in the Carolinas, dating in print to about 1885.

STICKY

Make pastry dough for 2 pies, roll out thin, and cut into 12 squares about 3 ½ in. across. Divide ½ lb. butter into 12 pieces, place on squares, and pour 1 c. sugar on pastry. Fold corners into center, close edges, place closely together on a greased pan, and bake at 350° until browned.

STICKY BUN. Also "honey bun." A yeast pastry topped with melted brown sugar or honey, cinnamon, and raisins, so called because it has a very sticky texture when eaten with the fingers. Although they are popular throughout the U.S., they are often associated with Philadelphia and sometimes called "Philadelphia sticky buns," although in Philadelphia itself they are called "cinnamon buns." The name dates in print to 1900.

STICKY BUN

Dissolve 1 pkg. yeast in ¼ c. lukewarm water. Scald 1 c. milk, then cool until lukewarm and add yeast and 1 ½ c. flour. Mix, cover, and let rise for 1 hr. Add 4 T. cooled melted butter, 2 beaten egg yolks, 4 T. sugar, 1 t. salt, the grated rind of 1 lemon, and 3 c. flour. Knead, then cover and let rise until doubled. Roll dough in a long, 1-in.-thick rectangle, brush with a mixture of melted butter, 2 T. brown sugar, 1 t. cinnamon, and 3 T. red currants (if desired). Roll and cut into 1-in. slices. Crumble ¾ c. brown sugar with 4 T. melted butter and spread in skillet. Place dough slices in skillet, let rise for another 60 min., or until doubled, then bake at 350° for 30 min. Turn out onto cooling rack. Makes 12 buns.

STIFLE. Also "stiffle." A New England stew made with salt pork and vegetables or seafood, dating in print to 1832. The word probably suggests the "stifling"—that is, smothering of the ingredients—in the cooking process. "Eel stiffle" is described by Josephine H. Pierce, in *Coast to Coast Cookery* (1951), as "a scalloped dish made with eels, onions, potatoes and salt pork. A favorite on Martha's Vineyard [in Massachusetts]." Pierce also notes that a similar stew without the eel is known on Cape Cod as "Halieluia," the biblical exclamation for good news, though this may be a bit of hyperbole or sarcasm.

STIRABOUT. A form of porridge whose name is formed from the words *stir* and *about*, dating in English print to 1691. The Pennsylvania Dutch of the nineteenth century made this dish with vegetables, saffron, and chicken broth, but in the mining towns of the Northwest it was a simpler affair, no more than a breakfast of oatmeal mush thinned with milk and salt. In the Federal Writers' Project volume entitled *Copper Camp: Stories of the Greatest Mining Town, Butte, Montana* (1943), the authors report that stirabout was brought to that locale by Irish miners and dished out at the Clarence Hotel and the Florence Hotel, where servings were "computed in tons" and every boarder ate two to three bowls each morning and carried more to the mines for lunch.

STIRABOUT

To a kettle of 6 c. boiling chicken broth, add 4 c. sliced peeled potatoes, 2 T. chopped parsley, 1 c. chopped celery, salt, pepper, and ⅛ t. saffron. Reduce heat and simmer for 20 min. Beat 2 eggs with ½ c. flour, drop into simmering broth by teaspoonfuls, then cover and boil another 7 min. Serves 6.

STONE BOILING. A Pueblo Indian method of cooking by placing hot stones into a basket with food.

STONE CRAB (*Menippe mercenaria*, although *Lithodes maja* is also known by this name). Also "moro" or "morro" crab. A crab with very hard claws filled with sweet white meat. "Stone crab" first appeared in print in 1713. The stone crab is one of the delicacies of the southern U.S. and particularly of Florida, where the main harvesting areas include Marathon Island, Crystal River, Biscayne Bay, and Naples.

Damon Runyon said of the crustacean, "The stone crab is much larger than the northern crab and has a shell harder than a landlord's heart." Before 1920, the crab was eaten only by Miamians and others in the Florida and Gulf Coast communities. The stone crab has become especially associated with a restaurant in Miami Beach that popularized the dish in the 1920s—Joe's Stone Crab, opened in 1913 by Joe Weiss and designated a historic landmark in 1975.

Since only the claws are eaten, fishermen twist them off and throw back the crab (usually only one claw is taken so that the creature can defend itself), which grows new claws (called "retreads") within eighteen months. By law, the claws must then be boiled for seven minutes, then either put on ice or frozen, because cooks have found that freezing removes the unpleasant taste of iodine frequently noticed in the meat. Chilled claws are then "floated" in a tank of water to determine which have the most meat ("lights" are unmeaty claws that float to the top). When served, the claws are cracked with a mallet and eaten with dipping sauces of either melted butter or mustard-mayonnaise. They are usually eaten cold.

The season lasts from October 15 through May 15. More than 2.5 million pounds are harvested yearly. The minimum size for selling claws is 2 to 2.75 ounces, called "mediums." "Large" claws are three to six ounces, and "jumbos" over six ounces.

JOE'S STONE CRAB MUSTARD-MAYONNAISE

Beat together 3 ½ t. dry mustard, 1 c. mayonnaise, 2 t. Worcestershire sauce, 1 t. A.1. steak sauce, 1 ½ T. light cream, and ⅛ t. salt. Chill and serve with stone crabs or other seafood. Makes ⅔ c.

STONE FENCE. Also "stonewall." An alcoholic drink made from apple cider or applejack and a whiskey such as rum. Washington Irving mentions the drink in his *History of New York…by Diedrich Knickerbocker* in 1809. According to the *Better Homes and Gardens Heritage Cook Book* (1975), "stonewall was the favorite drink of Ethan Allen and his Green Mountain Boys."

STONE FENCE

Combine 1 ½ oz. applejack with ½ oz. dark rum. It may be poured over crushed ice.

ST. PAUL SANDWICH. An egg sandwich of St. Paul, Minnesota, commonly made with egg foo young and pickles, on a bun, dating in print to 1943.

STRAIGHT. An alcoholic spirit of any kind drunk with no other ingredients except, in some cases, ice. Americans have used this word since at least the middle of the nineteenth century. In England a drinker would say "neat" instead. "Straight up" is a request for a cocktail to be served without ice cubes, usually in a martini glass.

STRAWBERRY. Any of a variety of plants in the genus *Fragaria* bearing a red berry with a soft, pulpy flesh. The word is from Old English *strēawberige*, possibly because the low-lying plant's runners resemble straw.

Strawberries have been eaten by humans for thousands of years, but little trouble was taken to cultivate them before the Renaissance in Europe. In the New World, strawberries were abundant, and the native people made them into bread and held feasts at the harvest of the fruit. Jacques Cartier mentioned seeing wild strawberries along the banks of the St. Lawrence River in Canada in 1534, and in 1536 a white strawberry was noted to be growing in Massachusetts and New York.

The "native American strawberry" (*F. virginiana*), also called the "Virginia strawberry," "meadow strawberry," or "scarlet strawberry" by the white settlers and *wuttahimneash* by the tribes of the eastern coast of America, was admired by the first colonists, and plants were soon sent back to Europe, perhaps as early as 1600. (France had samples as of 1624.) In 1607, Captain John Smith reported, "Captain Newport and my selfe with divers others, to the number of twenty-two persons, set forward to discover the [James] River, some fiftie or sixtie miles, finding it in some places broader, and in some narrower…the people in all places kindly intreating us, daunsing and feasting us with strawberries, Mulberries, Bread, Fish, and other their Countrie provisions." Roger Williams of Rhode Island marveled at the great size of his region's strawberries—"four times bigger than ours in England," he wrote.

A second American berry was discovered by the Spanish explorers of Central and South America, where they found Indians cultivating a very large berry the conquistadores called *frutilla*. This strawberry was of little interest until French navy engineer Amédée-François Frézier rediscovered it while exploring Peru and Chile in 1712 and sent some back to the royal gardens in France and to Brittany. This strawberry was widely proliferated throughout the Pacific coast, as far as Alaska, and also in Hawaii, and in English took the name "beach" or "Chilean" strawberry (*F. chiloensis*). Frézier's plants did not bear fruit in France, because he had unknowingly brought only female examples of a species that needed a separate male in order to breed. Thirty years later, an accidental crossing of these same berries with the already established Virginia strawberries in France resulted in an excellent hybrid that became known as the "pine" or "pineapple" strawberry (*F. ovalis*), now one of the major cultivated varieties.

In the U.S., few people bothered to cultivate berries, because they were so plentiful in the wild. After Englishman William Cobbett visited the U.S., he reported, in *A Year's Residence in the United States of America* (1818), that "strawberries grow wild in abundance; but no one will take the trouble to get them." By one estimate there were only fourteen hundred acres of cultivated strawberries in America at the beginning of the nineteenth century, and the strawberry patch was a well-established fixture in rural areas and home gardens. Cultivation did begin, however, in the early years of the nineteenth century, and strawberries became something of a luxury, especially when served with cream. President Martin Van Buren (1782–1862; held office, 1837–1841), who was often accused of trying to turn the White House into a highfalutin palace, was criticized before his election for using public money to grow strawberries for his delectation.

New York became a strawberry market after the Erie Railroad brought in eighty thousand baskets in a single night in June 1847, and wide-scale cultivation began in America four years later, with the development, by Albany, New York, horticulturist James Wilson, of the hardy Wilson variety. By the 1880s, more than one hundred thousand acres were under cultivation for the fruit, and the refrigerated railroad cars perfected in that era meant that the perishable strawberry could be shipped to the Midwest. A strawberry industry began to grow in Arkansas, Louisiana, northern Florida, and Tennessee, and today strawberries are grown in all fifty states, with 75 percent coming from California, which has a year-round harvest.

In 2010, U.S. production of strawberries was 1.433 million tons (30 percent of the world's production). Per capita U.S. consumption of strawberries is nearly nine pounds.

The main species is the hybrid *F. ovalis*, the main varieties of which include the Aroma, Beaver, Blakemore, Catskill, Dorset, Fairfax, Howard 17, Klondike, Klonmore, Lupton, Marshall, Massey, Missionary, Redheart, Fairpeake, Swanee, Tennessee Beauty, Florida Ninety, and Tioga.

Americans eat strawberries fresh or frozen in syrups, particularly on strawberry **sundaes** (first recorded in 1904), as well as in **strawberry shortcake** and as a flavoring for various desserts, especially ice cream. There are many strawberry festivals held throughout the U.S. each year, a tradition dating back to the 1850s.

STRAWBERRY SHORTCAKE. A dessert made with a biscuit pastry, strawberries, and whipped cream, though Americans commonly use store-bought spongecake instead of the biscuit pastry. The name derives from its being made "short," that is, crisp, by the use of lard or another fat, a meaning of the word that dates back to the fifteenth century. In the UK, "shortcake," mentioned in Shakespeare's *The Merry Wives of Windsor* (circa 1598), is usually synonymous with shortbread, which is a crisp cookie and a traditional specialty of Scotland. In America, however, "shortcake" meant a rich pastry enclosing fruits, to which Washington Irving, in his story "The Legend of Sleepy Hollow" (1821), may have been referring when he wrote of a table laid with "sweet cakes and short cakes, ginger cakes and crumbling cruller, and the whole family of cakes." By the 1830s, strawberry shortcake was known and soon became one of the best-loved American desserts, especially after the popularity of strawberries rose to the point that, in the 1850s, people spoke of "strawberry fever."

The recipe below is adapted from Marjorie Kinnan Rawlings's *Cross Creek Cookery* (1942).

STRAWBERRY SHORTCAKE

Sift twice 2 c. flour, ¼ c. sugar, 4 t. baking powder, and ½ t. salt. Work mixture with 6 T. butter until coarse and crumbly. Add 1 well-beaten egg, then ⅓ c. milk, and blend to make a dough. Turn into buttered pan and pat into shape. Bake 15–20 min. at 400°. An hour before serving, cut up 1 qt. fresh strawberries, saving about 1 doz. whole. Add ¼ c. brown sugar. Let stand in a warm place for 1 hr. Split the shortcake, hot from the oven, into 2 layers, butter each side, lay strawberries and juice on one half, cover with other shortcake layer, and top with whole strawberries and whipped cream.

STREAK-OF-LEAN. Also "streak-o-lean." A southern African American term for salt pork, in print since 1874.

STREETED. Restaurant workers' slang for the act of being thrown out into the street. In *The Girl from Rector's* (1927), restaurateur George Rector describes the action thus: "The process of being streeted meant that you were grasped by the slack of the trousers and the back of the neck and tossed out into the street."

STREUSEL. A crumb topping of flour, butter, and spices that is sprinkled and baked on breads, cakes, and muffins. The term is from the German, for "something strewn together," in English print since 1909, and these toppings are certainly of German origin, although they are sometimes referred to as Danish or Swedish.

STRING BEAN (*Phaseolus vulgaris*). Also called "snap bean" or "green bean." A long, slender green bean, so called because of its stringy tendrils. The term is first recorded in 1759, and "snap bean" (because of its crisp sound when cracked) was first recorded in 1770. String beans are widely eaten in the U.S., usually boiled and buttered.

The yellow variety of string bean is called the "wax bean," which dates in print to 1888.

STRIPED BASS (*Morone saxatilis*). Also "rockfish" and "striper." A North American fish whose name derives from the dark stripes along the length of its body, first in American print in 1787. They are considered one of the principal game fishes of the world. (For distinctions among **bass**, see main entry.)

The striped bass was one of the many fish early European settlers marveled at for its size and abundance, and Captain John Smith, who sailed into Chesapeake

Bay in 1607, wrote enthusiastically of striped bass "so large, the head of one will give a good eater a dinner, and for the daintinesse of diet they excell the Marybones of Beefe." The Pilgrims were nourished on striped bass heads and salted the bodies for winter, also using the fish for fertilizer to such an extent that the Massachusetts Bay Colony General Court put a stop to the practice in 1639 because the fishes were quickly dwindling in number. In those days, the striped bass grew to an enormous size, sometimes six feet long and well over a hundred pounds. The fish was introduced to the Pacific in 1879. By the nineteenth century the bass had become one of the sportsman's favorite fishes, and waters of both coasts were full of this elusive challenger to the talents of the best fishermen.

U.S. landings totaled 7.307 million pounds in 2010, valued at $17.233 million.

STROMBOLI. A sandwich made with pizza dough folded over a variety of ingredients, most often mozzarella and sliced pepperoni. The stromboli is a specialty of Philadelphia, though similar to an Italian creation called the **calzone** (which is far more commonly sold at pizzerias in the U.S. than the stromboli), whose dough pocket is somewhat puffier. The name may derive from the Italian island of Stromboli, but more probably refers to a very big, strong character in the fairy tale *The Adventures of Pinocchio* (1882), by Carlo Lorenzini, whose pen name was Collodi. The association with such a character may play off another Italian American sandwich, the **hero**.

STRUDEL. A rolled pastry filled with nuts, streusel mixture, fruit, or cheese, brought to America by German immigrants. The name is from Middle High German, meaning "whirlpool." "Apple strudel" is the most common form of the pastry. The word was first printed in English circa 1893.

STUFFING. A packed combination of meats, vegetables, grains, fats, or other ingredients inserted into the cavity of meat, poultry, or fish. The word comes from the verb *stuff*, a meaning that first appeared in English print in 1538, displacing the customary "forcemeat" (from the French *farcir*, "to stuff") used in the English tradition.

After the 1880s, however, Victorian propriety in America made the term "dressing" more acceptable; both "stuffing" and "dressing" are still used interchangeably today, with the former finding more adherents in the East and the South.

Turkeys and most roast poultry and game are stuffed, usually with bread or cornmeal crumbs and various seasonings. Oysters were a very popular nineteenth-century stuffing, and pecan or rice stuffings were often used in the South. Italian Americans may use a stuffing of sausage, onion, and mozzarella cheese, while dried fruit, potatoes, and apples are customary among German Americans.

OYSTER STUFFING

Drain 1 pt. oysters and retain liquid. Cut oysters in half. Sauté in 8 T. butter, 2 c. chopped onion, 1 ½ c. chopped celery, 1 c. chopped green pepper, 1 T. minced garlic, ½ t. thyme, ½ t. rosemary, 1 crushed bay leaf, and 1 c. chopped parsley. Cook with onion for about 5 min. Add oyster liquid, cook for 5 sec., remove from heat, and add 5 c. bread crumbs, salt and pepper, and 2 beaten eggs. Blend well, adding water if necessary for texture.

STURGEON. Any of a variety of fishes in the family Acipenseridae. It is a very large fish particularly known for its roe, which is turned into **caviar**. The name is from Germanic *sturjön* and has been used in English since at least 1300.

The sturgeon in North American waters amazed the early European settlers, who found two-hundred-pound examples in the Hudson River, and Captain John Smith, who explored the Virginia coastline in 1607, wrote, "We had more Sturgeon, than could be devoured by Dog and Man." Sturgeon was an everyday food for southerners: "The supplies seemed limitless," wrote Richard J. Hooker in *Food and Drink in America* (1981). "Stories were told of men becoming physically tired from pulling fish from the rivers, of catches with hooks of 600 sturgeon, and of immense takes on the rivers with seines, eelpots, weirs, and fish pots."

In the nineteenth century, the sturgeon became the source of a booming American caviar business, but by 1900 supplies of both the Atlantic and Pacific sturgeon

SUCCOTASH—SUFFERING BASTARD

were almost totally depleted. So far, the resurgence of the fish has been modest but encouraging, with most coming from the Northwest, though the "Atlantic sturgeon" (*A. oxyrhynchus*) is taken in the waters of South Carolina and Georgia. The main species marketed for consumption are the "white sturgeon" (*A. transmontanus*), the "green sturgeon" (*A. medirostris*), and the "lake sturgeon" (*A. fulvescens*). The white sturgeon is now being farm-raised. The largest sturgeon farm in the world is Sierra Aquafarms, begun in 1980 in Elverta, California, which now produces about 100,000 pounds of white sturgeon per month. Farm-raised sturgeon average about ten to twenty-five pounds, while wild sturgeon average between fifteen and eighty but may grow much larger.

Today most sturgeon that comes to market is smoked, frozen, or packed in jars with pickling spices.

SUCCOTASH. A cooked dish of corn and lima beans. More popular in the South these days than elsewhere, it is still often found in cafeterias.

The term made its first appearance in print in 1745, an Americanism formed from the Narragansett word *misickquatash* (and other Native American words, such as *sukquttahash* and *msakwitash*), referring to various ingredients in a stew pot and, more specifically in the Narragansett, to an ear of corn.

So American is the term that President Ronald Reagan once lumped "South Succotash" in with "Podunk" as epithets for an out-of-the-way, insignificant small town, which immediately got up the dander of the six hundred people who actually live in a place called Succotash Point, Rhode Island, on Narragansett Bay.

SUCCOTASH

Cook 1 c. fresh corn kernels until tender in boiling water. Do the same with 1 c. lima beans. Mix together with ½ t. salt, ⅛ t. pepper, 1 T. salt pork or butter, and ¼ c. milk and cook together until hot but not boiling. Serves 4.

A recipe for "Delaware succotash," appearing in *The American Heritage Cookbook* (1980), contains tomato and nutmeg.

SUCKER. Any of a variety of fish in the family Catostomidae. These fishes derive their name from their sucking, protractile mouth, that which attaches itself to whales, sharks, other fish, and boats. The freshwater varieties of sucker are so called because their method of eating is to suck up the algae and crustaceans of their diet. The first mention of such fish in print was in 1772, referring to species in the Hudson River.

The principal suckers of culinary interest include: "blue sucker" (*Cycleptus elongatus*), ranging throughout the Midwest and the South; the "bigmouth buffalo" (*Ictiobus cyprinellus*), also called "redmouth" and "gourdhead buffalo"; "black buffalo" (*I. niger*), also called "bugler," "Prairie buffalo," and "rooter"; "small-mouth buffalo" (*I. bubalus*), also called "highback," "channel buffalo," and "razorback"; "black redhorse" (*Moxostoma duguesnei*); "golden red-horse" (*M. erythrurum*), "spotted sucker" (*Minytrema melanops*); and "white sucker" (*Catostomos commersoni*).

Not related to these species is a marine fish of the family Echeneidae, the "remora," also called "suckerfish." The remora takes its name from the Latin *re-* (back) and *mora* (delay), because they held back and delayed a ship's passage.

SUCKLING PIG. A pig six to eight weeks old that is usually roasted on a spit or in the oven. In Louisiana, this dish goes by the name "*cochon de lait*" or "*cochon du lait*" (French for "suckling pig"). A "suckling" is any young animal being nursed, a usage dating in print to circa 1530. The pig is usually seasoned inside and out and then stuffed with apples or other ingredients.

SUELZE. Jellied, pressed meat, popular with German Americans. The word is German, dating in American print to 1918.

SUFFERING BASTARD. A name used for two entirely different cocktails. An American drink of this name was created by a Los Angeles restaurateur of the 1930s called Don the Beachcomber (born Ernest Raymond Beaumont-Gantt), who specialized in creating rum drinks like the "Missionary's Downfall," the "Vicious Virgin," and the "**Zombie**." His Suffering Bastard was made with lime juice, a half-ounce of curaçao, a quarter-ounce sugar syrup, a quarter-ounce orgeat syrup, an ounce of light rum, and an ounce of medium rum, all shaken with crushed ice and garnished with cucumber peel, fresh mint, lime shell, and a fruit stick.

The other "Suffering Bastard" is attributed to the bar at the Shepheard Hotel, in Cairo, Egypt, where it was originally called the "suffering bar steward." The name changed when it became associated with the hard-pressed World War II British and Australian defenders of Tobruk, in North Africa, in 1941. In this drink, two ounces of cognac or brandy, two ounces of dry sherry, and ginger ale are poured over ice in a tall tumbler and decorated with fresh mint.

SUGAR. There are more than a hundred substances that may be described as "sugars"—**honey**, dextrose, **corn syrup**, levulose, lactose, sorbitol, mannitol, maltitol, xylitol, total **invert sugar**, turbinado sugar, and scores of others—but common white sugar, called "sucrose," is the one most used in the American home. The word *sugar* (which derives ultimately from Sanskrit *sárkara*) refers to sweet, water-soluble carbohydrates extracted from plants such as sugarcane, sugar beets, maple sap, fruits, sorghum, and other sources.

Until the Middle Ages, honey was the only sweetener known in Europe, but sugarcane products, including molasses, were used in Asia at least as early as 800 B.C. The Arabs brought sugarcane to the West, and the Crusaders might have brought some back, too. By the fifteenth century Venice was importing it from Alexandria, and sugar became a sensation throughout Italy, where it was used to sweeten not only desserts but hors d'oeuvres, meats, and macaroni as well. In 1498, the Portuguese explorer Vasco da Gama brought sugarcane back from his voyage to India, heralding an expansion of sugarcane production into the Cape Verde and Canary islands and Madeira. But four years before that, Christopher Columbus had planted pieces of cane in the New World that were to flourish and change the course of Caribbean history, for soon the Spanish introduced the plant to Hispaniola, Cuba, and other islands, the Portuguese to Brazil, the English to Barbados, and the French to Martinique, establishing both a profitable sugar trade and a slave trade to support it. As Reay Tannahill points out, in *The Fine Art of Food* (1968), "Sugar became so

important to trade that in the 1670s the Dutch yielded New York to England in exchange for the captured sugar lands of Surinam, and in 1763 France was prepared to leave England with the whole of Canada, provided she had Guadeloupe returned to her." By 1520 there were at least sixty sugar factories on the island of St. Thomas alone. Whole native populations, such as the Caribs and Arawak of the Greater Antilles, were forced into slavery on the sugar plantations, causing the virtual extermination of these tribes. The Europeans then turned to Africa for slave labor, bringing more than ten million unfortunate souls to work the New World's plantations. Soon a reciprocal trade network was set up between the islands, the North American colonies, and Europe, with New England selling codfish (with which to feed the slaves) to the islands, the islands shipping sugar and molasses to New England and Europe, and New England sending cod and rum made from molasses to Africa in return for a fresh supply of slaves. "King Sugar" ruled an empire of human misery. Many abolitionists urged people to refrain from using sugar, and some sugar vendors advertised their product as "East India sugar not made by slaves."

France's loss of its "sugar islands" in the West Indies to England after 1761 severely crippled Louis XV's prosperity and was one of the significant reasons his successor entered America's War of Independence on the colonists' side. Despite the outcome of the war, however, France never regained much of the Caribbean sugar trade.

Sugarcane never brought North American farmers much profit, though it was grown in the South—in Louisiana, Alabama, Mississippi, Florida, and Georgia—until competition from the Caribbean and the Far East after the Civil War pretty much wiped out the domestic industry. Today only Florida, Hawaii, Louisiana, and Texas have a sugarcane industry, producing only a small percentage of the world's output. Some cane is still grown in other southern states to make sugar syrup.

Although white sugar was always popular with Americans, it was often more expensive than alternatives like molasses, maple syrup in the Northeast, and "muscovado" (from Portuguese *mascavado*, unrefined sugar), an unrefined product derived from sugarcane juice that was considerably cheaper than white sugar. In 1868, Claus Spreckels, of San Francisco, patented a method of refining sugar in eight hours, rather than the usual three weeks, and, after opening his California Sugar Refinery, became known as the "Sugar King."

After the lifting of sugar tariffs in the 1880s, sugar came down in price and afterwards became a cheap commodity all Americans could easily afford. Consumption doubled between 1880 and 1915.

Today Americans ingest about eighty pounds per capita, of which about half is cane sugar. The following list includes the most common sugars and sweeteners.

BROWN SUGAR. Less refined than white sugar, brown sugar consists of sugar crystals contained in molasses syrup with natural color and flavor. It may also be made by adding syrup to white sugar and blending. It can be found in groceries in either a light or dark brown shade, the latter having a somewhat stronger taste.

COLORED SUGAR. Also "confetti sugar." Any sugar variously colored for cake and dessert decoration.

CONFECTIONERS' SUGAR. A highly ground form of powdered sugar (which would be labeled "XXX") that is labeled "XXXX" and is ideal for making icings and other confections.

CORN SYRUP. See main entry.

DEXTROSE. Also "glucose" or "corn sugar." A commercial sugar made from the action of heat and acids, or enzymes, on starch. Dextrose is often blended with regular sugar.

FLAVORED SUGAR. Any sugar scented with aromatics such as lemon, vanilla, or cinnamon, often added to tea or coffee.

FRUCTOSE. Also "levulose." A commercial fruit sugar that is sweeter than sucrose and is used in cooking.

HONEY. See main entry.

LACTOSE. Also "milk sugar." Made from skim and whey milk for commercial purposes, lactose is found in mammals' milk and is used mainly by the pharmaceutical industry.

MAPLE SUGAR. See **maple syrup**.

RAW SUGAR. A coarse light brown granulated sugar evaporated from cane juice. Only purified raw sugar may be sold.

SUCROSE. Obtained from cane or sugar beets, sucrose is a compound of glucose and fructose, is 99.9 percent pure, and is sold granulated or powdered.

SUGAR ALCOHOL. Also "polyol." Any natural fruit sugars, like sorbitol, mannitol, maltitol, and xylitol, that are commercially produced from sources like dextrose.

TOTAL INVERT SUGAR. A mixture of glucose and fructose, made by a process called "inversion," by which acids or enzymes split sucrose. Total invert sugar is sweeter than sucrose and comes in liquid form; it helps to prolong the freshness of baked goods.

TURBINADO SUGAR. Produced by separating raw sugar crystals and washing them with steam, turbinado sugar must be refined to remove impurities.

SUKIYAKI. A **Japanese American** dish of meat and vegetables simmered together. Sukiyaki is a standard item in Japanese American restaurants. The word, which dates in print to 1920, translates as "broiled on the blade of a plow," from the practice of Japanese farmers who often cooked their meals in the fields on such a utensil. Today, however, the dish is not broiled but stir-fried and simmered.

SUNFISH. Any of a variety of North American freshwater fishes in the family Centrarchidae or marine fishes in the family Molidae. Their brightly colored bodies give these fishes their name, which was first mentioned in print in 1629, referring to the sea species, and in 1685 (by William Penn) referring to the North American freshwater variety. The most important sunfish for culinary use include: the "bluegill" (*Lepomis macrochirus*); the "black crappie" (*Pomoxis nigromaculatus*) and "white crappie" (*P. annularis*), also called "speckled perch," "calico bass," "strawberry bass," "bachelor perch," "bachelor," "papermouth," and, in Louisiana, "sac-à-lait" (Creole French for "milk sack"); "crappie" is from a Canadian French name for another fish, *crapet;* the "flier" (*Centrarchus macropterus*); the "green sunfish" (*L. cyanellus*); the "longer sunfish" (*L. megalotis*); the "pumpkinseed" (*L. gibbosus*); the "redbreast sunfish" (*L. auritus*), also called the "robin," "sun perch," and "yellow-belly sunfish"; the "redear sunfish" (*L. microlophus*), also called the "shellcracker"; the "rock bass" (*Ambloplites rupestris*), also called the "redeye bass" or "goggle-eye"; and the "warmouth" (*L. qulosus*), also called the "stump knocker."

SUNFLOWER. Any of a variety of plants in the genus *Helianthus*, especially the "common sunflower" (*H. annuus*), native to the New World, bearing seeds that are dried or roasted to be eaten as a snack or pressed to make an oil. The word derives from its bright yellow flowers surrounding a dark center and was first recorded in English in 1597. "Sunflower oil" is first mentioned in print in 1819.

Sunflowers were cultivated by the Native Americans long before the arrival of the Europeans, but Russia became the world's largest producer. Although the sunflower is the official state flower of Kansas, the states producing the largest sunflower crops are North Dakota, Minnesota, and California.

SUPERMARKET. A large self-service food market that also sells many nonfood items, first in print in 1931. The supermarket is the principal retail food store for Americans. The various items and brands are arranged on open shelves along long aisles, and customers line up at cash registers near the exit to unload their purchases from a rolling metal gridwork basket (a "shopping cart"). The items are totaled up by a cashier as they move along a conveyor belt and are then placed in brown paper or plastic bags by a store attendant called a "packer."

The supermarket is a specifically American notion, built on the ideas that efficiency is increased by self-service, that variety is a tempting and competitive manner of advertising on the spot, and that the mobile nature of the American consumer is conducive to shopping in large retail stores with easy access by automobiles. Such stores have become popular in globally, too, often under the same term, "supermarket," in various languages.

The first self-service market was opened in 1916, by Clarence Saunders, on Jefferson Street in Memphis, Tennessee, and a patent for a "self-service store" was issued to him on October 9, 1917. Items were prepackaged, labeled, and priced, and the store was kept impeccably clean, in contrast to the traditional rustic grocery store, where many items were sold loose, priced according to how much one bought, and often delivered to one's home.

The self-service idea did not really catch on, however, until the 1930s, when such stores were sometimes referred to as "cafeteria-type" markets. In August 1930, a grocery-chain manager named Michael Cullen opened the King Kullen Grocery in an abandoned garage in Jamaica, Queens, in New York City, that was ten times the size of the average grocery and cut prices radically by doing high-volume business, making it the first true "supermarket." By 1936 there were more than twelve hundred supermarkets under different names in eighty-four cities. In 1937, Sylvan N. Goldman, of Standard Food Stores in Oklahoma City, Oklahoma, debuted the first "shopping cart."

The first printed mentions of the word *supermarket* in America were in the 1920s, and the term became as firmly entrenched as the concept, so that by 1950 America had more than ten thousand supermarkets, their growth encouraged by the postwar baby boom and the movement of the middle class to the suburbs.

The average supermarket was by then more than thirty thousand square feet, with chains like A&P, Safeway, Grand Union, and others dominating the food-buying habits of the country. In significant ways, these large chains influenced what Americans ate to the extent that pretty much the same offerings in the West were enjoyed by those in the East, North, and South. By the 1960s supermarkets were carrying everything from imported foods to lawn furniture, and many had sections selling delicatessen-style items, fresh bread, and cooked foods.

But in the 1970s, competition and overexpansion caused the supermarkets to lose money, even though sales in 1981 totaled $150 billion. Profit margins, never very high, fell to half what they had been in the 1950s and 1960s, and some chains went bankrupt.

To some extent, many Americans began to regard the supermarket as depersonalized and lacking the nostalgic charm of the older neighborhood groceries, and in cities increasing numbers of "gourmet" or delicacy shops opened, carrying better-quality (and higher-priced) merchandise. Supermarkets in the 1980s and 1990s thereupon tried to meet this challenge by creating small delicacy shops, butchers, seafood sections, and takeout counters within the walls of the traditional supermarket structure. Many others started to carry **health food** and more organically grown produce. The size of supermarkets grew so large in the 1980s that many were called "hypermarkets" or "superstores." While many of these were dazzling in design and elaborateness, other supermarkets, called "warehouse stores," shed all but the most rudimentary amenities and decor, offering lower prices for high-volume purchases. These began in the Midwest in the 1960s, when wholesalers tried to unload excess merchandise, but their popularity rose during the recession of 1974–1975. A "club store" is a form of supermarket offering wholesale prices to members, with as many as 35 percent of such members being consumers, the rest wholesale business members.

SUPPER CLUB. An upscale restaurant serving dinner only, often with live entertainment and offering banquet rooms, dating in print to 1940.

SUPTION. A southern African American word for "flavor" in food, perhaps a variant of the words "sup" or "substance." The word dates in print to 1887.

SURF AND TURF. Also "surf 'n' turf." A dish of meat and seafood served on the same plate. The meat is usually beef, the seafood lobster. This combination has led to several colloquial variants, including "pier and steer," "lobsteer," "beef and reef," and others, used as menu listings or restaurant names. The term first appeared in print in 1961.

SURIMI. A minced-fish paste that can be molded and flavored to taste like higher-priced seafood such as crab, scallops, shrimp, or lobster. The term *surimi*, first in print in 1973, for the process of preserving fish this way, has long been used in Japan (though sometimes referred to as *kamaboko*, which is more specifically a form of surimi crab cake), where records mentioning the process date back to A.D. 720. Surimi was introduced into the U.S. in the early 1980s, and today between 160 and 175 million pounds are produced for the domestic market each year.

Surimi usually begins with an inexpensive fish, mostly Alaska pollack, which is skinned, filleted, minced, washed with water, then flash-frozen before being shipped to processors who add flavorings, natural binders and stabilizers (including starch, salt, egg white, or sugar), and natural coloring. The resulting paste is shaped into various analogs marketed under different brand names. Surimi is also sold in chunks and flakes (called "salad style"). One of the most popular forms of surimi is in imitation crab legs.

In the U.S., "surimi" is used to describe the raw material used in making "surimi seafood," which is the final product.

SWAGIN. A Maine bean soup, etymology unknown, dating in print to 1909.

SWEATY SADDLES. A winemakers' slang term for wine spoiled by *Brettanomyces* yeast.

SWEDISH MEATBALLS. A dish of seasoned pork or beef meatballs covered with a brown gravy. There are endless variations on this dish, which is most popular in the Midwest and derives from Swedish origins. Swedish meatballs are usually served at buffets and **smorgasbords**. Buttered noodles are the traditional accompaniment. "Swedish meatballs" dates in print to the 1920s.

SWEDISH MEATBALLS

Grind together ¾ lb. beef, ¼ lb. pork, and ¼ lb. veal. Soak 1½ c. soft bread cubes in 1 c. light cream for several min., then mash into meat with ½ c. mashed potatoes, ½ c. chopped onion, 1 beaten egg, salt, pepper, ¼ c. chopped parsley, and a dash of ginger and nutmeg. Form into meatballs about 1 in. in diameter. Sauté meatballs in 3 T. butter until browned, then remove. Melt 2 T. butter in same skillet, scrape meat drippings, stir in 2 T. flour, cook briefly, and add 1 ⅓ c. beef bouillon. Cook until thickened, return meatballs to skillet, and cook, basting often, for about 30 min. Serve with buttered noodles or rice.

SWEET AND SOUR. Any dish that combines the flavors of sweet and sour, usually achieved by the use of a sweetener, like sugar, corn syrup, or jelly, and a vinegar-based ingredient.

SWEET AND SOUR MEATBALLS

In a bowl combine 1 lb. ground beef, 1 beaten egg, 1 c. bread crumbs, 2 T. minced onions, 1 clove minced garlic, 1 t. salt, ½ t. black or white pepper, 2 T. milk, and 1 T. vegetable oil. Mix well and form into small meatballs. Brown meatballs in a pan with 3 T. vegetable oil and drain excess fat. Blend together ½ c. fruit jelly with ⅔ c. chili sauce and pour over meatballs. Simmer for about 10 minutes.

SWEET POTATO (*Ipomoea batatas*). A vine of the morning glory family, native to the New World tropics, the yellow or orange tuber of which is eaten as a side dish in various forms. Sweet potatoes may be baked, boiled, candied, mixed in a pie, pudding, or biscuits, or topped with marshmallows. They are an important crop of the American South, though grown elsewhere in the U.S., too, with two types being dominant: the "pale" sweet potato and another, darker-fleshed type called, erroneously, "yam." The true yam (*Dioscorea bulbifera*) is a different tropical vine, whose tuber may grow to lengths over seven feet and which is generally sweeter than the sweet potato. It is rarely seen in the U.S., except perhaps in Latin American markets, although it is called in regional English the "air potato." The confusion with the true yam came from the habit of slaves calling the American sweet potato by an African word (either Gullah *njam*, Senegal *nyami*, or Vai *djambi*), meaning "to eat." The word was first recorded in America in 1676.

The earliest records of the cultivation of the sweet potato, dated to around 750 B.C., come from Peru, but it was grown throughout South and Central America by the time Christopher Columbus arrived in the New World.

He found the tuber in St. Thomas, where it was called *aje* or *axi*; on Hispaniola (*ages*); in the Yucatán (*camote*); and in Arawak (*batatas*).

The Taino word *batata* was soon transformed into several European words, including the Spanish *patata*, French *patate*, and English "potato." These words first meant specifically the sweet potato, not the white potato, which was introduced much later to the North American colonies. John Gerard, in his *Herball* (1597), called sweet potatoes "common Potatoes," and according to the *OED*, he termed white potatoes "Virginia Potatoes" and, later, "Bastard Potatoes." But as Waverley Root points out, in *Food* (1980), Gerard could not have meant the white potato, for "not only did [it] not exist in Virginia, it did not exist anywhere in North America."

The sweet potato, meanwhile, had already been shipped back to the Old World, perhaps as early as 1493 on Columbus's ship, and was cultivated in Spain by the middle of the sixteenth century. England got its first taste of the tuber in 1564, when Sir John Hawkins brought it back from "the Indies of Nova Hispania," although Henry VII might have sampled some Spanish varieties earlier. By the turn of the century, Shakespeare wrote of them in *The Merry Wives of Windsor* (circa 1598), and "sweet potato pie" had become an English delicacy.

But the term "sweet potato" was not in use in America until the 1740s, distinguished from the white potato. Long before then, the sweet potato was being shipped to ports in Massachusetts from as far away as Bermuda. Root said the earliest evidence for the cultivation of the tuber in North America dates to 1648, and probably back to 1610. It was in cultivation in New England by 1764 and much earlier in Virginia. In the South, it was also called the "Carolina potato" or "dolley."

In the nineteenth century, George Washington Carver devised more than a hundred uses for the sweet potato, which he noted was also called the "Indian potato," the "Tuckahoe," and the "hog potato," and listed table varieties that included the "Dooley yam," "Triumph," "Pumpkin yam," "Porto Rico," and "Nancy Hall." By the 1880s Americans were enjoying candied sweet potatoes, along with less lavish preparations of boiled, roasted, or mashed tubers. Today some of the most popular market varieties include the "Centennial," "Goldrush," "Georgia Red," "Puerto Rico," "New Jersey," and "Velvet." The sweet potato has long been associated with southern and soul cooking, and it is still traditional to serve it with the Thanksgiving meal. Per capita U.S. consumption of sweet potatoes in 1997 was 4.1 pounds.

In *Invisible Man* (1952) Ralph Ellison reminisced about the sweet potatoes of his childhood:

> *At home we'd bake them in the hot coals of the fire-place, had carried them cold to school for lunch; munched them secretly, squeezing the sweet pulp from the soft peel as we hid from the teacher behind the largest book, the World's Geography. Yes, and we'd loved them candied, or baked, in a cobbler, deep-fat fried in a pocket of dough, or roasted with pork and glazed with the well-browned fat; had chewed them raw—yams and years ago. More yams than years ago, though the time seemed endlessly expanded, stretched thin as the spiraling smoke beyond all recall.*

SWEET POTATO PIE

Boil 1 lb. sweet potatoes, remove the skins, mash, and beat. Blend with ¾ c. brown sugar, ¼ t. salt, and 1 t. ground cinnamon. Beat in 3 eggs, ¾ c. milk, ¾ c. heavy cream, and 1 T. butter. Spoon into pie plate lined with a pastry crust and bake at 400° for about 45 min.

CANDIED SWEET POTATOES

Boil, peel, and cut up 6 sweet potatoes. Place in a buttered pan, sprinkle with ¾ c. brown sugar, ½ t. grated lemon rind, and 1 ½ T. lemon juice, and bake in 375° oven for about 20 min. Serves 4.

SWEETSOP. (*Annona squamosa*). Also called "sugar apple." A tropical American tree bearing a yellow-green fruit with sweet yellow pulp, grown to some extent in Florida. The word first appeared in print in 1696.

SWEET TEA. Pre-sweetened iced tea, long enjoyed in the South but dating in print only to 1989.

SWELLFISH (family Tetraodontidae). Any of a variety of fish that can inflate themselves with air or water, which gives them their name, in print since 1807, as well as others, like "puffer," "blowfish," "globefish," and "sea squab." Swellfish are often poisonous to eat. The two main American species are the "smooth puffer" (*Lagocephalus laevigatus*) and the "northern puffer" (*Sphoeroides maculatus*).

SWISS STEAK. Sliced **beef** rump or round baked with tomatoes, onions, peppers, and sometimes seasonings such as thyme, rosemary, basil, or chile. In England it would be called "**smothered** steak," but there is really no direct corollary for the dish in Switzerland, the closest being the carbonade. The name may derive instead from an English term, "swissing," which refers to a method of smoothing out cloth between a set of rollers, because Swiss steak is usually pounded and flattened before cooking. According to food historian Jean Anderson, the first known recipe for the dish appeared in 1915, though the *OED* cites the term's first appearance in print as 1932.

SWISS STEAK

Rub 2 lb. sliced round steak with ½ t. sugar and ½ lemon. Mix ½ c. flour, salt, and pepper, and pound into the meat. Sear the slices, then place in casserole. Sauté 2 sliced onions, 1 chopped green pepper, and 3 chopped celery stalks in 3 T. oil until tender. Add a 1-lb. can of stewed tomatoes, ¼ t. rosemary, and ¼ t. basil. Cook until tomatoes break down. Spoon over the meat, cover, and cook at 300° for 1 ½–2 hr. Serves 4.

SWITCHEL. A colonial drink made from molasses, vinegar, and water, dating in print to 1790. It is sometimes called "haymaker's punch." Brandy, cider, or rum was often added.

SWITCHEL

Combine 1 c. light brown sugar, 1 c. wine vinegar, ½ c. light molasses, 1 T. ground ginger, and 1 qt. cold water. Stir.

SWIZZLE. A tall drink, usually made with rum, dating in print to 1813. Its origins are unknown, but the term perhaps is onomatopoeia that refers to the sound of mixing the drink in a glass. Swizzle has been used to describe a drink since the early nineteenth century, and it also came to mean drunkenness. A "swizzle stick," first mentioned in print in 1875, is a kind of small paddle used to stir a drink.

SWORDFISH. Any of a variety of large marine fish in the family Xiphiidae. Swordfish is one of the great game fishes and is found throughout the world. The name refers to the fish's swordlike upper jaw and has been used in English since at least 1400. The fish usually referred to under this name is *Xiphias gladius*, which is found in the waters of both the Atlantic and Pacific coasts and is called *shutome* in Hawaii. Although expensive, because of the difficulty of landing the large, athletic fish, the swordfish has long been enjoyed by Americans, even though in the 1960s the Food and Drug Administration announced that it had found dangerously high levels of mercury in the majority of specimens it examined. This is no longer believed to be of major concern.

U.S. commercial landings of swordfish totaled 7.736 million pounds in 2010, valued at $21.745 million.

SYDNEY SMITH'S SALAD DRESSING. A salad dressing of potatoes, mustard, olive oil, egg yolks, onions, and anchovies. The recipe—which came from a doggerel poem by Sydney Smith (1771–1845), and English clergyman and founder of the *Edinburgh Review*—was quite popular among American cooks in the nineteenth century.

Two boiled potatoes strained through a kitchen sieve,
Softness and smoothness to the salad give,
Of mordant mustard take a single spoon,
Distrust the condiment that bites too soon!
Yet deem it not, thou man of taste, a fault

To add a double quantity of salt.
Four times the spoon with oil of Lucca crown,
And twice with vinegar procured from town;
True taste requires it and your poet begs
The pounded yellow of two well-boiled eggs.
Let onion's atoms lurk within the bowl
And, scarce suspected, animate the whole,
And lastly in the flavoured compound toss
A magic spoonful of anchovy sauce.
Oh, great and glorious! Oh, herbaceous meat!
'Twould tempt the dying Anchorite to eat,
Back to the world he'd turn his weary soul
And plunge his fingers in the salad bowl.

SYLLABUB. An eggnog made with wine. It was once a popular drink at American Christmas parties, though it is rarely seen today. *The American Heritage Cookbook* (1980) contends the name "is derived from wine that came from Sillery in the Champagne region of France, and from 'bub,' an Elizabethan slang word for bubbling drink," although sparkling champagne was not made until the seventeenth century; the *OED* says the word is of obscure origin. The term first appeared in print circa 1537.

SYLLABUB

Combine 2 c. white wine, 5 T. grated lemon rind, 1 c. sugar, and ⅓ c. lemon juice. When sugar is dissolved, add to a blend of 3 c. milk and 2 c. light cream, then beat until frothy. Beat 4 egg whites with ½ c. sugar until stiff. Pour wine mixture into bowl and top with mounds of egg white. Sprinkle with nutmeg.

T

TABASCO (*Capsicum frutescens*). A hot **chile** pepper whose name derives from the Mexican city of Tabasco. (*Tabasco* is a Mexican Indian word meaning "damp earth.") The chile was first cultivated in Louisiana by banker Maunsel White, who brought the seeds from Tabasco and gave them to Edmund McIlhenny, who in turn planted them on a hillock named Avery Island. In 1859, McIlhenny began producing a bottled **hot sauce** made by aging mashed chile peppers with salt and vinegar in casks for three years and sold it (in used perfume bottles) under the trademark name Tabasco sauce, which has become the most famous hot sauce in the world. Tabasco sauce is so thoroughly identified with hot sauces that many recipes specifically refer to this brand, and it is commonly set on tables in the South along with the salt and pepper shakers so that people can season their food according to their own taste. Today the McIlhenny family still makes the sauce, shipping fifty million bottles each year to more than a hundred countries.

TABLE-BOARD. A boardinghouse meal that does not include lodging, first mentioned in print in 1859.

TABLECLOTH RESTAURANT. Also "tableclother" and "white tablecloth restaurant." A restaurant-industry term for a full-service restaurant, usually set with tablecloths, offering a wide variety of foods and some level of formal dining. Such a restaurant would be distinguished from a **lunch counter**, diner, or other common eatery.

TACO. In Mexico, this refers to a stuffed and folded **tortilla**, but in the U.S. a "taco" is more commonly a crisp fried tortilla shaped into a U and filled with various stuffings. The word was first printed in English in 1914. Tacos are often served as a snack but also as a main course when accompanied by refried beans, rice, and hot sauce. The word is Mexican Spanish, meaning a "wad" or "plug," but colloquially refers to a light meal or snack. Small **Mexican American** restaurants, especially those found along the road, are often called "taco stands," which are usually fast-food restaurants in the United States. A "taco bender" is a slur term for a Mexican or Mexican American, dating in print to 1962.

A national chain of taco stands under the name Taco Bell was begun in 1962 by **Glen Bell** in Downey, California. It is now owned by PepsiCo Inc., of Purchase, New York, and has more than thirty-five hundred outlets.

"Taco shells" are usually bought in packages at a grocery and are quite crisp, though in Mexico they are generally more pliable. The various fillings for a taco, usually doused with a hot chile sauce, include ground beef, chicken, pork, fish, chorizo sausage, tomato, cheese, lettuce, guacamole, onion, and refried beans.

TAFFY. A confection made from sugar, butter, and flavorings that has a chewy texture obtained by twisting and pulling the cooked ingredients into elasticity.

The British term for such candy is "toffee" or "toffy," possibly from "tafia," a cheap West Indian rum made from molasses and used originally to flavor candy. The *OED* notes that "taffy" (the preferred word in Scotland, Northern England, and America), dating in print to 1817, seems to refer to an older form of the candy. By the 1850s "taffy pulls," at which young people would gather to stretch the candy between themselves, had become social occasions.

English toffees are often harder than American taffies. "Saltwater taffy," which at one point actually contained a small amount of salt water, was popularized as "Fralinger's Original Salt Water Taffy," established as a confectionery stand by Joseph Fralinger in 1885 on the Boardwalk in Atlantic City, New Jersey. The story of how the taffy got its name dates back a couple of years before that, to when one taffy stand was hit by an ocean wave, drenching the stock with salt water. According to legend, the next day a little girl tasted the candy and asked, "Is this saltwater taffy?"

TAILGATE PARTY. Also "tailgate picnic." A meal served outdoors, off the folded-down rear door, or tailgate, of a station wagon, an American car designed to carry several family members or a large load. The term "tailgate picnic" dates in print to at least 1941, although a photo in a spring 1936 English magazine and an illustration in a November 1936 NYC clothing advertisement both depict tailgate picnics.

The food is varied and of a kind found at any picnic—salads, sandwiches, fried chicken, beer, soft drinks, coffee, cakes, and anything else that strikes the fancy.

TAKEOUT. A term for food that is bought at a restaurant but taken elsewhere to be eaten. The term has been in use since at least the 1940s and is shown on the sign of the "Tail o' the Pup" hot dog stand, in L.A., in a 1949 photo. Synonyms include "carryout," "take-home," and "to go." While the majority of restaurants in the U.S. provide some form of takeout food, it is those restaurants with average checks of under twenty-five dollars that sell the most takeout food.

TAKE THE PLEDGE. An alcoholic's phrase for abstaining completely from alcohol.

TAMALE. A term describing a wide range of dishes based on a cornmeal-flour dough called **masa** that is placed inside cornhusks (sometimes a banana leaf) with fillings and then steamed. Tamales are of Mexican origin and were enjoyed by the Aztecs (the word comes from the Nahuatl *tamalli*) in several versions, from appetizer to sweet dessert, dating in American print to 1844. In Mexico they are traditionally served in restaurants on Sunday nights and as ceremonial food on All Saints' Day. As early as 1612, Englishman Captain John Smith

mentioned a kind of tamale made by the Indians of Virginia, and by 1691 note was made by others of a bean-filled tamale of the Southwest. A "tamale pie" is a dish of cornmeal mush filled with chopped meat and a hot chile sauce, dating in print to 1911.

TAMALE

Coarsely chop 2 lb. pork and cover with water, bring to a boil, then simmer until tender. Drain, reserving 1 ½ c. stock. Shred the pork and sauté in 4 T. oil until brown, then stir in 2 T. flour until brown. Stir in a sauce made from 1 chopped tomato, 1 chopped garlic clove, 1 chopped red or green chile pepper, 1 chopped onion, salt, and pepper pureed in a blender. Add 3 chopped green or red chile peppers, ¼ t. oregano, salt, and pepper and simmer for about 30 min. Make a dough by creaming 1 ½ c. lard with 1 ½ t. salt, mixing 4 ½ c. masa with 2 ½ c. warm water, and beating this mixture into the lard. Place portions of the dough into a dozen presoaked cornhusks, spread portions of meat mixture on dough, and fold opposite sides of husks toward center. Peel dough from husks and seal, then close husks around dough to seal into a packet. Steam for 1 ½ hr. Serves 12.

TANGELO (*Citrus tangelo*). A hybrid fruit obtained by crossing a grapefruit with a tangerine. The word entered English print in 1900 as a portmanteau of *tangerine* and *pomelo*. The main varieties grown in the U.S. are the "K Early," the "Nova," and the "Mineola" (called "honey belles" in Florida).

TANGLE CAKE. A deep-fried pastry of the Mid-Atlantic states, made from tangled strips of dough, dating in print to 1957.

TANSY. Also "tansey." A pudding made from the juice of the tansy plant (of the genus *Tanacetum*, especially *T. vulgare*) or any such confection made with a tart fruit. The word is from Middle English, derived from Old French *tanesie*, and, ultimately Greek *athanasia*, "immortality."

"Tansy cake" was known in England from at least the fifteenth century. As a pudding, tansy was first mentioned circa 1450, said to be eaten at Easter to commemorate the "bitter herbs" of the Passover.

In America, the dish often lacked the ingredient that gave it its name, a tart fruit such as the cherry being substituted. It was a popular dessert at George Washington's Mount Vernon home, in Virginia.

TAOS LIGHTNIN'. Also "Touse." A variety of distilled spirits originally made at San Fernández de Taos, now Taos, New Mexico, dating in American print to 1901. The Spanish called it *aquardiente*, or "burning water," and it was enjoyed by the early trappers in that region.

TARO (*Colocasia esculenta*, family Araceae). Also "dasheen," "eddo," and many other regional names. A tropical plant with broad leaves and a starchy, edible root, dating in print to 1769. The name comes from the Tahitian and Maori and was mentioned by Captain James Cook in 1779 after finding the plant in the Sandwich Islands of the Pacific. The plant is cultivated in the southern U.S., and there are at least one thousand varieties in the world.

Taro was a staple of the high islands of Polynesia and Hawaii, where it is called *kalo*, and treated with the respect that made it the islands' most important food. The corm of the plant was used for food, with some of the leaves and stalks occasionally cooked as greens. Taro's most important use in Hawaii to this day is in the preparation of **poi**, and it is also made into cakes and biscuits and fried in butter.

TARRAGON (*Artemisia dracunculus*). A Eurasian herb used as a seasoning in soups, sauces, salads, and other foods. The name is from the Greek *drákōntion*, "adderwort," which became in Middle English *tragonia* or *tarchon*, first in English print in 1538.

Although tarragon is used as a seasoning in the U.S., it is little grown here except in home gardens, where it was first reported in 1806. In many home gardens, the variety grown may actually be the "false" or "Russian" tarragon (*A. dracunculoides*), which has a less pungent flavor.

TARTE À LA BOUIE. A Creole or Cajun custard tart. The name is from the French for "boiled tart."

TASSO. A Cajun and Creole smoked, pickled pork that is usually used to flavor **gumbo**, **jambalaya**, and other dishes, dating in print to 1841. The word may derive from Spanish *tasajo*, "dried salt meat," or French *tasser*, "to shrink," because the pickled pork shrinks in size when it is dried. To make tasso, pickled pork is rubbed with a blend of herbs and spices, then air-dried and cold-smoked over an aromatic wood.

TASSY. According to Nathalie Dupree, in *New Southern Cooking* (1987), "Tassies are tiny tarts frequently served at weddings and special occasions which may require a finger-food dessert treat."

TAUTOG (*Tautoga onitis*). Also "blackfish." A fish of the wrasse family (Labridae), found on the Atlantic coast. It is of little commercial value. The name comes from the Narragansett *tautauog* and appeared in print as early as 1635.

TAVERN. A modest establishment that primarily serves alcoholic beverages, though most now serve food, too. The word is from Middle English and dates in print to the fourteenth century. Taverns were among the first structures to be erected in colonial settlements, and by 1714 the city of Boston had thirty-four taverns. The extension of good roads and turnpikes promoted the growth of taverns along those routes. Many offered lodgings, and some served as local post offices.

TAVERN. A loose-meat sandwich, such as a **sloppy joe**, dating in print to 1927.

TEA. A beverage made by steeping the leaves of various shrubs or herbs, but specifically of the shrub *Thea sinensis* (or *Camellia sinensis*). The word derives from the Ancient Chinese *d'a*, as transmuted by the early Dutch traders in that region. The word first appeared in English print in 1598 as "Chaa," in 1655 as "tay," and circa 1665 as "tea."

The first canisters of tea were brought from Bantam, in Java, to England in 1669 by the British East India Co., but they were merely a novelty until 1678, when larger quantities began to be imported. Thomas Twining, who already owned one coffeehouse in London, opened a second, called the Golden Lyon, in 1717 that also featured tea, which soon exceeded coffee in popularity.

Tea drinking caught on quickly in America soon afterwards and became a convenient product for the English to tax heavily. The passage of the Townshend Acts, in 1767—which levied a three-pence-per-pound tax on tea imported to the colonies—followed by the Tea Act, in 1773, which nearly gave the East India Co. a monopoly on the selling of tea, was cause for great dissent and opposition to British policies. Protests erupted in Boston on the night of December 16, 1773, when a group of colonists dressed in Indian outfits boarded three English ships and threw the tea shipments into the harbor. By the 1830s this had became known as the Boston Tea Party. Patriots took to drinking "liberty tea," made from loosestrife leaves, or turned to coffee.

After the Revolutionary War, U.S. shippers established a trade with China, in 1784, and within three years had shipped more than a billion pounds of tea. The British still dominated the tea trade, however, until 1859, when Americans George Huntington Hartford and George Gilman eliminated the wholesaler by buying tea directly from ships and selling it to their customers for one-third the price charged by their competitors. They established the "Great Atlantic and Pacific Tea Co.," later to grow into a chain of supermarkets under the name "A&P."

By the 1860s Americans were enjoying "iced tea," which was popularized at the 1904 Louisiana Purchase Exposition, in St. Louis, by Richard Blechynden, after finding he couldn't sell much hot tea in the summer's heat. Iced tea is especially popular in the South, where it is often presweetened before being iced and where hot tea is often prepared by heating up iced tea for those few who want a cup of the beverage. "Sun tea" is made by putting tea bags in cold water and leaving it to steep in the hot sun for several hours. It is thereafter iced. Instant iced tea was introduced in 1953, under the label White Rose Redi-Tea, by the Seeman Brothers of NYC.

The "tea bag" was first marketed in 1904, by Thomas Sullivan of NYC, and quickly replaced loose tea in the decoction of the leaves. Although few Americans adopted the British custom of having "afternoon tea," first enjoyed in the 1840s, by 1915 young women attended "tea dances" (see **thé dansant**), and afterwards many women invited their friends for "tea parties," often as part of a fashion show at a club.

By the 1930s Americans could buy instant tea, made from processed granules (and often containing sugar) that needed only water from the tap to produce the beverage.

Tea leaves have never been successfully cultivated in the U.S. (more than 50 percent is now imported from China, less than 30 percent each from Argentina and Indonesia), the last significant attempt having been made by C. U. Shepard and the Department of Agriculture at Summerville, South Carolina, from 1890 to 1916.

Herb (or herbal) teas made from sassafras, ginger, and other herbs have long been a part of American history. They received a great boost in popularity during the "natural foods" movement of the 1960s, when such decoctions were thought to be soothing and beneficial to one's health (for more information see **health food**).

The U.S. imports about 520 million pounds of tea annually, with sales of about $12 billion. About 50 percent of Americans drink tea—80 percent of which is iced tea, about 1.9 billion gallons.

Teas are generally named after their type and size of leaf or their region of origin; most are blends of several varieties. Some of the most common teas consumed in the U.S. include:

DARJEELING TEA. A costly Indian tea. The name comes from a Bengali town in northeastern India.

EARL GREY TEA. A blend of China teas flavored with bergamot, whose name derives from Charles Grey, the 2nd Earl Grey, prime minister of the United Kingdom from 1830 to 1834 under William IV. The blend was supposedly presented to Earl Grey and originally made by the Twinings tea company but never trademarked, so that various Earl Grey blends are now made by several tea companies.

ENGLISH BREAKFAST TEA. A blend of Ceylon and India teas whose "brisk" flavor is considered especially bracing at breakfast.

JASMINE TEA. Chinese tea scented with jasmine petals.

ORANGE PEKOE. A blend of Ceylon teas, whose name refers only to the color of the leaf. It is the largest-selling tea in the U.S.

TENDERIZER. A substance used to make meat more tender, usually taken from the enzyme papain, from the papaya plant. As a powder, this substance will partly digest up to three hundred times its weight in lean meat with which it comes in contact, but it is deactivated when heated. Although it is considered no substitute for proper aging, a powdered tenderizer can improve inferior cuts of meat.

TENDERLOIN. The most tender fillet of beef, cut from the hindquarter in the primal short loin. Tenderloin is almost entirely free from fat, marbling, or bone and sometimes is sold as part of the "porterhouse steak." Butchers may also refer to this cut as "filet mignon," "chateaubriand," and "tournedos." "Tenderloin" has been in American print since 1828.

Colloquially, the term has long been associated with sections of cities where vice and graft run rampant, originally referring to the Twenty-ninth Precinct of Manhattan, which extended from Seventh Avenue to Park and Fourth avenues and from Fourteenth to Forty-second streets. According to a deposition given to a committee investigating police corruption in 1894, police captain Alexander S. Williams testified that the term had been picked up by a reporter for the *New York Sun* from an interview with Williams, who, on being transferred to the Twenty-ninth in 1876, had said, "I have been living on rump steak in the Fourth District, I will have some tenderloin now."

TENNESSEE WHISKEY. A straight whiskey that must be made from at least 51 percent of a single grain, usually corn, and made by a sour-mash process similar to that used for bourbon. The term has been in use since at least the 1840s.

The most famous name in Tennessee whiskey is Jack Daniel's, a distillery set up in Lynchburg's Cave Spring Hollow by Jasper Newton "Jack" Daniel. Registered with the government in 1866, Jack Daniel Distillery claims to be the oldest registered distillery in the U.S. Three others make Tennessee Whiskey—George Dickel, Prichard's, and Collier & McKeel. NAFTA (the North American Free Trade Agreement) defines Tennessee whiskey as nothing more than a "straight bourbon whiskey produced in the state of Tennessee."

TEPARY (*Phaseolus acutifolius latifolius*). A New World vine bearing a bean, particularly grown in the Southwest and Mexico. The origin of the word is obscure, mentioned in Spanish and translated into English in 1716. It has been suggested that the name is from a Papago word, *'stāte pāve*, "wild pave."

TEQUILA. A liquor distilled from the Mexican blue **agave** (*Agave tequilana weber*, var. *azul*) plant, which dates in print to 1795, when the King of Spain granted José María Guadalupe Cuervo the first commercial licenses to produce tequila. The name comes from the Tequila district of Mexico, where the best tequila traditionally is made. The word was first printed in English in 1849, and the Bureau of Alcohol, Tobacco and Firearms recognized tequila as a distinctive product of Mexico in September 1975.

The agave plant contains a sweet sap at its heart called *aquamiel* ("honey water"), which is made into a brandy called *vino mezcal*, which is tequila. The fermented and double-distilled spirit is drawn off at 104 to 106 proof and reduced to 80 to 86 proof when shipped to the U.S., most of it unaged. The Mexican government allows a spirit to be labeled "tequila" if it has a minimum of 51 percent agave-derived sugar (the rest may be cane or corn sugar). Tequila at this level of agave sugar is called "white tequila" and is the most common variety used for mixed drinks. Tequila made from 100 percent agave is generally sipped on its own.

Tax records of the town of Tequila show that Don Cenobio Sauza shipped barrels of "mezcal wine" to the U.S. in 1873, and American troops brought it back from their campaign against Pancho Villa in 1916. During a gin shortage in this country in 1944, tequila enjoyed a brief popularity, but it was not until the 1960s, when it became a faddish drink among California university students, that sales of the spirit really grew, especially as the basis for the **margarita** cocktail. By 1990 shipments had soared to 5.1 million nine-liter cases; by 2011, shipments were 12 million cases, for revenues of $1.8 billion.

The "classic" way (sometimes called the "Mexican itch") to drink straight tequila, which required dried crushed worms from the agave plant in a shaker of salt, was described by Green Peyton, in his book *San Antonio: City in the Sun* (1946): "You gulp the Tequila, sprinkle the mummified condiment on the back of your hand, swallow it, suck on a small piece of lime, and then sit down for a while to recover your senses." The "worm" Peyton speaks of is a caterpillar or larva sometimes placed as a gimmick in a bottle of mezcal and drunk down as a show of bravado.

TEQUILA SUNRISE. A cocktail made from tequila, orange juice, and grenadine, dating in print to 1965, although it is claimed that the cocktail was created by Gene Sulit at the Arizona Biltmore hotel, in Phoenix, sometime before World War II. Another claim is that it might have originated at the Agua Caliente Racetrack bar, in Tijuana, Mexico, during the Prohibition era, when Californians would drive there to play the horses and drink. After a night of carousing, the visitors would need a pick-me-up at sunrise, and the addition of one's morning orange juice to tequila seemed appropriate. Yet another claim is that Bobby Lazoff and Billy Rice, of the Trident restaurant, in Sausalito, California, invented the drink in the early 1970s. In 1973, the band the Eagles recorded a song called "Tequila Sunrise."

TEQUILA SUNRISE

In a shaker with crushed ice combine 1 ½ oz. tequila, 1 oz. grenadine, and 3 oz. orange juice. Shake, strain into a wine-glass that has been chilled, and garnish with lime slice.

TEQUILA SUNSET

In a blender with crushed ice combine 1 ½ oz. orange juice, 1 oz. tequila, and 1 ½ oz. pineapple juice. Blend for about 30 sec. Pour, without straining, into a chilled wineglass whose rim has been sugared.

TEXAS TOAST. Toast that is cut one inch or more in thickness, so called because of the popular mythology that everything in Texas is bigger than anywhere else, dating in print to 1999. It may be spread with a cheese topping and baked in the oven.

TEX-MEX. A combination of "Texan" and "Mexican," first printed in 1945, that refers both to a Texan of Mexican heritage and to an adaptation of Mexican dishes by Texas cooks. It is difficult to be precise as to what distinguishes Tex-Mex from true Mexican food, except to say that the variety of the latter is wider and more regional, whereas Tex-Mex is a more standardized cookery popular throughout the state and, now, throughout the entire U.S. The best-known Tex-Mex dishes might be found at a roadside taco stand or at a fine home, and they might include **tacos** (which are more often the hard-shelled variety), **tortillas**, **chalupas**, **burritos**, corn bread, **tamales**, **tostadas**, **nachos**, **enchiladas**, and various forms of chili, the most specific Tex-Mex version being **chili con carne**, or, as Texans call it, "a bowl of red." Central to Tex-Mex cooking is the **chile** pepper, which may go into anything from bread to jelly, and a prominent use of **beef**, especially skirt steak, which is used in the dish called **fajitas**. See **Mexican American food**.

THANKSGIVING. A national American holiday centered on a family feast commemorating the first harvest of the Plymouth Colony, in 1621, after a winter of great suffering and near starvation, followed by a good harvest that autumn.

There had, in fact, been prior days of thanksgiving in the colonies, including when Spanish explorer Francisco Vasquez Coronado celebrated with his men in 1541 in what was to become Texas; in 1561 French Huguenots in what is now Jacksonville, Florida, also held a feast of thanksgiving, as did the settlers in Jamestown, Virginia, in 1610, after the arrival of supply ships from England. But it was the Plymouth Colony's feast that set the stage for the established holiday to follow.

The fifty-three members of the colony had settled the year before, and, in thanks to God for their survival, Governor William Bradford declared a feast be held between the settlers and the Native Americans of the region, led by Chief Massasoit of the Wampanoag tribe, which had signed a treaty with the Pilgrims. It is not known exactly when the feast was held, but it was most probably between September 21 and November 9. (It should be noted, however, that a year before the Pilgrims landed at Plymouth, a band of thirty-eight settlers arrived in Virginia at what is now the Berkeley

Plantation, on the James River, where, on December 4, 1619, Captain John Woodlief ordered that the day of the ship's arrival be "yearly and perpetually kept holy as a day of Thanksgiving to Almighty God.")

Massasoit arrived at the feast, which lasted three days, with ninety braves, bringing many of the dishes. Governor Bradford sent out four men to catch game, but it is not known for sure whether the fowl consumed on the first Thanksgiving included turkey, which has since become the traditional main course of Thanksgiving celebrations. It is known that oysters, cod, eel, corn bread, goose, venison, watercress, leeks, berries, and plums were eaten, all accompanied by sweet wine.

The next recorded Thanksgiving in the Plymouth Colony was on July 30, 1623, at which turkey was definitely served, along with cranberries and pumpkin pie. Thanksgiving was not held as a regular feast, but it became traditional in New England to give thanks on a day set aside for that purpose; Connecticut had its first Thanksgiving in 1649, the Massachusetts Bay Colony in 1669, and by the 1780s the feast day was popular throughout the region. President George Washington proclaimed the first nationally observed Thanksgiving on November 26, 1789.

In her 1827 novel *Northwood*, Mrs. Sarah Joseph Hall (author of the nursery rhyme "Mary Had a Little Lamb") expressed the hope that Thanksgiving would soon become a "national festival…[and] a grand spectacle of moral power and human happiness, such as the world has never witnessed." As editor of Philadelphia's *Godey's Lady's Book*, Hall campaigned as of 1846 to turn Thanksgiving into a national holiday. President Abraham Lincoln declared August 6 the appropriate day in 1863 but a few months later changed the date to the fourth Thursday of November. This tradition was maintained until 1939, when president Franklin D. Roosevelt changed the date to the third Thursday in November, in an effort to stimulate sales in retail stores by heralding the advent of the Christmas season a week earlier. In December 1941, Congress changed it back again to the fourth Thursday in November.

The traditional Thanksgiving meal for most Americans is eaten at home (45 percent at one's own, 42 percent at someone else's) and includes many of the same dishes enjoyed at the first Thanksgiving—the turkey having been well established as the feast's main course by the 1820s.

THÉ DANSANT. A term from the French, meaning "tea dance," to describe an afternoon tea with dancing, in print since 1819 and a fad in American hotels from 1914 to 1916. The practice originated in England, where the dances were often charity affairs, but in the U.S., more often than not, these became what restaurateur George Rector called "booze dansants," because liquor and cocktails were served in teacups.

THOMPSON SEEDLESS. A white vinifera grape used as a blending grape in sparkling wine and brandy, as well as a popular table grape. It was introduced in 1872 by farmer William Thompson, of Yuba City, California, and it became the most widely planted variety of grape in the state.

THOUSAND ISLANDS DRESSING. Also "Thousand Island" and "1000 Island." A salad dressing based on **Russian dressing**, with various additions of pickles, cream, green peppers, and other seasonings. The name dates in print to 1920 and probably derives from the place where the dressing may have first been concocted, the Thousand Islands in the St. Lawrence River, which cuts between New York and Ontario. According to Jane and Michael Stern, in *The Lexicon of Real American Food*, cookbook writer May Irwin, visiting friends in upstate New York, sampled the condiment made by Sophia LaLonde and gave the recipe to George Boldt, the owner of the Waldorf-Astoria Hotel in NYC, whose maître d', Oscar Tschirky, popularized it there.

It has also been suggested that the bits and pieces of seasonings and ingredients resemble a multitude of islands in a sea of dressing.

THOUSAND ISLANDS DRESSING

Fold 1 qt. mayonnaise into 1 qt. chili sauce, add 1 chopped pimiento, 5 chopped hard-boiled eggs, 1 pt. chopped sweet pickles, and 2 chopped green peppers. Mix well.

THREE SHEETS IN THE WIND. Also "three sheets to the wind." An expression meaning "drunk." It derives from a sailor's tacking of the sails by means of a chain or rope called a "sheet," attached to the lower corner of the sail. If the sail fluttered freely, it was said to be "in the wind." If three sheets were thus free, the sail would not be under control, causing the ship to weave and sway in the wind. The phrase "three sheets" dates in print to 1857; "sheet in the wind" to 1862.

THUMBPRINT COOKIE. A cookie with a depressed center filled with jam or another sweet filling, dating in print to 1950.

THYME. Any of a variety of herbs grown in New England in the genus *Thymus*, of the mint family, especially the "garden thyme" or "black thyme" (*T. vulgaris*), the "lemon thyme" (*T. citriodorus*), and the "wild thyme" (*T. serpyllum*). The word is from the Greek *thymon*, first entering English print circa 1440. Thyme is used as a seasoning in soups, sauces, salads, and other dishes. It is customarily added to chowder.

TI. Polynesian name for the tropical plant *Cordyline terminalis*, dating in print to 1825, whose leathery leaves are used to steam foods in the **imu** pit.

TILAPIA. Also "St. Peter's fish." Any of a variety of cichlids from the genus *Tilapia*, from African waters. The origins of the word are New Latin, in English print since 1849. In recent years it has become an important food fish in the American market, and aquaculturists have high hopes that the species can be successfully farmed. Market varieties are usually about ten to twenty ounces in weight and are usually broiled, steamed, or sautéed. Per capita U.S. consumption of tilapia is 1.5 pounds annually.

TILEFISH. Any of a variety of marine fish in the family Branchiostegidae, with four species in the U.S. The name is actually short for a species known in taxonomic Latin as *Lopholatilus chamaeleonticeps*, although the tile-like spots on the fish probably also influenced the name, which first appeared in print in 1849. This species is found from the Chesapeake Bay to Maine and was first noted off the New England coast in May 1879. In 1882, the fish had totally disappeared, possibly as a result of a

climatic change in the water temperature, but it came back in abundance five years later and is readily available at market today. The main species of culinary interest include the common tilefish named above, the "blackline tilefish" (*Caulolatilus cyanops*), the "sand tilefish" (*Malacanthus plumieri*), and the "ocean whitefish" (*C. princeps*). U.S. commercial landings of tilefish totaled 3.173 million pounds in 2010, valued at $7.677 million.

TIPSINNA. A breadroot, *Pediomelum esculentum*, consumed by Northwest Coast Indians, first in print in 1853.

TIPSY. Also "tipsy parson" in the South. A sponge cake spread with almonds, soaked in sherry, and served with custard, in print since 1570. It was a dish of the late nineteenth century. The name apparently refers to the alcohol content, which if taken in large doses would make the imbiber "tipsy" or slightly drunk.

TIPSY

Moisten a sponge cake with 1 c. sherry. Beat 3 egg yolks until light yellow and stir in 2 c. milk. In a saucepan heat the liquid until it coats the spoon and becomes a custard. Pour over the sponge cake. Sprinkle with ½ c. blanched almonds. Whip 3 egg whites with 2 T. powdered sugar, then blend in 1 c. cream and ¼ c. candied fruit. Pour over the sponge cake and spoon a little currant jelly in the center.

TISWIN. A fermented beverage made by the Apache Indians, dating in print to 1875. The name comes from the Spanish *tesquino*, derived from Cáhita, the language spoken by the Yaqui and Maya Indians of Sonora, Mexico. Is also spelled *tiswino* or *tesquino* by the New Mexican Indians. Tiswin is made by fermenting dried corn with water, **piloncillo** cones of brown sugar, and spices such as cinnamon and orange peel.

TOASTED RAVIOLI. A St. Louis specialty of meat-filled pasta dough that is deep-fried golden brown. Italian ravioli are boiled and served with a sauce, but toasted ravioli was supposedly first made in the 1930s at a St. Louis restaurant named Angelo Oldani's, when a German employee named Fritz accidentally threw freshly made ravioli into a pan of boiling oil. Owner Oldani tried to salvage them, brushed them with grated cheese, and served them to his customers, who loved them. Other claims from St. Louis chefs have also been made.

TOASTED RAVIOLI

In a shallow pan sprinkle a thin layer of bread crumbs. Dip meat ravioli into milk, place on top of the crumbs, dust the tops of the ravioli with more bread crumbs, and pat down to coat evenly. Heat oil to 375° and fry ravioli for about 3–4 min., until golden brown. Drain, sprinkle with Parmesan cheese, and serve plain or with tomato sauce or melted butter.

TODDY. Also "hot toddy." Although there are many variations, a toddy is usually a heated mug of whiskey flavored with citrus fruits and spices. The word, dating in print to 1786, in a poem by Robert Burns, comes from the Hindi *tāri*, for the fermented or fresh sap of a palm tree, and the English traders picked up the word in India. Originally the drink was served cold, but cold days at sea made the idea of a hot toddy more convivial on board.

TODDY

Dissolve 1 lump of sugar in a mug half-filled with boiling water and add 1 ½ oz. rum or whiskey, 2 cloves, a stick of cinnamon, and lemon rind.

TOGUE. A Maine term for a large lake trout, *Salvelinus namaycush*, first noted in print in 1839. The name is from the Canadian French, via Algonquian.

TOGUS. Also "togus bread." A New England dish of the nineteenth century made from milk, cornmeal, and molasses, whose name possibly derives from an Indian word, dating in American print to 1880. *The Pentucket Housewife* (1882) lists the ingredients as three cups milk, one cup sour milk, three cups cornmeal, one cup flour, one half-cup molasses, and one teaspoon baking soda. The dish is steamed for three hours and eaten with butter and sugar.

TOLL HOUSE COOKIE. A cookie made from flour, semisweet chocolate chips, brown sugar, and nuts. It is by far the most popular of American cookies. In 1930, Mrs. Ruth Wakefield and her husband purchased a 1709 tollhouse on the outskirts of Whitman, Massachusetts, a halfway point for travelers between Boston and New Bedford. Mrs. Wakefield turned the house into the Toll House Inn, and one day in her kitchen, while experimenting with an old American recipe for "Butter Drop-Do" cookies, she happened to cut up a bar of Nestlé semisweet chocolate into small chips and added them to the batter. Instead of melting, as she had expected, the chocolate bits retained their texture in the baking and gave the cookie a flavor that would soon make her famous. The Toll House cookie was born (Wakefield originally called it the "chocolate crunch cookie" or "chocolate crispies"), and, after the recipe appeared in a Boston newspaper in 1937, people began writing to her for the recipe. Sales of Nestlé's chocolate bar increased dramatically, and, with Wakefield's permission, the Nestlé Co. began printing the recipe on its semisweet chocolate-bar wrappers. In 1939, it began packaging bits of uniformly shaped chocolate chips called "Nestlé Semi-Sweet Chocolate Morsels." Today Nestlé produces 250 million morsels a day in three factories, and it has been estimated that half the cookies baked at home in America are chocolate chip, making them as famous as the proverbial apple pie. In fact, after Canadian diplomats had secretly helped six Americans escape from Iran during the hostage crisis of 1980, the grateful people of America sent a large bag of chocolate-chip cookies to the Canadian embassy in Washington. The recipe below is still printed on the Nestlé Semi-Sweet Chocolate Morsels package.

A "blondie" is a bar cookie of the same texture, made with the same dough (and no chocolate), in print since 1943.

TOLL HOUSE COOKIES

Combine in a bowl 2 ¼ c. unsifted flour, 1 t. baking soda, and 1 t. salt. In another bowl combine 1 c. butter, ¾ c. sugar, ¾ c. brown sugar, and 1 t. vanilla extract. Beat until creamy, then add 2 eggs. Gradually add the flour mixture and blend in well. Stir in 12 oz. Nestlé semisweet chocolate morsels (2 c.) and 1 c. chopped nuts. Drop by rounded teaspoons onto ungreased cookie sheet. Bake in and oven preheated to 375° for 8 to 10 min. Makes 100 2-in. cookies.

BLONDIES

A variation on the shape of Toll House cookies, achieved by spreading the dough into a greased 15-by-10-in. baking pan. Bake at 375° for 20 min., then cut into thirty-five 2-in. squares.

TOM AND JERRY. A beverage made from eggs, sugar, brandy or bourbon, and whiskey, topped with milk or boiling water. Some believe the name comes from *Pierce Egan's Life in London, or the Day and Night Scenes of Jerry Hawthorne, Esq., and his Elegant Friend Corinthian Tom* (1821), which did help establish "Tom-and-Jerrying" as a phrase connoting rowdy, drunken behavior, and a "Tom and Jerry shop" was a low beer-house of the day. But the first printed reference to the drink itself came in 1862, when American bartender "Professor" Jerry Thomas gave the first recipe for a Tom and Jerry in his *How to Mix Drinks: or, The Bon Vivant's Companion*, and Thomas has been credited with first serving the drink at St. Louis's Planter's Hotel. Thomas is said to have refused to make the drink in warm weather or to serve it before the first snowfall.

"Tom and Jerry mugs" were ceramic cups with handles.

TOM AND JERRY

Separate 6 eggs. Beat ¼ lb. sugar into yolks until the mixture is light yellow, then pour in 2 oz. whiskey. Beat egg whites until stiff and fold into mixture. Ladle into mugs, add 2 oz. brandy or bourbon to each, and fill with boiling milk or water. Stir and sprinkle on nutmeg and a dash of brandy, if desired.

TOMATILLO. A berry of the family Physalis that resembles a small unripe tomato. It is known under various names in Mexico—*tomate verde*, *tomate de cáscara*, and *fresadilla*—and canned in the U.S. as "tomatito verde" and "peeled green tomato." (There is also a shrub in Chile, of the genus *Solanaceous*, called "tomatillo.") When ripe, tomatillos turn yellow, but the green fruit is preferred for coloring sauces. The term has been in English print since about 1897.

TOMATO. The fleshy, juicy, usually bright red fruit of the plant *Lycopersicon esculentum*. Tomatoes are used in a wide variety of ways—including fresh in salads, in sauces, as juice, and in other preparations. The word is from the Nahuatl *tomatl* and first appeared in English print in 1604, though then the tomato was also referred to as a "love apple." (The Italian name for the fruit is *pomodoro*, "golden apple," because the first examples to reach Europe were yellow varieties.)

The tomato is probably native to Peru and Ecuador, but it was widely established throughout Central America by the time the Spanish arrived, in the early sixteenth century. Because the tomato is taxonomically a member of the nightshade family, Solanaceae, which includes deadly nightshade, Europeans approached the idea of eating the fruit with extreme caution. The Spaniards had brought the tomato back to their own country early in the century, and from there to Italy (though some authorities posit that the fruit may have gotten to Italy via Neapolitan sailors). Pietro Andrea Mattioli's 1544 translation of a botany text described the tomato as a kind of eggplant, but he later changed his description to "*mala insana*," "unhealthy apple." Indeed, most Europeans continued to believe the tomato was poisonous—or at the very least an exotic fruit or vegetable to be cooked cautiously and eaten sparingly.

Tomatoes were not cultivated in North America until the 1700s, and then only in home gardens. Thomas Jefferson was raising tomatoes by 1782 and noted that others in Virginia grew them for private consumption. Nevertheless, most people of that century paid little heed to tomatoes, and only in the next century did they make their way into American cookbooks, always with instructions that they be cooked for at least three hours or else, as Eliza Leslie wrote in her *Directions for Cookery* (1848), they "will not lose their raw taste." Nineteenth-century cooks used them in **ketchups** or in sauces but did not recommend eating them raw. Waverley Root, in *Food* (1980), notes that "the Thorbun seed catalog gave directions for growing tomatoes in 1817, but offered only one variety; by 1881 it would be selling thirty-one." By 1865 northern markets offered tomatoes year-round. In 1893, the Supreme Court decreed that, for trade purposes, the tomato could be classified as a vegetable, though it is in reality a fruit.

Tomato sauces became popular with the arrival of Italian immigrants in the late nineteenth and early twentieth centuries, and after 1900 the tomato itself finally gained credibility as a flavorful, healthy food, aided by southern farmers who began propagating the fruit on a widespread basis. By 1929 Americans were eating thirty-six pounds of tomatoes per capita per year. The tomato has become the most widely planted of all home-garden fruits or vegetables and is now grown in every state in the union.

Although fresh tomatoes are grown in every state, market varieties are most likely to come from Florida, California, New Jersey, Texas, or Alabama, with the principal varieties being Fireball, Big Boy, Manapal, Floradel, and Pinkshipper.

Tomatoes grown primarily for canning are raised in California and include the Bouncer, New Yorker, Red Top, Campbell 1327, and San Marzano. Homegrown varieties include the Red Cherry, Bonney Best, Marglobe, Jubilee, Rutgers, and Beefsteak.

Many Americans who have grown their own tomatoes or who remember the tomatoes of other decades believe that the various hybrids and commercially cultivated tomatoes marketed today have lost a great deal of their natural flavor in return for easy availability on a year-round basis and a high yield. As John L. and Karen Hess observed in *The Taste of America* (1977):

More and more of the produce grown in those far-off factories of the soil is harvested by machine. It is bred for rough handling, which it gets. A chemical is sprayed on trees to force all the fruit to "ripen"—that is, change color—at once, in time for a monster harvester to strike the tree and catch the fruit in its canvas maw. Tomatoes are picked hard green and gassed with ethylene in trucks or in chambers at the market, whereupon they turn a sort of neon red. Of course, they taste like nothing at all, but the taste of real tomatoes has so far faded from memory that, even for local markets, farmers now pick tomatoes that are just turning pink. This avoids the spoilage that occurred when they used to pick tomatoes red-ripe.

Industry terms for the ripening process of tomatoes include "green" (the surface of the tomato is completely green); "breakers" (a break in the color from green to yellow-pink or red on 10 percent of the surface); "turning"

(at least 10 but not more than 30 percent has changed color); and "pink" (30 to 60 percent has changed color). "Vine ripened" actually means that the tomato was harvested when it was turning pink, although greenhouse-grown tomatoes may well be shipped red. Tomatoes are also one of the most successful crops grown hydroponically. U.S. per capita consumption of tomatoes in 1997 was 16.1 pounds.

Green tomatoes are particularly popular in the South and the Midwest, where they are often fried or made into relishes or "green tomato pie."

GREEN TOMATO PIE

Chop up 8 peeled green tomatoes and place in a saucepan with 2 T. cider vinegar and 2 T. butter and cook on medium heat about 10 min. In a bowl combine 1 c. sugar, 2 T. cornstarch, and ½ t. cinnamon, then add to tomato mixture. Heat through, stirring, remove from heat, and pour into a pie crust. Layer over a top crust, slash the pastry a few times to release steam, and bake at 425° for 10 min. Reduce heat to 350° and bake for another 20 min. or until the crust is light brown.

TOM COLLINS. A cocktail made with gin, citrus juice, and soda water, customarily served in a tall glass called a "Tom Collins glass" or "Collins glass." The drink is supposedly named after the bartender who created it, though the moment of creation is highly speculative. The first printed reference was in 1888, in a bartender's manual; H. L. Mencken, in *The American Language* (1945), guessed that it came out of the post–Civil War era. The original Tom Collins was supposedly made with Old Tom gin, which was slightly sweet, but another drink, the "John Collins," was customarily made with Holland gin, with its more pronounced, aromatic flavor. The problem is that the first printed reference to a John Collins was in 1865, and, suggests the *OED*, it may be of American origins. Mencken writes of the John Collins, "Who John Collins was I do not know. Sidney J. Baker, author of *Popular Dictionary of Australian Slang* (1941), told me that the John Collins was known in Australia as long ago as 1865, but he does not list it in his dictionary." The "fizz" is a similar drink made with crushed ice in the blend and dates back to at least the 1860s.

Whichever cocktail came first, American bartenders at the beginning of the twentieth century mixed both, making a John Collins with dry London gin and a Tom Collins with Old Tom gin. This latter gin gradually disappeared from the American market, however, and the dry London gin replaced it. After a while, both drinks went by the name Tom Collins, and today the cocktail is made with dry gin.

Still later, a carbonated citrus soda appeared, called "Tom Collins mix," which most bartenders use instead of fresh citrus juice and sugar.

TOM COLLINS

In a glass with ice cubes stir 1 T. sugar syrup, the juice of 1 lemon, and 3–4 oz. gin. Fill glass with soda water or seltzer.

TOM FULLER. A dish of cooked corn, peas, beans, and dried venison that is similar to succotash. It was originally a Native American dish of the Mississippi region, called *sofkee*. The word derives from Choctaw *tafula*, "hominy," appearing in American print as of 1844.

TOM THUMB. A large sausage, sometimes made with the pig's intestine, dried, smoked, or boiled, dating in print to 1830. The name may derive from the English folktale *The History of Tom Thumb* (1621), about a child as big as a man's thumb whose adventures include being swallowed by a cow.

TORTILLA. A flat, unleavened bread made of cornmeal or white flour cooked on a griddle and used in a variety of dishes of Mexican origin, including as an accompaniment to a meal, in a casserole, or as a sandwich-like holder for other foods. Tortillas are a staple of **Mexican American** and **Tex-Mex** cookery. The word comes from the Spanish American diminutive for the Spanish *torta*, "round cake." (In Spain, the *tortilla española* is more like an omelet.) The word was first printed in English in 1699.

In the U.S., tortillas are usually bought in groceries and are rarely made at home, except in the Southwest. In Arizona, where a great deal of wheat is grown, they are often made from white flour and are called *tortillas*

de harina de trigo, as opposed to those made with corn **masa**, *tortillas de masa harina*. When a large flour tortilla is filled with meat, vegetables, or beans and rolled, it is called a **burrito**, which can be deep-fried to make a **chimichanga**. A **taco** is a smaller corn tortilla filled with meats and vegetables and folded over, often fried in hot lard, while an **enchilada** is somewhat more elaborate, smothered in **chile** sauce and cheese as well as other ingredients and baked. Tortillas now outsell bagels and English muffins in the U.S.

"Tortilla soup" is a southwestern dish made with chicken soup and seasonings, with a base of fried tortilla strips. "Tortilla chips" (or "taco chips") are cut-up fried pieces of tortilla, the first commercial example being "Doritos," which appeared in 1966 and are now produced by Frito-Lay Inc.

TORTILLA CHIP

Cut corn tortillas into wedges, fry in hot oil, drain, and sprinkle with salt and, if desired, minced garlic. Serve with guacamole and other appetizer dips or sauces.

TORTILLA SOUP

In a large pot heat 4 T. corn oil. Sauté 1 chopped large onion and 3 cloves chopped garlic for about 1 min. Cut 4 tortillas into ½-in. strips and fry in oil until crisp. Pour in 8 c. chicken broth, add 4 skinned, seeded, chopped tomatoes, ½ t. salt, ¼ t. black pepper, ¼ t. ground cumin, ¼ c. chopped cilantro, and 1 seeded jalapeño or serrano chile pepper. Bring to a boil and simmer for about 20–30 min. Serve in bowls with garnishes of shredded Monterey Jack cheese and more fried tortilla strips. Serves 6.

TORTONI. Also "biscuit tortoni." An Italian American ice cream with crushed almonds or macaroons sprinkled on top, dating in print, as "Tortoni pudding," to 1911. The confection originated in the eighteenth century, at the Café Napolitain, in Paris, and was named after the owner, Tortoni. After the arrival of Italian immigrants in NYC, the ice cream became featured in every Italian American restaurant (and often called "biscuit tortoni").

Tortoni can be made simply by mixing finely chopped almonds into vanilla ice cream and topping the cup with more chopped almonds before freezing. Macaroons may be substituted for the almonds.

TOSTADA. Also "tostado." A deep-fried flat corn tortilla popular in **Mexican American** and **Tex-Mex** cooking, where they are usually topped with beans, cheese, and meats. The name is from the Spanish for "toasted" and first appeared in English print in 1934.

TOUGH JACK. A kind of molasses candy, dating in print to 1957.

TRADE WHISKEY. Whiskey traded to the Indians in the nineteenth century. The term later became associated with any cheap, inferior spirit.

TRANSPARENT PIE. Also "transparent pudding." A nineteenth-century midwestern custard-style dessert made with a smooth filling, without nuts or fruits, giving the pie a semitranslucent appearance. It dates in print to 1786.

TRANSPARENT PIE

Beat 3 eggs until frothy, then add 2 T. sugar and 1 ½ c. heavy cream until well blended. Add 3 T. fruit jelly and stir in the zest of one lemon and 1 T. lemon juice. Pour the filling into a pastry crust and bake at 350° for 30–35 min., until set. Let cool on rack.

TRAPPERS' BUTTER. Trappers' term for bone marrow of a killed animal, which was often made into a thickened broth.

TRASH FISH. A fishermen's term, dating in print to 1940, for any fish that has no commercial value. The species of such fish may change whenever one comes into favor and another goes out. Trash fish are usually sold for animal fodder or manufactured products.

TREASURE CAVE. A blue-veined cheese, also called "Minnesota Blue," ripened in sandstone caves. It is produced by the company Caves of Faribault, in Faribault, Minnesota.

TRENTON CRACKER. A light, puffy round cracker made from wheat flour, vegetable shortening, salt, and yeast. It is a traditional eastern cracker used in oyster stews.

The Trenton cracker was first made in 1848, by Adam and John Exton, two English immigrants who created the item in their Trenton, New Jersey, bakery. They called it the "Exton Oyster and Butter Cracker and Wine Scroll Biscuit." Within a short time, more than thirty competitors were making imitations, including Ezekiel Pullen, owner of the Pullen Cracker Co., in Trenton, New Jersey. This company was later sold and in 1887 became the Original Trenton Cracker Co., which in 1962 bought exclusive rights to the Exton products. Today the crackers are stamped before baking with the company's initials, "O.T.C.," which is a trademark of the company, now located in Lambertville, New Jersey.

The crackers are still served in chowders and stews or eaten buttered with a small bit of horseradish. They are called "Trentons" for short.

TREVALLY. Any of a variety of six Pacific fish in the genus *Caranx*, but especially *C. georgianus*. The origins of its name are obscure, dating in print to 1883. In Hawaii, the fish is known as the *ulua*.

TRIGGERFISH. Also "leatherjacket." Any of a variety of fishes of the family Balistidae that is found in Atlantic waters and is enjoyed in the South as fillets. Triggerfish have a second, "trigger" spine that releases the first spine—hence the name, first in print in 1814.

TRIPE. The stomach of a cow, sheep, or pig. Its name is from the Old French and first appeared in English circa 1300.

Owing to its perishable nature and the difficulty of cleaning it, tripe has never been a popular meat with most Americans, although it has some ethnic interest among Mediterranean and Chinese immigrants in this country, as well as Mexican Americans, who use it to make *menudo* stew. The recipe of note, given below, was developed at Boston's Parker House Hotel.

TRIPE

Boil a piece of tripe (about 8 oz.) until tender, cool, then soak in milk for 2 hr. Sprinkle with 2 T. white wine, 1 T. oil, ½ c. bread crumbs, 1 t. vinegar, a dash of paprika, and salt, pepper, and thyme to taste. Broil until golden brown. Serve with a mustard sauce made by combining 1 c. demiglace, 2 t. Dijon mustard, 1 oz. white wine, ½ oz. white vinegar, 1 small shallot finely minced, peppercorns, and 2 T. heavy cream.

TROTTER, CHARLIE H. (1959–). Chef, restaurateur, author, media personality.

At a seminal point in the development of modern fine dining in America, Charlie Trotter brought his own sensibility and perfectionism to his namesake restaurant in Chicago, becoming one of the most respected chefs in the U.S. and an inspiration to a generation of chefs who later distinguished themselves.

Born in Chicago, Trotter earned a degree in political science at the University of Wisconsin at Madison and then began cooking at restaurants in Chicago, San Francisco, Florida, and Europe. In 1987, he opened Charlie Trotter's, in Chicago, immediately winning accolades, including a place on *Esquire's* Best New Restaurants of the Year, for his innovative blend of French nouvelle cuisine with global influences and an American spirit. Charlie Trotter's featured formal, multi-course meals served by a staff who would describe each dish; his 26,000-bottle wine list won many awards for its breadth and depth; in 2010, the restaurant was given two Michelin stars.

Reservations were for many years difficult to come by on short notice, and his kitchen was a training ground for chefs who regarded Trotter as a taskmaster for perfectionism. "On our worst day," said Trotter, "we're still in the top three restaurants in America." His popularity inspired him to institute "Dinner in Your Home," in which he would cook for the highest bidder in a charity auction, with one meal going for $180,000. He also invite a homeless person to dine at his restaurant once a week.

Trotter became one of the most respected celebrity chefs of the 1990s. He opened two restaurants, on separate occasions, in Las Vegas, winning excellent reviews, but both closed. In 2004, he also ran C, a seafood restaurant in Los Cabos, Mexico, which has since closed. Other plans for expansion fell through, including restaurants to be located in London and NYC.

In 1999, Trotter hosted *The Kitchen Sessions with Charlie Trotter* on PBS and made a cameo appearance playing himself in the film *My Best Friend's Wedding* (1997).

His books include *Charlie Trotter's* (1994), *Charlie Trotter's Vegetables* (1996), *Charlie Trotter's Seafood* (1997), *Gourmet Cooking for Dummies* (1997), *Charlie Trotter Cooks at Home* (2000), and *Homecooking with Charlie Trotter* (2009).

Upon announcing that after twenty-five years he would close his restaurant on August 31, 2012, to pursue a master's degree, Trotter said, "Life's too short. You can't do the same thing for too long or your head will explode." The restaurant's last dinner, August 31, for three hundred guests, was booked months in advance and covered as an international media event. The city of Chicago named a public street Charlie Trotter Way in advance of the dinner.

Trotter founded the philanthropic Charlie Trotter Culinary Education Foundation and was awarded the Humanitarian of the Year award in 2005 by the International Association of Culinary Professionals. He has earned ten **James Beard Foundation** awards.

TROUT. Any of a variety of fishes of the genera *Salvelinus* and *Salmo*, cultured throughout the world both for sport and for food. The name derives from the Latin *tructus*, first in English print circa 1050.

As did sturgeon and salmon in the colonial era, trout became an everyday food for the first settlers, and there seemed little reason to imitate the efforts of the French to propagate fish commercially, which culminated in 1852 with the construction of the first public-owned trout hatchery. American anglers merely had to dip their lines in the rivers and come up with large, beautiful fish perfect for pan-frying on the spot; America's first great fishing author, Frank Forester, complained in his *Fish and Fishing* (1849) that Americans did not take their fly-fishing with all due seriousness. A hatchery was set up in 1864 at Mumford, New York, by Seth Green, for the days when anglers filled their baskets with forty trout in an afternoon were almost over. When the end came—as a result of industrial pollution and invasion of the trout streams, as well as overfishing—it came quickly, and after the Civil War, the trout population decreased at a depressing rate. It was the introduction of the "German brown trout" (*Salmo trutta*) to North America in 1883, and Seth Green's stocking of his own hatcheries with that fish in 1886, that caused a comeback of the trout in America, and before long the native rainbow trout (*S. gairdneri*) was being introduced as far away as New Zealand and South Africa.

Protective measures also helped restore the trout populations, and, since American anglers had by then become serious about their sport, efforts were made to maintain the balance of nature in trout streams. U.S. commercial landings of trout totaled only 303,000 pounds in 1997.

Some of the finest literature on trout has come from American authors—from specialists like George Michel Lucien La Branche, Zebulon Southard, Arthur Flick, Sparse Grey Hackle, and Ernest Schwiebert to outdoorsmen like Zane Grey (who wrote mostly fishing books in his later life), John Steinbeck, and Ernest Hemingway, whose short story "Big Two-Hearted River" is a classic for its description of the challenge and beauty of the sport.

The trout species of the most culinary interest include: the "brook trout" (*Salvelinus fontinalis*), also called a "brookie" and other names, and the "brown trout" (*Salmop trutta morpha fario* and *S. trutta morpha lacustris*) both found in nearly every state in the union; the "cutthroat trout" (*Salmo clarki*), so called because of slash marks on the throat; the **Dolly Varden** (*Salvelinus malma*); the "golden trout" (*Salmo aquabonita*); the "lake trout" (*Salvelinus namaycush*), in Maine called the **togue** or the "mackinaw" (possibly from its coloring, which resembles a plaid mackinaw coat or cloth, which itself refers to the island of Mackinac, in Michigan) or the "gray trout" (in Canada); "salmon trout," and the "rainbow trout."

Trout in America is prepared in a variety of ways, from simple pan-frying or grilling to French recipes such as *amandine* (with almonds) and *meunière* (with browned butter) to the Swiss *truite au bleu*, by which a freshly caught trout is cooked in a court bouillon that turns the skin blue.

TRUCK FARM. Also "truck garden." Garden produce or a garden producing vegetables intended for sale in the market. Originally the word "truck," derived from an Old French word, *trogue*, for "barter," referred to the vegetables themselves. By the eighteenth century in America, people referred to "market truck," dating in print to 1784, meaning fresh produce brought to the market, while "truck garden" dates to 1855 and "truck farm" to 1866.

Truck farms became very important to the agricultural economy of the South, so that seasonal crops decreased small farmers' dependency on cash crops and agribusiness.

Much later, when motorized trucks began carrying fresh produce to city markets, it was quite natural for "truck farm" to take on a double meaning, both for the vegetables themselves and for the means of conveyance.

TRUFFLE. Any of a variety of subterranean ascomycetous fungi in the genus *Tuber*, from Middle French. The term has been in English print since 1591.

Truffles have long been a delicacy in Europe, where they are found by specially trained dogs and pigs under oak trees. The most famous truffles are the black variety (*T. melanosporum*), grown in France's Périgord region, and it is this truffle that American scientists have experimented with growing in a laboratory, which was first successfully done by Dr. Moshe Shifrine and Dr. Randy Dorian, in Woodland, California, in the late 1980s.

"Chocolate truffles" are chocolate candies (sometimes with a filling of chocolate ganache or other flavors) molded and dusted with powdered chocolate to look like black truffles.

TUCKAHOE. A starchy root vegetable of the Arum family (Araceae), chiefly *Peltandra virginica*, commonly used in colonial times as a flour additive or as a flour itself. The term dates in print to 1612, derived from a Virginia Native American word (*tockawoughe*), and came to have a pejorative reference to poor Virginians who could not afford wheat flour, although tuckahoe was also used as a starch in puddings and blancmange.

TUNA. Also "tuna fish." Any of a variety of marine fishes of the genus *Thunnus*, although the name is also applied to some related species. The name is derived from the

Latin *thunnus* and is a variation on the English name for the fish, "tunny." The *OED* says tuna is "American Spanish" and a "name in California for the tunny." The word dates in print to 1881.

The tuna is a member of the mackerel family (Scombridae), with six species available at market in the U.S., where most of the catch has been from Pacific waters. Not until 1960 were significant commercial catches made in the Atlantic, and the industry continues to be centered in California.

The most important species for culinary interest include: the "albacore" (*T. alalunga*), called "*tombo*" in Hawaii, the most desirable tuna for the canning industry, which labels its product "white-meat tuna"; the "bluefin tuna" (*T. thynnus*), the largest tuna, weighing up to sixteen hundred pounds; the "bonito" (*Sarda sarda* in the Atlantic and *S. chiliensis* in the Pacific), which cannot legally be labeled "tuna" and must be put in brine before cooking (its name is from the Spanish for "beautiful"); the "false albacore" (*Euthynnus alletteratus*), also called the "little tunny" or "bonito"; the "kawakawa" (*E. yaito*); the "skipjack tuna" (*E. pelamis*), also called "oceanic bonito," "watermelon," "oceanic skipjack," "Arctic bonito," and, in Hawaii, *aku*; and the "yellowfin tuna" (*T. albacares*), which in Hawaii is called "ahi" and which is the principal fish of the California tuna industry.

Canned tuna is designated as "solid" or "fancy" (with several large pieces), "chunk" (smaller pieces), and "flaked" or "grated." Tuna may be canned in oil or water and may be seasoned. The FDA standards of identity require that "white" tuna must be limited to albacore; "light," any tuna not darker than the Munsell color value 5.3; "dark," all tuna darker than the value 5.3. "Blended" applies to a blend of tuna flakes.

Americans have, since the 1980s, eaten an increasing amount of fresh tuna—3.6 pounds per capita, with landings of 531 million pounds in 2010, for sales of $382.8 million. It is usually grilled or sautéed as steaks, but most often it is served from a can as a filling for a tuna-fish sandwich or a tuna-fish salad, in both cases mixed with mayonnaise. A "tuna melt" is a grilled sandwich made with tuna fish and American cheese. The "tuna casserole" has long been a staple of the American dinner table, and the recipe given by the Campbell's Soup Co. on the back of its cans is considered a "classic."

TUNA CASSEROLE

In a casserole mix 1 can Campbell's Condensed Cream of Celery Soup with ½ c. milk. Add 1 c. peas, 2 T. chopped pimiento, and two 7-oz. cans drained, flaked tuna. Add 2 c. cooked egg noodles, if desired. Bake for 25 minutes at 425° until hot. In a saucepan combine 1 T. butter or margarine and 2 T. bread crumbs and sauté until brown. Top casserole with bread crumbs and bake for 5 more minutes.

TURKEY (*Meleagris gallopavo*). A large native North American game bird widely domesticated here and abroad. With its brownish feathers and wattled head and neck, the turkey is certainly an unattractive fowl, but its associations with colonial American history and its indigenous character throughout the U.S. caused Benjamin Franklin to remark, "I wish the Bald Eagle had not been chosen as the representation of our country....The turkey is...a much more respectable bird, and withal a true original native of America."

The turkey proliferated throughout Mexico, the Southwest, and the East. The Plains Indians and the New England tribes caught the bird in the wild with little trouble, whereas the Aztecs of Mexico, the Anasazi, and others of the Southwest had domesticated the birds very early so that by the time the Spaniards arrived in Mexico, the turkey was a staple part of the Native American diet.

It is not known who first brought the turkey back to Europe (according to Waverley Root, there is a turkey-like bird woven into the Bayeux Tapestry of 1087), but by the first quarter of the sixteenth century, Spanish explorers had brought the bird home. One English chronicler of the seventeenth century noted that turkeys were brought to England around 1524, giving rise to the ditty "Turkeys, Carps, Hoppes, Piccarell, and Beer, Came into England in one year." By 1570 Englishman Thomas Tusser could vouch that the domesticated turkey already formed part of the common farmer's "Christmas husbandlie fare," and across the channel the bird was highly esteemed.

It is not entirely clear how the bird got its name, dating in print to 1577 as "Turkicockes." The *American Heritage Cookbook* suggests the word is a corruption of *furkee*, a Native American name for the bird. But most authorities believe the name was the result of the bird's being confused with the guinea fowl, which the Portuguese had brought to Europe from Guinea, through the dominion of Turkey, so that both birds were called "turkeys" in the sixteenth century. Even after the confusion was cleared up and the American fowl took the name "turkey," the Linnaean system devised in the eighteenth century christened it with the Latin word for the guinea fowl, *Meleagris*.

The turkey thrived in Europe under various names. The French called it *d'inde* (later *dinde*), "of India"; the Germans called it *calecutische Hahn*, "Calcutta hen"; the Native Americans themselves called it *peru*, with no reference to the country of that name.

Captain John Smith, who explored the Virginia territory during the first two decades of the seventeenth century, spoke of turkeys brought to feasts by the Native Americans, but at least one authority doubts that they brought turkeys to the famous 1621 feast that initiated the tradition of **Thanksgiving** in the Plymouth Colony. It is curious that the colony's governor, William Bradford, did not mention the bird in his transcript of the feast's menu (which probably extended over days), but another attendee, Governor Edward Winslow, described how the settlers brought in their harvest and sent out "foure men on fowling," who "killed as much fowle as, with a little helpe beside [possibly from the Indians], served the Company almost a weeke." It is a safe assumption that these fowl included wild turkeys.

Turkey was certainly served at the Pilgrims' next Thanksgiving, on July 30, 1623. The term "Thanksgiving turkey" was in circulation by 1829, and Thanksgiving itself was referred to as "Turkey Day" by 1916.

In the early days, turkey was a frequently served dish, usually a wild bird, sometimes weighing up to forty pounds, and by 1820 turkeys were cheaper than chickens in Kentucky. In other parts of the colonies, however, the wild turkey was nearly wiped out by hunters, so that by the end of the eighteenth century the bird had virtually disappeared east of the Connecticut River. After World War II, the federal government began protecting the wild turkey, so that by 1991 the bird's population had risen from thirty thousand in the 1930s to more than four million today, and they are now found in forty-nine states. A small, seven-to-ten-pound breed called the "Bronze" is, however, marketed as "wild," even though it is, in fact, farm-raised. It tends to have a gamier taste but drier flesh than the more common farm-raised breeds.

Domesticated turkeys filled the void rapidly, and turkey was readily available to most people year-round. But the bird's association with Thanksgiving became so distinct after President Abraham Lincoln proclaimed the fourth Thursday in November as the official holiday that most Americans ate turkey only on that day and perhaps on Christmas. In 1935, the per capita consumption of turkey in the U.S. was only 1.7 pounds. But increased interest in turkey as a nutritious meat and the selling of various turkey products and parts not requiring the cooking of a whole bird have now raised the consumption figure to 18 pounds per person.

Today turkeys are raised on more than seven thousand farms (North Carolina leads the nation in turkey production), inspected by the USDA and sold both fresh-killed and frozen, their average weight being between eight and sixteen pounds. Most of these are young hens of the White Holland breed (first used for commercial production in the late 1950s), for mature "tom turkeys" are increasingly rare. Breast meat is the most valued part of the turkey by Americans, and one may buy such meat separately, sometimes smoked. Other turkey meat may be compressed into "turkey roll," used for sandwiches. There is even a "self-basting turkey," injected with oils beneath the skin. In some instances, the poultry producer also inserts a small plastic thermometer in the bird's skin that pops out when the turkey is cooked to the right temperature.

Ninety-two percent of turkeys consumed in the U.S. are eaten at home. Of the 3 percent consumed in restaurants, 74 percent are prepared as sandwiches, 26 percent as entrées.

American recipe writers have over the years come up with all manner of methods of cooking a turkey, from covering it with foil to placing it on a rack, from turning the bird on its back to cooking it in a very slow oven. The simplest way to cook a turkey is to wash and clean the bird, stuff it, baste it with butter, place it in a large roasting pan, and set it in a 450° oven for fifteen minutes. Turn down the heat to 350° and continue cooking and basting until a fork inserted in the leg joints shows the juices running clear.

In Cajun country, turkeys are often deep-fried.

Any number of side dishes are traditionally served with turkey—cranberry sauce, sweet potatoes, turnips, and, of course, the stuffing.

TURKEY DEVONSHIRE. A dish of turkey breast and bacon on toast with a cheddar cheese sauce, created in 1934 by Frank Blandi, a restaurateur in Pittsburgh. The sauce itself became so popular that it is often used on other dishes.

TURNIP (*Brassica rapa*). An Old World plant bearing a large yellow or white root that is usually boiled and served as a vegetable. The word comes from the Latin *nāpus*, which in Middle English became *nepe*, and was first recorded as "turnip" in 1539.

The turnip, native to Asia Minor, was eaten in Europe in the Middle Ages and cultivated in England by the seventeenth century. The French and English brought the plant to America, though the root was of little culinary interest until the eighteenth century. The "common turnip" (*B. rapa*), also called the "white turnip" for its coloring, is the most available variety in U.S. markets, though in the South the "rutabaga" (*B. napus rutabaga*), also called the "big yellow" or "Canadian turnip," is particularly well liked, often mashed and served with butter. (The name "rutabaga" comes from dialectical Swedish *rotabagge*, "baggy root.")

There are records of turnip cultivation in Canada as of 1540, and Virginia had them by 1609, but it took another century and more before they found their way into southern soil. They were very successful with the Native Americans, who preferred them to their native "Indian turnip" (*Arisaema dracontium*, also called "green dragon" or "dragonroot," and *A. triphyllum*, also called "Jack-in-the-pulpit," "starchwort," and "bog onion"). Today the turnip is widely planted throughout the U.S.

"Turnip greens" are often cooked with bacon as a vegetable.

TURNOVER. A pastry filled with fruit preserves, chopped meat, or cooked sauce, in print since 1605.

TURNPIKE CAKE. A cake of dried yeast, dating in print to 1834. According to a citation in *DARE* from 1869, the name comes from the story of a cook named Mrs. Fowler, who, during the building of the Windham Turnpike, in New York State, around 1805, solved the problem of carrying soft yeast to the site by drying it first.

TURTLE (order Testudinate). Any of a large number of fresh- or saltwater reptiles having a shell, a horny beak, and a wide array of colorings. There are about 225 species in the world, found at sea and in lakes, rivers, ponds, woodlands, fields, and pastures. The most treasured—and today one of the rarest—for the American connoisseur has always been the "diamondback terrapin" (*Malaclemys terrapin*), whose name comes from a Virginian Algonquian name, *toolepeiwa*, and its diamond-shaped polygonal scutes with concentric ridges on its back. The "green turtle" (*Chelonia mydas*) of the Caribbean is also eaten in the South with great favor, while other species—such as the southeastern "alligator snapping turtle" (*Macroclemys temminckii*), the "common snapping turtle" (*Chelydra serpentina*), the "caouanne" (*M. lacertina*), and the "loggerhead" (*Caretta caretta*)—are also considered good food turtles. The eggs from various species are also of culinary interest. A "queen turtle" is a soft-shell turtle.

The word *turtle*, dating in print to 1657, may derive from the French *tortues*, from which we also get "tortoise." "Cooter" (also "slider" in the Mississippi Valley) is a southern term derived from the African *kuta* (dating in print to 1832), for a variety of freshwater species of the genus *Chrysemys* found mainly in the eastern U.S. In *Hoppin' John's Lowcountry Cooking* (1992), John Martin Taylor notes that in the South the word "turtle" is reserved for sea turtles. Europeans have depended on the West Indies, South America, Africa, and Australia for these delicacies.

The earliest explorers of North America commented on the variety and numbers of turtles here, and Thomas Harriot, who wrote *A Briefe and True Report of the New Found Land of Virginia* (1588), spoke of turtles a yard in breadth and found the meat and eggs good eating. By the seventeenth century turtle meat was being exported back to England, where it became an expensive item of exotica. But in America, turtle was cooked by most coastal settlers, who used the meat as steaks, in stews, or in soups. So popular was the turtle that Eliza Leslie, in her *Directions for Cookery*, published in Philadelphia in 1837, noted that turtle soup was a time-consuming, difficult process best left to a "first-rate cook" or ordered in a "turtle-soup house." This appetite for turtle led quickly to the near extinction of several species, including the diamondback terrapin, and by the middle of the nineteenth century wealthy Americans had joined their European peers in the consumption of the few turtles that were caught. As a result, turtle dishes became the pride of the elite social clubs in cities like Baltimore and Philadelphia, whose wealthy citizens argued over the correct way to treat a tortoise. Marylanders insisted a turtle should be the base for a sherry-tinged clear consommé, while their northern neighbors preferred the turtle meat in a cream sauce. According to Evan Jones, members of Philadelphia's Rittenhouse Club and Baltimore's Maryland Club met with an impartial jury in 1893 to decide the matter of taste: The turtle consommé won.

By 1920 the prices for terrapin had grown so high that even the wealthy found them too much, and fortunately the species has since then been restored to a certain extent.

In other parts of the country, other species have been consumed; in Florida and the South, the green sea turtle has been prized as steak meat or used for turtle soup. Today sea turtles are being commercially raised, especially in the Cayman Islands. Turtle eggs are also a southern delicacy.

"Snapper soup," a specialty of Old Original Bookbinder's restaurant, in Philadelphia, where it was introduced in 1941, is made from farm-grown snapping turtles.

Turtle is today found frozen, canned, or in prepared soups.

TURTLE SOUP

Brown 1 lb. chopped turtle meat in a kettle, add 1 c. water, bring to a boil, then simmer, covered, until tender. In a saucepan mix 2 stalks chopped celery, 2 chopped carrots, 1 chopped onion, 2 c. chopped cabbage, 8 peppercorns, 3 sprigs parsley, 2 bay leaves, 2 cloves garlic, 1 ½ t. salt, and 5 c. water. Bring to a boil, cover, simmer for 1 hr., then strain. Stir in turtle meat, add ½ c. dry sherry, heat, and serve. Serves 6.

TUTTI-FRUTTI. A maceration of fruits and brandy especially popular in the South, where ladies would add one of each fruit of the season to one pint brandy, along with an amount of sugar equal to a quart of fruit. The mixture would be stirred each morning and kept for the season.

Tutti-frutti is also an ice cream or ice flavored with various fruits, dating in American print to 1834. The term is from the Italian, meaning "all fruits," and in America dates to 1875 in print. There was also a gum-ball candy known by this name in NYC in the 1880s. Today Tutti Frutti is a proprietary name for a fruit-flavored chewing gum.

TV DINNER. A meal of meat, poultry, or fish, together with vegetables and dessert, all precooked and packed on an aluminum plate, frozen, and sold in groceries and supermarkets. The meal has simply to be heated in the oven, and its self-contained character makes it easy to eat it away from the dining-room table while watching television. After World War II, many frozen foods appeared on the market, but the concept of a frozen, fully prepared meal under the name "TV Dinner" was marketed most successfully by Clarke and Gilbert Swanson of C. A. Swanson & Sons, of Omaha, Nebraska, who marketed a turkey-and-mashed-potatoes meal under the trademark "TV Dinner" in 1952. The name was later dropped in favor of "Frozen Dinner" by the end of the 1960s.

TWINKIES. Trademark name for a confection of small oblong sponge cakes with a creamy filling. They were created in 1930 by James A. Dewar, manager of Chicago's Continental Baking Co., and named after a billboard ad for Twinkle Toe shoes he'd seen in St. Louis. They were sold under the Hostess baked goods line. The first filling (originally done by hand) was a "banana creme," but it was changed in the 1940s to vanilla creme.

So associated with **junk food** were Twinkies that, in 1978, a San Francisco man named Dan White, who shot and killed the city's mayor, used what became known as the "Twinkie defense," suggesting that White's consumption of Twinkies and candy bars before the shooting had radically altered his frame of mind and made him momentarily insane. (White was convicted on a lesser charge and later committed suicide.)

Hostess declared bankruptcy in 2012, having sold 36 million packages in 2011, and closed its bakeries. In 2013, Twinkies and other Hostess brands were purchased by Apollo Global Management and Metropoulos & Co. for $410 million.

'ULA'ULA. A Hawaiian name, meaning "red," for any of several Pacific red snappers, especially *Etelis carbunculus* and *E. coruscans*, dating in print to 1899.

'ULU. A Hawaiian name for breadfruit (*Artocarpus altilis*), dating in print to 1888.

UNIVERSAL PRODUCT CODE. A printed series of symbols on a prepackaged food item in a retail store that identifies the type of product, manufacturer or distributor, contents, and price. The symbols are printed in binary forms that are scanned by a low-powered laser beam near the cash register. The laser converts these symbols into an electronic code that is then imprinted and tallied on the cash register's tape. This allows for fewer mistakes for the customer, higher efficiency for the store, and an automatic record of sales and inventory. There is even one Universal Product Code (UPC) scanner, called "POSitalker," that enunciates in a female voice the price of each item as it passes by the laser beam.

The UPC was devised by a committee formed in 1970 by manufacturers and grocers and began to appear on food products as of 1973.

UPAPALU. Hawaiian name for the cardinal fish (*Apogon taeriopterus* or *A. kallopterus*), dating in print to 1864.

UPSIDE-DOWN CAKE. A cake that is baked with its filling or flavoring on the bottom and then inverted before serving. The first mention in print of such a cake was in 1920, and it was so listed in the 1936 Sears, Roebuck catalog, but the cake is somewhat older.

Sometimes the cake is cooked in a skillet.

U'U. Hawaiian name for a fish of the Pacific reefs (*Myripristis murdjan*), dating in print to 1905.

V

VALLEY TAN. Traders' term for a whiskey made by the Mormons of Salt Lake Valley.

VALLONE, TONY (1944–). At a time in the 1970s when the Midwest was nearly bereft of fine dining, Tony Vallone made his eponymous restaurant, Tony's, in Houston, into one of the brightest stars in the nation for food, wine, and service, later adding to its luster by turning it into one of the best Italian restaurants in the U.S.

Vallone was born in Houston to a family in the restaurant and catering business. When he was a child, his grandmother had fed him the traditional food of her native Sicily.

When Vallone took over his father's restaurant, in the early 1960s, Houston was a dry city, and only "private clubs" could serve liquor by the glass (restaurants got around this law by making patrons "members" for the evening). Vallone said he felt "that Houston was going to boom and people with money would want to eat somewhere with class. They didn't just want to eat and drink at their country clubs anymore. They'd eaten in New York and Paris and Rome and would spend the money to get the same quality here in Houston."

Vallone opened his first namesake restaurant, Tony's, in 1965, with six tables, dancing, and a little Italian food on the primarily continental menu. By 1969, alcohol was allowed to be served in the Houston restaurant, so Tony's moved to much larger, more stylish quarters in 1972, where, emulating **Sirio Maccione** at Le Cirque in New York City, Vallone began to move away from the clichés of continental cuisine in favor of finer French and Italian food and wines.

Through the 1970s, Vallone's culinary ambitions were shackled by the poor availability of good Italian ingredients. "We couldn't get fresh clams," he remembers, "so we had to use canned clams with the linguine. I started doing it with oysters, which were abundant in the Gulf. Nobody sold calamari, so I had to go down to the fishing docks and buy it out of the guys' bait bags."

Over the next three decades, Tony's became the principal arena for Houston society, visiting U.S. presidents, Hollywood actors, and celebrity sports figures. Vallone once prepared takeout food for Frank Sinatra, and opera star Luciano Pavarotti once got up and sang two impromptu arias in the dining room.

Little by little, Vallone came within sight of his goal of serving authentic, modern Italian cuisine while building an award-winning wine cellar that compared with the best in NYC and California. Vallone branched out in Houston in the 1980s, with the more casual Grotto, then La Griglia, along with an Italian steakhouse named after his son Joey. By the end of the 1990s, his menus were almost entirely Italian, and his wine list heavy with Italian bottlings. "Little by little my clientele was being educated," says Vallone. "They'd ask me where to eat Italian food in New York and Italy. By 2005 I started playing to my heart and made my menu what I call 'progressive American' with a heavy Italian accent and world-class cooking."

Tony's next incarnation at a new location came in 2005, with a dramatic arched dining room, a twelve-foot free-form sculpture by Jesús Moroles and works by Robert Rauschenberg and other artists. He called his menu "European-style" that "shows its Italian roots with new creations that are developed each day, and rivals the best that you can find in New York, Milan, London, or Paris." He also wisely noted, for his faithful regulars, "But rest assured that your Tony's favorites are still available; we call them our 1801's (named after our previous address on Post Oak) and they are the classic dishes upon which our reputation for culinary excellence was built."

Vallone sits on the boards of the Texas Heart Institute, the University of Texas M.D. Anderson Cancer Center, and the University of Houston's Conrad N. Hilton College of Hotel and Restaurant Management. He was the first Texan inducted into the National Restaurant Association Hall of Fame, in 1982, as well as the first American-born board member of the famed Gruppo Ristoratori Italiani of Italy. Vallone was elected to the *Nation's Restaurant News* Hall of Fame and was elected to the Culinary Who's Who of Texas.

Vallone co-authored, with George Fuermann, *Tony's: The Cookbook*.

VANILLA (Vanilla planifolia). Also called "vanilla bean." The seed pod of a tropical American orchid. It is frequently used as a flavoring, especially in desserts.

The word is from the Spanish *vainilla*, "little sheath." Vanilla was brought to Europe by the Spanish conquistadores returning from Mexico. The word is first mentioned in English in 1662, as a flavoring used by the Native Americans with their chocolate, but although it became a highly desirable substance in France and England, Americans were not very familiar with vanilla until ice cream became popular, in the late eighteenth century. Thomas Jefferson discovered its virtues in France and on arriving back in the U.S. in 1789 sent for some pods from Paris, which must have originally come from Central America.

By the nineteenth century Americans had developed a passion for vanilla, especially as an ice cream flavoring (by 1932 it was estimated that 75 to 80 percent of all ice cream was vanilla), and today America uses more vanilla than any other country. The supply of vanilla beans, however, has never met demand, so substitutes, especially "vanilla extract," were developed. Vanilla extract (or "vanilla essence"), created by Joseph Burnett in 1847, was made by soaking vanilla beans in grain alcohol and water (requirements stipulate that bottled extract must contain at least 35 percent alcohol; "vanilla flavoring" may contain less than 35 percent alcohol). There is also a concentrated vanilla extract that may be used as a flavoring for regular vanilla extract. During Prohibition, some producers removed the alcohol from their product as a temperance precaution.

"Vanillin" is a flavoring obtained either from vanilla itself or from various balsams and resins; it is chemically a crystalline compound, $C_8H_8O_3$.

VEAL. The meat of a slaughtered calf. The word is from the Latin *vitellus*, which became, in Middle English, *veel*, first in print circa 1386.

Esteemed as a delicate meat since biblical times, veal achieved its greatest popularity in Italy. By the Renaissance it was valued in France, Germany, Austria, Holland, and elsewhere in Europe, where the high price of the meat never dissuaded connoisseurs from enjoying it. In America, where beef cattle were not plentiful until the middle of the nineteenth century, veal was not much appreciated. Also, the abundance of grass and fodder in America's Midwest promoted the raising of cattle to their full size for **beef**, while in Europe the availability of pastureland was severely restricted, thereby making the slaughter of an unweaned calf more the norm.

Veal was eaten, especially in the South and the Midwest, but it was often ill treated by overcooking. It was only with the arrival of Italian and German immigrants in the late nineteenth and early twentieth centuries that an appetite for veal developed in the eastern cities, with "schnitzels" and "veal scaloppini" showing up on restaurant menus. Consumption of veal by Americans in the 1940s was nearly ten pounds per capita per year, but, largely owing to the high cost of the meat, consumption has fallen to less than half a pound per person. It is still eaten mostly in Italian and French restaurants, where adaptations of Old World recipes have resulted in dishes like "**veal parmesan**" and "**veal francese**," whose names are unknown abroad.

The three basic categories of veal are "bob veal," usually the meat of a calf up to one month old; "veal," between one and three months; and "baby beef" or "calves' meat," between three and twelve months. These categories are not strict, however, and the terminology is inexact. A colloquial expression for a very young calf, especially a weakling, is "deacon."

The best veal is usually thought to be that from unweaned calves, which is called "milk-fed veal." A feeding system called the "Dutch method" (because it was developed in Holland) raises the calves on a special formula of milk solids, water, and nutrients, producing an anemic animal.

The main cuts of veal include the "primal leg" (for veal scallops), the "primal loin" (for chops), the "primal rib" (for chops and roasts), the "primal shoulder" (for veal rolls or blade roasts), the "primal shank" (for braised dishes like the Italian menu item "osso buco"), the "primal breast" (for riblets and veal breast), and the "primal flank" (for stew meat).

VEAL FRANCESE. An **Italian American** dish of pounded veal scallops cooked in butter and white wine. The cutlets are often dipped in egg and flour before cooking.

The name is Italian, meaning "veal French style," which seems to indicate nothing more than the use of white wine in the recipe and a lighter treatment than in many Italian American recipes for veal scallops, which are often covered with tomato sauce and cheese. There is no specific or traditional dish in Italy by this name.

VEAL FRANCESE

Pound 4 veal scallops until thin and tender, sauté in 2 t. butter until browned, then remove from skillet. Add to skillet 1 T. butter and ½ c. dry white wine, scraping brown bits from skillet. Reduce, burn off alcohol, pour sauce over veal scallops, and serve with a slice of lemon and a bit of chopped parsley.

VEAL PARMESAN. Also "veal parmigiana" and "veal alla parmigiana." An **Italian American** dish of pounded veal scallops that are breaded, sautéed, topped with mozzarella cheese and tomato sauce, and heated until the cheese is melted. Although it is a dish in the Italian style and a staple of Italian American restaurants, there is no dish specifically by this name in Italy. The name probably derives from Parmesan cheese, a grating cheese originally made in Parma, Italy, and now made in the U.S., though the dish does not necessarily contain Parmesan cheese.

VEAL PARMESAN

Dip veal scallops in an egg-and-milk mixture, then in bread crumbs. Sauté in butter or olive oil until browned. Top with a thin slice of mozzarella cheese and some tomato sauce, and either bake in a 400° oven or put under broiler until cheese is melted.

VEGETABLE LIVER. A Jewish American dish made of eggplant and seasonings as a substitute for chopped chicken liver, which is forbidden at certain times under **kosher** dietary laws.

VEGETABLE OIL. Any oil made from various vegetables and seeds, such as rapeseed, olive, safflower, corn, peanut, soy, and, sesame, used both for cooking and for salad dressings. These oils are pressed in large cylinders that squeeze out 95 percent of the oil in the seed or are extracted through a method invented in Germany in 1870 by which the seed is treated in a bath of a solvent such as hexane. The often seen term "cold-pressed" has no real authority, though it is often used by the food-processing industry to indicate a superior method of oil extraction. The fact is that all oils reach at least 130–150° Fahrenheit during pressing.

The usual distinction between an "oil" and a "fat" is that the former is liquid and the latter solid. Saturated oils are those in which each of the molecule's carbon atoms is paired with two attached hydrogen atoms; if there are fewer than two hydrogens per carbon, the oil is unsaturated, in which case adjacent carbon atoms make a double bond. If there is one double bond in the oil molecule, the oil is monounsaturated; if there are two or more double bonds, it is polyunsaturated. These differences are mainly the concerns of nutritionists, because the more saturated the oil, the greater the likelihood that it will be turned into cholesterol by the body. Generally speaking, most vegetable oils are polyunsaturated. A "hydrogenated oil" is one in which the polyunsaturated oils are saturated with hydrogen in order to stabilize them.

"Crude" or "virgin" oils are not processed after pressing.

VEGETABLE (PLANT) PROTEIN. According to the USDA guidelines, "Vegetable protein products derived from soybeans may be used as binders or extenders in such meat and poultry products as sausages, luncheon meats, soups, sauces, and gravies. Sometimes, they are the main ingredients in meat and poultry product substitutes."

VEGGIES. A slang term for vegetables, first appearing in English print in 1907.

VENDING MACHINE. A coin-operated dispenser of various items, but especially food like candy, snacks, soda, and coffee, dating in print to 1895. The idea actually dates back to Hero of Alexandria, who in the first century introduced a holy-water dispenser that required five drachmas. But the first modern food-vending machines were called Tutti Frutti machines, set up on NYC train platforms by the Adams gum company in 1897. The **Automat** was a restaurant that offered customers a wide range of foods set behind glass windows that opened when a coin was inserted into the slot. When candy rationing began in America during World War II, the Austin Baking Co. created the peanut-butter-and-cheese cracker for vending machines. Today vending machines dispense hot, cooked, microwaved foods like popcorn, pizza, and french-fried potatoes.

The National Automatic Merchandising Association has more than two thousand members.

VENISON. The flesh of the deer, which is usually marinated and cooked as a steak, a stew, or a barbecue. The word is from the Latin *venatio*, "hunting," dating in Middle English to circa 1300.

Venison was eaten by Native Americans, who stored it for the winter, as Captain John Smith noted on his travels in Virginia in 1607. The woods were filled with deer, and the early colonists followed the Native Americans' example of drying the meat by grilling it over fires. By the nineteenth century venison was a common meat in large cities' markets, but few could vouch for its freshness, and so treated the meat with marinades and heavy, highly seasoned sauces that lessened its gaminess. Venison with a pronounced gamy taste is colloquially called "balsam steak."

Today venison is readily available in restaurants during the season, but it is illegal to sell a deer freshly killed by a private hunter unless it has been inspected by government inspectors.

VERMOUTH. An aromatized wine flavored with various herbs and spices and made in both dry and sweet varieties. The word comes from the German *Wermut*, "wormwood," which was once customarily used in the manufacture of vermouth, though it is now considered poisonous. Today's vermouths are made with herbs and spices like cinnamon, gentian, cloves, artemisia, quinine, orange peel, chamomile, and angelica root.

France and Italy are generally credited with making the best vermouths, but some are made in the U.S., including some under license from European companies. The word *vermouth* was first printed in 1800.

VETO. A beverage of the 1840s. It was mentioned in the New Orleans *Picayune* in 1841, though it is not known precisely what the ingredients were or what the origin of the name was.

VICHYSSOISE. A potato-and-leek cream soup served cold. Vichyssoise was created by chef Louis Diat at the Ritz-Carlton Hotel in NYC. In *American Food* (1975), Evan Jones said the soup was first served in 1910, while *The American Heritage Cookbook* (1980) adds, "[The soup] was served for the first time to Charles Schwab, the steel magnate," for the opening of the hotel's roof garden. But there are several things wrong with these assertions: Diat did come to work at the Ritz-Carlton sometime in 1910, but the restaurant did not open until December 14 of that year, and this was not the roof-garden restaurant in any case. Nor was Charles M. Schwab (1862–1939) present. Also, the menu for that opening night's meal was listed in the *New York Times* the next day, and the soup served was a turtle soup, not leek and potato. The *Times* also noted that the meal had been overseen not by Diat but by Georges Auguste Escoffier, the renowned chef who had opened Ritz hotels in Paris and elsewhere. Finally, Diat himself remarked, in his book *French Cookbook for Americans* (1946), that "one of my earliest food memories is of my mother's good Leek and Potato soup made with plump, tender leeks I pulled myself from the garden....When I first came to this country I actually couldn't find any [leeks]. I finally persuaded one of my vegetable suppliers to find someone who would grow leeks for me." It is unlikely that Diat found someone to grow leeks quickly enough to have them in time for the opening in 1910. The *OED* dates the soup name's first appearance in print to 1939.

Curiously enough, Diat does not mention his famous soup by name in his 1946 cookbook, published at a time when many French chefs in NYC wanted to change the name to *crème gauloise* because of their hatred for the wartime government established at the city of Vichy, after which Diat had named the soup because he had grown up nearby. Nor did he give a date for the soup's creation in his earlier book *Cooking à la Ritz* (1941). Elizabeth David, however, in her *French Provincial Cooking* (1960), gave, without comment, the date 1917 as the year of the soup's creation.

The recipe below is from Diat's 1941 volume, in which the full, formal name of the soup is "crème vichyssoise glacée."

VICHYSSOISE

Finely slice the white parts of 4 leeks and 1 medium onion, brown very gently in 2 oz. sweet butter, then add 5 medium potatoes, also finely sliced. Add 1 qt. water or chicken broth and 1 T. salt. Boil for 35–40 min. Crush and rub through a fine strainer. Return to fire and add 2 c. milk and 2 c. medium cream. Season to taste and bring to a boil. Cool, then rub through a very fine strainer. When soup is cold, add 1 c. heavy cream. Chill before serving. Finely chopped chives may be added when serving. Serves 6.

VICTUALS. Also "vittles." Food provisions, from Latin *victualia*, first in Middle English in 1303. In American English the word is always used in the plural, dating in print to 1815, and "vittles" is common.

VILLAS, JAMES (1938–). Author. Born in Charlotte, North Carolina, James Villas grew up with his mother Martha Pearl Villas's good cooking. Villas described her as "a real character, basically a fun-loving, selfless lady but also a highly opinionated one for whom certain rules are simply not to be broken—or even modified," virtues Villas himself put into practice throughout his career.

After earning his Ph.D. in Romance languages and comparative literature from the University of North Carolina, he attended the University of Grenoble, France, as a Fulbright scholar and taught college for eight years at the University of Missouri, Rutgers University, and Hunter College, in NYC.

After sending a letter to *Esquire* magazine protesting a 1972 article on bourbon that he claimed was rife with errors, he was hired by the magazine to write food articles, largely on American subjects. He was hired in 1973 by *Town & Country* magazine as food and wine editor, a position he held for twenty-seven years, allowing him far more leeway to travel the world and write about the cuisine and restaurants of France, Italy, England, and other countries.

In his articles and books, Villas championed American food as often as he did haute cuisine, writing just as often about hamburgers and strawberry shortcake as he would cognac and **crème brûlée.** He raged against culinary fads like nouvelle cuisine, which he said "managed to dupe so many and shove our wonderful American regional dishes even further into oblivion by proclaiming a new style of cooking which is little more than the superficial application of tired *nouvelle* principles to native ingredients."

In the mid-1980s, Villas had tired of writing about a culinary world that he felt had become increasingly pretentious and trend-driven. He retired to his home in East Hampton, New York, to write cookbooks, which have included *American Taste* (1982); *Villas at Table* (1988); *James Villas' The Town & Country Cookbook* (1985); *The French Country Kitchen* (1992); *My Mother's Southern Kitchen* (1994); *The Glory of Southern Cooking* (2007); *The Bacon Cookbook* (2007); and *Pig: King of the Southern Table* (2010). His autobiography, *Between Bites: Memoirs of a Hungry Hedonist*, was published in 2003. He has published two novels, *Dancing in the Lowcountry* (2008) and *Hungry for Happiness* (2010).

Villas is listed in Who's Who of Food & Beverage in America.

VINEGAR. A pungent, sour, acidic solution of fermented wine, apple cider, or other substances. Vinegar is the result of a conversion by bacteria of alcoholic solutions into acetic acid. The word is from the Latin *vinum* (wine) plus *acer* (sharp), which in Middle English became *vinegre*, first in print circa 1315.

Vinegar is used as a flavoring, especially in salad dressings, and as a pickling solution. It is made by any of three methods: the "slow process," the "generator process," or the "submerged process" (this last developed since World War II). Homemade vinegar must utilize a starter known as "mother of vinegar."

In Europe, most vinegars are based on wine, and the U.S. produces this kind, too, sometimes by winemakers who age the vinegar in oak casks. "Distilled white vinegar" (also called "white vinegar," "grain vinegar," or "spirit vinegar") is made from grain alcohol diluted with water to a strength of about 5 percent acidity. The H. J. Heinz Co., established in 1869, claims to have produced the first bottled distilled white vinegar, which today is the biggest seller of its type in the U.S. The most commonly produced vinegar in this country, however, is "apple cider vinegar," diluted with water to a table strength of 5 percent acidity.

VINEGAR CANDY

A popular nineteenth-century confection made by combining 1 c. sugar, ½ c. water, 2 T. white vinegar, 1 T. molasses, 2 T. butter, and 1 T. chocolate. Boil for about 20 min. and turn out onto buttered sheet. Cut up into small candy pieces.

VINEGAR PIE. Also "red pie." A spiced pie made with vinegar, common in the North and the Midwest since the nineteenth century. In *America Eats*, written in the 1930s for the WPA Illinois Writers' Project but not published until 1992, Nelson Algren noted that as winter wore on, Midwestern settlers' systems craved fruit and tart flavors: "To satisfy their craving, ingenious housewives invented the vinegar pie....When baked in a pie tin, the resulting product was much relished and remained a favorite springtime dessert until young orchards coming into bearing provided real fruit pies to take its place."

VINEGAR PIE

Mix 1 beaten egg, 1 t. flour, 1 t. sugar, 1 T. white vinegar, 1 c. cold water, and a pinch of ground nutmeg. Pour into a pie crust, top with another pie crust, brush with cold water, and bake at 375° until filling is set and the crust is browned.

VODKA. A distilled spirit made from potatoes, corn, or other grains (1795). It is usually neutral in flavor and, in America, bottled at proofs between 80 and 100, although 60 is the legal minimum.

The word *vodka* is from a Russian diminutive, *vodka*, meaning "little water," first in English print circa 1802, and although some claim the spirit originated in Russia, other authorities believe its birthplace was Poland, at the end of the tenth century. *Zhizennia voda* ("water of life") is first mentioned in Russian records in the twelfth century, but the spirit was also being made in Finland, Czechoslovakia, and other regions of Eastern Europe. Its prominence in the czarist Russian courts was legendary, and in the sixteenth century Ivan the Terrible opened taverns where the general populace could enjoy vodka. Western Europeans became familiar with the spirit during the Crimean War (1854–1856), but vodka was still a rarity in the West until well into the twentieth century.

Vodka first came to America with Russian émigré Rudolph Kunnetchansky, son of a Ukrainian plantation owner who supplied the P.A. Smirnoff Co. (which supplied the czar's vodka) with grain-neutral spirits. Kunnetchansky fled Russia during the Revolution of 1917 and settled in the U.S., where he changed his name to Kunett and became a salesman for Standard Oil, then a manager for the Helena Rubinstein cosmetics company. He also bought the rights from Vladimir Smirnoff, then in Paris, for $2,500 to produce and sell Smirnoff vodka in the U.S., and with Smirnoff's help set up the first American vodka distillery, in Bethel, Connecticut, in 1934. In 1939, after years of poor sales, the Smirnoff Co. was sold to G. F. Heublein & Brother for $14,000 plus royalties.

Still, there was little interest in vodka among Americans, even though the **Bloody Mary** cocktail had achieved some success after the end of Prohibition. It was not until well after World War II that interest in the spirit picked up, and cocktails like the **Moscow Mule** helped spur a taste for vodka. By the 1960s vodka sales soared, buoyed by a new generation of young Americans who found the lack of a distinct flavor in the spirit perfectly suited to their taste, mixing vodka with all sorts of fruit juices and tonic waters. Even the vodka martini became faddish, especially after the success of Ian Fleming's series of spy books, in the 1960s, about James "007" Bond, a suave British agent who preferred vodka to gin in his **martinis**.

By 1975 vodka had become the bestselling spirit in the U.S. (a position it has held ever since), with about 63 million nine-liter cases now sold each year, accounting for 32 percent of industry volume, with revenues in 2011 of $412 million.

American vodkas are distilled to be odorless, colorless, and nearly tasteless, although a few flavored vodkas are made in small quantities. American vodkas are unaged, distilled from a fermented mash, and highly purified. If a vodka is colored, that fact must be noted on the bottle's label. There are today more than three hundred brands of vodka, both foreign and domestic, available on the U.S. market.

VOLSTEAD COCKTAIL. According to Harry MacElhone's *ABC of Mixing Cocktails* (reprinted in various editions from 1919 to 1939), "This cocktail was invented at Harry's Bar, Paris, in honour of Mr. Andrew J. Volstead (who brought out the Dry Act in the U.S.A.) and was the reason for sending such a large number of Americans to Europe to quench their thirst." (See **Prohibition**.) The drink is made with "$^1/_3$ Rye Whiskey, $^1/_3$ Swedish Punch, $^1/_6$ Orange Juice, $^1/_6$ Raspberry Syrup, 1 dash of Anisette."

VONGERICHTEN, JEAN-GEORGES (1956–). Chef, restaurateur, author. Alsatian-born chef Jean-Georges Vongerichten created a style of French cuisine highly personalized but buoyed by American and global influences that had a widespread and immediate influence on American gastronomy every time he opened a new concept restaurant.

Born near Strasbourg, France, Vongerichten began his culinary training with Paul Haeberlin, at L'Auberge de l'Ill, in Illhaeusern, then with chefs Paul Bocuse and Louis Outhier, who sent Vongerichten to Asia to open outposts in Bangkok, Singapore, and Hong Kong. In Asia, especially in Thailand, Vongerichten became fascinated with the regional cuisine, saying, "I was preparing all this French haute cuisine, but I was more interested in eating what the local cooking staff ate for house meals."

Outhier then sent Vongerichten to Boston in 1985 to open a fine dining restaurant, the Marquis de Lafayette, based on classic and nouvelle ideas, which were carried over to NYC at Lafayette restaurant, where they won four stars from the *New York Times*. With business partner Phil Suarez, Vongerichten struck out on his own with a series of groundbreaking NYC restaurants that included an innovative bistro called JoJo (1991) that was named Best New Restaurant of the Year by *Esquire*, which noted that "JoJo affirms the virtues of downscaling while proving the folly of merely cutting corners." He next opened a Thai-French restaurant called Vong and, in 1997, what would be his flagship, Jean-Georges, to which was attached a casual offshoot called Nougatine.

It was at Jean-Georges that Vongerichten debuted his very personalized style of modern French and American cuisine. Lighter and more focused on vegetables and spices, the menu reflected a new approach to cooking that went with a change in the diet of the upscale dining public in America. Its design, by Adam Tihany, shifted from the traditional French restaurant decor of the past to a more minimalist layout. In 2005, Jay McInerney, in *New York* magazine, wrote, "It's probably safe to say that in the past two decades, no single chef has had more influence on the way New Yorkers dine out—or on the way other chefs cook and other restaurants look."

Vongerichten and Suarez expanded in NYC with an Asian eatery named Spice Market (2004); a French American restaurant, Perry St. (2005); a Japanese soba noodle restaurant, Matsugen (2008, since closed); a modern French American restaurant called The Mark (2009); and J&G Steakhouses.

Vongerichten put Vong branches in Chicago, Hong Kong, and London; Market Bistro in Paris; Cafe Martinique and Dune in Nassau; Lagoon in Bora Bora; and Jean-Georges in Shanghai. By then, Vongerichten was taking criticism for opening restaurants he merely visited only occasionally, although most often he was cooking on the line at Jean-Georges in NYC.

In 2006, Vongerichten and Suarez partnered with Starwood Hotels and Resorts Worldwide Inc. and equity firm Catterton Partners to create a multinational restaurant and licensing business. Vongerichten and his wife, Marja, hosted a PBS travel and cooking series entitled *Kimchi Chronicles*.

Vongerichten's books including *Simple Cuisine: The Easy, New Approach to Four-Star Cooking* (1991); *Jean-Georges: Cooking at Home with a Four-Star Chef*, co-authored with Mark Bittman (1998); *Asian Flavors of Jean-Georges* (2007); and *Home Cooking with Jean-Georges*, co-authored with Genevieve Ko (2011).

WAFFLE. A light batter cake cooked on a griddle with a special weblike pattern. Waffles are a popular breakfast dish served with butter and maple syrup. The word is from the Dutch *wafel* and first appeared in English print in 1735. The item was known to the Pilgrims, who had spent time in Holland before sailing to America in 1620, and "waffle parties" became popular in the latter part of the eighteenth century. Thomas Jefferson returned from France with a waffle iron, a long-handled patterned griddle that encloses the batter and gives it its characteristic crispness and shape. A century later, vendors on city streets sold waffles hot and slathered with molasses or maple syrup.

Waffles continued to be extremely popular breakfast items in the twentieth century, and electric waffle irons made the timing of the cooking easier. Then, in 1953, Frank Dorsa introduced frozen waffles into supermarkets, calling them Eggo waffles. At the 1964 New York World's Fair, "Belgian waffles," made with yeast and thicker than the usual waffle, were an immediate sensation, and they are sold today at stands, county fairs, carnivals, and other fast-food outlets. In the South, waffles are also made with rice or cornmeal (sometimes called "Virginia waffles"). In Baltimore, kidney stew on waffles is a traditional Sunday specialty.

WAFFLE

Combine 1 c. flour, 1 ½ t. baking powder, a pinch of salt, ½ c. milk, and 1 beaten egg yolk. Mix in 1 T. cooled melted butter, then fold in 1 stiffly beaten egg white. Pour onto a well-buttered waffle iron and cook until golden brown. Serve with butter and maple syrup.

WALDORF SALAD. A salad with a mayonnaise dressing, apples, and celery, though walnuts are traditional too. The dish was supposedly created by maître d'hôtel Oscar Tschirky, of the Waldorf-Astoria Hotel, in NYC, which opened in 1893. By 1896, when Tschirky compiled *The Cook Book by "Oscar of the Waldorf,"* the recipe—given without comment—called for only apples, celery, and mayonnaise, and the salad later became a staple item in most hotel dining rooms and other restaurants. At some point in the next two decades, chopped walnuts were added, for they are listed by George Rector in the ingredients for the salad in *The Rector Cook Book*, which appeared in 1928, after which walnuts became standard in the recipe, including the one given in *The Waldorf-Astoria Cookbook* (1981), by Ted James and Rosalind Cole.

OSCAR'S ORIGINAL WALDORF SALAD RECIPE

Peel 2 raw apples, cut into small pieces about ½ in. square, cut some celery the same way, and mix with the apple. Add "a good mayonnaise."

WAHOO. Also "kingfish," "ono" (in Hawaii), and "queenfish." A warm-ocean fish (*Acanthocybium solandri*). The word, dating in print to 1884, is common in the Florida Keys.

WAIT ON THE TABLE. Appalachian term for saying grace before a meal, dating in print to 1911.

WALLEYE (*Stizostedion vitreum*). A North American freshwater fish whose wide, bright eyes give it its name, from the Middle English *wawil-eghed*, dating in American print, with reference to the fish, to 1888. It is sometimes called "yellow pike," "dory," and "pike perch," although it is not a pike or a John Dory. According to A. J. McClane, in *The Encyclopedia of Fish Cookery* (1977), the walleye was apparently introduced into the Chemung River, a tributary to the north branch of the Susquehanna at Elmira, New York, in 1812 by a Jesuit priest. "The reproduction of these walleyes," wrote McClane, "was so successful that they literally swarmed in the pools and eddies of the entire river system, and 'Susquehanna salmon' were soon in greater favor than shad." For a long while afterwards, the walleye was called a "salmon."

WALNUT. Any of a variety of trees in the genus *Juglans* bearing a nut that is eaten on its own, in pastries and desserts, in stuffings, and as a flavoring for ice cream, syrups, and other foods. Cordials and oils are also made from walnuts.

The word is from the Latin *nux Gallia*, "Gaulish nut" (referring to a nut from Gaul), which in Middle English became *walnotte*, appearing in print circa 1050.

The native "American black walnut" (*J. nigra*) was eaten by the Native Americans three thousand years ago, about the same time that the "Persian walnut" (*J. regia*) was being consumed in Babylon. Other native American varieties include the "butternut" or "white walnut" (*J. cinerea*), the "little walnut" (*J. microcarpa*), the "Arizona walnut" (*J. magor*), the "California walnut" (*J. californica*), and the "Hinds" (*J. hindsi*). Eleven other species are native to Central and South America. Nevertheless, nearly 100 percent of the walnuts produced in the U.S. come from California, where Spanish Franciscans brought the plant during the missionary period, the first commercial planting in the state having been done by Joseph Sexton, in Santa Barbara in 1867. Today about 217,000 tons are produced annually, but most of those are of the Persian variety, also called the "English walnut" because of its wide propagation by the English.

Walnuts are often combined with maple syrup or flavoring to make maple-walnut ice cream. Walnut fudge appeared just after World War I.

WANIGAN. The cook's boat that followed a river drive of logs. Wanigan was also used by sheepherders to describe the supply wagon. The word may come from the Ojibwa Indian *wannikan*, "man-made hole," because it originally referred to a large supply chest, or to Algonquian, for a storage place or "things carried around," or Montagnais *atawangan*, "to buy or sell," dating in American print to 1848.

WAPATULI. Also "wampa toole," "hairy buffalo," "trashcan punch," and "Jesus juice." A college-campus drink made by blending various alcoholic drinks and fruits in a trash can, dating in print to 1980, but older in common usage. The word also refers to the party, with each guest bringing his own alcohol, at which the drink is served. The recipe below, from the *Urban Dictionary*, is called "Standard Wapatuli." The origin of the name is unknown.

WAPATULI

Mix together 3 750 ml Bottles each Gin, Rum, Vodka, 5 Gallons Apple Cider, 5 Gallons Lemonade, 5 Gallons Orange Juice, 1 Case Beer, and 30 Lbs Ice. Chop up pineapple, oranges, melons, or your choice of fruit and add to mixture.

WASHINGTON PIE. Also "Martha Washington pie," "Washington cake," and other variants, dating in print to 1878. A cake of several layers spread with fruit jelly or marmalade. The name derives from Martha Washington (1732–1802), who in her day was a prominent hostess and fine cook, basing many of her preparations on two old recipe collections, *A Booke of Cookery* and *Booke of Sweetmeats*, given to her by her first husband, Daniel Custis, in 1749. These collections, passed on to her granddaughter, Nelly Custis, in 1799, were reprinted by Karen Hess as *Martha Washington's Booke of Cookery* (1981) and contain several cake recipes, none of which much resembles the Washington cakes of the nineteenth century that supposedly were variants of a cake Martha Washington was said to have made for her granddaughter's wedding in 1799. The recipe below is adapted from one of these nineteenth-century preparations.

Another kind of Washington pie was described by H. L. Mencken as being "about two inches thick and [sold] in blocks about two inches square. It was made of stale pies, gingercakes, etc., ground up and rebaked." The dish is mentioned in the Ladies of the First Baptist Church's *Pentucket Housewife* (1882).

WASHINGTON PIE

Beat together ½ lb. butter with ¾ lb. sugar until light. Add the rind of half a lemon, then beat in 6 eggs, one at a time. Mix 3 t. baking powder with ¾ c. cream, stir into batter, then add 4 c. flour and blend well. Pour into 4 cake pans and bake at 350° until an inserted knife comes out clean, about 30 min. Cool, then spread layers with fruit jelly or marmalade.

WATER. The most basic of drinks, H$_2$O, clean, pure water was one of the potables early colonists found in America in what seemed unlimited quantities. This was not true in European cities, where water was often contaminated, and in colonial America cities, water supplies were primitive, although one European traveler pronounced the waterworks of Bethlehem, Pennsylvania, "excellently contrived" as of 1783. For the most part, city water in the eighteenth century was supplied by hand pumps, and in NYC tank carts sold water from the so-called Tea Water Pump, noted for its purity. The first major city to provide its citizens with fresh, pure water was Philadelphia, when Benjamin Henry Latrobe installed a marble pumping station in Center Square in 1801. Fifty years later, more than eighty American cities had public water supplies, and New York's Croton system of aqueducts was one of the marvels of the age. Modern American water supplies are often treated with fluoride to help prevent tooth decay.

As concerns about the purity of American water grew in the 1970s, **bottled water** grew enormously popular, both in its "flat" and carbonated forms (see also **seltzer**). "Distilled water" is usually plain water from the tap that has had all minerals removed. "Mineral water" has five hundred parts per million of dissolved mineral salts and is taken from underground water sources. Bottled waters must meet the federal standards set by the Safe Drinking Water Act of 1974. Americans now consume more than nine billion gallons of bottled water annually.

WATERMELON (*Citrullus vulgaris*). A vine native to Africa bearing a large, green-skinned fruit with bright pink flesh and black seeds. The name derives from the great amount of watery juice in the fruit and first appeared in English in 1615.

Cultivated for thousands of years in the Middle East and Russia, the watermelon was brought to America by the African slaves. In fact, watermelons have long been associated with African Americans, not always in a complimentary way, for much of the graphic and cartoon art of the nineteenth century pictured African Americans as docile people content to walk barefoot and eat watermelon. The word itself has sometimes been used as a slur word for African Americans, and one slang term for the fruit is "nigger special." A colloquial name for the fruit is "August ham," because of its size and time of appearance. An "icebox melon" is a small watermelon that may be easily stored in the refrigerator. A "rattlesnake melon" is a cultivar with an outer skin resembling a rattlesnake's markings, dating in print to 1855.

Watermelons were grown in Massachusetts as of 1629, and there is some evidence that in Florida Native Americans cultivated the watermelon as early as 1664. The watermelon has been widely cultivated in California, Indiana, and Texas. It is usually eaten fresh in the summertime, although pickled watermelon rind is a traditional American relish. Per capita U.S. consumption of watermelons in 1997 was 14.5 pounds.

WATERMELON RIND OR PICKLE

Cut away 1 lb. of watermelon rind and cut into chunks. Cover with cold salted water and boil until softened. Drain, cover again with cold water, and cook until very tender. Dissolve ¾ lb. sugar in 1 c. hot water, add rind and 1 sliced lemon, bring to a rapid boil, and cook until rind turns transparent. Add 2 T. vinegar and ½ oz. whole cloves and cook until clear. Chill.

WATERS, ALICE LOUISE (1944–). Chef, restaurateur and author. Widely renowned as one of the seminal pioneers of modern American cuisine, Alice Waters helped change the way chefs and home cooks purchased and prepared food, championing fresh, local ingredients at a time in the 1970s when few actually had access to them.

Born in Chatham, New Jersey, Waters attended the University of California at Berkeley, where by 1964 she had become active in the campus's Free Speech Movement. In 1965, Waters matriculated at the Sorbonne, in Paris, where she fell in love with the city's gastronomy. She returned to Berkeley the following year and graduated with a degree in French cultural studies (1967). She taught at the Montessori school there and, a year later, in London, taking time to travel through Europe, Turkey, and Corfu.

Inspired by the cookbooks of British food writer Elizabeth David, Waters began cooking seriously upon her return to Berkeley, where she wrote a recurring food column for the *San Francisco Express Times* called Alice's Restaurant (named after the 1967 Arlo Guthrie song). With friends and investors, she decided to create her own little bistro of the kind she recalled from Provence. In 1971 she opened the doors to Chez Panisse (named after a beloved character in the 1930s French films of Marcel Pagnol).

From the beginning, Waters courted local organic farmers and sought out the best fish, meat, and cheeses available to put on her fixed-price, three- or four-course menus, determined each day solely by what was available. Fiercely proud of the quality of her ingredients, she would sometimes serve a single uncooked, unadorned peach for dessert, on the rationale that she could not improve on its taste.

Despite Waters's complete lack of business sense, which had her veering toward an early bankruptcy, the restaurant began to attract attention, at first local, then national, as a new kind of eating that, while based on French recipes, was wholly American in its ingredients and its casual decor and service. Guests could peer into the kitchen, where cooks would as soon wear headbands as white toques. Menus were written in French with English translations.

Waters also had a knack for finding fresh young culinary talent, usually untrained in cooking, many of whom had left other careers to work at Chez Panisse, including many who became well-known chefs in their own right, like underwater architect Jeremiah Tower, fine arts student Joyce Goldstein, and Asian Studies anthropologist Mark Miller.

In 1980, Waters opened a more casual, Italian-inflected, à la carte eatery, the Café at Chez Panisse, upstairs from the restaurant, where she gave her benediction to the humble pizza, and in 1984 she started Café Fanny (named after her daughter).

In 1992, she was honored as Best Chef in America by the James Beard Foundation. By then, however, Waters had turned over the day-to-day cooking to her staff as she became more socially active in projects through her Chez Panisse Foundation (1996), which established the Edible Schoolyard Program in Berkeley to involve young people in farming of sustainable foods at a garden at Berkeley's Martin Luther King Jr. Middle School. There are now five such programs around the country. This led to the School Lunch Initiative, out of a remodeled cafeteria, which provided wholesome lunches to the city's school district. Waters urged both the Clinton and Obama administrations to plant a White House vegetable garden, using **Thomas Jefferson**'s efforts as a model, and First Lady Michelle Obama incorporated the idea into her Let's Move! anti-obesity campaign.

Waters has also worked to create the Yale Sustainable Food Project, integrated with the school's dining services. She was an early supporter of the Slow Food movement, which began in Turin, Italy.

Once asked why her menus at Chez Panisse offered no choices, Waters responded, "It comes down to whether or not the tomatoes had rain on them that morning. To try to create and produce four or five perfect dishes, you have to think very hard about what to do with your ingredients. You see, it takes a lifetime just to understand a lima bean…It's a never-ending process of evolution."

Waters's award-winning books including *Chez Panisse Pasta, Pizza, Calzone* (1984), *Chez Panisse Menu Cookbook* (1995), *The Art of Simple Food* (2007), *Edible Schoolyard* (2008), and *In the Green Kitchen* (2010). With "Friends," Waters wrote a memoir entitled *40 Years of Chez Panisse: The Power of Gathering* (2011).

WEAKFISH (*Cynoscion regalis*). Also "sea trout" and "squeteague" (the latter from the Narragansett). A variety of marine fish found in the Atlantic, dating in print to 1791. It seemed to have vanished from American waters after 1800 and did not reappear in force until 1870, with remarkable numbers swarming off NYC's Rockaway Beach in 1881. The fish again disappeared in the 1950s and came back in 1972. It has since made progress as a desirable food fish in eastern restaurants. U.S. commercial landings of weakfish totaled 599,073 pounds in 2010, valued at $363,000.

The name is from an obsolete Dutch word, *weekvische*, probably referring to the soft mouth of the fish, although an English encyclopedia of the 1830s suggested that Americans called the fish by that name because it was "considered by some as a debilitating food."

WEEPER. Vinicultural slang for a bottle whose wine has leaked out from the cork to form a sticky substance around the neck, first in print in 1946. It is usually caused by keeping wines at too warm a temperature.

WENTE, CARL (1851–1934). German immigrant Carl Heinrich Wente established what is today the oldest continuously operated family-owned winery in the U.S. His marrying of European winemaking techniques to California soil resulted in major advances in white wine production, which including planting French chardonnay cuttings in 1912 that would become the "Wente Clone," which now accounts for 80 percent of all the chardonnay planted in California.

Moving to California's Napa Valley from his native Hanover, Germany, in 1880, Wente learned winemaking from Charles Krug, then, three years later, partnered with Dr. George Bernard, who owned a winery in Livermore, California, to produce white wines in bulk, which sold for more money than reds in those days.

In 1918, Wente's son Ernest joined his father as vineyard manager with his brother Herman, who became winemaker. The winery survived Prohibition making altar wine for Georges de Latour's Beaulieu winery, then after repeal Wente began bottling his own, under the label Valle de Oro, winning an award for his sauvignon blanc in 1939 at San Francisco's Golden Gate International Exposition. The name was later changed to Wente Vineyards. It was at that time that importer Frank Schoonmaker contracted to sell Wente's wines, which included Sémillon, gray Riesling, pinot blanc, and other white varietals.

Expansion brought the winery to the Salinas Valley, where they named their vineyard Arroyo Seco. The company was later passed on to Ernest's only son, Karl, and in 1977 Karl's young son Eric took the helm. Continuing the legacy, the winery is managed today by the fourth generation of the Wente family—Eric, Philip, Carolyn—and the fifth generation, Christine and Karl. The winery has grown to include more than two thousand acres of vineyards in the Livermore Valley, on San Francisco Bay, and eight hundred acres in Arroyo Seco, Monterey.

WESTERN. A sandwich composed of an omelet with green pepper, chopped ham, and onions on white bread or toast. First in print in 1908. It is sometimes called a "western omelet" (which first appeared in print in 1927; "western" in 1951) or, in Utah, a "Denver omelet" or "Denver sandwich," in print since 1925.

WET BAR. A small bar equipped to make drinks and cocktails at home or in a hotel room. The term dates in print to 1968.

WHEAT. One of the most important grains known to man, with several varieties in the genus *Triticum*. The word is from Old English *hwaete*.

There is no evidence that wheat existed in the New World before Columbus brought it to Isabela, on Hispaniola, in 1493, and it was introduced to Mexico by Hernán Cortés as of 1519. The Spanish missionaries brought the grain to Arizona and California in the eighteenth century. In the East, wheat was sown unsuccessfully by the Pilgrims, who made do with corn, and in Virginia tobacco was a more profitable crop, so wheat was relegated to a minor role in that colony. It was not until it was planted in the Mississippi Valley, in 1718, by the Company of the West, that wheat became an important American crop, increasingly so during the Civil War, when the mechanized Northern harvesters brought in far more wheat for their troops than the Southerners could with manual labor. The North was even able to export wheat and flour to Europe during the hostilities.

Today China is the leading producer of wheat, followed by the Russian Federation, then the U.S., which in recent years has exported a great deal of wheat to these countries.

Wheat is turned into flour, cereals, pasta, and enough kinds of food to provide one-quarter of the total food requirements of humanity. Americans' consumption of wheat flour today is 36.6 million tons, from 76.7 million tons grown in the U.S.

The principal varieties of U.S. wheat include:

DURUM WHEAT. High in gluten, durum wheat is ground to make semolina for pasta.

HARD RED SPRING WHEAT. High in protein and gluten, this is excellent for making bread flour.

HARD RED WINTER WHEAT. A thinner kernel than hard red spring wheat, also good for bread flour.

SOFT RED WINTER WHEAT. Starchier than hard wheat, this is good for pastry flour.

Commercial forms of wheat include:

BRAN. The outer covering of the wheat kernel, used to make cereals.

BULGUR. Also called "wheat pilaf," bulgur is the ground whole kernel, often used in Middle Eastern dishes.

CRACKED WHEAT. Another form of crushed whole-wheat kernels.

WHEAT GERM. The embryo of the wheat kernel, often used as a nutritional supplement for cereal and other foods. The word first saw print around 1903, when Charles Kretschmer and his son Charles Jr. began toasting wheat germ, which was then bottled and sold as a cereal and nutritious food additive.

WHELK. Any of a variety of marine snails in the family Buccinidae having a thick, turreted shell and a large foot, that is used as food. The name is from Old English *weoloc*. The two species of culinary interest are the "waved whelk" (*Buccinum undatum*) and the "channeled whelk" (*Busycon canaliculatum*).

Whelk is usually prepared with garlic and tomato sauce or served with lemon, oil, and vinegar as part of a cold salad.

WHIP. A dessert of whipped cream to which have been added sugar and lemon juice.

~~~~~~

WHIP

~~~~~~

Combine 1 c. sugar with the juice of 3 lemons. Add 1 pt. heavy cream and whip until stiff. Serve in glasses.

WHISKEY. An alcoholic distilled spirit from grains such as corn, barley, or rye. In the U.S., several grain spirits are produced, but the only true American whiskeys (that is, those that are produced only within the U.S.) are **bourbon**, **Tennessee whiskey**, and **blended whiskey** (often erroneously called **rye**), each of which should be consulted under those names. Minimum proof for whiskey is 60.

The word *whiskey* comes from the Gaelic *uisqebeatha*, "water of life," dating in print to 1715. When it specifically refers to Scotch (produced only in Scotland), the word is spelled without the *e*, although this spelling has been adopted as standard for all domestic whiskeys by the ATF. Still, Americans continue to spell domestic and Irish grain spirits "whiskey." The earliest European settlers in America brought distilled spirits with them, and rum was commercially produced in New England very early. By 1640 there was a distillery on NYC's Staten Island, but the industry grew rather slowly, with rye and barley the principal grains used. Many farmers used their excess grain to this end, and during the Revolutionary War whiskey was used as a medium of exchange.

In 1791, Alexander Hamilton passed a federal excise tax on whiskey that resulted, three years later, in an uprising of mostly Scottish-Irish farmers in western Pennsylvania who opposed this incursion into their livelihoods. President George Washington was forced to call out the militia to quell the revolt, called the Whisky Rebellion, thereby demonstrating the federal government's resolve in enforcing the new laws of the land.

Today the best American whiskeys continue to come from those regions where the water passes through layers of limestone, as it does in the principal whiskey-producing states of Pennsylvania, Indiana, Tennessee, Maryland, and Kentucky.

The principal types of American whiskey are defined as:

STRAIGHT WHISKEY. Whiskey distilled at 160 **proof** or less, aged at least two years in new white charred-oak barrels. The addition of water brings the alcohol down to no lower than 80 proof, with a minimum of 51 percent of the volume being the grain. A spirit that has reached a proof above 160 is called a "neutral spirit" and should not possess any discernible flavor, aroma, or body. About half the whiskey consumed in the U.S. is straight whiskey.

BOTTLED-IN-BOND. Only straight whiskeys are thus called, a term that has nothing to do with guaranteeing quality but is instead a means of aging whiskey without having to pay tax on it until the spirit is ready for sale. The Bottled-in-Bond Act of 1894 required that the whiskey be aged at least four years (usually higher in practice), bottled at a minimum of 100 proof, and kept under the supervision of the Internal Revenue Service in a "bonded warehouse." When the distiller removes the whiskey from the warehouse, he then pays the tax.

LIGHT WHISKEY. Whiskey distilled at 161 to 189 proof, stored in used or uncharred new oak containers. This category was established in 1972. Most light whiskey is made from corn, and it may be called a "blended light whiskey" if mixed with less than 20 percent straight whiskey on a proof-gallon basis.

WHISKEY MILL. A frontier saloon.

WHITE BASS (*Morone chrysops*). A freshwater fish similar to the **striped bass**. White bass are particularly popular in lake and river regions of the Midwest, where pan-frying is the most usual preparation. The name dates in American print to 1869.

WHITE CHOCOLATE MOUSSE. A dessert made from white chocolate, cream, egg whites, and sugar. It was created by chef Michel Fitoussi in 1977, on the occasion of the second anniversary of the Palace Restaurant, in NYC, and quickly became popular in other restaurants around the U.S.; it also began an interest in white chocolate (actually a form of flavored cocoa butter) as a confectionary ingredient. *Mousse* is French, first appearing in English print, in reference to the foamy bubbles in champagne, in 1777.

WHITE CHOCOLATE MOUSSE

Whip 1 qt. heavy cream until stiff. Chill in refrigerator. Cook 1 lb. sugar with 1 c. water to 250° on a candy thermometer. Beat 1 c. egg whites until almost stiff, pour in sugar syrup, and blend until almost cool. Cut 2 lb. white chocolate into small cubes. Melt white chocolate, then fold in egg whites and whipped cream. Puree 4 pt. strawberries with sugar to taste and a little kirsch. Spoon sauce onto plate, spoon mousse onto sauce, and top with strawberry or raspberry. Serves 10.

WHITEFISH. Any of a variety of freshwater fishes in the genus *Coregonus*, although other related species are usually called by this name. The word first appeared in American print in 1748. Whitefish are members of the salmon family, and the most important species gastronomically include the "cisco," whose name derives from the Ojibwa *pemitewiskawet*, "oily-skinned fish," and of which there are several species—the "cisco" (*C. artedii*), also called "lake herring"; the "deepwater cisco" (*C. johannae*); the "longjaw cisco" (*C. alpenae*); the "shortjaw cisco" (*C. zenithicus*); the "shortnose cisco" (*C. reighardi*); and the "blackfin cisco" (*C. nigripinnis*); the "lake whitefish" (*C. culpeaformis*); the "mountain whitefish" (*Prosopium williamsoni*), also called the "Rocky Mountain whitefish"; and the "round whitefish" (*P. cylindraceum*), also called "Menominee whitefish" (after the Menominee River, in Michigan). U.S. commercial landings of whitefish totaled 10.324 million pounds in 2010, valued at $11.113 million.

WHITE LADY. A drink of equal parts lemon juice, white crème de menthe, and Cointreau, shaken over ice and strained into a cocktail glass. The original was created by bartender Harry MacElhone in 1919, at London's Ciro's Club, but he changed the formula in 1929 at Harry's New York Bar, in Paris, substituting gin, which is more readily found today, for the white crème de menthe. Sometimes the drink is made with the addition of half an egg white. As "White Lady," the name dates in print to 1930.

WHITE LIGHTNING. Also "white lightnin'" and "white mule." White liquor, especially moonshine, dates in print to 1904.

WHITES. Restaurant workers' slang for the white jackets traditionally worn by chefs and cooks.

WHITE SAUCE. This term may refer to a sauce made from a roux of flour, butter, and milk or cream, in English print since 1845 in reference to a béchamel, and since 1981 in reference to a light, clear sauce made with clams and clam broth that goes with linguine. The former usage is far older than the latter, which has been heard in Italian American restaurants only since World War II. See also **red sauce**.

WHITE CLAM SAUCE

In ¼ c. olive oil sauté 1 sliced clove garlic for 1 min. Add ¼ c. water, stir in ½ t. chopped parsley, salt and pepper, ½ c. minced clams, and 1 c. clam broth. Simmer until tender.

WHOOPIE PIE. A Pennsylvania Dutch confection resembling a cupcake. It is usually made with chocolate batter and a white icing filling, though there are many flavor variations. According to cookbook author and Pennsylvania restaurateur Betty Groff, whoopie pies might have originated with mothers who used leftover batter from more traditional cakes to make little cakes on cookie sheets for their children. The origin of the name, in print since 1931, is obscure, perhaps simply related to the whoop of joy uttered by children upon receiving such an unexpected sweet.

WILD BOAR (*Sus scrofa*). A Eurasian swine with a thick, short, powerful body and upcurved tusks, dating in print to about 1225. It was domesticated in Europe around 1500 B.C. and introduced in its wild state to the U.S. by sportsmen. Waverley Root and Richard de Rochemont noted in *Eating in America* (1976) that Hernando de Soto "landed near what is now Tampa [Florida] in 1542 with thirteen porkers in his supply train, and although other explorers and settlers of the American South brought pigs which eventually ran wild, Louisianans like to think of their wild boar as having a true Creole ancestry, that is to say, in this case, Spanish, with no native intermixture." Yet de Soto's swine were obviously domesticated boars or, more probably, simple hogs.

Wild boars proliferated throughout New Hampshire, North Carolina, and Texas. They are still hunted and, when taken, cooked in a stew or as a roast.

WILD RICE (*Zizania aquatica*). Also called "Indian rice," "Tuscarora rice," and "Canadian rice." Not a true rice, but the grain of a tall aquatic grass grown in the northern part of the U.S. The Native Americans of that region called it *manomin* or *Meneninee*. It was called "crazy oats" by the French and "wild rice" by Americans as of 1748. Later, it was also referred to as "water oats" or "water rice."

Wild rice is now cultivated in rice paddies, mostly in Minnesota, though increasingly in California, where it is most often cooked by the following method.

WILD RICE

Cover 1 c. wild rice with boiling water, cover the pot, and let stand for 20 min. Drain, repeat process three more times. Add salt to taste, drain, then dry briefly over a low heat. It is usually served with butter, but sliced almonds, mushrooms, or onions may be added also.

WILLIAMS, CHUCK (1915–). As founder of Williams-Sonoma Inc., Chuck Williams developed a kitchenware business that set many of the standards and styles for home cooks in the postwar era, when Americans were becoming more sophisticated about culinary technique and gourmet cooking.

Williams was born in Florida, but when his father's auto maintenance business failed during the Depression, the family moved to California, where his father abandoned his wife and children. Williams worked on a date farm and a gift shop near Palm Springs while attending high school (his sister died in 1933, and his mother returned to Florida). He moved to Los Angeles to work in shipping at the I. Magnin department store, then became an airplane mechanic in India and East Africa during the war, afterwards moving to Sonoma to became a building contractor.

After a trip to Paris in 1953, he became a dedicated Francophile, committed to bringing some of the French lifestyle to Americans through the kitchen. "I started the store because I wanted to create something that nobody else had done," he said, "bring over things people in America hadn't been exposed to. The average person going to France wouldn't have seen them readily, either." In 1956, he opened his housewares store, selling professional-quality products displayed in brilliant colors against white walls. He encouraged customers to interact with store employees by putting merchandise just out of reach. Success brought him to open a store in 1958 in San Francisco, on Sutter Street, that was at first a local sensation, then a requisite stop for tourists in the city.

In 1972, with increasing pressure to expand, Williams took on partner Edward Marcus, owner of the Neiman Marcus department stores. Together they opened more stores and brought out an enormously successful catalog. After Marcus died, in 1977, Williams sold the company in 1978 to multi-millionaire Howard Lester and furniture store entrepreneur Jay McMahan, who expanded stores even more rapidly, with Williams staying on as buyer. "From the catalog business, we knew where our customers were so we put retail stores there," Mr. Williams told the *New York Times*. "We followed the ZIP codes." By 2010 Williams-Sonoma was accruing annual sales of $3.4 billion and had acquired Pottery Barn, Pottery Barn Kids, PBteen, and West Elm. (Lester died in 2010.)

Since selling the company, Williams has edited a series of Williams-Sonoma books that have sold millions of copies.

WINE. Fermented grape juice, although wine may also be made from other fruits. The word is from the Latin *vinum*.

The story of wine in most wine-producing countries is the history of a culture, but in America the story of wine is a spotty narrative of fits and starts, blind alleys, and intermittent, slow progress. Viticulture in this country has been a series of vignettes rather than a saga. Only within the past twenty years have Americans begun to appreciate wine as an ordinary beverage with some extraordinary characteristics.

The earliest settlers in this country set about making wine almost as soon as they arrived. These were wines made from wild American grapes, the **muscadine** (*Vitis rotundifolia*) and "labrusca," strong-flavored wines that were unfamiliar to the Europeans' taste. But the French Huguenots made wine from these grapes in the 1560s near Jacksonville, Florida, and Captain John Hawkins noted in 1565 that the Spanish settlers in Florida had made their own wine there. By the early 1600s Captain John Smith, of Virginia, could report "a great abundance [of vines] in many parts, that climbe the toppes of highest trees in some places.…Of these hedge grapes we made neere twentie gallons of wine, which was like our British wine, but certainly they would prove good were they well manured."

There was certainly wine at the first **Thanksgiving** feast, in 1621. Lord Delaware brought French vines to Virginia in 1619, and the Virginia general assembly required landowners to plant ten vines and offered prizes for the best wines.

In the seventeenth century, there were several failed attempts throughout the eastern colonies to grow wine grapes—in Maryland, Massachusetts, Pennsylvania, Rhode Island, and New York and throughout the South. Thomas Jefferson's wine-producing attempts at Monticello in 1773 were unsuccessful, too, largely because he, like the other farmers of the day, tried to plant European vinifera grapes that were not resistant to American disease, pests, and cold winters.

Meanwhile, wines were being successfully introduced in the West, particularly in California. As early as 1518, the Spanish explorer Hernán Cortés ordered grapes to be grown for wine in Mexico, a program that so swiftly became successful that the Spanish wine producers feared the competition and decreed that New World wines would be considered contraband. Nevertheless, the wines prospered. Franciscan friar Augustin Rodriguez is said to have brought grape vines to southern New Mexico around 1580, and by 1662 sacramental wine was being produced in that territory's Mesilla Valley.

Legend has it that wine vines were introduced into California by a Franciscan priest named **Junípero Serra** in 1769, when he founded the Mission San Diego de Alcalá. Research now shows that it probably did not occur this early. In a 1979 article in *New West* magazine, Roy Brady showed that Father Serra did not choose the San Diego site until July 16, 1769, too late in the year to plant vines for successful propagation, and in 1772 Serra lamented the lack of wine at the mission in his letters to his superior. By 1777 Serra was certain that wine could be made at the mission, and in a letter of March 15, 1779, Father Pablo de Mugártegui refers to plantings of "vine cuttings which at your request were sent to us from the lower country." Brady surmised that the first vines actually arrived in 1778, brought aboard Don José Camacho's ship, the *San Antonio*, and were planted at San Juan Capistrano, and that the first wines were ready for drinking in 1783, from a year-old vintage.

The grape the Spanish used in California was a type of vinifera called "Mission" or "Criolla." Leon D. Adams noted in *The Wines of America* (1978) that "ampelographers say it probably grew from a seed brought from Spain via Mexico by the conquistadores," since there is no precise counterpart for the grape in Europe.

Until the late nineteenth century, New Mexico continued to produce more wine than California, but a series of natural and man-made disasters killed off the industry. After the devastating flood of 1897 and a bad drought that followed, many vintners switched to the more profitable cotton crop. When Prohibition arrived, New Mexico's wine industry, which had been producing nearly a million gallons per year as of 1880, all but disappeared.

Native American grapes were propagated back east, with the first plantings of an indigenous grape made by James Alexander, of Pennsylvania, and named after him, in the 1730s. By 1793 the first commercial wine producing was being done northwest of Philadelphia, along the Susquehanna River, by the Pennsylvania Vine Co. Grape growing for wine had expanded into the Midwest by 1804, when Jean Jacques Dufour planted Alexander grapes at Vevay, Indiana. By the 1820s there were vineyards in Ohio, the Hudson Valley of New York, Missouri, and North Carolina.

All these were wines made from varieties of labrusca, which possess a very grapey flavor Americans called "foxy." This term, considered derogatory by growers of labrusca, refers to the fox grape, *Vitis labrusca*, of the eastern U.S. (Actually, all eastern wine grapes are by now crossbreeds, more properly called *Vitis labruscana*.) Purplish and large, the fox grape was first mentioned in 1657 and was described in 1682 by William Penn as "the great red grape (now ripe) called by ignorance, 'The foxgrape,' (because of the relish it hath with unskilful palates)." By 1864 Webster defined "foxy" as "having the coarse flavor of the fox grape."

Vinifera grapes had failed consistently in the East, but in 1833 Jean-Louis Vignes brought French vines to Los Angeles and grew them successfully, spurring more farmers to plant such varieties. After the Gold Rush of 1849, many failed miners stayed on in California to plant grapes, so that by 1863 there were more than twelve million vines in the state. There was even an industry bust in 1858 and 1859, and another in 1876, owing to an overproduction of wine. American wines by then were being shipped abroad in increasing numbers, and the French even feared U.S. competition in viticulture.

A great deal of credit for improving the California wine industry has been given to Hungarian-born **Ágoston Haraszthy**, who in 1857 opened a successful winery (still in operation) called the Buena Vista Winery in California's Sonoma County, then returned to Europe, with the approval of the state legislature, to bring back one hundred thousand vine cuttings. It has often been charged that the legislature reneged on a promise to reimburse Haraszthy (who called himself "Count," with no documentation to back up the title) for his trip and cuttings, but Charles L. Sullivan showed, in his article "Viticultural Mystery Solved: The Historical Origins of Zinfandel in California," in *California History* (Summer 1978), not only that Haraszthy did not bring back the Green Hungarian and **zinfandel** grapes that would eventually become important varieties in California viticulture, but that he guaranteed the legislature his trip would not cost them a cent. Haraszthy's contributions to viticulture in the state were considerable in terms of technical methods and improved propagation, but there seems little reason now to christen him the "Father of California's Wine Industry," as some have in the past.

Sometime between 1858 and 1863, American vines were imported by Europeans for experimental purposes. These labrusca vines carried with them a louse, the *Phylloxera vastatrix*, that attacked the susceptible European vines, almost completely destroying the vineyards over the next fifty years and eventually affecting the vines of Russia and Australia as well. Ironically, the vines of the eastern U.S. were resistant to the phylloxera, but those of California had never built up such a resistance; in 1873 the lice attacked the vines in Sonoma and devastated many vineyards throughout Northern California before it was checked at the turn of the century.

The phylloxera had been stopped in Europe by grafting European vines onto resistant American roots, principally from the Midwest, so California vineyards began replantings with these same roots, halting the ravages of the lice. (Another infestation began in the California vineyards in 1985, with the arrival of a strain called "biotype B," and it is estimated that more than 75 percent of Napa and Sonoma Valley vineyards have had to be replanted since then.)

In 1880, the California state legislature ordered the University of California to undertake a continuing program of intensive research in viticulture, a tradition that has made the school preeminent in the world today. California surpassed Ohio and Missouri as the largest wine-producing state in 1870, but wineries were thriving in the South, the Midwest, the Northwest, and even Utah. After 1860, New York State's Finger Lakes became an important wine-producing region, and by 1876 American wines were winning medals in international expositions. American **champagne** was first made in Ohio in 1842, and a sparkling wine made from Catawba grapes, by New York's Pleasant Valley Winery, in 1865, won an honorable mention at the Paris Exposition two years later.

American wines had earned international respect, but Americans themselves drank very little wine, and what was available was usually sold in bulk. Italian immigrants set up wineries in New York and California and made wine according to Old World methods, which sometimes included pressing the grapes with their feet, leading to appellations that were sometimes facetious, such as calling the harsh red wines of Northern California "Chateau La Feet" (a pun on the prestigious French Bordeaux wine Château Lafite) or, with a somewhat more belittling tone, "dago red" (from the ethnic slur "dago," which originally derived from the common Spanish name "Diego" but which by 1887 referred to an Italian). "Dago red" (used in print at least as early as 1906) was used as a general term for red wines made from zinfandel and other grapes and often marketed under the name Chianti (a red wine made in Italy's Tuscany region from Sangiovese and other grapes).

It was not the low reputation of more ordinary American wines that kept Americans from building a palate for table wine, but instead the growing temperance movement of the early twentieth century that first demonstrated its power in individual counties, then states, with Kansas having declared itself "dry" as early as 1880.

By World War I, thirty-three of the forty-eight states forbade the sale of spirits and wine, and the passage of the Volstead Act, in 1919, effectively crippled the rapidly developing wine industry, causing growers to switch to the production of "sacramental wine," used for religious rituals, or supplying home winemakers (as well as bootleggers) with grapes. One provision of the Volstead Act (Section 29), added at the behest of Virginia apple farmers, allowed private citizens to make up to two hundred gallons a year of homemade cider or non-intoxicating fruit juice, and the Department of Agriculture even amended its own crop reports to read "juice grapes" instead of "wine grapes." The popularity of homemade wine was so great that the California grape growers suddenly found that what they thought was a disaster had turned into an astounding boom for their industry. By the end of **Prohibition**, grape acreage in California was 35 percent greater than it had been when the Volstead Act was passed, and more than ninety million gallons of "nonintoxicating fruit juice" were being made at home each year, though the majority was made from inferior grapes the industry had been quick to provide.

Owing to an oversupply, there was a collapse of the California grape market in 1925, and many growers switched to other fruits, like apricots. But most wineries went out of business during Prohibition, with only a hundred or so surviving the Great Experiment.

During this period, wineries sold sacramental wine, wine bricks (compressed grapes), grape juice, and "Vine-Glow," a syrupy concentrate marketed in 1931 for the home winemaker (this last product was denounced in public forums and removed from the market soon afterwards). In 1932, on the verge of repeal, Senator William Gibbs McAdoo of California proposed to allow wine and beer to be sold at 3.2 percent alcohol, and the little wine that was made according to this formula was scornfully called "McAdoo wine."

Even after repeal, the wine industry took a long while to recover, largely because the growers had already switched to other crops or to inferior grapes. Sweet dessert wines gained in popularity, as did high-alcohol "fortified wines," with a 20 percent alcoholic content boosted by brandy. And, too, the legacy of Prohibition was still manifest in many states that chose to remain "dry" after repeal.

In 1935, however, Philip Wagner of Baltimore began bringing in hybrid grapes from France. A home winemaker himself, Wagner could not obtain his preferred zinfandel and Carignane grapes from California after 1933, and he did not care for the labrusca flavors of eastern grapes. He therefore imported the new French hybrids and began making wines that did indeed taste more like European wines. Wagner's first hybrids, created by Maurice Baco and Albert Seibel, became the basis for wide-ranging experimentation in New York during the 1960s, revitalizing the industry in that state, where sweet labrusca wines had been made almost exclusively.

A small but ultimately significant boost was given to American wines when NYC journalist **Frank Schoonmaker** began importing the best wines of California, Ohio, and New York and labeling them not with imitative and misleading names like Burgundy, Chianti, and Sauterne (American winemakers commonly spell the French wine Sauternes without the final *s*), but with varietal names based on the principal grape used—"**cabernet**," "Catawba," "Riesling," "Grenache Rosé," and others, sold at premium prices to the best restaurants and wine stores. Together with Tom Marvel, Schoonmaker also published *American Wines* in 1941, which tried to interest more Americans in drinking wine by removing the pompous snobbism of connoisseurship—what they called "Wine Hokum."

In 1934, the California Wine Institute was formed to work toward national standards for winemaking in the U.S. In 1938, the word "fortified" (which had a connotation of alcohol abuse) was banned from labels and advertising, and by 1954 the term was removed completely from federal regulations regarding wine. By the 1950s, the prestige of the University of California's enology school at Davis was unparalleled in the world, and, thanks to its efforts, American wines improved year by year.

Still, Americans continued to drink more dessert wines than table wines, and by the mid-1950s per capita consumption was less than a gallon per year, much of that being softer versions of red wine, called "vino" in an attempt to imbue such wines with an Italian cachet. Flavored wines with high alcohol and strange proprietary names like "Pagan Pink Ripple" and "Thunderbird" seemed ideal for the soda-pop palate of the postwar generation. Dozens of "pop wines" made from fruit juices and other flavorings became extremely popular in the 1960s. **Wine coolers**, made with fruit juices, became popular in the 1980s, especially among young drinkers.

It was during the same decade, however, that American wines took an astonishing leap in quality and reputation. In California, established wine-producing families and individuals like Sam Sebastiani, Robert Mondavi, André Tchelistcheff, Joe Heitz, and others pioneered the new technologies that utterly transformed the industry into a modern, efficient system capable of turning out varietal vinifera wines of great character, long-livedness, and prices competitive with the best French wines. Indeed, the taste for European varietals grew so much in the 1980s that native American varieties fell in popularity and were often replaced by European varietals, with **chardonnay** and **cabernet sauvignon** now accounting for 50 percent of the total vinifera grapes crushed in 1991.

This rise in quality, coupled with a growing interest on the part of American consumers in their own wines, boosted the sales of table wines over dessert wines for the first time in 1968, and by 1972 per capita consumption had risen to a gallon and a half per year. Land prices in the Napa and Sonoma valleys soared, investors bought up farms in an increasing number of wine regions in California, Washington, Idaho, and elsewhere, and there was increased activity in wine culture along the Hudson Valley, in New York, as well as renewed efforts in Maryland, Virginia, Connecticut, Texas, and other states that had all but abandoned winemaking on a commercial scale. Even on the island of Maui, in Hawaii, a winery was opened by Emil Tedeschi, who used a hybrid called "Carnelian," made from grenache, cabernet sauvignon, and Carignane grapes that flourished in the Pacific heat.

By the mid-1980s, however, many California winemakers showed a renewed interest in blending grapes to achieve more multidimensional wines and formed a group called the Meritage Association to develop wines made with a mix of traditional Bordeaux wine grapes. An increasing number of Americans are buying "light wines," which may have one-third fewer calories than regular wine. Light wines are produced in various ways, but most winemakers pick their grapes earlier, when the sugar level is lower than that at full ripening, thereby decreasing the alcohol content before fermentation.

Other producers remove the alcohol after fermentation is completed. Light wines have been made commercially since December 1979, when California laws permitted a reduction of alcohol from a previous minimum of 10 percent down to as low as 7 percent, and in February 1981 vintners won the right in federal court to use the term "light" on their labels. "Nonalcoholic," "alcohol-free" or "de-alcoholized" wines may contain no more than 0.5 percent alcohol (about the same as orange juice).

Varietal wines must contain, under federal regulations that went into effect on January 1, 1983, a minimum of 75 percent of the grape variety named on the label, although premium varietals have often been made using 100 percent of the grape named. Multivarietal labels listing two different grapes are also allowed, as long as the exact percentages appear on the label. "Fighting varietal" is a wine producer's term from the 1980s for a varietal wine that can be produced in sufficient volume to sell at a price considerably cheaper than such varietals usually do.

"Estate bottled" may be printed on wine labels when both the vineyard and the winery are in the same **American Viticultural Areas**, according to federal regulations; furthermore, the winery must own its own vineyard or have it under long-term lease, and all winemaking activities must occur on the premises. A specific geographical region—for instance, "Napa Valley" or "Western Connecticut Highlands"—may be listed on the label only if 85 percent of the grapes have been grown in that region. If a county is named—for instance, "Mendocino"—85 percent of the grapes must be grown in that county. The same percentage applies to state names appearing on labels (although California law mandates that 100 percent of the grapes come from the state for a California appellation).

"Chaptalization" (after a Napoleonic minister named Chaptal), a process of adding sugar to wine in order to increase its alcohol content through fermentation, has been forbidden in California since 1887 but is permitted in New York.

Home winemaking is allowed by the federal government if no more than one hundred gallons per year per adult—or two hundred gallons per household with two or more adults—are produced.

The U.S. produced 347 million cases in 2011, with 90 percent produced in California, which had 3,540 bonded wineries and 4,600 grape growers that in 2011 made 211.9 million cases, for sales of $19.9 billion. Washington, New York, and Oregon are the next largest. Wine exports in 2011 made up $1.39 billion in sales.

Americans still do not drink much wine, however, compared with other countries: 2.54 gallons per capita (even Vatican City and Luxembourg drink far more). Indeed, the U.S. is fifty-seventh in terms of consumption among wine-drinking countries.

The most popular varietals of American wines are chardonnay (21 percent share), cabernet (12 percent), and merlot (10 percent).

The following is a list of the principal grape varieties grown in the U.S. for making wine. Those printed in bold are major varieties having their own entries elsewhere in this book. A name preceding numerals indicates the creator of the hybrid.

Aleatico (red vinifera)

Alicante Bouschet (red vinifera)

Aligoté (white vinifera)

Aurora (also "Aurore"; white hybrid; Seibel 5279)

Baco Noir (red hybrid; Baco No. 1)

Barbera (red vinifera)

Cabernet Franc (red vinifera)

Cabernet Sauvignon (red vinifera)

Carignane (red vinifera)

Cascade (red hybrid; Seibel 13053)

Catawba (native red labrusca American hybrid)

Cayuga White (white hybrid)

Chancellor (also "Chancellor Noir"; red hybrid; Seibel 7053)

Charbono (red hybrid)

Chardonel (white vinifera hybrid)

Chardonnay (white vinifera)

Chelois (red hybrid)

Chenin Blanc (white vinifera)

Concord (red labrusca hybrid)

Cynthiana (also "Norton" and "Virginia Seedling"; red hybrid)

De Chaunac (red hybrid; Seibel 9549)

Delaware (red labrusca hybrid)

Diamond (white labrusca hybrid)

Dutchess (white labrusca hybrid)

Emerald Riesling (white vinifera)

Flora (white vinifera)

Foch (also "Maréchal Foch"; red hybrid; Kuhlmann 188–2)

Folle Blanche (white vinifera)

French Colombard (also "Colombard"; white vinifera)

Gamay (also "Napa Gamay"; red vinifera)

Gamay Beaujolais (red vinifera)

Gewürztraminer (white vinifera)

Green Hungarian (white vinifera)

Grenache (red vinifera)

Gray Riesling (white vinifera)

Grignolino (red vinifera)

Johannisberg Riesling (also "White Riesling"; white vinifera)

Leon Millot (red hybrid; Kulhmann 192–2)

Malbec (red vinifera)

Merlot (red vinifera)

Mission (red vinifera)

Moscato (white vinifera)

Müller-Thurgau (white vinifera)

Muscadine (gold or reddish black labrusca)

Napa Gamay (red vinifera)

Nebbiolo (red vinifera)

Niagara (white hybrid)

Palomino (also "Golden Chasselas"; white vinifera)

Petite Sirah (also "Petite Syrah"; red vinifera)

Pinot Blanc (white vinifera)

Pinot Gris (white vinifera)

Pinot Noir (red vinifera)

Ruby Cabernet (red vinifera)

Sauvignon Blanc (white vinifera)

Sémillon (white vinifera)

Seyval Blanc (also "Seyval"; white hybrid; Seyve-Villard 5–276)

Sylvaner (also "Sylvaner Riesling" or Franken Riesling"; white vinifera)

Thompson Seedless (white vinifera)

Tinta Madeira (red vinifera)

Vidal Blanc (white hybrid; Vidal 256)

Villard Blanc (white hybrid; Seyve-Villard 12–375)

Zinfandel (red vinifera)

WINE BRICK. Dehydrated grapes pressed into a brick and later put in water for homemade wine, used during Prohibition.

WINE COOLER. Beverages made from wine and citrus-fruit juices, first in print in 1941. The first branded wine cooler was called "California Cooler," introduced in 1981. The popularity of wine coolers soared, especially among Americans under thirty years of age, during the 1980s, reaching a peak of seventy-one million cases sold in 1986, but interest in the category has declined since then.

The term also refers to a room or vessel in which to cool wines, in print since 1815.

WISCONSIN CAKE. A popular nineteenth-century **muffin** baked in cast-iron "Wisconsin cake pans" made by Nathaniel Waterman, of Boston, as of 1859.

WISCONSIN CAKE

Sift together 1 c. whole-wheat flour with ½ c. white flour, 1 t. baking powder, and ½ t. salt. In a bowl beat 2 egg yolks, add 1 c. milk, and 2 T. maple syrup, then add to dry ingredients. Beat 2 egg whites until stiff, fold into batter, fill greased cast-iron muffin cups to two-thirds, and bake at 350° for about 20 min.

WITCH. A nineteenth-century New England cookie described in *The Pentucket Housewife* (1882) as containing two eggs, one and a half cups sugar, half a cup of butter, one tablespoon of milk, half a teaspoon of baking soda, and one teaspoon each of cinnamon, cloves, and allspice.

WOHAW. Native American term for the cattle that the native people first saw with the arrival of Europeans. The story goes that the Indians combined the trail calls "Whoa!" and "Haw!" into a general name for the beasts.

WOLF FISH. Also "wolffish." Any of a variety of marine fishes in the genus *Anarhichas* having sharp teeth and an ugly appearance that has kept it from becoming a popular food fish. The name, derived from its appearance, is sometimes changed at the market to "ocean catfish." The first appearance in print of "wolf fish" was in 1569.

In the U.S., the "Atlantic wolffish" (*A. lupus*) is found from Labrador to Nantucket.

U.S. landings totaled only six thousand pounds in 2010, valued at $6,000.

WOP SALAD. A salad of lettuce made with olives, oregano, capers, anchovies, garlic, and oil. It is a Louisiana specialty whose name, in print since 1930, derives from "wop," an ethnic slur against Italians, from a Neapolitan word *guappo*, "ruffian," used since the 1890s.

WRASS. Any of a large variety of tropical, large-scaled fish in the family Labridae, dating in print to 1686, including the "cunner" (*Tautogolabrus adspersus*) and the **tautog**, in eastern waters, and, in the West, the "señorita" (*Oxyjulis californica*), the "Pacific sandfish" (*Trichoden trichodon*), the "kelpfish" (*Halichoeres semicinctus*), and the "California sheephead" (*Semicossyphus pulcher*).

Y

YAKITORI. A Japanese dish of skewered broiled chicken pieces that have been dipped in a soy-sauce marinade, in print since 1962. Yakitori is a staple of Japanese American restaurants. The word in Japanese means "grilled bird."

YALE BOAT PIE. A dish made with layers of meat, poultry, and shellfish set in a pastry crust. The name comes from Yale University, in New Haven, Connecticut, and the recipe below is from *Jennie June's American Cookery Book* (1866), by J. C. Croly, who says, "This pie is excellent for a picnic or water excursion."

YALE BOAT PIE

Season with salt and pepper 3–4 lb. beefsteak, then place in a large baking dish. Cut 2 chickens into pieces and place on top of steak, then add 1 ½ doz. oysters (without their liquid) and 6 sliced hard-boiled eggs. Dampen the bottom of the dish with ale and cover with mushrooms and ½ lb. meat glaze. Top with a pastry crust and bake at 400° until bubbling inside.

YALE COCKTAIL. A drink made by mixing three dashes of orange bitters, one dash Angostura bitters, and two ounces of gin with ice and garnishing with lemon peel. Named after Yale University, in New Haven, Connecticut, though its origins are unknown; it probably dates from the post-Prohibition era of the 1930s.

YEAST. Any of a number of fungi in the phylum Ascomycota that may be fermented into alcohol and carbon dioxide, or any number of fungi of the genus *Saccharomyces* that may be used as a leavening agent in making bread and brewing. The word is from Middle English *yest* and Old English *gist*. The term also refers to commercial products of dried yeast cells pressed into "yeast cakes" or "moist yeast," which was first produced in the U.S. by Charles and Maximilian Fleischmann and James Gaff, of Cincinnati, in 1868. The Fleischmanns also introduced packages of dry yeast in 1942, for use in the military, and in 1984 introduced RapidRise Yeast, which acted quickly to leaven dough. **Sourdough** breads are leavened with yeast and *Lactobacillus sanfranciscensis*, a lactic-acid bacterium named after the city where sourdough starters were extensively used during the Gold Rush.

Turnpike Cakes or "hard yeast" were described by **Lafcadio Hearn** in *La Cuisine Créole* (1885) as dried cakes made by mixing hops with water, then boiling, straining, and pouring over cornmeal to which is added baker's yeast.

In the Midwest, generations of families have used a yeast called **Herman** for sweet confections, and in central Texas a yeast that is passed on by saving a remnant for a new batch is called "everlasting yeast."

Wild yeasts are often used in the production of wine and beer.

YOGURT. A creamy food made from **milk** curdled with bacteria such as *Lactobacillus bulgaricus* and *Streptococcus thermophilus*. The word is Turkish, first mentioned in English in 1625.

Yogurt is a very old food, probably of Middle Eastern origins. Turkish immigrants are said to have brought yogurt to the U.S. in 1784, but its popularity dates only from the 1940s, when Daniel Carasso emigrated to the U.S. and took over a small yogurt factory in the Bronx, NYC. He was soon joined by Juan Metzger, and the two sold their yogurt under the name Dannon (originally Danone, after Daniel Carasso, whose father was a Barcelona yogurt maker). In 1947, the company added strawberry fruit preserves to make the first "sundae-style yogurt." When nutrition promoter Benjamin Gayelord Hauser published an excerpt from his book *Look Younger, Live Longer* (1950) in the October 1950 issue of *Reader's Digest*, extolling the health virtues of yogurt, the product's sales soared. They leaped again—500 percent from 1958 to 1968—when so-called health foods were popularized by the counterculture of the 1960s. Aside from the obvious nutritive values of the milk used, the health benefits of yogurt have not been conclusively proven, and in 1962 the FDA forbade claims that yogurt had any therapeutic or weight-reducing value.

Today Americans eat about a billion cups of yogurt a year (or 5.1 pounds per person), often as a light lunch or dessert, and increasingly as frozen yogurt. Yogurt is also made at home, usually with a simple yogurt machine that uses already made commercial yogurt as a culture starter. "Swiss" or "French-style" yogurts usually have the fruit flavors already mixed in, rather than in a separate layer at the bottom of the cup. Strawberry yogurt is the most popular of all flavors.

YORKSHIRE PUDDING. A puffy, breadlike side dish made by cooking an egg-and-milk batter in the hot fat and pan drippings from a roast beef. It is a traditional English dish named after a northern county in England. The first recipe for Yorkshire pudding appeared in Mrs. Hannah Glasse's *Art of Cookery*, printed in England in 1747 and widely circulated in America. The dish is now a traditional accompaniment to roast beef in this country as well.

YORKSHIRE PUDDING

Combine 1 c. flour, ¼ t. salt, and 1 c. milk. Add 2 beaten eggs, make a smooth batter, and let stand until roast beef is done. Pour off the hot fat, retaining about ½ in. in the pan. Pour in the batter evenly and bake at 450° until browned and puffy. Cut into wedges and serve with beef.

YUCCA. Also "Indian cabbage," "Our Lord's candle," and "Joshua palm." Any of a wide variety of plants in the genus *Yucca*, of the **agave** family. The word is from the Spanish and first appeared in English print in about 1655. It has a bananalike fruit and is eaten raw, dried, or cooked. It is most appreciated in the Southwest, where the "banana yucca" (*Y. baccata*), also called "soap plant" and "Spanish bayonet," is widely used. The "yuca" (*Manihot esculenta*), also known as "cassava" and "manioc," is an unrelated starchy tuber grown in South America that is made into meal and sweet desserts.

Z

ZAGAT SURVEYS. Launched in 1979 by lawyers Tim and Nina Zagat, the Zagat Survey began as a New York City restaurant guide printed on mimeographed sheets of legal-size paper, compiled by the Zagats for their friends who dined out often. This was expanded in the first published guide, which contained ratings, from 0 to 30 points, based on thousands of responses from people who dined out often, which distinguished it from previous guides written by professional restaurant critics.

After a 1985 cover story in *New York* magazine about the novelty of such an "everyman's guide," the success of the NYC edition led to scores of surveys for other cities. The Zagats expanded to volumes on hotels, shopping, theater, movies, and wine. In 2011, the company was acquired by Google for $151 million in cash.

ZEPHRINA. A North Carolina cookie baked by both the Native Americans and the early settlers of the territory. The name derives from Latin *zephyrus*, for "wind," because of its light, airy quality.

ZEPHRINA

Combine 2 c. flour, 1 T. butter, salt, and enough water to make an elastic dough. Roll thin, cut into rounds, prick with fork, and bake until browned in a 375° oven.

ZEPOS, DAPHNE (1959–2012). Teacher. Daphne Zepos was one of America's leading authorities and promoters of the artisanal cheese movement.

Zepos was born in Athens, Greece. She was the daughter of a Greek diplomat and grew up in Athens, London, Geneva, and Brussels. She studied medieval history at the University of Kent, in England, and architecture at the Architectural Association, in London.

When her father was appointed the Greek ambassador to the UN, the family moved to NYC, where in 1987 she studied at Peter Kump's New York Cooking School. After graduating, Zepos moved to San Francisco to run the cheese service work at the Campton Place hotel, where she began her lifelong passion for cheese. From 2002 to 2005, she was associated with the Artisanal Premium Cheese Center, in NYC, where she initiated an internship program and ran a master class program. There she oversaw the selection and maturing of more than three hundred cheeses.

In 2006, she helped found NYC's Essex St. Cheese Co., an importer of European cheeses. She was also involved with the advocacy group Cheese of Choice Coalition, to preserve raw-milk and artisan cheeses. She became co-owner of the Cheese School of San Francisco in 2011.

Zepos lectured widely and taught at Slow Food's biannual "Cheese" conference, in Bra, Italy, and at the College of Marin, in California. Her writings on cheese appeared regularly in the *Atlantic*.

In 2012, Zepos was awarded the Lifetime Achievement Award by the American Cheese Society, which said, "Daphne's work to educate retailers, chefs, cheese mongers and cheese makers has contributed enormously to a huge improvement in the quality of the cheese on counters across the country. Her passion, the poetry of her cheese descriptions, her never-ending drive for better flavor, for teaching people what makes good cheese good, and for making already-good cheese even better is truly unrivaled."

Zepos died of cancer at the age of fifty-two, in San Francisco.

ZINFANDEL. Also "zin" for short. A red vinifera grape that is usually made into a robust, fruity, tannic wine. It is the most widely propagated grape in California, growing in nearly every wine region in the state, and one of American viticulture's most distinctive wines.

There has been a great deal of speculation as to the origins of the zinfandel. Once thought to be indigenous to the U.S., it is now generally believed to have been brought to this country. There is a record of William Robert Prince growing a "Black Zinfandel" grape on Long Island, New York, as early as 1830, one that he said had come from Hungary. Four years later, a zinfandel grape was exhibited by Samuel J. Perkins, of Boston. In California, where the grape thrived, it was generally classified as a claret.

It has long been legend that Hungarian viticulturist **Ágoston Haraszthy** brought the grape with him to San Diego, where he supposedly planted vines in 1852. But in his own *Report on Grapes and Wine of California*, six years later, he did not mention zinfandel at all, nor did he include it in his 1861 list of 156 imported Hungarian wines. Nevertheless, Miles Lambert-Gocs, in his article "On the Trail of the Zinfandel," in *The Journal of Gastronomy* (1986), contended that zinfandel was indeed a Hungarian name for a grape better known as the "Blaufrankisch/Kekfrankos," and that Haraszthy did receive zinfandel from Dalmatia. In 1854, Antoine Delmas was said to have brought "Black St. Peter's" vines to California from France, which Lambert-Gocs believed must have been Blaufrankisch. Other historians believe Black St. Peter's might have been zinfandel brought from New England vineyards. But the eastern zinfandel, according to John W. McConnell, of the Shields Library, at the University of California at Davis, was a table grape, not a wine grape. Even if zinfandel wine grapes had been grown in the East, it is still not known how or when they arrived there from Europe. In separate opinions on the origin of the name "zinfandel," wine writer Gerald Asher and etymologist David L. Gold believe the word derives from the Czech *cinifádl* (Gold also mentions the possibility of the German *Zinifal*), though those may not be the same grape as the American varietal. Croatian-born California winemaker **Mike Grgich**, quoted in a 1996 article in *Wine Enthusiast* by Terry Robards, asserted that the precursor of the American zinfandel is a clone of a Croatian grape named Plavač Mali or Mali Plaveč. Meanwhile, David Darlington in his book *Angels' Visits: An Inquiry into the Mystery of Zinfandel* (1991) notes that when Haraszthy lived in Hungary, Dalmatia was part of Hungary and may well have provided the grapes he brought to America.

In 1967, ampelographer Austin Goheen identified zinfandel as being identical to a grape known in Italy's Puglia region as Primitivo di Gioia (also called Zingarello), believed to have come originally from Greece. But wine writer Sheldon Wasserman later showed that zinfandel had been introduced to Italy forty or fifty years after its first appearances in the U.S. Today some Italian and other European winemakers produce a wine they call "Zinfandel," but it has been banned from importation by the ATF.

While the mystery of zinfandel's origins may never be known, the variety has flourished and attained great popularity in Northern California, which has medium to warm coastal climates. The grape, grown for decades in California by Italian immigrants, was sometimes characterized as undistinguished "dago red," but today zinfandels are among the most sought-after and respected California bottlings. Zinfandel is also blended with other grapes to make a **port** or rosé, or made into a rosé itself, "blanc de noir." The first varietal labeled "rosé" was a zinfandel introduced in 1958 by J. Pedroncelli Winery, in Sonoma. So-called white zinfandel, made with little skin contact and therefore a very pale rose color, was first made by George West in California, in 1869, but not successfully marketed until the 1980s (by Sutter Home Winery, of St. Helena, California). Occasionally one finds a "late-harvest zinfandel" that is a sweet dessert wine. Some light varieties are made in a fruitier style.

ZIP-CODE WINE. A wine-industry term to describe a French wine made from grapes not grown in a prestigious region like Burgundy but whose shipper's office is in such a region. Under French law, only the regional zip code may be used on the label, not the region's name.

ZITTERLI. Pennsylvania Dutch headcheese or calf's foot jelly, dating in print to 1872.

ZOMBIE. A cocktail made from various rums, liqueurs, and citrus juices. It was created in the late 1930s, by Don the Beachcomber (born Ernest Raymond Beaumont-Gantt), whose restaurant in Los Angeles was known for its rum-based concoctions. The story goes that the Zombie was created to cure a customer of his hangover. Several weeks later, the customer showed up again and, when asked how he'd enjoyed the drink, replied, "I felt like the living dead." The cocktail was thereafter called the Zombie, after the legendary spirits that reanimate the bodies of dead people in voodoo mythology. The cocktail dates in print to 1942. The word is from Kongo *zumbi*, "fetish."

ZOMBIE

Shake together ¾ oz. lime juice, 1 oz. pineapple juice, 1 t. sugar syrup, 1 oz. light rum, 2 oz. medium rum, 1 oz. Jamaican rum, ½ oz. 151-proof Demerara rum, and ½ oz. apricot liqueur. Pour into a tall glass with shaved ice and garnish with a slice of orange and sprigs of mint. Serve with straw.

ZOO. Hotel workers' slang word for the place where the help eats.

ZUCCHINI. Also "Italian squash." A summer **squash** of the species *Cucurbita pepo*, which measures from four to six inches in length, has a smooth green skin, and grows from flowers that themselves are sometimes battered and fried, dating in American print to 1929. The word is derived from the Italian *zucchino*, for a small squash. Zucchini became known to Americans only in the 1920s. By the 1950s it was a staple of Italian American restaurant menus and served either stewed with tomatoes, battered and fried in olive oil, or cut into salads. A dip made with zucchini and anchovies is sometimes referred to as "poor man's caviar."

ZWIEBACK. Dry toasted bread slices, long popular for their digestibility and often served to young children. The word is from the German for "twice baked" and first appeared in English print in 1894. Zwieback is usually bought at the grocery.

A BIBLIOGRAPHIC GUIDE

Since bibliographic items of specific interest or particular scholarship are cited and credited in the text of this book, it would be repetitious to list all references again in a complete bibliography of everything I have read or looked at during my research. I have decided, therefore, to provide both the scholar and the general reader with a brief guide to the best and most important sources for my research, giving credit where it is heavily due while establishing a working bibliography for future scholarship in the field of American studies.

Biographies

It is fortunate that so many of those who have contributed in important ways to American gastronomy are still doing so as of this writing and that nearly every one of them was forthcoming with biographical information and confirming what I'd written about them.

For those who are no longer alive, I used a variety of resources, including the most recent, authoritative biographies, magazine articles, and, whenever possible, newspaper obituaries from newspapers in the cities those individuals were connected with. The availability of the complete obituaries published since 1851 by the *New York Times* was invaluable.

Etymology

The American Heritage Dictionary of the English Language (2011) was a primary source for American words, checked for etymology and first appearance in English in the *OED*. *The Random House Dictionary of the English Language* (1987), which added to and altered much of the material found in *A Dictionary of Americanisms* (1951), *The Dictionary of American English*, which appeared from 1936 to 1944, and *The Oxford Dictionary of New Words*

(1991) were used to a lesser degree in my research. For slang, I found invaluable Eric Partridge's *Dictionary of Slang and Unconventional English* (eighth edition, 1984), Harold Wentworth and Stuart Berg Flexner's *Dictionary of American Slang* (second supplemented edition, 1975) and its revision, the *New Dictionary of American Slang*, edited by Robert L. Chapman (1986). Also of interest was *The American Thesaurus of Slang*, edited by Lester V. Berrey and Melvin Van den Bark (second edition, 1953). The first two volumes of the *Random House Historical Dictionary of American Slang*, edited by J. E. Lighter (1994 and 1997), have enriched American linguistic studies immeasurably, but sadly the project never published past the letter H. Happily, however, the superb *Dictionary of American Regional English* (*DARE*), edited by Frederic G. Cassidy and, later, Joan Houston Hall, was finished in 2012. (I cannot repress joy in finding my own *Encyclopedia* quoted in both *DARE* and the *OED*!)

Every lover of words is equally a lover of H. L. Mencken's *The American Language*, first published in 1919, followed by a greatly expanded fourth edition, in 1936, and two massive supplements, in 1945 and 1948. All of this material was revised, brought up to date, and abridged by Raven I. McDavid Jr. in a one-volume edition that appeared in 1963.

Mencken made American linguistic studies exciting for the student and fascinating for the general reader, a tradition that was admirably maintained by Stuart Berg Flexner in two remarkable works on Americana—*I Hear America Talking* (1976) and *Listening to America* (1982)—which in both narrative and illustration, with scrupulous attention to detail and a fine eye for anecdote, make the study of the American language as much a social history as an analysis of word origins. And, of course, there is much pleasure and information found nowhere else to be derived from perusing various numbers of *American Speech*.

The Morris Dictionary of Word and Phrase Origins, by William and Mary Morris (1977), has the same delight in it for the general reader, as does *The Merriam-Webster Book of Word Histories* (1976).

For the language of cowboys, miners, trappers, loggers, and other westerners, I turned most often to Ramon F. Adams's *Western Words: A Dictionary of the American West* (1968), and for the language of African Americans I consulted Clarence Major's *Dictionary of Afro-American Slang* (1970). For Jewish American words, *The Joys of Yiddish*, by Leo Rosten (1968), wholly lives up to its title.

Encyclopedias, Dictionaries, Etc.

The advances in serious food scholarship over the past decade have made my research far more enjoyable and easier than have could have been imagined in 1985, when the first edition of this encyclopedia (titled *The Dictionary of American Food and Drink*) was produced. Foremost was the monumental *Cambridge World History of Food* (two volumes), edited by Kenneth F. Kiple and Kriemhild Coneè Ornelas (2000), and the wonderfully engaging *Oxford Companion to Food* (1999), by the late Alan Davidson.

For information on animals, birds, and fish, I relied first on *Harper & Row's Complete Field Guide to North American Wildlife* (two volumes, 1981). *The Oxford Book of Food Plants*, by G. B. Masefield, M. Wallis, S. G. Harrison, and B. E. Nicholson, was consulted for fruits and vegetables, while A. J. McClane's *Encyclopedia of Fish Cookery* (1977) was an inexhaustible source of information on edible marine life. For the beauty of Charlotte Knox's illustrations and for superb scholarship and writing by Alan Davidson, *Seafood: A Connoisseur's Guide and Cookbook* (1989) is a joy to read.

I constantly turned to the following books for general information on cooking, ingredients, and origins of dishes: Theodora FitzGibbon's *Food of the Western World* (1976); André L. Simon's *Concise Encyclopedia of Gastronomy* (1952) and its revision by Robin Howe, *A Dictionary of Gastronomy* (1962). The English-language edition of *Larousse Gastronomique* (2001) was a standard source, and I relied often on the *World Encyclopedia*

of Food, by Patrick L. Coyle Jr. (1982); Tom Stobart's *Cook's Encyclopedia* (1980); Craig Claiborne's *The New York Times Food Encyclopedia* (1985), compiled by Joan Whitman; and Harold McGee's *On Food and Cooking* (1984) and *The Curious Cook* (1990). Special credit must be given to the late Waverley Root, who published not only excellent studies of the cuisines of France and Italy, but also the beautifully written and lavishly illustrated *Food* (1980), an example to all food writers for style, wit, personality, and breathtaking scholarship.

There is also much good information to be dug out of a quirky hodgepodge entitled *The Enriched, Fortified, Concentrated, Country-Fresh, Lip-Smacking, Finger-Licking, International, Unexpurgated Foodbook*, by James Trager (1970), as well as the same author's *The Food Chronology* (1995).

The scholar may wish to consult Eleanor Lowenstein's *Bibliography of American Cookery Books, 1742–1860* (1972), Katherine Golden Bitting's *Gastronomic Bibliography* (1939), and Anne Willan's *The Cookbook Library* (2012).

Individual Topics

The value of Elizabeth Schneider's *Uncommon Fruits & Vegetables: A Commonsense Guide* (1986) cannot be overstressed when it comes to puzzling out the vagaries of botanical edibles, and *The Encyclopedia of Herbs, Spices & Flavorings*, by Elisabeth Lambert Ortiz (1992), is equally rewarding. For cheese history and description of types throughout the world, I consulted most often *Cheese Primer* (1996), by Steven Jenkins, and *The World of Cheese* (1979), by Evan Jones, whose *Book of Bread*, written with his wife, Judith Jones (1982), is just as good on the subject of baked goods. H. E. Jacob's *Six Thousand Years of Bread* (1944) is a profound study of the importance of this human staple. The subject of ice cream confections is lovingly covered in Paul Dickson's *The Great American Ice Cream Book* (1972), while Ray Broekel's *Great American Candy Bar Book* (1982) is just as important and just as much fun on the subject of the Milky Way, the Tootsie Roll, and Hershey's chocolate.

Grossman's Guide to Wines, Beers, and Spirits (seventh revised edition, 1983), by Harriet Lembeck, is still a good source of basic information. The whole story of American viticulture is comprehensively told in

Leon D. Adams's *Wines of America* (second revised edition, 1978). The publication of *The Oxford Companion to Wine*, edited by Jancis Robinson (third edition, 2006), pulls together the most scholarly information on wines and winemaking around the world. I also recommend *From Demon to Darling: A Legal History of Wine in America* (2009), by Richard Mendelson, and *Ambitious Brew: The Story of American Beer* (2007), by Maureen Ogle.

For cocktails and mixed drinks, I found the following extremely helpful for information and recipes: *Straight Up or On the Rocks*, by William Grimes (1993); *The Fine Art of Mixing Drinks*, by David A. Embury (third American edition, 1958); and *Trader Vic's Bartender Guide*, by Victor J. Bergeron (revised, 1972). Best of all is David Wondrich's *Imbibe! From Absinthe to Whiskey Smash…* (2007).

Histories, Reminiscences, and Essays

Little academic attention has been paid to American gastronomy in standard histories until recently, and few history texts spend any time at all on the subject, the exception being Daniel J. Boorstin's *The Americans: The Colonial Experience* (1958), *The Americans: The National Experience* (1965), and *The Americans: The Democratic Experience* (1973). I consider it a serious omission that the *Harvard Encyclopedia of American Ethnic Groups*, edited by Stephan Thernstrom (1980), barely mentions the foods and culinary traditions of the immigrants to this country. If not much concerned with immigrants' food cultures, the statistical information compiled by Roger Daniels in his *Coming to America: A History of Immigration and Ethnicity in American Life* (second edition, 2002) was invaluable.

The full history of American gastronomy is told admirably in *Eating in America*, by **Waverley Root** and Richard de Rochemont (1976). Evan Jones's *American Food: The Gastronomic Story* (second edition, 1981) is eminently readable and full of fine recipes. Often overlooked but extremely valuable is Richard J. Hooker's *Food and Drink in America: A History* (1981), and there is much useful information in *The American Heritage Cookbook*, by Helen McCully and Helen Duprey Bullock (1964), and in *The Better Homes and Gardens Heritage Cook Book* (1975), both of which have excellent historical recipes. For an idiosyncratic but fascinating study

of the role of food in human civilization, Maguelonne Toussaint-Samat's *History of Food*, translated from the French by Anthea Bell (1992), is not to be ignored, nor is Reay Tannahill's *Food in History* (1988). The sheer delight in reading Margaret Visser's *Much Depends on Dinner* (1986) is balanced by some of the most erudite scholarship in the field. The same might be said of *Good to Eat*, by Marvin Harris (1985). There's worthwhile cogent social history to be found in Donna R. Gabaccia's *We Are What We Eat* (1998), about the influence and interchange of ethnic foods in America, and Richard Pillsbury's *No Foreign Food: The American Diet in Time and Place* (1998). I also learned much from *Hungering for America: Italian, Irish, and Jewish Foodways in the Age of Immigration* (2001), by Hasia R. Diner.

The Time-Life series *American Cooking* (seven volumes, 1970–1973) was a landmark in American studies of our food and culture. Various numbers of John Thorne's intermittently published booklets collected in *Simple Cooking* (1987), on subjects like chili, chowder, and the English muffin, are exhaustive commentaries on those items. Raymond Sokolov's *Fading Feast* (1981), originally commissioned as a series of articles for *Natural History* magazine, has much of the same flavor and treats many dishes and traditions that are indeed fast fading in this country for a variety of reasons. **Jane and Michael Stern**'s *Roadfood and Goodfood* (1986) and its revisions, *Roadfood* (1992) and *Eat Your Way Across the U.S.A.* (1997), constitute a rich store of Americana and anecdote, along with serving the practical object of pointing the reader to the best American regional restaurants. John A. Jakle and Keith A. Sculle's *Fat Food: Roadside Restaurants in the Automobile Age* (1999) is the best of the academic studies on the subject.

The Taste of America, by John L. and Karen Hess (1977), is an instructive and disturbing jeremiad aimed at those who would corrupt the traditions of American cookery, and it includes an excellent bibliography of eighteenth- and nineteenth-century works on cookery.

A book with a similar name but a more engaging author is *American Taste*, by **James Villas** (1982), one of a number of southern writers who have fondly kept alive the lore and traditions of southern cooking. This group would also include **Craig Claiborne**, whose *A Feast Made for Laughter* (1982) is an excellent memoir of a

Mississippi childhood; **Edna Lewis**, who, in *The Taste of Country Cooking* (1976), recalls Virginia; and Norma Jean and Carole Darden, who write of North Carolina in *Spoonbread and Strawberry Wine* (1978). Most comprehensive of all is **John Egerton**'s evocative *Southern Food* (1987).

What these southerners lovingly did for their region's culinary heritage, James Beard did for Oregon, in *Delights and Prejudices* (1964), E. Mae Fritz for Nebraska, in *Prairie Kitchen Sampler* (1988), and Nelson Algren for Illinois, in a work compiled for the Illinois Writers' Project, under the Works Progress Administration of the 1930s, but not published until 1992, under the title *America Eats*. An excellent study of New York City's culinary and social history will be found in **Michael and Ariane Batterberry**'s *On the Town in New York* (1973, revised 1999) and William Grimes's *Appetite City: A Culinary History of New York* (2010). A look at dining out nationally is provided by Andrew P. Haley's *Turning the Tables: Restaurants and the Rise of the American Middle Class, 1880–1920* (2011).

For some of the best and most affectionate writing on American regional dishes, I turn to Calvin Trillin's *American Fried* (1974) and *Third Helpings* (1983), as well as to Jean Anderson's *American Century Cookbook* (1997). Readers may also find of interest my own *America Eats Out: An Illustrated History of Restaurants, Taverns, Coffee Shops, Speakeasies, and Other Establishments That Have Fed Us for 350 Years* (1991).

ACKNOWLEDGMENTS

Because of the addition of bios to this edition of the *Encyclopedia*, I was delighted by the prospect of contacting directly old friends and people I have always admired to gather the information to write about them and to check facts. In almost every case of a living person, I was able to speak or write to them, so I am very grateful for their participation in this project.

I have to thank my editor, Kathy Belden, whose idea it was to update a fourteen-year-old encyclopedia and this time to include bios.

Thanks, too, go to production editor Laura Phillips and copy editor Will Palmer, who saved me from making both large and small mistakes and whose close reading of every entry, every statistic, and every opinion has resulted in a much better and better-written book than it would have been.

INDEX